The Billboard

TOP 40
Country
HITS

JOEL WHITBURN

BILLBOARD BOOKS
An imprint of Watson-Guptill Publications/New York

Editor: Amy Handy
Senior Editor: Bob Nirkind
Photo captions: Dave DiMartino
Picture sleeves selected from Joel Whitburn's personal collection
Book and cover design: Bob Fillie, Graphiti Graphics
Graphic production: Ellen Greene

First published 1996 by Billboard Publications, Inc.
1515 Broadway, New York, NY 10036.
ISBN 8230-8289-X

Library of Congress Cataloging-in-Publication Data
Whitburn, Joel
      The Billboard book of top 40 country hits/Joel Whitburn.
          p.   cm.
      ISBN 0-8230-7632-6
      1. Country music—Discography. I. Billboard (Cincinnati, Ohio: 1963).
II. Title. III. Title: Billboard book of top 40 country hits. IV. Title: Top forty
country hits.
ML156.4.C7W45   1996
016.78242164'2'0266—DC20   96-42931
                                       CIP
                                       MN

Manufactured in the United States of America

First printing, 1996

1 2 3 4 5 6 7 8 9 10 / 99 98 97 96

To my Country heroes of the '50s:
Marty Robbins, Johnny Cash, Don Gibson,
Jim Reeves and Johnny Horton...
Thank you for opening my ears to
some of the greatest songs on earth.

The author wishes to give thanks
to the staff of Record Research:

Bill Hathaway
Kim Bloxdorf
Fran Whitburn
Brent Olynick
Joanne Wagner
Troy Kluess
Jeanne Olynick
Paul Haney
Oscar Vidotto
Bobby DeSai

CONTENTS

ABOUT THE AUTHOR

When Joel Whitburn spun his first 78 rpm single back in 1950, little did he know that his part-time passion would spin off into a lifelong career and the uncontested title of "The World's #1 Chart Authority."

From a few chart facts scribbled on 3x5 note cards as a hobby to help organize his personal record collection, to a vast computerized database encompassing over a century of charted music, Joel's research has developed a richness and diversity rivaling that of the music it documents.

Joel published his first book—a slim, 104-page volume on Pop music singles—in 1970. The first edition of *Top 40 Hits* was released in 1983; the book you now hold in your hands is the sixth edition of this title. With over 60 Record Research volumes published to date, Joel has proven himself to be a prolific compiler of chart research books. He has also delved into *Billboard's* charts covering Pop albums, Country singles, R&B singles, Adult Contemporary singles, and Album Rock and Modern Rock tracks. His research on the music charts stretches back to 1890, and his book formats run the gamut from yearly record rankings to artist-by-artist compilations of charted record data to reproductions of the original charts themselves.

Joel's ongoing collaborations with Rhino Records have also produced well over 100 yearly CD compilations featuring his personal picks of *Billboard's* top Country, Pop, Rock and Roll, R&B, Dance, and Christmas hits.

SYNOPSIS OF BILLBOARD'S COUNTRY SINGLES CHARTS 1944-1996

Date	Positions	Chart Title
	JUKE BOX	
1/8/44	2-8	Most Played Juke Box Folk Records (9/6/47-11/1/47 shown as Most-Played Juke Box Hillbilly Records)
1/31/48	9-15	Most Played Juke Box Folk Records
6/25/49	7-15	Most Played Juke Box (Country & Western) Records
11/4/50	6-10	Most Played Juke Box Folk (Country & Western) Records
11/15/52	8-10	Most Played in Juke Boxes
6/30/56	9-10	Most Played C&W in Juke Boxes
6/17/57	final chart	
	BEST SELLERS	
5/15/48	10-15	Best Selling Retail Folk Records
6/25/49	5-15	Best Selling Retail Folk (Country & Western) Records
11/15/52	8-10	National Best Sellers
2/20/54	9-15	Best Sellers in Stores
6/30/56	13-20	C&W Best Sellers in Stores
10/13/58	final chart	

Date	Positions	Chart Title
12/10/49	8-10	Country & Western Records Most Played By Folk Disk Jockeys
11/15/52	9-15	Most Played by Jockeys
6/30/56	12-15	Most Played C&W by Jockeys
10/13/58	final chart	
		HOT COUNTRY SINGLES
10/20/58	30	Hot C&W Sides
11/3/62	30	Hot Country Singles
1/11/64	50	Hot Country Singles
10/15/66	75	Hot Country Singles
7/14/73	100	Hot Country Singles
1/20/90	75	Hot Country Singles (Billboard begins compiling their country singles chart entirely from information provided by Broadcast Data Systems, which electronically monitors actual radio airplay)
2/17/90	75	Hot Country Singles & Tracks

RESEARCHING THE CHARTS

This book includes every Top 40 single that debuted on *Billboard*'s country singles charts from 1944 through May 25, 1996. Over 9,450 charted hits and over 960 artists are listed in all.

CHART DATES

All dates refer to *Billboard*'s actual issue dates and are not the "week ending"dates that appeared on the earlier charts when originally published. The issue and week ending dates were different until January 13, 1962, when Billboard began using one date system for both the issue and the charts inside.

BEST SELLERS / JOCKEYS / JUKE BOX CHARTS

Billboard published its first country singles chart, Juke Box Folk Records, on January 8, 1944. On May 15, 1948, *Billboard* introduced a second country chart, Best Selling Retail Folk Records. On December 10, 1949, their Most Played by Folk Disk Jockeys chart made its debut. All of these charts were published on a weekly basis and each focused on specific areas of the music trade. (See the Synopsis of *Billboard*'s Country Singles Charts on the previous page for a detailed history of these charts.) For years in which *Billboard* published multiple Country singles charts, 1948 to 1958, many records hit more than one of these charts. A chart-by-chart breakdown of the highest position a record attained on any of the multiple *Billboard* country singles charts is listed below the title. The following rules apply to the chart data of such records:

>   **DATE:** the earliest of the dates charted in the Top 40.

>   **POS:** the highest ranking achieved on any of the charts. (The total weeks a single held the #1 or #2 position are shown in parentheses after the peak position, and are from the chart on which it achieved its highest total.)

WKS: from the chart on which a single achieved it most weeks in the Top 40.

ALL-ENCOMPASSING CHART

With the end of the multiple charts, *Billboard* introduced one all-encompassing top 30 country singles chart on October 20, 1958. Initially titled Hot C&W Sides, the chart has had several names over the past 38 years and is known today as the 75-position Hot Country Singles & Tracks chart.

NEW CHART METHODOLOGY

For decades, the country charts were compiled from playlists reported by radio stations. On January 20, 1990, with the aid of a new technology, *Billboard* initiated an even more accurate method of gathering data. On that date, *Billboard* began compiling their country singles charts entirely from play totals gathered by Broadcast Data Systems (BDS). BDS is a subsidiary of *Billboard* that electronically monitors actual radio airplay. They have installed monitors throughout the country that track the airplay of songs 24 hours a day, seven days a week. These monitors can identify each song played by an encoded audio "fingerprint."

Because of this electronic monitoring system, *Billboard* now includes album tracks on the renamed Hot Country Singles & Tracks. In this book, all charted album tracks are identified by the words "LP Cut" next to their label name in the "Label & Number" column (ex.: Capitol LP Cut). The album that the track is from is noted below the track title.

AUTHOR'S NOTE

As a Country music fan, you are one of the most loyal of all music fans. You know that Country stardom does not come to an artist by gimmick or trend but by talent and hard work. The artists that you admire come from backgrounds not so different from your own. From their pre-chart days, they know what it means to earn an honest day's work. They may have worked as a carpenter, salesman, teacher, painter, housewife, truck driver, accountant or secretary. Their songs speak to your concerns. With their relentless touring schedules, you've probably seen them perform in or near your hometown. Go to Nashville's annual Fan Fair in June and you can meet them. So if you're a fan of Garth, Reba, Hank, Dolly, George, Shania, Merle, Loretta, Buck, Randy, Wynonna, Alan or Clint, you'll probably be a fan for life.

Chances are that your introduction to Country music came by radio. Of the nearly 12,800 radio stations currently active in the United States, the format with the greatest number of stations (2,600+) belongs to Country. Over the runners-up's formats of News/Talk and Adult Contemporary, Country radio maintains a strong 2-to-1 lead.

The pervasive appeal of Country music is that it is pure Americana. The Country song's common themes of life are told in honest, real and sometimes humorous ways by artists whose own stories are equally as compelling. Many make their pilgrimages from places like Quick Sand, Paw Paw, Blue Lick, Wolf Bayou and Bulls Gap, to the Country music capital, Nashville. After spending years pounding Music Row's pavement, a fortunate few eventually break through.

Top 40 Country Hits chronicles the artists and their songs that broke through, made Country radio playlists coast to coast and cracked the Top 40 of *Billboard* magazine's Country singles charts. In here, you'll find everything that fits under the umbrella of Country music: bluegrass, honkytonk, ballad, outlaw, folk and Western Swing. And you'll know every Top 40 Country hit of your favorite artists from Gene Autry to Trisha Yearwood. I am proud to introduce the first edition of *Top 40 Country Hits*.

JOEL WHITBURN

THE ARTISTS

HOW TO USE THIS SECTION

This section lists, alphabetically by artist name, every single that charted in the Top 40 on *Billboard*'s country singles charts from January 8, 1944, through May 25, 1996.

Each artist's Top 40 hits are listed in chronological order. A sequential number is shown in front of each song title to indicate that artist's number of Top 40 hits. All Top 10 hits are highlighted in dark type.

EXPLANATION OF COLUMNAR HEADINGS

DATE: Date single debuted in the Top 40

POS: Single's highest charted position (highlighted in bold type)

WKS: Total weeks charted in the Top 40

LABEL & NO.: Original label and catalog number at the time single charted

EXPLANATION OF SYMBOLS

(1)   Number in parentheses to the right of a #1 or #2 peak position is the total weeks the single held that position

+   Indicates single peaked in the year after it first charted (symbol shown next to date)

●   Gold single*

▲   Platinum single*
* The primary source used to determine gold and platinum singles is the Recording Industry Association of America (RIAA), which began certifying gold singles in 1958 and platinum singles in 1976. From 1958 through 1988, RIAA required sales of one million units for a gold single and two million units for a platinum single; however, as of January 1, 1989, RIAA lowered the certification requirements for gold singles to sales of 500,000 units and for platinum to one million units. Please keep in mind that some record labels have never requested RIAA certifications for their hits. In order to fill in the gaps, especially during the period prior to 1958, various other trade publications and reports were used to supplement RIAA's certifications.

/   Divides a two-sided hit. Complete chart data (date, peak position, etc.) is shown for both sides if each side achieved its own peak position. If a title was shown only as the B-side, then only the weeks it was shown as a "tag along" are listed.

↑   Indicates the weeks charted data is subject to change since the single was still charted as of the 7/20/96 cut-off date

LETTER(S) IN BRACKETS AFTER TITLES

[I]   Instrumental recording

[N]   Novelty recording

[C]   Comedy recording

[S]   Spoken recording

[F]   Foreign language recording

[X]   Christmas recording

[R]   Re-entry, reissue, remix or re-recording of a previous hit by that artist

See RESEARCHING THE CHARTS for an explanation of the chart names listed below titles from 1948 to 1958.

ARTIST AND TITLE NOTES

Below nearly every artist name are brief notes about the artist. Directly under some song titles are notes indicating backing vocalists, guest instrumentalists, the title of the movie in which the song was featured, the name of a famous songwriter or producer, and so on. Duets and other important name variations are shown in bold capital letters. All movie, TV and album titles, and other major works are shown in italics. In the title notes "Bubbled Under" refers to *Billboard*'s Bubbling Under The Hot 100 chart.

DUETS

Duets are generally mixed in with an artist's solo hits, and the duet name is shown in bold capital letters below the title. If an artist charted a number of duets in a row, the duet name is shown under their last chart hit, with a note in parentheses indicating the number of titles charted consecutively by that team. Example:

JIM REEVES/DEBORAH ALLEN (above 3)

A special coding system is used for artists who have numerous duets mixed in with their solo hits. A letter code is shown after each duet title to identify the recording partners. An index of recording partners (with the corresponding letter code) is listed after the artist's biographical notes.

DATE	POS	WKS	ARTIST–RECORD TITLE	LABEL & NO.

A

ACUFF, Roy, and His Smoky Mountain Boys

Born Roy Claxton Acuff on 9/15/03 in Maynardsville, Tennessee. Died of congestive heart failure on 11/23/92. Moved to Knoxville in 1919. An attack of sunstroke kept him from pursuing a career in baseball. Worked with a medicine show, 1932-33, then had own band, the Tennessee Crackerjacks, on WROL-Knoxville. New band, the Crazy Tennesseans, appeared on WNOX-Knoxville in 1935. First recorded for ARC (later merged with Columbia) in 1936, and this session included "Great Speckle Bird" and "Wabash Cannonball." Began appearing on the *Grand Ole Opry* in 1937, then changed band name to Smoky Mountain Boys. In 1942, formed Acuff-Rose music publishing company with composer Fred Rose (died 12/1/54). They also formed the Hickory label in 1953. In the 1940s, twice ran for Tennessee governor as a Republican. First living artist elected to the Country Music Hall of Fame in 1962. Won Grammy's Lifetime Achievement Award in 1987. Fondly known as "The King Of Country Music."

DATE	POS	WKS	ARTIST–RECORD TITLE	LABEL & NO.
2/12/44	4	2	1. **The Prodigal Son**	Okeh 6716
11/4/44	3	8	2. **I'll Forgive You But I Can't Forget/**	
11/11/44	6	4	3. **Write Me Sweetheart**	Okeh 6723
4/19/47	4	6	4. **(Our Own) Jole Blon**	Columbia 37287
2/7/48	8	5	5. **The Waltz Of The Wind** Juke Box #8 / Best Seller #13	Columbia 38042
6/19/48	14	2	6. Unloved And Unclaimed Best Seller #14	Columbia 20425
8/7/48	12	1	7. This World Can't Stand Long Best Seller #12	Columbia 20454
11/6/48	12	1	8. Tennessee Waltz Juke Box #12	Columbia 20551
12/18/48	14	1	9. A Sinner's Death Best Seller #14	Columbia 20475
3/31/58	8	7	10. **Once More** Jockey #8	Hickory 1073
12/29/58+	16	11	11. So Many Times	Hickory 1090
6/15/59	20	3	12. Come And Knock (On The Door Of My Heart)	Hickory 1097

ADAMS, Don

Born on 1/4/41 in Ross County, Ohio. Worked with George Jones. Don's brother Dime (real name: Gary) played lead guitar for Faron Young.

DATE	POS	WKS	ARTIST–RECORD TITLE	LABEL & NO.
1/5/74	34	4	1. I've Already Stayed Too Long	Atlantic 4009

ADAMS, Kay

Born Princetta Kay Adams on 4/9/41 in Knox City, Texas.

DATE	POS	WKS	ARTIST–RECORD TITLE	LABEL & NO.
11/5/66	30	3	1. Little Pink Mack **KAY ADAMS with The Cliffie Stone Group**	Tower 269

AKINS, Rhett

Born on 10/23/69 in Valdosta, Georgia. Singer/songwriter/guitarist.

DATE	POS	WKS	ARTIST–RECORD TITLE	LABEL & NO.
12/10/94	35	3	1. What They're Talkin' About	Decca 54910
2/25/95	36	4	2. I Brake For Brunettes	Decca 54974

DATE	POS	WKS	ARTIST–RECORD TITLE		LABEL & NO.
7/8/95	**3**	13	3. **That Ain't My Truck**		Decca 55034
1/13/96	**17**	10	4. She Said Yes		Decca 55085
5/4/96	**4**↑	12↑	5. **Don't Get Me Started**		Decca 55166
			ALABAMA		
			Group formed in Fort Payne, Alabama, in 1969 as Wildcountry. Consisted of Randy Owen (born 12/13/49; guitar), Jeff Cook (born 8/27/49; keyboards, fiddle), Teddy Gentry (born 1/22/52; bass) and Bennett Vartanian (drums). Owen, Cook and Gentry are cousins. Worked local clubs in Myrtle Beach, South Carolina, beginning in 1973. Jackie Owen (another cousin) replaced Vartanian briefly in 1976; Rick Scott then took over as drummer later that same year. Mark Herndon (born 5/11/55) replaced Scott as drummer in 1979. Adopted the name Alabama in 1977. CMA Awards: 1981, 1982 and 1983 Vocal Group of the Year; 1982, 1983 and 1984 Entertainer of the Year.		
11/17/79	**33**	4	1. I Wanna' Come Over originally released on Limbo International label		MDJ 7906
2/16/80	**17**	9	2. My Home's In Alabama later released on RCA 12008		MDJ 1002
6/7/80	**1** (1)	13	3. **Tennessee River**		RCA 12018
10/11/80	**1** (1)	13	4. **Why Lady Why** first released as the B-side of #2 above		RCA 12091
2/14/81	**1** (1)	11	5. **Old Flame**		RCA 12169
5/30/81	**1** (2)	9	6. **Feels So Right**		RCA 12236
10/31/81	**1** (2)	11	7. **Love In The First Degree**		RCA 12288
3/13/82	**1** (1)	13	8. **Mountain Music**		RCA 13019
5/29/82	**1** (1)	13	9. **Take Me Down**		RCA 13210
9/11/82	**1** (1)	11	10. **Close Enough To Perfect**		RCA 13294
12/25/82	**35**	2	11. Christmas In Dixie [X] flip side of the Louise Mandrell/RC Bannon Christmas single		RCA 13358
2/19/83	**1** (1)	13	12. **Dixieland Delight**		RCA 13446
5/21/83	**1** (1)	12	13. **The Closer You Get**		RCA 13524
8/27/83	**1** (1)	13	14. **Lady Down On Love**		RCA 13590
2/4/84	**1** (1)	11	15. **Roll On (Eighteen Wheeler)**		RCA 13716
4/28/84	**1** (1)	13	16. **When We Make Love**		RCA 13763
8/11/84	**1** (1)	14	17. **If You're Gonna Play In Texas (You Gotta Have A Fiddle In The Band)/**		
		1	18. I'm Not That Way Anymore		RCA 13840
11/24/84+	**1** (1)	12	19. **(There's A) Fire In The Night**		RCA 13926
2/23/85	**1** (1)	13	20. **There's No Way**		RCA 13992
5/25/85	**1** (1)	13	21. **Forty Hour Week (For A Livin')**		RCA 14085
8/31/85	**1** (1)	14	22. **Can't Keep A Good Man Down**		RCA 14165
2/8/86	**1** (1)	13	23. **She And I**		RCA 14281
9/20/86	**1** (1)	14	24. **Touch Me When We're Dancing** #16 Pop hit for the Carpenters in 1981		RCA 5003
12/6/86+	**10**	9	25. **Deep River Woman** **LIONEL RICHIE with Alabama** flip side "Ballerina Girl" by Richie made #7 on the *Hot 100*		Motown 1873
1/31/87	**1** (1)	14	26. **"You've Got" The Touch**		RCA 5081
8/29/87	**7**	12	27. **Tar Top** title refers to Randy Owen's nickname		RCA 5222
12/12/87+	**1** (1)	15	28. **Face To Face** K.T. Oslin (guest vocal)		RCA 5328

DATE	POS	WKS	ARTIST–RECORD TITLE	LABEL & NO.
4/30/88	1 (1)	14	29. **Fallin' Again**	RCA 6902
12/3/88+	1 (1)	14	30. **Song Of The South**	RCA 8744
3/18/89	1 (1)	13	31. **If I Had You**	RCA 8817
8/19/89	1 (1)	14	32. **High Cotton**	RCA 8948
12/16/89+	1 (1)	19	33. **Southern Star**	RCA 9083
5/5/90	3	15	34. **Pass It On Down**	RCA 2519
			written in honor of Earth Day	
8/4/90	1 (4)	19	35. **Jukebox In My Mind**	RCA 2643
11/17/90+	1 (1)	20	36. **Forever's As Far As I'll Go**	RCA 2706
3/2/91	1 (3)	19	37. **Down Home**	RCA 2778
6/15/91	2 (1)	19	38. **Here We Are**	RCA 2828
			co-written by Vince Gill and Beth Nielsen Chapman	
10/5/91	4	16	39. **Then Again**	RCA 62059
1/25/92	2 (1)	18	40. **Born Country**	RCA 62168
6/20/92	2 (1)	16	41. **Take A Little Trip**	RCA 62253
10/3/92	1 (2)	19	42. **I'm In A Hurry (And Don't Know Why)**	RCA 62336
1/9/93	3	15	43. **Once Upon A Lifetime**	RCA 62428
4/17/93	3	16	44. **Hometown Honeymoon**	RCA 62495
9/18/93	1 (1)	19	45. **Reckless**	RCA 62636
1/1/94	7	14	46. **T.L.C. A.S.A.P.**	RCA 62712
5/7/94	13	10	47. The Cheap Seats	RCA 62623
10/1/94	6	14	48. **We Can't Love Like This Anymore**	RCA 62897
12/31/94	28	1	49. Angels Among Us [X-R]	RCA 62643
			made #51 in 1993	
2/25/95	3	17	50. **Give Me One More Shot**	RCA 64273
7/8/95	2 (1)	13	51. **She Ain't Your Ordinary Girl**	RCA 64346
10/7/95	4	16	52. **In Pictures**	RCA 64419
2/3/96	19	12	53. It Works	RCA 64473

ALAN, Buddy

Born Alvis Alan Owens on 5/22/48 in Tempe, Arizona; son of Buck and Bonnie Owens.

DATE	POS	WKS	ARTIST–RECORD TITLE	LABEL & NO.
8/10/68	7	12	1. **Let The World Keep On A Turnin'** **BUCK OWENS AND BUDDY ALAN AND THE BUCKAROOS**	Capitol 2237
11/15/69	23	7	2. Lodi	Capitol 2653
			#52 Pop hit for Creedence Clearwater Revival in 1969	
2/21/70	23	5	3. Big Mama's Medicine Show	Capitol 2715
5/30/70	38	2	4. Down In New Orleans	Capitol 2784
11/21/70	19	8	5. Cowboy Convention **BUDDY ALAN & DON RICH**	Capitol 2928
2/6/71	37	2	6. Lookin' Out My Back Door	Capitol 3010
			#2 Pop hit for Creedence Clearwater Revival in 1970	
12/25/71+	29	5	7. Too Old To Cut The Mustard **BUCK & BUDDY**	Capitol 3215
4/5/75	35	3	8. Chains	Capitol 4019
			#17 Pop hit for The Cookies in 1962	

ALEXANDER, Daniele

Born on 12/2/54 in Fort Worth, Texas.

DATE	POS	WKS	ARTIST–RECORD TITLE	LABEL & NO.
9/9/89	19	6	1. She's There	Mercury 874330

DATE	POS	WKS	ARTIST—RECORD TITLE	LABEL & NO.
			ALLANSON, Susie	
			Born on 3/17/52 in Minneapolis. Performed in the musicals *Hair* and *Jesus Christ Superstar*. Also appeared in the film *Jesus Christ Superstar*. Formerly married to Oak Records owner Ray Ruff, who was also married to Stephanie Winslow and Carlette.	
8/20/77	23	6	1. Baby, Don't Keep Me Hangin' On later released on Warner 8429	Oak 1001
12/3/77+	20	7	2. Baby, Last Night Made My Day	Warner/Curb 8473
3/18/78	7	9	3. **Maybe Baby** #17 Pop hit for Buddy Holly & The Crickets in 1958	Warner/Curb 8534
6/24/78	2 (2)	11	4. **We Belong Together**	Warner/Curb 8597
11/11/78	17	8	5. Back To The Love	Warner/Curb 8686
2/3/79	8	8	6. **Words** #15 Pop hit for the Bee Gees in 1968	Elektra/Curb 46009
5/5/79	6	10	7. **Two Steps Forward And Three Steps Back**	Elektra/Curb 46036
1/5/80	38	3	8. I Must Be Crazy	Elektra/Curb 46565
9/6/80	31	5	9. While I Was Makin' Love To You	United Art. 1365
12/6/80+	23	7	10. Dance The Two Step	Liberty 1383
			ALLEN, Deborah	
			Born Deborah Lynn Thurmond on 9/30/53 in Memphis. Successful songwriter; wrote "Don't Worry 'Bout Me, Baby" for Janie Fricke, "You Do It" for Sheena Easton, "Can I See You Tonight" for Tanya Tucker, and many others in country and soul. Married to songwriter Rafe Van Hoy. Appeared on *The River Rat* movie soundtrack. Regular on TV's *The Jim Stafford Show* in 1975.	
7/7/79	10	8	1. **Don't Let Me Cross Over**	RCA 11564
11/17/79+	6	11	2. **Oh, How I Miss You Tonight**	RCA 11737
5/3/80	10	10	3. **Take Me In Your Arms And Hold Me** **JIM REEVES/DEBORAH ALLEN (above 3)**	RCA 11946
1/10/81	24	5	4. Nobody's Fool	Capitol 4945
9/5/81	20	5	5. You (Make Me Wonder Why)	Capitol 5014
2/6/82	33	3	6. You Look Like The One I Love	Capitol 5080
9/24/83	4	15	7. **Baby I Lied**	RCA 13600
2/11/84	2 (2)	13	8. **I've Been Wrong Before**	RCA 13694
6/23/84	10	11	9. **I Hurt For You**	RCA 13776
11/17/84	23	7	10. Heartache And A Half	RCA 13921
1/23/93	29	7	11. Rock Me (In The Cradle Of Love)	Giant 18566
			ALLEN, Red—see OSBORNE BROTHERS	
			ALLEN, Rex	
			Born on 12/31/20 in Wilcox, Arizona. Singer/guitarist/actor. Professional rodeo rider as a teenager. Had own radio show on WTTM-Trenton, New Jersey, in 1944. With the Sleepy Hollow Gang in Allentown, Pennsylvania, in 1944. On the *National Barn Dance*, 1945-49; CBS network radio from Hollywood in 1949. Signed to Republic Pictures, made 32 westerns, 1950-57. His first movie was *The Arizona Cowboy* in 1950. Own TV series, *Frontier Doctor*, in 1954. Narrator for over 80 Walt Disney movies. Elected to the Cowboy Hall of Fame in 1968.	
9/3/49	14	1	1. Afraid **REX ALLEN and The Arizona Wranglers with Jerry Byrd** Juke Box #14	Mercury 6192

DATE	POS	WKS	ARTIST–RECORD TITLE	LABEL & NO.
4/21/51	**10**	1	2. **Sparrow In The Tree Top** Juke Box #10; Harry Geller (orch.); Jud Conlon Singers (backing vocals)	Mercury 5597
8/8/53	**4**	13	3. **Crying In The Chapel** Best Seller #4 / Juke Box #4 / Jockey #6; #3 Pop hit for Elvis Presley in 1965	Decca 28758
8/14/61	**21**	4	4. Marines, Let's Go	Mercury 71844
9/29/62	**4**	13	5. **Don't Go Near The Indians**	Mercury 71997

ALLEN, Rex, Jr.

Born on 8/23/47 in Chicago; son of Rex Allen. Traveled with father from age six; played rhythm guitar and worked as a rodeo clown. Moved to Nashville in the late '60s. Regular on *The Statler Brothers Show* on TNN since 1991.

DATE	POS	WKS	ARTIST–RECORD TITLE	LABEL & NO.
6/1/74	**19**	6	1. Goodbye	Warner 7788
10/12/74	**31**	5	2. Another Goodbye Song	Warner 8000
1/25/75	**36**	2	3. Never Coming Back Again	Warner 8046
2/28/76	**34**	3	4. Play Me No Sad Songs	Warner 8171
5/22/76	**17**	7	5. Can You Hear Those Pioneers Rex Allen, Sr. and The Sons of The Pioneers (backing vocals)	Warner 8204
8/28/76	**18**	8	6. Teardrops In My Heart	Warner 8236
1/8/77	**8**	11	7. **Two Less Lonely People**	Warner 8297
4/23/77	**10**	8	8. **I'm Getting Good At Missing You (Solitaire)**	Warner 8354
8/20/77	**15**	7	9. Don't Say Goodbye	Warner 8418
11/26/77+	**8**	11	10. **Lonely Street** #5 Pop hit for Andy Williams in 1959	Warner 8482
4/8/78	**8**	10	11. **No, No, No (I'd Rather Be Free)**	Warner 8541
8/5/78	**10**	8	12. **With Love**	Warner 8608
12/9/78+	**12**	9	13. It's Time We Talk Things Over	Warner 8697
4/21/79	**9**	10	14. **Me And My Broken Heart**	Warner 8786
8/18/79	**18**	8	15. If I Fell In Love With You	Warner 49020
3/8/80	**25**	5	16. Yippy Cry Yi	Warner 49168
6/14/80	**14**	8	17. It's Over	Warner 49128
10/25/80	**25**	6	18. Drink It Down, Lady	Warner 49562
1/17/81	**12**	7	19. Cup Of Tea	Warner 49626
4/18/81	**35**	2	20. Just A Country Boy	Warner 49682
7/4/81	**26**	6	21. While The Feeling's Good	Warner 49738
			REX ALLEN, JR. & MARGO SMITH (#19 & 21)	
12/10/83	**37**	4	22. The Air That I Breathe #6 Pop hit for The Hollies in 1974	Moon Shine 3017
8/18/84	**18**	8	23. Dream On Texas Ladies	Moon Shine 3030
12/22/84+	**24**	8	24. Running Down Memory Lane	Moon Shine 3034

ALLEN, Rosalie

Born Julie Marlene Bedra on 6/27/24 in Old Forge, Pennsylvania. Moved to New York in the late '30s and worked with Denver Darling's *Swing Billies* radio show. Teamed with Elton Britt on Zeke Manners's radio shows. Had own TV show in New York in the early '50s and later worked as a DJ on WOV-New York. One of the first female Country stars; known as "The Prairie Star" and "Queen Of The Yodelers."

DATE	POS	WKS	ARTIST–RECORD TITLE	LABEL & NO.
8/17/46	**3**	4	1. **Guitar Polka (Old Monterey)/**	
8/10/46	**5**	1	2. **I Want To Be A Cowboy's Sweetheart**	RCA Victor 1924

DATE	POS	WKS	ARTIST—RECORD TITLE	LABEL & NO.
2/4/50	7	4	3. **Beyond The Sunset** **THE THREE SUNS with ROSALIE ALLEN and ELTON BRITT** Jockey #7; 45 rpm: 47-3105	RCA Victor 3599
2/25/50	3	10	4. **Quicksilver** **ELTON BRITT and ROSALIE ALLEN with The Skytoppers** Jockey #3 / Juke Box #6 / Best Seller #9; 45 rpm: 48-0168	RCA Victor 0157

AMAZING RHYTHM ACES, The

Memphis group consisting of Russell Smith (lead vocals, guitar), Barry "Byrd" Burton (guitar, dobro), Billy Earhart III (keyboards), Jeff Davis (bass) and Butch McDade (drums). Davis and McDade had been with Jesse Winchester. Disbanded in 1980. Smith went on to a solo career, then with Run C&W. Earhart joined The Bama Band in 1986.

DATE	POS	WKS	ARTIST—RECORD TITLE	LABEL & NO.
8/2/75	11	9	1. Third Rate Romance	ABC 12078
12/20/75+	9	10	2. **Amazing Grace (Used To Be Her Favorite Song)**	ABC 12142
8/28/76	12	10	3. The End Is Not In Sight (The Cowboy Tune)	ABC 12202

ANDERSON, Bill

Born James William Anderson III on 11/1/37 in Columbia, South Carolina. Worked as a sportswriter and DJ in Commerce, Georgia, in 1957. Wrote "City Lights" hit for Ray Price and "Once A Day" for Connie Smith. Co-wrote "Saginaw, Michigan" for Lefty Frizzell. Hosted TNN's game show *Fandango*. Appeared in the movies *Las Vegas Hillbillies, Forty Acre Farm, Road To Nashville* and several others. Member of the *Grand Ole Opry* since 1961. Currently co-hosts TNN's *Opry Backstage*. Known as "Whispering Bill."

(a) BILL ANDERSON & JAN HOWARD
(b) BILL ANDERSON & MARY LOU TURNER

DATE	POS	WKS	ARTIST—RECORD TITLE	LABEL & NO.
12/29/58+	12	17	1. That's What It's Like To Be Lonesome	Decca 30773
7/6/59	13	19	2. Ninety-Nine	Decca 30914
12/28/59+	19	8	3. Dead Or Alive	Decca 30993
6/20/60	7	18	4. **The Tip Of My Fingers**	Decca 31092
12/26/60+	9	14	5. **Walk Out Backwards**	Decca 31168
7/10/61	9	19	6. **Po' Folks**	Decca 31262
4/21/62	14	10	7. Get A Little Dirt On Your Hands	Decca 31358
7/28/62	1 (7)	27	8. **Mama Sang A Song**	Decca 31404
2/23/63	1 (7)	27	9. **Still**	Decca 31458
8/24/63	2 (2)	22	10. **8 X 10**	Decca 31521
1/25/64	5	18	11. **Five Little Fingers/**	
2/22/64	14	19	12. Easy Come-Easy Go	Decca 31577
7/25/64	8	14	13. **Me**	Decca 31630
11/14/64+	8	18	14. **Three A.M./**	
11/21/64	38	3	15. In Case You Ever Change Your Mind	Decca 31681
4/17/65	12	13	16. Certain	Decca 31743
9/18/65	11	13	17. Bright Lights And Country Music	Decca 31825
2/19/66	4	22	18. **I Love You Drops/** #30 Pop hit for Vic Dana in 1966	
1/29/66	11	12	19. Golden Guitar	Decca 31890
3/12/66	29	5	20. I Know You're Married (But I Love You Still) (a)	Decca 31884
8/27/66	1 (1)	19	21. **I Get The Fever**	Decca 31999
2/4/67	5	16	22. **Get While The Gettin's Good**	Decca 32077
7/22/67	10	16	23. **No One's Gonna Hurt You Anymore**	Decca 32146

DATE	POS	WKS	ARTIST–RECORD TITLE		LABEL & NO.
11/11/67	1 (4)	18	24. For Loving You (a)		Decca 32197
3/23/68	2 (1)	16	25. Wild Week-End		Decca 32276
8/24/68	2 (2)	15	26. Happy State Of Mind		Decca 32360
3/22/69	1 (2)	16	27. My Life (Throw It Away If I Want To)		Decca 32445
7/26/69	2 (3)	13	28. But You Know I Love You		Decca 32514
			#19 Pop hit for Kenny Rogers & The First Edition in 1969		
11/22/69+	2 (1)	14	29. If It's All The Same To You (a)		Decca 32511
3/21/70	5	13	30. Love Is A Sometimes Thing		Decca 32643
6/27/70	4	13	31. Someday We'll Be Together (a)		Decca 32689
			#1 Pop hit for Diana Ross & The Supremes in 1969		
10/24/70	6	12	32. Where Have All Our Heroes Gone	[S]	Decca 32744
3/20/71	6	14	33. Always Remember		Decca 32793
7/24/71	3	17	34. Quits		Decca 32850
10/23/71	4	13	35. Dis-Satisfied (a)		Decca 32877
4/1/72	5	13	36. All The Lonely Women In The World		Decca 32930
9/23/72	2 (2)	14	37. Don't She Look Good		Decca 33002
3/17/73	2 (1)	11	38. If You Can Live With It (I Can Live Without It)		MCA 40004
7/14/73	2 (3)	14	39. The Corner Of My Life		MCA 40070
12/29/73+	1 (1)	12	40. World Of Make Believe		MCA 40164
7/13/74	24	5	41. Can I Come Home To You		MCA 40243
11/2/74	7	8	42. Every Time I Turn The Radio On		MCA 40304
3/8/75	14	6	43. I Still Feel The Same About You		MCA 40351
6/14/75	36	3	44. Country D.J.		MCA 40404
9/27/75	24	5	45. Thanks		MCA 40443
12/20/75+	1 (1)	11	46. Sometimes (b)		MCA 40488
4/10/76	7	9	47. That's What Made Me Love You (b)		MCA 40533
9/4/76	10	10	48. Peanuts And Diamonds		MCA 40595
12/18/76+	6	11	49. Liars One, Believers Zero		MCA 40661
5/21/77	7	9	50. Head To Toe		MCA 40713
8/6/77	18	7	51. Where Are You Going, Billy Boy (b)		MCA 40753
10/8/77	11	9	52. Still The One		MCA 40794
			#5 Pop hit for Orleans in 1976		
2/18/78	25	4	53. I'm Way Ahead Of You (b)		MCA 40852
5/13/78	4	9	54. I Can't Wait Any Longer		MCA 40893
12/2/78	30	3	55. Double S		MCA 40964
3/17/79	20	6	56. This Is A Love Song		MCA 40992
8/25/79	40	2	57. The Dream Never Dies		MCA 41060
			BILL ANDERSON & THE PO' FOLKS		
			#48 Pop hit for The Cooper Brothers in 1978		
5/17/80	35	2	58. Make Mine Night Time		MCA 41212
			# ANDERSON, Ivie		
			Born in 1904 in Gilroy, California. Died on 12/28/49. Duke Ellington's featured vocalist, 1931-42.		
4/8/44	4	2	1. Mexico Joe		Exclusive 3113
			Ceele Burke (orch.)		

DATE	POS	WKS	ARTIST–RECORD TITLE	LABEL & NO.
			## ANDERSON, John	
			Born John David Anderson on 12/13/54 in Orlando and raised in Apopka, Florida. Played guitar from age seven. Had own band, Living End, while still a teenager. Sang with sister Donna in the early '70s. Moved to Nashville in 1972; became staff writer for Gallico Music. First recorded for Ace of Hearts label in 1974. CMA Award: 1983 Horizon Award.	
12/23/78	40	2	1. The Girl At The End Of The Bar	Warner 8705
8/18/79	31	4	2. Low Dog Blues	Warner 8863
11/17/79+	15	11	3. Your Lying Blue Eyes	Warner 49089
4/5/80	13	9	4. She Just Started Liking Cheatin' Songs	Warner 49191
8/30/80	21	6	5. If There Were No Memories	Warner 49275
12/20/80+	7	9	6. **1959**	Warner 49582
4/11/81	4	11	7. **I'm Just An Old Chunk Of Coal (But I'm Gonna Be A Diamond Someday)**	Warner 49699
8/15/81	8	10	8. **Chicken Truck**	Warner 49772
12/12/81+	7	11	9. **I Just Came Home To Count The Memories**	Warner 49860
5/15/82	6	12	10. **Would You Catch A Falling Star**	Warner 50043
10/30/82	1 (2)	11	11. **Wild And Blue**	Warner 29917
1/29/83	1 (1)	12	● 12. **Swingin'** CMA Award: Single of the Year	Warner 29788
7/9/83	5	11	13. **Goin' Down Hill**	Warner 29585
10/15/83	1 (1)	14	14. **Black Sheep**	Warner 29497
2/4/84	10	10	15. **Let Somebody Else Drive**	Warner 29385
6/2/84	14	9	16. I Wish I Could Write You A Song	Warner 29276
9/8/84	3	12	17. **She Sure Got Away With My Heart**	Warner 29207
1/12/85	20	8	18. Eye Of A Hurricane	Warner 29127
5/25/85	15	10	19. It's All Over Now #26 Pop hit for The Rolling Stones in 1964	Warner 29002
9/28/85	30	4	20. Toyko, Oklahoma	Warner 28916
12/14/85+	12	11	21. Down In Tennessee	Warner 28855
4/19/86	31	4	22. You Can't Keep A Good Memory Down	Warner 28748
9/6/86	10	12	23. **Honky Tonk Crowd**	Warner 28639
1/9/88	23	7	24. Somewhere Between Ragged And Right Waylon Jennings (guest vocal)	MCA 53226
8/13/88	35	3	25. If It Ain't Broke Don't Fix It	MCA 53366
1/18/92	1 (1)	16	26. **Straight Tequila Night**	BNA 62140
5/9/92	3	17	27. **When It Comes To You** written by Mark Knopfler of the rock group Dire Straits	BNA 62235
9/5/92	2 (2)	17	28. **Seminole Wind**	BNA 62312
12/12/92+	7	14	29. **Let Go Of The Stone**	BNA 62410
5/15/93	1 (1)	18	30. **Money In The Bank**	BNA 62443
9/18/93	13	11	31. I Fell In The Water	BNA 62621
1/1/94	3	17	32. **I've Got It Made**	BNA 62709
5/14/94	4	17	33. **I Wish I Could Have Been There**	BNA 62795
10/29/94	35	4	34. Country 'Til I Die	BNA 62935
12/31/94+	3	15	35. **Bend It Until It Breaks**	BNA 64260
5/13/95	15	11	36. Mississippi Moon	BNA 64274
12/30/95+	26	10	37. Paradise	BNA 64465

DATE	POS	WKS	ARTIST—RECORD TITLE	LABEL & NO.
			ANDERSON, Liz	
			Born Elizabeth Jane Haaby on 3/13/30 in Roseau, Minnesota; raised in Grand Forks, North Dakota. Wrote "(My Friends Are Gonna Be) Strangers" and "The Fugitive" for Merle Haggard, and many others. Mother of Lynn Anderson.	
4/16/66	23	8	1. Go Now Pay Later	RCA 8778
10/29/66	5	14	2. **The Game Of Triangles**	RCA 8963
			BOBBY BARE, NORMA JEAN, LIZ ANDERSON	
12/31/66+	22	8	3. The Wife Of The Party	RCA 8999
5/13/67	5	14	4. **Mama Spank**	RCA 9163
10/7/67	24	6	5. Tiny Tears	RCA 9271
3/9/68	21	9	6. Mother, May I	RCA 9445
			LIZ ANDERSON and LYNN ANDERSON	
3/9/68	40	1	7. Thanks A Lot For Tryin' Anyway	RCA 9378
2/28/70	26	6	8. Husband Hunting	RCA 9796
			ANDERSON, Lynn	
			Born on 9/26/47 in Grand Forks, North Dakota; raised in Sacramento. Daughter of Liz Anderson. An accomplished equestrian, Lynn was the California Horse Show Queen in 1966. On *American Swingaround* in Chicago, 1967-68. Regular on TV's *The Lawrence Welk Show* from 1968. Appeared on three Bob Hope specials, acted in *Starsky & Hutch* TV show and in the movie *Country Gold*. Formerly married to songwriter/singer Glenn Sutton. CMA Award: 1971 Female Vocalist of the Year.	
1/7/67	36	4	1. Ride, Ride, Ride	Chart 1375
4/1/67	5	17	2. **If I Kiss You (Will You Go Away)**	Chart 1430
9/9/67	28	9	3. Too Much Of You	Chart 1475
12/16/67+	4	15	4. **Promises, Promises**	Chart 1010
3/9/68	21	9	5. Mother, May I	RCA 9445
			LIZ ANDERSON and LYNN ANDERSON	
4/27/68	8	10	6. **No Another Time**	Chart 1026
8/17/68	12	12	7. Big Girls Don't Cry	Chart 1042
12/14/68+	11	12	8. Flattery Will Get You Everywhere	Chart 1059
3/22/69	18	10	9. Our House Is Not A Home (If It's Never Been Loved In)	Chart 5001
8/16/69	2 (2)	13	10. **That's A No No**	Chart 5021
12/13/69+	15	9	11. He'd Still Love Me	Chart 5040
2/28/70	16	7	12. I've Been Everywhere	Chart 5053
4/4/70	7	14	13. **Stay There 'Til I Get There**	Columbia 45101
6/20/70	17	7	14. Rocky Top	Chart 5068
8/8/70	15	11	15. No Love At All/	
			#16 Pop hit for B.J. Thomas in 1971	
		11	16. I Found You Just In Time	Columbia 45190
11/14/70	1 (5)	19	● 17. **Rose Garden**	Columbia 45252
11/21/70	20	6	18. I'm Alright	Chart 5098
3/6/71	20	8	19. It Wasn't God Who Made Honky Tonk Angels	Chart 5113
5/15/71	1 (2)	13	20. **You're My Man**	Columbia 45356
			written by Glenn Sutton	
8/28/71	1 (3)	14	21. **How Can I Unlove You**	Columbia 45429
2/5/72	3	14	22. **Cry**	Columbia 45529
			#1 Pop hit for Johnnie Ray in 1951	
6/10/72	4	13	23. **Listen To A Country Song**	Columbia 45615

DATE	POS	WKS	ARTIST-RECORD TITLE	LABEL & NO.
10/21/72	4	13	24. **Fool Me** #78 Pop hit for Joe South in 1971	Columbia 45692
2/10/73	1 (1)	12	25. **Keep Me In Mind**	Columbia 45768
6/16/73	2 (1)	13	26. **Top Of The World** #1 Pop hit for the Carpenters in 1973	Columbia 45857
10/6/73	3	13	27. **Sing About Love**	Columbia 45918
3/30/74	15	9	28. Smile For Me	Columbia 46009
7/27/74	7	9	29. **Talkin' To The Wall**	Columbia 46056
11/16/74	1 (1)	9	30. **What A Man, My Man Is**	Columbia 10041
3/29/75	13	8	31. He Turns It Into Love Again	Columbia 10100
7/19/75	14	8	32. I've Never Loved Anyone More	Columbia 10160
12/27/75+	26	5	33. Paradise	Columbia 10240
3/6/76	20	8	34. All The King's Horses	Columbia 10280
10/16/76	23	6	35. Sweet Talkin' Man	Columbia 10401
2/12/77	12	8	36. Wrap Your Love All Around Your Man	Columbia 10467
6/11/77	22	6	37. I Love What Love Is Doing To Me	Columbia 10545
9/24/77	19	7	38. He Ain't You	Columbia 10597
12/24/77+	26	8	39. We Got Love	Columbia 10650
3/24/79	10	8	40. **Isn't It Always Love**	Columbia 10909
7/7/79	18	7	41. I Love How You Love Me #5 Pop hit for The Paris Sisters in 1961	Columbia 11006
11/10/79	33	3	42. Sea Of Heartbreak	Columbia 11104
8/9/80	26	5	43. Even Cowgirls Get The Blues	Columbia 11296
11/29/80	27	4	44. Blue Baby Blue	Columbia 11374
8/27/83	18	7	45. What I Learned From Loving You	Permian 82001
1/28/84	9	10	46. **You're Welcome To Tonight** **LYNN ANDERSON & GARY MORRIS**	Permian 82003
11/7/87	38	3	47. Read Between The Lines	Mercury 888839
9/3/88	24	7	48. Under The Boardwalk #4 Pop hit for The Drifters in 1964	Mercury 870528
			ANDREWS SISTERS	
			Patty, Maxene and LaVerne Andrews emerged from Minneapolis to become the most popular female vocal group of the entire pre-1955 era. LaVerne died on 5/8/67 (age 52). Maxene died on 10/21/95 (age 79). The trio appeared in many '40s movies.	
1/8/44	1 (5)	11	● 1. **Pistol Packin' Mama** **BING CROSBY and the ANDREWS SISTERS**	Decca 23277
4/9/49	2 (1)	16	2. **I'm Biting My Fingernails And Thinking Of You/** **ANDREWS SISTERS & ERNEST TUBB with The Texas Troubadors** Juke Box #2 / Best Seller #4	
4/16/49	6	5	3. **Don't Rob Another Man's Castle** **ERNEST TUBB & ANDREWS SISTERS with The Texas Troubadors** Juke Box #6 / Best Seller #10	Decca 24592
			ANTHONY, Rayburn	
			Born in Jackson, Tennessee. Bass player. Worked with Billy Walker; wrote Walker's hit "Sing Me A Love Song To Baby." Backed up Bobby Bare for two years.	
4/30/77	39	2	1. Lonely Eyes	Polydor 14380

DATE	POS	WKS	ARTIST–RECORD TITLE	LABEL & NO.
4/15/78	**31**	5	2. Maybe I Should've Been Listenin'	Polydor 14457
2/24/79	**28**	6	3. Shadows Of Love	Mercury 55053

ANTON, Susan—see KNOBLOCK, Fred

ARCHER PARK

Duo of Randy Archer (from Swainsboro, Georgia) and Johnny Park (from Arlington, Texas).

DATE	POS	WKS	ARTIST–RECORD TITLE	LABEL & NO.
9/10/94	**29**	8	1. Where There's Smoke	Atlantic 87211

ARNOLD, Eddy

Born Richard Edward Arnold on 5/15/18 near Henderson, Tennessee. Became popular on Nashville's *Grand Ole Opry* as a singer with Pee Wee King, 1940-43. Nicknamed "The Tennessee Plowboy" on all RCA recordings through 1954. Elected to the Country Music Hall of Fame in 1966. CMA Award: 1967 Entertainer of the Year.

EDDY ARNOLD AND HIS TENNESSEE PLOWBOYS:

DATE	POS	WKS	ARTIST–RECORD TITLE	LABEL & NO.
6/30/45	**5**	2	1. **Each Minute Seems A Million Years**	Bluebird 33-0527
7/13/46	**7**	1	2. **All Alone In This World Without You**	RCA Victor 1855
10/12/46	**2 (4)**	17	3. **That's How Much I Love You/**	
10/12/46	**3**	2	4. **Chained To A Memory**	RCA Victor 1948
3/1/47	**1 (1)**	22	5. **What Is Life Without Love**	RCA Victor 2058
5/31/47	**1 (5)**	38	6. **It's A Sin/**	
6/21/47	**4**	2	7. **I Couldn't Believe It Was True**	RCA Victor 2241
8/23/47	**1 (21)**	46	8. **I'll Hold You In My Heart (Till I Can Hold You In My Arms)** Juke Box #1 / Best Seller #7	RCA Victor 2332
11/8/47	**2 (2)**	15	9. **To My Sorrow** Juke Box #2	RCA Victor 2481
2/7/48	**10**	2	10. **Molly Darling** Juke Box #10 / Best Seller #14	RCA Victor 2489
3/20/48	**1 (9)**	39	11. **Anytime/** Juke Box #1(9) / Best Seller #1(3); #2 Pop hit for Eddie Fisher in 1952	
3/27/48	**2 (5)**	21	12. **What A Fool I Was** Juke Box #2 / Best Seller #7; 45 rpm: 48-0002	RCA Victor 2700
5/15/48	**1 (19)**	54	● 13. **Bouquet Of Roses/** Best Seller #1(19) / Juke Box #1(18)	
5/15/48	**1 (3)**	26	14. **Texarkana Baby** Juke Box #1(3) / Best Seller #1(1); 45 rpm: 48-0001	RCA Victor 2806

EDDY ARNOLD, THE TENNESSEE PLOWBOY AND HIS GUITAR:

DATE	POS	WKS	ARTIST–RECORD TITLE	LABEL & NO.
8/28/48	**1 (8)**	32	15. **Just A Little Lovin' (Will Go A Long, Long Way)/** Juke Box #1(8) / Best Seller #1(4)	
8/28/48	**5**	19	16. **My Daddy Is Only A Picture** Best Seller #5 / Juke Box #6; 45 rpm: 48-0026	RCA Victor 3013
11/20/48	**1 (1)**	21	17. **A Heart Full Of Love (For a Handful of Kisses)/** Best Seller #1 / Juke Box #3	
11/20/48+	**2 (1)**	17	18. **Then I Turned And Walked Slowly Away** Juke Box #2 / Best Seller #4; 45 rpm: 48-0025	RCA Victor 3174

DATE	POS	WKS	ARTIST—RECORD TITLE	LABEL & NO.
2/5/49	**10**	1	19. **Many Tears Ago** [R] Juke Box #10; originally released in 1946	RCA Victor 1871
2/19/49	**1** (12)	31	20. **Don't Rob Another Man's Castle/** Juke Box #1(12) / Best Seller #1(6); 45 rpm: 48-0042	
2/12/49	**3**	10	21. **There's Not A Thing (I Wouldn't Do For You)** Juke Box #3 / Best Seller #7	RCA Victor 0002
5/14/49	**1** (3)	22	22. **One Kiss Too Many/** Juke Box #1 / Best Seller #2	
5/21/49	**2** (3)	19	23. **The Echo Of Your Footsteps** Best Seller #2 / Juke Box #3; 45 rpm: 48-0083	RCA Victor 0051
7/2/49	**1** (4)	22	24. **I'm Throwing Rice (At the Girl That I Love)/** Best Seller #1(4) / Juke Box #1(3)	
7/16/49	**7**	4	25. **Show Me The Way Back To Your Heart** Best Seller #7 / Juke Box #11; 45 rpm: 48-0080	RCA Victor 0083
12/10/49	**5**	4	26. **Will Santy Come To Shanty Town/** [X] Jockey #5 / Juke Box #6 / Best Seller #8; 45 rpm: 48-0127	
11/19/49	**7**	8	27. **C-H-R-I-S-T-M-A-S** [X] Best Seller #7 / Jockey #7 / Juke Box #9	RCA Victor 0124
12/17/49+	6	2	28. **There's No Wings On My Angel** Juke Box #6 / Best Seller #11; 45 rpm: 48-0137; from the movie *Feudin' Rhythm*	RCA Victor 0134
12/31/49+	**1** (1)	17	29. **Take Me In Your Arms And Hold Me/** Juke Box #1 / Jockey #4 / Best Seller #5; answer song to #8 above	
1/14/50	6	7	30. **Mama And Daddy Broke My Heart** Best Seller #6 / Juke Box #8; 45 rpm: 48-0150	RCA Victor 0146
4/15/50	**3**	12	31. **Little Angel With The Dirty Face/** Best Seller #3 / Juke Box #7 / Jockey #10	
4/22/50	**3**	13	32. **Why Should I Cry?** Juke Box #3 / Best Seller #5 / Jockey #5	RCA Victor 0300
7/1/50	**2** (2)	17	33. **Cuddle Buggin' Baby/** Best Seller #2 / Juke Box #3 / Jockey #4	
7/1/50	6	12	34. **Enclosed, One Broken Heart** Juke Box #6 / Best Seller #7 / Jockey #7	RCA Victor 0342
9/30/50	**2** (8)	16	35. **The Lovebug Itch/** Best Seller #2 / Jockey #2 / Juke Box #2	
12/9/50	**10**	1	36. **A Prison Without Walls** Juke Box #10	RCA Victor 0382
1/13/51	**1** (11)	23	37. **There's Been A Change In Me** Jockey #1(11) / Best Seller #1(4) / Juke Box #2	RCA 0412
2/24/51	8	5	38. **May The Good Lord Bless And Keep You** Best Seller #8 / Jockey #10	RCA 0425
4/14/51	**1** (3)	17	39. **Kentucky Waltz** Best Seller #1(3) / Juke Box #1(3) / Jockey #4	RCA 0444
6/23/51	**1** (11)	24	40. **I Wanna Play House With You/** Juke Box #1(11) / Best Seller #1(6) / Jockey #2	
7/7/51	**4**	9	41. **Something Old, Something New** Juke Box #4 / Best Seller #7	RCA 0476
10/27/51	**2** (1)	16	42. **Somebody's Been Beating My Time/** Juke Box #2 / Jockey #3 / Best Seller #5	
10/27/51	**5**	12	43. **Heart Strings** Best Seller #5 / Juke Box #8	RCA 4273

DATE	POS	WKS	ARTIST–RECORD TITLE		LABEL & NO.
1/26/52	**4**	12	44. **Bundle Of Southern Sunshine/** Best Seller #4 / Juke Box #4 / Jockey #5		
2/23/52	**9**	1	45. **Call Her Your Sweetheart** Jockey #9		RCA 4413
4/5/52	**1** (1)	14	46. **Easy On The Eyes** Best Seller #1 / Jockey #4 / Juke Box #6		RCA 4569
7/19/52	**1** (4)	18	47. **A Full Time Job** Jockey #1 / Best Seller #3 / Juke Box #3		RCA 4787
10/25/52	**3**	11	48. **Older And Bolder/** Best Seller #3 / Juke Box #4 / Jockey #7		
12/6/52	**9**	1	49. **I'd Trade All Of My Tomorrows (For Just One** **Yesterday)** Juke Box #9		RCA 4954
1/24/53	**1** (3)	13	50. **Eddy's Song** Best Seller #1 / Juke Box #2 / Jockey #5; tune includes titles of many of Eddy's past hits		RCA 5108
6/20/53	**4**	9	51. **Free Home Demonstration/** Best Seller #4 / Jockey #5 / Juke Box #5		
7/18/53	**4**	10	52. **How's The World Treating You** Jockey #4 / Juke Box #7		RCA 5305
10/3/53	**4**	10	53. **Mama, Come Get Your Baby Boy** Jockey #4 / Best Seller #9 / Juke Box #9		RCA 5415
1/9/54	**1** (1)	37	54. **I Really Don't Want To Know** Juke Box #1 / Best Seller #2 / Jockey #2; there have been 6 Pop charted versions of this song, 1954-71		RCA 5525
4/10/54	**7**	9	55. **My Everything** Best Seller #7 / Jockey #7		RCA 5634
8/28/54	**3**	23	56. **This Is The Thanks I Get (For Loving You)/** Best Seller #3 / Jockey #3 / Juke Box #3		
			EDDY ARNOLD AND HIS GUITAR:		
8/21/54	**7**	14	57. **Hep Cat Baby** Juke Box #7 / Best Seller #9 / Jockey #14		RCA 5805
12/18/54	**12**	3	58. Christmas Can't Be Far Away Jockey #12	[X]	RCA 5905
1/29/55	**2** (4)	25	59. **I've Been Thinking/** Juke Box #2 / Best Seller #3 / Jockey #4		
2/5/55	**12**	7	60. Don't Forget Best Seller #12		RCA 6000
4/23/55	**6**	9	61. **In Time/** Jockey #6 / Best Seller #7		
4/23/55	**9**	8	62. **Two Kinds Of Love** Best Seller #9 / Juke Box #9		RCA 6069
6/25/55	**1** (2)	26	63. **The Cattle Call/** Best Seller #1 / Juke Box #2 / Jockey #4		
7/9/55	**8**	7	64. **The Kentuckian Song** Juke Box #8; from the movie The Kentuckian starring Burt Lancaster		RCA 6139
8/20/55	**1** (2)	15	65. **That Do Make It Nice/** Juke Box #1 / Jockey #4 / Best Seller #11		
8/20/55	**2** (7)	31	66. **Just Call Me Lonesome** Juke Box #2 / Best Seller #2 / Jockey #2		RCA 6198
11/26/55	**6**	8	67. **I Walked Alone Last Night/** Best Seller #6		
11/12/55	**10**	10	68. **The Richest Man (In The World)** Best Seller #10 / Jockey #14		RCA 6290

DATE	POS	WKS	ARTIST—RECORD TITLE	LABEL & NO.
1/28/56	7	3	69. **Trouble In Mind** Best Seller #7	RCA 6365
			EDDY ARNOLD:	
8/25/56	15	1	70. Casey Jones (The Brave Engineer) Jockey #15; written in 1909 about the engineer of the "Cannonball Express"	RCA 6601
9/1/56	10	8	71. **You Don't Know Me** Best Seller #10 / Jockey #15; Charles Grean (orch.)	RCA 6502
5/27/57	12	3	72. Gonna Find Me A Bluebird Jockey #12 / Best Seller #15	RCA 6905
3/16/59	12	9	73. Chip Off The Old Block	RCA 7435
6/22/59	5	19	74. **Tennessee Stud**	RCA 7542
1/9/61	23	3	75. Before This Day Ends	RCA 7794
5/29/61	27	1	76. (Jim) I Wore A Tie Today	RCA 7861
10/16/61	17	10	77. One Grain Of Sand	RCA 7926
3/17/62	7	10	78. **Tears Broke Out On Me**	RCA 7984
6/30/62	3	19	79. **A Little Heartache/**	
8/4/62	7	19	80. **After Loving You**	RCA 8048
12/8/62+	5	15	81. **Does He Mean That Much To You?**	RCA 8102
4/27/63	11	10	82. Yesterday's Memories	RCA 8160
8/10/63	13	12	83. A Million Years Or So	RCA 8207
12/7/63+	12	12	84. Jealous Hearted Me	RCA 8253
2/15/64	5	18	85. **Molly** **EDDY ARNOLD and The Needmore Creek Singers**	RCA 8296
8/1/64	26	11	86. Sweet Adorable You	RCA 8363
11/14/64+	8	18	87. **I Thank My Lucky Stars**	RCA 8445
4/3/65	1 (2)	24	88. **What's He Doing In My World**	RCA 8516
9/25/65	15	8	89. I'm Letting You Go	RCA 8632
10/16/65	1 (3)	23	90. **Make The World Go Away**	RCA 8679
2/26/66	1 (6)	17	91. **I Want To Go With You**	RCA 8749
5/21/66	2 (1)	15	92. **The Last Word In Lonesome Is Me** written by Roger Miller	RCA 8818
7/30/66	3	14	93. **The Tip Of My Fingers**	RCA 8869
10/22/66	1 (4)	18	94. **Somebody Like Me**	RCA 8965
2/25/67	1 (2)	15	95. **Lonely Again**	RCA 9080
5/20/67	3	13	96. **Misty Blue** #3 Pop hit for Dorothy Moore in 1976	RCA 9182
9/9/67	1 (1)	14	97. **Turn The World Around**	RCA 9265
12/9/67+	2 (2)	14	98. **Here Comes Heaven**	RCA 9368
2/24/68	4	13	99. **Here Comes The Rain, Baby**	RCA 9437
6/8/68	4	11	100. **It's Over** #37 Pop hit for Jimmie Rodgers in 1966	RCA 9525
9/7/68	1 (2)	13	101. **Then You Can Tell Me Goodbye** #6 Pop hit for The Casinos in 1967	RCA 9606
12/7/68+	10	11	102. **They Don't Make Love Like They Used To**	RCA 9667
4/19/69	10	10	103. **Please Don't Go**	RCA 0120
7/12/69	19	9	104. But For Love	RCA 0175
3/14/70	22	7	105. Soul Deep #18 Pop hit for The Box Tops in 1969	RCA 9801

DATE	POS	WKS	ARTIST–RECORD TITLE	LABEL & NO.
7/11/70	28	5	106. A Man's Kind Of Woman/	
		5	107. Living Under Pressure	RCA 9848
9/19/70	22	8	108. From Heaven To Heartache	RCA 9889
1/23/71	26	8	109. Portrait Of My Woman	RCA 9935
7/24/71	34	3	110. Welcome To My World	RCA 9993
4/8/72	38	2	111. Lonely People	RCA 0641
2/24/73	28	7	112. So Many Ways	MGM 14478
			#6 Pop hit for Brook Benton in 1959	
9/29/73	29	5	113. Oh, Oh, I'm Falling In Love Again	MGM 14600
1/19/74	24	6	114. She's Got Everything I Need	MGM 14672
9/7/74	19	6	115. I Wish That I Had Loved You Better	MGM 14734
7/17/76	13	7	116. Cowboy	RCA 10701
4/2/77	22	7	117. (I Need You) All The Time	RCA 10899
5/20/78	23	5	118. Country Lovin'	RCA 11257
1/6/79	13	8	119. If Everyone Had Someone Like You	RCA 11422
5/5/79	21	6	120. What In Her World Did I Do	RCA 11537
8/25/79	22	5	121. Goodbye	RCA 11668
12/15/79+	28	6	122. If I Ever Had To Say Goodbye To You	RCA 11752
3/22/80	6	9	123. **Let's Get It While The Gettin's Good**	RCA 11918
7/26/80	10	9	124. **That's What I Get For Loving You**	RCA 12039
12/27/80+	11	10	125. Don't Look Now (But We Just Fell In Love)	RCA 12136
6/13/81	32	3	126. Bally-Hoo Days/	
		2	127. Two Hearts Beat Better Than One	RCA 12226
1/16/82	30	3	128. All I'm Missing Is You	RCA 13000

ASHLEY, Leon

Born near Covington, Georgia. Emcee of his own country music radio show at age 11. Married Margie Singleton in 1965. Formed own label, Ashley, in 1967. Known in the radio industry as Leon Walton, owner of several radio stations.

DATE	POS	WKS	ARTIST–RECORD TITLE	LABEL & NO.
8/12/67	1 (1)	15	1. **Laura (What's He Got That I Ain't Got)**	Ashley 2003
12/30/67+	28	8	2. Anna, I'm Taking You Home	Ashley 2025
4/13/68	14	12	3. Mental Journey	Ashley 2075
8/10/68	8	13	4. **Flower Of Love**	Ashley 4000
1/18/69	25	8	5. While Your Lover Sleeps	Ashley 7000
5/10/69	23	7	6. Walkin' Back To Birmingham	Ashley 9000

ASHWORTH, Ernest

Born on 12/15/28 in Huntsville, Alabama. Worked on local radio stations, then WSIX-Nashville. Recorded for MGM as Billy Worth in 1955. Out of music until 1960. A regular on the *Grand Ole Opry* since 1964. Appeared in the movie *The Farmer's Other Daughter*.

DATE	POS	WKS	ARTIST–RECORD TITLE	LABEL & NO.
5/30/60	4	16	1. **Each Moment ('Spent With You)**	Decca 31085
10/24/60	8	20	2. **You Can't Pick A Rose In December**	Decca 31156
5/15/61	15	2	3. Forever Gone	Decca 31237
6/30/62	3	20	4. **Everybody But Me**	Hickory 1170
12/29/62+	7	15	5. **I Take The Chance**	Hickory 1189
6/22/63	1 (1)	35	6. **Talk Back Trembling Lips**	Hickory 1214
2/8/64	10	19	7. **A Week In The Country**	Hickory 1237

DATE	POS	WKS	ARTIST–RECORD TITLE	LABEL & NO.
6/27/64	4	21	8. **I Love To Dance With Annie**	Hickory 1265
11/14/64+	11	20	9. Pushed In A Corner	Hickory 1281
5/15/65	18	13	10. Because I Cared	Hickory 1304
8/14/65	8	18	11. **The DJ Cried**	Hickory 1325
			ERNIE ASHWORTH:	
2/12/66	28	9	12. I Wish	Hickory 1358
7/16/66	13	16	13. At Ease Heart	Hickory 1400
12/31/66+	31	4	14. Sad Face	Hickory 1428
6/29/68	39	2	15. A New Heart	Hickory 1503
			## ASLEEP AT THE WHEEL	
			Group formed in Paw Paw, West Virginia, in 1970. Consisted of Ray Benson (vocals, guitar), Reuben "Lucky Oceans" Gosfield (steel guitar), Danny Levin (fiddle, mandolin) and Chris O'Connell (vocals, guitar). Worked local clubs in West Virginia and Washington, D.C., then moved to San Francisco in 1973, where they were joined by Floyd Domino (keyboards). Relocated to Austin in 1974. Personnel in 1987 included Benson, Larry Franklin (fiddle), Michael Francis (sax), John Ely (steel guitar), Tim Alexander (keyboards), Dave Dawson (bass) and David Sanger (drums). Dawson left by 1991, replaced by Jon Mitchell. By 1994, Franklin replaced by Ricky Turpin, Ely by Cindy Cashdollar, Mitchell by David Earl Miller and Sanger by Tommy Beavers.	
10/4/75	10	8	1. **The Letter That Johnny Walker Read**	Capitol 4115
1/10/76	31	6	2. Bump Bounce Boogie	Capitol 4187
5/8/76	35	4	3. Nothin' Takes The Place Of You	Capitol 4238
1/8/77	38	2	4. Miles And Miles Of Texas	Capitol 4357
4/4/87	39	1	5. Way Down Texas Way	Epic 06671
7/4/87	17	9	6. House Of Blue Lights #9 Pop hit for Chuck Miller in 1955	Epic 07125
			## ATCHER, Bob	
			Born Robert Owen Atcher on 5/11/14 in Hardin County, Kentucky; raised in North Dakota. Died on 10/30/93. Worked on WHAS-Louisville in the mid-1930s and Chicago radio, 1931-48. First recorded for Columbia in 1937. With the WLS *National Barn Dance*, 1948-70, and had own TV show. Mayor of Schaumburg, Illinois, for 16 years.	
7/13/46	7	1	1. **I Must Have Been Wrong**	Columbia 36983
1/31/48	6	11	2. **Signed, Sealed And Delivered**	Columbia 37991
5/7/49	12	1	3. Tennessee Border Juke Box #12	Columbia 20557
10/8/49	9	2	4. **Why Don't You Haul Off And Love Me** Juke Box #9	Columbia 20611
			## ATKINS, Chet	
			Born Chester Burton Atkins on 6/20/24 in Luttrell, Tennessee. First worked on WNOX-Knoxville, 1942-44, and toured with Archie Campbell and Bill Carlisle. On WLW-Cincinnati, 1944-46; Red Foley's radio show in Chicago in 1946. Recorded with Wally Fowler's Georgia Clodhoppers for Capitol in 1946. Recorded solo for Bullet in 1946. Began recording for RCA in 1947. Moved to Nashville in 1950 and became prolific studio musician and producer. RCA's A&R manager in Nashville, 1960-68; RCA vice president, 1968-82. Revered as an exceptional guitarist in all fields of music. Entered the Country Music Hall of Fame in 1973 as the youngest inductee (age 49). Won Grammy's Lifetime Achievement Award in 1993.	

DATE	POS	WKS	ARTIST–RECORD TITLE	LABEL & NO.
1/15/55	13	2	1. Mister Sandman [I] **CHET ATKINS and his Gallopin' Guitar** Jockey #13 / Best Seller #15; #1 Pop hit for The Chordettes in 1954	RCA 5956
4/2/55	15	1	2. Silver Bell [I] **HANK SNOW and CHET ATKINS** Best Seller #15	RCA 5995
7/3/65	4	18	3. **Yakety Axe** [I] same tune as Boots Randolph's Pop hit "Yakety Sax"	RCA 8590
11/12/66	30	5	4. Prissy [I]	RCA 8927
8/14/76	40	1	5. Frog Kissin' [N]	RCA 10614
1/21/84	6	10	6. **We Didn't See A Thing** **RAY CHARLES & GEORGE JONES featuring Chet Atkins**	Columbia 04297

ATLANTA

Group formed in Atlanta in 1983. Consisted of Brad Griffis, Dick Stevens, Bill Packard, Allen Collay, Jeff Baker, Tony Ingram (ex-Spurzz), Bill Davidson, John Holder and Allen David. Future members included Darrell "Boo Boo" McAfee and Jody Warrell. Griffis, Stevens, Packard and Davidson had been in pop group The Vogues in the late '70s. Collay had worked with jazz clarinetist Pete Fountain.

DATE	POS	WKS	ARTIST–RECORD TITLE	LABEL & NO.
6/18/83	9	10	1. **Atlanta Burned Again Last Night**	MDJ 4831
10/15/83	11	9	2. Dixie Dreaming	MDJ 4832
3/3/84	5	12	3. **Sweet Country Music**	MCA 52336
7/28/84	35	2	4. Pictures	MCA 52391
10/13/84	22	6	5. Wishful Drinkin' from the movie *Ellie* starring Shelley Winters	MCA 52452

AUSTIN, Bobby

Born on 5/5/33 in Wenatchee, Washington. Session fiddler. Had own band in Vancouver, Washington. Member of Wynn Stewart's band in Las Vegas.

DATE	POS	WKS	ARTIST–RECORD TITLE	LABEL & NO.
10/8/66	21	11	1. Apartment #9	Tally 500
12/16/72	39	2	2. Knoxville Station	Atlantic 2913

AUTRY, Gene

Born Orvon Gene Autry on 9/29/07 in Tioga Springs, Texas. Worked as a cowboy and telegrapher for the Frisco Railroad after attending Ravia High School in Oklahoma. Played saxophone with the Fields Brothers Medicine Show, then switched to guitar so he could sing along. Sang on KVOO-Tulsa, 1929-30, recorded for ARC and Victor. Worked the WLS *National Barn Dance* and vaudeville, 1930-34. First movie appearance in 1934, in *Old Santa Fe*. Made over 90 other starring movies beginning with *Tumbling Tumbleweeds*. Very popular *Melody Ranch* radio series began on CBS on 1/7/40. Enlisted in the Army Air Corps; returned to radio from September 1945 until 1956. Owner of several record companies and the California Angels baseball team. Wrote "That Silver-Haired Daddy Of Mine," "Back In The Saddle Again," "Here Comes Santa Claus," and many others. Elected to the Country Music Hall of Fame in 1969.

DATE	POS	WKS	ARTIST–RECORD TITLE	LABEL & NO.
1/29/44	3	9	1. **I'm Thinking Tonight Of My Blue Eyes**	Okeh 06648
4/29/44	4	1	2. **I Hang My Head And Cry**	Okeh 06627
2/10/45	2 (1)	8	3. **Gonna Build A Big Fence Around Texas/**	
2/17/45	4	3	4. **Don't Fence Me In** from the movie *Hollywood Canteen* starring Bette Davis	Okeh 6728
4/28/45	1 (8)	22	5. **At Mail Call Today/**	
4/28/45	7	2	6. **I'll Be Back**	Okeh 6737

DATE	POS	WKS	ARTIST–RECORD TITLE	LABEL & NO.
10/27/45	4	2	7. **Don't Hang Around Me Anymore**	Columbia 36840
12/29/45	4	1	8. **Don't Live A Lie/**	
12/29/45	4	1	9. **I Want To Be Sure**	Columbia 36880
2/23/46	4	5	10. **Silver Spurs (On The Golden Stairs)**	Columbia 36904
5/25/46	3	7	11. **I Wish I Had Never Met Sunshine**	Columbia 36970
6/15/46	4	8	12. **Wave To Me, My Lady**	Columbia 36984
7/6/46	7	1	13. **You Only Want Me When You're Lonely**	Columbia 36970
10/19/46	3	12	14. **Have I Told You Lately That I Love You/**	
10/26/46	4	3	15. **Someday You'll Want Me To Want You**	Columbia 37079
3/8/47	3	2	16. **You're Not My Darlin' Anymore**	Columbia 37201
12/27/47	5	1	● 17. **Here Comes Santa Claus (Down Santa Claus Lane)** [X]	Columbia 37942
10/9/48	6	12	18. **Buttons And Bows** Best Seller #6 / Juke Box #6; from the movie The Paleface starring Bob Hope	Columbia 20469
11/27/48	4	7	19. **Here Comes Santa Claus (Down Santa Claus Lane)** [X-R] Best Seller #4 / Juke Box #7	Columbia 20377
12/10/49	1 (1)	5	● 20. **Rudolph, The Red-Nosed Reindeer** [X] **GENE AUTRY and The Pinafores** Jockey #1 / Best Seller #4 / Juke Box #7; 7" 33-1/3 rpm: 1-375	Columbia 38610
12/10/49	8	3	21. **Here Comes Santa Claus (Down Santa Claus Lane)** [X-R] Jockey #8 / Best Seller #13	Columbia 20377
4/8/50	3	4	● 22. **Peter Cottontail** Best Seller #3 / Jockey #5 / Juke Box #7; 7" 33-1/3 rpm: 1-575	Columbia 38750
12/9/50	4	4	● 23. **Frosty The Snow Man** [X] Best Seller #4; The Cass County Boys (vocals); Carl Cotner (orch.); 45 rpm: 6-742	Columbia 38907
12/16/50	5	3	24. **Rudolph, The Red-Nosed Reindeer** [X-R] Best Seller #5 / Jockey #5 / Juke Box #5	Columbia 38610
6/9/51	9	1	25. **Old Soldiers Never Die** Jockey #9; Carl Cotner (orch.)	Columbia 39405
			AXTON, Hoyt	
			Born on 3/25/38 in Duncan, Oklahoma; son of songwriter Mae Axton ("Heartbreak Hotel"). First worked as a folk singer on the West Coast in the late '50s. Started own Jeremiah label in 1978. Acted in the movies The Black Stallion and Gremlins.	
4/27/74	10	10	1. **When The Morning Comes**	A&M 1497
9/21/74	8	9	2. **Boney Fingers** Renee Armand (female vocal)	A&M 1607
6/19/76	18	8	3. Flash Of Fire	A&M 1811
6/9/79	17	7	4. Della And The Dealer	Jeremiah 1000
10/27/79	14	8	5. A Rusty Old Halo	Jeremiah 1001
2/2/80	21	6	6. Wild Bull Rider	Jeremiah 1003
5/24/80	37	3	7. Evangelina	Jeremiah 1005

DATE	POS	WKS	ARTIST–RECORD TITLE	LABEL & NO.

B

BAILEY, Judy—see BANDY, Moe

BAILEY, Razzy

Born Rasie Michael Bailey on 2/14/39 in Five Points, Alabama. Own pop group, Daily Bread, in 1958; recorded with the Aquarians for MGM in 1972. Also recorded only as Razzy on MGM in 1974. Wrote "9,999,999 Tears" hit for Dickey Lee.

DATE	POS	WKS	ARTIST–RECORD TITLE	LABEL & NO.
9/2/78	9	11	1. **What Time Do You Have To Be Back To Heaven**	RCA 11338
1/6/79	6	10	2. **Tonight She's Gonna Love Me (Like There Was No Tomorrow)**	RCA 11446
5/5/79	6	9	3. **If Love Had A Face**	RCA 11536
9/8/79	10	9	4. **I Ain't Got No Business Doin' Business Today**	RCA 11682
1/5/80	5	10	5. **I Can't Get Enough Of You**	RCA 11885
5/10/80	13	8	6. Too Old To Play Cowboy	RCA 11954
8/16/80	1 (1)	10	7. **Loving Up A Storm**	RCA 12062
11/29/80+	1 (1)	13	8. **I Keep Coming Back/**	
		13	9. True Life Country Music	RCA 12120
4/4/81	1 (1)	12	10. **Friends/**	
		12	11. Anywhere There's A Jukebox	RCA 12199
7/25/81	1 (1)	12	12. **Midnight Hauler/**	
7/25/81	8	12	13. **Scratch My Back (And Whisper in My Ear)**	RCA 12268
1/9/82	1 (1)	14	14. **She Left Love All Over Me**	RCA 13007
4/24/82	10	10	15. **Everytime You Cross My Mind (You Break My Heart)**	RCA 13084
9/11/82	8	11	16. **Love's Gonna Fall Here Tonight**	RCA 13290
1/29/83	30	3	17. Poor Boy	RCA 13383
5/28/83	19	7	18. After The Great Depression	RCA 13512
3/24/84	14	8	19. In The Midnight Hour	RCA 13718
			#21 Pop hit for Wilson Pickett in 1965	
9/8/84	29	5	20. Knock On Wood	MCA 52421
			#1 Pop hit for Amii Stewart in 1979	

BAILLIE AND THE BOYS

Trio of songwriters/session vocalsits: Kathie Baillie (born 2/20/51, Morristown, New Jersey) and husband Michael Bonagura (born 3/26/53, Newark, New Jersey) with Alan LeBoeuf. LeBoeuf starred in the Broadway show *Beatlemania*. Group became a duo when LeBoeuf left in 1988.

DATE	POS	WKS	ARTIST–RECORD TITLE	LABEL & NO.
5/16/87	9	12	1. **Oh Heart**	RCA 5130
9/12/87	18	8	2. He's Letting Go	RCA 5227
1/23/88	9	10	3. **Wilder Days**	RCA 5327
10/22/88+	5	15	4. **Long Shot**	RCA 8631
3/4/89	8	12	5. **She Deserves You**	RCA 8796
7/22/89	4	15	6. **(I Wish I Had A) Heart Of Stone**	RCA 8944
11/25/89+	9	19	7. **I Can't Turn The Tide**	RCA 9076
5/19/90	23	7	8. Perfect	RCA 2500
9/8/90	5	17	9. **Fool Such As I**	RCA 2641
1/19/91	18	15	10. Treat Me Like A Stranger	RCA 2720

DATE	POS	WKS	ARTIST–RECORD TITLE	LABEL & NO.
			BAKER, George, Selection	
			Baker is Johannes Bouwens (born 12/9/44). Pop vocalist/guitarist/ keyboardist of Dutch group.	
2/28/76	**33**	5	1. Paloma Blanca	Warner 8115
			BAKER, Two Ton—see HOOSIER HOT SHOTS	
			BALL, David	
			Born on 7/9/53 in Rock Hill, South Carolina.	
5/28/94	**2** (1)	14	1. **Thinkin' Problem**	Warner 18250
10/1/94	**7**	17	2. **When The Thought Of You Catches Up With Me**	Warner 18081
2/11/95	**11**	13	3. Look What Followed Me Home	Warner 17977
			BANDANA	
			Formed in Nashville in 1981 by lead vocalist Lonnie Wilson and bassist Jerry Fox. Originally included Tim Mensy (guitar), Joe Van Dyke (keyboards) and Jerry Ray Johnston (drums). In 1986 group consisted of Wilson, Fox, Michael Black and Billy Kemp (guitars) and Bob Mummert (drums).	
2/20/82	**37**	2	1. Guilty Eyes	Warner 49872
9/18/82	**17**	10	2. The Killin' Kind	Warner 29936
2/5/83	**29**	3	3. I Can't Get Over You (Getting Over Me)	Warner 29831
10/8/83	**18**	8	4. Outside Lookin' In	Warner 29524
5/19/84	**26**	5	5. Better Our Hearts Should Bend (Than Break)	Warner 29315
10/26/85	**37**	2	6. Lovin' Up A Storm	Warner 28939
			BANDY, Moe	
			Born Marion Franklin Bandy, Jr., on 2/12/44 in Meridian, Mississippi; raised in San Antonio. Played with father's band, the Mission City Playboys, in San Antonio; also worked as a rodeo rider. Own TV show with The Mavericks in the early '70s; went solo in 1973. CMA Award: 1980 Vocal Duo of the Year (with Joe Stampley).	
			(a) MOE BANDY & JOE STAMPLEY	
4/27/74	**17**	10	1. I Just Started Hatin' Cheatin' Songs Today	GRC 2006
			originally issued on Footprint 1006	
9/7/74	**24**	5	2. Honky Tonk Amnesia	GRC 2024
12/21/74+	**7**	9	3. **It Was Always So Easy (To Find An Unhappy Woman)**	GRC 2036
4/12/75	**13**	7	4. Don't Anyone Make Love At Home Anymore	GRC 2055
7/26/75	**7**	11	5. **Bandy The Rodeo Clown**	GRC 2070
1/3/76	**2** (2)	11	6. **Hank Williams, You Wrote My Life**	Columbia 10265
			lyrics feature titles to many Hank Williams songs	
5/8/76	**27**	6	7. The Biggest Airport In The World	Columbia 10313
7/24/76	**11**	9	8. Here I Am Drunk Again	Columbia 10361
11/27/76+	**11**	10	9. She Took More Than Her Share	Columbia 10428
3/26/77	**9**	9	10. **I'm Sorry For You, My Friend**	Columbia 10487
			written in 1952 by Hank Williams	
7/2/77	**13**	8	11. Cowboys Ain't Supposed To Cry	Columbia 10558
10/29/77	**11**	7	12. She Just Loved The Cheatin' Out Of Me	Columbia 10619
2/11/78	**13**	8	13. Soft Lights And Hard Country Music	Columbia 10671
6/10/78	**11**	9	14. That's What Makes The Juke Box Play	Columbia 10735
9/30/78	**7**	9	15. **Two Lonely People**	Columbia 10820

DATE	POS	WKS	ARTIST–RECORD TITLE	LABEL & NO.
2/10/79	2 (2)	10	16. **It's A Cheating Situation** Janie Fricke (backing vocal)	Columbia 10889
6/30/79	9	8	17. **Barstool Mountain**	Columbia 10974
7/28/79	1 (1)	11	18. **Just Good Ol' Boys** (a)	Columbia 11027
10/13/79	1 (1)	10	19. **I Cheated Me Right Out Of You**	Columbia 11090
12/1/79+	7	9	20. **Holding The Bag** (a)	Columbia 11147
2/9/80	13	9	21. One Of A Kind	Columbia 11184
5/3/80	11	10	22. Tell Ole I Ain't Here, He Better Get On Home (a)	Columbia 11244
5/24/80	22	6	23. The Champ	Columbia 11255
8/23/80	10	9	24. Yesterday Once More	Columbia 11305
12/20/80+	10	8	25. **Following The Feeling** **MOE BANDY featuring JUDY BAILEY**	Columbia 11395
3/28/81	10	9	26. Hey Joe (Hey Moe) (a)	Columbia 60508
5/9/81	15	9	27. My Woman Loves The Devil Out Of Me	Columbia 02039
8/15/81	12	8	28. Honky Tonk Queen (a)	Columbia 02198
10/31/81+	10	11	29. **Rodeo Romeo**	Columbia 02532
3/20/82	21	10	30. Someday Soon	Columbia 02735
7/3/82	4	14	31. **She's Not Really Cheatin' (She's Just Gettin' Even)**	Columbia 02966
11/20/82+	12	12	32. Only If There Is Another You	Columbia 03309
3/26/83	19	8	33. I Still Love You In The Same Ol' Way	Columbia 03625
7/23/83	10	10	34. **Let's Get Over Them Together** **MOE BANDY featuring BECKY HOBBS**	Columbia 03970
12/10/83	34	2	35. You're Gonna Lose Her Like That	Columbia 04204
3/24/84	31	4	36. It Took A Lot Of Drinkin' (To Get That Woman Over Me)	Columbia 04353
6/23/84	8	9	37. **Where's The Dress** (a) [N] parody about Pop singer Boy George of the group Culture Club	Columbia 04477
9/1/84	12	11	38. Woman Your Love	Columbia 04466
11/10/84	36	2	39. The Boy's Night Out (a)	Columbia 04601
3/28/87	6	14	40. **Till I'm Too Old To Die Young**	MCA/Curb 53033
9/5/87	11	11	41. You Haven't Heard The Last Of Me	MCA/Curb 53132
3/5/88	8	11	42. **Americana**	Curb 10504
10/22/88	21	7	43. I Just Can't Say No To You #42 Pop hit for Parker McGee in 1977	Curb 10513
4/15/89	34	2	44. Many Mansions	Curb 10524

BANNON, R.C.

Born Dan Shipley on 5/2/45 in Dallas. Worked with rock and soul bands and as a disc jockey in Seattle. Toured with Marty Robbins in 1973. Moved to Nashville in 1976, worked as a staff writer for Warner Records. Married Louise Mandrell in February 1979; later divorced. Music director for Barbara Mandrell's TV show.

DATE	POS	WKS	ARTIST–RECORD TITLE	LABEL & NO.
2/4/78	33	3	1. It Doesn't Matter Anymore written by Paul Anka; #13 Pop hit for Buddy Holly in 1959	Columbia 10655
6/16/79	13	7	2. Reunited #1 Pop hit for Peaches & Herb in 1979	Epic 50717
10/20/79	26	4	3. Winners And Losers	Columbia 11081
10/18/80	36	2	4. Never Be Anyone Else #6 Pop hit for Ricky Nelson in 1959	Columbia 11346
1/16/82	35	2	5. Where There's Smoke There's Fire	RCA 12359

DATE	POS	WKS	ARTIST–RECORD TITLE	LABEL & NO.
12/25/82	35	2	6. Christmas Is Just A Song For Us This Year [X] **LOUISE MANDRELL & R.C. BANNON** (#2, 5, 6) flip side of Alabama's Christmas single	RCA 13358
			BARBER, Ava	
			Born on 6/28/54 in Knoxville. Singing professionally since age 10. Regular on TV's *The Lawrence Welk Show*, 1974-82.	
3/4/78	14	7	1. Bucket To The South	Ranwood 1083
			BARBER, Glenn	
			Born on 2/2/35 in Hollis, Oklahoma. Raised in Pasadena, Texas.	
9/12/64	27	5	1. Stronger Than Dirt	Starday 676
10/11/69	24	8	2. Kissed By The Rain, Warmed By The Sun	Hickory 1545
2/14/70	28	5	3. She Cheats On Me	Hickory 1557
5/6/72	28	6	4. I'm The Man On Susie's Mind	Hickory 1626
8/19/72	23	10	5. Unexpected Goodbye	Hickory 1645
11/4/78	30	4	6. What's The Name Of That Song?	Century 21 100
1/27/79	27	5	7. Love Songs Just For You	Century 21 101
			BARE, Bobby	
			Born Robert Joseph Bare on 4/7/35 in Ironton, Ohio. Worked with local bands in the early '50s; worked in California and Hawaii in 1953. First recorded for Capitol in 1956. Drafted by the Army in 1958; left a demo tape of "The All American Boy" with Fraternity Records. The song was released erroneously as by Bill Parsons. Wrote songs for the movie *Teenage Millionaire* and acted in the movie *A Distant Trumpet* in 1964. His daughter Cari, heard on "Singin' In The Kitchen," died of heart failure in 1976 at the age of 15. Own TV series in the mid-1980s.	
9/15/62	18	8	1. Shame On Me	RCA 8032
7/6/63	6	18	2. **Detroit City**	RCA 8183
10/26/63+	5	16	3. **500 Miles Away From Home**	RCA 8238
2/8/64	4	16	4. **Miller's Cave**	RCA 8294
11/28/64+	3	16	5. **Four Strong Winds**	RCA 8443
3/20/65	11	11	6. A Dear John Letter **SKEETER DAVIS & BOBBY BARE** #44 Pop hit for Pat Boone in 1960	RCA 8496
4/3/65	30	7	7. Times Are Gettin' Hard	RCA 8509
6/12/65	7	15	8. **It's Alright**	RCA 8571
10/30/65	31	1	9. Just To Satisfy You	RCA 8654
11/27/65+	26	11	10. Talk Me Some Sense	RCA 8699
5/7/66	34	2	11. In The Same Old Way	RCA 8758
6/25/66	5	19	12. **The Streets Of Baltimore**	RCA 8851
10/29/66	5	14	13. **The Game Of Triangles** **BOBBY BARE, NORMA JEAN, LIZ ANDERSON**	RCA 8963
12/10/66	38	3	14. Homesick	RCA 8988
4/1/67	16	9	15. Charleston Railroad Tavern	RCA 9098
6/17/67	14	10	16. Come Kiss Me Love	RCA 9191
11/4/67	15	9	17. The Piney Wood Hills	RCA 9314
3/23/68	15	8	18. Find Out What's Happening	RCA 9450
8/17/68	14	10	19. A Little Bit Later On Down The Line	RCA 9568
11/23/68	16	8	20. The Town That Broke My Heart	RCA 9643

DATE	POS	WKS	ARTIST—RECORD TITLE		LABEL & NO.
3/22/69	**4**	16	21. **(Margie's At) The Lincoln Park Inn**		RCA 0110
8/30/69	**19**	7	22. Which One Will It Be		RCA 0202
11/29/69	**16**	10	23. God Bless America Again		RCA 0264
2/14/70	**22**	4	24. Your Husband, My Wife		RCA 9789
			BOBBY BARE and SKEETER DAVIS		
8/22/70	**3**	12	25. **How I Got To Memphis**		Mercury 73097
1/16/71	**7**	13	26. **Come Sundown**		Mercury 73148
			written by Kris Kristofferson		
6/5/71	**8**	11	27. **Please Don't Tell Me How The Story Ends**		Mercury 73203
4/29/72	**13**	10	28. What Am I Gonna Do		Mercury 73279
9/23/72	**12**	10	29. Sylvia's Mother		Mercury 73317
			#5 Pop hit for Dr. Hook in 1972		
2/3/73	**25**	7	30. I Hate Goodbyes		RCA 0866
5/12/73	**11**	10	31. Ride Me Down Easy		RCA 0918
9/29/73	**30**	6	32. You Know Who		RCA 0063
1/19/74	**2** (2)	11	33. **Daddy What If**	[N]	RCA 0197
			with 5-year-old son, Bobby, Jr.		
6/1/74	**1** (1)	13	34. **Marie Laveau**		RCA 0261
12/28/74+	**29**	6	35. Singin' In The Kitchen	[N]	RCA 10096
			BOBBY BARE and THE FAMILY		
4/19/75	**23**	5	36. Back In Huntsville Again		RCA 10223
8/16/75	**18**	7	37. Alimony		RCA 10318
11/22/75	**29**	6	38. Cowboys And Daddys		RCA 10409
4/10/76	**13**	9	39. The Winner		RCA 10556
8/7/76	**23**	6	40. Put A Little Lovin' On Me		RCA 10718
10/30/76	**17**	7	41. Dropkick Me, Jesus		RCA 10790
2/5/77	**30**	3	42. Vegas		RCA 10852
			BOBBY and JEANNIE BARE		
4/2/77	**21**	9	43. Look Who I'm Cheating On Tonight/		
		9	44. If You Think I'm Crazy Now (You Should Have		
			Seen Me When I Was A Kid)		RCA 10902
5/13/78	**29**	4	45. Too Many Nights Alone		Columbia 10690
10/21/78	**11**	9	46. Sleep Tight, Good Night Man		Columbia 10831
2/10/79	**23**	7	47. Healin'		Columbia 10891
9/22/79	**17**	7	48. No Memories Hangin' Round		Columbia 11045
			ROSANNE CASH with BOBBY BARE		
2/2/80	**11**	7	49. Numbers	[N]	Columbia 11170
5/31/80	**31**	5	50. Tequila Sheila		Columbia 11259
1/17/81	**19**	5	51. Willie Jones		Columbia 11408
			Charlie Daniels (backing vocal, fiddle)		
5/23/81	**28**	6	52. Learning To Live Again		Columbia 02038
9/5/81	**28**	4	53. Take Me As I Am (Or Let Me Go)		Columbia 02414
12/5/81	**35**	3	54. Dropping Out Of Sight		Columbia 02577
2/20/82	**18**	9	55. New Cut Road		Columbia 02690
6/26/82	**31**	3	56. If You Ain't Got Nothin' (You Ain't Got Nothin'		
			To Lose)		Columbia 02895
10/2/82	**37**	2	57. (I'm Not) A Candle In The Wind		Columbia 03149
4/9/83	**30**	5	58. It's A Dirty Job		Columbia 03628
			BOBBY BARE & LACY J. DALTON		
7/2/83	**29**	5	59. The Jogger	[N]	Columbia 03809

DATE	POS	WKS	ARTIST—RECORD TITLE	LABEL & NO.
			BAREFOOT JERRY—see McCOY, Charlie	
			BARLOW, Jack	
			Born Jack Butcher in Muscatine, Iowa. Worked as a DJ on WQUA-Moline and WIRE-Indianapolis. Staff writer for Tree Music. Also recorded as Zoot Fenster.	
11/9/68	40	1	1. Baby, Ain't That Love	Dot 17139
12/4/71+	26	8	2. Catch The Wind	Dot 17396
12/13/75	30	4	3. The Man On Page 602 [N]	Antique 106
			ZOOT FENSTER	
			title refers to a revealing photo in a Sear's catalog	
			BARLOW, Randy	
			Singer from Detroit. Worked as emcee with Dick Clark's Caravan Of Stars. Settled in Los Angeles in 1965, worked local clubs.	
12/25/76+	18	9	1. Twenty-Four Hours From Tulsa	Gazelle 330
			#10 Pop hit for Gene Pitney in 1963	
4/16/77	26	6	2. Kentucky Woman	Gazelle 381
			#22 Pop hit for Neil Diamond in 1967	
7/23/77	31	4	3. California Lady	Gazelle 413
4/29/78	10	9	4. **Slow And Easy**	Republic 017
8/26/78	10	10	5. **No Sleep Tonight**	Republic 024
1/6/79	10	8	6. **Fall In Love With Me Tonight**	Republic 034
4/14/79	10	9	7. **Sweet Melinda**	Republic 039
9/1/79	25	5	8. Another Easy Lovin' Night	Republic 044
11/17/79+	13	9	9. Lay Back In The Arms Of Someone	Republic 049
2/7/81	25	5	10. Dixie Man	Paid 116
5/9/81	13	10	11. Love Dies Hard	Paid 133
10/10/81	32	3	12. Try Me	Paid 144
1/30/82	30	4	13. Love Was Born	Jamex 002
			BARNES, Benny	
			Born Ben M. Barnes, Jr., in Beaumont, Texas. Also recorded as Hank Smith.	
9/29/56	2 (1)	17	1. **Poor Man's Riches**	Starday 262
			Juke Box #2 / Jockey #8 / Best Seller #15	
6/12/61	22	4	2. Yearning	Mercury 71806
			BARNES, Kathy	
			Born in Henderson, Kentucky; singing since age seven. Sang in duo with brother Larry, and later worked with Gene Autry. Went solo in 1975. In 1978, she had two R&B-style records that made *Billboard's Hot Soul Singles* chart.	
10/30/76	39	3	1. Someday Soon	Republic 293
2/12/77	37	3	2. Good 'N' Country	Republic 338
			BARNETT, Bobby	
			Born on 2/15/36 in Cushing, Oklahoma.	
10/10/60	24	1	1. This Old Heart	Razorback 306
9/21/68	14	8	2. Love Me, Love Me	Columbia 44589

DATE	POS	WKS	ARTIST—RECORD TITLE	LABEL & NO.
			BAUGH, Phil	
			Born in Olivehurst, California. Died on 11/4/90 (age 53). Session guitarist; moved to Nashville in 1975. Worked in the Nashville Superpickers. Once owned Soundwaves Records.	
7/3/65	**16**	11	1. Country Guitar [N] Vern Stovall (vocal)	Longhorn 559
11/20/65	**27**	5	2. One Man Band [N]	Longhorn 563
			BAXTER, Les—see WAKELY, Jimmy	
			BEAVERS, Clyde	
			Born on 6/8/32 in Tennega, Georgia. Worked as a DJ in Atlanta during the mid-1950s.	
10/24/60	**13**	15	1. Here I Am Drunk Again	Decca 31173
3/16/63	**27**	2	2. Still Loving You	Tempwood 1039
8/3/63	**21**	1	3. Sukiyaki (I Look Up When I Walk) #1 Pop hit for Kyu Sakamoto in 1963	Tempwood 1044
			BEE GEES	
			Pop trio of brothers from Manchester, England: Barry (b: 9/1/47) and twins Robin and Maurice Gibb (b: 12/22/49). Extremely popular disco artists of the 1970s.	
1/13/79	**39**	2	1. Rest Your Love On Me flip side "Too Much Heaven" made #1 on the *Hot 100*	RSO 913
			BELEW, Carl	
			Born on 4/21/31 in Salina, Oklahoma. Died on 10/31/90. Worked on *Louisiana Hayride* in the early 1950s. Wrote hits "Lonely Street" for Andy Williams, "Stop The World" for Johnnie & Jack, and "What's He Doing In My World" for Eddy Arnold.	
4/6/59	**9**	20	1. **Am I That Easy To Forget** #25 Pop hit for Debbie Reynolds in 1960	Decca 30842
6/13/60	**19**	15	2. Too Much To Lose	Decca 31086
9/29/62	**8**	12	3. **Hello Out There**	RCA 8058
10/10/64	**23**	11	4. In The Middle Of A Memory	RCA 8406
9/11/65	**12**	13	5. Crystal Chandelier	RCA 8633
			BELLAMY BROTHERS	
			Duo from Darby, Florida: brothers Howard (born 2/2/46; guitar) and David Bellamy (born 9/16/50; guitar, keyboards). Made their professional debut in 1958. David played with the Accidents and wrote "Spiders And Snakes" for Jim Stafford. Both worked in the band Jericho, 1968-71.	
4/17/76	**21**	6	1. Let Your Love Flow	Warner/Curb 8169
5/20/78	**19**	6	2. Slippin' Away	Warner/Curb 8558
12/9/78+	**16**	9	3. Lovin' On	Warner/Curb 8692
4/7/79	**1** (3)	10	4. **If I Said You Have A Beautiful Body Would You Hold It Against Me**	Warner/Curb 8790
9/1/79	**5**	9	5. **You Ain't Just Whistlin' Dixie**	Warner/Curb 49032
2/9/80	**1** (1)	11	6. **Sugar Daddy**	Warner/Curb 49160
5/31/80	**1** (1)	14	7. **Dancin' Cowboys**	Warner/Curb 49241
10/18/80	**3**	13	8. **Lovers Live Longer**	Warner/Curb 49573
1/24/81	**1** (1)	9	9. **Do You Love As Good As You Look**	Warner/Curb 49639

DATE	POS	WKS	ARTIST-RECORD TITLE	LABEL & NO.
6/13/81	12	8	10. They Could Put Me In Jail	Warner/Curb 49729
10/17/81	7	13	11. **You're My Favorite Star**	Warner/Curb 49815
4/10/82	**1 (1)**	12	12. **For All The Wrong Reasons**	Elektra/Curb 47431
8/7/82	21	7	13. Get Into Reggae Cowboy	Elektra/Curb 69999
10/16/82	**1 (1)**	12	14. **Redneck Girl**	Warner/Curb 29923
1/29/83	**1 (1)**	12	15. **When I'm Away From You**	Elektra/Curb 69850
6/11/83	4	11	16. **I Love Her Mind**	Warner/Curb 29645
10/8/83	15	8	17. Strong Weakness	Warner/Curb 29514
6/16/84	5	12	18. **Forget About Me**	Curb 52380
10/13/84	6	13	19. **World's Greatest Lover**	Curb 52446
2/9/85	**1 (1)**	14	20. **I Need More Of You**	Curb 52518
5/25/85	**2 (2)**	14	21. **Old Hippie**	Curb 52579
10/5/85	**2 (1)**	14	22. **Lie To You For Your Love**	Curb 52668
2/22/86	**2 (1)**	13	23. **Feelin' The Feelin'**	Curb 52747
10/4/86	**1 (1)**	15	24. **Too Much Is Not Enough**	Curb 52917
			THE BELLAMY BROTHERS with THE FORESTER SISTERS	
1/31/87	**1 (1)**	14	25. **Kids Of The Baby Boom**	Curb 53018
5/30/87	31	3	26. Country Rap	Curb 52834
8/29/87	3	14	27. **Crazy From The Heart**	Curb/MCA 53154
1/30/88	5	12	28. **Santa Fe**	Curb/MCA 53222
6/4/88	6	12	29. **I'll Give You All My Love Tonight**	Curb/MCA 53310
10/1/88	9	11	30. **Rebels Without A Clue**	Curb/MCA 53399
2/4/89	5	11	31. **Big Love**	Curb/MCA 53478
8/5/89	10	13	32. **You'll Never Be Sorry**	Curb/MCA 53672
12/23/89	37	3	33. The Center Of My Universe	Curb/MCA 53719
7/28/90	7	14	34. **I Could Be Persuaded**	Curb/MCA 79019
7/18/92	23	8	35. Cowboy Beat	Bellamy Br. LP Cut
			from the album *The Latest And The Greatest* on Bellamy Br. 9108	

BENEDICT, Ernie, and His Polkateers

DATE	POS	WKS	ARTIST-RECORD TITLE	LABEL & NO.
10/8/49	15	1	1. Over Three Hills	RCA Victor 3389
			Juke Box #15; The Kendall Sisters (vocals)	

BENTLEY, Stephanie

DATE	POS	WKS	ARTIST-RECORD TITLE	LABEL & NO.
12/16/95+	21	9	1. Heart Half Empty	Epic 78073
			TY HERNDON featuring Stephanie Bentley	
4/6/96	32	5	2. Who's That Girl	Epic 78234

BENTON, Barbi

Born Barbara Klein on 1/28/50 in Sacramento, California. Ex-Playboy model.

DATE	POS	WKS	ARTIST-RECORD TITLE	LABEL & NO.
4/12/75	5	9	1. **Brass Buckles**	Playboy 6032
11/15/75	32	4	2. Roll You Like A Wheel	Playboy 6045
			MICKEY GILLEY & BARBI BENTON	

DATE	POS	WKS	ARTIST–RECORD TITLE	LABEL & NO.
			BERG, Matraca	
			First name pronounced: Muh-TRAY-suh. Born on 2/3/64 in Nashville. Her mother was the late Nashville session singer/songwriter Icee Berg. Matraca wrote Reba McEntire's "The Last One To Know" and co-wrote with Bobby Braddock "Faking Love" for T.G. Sheppard & Karen Brooks.	
7/14/90	36	3	1. Baby, Walk On	RCA 2504
11/3/90	36	2	2. The Things You Left Undone	RCA 2644
			BERRY, John	
			Born in South Carolina and raised in Atlanta. Underwent surgery for drainage of a benign cyst in his brain on 5/17/94.	
11/20/93	22	7	1. Kiss Me In The Car	Liberty 17518
3/19/94	1 (1)	15	2. **Your Love Amazes Me**	Liberty LP Cut
7/23/94	5	14	3. **What's In It For Me**	Liberty 58212
11/26/94+	4	14	4. **You And Only You**	Liberty 18137
			all of above from the album *John Berry* on Liberty 80472	
4/1/95	2 (1)	16	5. **Standing On The Edge Of Goodbye**	Patriot 18401
7/22/95	4	14	6. **I Think About It All The Time**	Patriot LP Cut
11/18/95	25	11	7. If I Had Any Pride Left At All	Capitol 18843
3/9/96	34	6	8. Every Time My Heart Calls Your Name	Capitol LP Cut
			above 4 from the album *Standing On The Edge* on Patriot 28495	
			BILLY HILL	
			Nashville-based band made up of sessionmen/songwriters Dennis Robbins (vocals), Bob DiPiero, John Scott Sherrill, Reno Kling and Martin Parker. Namesake of band was a reclusive drifter that the band members claimed to know. DiPiero is married to Pam Tillis.	
8/19/89	25	6	1. Too Much Month At The End Of The Money	Reprise 22942
			BLACK('S), Bill, Combo	
			Black was born on 9/17/26 in Memphis. Died of a brain tumor on 10/21/65. Bass guitarist. Backed Elvis Presley (with Scotty Moore, guitar; D.J. Fontana, drums) on most of his early records. Formed own band in 1959. Labeled "The Untouchable Sound." Group led by Bob Tucker in the 1970s.	
5/24/75	29	4	1. Boilin' Cabbage [I]	Hi 2283
			BLACK, Clint	
			Born Clint Patrick Black on 2/4/62 in Long Branch, New Jersey; raised in Houston. Former construction worker. Married actress Lisa Hartman (TV's *Knot's Landing, Tabitha*) on 10/20/91. Joined the *Grand Ole Opry* in 1991. CMA Awards: 1989 Horizon Award; 1990 Male Vocalist of the Year.	
3/25/89	1 (1)	15	1. **Better Man**	RCA 8781
7/29/89	1 (1)	14	2. **Killin' Time**	RCA 8945
11/25/89+	1 (3)	23	3. **Nobody's Home**	RCA 9078
3/31/90	1 (2)	18	4. **Walkin' Away**	RCA 2520
7/7/90	3	21	5. **Nothing's News**	RCA 2596
11/3/90	4	13	6. **Put Yourself In My Shoes**	RCA 2678
2/2/91	1 (2)	19	7. **Loving Blind**	RCA 2749
4/27/91	7	13	8. **One More Payment**	RCA 2819
8/10/91	1 (2)	18	9. **Where Are You Now**	RCA 62016
6/27/92	2 (2)	19	10. **We Tell Ourselves**	RCA 62194

DATE	POS	WKS	ARTIST–RECORD TITLE	LABEL & NO.
10/24/92	**4**	16	11. **Burn One Down**	RCA 62337
2/6/93	**1** (2)	16	12. **When My Ship Comes In**	RCA 62429
5/22/93	**2** (1)	15	13. **A Bad Goodbye**	RCA 62503
			CLINT BLACK (with Wynonna)	
8/21/93	**3**	18	14. **No Time To Kill**	RCA 62609
11/27/93+	**2** (2)	19	15. **State Of Mind**	RCA 62700
3/19/94	**1** (1)	18	16. **A Good Run Of Bad Luck**	RCA 62762
7/2/94	**4**	13	17. **Half The Man**	RCA 62878
10/8/94	**4**	15	18. **Untanglin' My Mind**	RCA 62933
1/21/95	**3**	16	19. **Wherever You Go**	RCA 64267
4/15/95	**1** (3)	18	20. **Summer's Comin'**	RCA 64281
7/22/95	**2** (2)	15	21. **One Emotion**	RCA 64381
10/28/95	**4**	18	22. **Life Gets Away**	RCA 64442

BLACK, Jeanne

Born Gloria Jeanne Black on 10/25/37 in Pomona, California.

DATE	POS	WKS	ARTIST–RECORD TITLE	LABEL & NO.
5/2/60	**6**	12	● 1. **He'll Have To Stay**	Capitol 4368
			answer song to "He'll Have To Go" by Jim Reeves	

BLACKHAWK

Trio of music veterans Henry Paul (member of Southern-rock bands The Outlaws and Henry Paul Band) with the songwriting team of Dave Robbins and Van Stephenson (hit pop charts with rock songs in early '80s). Robbins and Stephenson co-wrote several Restless Heart hits.

DATE	POS	WKS	ARTIST–RECORD TITLE	LABEL & NO.
1/8/94	**11**	13	1. **Goodbye Says It All**	Arista 12568
5/7/94	**2** (1)	17	2. **Every Once In A While**	Arista 12668
9/3/94	**9**	15	3. **I Sure Can Smell The Rain**	Arista 12718
1/21/95	**10**	12	4. **Down In Flames**	Arista 12769
5/13/95	**7**	16	5. **That's Just About Right**	Arista 12813
8/26/95	**2** (2)	16	6. **I'm Not Strong Enough To Say No**	Arista 12857
12/9/95+	**3**	16	7. **Like There Ain't No Yesterday**	Arista 12897
3/16/96	**11**	15	8. **Almost A Memory Now**	Arista 12975

BLACKWOOD, R.W., and The Blackwood Singers

Born in Memphis. Member of the Blackwood Boys gospel group.

DATE	POS	WKS	ARTIST–RECORD TITLE	LABEL & NO.
9/4/76	**32**	4	1. **Sunday Afternoon Boatride In The Park On The Lake**	Capitol 4302

BLANCH, Jewel

Born Jewel Evelyn Blanch. Singer/actress from Australia. Daughter of Berice and Arthur Blanch; member of family group. Appeared in the 1975 movie *Against A Crooked Sky*.

DATE	POS	WKS	ARTIST–RECORD TITLE	LABEL & NO.
3/24/79	**33**	4	1. **Can I See You Tonight**	RCA 11464

BLANCHARD, Jack, & Misty Morgan

Husband-and-wife team. Both born in Buffalo. Jack (born 5/8/42) plays saxophone and keyboards. Misty (born 5/23/45) plays keyboards. Met and married while working in Florida.

DATE	POS	WKS	ARTIST–RECORD TITLE	LABEL & NO.
2/14/70	**1** (2)	16	1. **Tennessee Bird Walk** [N]	Wayside 010
7/4/70	**5**	11	2. **Humphrey The Camel** [N]	Wayside 013

DATE	POS	WKS	ARTIST–RECORD TITLE	LABEL & NO.
10/24/70	27	4	3. You've Got Your Troubles (I've Got Mine) #7 Pop hit for The Fortunes in 1965	Wayside 015
8/21/71	25	9	4. There Must Be More To Life (Than Growing Old)	Mega 0031
11/27/71+	15	10	5. Somewhere In Virginia In The Rain	Mega 0046
5/6/72	38	2	6. The Legendary Chicken Fairy [N]	Mega 0063
1/5/74	23	7	7. Just One More Song	Epic 11058

BOGGUSS, Suzy

Born Susan Kay Bogguss on 12/30/56 in Aledo, Illinois. Earned a metalsmithery degree at Illinois State University. Married to songwriter/engineer Doug Crider. CMA Award: 1992 Horizon Award.

DATE	POS	WKS	ARTIST–RECORD TITLE	LABEL & NO.
7/15/89	14	13	1. Cross My Broken Heart	Capitol 44399
11/25/89	38	1	2. My Sweet Love Ain't Around	Capitol 79788
6/29/91	12	13	3. Hopelessly Yours **LEE GREENWOOD with Suzy Bogguss** from Greenwood's album *A Perfect 10* on Capitol 95541; later available as the B-side of #6 below	Capitol LP Cut
10/5/91	12	16	4. Someday Soon	Capitol 44772
2/1/92	9	12	5. **Outbound Plane**	Capitol 57753
5/9/92	9	15	6. **Aces**	Liberty 57764
9/5/92	6	14	7. **Letting Go**	Liberty 57801
12/19/92+	2 (1)	16	8. **Drive South** written by John Hiatt	Liberty 56786
4/24/93	23	8	9. Heartache	Liberty 56972
9/4/93	5	15	10. **Just Like The Weather**	Liberty 17495
12/25/93+	5	13	11. **Hey Cinderella**	Liberty 17641

BONAMY, James

Singer from Winter Park, Florida.

DATE	POS	WKS	ARTIST–RECORD TITLE	LABEL & NO.
3/2/96	26	7	1. She's Got A Mind Of Her Own	Epic 78220

BOND, Johnny

Born Cyrus Whitfield Bond on 6/1/15 in Enville, Oklahoma. Died of a heart attack on 6/12/78. Singer/songwriter/actor/author; worked on radio from age 19. Appeared with Jimmy Wakely in 1937 and joined *Gene Autry's Melody Ranch* in 1940. Appeared in many movies, including *Wilson, Gallant Bess* and *Duel In The Sun*. Worked *Town Hall Party* TV shows from Compton, California. Wrote the books *Reflections* (his autobiography) and *The Tex Ritter Story*. Famous for his novelty recordings about drunkenness.

DATE	POS	WKS	ARTIST–RECORD TITLE	LABEL & NO.
2/22/47	4	1	1. **Divorce Me C.O.D.**	Columbia 37217
3/8/47	3	5	2. **So Round, So Firm, So Fully Packed**	Columbia 37255
8/16/47	4	3	3. **The Daughter Of Jole Blon** **JOHNNY BOND and his Red River Valley Boys (above 3)**	Columbia 37566
6/12/48	9	6	4. Oklahoma Waltz Juke Box #9; Dick Reinhart (backing vocal)	Columbia 38160
4/9/49	12	2	5. Till The End Of The World Juke Box #12	Columbia 20549
7/23/49	11	1	6. Tennessee Saturday Night Juke Box #11	Columbia 20545
4/15/50	8	2	7. **Love Song In 32 Bars** **JOHNNY BOND and his Red River Valley Boys** Juke Box #8	Columbia 20671

DATE	POS	WKS	ARTIST-RECORD TITLE	LABEL & NO.
8/4/51	7	3	8. **Sick, Sober And Sorry** Juke Box #7	Columbia 20808
11/2/63	30	1	9. Three Sheets In The Wind	Starday 649
2/20/65	2 (4)	18	10. **10 Little Bottles** [N-R] originally released by Bond on Columbia 21222 in 1954	Starday 704

BONNIE LOU

Born Bonnie Lou Kath on 10/27/24 in Talawanda, Illinois. Worked on radio KMBC-Kansas City and WLW-Cincinnati. On *Midwestern Hayride* for over 20 years.

DATE	POS	WKS	ARTIST-RECORD TITLE	LABEL & NO.
5/9/53	7	5	1. **Seven Lonely Days** Jockey #7 / Best Seller #8 / Juke Box #9; #5 Pop hit for Georgia Gibbs in 1953	King 1192
9/19/53	6	9	2. **Tennessee Wig Walk** Best Seller #6 / Juke Box #6	King 1237

BONSALL, "Cat" Joe—see SAWYER BROWN

BOONE, Debby

Born on 9/22/56 in Hackensack, New Jersey. Third daughter of Shirley and Pat Boone and granddaughter of Red Foley. Worked with the Boone Family from 1969, sang with sisters in the Boones' gospel quartet. Went solo in 1977. Winner of three Grammys including Best New Artist of 1977. Popular Contemporary Christian artist. Married Gabriel Ferrer, son of Rosemary Clooney and Jose Ferrer, in 1982.

DATE	POS	WKS	ARTIST-RECORD TITLE	LABEL & NO.
11/5/77	4	10	▲ 1. **You Light Up My Life** title song from the movie starring Didi Conn; originally released on Warner 8446	Warner/Curb 8455
5/27/78	22	5	2. God Knows/	
5/27/78	33	5	3. Baby, I'm Yours	Warner/Curb 8554
2/3/79	11	8	4. My Heart Has A Mind Of Its Own #1 Pop hit for Connie Francis in 1960	Warner/Curb 8739
6/16/79	25	5	5. Breakin' In A Brand New Broken Heart #7 Pop hit for Connie Francis in 1961	Warner/Curb 8814
3/8/80	1 (1)	10	6. **Are You On The Road To Lovin' Me Again**	Warner/Curb 49176
8/16/80	14	7	7. Free To Be Lonely Again	Warner/Curb 49281
2/21/81	23	6	8. Perfect Fool	Warner/Curb 49652

BOONE, Larry

Born on 6/7/56 in Cooper City, Florida. Former substitute teacher. Wrote Don Williams' "Old Coyote Town."

DATE	POS	WKS	ARTIST-RECORD TITLE	LABEL & NO.
7/16/88	10	12	1. **Don't Give Candy To A Stranger**	Mercury 870454
12/17/88+	16	11	2. I Just Called To Say Goodbye Again	Mercury 872046
4/22/89	19	7	3. Wine Me Up	Mercury 872728
8/12/89	39	1	4. Fool's Paradise	Mercury 874538
7/27/91	34	4	5. To Be With You	Columbia 73813

BOONE, Pat

Born Charles Eugene Boone on 6/1/34 in Jacksonville, Florida. Married Red Foley's daughter, Shirley, in 1954. His pop chart success during the '50s was eclipsed only by Elvis Presley.

DATE	POS	WKS	ARTIST-RECORD TITLE	LABEL & NO.
8/21/76	34	3	1. Texas Woman	Hitsville 6037

DATE	POS	WKS	ARTIST—RECORD TITLE	LABEL & NO.
			BOOTH, Tony	
			Born on 2/7/43 in Tampa, Florida. Leader of Gene Watson's Farewell Party Band. Larry Booth is his brother.	
4/22/72	15	10	1. The Key's In The Mailbox	Capitol 3269
7/15/72	18	9	2. A Whole Lot Of Somethin'	Capitol 3356
10/21/72	16	10	3. Lonesome 7-7203	Capitol 3441
2/24/73	32	6	4. When A Man Loves A Woman (The Way That I Love You)	Capitol 3515
10/5/74	27	7	5. Workin' At The Car Wash Blues	Capitol 3943
			#32 Pop hit for Jim Croce in 1976	
			BORCHERS, Bobby	
			Born in Cincinnati; raised in Kentucky. Singer/songwriter.	
4/3/76	29	4	1. Someone's With Your Wife Tonight, Mister	Playboy 6065
9/11/76	32	5	2. They Don't Make 'Em Like That Anymore	Playboy 6083
1/8/77	12	9	3. Whispers	Playboy 6092
5/28/77	7	11	4. **Cheap Perfume And Candlelight**	Playboy 5803
9/17/77	18	7	5. What A Way To Go	Playboy 5816
1/7/78	18	6	6. I Promised Her A Rainbow	Playboy 5823
4/29/78	23	5	7. I Like Ladies In Long Black Dresses	Playboy 5827
9/2/78	20	6	8. Sweet Fantasy	Epic 50585
2/3/79	32	3	9. Wishing I Had Listened To Your Song	Epic 50650
			BOUCHER, Jessica—see STAMPLEY, Joe	
			BOWES, Margie	
			Born on 3/18/41 in Roxboro, North Carolina. Appeared on local radio beginning at age 13. Worked on the *Virginia Barn Dance*. With the *Grand Ole Opry* from 1958. Appeared on *Jubilee USA* TV series on ABC. In the movie *Gold Guitar*. Married for a time to Doyle Wilburn (Wilburn Brothers).	
3/23/59	10	16	1. **Poor Old Heartsick Me**	Hickory 1094
8/31/59	15	14	2. My Love And Little Me	Hickory 1102
			written by Phil Everly	
7/24/61	21	6	3. Little Miss Belong To No One	Mercury 71845
1/18/64	33	2	4. Our Things	Decca 31557
6/6/64	26	5	5. Understand Your Gal	Decca 31606
			answer song to "Understand Your Man" by Johnny Cash	
			BOWLING, Roger	
			Born in Harlan, Kentucky. Died on 12/26/82 (age 38). Wrote "Lucille" for Kenny Rogers and "Blanket On The Ground" for Billie Jo Spears.	
1/24/81	30	4	1. Yellow Pages	NSD 71
			later released on Mercury 57042	
			BOWMAN, Don	
			Born on 8/26/37 in Lubbock, Texas. Worked as a DJ, then with Waylon Jennings in local clubs. Discovered by Chet Atkins. Original host of radio's *American Country Countdown*.	
7/25/64	14	15	1. Chit Akins, Make Me A Star [N]	RCA 8384

DATE	POS	WKS	ARTIST–RECORD TITLE	LABEL & NO.
			BOXCAR WILLIE	
5/1/82	36	3	Born Lecil Travis Martin on 9/1/31 in Sterratt, Texas. Sang on local radio beginning at age 10, then worked as a DJ. Re-entered music in 1975 and scored a big success at the Wembly Festival Of Country Music in England in 1979. Joined the *Grand Ole Opry* in 1981. 1. Bad News	Main Street 951
			BOYD, Bill, & His Cowboy Ramblers	

9/8/45
8/24/46
	4
	5
		2
		1
			Born on 9/29/10 in Fannin County, Texas. Died on 12/7/77. Singer/actor. Own band with his brother Jim in the '20s, which became the Cowboy Ramblers and recorded for Bluebird in 1934. Own radio show on WRR-Dallas from 1932 into the '60s. Not to be confused with William "Hopalong Cassidy" Boyd.
			   1. **Shame On You**
			   2. **New Steel Guitar Rag**
				Bluebird 33-0530
				Victor 20-1907

			BOYD, Jimmy	
12/20/52	7	3	Born on 1/9/40 in McComb, Mississippi. "I Saw Mommy Kissing Santa Claus" sold 250,000 copies in one day. Portrayed Howard Meechim in TV's *Bachelor Father*, 1958-61. ● 1. **I Saw Mommy Kissing Santa Claus** [X-N] Jockey #7 / Juke Box #7	Columbia 39871
			BOY HOWDY	

7/31/93
 	
12/4/93+
 	
5/7/94
 	
1/28/95
	12
	
	4
	
	2 (1)
	
	23
		10
		
		16
		
		15
		
		9
			Four-man band formed in Los Angeles: vocalist/bassist Jeffrey Steele, guitarists Cary and Larry Park, and drummer Hugh Wright (seriously injured in 1992 after assisting at the scene of a car crash). The Parks are the sons of noted bluegrass fiddler Ray Park.
			   1. A Cowboy's Born With A Broken Heart
			     from the album *Welcome To Howdywood* on Curb 77562
			   2. **She'd Give Anything**
			     #28 Pop hit for Gerald Levert in 1994 ("I'd Give Anything")
			   3. **They Don't Make 'Em Like That Anymore**
			     above 2 from the album *She'd Give Anything* on Curb 77656
			   4. True To His Word
				Curb LP Cut
				
				Curb LP Cut
				
				Curb LP Cut
				
				Curb 76934

			BRADLEY, Owen, Quintet	

12/3/49+	7	4	Born on 10/21/15 in Westmoreland, Tennessee. Music director at WSM-Nashville, 1940-58. Leader of popular dance band; Nashville producer for Decca from 1947. Country A&R director for Decca, 1958-68. Vice president of MCA from 1968. Elected to the Country Music Hall of Fame in 1974.
			   1. **Blues Stay Away From Me**
			     Jockey #7 / Juke Box #8 / Best Seller #9; Jack Shook and Dottie Dillard (vocals); #36 Pop hit for Ace Cannon in 1962
				Coral 60107

			BRADSHAW, Carolyn	
8/22/53	10	1	1. **Marriage Of Mexican Joe** Juke Box #10; follow-up song to Jim Reeves's "Mexican Joe"	Abbott 141

DATE	POS	WKS	ARTIST–RECORD TITLE	LABEL & NO.
			BRADSHAW, Terry	
			Born on 9/2/48 in Shreveport, Louisiana. Pro football quarterback with the Pittsburgh Steelers, 1970-83. Appeared in the movies *Hooper, Smokey and the Bandit II* and *Cannonball Run*.	
3/6/76	17	8	1. I'm So Lonesome I Could Cry written by Hank Williams in 1949	Mercury 73760
			BRANDT, Paul	
			Born and raised in Calgary, Alberta, Canada. Singer/songwriter.	
4/27/96	5↑	13↑	1. My Heart Has A History	Reprise 17683
			BRANNON, Kippi	
			Born Kippi Brinkley in Nashville; 15 years old in 1981. Female singer.	
11/7/81	37	2	1. Slowly	MCA 51166
			BRENNAN, Walter	
			Born on 7/25/1894 in Swampscott, Massachusetts. Died on 9/21/74. Beloved character actor. First movie role in 1924. Three-time Oscar winner. Played Grandpa on *The Real McCoys* TV series.	
5/5/62	3	13	1. **Old Rivers** [S]	Liberty 55436
			BRESH, Tom	
			Singer/actor born in Hollywood. Worked as a stuntman as a child. Performed with Hank Penny in the early '60s. Appeared on the TV shows *Gunsmoke* and *Cheyenne*; and in the stage shows *Finian's Rainbow, Harvey* and *The Music Man*. Own TV series, *Nashville Swing*, in Canada. Moved to Nashville in 1983.	
5/22/76	6	10	1. **Home Made Love**	Farr 004
9/4/76	17	7	2. Sad Country Love Song	Farr 009
12/25/76+	33	4	3. Hey Daisy (Where Have All The Good Times Gone)	Farr 012
			BRITT, Elton	
			Born James Britt Baker on 6/27/17 in Marshall, Arkansas. Died on 6/23/72. Raised in Oklahoma; moved to Los Angeles in 1932 and began a radio series. Recorded with The Beverly Hillbillies. Appeared in the movies *Laramie, The Last Doggie* and *The Prodigal Son*. His 1942 hit "There's A Star-Spangled Banner Waving Somewhere" was one of the biggest-selling Country records up to that time.	
1/27/45	7	1	1. **I'm A Convict With Old Glory In My Heart**	Bluebird 33-0517
1/26/46	2 (5)	18	2. **Someday**	Bluebird 33-0521
3/16/46	3	9	3. **Wave To Me, My Lady/**	
4/13/46	4	1	4. **Blueberry Lane**	Victor 20-1789
5/11/46	5	1	5. **Detour**	Victor 20-1817
7/27/46	6	1	6. **Blue Texas Moonlight**	Victor 20-1873
			ELTON BRITT & THE SKYTOPPERS	
8/24/46	4	1	7. **Gotta Get Together With My Gal**	Victor 20-1927
10/30/48	6	6	8. **Chime Bells**	Victor 20-3090
			Best Seller #6 / Juke Box #12; 45 rpm: 48-0143	
3/19/49	4	12	9. **Candy Kisses**	RCA Victor 0006
			ELTON BRITT & THE SKYTOPPERS (above 2) Best Seller #4 / Juke Box #12	

DATE	POS	WKS	ARTIST–RECORD TITLE	LABEL & NO.
2/4/50	7	4	10. **Beyond The Sunset** **THE THREE SUNS with ROSALIE ALLEN and ELTON BRITT** Jockey #7; 45 rpm: 47-3105	RCA Victor 3599
2/25/50	3	10	11. **Quicksilver** **ELTON BRITT and ROSALIE ALLEN with The Skytoppers** Jockey #3 / Juke Box #6 / Best Seller #9; 45 rpm: 48-0168	RCA Victor 0157
6/1/68	26	6	12. The Jimmie Rodgers Blues	RCA 9503

BRODY, Lane

Born Eleni Connie Voorlas in Oak Park, Illinois; raised in Racine, Wisconsin. Played guitar from age 12, worked in local bands while a teenager. Had her own band, Sargasso, while attending the University of Wisconsin. Moved to Los Angeles in 1977. Appeared on *Taxi* TV series in 1979. Moved to Nashville in 1983. Acted in *Heart Of The City* TV series.

DATE	POS	WKS	ARTIST–RECORD TITLE	LABEL & NO.
7/2/83	15	9	1. **Over You** from the movie *Tender Mercies* starring Robert Duvall	Liberty 1498
2/25/84	1 (1)	12	2. **The Yellow Rose** **JOHNNY LEE with LANE BRODY** theme from the TV series starring Cybill Shepherd	Warner 29375
6/22/85	29	5	3. He Burns Me Up	EMI America 8266

BROOKS, Garth

Born Troyal Garth Brooks on 2/7/62 in Luba, Oklahoma; raised in Yukon, Oklahoma. Attended Oklahoma State on a track scholarship (javelin). His mother, Colleen Carroll, recorded with Capitol in 1954 and was a regular on Red Foley's *Ozark Jubilee* TV show. Joined the *Grand Ole Opry* in 1990. CMA Awards: 1990 Horizon Award; 1991 and 1992 Entertainer of the Year.

DATE	POS	WKS	ARTIST–RECORD TITLE	LABEL & NO.
5/13/89	8	14	1. **Much Too Young (To Feel This Damn Old)**	Capitol 44342
9/23/89	1 (1)	23	2. **If Tomorrow Never Comes**	Capitol 44430
2/3/90	2 (1)	17	3. **Not Counting You**	Capitol 44492
5/26/90	1 (3)	18	4. **The Dance**	Capitol 44629
8/25/90	1 (4)	19	5. **Friends In Low Places** CMA Award: Single of the Year	Capitol 44647
11/10/90+	1 (2)	19	6. **Unanswered Prayers**	Capitol 44650
2/16/91	1 (1)	19	7. **Two Of A Kind, Workin' On A Full House**	Capitol 44701
5/18/91	1 (2)	16	8. **The Thunder Rolls**	Capitol 44727
8/17/91	3	13	9. **Rodeo**	Capitol 44771
10/19/91	1 (2)	20	10. **Shameless** written by Billy Joel	Capitol 44800
1/11/92	1 (4)	19	11. **What She's Doing Now**	Liberty 57733
3/28/92	3	14	12. **Papa Loved Mama**	Liberty 57734
6/13/92	1 (1)	14	13. **The River**	Liberty 57765
9/12/92	12	10	14. We Shall Be Free inspired by the verdict in the Rodney King case	Liberty 57994
11/21/92+	1 (1)	14	15. **Somewhere Other Than The Night**	Liberty 56824
2/13/93	2 (1)	14	16. **Learning To Live Again**	Liberty 56973
5/15/93	1 (1)	16	17. **That Summer**	Liberty 17324
8/7/93	1 (2)	17	18. **Ain't Going Down (Til The Sun Comes Up)**	Liberty 17496
10/23/93	1 (1)	14	19. **American Honky-Tonk Bar Association**	Liberty 17639
1/29/94	3	14	20. **Standing Outside The Fire**	Liberty 17802
5/21/94	7	12	21. **One Night A Day**	Liberty 17972
8/20/94	2 (1)	13	22. **Callin' Baton Rouge**	Liberty 18136

DATE	POS	WKS	ARTIST–RECORD TITLE	LABEL & NO.
9/9/95	**1 (1)**	16	23. **She's Every Woman**	Capitol 18842
11/25/95	**23**	6	24. The Fever	Capitol 18948
			originally recorded by Aerosmith on the 1993 album *Get A Grip*; Brooks's version includes additional lyrics	
1/13/96	**1 (1)**	15	25. **The Beaches Of Cheyenne**	Capitol 19022
4/13/96	**19**	9	26. The Change	Capitol LP Cut
			above 4 from the album *Fresh Horses* on Capitol 32080	

BROOKS, Karen

Born on 4/29/54 in Dallas. Sang in clubs in Austin, then joined Rodney Crowell as backup vocalist. Wrote hits "Couldn't Do Nothin' Right" for Rosanne Cash, "Tennessee Rose" for Emmylou Harris and "Girls Like Me" for Tanya Tucker.

DATE	POS	WKS	ARTIST–RECORD TITLE	LABEL & NO.
9/11/82	**17**	9	1. New Way Out	Warner 29958
12/18/82+	**1 (1)**	13	2. **Faking Love**	Warner/Curb 29854
			T.G. SHEPPARD and KAREN BROOKS	
3/12/83	**21**	6	3. If That's What You're Thinking	Warner 29789
7/23/83	**30**	4	4. Walk On	Warner 29644
6/9/84	**40**	1	5. Born To Love You	Warner 29302
8/25/84	**19**	7	6. Tonight I'm Here With Someone Else	Warner 29225

BROOKS & DUNN

Duo of Kix Brooks and Ronnie Dunn. Both had solo hits in the 1980s. CMA Awards: 1992, 1993, 1994 and 1995 Vocal Duo of the Year.

DATE	POS	WKS	ARTIST–RECORD TITLE	LABEL & NO.
7/20/91	**1 (2)**	16	1. **Brand New Man**	Arista 2232
11/2/91	**1 (2)**	17	2. **My Next Broken Heart**	Arista 12337
3/14/92	**1 (2)**	17	3. **Neon Moon**	Arista 12388
6/20/92	**1 (4)**	16	4. **Boot Scootin' Boogie**	Arista 12440
			originally available as the B-side of #2 above	
10/17/92	**6**	16	5. **Lost And Found**	Arista 12460
2/13/93	**4**	15	6. **Hard Workin' Man**	Arista 12513
5/29/93	**2 (2)**	18	7. **We'll Burn That Bridge**	Arista 12563
9/18/93	**1 (1)**	17	8. **She Used To Be Mine**	Arista 12602
12/25/93+	**2 (2)**	18	9. **Rock My World (Little Country Girl)**	Arista 12636
4/23/94	**1 (1)**	17	10. **That Ain't No Way To Go**	Arista 12669
9/3/94	**1 (2)**	18	11. **She's Not The Cheatin' Kind**	Arista 12740
11/19/94+	**6**	14	12. **I'll Never Forgive My Heart**	Arista 12779
3/11/95	**1 (1)**	17	13. **Little Miss Honky Tonk**	Arista 12790
7/1/95	**1 (2)**	17	14. **You're Gonna Miss Me When I'm Gone**	Arista 12831
9/30/95	**5**	13	15. **Whiskey Under The Bridge**	Arista 12770
4/6/96	**1 (3)**	16↑	16. **My Maria**	Arista 12993
			#9 Pop hit for B.W. Stevenson in 1973	

BROTHER PHELPS

Duo of brothers Ricky Lee (born 10/8/53) and Doug (born 12/16/60) Phelps, formerly with The Kentucky Headhunters.

DATE	POS	WKS	ARTIST–RECORD TITLE	LABEL & NO.
8/7/93	**6**	14	1. **Let Go**	Asylum 64614
12/25/93+	**28**	7	2. Were You Really Livin'	Asylum 64598

DATE	POS	WKS	ARTIST–RECORD TITLE	LABEL & NO.
			BROWN, Jim Ed	
			Born on 4/1/34 in Sparkman, Arkansas. Appeared with older sister Maxine on KCLA-Pine Bluff in the late 1940s and KLRA-Little Rock's *Barnyard Frolics* in the early '50s. Recorded in duo with Maxine in 1953, joined by younger sister Bonnie in 1955. Began solo recording in 1965. Host of TNN's *You Can Be A Star!* and *Going Our Way*. Member of the *Grand Ole Opry* since 1963. CMA Award: 1977 Vocal Duo of the Year (with Helen Cornelius).	
			JIM EDWARD BROWN:	
7/31/65	33	4	1. I Heard From A Memory Last Night	RCA 8566
10/23/65	37	3	2. I'm Just A Country Boy	RCA 8644
8/13/66	23	8	3. A Taste Of Heaven	RCA 8867
3/4/67	18	7	4. You Can Have Her	RCA 9077
			#12 Pop hit for Roy Hamilton in 1961	
			JIM ED BROWN:	
6/17/67	3	15	5. **Pop A Top**	RCA 9192
11/4/67	13	10	6. Bottle, Bottle	RCA 9329
3/9/68	23	7	7. The Cajun Stripper	RCA 9434
6/8/68	13	10	8. The Enemy	RCA 9518
2/8/69	35	3	9. Longest Beer Of The Night	RCA 9677
4/12/69	17	8	10. Man And Wife Time	RCA 0144
8/23/69	29	5	11. The Three Bells	RCA 0190
			new version of Jim's #1 hit with The Browns in 1959	
12/27/69+	35	4	12. Ginger Is Gentle And Waiting For Me/	
		4	13. Drink Boys, Drink	RCA 0274
8/8/70	31	4	14. Baby, I Tried	RCA 9858
11/14/70	4	15	15. **Morning**	RCA 9909
4/17/71	13	11	16. Angel's Sunday	RCA 9965
11/6/71	37	4	17. She's Leavin' (Bonnie, Please Don't Go)	RCA 0509
1/20/73	29	7	18. Unbelievable Love	RCA 0846
5/19/73	6	12	19. **Southern Loving**	RCA 0928
9/22/73	15	10	20. Broad-Minded Man	RCA 0059
1/12/74	10	10	21. **Sometime Sunshine**	RCA 0180
6/1/74	10	10	22. **It's That Time Of Night**	RCA 0267
2/7/76	24	5	23. Another Morning	RCA 10531
			JIM ED BROWN/HELEN CORNELIUS:	
8/7/76	1 (2)	10	24. **I Don't Want To Have To Marry You**	RCA 10711
12/11/76+	2 (1)	13	25. **Saying Hello, Saying I Love You, Saying Goodbye**	RCA 10822
5/21/77	12	9	26. Born Believer	RCA 10967
9/3/77	12	8	27. If It Ain't Love By Now	RCA 11044
3/25/78	11	9	28. I'll Never Be Free	RCA 11220
8/12/78	6	11	29. **If The World Ran Out Of Love Tonight**	RCA 11304
12/9/78+	10	9	30. **You Don't Bring Me Flowers**	RCA 11435
3/31/79	2 (2)	10	31. **Lying In Love With You**	RCA 11532
8/11/79	3	10	32. Fools	RCA 11672
12/1/79	38	2	33. You're The Part Of Me	RCA 11742
			JIM ED BROWN	
3/29/80	5	9	34. **Morning Comes Too Early**	RCA 11927

DATE	POS	WKS	ARTIST–RECORD TITLE	LABEL & NO.
8/16/80	**24**	5	35. The Bedroom	RCA 12037
5/30/81	**13**	8	36. Don't Bother To Knock	RCA 12220

BROWN, Roy, and His Orchestra

Born on 9/10/25 in New Orleans. Died of a heart attack on 5/25/81 in Los Angeles. R&B vocalist/pianist. One of the originators of the New Orleans R&B sound. Wrote "Good Rocking Tonight."

DATE	POS	WKS	ARTIST–RECORD TITLE	LABEL & NO.
12/25/48	**12**	1	1. 'Fore Day In The Morning Juke Box #12	DeLuxe 3198

BROWN, T. Graham

Born Anthony Graham Brown on 10/30/54 in Atlanta; raised in Arabi, Georgia. Played baseball for the University of Georgia. Worked local clubs, toured with Dirk Howell as Dirk & Tony. Formed own country band, REO Diamond. Had soul band, Rack Of Spam, in 1979. Worked as staff writer for CBS songs. Appeared in the movies *Greased Lightning*, *The Farm* and *Heartbreak Hotel*. Former jingle singer for McDonald's, Taco Bell, Miller and Budweiser beer.

DATE	POS	WKS	ARTIST–RECORD TITLE	LABEL & NO.
9/7/85	**39**	1	1. Drowning In Memories	Capitol 5499
11/23/85+	**7**	14	2. **I Tell It Like It Used To Be**	Capitol 5524
5/17/86	**3**	13	3. **I Wish That I Could Hurt That Way Again**	Capitol 5571
9/27/86	**1** (1)	15	4. **Hell And High Water**	Capitol 5621
2/14/87	**1** (1)	14	5. **Don't Go To Strangers**	Capitol 5664
6/20/87	**9**	12	6. **Brilliant Conversationalist**	Capitol 44008
9/26/87	**4**	15	7. **She Couldn't Love Me Anymore**	Capitol 44061
2/20/88	**4**	12	8. **The Last Resort**	Capitol 44125
8/20/88	**1** (1)	14	9. **Darlene**	Capitol 44205
1/7/89	**7**	13	10. **Come As You Were**	Capitol 44273
6/3/89	**30**	3	11. Never Say Never	Capitol 44349
5/12/90	**6**	16	12. **If You Could Only See Me Now**	Capitol 44534
7/14/90	**6**	14	13. **Don't Go Out** **TANYA TUCKER with T. Graham Brown**	Capitol 44586
10/20/90	**18**	8	14. Moonshadow Road from the album *Bumper To Bumper* on Capitol 91780	Capitol LP Cut
5/25/91	**31**	4	15. With This Ring from the album *You Can't Take It With You* on Capitol 93547; #14 Pop hit for The Platters in 1967	Capitol LP Cut

BROWNE, Jann

Born on 3/14/54 in Anderson, Indiana; raised in Shelbyville, Indiana. To Southern California in 1977. Vocalist with Asleep At The Wheel, 1981-83. Married songwriter Roger Stebner in 1985.

DATE	POS	WKS	ARTIST–RECORD TITLE	LABEL & NO.
8/26/89	**19**	7	1. You Ain't Down Home	Curb 10530
12/23/89+	**18**	16	2. Tell Me Why	Curb 10568

DATE	POS	WKS	ARTIST–RECORD TITLE	LABEL & NO.
			## BROWNS, The	
			Brother-and-sister trio consisting of Jim Edward (born 4/1/34, Sparkman, Arkansas), Ella Maxine (born 4/27/32, Samti, Louisiana) and Bonnie (born 7/31/37, Sparkman, Arkansas). Maxine and Jim Ed had worked as a duo from the late 1940s and Bonnie joined them in 1955. The trio worked Red Foley's *Arkansas Jamboree* radio shows. Sister Norma subbed for Jim Ed while he was in the service. Joined the *Grand Ole Opry* in 1963. The trio disbanded in 1967, with Jim Ed and Maxine continuing as solo artists.	
			JIM EDWARD & MAXINE BROWN:	
6/26/54	8	15	1. **Looking Back To See** Jockey #8	Fabor 107
			JIM EDWARD, MAXINE & BONNIE BROWN:	
11/12/55	7	7	2. **Here Today And Gone Tomorrow** Jockey #7	Fabor 126
4/28/56	2 (1)	24	3. **I Take The Chance** Jockey #2 / Best Seller #6 / Juke Box #9	RCA 6480
9/22/56	11	2	4. Just As Long As You Love Me Jockey #11	RCA 6631
3/23/57	15	1	5. Money Jockey #15	RCA 6823
9/2/57	4	17	6. **I Heard The Bluebirds Sing** Jockey #4 / Best Seller #15	RCA 6995
			THE BROWNS:	
10/20/58	13	2	7. Would You Care	RCA 7311
2/23/59	11	12	8. Beyond The Shadow	RCA 7427
8/3/59	1 (10)	19	● 9. **The Three Bells**	RCA 7555
11/9/59+	7	16	10. **Scarlet Ribbons (For Her Hair)**	RCA 7614
			THE BROWNS FEATURING JIM EDWARD BROWN:	
4/11/60	20	7	11. The Old Lamplighter	RCA 7700
12/31/60	23	3	12. Send Me The Pillow You Dream On	RCA 7804
5/23/64	12	24	13. Then I'll Stop Loving You	RCA 8348
11/21/64	40	2	14. Everybody's Darlin', Plus Mine	RCA 8423
			THE BROWNS:	
7/16/66	16	11	15. I'd Just Be Fool Enough	RCA 8838
10/8/66	19	9	16. Coming Back To You	RCA 8942
			## BRUCE, Ed	
			Born William Edwin Bruce, Jr., on 12/29/40 in Keiser, Arkansas; raised in Memphis. Recorded for Sun in 1957. Moved to Nashville in 1964 and worked with the Marijohn Wilkins Singers. Did TV commercials as The Tennessean; appeared in *Maverick* TV series. Wrote "Mammas Don't Let Your Babies Grow Up To Be Cowboys," "The Man That Turned My Mama On," "Working Man's Prayer," and many others.	
12/13/75+	15	8	1. Mammas Don't Let Your Babies Grow Up To Be Cowboys	United Art. 732
4/24/76	32	3	2. The Littlest Cowboy Rides Again	United Art. 774
10/30/76	36	3	3. For Love's Own Sake	United Art. 862
4/12/80	21	7	4. Diane	MCA 41201

DATE	POS	WKS	ARTIST–RECORD TITLE	LABEL & NO.
8/9/80	**12**	8	5. The Last Cowboy Song Willie Nelson (guest vocal)	MCA 41273
11/29/80+	**14**	10	6. Girls, Women And Ladies	MCA 51018
5/2/81	**24**	6	7. Evil Angel	MCA 51076
8/15/81	**14**	9	8. (When You Fall In Love) Everything's A Waltz	MCA 51139
12/12/81+	**1 (1)**	14	9. **You're The Best Break This Old Heart Ever Had**	MCA 51210
5/15/82	**13**	9	10. Love's Found You And Me	MCA 52036
9/18/82	**4**	12	11. **Ever, Never Lovin' You**	MCA 52109
2/12/83	**6**	12	12. **My First Taste Of Texas**	MCA 52156
6/4/83	**21**	8	13. You're Not Leavin' Here Tonight	MCA 52210
8/27/83	**19**	8	14. If It Was Easy	MCA 52251
12/3/83+	**4**	13	15. **After All**	MCA 52295
12/1/84+	**3**	15	16. **You Turn Me On (Like a Radio)**	RCA 13937
4/20/85	**17**	9	17. When Givin' Up Was Easy	RCA 14037
8/31/85	**20**	8	18. If It Ain't Love originally the B-side of #16 above	RCA 14150
5/3/86	**4**	13	19. **Nights**	RCA 14305
1/24/87	**36**	2	20. Quietly Crazy	RCA 5077

BRYCE, Sherry

Born in Duncanville, Alabama. She and husband, Mack Sanders, owned the Pilot label.

MEL TILLIS & SHERRY BRYCE WITH THE STATESIDERS:

DATE	POS	WKS	ARTIST–RECORD TITLE	LABEL & NO.
6/12/71	**8**	12	1. **Take My Hand**	MGM 14255
11/20/71	**9**	10	2. **Living And Learning**	MGM 14303
5/6/72	**38**	3	3. Anything's Better Than Nothing	MGM 14365
12/22/73+	**26**	6	4. Let's Go All The Way Tonight	MGM 14660
5/4/74	**11**	9	5. Don't Let Go #13 Pop hit for Roy Hamilton in 1958	MGM 14714
2/1/75	**14**	7	6. You Are The One	MGM 14776
6/28/75	**32**	6	7. Mr. Right And Mrs. Wrong	MGM 14803

BUCHANAN BROTHERS

Chester and Lester Buchanan from Trenton, Georgia.

DATE	POS	WKS	ARTIST–RECORD TITLE	LABEL & NO.
6/29/46	**6**	3	1. **Atomic Power**	Victor 20-1850

BUCK, Gary

Born on 3/21/40 in Sault Sainte Marie, Canada. Had own band, the Rock-A-Billies, while a teenager. First recorded for Chateau in 1962. Member of The Four Guys until 1980. Once married to Louise Mandrell.

DATE	POS	WKS	ARTIST–RECORD TITLE	LABEL & NO.
6/29/63	**11**	17	1. Happy To Be Unhappy	Petal 1011
4/11/64	**37**	2	2. The Wheel Song	Petal 1500

DATE	POS	WKS	ARTIST–RECORD TITLE	LABEL & NO.
			BUCKAROOS, The	
			Backing band for Buck Owens. Included Don Rich (lead guitar, vocals), Tom Brumley (steel guitar), Doyle Holly (bass) and Willie Cantu (drums). Don Rich (real name: Don Ulrich) was killed in a motorcycle accident on 7/17/74. Also see Buddy Alan and Buck Owens.	
11/6/65	**1** (2)	16	1. **Buckaroo** [I] **BUCK OWENS & THE BUCKAROOS**	Capitol 5517
7/6/68	38	5	2. I'm Coming Back Home To Stay **BUCK OWENS' BUCKAROOS Featuring DON RICH**	Capitol 2173
			BUFF, Beverly	
			Born in Washington, Georgia.	
11/24/62+	22	3	1. I'll Sign	Bethlehem 3027
3/30/63	23	5	2. Forgive Me	Bethlehem 3065
			BUFFETT, Jimmy	
			Born on 12/25/46 in Pascagoula, Mississippi; raised in Mobile, Alabama. Has BS degree in journalism from the University of Southern Mississippi. After working in New Orleans, moved to Nashville in 1969. Nashville correspondant for *Billboard* magazine, 1969-70. Settled in Key West in 1971. Owns a store called Margaritaville and has his own line of tropical clothing.	
6/4/77	13	10	1. Margaritaville	ABC 12254
10/22/77	24	5	2. Changes In Latitudes, Changes In Attitudes	ABC 12305
5/4/85	37	3	3. Who's The Blonde Stranger?	MCA 52550
10/12/85	16	10	4. If The Phone Doesn't Ring, It's Me	MCA 52664
			BURCH SISTERS, The	
			Sisters Cathy (born 12/28/60), Charlene (born 9/19/62) and Cindy (born 8/1/63) Burch. All were born in Jacksonville, Florida. Later based out of Screven, Georgia.	
7/16/88	23	6	1. Everytime You Go Outside I Hope It Rains	Mercury 870362
			BURGESS, Wilma	
			Born on 6/11/39 in Orlando, Florida. Attended Stetson University, majoring in physical education. Started work as a demo singer in Nashville in 1960.	
12/18/65+	7	17	1. **Baby**	Decca 31862
5/21/66	12	15	2. Don't Touch Me	Decca 31941
11/12/66	4	16	3. **Misty Blue** #3 Pop hit for Dorothy Moore in 1976	Decca 32027
4/22/67	24	10	4. Fifteen Days	Decca 32105
9/23/67	16	11	5. Tear Time	Decca 32178
2/9/74	14	10	6. Wake Me Into Love **BUD LOGAN & WILMA BURGESS**	Shannon 816
			BURKE, Fiddlin' Frenchie, and The Outlaws	
			Burke born Leon Bourke in Kaplan, Louisiana. Cajun fiddler from age 11; worked with Johnny Bush, Jimmy Dickens and Ray Price. Formed own band, The Song Masters.	
2/8/75	39	2	1. Big Mamou **FIDDLIN' FRENCHIE BOURQUE and THE OUTLAWS**	20th Century 2152
5/17/75	30	3	2. Colinda	20th Century 2182

DATE	POS	WKS	ARTIST–RECORD TITLE	LABEL & NO.

BURNETTE, Dorsey

Born on 12/28/32 in Memphis. Died of a heart attack on 8/19/79 in Canoga Park, California. Older brother of Johnny Burnette, father of Billy Burnette. Was a Golden Gloves contender in 1949. Worked on KWEM-Memphis *West Memphis Jamboree* with Johnny and Paul Burlison as the Johnny Burnette Rock 'N Roll Trio. Recorded for Von in 1954. Winner on the *Ted Mack Amateur Hour* and appeared at Madison Square Garden with trio in September 1956. Went solo in 1958.

DATE	POS	WKS	ARTIST–RECORD TITLE	LABEL & NO.
6/3/72	21	9	1. In The Spring (The Roses Always Turn Red)	Capitol 3307
10/14/72	40	1	2. I Just Couldn't Let Her Walk Away	Capitol 3404
9/22/73	26	7	3. Darlin' (Don't Come Back)	Capitol 3678
			DORSEY BURNETTE with Sound Company	
6/28/75	28	4	4. Molly (I Ain't Gettin' Any Younger)	Melodyland 6007
8/13/77	31	4	5. Things I Treasure	Calliope 8004

BURNS, George

Born Nathan Birnbaum on 1/20/1896 in New York City. Died on 3/9/96. Top radio, movie and TV comedian. Starred in several movies including *The Sunshine Boys* and *Oh God*.

DATE	POS	WKS	ARTIST–RECORD TITLE	LABEL & NO.
2/2/80	15	8	1. I Wish I Was Eighteen Again	Mercury 57011

BURRITO BROTHERS

Originally formed in 1968 in California as The Flying Burrito Brothers by Chris Hillman and Gram Parsons, ex-members of the folk-rock band The Byrds. By 1980, consisted of "Sneaky" Pete Kleinow (steel guitar), Floyd "Gib" Guilbeau (fiddle; father of Ronnie Guilbeau of Palomino Road), Skip Battin (bass), Greg Harris (guitar) and Ed Ponder (drums). In 1981, relocated to Nashville, dropped "Flying" from band name, Harris and Ponder left and John Beland (guitar) joined. By late 1981, reduced to a duo of Guilbeau and Beland. Kleinow, Battin, Harris and Jim Goodall recorded as The Flying Brothers, 1985-88.

DATE	POS	WKS	ARTIST–RECORD TITLE	LABEL & NO.
5/23/81	20	5	1. Does She Wish She Was Single Again	Curb 01011
8/29/81	16	7	2. She Belongs To Everyone But Me	Curb 02243
1/30/82	27	5	3. If Something Should Come Between Us (Let It Be Love)	Curb 02641
5/29/82	40	2	4. Closer To You	Curb 02835
9/4/82	39	1	5. I'm Drinkin' Canada Dry	Curb 03023

BUSH, Johnny

Born John Bush Shin III on 2/17/35 in Houston. Guitarist/drummer. Worked local clubs in San Antonio from 1952. Worked with Willie Nelson and Ray Price in the early '60s. Joined Willie Nelson's band in the mid-1960s. Went solo in 1967. Known as "The Country Caruso."

DATE	POS	WKS	ARTIST–RECORD TITLE	LABEL & NO.
5/4/68	29	5	1. What A Way To Live	Stop 160
8/31/68	10	12	2. **Undo The Right**	Stop 193
2/1/69	16	8	3. Each Time	Stop 232
			written by Ray Price	
4/5/69	7	12	4. **You Gave Me A Mountain**	Stop 257
			#24 Pop hit for Frankie Laine in 1969	
9/6/69	26	6	5. My Cup Runneth Over	Stop 310
			#8 Pop hit for Ed Ames in 1967	
6/6/70	25	7	6. Warmth Of The Wine	Stop 371
5/20/72	17	8	7. I'll Be There	Million 1
8/12/72	14	12	8. Whiskey River	RCA 0745
			Willie Nelson's theme song	

DATE	POS	WKS	ARTIST-RECORD TITLE	LABEL & NO.
2/10/73	**34**	2	9. There Stands The Glass	RCA 0867
6/23/73	**38**	2	10. Here Comes The World Again	RCA 0931
1/12/74	**37**	2	11. We're Back In Love Again	RCA 0164
			BUTLER, Carl, and Pearl	
			Carl Butler born on 6/2/27 in Knoxville, Tennessee. Died on 9/4/92. Singing since age 12. Joined by wife Pearl (born Pearl Dee Jones on 9/20/27; died 3/1/88) as a duo in 1962. Appeared in the movie *Second Fiddle To A Steel Guitar* in 1967.	
8/7/61	**25**	2	1. Honky Tonkitis	Columbia 41997
			CARL BUTLER	
12/8/62	**1** (11)	24	2. **Don't Let Me Cross Over**	Columbia 42593
7/6/63	**14**	14	3. Loving Arms	Columbia 42778
1/11/64	**9**	4	4. **Too Late To Try Again/**	
1/11/64	**36**	1	5. My Tears Don't Show	Columbia 42892
6/6/64	**14**	16	6. I'm Hanging Up The Phone	Columbia 43030
10/3/64	**23**	9	7. Forbidden Street	Columbia 43102
4/10/65	**22**	9	8. Just Thought I'd Let You Know/	
4/3/65	**38**	1	9. We'd Destroy Each Other	Columbia 43210
9/3/66	**31**	3	10. Little Pedro	Columbia 43685
9/28/68	**28**	6	11. Punish Me Tomorrow	Columbia 44587
			BYRD, Jerry—see ALLEN, Rex, and KIRK, Red	
			BYRD, Tracy	
			Born on 12/18/66 in Vidor, Texas. Male singer.	
7/24/93	**1** (1)	15	1. **Holdin' Heaven**	MCA 54659
12/25/93	**39**	2	2. Why Don't That Telephone Ring	MCA 54735
5/14/94	**4**	16	3. **Lifestyles Of The Not So Rich And Famous**	MCA 54778
9/3/94	**4**	12	4. **Watermelon Crawl**	MCA 54889
12/17/94+	**5**	13	5. **The First Step**	MCA 54945
3/11/95	**2** (2)	13	6. **The Keeper Of The Stars**	MCA 54988
6/24/95	**15**	9	7. Walking To Jerusalem	MCA 55049
10/14/95	**9**	15	8. **Love Lessons**	MCA 55102
2/24/96	**14**	11	9. Heaven In My Woman's Eyes	MCA 55155
			C	
			CAGLE, Buddy	
			Born on 2/8/36 in Concord, North Carolina. Raised in the Children's Home in Winston-Salem. Worked with Hank Thompson's Brazos Valley Boys.	
5/18/63	**29**	3	1. Your Mother's Prayer	Capitol 4923
11/16/63	**26**	2	2. Sing A Sad Song	Capitol 5043
10/2/65	**37**	3	3. Honky Tonkin' Again	Mercury 72452
5/7/66	**31**	8	4. Tonight I'm Coming Home	Imperial 66161

DATE	POS	WKS	ARTIST–RECORD TITLE	LABEL & NO.
			CAMP, Shawn	
			Male singer/songwriter/guitarist/fiddle player from Perryville, Arkansas.	
10/16/93	39	1	1. Fallin' Never Felt So Good	Reprise 18465
1/22/94	39	1	2. Confessin' My Love	Reprise 18331
			CAMPBELL, Archie	
			Born on 11/7/14 in Bulls Gap, Tennessee. Died on 8/29/87 in Knoxville. From the late '30s to early '40s, worked on the *Mid-Day Merry-Go-Round* radio show, WNOX-Knoxville. Served in U.S. Navy in World War II. Returned to radio, then own TV show on WATE-Knoxville, 1952-58. Joined the *Grand Ole Opry* in 1968. Chief writer and a star of the *Hee Haw* TV series. Hosted TNN's interview show *Yesteryear in Nashville*.	
3/14/60	24	4	1. Trouble In The Amen Corner	RCA 7660
1/29/66	16	7	2. The Men In My Little Girl's Life	RCA 8741
			#6 Pop hit for Mike Douglas in 1960	
			ARCHIE CAMPBELL AND LORENE MANN:	
2/10/68	24	9	3. The Dark End Of The Street	RCA 9401
7/27/68	31	6	4. Tell It Like It Is	RCA 9549
			#2 Pop hit for Aaron Neville in 1967	
1/18/69	36	6	5. My Special Prayer	RCA 9691
			CAMPBELL('S), Cecil, Tennessee Ramblers	
			Campbell born on 3/22/11 in Danbury, North Carolina; raised in Belews Creek, North Carolina. Died on 6/18/89. Appeared in the movies *My Darling Clementine* and *Swing Your Partner*.	
5/21/49	9	1	1. **Steel Guitar Ramble**	RCA Victor 0014
			Juke Box #9	
			CAMPBELL, Glen	
			Born on 4/22/36 in Billstown, Arkansas. Vocalist/guitarist/composer. With his uncle Dick Bills's band, 1954-58. To Los Angeles; recorded with The Champs in 1960. Became prolific studio musician; with The Hondells in 1964, The Beach Boys in 1965 and Sagittarius in 1967. Own TV show, *The Glen Campbell Goodtime Hour*, 1968-72. Appeared in the movies *True Grit*, *Norwood* and *Strange Homecoming*; voice in the animated movie *Rock-A-Doodle*. CMA Awards: 1968 Male Vocalist of the Year; 1968 Entertainer of the Year.	
12/29/62	20	5	1. Kentucky Means Paradise	Capitol 4867
			THE GREEN RIVER BOYS featuring GLEN CAMPBELL	
1/14/67	18	7	2. Burning Bridges	Capitol 5773
			#3 Pop hit for Jack Scott in 1960	
8/26/67	30	3	3. Gentle On My Mind	Capitol 5939
11/18/67+	2 (2)	15	4. **By The Time I Get To Phoenix**	Capitol 2015
2/24/68	13	8	5. Hey Little One	Capitol 2076
4/20/68	1 (3)	15	6. **I Wanna Live**	Capitol 2146
7/6/68	3	14	7. **Dreams Of The Everyday Housewife**	Capitol 2224
11/9/68	1 (2)	15	● 8. **Wichita Lineman**	Capitol 2302
2/15/69	14	11	9. Let It Be Me	Capitol 2387
			GLEN CAMPBELL and BOBBIE GENTRY	
3/22/69	1 (3)	13	● 10. **Galveston**	Capitol 2428
5/24/69	28	7	11. Where's The Playground Susie	Capitol 2494

DATE	POS	WKS	ARTIST–RECORD TITLE	LABEL & NO.
8/2/69	9	11	12. **True Grit** title song from the movie starring John Wayne and Campbell	Capitol 2573
11/1/69	2 (1)	12	13. **Try A Little Kindness**	Capitol 2659
1/31/70	2 (3)	12	14. **Honey Come Back**	Capitol 2718
3/7/70	6	11	15. **All I Have To Do Is Dream** **BOBBIE GENTRY & GLEN CAMPBELL**	Capitol 2745
5/9/70	25	7	16. Oh Happy Day	Capitol 2787
7/25/70	5	10	17. **Everything A Man Could Ever Need** from the movie *Norwood* starring Campbell	Capitol 2843
10/3/70	3	13	18. **It's Only Make Believe** #1 Pop hit for Conway Twitty in 1958	Capitol 2905
3/20/71	7	13	19. **Dream Baby (How Long Must I Dream)**	Capitol 3062
7/24/71	21	10	20. The Last Time I Saw Her written by Gordon Lightfoot	Capitol 3123
11/20/71	40	2	21. I Say A Little Prayer/By The Time I Get To Phoenix **GLEN CAMPBELL/ANNE MURRAY**	Capitol 3200
1/29/72	15	9	22. Oklahoma Sunday Morning	Capitol 3254
4/15/72	6	11	23. **Manhattan Kansas**	Capitol 3305
1/27/73	33	3	24. One Last Time	Capitol 3483
11/24/73	20	5	25. Wherefore And Why written by Gordon Lightfoot	Capitol 3735
2/23/74	20	6	26. Houston (I'm Comin' To See You)	Capitol 3808
8/31/74	3	13	27. **Bonaparte's Retreat** written in 1950 by Pee Wee King	Capitol 3926
1/18/75	16	7	28. It's A Sin When You Love Somebody	Capitol 3988
7/5/75	1 (3)	14	● 29. **Rhinestone Cowboy**	Capitol 4095
11/22/75	3	11	30. **Country Boy (You Got Your Feet In L.A.)**	Capitol 4155
4/24/76	4	9	31. **Don't Pull Your Love/Then You Can Tell Me** **Goodbye** medley of #4 Pop hit for Hamilton, Joe Frank & Reynolds in 1971 and #6 Pop hit for The Casinos in 1967	Capitol 4245
7/31/76	18	6	32. See You On Sunday	Capitol 4288
2/12/77	1 (2)	10	● 33. **Southern Nights**	Capitol 4376
7/16/77	4	10	34. **Sunflower** written by Neil Diamond	Capitol 4445
1/7/78	39	2	35. God Must Have Blessed America	Capitol 4515
7/8/78	21	6	36. Another Fine Mess from the movie *The End* starring Burt Reynolds	Capitol 4584
10/21/78	16	9	37. Can You Fool originally released as the B-side of #36 above	Capitol 4638
2/24/79	13	8	38. I'm Gonna Love You	Capitol 4682
9/15/79	25	6	39. Hound Dog Man #58 Pop hit for Lenny LeBlanc in 1977	Capitol 4769
12/20/80+	10	11	40. **Any Which Way You Can** title song from the movie starring Clint Eastwood	Warner 49609
8/29/81	15	7	41. I Love My Truck from the movie *The Night The Lights Went Out In Georgia* starring Kristy McNichol	Mirage 3845
2/19/83	17	8	42. I Love How You Love Me #5 Pop hit for The Paris Sisters in 1961	Atln. Am. 99930
7/21/84	10	10	43. **Faithless Love**	Atln. Am. 99768
12/22/84+	4	14	44. **A Lady Like You**	Atln. Am. 99691

DATE	POS	WKS	ARTIST–RECORD TITLE	LABEL & NO.
6/15/85	**14**	10	45. (Love Always) Letter To Home	Atln. Am. 99647
12/14/85+	**7**	12	46. **It's Just A Matter Of Time**	Atln. Am. 99600
			#3 Pop hit for Brook Benton in 1959	
5/24/86	**38**	2	47. Cowpoke	Atln. Am. 99559
7/4/87	**6**	14	48. **The Hand That Rocks The Cradle**	MCA 53108
			GLEN CAMPBELL with STEVE WARINER	
10/31/87+	**5**	14	49. **Still Within The Sound Of My Voice**	MCA 53172
3/26/88	**32**	3	50. I Remember You	MCA 53245
			#5 Pop hit for Frank Ifield in 1962	
6/18/88	**7**	13	51. **I Have You**	MCA 53218
11/19/88	**35**	2	52. Light Years	MCA 53426
10/14/89	**6**	16	53. **She's Gone, Gone, Gone**	Universal 66024
3/16/91	**27**	6	54. Unconditional Love	Capitol LP Cut
			from the album *Unconditional Love* on Capitol 90992	
			CAMPBELL, Jo Ann	
			Born on 7/20/38 in Jacksonville, Florida. First recorded for El Dorado in 1957. Appeared in the movies *Johnny Melody, Go Johnny Go* and *Hey, Let's Twist.* Married singer Troy Seals in the early 1960s; recorded together as Jo Ann & Troy in 1964.	
9/22/62	**24**	3	1. (I'm The Girl On) Wolverton Mountain	Cameo 223
			answer song to "Wolverton Mountain" by Claude King; some pressings titled "I'm The Girl From Wolverton Mountain"	
			CANYON	
			Texas group featuring Steve "Coop" Cooper, lead vocals.	
9/30/89	**40**	1	1. Hot Nights	16th Ave. 70433
			CAPITALS, The	
			Vocal quartet from Columbus, Ohio: Arti Portilla, Ronnie Cochran, Terry Kaufman and Jack Crum.	
11/1/80	**29**	4	1. A Little Ground In Texas	Ridgetop 01080
			CAPPS, Hank	
11/4/72	**33**	5	1. Bowling Green	Capitol 3416
			CAPTAIN STUBBY & THE BUCCANEERS	
			Band led by Tom C. "Captain Stubby" Fouts (born 11/24/18, Carroll County, Indiana). Worked on WLW-Cincinnati, own band from 1937. On WLS *National Barn Dance* for 10 years; made appearances on Don McNeil's *Breakfast Club.* Own *Polka-Go-Round* TV series on ABC, 1965-68. Later worked as a DJ on WLS-Chicago.	
2/12/49	**13**	1	1. Lavender Blue (Dilly Dilly)	Decca 24547
			BURL IVES with Captain Stubby & The Buccaneers	
			Best Seller #13	
			STUBBY AND THE BUCCANEERS:	
7/16/49	**12**	1	2. Money, Marbles And Chalk	Decca 46149
			Juke Box #12; Windy Breeze (vocal)	
7/23/49	**14**	1	3. Come Wet Your Mustache With Me	Decca 46169
			Juke Box #14	

DATE	POS	WKS	ARTIST–RECORD TITLE	LABEL & NO.
			CARDWELL, Jack	
			Born on 11/9/30 near Chapman, Alabama; raised in Mobile. Own band while a teenager; worked as a singing DJ with Tom Jackson as Tom & Jack, on WKAB-Mobile, in the late '40s.	
2/14/53	**3**	9	1. **The Death Of Hank Williams** Best Seller #3 / Jockey #4 / Juke Box #5	King 1172
9/26/53	**7**	2	2. **Dear Joan** Best Seller #7	King 1269
			CARGILL, Henson	
			Born on 2/5/41 in Oklahoma City. Studied animal husbandry at Colorado State; worked as a deputy sheriff in Oklahoma County. Performed with The Kimberleys in the mid-1960s. Appeared on the TV series *Country Hayride* in Cincinnati. Operates a large cattle ranch in Stillwater, Oklahoma.	
12/23/67+	**1** (5)	16	1. **Skip A Rope**	Monument 1041
5/11/68	**11**	10	2. Row Row Row	Monument 1065
9/14/68	**39**	1	3. She Thinks I'm On That Train	Monument 1084
2/1/69	**8**	13	4. **None Of My Business**	Monument 1122
7/12/69	**40**	1	5. This Generation Shall Not Pass	Monument 1142
10/18/69	**32**	4	6. Then The Baby Came	Monument 1158
5/30/70	**18**	8	7. The Most Uncomplicated Goodbye I've Ever Heard	Monument 1198
12/1/73	**28**	5	8. Some Old California Memory	Atlantic 4007
7/6/74	**29**	5	9. Stop And Smell The Roses	Atlantic 4021
2/2/80	**29**	5	10. Silence On The Line	Copper Mt. 201
			CARLILE, Tom	
			Born in Miami in 1943.	
9/4/82	**39**	2	1. Back In Debbie's Arms	Door Knob 180
12/11/82	**37**	2	2. Green Eyes	Door Knob 187
			CARLISLE, Bill	
			Born on 12/19/08 in Wakefield, Kentucky. Brother of Cliff Carlisle; performed as a team, 1930-47. On WLAP-Lexington from 1931, with own show starting in 1937. Cliff retired in 1947, and Bill formed and led The Carlisles, who were noted for their humorous recordings. Member of the *Grand Ole Opry* since 1953.	
6/19/48	**14**	2	1. Tramp On The Street [N] Best Seller #14 / Juke Box #14	King 697
12/18/65+	**4**	16	2. **What Kinda Deal Is This** [N]	Hickory 1348
			CARLISLES, The	
			Group formed by Bill Carlisle in 1951. Bill performed with his brother Cliff as the Carlisle Brothers, 1930-47.	
10/26/46	**5**	1	1. **Rainbow At Midnight** [N] **CARLISLE BROTHERS**	King 535
12/15/51+	**6**	8	2. **Too Old To Cut The Mustard** Jockey #6	Mercury 6348
1/10/53	**1** (4)	24	3. **No Help Wanted** Jockey #1(4) / Juke Box #1(4) / Best Seller #2	Mercury 70028
4/11/53	**3**	13	4. **Knothole** [N] Jockey #3 / Best Seller #8	Mercury 70109

DATE	POS	WKS	ARTIST–RECORD TITLE	LABEL & NO.
7/25/53	**2** (1)	8	5. **Is Zat You, Myrtle** [N] Jockey #2 / Best Seller #9	Mercury 70174
11/7/53+	**5**	6	6. **Tain't Nice (To Talk Like That)** **BILL CARLISLE & THE CARLISLES** Jockey #5 / Juke Box #6	Mercury 70232
7/3/54	**15**	1	7. Shake-A-Leg Jockey #15	Mercury 70351
10/9/54	**12**	5	8. Honey Love Jockey #12	Mercury 70435

CARLSON, Paulette

Born on 10/11/53 in Northfield, Minnesota. Sang backup with Gail Davies. Formed own band, Highway 101, in 1986. Resumed solo career in 1991.

DATE	POS	WKS	ARTIST–RECORD TITLE	LABEL & NO.
1/11/92	**21**	9	1. I'll Start With You from the album *Love Goes On* on Capitol 97711	Capitol LP Cut

CARNES, Kim—see ROGERS, Kenny

CARNES, Rick & Janis

Husband-and-wife team: Rick (born 6/30/50 in Fayetteville, Arkansas; guitar) and Janis (born 5/21/47 in Shelbyville, Tennessee; keyboards). Married in 1973; moved to Nashville in 1978.

DATE	POS	WKS	ARTIST–RECORD TITLE	LABEL & NO.
1/7/84	**32**	3	1. Does He Ever Mention My Name	Warner 29448

CARPENTER, Mary-Chapin

Born on 2/21/58 in Princeton, New Jersey. Moved to Washington, D.C., in 1974. Graduated from Brown University with an American Civilization degree. Pursued folk music before she became a top Country vocalist. CMA Awards: 1992 and 1993 Female Vocalist of the Year.

DATE	POS	WKS	ARTIST–RECORD TITLE	LABEL & NO.
6/10/89	**19**	8	1. How Do	Columbia 68677
9/23/89	**8**	13	2. **Never Had It So Good**	Columbia 69050
2/17/90	**7**	14	3. **Quittin' Time**	Columbia 73202
7/21/90	**14**	9	4. Something Of A Dreamer	Columbia 73361
11/24/90+	**16**	11	5. You Win Again	Columbia 73567
3/9/91	**15**	10	6. Right Now	Columbia 73699
7/13/91	**2** (1)	15	7. **Down At The Twist And Shout**	Columbia 73838
11/16/91+	**14**	11	8. Going Out Tonight	Columbia 74038
6/13/92	**4**	18	9. **I Feel Lucky**	Columbia 74345
10/10/92	**15**	11	10. Not Too Much To Ask **MARY-CHAPIN CARPENTER with Joe Diffie**	Columbia 74485
1/9/93	**4**	14	11. **Passionate Kisses**	Columbia 74795
5/8/93	**11**	13	12. The Hard Way	Columbia 74930
9/11/93	**16**	12	13. The Bug written by Mark Knopfler of the rock group Dire Straits	Columbia 77134
1/8/94	**2** (1)	17	14. **He Thinks He'll Keep Her**	Columbia 77316
5/14/94	**2** (1)	14	15. **I Take My Chances**	Columbia 77476
9/17/94	**1** (1)	15	16. **Shut Up And Kiss Me**	Columbia 77696
12/24/94+	**6**	12	17. **Tender When I Want To Be**	Columbia 77780
4/15/95	**21**	8	18. House Of Cards	Columbia 77826

DATE	POS	WKS	ARTIST—RECORD TITLE	LABEL & NO.
			CARPENTERS	
			Brother-sister duo from New Haven, Connecticut: Richard (born 10/15/46) and Karen Carpenter (born 3/2/50; died 2/4/83 of heart failure due to anorexia nervosa). Won the 1970 Best New Artist Grammy Award.	
3/11/78	8	8	1. **Sweet, Sweet Smile** written by Juice Newton	A&M 2008
			CARSON, Jeff	
			Born in Tulsa, Oklahoma. Singer/songwriter/guitarist.	
7/1/95	**1** (1)	16	1. **Not On Your Love**	MCG/Curb 76954
11/4/95	**3**	16	2. **The Car/**	
4/20/96	6	13	3. Holdin' Onto Something	MCG/Curb 76970
			CARSON, Joe	
			Singer from Brownwood, Texas. Died in an automobile accident in February 1964.	
8/3/63	27	2	1. I Gotta Get Drunk (And I Shore Do Dread It) written by Willie Nelson	Liberty 55578
11/9/63+	19	9	2. Helpless	Liberty 55614
3/21/64	34	7	3. Double Life	Liberty 55664
			CARTER, Anita	
			Born on 3/31/33 in Maces Spring, Virginia. Member of The Carter Family. Daughter of Maybelle and Ezra Carter; sister of June and Helen. Member of Nita, Rita & Ruby trio, which included Ruby Wright.	
5/19/51	**2** (1)	14	1. **Down The Trail Of Achin' Hearts/** Juke Box #2 / Best Seller #7 / Jockey #7	
4/21/51	4	11	2. **Bluebird Island** **HANK SNOW (The Singing Ranger) with ANITA CARTER and TheRainbow Ranch Boys (above 2)**	RCA 0441
4/13/68	4	13	3. I Got You **WAYLON JENNINGS & ANITA CARTER**	RCA 9480
			CARTER, Benny, And His Orchestra	
			Born Bennett Lester Carter on 8/8/07 in New York City. Alto saxophonist/trumpeter/clarinetist/pianist. Played in several bands, including Duke Ellington, until 1935. Own band to 1946. Moved to Los Angeles and did movie soundtrack work. Appeared in the movie *The Snows Of Kilimanjaro* in 1952. Won Grammy's Lifetime Achievement Award in 1987.	
2/19/44	**2** (1)	5	1. **Hurry, Hurry!** Savannah Churchill (vocal)	Capitol 144
			CARTER, Carlene	
			Born Rebecca Carlene Smith on 9/26/55 in Madison, Tennessee; daughter of June Carter and Carl Smith. Worked with The Carter Family from the late '60s into the early '70s. Went solo thereafter. Appeared in the London production of *Pump Boys And Dinettes*. Once married to rocker Nick Lowe; later to Howie Epstein of the rock group Tom Petty & The Heartbreakers.	
1/13/90	26	8	1. Time's Up **SOUTHERN PACIFIC and CARLENE CARTER**	Warner 22714
8/4/90	**3**	18	2. **I Fell In Love**	Reprise 19915
11/24/90+	**3**	16	3. **Come On Back**	Reprise 19564

DATE	POS	WKS	ARTIST–RECORD TITLE	LABEL & NO.
4/20/91	**25**	7	4. The Sweetest Thing	Reprise 19398
8/24/91	**33**	7	5. One Love	Reprise 19255
6/19/93	**3**	17	6. **Every Little Thing**	Giant 18527

CARTER, June

Born on 6/23/29 in Maces Spring, Virginia. Member of famous Carter Family group. Daughter of Maybelle and Ezra Carter, sister of Anita and Helen. Worked with Elvis Presley, then joined the Johnny Cash road show in 1961. Married Cash in 1968. CMA Award: 1969 Vocal Group of the Year (with Johnny Cash).

DATE	POS	WKS	ARTIST–RECORD TITLE	LABEL & NO.
8/27/49	**9**	1	1. **Baby, It's Cold Outside** [N] **HOMER and JETHRO with June Carter** Best Seller #9; 45 rpm: 48-0075	RCA Victor 0078

JOHNNY CASH & JUNE CARTER:

DATE	POS	WKS	ARTIST–RECORD TITLE	LABEL & NO.
11/14/64+	**4**	20	2. **It Ain't Me, Babe** #8 Pop hit for The Turtles in 1965	Columbia 43145
3/18/67	**2 (1)**	15	3. **Jackson** #14 Pop hit for Nancy Sinatra & Lee Hazlewood in 1967	Columbia 44011
7/8/67	**6**	14	4. **Long-Legged Guitar Pickin' Man**	Columbia 44158
1/31/70	**2 (1)**	13	5. **If I Were A Carpenter** #8 Pop hit for Bobby Darin in 1966	Columbia 45064
5/1/71	**27**	5	6. A Good Man **JUNE CARTER CASH**	Columbia 45338
9/18/71	**15**	11	7. No Need To Worry	Columbia 45431
7/29/72	**29**	5	8. If I Had A Hammer #10 Pop hit for Peter, Paul & Mary in 1962	Columbia 45631
2/10/73	**27**	6	9. The Loving Gift	Columbia 45758
12/18/76+	**26**	5	10. Old Time Feeling	Columbia 10436

CARTER, Woody, and his Hoedown Boys

DATE	POS	WKS	ARTIST–RECORD TITLE	LABEL & NO.
9/17/49	**14**	1	1. Sittin' On The Doorstep Juke Box #14	Macy's Rec. 100

CARTER FAMILY, The

"The First Family of Country Music." Influential Virginia family group, first recorded in August 1927. Founded by Alvin Pleasant "A.P." Carter (born 4/15/1891, Maces Spring, Virginia; died 11/7/60); with wife Sara Dougherty (born 7/21/1898) and sister-in-law Maybelle Addington (born 5/10/09; died 10/23/78). Joined 1936-39 by Maybelle's daughters Anita, June and Helen, and A.P.'s children Janette and Joe. This group disbanded in 1943 and was re-formed by Maybelle and her daughters as the Carter Sisters and Mother Maybelle. Worked on the *Tennessee Barn Dance*, WRVA-Richmond, 1943-48. Joined the *Grand Ole Opry* in 1948. Joined Johnny Cash's road show in 1961. Original group entered the Country Music Hall of Fame in 1970. Chart hits feature Maybelle and her daughters.

DATE	POS	WKS	ARTIST–RECORD TITLE	LABEL & NO.
4/6/63	**13**	3	1. Busted **JOHNNY CASH with The Carter Family** #4 Pop hit for Ray Charles in 1963	Columbia 42665
10/2/71	**37**	3	2. A Song To Mama Johnny Cash (narration and vocal backing)	Columbia 45428
10/28/72	**35**	4	3. The World Needs A Melody **THE CARTER FAMILY with JOHNNY CASH**	Columbia 45679

DATE	POS	WKS	ARTIST–RECORD TITLE	LABEL & NO.
			CARTWRIGHT, Lionel	
			Born on 2/10/60 in Gallipolis, Ohio. Raised in West Virginia. Starred on TNN's *I-40 Paradise* and *Pickin' At The Paradise*; also a songwriter/musical director/arranger for both shows.	
3/25/89	14	11	1. Like Father Like Son	MCA 53498
7/8/89	3	14	2. **Give Me His Last Chance**	MCA 53651
11/18/89+	12	14	3. In My Eyes	MCA 53723
4/7/90	8	17	4. **I Watched It All (On My Radio)**	MCA 53779
8/25/90	7	12	5. **My Heart Is Set On You**	MCA 79046
1/12/91	31	6	6. Say It's Not True	MCA 53955
7/27/91	1 (1)	17	7. **Leap Of Faith**	MCA 54078
12/21/91+	24	10	8. What Kind Of Fool	MCA 54237
			CARVER, Johnny	
			Born John David Carver on 11/24/40 in Jackson, Mississippi. Sang with family gospel group from age five, had own band in high school. Lived in Milwaukee, 1961-65, then worked in Los Angeles as singer with the house band at The Palomino in Hollywood.	
1/27/68	21	7	1. Your Lily White Hands	Imperial 66268
1/4/69	32	3	2. Hold Me Tight	Imperial 66341
			#5 Pop hit for Johnny Nash in 1968	
4/26/69	26	6	3. Sweet Wine	Imperial 66361
9/25/71	34	5	4. If You Think That It's All Right	Epic 10760
1/15/72	27	7	5. I Start Thinking About You	Epic 10813
8/5/72	35	2	6. I Want You	Epic 10872
5/5/73	5	12	7. **Yellow Ribbon**	ABC 11357
			also known as "Tie A Yellow Ribbon Round The Ole Oak Tree"; #1 Pop hit for Tony Orlando & Dawn in 1973	
8/18/73	6	10	8. **You Really Haven't Changed**	ABC 11374
1/19/74	12	10	9. Tonight Someone's Falling In Love	ABC 11403
5/11/74	27	6	10. Country Lullabye	ABC 11425
9/21/74	10	10	11. **Don't Tell (That Sweet Ole Lady Of Mine)**	ABC 12017
3/1/75	39	1	12. January Jones	ABC 12052
7/31/76	9	9	13. **Afternoon Delight**	ABC/Dot 17640
4/9/77	29	4	14. Living Next Door To Alice	ABC/Dot 17685
			#25 Pop hit for Smokie in 1977	
7/16/77	36	4	15. Down At The Pool	ABC/Dot 17707
			CASH, Johnny	
			Born on 2/26/32 in Kingsland, Arkansas. To Dyess, Arkansas at age three. Brother Roy led the Dixie Rhythm Ramblers band in late 1940s. In U.S. Air Force, 1950-54. Formed trio with Luther Perkins (guitar) and Marshall Grant (bass) in 1955. First recorded for Sun in 1955. On *Louisiana Hayride* and *Grand Ole Opry* in 1957. Own TV show for ABC, 1969-71. Worked with June Carter from 1961, married her in March 1968. Daughter Rosanne Cash and stepdaughter Carlene Carter currently enjoying successful singing careers. CMA Awards: 1969 Vocal Group of the Year (with June Carter); 1969 Male Vocalist of the Year; 1969 Entertainer of the Year. Elected to the Country Music Hall of Fame in 1980. Won Grammy's Living Legends Award in 1990. (a) JOHNNY CASH & JUNE CARTER (b) JOHNNY CASH & WAYLON JENNINGS (c) WAYLON JENNINGS, WILLIE NELSON, JOHNNY CASH, KRIS KRISTOFFERSON	

DATE	POS	WKS	ARTIST–RECORD TITLE	LABEL & NO.
11/26/55	**14**	1	1. Cry! Cry! Cry! Best Seller #14	Sun 221
2/4/56	**4**	23	2. **So Doggone Lonesome/** Juke Box #4 / Best Seller #6 / Jockey #6	
2/11/56	**4**	20	3. **Folsom Prison Blues** Jockey #4 / Juke Box #5 / Best Seller #5	Sun 232
6/9/56	**1 (6)**	43	4. **I Walk The Line/** Juke Box #1(6) / Jockey #1(1) / Best Seller #2	
		9	5. Get Rhythm Juke Box flip / Best Seller flip	Sun 241
12/22/56+	**1 (5)**	28	6. **There You Go/** Juke Box #1 / Best Seller #2 / Jockey #2	
12/22/56+	**7**	24	7. **Train Of Love** Jockey #7 / Best Seller #13	Sun 258
5/27/57	**9**	15	8. **Next In Line/** Best Seller #9 / Jockey #9	
		9	9. Don't Make Me Go Best Seller flip	Sun 266
9/16/57	**3**	23	10. **Home Of The Blues/** Jockey #3 / Best Seller #5	
10/7/57	**13**	2	11. Give My Love To Rose Jockey #13	Sun 279
1/20/58	**1 (10)**	23	12. **Ballad Of A Teenage Queen/** Jockey #1(10) / Best Seller #1(8)	
2/10/58	**4**	14	13. **Big River** Jockey #4	Sun 283
5/26/58	**1 (8)**	24	14. **Guess Things Happen That Way/** Best Seller #1(8) / Jockey #1(3)	
6/2/58	**6**	13	15. **Come In Stranger** Jockey #6	Sun 295
8/25/58	**2 (4)**	16	16. **The Ways Of A Woman In Love/** Best Seller #2 / Jockey #2; written by Charlie Rich	
9/1/58	**5**	16	17. **You're The Nearest Thing To Heaven**	Sun 302
10/13/58	**4**	19	18. **All Over Again/**	
10/13/58	**7**	15	19. **What Do I Care**	Columbia 41251
1/19/59	**1 (6)**	20	20. **Don't Take Your Guns To Town**	Columbia 41313
1/19/59	**30**	1	21. It's Just About Time	Sun 309
3/30/59	**8**	13	22. **Luther Played The Boogie/**	
3/30/59	**12**	9	23. Thanks A Lot	Sun 316
5/4/59	**9**	11	24. **Frankie's Man, Johnny/** new version of tune written in 1870, "Frankie & Johnny"	
5/11/59	**13**	11	25. You Dreamer You	Columbia 41371
7/20/59	**11**	11	26. Katy Too	Sun 321
8/10/59	**4**	20	27. **I Got Stripes/**	
8/24/59	**14**	9	28. Five Feet High And Rising	Columbia 41427
11/9/59	**22**	5	29. Goodby Little Darlin' written and recorded in 1946 by Gene Autry	Sun 331
12/28/59	**24**	1	30. The Little Drummer Boy [X]	Columbia 41481
2/15/60	**16**	10	31. Straight A's In Love/	
3/7/60	**20**	2	32. I Love You Because	Sun 334
4/25/60	**10**	15	33. **Seasons Of My Heart/**	
5/9/60	**13**	7	34. Smiling Bill McCall	Columbia 41618

DATE	POS	WKS		ARTIST–RECORD TITLE		LABEL & NO.
8/22/60	**15**	7	35.	Second Honeymoon		Columbia 41707
12/26/60	**30**	1	36.	Mean Eyed Cat		Sun 347
2/6/61	**13**	9	37.	Oh Lonesome Me		Sun 355
				The Gene Lowery Singers (backing vocals: 32, 37); all of above Sun recordings with The Tennessee Two (Luther Perkins & Marshall Grant, instrumental backing)		
6/12/61	**24**	2	38.	The Rebel - Johnny Yuma		Columbia 41995
				theme from TV series *The Rebel* starring Nick Adams		
12/18/61+	**11**	14	39.	Tennessee Flat-Top Box		Columbia 42147
3/31/62	**24**	3	40.	The Big Battle		Columbia 42301
7/14/62	**8**	10	41.	**In The Jailhouse Now**		Columbia 42425
				#14 Pop hit for Jimmie Rodgers in 1928		
4/6/63	**13**	3	42.	Busted		Columbia 42665
				JOHNNY CASH with The Carter Family		
				#4 Pop hit for Ray Charles in 1963		
6/8/63	**1 (7)**	26	43.	**Ring Of Fire**		Columbia 42788
11/9/63	**2 (3)**	16	44.	**The Matador**		Columbia 42880
2/22/64	**1 (6)**	22	45.	**Understand Your Man**		Columbia 42964
7/18/64	**3**	18	46.	**The Ballad Of Ira Hayes/**		
				Hayes: Indian who helped raise the flag at Iwo Jima in WWII		
7/25/64	**8**	14	47.	**Bad News**		Columbia 43058
11/14/64+	**4**	20	48.	**It Ain't Me, Babe** (a)		Columbia 43145
				#8 Pop hit for The Turtles in 1965		
2/27/65	**3**	15	49.	**Orange Blossom Special**		Columbia 43206
7/17/65	**15**	12	50.	Mister Garfield		Columbia 43313
				ballad about President Garfield's assassination; flip side "The Streets Of Laredo" Bubbled Under (#124)		
9/11/65	**10**	8	51.	**The Sons Of Katie Elder**		Columbia 43342
				title song from the movie starring John Wayne		
11/27/65+	**9**	12	52.	**Happy To Be With You**		Columbia 43420
2/26/66	**2 (2)**	16	53.	**The One On The Right Is On The Left**		Columbia 43496
7/9/66	**17**	8	54.	Everybody Loves A Nut		Columbia 43673
9/17/66	**39**	2	55.	Boa Constrictor	[N]	Columbia 43763
1/21/67	**20**	8	56.	You Beat All I Ever Saw		Columbia 43921
3/18/67	**2 (1)**	15	57.	**Jackson** (a)		Columbia 44011
				#14 Pop hit for Nancy Sinatra & Lee Hazlewood in 1967		
7/8/67	**6**	14	58.	**Long-Legged Guitar Pickin' Man** (a)		Columbia 44158
12/30/67+	**2 (2)**	14	59.	**Rosanna's Going Wild**		Columbia 44373
6/15/68	**1 (4)**	16	60.	**Folsom Prison Blues**	[R]	Columbia 44513
				"live" version of #3 above; recorded at Folsom Prison		
12/14/68+	**1 (6)**	19	61.	**Daddy Sang Bass**		Columbia 44689
8/9/69	**1 (5)**	12	● 62.	**A Boy Named Sue**	[N]	Columbia 44944
				recorded "live" at San Quentin prison; CMA Award: Single of the Year		
11/1/69	**23**	6	63.	Get Rhythm	[R]	Sun 1103
				reissue of #5 above; "live" effects dubbed in		
12/6/69	**4**	10	64.	**Blistered/**		
		10	65.	See Ruby Fall		Columbia 45020
1/31/70	**2 (1)**	13	66.	**If I Were A Carpenter** (a)		Columbia 45064
				#8 Pop hit for Bobby Darin in 1966		
3/14/70	**35**	2	67.	Rock Island Line		Sun 1111
				#8 Pop hit for Lonnie Donegan in 1956		
4/18/70	**3**	13	68.	**What Is Truth**		Columbia 45134

DATE	POS	WKS	ARTIST–RECORD TITLE	LABEL & NO.
9/5/70	**1 (2)**	14	69. **Sunday Morning Coming Down**	Columbia 45211
12/19/70+	**1 (1)**	13	70. **Flesh And Blood**	Columbia 45269
			from the movie *I Walk The Line* starring Gregory Peck	
3/27/71	**3**	13	71. **Man In Black**	Columbia 45339
7/10/71	18	7	72. Singing In Viet Nam Talking Blues	Columbia 45393
9/18/71	15	11	73. No Need To Worry (a)	Columbia 45431
11/6/71	16	8	74. Papa Was A Good Man	Columbia 45460
2/5/72	**2 (1)**	13	75. **A Thing Called Love**	Columbia 45534
			The Evangel Temple Choir (backing vocals, above 2)	
5/13/72	**2 (3)**	11	76. **Kate**	Columbia 45590
			written by Marty Robbins	
7/29/72	29	5	77. If I Had A Hammer (a)	Columbia 45631
			#10 Pop hit for Peter, Paul & Mary in 1962	
9/9/72	**2 (2)**	14	78. **Oney**	Columbia 45660
10/28/72	35	4	79. The World Needs A Melody	Columbia 45679
			THE CARTER FAMILY with JOHNNY CASH	
12/30/72+	**3**	14	80. **Any Old Wind That Blows**	Columbia 45740
2/10/73	27	6	81. The Loving Gift (a)	Columbia 45758
5/19/73	30	5	82. Children	Columbia 45786
			from the movie *The Gospel Road* starring Cash	
12/29/73+	34	2	83. Pick The Wildwood Flower	Columbia 45938
			JOHNNY CASH with MOTHER MAYBELLE CARTER	
6/1/74	31	4	84. Ragged Old Flag	Columbia 46028
1/4/75	14	7	85. Lady Came From Baltimore	Columbia 10066
8/30/75	17	6	86. Look At Them Beans	Columbia 10177
12/20/75+	35	4	87. Texas - 1947	Columbia 10237
4/24/76	**1 (2)**	11	88. **One Piece At A Time** [N]	Columbia 10321
8/14/76	29	3	89. Sold Out Of Flagpoles	Columbia 10381
12/18/76+	26	5	90. Old Time Feeling (a)	Columbia 10436
3/26/77	38	3	91. The Last Gunfighter Ballad	Columbia 10483
11/19/77	32	4	92. After The Ball	Columbia 10623
2/25/78	12	8	93. I Would Like To See You Again	Columbia 10681
5/27/78	**2 (2)**	10	94. **There Ain't No Good Chain Gang** (b)/	
12/1/79+	22	8	95. I Wish I Was Crazy Again (b)	Columbia 10742
2/10/79	21	6	96. I Will Rock And Roll With You	Columbia 10888
6/2/79	**2 (1)**	10	97. **(Ghost) Riders In The Sky**	Columbia 10961
4/11/81	**10**	9	98. **The Baron**	Columbia 60516
5/1/82	26	6	99. The General Lee	Scotti Br. 02803
			title refers to TV's *Dukes Of Hazzard* car	
6/1/85	**1 (1)**	14	100. **Highwayman** (c)	Columbia 04881
10/5/85	15	9	101. Desperados Waiting For A Train (c)	Columbia 05594
6/28/86	35	2	102. Even Cowgirls Get The Blues (b)	Columbia 05896
10/29/88	21	8	103. That Old Wheel	Mercury 870688
			JOHNNY CASH with HANK WILLIAMS, JR.	
3/31/90	25	7	104. Silver Stallion (c)	Columbia 73233

DATE	POS	WKS	ARTIST–RECORD TITLE	LABEL & NO.
			CASH, Rosanne	
			Born on 5/24/55 in Memphis. Daughter of Johnny Cash and Vivian Liberto. Raised by her mother in California, then moved to Nashville after high school graduation. Worked in the Johnny Cash Road Show. Married to Rodney Crowell, 1979-92; later married to producer John Leventhal. Released short-story collection *Bodies Of Water* in 1996.	
9/22/79	17	7	1. No Memories Hangin' Round **ROSANNE CASH with BOBBY BARE**	Columbia 11045
2/23/80	15	9	2. Couldn't Do Nothin' Right	Columbia 11188
6/21/80	25	6	3. Take Me, Take Me	Columbia 11268
3/14/81	1 (1)	13	4. **Seven Year Ache**	Columbia 11426
9/12/81	1 (1)	11	5. **My Baby Thinks He's A Train**	Columbia 02463
1/9/82	1 (1)	11	6. **Blue Moon With Heartache** also released as the B-side of #4 above	Columbia 02659
6/12/82	4	13	7. **Ain't No Money**	Columbia 02937
10/30/82+	8	13	8. **I Wonder**	Columbia 03283
4/2/83	14	9	9. It Hasn't Happened Yet	Columbia 03705
6/22/85	1 (1)	15	10. **I Don't Know Why You Don't Want Me**	Columbia 04809
10/26/85+	1 (1)	16	11. **Never Be You**	Columbia 05621
3/15/86	5	13	12. **Hold On**	Columbia 05794
8/2/86	5	14	13. **Second To No One**	Columbia 06159
7/18/87	1 (1)	15	14. **The Way We Make A Broken Heart** written by John Hiatt	Columbia 07200
11/28/87+	1 (1)	15	15. **Tennessee Flat Top Box**	Columbia 07624
2/20/88	1 (1)	13	16. **It's Such A Small World** **RODNEY CROWELL & ROSANNE CASH**	Columbia 07693
4/23/88	1 (1)	15	17. **If You Change Your Mind**	Columbia 07746
9/3/88	1 (1)	14	18. **Runaway Train** all of above produced by Rodney Crowell	Columbia 07988
4/8/89	1 (1)	14	19. **I Don't Want To Spoil The Party** written by John Lennon and Paul McCartney; #39 Pop hit for The Beatles in 1965	Columbia 68599
12/16/89	37	1	20. Black And White	Columbia 73054
11/17/90	39	1	21. What We Really Want	Columbia 73517
			CASH, Tommy	
			Born on 4/5/40 in Dyess, Arkansas; younger brother of Johnny Cash. Own band at Treadwell High School in 1957. DJ for U.S. Army in Frankfurt, Germany, in 1958. Worked with Hank Williams, Jr., in the mid-1960s.	
12/13/69+	4	13	1. **Six White Horses** tribute to John F. Kennedy, Robert Kennedy and Martin Luther King	Epic 10540
4/11/70	9	12	2. **Rise And Shine**	Epic 10590
7/25/70	9	11	3. **One Song Away**	Epic 10630
12/19/70	36	3	4. The Tears On Lincoln's Face	Epic 10673
4/3/71	20	7	5. So This Is Love	Epic 10700
7/31/71	28	6	6. I'm Gonna Write A Song	Epic 10756
5/13/72	32	2	7. You're Everything	Epic 10838
7/29/72	22	9	8. That Certain One	Epic 10885
11/18/72	24	8	9. Listen	Epic 10915
5/5/73	37	3	10. Workin' On A Feelin'	Epic 10964
9/1/73	16	8	11. I Recall A Gypsy Woman	Epic 11026
12/22/73+	21	7	12. She Met A Stranger, I Met A Train	Epic 11057

DATE	POS	WKS	ARTIST – RECORD TITLE	LABEL & NO.
			CATES SISTERS, The	
			Duo of fiddlers Margie and Marcy Cates. Worked as backup act for Jim Ed Brown.	
10/29/77	30	6	1. I'll Always Love You	Caprice 2036
1/28/78	29	4	2. I've Been Loved	Caprice 2041
10/7/78	39	2	3. Lovin' You Off My Mind	Caprice 2051
			CATO, Connie	
			Born Connie Ann Cato on 3/30/55 in Carlinville, Illinois.	
4/6/74	33	4	1. Superskirt	Capitol 3788
4/12/75	14	8	2. Hurt	Capitol 4035
			#4 Pop hit for Timi Yuro in 1961	
			CHANCE	
			Quintet originally named Texas Pride. Consisted of brothers Jeff (vocals, steel guitar, fiddle, sax) and Mick (vocals, drums) Barosh, Jon Mulligan (keyboards), John Buckley (vocals, guitar) and Billy Hafer (bass). Jeff began solo recording career as Jeff Chance in 1988.	
6/8/85	35	2	1. To Be Lovers	Mercury 880555
11/30/85	30	6	2. She Told Me Yes	Mercury 884178
			CHARLES, Kim	
			Male singer.	
3/10/79	35	3	1. I Want To Thank You	MCA 40987
			title also shown as simply "Want To Thank You"	
			CHARLES, Ray	
			Born Ray Charles Robinson on 9/23/30 in Albany, Georgia. To Greenville, Florida while still an infant. Partially blind at age five, completely blind at seven (glaucoma). Studied classical piano and clarinet at State School for Deaf and Blind Children, St. Augustine, Florida, 1937-45. With local Florida bands; moved to Seattle in 1948. Formed the McSon Trio (also known as the Maxim Trio and the Maxine Trio) with Gossady McGhee (guitar) and Milton Garret (bass). First recordings were very much in the King Cole Trio style. Formed own band in 1954. The 1950s female vocal group, The Cookies, became his backing group, The Raeletts. Inducted into the Rock and Roll Hall of Fame in 1986. Won Grammy's Lifetime Achievement Award in 1987. Popular performer with many TV and movie appearances.	
2/5/83	20	7	1. Born To Love Me	Columbia 03429
6/4/83	37	1	2. 3/4 Time	Columbia 03810
1/21/84	6	10	3. **We Didn't See A Thing** **RAY CHARLES & GEORGE JONES featuring Chet Atkins**	Columbia 04297
9/1/84	14	9	4. Rock And Roll Shoes **RAY CHARLES with B.J. THOMAS**	Columbia 04531
1/26/85	1 (1)	12	5. **Seven Spanish Angels** **RAY CHARLES with WILLIE NELSON**	Columbia 04715
5/25/85	12	9	6. It Ain't Gonna Worry My Mind **RAY CHARLES with MICKEY GILLEY**	Columbia 04860
9/28/85	14	8	7. Two Old Cats Like Us **RAY CHARLES with HANK WILLIAMS, JR.**	Columbia 05575
8/23/86	34	3	8. The Pages Of My Mind	Columbia 06172

Alabama was inarguably the hottest Country act of the '80s. Beginning with 1980's "Tennessee River," the group released an astounding string of 20 consecutive No. 1 singles, leaving previous record-holder Sonny James well in the dust. "Forty Hour Week (For A Livin')" of 1985 was one of the 20.

Rex Allen, Jr.'s real-life roots were ably displayed on his 1982 single "Last Of The Silver Screen Cowboys." The track, which reached No. 43, featured "guest stars" Roy Rogers and Allen's own distinguished actor/singer father, Rex Allen, Sr.

Eddy Arnold's massive sales success and career longevity made him a true titan of Country music: The singer released 58 consecutive Top 10 records between 1945 and 1954. "A Million Years Or So" climbed to No. 13 in 1963.

Asleep At The Wheel—a long-lived aggregation of players that originally formed in West Virginia in 1970—returned to their former label, Epic Records, in the mid-'80s and nabbed their first chart hit in nine years: 1987's "Way Down Texas Way."

Razzy Bailey rode a brief wave of enormous popularity in the early '80s that nearly ended as swiftly as it arrived. Between August 1980 and December 1981, he scored five No. 1 hits, "I Keep Coming Back" among them.

Moe Bandy & Joe Stampley, better known as the Good Ol' Boys, played up their good-timey image to great success in the late '70s. "The Boy's Night Out" of 1984 followed their inimitable Top 10 parody of Pop singer Boy George, titled "Where's The Dress."

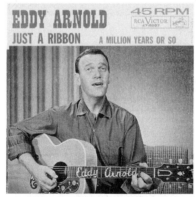

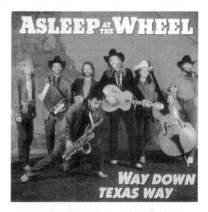

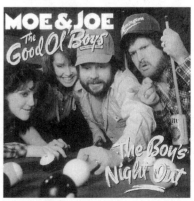

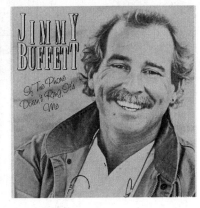

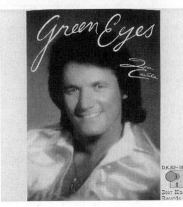

Thom Bresh, a singer and actor who'd appeared on TV Westerns like "Gunsmoke" as well as on the stage, moved to Nashville in 1983—at which point, oddly enough, he never released a charting single again. His last, 1982's "When It Comes To Love," was a duet with singer Lane Brody.

T. Graham Brown's finger was clearly on the pulse of middle America during the '80s: The Georgia-born singer was a one-time jingle-singer for the likes of McDonalds and Budweiser. "She Couldn't Love Me Anymore" was one of three Top 10 singles he released in 1987.

Jimmy Buffett's evolution from little-known Country good-timer to record-breaking concert attraction is one of the most fascinating stories in the industry. His 1985 No. 16 hit "If The Phone Doesn't Ring, It's Me" is included in MCA's 1992 4-CD collection *Boats, Beaches, Bars & Ballads*—the biggest-selling boxed set in MCA's history.

Glen Campbell's singing and notable guitar playing have been fixtures on the Pop and Country charts since 1962. The versatile actor-TV star met Top 10 success in 1985 covering another yet Pop institution—Brook Benton and his 1959 Pop hit "It's Just A Matter Of Time."

Tom Carlile's "Green Eyes" provided the second-to-last chart appearance for the Florida-based singer in 1982. The track, issued on the small Door Knob Records label, reached No. 37—his all-time high.

Johnny Cash's masterful recording career has boasted more than one prison-themed song or album. From the singer of "Folsom Prison Blues" came this 1962 cover of Jimmie Rodgers's "In The Jailhouse Now," which swiftly climbed to No. 8.

DATE	POS	WKS	ARTIST—RECORD TITLE	LABEL & NO.
			CHASE, Carol	
			Born Carol Schulte in Stanley, North Dakota. Graduated from University of North Dakota in 1971. Wrote "We Belong Together" for Susie Allanson.	
12/15/79+	32	5	1. This Must Be My Ship	Casabl. W. 4501
			CHESNEY, Kenny	
			Born on 3/26/68 in Knoxville; raised in Luttrell, Tennessee.	
4/29/95	6	15	1. **Fall In Love**	BNA 64278
8/26/95	8	14	2. **All I Need To Know**	BNA 64347
12/30/95+	23	9	3. Grandpa Told Me So	BNA 64352
			CHESNUT, Jim	
			Born on 12/1/44 in Midland, Texas. Former DJ and TV weatherman. One-time member of The Dan Blocker Singers.	
10/13/79	27	5	1. Let's Take The Time To Fall In Love Again	MCA 41106
7/11/81	36	2	2. Bedtime Stories	Liberty 1405
			CHESNUTT, Mark	
			Born on 9/6/63 in Beaumont, Texas. Son of regional Texas star Bob Chesnutt. First recorded for Axbar label in the mid-1980s. CMA Award: 1993 Horizon Award.	
8/11/90	3	19	1. **Too Cold At Home**	MCA 79054
12/15/90+	1 (2)	17	2. **Brother Jukebox**	MCA 53965
4/13/91	5	15	3. **Blame It On Texas**	MCA 54053
8/3/91	3	17	4. **Your Love Is A Miracle**	MCA 54136
11/23/91+	10	14	5. **Broken Promise Land**	MCA 54256
3/7/92	5	19	6. **Old Flames Have New Names**	MCA 54334
7/4/92	1 (1)	17	7. **I'll Think Of Something**	MCA 54395
10/3/92	4	10	8. **Bubba Shot The Jukebox**	MCA 54471
1/30/93	4	14	9. **Old Country**	MCA 54539
6/5/93	1 (1)	18	10. **It Sure Is Monday**	MCA 54630
9/25/93	1 (1)	17	11. **Almost Goodbye**	MCA 54718
12/25/93+	1 (1)	18	12. **I Just Wanted You To Know**	MCA 54768
4/30/94	21	8	13. Woman, Sensuous Woman	MCA 54822
8/6/94	6	14	14. **She Dreams**	Decca 54887
11/12/94+	2 (2)	17	15. **Goin' Through The Big D**	Decca 54941
3/18/95	1 (1)	17	16. **Gonna Get A Life**	Decca 54978
7/15/95	23	8	17. Down In Tennessee	Decca 55050
10/21/95	18	9	18. Trouble	Decca 55103
1/27/96	7	16	19. **It Wouldn't Hurt To Have Wings**	Decca 55164
			CHICK AND HIS HOT RODS—see RENO & SMILEY	
			CHOATES, Harry	
			Born on 12/26/22 in Rayne, Louisiana. Died in jail on 7/17/51 in Austin, Texas. Cajun fiddler. Label misspelled last name as Coates.	
1/4/47	4	2	1. Jole Blon **HARRY COATES** first released in 1946 on Gold Star 1314	Modern Mt. 511

DATE	POS	WKS	ARTIST– RECORD TITLE	LABEL & NO.
			CLANTON, Darrell	
			Indianapolis-born guitarist/bassist/banjo player. Played in father's band from age nine. From age 17 to 22, worked in the Florida trio Just Us Brothers.	
12/3/83+	24	7	1. Lonesome 7-7203	Audiograph 474
			CLAPTON, Eric	
			Born Eric Patrick Clapp on 3/30/45 in Ripley, England. Prolific rock-blues guitarist/vocalist. A member of The Roosters, The Yardbirds and John Mayall's Bluesbreakers. Founder of Cream and Blind Faith.	
4/8/78	26	4	● 1. Lay Down Sally	RSO 886
			CLARK, Guy	
			Born on 11/6/41 in Monahans, Texas; raised in Rockport, Texas. Moved to Nashville in 1971. Wrote "Desperados Waiting For A Train," "The Last Gunfighter Ballad," "L.A. Freeway" and many others.	
8/29/81	38	1	1. The Partner Nobody Chose	Warner 49740
			CLARK, Petula	
			Born on 11/15/32 in Epsom, England. Pop singer/actress.	
3/6/82	20	7	1. Natural Love	Scotti Br. 02676
			CLARK, Roy	
			Born Roy Linwood Clark on 4/15/33 in Meherrin, Virginia. Multi-instrumentalist. Won National Country Music Banjo Competition twice in the late 1940s. Moved to Washington, D.C., and worked with the Clark family group, appearing on the *Hayloft Conservatory Of Musical Interpretation* TV series in 1948. Worked on the Jimmy Dean and George Hamilton IV TV shows. Acted in *The Beverly Hillbillies* TV series, appearing as both Cousin Roy and Roy's mother Big Mama Halsey. With the *Hee-Haw* TV series from the first show in 1969. Joined the *Grand Ole Opry* in 1987. CMA Award: 1973 Entertainer of the Year.	
7/6/63	10	16	1. **Tips Of My Fingers**	Capitol 4956
2/8/64	31	3	2. Through The Eyes Of A Fool written by Bobby Bare	Capitol 5099
4/3/65	37	5	3. When The Wind Blows In Chicago co-written by actor Audie Murphy	Capitol 5350
7/5/69	9	12	4. **Yesterday, When I Was Young**	Dot 17246
10/18/69	40	2	5. September Song first popularized by actor Walter Huston in 1939	Dot 17299
12/27/69+	21	6	6. Right Or Left At Oak Street	Dot 17324
2/21/70	31	3	7. Then She's A Lover	Dot 17335
6/27/70	5	11	8. **I Never Picked Cotton**	Dot 17349
10/3/70	6	12	9. **Thank God And Greyhound**	Dot 17355
12/11/71	39	1	10. Magnificent Sanctuary Band written by Dorsey Burnette	Dot 17395
9/16/72	9	10	11. **The Lawrence Welk - Hee Haw Counter-Revolution Polka** [N]	Dot 17426
3/10/73	1 (1)	13	12. **Come Live With Me**	Dot 17449
7/28/73	27	7	13. Riders In The Sky [I]	Dot 17458
11/17/73+	2 (1)	12	14. **Somewhere Between Love And Tomorrow**	Dot 17480
4/6/74	4	12	15. **Honeymoon Feelin'**	Dot 17498
9/21/74	12	10	16. The Great Divide	Dot 17518

DATE	POS	WKS	ARTIST – RECORD TITLE	LABEL & NO.
5/3/75	35	3	17. You're Gonna Love Yourself In The Morning	ABC/Dot 17545
9/13/75	16	7	18. Heart To Heart	ABC/Dot 17565
2/7/76	2 (2)	12	19. **If I Had It To Do All Over Again**	ABC/Dot 17605
6/26/76	21	7	20. Think Summer	ABC/Dot 17626
1/29/77	26	4	21. I Have A Dream, I Have A Dream	ABC/Dot 17667
9/24/77	40	2	22. We Can't Build A Fire In The Rain	ABC/Dot 17712
3/24/79	34	3	23. Shoulder To Shoulder (Arm and Arm)	ABC 12402
1/19/80	21	6	24. Chain Gang Of Love	MCA 41153

CLARK, Sanford

Born in 1935 in Tulsa, Oklahoma. Moved to Phoenix in his teens.

DATE	POS	WKS	ARTIST – RECORD TITLE	LABEL & NO.
10/6/56	14	1	1. The Fool Jockey #14; first released on MCI 1003 in 1956	Dot 15481

CLARK, Terri

Born and raised in Medicine Hat, Alberta, Canada. Female singer.

DATE	POS	WKS	ARTIST – RECORD TITLE	LABEL & NO.
8/19/95	3	15	1. **Better Things To Do**	Mercury 852046
11/18/95+	3	17	2. **When Boy Meets Girl**	Mercury 852388
3/23/96	8	18	3. If I Were You	Mercury 852708

CLIFFORD, Buzz

Born Reese Francis Clifford III on 10/8/42 in Berwyn, Illinois.

DATE	POS	WKS	ARTIST – RECORD TITLE	LABEL & NO.
3/20/61	28	1	1. Baby Sittin' Boogie **[N]** babies' voices are by the children (boy and girl) of the producer	Columbia 41876

CLINE, Patsy

Born Virginia Patterson Hensley on 9/8/32 in Winchester, Virginia. Died in a plane crash on 3/5/63 near Camden, Tennessee. Worked local clubs as a singer, and briefly in Nashville in 1948. On *Arthur Godfrey's Talent Scouts* TV show in January 1957. With the *Grand Ole Opry* from 1961. Plane crash also claimed the lives of Hawkshaw Hawkins and Cowboy Copas. Elected to the Country Music Hall of Fame in 1973. Movie *Sweet Dreams*, based on her life, was produced in 1985.

DATE	POS	WKS	ARTIST – RECORD TITLE	LABEL & NO.
3/2/57	2 (2)	19	1. **Walkin' After Midnight/** Juke Box #2 / Best Seller #3 / Jockey #3	
6/10/57	14	1	2. A Poor Man's Roses (Or A Rich Man's Gold) Jockey #14	Decca 30221
4/3/61	1 (2)	39	3. **I Fall To Pieces**	Decca 31205
11/13/61+	2 (2)	21	4. **Crazy** written by Willie Nelson	Decca 31317
3/3/62	1 (5)	19	5. **She's Got You**	Decca 31354
6/2/62	10	12	6. **When I Get Thru With You (You'll Love Me Too)/**	
6/30/62	21	3	7. Imagine That	Decca 31377
8/25/62	14	10	8. So Wrong	Decca 31406
2/16/63	8	17	9. **Leavin' On Your Mind**	Decca 31455
5/11/63	5	16	10. **Sweet Dreams (Of You)**	Decca 31483
9/14/63	7	13	11. **Faded Love**	Decca 31522
11/7/64	23	11	12. He Called Me Baby	Decca 31671
9/27/80	18	5	13. Always **[R]** first released on Decca 25732; there have been 10 Pop charted versions of this Irving Berlin tune	MCA 41303

DATE	POS	WKS	ARTIST–RECORD TITLE	LABEL & NO.
11/28/81+	5	11	14. **Have You Ever Been Lonely (Have You Ever Been Blue)** **JIM REEVES and PATSY CLINE** *Cline and Reeves never recorded together; their voices were spliced together electronically*	RCA 12346
			COCHRAN, Cliff	
			Born in Pascagoula, Mississippi; raised in Greenville, Mississippi. Cousin of Hank Cochran. In duo with brother Bob in the mid-1960s. Moved to Nashville in 1967.	
6/23/79	24	7	1. Love Me Like A Stranger	RCA 11562
10/13/79	29	5	2. First Thing Each Morning (Last Thing at Night)	RCA 11711
			COCHRAN, Hank	
			Born Garland Perry on 8/2/35 in Isola, Mississippi. Worked in oil fields in New Mexico until moving to Los Angeles in the early '50s. Worked local clubs and teamed with Eddie Cochran (no relation) as the Cochran Brothers. Recorded for Ekko. Duo disbanded, Hank worked on the *California Hayride*. Moved to Nashville in 1959. Wrote "I Fall To Pieces," "She's Got You," "Funny Way Of Laughin'," "Make The World Go Away" and many others. Once married to Jeannie Seeley (since divorced).	
9/1/62	20	5	1. Sally Was A Good Old Girl	Liberty 55461
11/10/62	23	2	2. I'd Fight The World	Liberty 55498
10/5/63	25	1	3. A Good Country Song	Gaylord 6431
			CODY, Betty	
			Born Rita M. Cote in Auburn, Maine. Worked on SCOU-Lewiston, Maine, at age 15. Featured vocalist on the WWVA-Wheeling *Jamboree*. Married to Harold "Lone Pine" Breau.	
12/26/53	10	1	1. **I Found Out More Than You Ever Knew** *Juke Box #10; answer song to "I Forgot More Than You'll Ever Know"*	RCA 5462
			COE, David Allan	
			Born on 9/6/39 in Akron, Ohio. Billed as "The Mysterious Rhinestone Cowboy" until 1978. Wrote hit "Would You Lay With Me (In A Field Of Stone)" for Tanya Tucker. Appeared in the movies *Take This Job And Shove It* (also wrote the title tune for Johnny Paycheck) and *Last Days Of Frank And Jesse James*. Acted in and co-wrote the music for the movie *Stagecoach*.	
8/2/75	8	12	1. **You Never Even Called Me By My Name**	Columbia 10159
1/17/76	17	7	2. Longhaired Redneck	Columbia 10254
10/23/76	25	5	3. Willie, Waylon And Me　　　　　　　　　　[N]	Columbia 10395
4/9/83	4	13	4. **The Ride**	Columbia 03778
4/7/84	2 (1)	13	5. **Mona Lisa Lost Her Smile**	Columbia 04396
1/19/85	11	9	6. She Used To Love Me A Lot	Columbia 04688
5/18/85	29	4	7. Don't Cry Darlin' *George Jones (recitation)*	Columbia 04846
3/21/87	34	4	8. Need A Little Time Off For Bad Behavior	Columbia 06661
			COLDER, Ben—see WOOLEY, Sheb	
			COLE, Nat "King"—see KING COLE TRIO, The	

DATE	POS	WKS	ARTIST–RECORD TITLE	LABEL & NO.
			COLLIE, Mark	
			Born George Mark Collie on 1/18/56 in Waynesboro, Tennessee.	
7/28/90	35	3	1. Looks Aren't Everything	MCA 79023
3/16/91	18	11	2. Let Her Go	MCA 53971
8/10/91	31	8	3. Calloused Hands	MCA 54079
12/7/91+	28	8	4. She's Never Comin' Back	MCA 54244
10/3/92	5	15	5. **Even The Man In The Moon Is Crying**	MCA 54448
2/20/93	6	15	6. **Born To Love You**	MCA 54515
7/17/93	26	6	7. Shame Shame Shame Shame	MCA 54668
11/6/93	24	7	8. Something's Gonna Change Her Mind	MCA 54720
11/26/94+	13	9	9. Hard Lovin' Woman	MCA 54907
8/12/95	25	9	10. Three Words, Two Hearts, One Night	Giant 17855
			COLLIE, Shirley	
			Born Shirley Caddell on 3/16/31 in Chillicothe, Missouri. Worked on the *Brush Creek Follies*, KMBC-Kansas City. Formerly married to DJ Biff Collie and Willie Nelson.	
6/12/61	25	5	1. Dime A Dozen	Liberty 55324
9/11/61	23	3	2. Why, Baby, Why	Liberty 55361
			WARREN SMITH and SHIRLEY COLLIE	
3/17/62	10	13	3. **Willingly**	Liberty 55403
			WILLIE NELSON & SHIRLEY COLLIE	
			COLLINS, Brian	
			Born on 10/19/50 in Baltimore; raised in Texas City, Texas. Played in local bands from age 11. Had own band, The Nomads, while in junior high school. Discovered by Dolly Parton in 1969.	
8/18/73	24	8	1. I Wish (You Had Stayed)	Dot 17466
6/15/74	10	10	2. **Statue Of A Fool**	Dot 17499
12/28/74+	23	6	3. That's The Way Love Should Be	ABC/Dot 17527
			COLLINS, Gwen & Jerry	
			Husband-and-wife duo from Miami.	
2/7/70	34	2	1. Get Together	Capitol 2710
			#5 Pop hit for The Youngbloods in 1969	
			COLLINS, Tommy	
			Born Leonard Raymond Sipes on 9/28/30 in Oklahoma City. Worked local radio stations, first with KLPR-Oklahoma City. Served in U.S. Marines, then moved to Los Angeles after discharge. Worked on *Town Hall Party* radio series in the early 1950s. First recorded for Capitol in 1953. Married Wanda Shahan in 1955 and sang duets with her. Own band with Buck Owens as lead guitarist. Minister, 1961-64; joined Buck Owens' show in 1964. The song "Leonard" by Merle Haggard in 1981 was about Collins. Wrote several of Haggard's hits.	
2/20/54	2 (7)	21	1. **You Better Not Do That**	Capitol 2701
			Jockey #2 / Juke Box #2 / Best Seller #2	
9/4/54	4	15	2. **Whatcha Gonna Do Now**	Capitol 2891
			Jockey #4 / Best Seller #7	
2/5/55	10	1	3. **Untied**	Capitol 3017
			Juke Box #10 / Best Seller #15	

DATE	POS	WKS	ARTIST–RECORD TITLE	LABEL & NO.
4/30/55	5	9	4. **It Tickles** Juke Box #5 / Jockey #9 / Best Seller #10	Capitol 3082
10/1/55	13	2	5. I Guess I'm Crazy/ Best Seller #13	
10/1/55	15	2	6. You Oughta See Pickles Now Best Seller #15	Capitol 3190
2/19/66	7	11	7. **If You Can't Bite, Don't Growl**	Columbia 43489

COLTER, Jessi

Born Miriam Johnson on 5/25/47 in Phoenix. Played piano in church from age 11. Worked with Duane Eddy from 1961; married to him, 1962-68. With Waylon Jennings from 1969, married him in October 1969.

(a) WAYLON & JESSI

DATE	POS	WKS	ARTIST–RECORD TITLE	LABEL & NO.
12/12/70	25	4	1. Suspicious Minds (a) #1 Pop hit for Elvis Presley in 1969	RCA 9920
7/24/71	39	1	2. Under Your Spell Again (a)	RCA 9992
3/29/75	1 (1)	11	3. **I'm Not Lisa**	Capitol 4009
9/13/75	5	12	4. **What's Happened To Blue Eyes**	Capitol 4087
1/24/76	11	9	5. **It's Morning (And I Still Love You)**	Capitol 4200
5/15/76	2 (1)	11	6. **Suspicious Minds** (a) [R]	RCA 10653
10/9/76	29	5	7. I Thought I Heard You Calling My Name	Capitol 4325
3/7/81	17	7	8. Storms Never Last (a)	RCA 12176
6/20/81	10	8	9. **Wild Side Of Life/It Wasn't God Who Made Honky Tonk Angels** (a)	RCA 12245

COMPTON BROTHERS, The

Harry and Bill Compton from St. Louis, Missouri. Won a Columbia Records talent contest in 1965. Operate their own publishing company, Wepedol Music.

DATE	POS	WKS	ARTIST–RECORD TITLE	LABEL & NO.
10/4/69	11	10	1. Haunted House #11 Pop hit for Gene Simmons in 1964	Dot 17294
2/7/70	16	8	2. Charlie Brown #2 Pop hit for The Coasters in 1959	Dot 17336

CONFEDERATE RAILROAD

Southern country-rock band: Danny Shirley, Chris McDaniel, Michael Lamb, Wayne Secrest, Gates Nichols and Mark DuFresne. Worked as house band at Miss Kitty's in Marietta, Georgia. Jimmy Dormire replaced Lamb by 1995.

DATE	POS	WKS	ARTIST–RECORD TITLE	LABEL & NO.
5/30/92	37	3	1. She Took It Like A Man	Atlantic LP Cut
8/15/92	4	14	2. **Jesus And Mama** later available as the B-side of #3 below	Atlantic LP Cut
12/19/92+	2 (1)	16	3. **Queen Of Memphis**	Atlantic 87404
8/28/93	10	13	4. **Trashy Women/**	
5/29/93	14	11	5. When You Leave That Way You Can Never Go Back	Atlantic 87357
1/15/94	27	8	6. She Never Cried all of above from the album *Confederate Railroad* on Atlantic 82335	Atlantic LP Cut
4/9/94	9	14	7. **Daddy Never Was The Cadillac Kind**	Atlantic 87273
8/6/94	20	9	8. Elvis And Andy	Atlantic 87229
6/24/95	24	9	9. When And Where from the album *When And Where* on Atlantic 82774	Atlantic LP Cut

DATE	POS	WKS	ARTIST– RECORD TITLE	LABEL & NO.
			CONLEE, John	
			Born on 8/11/46 in Versailles, Kentucky. Worked as a mortician for six years, then a newsreader in Fort Knox. Moved to WLAC-Nashville in 1971; worked as a DJ and music director. Joined the *Grand Ole Opry* in 1981. Chairman of the Family Farm Defense Fund.	
6/24/78	5	10	1. **Rose Colored Glasses**	ABC 12356
11/11/78+	1 (1)	12	2. **Lady Lay Down**	ABC 12420
3/10/79	1 (1)	11	3. **Backside Of Thirty**	ABC 12455
8/18/79	2 (2)	12	4. **Before My Time**	MCA 41072
12/22/79+	7	11	5. **Baby, You're Something**	MCA 41163
5/24/80	2 (2)	11	6. **Friday Night Blues**	MCA 41233
10/4/80	2 (2)	10	7. **She Can't Say That Anymore**	MCA 41321
2/7/81	12	9	8. What I Had With You	MCA 51044
7/4/81	26	4	9. Could You Love Me (One More Time)	MCA 51112
9/26/81	2 (2)	11	10. **Miss Emily's Picture**	MCA 51164
3/6/82	6	13	11. **Busted**	MCA 52008
			#4 Pop hit for Ray Charles in 1963	
7/24/82	26	7	12. Nothing Behind You, Nothing In Sight	MCA 52070
11/6/82+	10	12	13. **I Don't Remember Loving You**	MCA 52116
3/19/83	1 (1)	13	14. **Common Man**	MCA 52178
7/16/83	1 (1)	12	15. **I'm Only In It For The Love**	MCA 52231
11/12/83+	1 (1)	15	16. **In My Eyes**	MCA 52282
3/31/84	1 (1)	12	17. **As Long As I'm Rockin' With You**	MCA 52351
7/14/84	4	12	18. **Way Back**	MCA 52403
11/10/84+	2 (2)	14	19. **Years After You**	MCA 52470
3/23/85	7	11	20. **Working Man**	MCA 52543
8/3/85	15	9	21. Blue Highway	MCA 52625
11/23/85+	5	13	22. **Old School**	MCA 52695
3/22/86	10	11	23. **Harmony**	Columbia 05778
7/5/86	1 (1)	14	24. **Got My Heart Set On You**	Columbia 06104
11/15/86+	6	13	25. **The Carpenter**	Columbia 06311
3/21/87	4	13	26. **Domestic Life**	Columbia 06707
8/8/87	11	12	27. Mama's Rockin' Chair	Columbia 07203
			CONLEY, Earl Thomas	
			Born on 10/17/41 in Portsmouth, Ohio. Worked clubs in Huntsville, Alabama, in the early '70s, wrote songs for Billy Larkin and Bobby G. Rice. Wrote hits "Smokey Mountain Memories" for Mel Street, and "This Time I've Hurt Her More Than She Loves Me" for Conway Twitty. Also recorded as The ETC Band.	
2/10/79	32	5	1. Dreamin's All I Do **EARL CONLEY**	Warner 8717
10/27/79	26	6	2. Stranded On A Dead End Street **THE ETC BAND**	Warner 49072
12/20/80+	7	11	3. **Silent Treatment**	Sunbird 7556
4/25/81	1 (1)	14	4. **Fire & Smoke**	Sunbird 7561
11/7/81+	10	12	5. **Tell Me Why**	RCA 12344
2/27/82	16	7	6. After The Love Slips Away/	
		7	7. Smokey Mountain Memories	RCA 13053
7/3/82	8	11	8. **Heavenly Bodies**	RCA 13246

DATE	POS	WKS	ARTIST– RECORD TITLE	LABEL & NO.
10/16/82	**1** (1)	13	9. **Somewhere Between Right And Wrong**	RCA 13320
2/5/83	**2** (2)	13	10. **I Have Loved You, Girl (But Not Like This Before)**[R]	RCA 13414
			new version of Conley's first hit (#87 in 1975)	
5/28/83	**1** (1)	13	11. **Your Love's On The Line**	RCA 13525
10/1/83	**1** (1)	14	12. **Holding Her And Loving You**	RCA 13596
2/4/84	**1** (1)	12	13. **Don't Make It Easy For Me**	RCA 13702
5/19/84	**1** (1)	13	14. **Angel In Disguise**	RCA 13758
9/29/84	**1** (1)	14	15. **Chance Of Lovin' You**	RCA 13877
12/15/84+	**8**	13	16. **All Tangled Up In Love**	RCA 13938
			GUS HARDIN with **EARL THOMAS CONLEY**	
2/2/85	**1** (1)	13	17. **Honor Bound**	RCA 13960
5/18/85	**1** (1)	13	18. **Love Don't Care (Whose Heart It Breaks)**	RCA 14060
10/5/85	**1** (1)	15	19. **Nobody Falls Like A Fool**	RCA 14172
2/15/86	**1** (1)	14	20. **Once In A Blue Moon**	RCA 14282
8/16/86	**2** (1)	14	21. **Too Many Times**	RCA 14380
			EARL THOMAS CONLEY and ANITA POINTER	
12/20/86+	**1** (1)	13	22. **I Can't Win For Losin' You**	RCA 5064
4/25/87	**1** (1)	13	23. **That Was A Close One**	RCA 5129
8/15/87	**1** (1)	14	24. **Right From The Start**	RCA 5226
4/2/88	**1** (1)	13	25. **What She Is (Is A Woman In Love)**	RCA 6894
7/16/88	**1** (1)	15	26. **We Believe In Happy Endings**	RCA 8632
			EARL THOMAS CONLEY with EMMYLOU HARRIS	
11/26/88+	**1** (1)	14	27. **What I'd Say**	RCA 8717
4/1/89	**1** (1)	15	28. **Love Out Loud**	RCA 8824
10/21/89	**26**	8	29. **You Must Not Be Drinking Enough**	RCA 8973
3/24/90	**11**	11	30. **Bring Back Your Love To Me**	RCA 9121
7/6/91	**8**	15	31. **Shadow Of A Doubt**	RCA 2826
9/21/91	**2** (1)	18	32. **Brotherly Love**	RCA 62037
			KEITH WHITLEY & EARL THOMAS CONLEY	
2/29/92	**36**	2	33. **Hard Days And Honky Tonk Nights**	RCA 62167

COOLEY, Spade, and his Orchestra

Cooley was born Donnell Clyde Cooley on 2/22/10 in Grand, Oklahoma. Died of a heart attack on 11/23/69. Played fiddle at square dances from age eight. Moved to Hollywood in the mid-1930s and worked as an actor in Roy Rogers movies. Worked with Cal Shrum, sang with the Riders Of The Purple Sage. From 1941, led big band at the Venice Ballroom, including Tex Williams. Appeared in many movies including own short subjects *King Of Western Swing* and *Spade Cooley & His Orchestra* in 1949. Own TV shows from the late '40s to 1958. Married Ella Mae Evans in 1945, convicted of her murder in April 1961. Sentenced to life imprisonment at Vacaville, California. Died performing at the Oakland Deputy Sheriff's Show two months before he was to be paroled.

DATE	POS	WKS	ARTIST– RECORD TITLE	LABEL & NO.
3/3/45	**1** (9)	31	1. **Shame On You/**	
			Tex Williams and Oakie (vocals)	
4/28/45	**8**	1	2. **A Pair Of Broken Hearts**	Okeh 6731
10/6/45	**4**	1	3. **I've Taken All I'm Gonna Take From You**	Okeh 6746
3/16/46	**2** (1)	11	4. **Detour/**	
			Oakie, Arkie and Tex Williams (vocals)	
4/20/46	**3**	11	5. **You Can't Break My Heart**	Columbia 36935
3/8/47	**4**	1	6. **Crazy 'Cause I Love You**	Columbia 37058
			Tex Williams (vocal: #2,3,5,6)	

DATE	POS	WKS	ARTIST– RECORD TITLE	LABEL & NO.
			## COOLIDGE, Rita	
			Born on 5/1/44 in Nashville. Had own group, R.C. and the Moonpies, at Florida State University. Moved to Los Angeles in the late '60s. Did backup work for Delaney & Bonnie, Leon Russell, Joe Cocker and Eric Clapton. With Kris Kristofferson from 1971; married to him, 1973-80. Known as "The Delta Lady," for whom Leon Russell wrote the song of the same name. Appeared in the 1983 movie *Club Med*.	
1/26/80	**32**	3	1. I'd Rather Leave While I'm In Love	A&M 2199
			## COOPER, Wilma Lee & Stoney	
			Husband-and-wife duo: Wilma Lee Leary (born 2/7/21, Valley Head, West Virginia), vocals, guitar, banjo, piano; and Dale T. "Stoney" Cooper (born 10/16/18, Harman, West Virginia; died of a heart attack 3/22/77), vocals, fiddle. Wilma was with the Leary Family gospel group when Stoney joined the group as a fiddler. With the Leary Family until the mid-1940s. On the WWVA-Wheeling *Jamboree*, 1947-57. Joined the *Grand Ole Opry* in 1957. Own band, the Clinch Mountain Clan. Daughter Carolee Cooper is leader of The Carol Lee Singers.	
			WILMA LEE & STONEY COOPER AND THE CLINCH MOUNTAIN CLAN:	
9/29/56	**14**	1	1. Cheated Too Jockey #14	Hickory 1051
12/15/58+	**4**	26	2. **Come Walk With Me** **WILMA LEE & STONEY COOPER With Carolee and The Clinch Mountain** Clan	Hickory 1085
5/25/59	**4**	23	3. **Big Midnight Special** Paul Evans' "Midnite Special" was a #16 Pop hit in 1960	Hickory 1098
10/19/59	**3**	24	4. **There's A Big Wheel** written by Don Gibson	Hickory 1107
5/16/60	**17**	8	5. Johnny, My Love (Grandma's Diary)	Hickory 1118
9/12/60	**16**	14	6. This Ole House #1 Pop hit for Rosemary Clooney in 1954	Hickory 1126
6/12/61	**8**	7	7. **Wreck On The Highway**	Hickory 1147
			## COPAS, Cowboy	
			Born Lloyd Estel Copas on 7/15/13 in Muskogee, Oklahoma. Died in a plane crash on 3/5/63 near Camden, Tennessee. Fiddler and guitarist from age 10. Moved to Cincinnati in 1929 and formed duo with Indian fiddler Natchee. Went solo in 1940, performed on *Midwest Hayride* radio show, Cincinnati, in the early 1940s. With Pee Wee King on the *Grand Ole Opry* in the late '40s. Career waned in the '50s, but recovered with hit "Alabam" in 1960. Plane crash also killed Patsy Cline, Hawkshaw Hawkins, and Copas's son-in-law, pilot Randy Hughes.	
8/31/46	**4**	1	1. **Filipino Baby** **COWBOY (PAPPY) COPAS**	King 505
1/3/48	**2** (3)	20	2. **Signed Sealed And Delivered**	King 658
5/1/48	**3**	17	3. **Tennessee Waltz** Best Seller #3 / Juke Box #4	King 696
7/3/48	**7**	9	4. **Tennessee Moon** Best Seller #7 / Juke Box #7	King 714
9/18/48	**12**	1	5. Breeze Juke Box #12	King 618
2/12/49	**12**	1	6. I'm Waltzing With Tears In My Eyes Best Seller #12	King 775

DATE	POS	WKS	ARTIST– RECORD TITLE	LABEL & NO.
2/19/49	**5**	13	7. **Candy Kisses**	King 777
			Juke Box #5 / Best Seller #7	
11/12/49	**14**	2	8. Hangman's Boogie	King 811
			Best Seller #14 / Juke Box #14; from the movie Square Dance Jubilee	
4/28/51	**5**	11	9. **The Strange Little Girl**	King 951
			Jockey #5 / Best Seller #7 / Juke Box #10	
1/19/52	**8**	3	10. **'Tis Sweet To Be Remembered**	King 1000
			Jockey #8	
7/4/60	**1** (12)	34	11. **Alabam**	Starday 501
4/24/61	**9**	8	12. **Flat Top**	Starday 542
7/31/61	**12**	10	13. Sunny Tennessee	Starday 552
9/11/61	**10**	8	14. **Signed Sealed And Delivered** [R]	Starday 559
4/27/63	**12**	14	15. Goodbye Kisses	Starday 621

CORNELIUS, Helen

Born on 12/6/41 in Hannibal, Missouri. Performed in vocal group with sisters Judy and Sharon while in high school. Went solo and won on the *Ted Mack Amateur Hour.* Staff writer with Screen Gems in 1970. Teamed with Jim Ed Brown and appeared on the *Nashville On The Road* TV series, 1976-80, when she again went solo. Reunited with Brown in February 1988. CMA Award: 1977 Vocal Duo of the Year (with Jim Ed Brown).

JIM ED BROWN/HELEN CORNELIUS:

DATE	POS	WKS	ARTIST– RECORD TITLE	LABEL & NO.
8/7/76	**1** (2)	10	1. **I Don't Want To Have To Marry You**	RCA 10711
12/11/76+	**2** (1)	13	2. **Saying Hello, Saying I Love You, Saying Goodbye**	RCA 10822
5/21/77	**12**	9	3. Born Believer	RCA 10967
9/3/77	**12**	8	4. If It Ain't Love By Now	RCA 11044
3/25/78	**11**	9	5. I'll Never Be Free	RCA 11220
8/12/78	**6**	11	6. **If The World Ran Out Of Love Tonight**	RCA 11304
10/21/78	**30**	4	7. What Cha Doin' After Midnight, Baby	RCA 11375
			HELEN CORNELIUS	
12/9/78+	**10**	9	8. **You Don't Bring Me Flowers**	RCA 11435
3/31/79	**2** (2)	10	9. **Lying In Love With You**	RCA 11532
8/11/79	**3**	10	10. **Fools**	RCA 11672
3/29/80	**5**	9	11. **Morning Comes Too Early**	RCA 11927
8/16/80	**24**	5	12. The Bedroom	RCA 12037
5/30/81	**13**	8	13. **Don't Bother To Knock**	RCA 12220

CORNOR, Randy

Born in 1954 in Houston. Played guitar with Gene Watson at age 13. With Frenchie Burke for three years. Top session guitarist in Houston.

DATE	POS	WKS	ARTIST– RECORD TITLE	LABEL & NO.
12/6/75+	**9**	9	1. **Sometimes I Talk In My Sleep**	ABC/Dot 17592
			written by Eddy Raven	
6/12/76	**33**	4	2. Heart Don't Fail Me Now	ABC/Dot 17625

COUCH, Orville

Born in Ferris, Texas. First recorded for Derby in 1954.

DATE	POS	WKS	ARTIST– RECORD TITLE	LABEL & NO.
11/24/62+	**5**	21	1. **Hello Trouble** [R]	Vee Jay 470
			originally released on Custom label	
9/28/63	**25**	1	2. Did I Miss You?	Vee Jay 528

DATE	POS	WKS	ARTIST—RECORD TITLE	LABEL & NO.
			CRADDOCK, Billy "Crash"	
			Born on 6/16/39 in Greensboro, North Carolina. With his brother Ronald in rock band the Four Rebels, in the mid-1950s. First recorded for Colonial in 1957. Semi-retired from recording and worked outside of music in Greensboro, 1960-69. Known as "Mr. Country Rock."	
2/27/71	3	13	1. **Knock Three Times** #1 Pop hit for Dawn in 1971	Cartwheel 193
7/3/71	5	12	2. **Dream Lover** #2 Pop hit for Bobby Darin in 1959	Cartwheel 196
11/27/71	10	10	3. **You Better Move On** #24 Pop hit for Arthur Alexander in 1962	Cartwheel 201
3/25/72	10	13	4. **Ain't Nothin' Shakin' (But the Leaves on the Trees)**	Cartwheel 210
7/8/72	5	15	5. **I'm Gonna Knock On Your Door** #12 Pop hit for Eddie Hodges in 1961	Cartwheel 216
12/9/72+	22	8	6. Afraid I'll Want To Love Her One More Time originally released on Cartwheel 222	ABC 11342
3/31/73	33	4	7. Don't Be Angry	ABC 11349
6/16/73	14	8	8. Slippin' And Slidin' #33 Pop hit for Little Richard in 1956	ABC 11364
9/22/73	8	11	9. **'Till The Water Stops Runnin'**	ABC 11379
1/26/74	3	12	10. **Sweet Magnolia Blossom**	ABC 11412
6/22/74	1 (2)	12	11. **Rub It In**	ABC 12013
11/30/74+	1 (1)	10	12. **Ruby, Baby** #2 Pop hit for Dion in 1963	ABC 12036
3/15/75	4	9	13. **Still Thinkin' 'Bout You**	ABC 12068
7/12/75	10	10	14. **I Love The Blues And The Boogie Woogie**	ABC 12104
11/8/75	2 (3)	12	15. **Easy As Pie**	ABC/Dot 17584
4/17/76	7	10	16. **Walk Softly**	ABC/Dot 17619
7/17/76	4	10	17. **You Rubbed It In All Wrong**	ABC/Dot 17635
11/13/76+	1 (1)	12	18. **Broken Down In Tiny Pieces**	ABC/Dot 17659
4/2/77	28	4	19. Just A Little Thing	ABC/Dot 17682
6/18/77	7	10	20. **A Tear Fell** #5 Pop hit for Teresa Brewer in 1956	ABC/Dot 17701
11/26/77+	10	11	21. **The First Time**	ABC/Dot 17725
2/18/78	4	10	22. **I Cheated On A Good Woman's Love**	Capitol 4545
6/17/78	28	5	23. I've Been Too Long Lonely Baby	Capitol 4575
10/7/78	14	7	24. Hubba Hubba	Capitol 4624
1/20/79	4	9	25. **If I Could Write A Song As Beautiful As You**	Capitol 4672
5/26/79	28	4	26. My Mama Never Heard Me Sing	Capitol 4707
8/25/79	16	6	27. Robinhood	Capitol 4753
12/8/79+	24	8	28. Till I Stop Shaking	Capitol 4792
4/5/80	22	6	29. I Just Had You On My Mind	Capitol 4838
11/8/80	20	6	30. A Real Cowboy (You Say You're)	Capitol 4935
3/14/81	37	3	31. It Was You	Capitol 4972
7/11/81	11	9	32. I Just Need You For Tonight	Capitol 5011
11/21/81	38	2	33. Now That The Feeling's Gone	Capitol 5051
8/14/82	28	5	34. Love Busted	Capitol 5139

DATE	POS	WKS	ARTIST–RECORD TITLE	LABEL & NO.
			CRAMER, Floyd	
			Born on 10/27/33 in Samti, Louisiana; raised in Huttig, Arkansas. Played piano from age five. Joined KWKH-Shreveport *Louisiana Hayride* in 1951. Staff musician for Abbott Records, toured with Elvis Presley. Moved to Nashville in 1955. Top session pianist.	
11/7/60+	**11**	18	● 1. Last Date [I]	RCA 7775
6/19/61	**8**	10	2. **San Antonio Rose** [I]	RCA 7893
			written by Bob Wills in 1938	
4/12/80	**32**	4	3. Dallas [I]	RCA 11916
			theme song from the TV series starring Larry Hagman	
			CREECH, Alice	
			Vocalist from Panther Branch, North Carolina.	
12/4/71	**33**	5	1. The Night They Drove Old Dixie Down	Target 0138
			#3 Pop hit for Joan Baez in 1971	
3/18/72	**34**	4	2. We'll Sing In The Sunshine	Target 0144
			CROSBY, Bing	
			One of the most popular entertainers of the 20th century's first 50 years. Born Harry Lillis Crosby on 5/3/03 in Tacoma, Washington. Died of a heart attack on a golf course near Madrid, Spain, on 10/14/77.	
1/8/44	**1** (5)	11	● 1. **Pistol Packin' Mama**	Decca 23277
			BING CROSBY and the ANDREWS SISTERS	
8/30/52	**10**	1	2. **Till The End Of The World**	Decca 28265
			BING CROSBY and GRADY MARTIN and His Slew Foot Five	
			Juke Box #10	
			CROSBY, Eddie	
12/10/49	**7**	2	1. **Blues, Stay Away From Me**	Decca 46180
			Jockey #7 / Juke Box #10	
			CROSBY, Rob	
			Born Robert Crosby Hoar on 4/25/54 in Sumter, South Carolina. Co-wrote "Holdin' A Good Hand."	
12/15/90+	**12**	13	1. Love Will Bring Her Around	Arista 2124
6/8/91	**15**	12	2. She's A Natural	Arista 2180
11/2/91	**20**	10	3. Still Burnin' For You	Arista 12336
3/7/92	**28**	5	4. Working Woman	Arista 12397
			CROWELL, Rodney	
			Born on 8/7/50 in Houston. Had own band, the Arbitrators, in 1965. Moved to Nashville in 1972 and worked as staff writer for Jerry Reed. Worked with Emmylou Harris, 1975-77. Wrote "Till I Gain Control Again" hit for Harris, "Leavin' Louisiana In The Broad Daylight" for the Oak Ridge Boys, "I Ain't Livin' Long Like This" for Waylon Jennings and "An American Dream" for The Dirt Band. Married to Rosanne Cash, 1979-92.	
11/14/81	**30**	3	1. Stars On The Water	Warner 49810
3/13/82	**34**	5	2. Victim Or A Fool	Warner 50008
12/27/86+	**38**	3	3. When I'm Free Again	Columbia 06415
2/20/88	**1** (1)	13	4. **It's Such A Small World**	Columbia 07693
			RODNEY CROWELL & ROSANNE CASH	

DATE	POS	WKS	ARTIST – RECORD TITLE	LABEL & NO.
6/25/88	**1 (1)**	13	5. **I Couldn't Leave You If I Tried**	Columbia 07918
11/5/88+	**1 (1)**	14	6. **She's Crazy For Leavin'**	Columbia 08080
3/11/89	**1 (1)**	15	7. **After All This Time**	Columbia 68585
7/15/89	**1 (1)**	14	8. **Above And Beyond**	Columbia 68948
11/4/89+	**3**	16	9. **Many A Long & Lonesome Highway**	Columbia 73042
3/31/90	**6**	11	10. **If Looks Could Kill**	Columbia 73254
8/4/90	**22**	8	11. My Past Is Present	Columbia 73423
11/24/90+	**17**	11	12. Now That We're Alone	Columbia 73569
3/28/92	**10**	13	13. **Lovin' All Night**	Columbia 74250
7/25/92	**11**	11	14. What Kind Of Love	Columbia 74360
			co-written by Roy Orbison	

CROWLEY, J.C.

Born on 11/13/47 in Houston. During the late 1970s, was a member of the pop group Player; co-wrote their #1 pop hit "Baby Come Back."

DATE	POS	WKS	ARTIST – RECORD TITLE	LABEL & NO.
12/10/88+	**13**	10	1. **Paint The Town And Hang The Moon Tonight**	RCA 8747
4/29/89	**21**	8	2. I Know What I've Got	RCA 8822

CRUM, Simon—see HUSKY, Ferlin

CUMMINGS, Burton

Born on 12/31/47 in Winnipeg, Canada. Lead singer of rock group The Guess Who.

DATE	POS	WKS	ARTIST – RECORD TITLE	LABEL & NO.
4/21/79	**33**	3	1. Takes A Fool To Love A Fool	Portrait 70024

CURB, Mike, Congregation

Curb was born on 12/24/44 in Savannah, Georgia. Pop music mogul and politician. President of MGM Records, 1969-73. Elected lieutenant governor of California in 1978; served as governor of California, 1980. Formed own company, Sidewalk Records, in 1964, became Curb Records in 1974. Currently resides in Nashville.

DATE	POS	WKS	ARTIST – RECORD TITLE	LABEL & NO.
8/1/70	**1 (2)**	15	1. **All For The Love Of Sunshine**	MGM 14152
			from the movie Kelly's Heroes starring Clint Eastwood	
12/26/70+	**3**	13	2. **Rainin' In My Heart**	MGM 14194
1/1/72	**7**	11	3. **Ain't That A Shame**	MGM 14317
			HANK WILLIAMS, JR. With THE MIKE CURB CONGREGATION (above 3)	
			#1 R&B hit for Fats Domino in 1955	
6/24/72	**24**	6	4. Gone (Our Endless Love)	MGM 14377
			BILLY WALKER with The Mike Curb Congregation	

CURLESS, Dick

Born on 3/17/32 in Fort Fairfield, Maine. Died on 5/25/95. With the Trail Blazers band in the early '40s. Had his own radio show as the "Tumbleweed kid" in Ware, Massachusetts, in 1948. On Armed Forces Radio Network as "The Rice-Paddy Ranger," 1951-54. Worked in Las Vegas and Hollywood clubs in the late 1950s, toured with Buck Owens' All-American Show. Heard on the soundtrack for the movie *Killer's Three* in 1968. Father-in-law of Billy Chinnock.

DATE	POS	WKS	ARTIST – RECORD TITLE	LABEL & NO.
3/20/65	**5**	16	1. **A Tombstone Every Mile**	Tower 124
			first released on Allagash 101	
6/19/65	**12**	11	2. Six Times A Day (The Trains Came Down)	Tower 135
2/25/67	**28**	4	3. All Of Me Belongs To You	Tower 306

DATE	POS	WKS	ARTIST–RECORD TITLE	LABEL & NO.
7/13/68	34	4	4. I Ain't Got Nobody	Tower 415
5/23/70	27	7	5. Big Wheel Cannonball	Capitol 2780
			new version of Vaughn Horton's "Wabash Cannonball"	
8/29/70	31	7	6. Hard, Hard Traveling Man	Capitol 2848
11/28/70	29	6	7. Drag 'Em Off The Interstate, Sock It To 'Em, J.P.	
			Blues	Capitol 2949
8/21/71	36	5	8. Loser's Cocktail	Capitol 3105
11/6/71	40	2	9. Snap Your Fingers	Capitol 3182
			#8 Pop hit for Joe Henderson in 1962	
3/25/72	34	4	10. January, April And Me	Capitol 3267
7/22/72	31	6	11. Stonin' Around	Capitol 3354

CURTIS, Mac

Born Wesley Erwin Curtis on 1/16/39 in Fort Worth, Texas; raised in Olney, Texas. Moved to Weatherford, Texas, in 1954 and formed his own band. On KNOK radio in 1955. Had rockabilly hits starting in 1956 and worked Alan Freed shows in New York. Toured with Little Richard and George Hamilton IV. In the service, 1957-60; worked as Armed Forces radio and TV broadcaster. Worked as a DJ in Dallas and on WPLO-Atlanta into the late '60s. Moved to Los Angeles in 1971.

DATE	POS	WKS	ARTIST–RECORD TITLE	LABEL & NO.
11/21/70	35	2	1. Early In The Morning	GRT 26
			recorded by Bobby Darin (Rinky-Dinks) and Buddy Holly in 1958	

CURTIS, Sonny

Born in Meadow, Texas. Original fiddler/guitarist in 1956 with Buddy Holly & The Three Tunes. Wrote "I Fought The Law" pop hit for Bobby Fuller, and the themes for TV's *The Mary Tyler Moore Show* and *Evening Shade*.

DATE	POS	WKS	ARTIST–RECORD TITLE	LABEL & NO.
4/20/68	36	2	1. Atlanta Georgia Stray	Viva 626
5/3/80	38	3	2. The Real Buddy Holly Story	Elektra 46616
			Curtis recalls Holly's rise to fame	
8/16/80	29	4	3. Love Is All Around	Elektra 46663
			theme from TV's *The Mary Tyler Moore Show*	
5/23/81	15	9	4. Good Ol' Girls	Elektra 47129
9/19/81	33	3	5. Married Women	Elektra 47176

CYRUS, Billy Ray

Born on 8/25/61 in Flatwoods, Kentucky.

DATE	POS	WKS	ARTIST–RECORD TITLE	LABEL & NO.
5/2/92	1 (5)	16	▲ 1. **Achy Breaky Heart**	Mercury 866522
			CMA Award: Single of the Year	
			recorded by The Marcy Brothers in 1991 as "Don't Tell My Heart"	
7/18/92	2 (1)	15	2. **Could've Been Me**	Mercury 866998
11/7/92	23	7	3. Wher'm I Gonna Live?	Mercury 864502
			originally the B-side of #1 above	
2/6/93	6	14	4. **She's Not Cryin' Anymore**	Mercury 864778
7/10/93	3	16	5. **In The Heart Of A Woman**	Mercury 862448
10/30/93	9	14	6. **Somebody New**	Mercury 862754
2/19/94	12	12	7. Words By Heart	Mercury 858132
12/3/94	33	4	8. Storm In The Heartland	Mercury 856260

DATE	POS	WKS	ARTIST– RECORD TITLE	LABEL & NO.

D

DAFFAN('S), Ted, Texans

Born Theron Eugene Daffan on 9/21/12 in Beauregard Parish, Louisiana; raised in Houston. Played with the Blue Islanders and Blue Ridge Playboys, 1934-36; Bar-X Cowboys, 1936-40. Had own band, the Texans, from 1940 to late '50s. Wrote "Truck Driver's Blues," "A Worried Mind," "Born To Lose," "I'm A Fool To Care" and "No Letter Today," all between 1939 and 1942. Worked Venice Pier Ballroom in Venice, California, until 1946, then formed new band in Houston. Had publishing company with Hank Snow in Nashville in 1958, and own company in Houston from 1961.

DATE	POS	WKS	ARTIST– RECORD TITLE	LABEL & NO.
1/8/44	2 (3)	8	1. **No Letter Today/** Chuck Keeshan and Leon Seago (vocals)	
1/15/44	3	21	2. **Born To Lose** #41 Pop hit for Ray Charles in 1962	Okeh 6706
6/3/44	4	2	3. **Look Who's Talkin'** Leon Seago (vocal, above 2)	Okeh 6719
3/3/45	5	3	4. **You're Breaking My Heart/**	
2/24/45	6	2	5. **Time Won't Heal My Broken Heart**	Okeh 6729
9/1/45	2 (3)	13	6. **Headin' Down The Wrong Highway/**	
8/25/45	5	3	7. **Shadow On My Heart** "Idaho" (vocal, above 2)	Okeh 6744
10/26/46	5	3	8. **Shut That Gate** **TED DAFFAN and his TEXANS** George Strange (vocal)	Columbia 37087

DAISY, Pat

Born Patricia Key Deasy on 10/10/44 in Gallatin, Tennessee. Moved to Huntsville, Alabama, in 1966; worked in a folk group.

DATE	POS	WKS	ARTIST– RECORD TITLE	LABEL & NO.
3/11/72	20	10	1. **Everybody's Reaching Out For Someone** The Jordanaires (backing vocals)	RCA 0637

DALE, Kenny

Singer from Artesia, New Mexico. Worked clubs in Houston; first recorded in 1976.

DATE	POS	WKS	ARTIST– RECORD TITLE	LABEL & NO.
4/2/77	11	10	1. Bluest Heartache Of The Year originally released on Earthrider label in 1976	Capitol 4389
8/27/77	11	8	2. Shame, Shame On Me (I Had Planned To Be Your Man)	Capitol 4457
2/18/78	17	8	3. Red Hot Memory	Capitol 4528
6/3/78	28	4	4. The Loser	Capitol 4570
9/23/78	18	7	5. Two Hearts Tangled In Love	Capitol 4619
5/5/79	16	8	6. Down To Earth Woman	Capitol 4704
8/4/79	7	9	7. **Only Love Can Break A Heart** #2 Pop hit for Gene Pitney in 1962	Capitol 4746
11/17/79	15	8	8. Sharing	Capitol 4788
3/15/80	23	5	9. Let Me In	Capitol 4829
8/9/80	33	3	10. Thank You, Ever-Lovin'	Capitol 4882
1/10/81	31	3	11. When It's Just You And Me	Capitol 4943

DATE	POS	WKS	ARTIST–RECORD TITLE	LABEL & NO.
			DALTON, Lacy J.	
			Born Jill Byrem on 10/13/46 in Bloomsburg, Pennsylvania. Began career as a folk singer. Moved to Santa Cruz, California, in the late 1960s. Sang with the rock group Office in the early 1970s. First recorded for Harbor in 1978, as Jill Croston.	
10/27/79	17	8	1. Crazy Blue Eyes	Columbia 11107
2/16/80	18	7	2. Tennessee Waltz	Columbia 11190
5/17/80	14	9	3. Losing Kind Of Love	Columbia 11253
9/20/80	7	9	4. **Hard Times**	Columbia 11343
12/27/80+	8	10	5. **Hillbilly Girl With The Blues**	Columbia 11410
4/25/81	10	9	6. **Whisper**	Columbia 01036
8/8/81	2 (2)	12	7. **Takin' It Easy**	Columbia 02188
12/26/81+	5	10	8. **Everybody Makes Mistakes/**	
		9	9. Wild Turkey	Columbia 02637
5/22/82	13	10	10. Slow Down	Columbia 02847
10/9/82	7	13	11. **16th Avenue**	Columbia 03184
4/9/83	30	5	12. It's A Dirty Job	Columbia 03628
			BOBBY BARE & LACY J. DALTON	
7/9/83	9	11	13. **Dream Baby (How Long Must I Dream)**	Columbia 03926
			#4 Pop hit for Roy Orbison in 1962	
1/5/85	15	9	14. If That Ain't Love	Columbia 04696
5/25/85	19	7	15. Size Seven Round (Made Of Gold)	Epic 04876
			GEORGE JONES and LACY J. DALTON	
7/13/85	20	8	16. You Can't Run Away From Your Heart	Columbia 04884
7/19/86	16	9	17. Working Class Man	Columbia 06098
			#74 Pop hit for Jimmy Barnes in 1986	
1/31/87	33	3	18. This Ol' Town	Columbia 06360
2/18/89	13	10	19. The Heart	Universal 53487
8/26/89	38	3	20. Hard Luck Ace	Universal 66015
4/21/90	15	13	21. Black Coffee	Capitol 44519
			DANIEL, Davis	
			Born Robert Andrykowski on 3/1/61 in Arlington Heights, Illinois. Raised in Nebraska. Moved to Nashville in 1987.	
7/13/91	28	4	1. Picture Me	Mercury 878972
9/28/91	13	14	2. For Crying Out Loud	Mercury 868544
2/29/92	27	5	3. Fighting Fire With Fire	Mercury 866132
			DANIELS, Charlie, Band	
			Daniels (born 10/28/36, Wilmington, North Carolina; vocals, guitar, fiddle) formed band in Nashville in 1971. Included Tom Crain (guitar), Joe "Taz" DiGregorio (keyboards), Charles Hayward (bass), and James W. Marshall and Fred Edwards (drums). Marshall and Edwards left in 1986; replaced by Jack Gavin. Daniels led the Jaguars, 1958-67. Went solo in 1968 and worked as a session musician in Nashville. Played on Bob Dylan's *Nashville Skyline* hit album. In the movie *Urban Cowboy*.	
3/13/76	36	3	1. Texas	Kama Sutra 607
7/24/76	22	5	2. Wichita Jail	Epic 50243
7/21/79	1 (1)	7	▲ 3. **The Devil Went Down To Georgia**	Epic 50700
			CMA Award: Single of the Year	
10/27/79	19	6	4. Mississippi	Epic 50768

DATE	POS	WKS	ARTIST– RECORD TITLE	LABEL & NO.
3/22/80	27	5	5. Long Haired Country Boy [R] #56 Pop hit in 1975 (Kama Sutra 601)	Epic 50845
6/14/80	13	8	6. In America	Epic 50888
1/18/86	33	4	7. Still Hurtin' Me	Epic 05699
4/19/86	8	12	8. **Drinkin' My Baby Goodbye**	Epic 05835
9/10/88	10	11	9. **Boogie Woogie Fiddle Country Blues**	Epic 08002
3/4/89	36	3	10. Cowboy Hat In Dallas	Epic 68542
10/28/89+	12	13	11. Simple Man	Epic 73030
4/28/90	34	4	12. Mister DJ	Epic 73236

DARIN, Bobby

Born Walden Robert Cassotto on 5/14/36 in the Bronx, New York. Died of heart failure on 12/20/73.

DATE	POS	WKS	ARTIST– RECORD TITLE	LABEL & NO.
8/4/58	14	3	● 1. Splish Splash Best Seller #14	Atco 6117

DARRELL, Johnny

Born on 7/23/40 in Hopewell, Alabama.

DATE	POS	WKS	ARTIST– RECORD TITLE	LABEL & NO.
1/8/66	30	4	1. As Long As The Wind Blows	United Art. 943
4/22/67	9	12	2. **Ruby, Don't Take Your Love To Town**	United Art. 50126
11/18/67	37	2	3. Come See What's Left Of Your Man	United Art. 50207
1/13/68	22	10	4. The Son Of Hickory Holler's Tramp #40 Pop hit for O.C. Smith in 1968	United Art. 50235
5/11/68	3	15	5. **With Pen In Hand** written by Bobby Goldsboro; Billy Vera and Vikki Carr both had Pop hits	United Art. 50292
10/12/68	27	7	6. I Ain't Buying	United Art. 50442
12/7/68+	20	10	7. Woman Without Love	United Art. 50481
5/3/69	17	12	8. Why You Been Gone So Long	United Art. 50518
10/4/69	23	7	9. River Bottom	United Art. 50572

DAVE & SUGAR

Trio consisting of David Rowland (born 1/26/42, Los Angeles), Vicki Hackeman and Jackie Frantz. Rowland had been with the Stamps Quartet. Trio worked as backup singers for Charley Pride. Frantz was replaced by Sue Powell in 1977. Hackeman was replaced by Melissa Dean in 1979. Powell was replaced by Jamie Jaye in 1980. Rowland went solo in 1982.

DATE	POS	WKS	ARTIST– RECORD TITLE	LABEL & NO.
12/27/75+	25	9	1. Queen Of The Silver Dollar	RCA 10425
5/8/76	1 (1)	14	2. **The Door Is Always Open**	RCA 10625
9/25/76	3	12	3. **I'm Gonna Love You**	RCA 10768
2/26/77	5	9	4. **Don't Throw It All Away**	RCA 10876
7/23/77	7	10	5. **That's The Way Love Should Be**	RCA 11034
11/5/77	2 (4)	12	6. **I'm Knee Deep In Loving You**	RCA 11141
4/22/78	4	9	7. **Gotta' Quit Lookin' At You Baby**	RCA 11251
8/26/78	1 (1)	11	8. **Tear Time**	RCA 11322
1/20/79	1 (3)	12	9. **Golden Tears**	RCA 11427
7/7/79	6	9	10. **Stay With Me**	RCA 11654
11/3/79	4	9	11. **My World Begins And Ends With You/**	
		9	12. Why Did You Have To Be So Good	RCA 11749
4/26/80	18	7	13. New York Wine And Tennessee Shine	RCA 11947

DATE	POS	WKS	ARTIST—RECORD TITLE	LABEL & NO.
9/20/80	40	1	14. A Love Song	RCA 12063
2/28/81	32	4	15. It's A Heartache	RCA 12168
5/23/81	6	10	16. **Fool By Your Side**	Elektra 47135
9/19/81	32	4	17. The Pleasure's All Mine	Elektra 47177

DAVIES, Gail

Born Patricia Gail Dickerson on 4/4/48 in Broken Bow, Oklahoma. Moved to Seattle, worked as a jazz vocalist. In a duo with brother Ron in the early '70s. Did session work in Los Angeles and worked as a staff writer for Vogue Music. Moved to Nashville in the mid-1970s. Wrote "Bucket To The South" for Ava Barber. Lead singer with the Wild Choir in 1986.

DATE	POS	WKS	ARTIST—RECORD TITLE	LABEL & NO.
8/12/78	26	4	1. No Love Have I	Lifesong 1771
11/25/78	27	6	2. Poison Love	Lifesong 1777
3/10/79	11	8	3. Someone Is Looking For Someone Like You	Lifesong 1784
12/8/79+	7	10	4. **Blue Heartache**	Warner 49108
4/5/80	21	7	5. Like Strangers	Warner 49199
			#22 Pop hit for The Everly Brothers in 1960	
8/2/80	21	5	6. Good Lovin' Man	Warner 49263
12/13/80+	4	11	7. **I'll Be There (If You Ever Want Me)**	Warner 49592
4/18/81	5	13	8. **It's A Lovely, Lovely World**	Warner 49694
9/5/81	9	9	9. **Grandma's Song**	Warner 49790
2/27/82	9	13	10. **'Round The Clock Lovin'**	Warner 50004
7/17/82	17	8	11. You Turn Me On I'm A Radio	Warner 29972
			#25 Pop hit for Joni Mitchell in 1973	
11/27/82+	24	8	12. Hold On	Warner 29892
4/23/83	17	8	13. Singing The Blues	Warner 29726
			#1 Pop hit for Guy Mitchell in 1956	
11/19/83	18	9	14. You're A Hard Dog (To Keep Under The Porch)	Warner 29472
3/31/84	19	7	15. Boys Like You	Warner 29374
11/10/84	20	9	16. Jagged Edge Of A Broken Heart	RCA 13912
3/30/85	37	6	17. Nothing Can Hurt Me Now	RCA 14017
10/26/85	15	9	18. Break Away	RCA 14184

DAVIS, Danny, & The Nashville Brass

Born George Nowlan on 4/29/25 in Dorchester, Massachusetts. Trumpet player/leader educated at the New England Conservatory of Music. Played and sang in swing bands including Gene Krupa, Bob Crosby, Freddy Martin, Blue Barron and Sammy Kaye. Producer for Joy and MGM Records in the late '50s. Production assistant to Chet Atkins in 1965. Formed The Nashville Brass in 1968.

DATE	POS	WKS	ARTIST—RECORD TITLE	LABEL & NO.
3/1/80	20	7	1. Night Life	RCA 11893
			DANNY DAVIS and WILLIE NELSON with THE NASHVILLE BRASS	

DAVIS, Jimmie

Born on 9/11/02 in Beech Grove, Louisiana. Sang in college group the Tiger Four and appeared on KWKH-Shreveport. Taught history at Dodd College in the late '20s. Recorded for Victor, 1929-34, then switched to Decca. Wrote "You Are My Sunshine" with Charles Mitchell in 1940. Also wrote "Nobody's Darlin' But Mine." Appeared in the movies *Strictly In The Groove, Frontier Fury, Louisiana* and *Square Dance Katy*. Governor of Louisiana, 1944-48 and 1960-64. Elected to the Country Music Hall of Fame in 1972.

DATE	POS	WKS	ARTIST—RECORD TITLE	LABEL & NO.
9/2/44	3	2	1. **Is It Too Late Now/**	
9/30/44	4	2	2. **There's A Chill On The Hill Tonight**	Decca 6100

DATE	POS	WKS	ARTIST– RECORD TITLE	LABEL & NO.
2/17/45	**1** (1)	18	3. **There's A New Moon Over My Shoulder**	Decca 6105
3/2/46	**4**	1	4. **Grievin' My Heart Out For You**	Decca 18756
1/18/47	**4**	2	5. **Bang Bang**	Decca 46016
6/16/62	**15**	9	6. Where The Old Red River Flows	Decca 31368

DAVIS, Linda

Born on 11/26/62 in Dodson, Texas. In duo Skip & Linda, with Skip Eaton. Sang Dr. Pepper and Kentucky Fried Chicken jingles. Married to Lang Scott.

DATE	POS	WKS	ARTIST– RECORD TITLE	LABEL & NO.
9/4/93	**1** (1)	16	1. **Does He Love You** **REBA McENTIRE (with Linda Davis)**	MCA 54719
1/6/96	**13**	14	2. Some Things Are Meant To Be	Arista 12896

DAVIS, Mac

Born on 1/21/42 in Lubbock, Texas. Vocalist/guitarist/composer. Worked as a regional rep for Vee-Jay and Liberty Records. Wrote "In The Ghetto" and "Don't Cry Daddy," hits for Elvis Presley. Host of own musical variety TV series, 1974-76. Appeared in several movies, including *North Dallas Forty* in 1979.

DATE	POS	WKS	ARTIST– RECORD TITLE	LABEL & NO.
9/23/72	**26**	7	● 1. Baby Don't Get Hooked On Me	Columbia 45618
6/16/73	**36**	4	2. Your Side Of The Bed	Columbia 45839
10/20/73	**29**	6	3. Kiss It And Make It Better	Columbia 45911
11/2/74	**40**	1	4. Stop And Smell The Roses	Columbia 10018
2/1/75	**29**	4	5. Rock N' Roll (I Gave You The Best Years Of My Life)	Columbia 10070
7/12/75	**31**	4	6. Burnin' Thing	Columbia 10148
4/24/76	**17**	8	7. Forever Lovers	Columbia 10304
11/6/76	**34**	4	8. Every Now And Then	Columbia 10418
4/19/80	**10**	6	9. **It's Hard To Be Humble** [N]	Casablanca 2244
8/2/80	**10**	10	10. **Let's Keep It That Way**	Casablanca 2286
11/1/80	**9**	10	11. **Texas In My Rear View Mirror**	Casablanca 2305
3/7/81	**2** (2)	11	12. **Hooked On Music**	Casablanca 2327
11/14/81+	**5**	12	13. **You're My Bestest Friend**	Casablanca 2341
7/3/82	**37**	2	14. Rodeo Clown	Casablanca 2350
6/22/85	**10**	14	15. **I Never Made Love (Till I Made Love With You)**	MCA 52573
11/16/85	**34**	3	16. I Feel The Country Callin' Me	MCA 52669

DAVIS, Paul

DATE	POS	WKS	ARTIST– RECORD TITLE	LABEL & NO.
7/18/60	**28**	5	1. One Of Her Fools	Doke 107

DAVIS, Paul

Born on 4/21/48 in Meridian, Mississippi. Singer/songwriter/producer. Charted several Pop hits in the 1970s. Survived a shooting in Nashville on 7/30/86.

DATE	POS	WKS	ARTIST– RECORD TITLE	LABEL & NO.
9/13/86	**1** (1)	13	1. **You're Still New To Me**	Capitol/Curb 5613
12/12/87+	**1** (1)	15	2. **I Won't Take Less Than Your Love** **TANYA TUCKER with PAUL DAVIS & PAUL OVERSTREET**	Capitol 44100

DATE	POS	WKS	ARTIST–RECORD TITLE	LABEL & NO.
			DAVIS, Skeeter	
			Born Mary Frances Penick on 12/30/31 in Dry Ridge, Kentucky. Worked in duo with close friend Betty Jack Davis, and later with Georgia Davis. Went solo in 1956. Toured with Eddy Arnold and Elvis Presley. Joined the *Grand Ole Opry* in 1959. Married to TV's *Nashville Now* host, Ralph Emery, 1960-64. Later married Joey Spampinato, bassist of the jazz-rock band NRBQ.	
2/24/58	15	1	1. Lost To A Geisha Girl	RCA 7084
			Jockey #15; answer song to Hank Locklin's "Geisha Girl"	
3/30/59	5	17	2. **Set Him Free**	RCA 7471
9/21/59	15	13	3. Homebreaker	RCA 7570
3/7/60	11	12	4. Am I That Easy To Forget?	RCA 7671
8/29/60	2 (3)	16	5. **(I Can't Help You) I'm Falling Too**	RCA 7767
			answer song to Hank Locklin's "Please Help Me, I'm Falling"	
12/31/60+	5	13	6. **My Last Date (With You)**	RCA 7825
			vocal version of Floyd Cramer's "Last Date"	
4/24/61	11	11	7. The Hand You're Holding Now	RCA 7863
10/16/61	10	11	8. **Optimistic**	RCA 7928
3/10/62	9	9	9. **Where I Ought To Be/**	RCA 7979
6/2/62	23	3	10. Something Precious	
9/8/62	22	1	11. The Little Music Box	RCA 8055
12/15/62+	2 (3)	24	12. **The End Of The World**	RCA 8098
5/25/63	9	14	13. **I'm Saving My Love**	RCA 8176
10/12/63	14	10	14. I Can't Stay Mad At You	RCA 8219
1/25/64	17	14	15. He Says The Same Things To Me	RCA 8288
5/23/64	8	12	16. **Gonna Get Along Without You Now**	RCA 8347
12/5/64	38	2	17. What Am I Gonna Do With You	RCA 8450
3/20/65	11	11	18. A Dear John Letter	RCA 8496
			SKEETER DAVIS & BOBBY BARE	
			#44 Pop hit for Pat Boone in 1960	
9/25/65	30	5	19. Sun Glasses	RCA 8642
11/5/66	36	5	20. Goin' Down The Road (Feelin' Bad)	RCA 8932
2/18/67	11	13	21. Fuel To The Flame	RCA 9058
			written by Dolly Parton and Dolly's uncle, Bill Owens	
8/19/67	5	14	22. **What Does It Take (To Keep A Man Like You**	
			Satisfied)	RCA 9242
7/13/68	16	47	23. There's A Fool Born Every Minute	RCA 9543
1/3/70	9	11	24. **I'm A Lover (Not a Fighter)**	RCA 0292
2/14/70	22	4	25. Your Husband, My Wife	RCA 9789
			BOBBY BARE and SKEETER DAVIS	
3/27/71	21	9	26. Bus Fare To Kentucky	RCA 9961
7/14/73	12	12	27. I Can't Believe That It's All Over	RCA 0968
			DAVIS SISTERS, The	
			Duo from Lexington, Kentucky, formed in 1949. Consisted of Mary Frances "Skeeter Davis" Penick and Betty Jack Davis (killed in an auto accident on 8/2/53). The two were not related. First recorded for Fortune in 1952. Skeeter was seriously injured in the wreck that killed Betty Jack. Betty Jack was replaced by her sister Georgia.	
8/15/53	1 (8)	26	1. **I Forgot More Than You'll Ever Know**	RCA 5345
			Jockey #1(8) / Best Seller #1(6) / Juke Box #1(2)	

DATE	POS	WKS	ARTIST– RECORD TITLE	LABEL & NO.
			DEAN, Billy	
			Born on 4/2/62 in Quincy, Florida. Attended college in Decatur, Mississippi, on a basketball scholarship.	
2/23/91	3	13	1. **Only Here For A Little While**	Capitol LP Cut
5/25/91	3	17	2. **Somewhere In My Broken Heart**	Cap./SBK 44757
			<div align="center">above 2 from the album *Young Man* on Capitol 94302</div>	
10/5/91	4	17	3. **You Don't Count The Cost**	Cap./SBK 44773
2/1/92	4	16	4. **Only The Wind**	Cap./SBK 44803
6/6/92	4	17	5. **Billy The Kid**	SBK/Liberty 57745
9/26/92	3	16	6. **If There Hadn't Been You**	SBK/Liberty 57884
1/2/93	6	14	7. **Tryin' To Hide A Fire In The Dark**	SBK/Liberty 56804
5/8/93	22	9	8. I Wanna Take Care Of You	SBK/Liberty 56984
10/16/93	34	2	9. I'm Not Built That Way	SBK/Liberty LP Cut
			<div align="center">also available as the B-side of #8 above</div>	
12/11/93+	9	14	10. **We Just Disagree**	SBK/Liberty LP Cut
			<div align="center">#12 Pop hit for Dave Mason in 1977;</div><div align="center">above 4 from the album *Fire In The Dark* on SBK/Liberty 98947</div>	
7/23/94	24	7	11. Cowboy Band	Liberty 58189
3/2/96	5	16	12. **It's What I Do**	Capitol 58526
			DEAN, Eddie	
			Born Edgar Dean Glosup on 7/9/07 in Posey, Texas. Teamed with older brother Jimmy and worked the WLS-Chicago *National Barn Dance*. Moved to Los Angeles in 1937; made movies with Gene Autry and did his own movie series, 1946-48. Featured on the Judy Canova network radio show.	
9/25/48	11	1	1. One Has My Name (The Other Has My Heart)	Crystal 132
			<div align="center">Best Seller #11</div>	
1/22/55	10	3	2. **I Dreamed Of A Hill-Billy Heaven**	Sage & Sand 180
			<div align="center">Juke Box #10 / Jockey #10 / Best Seller #15;</div><div align="center">The Frontiersmen (instrumental backing: above 2)</div>	
			DEAN, Jimmy	
			Born on 8/10/28 in Plainview, Texas. With the Tennessee Haymakers in Washington, D.C., in 1948. Own Texas Wildcats in 1952. Recorded for 4 Star in 1952. Own CBS-TV series, 1957-58; ABC-TV series, 1963-66. Business interests include a restaurant chain and a line of pork sausage. Married Donna Meade on 10/27/91.	
3/7/53	5	7	1. **Bumming Around**	4 Star 1613
			JIMMIE DEAN	
			<div align="center">Jockey #5 / Best Seller #9 / Juke Box #10</div>	
10/16/61	1 (2)	22	● 2. **Big Bad John**	Columbia 42175
2/3/62	9	10	3. **Dear Ivan** [S]	Columbia 42259
			<div align="center">background tune: "Battle Hymn Of The Republic"</div>	
3/10/62	15	6	4. To A Sleeping Beauty/ [S]	
			<div align="center">background tune: "Memories"</div>	
2/10/62	16	10	5. The Cajun Queen [S]	Columbia 42282
4/21/62	3	13	6. P.T. 109	Columbia 42338
			<div align="center">based on the sinking of John F. Kennedy's torpedo boat in 1943</div>	
9/29/62	10	11	7. **Little Black Book**	Columbia 42529
2/29/64	35	2	8. Mind Your Own Business	Columbia 42934
			<div align="center">written and popularized in 1949 by Hank Williams</div>	
6/12/65	1 (2)	16	9. **The First Thing Ev'ry Morning (And The Last Thing Ev'ry Night)**	Columbia 43263

DATE	POS	WKS	ARTIST– RECORD TITLE	LABEL & NO.
10/30/65	35	5	10. Harvest Of Sunshine	Columbia 43382
11/5/66	10	15	11. **Stand Beside Me**	RCA 8971
3/11/67	16	11	12. Sweet Misery	RCA 9091
12/23/67+	30	5	13. I'm A Swinger	RCA 9350
4/6/68	21	10	14. A Thing Called Love	RCA 9454
11/16/68	22	8	15. A Hammer And Nails	RCA 9652
2/27/71	29	5	16. Slowly	RCA 9947
			JIMMY DEAN and DOTTIE WEST	
2/19/72	38	3	17. The One You Say Good Mornin' To	RCA 0600
5/22/76	9	4	● 18. **I.O.U.** [S]	Casino 052
			Jimmy Dean's ode of thanks to his mother	
			DEE, Duane	
			Born Duane DeRosia in Hartford, Wisconsin. Discovered by DJ Bill Ericksen. Worked in Milwaukee clubs. Appeared on Bobby Lord's TV show, *Midwestern Hayride*.	
12/4/71	36	3	1. How Can You Mend A Broken Heart	Cartwheel 200
			#1 Pop hit for the Bee Gees in 1971	
			DEE, Kathy	
			Born Kathleen Dearth in Moundsville, West Virginia. Own group, Kathy's Clowns, 1963-68. Died on 11/3/68.	
9/21/63	18	3	1. Unkind Words	United Art. 627
			DeHAVEN, Penny	
			Born Charlotte DeHaven on 5/17/48 in Winchester, Virginia. Appeared in the movies *Valley Of Blood, Traveling Light* and *Country Music Story*. Also recorded as Penny Starr.	
9/6/69	34	4	1. Mama Lou	Imperial 66388
12/20/69	37	3	2. Down In The Boondocks	Imperial 66421
			#9 Pop hit for Billy Joe Royal in 1965	
6/27/70	20	7	3. Land Mark Tavern	United Art. 50669
			DEL REEVES & PENNY DeHAVEN	
			DELMORE BROTHERS	
			Duo from Elkmont, Alabama, formed in the '20s. Consisted of brothers Alton (born 12/25/08; died 6/8/64, Huntsville, Alabama) and Rabon (born 12/3/16; died 12/4/52, Athens, Alabama). Both played guitars and fiddles. On the *Grand Ole Opry*, 1932-38. Moved to Houston in the late '40s. After Rabon's death, Alton moved to Huntsville, Alabama, and taught music. Duo elected to the Songwriter's Hall of Fame in 1971.	
12/14/46	2 (1)	4	1. **Freight Train Boogie**	King 570
9/17/49+	1 (1)	23	2. **Blues Stay Away From Me**	King 803
			Juke Box #1 / Best Seller #2 / Jockey #3	
2/18/50	7	1	3. **Pan American Boogie**	King 826
			Juke Box #7	
			DELRAY, Martin	
			Born Michael Ray Martin on 9/26/49 in Texarkana, Arkansas. Also recorded under real name, Mike Martin.	
4/6/91	27	7	1. Get Rhythm	Atlantic 87869
			Johnny Cash (guest vocal)	

DATE	POS	WKS	ARTIST– RECORD TITLE	LABEL & NO.
			DENVER, John	
			Born John Henry Deutschendorf on 12/31/43 in Roswell, New Mexico. To Los Angeles in 1964. With the Chad Mitchell Trio, 1965-68. Wrote "Leaving On A Jet Plane." Starred in the 1977 movie *Oh, God*. Won an Emmy in 1975 for the TV special *An Evening with John Denver*. CMA Award: 1975 Entertainer of the Year.	
7/20/74	**9**	7	● 1. **Annie's Song**	RCA 0295
			written by Denver for his wife Ann Martell (married 1967-83)	
10/19/74	**1 (1)**	10	● 2. **Back Home Again**	RCA 10065
1/25/75	**7**	7	3. Sweet Surrender	RCA 10148
4/19/75	**1 (1)**	9	● 4. **Thank God I'm A Country Boy**	RCA 10239
			above 2 recorded "live" at Universal City Amphitheater, California	
9/6/75	**1 (1)**	14	● 5. **I'm Sorry**	RCA 10353
			flip side "Calypso" made #2 on the *Hot 100*	
12/27/75+	**12**	8	6. Fly Away	RCA 10517
			Olivia Newton-John (backing vocal)	
4/10/76	**30**	4	7. Looking For Space	RCA 10586
10/16/76	**34**	2	8. Like A Sad Song	RCA 10774
1/15/77	**22**	5	9. Baby, You Look Good To Me Tonight	RCA 10854
12/17/77+	**22**	7	10. How Can I Leave You Again	RCA 11036
7/18/81	**10**	9	11. **Some Days Are Diamonds (Some Days Are Stone)**	RCA 12246
8/13/83	**14**	8	12. Wild Montana Skies	RCA 13562
			JOHN DENVER and EMMYLOU HARRIS	
1/18/86	**9**	10	13. **Dreamland Express**	RCA 14227
7/1/89	**14**	10	14. And So It Goes	Universal 66008
			JOHN DENVER and THE NITTY GRITTY DIRT BAND	
			DESERT ROSE BAND, The	
			Nucleus of band: Southern California natives Chris Hillman, John Jorgenson and Herb Pedersen. Hillman was a founding member of The Byrds and the Flying Burrito Brothers. Jorgenson left in 1992. Disbanded in early 1994.	
5/9/87	**26**	4	1. Ashes Of Love	Curb/MCA 53048
8/8/87	**6**	13	2. **Love Reunited**	Curb/MCA 53142
11/28/87+	**2 (1)**	14	3. **One Step Forward**	Curb/MCA 53201
4/9/88	**1 (1)**	14	4. **He's Back And I'm Blue**	Curb/MCA 53274
8/20/88	**2 (1)**	14	5. **Summer Wind**	Curb/MCA 53354
12/10/88+	**1 (1)**	15	6. **I Still Believe In You**	Curb/MCA 53454
4/1/89	**3**	14	7. **She Don't Love Nobody**	Curb/MCA 53616
7/29/89	**11**	11	8. Hello Trouble	Curb/MCA 53671
11/25/89+	**6**	19	9. **Start All Over Again**	Curb/MCA 53746
4/21/90	**13**	11	10. In Another Lifetime	Curb/MCA 53804
8/18/90	**10**	12	11. **Story Of Love**	Curb/MCA 79052
3/23/91	**37**	3	12. Will This Be The Day	Curb/MCA 54002
			DEXTER, Al, and his Troopers	
			Born Clarence Albert Poindexter on 5/4/02 in Troup, Texas. Died on 1/28/84. Vocalist/guitarist/violinist/composer.	
1/8/44	**1 (3)**	10	● 1. **Pistol Packin' Mama/**	
1/8/44	**1 (1)**	25	2. **Rosalita**	Okeh 6708
3/11/44	**1 (13)**	30	3. **So Long Pal/**	
3/11/44	**1 (2)**	30	4. **Too Late To Worry, Too Blue To Cry**	Okeh 6718

DATE	POS	WKS	ARTIST–RECORD TITLE	LABEL & NO.
1/20/45	1 (7)	21	5. **I'm Losing My Mind Over You/**	
1/27/45	2 (1)	10	6. **I'll Wait For You Dear**	Okeh 6727
7/7/45	2 (5)	11	7. **Triflin' Gal/**	
8/25/45	5	3	8. **I'm Lost Without You**	Okeh 6740
2/2/46	1 (16)	29	9. **Guitar Polka/** [I]	
2/9/46	2 (1)	8	10. **Honey Do You Think It's Wrong**	Columbia 36898
8/31/46	1 (5)	13	11. **Wine, Women And Song/**	
9/14/46	3	5	12. **It's Up To You**	Columbia 37062
1/25/47	4	1	13. **Kokomo Island**	Columbia 37200
5/10/47	4	7	14. **Down At The Roadside Inn**	Columbia 37303
7/3/48	14	1	15. Rock And Rye Rag Juke Box #14	Columbia 20422
9/18/48	11	2	16. Calico Rag Juke Box #11	Columbia 20438

DIAMOND RIO

Six-man band: Marty Roe (vocals), Jimmy Olander (guitar), Gene Johnson (mandolin), Dan Truman (piano), Dana Williams (bass) and Brian Prout (drums; married to Nancy Given, drummer for Wild Rose). CMA Awards: 1992, 1993 and 1994 Vocal Group of the Year.

DATE	POS	WKS	ARTIST–RECORD TITLE	LABEL & NO.
4/6/91	1 (2)	18	1. **Meet In The Middle**	Arista 2182
8/3/91	3	18	2. **Mirror Mirror**	Arista 2262
12/7/91+	9	17	3. **Mama Don't Forget To Pray For Me**	Arista 2258
4/25/92	2 (2)	16	4. **Norma Jean Riley** originally released as the B-side of #3 above	Arista 12407
8/1/92	7	16	5. **Nowhere Bound**	Arista 12441
12/5/92+	2 (2)	17	6. **In A Week Or Two**	Arista 12457
4/24/93	5	13	7. **Oh Me, Oh My, Sweet Baby**	Arista 12464
8/14/93	13	11	8. This Romeo Ain't Got Julie Yet	Arista 12580
1/1/94	21	8	9. Sawmill Road	Arista 12610
6/18/94	2 (2)	17	10. **Love A Little Stronger**	Arista 12696
11/12/94+	9	15	11. **Night Is Fallin' In My Heart**	Arista 12764
2/25/95	16	10	12. Bubba Hyde	Arista 12787
6/17/95	19	11	13. Finish What We Started	Arista 12739
1/6/96	2 (1)	17	14. **Walkin' Away**	Arista 12934
5/18/96	8 ↑	10 ↑	15. That's What I Get For Lovin' You	Arista 12992

DIANA

Born Diana Murrell on 5/26/55 in Cincinnati. Sister of Jimmy Murrell, leader of Tom T. Hall's band.

DATE	POS	WKS	ARTIST–RECORD TITLE	LABEL & NO.
7/28/79	40	1	1. Just When I Needed You Most	Elektra 46061
8/29/81	29	5	2. He's The Fire	Sunbird 7564

DICKENS, "Little" Jimmy

Born James Cecil Dickens on 12/19/20 in Bolt, West Virginia. Stands only 4'11" tall. First worked as Jimmy The Kid with Johnny Bailes & His Happy Valley Boys in 1942. Worked radio stations in Indianapolis, Cincinnati and Saginaw. With the *Grand Ole Opry* since 1948. Nicknamed "Tater." Elected to the Country Music Hall of Fame in 1982.

DATE	POS	WKS	ARTIST–RECORD TITLE	LABEL & NO.

4/16/49	7	7	1. **Take An Old Cold 'Tater (And Wait)** [N]
			    JIMMIE DICKENS
			    Best Seller #7 / Juke Box #11
				Columbia 20548

DATE	POS	WKS	ARTIST– RECORD TITLE	LABEL & NO.
6/25/49	**7**	10	2. **Country Boy** Best Seller #7 / Juke Box #8	Columbia 20585
9/3/49	**12**	1	3. Pennies For Papa Best Seller #12	Columbia 20548
9/24/49	**10**	1	4. **My Heart's Bouquet** Juke Box #10	Columbia 20598
1/14/50	**6**	3	5. **A-Sleeping At The Foot Of The Bed** Best Seller #6 / Jockey #7	Columbia 20644
4/22/50	**3**	10	6. **Hillbilly Fever** Jockey #3 / Best Seller #5 / Juke Box #9	Columbia 20677
8/7/54	**9**	7	7. **Out Behind The Barn** Jockey #9	Columbia 21247
11/3/62	**10**	8	8. **The Violet And A Rose**	Columbia 42485
12/14/63	**28**	2	9. Another Bridge To Burn	Columbia 42845
5/8/65	**21**	13	10. He Stands Real Tall	Columbia 43243
10/9/65	**1** (2)	18	11. **May The Bird Of Paradise Fly Up Your Nose** [N]	Columbia 43388
2/26/66	**27**	8	12. When The Ship Hit The Sand [N]	Columbia 43514
4/1/67	**23**	10	13. Country Music Lover [N]	Columbia 44025

DIFFIE, Joe

Born Joe Logan Diffie on 12/28/58 in Tulsa; raised in Duncan, Oklahoma. Co-wrote "There Goes My Heart Again" by Holly Dunn. Joined the *Grand Ole Opry* in 1993.

DATE	POS	WKS	ARTIST– RECORD TITLE	LABEL & NO.
9/8/90	**1** (1)	18	1. **Home**	Epic 73447
1/5/91 *	**2** (2)	17	2. **If You Want Me To**	Epic 73637
4/13/91	**1** (1)	19	3. **If The Devil Danced (In Empty Pockets)**	Epic 73747
8/17/91	**2** (2)	18	4. **New Way (To Light Up An Old Flame)**	Epic 73935
1/4/92	**5**	16	5. **Is It Cold In Here**	Epic 74123
5/16/92	**5**	16	6. **Ships That Don't Come In**	Epic 74285
8/29/92	**16**	11	7. Next Thing Smokin'	Epic 74415
10/10/92	**15**	11	8. Not Too Much To Ask **MARY-CHAPIN CARPENTER with Joe Diffie**	Columbia 74485
4/10/93	**5**	16	9. **Honky Tonk Attitude**	Epic 74911
8/14/93	**3**	16	10. **Prop Me Up Beside The Jukebox (If I Die)**	Epic 77071
11/27/93+	**5**	17	11. **John Deere Green**	Epic 77235
4/2/94	**19**	11	12. In My Own Backyard	Epic 77380
7/30/94	**1** (2)	18	13. **Third Rock From The Sun**	Epic 77577
10/29/94	**1** (4)	19	14. **Pickup Man**	Epic 77715
2/18/95	**2** (2)	16	15. **So Help Me Girl**	Epic 77808
6/10/95	**21**	8	16. I'm In Love With A Capital "U"	Epic 77902
10/7/95	**40**	1	17. That Road Not Taken	Epic 77978
12/16/95+	**1** (2)	18	18. **Bigger Than The Beatles**	Epic 78202
12/30/95	**33**	1	19. Leroy The Redneck Reindeer [X-C]	Epic 78201
3/30/96	**23**	9	20. C-O-U-N-T-R-Y	Epic 78246

DILLINGHAM, Craig

Born in Brownwood, Texas. Sang in a group with his sisters from age eight. Worked with Ray Price. Appeared on *Louisiana Hayride* from 1976.

DATE	POS	WKS	ARTIST– RECORD TITLE	LABEL & NO.
1/28/84	**32**	4	1. Have You Loved Your Woman Today	MCA/Curb 52301

DATE	POS	WKS	ARTIST– RECORD TITLE	LABEL & NO.
			DILLON, Dean	
			Born on 3/26/55 in Lake City, Tennessee. Wrote "Lying In Love With You" hit for Jim Ed Brown and Helen Cornelius. Also wrote many hits for George Strait.	
1/26/80	30	4	1. I'm Into The Bottle (To Get You Out of My Mind)	RCA 11881
7/12/80	28	4	2. What Good Is A Heart	RCA 12003
12/6/80+	25	7	3. Nobody In His Right Mind (Would've Left Her)	RCA 12109
11/5/88	39	1	4. I Go To Pieces	Capitol 44239
			#9 Pop hit for Peter & Gordon in 1965	
8/3/91	39	2	5. Friday Night's Woman	Atlantic 87794
			DIXIANA	
			Band based in Greenville, South Carolina, consisting of Cindy Murphy (vocals), brothers Mark and Phil Lister, Randall Griffith and Colonel Shuford. The Listers hosted own regional TV program in the mid-1970s.	
4/25/92	39	3	1. Waitin' For The Deal To Go Down	Epic 74221
8/22/92	40	1	2. That's What I'm Working On Tonight	Epic 74361
			DR. HOOK	
			Pop group formed in New Jersey in 1968. Fronted by Ray Sawyer (known as Dr. Hook because of eye patch) and Dennis Locorriere.	
1/8/77	26	5	1. If Not You	Capitol 4364
			DOLAN, Ramblin' Jimmie	
			Born in Missouri in 1924. Died on 7/31/94. First worked on KWK-St. Louis. In U.S. Navy, 1941-45. Formed own band in 1946. Known as "America's Country Troubador."	
2/3/51	7	4	1. **Hot Rod Race** [N]	Capitol 1322
			Best Seller #7	
			DOLLAR, Johnny	
			Born John Washington Dollar, Jr., on 3/8/33 in Kilgore, Texas. Died on 4/13/86. Leader of the Texas Sons, worked on radio in Dallas and Shreveport, 1953-54.	
3/26/66	15	14	1. Stop The Start (Of Tears In My Heart)	Columbia 43537
			DOTTSY	
			Born Dottsy Brodt on 4/6/53 in Seguin, Texas. Won talent contest on KBER-San Antonio in 1966. Had her own TV show, *San Antonio*, in 1968.	
7/19/75	17	7	1. Storms Never Last	RCA 10280
12/20/75+	12	9	2. I'll Be Your San Antone Rose	RCA 10423
7/2/77	10	9	3. **(After Sweet Memories) Play Born To Lose Again**	RCA 10982
11/26/77	22	6	4. It Should Have Been Easy	RCA 11138
3/4/78	20	7	5. Here In Love	RCA 11203
8/5/78	21	4	6. I Just Had You On My Mind	RCA 11293
			The Holladay Sisters (backing vocals: 3 & 6)	
2/3/79	12	9	7. Tryin' To Satisfy You	RCA 11448
			Waylon Jennings (backing vocal)	
7/7/79	22	5	8. Slip Away	RCA 11610
12/8/79	34	2	9. When I'm Gone	RCA 11743
			The Lea Jane Singers (backing vocals: 1, 2, 4, 5, 9)	
8/1/81	32	4	10. Somebody's Darling, Somebody's Wife	Tanglewood 1908

DATE	POS	WKS	ARTIST– RECORD TITLE	LABEL & NO.
			DOUGLAS, Tony	
			Born in Martins Mill, Texas, on 4/12/29. Member of *Louisiana Hayride* for three years.	Vee Jay 481
3/30/63	23	1	1. His And Hers	Vee Jay 481
2/24/73	35	6	2. Thank You For Touching My Life	Dot 17443
8/11/73	37	1	3. My Last Day	Dot 17464
			DOUGLASS, Lew—see NOBLE, Nick	
			DOVE, Ronnie	
			Born on 9/7/40 in Herndon, Virginia; raised in Baltimore. Sang in rock vocal group while in high school. Served in U.S. Coast Guard. Worked clubs in Baltimore. Had several Pop hits in the 1960s.	
7/19/75	25	5	1. Things #3 Pop hit for Bobby Darin in 1962	Melodyland 6011
			DOWNING, Big Al	
			Born on 1/9/40 in Lenapah, Oklahoma. Black vocalist/pianist. Session work with Wanda Jackson. First recorded for White Rock in 1958.	
12/16/78+	20	7	1. Mr. Jones	Warner 8716
5/19/79	18	8	2. Touch Me (I'll Be Your Fool Once More)	Warner 8787
3/1/80	33	4	3. The Story Behind The Story	Warner 49161
8/16/80	20	5	4. Bring It On Home	Warner 49270
3/26/83	38	2	5. It Takes Love	Team 1004
			DOWNS, Laverne	
7/4/60	16	7	1. But You Use To	Peach 735
			DRAKE, Guy	
			Humorist from Weir, Kentucky. Worked as a high school band director in Central City, Kentucky, in 1947. Own western swing band in the late 1940s.	
2/7/70	6	10	1. **Welfare Cadilac** [N]	Royal Amer. 1
			DRAPER, Rusty	
			Born Farrell Draper in Kirksville, Missouri. In show business from age 12; worked radio stations in Tulsa, Des Moines, and Quincy, Illinois. Singing emcee at the Mel Hertz Club in San Francisco for seven years.	
8/29/53	6	5	● 1. **Gambler's Guitar** Best Seller #6 / Juke Box #6	Mercury 70167
			DRIFTWOOD, Jimmie	
			Born James Corbett Morris on 6/20/07 in Mountain View, Arkansas. Added his own lyrics to square dance tune "The Eighth Of January" to create song "The Battle Of New Orleans," a giant #1 hit for Johnny Horton in 1959.	
6/8/59	24	3	1. The Battle Of New Orleans	RCA 7534
			DRUMM, Don	
			Pianist/guitarist/singer from Springfield, Massachusetts.	
2/4/78	18	7	1. Bedroom Eyes	Churchill 7704
6/24/78	35	3	2. Just Another Rhinestone	Churchill 7710

DATE	POS	WKS	ARTIST – RECORD TITLE	LABEL & NO.
			DRUSKY, Roy	
			Born on 6/22/30 in Atlanta. Learned to play guitar while in U.S. Navy in the late 1940s. Attended Emory College School of Veterinary Medicine in 1950; formed band, The Southern Ranch Boys, to earn money for his education. Worked as a DJ on WEAS-Decatur, Georgia. First recorded for Starday in 1955. Moved to Minneapolis and worked as a DJ while singing in local clubs. With the *Grand Ole Opry* since 1958. Wrote "Alone With You" hit for Faron Young. Appeared in the movies *The Golden Guitar* and *Forty-Acre Feud*.	
1/18/60	2 (3)	24	1. **Another**	Decca 31024
7/11/60	3	20	2. **Anymore**	Decca 31109
12/19/60	26	3	3. I Can't Tell My Heart That	Decca 31164
			KITTY WELLS and ROY DRUSKY	
3/13/61	2 (4)	27	4. **Three Hearts In A Tangle/**	
2/20/61	10	12	5. **I'd Rather Loan You Out**	Decca 31193
9/11/61	9	20	6. **I Went Out Of My Way (To Make You Happy)**	Decca 31297
			title also shown as simply "I Went Out Of My Way"	
4/21/62	17	2	7. There's Always One (Who Loves A Lot)	Decca 31366
12/22/62+	3	21	8. **Second Hand Rose**	Decca 31443
12/7/63+	8	19	9. **Peel Me A Nanner**	Mercury 72204
			written by Bill Anderson	
5/9/64	13	16	10. Pick Of The Week	Mercury 72265
			written by Liz Anderson	
1/23/65	6	20	11. **(From Now On All My Friends Are Gonna Be)**	
			Strangers	Mercury 72376
5/29/65	1 (2)	23	12. **Yes, Mr. Peters**	Mercury 72416
			ROY DRUSKY & PRISCILLA MITCHELL	
11/6/65	21	12	13. White Lightnin' Express	Mercury 72471
3/5/66	20	12	14. Rainbows And Roses	Mercury 72532
8/6/66	10	11	15. **The World Is Round**	Mercury 72586
12/17/66+	12	10	16. If The Whole World Stopped Lovin'	Mercury 72627
7/29/67	25	6	17. New Lips	Mercury 72689
12/30/67+	18	9	18. Weakness In A Man	Mercury 72742
4/20/68	28	8	19. You Better Sit Down Kids	Mercury 72784
			#9 Pop hit for Cher in 1967	
8/10/68	24	8	20. Jody And The Kid	Mercury 72823
			written by Kris Kristofferson	
2/8/69	10	13	21. **Where The Blue And Lonely Go**	Mercury 72886
6/21/69	14	9	22. My Grass Is Green	Mercury 72928
10/18/69	7	9	23. **Such A Fool**	Mercury 72964
1/31/70	11	9	24. I'll Make Amends	Mercury 73007
5/16/70	5	14	25. **Long Long Texas Road**	Mercury 73056
10/10/70	9	9	26. **All My Hard Times**	Mercury 73111
3/20/71	15	9	27. I Love The Way That You've Been Lovin' Me	Mercury 73178
8/7/71	37	3	28. I Can't Go On Loving You	Mercury 73212
1/1/72	17	10	29. Red Red Wine	Mercury 73252
			written by Neil Diamond; #1 Pop hit for UB40 in 1988	
9/9/72	25	8	30. The Last Time I Called Somebody Darlin'	Mercury 73314
2/17/73	32	5	31. I Must Be Doin' Something Right	Mercury 73356
9/1/73	25	6	32. Satisfied Mind	Mercury 73405

DATE	POS	WKS	ARTIST– RECORD TITLE	LABEL & NO.
			DUCAS, George	
			Born on 8/1/66 in Texas City, Texas; raised in San Diego and Houston.	
10/29/94	38	3	1. Teardrops	Liberty 18093
2/4/95	9	12	2. **Lipstick Promises**	Liberty 18306
			DUDLEY, Dave	
			Born David Pedruska on 5/3/28 in Spencer, Wisconsin. Played baseball for semi-pro team in Wausau, Wisconsin, and with the Gainesville Texas Owls. After injury to his arm, he worked as a DJ and singer at WTWT-Wausau in 1950. Formed his own trio and worked throughout the Midwest. He has a gold card from the Nashville truck driver's union in recognition of his trucking songs.	
10/16/61	28	2	1. Maybe I Do	Vee 7003
9/15/62	18	9	2. Under Cover Of The Night	Jubilee 5436
6/1/63	2 (2)	21	3. **Six Days On The Road**	Golden Wing 3020
10/5/63	3	20	4. **Cowboy Boots**	Golden Ring 3030
12/14/63+	7	16	5. **Last Day In The Mines**	Mercury 72212
10/17/64	6	15	6. **Mad**	Mercury 72308
3/27/65	15	14	7. Two Six Packs Away	Mercury 72384
7/31/65	3	18	8. **Truck Drivin' Son-Of-A-Gun**	Mercury 72442
11/20/65+	4	16	9. **What We're Fighting For**	Mercury 72500
3/12/66	12	12	10. Viet Nam Blues [S] written by Kris Kristofferson	Mercury 72550
7/9/66	13	12	11. Lonelyville	Mercury 72585
10/8/66	15	12	12. Long Time Gone	Mercury 72618
3/18/67	12	11	13. My Kind Of Love	Mercury 72655
8/5/67	23	10	14. Trucker's Prayer	Mercury 72697
12/2/67+	12	11	15. Anything Leaving Town Today	Mercury 72741
3/16/68	10	11	16. **There Ain't No Easy Run**	Mercury 72779
7/13/68	14	11	17. I Keep Coming Back For More	Mercury 72818
11/30/68+	10	14	18. **Please Let Me Prove (My Love For You)**	Mercury 72856
4/26/69	12	11	19. One More Mile	Mercury 72902
9/13/69	10	11	20. **George (And The North Woods)**	Mercury 72952
3/21/70	1 (1)	14	21. **The Pool Shark**	Mercury 73029
8/15/70	20	9	22. This Night (Ain't Fit For Nothing But Drinking)	Mercury 73089
12/5/70	23	9	23. Day Drinkin' **DAVE DUDLEY & TOM T. HALL**	Mercury 73139
1/9/71	15	9	24. Listen Betty (I'm Singing Your Song)	Mercury 73138
5/8/71	8	10	25. **Comin' Down**	Mercury 73193
9/4/71	8	12	26. **Fly Away Again**	Mercury 73225
4/8/72	14	11	27. If It Feels Good Do It	Mercury 73274
8/19/72	12	12	28. You've Gotta Cry Girl	Mercury 73309
1/27/73	40	2	29. We Know It's Over **DAVE DUDLEY & KAREN O'DONNAL**	Mercury 73345
3/31/73	19	7	30. Keep On Truckin'	Mercury 73367
9/22/73	37	1	31. It Takes Time	Mercury 73404
5/24/75	21	6	32. Fireball Rolled A Seven	United Art. 630
11/22/75+	12	9	33. Me And Ole C.B.	United Art. 722

DATE	POS	WKS	ARTIST—RECORD TITLE	LABEL & NO.
			DUFF, Arlie	
			Born Arleigh Elton Duff on 3/28/24 in Jack's Branch, near Warren, Texas. Longtime DJ in Colorado and Texas.	
12/5/53+	7	10	1. **You All Come** Best Seller #7 / Jockey #7 / Juke Box #8	Starday 104
			DUNCAN, Johnny	
			Born on 10/5/38 in Dublin, Texas. Attended Texas Christian University and lived in Clovis, New Mexico, 1959-64. Moved to Nashville in 1964 and worked as a DJ on WAGG-Franklin, Tennessee. Appeared on WSM-TV shows with Ralph Emery. Cousin of Dan Seals and Jim Seals (Seals & Crofts).	
10/26/68	21	7	1. Jackson Ain't A Very Big Town **JOHNNY DUNCAN & JUNE STEARNS**	Columbia 44656
7/19/69	30	7	2. When She Touches Me	Columbia 44864
6/20/70	39	2	3. You're Gonna Need A Man	Columbia 45124
11/28/70	27	7	4. Let Me Go (Set Me Free)	Columbia 45227
4/3/71	19	8	5. There's Something About A Lady	Columbia 45319
8/21/71	39	3	6. One Night Of Love	Columbia 45418
12/11/71+	12	9	7. Baby's Smile, Woman's Kiss	Columbia 45479
4/8/72	19	9	8. Fools	Columbia 45556
4/21/73	6	12	9. **Sweet Country Woman**	Columbia 45818
9/29/73	18	10	10. Talkin' With My Lady	Columbia 45917
10/11/75	26	5	11. Jo And The Cowboy Janie Fricke (guest vocal)	Columbia 10182
5/1/76	4	14	12. **Stranger**	Columbia 10302
10/16/76	1 (2)	13	13. **Thinkin' Of A Rendezvous**	Columbia 10417
2/19/77	1 (1)	11	14. **It Couldn't Have Been Any Better** Janie Fricke (harmony vocal, above 3)	Columbia 10474
6/18/77	5	12	15. **A Song In The Night**	Columbia 10554
11/5/77+	4	12	16. **Come A Little Bit Closer** **JOHNNY DUNCAN with JANIE FRICKE** #3 Pop hit for Jay & The Americans in 1964	Columbia 10634
3/25/78	1 (1)	10	17. **She Can Put Her Shoes Under My Bed (Anytime)**	Columbia 10694
7/29/78	4	9	18. **Hello Mexico (And Adios Baby To You)**	Columbia 10783
3/10/79	6	9	19. **Slow Dancing** #10 Pop hit for Johnny Rivers in 1977 as "Swayin' To The Music (Slow Dancin')"	Columbia 10915
10/6/79	9	10	20. **The Lady In The Blue Mercedes**	Columbia 11097
2/2/80	17	8	21. Play Another Slow Song	Columbia 11185
6/28/80	17	8	22. I'm Gonna Love You Tonight (In My Dreams)	Columbia 11280
8/16/80	17	7	23. He's Out Of My Life **JOHNNY DUNCAN and JANIE FRICKE** #10 Pop hit for Michael Jackson in 1980 as "She's Out Of My Life"	Columbia 11312
11/29/80+	16	9	24. Acapulco	Columbia 11385
12/5/81	40	1	25. All Night Long	Columbia 02570

DATE	POS	WKS	ARTIST– RECORD TITLE	LABEL & NO.
			DUNCAN, Tommy, And His Western All Stars	
			Born on 1/11/11 in Hillsboro, Texas. Died of a heart attack on 7/24/67. Sang with Bob Wills in the Light Crust Doughboys, 1932-33. Vocalist on 17 hits of Bob Wills's Texas Playboys from 1933 on. Own band, the Western All Stars, 1948-49.	
8/13/49	**8**	3	1. **Gamblin' Polka Dot Blues** Best Seller #8 / Juke Box #8	Capitol 40178
1/23/61	**26**	1	2. The Image Of Me **BOB WILLS & TOMMY DUNCAN**	Liberty 55264
			DUNN, Holly	
			Born on 8/22/57 in San Antonio, Texas. Sister of composer Chris Waters. Guitarist/drummer; lead vocalist with the Freedom Folk Singers, 1975-76. Attended Abiline Christian University. Formed songwriting team with brother Chris. Former staff writer at CBS and MTM Records. Joined the *Grand Ole Opry* in 1989. CMA Award: 1987 Horizon Award.	
7/5/86	**39**	2	1. Two Too Many	MTM 72064
9/27/86	**7**	12	2. **Daddy's Hands**	MTM 72075
2/14/87	**4**	14	3. **A Face In The Crowd** **MICHAEL MARTIN MURPHEY and HOLLY DUNN**	Warner 28471
5/23/87	**2** (2)	14	4. **Love Someone Like Me**	MTM 72082
9/19/87	**4**	13	5. **Only When I Love**	MTM 72091
2/20/88	**7**	11	6. **Strangers Again**	MTM 72093
7/16/88	**5**	12	7. **That's What Your Love Does To Me**	MTM 72108
12/3/88+	**11**	12	8. (It's Always Gonna Be) Someday	MTM 72116
6/17/89	**1** (1)	14	9. **Are You Ever Gonna Love Me**	Warner 22957
10/7/89	**4**	19	10. **There Goes My Heart Again**	Warner 22796
2/24/90	**25**	6	11. Maybe **KENNY ROGERS with Holly Dunn**	Reprise 19972
9/22/90	**1** (1)	17	12. **You Really Had Me Going**	Warner 19756
1/26/91	**19**	12	13. Heart Full Of Love	Warner 19472
			E	
			EAGLES	
			Rock-country group based in Los Angeles: Glenn Frey (vocals, guitar), Randy Meisner (bass), Don Henley (drums) and Bernie Leadon (guitar). Meisner founded Poco. Leadon had been in the Flying Burrito Brothers. Frey and Henley were with Linda Ronstadt. Don Felder (guitar) added in 1975. Leadon replaced by Joe Walsh in 1975. Meisner replaced by Timothy B. Schmit in 1977. Disbanded in 1982. Various Country artists saluted the band with the 1993 tribute album *Common Thread: The Songs Of The Eagles*. Henley, Frey, Felder, Walsh and Schmit reunited in 1994.	
11/1/75	**8**	9	1. **Lyin' Eyes**	Asylum 45279
			EARLE, Steve	
			Born on 1/17/55 in Fort Monroe, Virginia; raised in Schertz, Texas. To Nashville in 1974. Had bit part in the movie *Nashville*. Worked local clubs. Lived in Mexico, 1980-81. Worked as the manager of a music publishing company in Nashville, sang on demos. Began serving a year-long sentence for heroin possession in September 1994.	

DATE	POS	WKS	ARTIST–RECORD TITLE	LABEL & NO.
5/3/86	37	2	1. Hillbilly Highway	MCA 52785
7/26/86	**7**	13	2. **Guitar Town**	MCA 52856
11/15/86	28	6	3. Someday	MCA 52920
3/7/87	**8**	11	4. **Goodbyes All We've Got Left**	MCA 53011
7/11/87	20	8	5. Nowhere Road	MCA 53103
			STEVE EARLE & THE DUKES:	
11/28/87	37	2	6. Sweet Little '66	MCA 53182
2/6/88	29	5	7. Six Days On The Road	MCA 53249
			from the John Hughes movie Planes, Trains & Automobiles	

EARWOOD, Mundo

Mundo pronounced: moon-doe. Born Raymond Earwood on 10/13/52 in Del Rio, Texas. Own band, Tumbling Tumbleweeds, in 9th grade. Attended San Jacinto College; majored in business administration.

DATE	POS	WKS	ARTIST–RECORD TITLE	LABEL & NO.
8/13/77	32	4	1. Behind Blue Eyes [R]	True 104
7/8/78	36	2	2. When I Get You Alone	GMC 102
9/23/78	18	8	3. Things I'd Do For You	GMC 104
1/6/79	25	6	4. Fooled Around And Fell In Love	GMC 105
6/9/79	38	2	5. My Heart Is Not My Own	GMC 106
9/1/79	34	3	6. We Got Love	GMC 107
5/24/80	27	4	7. You're In Love With The Wrong Man	GMC 109
			Mel Tillis (harmony vocal)	
10/25/80	26	6	8. Can't Keep My Mind Off Of Her	GMC 111
3/28/81	40	1	9. Blue Collar Blues	Excelsior 1005
6/20/81	32	3	10. Angela	Excelsior 1010

EASTON, Sheena—see ROGERS, Kenny

EATON, Connie

Born on 3/1/50 in Nashville. Performing since age 14. Appeared on *Arthur Godfrey*, *Lawrence Welk* and *Hee-Haw* TV shows in the late '60s.

DATE	POS	WKS	ARTIST–RECORD TITLE	LABEL & NO.
3/7/70	34	2	1. Angel Of The Morning	Chart 5048
			#7 Pop hit for Merrilee Rush in 1968	
3/8/75	23	6	2. Lonely Men, Lonely Women	Dunhill 15022

EBERLY, Bob, & The Sunshine Serenaders

Eberly was born Robert Eberle on 7/24/16 in Mechanicsville, New York. Died on 11/17/81. Vocalist with Jimmy Dorsey, 1935-43. Made popular duets with Helen O'Connell.

DATE	POS	WKS	ARTIST–RECORD TITLE	LABEL & NO.
1/1/49	**8**	1	1. **One Has My Name The Other Has My Heart**	Decca 24492
			Juke Box #8 / Best Seller #15	

EDDY, Duane

Born on 4/26/38 in Corning, New York. Duane originated the "twangy" guitar sound and is rock and roll's all-time #1 instrumentalist. Married to Jessi Colter, 1962-68. Inducted into the Rock and Roll Hall of Fame in 1994.

DATE	POS	WKS	ARTIST–RECORD TITLE	LABEL & NO.
8/4/58	17	5	1. Rebel-'Rouser [I]	Jamie 1104
			Best Seller #17; The Sharps (later known as The Rivingtons, rebel yells)	

DATE	POS	WKS	ARTIST– RECORD TITLE	LABEL & NO.
			EDWARDS, Bobby	
			Born Robert Moncrief in Anniston, Alabama. Own band, The Four Young Men.	
9/4/61	**4**	24	1. **You're The Reason**	Crest 1075
			The Four Young Men (backing vocals)	
9/14/63	23	2	2. Don't Pretend	Capitol 5006
			EDWARDS, Jimmy	
			Born James Bullington on 2/9/33 in Senath, Missouri.	
11/11/57+	**12**	6	1. Love Bug Crawl	Mercury 71209
			Jockey #12	
			EDWARDS, Stoney	
			Born Frenchy Edwards on 12/24/29 in Seminole, Oklahoma. Played guitar from age 15. Moved to California in 1950; worked outside of music. First recorded for Capitol in 1970. Moved to San Antonio in the late '70s. One of the few successful black country singers.	
12/16/72+	20	9	1. She's My Rock	Capitol 3462
9/22/73	39	2	2. Hank And Lefty Raised My Country Soul	Capitol 3671
5/17/75	20	7	3. Mississippi You're On My Mind	Capitol 4051
			EMERY, Ralph	
			Born Walter Ralph Emery on 3/10/33 in McEwen, Tennessee. Popular host of TNN's *Nashville Now*. Married to Skeeter Davis, 1960-64. Retired from *Nashville Now* in October 1993.	
8/28/61	**4**	15	1. **Hello Fool** [S]	Liberty 55352
			answer song to Faron Young's "Hello Walls"	
			EMILIO	
			Born Emilio Navaira in San Antonio.	
10/14/95	27	11	1. It's Not The End Of The World	Capitol 18846
			ENGLAND, Ty	
			College roommate of Garth Brooks. Member of Brooks's touring band.	
7/8/95	**3**	16	1. **Should've Asked Her Faster**	RCA 64280
			ESMERELDY and Her Novelty Band	
			Esmereldy married to opera singer Harry Boersma. Mother of Pop singer Amy Holland.	
3/20/48	10	1	1. **Slap Her Down Again Paw** [N]	Musicraft 524
			EVERETTE, Leon	
			Born Leon Everette Baughman on 6/21/48 in Aiken, South Carolina; raised in New York City. First recorded for Doral Records.	
7/14/79	33	3	1. Don't Feel Like The Lone Ranger	Orlando 103
1/19/80	28	4	2. I Love That Woman (Like The Devil Loves Sin) [R]	Orlando 105
			new version of Everette's #84 hit in 1977	
3/29/80	30	5	3. I Don't Want To Lose	Orlando 106
6/21/80	10	11	4. **Over**	Orlando 107

DATE	POS	WKS	ARTIST–RECORD TITLE	LABEL & NO.
11/1/80+	5	13	5. **Giving Up Easy** [R] reissue (same version) of Everette's #81 hit in 1979	RCA 12111
3/21/81	11	9	6. If I Keep On Going Crazy	RCA 12177
8/8/81	4	11	7. **Hurricane**	RCA 12270
11/28/81+	9	11	8. **Midnight Rodeo**	RCA 12355
4/17/82	7	12	9. **Just Give Me What You Think Is Fair**	RCA 13079
8/28/82	10	11	10. **Soul Searchin'**	RCA 13282
1/15/83	15	7	11. Shadows Of My Mind	RCA 13391
4/23/83	9	9	12. **My Lady Loves Me (Just As I Am)**	RCA 13466
9/17/83	31	4	13. The Lady, She's Right Rex Gosdin (harmony vocal)	RCA 13584
2/25/84	6	12	14. **I Could'a Had You**	RCA 13717
8/4/84	30	5	15. Shot In The Dark	RCA 13834

EVERLY, Phil

Born on 1/19/39 in Chicago. Younger member of The Everly Brothers duo. Married for a time to the daughter of Janet Bleyer (member of '50s pop vocal group The Chordettes).

DATE	POS	WKS	ARTIST–RECORD TITLE	LABEL & NO.
3/26/83	37	2	1. Who's Gonna Keep Me Warm	Capitol 5197

EVERLY BROTHERS, The

Duo of vocalists/guitarists/songwriters Don and Phil. Don (beginning at age eight) and Phil (age six) sang with parents through high school. Invited to Nashville by Chet Atkins and first recorded there for Columbia in 1955. Signed to Archie Bleyer's Cadence Records in 1957. Duo split up in July 1973 and reunited in September 1983. Inducted into the Rock and Roll Hall of Fame in 1986.

DATE	POS	WKS	ARTIST–RECORD TITLE	LABEL & NO.
5/13/57	1 (7)	26	● 1. **Bye Bye Love** Best Seller #1(7) / Jockey #1(7)	Cadence 1315
9/30/57	1 (8)	22	● 2. **Wake Up Little Susie** Jockey #1(8) / Best Seller #1(7)	Cadence 1337
2/10/58	4	13	3. **This Little Girl Of Mine/** Best Seller #4 / Jockey #5; #9 R&B hit for Ray Charles in 1955	
3/24/58	10	1	4. **Should We Tell Him** Jockey #10	Cadence 1342
4/28/58	1 (3)	20	● 5. **All I Have To Do Is Dream/** Best Seller #1(3) / Jockey #1(1)	
6/16/58	15	1	6. Claudette Jockey #15; written by Roy Orbison	Cadence 1348
8/18/58	1 (6)	13	● 7. **Bird Dog/** Best Seller #1 / Jockey #3	
9/1/58	7	5	8. **Devoted To You** Jockey #7	Cadence 1350
12/1/58+	17	7	9. Problems	Cadence 1355
8/31/59	8	12	10. ('Til) I Kissed You	Cadence 1369
3/6/61	25	3	11. Ebony Eyes	Warner 5199
4/5/86	17	9	12. Born Yesterday	Mercury 884428

EWING, Skip

Born Donald R. Ewing on 3/6/64 in Redlands, California. Moved to Nashville in 1984.

DATE	POS	WKS	ARTIST–RECORD TITLE	LABEL & NO.
4/9/88	17	8	1. Your Memory Wins Again	MCA 53271

DATE	POS	WKS	ARTIST– RECORD TITLE	LABEL & NO.
7/30/88	8	13	2. **I Don't Have Far To Fall**	MCA 53353
11/26/88+	3	14	3. **Burnin' A Hole In My Heart**	MCA 53435
4/1/89	10	11	4. **The Gospel According To Luke**	MCA 53481
7/22/89	15	10	5. The Coast Of Colorado	MCA 53663
11/4/89+	5	17	6. **It's You Again**	MCA 53732

EXILE

Band formed in Lexington, Kentucky, in 1963 as The Exiles. Toured with Dick Clark in 1965. Changed name to Exile in 1973. Had several Pop hits in the late '70s. In 1983, the group consisted of J.P. Pennington (vocals, lead guitar), Les Taylor (rhythm guitar), Marlon Hargis (keyboards), Sonny Lemaire (bass) and Steve Goetzman (drums). Hargis was replaced by Lee Carroll in 1985. Carroll was in the Hatfield Clan and worked as music director for the Judds. Pennington wrote "Take Me Down" and "The Closer You Get" for Alabama; left band in early 1989. Paul Martin replaced Pennington. Taylor began solo career in 1989.

DATE	POS	WKS	ARTIST– RECORD TITLE	LABEL & NO.
10/1/83	27	6	1. High Cost Of Leaving	Epic 04041
1/7/84	1 (1)	12	2. **Woke Up In Love**	Epic 04247
4/28/84	1 (1)	14	3. **I Don't Want To Be A Memory**	Epic 04421
9/1/84	1 (1)	15	4. **Give Me One More Chance**	Epic 04567
1/5/85	1 (1)	13	5. **Crazy For Your Love**	Epic 04722
4/27/85	1 (1)	13	6. **She's A Miracle**	Epic 04864
8/31/85	1 (1)	15	7. **Hang On To Your Heart**	Epic 05580
12/28/85+	1 (1)	14	8. **I Could Get Used To You**	Epic 05723
4/26/86	14	9	9. Super Love	Epic 05860
8/9/86	1 (1)	15	10. **It'll Be Me**	Epic 06229
1/24/87+	1 (1)	14	11. **I Can't Get Close Enough**	Epic 07597
6/27/87	1 (1)	14	12. **She's Too Good To Be True**	Epic 07135
5/14/88	9	12	13. **Just One Kiss**	Epic 07775
10/8/88	21	7	14. It's You Again	Epic 08020
1/13/90	17	11	15. Keep It In The Middle Of The Road	Arista 9911
6/2/90	2 (1)	14	16. **Nobody's Talking**	Arista 2009
9/29/90	7	16	17. **Yet**	Arista 2075
2/16/91	32	4	18. There You Go	Arista 2139
7/13/91	16	11	19. Even Now	Arista 2228

F

FAIRCHILD, Barbara

Born on 11/12/50 in Lafe, Arkansas; raised in Knobel, Arkansas. Moved to St. Louis in 1963, worked on TV from 1965. First recorded for Norman Records in 1965. Moved to Nashville in 1968 and worked as a songwriter. Lived in Texas, 1980-85, then returned to Nashville.

DATE	POS	WKS	ARTIST– RECORD TITLE	LABEL & NO.
3/14/70	26	5	1. A Girl Who'll Satisfy Her Man *The Town & Country Singers (backing vocals)*	Columbia 45063
1/30/71	33	4	2. (Loving You Is) Sunshine	Columbia 45272
9/4/71	28	7	3. Love's Old Song	Columbia 45422
2/5/72	38	3	4. Color My World *#16 Pop hit for Petula Clark in 1967*	Columbia 45522

DATE	POS	WKS	ARTIST–RECORD TITLE	LABEL & NO.
6/17/72	29	6	5. Thanks For The Mem'ries	Columbia 45589
1/27/73	1 (2)	15	6. **Teddy Bear Song**	Columbia 45743
8/18/73	2 (2)	13	7. **Kid Stuff**	Columbia 45903
2/23/74	6	9	8. **Baby Doll**	Columbia 45988
8/3/74	17	7	9. Standing In Your Line	Columbia 46053
12/7/74	31	4	10. Little Girl Feeling	Columbia 10047
8/28/76	31	3	11. Mississippi	Columbia 10378
11/27/76	15	7	12. Cheatin' Is	Columbia 10423
4/9/77	22	8	13. Let Me Love You Once Before You Go	Columbia 10485
			#48 Pop hit for Greg Lake in 1981 as "Let Me Love You Once"	

FALLS, Ruby

Born in Jackson, Tennessee. Died on 6/15/86. Moved to Milwaukee, sang with local bands. Appeared on many TV music shows. One of the very few black female Country singers.

DATE	POS	WKS	ARTIST–RECORD TITLE	LABEL & NO.
10/29/77	40	1	1. You've Got To Mend This Heartache	50 States 56

FAMILY BROWN

Canadian group featuring Tracey and Barry Brown.

DATE	POS	WKS	ARTIST–RECORD TITLE	LABEL & NO.
2/13/82	30	4	1. But It's Cheating	RCA 13015

FARGO, Donna

Born Yvonne Vaughan on 11/10/49 in Mount Airy, North Carolina. Taught high school in Covina, California, while working local clubs as Donna Fargo. Recorded for Ramco in 1969. Quit teaching in June 1972. Stricken with multiple sclerosis in 1979. Has own music publishing company.

DATE	POS	WKS	ARTIST–RECORD TITLE	LABEL & NO.
4/22/72	1 (3)	17	● 1. **The Happiest Girl In The Whole U.S.A.**	Dot 17409
			CMA Award: Single of the Year	
9/9/72	1 (3)	14	● 2. **Funny Face**	Dot 17429
2/17/73	1 (1)	14	3. **Superman**	Dot 17444
6/9/73	1 (1)	12	4. **You Were Always There**	Dot 17460
10/13/73	2 (1)	11	5. **Little Girl Gone**	Dot 17476
3/9/74	6	10	6. **I'll Try A Little Bit Harder**	Dot 17491
6/29/74	1 (1)	11	7. **You Can't Be A Beacon (If Your Light Don't Shine)**	Dot 17506
11/9/74+	9	10	8. **U.S. of A**	ABC/Dot 17523
3/1/75	7	8	9. **It Do Feel Good**	ABC/Dot 17541
6/28/75	14	8	10. Hello Little Bluebird	ABC/Dot 17557
11/15/75	38	3	11. Whatever I Say	ABC/Dot 17579
4/24/76	20	7	12. Mr. Doodles	Warner 8186
7/31/76	15	9	13. I've Loved You All The Way	Warner 8227
11/27/76+	3	12	14. **Don't Be Angry**	ABC/Dot 17660
2/26/77	9	9	15. **Mockingbird Hill**	Warner 8305
			#2 Pop hit for Patti Page in 1951	
5/14/77	1 (1)	11	16. **That Was Yesterday**	Warner 8375
9/24/77	8	11	17. **Shame On Me**	Warner 8431
1/14/78	2 (2)	11	18. **Do I Love You (Yes In Every Way)**	Warner 8509
6/10/78	19	7	19. Ragamuffin Man	Warner 8578
9/9/78	10	10	20. **Another Goodbye**	Warner 8643
1/20/79	6	11	21. **Somebody Special**	Warner 8722

DATE	POS	WKS	ARTIST– RECORD TITLE	LABEL & NO.
8/4/79	14	8	22. Daddy [R] first issued on Challange 59387 and then on Decca 33001 in 1972	Warner 8867
8/14/82	40	1	23. It's Hard To Be The Dreamer (When I Used to be the Dream)	RCA 13264
12/27/86+	29	5	24. Me And You	Mercury 888093
8/1/87	23	7	25. Members Only **DONNA FARGO and BILLY JOE ROYAL**	Mercury 888680
			## FELL, Terry, & the Fellers	
			Born on 5/13/21 in Dora, Alabama. Wrote "You're The Reason" for Bobby Edwards	
8/7/54	4	11	1. **Don't Drop It** Juke Box #4 / Best Seller #11 / Jockey #12	"X" 0010
			## FELLER, Dick	
			Born on 1/2/43 in Bronaugh, Missouri. Moved to Nashville in 1966, worked sessions with Mel Tillis, Warner Mack, Skeeter Davis and Stu Phillips. Staff writer for Johnny Cash in the early '70s.	
12/15/73+	22	6	1. Biff, The Friendly Purple Bear [S]	United Art. 316
7/6/74	11	8	2. Makin' The Best Of A Bad Situation [N]	Asylum 11037
10/19/74	10	10	3. **The Credit Card Song** [N]	United Art. 535
			## FELTS, Narvel	
			Born Albert Narvel Felts on 11/11/38 near Keiser, Arkansas. Rockabilly-Country singer/guitarist. Began recording career in 1957 on Sun. Served in the Army National Guard, 1961-67. Member of The Wolfpack.	
7/21/73	8	11	1. **Drift Away** #5 Pop hit for Dobie Gray in 1973	Cinnamon 763
11/10/73	13	8	2. All In The Name Of Love	Cinnamon 771
2/16/74	14	9	3. When Your Good Love Was Mine	Cinnamon 779
6/15/74	39	2	4. Until The End Of Time **NARVEL FELTS and SHARON VAUGHN**	Cinnamon 793
6/22/74	26	5	5. I Want To Stay	Cinnamon 798
10/26/74	33	4	6. Raindrops #2 Pop hit for Dee Clark in 1961	Cinnamon 809
5/3/75	2 (1)	14	7. **Reconsider Me**	ABC/Dot 17549
9/20/75	12	9	8. Funny How Time Slips Away written by Willie Nelson (5 Pop hit versions, 1962-83)	ABC/Dot 17569
12/27/75+	10	11	9. **Somebody Hold Me (Until She Passes By)**	ABC/Dot 17598
4/24/76	5	11	10. **Lonely Teardrops** #7 Pop hit for Jackie Wilson in 1959	ABC/Dot 17620
8/21/76	14	6	11. My Prayer #1 Pop hit for The Platters in 1956	ABC/Dot 17643
12/4/76+	20	7	12. My Good Thing's Gone	ABC/Dot 17664
3/19/77	19	6	13. The Feeling's Right	ABC/Dot 17680
7/2/77	37	2	14. I Don't Hurt Anymore	ABC/Dot 17700
9/10/77	22	6	15. To Love Somebody #17 Pop hit for the Bee Gees in 1967	ABC/Dot 17715
1/14/78	34	3	16. Please/	
		3	17. Blue Darlin'	ABC/Dot 17731

DATE	POS	WKS	ARTIST – RECORD TITLE	LABEL & NO.
4/15/78	**30**	5	18. Runaway #1 Pop hit for Del Shannon in 1961	ABC 12338
7/29/78	**31**	3	19. Just Keep It Up #18 Pop hit for Dee Clark in 1959	ABC 12374
11/18/78	**26**	5	20. One Run For The Roses	ABC 12414
1/6/79	**14**	9	21. Everlasting Love Robert Knight and Carl Carlton had Pop hit versions	ABC 12441
8/4/79	**33**	3	22. Tower Of Strength #5 Pop hit for Gene McDaniels in 1961	MCA 41055

FENDER, Freddy

Born Baldemar G. Huerta on 6/4/37 in San Benito, Texas. First recorded in Spanish under his real name for Falcon in 1956. In Angola State Prison for marijuana possession, 1960-63. Did session work in New Orleans after parole. Out of music, 1969-74. Appeared in the movie *The Milagro Beanfield War*. Joined the Texas Tornados in 1990.

DATE	POS	WKS	ARTIST – RECORD TITLE	LABEL & NO.
2/8/75	**1 (2)**	10	● 1. **Before The Next Teardrop Falls** CMA Award: Single of the Year	ABC/Dot 17540
7/5/75	**1 (2)**	11	● 2. **Wasted Days And Wasted Nights** originally recorded by Fender on the Duncan label in 1959	ABC/Dot 17558
10/25/75	**1 (1)**	12	3. **Secret Love** #1 Pop hit for Doris Day in 1954	ABC/Dot 17585
11/1/75	**10**	9	4. **Since I Met You Baby** #12 Pop hit for Ivory Joe Hunter in 1956	GRT 031
1/31/76	**13**	7	5. Wild Side Of Life	GRT 039
2/21/76	**1 (1)**	11	6. **You'll Lose A Good Thing** #8 Pop hit for Barbara Lynn in 1962	ABC/Dot 17607
6/5/76	**7**	10	7. **Vaya Con Dios** #1 Pop hit for Les Paul & Mary Ford in 1953	ABC/Dot 17627
10/2/76	**2 (2)**	11	8. **Living It Down**	ABC/Dot 17652
4/2/77	**4**	11	9. **The Rains Came/** #31 Pop hit for Sir Douglas Quintet in 1966	
		11	10. Sugar Coated Love	ABC/Dot 17686
8/13/77	**11**	8	11. If You Don't Love Me (Why Don't You Just Leave Me Alone)	ABC/Dot 17713
12/10/77+	**18**	7	12. Think About Me	ABC/Dot 17730
4/8/78	**34**	3	13. If You're Looking For A Fool	ABC 12339
7/1/78	**13**	8	14. Talk To Me #20 Pop hit for Little Willie John in 1958	ABC 12370
11/4/78	**26**	5	15. I'm Leaving It All Up To You #1 Pop hit for Dale & Grace in 1963	ABC 12415
3/17/79	**22**	7	16. Walking Piece Of Heaven	ABC 12453
7/14/79	**22**	5	17. Yours	Starflite 4900

FENDERMEN, The

Duo of Jim Sundquist (from Niagara, Wisconsin) and Phil Humphrey (from Stoughton, Wisconsin). Both guitarists were born on 11/26/37. Formed at the University of Wisconsin-Madison in 1959. John Howard (drums) added in 1960.

DATE	POS	WKS	ARTIST – RECORD TITLE	LABEL & NO.

7/11/60	**16**	8	1. Mule Skinner Blues
			     originally recorded in 1959 on the Cuca label; tune written and
			     recorded by Jimmie Rodgers in 1930 (Victor 23503)
				Soma 1137

DATE	POS	WKS	ARTIST–RECORD TITLE	LABEL & NO.
			FENSTER, Zoot—see BARLOW, Jack	
			FITZGERALD, Ella, And Her Famous Orchestra	
			Born on 4/25/18 in Newport News, Virginia. The most honored jazz singer of all time.	
3/18/44	2 (1)	1	1. **When My Sugar Walks Down The Street** #2 Pop hit for Aileen Stanley & Gene Austin in 1925	Decca 18587
			5 RED CAPS	
			R&B group formed as the Toppers in Los Angeles in 1938. Consisted of Steve Gibson, Emmett Matthews, Dave Patillo, Jimmy Springs and Romaine Brown. Also known as Steve Gibson's Red Caps.	
4/29/44	2 (1)	8	1. **I Learned A Lesson, I'll Never Forget**	Beacon 7120
			FLATT & SCRUGGS	
			Bluegrass duo of Lester Raymond Flatt (born 6/19/14, Overton County, Tennessee; died 5/11/79), guitar, mandolin; and Earl Eugene Scruggs (born 1/6/24, Flintville, North Carolina), banjo. Flatt had been in the Harmonizers and Charlie Monroe's Band and joined Bill Monroe in 1944. Scruggs had been in the Carolina Wildcats and the Morris Brothers, and had broadcast with Lost John Miller on WSM-Nashville in 1945. He joined Bill Monroe in 1945. The duo left Monroe in 1948 and formed their own Foggy Mountain Boys, which included Mac Wiseman. Worked on WCYB-Bristol, Tennessee, until 1949. Toured with Ernest Tubb and Lefty Frizzell in the early '50s. Own radio series, *Martha White Biscuit Time*, on WSM from 1953. Own TV show for a time, and joined the *Grand Ole Opry* in 1955. Disbanded in 1969; Flatt formed Nashville Grass and Scruggs started his Earl Scruggs Revue. Elected to the Country Music Hall of Fame in 1985.	
			LESTER FLATT, EARL SCRUGGS & THE FOGGY MOUNTAIN BOYS:	
2/2/52	9	1	1. **'Tis Sweet To Be Remembered** Jockey #9; Lester Flatt and Everett Lilly (vocals)	Columbia 20886
6/8/59	9	30	2. **Cabin In The Hills**	Columbia 41389
2/1/60	21	6	3. Crying My Heart Out Over You	Columbia 41518
12/5/60+	12	14	4. Polka On A Banjo	Columbia 41786
10/9/61	10	16	5. **Go Home**	Columbia 42141
4/7/62	16	8	6. Just Ain't	Columbia 42280
6/23/62	27	1	7. The Legend Of The Johnson Boys	Columbia 42413
12/8/62+	1 (3)	20	8. **The Ballad Of Jed Clampett** theme song from the TV series *The Beverly Hillbillies*	Columbia 42606
5/11/63	8	11	9. **Pearl Pearl Pearl** featured on the TV series *The Beverly Hillbillies*	Columbia 42755
9/28/63	26	3	10. New York Town	Columbia 42840
2/22/64	12	15	11. You Are My Flower/	
2/22/64	40	2	12. My Saro Jane	Columbia 42954
3/14/64	14	9	13. Petticoat Junction theme from the TV series starring Edgar Buchanan	Columbia 42982
8/22/64	21	12	14. Workin' It Out	Columbia 43080
9/2/67	20	8	15. California Up Tight Band **LESTER FLATT & EARL SCRUGGS (#13 & 15)**	Columbia 44194

DATE	POS	WKS	ARTIST– RECORD TITLE	LABEL & NO.
			FOGELBERG, Dan	
			Born on 8/13/51 in Peoria, Illinois. Vocalist/composer. Worked as a folk singer in Los Angeles. With Van Morrison in the early '70s. Session work in Nashville.	
9/28/85	33	4	1. Down The Road Mountain Pass	Full Moon 05446
			FOGERTY, John	
			Born on 5/28/45 in Berkeley, California. Leader of Creedence Clearwater Revival.	
3/9/85	38	2	1. Big Train (From Memphis) flip side of the #10 Pop hit "The Old Man Down The Road"	Warner 29100
			FOLEY, Betty	
			Born on 2/3/33 in Chicago; raised in Berea, Kentucky. Daughter of Pauline and Red Foley. Worked on the *Renfro Valley Barn Dance*, 1950-54; the *Grand Ole Opry*, 1956-57, and the *Louisiana Hayride* in 1958. With her father on the TV series *Jubilee USA*.	
3/6/54	8	10	1. As Far As I'm Concerned Juke Box #8 / Jockey #8 / Best Seller #11	Decca 29000
6/25/55	3	23	2. Satisfied Mind **RED FOLEY & BETTY FOLEY** (above 2) Juke Box #3 / Best Seller #4 / Jockey #6	Decca 29526
8/31/59	7	12	3. Old Moon	Bandera 1304
			FOLEY, Red	
			Born Clyde Julian Foley on 6/17/10 in Blue Lick, Kentucky. Died of a heart attack on 9/19/68 in Fort Wayne, Indiana. On the WLS *National Barn Dance*, 1930-37, and the *Renfro Valley Show*, 1937-39. Member of the *Grand Ole Opry*, 1946-54. Hosted the ABC-TV series *Ozark Jubilee*, 1954-60. Co-starred with Fess Parker in the TV series *Mr. Smith Goes To Washington* in the early '60s. His daughter Shirley married Pat Boone in 1953. Elected to the Country Music Hall of Fame in 1967. (a) ERNEST TUBB & RED FOLEY (b) KITTY WELLS and RED FOLEY	
8/26/44	1 (13)	27	1. Smoke On The Water/	Decca 6102
9/30/44	5	1	2. There's A Blue Star Shining Bright	
6/23/45	4	2	3. Hang Your Head In Shame/	Decca 6108
6/23/45	5	1	4. I'll Never Let You Worry My Mind	
9/8/45	1 (1)	14	5. Shame On You/	Decca 18698
11/10/45	3	2	6. At Mail Call Today **LAWRENCE WELK AND HIS ORCHESTRA with RED FOLEY (above 2)**	
5/4/46	4	1	7. Harriet	Decca 9003
11/30/46	5	1	8. Have I Told You Lately That I Love You **RED FOLEY with ROY ROSS & HIS RAMBLERS** (above 2) from the movie *Over The Trail*	Decca 46014
			RED FOLEY AND THE CUMBERLAND VALLEY BOYS:	
3/15/47	4	1	9. That's How Much I Love You	Decca 46028
4/5/47	1 (2)	16	10. New Jolie Blonde (New Pretty Blonde)	Decca 46034
6/21/47	5	1	11. Freight Train Boogie	Decca 46035
11/22/47	2 (1)	13	12. Never Trust A Woman	Decca 46074

DATE	POS	WKS	ARTIST– RECORD TITLE	LABEL & NO.
10/2/48+	**1** (1)	40	13. **Tennessee Saturday Night/** Juke Box #1 / Best Seller #3	
5/14/49	**15**	1	14. Blues In My Heart Best Seller #15	Decca 46136
4/2/49	**3**	21	15. **Tennessee Border/** Juke Box #3 / Best Seller #4	
3/26/49	**4**	15	16. **Candy Kisses** Juke Box #4 / Best Seller #6	Decca 46151

RED FOLEY:

DATE	POS	WKS	ARTIST– RECORD TITLE	LABEL & NO.
6/25/49	**4**	13	17. **Tennessee Polka/** Juke Box #4 / Best Seller #6	
7/23/49	**11**	2	18. I'm Throwing Rice (At The Girl I Love) Best Seller #11 / Juke Box #14	Decca 46170
8/6/49	**8**	4	19. **Two Cents, Three Eggs And A Postcard** Juke Box #8	Decca 46165
12/17/49+	**3**	6	20. **Sunday Down In Tennessee** Jockey #3 / Juke Box #3 / Best Seller #10	Decca 46197
12/31/49+	**2** (2)	10	21. **Tennessee Border No. 2** (a)/ Best Seller #2 / Juke Box #2	
1/21/50	**7**	2	22. Don't Be Ashamed Of Your Age (a) Juke Box #7 / Jockey #9	Decca 46200
1/14/50	**8**	1	23. **Careless Kisses/** Juke Box #8 / Best Seller #14	
1/7/50	**10**	1	24. I Gotta Have My Baby Back Juke Box #10 / Best Seller #13	Decca 46201
1/21/50	**1** (13)	20	● 25. Chattanoogie Shoe Shine Boy Jockey #1(13) / Juke Box #1(13) / Best Seller #1(12); #34 Pop hit for Freddy Cannon in 1960	
2/18/50	**4**	11	26. **Sugarfoot Rag** Juke Box #4 / Jockey #8; Hank "Sugarfoot" Garland (guitar solo)	Decca 46205
5/6/50	**9**	1	27. Steal Away/ Best Seller #9	
7/22/50	**9**	5	28. **Just A Closer Walk With Thee** Best Seller #9; released on the Decca Faith Series label (also #31 below)	Decca 14505
5/13/50	**1** (4)	15	29. **Birmingham Bounce/** Best Seller #1(4) / Juke Box #1(3) / Jockey #4	
6/3/50	**5**	4	30. Choc'late Ice Cream Cone Jockey #5 / Juke Box #8 / Best Seller #10; The Dixie Dons (female backing vocals, above 2)	Decca 46234
6/3/50	**1** (1)	13	31. Mississippi Juke Box #1 / Best Seller #2 / Jockey #3	Decca 46241
8/12/50	**1** (3)	15	32. Goodnight Irene (a)/ Juke Box #1(3) / Best Seller #1(2) / Jockey #2; The Sunshine Trio (female backing vocals)	
9/2/50	**9**	2	33. Hillbilly Fever No. 2 (a) Juke Box #9	Decca 46255
9/9/50	**2** (1)	12	34. **Cincinnati Dancing Pig** Best Seller #2 / Juke Box #3 / Jockey #6	Decca 46261
11/4/50	**8**	4	35. **Our Lady Of Fatima** Best Seller #8	Decca 14526
2/17/51	**6**	1	36. **My Heart Cries For You** **EVELYN KNIGHT and RED FOLEY** Jockey #6; Alcyone Beasley Singers (backing vocals)	Decca 27378

DATE	POS	WKS	ARTIST–RECORD TITLE	LABEL & NO.
2/17/51	7	3	37. **Hot Rod Race** Best Seller #7 / Juke Box #8 / Jockey #10	Decca 46286
5/12/51	8	3	38. **Hobo Boogie** Juke Box #8	Decca 46304
5/19/51	9	1	39. **The Strange Little Girl** (a) Juke Box #9; Anita Kerr Singers (backing vocals: #31, 43, 46, 53)	Decca 46311
7/7/51	5	11	● 40. **(There'll Be) Peace In The Valley (For Me)** Jockey #5 / Juke Box #5 / Best Seller #7; The Sunshine Boys Quartet (backing vocals)	Decca 46319
11/24/51	3	16	41. **Alabama Jubilee** Juke Box #3 / Best Seller #5 / Jockey #6; The Nashville Dixielanders (dixieland backing - feat. Francis Craig on bones)	Decca 27810
2/2/52	5	9	42. **Too Old To Cut The Mustard** (a) Best Seller #5 / Juke Box #8 / Jockey #10	Decca 46387
3/8/52	8	3	43. **Milk Bucket Boogie/** Juke Box #8	
3/29/52	8	2	44. **Salty Dog Rag** Juke Box #8	Decca 27981
11/15/52+	1 (1)	10	45. **Midnight** Best Seller #1 / Juke Box #2 / Jockey #5; co-written by Chet Atkins	Decca 28420
1/10/53	8	2	46. **Don't Let The Stars Get In Your Eyes** Best Seller #8	Decca 28460
3/21/53	6	4	47. **Hot Toddy** Juke Box #6 / Best Seller #10	Decca 28587
4/18/53	7	2	48. **No Help Wanted #2** (a) Best Seller #7 / Juke Box #9	Decca 28634
5/9/53	8	1	49. **Slaves Of A Hopeless Love Affair** Juke Box #8	Decca 28567
10/10/53	6	4	50. **Shake A Hand** Best Seller #6 / Juke Box #7 / Jockey #10	Decca 28839
3/6/54	8	10	51. **As Far As I'm Concerned** **RED FOLEY & BETTY FOLEY** Juke Box #8 / Jockey #8 / Best Seller #11; #1 R&B hit for Faye Adams in 1953	Decca 29000
5/8/54	7	4	52. **Jilted** Juke Box #7 / Best Seller #9	Decca 29100
5/22/54	1 (1)	34	53. **One By One** (b)/ Juke Box #1 / Best Seller #2 / Jockey #2	
7/10/54	12	1	54. **I'm A Stranger In My Home** (b) Jockey #12 / Best Seller #15	Decca 29065
1/8/55	4	15	55. **Hearts Of Stone** Jockey #4 / Juke Box #4 / Best Seller #6; #1 Pop hit for The Fontane Sisters in 1955	Decca 29375
2/26/55	3	16	56. **As Long As I Live** (b)/ Juke Box #3 / Best Seller #7 / Jockey #8	
2/26/55	6	17	57. **Make Believe ('Til We Can Make It Come True)** (b) Juke Box #6 / Best Seller #7 / Jockey #14	Decca 29390
6/25/55	3	23	58. **Satisfied Mind** Juke Box #3 / Best Seller #4 / Jockey #6 **RED FOLEY & BETTY FOLEY**	Decca 29526
1/28/56	3	31	59. **You And Me** (b)/ Best Seller #3 / Jockey #3 / Juke Box #6	
		6	60. No One But You (b) Best Seller flip / Juke Box flip	Decca 29740
6/29/59	29	1	61. Travelin' Man	Decca 30882

DATE	POS	WKS	ARTIST–RECORD TITLE	LABEL & NO.
			FORD, "Tennessee" Ernie	
			Born Ernest Jennings Ford on 2/13/19 in Bristol, Tennessee. Died on 10/17/91 from liver disease. Worked as staff announcer on WOAI-Bristol in 1937. Worked as a DJ in Atlanta and Knoxville in the early '40s. Served as an Air Corps bombardier during the war. Worked as a DJ in San Bernadino and Pasadena, California. Sang with Cliffie Stone's quartet on *Hometown Jamboree* radio shows. First recorded for Capitol in 1948. Own TV series, 1955-65. Later turned to inspirational music. Elected to the Country Music Hall of Fame in 1990.	
			TENNESSEE ERNIE:	
4/30/49	8	1	1. **Tennessee Border** Juke Box #8 / Best Seller #15	Capitol 15400
5/28/49	14	1	2. Country Junction Juke Box #14	Capitol 15430
9/10/49	8	4	3. **Smokey Mountain Boogie** Best Seller #8 / Juke Box #13	Capitol 40212
11/26/49	1 (4)	10	4. **Mule Train/** Jockey #1 / Juke Box #3 / Best Seller #4	
12/10/49	3	11	5. **Anticipation Blues** Jockey #3 / Best Seller #5 / Juke Box #8	Capitol 40258
2/11/50	2 (2)	10	6. **The Cry Of The Wild Goose** Best Seller #2 / Jockey #3 / Juke Box #5	Capitol 40280
9/16/50	2 (1)	16	7. **I'll Never Be Free/** Jockey #2 / Juke Box #2 / Best Seller #4	
8/26/50	5	6	8. **Ain't Nobody's Business But My Own** **KAY STARR and TENNESSEE ERNIE** (above 2) Jockey #5 / Juke Box #10	Capitol 1124
12/16/50+	1 (14)	25	9. **The Shot Gun Boogie** Juke Box #1(14) / Best Seller #1(3) / Jockey #1(1)	Capitol 1295
3/3/51	8	2	10. Tailor Made Woman **TENNESSEE ERNIE and JOE "FINGERS" CARR** Juke Box #8	Capitol 1349
6/16/51	2 (1)	7	11. **Mr. And Mississippi** Jockey #2 / Best Seller #4 / Juke Box #6	Capitol 1521
6/16/51	9	1	12. **The Strange Little Girl** Best Seller #9	Capitol 1470
9/20/52	6	7	13. **Blackberry Boogie** Juke Box #6 / Best Seller #9 / Jockey #9	Capitol 2170
6/6/53	8	3	14. **Hey, Mr. Cotton Picker** Juke Box #8; Cliffie Stone (orch.)	Capitol 2443
			TENNESSEE ERNIE FORD:	
8/14/54	9	9	15. **River Of No Return** Best Seller #9; title song from the movie starring Robert Mitchum	Capitol 2810
3/26/55	4	16	16. **Ballad Of Davy Crockett** Best Seller #4 / Juke Box #5 / Jockey #6; from the ABC-TV *Disneyland* series which featured 3 "Davy Crockett" segments (Dec. '54 - Feb. '55)	Capitol 3058
7/9/55	13	2	17. His Hands Best Seller #13	Capitol 3135
11/12/55	1 (10)	21	● 18. **Sixteen Tons** Best Seller #1(10) / Juke Box #1(7) / Jockey #1(3)	Capitol 3262
3/17/56	12	5	19. That's All Best Seller #12	Capitol 3343
7/17/65	9	13	20. **Hicktown**	Capitol 5425

DATE	POS	WKS	ARTIST–RECORD TITLE	LABEL & NO.
			FORESTER SISTERS, The	
			Family group from Lookout Mountain, Georgia: Kathy (born 1/4/55; lead), Kim (born 11/4/60; second lead), June (born 9/22/56), and Christy (born 12/21/62). The three eldest sisters had sung with small bands since leaving college. Worked as opening act for The Gatlin Brothers. Christy joined them in 1982.	
3/2/85	10	12	1. **(That's What You Do) When You're In Love**	Warner 29114
7/13/85	1 (1)	14	2. **I Fell In Love Again Last Night**	Warner 28988
11/23/85+	1 (1)	13	3. **Just In Case**	Warner 28875
3/29/86	1 (1)	15	4. **Mama's Never Seen Those Eyes**	Warner 28795
7/19/86	2 (2)	15	5. **Lonely Alone**	Warner 28687
10/4/86	1 (1)	15	6. **Too Much Is Not Enough**	Curb 52917
			THE BELLAMY BROTHERS with THE FORESTER SISTERS	
3/28/87	5	12	7. **Too Many Rivers**	Warner 28442
			#13 Pop hit for Brenda Lee in 1965	
7/18/87	1 (1)	14	8. **You Again**	Warner 28368
11/21/87+	5	14	9. **Lyin' In His Arms Again**	Warner 28208
7/16/88	9	13	10. **Letter Home**	Warner 27839
12/10/88+	8	10	11. **Sincerely**	Warner 27686
			#1 Pop hit for The McGuire Sisters in 1955	
3/18/89	7	12	12. **Love Will**	Warner 27575
7/15/89	9	12	13. **Don't You**	Warner 22943
12/16/89+	7	18	14. **Leave It Alone**	Warner 22773
2/16/91	8	12	15. **Men**	Warner 19450
			FOSTER, Lloyd David	
			Born in 1952 in Wills Point, Texas. Played guitar since his teens. Drove a beer truck in Dallas while working clubs on weekends. First recorded for Autumn Leaves in 1981.	
7/31/82	32	3	1. Blue Rendezvous	MCA 52061
4/9/83	32	3	2. Unfinished Business	MCA 52173
			FOSTER, Radney	
			Born on 7/20/59 in Del Rio, Texas. Half of Foster & Lloyd duo. Graduated from the University of the South in Sewanee, Texas.	
10/3/92	10	12	1. **Just Call Me Lonesome**	Arista 12448
2/13/93	2 (2)	17	2. **Nobody Wins**	Arista 12512
7/24/93	20	8	3. Easier Said Than Done	Arista 12564
11/13/93	34	4	4. Hammer And Nails	Arista 12608
			FOSTER, Sally—see HOOSIER HOT SHOTS	
			FOSTER & LLOYD	
			Vocal duo of songwriters Radney Foster (see previous entry) and Bill Lloyd (born 12/6/55 in Fort Hood, Texas). Wrote "Love Someone Like Me" for Holly Dunn. Foster went solo in 1992.	
8/1/87	4	14	1. **Crazy Over You**	RCA 5210
11/28/87+	8	14	2. **Sure Thing**	RCA 5281
5/7/88	18	8	3. Texas In 1880	RCA 6900
9/3/88	6	12	4. **What Do You Want From Me This Time**	RCA 8633
2/11/89	5	13	5. **Fair Shake**	RCA 8795

DATE	POS	WKS	ARTIST– RECORD TITLE	LABEL & NO.
1/19/91	38	2	6. Can't Have Nothin'	RCA 2635
			4 RUNNER	
4/22/95	26	7	Vocal quartet: Craig Morris, Billy Crittenden, Lee Hilliard and Jim Chapman. 1. Cain's Blood	Polydor 851622
			FOXFIRE	
6/30/79 5/24/80	30 38	5 3	Nashville-based trio: Dave Hall, Russ Allison and Don Miller. 1. Fell Into Love 2. I Can See Forever Loving You	NSD 24 Elektra 46625
			FOXWORTHY, Jeff	
12/23/95	18	3	Born and raised in Hapeville, Georgia. Comedian/actor. Worked as a computer engineer for IBM. 1. Redneck 12 Days Of Christmas [X-C] <center>available only as a promotional CD single</center>	Warner 7967
			FRANCIS, Connie	
7/25/60 3/29/69	24 33	3 5	Born Concetta Rosa Maria Franconero on 12/12/38 in Newark, New Jersey. Pop music's #1 female vocalist from the late 1950s to the mid-1960s. ● 1. Everybody's Somebody's Fool 2. The Wedding Cake	MGM 12899 MGM 14034
			FRANKLIN, Bill—see MESSNER, Bud	
			FRANKS, Tillman	
12/21/63 5/16/64	30 30	2 4	Born on 9/29/20 in Stamps, Arkansas. Singer/guitarist. Debuted on *Louisiana Hayride* in 1947. Became artist manager; clients included Slim Whitman, Johnny Horton, Webb Pierce and David Houston. Wrote "Sink The Bismark." Was in the car crash that killed Horton in 1960. 1. Tadpole [I] **TILLMAN FRANKS and the Cedar Grove Three** 2. When The World's On Fire **TILLMAN FRANKS SINGERS**	Starday 651 Starday 670
			FRAZIER, Dallas	
12/16/67+	28	6	Born on 10/27/39 in Spiro, Oklahoma; raised in Bakersfield, California. Toured with Ferlin Husky at age 12. Appeared on Cliffie Stone's TV series *Hometown Jamboree*. Wrote "Alley Oop," "There Goes My Everything," "Son Of Hickory Holler's Tramp," "Elvira" and many others. 1. Everybody Oughta Sing A Song	Capitol 2011
			FREEMAN, Ernie	
1/13/58	11	2	Born on 8/16/22 in Cleveland. Died of a heart attack on 5/16/81 in North Hollywood. Pianist/composer/conductor for many top artists, including Frank Sinatra. 1. Raunchy [I] <center>Best Seller #11</center>	Imperial 5474

DATE	POS	WKS	ARTIST—RECORD TITLE	LABEL & NO.
			FRICKE, Janie	
			Born on 12/19/47 in South Whitney, Indiana. Worked as a backup singer in Dallas, Memphis and Los Angeles in the early '70s. With Judy Rodman and Karen Taylor-Good in Phase II in Memphis, in the late '70s. Moved to Nashville and sang backup for Dolly Parton, Elvis Presley, Billy Swan, Ronnie Milsap, Crystal Gayle, Johnny Duncan and others. Made numerous commercial jingles. Own TV special in 1983. Currently a regular on TNN's *The Statler Brothers Show.* Occasionally spells her name "Frickie." CMA Awards: 1982 and 1983 Female Vocalist of the Year.	
10/8/77	21	7	1. What're You Doing Tonight	Columbia 10605
11/5/77+	4	12	2. **Come A Little Bit Closer**	Columbia 10634
			JOHNNY DUNCAN with JANIE FRICKE	
			#3 Pop hit for Jay & The Americans in 1964	
4/1/78	21	6	3. Baby It's You	Columbia 10695
6/17/78	12	9	4. Please Help Me, I'm Falling (In Love With You)	Columbia 10743
10/14/78	1 (1)	10	5. **On My Knees**	Epic 50616
			CHARLIE RICH with JANIE FRICKE	
12/2/78+	22	6	6. Playin' Hard To Get	Columbia 10849
3/17/79	14	8	7. I'll Love Away Your Troubles For Awhile	Columbia 10910
7/28/79	28	4	8. Let's Try Again	Columbia 11029
12/8/79+	26	7	9. But Love Me	Columbia 11139
4/12/80	22	6	10. Pass Me By (If You're Only Passing Through)	Columbia 11224
8/16/80	17	7	11. He's Out Of My Life	Columbia 11312
			JOHNNY DUNCAN and JANIE FRICKE	
			#10 Pop hit for Michael Jackson in 1980 as "She's Out Of My Life"	
11/15/80+	2 (1)	12	12. **Down To My Last Broken Heart**	Columbia 11384
4/4/81	12	8	13. Pride	Columbia 60509
8/8/81	4	13	14. **I'll Need Someone To Hold Me (When I Cry)**	Columbia 02197
12/26/81+	4	13	15. **Do Me With Love**	Columbia 02644
5/22/82	1 (1)	12	16. **Don't Worry 'Bout Me Baby**	Columbia 02859
10/9/82	1 (1)	13	17. **It Ain't Easy Bein' Easy**	Columbia 03214
2/5/83	4	12	18. **You Don't Know Love**	Columbia 03498
			Bill Warren (backing vocal)	
6/11/83	1 (1)	13	19. **He's A Heartache (Looking For A Place To Happen)**	Columbia 03899
10/15/83	1 (1)	13	20. **Tell Me A Lie**	Columbia 04091
2/4/84	1 (1)	12	21. **Let's Stop Talkin' About It**	Columbia 04317
5/26/84	8	11	22. If The Fall Don't Get You	Columbia 04454
9/22/84	1 (1)	13	23. **Your Heart's Not In It**	Columbia 04578
11/17/84+	1 (1)	14	24. **A Place To Fall Apart**	Epic 04663
			MERLE HAGGARD with JANIE FRICKE	
2/2/85	7	11	25. The First Word In Memory Is Me	Columbia 04731
6/8/85	2 (1)	15	26. **She's Single Again**	Columbia 04896
10/19/85	4	14	27. Somebody Else's Fire	Columbia 05617
2/22/86	5	14	28. **Easy To Please**	Columbia 05781
			JANIE FRICKIE:	
7/19/86	1 (1)	14	29. **Always Have Always Will**	Columbia 06144
12/13/86+	20	8	30. When A Woman Cries	Columbia 06417
4/11/87	32	4	31. Are You Satisfied	Columbia 06985
			#11 Pop hit for Rusty Draper in 1956	
5/30/87	21	6	32. From Time To Time (It Feels Like Love Again)	Columbia 07088
			LARRY GATLIN & JANIE FRICKIE (with The Gatlin Brothers)	

DATE	POS	WKS	ARTIST— RECORD TITLE	LABEL & NO.

FRIZZELL, David

Born on 9/26/41 in El Dorado, Arkansas; younger brother of Lefty Frizzell and older brother of Allen Frizzell. Toured with Lefty while a teenager. Worked with Buck Owens in the early '70s. Made a series of successful duets with his sister-in-law Shelly West. CMA Awards: 1981 & 1982 Vocal Duo of the Year (with Shelly West).

(a) DAVID FRIZZELL & SHELLY WEST

DATE	POS	WKS	ARTIST— RECORD TITLE	LABEL & NO.
12/5/70	36	2	1. I Just Can't Help Believing #9 Pop hit for B.J. Thomas in 1970	Columbia 45238
2/7/81	1 (1)	11	2. **You're The Reason God Made Oklahoma** (a) from the movie *Any Which Way You Can* starring Clint Eastwood	Warner 49650
7/11/81	9	8	3. **A Texas State Of Mind** (a)	Warner 49745
10/31/81	16	10	4. Husbands And Wives (a)	Warner 49825
2/20/82	8	13	5. **Another Honky-Tonk Night On Broadway** (a)	Warner 50007
6/19/82	1 (1)	14	6. **I'm Gonna Hire A Wino To Decorate Our Home**	Warner 50063
7/31/82	4	13	7. **I Just Came Here To Dance** (a)	Warner 29980
10/30/82+	5	14	8. **Lost My Baby Blues**	Warner 29901
6/25/83	10	9	9. **Where Are You Spending Your Nights These Days**	Viva 29617
11/19/83	39	1	10. A Million Light Beers Ago	Viva 29498
3/3/84	20	7	11. Silent Partners (a)	Viva 29404
10/20/84	13	9	12. It's A Be Together Night (a)	Viva 29187

FRIZZELL, Lefty

Born William Orville Frizzell on 3/31/28 in Corsicana, Texas. Died of a stroke on 7/19/75 in Nashville. Nicknamed "Lefty" during amateur boxing career. Worked local clubs in Waco and Dallas. Appeared on the TV shows *Town Hall Party* and *Country America*. Moved to Nashville in 1962. Recorded with June Stearns as Agnes & Orville on Columbia in 1968. Older brother of Allen and David Frizzell. Elected to the Country Music Hall of Fame in 1982.

DATE	POS	WKS	ARTIST— RECORD TITLE	LABEL & NO.
10/28/50	1 (3)	22	1. **If You've Got The Money I've Got The Time/** Juke Box #1 / Best Seller #2 / Jockey #2	
11/4/50+	1 (3)	32	2. **I Love You A Thousand Ways** Jockey #1 / Juke Box #3 / Best Seller #5; 45 rpm: 9-770	Columbia 20739
3/3/51	4	12	3. **Look What Thoughts Will Do/** Jockey #4 / Best Seller #9 / Juke Box #9	
3/10/51	7	2	4. **Shine, Shave, Shower (It's Saturday)** Juke Box #7	Columbia 20772
4/14/51	1 (11)	27	5. **I Want To Be With You Always** Jockey #1(11) / Best Seller #1(6) / Juke Box #1(5)	Columbia 20799
8/4/51	1 (12)	28	6. **Always Late (With Your Kisses)/** Best Seller #1(12) / Jockey #1(6) / Juke Box #1(6)	
8/18/51	2 (8)	29	7. **Mom And Dad's Waltz** Best Seller #2 / Jockey #2 / Juke Box #3	Columbia 20837
10/13/51	6	9	8. **Travellin' Blues** Best Seller #6 / Juke Box #7 / Jockey #8	Columbia 20842
12/22/51+	1 (3)	21	9. **Give Me More, More, More (Of Your Kisses)/** Jockey #1(3) / Juke Box #1(3) / Best Seller #3	
1/12/52	7	5	10. **How Long Will It Take (To Stop Loving You)** Jockey #7	Columbia 20885
4/12/52	2 (1)	12	11. **Don't Stay Away (Till Love Grows Cold)** Best Seller #2 / Juke Box #2 / Jockey #4	Columbia 20911

DATE	POS	WKS	ARTIST–RECORD TITLE	LABEL & NO.
9/27/52	6	5	12. **Forever (And Always)** Best Seller #6	Columbia 20997
12/6/52+	3	9	13. **I'm An Old, Old Man (Tryin' To Live While I Can)** Best Seller #3 / Juke Box #4	Columbia 21034
5/23/53	8	1	14. **(Honey, Baby, Hurry!) Bring Your Sweet Self Back To Me** Jockey #8	Columbia 21084
2/20/54	8	2	15. **Run 'Em Off** Juke Box #8	Columbia 21194
1/15/55	11	4	16. I Love You Mostly Best Seller #11 / Jockey #13	Columbia 21328
11/24/58+	13	11	17. Cigarettes And Coffee Blues written by Marty Robbins	Columbia 41268
6/8/59	6	15	18. **The Long Black Veil**	Columbia 41384
4/27/63	23	2	19. Forbidden Lovers	Columbia 42676
11/9/63	30	1	20. Don't Let Her See Me Cry	Columbia 42839
1/18/64	1 (4)	23	21. **Saginaw, Michigan**	Columbia 42924
9/5/64	28	6	22. The Nester	Columbia 43051
5/15/65	12	13	23. She's Gone Gone Gone	Columbia 43256
10/30/65	36	2	24. A Little Unfair	Columbia 43364
3/30/74	25	5	25. I Never Go Around Mirrors	ABC 11416
11/2/74	21	6	26. Lucky Arms	ABC 12023

GALLION, Bob

Born on 4/22/31 in Ashland, Kentucky. Own band, the Country Boys; worked on the *Louisiana Hayride* and WWVA-Wheeling Jamboree, 1952-55. Performed with Stoney Cooper's Clinch Mountain Clan.

DATE	POS	WKS	ARTIST–RECORD TITLE	LABEL & NO.
11/3/58	28	1	1. That's What I Tell My Heart	MGM 12700
5/18/59	18	9	2. You Take The Table And I'll Take The Chairs	MGM 12777
11/28/60+	7	22	3. **Loving You (Was Worth This Broken Heart)**	Hickory 1130
6/19/61	20	4	4. One Way Street	Hickory 1145
12/4/61	20	2	5. Sweethearts Again	Hickory 1154
11/10/62	5	15	6. **Wall To Wall Love**	Hickory 1181
8/31/63	23	2	7. Ain't Got Time For Nothin'	Hickory 1220

GARRON, Jess

DATE	POS	WKS	ARTIST–RECORD TITLE	LABEL & NO.
5/5/79	30	4	1. Lo Que Sea (What Ever May The Future Be)	Charta 131

DATE	POS	WKS	ARTIST–RECORD TITLE	LABEL & NO.
			GATLIN, Larry, & The Gatlin Brothers Band	
			Trio of brothers reared in several West Texas towns: Larry (born 5/2/48, Seminole, Texas), Steve (born 4/4/51, Olney, Texas) and Rudy (born 8/20/52, Olney, Texas). Worked as a gospel trio and had their own TV series in Abilene. Joined by younger sister LaDonna. Larry was a staff writer for Dottie West. He moved to Nashville in 1972. Also wrote for Elvis Presley, Tom Jones, Kris Kristofferson and Glen Campbell. His songs were used in the Johnny Cash movie *The Glory Road*. Steve, Rudy, LaDonna and her husband, Tim Johnson, worked as "Young Country," did backup for Tammy Wynette. The brothers rejoined Larry after finishing college. Own ABC-TV special in 1981. Members of the *Grand Ole Opry* since 1976. (a) LARRY GATLIN (b) LARRY GATLIN with Family & Friends	
12/29/73	40	1	1. Sweet Becky Walker (a)	Monument 8584
10/5/74	14	9	2. Delta Dirt (a)	Monument 8622
1/24/76	5	13	3. **Broken Lady** (b)	Monument 8680
11/20/76+	5	11	4. **Statues Without Hearts** (b)	Monument 201
3/12/77	12	7	5. **Anything But Leavin'** (b)	Monument 212
6/11/77	3	12	6. **I Don't Wanna Cry** (b)	Monument 221
9/24/77	3	10	7. **Love Is Just A Game** (b)	Monument 226
12/17/77+	1 (1)	11	8. **I Just Wish You Were Someone I Love** **LARRY GATLIN with Brothers and Friends**	Monument 234
4/22/78	2 (2)	10	9. **Night Time Magic** (a)	Monument 249
8/26/78	13	7	10. Do It Again Tonight (a)	Monument 259
11/18/78+	7	10	11. **I've Done Enough Dyin' Today** (a)	Monument 270
9/8/79	1 (2)	10	12. **All The Gold In California**	Columbia 11066
3/22/80	12	8	13. Taking Somebody With Me When I Fall	Columbia 11219
7/5/80	18	6	14. We're Number One	Columbia 11282
10/18/80	5	10	15. **Take Me To Your Lovin' Place**	Columbia 11369
3/14/81	25	5	16. It Don't Get No Better Than This	Columbia 11438
7/4/81	20	5	17. Wind Is Bound To Change	Columbia 02123
10/10/81	4	13	18. **What Are We Doin' Lonesome**	Columbia 02522
2/27/82	15	7	19. In Like With Each Other	Columbia 02698
6/12/82	19	7	20. She Used To Sing On Sunday	Columbia 02910
10/2/82	5	12	21. **Sure Feels Like Love**	Columbia 03159
2/26/83	20	6	22. Almost Called Her Baby By Mistake	Columbia 03517
6/25/83	32	3	23. Easy On The Eye	Columbia 03885
10/15/83	1 (2)	15	24. **Houston (Means I'm One Day Closer To You)**	Columbia 04105
4/14/84	7	11	25. **Denver**	Columbia 04395
8/11/84	3	13	26. **The Lady Takes The Cowboy Everytime**	Columbia 04533
2/15/86	12	10	27. Nothing But Your Love Matters	Columbia 05764
9/13/86	2 (1)	14	28. **She Used To Be Somebody's Baby**	Columbia 06252
1/24/87	4	12	29. **Talkin' To The Moon**	Columbia 06592
5/30/87	21	6	30. From Time To Time (It Feels Like Love Again) **LARRY GATLIN & JANIE FRICKIE (with The Gatlin Brothers)**	Columbia 07088
9/12/87	16	8	31. Changin' Partners	Columbia 07320
4/16/88	4	13	32. **Love Of A Lifetime** **THE GATLIN BROS.**	Columbia 07747
9/17/88	34	4	33. Alive And Well	Columbia 07998
6/10/89	37	3	34. I Might Be What You're Looking For	Universal 66005

DATE	POS	WKS	ARTIST–RECORD TITLE	LABEL & NO.
			GAYLE, Crystal	
			Born Brenda Gail Webb on 1/9/51 in Paintsville, Kentucky; raised in Wabash, Indiana. Sister of Loretta Lynn, Peggy Sue and Jay Lee Webb; distant cousin of Patty Loveless. Worked with the Loretta Lynn Road Show from age 16. First country artist to tour China (1979). On soundtrack of the movie *One From The Heart*. At times, her hair is over five feet long. CMA Awards: 1977 and 1978 Female Vocalist of the Year.	
10/17/70	23	8	1. I've Cried (The Blues Right Out Of My Eyes)	Decca 32721
7/27/74	39	1	2. Restless	United Art. 428
12/14/74+	6	12	3. **Wrong Road Again**	United Art. 555
5/10/75	27	4	4. Beyond You	United Art. 600
8/30/75	21	8	5. This Is My Year For Mexico	United Art. 680
12/27/75+	8	11	6. **Somebody Loves You**	United Art. 740
4/17/76	1 (1)	14	7. **I'll Get Over You**	United Art. 781
9/11/76	31	5	8. One More Time (Karneval)	United Art. 838
11/20/76+	1 (1)	12	9. **You Never Miss A Real Good Thing (Till He Says Goodbye)**	United Art. 883
4/9/77	2 (2)	11	10. **I'll Do It All Over Again**	United Art. 948
7/16/77	1 (4)	15	● 11. **Don't It Make My Brown Eyes Blue**	United Art. 1016
1/28/78	40	1	12. I've Cried (The Blues Right Out Of My Eyes)　　　　[R]	MCA 40837
2/18/78	1 (1)	10	13. **Ready For The Times To Get Better**	United Art. 1136
7/1/78	1 (2)	10	14. **Talking In Your Sleep**	United Art. 1214
12/9/78+	1 (2)	10	15. **Why Have You Left The One You Left Me For**	United Art. 1259
4/21/79	3	10	16. **When I Dream**	United Art. 1288
7/28/79	7	8	17. **Your Kisses Will**	United Art. 1306
9/15/79	2 (3)	11	18. **Half The Way**	Columbia 11087
12/22/79+	5	9	19. **Your Old Cold Shoulder**	United Art. 1329
2/16/80	1 (1)	11	20. **It's Like We Never Said Goodbye**	Columbia 11198
5/31/80	8	9	21. **The Blue Side**	Columbia 11270
10/4/80	1 (1)	10	22. **If You Ever Change Your Mind**	Columbia 11359
2/21/81	17	8	23. Take It Easy	Columbia 11436
6/13/81	1 (1)	11	24. **Too Many Lovers**	Columbia 02078
10/17/81	3	15	25. **The Woman In Me**	Columbia 02523
3/6/82	5	14	26. **You Never Gave Up On Me**	Columbia 02718
8/21/82	9	10	27. **Livin' In These Troubled Times**	Columbia 03048
10/23/82	1 (1)	12	28. **You And I**	Elektra 69936
			EDDIE RABBITT with CRYSTAL GAYLE	
12/18/82+	1 (1)	12	29. **'Til I Gain Control Again**	Elektra 69893
4/16/83	1 (1)	12	30. **Our Love Is On The Faultline**	Warner 29719
7/30/83	1 (1)	12	31. **Baby, What About You**	Warner 29582
11/19/83+	1 (1)	14	32. **The Sound Of Goodbye**	Warner 29452
3/17/84	2 (2)	13	33. **I Don't Wanna Lose Your Love**	Warner 29356
7/21/84	1 (1)	13	34. **Turning Away**	Warner 29254
11/17/84+	4	13	35. **Me Against The Night**	Warner 29151
4/13/85	3	13	36. **Nobody Wants To Be Alone**	Warner 29050
8/24/85	5	13	37. **A Long And Lasting Love**	Warner 28963
11/30/85+	1 (1)	14	38. **Makin' Up For Lost Time (The Dallas Lovers' Song)** from the TV series *Dallas* starring Larry Hagman	Warner 28856
8/9/86	1 (1)	14	39. **Cry** #1 Pop hit for Johnnie Ray in 1951	Warner 28689

DATE	POS	WKS	ARTIST–RECORD TITLE	LABEL & NO.
12/6/86+	**1** (1)	14	40. **Straight To The Heart**	Warner 28518
5/9/87	**4**	12	41. **Another World**	Warner 28373
			theme from the daytime-TV serial	
8/22/87	26	4	42. Nobody Should Have To Love This Way	Warner 28409
11/14/87+	**11**	11	43. Only Love Can Save Me Now	Warner 28209
3/12/88	26	6	44. All Of This & More	Warner 28106
			CRYSTAL GAYLE & GARY MORRIS (#38, 41, 44)	
10/1/88	22	7	45. Nobody's Angel	Warner 27811

GENTRY, Bobbie

Born Roberta Streeter on 7/27/44 in Chickasaw County, Mississippi; raised in Greenwood, Mississippi. Guitarist/pianist/bassist/banjo player. Moved to Palm Springs, California, while still in high school. Own TV series in England in the late '60s. Own production company in Los Angeles. Married Jim Stafford on 10/15/78.

DATE	POS	WKS	ARTIST–RECORD TITLE	LABEL & NO.
9/23/67	17	6	● 1. Ode To Billie Joe	Capitol 5950
2/15/69	14	11	2. Let It Be Me	Capitol 2387
			GLEN CAMPBELL and BOBBIE GENTRY	
1/24/70	26	3	3. Fancy	Capitol 2674
3/7/70	6	11	4. **All I Have To Do Is Dream**	Capitol 2745
			BOBBIE GENTRY & GLEN CAMPBELL	

GIBBS, Terri

Born on 6/15/54 in Augusta, Georgia. Female vocalist/pianist. Blind since birth. Sang gospel as a child and had own band, Sound Dimension, from 1974. Worked at the Steak & Ale in Augusta, 1975-80. CMA Award: 1981 Horizon Award.

DATE	POS	WKS	ARTIST–RECORD TITLE	LABEL & NO.
11/8/80+	8	13	1. **Somebody's Knockin'**	MCA 41309
6/27/81	19	6	2. **Rich Man**	MCA 51119
10/24/81	38	3	3. I Wanna Be Around	MCA 51180
			#14 Pop hit for Tony Bennett in 1963	
1/23/82	12	8	4. Mis'ry River	MCA 51225
5/22/82	19	7	5. Ashes To Ashes	MCA 52040
1/8/83	33	3	6. Baby I'm Gone	MCA 52134
9/17/83	17	7	7. Anybody Else's Heart But Mine	MCA 52252

GIBSON, Don

Born Donald Eugene Gibson on 4/3/28 in Shelby, North Carolina. Worked local clubs and radio while still in high school. Moved to Knoxville in 1953 and worked on the WNOX *Barn Dance* radio series. Wrote "Sweet Dreams," "I Can't Stop Loving You," "Oh Lonesome Me" and many of his other hits. Joined the *Grand Ole Opry* in 1958.

(a) DOTTIE WEST & DON GIBSON
(b) DON GIBSON & SUE THOMPSON

DATE	POS	WKS	ARTIST–RECORD TITLE	LABEL & NO.
8/11/56	9	1	1. **Sweet Dreams**	MGM 12194
			Jockey #9; also see #15 below	
2/17/58	**1** (8)	34	2. **Oh Lonesome Me/**	
			Best Seller #1(8) / Jockey #1(8)	
3/17/58	7	14	3. **I Can't Stop Lovin' You**	RCA 7133
			Jockey #7	
6/9/58	**1** (2)	24	4. **Blue Blue Day**	RCA 7010
			Best Seller #1 / Jockey #2	

DATE	POS	WKS	ARTIST–RECORD TITLE		LABEL & NO.
9/29/58	5	19	5. **Give Myself A Party/**		
10/6/58	8	9	6. **Look Who's Blue**		RCA 7330
			Jockey #8		
2/2/59	3	16	7. **Who Cares/**		
2/23/59	27	2	8. A Stranger To Me		RCA 7437
5/11/59	11	13	9. Lonesome Old House		RCA 7505
8/17/59	5	16	10. **Don't Tell Me Your Troubles**		RCA 7566
12/7/59+	14	9	11. I'm Movin' On/		
1/4/60	29	1	12. Big Hearted Me		RCA 7629
3/7/60	2 (1)	21	13. **Just One Time**		RCA 7690
8/8/60	11	11	14. Far, Far Away		RCA 7762
11/28/60+	6	16	15. **Sweet Dreams**	[R]	RCA 7805
			new version of #1 above		
3/13/61	22	6	16. What About Me		RCA 7841
6/19/61	2 (1)	26	17. **Sea Of Heartbreak**		RCA 7890
12/18/61+	2 (1)	21	18. **Lonesome Number One**		RCA 7959
5/19/62	5	14	19. **I Can Mend Your Broken Heart**		RCA 8017
11/17/62	22	4	20. So How Come (No One Loves Me)		RCA 8085
4/6/63	12	10	21. Head Over Heels In Love With You		RCA 8144
8/31/63	22	5	22. Anything New Gets Old (Except My Love For You)		RCA 8192
12/26/64+	23	11	23. Cause I Believe In You		RCA 8456
7/24/65	19	9	24. Again		RCA 8589
11/13/65	10	10	25. **Watch Where You're Going**		RCA 8678
2/5/66	12	10	26. A Born Loser		RCA 8732
5/14/66	6	16	27. **(Yes) I'm Hurting**		RCA 8812
12/3/66+	8	13	28. **Funny, Familiar, Forgotten, Feelings**		RCA 8975
9/9/67	23	10	29. All My Love		RCA 9266
4/6/68	37	4	30. Ashes Of Love		RCA 9460
8/3/68	12	11	31. It's A Long, Long Way To Georgia		RCA 9563
12/21/68+	30	5	32. Ever Changing Mind		RCA 9663
3/8/69	2 (1)	15	33. **Rings Of Gold** (a)		RCA 9715
5/17/69	28	7	34. Solitary		RCA 0143
8/16/69	32	4	35. Sweet Memories (a)		RCA 0178
9/20/69	21	6	36. I Will Always		RCA 0219
12/20/69+	7	11	37. **There's A Story (Goin' 'Round)** (a)		RCA 0291
3/28/70	17	9	38. Don't Take All Your Loving		Hickory 1559
7/18/70	16	9	39. A Perfect Mountain		Hickory 1571
11/7/70	37	2	40. Someway		Hickory 1579
2/13/71	19	8	41. Guess Away The Blues		Hickory 1588
6/26/71	29	4	42. (I Heard That) Lonesome Whistle		Hickory 1598
			written by Hank Williams and Jimmie Davis		
11/13/71	5	13	43. **Country Green**		Hickory 1614
			written by Eddy Raven		
3/11/72	12	9	44. Far, Far Away	[R]	Hickory 1623
			new version of #14 above		
6/24/72	1 (1)	16	45. **Woman (Sensuous Woman)**		Hickory 1638
9/23/72	37	4	46. I Think They Call It Love (b)		Hickory 1646
11/11/72	11	10	47. Is This The Best I'm Gonna Feel		Hickory 1651
3/17/73	26	7	48. If You're Goin' Girl		Hickory 1661

DATE	POS	WKS	ARTIST– RECORD TITLE	LABEL & NO.
6/9/73	6	11	49. **Touch The Morning** written by Eddy Raven	Hickory 1671
11/10/73	30	5	50. That's What I'll Do	Hickory 306
1/26/74	12	9	51. Snap Your Fingers #8 Pop hit for Joe Henderson in 1962	Hickory 312
6/1/74	8	10	52. **One Day At A Time**	Hickory 318
9/21/74	31	5	53. Good Old Fashioned Country Love (b)	Hickory 324
9/28/74	9	12	54. **Bring Back Your Love To Me**	Hickory 327
2/15/75	27	4	55. I'll Sing For You	Hickory 338
5/17/75	24	6	56. (There She Goes) I Wish Her Well	Hickory 345
9/6/75	36	4	57. Oh, How Love Changes (b)	Hickory 350
7/17/76	39	2	58. Doing My Time	Hickory 372
12/4/76	23	6	59. I'm All Wrapped Up In You	ABC/Hick. 54001
4/9/77	30	4	60. Fan The Flame, Feed The Fire	ABC/Hick. 54010
7/23/77	16	8	61. If You Ever Get To Houston (Look Me Down)	ABC/Hick. 54014
3/4/78	16	8	62. Starting All Over Again #19 Pop hit for Mel & Tim in 1972	ABC/Hick. 54024
6/24/78	22	6	63. The Fool #7 Pop hit for Sanford Clark in 1956	ABC/Hick. 54029
1/27/79	26	5	64. Any Day Now #23 Pop hit for Chuck Jackson in 1962	ABC/Hick. 54039
7/21/79	37	2	65. Forever One Day At A Time written by Eddy Raven	MCA 41031

GIBSON/MILLER BAND

Five-man band led by Nashville songwriter Dave Gibson and Detroit rock guitarist Bill "Blue" Miller. Includes Bryan Grassmeyer, Steve Grossman and Mike Daly. Gibson wrote Joe Diffie's "Ships That Don't Come In," Alabama's "Jukebox In My Mind," Tanya Tucker's "If It Don't Come Easy" and others.

DATE	POS	WKS	ARTIST– RECORD TITLE	LABEL & NO.
1/16/93	37	5	1. Big Heart	Epic 74739
3/20/93	20	10	2. High Rollin'	Epic 74856
7/10/93	22	7	3. Texas Tattoo	Epic 74991
3/12/94	40	1	4. Stone Cold Country	Epic 77355

GILKYSON, Terry—see WEAVERS, The

GILL, Vince

Born Vincent Grant Gill on 4/12/57 in Norman, Oklahoma. Guitarist from age 10; vocalist/lead guitarist for his own band at age 15. Worked with Mountain Smoke while still in high school. Moved to Louisville in 1975; played with Bluegrass Alliance. With Pure Prairie League from 1979. With Rodney Crowell and Rosanne Cash in the Cherry Bombs. Session work in Nashville; solo since 1983. Married to Janis Oliver of the Sweethearts Of The Rodeo. CMA Awards: 1991, 1992, 1993, 1994 and 1995 Male Vocalist of the Year; 1993 and 1994 Entertainer of the Year.

DATE	POS	WKS	ARTIST– RECORD TITLE	LABEL & NO.
3/31/84	40	1	1. Victim Of Life's Circumstances	RCA 13731
6/30/84	38	1	2. Oh Carolina	RCA 13809
11/3/84	39	1	3. Turn Me Loose	RCA 13860
4/20/85	32	5	4. True Love	RCA 14020
8/10/85	10	11	5. **If It Weren't For Him** Rosanne Cash (guest vocal)	RCA 14140
12/28/85+	9	12	6. **Oklahoma Borderline**	RCA 14216
7/19/86	33	2	7. With You	RCA 14371

DATE	POS	WKS	ARTIST– RECORD TITLE	LABEL & NO.
5/23/87	5	13	8. **Cinderella**	RCA 5131
10/17/87	16	9	9. Let's Do Something	RCA 5257
2/27/88	11	10	10. Everybody's Sweetheart	RCA 5331
7/2/88	39	2	11. The Radio	RCA 8301
10/14/89	22	9	12. Never Alone	MCA 53717
2/17/90	13	11	13. Oklahoma Swing	MCA 53780
			VINCE GILL with Reba McEntire	
6/30/90	2 (2)	16	14. **When I Call Your Name**	MCA 79011
			Patty Loveless (backing vocal); CMA Award: Single of the Year	
10/27/90	3	16	15. **Never Knew Lonely**	MCA 53892
3/9/91	7	13	16. **Pocket Full Of Gold**	MCA 54026
4/27/91	25	8	17. Restless	Warner 19354
			MARK O'CONNOR-THE NEW NASHVILLE CATS Featuring STEVE WARINER, RICKY SKAGGS AND VINCE GILL	
6/22/91	7	13	18. **Liza Jane**	MCA 54123
11/2/91+	4	14	19. **Look At Us**	MCA 54179
2/15/92	2 (2)	16	20. **Take Your Memory With You**	MCA 54282
7/11/92	1 (2)	19	21. **I Still Believe In You**	MCA 54406
10/31/92	1 (3)	18	22. **Don't Let Our Love Start Slippin' Away**	MCA 54489
2/27/93	1 (2)	16	23. **The Heart Won't Lie**	MCA 54599
			REBA McENTIRE and VINCE GILL co-written by Kim Carnes	
4/24/93	3	15	24. **No Future In The Past**	MCA 54540
8/14/93	1 (1)	18	25. **One More Last Chance**	MCA 54715
1/22/94	1 (1)	15	26. **Tryin' To Get Over You**	MCA 54706
4/30/94	2 (3)	14	27. **Whenever You Come Around**	MCA 54833
7/23/94	2 (2)	17	28. **What The Cowgirls Do**	MCA 54879
10/22/94	3	17	29. **When Love Finds You**	MCA 54937
2/11/95	4	13	30. **Which Bridge To Cross (Which Bridge To Burn)**	MCA 54976
5/27/95	2 (1)	14	31. **You Better Think Twice**	MCA 55035
9/30/95	15	11	32. I Will Always Love You [R]	Columbia 78079
			DOLLY PARTON WITH SPECIAL GUEST VINCE GILL 2 previous versions by Parton hit #1 in 1974 and 1982; #1 Pop hit for Whitney Houston in 1992	
10/7/95	14	14	33. Go Rest High On That Mountain	MCA 55098
4/20/96	12	12	34. High Lonesome Sound	MCA 55188

GILLEY, Mickey

DATE	POS	WKS	ARTIST– RECORD TITLE	LABEL & NO.
			Born on 3/9/36 in Natchez, Louisiana. Raised in Ferriday, Lousiana. Worked local clubs, moved to Houston in the early '50s. Recorded for Minor in 1953. Worked in construction for a time. Had own record label, Astro, in 1964. Played at the Nesadel Club in Houston throughout the '60s. Co-owner with Sherwood Cryer of Gilleys nightclub in Pasadena, Texas, from 1971. Club closed in 1989. Gilley and the club were featured in the movie *Urban Cowboy.* Cousin of Jerry Lee Lewis and Reverend Jimmy Swaggart.	
5/11/74	1 (1)	11	1. **Room Full Of Roses** first released on Astro 10003	Playboy 50056
8/31/74	1 (1)	14	2. **I Overlooked An Orchid**	Playboy 6004
12/21/74+	1 (1)	9	3. **City Lights**	Playboy 6015
4/5/75	1 (1)	12	4. **Window Up Above**	Playboy 6031
7/26/75	11	9	5. Bouquet Of Roses	Playboy 6041

Rosanne Cash, daughter of Country legend Johnny, often walked the line between Country and Pop, but her 1985 album *Rhythm & Romance* bore four Top 5 Country hits: "Hold On," "Second To No One," and the dual No. 1 smashes "I Don't Know Why You Don't Want Me" and "Never Be You."

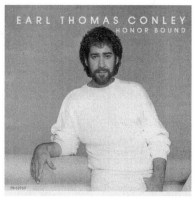

Earl Thomas Conley's dominance of the '80s chart was amply evidenced by the rapid ascension to No. 1 of 1985's "Honor Bound." All told, the Ohio-born Conley made 18 No. 1 records between 1981 and 1989.

The Charlie Daniels Band drew the same fans that made rock and roll heroes of such Southern bands as the Allman Brothers and Lynyrd Skynyrd. "Still Hurtin' Me," which reached No. 33 in 1985, was immediately followed by the group's second Top 10 hit, "Drinkin' My Baby Goodbye." Their first had been 1979's memorable No. 1 track "The Devil Went Down To Georgia."

Johnny Darrell's 1967 single "The Son Of Hickory Holler's Tramp" reached No. 22—then met Pop success the next year when covered by black crooner O.C. ("Little Green Apples") Smith.

Skip Ewing, a California-born singer who moved to Nashville in the mid-'80s, got his first taste of chart success in 1988 with the No. 22 hit "Your Memory Wins Again."

Exile—a Kentucky band once known as The Exiles—met initial success on the Pop charts with their 1978 hit "Kiss You All Over." Soon shifting full-time to Country, the band scored a red-hot streak of No. 1 hits during the '80s. "Give Me One More Chance," their third, hit the top spot in 1984.

Flatt & Scruggs, known nationwide simply for singing the theme from TV's "Beverly Hillbillies," later acknowledged another set of '60s tube icons: The B-side to their Top 20 hit "California Up Tight Band" was a cover of the Monkees hit "Last Train To Clarksville."

The Forester Sisters—individually known as Kathy, June, Kim and Christy—were a constant fixture in the mid-'80s singles chart. "Don't You" made the Top 10, but simply couldn't match the sucess of the group's previous No. 1 hit, 1987's "You Again."

Janie Frickie changed her last name from its original spelling of "Fricke" to alleviate the constant pronunciation problems she encountered. Her 1986 track "Always Have Always Will" was the last of nine No. 1 hits she produced.

Larry Gatlin, a well-respected song-writer who'd penned works for Dottie West, Elvis Presley and Tom Jones, reached No. 1 for the very first time himself with 1977's "I Just Wish You Were Someone I Love."

Crystal Gayle, youngest sister of Loretta Lynn—17 years her senior—was a powerhouse chart presence through-out the '70s and '80s. Eight No. 1 hits after her all-time smash "Don't It Make My Brown Eyes Blue" came 1982's chart-topping "'Til I Gain Control Again."

Don Gibson's stellar reputation as a songwriter is unequaled in its diversity: He penned "Sweet Dreams," "I Can't Stop Loving You" and "Oh Lonesome Me," respectively covered by Patsy Cline, Ray Charles and Neil Young, among others. A prolific hitmaker him-self, he produced the No. 22 hit "So How Come (No One Loves Me)" in 1962.

DATE	POS	WKS	ARTIST–RECORD TITLE	LABEL & NO.
11/15/75	**32**	4	6. Roll You Like A Wheel **MICKEY GILLEY & BARBI BENTON**	Playboy 6045
12/13/75+	**7**	9	7. **Overnight Sensation**	Playboy 6055
3/6/76	**1** (1)	12	8. **Don't The Girls All Get Prettier At Closing Time**	Playboy 6063
7/10/76	**1** (1)	10	9. **Bring It On Home To Me** #13 Pop hit for Sam Cooke in 1962	Playboy 6075
10/30/76	**3**	10	10. **Lawdy Miss Clawdy** #1 R&B hit for Lloyd Price in 1952	Playboy 6089
3/5/77	**1** (1)	13	11. **She's Pulling Me Back Again**	Playboy 6100
6/25/77	**4**	9	12. **Honky Tonk Memories**	Playboy 5807
11/12/77	**9**	10	13. **Chains Of Love** #1 R&B hit for Joe Turner in 1951	Playboy 5818
4/1/78	**8**	8	14. **The Power Of Positive Drinkin'**	Playboy 5826
8/19/78	**9**	10	15. **Here Comes The Hurt Again**	Epic 50580
12/9/78+	**13**	9	16. The Song We Made Love To	Epic 50631
3/31/79	**10**	9	17. **Just Long Enough To Say Goodbye**	Epic 50672
8/4/79	**8**	9	18. **My Silver Lining**	Epic 50740
12/8/79+	**17**	8	19. A Little Getting Used To	Epic 50801
5/24/80	**1** (1)	12	20. **True Love Ways** #14 Pop hit for Peter & Gordon in 1965; written by Buddy Holly and Norman Petty	Epic 50876
6/14/80	**1** (1)	12	21. **Stand By Me** from the movie *Urban Cowboy* starring John Travolta	Full Moon 46640
10/25/80	**1** (1)	11	22. **That's All That Matters**	Epic 50940
2/21/81	**1** (1)	12	23. **A Headache Tomorrow (Or A Heartache Tonight)**	Epic 50973
7/18/81	**1** (1)	10	24. **You Don't Know Me** #2 Pop hit for Ray Charles in 1962	Epic 02172
11/21/81+	**1** (1)	13	25. **Lonely Nights**	Epic 02578
4/3/82	**3**	13	26. **Tears Of The Lonely**	Epic 02774
8/7/82	**1** (1)	12	27. **Put Your Dreams Away**	Epic 03055
11/27/82+	**1** (1)	13	28. **Talk To Me** #20 Pop hit for Little Willie John in 1958	Epic 03326
4/23/83	**1** (1)	12	29. **Fool For Your Love**	Epic 03783
8/6/83	**1** (1)	13	30. **Paradise Tonight** **CHARLY McCLAIN & MICKEY GILLEY**	Epic 04007
9/24/83	**5**	11	31. **Your Love Shines Through**	Epic 04018
1/28/84	**2** (1)	12	32. **You've Really Got A Hold On Me** #8 Pop hit for The Miracles in 1963	Epic 04269
3/10/84	**5**	11	33. **Candy Man** **MICKEY GILLEY and CHARLY McCLAIN** #25 Pop hit for Roy Orbison in 1961	Epic 04368
7/14/84	**14**	9	34. The Right Stuff **CHARLY McCLAIN & MICKEY GILLEY**	Epic 04489
9/29/84	**4**	14	35. **Too Good To Stop Now**	Epic 04563
2/16/85	**10**	12	36. **I'm The One Mama Warned You About**	Epic 04746
5/25/85	**12**	9	37. It Ain't Gonna Worry My Mind **RAY CHARLES with MICKEY GILLEY**	Columbia 04860
9/14/85	**10**	11	38. **You've Got Something On Your Mind**	Epic 05460
1/25/86	**5**	10	39. **Your Memory Ain't What It Used To Be**	Epic 05744
8/16/86	**6**	13	40. **Doo-Wah Days**	Epic 06184
5/2/87	**16**	8	41. Full Grown Fool	Epic 07009
12/17/88+	**23**	8	42. She Reminded Me Of You	Airborne 10008

DATE	POS	WKS	ARTIST– RECORD TITLE	LABEL & NO.
			GIRLS NEXT DOOR	
			Group formed as Belle in 1982. Consisted of Doris King (born 2/13/57, Nashville), first alto; Diane Williams (born 8/9/59, Hahn AFB, Germany), first soprano; Cindy Nixon (born 8/3/58, Nashville), second alto, and Tammy Stephens (born 4/13/61, Arlington, Texas), second soprano. Stephens had sung with family gospel group, the Wills Family, from age six. Married to Jeff Smith of the TV series *Hee-Haw*. All had worked in different shows at Opryland and as backup vocalists. Disbanded in 1991.	
3/8/86	**14**	12	1. Love Will Get You Through Times With No Money	MTM 72059
7/12/86	**8**	12	2. **Slow Boat To China**	MTM 72068
			written by Mike Ragogna of The Almost Brothers	
11/22/86	**26**	7	3. Baby I Want It	MTM 72078
3/14/87	**28**	4	4. Walk Me In The Rain	MTM 72084
			GLASER, Jim	
			Born on 12/16/37 in Spalding, Nebraska. Tenor and youngest of The Glaser Brothers. Co-wrote "Woman, Woman," pop hit for Gary Puckett & The Union Gap.	
9/28/68	**32**	4	1. God Help You Woman	RCA 9587
3/1/69	**40**	1	2. Please Take Me Back	RCA 9696
1/15/83	**16**	8	3. When You're Not A Lady	Noble Vision 101
5/7/83	**28**	5	4. You Got Me Running	Noble Vision 102
10/1/83	**17**	10	5. The Man In The Mirror	Noble Vision 103
2/18/84	**10**	11	6. **If I Could Only Dance With You**	Noble Vision 104
7/7/84	**1** (1)	14	7. **You're Gettin' To Me Again**	Noble Vision 105
12/15/84+	**16**	10	8. Let Me Down Easy	Noble Vision 107
10/19/85	**27**	5	9. In Another Minute	MCA 52672
6/14/86	**40**	1	10. The Lights Of Albuquerque	MCA 52808
			GLASER, Tompall	
			Born Thomas Paul Glaser on 9/3/33 in Spalding, Nebraska. Lead singer and oldest of The Glaser Brothers. Formed own Outlaw Band; toured with Waylon Jennings and Willie Nelson.	
7/26/75	**21**	8	1. Put Another Log On The Fire (Male Chauvinist National Anthem) **TOMPALL**	MGM 14800
5/29/76	**36**	3	2. T For Texas **TOMPALL And His Outlaw Band** originally recorded in 1927 as "Blue Yodel" by Jimmie Rodgers	Polydor 14314
			GLASER BROTHERS, Tompall & The	
			Brothers Tompall, Chuck and Jim Glaser performed at local fairs and festivals in their home state of Nebraska. Signed by Marty Robbins to his Robbins label in 1957. Signed with Decca in 1959 as Tompall & The Glaser Brothers; then hooked up with producer Jack Clement and MGM in 1965. Opened own recording studio in Nashville in 1969, which was a hangout for the budding "outlaw" music movement. Trio split up in 1973 to follow separate careers. Reunited in 1979 and then split up once again in 1982. CMA Award: 1970 Vocal Group of the Year.	
2/4/67	**24**	9	1. Gone, On The Other Hand	MGM 13611
8/26/67	**27**	10	2. Through The Eyes Of Love	MGM 13754
9/7/68	**36**	4	3. One Of These Days	MGM 13954
4/26/69	**11**	10	4. California Girl (And The Tennessee Square)	MGM 14036

DATE	POS	WKS	ARTIST– RECORD TITLE	LABEL & NO.
8/16/69	**24**	7	5. Wicked California	MGM 14064
1/10/70	**30**	5	6. Walk Unashamed	MGM 14096
5/2/70	**33**	4	7. All That Keeps Ya Goin'	MGM 14113
			from the movie ...tick...tick...tick... starring George Kennedy; also on the B-side of #4 above	
11/14/70	**23**	8	8. Gone Girl	MGM 14169
7/3/71	**22**	4	9. Faded Love	MGM 14249
			TOMPALL AND THE GLASER BROTHERS WITH LEON McAULIFFE AND THE CIMARRON BOYS	
9/18/71	**7**	12	10. **Rings**	MGM 14291
			#17 Pop hit for Cymarron in 1971	
2/12/72	**23**	7	11. Sweet, Love Me Good Woman	MGM 14339
7/15/72	**15**	11	12. Ain't It All Worth Living For	MGM 14390
			The London Symphony (orch.)	
12/6/80	**34**	3	13. Sweet City Woman	Elektra 47056
			#8 Pop hit for the Stampeders in 1971	
5/16/81	**2** (2)	11	14. **Lovin' Her Was Easier (Than Anything I'll Ever Do Again)**	Elektra 47134
			#26 Pop hit for Kris Kristofferson in 1971	
10/17/81	**17**	7	15. Just One Time	Elektra 47193
3/6/82	**19**	7	16. It'll Be Her [R]	Elektra 47405
			new version of Tompall's #45 solo hit from 1977	
7/3/82	**28**	5	17. I Still Love You (After All These Years)	Elektra 47461
			GLENN, Darrell	
			Born on 12/7/35 in Waco, Texas. Died of cancer on 4/9/90. Son of Artie Glenn, who wrote "Crying In The Chapel." Became a recording engineer and producer.	
7/25/53	**4**	13	1. **Crying In The Chapel**	Valley 105
			Jockey #4 / Juke Box #4 / Best Seller #7	
			GODFREY, Ray	
			Born Arnold Godfrey in Copperville, Tennessee.	
6/27/60	**8**	15	1. **The Picture**	Savoy 3021
			originally released on J&J 001	
			GODFREY, Ray	
12/29/62+	**20**	6	1. Better Times A Comin'	Sims 130
			GOLDSBORO, Bobby	
			Born on 1/18/41 in Marianna, Florida. Singer/songwriter/guitarist. To Dothan, Alabama, in 1956. Toured with Roy Orbison, 1962-64. Own syndicated TV show, *The Bobby Goldsboro Show*, 1972-75.	
4/20/68	**1** (3)	12	● 1. **Honey**	United Art. 50283
7/27/68	**15**	9	2. Autumn Of My Life	United Art. 50318
11/16/68	**37**	6	3. The Straight Life	United Art. 50461
5/24/69	**22**	8	4. I'm A Drifter	United Art. 50525
9/13/69	**15**	8	5. Muddy Mississippi Line	United Art. 50565
11/22/69	**31**	3	6. Take A Little Good Will Home	United Art. 50591
			BOBBY GOLDSBORO & DEL REEVES	

DATE	POS	WKS	ARTIST–RECORD TITLE	LABEL & NO.
1/23/71	**7**	12	7. **Watching Scotty Grow**	United Art. 50727
6/19/76	**22**	7	8. A Butterfly For Bucky	United Art. 793
11/22/80+	**17**	9	9. Goodbye Marie	Curb 5400
3/28/81	**20**	6	10. Alice Doesn't Love Here Anymore	Curb 70052
8/1/81	**19**	7	11. Love Ain't Never Hurt Nobody	Curb 02117
12/12/81	**31**	4	12. The Round-Up Saloon	Curb 02583

GOODWIN, Bill

Born on 6/2/30 in Cumberland City, Tennessee. First recorded for Chart.

DATE	POS	WKS	ARTIST–RECORD TITLE	LABEL & NO.
5/11/63	**17**	8	1. Shoes Of A Fool	Vee Jay 501

GORDON, Luke

Born on 4/15/32 in Quincy, Kentucky. Worked on WPAY-Portsmouth, Ohio. Toured with Jimmy Dean in 1953. First recorded for Starday in 1953.

DATE	POS	WKS	ARTIST–RECORD TITLE	LABEL & NO.
12/22/58+	**13**	7	1. Dark Hollow	Island 0640

GOSDIN, Vern

Born on 8/5/34 in Woodland, Alabama. Joined the Gosdin Family Gospel radio show from Birmingham in the early '50s. Moved to California in 1960 and formed The Golden State Boys with his brother Rex Gosdin. Out of music, 1962-76. Hospitalized for quintuple coronary bypass operation in October 1990.

DATE	POS	WKS	ARTIST–RECORD TITLE	LABEL & NO.
3/19/77	**9**	11	1. **Yesterday's Gone/**	
11/27/76+	**16**	9	2. Hangin' On [R]	Elektra 45353
			new version of his hit with The Gosdin Bros.; Emmylou Harris (harmony vocal, above 2)	
7/9/77	**7**	10	3. **Till The End**	Elektra 45411
11/12/77	**17**	8	4. Mother Country Music	Elektra 45436
2/25/78	**23**	3	5. It Started All Over Again	Elektra 45411
6/3/78	**9**	9	6. **Never My Love**	Elektra 45483
			#2 Pop hit for The Association in 1967; Janie Fricke (harmony vocal: #4 & 6)	
10/14/78	**13**	8	7. Break My Mind	Elektra 45532
3/31/79	**16**	7	8. You've Got Somebody, I've Got Somebody	Elektra 46021
8/4/79	**21**	7	9. All I Want And Need Forever	Elektra 46052
2/21/81	**28**	5	10. Too Long Gone	Ovation 1163
6/6/81	**7**	10	11. **Dream Of Me**	Ovation 1171
2/13/82	**28**	6	12. Don't Ever Leave Me Again	AMI 1302
8/14/82	**22**	7	13. Your Bedroom Eyes	AMI 1307
11/27/82+	**10**	11	14. **Today My World Slipped Away**	AMI 1310
3/12/83	**5**	11	15. **If You're Gonna Do Me Wrong (Do It Right)**	Compleat 102
7/2/83	**5**	11	16. **Way Down Deep**	Compleat 108
10/29/83	**10**	12	17. **I Wonder Where We'd Be Tonight**	Compleat 115
4/21/84	**1** (1)	14	18. **I Can Tell By The Way You Dance (You're Gonna Love Me Tonight)**	Compleat 122
8/18/84	**10**	10	19. **What Would Your Memories Do**	Compleat 126
1/5/85	**10**	12	20. **Slow Burning Memory**	Compleat 135
6/8/85	**20**	8	21. Dim Lights, Thick Smoke (And Loud, Loud Music)	Compleat 142
			Lou Reid (harmony vocal)	
10/5/85	**35**	3	22. I Know The Way To You By Heart	Compleat 145

DATE	POS	WKS	ARTIST– RECORD TITLE	LABEL & NO.
12/5/87+	4	15	23. **Do You Believe Me Now**	Columbia 07627
4/30/88	1 (1)	15	24. **Set 'Em Up Joe**	Columbia 07762
			tribute to Ernest Tubb	
9/17/88	6	14	25. **Chiseled In Stone**	Columbia 08003
2/4/89	2 (1)	13	26. **Who You Gonna Blame It On This Time**	Columbia 08528
6/24/89	1 (1)	14	27. **I'm Still Crazy**	Columbia 68888
10/21/89+	4	20	28. **That Just About Does It**	Columbia 69084
3/10/90	10	10	29. **Right In The Wrong Direction**	Columbia 73221
9/29/90	14	11	30. This Ain't My First Rodeo	Columbia 73491
1/12/91	10	14	31. **Is It Raining At Your House**	Columbia 73632
			GOSDIN BROS., The	
			Duo from Woodland, Alabama: Vern and Rex Gosdin.	
11/18/67	37	3	1. Hangin' On	Bakers. I. 1002
			GRAMMER, Billy	
			Born on 8/28/25 in Benton, Illinois. Worked on WRAL-Arlington, Virginia, in 1947. First recorded for Plaza in 1949. Toured with T. Texas Tyler and Hawkshaw Hawkins in the early '50s. On the Jimmy Dean TV show from 1955; on the *Grand Ole Opry* since 1959. Designed the Grammer Flat-Top guitar, the first model of which was added to the Country Music Hall Of Fame in 1969. Prominent session musician in Nashville.	
1/5/59	5	13	1. **Gotta Travel On**	Monument 400
			based on 19th-century tune that originated in the British Isles	
1/19/63	18	5	2. I Wanna Go Home	Decca 31449
			Bobby Bare recorded this tune as "Detroit City" in 1963	
8/27/66	35	3	3. Bottles	Epic 10052
2/11/67	30	6	4. The Real Thing	Epic 10103
			GRANT, Tom	
			Born on 8/28/50 in Milwaukee. Sang in trio with his brothers from age eight. Own Country band at age 16. Moved to Nashville in 1977; worked on WSM *Waking Crew*, *The Noon Show* and the *Ralph Emery Show*. Member of Trinity Lane.	
3/3/79	40	1	1. If You Could See You Through My Eyes	Republic 036
9/22/79	16	7	2. Sail On	Republic 045
			#4 Pop hit for the Commodores in 1979	
			GRAY, Claude	
			Born on 1/26/32 in Henderson, Texas. Worked as a DJ on WDAL-Meridian, Mississippi in the late '50s. Stands 6'5"; known as "The Tall Texan."	
3/21/60	10	13	1. **Family Bible**	D 1118
			written by Willie Nelson	
1/9/61	4	23	2. **I'll Just Have A Cup Of Coffee (Then I'll Go)**	Mercury 71732
6/26/61	3	19	3. **My Ears Should Burn (When Fools Are Talked About)**	Mercury 71826
			written by Roger Miller	
1/13/62	26	1	4. Let's End It Before It Begins	Mercury 71898
10/20/62	20	5	5. Daddy Stopped In	Mercury 72001
2/9/63	18	6	6. Knock Again, True Love	Mercury 72063
8/6/66	22	8	7. Mean Old Woman	Columbia 43614
12/17/66+	9	15	8. **I Never Had The One I Wanted**	Decca 32039

DATE	POS	WKS	ARTIST–RECORD TITLE	LABEL & NO.
10/21/67	**12**	10	9. How Fast Them Trucks Can Go	Decca 32180
6/15/68	**31**	8	10. Night Life	Decca 32312
11/22/69	**34**	2	11. Take Off Time	Decca 32566
8/22/70	**40**	1	12. Everything Will Be Alright	Decca 32697

GRAY, Dobie

Born Lawrence Darrow Brown on 7/26/40 in Brookshire/Simonton, Texas. Moved to Los Angeles in 1960. Recorded under various names: Leonard Victor Ainsworth, Larry Curtis and Larry Dennis. Acted in the Los Angeles production of *Hair*. Lead singer of Pollution in 1971.

DATE	POS	WKS	ARTIST–RECORD TITLE	LABEL & NO.
4/26/86	**35**	2	1. That's One To Grow On	Capitol 5562

GRAY, Mark

Born on 10/24/52 in Vicksburg, Mississippi. Played piano from age 12. Own gospel group at age 19. Worked in the office for the Oak Ridge Boys. Worked as a writer for Troy Seals. One-time member of Exile.

DATE	POS	WKS	ARTIST–RECORD TITLE	LABEL & NO.
7/16/83	**25**	6	1. It Ain't Real (If It Ain't You)	Columbia 03893
11/26/83+	**18**	9	2. Wounded Hearts	Columbia 04137
3/3/84	**10**	10	3. **Left Side Of The Bed**	Columbia 04324
6/23/84	**9**	10	4. **If All The Magic Is Gone**	Columbia 04464
10/27/84	**9**	12	5. **Diamond In The Dust**	Columbia 04610
3/23/85	**6**	12	6. **Sometimes When We Touch** **MARK GRAY and TAMMY WYNETTE** #3 Pop hit for Dan Hill in 1978	Columbia 04782
12/21/85+	**7**	14	7. **Please Be Love**	Columbia 05695
5/17/86	**14**	8	8. Back When Love Was Enough	Columbia 05857

GRAYSON, Jack, and Blackjack

Grayson was staff writer for ABC/Dot records in the 1970s. Wrote "Super Kind Of Woman" for Freddie Hart. Also recorded under his given name, Jack Lebsock. Changed last name in honor of his mother, Grace.

DATE	POS	WKS	ARTIST–RECORD TITLE	LABEL & NO.
1/31/81	**37**	4	1. A Loser's Night Out	Koala 328
1/23/82	**18**	7	2. When A Man Loves A Woman #1 Pop hit for Percy Sledge in 1966	Koala 340
7/10/82	**38**	1	3. Tonight I'm Feeling You (All Over Again) [R] **JACK GRAYSON** originally charted at #65 in 1980 on Hitbound 4501	Joe-Wes 81000

GREEN, Lloyd

Born on 10/4/37 in Mobile, Alabama. Leading session steel guitarist. Attended the University of Mississippi, 1954-56. Moved to Nashville in 1956 and worked as a session musician. Toured with Faron Young, 1956-58, and recorded with George Jones. Featured on *Sweetheart Of The Rodeo* album by the Byrds.

DATE	POS	WKS	ARTIST–RECORD TITLE	LABEL & NO.
3/24/73	**36**	4	1. I Can See Clearly Now [I] #1 Pop hit for Johnny Nash in 1972	Monument 8562

DATE	POS	WKS	ARTIST– RECORD TITLE	LABEL & NO.
			GREENE, Jack	
			Born on 1/7/30 in Maryville, Tennessee. Worked with the Cherokee Trio in Atlanta in the '40s. On radio with Clyde Grubbs in Maryville and worked as a drummer with the Rhythm Ranch Boys in the early '50s. Played with the Peachtree Cowboys in the mid-1950s. Joined Ernest Tubb in 1962. Own band, the Jolly Green Giants, later named the Renegades, since 1965. Joined the *Grand Ole Opry* in 1967. Known as the "Jolly Green Giant." CMA Award: 1967 Male Vocalist of the Year. (a) JACK GREENE/JEANNIE SEELY	
1/22/66	37	3	1. Ever Since My Baby Went Away	Decca 31856
11/5/66	1 (7)	21	2. **There Goes My Everything** CMA Award: Single of the Year	Decca 32023
5/6/67	1 (5)	17	3. **All The Time**	Decca 32123
10/21/67	2 (4)	17	4. **What Locks The Door**	Decca 32190
3/2/68	1 (1)	12	5. **You Are My Treasure**	Decca 32261
7/20/68	4	16	6. **Love Takes Care Of Me**	Decca 32352
1/4/69	1 (2)	13	7. **Until My Dreams Come True**	Decca 32423
5/24/69	1 (2)	15	8. **Statue Of A Fool**	Decca 32490
10/25/69	4	10	9. **Back In The Arms Of Love**	Decca 32558
11/29/69+	2 (2)	13	10. **Wish I Didn't Have To Miss You** (a)	Decca 32580
3/28/70	16	9	11. Lord Is That Me	Decca 32631
7/25/70	14	11	12. The Whole World Comes To Me/	
		11	13. If This Is Love	Decca 32699
11/28/70	15	8	14. Something Unseen	Decca 32755
5/1/71	13	11	15. There's A Whole Lot About A Woman (A Man Don't Know)/	
		10	16. Makin' Up His Mind	Decca 32823
10/2/71	26	6	17. Hanging Over Me	Decca 32863
1/1/72	15	9	18. Much Oblige (a)	Decca 32898
4/22/72	31	7	19. If You Ever Need My Love	Decca 32939
9/2/72	19	9	20. What In The World Has Gone Wrong With Our Love (a)	Decca 32991
12/30/72+	17	9	21. Satisfaction	Decca 33008
6/9/73	40	1	22. The Fool I've Been Today	MCA 40035
9/8/73	11	12	23. I Need Somebody Bad	MCA 40108
3/9/74	13	8	24. It's Time To Cross That Bridge	MCA 40179
2/2/80	28	5	25. Yours For The Taking	Frontline 704
			GREENE, Lorne	
			Born on 2/12/14 in Ottawa, Canada. Died on 9/11/87 of cardiac arrest. Studied acting; appeared in the movies *The Silver Chalice* and *Tight Spot*; starred on TV's *Bonanza* and *Battlestar Galactica*.	
12/5/64	21	9	1. Ringo [S]	RCA 8444

DATE	POS	WKS	ARTIST – RECORD TITLE	LABEL & NO.
			GREENWOOD, Lee	
			Born Melvin Lee Greenwood on 10/27/42 in Southgate, California; raised in Sacramento. Own band, the Moonbeams, while in high school. Toured with Del Reeves and own band, the Apollos, in the early '60s. Worked in Las Vegas as a sax and piano player. With Felix Cavaliere (later of the Young Rascals) in The Scotties. Worked as a dealer in Vegas casinos until 1981. Has own band, Trick. Married former Miss Tennessee, Kimberly Payne, on 4/11/92. CMA Awards: 1983 and 1984 Male Vocalist of the Year.	
11/21/81+	17	10	1. It Turns Me Inside Out	MCA 51159
4/24/82	5	11	2. **Ring On Her Finger, Time On Her Hands**	MCA 52026
8/28/82	7	11	3. **She's Lying**	MCA 52087
1/22/83	7	10	4. **Ain't No Trick (It Takes Magic)**	MCA 52150
4/30/83	6	13	5. **I.O.U.**	MCA 52199
9/10/83	1 (1)	13	6. **Somebody's Gonna Love You**	MCA 52257
1/14/84	1 (1)	12	7. **Going, Going, Gone**	MCA 52322
6/9/84	7	10	8. **God Bless The USA**	MCA 52386
7/28/84	3	14	9. **To Me**	MCA 52415
9/15/84	3	12	10. **Fool's Gold**	MCA 52426
1/19/85	9	11	11. **You've Got A Good Love Comin'**	MCA 52509
2/23/85	19	7	12. It Should Have Been Love By Now	MCA 52525
			BARBARA MANDRELL/LEE GREENWOOD (#9 & 12)	
5/4/85	1 (1)	14	13. **Dixie Road**	MCA 52564
9/14/85	1 (1)	12	14. **I Don't Mind The Thorns (If You're The Rose)**	MCA 52656
1/25/86	1 (1)	12	15. **Don't Underestimate My Love For You**	MCA 52741
5/3/86	1 (1)	14	16. **Hearts Aren't Made To Break (They're Made To Love)**	MCA 52807
8/23/86	10	11	17. **Didn't We**	MCA 52896
12/13/86+	1 (1)	15	18. **Mornin' Ride**	MCA 52984
5/23/87	5	12	19. **Someone**	MCA 53096
9/19/87	9	11	20. **If There's Any Justice**	MCA 53156
1/23/88	5	11	21. **Touch And Go Crazy**	MCA 53234
6/4/88	12	10	22. I Still Believe	MCA 53312
9/10/88	20	9	23. You Can't Fall In Love When You're Cryin'	MCA 53386
2/18/89	16	10	24. I'll Be Lovin' You	MCA 53475
8/4/90	2 (1)	17	25. **Holdin' A Good Hand**	Capitol 44576
12/1/90+	14	13	26. We've Got It Made	Capitol LP Cut
			above 2 from the album *Holdin' A Good Hand* on Capitol 94153	
6/29/91	12	13	27. Hopelessly Yours	Capitol LP Cut
			LEE GREENWOOD with Suzy Bogguss	
			from Greenwood's album *A Perfect 10* on Capitol 95541	
			GREGG, Ricky Lynn	
			Country-rock singer/songwriter/guitarist. Native of Longview, Texas. Part Native American Indian.	
6/5/93	36	3	1. If I Had A Cheatin' Heart	Liberty 17323
			GREGORY, Clinton	
			Born on 3/1/66 in Martinsville, Virginia. Singer/fiddle player. Teamed with John & Audrey Wiggins, 1979-87.	
5/4/91	26	9	1. (If It Weren't For Country Music) I'd Go Crazy	Step One 427
3/28/92	25	7	2. Play, Ruby, Play	Step One 437
11/21/92	29	5	3. Who Needs It	Step One 444

DATE	POS	WKS	ARTIST–RECORD TITLE	LABEL & NO.

GREGORY, Terry

Born Teresa Ann Gregory Burdine on 4/30/56 in Takoma Park, Maryland. Moved to Berkeley Springs, West Virginia, at age 16. Made professional debut at age 18. Toured with the rock band Fire And Ice. Moved to Hollywood in the late '70s.

DATE	POS	WKS	ARTIST–RECORD TITLE	LABEL & NO.
5/30/81	16	8	1. Just Like Me	Handshake 70071
12/19/81+	30	5	2. I Can't Say Goodbye To You	Handshake 02563
			written by Becky Hobbs	

GRIFF, Ray

Born John Ray Griff on 4/22/40 in Vancouver; raised in Winfield, Alberta. Guitarist/pianist/drummer. Played drums in the Winfield Amateurs from age six. Appeared on Calgary TV with own band, The Blue Echoes. Wrote "Mr. Moonlight" for Johnny Horton; "Where Do I Go" for Jim Reeves. Moved to Nashville in 1964. Own TV series on CBC.

DATE	POS	WKS	ARTIST–RECORD TITLE	LABEL & NO.
10/31/70	26	4	1. Patches	Royal Amer. 19
			#4 Pop hit for Clarence Carter in 1970	
12/11/71+	14	11	2. The Mornin' After Baby Let Me Down	Royal Amer. 46
10/18/75	16	9	3. You Ring My Bell	Capitol 4126
2/21/76	11	9	4. If I Let Her Come In	Capitol 4208
7/4/76	40	2	5. I Love The Way That You Love Me	Capitol 4266
9/25/76	24	7	6. That's What I Get (For Doin' My Own Thinkin')	Capitol 4320
1/22/77	27	5	7. The Last Of The Winfield Amateurs/	
		5	8. You Put The Bounce Back Into My Step	Capitol 4368
5/21/77	28	4	9. A Passing Thing	Capitol 4415

GRIFFITH, Nanci

Born on 7/16/54 in Austin, Texas; raised in southern Louisiana and Dallas. "Folkabilly" (term coined by Griffith for fusion of folk and hillbilly music) singer. First recorded for B.F. Deal records in 1977. Wrote Kathy Mattea's "Love At The Five & Dime."

DATE	POS	WKS	ARTIST–RECORD TITLE	LABEL & NO.
2/28/87	36	2	1. Lone Star State Of Mind	MCA 53008
5/28/88	37	3	2. I Knew Love	MCA 53306

GUITAR, Bonnie

Born Bonnie Buckingham on 3/25/23 in Seattle. Own group in the early 1950s. Worked as session guitarist in Los Angeles in the mid-1950s. Owner of Dolphin/Dolton Records in Seattle in 1958. Director of country music A&R for Dot and ABC-Paramount.

DATE	POS	WKS	ARTIST–RECORD TITLE	LABEL & NO.
6/10/57	14	1	1. Dark Moon	Dot 15550
			Jockey #14	
11/11/57	15	1	2. Mister Fire Eyes	Dot 15612
			Jockey #15	
3/12/66	9	15	3. **I'm Living In Two Worlds**	Dot 16811
7/30/66	14	8	4. Get Your Lie The Way You Want It	Dot 16872
10/15/66	24	9	5. The Tallest Tree	Dot 16919
6/10/67	33	5	6. You Can Steal Me	Dot 17007
8/26/67	4	14	7. **A Woman In Love**	Dot 17029
1/20/68	13	12	8. Stop The Sun	Dot 17057
6/15/68	10	13	9. **I Believe In Love**	Dot 17097
9/20/69	36	3	10. That See Me Later Look	Dot 17276

DATE	POS	WKS	ARTIST–RECORD TITLE	LABEL & NO.
			GUTHRIE, Jack, and his Oklahomans	
			Born Leon Guthrie on 11/13/15 in Olive, Oklahoma. Died on 1/15/48. Moved to California in 1932 and worked on radio stations in Marysville and Chico. He was in the service in the South Pacific when "Oklahoma Hills" became a hit. Cousin of Woody Guthrie.	
7/7/45	1 (6)	19	1. **Oklahoma Hills/**	Capitol 201
7/21/45	5	2	2. **I'm A Brandin' My Darlin' With My Heart**	
3/1/47	3	3	3. **Oakie Boogie**	Capitol 341

H

DATE	POS	WKS	ARTIST–RECORD TITLE	LABEL & NO.
			HAGGARD, Merle	
			Born Merle Ronald Haggard on 4/6/37 in Bakersfield, California. Served nearly three years in San Quentin prison for burglary, 1957-60. Granted full pardon by Governor Ronald Reagan on 3/14/72. Worked in local clubs from 1960. First recorded for Tally in 1962. Signed to Capitol Records in 1965 and formed his backing band, The Strangers. Appeared in the movies *Bronco Billy*, *Huckleberry Finn*, *Killers Three* and *Doc Elliot*. Appeared on the TV series *The Waltons* and *Centennial*. Formerly married to Country singers Bonnie Owens and Leona Williams. Wrote the majority of his hits. Elected to the Country Music Hall of Fame in 1994. CMA Awards: 1970 Male Vocalist of the Year; 1970 Entertainer of the Year; 1983 Vocal Duo of the Year (with Willie Nelson).	
12/28/63+	19	3	1. Sing A Sad Song	Tally 155
9/19/64	28	24	2. Just Between The Two Of Us	Tally 181
			MERLE HAGGARD and BONNIE OWENS	
1/9/65	10	21	3. **(My Friends Are Gonna Be) Strangers**	Tally 179
			MERLE HAGGARD & THE STRANGERS:	
4/16/66	5	26	4. **Swinging Doors**	Capitol 5600
8/27/66	3	20	5. **The Bottle Let Me Down**	Capitol 5704
1/7/67	1 (1)	15	6. **The Fugitive/**	Capitol 5803
			later titled "I'm A Lonesome Fugitive"	
1/28/67	32	5	7. Someone Told My Story	
4/8/67	2 (2)	15	8. **I Threw Away The Rose**	Capitol 5844
7/15/67	1 (1)	15	9. **Branded Man**	Capitol 5931
12/9/67+	1 (2)	17	10. **Sing Me Back Home**	Capitol 2017
3/16/68	1 (2)	14	11. **The Legend Of Bonnie And Clyde**	Capitol 2123
			flip side is the classic "Today I Started Loving You Again"	
7/27/68	1 (4)	15	12. **Mama Tried**	Capitol 2219
			ballad from the movie *Killers Three* starring Haggard	
11/9/68+	3	16	13. **I Take A Lot Of Pride In What I Am**	Capitol 2289
3/8/69	1 (1)	15	14. **Hungry Eyes**	Capitol 2383
7/19/69	1 (1)	13	15. **Workin' Man Blues**	Capitol 2503
10/18/69	1 (4)	15	16. **Okie From Muskogee**	Capitol 2626
			CMA Award: Single of the Year	
2/7/70	1 (3)	14	17. **The Fightin' Side Of Me**	Capitol 2719
5/2/70	9	10	18. **Street Singer** [I]	Capitol 2778
6/20/70	3	13	19. **Jesus, Take A Hold**	Capitol 2838

DATE	POS	WKS	ARTIST-RECORD TITLE		LABEL & NO.
10/24/70	**3**	15	20. **I Can't Be Myself**/		
		15	21. Sidewalks Of Chicago		Capitol 2891
2/20/71	**3**	12	22. **Soldier's Last Letter**		Capitol 3024
7/3/71	**2** (2)	14	23. **Someday We'll Look Back**		Capitol 3112
10/23/71	**1** (2)	13	24. **Daddy Frank (The Guitar Man)**		Capitol 3198
12/11/71+	**1** (3)	15	25. **Carolyn**		Capitol 3222
4/1/72	**1** (2)	14	26. **Grandma Harp**/		
		10	27. Turnin' Off A Memory		Capitol 3294
9/16/72	**1** (1)	12	28. **It's Not Love (But It's Not Bad)**		Capitol 3419
12/16/72+	**1** (1)	13	29. **I Wonder If They Ever Think Of Me**		Capitol 3488
3/24/73	**3**	12	30. **The Emptiest Arms In The World**		Capitol 3552
7/7/73	**1** (2)	15	31. **Everybody's Had The Blues**		Capitol 3641
11/10/73	**1** (4)	14	32. **If We Make It Through December**	[X]	Capitol 3746
3/23/74	**1** (1)	10	33. **Things Aren't Funny Anymore**		Capitol 3830
7/20/74	**1** (1)	10	34. **Old Man From The Mountain**		Capitol 3900
11/30/74+	**1** (1)	11	35. **Kentucky Gambler**		Capitol 3974
			written by Dolly Parton		
3/8/75	**1** (2)	10	36. **Always Wanting You**		Capitol 4027
6/14/75	**1** (1)	9	37. **Movin' On**		Capitol 4085
			theme from the TV series starring Claude Akins		
10/11/75	**1** (1)	13	38. **It's All In The Movies**		Capitol 4141
1/31/76	**1** (1)	10	39. **The Roots Of My Raising**		Capitol 4204
5/29/76	**10**	9	40. **Here Comes The Freedom Train**		Capitol 4267
9/18/76	**1** (1)	11	41. **Cherokee Maiden**/		
			tune originally written and recorded in 1941 by Bob Wills		
		11	42. What Have You Got Planned Tonight Diana		Capitol 4326
			MERLE HAGGARD:		
4/9/77	**2** (2)	12	43. **If We're Not Back In Love By Monday**		MCA 40700
7/9/77	**2** (2)	11	44. **Ramblin' Fever**/		
		10	45. When My Blue Moon Turns To Gold Again		MCA 40743
			#19 Pop hit for Elvis Presley in 1956		
9/24/77	**16**	8	46. A Working Man Can't Get Nowhere Today		Capitol 4477
10/15/77	**4**	9	47. **From Graceland To The Promised Land**		MCA 40804
			an Elvis Presley tribute; The Jordanaires (backing vocals)		
1/28/78	**12**	8	48. Running Kind/		
		7	49. Making Believe		Capitol 4525
3/25/78	**2** (2)	11	50. **I'm Always On A Mountain When I Fall**		MCA 40869
8/19/78	**2** (3)	11	51. **It's Been A Great Afternoon**/		
		6	52. Love Me When You Can		MCA 40936
11/4/78	**8**	7	53. **The Bull And The Beaver**		MCA 40962
			MERLE HAGGARD/LEONA WILLIAMS		
4/28/79	**4**	10	54. **Red Bandana**/		
		10	55. I Must Have Done Something Bad		MCA 41007
9/22/79	**4**	10	56. **My Own Kind Of Hat**/		
		10	57. Heaven Was A Drink Of Wine		MCA 41112
3/29/80	**2** (2)	11	58. **The Way I Am**		MCA 41200
5/31/80	**1** (1)	13	59. **Bar Room Buddies**		Elektra 46634
			MERLE HAGGARD and CLINT EASTWOOD		

DATE	POS	WKS	ARTIST – RECORD TITLE	LABEL & NO.
7/19/80	3	10	60. Misery And Gin	MCA 41255
			above 2 from the movie Bronco Billy _starring Clint Eastwood_	
11/8/80+	1 (1)	12	61. I Think I'll Just Stay Here And Drink	MCA 51014
2/28/81	9	9	62. Leonard	MCA 51048
			an ode of thanks to songwriter Leonard "Tommy Collins" Sipes	
6/27/81	4	10	63. Rainbow Stew	MCA 51120
10/3/81	1 (1)	10	64. My Favorite Memory	Epic 02504
1/30/82	1 (1)	13	65. Big City	Epic 02686
			Leona Williams (harmony vocal)	
5/29/82	2 (2)	13	66. Are The Good Times Really Over (I Wish A Buck Was Still Silver)	Epic 02894
8/21/82	1 (1)	10	67. Yesterday's Wine	Epic 03072
			MERLE HAGGARD/GEORGE JONES	
11/13/82+	1 (1)	13	68. Going Where The Lonely Go	Epic 03315
1/8/83	10	10	69. C.C. Waterback	Epic 03405
			GEORGE JONES/MERLE HAGGARD	
2/5/83	6	11	70. Reasons To Quit	Epic 03494
			MERLE HAGGARD and WILLIE NELSON	
3/26/83	1 (1)	13	71. You Take Me For Granted	Epic 03723
5/14/83	1 (1)	14	72. Pancho And Lefty	Epic 03842
			WILLIE NELSON and MERLE HAGGARD	
8/13/83	3	12	73. What Am I Gonna Do (With The Rest Of My Life)	Epic 04006
12/3/83+	1 (1)	14	74. That's The Way Love Goes	Epic 04226
4/7/84	1 (1)	13	75. Someday When Things Are Good	Epic 04402
7/28/84	1 (1)	12	76. Let's Chase Each Other Around The Room	Epic 04512
11/17/84+	1 (1)	14	77. A Place To Fall Apart	Epic 04663
			MERLE HAGGARD with JANIE FRICKE	
4/6/85	1 (1)	12	78. Natural High	Epic 04830
			Janie Frickie (guest vocal)	
8/3/85	10	10	79. Kern River	Epic 05426
10/26/85	36	2	80. Amber Waves Of Grain	Epic 05659
2/15/86	5	14	81. I Had A Beautiful Time	Epic 05782
6/28/86	9	11	82. A Friend In California	Epic 06097
11/8/86	21	7	83. Out Among The Stars	Epic 06344
12/5/87+	1 (1)	15	84. Twinkle, Twinkle Lucky Star	Epic 07631
4/9/88	9	10	85. Chill Factor	Epic 07754
8/13/88	22	7	86. We Never Touch At All	Epic 07944
12/17/88+	23	9	87. You Babe	Epic 08111
5/6/89	18	14	88. 5:01 Blues	Epic 68598
8/19/89	4	14	89. A Better Love Next Time	Epic 68979
1/6/90	23	9	90. If You Want To Be My Woman	Epic 73076

HALL, Connie

Born on 6/24/29 in Walden, Kentucky; raised in Cincinnati. Worked on WZIP-Covington, Kentucky. With the _Jimmie Skinner Show_, WNOP-Newport, Kentucky, in 1954.

DATE	POS	WKS	ARTIST – RECORD TITLE	LABEL & NO.
2/15/60	21	4	1. The Bottle Or Me	Mercury 71540
10/17/60	17	2	2. It's Not Wrong/	
			answer song to "Is It Wrong (For Loving You)"	
10/10/60	25	2	3. The Poison In Your Hand	Decca 31130
4/24/61	20	5	4. Sleep, Baby, Sleep	Decca 31208

DATE	POS	WKS	ARTIST– RECORD TITLE	LABEL & NO.
1/20/62	23	5	5. What A Pleasure	Decca 31310
1/5/63	14	3	6. Fool Me Once	Decca 31438
			HALL, Tom T.	
			Born Thomas Hall on 5/25/36 in Olive Hill, Kentucky. Played guitar from age eight; own band, the Kentucky Travelers, at age 16. Worked as a DJ on WMOR-Morehead, Kentucky. Worked on Armed Forces Radio in Germany while in service, 1957-61. Moved to Nashville in 1964. Wrote "Harper Valley P.T.A." hit for Jeannie C. Riley. Host of the TV series *Pop Goes The Country*. Joined the *Grand Ole Opry* in 1980. Added "T" to his name when he began his singing career. Famous for his storytelling style of writing and singing.	
8/26/67	30	6	1. I Washed My Face In The Morning Dew	Mercury 72700
11/30/68+	4	16	2. **Ballad Of Forty Dollars**	Mercury 72863
6/21/69	40	1	3. Strawberry Farms	Mercury 72913
9/13/69	5	12	4. **Homecoming**	Mercury 72951
12/27/69+	1 (2)	13	5. **A Week In A Country Jail**	Mercury 72998
4/11/70	8	11	6. **Shoeshine Man**	Mercury 73039
7/18/70	8	11	7. **Salute To A Switchblade**	Mercury 73078
12/5/70	23	9	8. Day Drinkin' **DAVE DUDLEY & TOM T. HALL**	Mercury 73139
1/9/71	14	9	9. One Hundred Children	Mercury 73140
4/24/71	21	7	10. Ode To A Half A Pound Of Ground Round	Mercury 73189
7/17/71	1 (2)	18	11. **The Year That Clayton Delaney Died**	Mercury 73221
4/1/72	8	13	12. **Me And Jesus** The Mt. Pisgah United Methodist Church Choir (backing vocals)	Mercury 73278
7/15/72	11	10	13. The Monkey That Became President	Mercury 73297
10/28/72	26	6	14. More About John Henry	Mercury 73327
12/16/72+	1 (1)	13	15. **(Old Dogs-Children And) Watermelon Wine**	Mercury 73346
1/13/73	14	8	16. Hello We're Lonely **PATTI PAGE & TOM T. HALL**	Mercury 73347
5/19/73	3	11	17. **Ravishing Ruby**	Mercury 73377
7/28/73	16	6	18. Watergate Blues/	
		6	19. Spokane Motel Blues	Mercury 73394
11/24/73+	1 (2)	15	20. **I Love**	Mercury 73436
6/15/74	2 (2)	11	21. **That Song Is Driving Me Crazy**	Mercury 73488
10/12/74	1 (1)	11	22. **Country Is**	Mercury 73617
1/4/75	1 (1)	10	23. **I Care**	Mercury 73641
6/21/75	8	10	24. **Deal**	Mercury 73686
9/20/75	4	13	25. **I Like Beer**	Mercury 73704
1/24/76	1 (1)	13	26. **Faster Horses (The Cowboy And The Poet)**	Mercury 73755
6/5/76	24	7	27. Negatory Romance	Mercury 73795
10/30/76	9	10	28. **Fox On The Run**	Mercury 73850
4/23/77	4	12	29. **Your Man Loves You, Honey**	Mercury 73899
8/20/77	12	8	30. It's All In The Game #1 Pop hit for Tommy Edwards in 1958	Mercury 55001
12/17/77+	13	9	31. May The Force Be With You Always inspired by the movie *Star Wars*	RCA 11158
4/22/78	13	9	32. I Wish I Loved Somebody Else Bonnie & Maxine Brown (backing vocals, above 2)	RCA 11253
9/30/78	9	8	33. **What Have You Got To Lose**	RCA 11376

DATE	POS	WKS	ARTIST – RECORD TITLE	LABEL & NO.
2/3/79	14	7	34. Son Of Clayton Delaney	RCA 11453
6/2/79	20	6	35. There Is A Miracle In You	RCA 11568
10/6/79	11	10	36. You Show Me Your Heart (And I'll Show You Mine)	RCA 11713
1/19/80	9	9	37. **The Old Side Of Town/**	
		9	38. Jesus On The Radio (Daddy on the Phone)	RCA 11888
9/20/80	36	3	39. Back When Gas Was Thirty Cents A Gallon	RCA 12066
10/6/84	8	10	40. **P.S. I Love You**	Mercury 880216
			#12 Pop hit for Rudy Vallee in 1934	
6/29/85	40	1	41. A Bar With No Beer	Mercury 880690

HAMBLEN, Stuart

Born Carl Stuart Hamblen on 10/20/08 in Kellerville, Texas. Died on 3/8/89. Singer/actor. On radio from age 17. Moved to Hollywood in the early 1930s and appeared in many Western movies and on radio with own band. Wrote "It Is No Secret (What God Can Do)," "This Ole House," "Open Up Your Heart (And Let The Sunshine In)" and many others. Ran for president on Prohibition Party ticket in 1952.

DATE	POS	WKS	ARTIST – RECORD TITLE	LABEL & NO.
11/12/49+	3	7	1. **(I Won't Go Huntin', Jake) But I'll Go Chasin' Women** Juke Box #3 / Best Seller #9	Columbia 20625
8/5/50	2 (9)	26	2. **(Remember Me) I'm The One Who Loves You** Jockey #2 / Best Seller #3 / Juke Box #4; 45 rpm: 9-692; #32 Pop hit for Dean Martin in 1965	Columbia 20714
1/6/51	8	2	3. **It's No Secret** Jockey #8	Columbia 20724
8/21/54	2 (1)	30	4. **This Ole House** Jockey #2 / Best Seller #3 / Juke Box #5	RCA 5739

HAMILTON, George, IV

Born on 7/19/37 in Winston-Salem, North Carolina. Recorded "A Rose And A Baby Ruth" for Colonial in 1956. Toured with Buddy Holly, Gene Vincent and The Everly Brothers. Moved to Nashville in 1959 and joined the *Grand Ole Opry* in 1960. Own TV series on ABC in 1959, and in Canada in the late 1970s.

DATE	POS	WKS	ARTIST – RECORD TITLE	LABEL & NO.
10/10/60	4	17	1. **Before This Day Ends**	ABC-Para. 10125
6/12/61	9	13	2. **Three Steps To The Phone (Millions of Miles)**	RCA 7881
11/13/61	13	8	3. To You And Yours (From Me and Mine)	RCA 7934
6/16/62	22	2	4. China Doll #38 Pop hit for The Ames Brothers in 1960	RCA 8001
8/25/62	6	14	5. **If You Don't Know I Ain't Gonna Tell You**	RCA 8062
1/19/63	21	5	6. In This Very Same Room	RCA 8118
6/15/63	1 (4)	24	7. **Abilene**	RCA 8181
1/25/64	21	6	8. There's More Pretty Girls Than One	RCA 8250
3/28/64	25	7	9. Linda With The Lonely Eyes/	
4/18/64	28	6	10. Fair And Tender Ladies	RCA 8304
9/5/64	9	13	11. **Fort Worth, Dallas Or Houston**	RCA 8392
12/26/64+	11	15	12. Truck Driving Man	RCA 8462
8/7/65	18	12	13. Walking The Floor Over You Ernest Tubb's classic hit of the early '40s	RCA 8608
12/11/65+	16	11	14. Write Me A Picture	RCA 8690
5/14/66	15	14	15. Steel Rail Blues	RCA 8797
9/24/66	9	13	16. **Early Morning Rain**	RCA 8924
2/18/67	7	15	17. **Urge For Going** written by Joni Mitchell	RCA 9059

DATE	POS	WKS	ARTIST—RECORD TITLE	LABEL & NO.
7/22/67	6	14	18. **Break My Mind**	RCA 9239
1/13/68	18	9	19. Little World Girl	RCA 9385
12/7/68	38	3	20. Take My Hand For Awhile	RCA 9637
3/22/69	26	9	21. Back to Denver	RCA 0100
7/12/69	25	9	22. Canadian Pacific	RCA 0171
12/6/69	29	4	23. Carolina In My Mind	RCA 0256
			written by James Taylor	
5/16/70	3	14	24. **She's A Little Bit Country**	RCA 9829
9/19/70	16	8	25. Back Where It's At	RCA 9886
2/20/71	13	8	26. Anyway	RCA 9945
6/26/71	35	4	27. Countryfied	RCA 0469
10/16/71	23	8	28. West Texas Highway	RCA 0531
3/4/72	33	3	29. 10 Degrees & Getting Colder	RCA 0622
1/27/73	22	8	30. Blue Train (Of The Heartbreak Line)	RCA 0854
7/7/73	38	2	31. Dirty Old Man	RCA 0948

HARDEN, Arlene

Born Ava A. Harden on 3/1/45 in England, Arkansas. Part of The Harden Trio with brother Bobby and sister Robbie; appeared on the *Grand Ole Opry* from 1966, went solo in 1967. Made appearances on the Porter Wagoner and Wilburn Brothers TV shows, and *Midwestern Hayride*.

DATE	POS	WKS	ARTIST—RECORD TITLE	LABEL & NO.
5/18/68	32	4	1. He's A Good Ole Boy	Columbia 44461
5/2/70	13	12	2. Lovin' Man (Oh Pretty Woman)	Columbia 45120
			female version of Roy Orbison's #1 Pop hit in 1964	
10/3/70	28	5	3. Crying	Columbia 45203
			#2 Pop hit for Roy Orbison in 1961	
1/30/71	22	8	4. True Love Is Greater Than Friendship	Columbia 45287
			from the movie *Little Fauss And Big Halsy* starring Robert Redford	
5/29/71	25	7	5. Married To A Memory	Columbia 45365
5/27/72	29	6	6. A Special Day	Columbia 45577
7/28/73	21	9	7. Would You Walk With Me Jimmy	Columbia 45845

HARDEN TRIO, The

Family trio from England, Arkansas: Bobby and sisters Robbie and Arlene Harden. On *Barnyard Frolics* in Little Rock while still teenagers. Worked on *Ozark Jubilee*, *Louisiana Hayride* and *Grand Ole Opry*. Disbanded in 1968.

DATE	POS	WKS	ARTIST—RECORD TITLE	LABEL & NO.
2/19/66	2 (1)	20	1. **Tippy Toeing**	Columbia 43463
12/10/66	28	4	2. Seven Days Of Crying (Makes One Weak)	Columbia 43844
5/20/67	16	10	3. Sneaking 'Cross The Border	Columbia 44059

HARDIN, Gus

Born Carolyn Ann Blankenship on 4/9/45 in Tulsa. Female singer. Longtime favorite in Tulsa Clubs.

DATE	POS	WKS	ARTIST—RECORD TITLE	LABEL & NO.
3/19/83	10	9	1. **After The Last Goodbye**	RCA 13445
7/9/83	26	6	2. If I Didn't Love You	RCA 13532
11/5/83	32	4	3. Loving You Hurts	RCA 13597
12/15/84+	8	13	4. **All Tangled Up In Love**	RCA 13938
			GUS HARDIN with EARL THOMAS CONLEY	

DATE	POS	WKS	ARTIST–RECORD TITLE	LABEL & NO.
			HARDY, Johnny	
2/13/61	**17**	10	Born in Rockmont, Georgia. 1. In Memory Of Johnny Horton	J&J 003
			HARGROVE, Linda	
1/10/76	**39**	1	Born on 2/3/51 in Tallahasee. Moved to Nashville in 1970 and worked as a songwriter and session musician. Turned to gospel music in 1978. Now known as Linda Bartholemew. 1. Love Was (Once Around The Dance Floor)	Capitol 4153
			HARMS, Joni	
4/22/89	**34**	2	Born on 11/5/59 in Canby, Oregon. Won Miss Northwest Rodeo title in 1979. 1. I Need A Wife	Universal 53492
			HARRIS, Emmylou	
			Born on 4/2/47 in Birmingham, Alabama. Worked as a folk singer in Washington, D.C., in the late '60s. First recorded for Jubilee in 1969. Toured with the Flying Burrito Brothers and Gram Parsons until 1973. Own band from 1975. Married British songwriter Paul Kennerley in 1985 (since divorced). Joined the *Grand Ole Opry* in 1992. Also see Southern Pacific. CMA Award: 1980 Female Vocalist of the Year.	
8/9/75	**4**	11	1. **If I Could Only Win Your Love**	Reprise 1332
1/17/76	**12**	8	2. **The Sweetest Gift** **LINDA RONSTADT and EMMYLOU HARRIS**	Asylum 45295
3/20/76	**1 (1)**	11	3. **Together Again** flip side "Here, There And Everywhere" made #65 on the *Hot 100*	Reprise 1346
6/19/76	**3**	13	4. **One Of These Days**	Reprise 1353
11/6/76	**1 (2)**	11	5. **Sweet Dreams**	Reprise 1371
3/12/77	**6**	10	6. **(You Never Can Tell) C'est La Vie** #14 Pop hit for Chuck Berry in 1964	Warner 8329
6/11/77	**8**	10	7. **Making Believe** Herb Pedersen (harmony vocal: #1 & 7)	Warner 8388
12/10/77+	**3**	11	8. **To Daddy** written by Dolly Parton	Warner 8498
4/29/78	**1 (1)**	10	9. **Two More Bottles Of Wine**	Warner 8553
8/19/78	**12**	8	10. Easy From Now On	Warner 8623
2/17/79	**13**	8	11. Too Far Gone [R] originally hit #73 in 1975 on Reprise 1326	Warner 8732
5/26/79	**11**	9	12. Play Together Again Again **BUCK OWENS with EMMYLOU HARRIS** title refers to Owens's classic "Together Again"	Warner 8830
6/9/79	**4**	9	13. **Save The Last Dance For Me** #1 Pop hit for The Drifters in 1960	Warner 8815
9/29/79	**6**	8	14. **Blue Kentucky Girl**	Warner 49056
3/8/80	**1 (1)**	12	15. **Beneath Still Waters**	Warner 49164
6/14/80	**7**	11	16. **Wayfaring Stranger**	Warner 49239
7/19/80	**6**	9	17. **That Lovin' You Feelin' Again** **ROY ORBISON & EMMYLOU HARRIS** from the movie *Roadie* starring Meat Loaf	Warner 49262
10/4/80	**13**	7	18. The Boxer #7 Pop hit for Simon & Garfunkel in 1969	Warner 49551

DATE	POS	WKS	ARTIST– RECORD TITLE	LABEL & NO.
3/28/81	10	7	19. **Mister Sandman** #1 Pop hit for The Chordettes in 1954	Warner 49684
10/10/81	3	9	20. **If I Needed You** **EMMYLOU HARRIS & DON WILLIAMS**	Warner 49809
2/6/82	9	10	21. **Tennessee Rose** Cheryl and Sharon White (backing vocals)	Warner 49892
6/12/82	3	12	22. **Born To Run**	Warner 29993
11/13/82+	1 (1)	14	23. **(Lost His Love) On Our Last Date** vocal version of Floyd Cramer's "Last Date"	Warner 29898
4/2/83	5	11	24. **I'm Movin' On**	Warner 29729
8/6/83	28	4	25. **So Sad (To Watch Good Love Go Bad)** #7 Pop hit for The Everly Brothers in 1960	Warner 29583
8/13/83	14	8	26. Wild Montana Skies **JOHN DENVER and EMMYLOU HARRIS**	RCA 13562
12/17/83+	26	6	27. Drivin' Wheel	Warner 29443
4/14/84	9	11	28. **In My Dreams**	Warner 29329
9/1/84	9	12	29. **Pledging My Love** #17 Pop hit for Johnny Ace in 1955	Warner 29218
1/5/85	26	6	30. Someone Like You	Warner 29138
4/20/85	14	9	31. White Line	Warner 29041
2/28/87	1 (1)	14	32. **To Know Him Is To Love Him** #1 Pop hit for The Teddy Bears in 1958	Warner 28492
6/13/87	3	11	33. **Telling Me Lies**	Warner 28371
10/10/87	5	13	34. **Those Memories Of You**	Warner 28248
4/16/88	6	11	35. **Wildflowers** **DOLLY PARTON, LINDA RONSTADT, EMMYLOU HARRIS** **(above 4)**	Warner 27970
7/16/88	1 (1)	15	36. **We Believe In Happy Endings** **EARL THOMAS CONLEY with EMMYLOU HARRIS**	RCA 8632
1/28/89	8	11	37. **Heartbreak Hill**	Reprise 27635
6/3/89	16	9	38. Heaven Only Knows	Reprise 22999

HART, Clay

Born Henry Clay Hart III in Providence, Rhode Island. Attended Amherst College. Worked as an engineer in studios in Tampa, Florida. Appeared on the TV series *The Lawrence Welk Show*, 1969-75. Wife Sally Flynn was on Welk shows in duo with Sandy Jensen.

DATE	POS	WKS	ARTIST– RECORD TITLE	LABEL & NO.
6/28/69	30	6	1. Spring	Metromedia 119
10/11/69	25	6	2. Another Day, Another Mile, Another Highway	Metromedia 140

HART, Freddie

Born Fred Segrest on 12/21/26 in Lochapoka, Alabama. Served in U.S. Marines during World War II. Moved to Phoenix in 1950 and worked with Lefty Frizzell, 1951-52. Appeared on the TV series *Home Town Jamboree*. Operates a trucking company and school for handicapped children in Burbank, California.

DATE	POS	WKS	ARTIST– RECORD TITLE	LABEL & NO.
4/20/59	24	4	1. The Wall	Columbia 41345
11/16/59	17	4	2. Chain Gang	Columbia 41456
5/2/60	18	11	3. The Key's In The Mailbox	Columbia 41597
1/9/61	27	2	4. Lying Again	Columbia 41805
11/6/61	23	2	5. What A Laugh!	Columbia 42146
11/6/65	23	10	6. Hank Williams' Guitar	Kapp 694

DATE	POS	WKS	ARTIST– RECORD TITLE	LABEL & NO.
2/3/68	**24**	7	7. Togetherness	Kapp 879
7/27/68	**21**	7	8. Born A Fool	Kapp 910
1/17/70	**27**	6	9. The Whole World Holding Hands	Capitol 2692
7/17/71	**1** (3)	22	● 10. **Easy Loving**	Capitol 3115
2/5/72	**1** (6)	18	11. **My Hang-Up Is You**	Capitol 3261
			FREDDIE HART AND THE HEARTBEATS:	
7/1/72	**1** (2)	13	12. **Bless Your Heart**	Capitol 3353
10/21/72	**1** (3)	16	13. **Got The All Overs For You (All Over Me)**	Capitol 3453
2/17/73	**1** (1)	12	14. **Super Kind Of Woman**	Capitol 3524
6/16/73	**1** (1)	13	15. **Trip To Heaven**	Capitol 3612
10/20/73	**3**	13	16. If You Can't Feel It (It Ain't There)	Capitol 3730
3/9/74	**2** (1)	9	17. **Hang In There Girl** **FREDDIE HART**	Capitol 3827
7/6/74	**3**	12	18. **The Want-To's**	Capitol 3898
11/30/74+	**3**	11	19. **My Woman's Man**	Capitol 3970
3/22/75	**5**	11	20. **I'd Like To Sleep Til I Get Over You**	Capitol 4031
7/19/75	**2** (2)	12	21. **The First Time**	Capitol 4099
11/15/75	**6**	9	22. **Warm Side Of You**	Capitol 4152
2/14/76	**11**	8	23. You Are The Song (Inside Of Me)	Capitol 4210
5/1/76	**12**	9	24. She'll Throw Stones At You	Capitol 4251
9/11/76	**11**	9	25. That Look In Her Eyes	Capitol 4313
12/18/76+	**8**	10	26. **Why Lovers Turn To Strangers**	Capitol 4363
			FREDDIE HART:	
4/30/77	**11**	7	27. **Thank God She's Mine**	Capitol 4409
7/30/77	**13**	8	28. The Pleasure's Been All Mine/	
		8	29. It's Heaven Loving You	Capitol 4448
2/18/78	**27**	4	30. So Good, So Rare, So Fine	Capitol 4530
5/27/78	**34**	2	31. Only You #1 Pop hit for The Platters in 1955	Capitol 4561
9/9/78	**21**	7	32. Toe To Toe	Capitol 4609
3/31/79	**40**	1	33. My Lady	Capitol 4684
6/30/79	**28**	5	34. Wasn't It Easy Baby	Capitol 4720
6/21/80	**15**	8	35. Sure Thing	Sunbird 7550
10/11/80	**33**	3	36. Rose's Are Red	Sunbird 7553
5/16/81	**31**	3	37. You're Crazy Man	Sunbird 7560
10/17/81	**38**	1	38. You Were There	Sunbird 7565
			HART, Rod Born in Beulah, Michigan. Appeared in the Steve McQueen movie *Junior Bonner*.	
12/18/76+	**23**	6	1. C.B. Savage [N]	Plantation 144
			HARVELL, Nate Singer/songwriter from Alabama.	
8/19/78	**23**	5	1. Three Times A Lady #1 Pop hit for the Commodores in 1978	Republic 025

DATE	POS	WKS	ARTIST– RECORD TITLE	LABEL & NO.
			HAWKINS, Erskine, & His Orchestra	
			Hawkins was born on 7/26/14 in Birmingham, Alabama. Died on 11/11/93. Trumpeter/bandleader/composer.	
2/5/44	6	1	1. **Don't Cry, Baby**	Bluebird 30-0813
			HAWKINS, Hawkshaw	
			Born Harold Franklin Hawkins on 12/22/21 in Huntington, West Virginia. Died in a plane crash on 3/5/63 near Camden, Tennessee. Worked on local radio from age 15. In service during World War II. Worked on WWVA-Wheeling *Jamboree* from 1946. With the *Grand Ole Opry* from 1955. Married to Jean Shepard. Plane crash also killed Patsy Cline, Cowboy Copas and pilot Randy Hughes.	
5/1/48	9	4	1. **Pan American** Juke Box #9	King 689
8/21/48	6	15	2. **Dog House Boogie** Juke Box #6 / Best Seller #12	King 720
12/24/49	15	1	3. I Wasted A Nickel Best Seller #15	King 821
3/17/51	8	1	4. **I Love You A Thousand Ways** Jockey #8	King 918
10/13/51	8	2	5. **I'm Waiting Just For You** Jockey #8	King 969
12/8/51+	7	4	6. **Slow Poke** Juke Box #7 / Best Seller #8	King 998
8/10/59	15	7	7. Soldier's Joy	Columbia 41419
3/2/63	1 (4)	25	8. **Lonesome 7-7203**	King 5712
			HAYES, Wade	
			Singer/songwriter from Bethel Acres, Oklahoma.	
12/17/94+	1 (2)	16	1. **Old Enough To Know Better**	Columbia 77739
4/8/95	4	14	2. **I'm Still Dancin' With You**	Columbia 77842
7/29/95	10	12	3. **Don't Stop**	Columbia 77954
12/16/95+	5	13	4. **What I Meant To Say**	Columbia 78087
5/25/96	10 ↑	9 ↑	5. On A Good Night	Columbia 78312
			HEAD, Roy	
			Born on 9/1/41 in Three Rivers, Texas. Had Pop career in the mid-1960s.	
5/17/75	19	6	1. The Most Wanted Woman In Town	Shannon 829
3/13/76	28	5	2. The Door I Used To Close	ABC/Dot 17608
12/3/77+	16	9	3. Come To Me	ABC/Dot 17722
4/29/78	19	6	4. Now You See 'Em, Now You Don't	ABC 12346
8/19/78	28	3	5. Tonight's The Night (It's Gonna Be Alright) #1 Pop hit for Rod Stewart in 1976	ABC 12383
			HEAP, Jimmy, And The Melody Masters with Perk Williams	
			Heap born James Arthur Heap on 3/3/22 in Taylor, Texas. Died on 12/4/77. Worked on KTAE-Taylor, 1948-58. Worked on *Big D Jamboree*, KRLD-Dallas. Had own band, The Melody Masters, featuring lead singer Perk Williams.	
1/9/54	5	13	1. **Release Me** Best Seller #5 / Juke Box #8 / Jockey #10; Esther Phillips and Engelbert Humperdinck had Pop hit versions	Capitol 2518

DATE	POS	WKS	ARTIST–RECORD TITLE	LABEL & NO.
			HEATH, Boyd	
			Emcee of the NBC-TV show *Saturday Night Jamboree* in 1949.	
5/5/45	**7**	1	1. **Smoke On The Water**	Bluebird 33-0522
			HELMS, Bobby	
			Born on 8/15/36 in Bloomington, Indiana. Singer/guitarist. Appeared on father's local TV show for six years.	
3/30/57	**1 (4)**	52	1. **Fraulein**	Decca 30194
			Jockey #1(4) / Best Seller #1(3) / Juke Box #9	
10/14/57	**1 (4)**	26	● 2. **My Special Angel**	Decca 30423
			Best Seller #1(4) / Jockey #1(1)	
12/23/57	**13**	1	3. Jingle Bell Rock [X]	Decca 30513
			Jockey #13	
3/3/58	**10**	9	4. **Just A Little Lonesome**	Decca 30557
			Best Seller #10 / Jockey #12	
5/12/58	**5**	12	5. **Jacqueline**	Decca 30619
			Best Seller #5; from the movie *The Case Against Brooklyn* starring Darren McGavin	
3/30/59	**26**	3	6. New River Train	Decca 30831
10/24/60	**16**	4	7. Lonely River Rhine	Decca 31148
			HENHOUSE FIVE PLUS TOO—see STEVENS, Ray	
			HERNDON, Ty	
			Singer from Butler, Alabama. Sentenced to five years probation for felony drug possession after an incident in a park in Fort Worth, Texas, on 6/13/95.	
3/18/95	**1 (1)**	16	1. **What Mattered Most**	Epic 77843
6/24/95	**7**	17	2. **I Want My Goodbye Back**	Epic 77946
12/16/95+	**21**	9	3. Heart Half Empty	Epic 78073
			TY HERNDON featuring Stephanie Bentley	
			HERRING, Red	
7/4/60	**27**	2	1. Wasted Love	Country Jub. 533
			HEWITT, Dolph	
			Born Dolph Edward Hewitt on 7/15/14 in West Finley, Pennsylvania. Regular on the WLS *National Barn Dance*, 1946-60.	
12/17/49	**8**	1	1. **I Wish I Knew**	RCA Victor 0107
			Jockey #8	
			HIGHWAY 101	
			Quartet consisting of Paulette Carlson (lead vocals, guitar), Scott "Cactus" Moser (vocals, drums), Curtis Stone (vocals, bass) and Jack Daniels (vocals, guitar). Formed in late 1986 in Los Angeles. Stone is the son of Cliffie Stone. Carlson left the group in late 1990. Nikki Nelson joined in early 1991 as female lead singer. CMA Awards: 1988 and 1989 Vocal Group of the Year.	
2/7/87	**4**	13	1. **The Bed You Made For Me**	Warner 28483
6/6/87	**2 (1)**	15	2. **Whiskey, If You Were A Woman**	Warner 28372
10/17/87	**1 (2)**	14	3. **Somewhere Tonight**	Warner 28223

DATE	POS	WKS	ARTIST– RECORD TITLE	LABEL & NO.
2/27/88	**1** (1)	13	4. **Cry, Cry, Cry**	Warner 28105
7/2/88	**1** (1)	14	5. **(Do You Love Me) Just Say Yes**	Warner 27867
11/12/88+	**5**	13	6. **All The Reasons Why**	Warner 27735
3/4/89	**7**	11	7. **Setting Me Up**	Warner 27581
			written by Mark Knopfler of the rock group Dire Straits	
7/8/89	**6**	13	8. **Honky Tonk Heart**	Warner 22955
10/14/89+	**1** (1)	17	9. **Who's Lonely Now**	Warner 22779
3/3/90	**4**	14	10. **Walkin', Talkin', Cryin', Barely Beatin' Broken**	
			Heart	Warner 19968
			written by Roger Miller and Justin Tubb	
6/16/90	**11**	10	11. This Side Of Goodbye	Warner 19829
10/20/90	**14**	14	12. Someone Else's Trouble Now	Warner 19593
4/27/91	**14**	12	13. Bing Bang Boom	Warner 19346
			first release with new vocalist, Nikki Nelson	
11/2/91	**31**	4	14. The Blame	Warner 19203
2/22/92	**22**	7	15. Baby, I'm Missing You	Warner 19043
			HILL, Billy—see BILLY	
			HILL, Faith	
			Born on 9/21/67 in Jackson, Mississippi. Adopted at less than a week old and raised as Audrey Faith Perry in Star, Mississippi.	
11/6/93+	**1** (4)	17	1. **Wild One**	Warner 18411
2/26/94	**1** (1)	18	2. **Piece Of My Heart**	Warner 18261
			#12 Pop hit for Big Brother And The Holding Company (Janis Joplin) in 1968	
7/16/94	**35**	3	3. But I Will	Warner 18179
10/15/94	**2** (2)	17	4. **Take Me As I Am**	Warner LP Cut
			above 4 from the album Take Me As I Am on Warner 45389	
8/19/95	**5**	13	5. **Let's Go To Vegas**	Warner 17817
11/25/95+	**1** (3)	18	6. **It Matters To Me**	Warner 17718
3/9/96	**3**	18	7. **Someone Else's Dream**	Warner LP Cut
			above 3 from the album It Matters To Me on Warner 45872	
			HILL, Goldie	
			Born Argolda Voncile Hill on 1/11/33 in Karnes City, Texas. Appeared on the *Louisiana Hayride* radio shows starting in the early '50s. Married Carl Smith in 1957. Billed as "The Golden Hillbilly."	
1/10/53	**1** (3)	9	1. **I Let The Stars Get In My Eyes**	Decca 28473
			GOLDIE HILL (The Golden Hillbilly)	
			Juke Box #1 / Best Seller #4;	
			answer song to Slim Willet's "Don't Let The Stars Get In Your Eyes"	
7/3/54	**4**	21	2. **Looking Back To See**	Decca 29145
			GOLDIE HILL - JUSTIN TUBB	
			Juke Box #4 / Best Seller #5 / Jockey #5	
1/8/55	**11**	2	3. Sure Fire Kisses	Decca 29349
			JUSTIN TUBB - GOLDIE HILL	
			Jockey #11 / Best Seller #13	
3/26/55	**14**	2	4. Are You Mine	Decca 29411
			RED SOVINE - GOLDIE HILL	
			Best Seller #14	
2/23/59	**17**	4	5. Yankee, Go Home	Decca 30826
			Red Sovine (narration)	

DATE	POS	WKS	ARTIST– RECORD TITLE	LABEL & NO.
			### HILL, Tiny, and His Orchestra	
			Hill born Harry Hill on 7/19/06 in Sullivan Township, Illinois. Died in 1972. Nicknamed Tiny because of his weight (350 pounds). Formed his own trio in 1931, later had The Five Jacks. Own big band in 1933. Worked as drummer with Byron Dunbar in the mid-1930s.	
1/26/46	3	4	1. **Sioux City Sue**	Mercury 2024
1/10/48	5	1	2. **Never Trust A Woman** **TINY HILL And the Cactus Cutups**	Mercury 6062
2/3/51	7	2	3. **Hot Rod Race** [N] Best Seller #7	Mercury 5547
3/24/51	10	1	4. **I'll Sail My Ship Alone** Juke Box #10	Mercury 5508
			### HILLMAN, Chris	
			Born on 12/4/44 in San Diego County, California. Member of The Byrds, 1964-68. Formed the Flying Burrito Brothers with Gram Parsons in 1968. Went solo in 1972. Married Connie Pappas, Elton John's former manager and head of his Rocket Records. Formed country group The Desert Rose Band in 1986.	
5/27/89	6	13	1. **You Ain't Going Nowhere** **CHRIS HILLMAN & ROGER McGUINN** written by Bob Dylan	Universal 66006
			### HITCHCOCK, Stan	
			Born on 3/21/37 in Pleasant Hope, Missouri. Worked as a DJ on KWTO and KTTS in Springfield, Missouri. Moved to Nashville in 1962. Own TV series in the mid-1960s. One-time program director for Country Music Television.	
11/1/69	17	8	1. Honey, I'm Home	Epic 10525
			### HOBBS, Becky	
			Born Rebecca Ann Hobbs on 1/24/50 in Bartlesville, Oklahoma. In all-girl band, Surprise Package, while attending Tulsa University. Moved to Baton Rouge; performed with Swamp Fox, 1971-73. Moved to Los Angeles in 1973 and wrote songs for Helen Reddy, Shirley Bassey, Jane Olivor and others. Moved to Nashville in 1982.	
7/23/83	10	10	1. **Let's Get Over Them Together** **MOE BANDY featuring BECKY HOBBS**	Columbia 03970
7/27/85	37	2	2. Hottest "Ex" In Texas	EMI America 8273
4/23/88	31	4	3. Jones On The Jukebox title refers to George Jones	MTM 72104
9/9/89	39	2	4. Do You Feel The Same Way Too?	RCA 8974
			### HOBBS, Bud, with His Trail Herders	
			Vocalist/guitarist. Own radio show in San Francisco during the mid-1940s.	
9/25/48	13	1	1. Lazy Mary Juke Box #13	MGM 10206
1/29/49	12	4	2. I Heard About You Juke Box #12 / Best Seller #13	MGM 10305
5/21/49	12	1	3. Candy Kisses Juke Box #12 / Best Seller #15	MGM 10366

DATE	POS	WKS	ARTIST– RECORD TITLE	LABEL & NO.
			HOGSED, Roy	
			Born on 12/24/19 in Flippin, Arkansas.	Capitol 40120
8/21/48	**15**	1	1. Cocaine Blues Juke Box #15	
			HOLLOWELL, Terri	
			Born on 7/2/56 in Jeffersonville, Indiana. Female vocalist.	Con Brio 150
5/5/79	**35**	3	1. May I	
			HOLLY, Doyle	
			Born Hoyle F. Hendricks on 6/30/36 in Perkins, Oklahoma. Worked oilfields in Oklahoma, Kansas and California. Played for a time with the Johnny Burnette band. Worked with Buck Owens's Buckaroos, 1963-70. Own band, the Vanishing Breed, from 1970.	
8/4/73	**29**	6	1. Queen Of The Silver Dollar	Barnaby 5018
11/10/73	**17**	7	2. Lila	Barnaby 5027
			HOMER AND JETHRO	
			Comedy duo of Henry D. "Homer" Haynes (born 7/29/17, Knoxville; died 8/7/71), guitar; and Kenneth C. "Jethro" Burns (born 3/10/23, Knoxville; died 2/4/89), mandolin. Duo formed in 1932 and worked local radio shows and fairs. Appeared on WLS *National Barn Dance* beginning in 1950. Worked with Chet Atkins as the Nashville String Band.	
3/26/49	**14**	1	1. I Feel That Old Age Creeping On [N] Juke Box #14	King 749
8/27/49	**9**	1	2. **Baby, It's Cold Outside** [N] **HOMER and JETHRO with June Carter** Best Seller #9; 45 rpm: 48-0075	RCA Victor 0078
11/5/49	**14**	1	3. Tennessee Border—No. 2 [N] Juke Box #14; 45 rpm: 48-0113	RCA Victor 0110
5/23/53	**2** (2)	9	4. **(How Much Is) That Hound Dog In The Window**[N] Best Seller #2 / Juke Box #3 / Jockey #10	RCA 5280
8/14/54	**14**	1	5. Hernando's Hideaway [N] Best Seller #14	RCA 5788
10/19/59	**26**	3	6. The Battle Of Kookamonga [N] a parody of "The Battle Of New Orleans"	RCA 7585
			HOOSIER HOT SHOTS	
			Novelty group from Fort Wayne, Indiana. Consisted of Paul "Hezzie" Trietsch (song whistle, washboard, drums, alto horn), Kenneth "Rudy" Trietsch (banjo, guitar, bass horn), Charles Otto "Gabe" Ward (clarinet, saxophone, fife) and Frank Kettering (banjo, guitar, flute, piano, bass fiddle). Regulars on WLS-Chicago *National Barn Dance*, 1933-42. Also appeared in several Western movies. Group disbanded in the mid-1950s.	
6/17/44	**3**	2	1. **She Broke My Heart In Three Places** [N]	Decca 4442
1/26/46	**3**	10	2. **Someday (You'll Want Me To Want You)** [N] **HOOSIER HOT SHOTS and SALLY FOSTER** Sally Foster and Gil Taylor (vocals)	Decca 18738
2/9/46	**2** (1)	16	3. **Sioux City Sue** [N] **HOOSIER HOT SHOTS and TWO TON BAKER**	Decca 18745

DATE	POS	WKS	ARTIST– RECORD TITLE	LABEL & NO.
			HORNSBY, Bruce, And The Range	
			Born on 11/23/54 in Williamsburg, Virginia. Singer/pianist/songwriter/ leader of jazz-influenced Pop quintet The Range. Formed The Range in 1984 with George Marinelli, Jr., Joe Puerta, John Molo and David Mansfield (replaced by Peter Harris by 1990). Won the 1986 Best New Artist Grammy Award.	
4/18/87	38	2	1. Mandolin Rain	RCA 5087
			HORTON, Billie Jean	
			Billie-Jean Jones Eshlimar from Bossier City, Louisiana. Married to Hank Williams from 10/18/52 until his death 10 weeks later. Married to Johnny Horton from September 1953 until his death on 11/5/60.	
8/28/61	29	3	1. Ocean Of Tears	Fox 266
			HORTON, Johnny	
			Born on 4/30/25 in Los Angeles; raised in Tyler, Texas. Died in an automobile accident on 11/5/60. Attended Baylor University and University of Seattle on athletic scholarships. Worked in the fishing industry in Alaska. Appeared on *Hometown Jamboree*, KLAC-Los Angeles, and KXLA-Pasadena. Billed as "The Singing Fisherman." Joined the *Louisiana Hayride* in 1951. First recorded for Cormac in 1951. On KLTV-Tyler radio in the mid-1950s. Married to Billie Jean Jones Eshlimar (Billie Jean Horton), widow of Hank Williams, from September 1953 until his death.	
5/5/56	9	12	1. **Honky-Tonk Man** Jockey #9 / Best Seller #14	Columbia 21504
9/8/56	7	13	2. **I'm A One-Woman Man** Jockey #7 / Best Seller #9 / Juke Box #9	Columbia 21538
2/23/57	11	5	3. **I'm Coming Home** Jockey #11 / Best Seller #15	Columbia 40813
5/27/57	9	1	4. **The Woman I Need** Juke Box #9	Columbia 40919
9/29/58	8	8	5. **All Grown Up** Jockey #8	Columbia 41210
1/12/59	1 (1)	23	6. **When It's Springtime In Alaska (It's Forty Below)**	Columbia 41308
4/27/59	1 (10)	21	● 7. **The Battle Of New Orleans** original melody written in celebration of the final battle of the War of 1812	Columbia 41339
9/7/59	10	9	8. **Johnny Reb/**	
9/7/59	19	7	9. Sal's Got A Sugar Lip	Columbia 41437
3/28/60	6	15	10. **Sink The Bismarck** inspired by the movie starring Kenneth Moore, which is based on the sinking of the German battleship in World War II	Columbia 41568
11/14/60+	1 (5)	22	11. **North To Alaska** title song from the movie starring John Wayne	Columbia 41782
4/24/61	9	8	12. **Sleepy-Eyed John**	Columbia 41963
4/14/62	11	12	13. Honky-Tonk Man [R]	Columbia 42302
2/9/63	26	5	14. All Grown Up [R]	Columbia 42653
			HOUSE, James	
			Born on 3/21/55 in Sacramento, California. Vocal coach for actor Dustin Hoffman for the movie *Ishtar*.	
4/29/89	25	7	1. Don't Quit Me Now	MCA 53510
2/11/95	25	6	2. Little By Little	Epic 77752
6/10/95	6	14	3. **This Is Me Missing You**	Epic 77870

DATE	POS	WKS	ARTIST–RECORD TITLE	LABEL & NO.
			HOUSTON, David	
			Born on 12/9/38 in Bossier City, Louisiana. Died on 11/30/93 after suffering a ruptured brain aneurysm on 11/25/93. Godson of 1920s Pop star Gene Austin, and descended from Sam Houston and Robert E. Lee. Worked on *Louisiana Hayride* radio shows from age 12. Appeared in the 1967 movie *Cottonpickin' Chicken-Pluckers*. With the *Grand Ole Opry* since 1972.	
			(a) DAVID HOUSTON & TAMMY WYNETTE	
			(b) DAVID HOUSTON and BARBARA MANDRELL	
10/19/63	**2** (1)	18	1. **Mountain Of Love**	Epic 9625
4/4/64	**17**	12	2. Chickashay/	
3/7/64	**37**	4	3. Passing Through	Epic 9658
7/11/64	**11**	15	4. One If For Him, Two If For Me	Epic 9690
10/24/64	**17**	12	5. Love Looks Good On You	Epic 9720
3/6/65	**18**	12	6. Sweet, Sweet Judy	Epic 9746
9/18/65	**3**	16	7. **Livin' In A House Full Of Love**	Epic 9831
6/25/66	**1** (9)	24	8. **Almost Persuaded**	Epic 10025
1/7/67	**3**	14	9. **A Loser's Cathedral/**	
12/24/66+	**14**	9	10. Where Could I Go? (But To Her)	Epic 10102
5/13/67	**1** (1)	15	11. **With One Exception**	Epic 10154
7/29/67	**1** (2)	16	12. **My Elusive Dreams** (a)	Epic 10194
9/30/67	**1** (2)	16	13. **You Mean The World To Me**	Epic 10224
2/10/68	**11**	11	14. It's All Over (a)	Epic 10274
3/16/68	**1** (1)	13	15. **Have A Little Faith**	Epic 10291
6/22/68	**1** (1)	15	16. **Already It's Heaven**	Epic 10338
10/19/68	**2** (2)	14	17. **Where Love Used To Live**	Epic 10394
1/25/69	**4**	16	18. **My Woman's Good To Me**	Epic 10430
7/12/69	**3**	14	19. **I'm Down To My Last "I Love You"**	Epic 10488
11/15/69+	**1** (4)	16	20. **Baby, Baby (I Know You're A Lady)**	Epic 10539
4/18/70	**3**	14	21. **I Do My Swinging At Home**	Epic 10596
8/15/70	**6**	14	22. **Wonders Of The Wine**	Epic 10643
10/17/70	**6**	11	23. **After Closing Time** (b)	Epic 10656
1/23/71	**2** (4)	13	24. **A Woman Always Knows**	Epic 10696
7/3/71	**9**	10	25. **Nashville**	Epic 10748
10/23/71	**10**	12	26. **Maiden's Prayer/**	
10/23/71	**32**	12	27. Home Sweet Home	Epic 10778
10/30/71	**20**	7	28. We've Got Everything But Love (b)	Epic 10779
3/11/72	**18**	8	29. The Day That Love Walked In	Epic 10830
6/24/72	**8**	10	30. **Soft, Sweet And Warm**	Epic 10870
10/7/72	**24**	10	31. A Perfect Match (b)	Epic 10908
1/27/73	**2** (2)	12	32. **Good Things**	Epic 10939
6/23/73	**3**	11	33. **She's All Woman**	Epic 10995
12/1/73	**22**	6	34. The Lady Of The Night	Epic 11048
1/19/74	**6**	12	35. **I Love You, I Love You** (b)	Epic 11068
5/18/74	**33**	4	36. That Same Ol' Look Of Love	Epic 11096
7/6/74	**40**	2	37. Lovin' You Is Worth It (b)	Epic 11120
9/21/74	**14**	9	38. Ten Commandments Of Love (b)	Epic 20005
			#22 Pop hit for Harvey & The Moonglows in 1958	

DATE	POS	WKS	ARTIST–RECORD TITLE	LABEL & NO.
10/12/74	9	11	39. **Can't You Feel It**	Epic 50009
4/19/75	36	2	40. A Man Needs Love	Epic 50066
7/26/75	40	1	41. I'll Be Your Steppin' Stone	Epic 50113
12/13/75	35	2	42. The Woman On My Mind	Epic 50156
10/23/76	24	6	43. Come On Down (To Our Favorite Forget-About-Her Place)	Epic 50275
5/28/77	33	4	44. So Many Ways #6 Pop hit for Brook Benton in 1959	Gusto/Starday 156
5/12/79	33	4	45. Faded Love And Winter Roses	Elektra 46028
			HOWARD, Eddy	
			Born on 9/12/14 in Woodland, California. Died on 5/23/63. One of the top Pop singers of the '40s and early '50s.	
8/9/47	5	1	1. **Ragtime Cowboy Joe**	Majestic 1155
			HOWARD, Harlan	
			Born on 9/8/27 in Lexington, Kentucky; raised in Detroit. Moved to Los Angeles in the mid-1950s. Hit songwriter; won 10 BMI awards in 1961. Married for a time to Jan Howard.	
5/8/71	38	4	1. Sunday Morning Christian	Nugget 1058
			HOWARD, Jan	
			Born Lula Grace Johnson on 3/13/30 in West Plains, Missouri. Moved to Los Angeles in 1953. Married songwriter Harlan Howard. Moved to Nashville in the mid-1960s; did tours and TV shows with Bill Anderson for seven years. Worked with the Johnny Cash and Tammy Wynette shows. Two of her three sons from a previous marriage have died, one in Vietnam shortly after the release of her song "My Son." Joined the *Grand Ole Opry* in 1971. (a) BILL ANDERSON & JAN HOWARD	
1/11/60	13	12	1. The One You Slip Around With	Challenge 59059
5/30/60	26	2	2. Wrong Company **WYNN STEWART and JAN HOWARD**	Challenge 59071
11/16/63	27	3	3. I Wish I Was A Single Girl Again	Capitol 5035
1/30/65	25	11	4. What Makes A Man Wander?	Decca 31701
3/12/66	29	5	5. I Know You're Married (But I Love You Still (a)	Decca 31884
5/28/66	5	15	6. **Evil On Your Mind**	Decca 31933
10/8/66	10	12	7. **Bad Seed**	Decca 32016
4/22/67	32	4	8. Any Old Way You Do	Decca 32096
8/26/67	26	5	9. Roll Over And Play Dead	Decca 32154
11/11/67	1 (4)	10	10. **For Loving You** (a)	Decca 32197
3/30/68	16	10	11. Count Your Blessings, Woman	Decca 32269
8/24/68	27	9	12. I Still Believe In Love	Decca 32357
11/30/68+	15	12	13. My Son	Decca 32407
3/22/69	24	9	14. When We Tried	Decca 32447
10/11/69	20	5	15. We Had All The Good Things Going	Decca 32543
11/22/69+	2 (1)	14	16. **If It's All The Same To You** (a)	Decca 32511
4/18/70	26	5	17. Rock Me Back To Little Rock	Decca 32636
6/27/70	4	13	18. **Someday We'll Be Together** (a) #1 Pop hit for Diana Ross & The Supremes in 1969	Decca 32689

DATE	POS	WKS	ARTIST– RECORD TITLE	LABEL & NO.
10/23/71	**4**	13	19. **Dis-Satisfied** (a)	Decca 32877
2/5/72	**36**	3	20. Love Is Like A Spinning Wheel	Decca 32905
			HOWARD, Jim	
7/25/64	**38**	6	1. Meet Me Tonight Outside Of Town	Del-Mar 1013
			HUDSON, Larry G.	
			Born on 12/19/49 in Hawkinsville, Georgia; raised in Unadilla, Georgia. Guitarist at age 11 in Future Farmer's Of America String Band. Replaced Razzy Bailey at the Nashville South Club, in Macon, Georgia in 1974.	
11/25/78	**37**	3	1. Just Out Of Reach Of My Two Open Arms #24 Pop hit for Solomon Burke in 1961	Lone Star 702
2/17/79	**31**	5	2. Loving You Is A Natural High	Lone Star 706
4/19/80	**34**	4	3. I Can't Cheat	Mercury 57015
9/20/80	**39**	2	4. I'm Still In Love With You	Mercury 57029
			HUMMERS, The	
8/25/73	**38**	1	1. Old Betsy Goes Boing, Boing, Boing adapted from a Mazda jingle	Capitol 3646
			HUMPERDINCK, Engelbert	
			Born Arnold George Dorsey on 5/2/36 in Madras, India. To Leicester, England, in 1947. First recorded for Decca in 1958. Met Tom Jones's manager, Gordon Mills, in 1965, who suggested his name change to Engelbert Humperdinck (a famous German opera composer). Starred in his own musical variety TV series in 1970.	
2/26/77	**40**	2	● 1. After The Lovin'	Epic 50270
6/25/83	**39**	1	2. Til You And Your Lover Are Lovers Again	Epic 03817
			HUNLEY, Con	
			Born Conrad Logan Hunley on 4/9/45 in Luttrell, Tennessee. Worked local clubs in Knoxville and formed his own band in 1976. Moved to Nashville in 1978 and worked at George Jones's Possum Holler Club.	
2/25/78	**34**	5	1. Cry Cry Darling	Warner 8520
5/27/78	**13**	9	2. Week-End Friend	Warner 8572
10/21/78	**14**	7	3. You've Still Got A Place In My Heart	Warner 8671
2/10/79	**14**	9	4. I've Been Waiting For You All Of My Life #48 Pop hit for Paul Anka in 1981	Warner 8723
6/16/79	**20**	6	5. Since I Fell For You #4 Pop hit for Lenny Welch in 1963	Warner 8812
12/1/79+	**20**	7	6. I Don't Want To Lose You	Warner 49090
3/29/80	**19**	7	7. You Lay A Whole Lot Of Love On Me	Warner 49187
9/20/80	**19**	5	8. They Never Lost You	Warner 49528
1/17/81	**11**	9	9. What's New With You	Warner 49613
10/3/81	**17**	6	10. She's Steppin' Out	Warner 49800
1/30/82	**20**	6	11. No Relief In Sight	Warner 49887
6/5/82	**12**	10	12. Oh Girl #1 Pop hit for The Chi-Lites in 1972; The Oak Ridge Boys (backing vocals)	Warner 50058

DATE	POS	WKS	ARTIST–RECORD TITLE	LABEL & NO.
			HURT, Cindy	
			Born in 1956 in Mundelein, Illinois. Studied music, drama and voice at Butler University in Indianapolis. Did commercials in Chicago; worked with all-girl quartet, Magic. Toured with the musical *Sophisticated Ladies* in 1980.	
2/27/82	**28**	5	1. Don't Come Knockin	Churchill 94000
7/17/82	**35**	3	2. Talk To Me Loneliness	Churchill 94004
			HUSKY, Ferlin	
			Born on 12/3/25 near Flat River, Missouri. Spent five years in U.S. Merchant Marines during World War II. After discharge, worked clubs in Bakersfield. Recorded as Terry Preston in the early 1950s; also did humorous recordings as Simon Crum. Worked with Tennessee Ernie Ford in the early 1950s. Appeared as a dramatic actor on Kraft TV theater. Appeared in the movies *Mr. Rock & Roll* (1957) and *Country Music Holiday* (1958). Married six times; has seven children. Had a heart operation in 1977. Backing group called The Hushpuppies.	
			JEAN SHEPARD & FERLIN HUSKEY:	
7/25/53	**1** (6)	23	1. **A Dear John Letter** Best Seller #1(6) / Juke Box #1(4) / Jockey #2	Capitol 2502
10/10/53	**4**	7	2. **Forgive Me John** Best Seller #4 / Juke Box #6 / Jockey #8	Capitol 2586
			FERLIN HUSKEY:	
1/15/55	**6**	10	3. **I Feel Better All Over (More Than Anywhere's Else)/** Jockey #6 / Best Seller #15	
1/15/55	**7**	8	4. **Little Tom** Jockey #7	Capitol 3001
4/16/55	**5**	15	5. **Cuzz Yore So Sweet** [N] **SIMON CRUM** Jockey #5	Capitol 3063
5/28/55	**14**	1	6. I'll Baby Sit With You **FERLIN HUSKEY and His Hush Puppies** Best Seller #14	Capitol 3097
			FERLIN HUSKY:	
2/23/57	**1** (10)	27	7. **Gone** Best Seller #1(10) / Jockey #1(9) / Juke Box #1(5); originally recorded by Husky in 1952 as by Terry Preston	Capitol 3628
7/1/57	**8**	13	8. **A Fallen Star/** Best Seller #8 / Jockey #8	
7/15/57	**12**	1	9. Prize Possession Jockey #12	Capitol 3742
10/27/58	**23**	1	10. I Will	Capitol 4046
11/3/58+	**2** (3)	24	11. **Country Music Is Here To Stay** [N] **SIMON CRUM**	Capitol 4073
2/16/59	**14**	12	12. My Reason For Living	Capitol 4123
6/1/59	**11**	10	13. Draggin' The River	Capitol 4186
11/16/59	**21**	8	14. Black Sheep	Capitol 4278
9/5/60	**1** (10)	36	15. **Wings Of A Dove**	Capitol 4406
10/9/61	**23**	1	16. Willow Tree	Capitol 4594
1/27/62	**13**	10	17. The Waltz You Saved For Me Wayne King's familiar theme song - written by King in 1930	Capitol 4650
5/26/62	**16**	11	18. Somebody Save Me	Capitol 4721

DATE	POS	WKS	ARTIST–RECORD TITLE	LABEL & NO.
9/22/62	**28**	1	19. Stand Up	Capitol 4779
12/1/62	**21**	2	20. It Was You	Capitol 4853
2/22/64	**13**	20	21. Timber I'm Falling	Capitol 5111
6/4/66	**27**	5	22. I Could Sing All Night	Capitol 5615
8/27/66	**17**	8	23. I Hear Little Rock Calling	Capitol 5679
12/24/66+	**4**	14	24. **Once**	Capitol 5775
4/29/67	**37**	3	25. What Am I Gonna Do Now	Capitol 5852
8/12/67	**14**	11	26. You Pushed Me Too Far	Capitol 5938
1/13/68	**4**	15	27. **Just For You**	Capitol 2048
6/8/68	**26**	8	28. I Promised You The World	Capitol 2154
11/9/68	**25**	7	29. White Fences And Evergreen Trees	Capitol 2288
4/19/69	**33**	2	30. Flat River, Mo.	Capitol 2411
7/12/69	**16**	11	31. That's Why I Love You So Much	Capitol 2512
12/13/69	**21**	7	32. Every Step Of The Way	Capitol 2666
5/23/70	**11**	11	33. Heavenly Sunshine	Capitol 2793
1/16/71	**14**	7	34. Sweet Misery	Capitol 2999
4/17/71	**28**	7	35. One More Time	Capitol 3069
5/20/72	**39**	4	36. Just Plain Lonely	Capitol 3308
2/17/73	**35**	4	37. True True Lovin' [R]	ABC 11345
			originally made #46 in 1965 on Capitol 5355	
12/8/73+	**17**	6	38. Rosie Cries A Lot	ABC 11395
6/22/74	**26**	6	39. Freckles And Polliwog Days	ABC 11432
2/8/75	**34**	3	40. Champagne Ladies And Blue Ribbon Babies	ABC 12048
6/7/75	**37**	2	41. Burning	ABC 12085

IFIELD, Frank

Born on 11/30/37 in Coventry, England. Began career as a teenager in Australia with his own radio and TV shows. Signed to Columbia Records in England in 1959.

DATE	POS	WKS	ARTIST–RECORD TITLE	LABEL & NO.
11/19/66	**28**	8	1. Call Her Your Sweetheart	Hickory 1411

IGLESIAS, Julio

Born on 9/23/43 in Madrid. Spanish singer, immensely popular worldwide. Soccer goalie for the pro Real Madrid team until temporary paralysis from a car crash. CMA Award: Vocal Duo of the Year (with Willie Nelson).

DATE	POS	WKS	ARTIST–RECORD TITLE	LABEL & NO.
3/17/84	**1** (2)	13	● 1. **To All The Girls I've Loved Before** **JULIO IGLESIAS & WILLIE NELSON**	Columbia 04217
10/15/88	**8**	12	2. **Spanish Eyes** **WILLIE NELSON with JULIO IGLESIAS**	Columbia 08066

INGLE, Red, & The Natural Seven

Red's real name is Ernest I. Ingle. Performed into the '50s, now reportedly deceased. Comic singer/violinist/clarinetist/saxophonist.

DATE	POS	WKS	ARTIST–RECORD TITLE	LABEL & NO.
6/21/47	**2** (11)	18	1. **Temptation (Tim-Tayshun)** [N] Jo Stafford as Cinderella G. Stump (vocal)	Capitol 412

DATE	POS	WKS	ARTIST–RECORD TITLE	LABEL & NO.
			INMAN, Autry	
			Born Robert Autry Inman on 1/6/29 in Florence, Alabama. Died on 9/6/88. Worked on WLAY-Muscle Shoals and WWVA-Wheeling *Jamboree*. With Cowboy Copas' Oklahoma Cowboys, 1949-50. Played bass for George Morgan's Candy Kids, 1950-52.	
7/11/53	4	4	1. **That's All Right** Juke Box #4	Decca 28629
4/13/63	22	3	2. The Volunteer	Sims 131
11/16/68	14	12	3. Ballad Of Two Brothers patriotic-styled narrative, featuring strains of "The Battle Hymn Of The Republic"	Epic 10389
			IRBY, Jerry, And His Texas Ranchers	
			Irby is the owner of Jerry Irby's Texas Corral restaurant in his native city of Houston.	
6/19/48	11	2	1. Cryin' In My Beer Juke Box #11	MGM 10151
7/3/48	10	1	2. **Great Long Pistol** Juke Box #10	MGM 10188
			IRVING, Lonnie	
			Born on 6/11/32 in Stoneville, North Carolina. Died of leukemia on 12/2/60.	
3/14/60	13	15	1. Pinball Machine first issued on Lonnie Irving label	Starday 486
			IVES, Burl	
			Born on 6/14/09 in Huntington Township, Illinois. Died on 4/14/95. Actor/author/singer. Played semi-pro football. Began Broadway career in the late 1930s. Worked in *This Is The Army* service show during World War II. Own CBS radio show *The Wayfaring Stranger* in 1944. Appeared in many movies, including *Our Man In Havana*, *East Of Eden*, *Cat On A Hot Tin Roof* and *The Big Country*. Narrated the kids' TV classic *Rudolph The Red-Nosed Reindeer*. Worked on the TV series *The Bold Ones* in the early 1970s.	
2/12/49	13	1	1. **Lavender Blue (Dilly Dilly)** **BURL IVES with Captain Stubby & The Buccaneers** Best Seller #13	Decca 24547
5/21/49	8	5	2. **Riders In The Sky (Cowboy Legend)** Juke Box #8 / Best Seller #15	Columbia 38445
7/26/52	6	4	3. **Wild Side Of Life** **BURL IVES and GRADY MARTIN And His Slew Foot Five** Juke Box #6 / Best Seller #10	Decca 28055
2/3/62	2 (2)	17	4. **A Little Bitty Tear**	Decca 31330
4/28/62	9	13	5. **Funny Way Of Laughin'**	Decca 31371
8/11/62	3	11	6. **Call Me Mr. In-Between**	Decca 31405
12/1/62+	12	7	7. Mary Ann Regrets	Decca 31433

DATE	POS	WKS	ARTIST– RECORD TITLE	LABEL & NO.

J

JACKSON, Alan

Born Alan Eugene Jackson on 10/17/58 in Newnan, Georgia. Worked as a car salesman and carpenter before signing with Glen Campbell's publishing company. Joined the *Grand Ole Opry* in 1991. CMA Award: 1995 Entertainer of the Year.

DATE	POS	WKS	ARTIST– RECORD TITLE	LABEL & NO.
2/17/90	3	21	1. **Here In The Real World**	Arista 9922
7/7/90	3	18	2. **Wanted**	Arista 2032
10/20/90	2 (2)	18	3. **Chasin' That Neon Rainbow**	Arista 2095
2/2/91	1 (2)	18	4. **I'd Love You All Over Again**	Arista 2166
5/25/91	1 (3)	19	5. **Don't Rock The Jukebox**	Arista 2220
9/7/91	1 (1)	19	6. **Someday**	Arista 12335
1/25/92	1 (1)	18	7. **Dallas**	Arista 12385
5/9/92	3	17	8. **Midnight In Montgomery**	Arista 12418
8/8/92	1 (2)	17	9. **Love's Got A Hold On You**	Arista 12447
10/31/92	1 (1)	17	10. **She's Got The Rhythm (And I Got The Blues)**	Arista 12463
2/27/93	4	14	11. **Tonight I Climbed The Wall**	Arista 12514
6/12/93	1 (4)	16	● 12. **Chattahoochee** *CMA Award: Single of the Year*	Arista 12573
10/2/93	2 (1)	13	13. **Mercury Blues**	Arista 12607
2/5/94	4	15	14. **(Who Says) You Can't Have It All**	Arista 12649
6/25/94	1 (3)	14	15. **Summertime Blues** *#8 Pop hit for Eddie Cochran in 1958*	Arista 12697
9/24/94	1 (3)	17	16. **Livin' On Love**	Arista 12745
12/10/94+	1 (1)	11	17. **Gone Country**	Arista 12778
3/4/95	6	14	18. **Song For The Life**	Arista 12792
6/10/95	1 (1)	16	19. **I Don't Even Know Your Name**	Arista 12830
10/28/95	1 (2)	19	20. **Tall, Tall Trees** *written by George Jones and Roger Miller*	Arista 12879
1/13/96	1 (1)	18	21. **I'll Try** *from the album The Greatest Hits Collection on Arista 18801*	Arista LP Cut
5/4/96	3	12 ↑	22. **Home**	Arista 12942

JACKSON, Stonewall

His real name (he is descended from General Thomas Jonathan "Stonewall" Jackson). Born on 11/6/32 in Emerson, North Carolina. Singer/guitarist/pianist. In U.S. Army in 1948; served in U.S. Navy, 1949-54. Had own log-trucking company in Georgia in 1955. Moved to Nashville in 1956; discovered by Wesley Rose of Acuff-Rose. With the *Grand Ole Opry* since 1956.

DATE	POS	WKS	ARTIST– RECORD TITLE	LABEL & NO.
11/3/58+	2 (1)	23	1. **Life To Go** *written by George Jones*	Columbia 41257
6/8/59	1 (5)	19	2. **Waterloo**/	
6/29/59	24	5	3. Smoke Along The Track	Columbia 41393
11/23/59	29	1	4. Igmoo (The Pride Of South Central High)	Columbia 41488
1/18/60	12	12	5. Mary Don't You Weep	Columbia 41533
4/4/60	6	17	6. **Why I'm Walkin'**/	
4/25/60	15	5	7. Life Of A Poor Boy	Columbia 41591

DATE	POS	WKS	ARTIST– RECORD TITLE	LABEL & NO.
11/7/60	13	15	8. A Little Guy Called Joe	Columbia 41785
3/13/61	26	6	9. Greener Pastures	Columbia 41932
8/7/61	27	2	10. Hungry For Love written by Mel Tillis	Columbia 42028
1/20/62	3	22	11. **A Wound Time Can't Erase/**	
2/3/62	18	3	12. Second Choice	Columbia 42229
7/21/62	9	7	13. **Leona/**	
6/30/62	11	10	14. One Look At Heaven	Columbia 42426
1/26/63	11	10	15. Can't Hang Up The Phone	Columbia 42628
5/18/63	8	14	16. **Old Showboat**	Columbia 42765
11/9/63	15	8	17. Wild Wild Wind	Columbia 42846
12/7/63+	1 (1)	22	18. **B.J. The D.J.**	Columbia 42889
4/25/64	24	7	19. Not My Kind Of People	Columbia 43011
9/5/64	4	23	20. **Don't Be Angry** [R] first released on Columbia 40883	Columbia 43076
3/20/65	8	16	21. **I Washed My Hands In Muddy Water** #19 Pop hit for Johnny Rivers in 1966	Columbia 43197
8/28/65	22	5	22. Lost In The Shuffle/	
7/31/65	30	6	23. Trouble And Me	Columbia 43304
12/4/65+	24	11	24. If This House Could Talk	Columbia 43411
5/7/66	24	7	25. The Minute Men (Are Turning In Their Graves)	Columbia 43552
8/20/66	12	12	26. Blues Plus Booze (Means I Lose)	Columbia 43718
2/18/67	5	14	27. **Stamp Out Loneliness**	Columbia 43966
6/24/67	15	12	28. Promises And Hearts (Were Made To Break)	Columbia 44121
11/4/67	27	7	29. This World Holds Nothing (Since You're Gone)	Columbia 44283
3/30/68	39	2	30. Nothing Takes The Place Of Loving You	Columbia 44416
6/29/68	31	4	31. I Believe In Love	Columbia 44501
11/2/68	16	9	32. Angry Words	Columbia 44625
6/28/69	25	5	33. "Never More" Quote The Raven	Columbia 44863
11/1/69	19	6	34. Ship In The Bottle	Columbia 44976
6/5/71	7	11	35. **Me And You And A Dog Named Boo** #5 Pop hit for Lobo in 1971	Columbia 45381

JACKSON, Wanda

Born on 10/20/37 in Maud, Oklahoma. Moved to Bakersfield, California, in 1941. Guitarist/pianist from age nine. Moved to Oklahoma City in 1949. Own radio show on KLPR-Oklahoma City in 1950. Recorded with Hank Thompson in 1954. Had three solo records released while still in high school. Worked with Red Foley's *Ozark Jubilee*, 1955-62; toured with Elvis Presley in 1955 and 1956.

DATE	POS	WKS	ARTIST– RECORD TITLE	LABEL & NO.
7/24/54	8	8	1. **You Can't Have My Love** **WANDA JACKSON and BILLY GRAY** Best Seller #8 / Jockey #8 / Juke Box #10	Decca 29140
10/20/56	15	1	2. I Gotta Know Jockey #15	Capitol 3485
7/31/61	9	14	3. **Right Or Wrong**	Capitol 4553
11/20/61+	6	15	4. **In The Middle Of A Heartache**	Capitol 4635
6/9/62	28	1	5. If I Cried Every Time You Hurt Me	Capitol 4723
6/20/64	36	4	6. The Violet And A Rose	Capitol 5142
3/5/66	18	10	7. The Box It Came In	Capitol 5559
7/2/66	28	6	8. Because It's You	Capitol 5645

DATE	POS	WKS	ARTIST– RECORD TITLE	LABEL & NO.
1/21/67	**11**	12	9. Tears Will Be The Chaser For Your Wine	Capitol 5789
5/27/67	**21**	6	10. Both Sides Of The Line	Capitol 5863
12/23/67+	**22**	6	11. A Girl Don't Have To Drink To Have Fun	Capitol 2021
6/1/68	**34**	5	12. My Baby Walked Right Out On Me	Capitol 2151
10/25/69	**20**	7	13. My Big Iron Skillet	Capitol 2614
2/7/70	**35**	2	14. Two Separate Bar Stools	Capitol 2693
4/25/70	**17**	8	15. A Woman Lives For Love	Capitol 2761
1/2/71	**13**	8	16. Fancy Satin Pillows	Capitol 2986
9/25/71	**25**	3	17. Back Then	Capitol 3143
1/15/72	**35**	3	18. I Already Know (What I'm Getting For My Birthday)	Capitol 3218

JAMES, Sonny

Born James Hugh Loden on 5/1/29 in Hackleburg, Alabama. Singer/songwriter/guitarist. Sang with his four sisters in the Loden Family group from age four. Own radio show in Birmingham, Alabama, while still a teenager. Performed while in the service in the early 1950s. Appeared in the movies *Second Fiddle To A Steel Guitar*, *Nashville Rebel*, *Las Vegas Hillbillies* and *Hillbillys In A Haunted House*. Billed as "The Southern Gentleman" on most of his records.

DATE	POS	WKS	ARTIST– RECORD TITLE	LABEL & NO.
2/7/53	**9**	1	1. **That's Me Without You** Jockey #9	Capitol 2259
11/20/54	**14**	1	2. She Done Give Her Heart To Me Jockey #14	Capitol 2906
3/24/56	**7**	11	3. **For Rent (One Empty Heart)** Jockey #7 / Juke Box #8 / Best Seller #12	Capitol 3357
6/30/56	**11**	6	4. Twenty Feet Of Muddy Water Jockey #11	Capitol 3441
11/10/56	**12**	1	5. The Cat Came Back Jockey #12	Capitol 3542
12/22/56+	**1 (9)**	24	● 6. **Young Love/** Jockey #1(9) / Best Seller #1(7) / Juke Box #1(3)	
1/26/57	**6**	12	7. **You're The Reason I'm In Love** Jockey #6	Capitol 3602
4/13/57	**9**	9	8. **First Date, First Kiss, First Love** Best Seller #9 / Jockey #9	Capitol 3674
8/12/57	**15**	1	9. Lovesick Blues Jockey #15	Capitol 3734
1/6/58	**8**	5	10. **Uh-Huh—mm** Jockey #8 / Best Seller #14	Capitol 3840
5/9/60	**22**	6	11. Jenny Lou	NRC 050
7/20/63	**9**	15	12. **The Minute You're Gone**	Capitol 4969
12/21/63	**17**	9	13. Going Through The Motions (Of Living)	Capitol 5057
3/28/64	**6**	17	14. **Baltimore**	Capitol 5129
8/15/64	**19**	10	15. Ask Marie/	
7/18/64	**27**	6	16. Sugar Lump	Capitol 5197
11/14/64+	**1 (4)**	24	17. **You're The Only World I Know**	Capitol 5280
4/10/65	**2 (1)**	19	18. **I'll Keep Holding On (Just To Your Love)**	Capitol 5375
8/21/65	**1 (3)**	20	19. **Behind The Tear**	Capitol 5454
12/11/65+	**3**	18	20. **True Love's A Blessing**	Capitol 5536
4/16/66	**1 (2)**	19	21. **Take Good Care Of Her** #7 Pop hit for Adam Wade in 1961	Capitol 5612
8/13/66	**2 (2)**	20	22. **Room In Your Heart**	Capitol 5690

DATE	POS	WKS	ARTIST– RECORD TITLE	LABEL & NO.
3/4/67	**1** (2)	17	23. **Need You**	Capitol 5833
6/24/67	**1** (4)	15	24. **I'll Never Find Another You** #4 Pop hit for The Seekers in 1965	Capitol 5914
10/14/67	**1** (5)	14	25. **It's The Little Things**	Capitol 5987
2/3/68	**1** (3)	15	26. **A World Of Our Own** #19 Pop hit for The Seekers in 1965	Capitol 2067
6/8/68	**1** (1)	16	27. **Heaven Says Hello**	Capitol 2155
10/12/68	**1** (1)	16	28. **Born To Be With You** #5 Pop hit for The Chordettes in 1956	Capitol 2271
1/25/69	**1** (3)	15	29. **Only The Lonely** #2 Pop hit for Roy Orbison in 1960	Capitol 2370
5/17/69	**1** (3)	14	30. **Running Bear** #1 Pop hit for Johnny Preston in 1960	Capitol 2486
9/13/69	**1** (3)	14	31. **Since I Met You, Baby** #12 Pop hit for Ivory Joe Hunter in 1956	Capitol 2595
1/24/70	**1** (4)	13	32. **It's Just A Matter Of Time** #3 Pop hit for Brook Benton in 1959	Capitol 2700
4/18/70	**1** (3)	13	33. **My Love** #1 Pop hit for Petula Clark in 1966	Capitol 2782
7/11/70	**1** (4)	14	34. **Don't Keep Me Hangin' On**	Capitol 2834
10/24/70	**1** (3)	14	35. **Endlessly** #12 Pop hit for Brook Benton in 1959	Capitol 2914
3/6/71	**1** (4)	15	36. **Empty Arms** #13 Pop hit for Teresa Brewer in 1957	Capitol 3015
6/19/71	**1** (1)	13	37. **Bright Lights, Big City** #58 Pop hit for Jimmy Reed in 1961	Capitol 3114
10/9/71	**1** (1)	14	38. **Here Comes Honey Again**	Capitol 3174
1/22/72	**2** (2)	14	39. **Only Love Can Break A Heart** #2 Pop hit for Gene Pitney in 1962	Capitol 3232
5/13/72	**1** (1)	11	40. **That's Why I Love You Like I Do**	Capitol 3322
7/29/72	**1** (1)	14	41. **When The Snow Is On The Roses**	Columbia 45644
9/30/72	**30**	4	42. Traces #2 Pop hit for the Classics IV in 1969	Capitol 3398
11/4/72	**5**	11	43. **White Silver Sands** #7 Pop hit for Don Rondo in 1957	Columbia 45706
1/6/73	**32**	3	44. Downfall Of Me	Capitol 3475
2/17/73	**4**	13	45. **I Love You More And More Everyday** #9 Pop hit for Al Martino in 1964	Columbia 45770
7/7/73	**15**	6	46. If She Just Helps Me Get Over You	Columbia 45871
3/23/74	**1** (1)	11	47. **Is It Wrong (For Loving You)**	Columbia 46003
8/24/74	**4**	12	48. **A Mi Esposa Con Amor (To My Wife With Love)**	Columbia 10001
2/15/75	**6**	8	49. **A Little Bit South Of Saskatoon**	Columbia 10072
5/17/75	**5**	10	50. **Little Band Of Gold** #21 Pop hit for James Gilreath in 1963	Columbia 10121
9/6/75	**10**	10	51. **What In The World's Come Over You** #5 Pop hit for Jack Scott in 1960	Columbia 10184
2/21/76	**14**	9	52. The Prisoner's Song/ million-selling song for Vernon Dalhart in 1925	
		9	53. Back In The Saddle Again Gene Autry's theme song	Columbia 10276
6/5/76	**6**	11	54. **When Something Is Wrong With My Baby** #42 Pop hit for Sam & Dave in 1967	Columbia 10335
9/11/76	**8**	11	55. **Come On In**	Columbia 10392

DATE	POS	WKS	ARTIST–RECORD TITLE	LABEL & NO.
2/12/77	**9**	9	56. **You're Free To Go**	Columbia 10466
7/2/77	**15**	7	57. In The Jailhouse Now	Columbia 10551
			written and recorded by Jimmie Rodgers in 1928	
11/12/77	**24**	5	58. Abilene	Columbia 10628
			SONNY JAMES with His Tennessee State Prison Band	
			above 2 are live recordings at the Tennessee State Prison	
4/8/78	**16**	7	59. This Is The Love	Columbia 10703
8/12/78	**18**	6	60. Caribbean	Columbia 10764
1/6/79	**30**	4	61. Building Memories	Columbia 10852
5/5/79	**36**	2	62. Hold What You've Got	Monument 280
			#5 Pop hit for Joe Tex in 1965	
1/30/82	**19**	6	63. Innocent Lies	Dimension 1026
			SONNY JAMES and His Southern Gentlemen	
2/12/83	**33**	3	64. The Fool In Me	Dimension 1040
			SONNY JAMES & SILVER	

JAYE, Jerry

Born Gerald Jaye Hatley on 10/19/37 in Manila, Arkansas.

DATE	POS	WKS	ARTIST–RECORD TITLE	LABEL & NO.
7/31/76	**32**	5	1. Honky Tonk Women Love Red Neck Men	Hi 2310

JEAN—see NORMA JEAN

JENNINGS, Bob

Born on 9/26/24 in Liberty, Tennessee. Own bands, the Eagle Rangers, 1947-49; the Radio Playboys, 1949-52, and the Farm Hands, 1952-55.

DATE	POS	WKS	ARTIST–RECORD TITLE	LABEL & NO.
5/9/64	**32**	7	1. The First Step Down (Is The Longest)	Sims 161
11/28/64	**34**	5	2. Leave A Little Play (In The Chain Of Love)	Sims 202

JENNINGS, Waylon

Born on 6/15/37 in Littlefield, Texas. On local radio from age 12. Moved to Lubbock, Texas, in 1954 and worked as a DJ. Toured with Buddy Holly as his bass player, 1958-59. Moved to Phoenix and formed his own band, the Waylors, in 1960. Recorded for Trend in 1961. Moved to Nashville in 1965. Established himself in the mid-1970s as a leader of the "outlaw" movement in Country music. Married to Jessi Colter since 1969. Appeared in the movies *Nashville Rebel* and *MacKintosh And T.J.* Narrator for TV's *The Dukes Of Hazzard*. CMA Awards: 1975 Male Vocalist of the Year; 1976 Vocal Duo of the Year (with Willie Nelson).

(a) WAYLON & JESSI
(b) WAYLON & WILLIE
(c) JOHNNY CASH & WAYLON JENNINGS
(d) WAYLON JENNINGS, WILLIE NELSON, JOHNNY CASH, KRIS KRISTOFFERSON
(#51-64) WAYLON

DATE	POS	WKS	ARTIST–RECORD TITLE	LABEL & NO.
10/9/65	**16**	11	1. Stop The World (And Let Me Off)	RCA 8652
2/5/66	**17**	12	2. Anita, You're Dreaming	RCA 8729
6/4/66	**17**	13	3. Time To Bum Again	RCA 8822
9/3/66	**9**	18	4. **(That's What You Get) For Lovin' Me**	RCA 8917
			#30 Pop hit for Peter, Paul & Mary in 1965	
1/7/67	**11**	12	5. Green River	RCA 9025
			from the movie *Nashville Rebel*	
5/6/67	**12**	11	6. Mental Revenge	RCA 9146
			written by Mel Tillis	

DATE	POS	WKS	ARTIST–RECORD TITLE		LABEL & NO.
9/9/67	8	14	7. **The Chokin' Kind** **WAYLON JENNINGS AND THE WAYLORS** #13 Pop hit for Joe Simon in 1969		RCA 9259
2/17/68	5	13	8. **Walk On Out Of My Mind**		RCA 9414
4/13/68	4	13	9. **I Got You** **WAYLON JENNINGS & ANITA CARTER**		RCA 9480
7/13/68	2 (5)	18	10. **Only Daddy That'll Walk The Line**		RCA 9561
11/23/68+	5	16	11. **Yours Love**		RCA 9642
3/29/69	19	9	12. Something's Wrong In California		RCA 0105
6/14/69	20	9	13. The Days Of Sand And Shovels/ #34 Pop hit for Bobby Vinton in 1969		
6/21/69	37	2	14. Delia's Gone		RCA 0157
10/4/69	23	3	15. MacArthur Park **WAYLON JENNINGS AND THE KIMBERLYS** #2 Pop hit for Richard Harris in 1968		RCA 0210
12/13/69+	3	13	16. **Brown Eyed Handsome Man** written and recorded by Chuck Berry in 1956		RCA 0281
4/18/70	12	13	17. Singer Of Sad Songs		RCA 9819
9/5/70	5	14	18. **The Taker**		RCA 9885
12/12/70	25	4	19. Suspicious Minds (a) #1 Pop hit for Elvis Presley in 1969		RCA 9920
12/19/70+	16	9	20. (Don't Let the Sun Set on You) Tulsa		RCA 9925
4/24/71	14	10	21. Mississippi Woman		RCA 9967
7/24/71	39	1	22. Under Your Spell Again (a)		RCA 9992
8/28/71	12	11	23. Cedartown, Georgia		RCA 1003
1/22/72	3	15	24. **Good Hearted Woman** also see version by Waylon & Willie - #37 below		RCA 0615
6/17/72	7	12	25. **Sweet Dream Woman**		RCA 0716
11/11/72	6	12	26. **Pretend I Never Happened**		RCA 0808
3/10/73	7	11	27. **You Can Have Her** #12 Pop hit for Roy Hamilton in 1961		RCA 0886
6/16/73	28	7	28. We Had It All		RCA 0961
10/27/73	8	12	29. **You Ask Me To**		RCA 0086
5/18/74	1 (1)	9	30. **This Time**		RCA 0251
8/31/74	1 (1)	9	31. **I'm A Ramblin' Man**		RCA 10020
1/4/75	2 (1)	11	32. **Rainy Day Woman/**		
		10	33. Let's All Help The Cowboys (Sing The Blues)		RCA 10142
5/31/75	10	7	34. **Dreaming My Dreams With You** flip side "Waymore's Blues" Bubbled Under (POS 110)		RCA 10270
9/20/75	1 (1)	13	35. **Are You Sure Hank Done It This Way/** tribute to Hank Williams		
		13	36. Bob Wills Is Still The King tribute to Bob Wills		RCA 10379
1/10/76	1 (3)	13	37. **Good Hearted Woman** (b) CMA Award: Single of the Year	[R]	RCA 10529
5/15/76	2 (1)	11	38. **Suspicious Minds** (a)	[R]	RCA 10653
8/14/76	4	11	39. **Can't You See/**		
		7	40. I'll Go Back To Her		RCA 10721
12/4/76+	7	11	41. **Are You Ready For The Country/**		
		11	42. So Good Woman		RCA 10842

DATE	POS	WKS	ARTIST– RECORD TITLE	LABEL & NO.
4/23/77	1 (6)	14	43. **Luckenbach, Texas (Back to the Basics of Love)** Willie Nelson (ending vocal)	RCA 10924
10/8/77	1 (2)	11	44. **The Wurlitzer Prize (I Don't Want to Get Over You)/**	
		11	45. Lookin' For A Feeling	RCA 11118
1/21/78	1 (4)	12	46. **Mammas Don't Let Your Babies Grow Up To Be Cowboys (b)/**	
		11	47. I Can Get Off On You (b)	RCA 11198
5/27/78	2 (2)	10	48. **There Ain't No Good Chain Gang (c)/**	
12/1/79+	22	8	49. I Wish I Was Crazy Again (c)	Columbia 10742
7/29/78	1 (3)	11	50. **I've Always Been Crazy**	RCA 11344
10/28/78	5	10	51. **Don't You Think This Outlaw Bit's Done Got Out Of Hand/**	
		8	52. Girl I Can Tell (You're Trying To Work It Out)	RCA 11390
5/19/79	1 (3)	11	53. **Amanda**	RCA 11596
9/22/79	1 (2)	12	54. **Come With Me**	RCA 11723
1/12/80	1 (1)	11	55. **I Ain't Living Long Like This**	RCA 11898
6/14/80	7	9	56. **Clyde**	RCA 12007
8/30/80	1 (1)	12	● 57. **Theme From The Dukes Of Hazzard (Good Ol' Boys)** from *The Dukes Of Hazzard* TV series starring John Schneider and Tom Wopat	RCA 12067
3/7/81	17	7	58. Storms Never Last	RCA 12176
6/20/81	10	8	59. **Wild Side Of Life/It Wasn't God Who Made Honky Tonk Angels (a)**	RCA 12245
12/12/81+	5	12	60. **Shine**	RCA 12367
3/27/82	1 (2)	12	61. **Just To Satisfy You (b)**	RCA 13073
7/3/82	4	14	62. **Women Do Know How To Carry On**	RCA 13257
11/6/82	13	11	63. (Sittin' On) The Dock Of The Bay (b) #1 Pop hit for Otis Redding in 1968	RCA 13319
4/2/83	1 (1)	12	64. **Lucille (You Won't Do Your Daddy's Will)** #21 Pop hit for Little Richard in 1957	RCA 13465
7/23/83	10	9	65. **Breakin' Down**	RCA 13543
9/3/83	20	6	66. Hold On, I'm Comin' **WAYLON JENNINGS & JERRY REED** #21 Pop hit for Sam & Dave in 1966	RCA 13580
10/29/83	8	11	67. Take It To The Limit (b) #4 Pop hit for the Eagles in 1976	Columbia 04131
11/19/83	15	9	68. The Conversation **WAYLON JENNINGS with HANK WILLIAMS, JR.** originally released on a Hank Williams, Jr. album in 1979	RCA 13631
3/24/84	4	11	69. **I May Be Used (But Baby I Ain't Used Up)**	RCA 13729
7/7/84	6	11	70. **Never Could Toe The Mark**	RCA 13827
10/20/84	6	14	71. **America**	RCA 13908
2/16/85	10	11	72. **Waltz Me To Heaven** written by Dolly Parton	RCA 13984
6/1/85	1 (1)	14	73. **Highwayman (d)**	Columbia 04881
7/13/85	2 (2)	14	74. **Drinkin' And Dreamin'**	RCA 14094
10/5/85	15	9	75. Desperados Waiting For A Train (d)	Columbia 05594
12/14/85+	13	9	76. The Devil's On The Loose	RCA 14215
3/1/86	7	12	77. **Working Without A Net**	MCA 52776

DATE	POS	WKS	ARTIST– RECORD TITLE	LABEL & NO.
6/14/86	5	12	78. **Will The Wolf Survive** #78 Pop hit for Los Lobos in 1985	MCA 52830
6/28/86	35	2	79. Even Cowgirls Get The Blues (c)	Columbia 05896
10/11/86	8	13	80. **What You'll Do When I'm Gone**	MCA 52915
2/7/87	1 (1)	14	81. **Rose In Paradise**	MCA 53009
6/6/87	8	12	82. **Fallin' Out**	MCA 53088
10/10/87	6	13	83. **My Rough And Rowdy Days**	MCA 53158
2/27/88	16	8	84. If Ole Hank Could Only See Us Now (Chapter Five...Nashville)	MCA 53243
10/29/88	38	2	85. How Much Is It Worth To Live In L.A.	MCA 53314
2/11/89	28	4	86. Which Way Do I Go (Now That I'm Gone)	MCA 53476
3/31/90	25	7	87. Silver Stallion (d)	Columbia 73233
6/30/90	5	15	88. **Wrong**	Epic 73352
2/16/91	22	7	89. The Eagle	Epic 73718

JIM & JESSE

Duo of brothers from Coeburn, Virginia: Jim (born 2/13/27, guitar) and Jesse McReynolds (born 7/9/29, mandolin). Worked on radio in Norton, Virginia, then on WNOX-Knoxville *Tennessee Barn Dance*. Regulars on the *Grand Ole Opry* since 1964.

DATE	POS	WKS	ARTIST– RECORD TITLE	LABEL & NO.
1/16/65	39	1	1. Better Times A-Coming	Epic 9729
5/20/67	18	9	2. Diesel On My Tail **JIM & JESSE And The Virginia Boys (above 2)**	Epic 10138
2/21/70	38	1	3. The Golden Rocket	Epic 10563

JIMMY & JOHNNY

Duo of Jimmy Lee Fautheree (born 1934, El Dorado, Arkansas) and Country Johnny Mathis.

DATE	POS	WKS	ARTIST– RECORD TITLE	LABEL & NO.
9/25/54	3	18	1. **If You Don't Somebody Else Will** Juke Box #3 / Jockey #5 / Best Seller #6	Chess 4859

JOHNNIE & JACK

Duo of Johnnie Wright (born 5/13/14, Mount Juliet, Tennessee) and Jack Anglin (born 5/13/16, Columbia, Tennessee; died 3/8/63 in car crash, en route to Patsy Cline's memorial service). The team was formed in 1938 and worked WSIX-Nashville. Wright married Kitty Wells in 1938. First recorded for Apollo in 1947. Worked as a team with Wells from 1948. On the *Louisiana Hayride*, 1948-52; switched to the *Grand Ole Opry* in 1952. Wright continued as a solo.

DATE	POS	WKS	ARTIST– RECORD TITLE	LABEL & NO.
1/20/51	4	17	1. **Poison Love** Jockey #4 / Best Seller #5 / Juke Box #9	RCA 0377
8/4/51	5	11	2. **Cryin' Heart Blues** Juke Box #5 / Jockey #6 / Best Seller #10	RCA 0478
5/10/52	7	5	3. **Three Ways Of Knowing** **JOHNNIE and JACK and Their Tennessee Mountain Boys** (above 3) Juke Box #7	RCA 4555
4/10/54	1 (2)	18	4. **(Oh Baby Mine) I Get So Lonely** Jockey #1 / Best Seller #5	RCA 5681
7/17/54	3	17	5. **Goodnight, Sweetheart, Goodnight/** Jockey #3 / Best Seller #4 / Juke Box #4	
8/7/54	15	1	6. Honey, I Need You Jockey #15	RCA 5775

DATE	POS	WKS	ARTIST– RECORD TITLE	LABEL & NO.
11/27/54+	7	4	7. **Kiss-Crazy Baby/** Juke Box #7 / Best Seller #13	
11/13/54	9	10	8. **Beware Of "It"** Best Seller #9 / Juke Box #9 / Jockey #10	RCA 5880
5/21/55	14	3	9. No One Dear But You Jockey #14	RCA 6094
12/17/55	15	1	10. S.O.S. Jockey #15	RCA 6295
3/3/56	13	3	11. I Want To Be Loved **JOHNNIE & JACK with Ruby Wells** Jockey #13	RCA 6395
2/24/58	7	18	12. **Stop The World (And Let Me Off)** Best Seller #7 / Jockey #9	RCA 7137
10/20/58	18	3	13. Lonely Island Pearl	RCA 7324
8/10/59	16	12	14. Sailor Man	RCA 7545
8/11/62	17	4	15. Slow Poison [R] **JOHNNY AND JACK** first issued on RCA 4765 in 1962	Decca 31397
			JOHNSON, Buddy, and His Orchestra Johnson born Woodrow Wilson Johnson on 1/10/15 in Darlington, South Carolina. Died on 2/9/77 of a brain tumor. R&B band leader from 1940s to '60s whose vocalists included Arthur Prysock and Buddy's sister, Ella Johnson. Composer of "Since I Fell For You."	
3/11/44	2 (2)	7	1. **When My Man Comes Home** Ella Johnson (vocal)	Decca 8655
			JOHNSON, Lois Born in Knoxville, Tennessee. Worked on local radio from age 11. Regular appearances on WWVA-Wheeling *Jamboree*. Toured for four years with Hank Williams, Jr.	
7/18/70	23	7	1. Removing The Shadow	MGM 14136
10/24/70	12	9	2. So Sad (To Watch Good Love Go Bad)	MGM 14164
4/22/72	14	11	3. Send Me Some Lovin'	MGM 14356
12/2/72+	22	8	4. Whole Lotta Loving #6 Pop hit for Fats Domino in 1959 **HANK WILLIAMS, JR. and LOIS JOHNSON (above 4)**	MGM 14443
9/21/74	19	9	5. Come On In And Let Me Love You	20th Century 2106
2/8/75	6	7	6. **Loving You Will Never Grow Old**	20th Century 2151
2/12/77	20	7	7. Your Pretty Roses Came Too Late	Polydor 14371
6/18/77	40	2	8. I Hate Goodbyes	Polydor 14392
			JOHNSON, Michael Born on 8/8/44 in Alamosa, Colorado; raised in Denver. Studied classical guitar in 1966 in Spain. In the Chad Mitchell Trio with John Denver in 1968. Pop career in the late 1970's. Members of his session band later formed Great Plains.	
12/21/85+	9	11	1. I Love You By Heart **SYLVIA & MICHAEL JOHNSON**	RCA 14217
5/24/86	12	10	2. Gotta Learn To Love Without You	RCA 14294
10/11/86+	1 (1)	16	3. **Give Me Wings**	RCA 14412
2/14/87	1 (1)	15	4. **The Moon Is Still Over Her Shoulder**	RCA 5091
7/11/87	26	5	5. Ponies	RCA 5171
11/7/87+	4	14	6. **Crying Shame**	RCA 5279

DATE	POS	WKS	ARTIST– RECORD TITLE	LABEL & NO.
5/7/88	7	11	7. **I Will Whisper Your Name**	RCA 6833
10/1/88	9	10	8. **That's That**	RCA 8650
			JOHNSON, Roland	
3/2/59	25	3	1. I Traded Her Love (For Deep Purple Wine)	Brunswick 55110
			JONES, Ann	
			Born Ann Matthews in Hutchison, Kansas; raised in Enid, Oklahoma. On WCRL-Enid radio shows at age 14.	
10/15/49	15	1	1. Give Me A Hundred Reasons Juke Box #15	Capitol 15414
			JONES, Anthony Armstrong	
			Born Ronnie Jones on 6/2/49 in Ada, Oklahoma. Professional golfer. Discovered by Conway Twitty in 1962; worked with Twitty's band. Stage name came from the English photographer who married Princess Margaret.	
8/2/69	22	7	1. Proud Mary #2 Pop hit for Creedence Clearwater Revival in 1969	Chart 5017
11/15/69	28	3	2. New Orleans #6 Pop hit for U.S. Bonds in 1960	Chart 5033
1/17/70	8	9	3. **Take A Letter Maria** #2 Pop hit for R.B. Greaves in 1969	Chart 5045
8/15/70	38	4	4. Sugar In The Flowers	Chart 5083
12/12/70	40	2	5. Sweet Caroline #4 Pop hit for Neil Diamond in 1969	Chart 5100
8/11/73	33	3	6. Bad, Bad Leroy Brown #1 Pop hit for Jim Croce in 1973	Epic 11002
			JONES, David Lynn	
			Born on 1/15/50 in Bexar, Arkansas. Wrote "Living In The Promiseland" for Willie Nelson.	
9/26/87	10	11	1. **Bonnie Jean (Little Sister)**	Mercury 888733
4/23/88	14	10	2. High Ridin' Heroes Waylon Jennings (guest vocal)	Mercury 870128
9/10/88	36	2	3. The Rogue	Mercury 870525
			JONES, George	
			Born George Glenn Jones on 9/12/31 in Saratoga, Texas. Worked on KTXJ-Jasper, Texas. Worked with Eddie & Pearl on KRIC-Beaumont, Texas in 1947. Served in U.S. Marines, 1950-52. First recorded for Starday in 1953. Appeared on KNUZ-Houston Jamboree and worked as a DJ on KTRM-Beaumont in the early '50s. Appearances on *Louisiana Hayride* in 1956. Also recorded rockabilly as Thumper Jones and Hank Smith. Recorded with Gene Pitney as George & Gene. Married to Tammy Wynette, 1969-75. Joined the *Grand Ole Opry* in 1969. Underwent triple-bypass surgery on 9/12/94. Fondly known as the "Rolls Royce of Country Singers." CMA Awards: 1980 and 1981 Male Vocalist of the Year. Elected to the Country Music Hall of Fame in 1992. (a) GEORGE JONES & MARGIE SINGLETON (b) GEORGE JONES & MELBA MONTGOMERY (c) GEORGE & GENE (d) GEORGE JONES & TAMMY WYNETTE (e) GEORGE JONES and JOHNNY PAYCHECK	
10/29/55	4	18	1. **Why Baby Why** Juke Box #4 / Best Seller #4 / Jockey #4	Starday 202

DATE	POS	WKS	ARTIST– RECORD TITLE	LABEL & NO.
1/28/56	**7**	7	2. **What Am I Worth** Juke Box #7 / Jockey #10 / Best Seller #14	Starday 216
7/14/56	**7**	8	3. **You Gotta Be My Baby** Juke Box #7 / Jockey #10	Starday 247
10/20/56	**3**	11	4. **Just One More/** Juke Box #3	
		5	5. Gonna Come Get You Juke Box flip	Starday 264
1/26/57	**10**	1	6. **Yearning** **GEORGE JONES and JEANETTE HICKS** Juke Box #10	Starday 279
3/9/57	**10**	2	7. **Don't Stop The Music/** Juke Box #10 / Best Seller #15 / Jockey #15	
		1	8. Uh, Uh, No Juke Box flip	Mercury 71029
6/10/57	**13**	6	9. Too Much Water Best Seller #13; written by Jones and Sonny James	Mercury 71096
4/14/58	**7**	10	10. **Color Of The Blues** Jockey #7 / Best Seller #18	Mercury 71257
11/17/58	**6**	16	11. **Treasure Of Love/**	
12/8/58	**29**	1	12. If I Don't Love You (Grits Ain't Groceries)	Mercury 71373
3/9/59	**1** (5)	22	13. **White Lightning** written by the Big Bopper (J.P. Richardson)	Mercury 71406
7/20/59	**7**	13	14. **Who Shot Sam**	Mercury 71464
11/23/59+	**15**	12	15. Money To Burn/	
11/23/59	**19**	12	16. Big Harlan Taylor written by Roger Miller	Mercury 71514
4/4/60	**16**	12	17. Accidently On Purpose/	
4/25/60	**30**	1	18. Sparkling Brown Eyes	Mercury 71583
8/22/60	**25**	2	19. Out Of Control	Mercury 71641
11/7/60+	**2** (1)	34	20. **The Window Up Above**	Mercury 71700
5/29/61	**16**	2	21. Family Bible	Mercury 71721
6/19/61	**1** (7)	32	22. **Tender Years**	Mercury 71804
9/18/61	**15**	3	23. Did I Ever Tell You (a)	Mercury 71856
2/24/62	**5**	12	24. **Aching, Breaking Heart**	Mercury 71910
4/14/62	**1** (6)	23	25. **She Thinks I Still Care/**	
4/28/62	**17**	5	26. Sometimes You Just Can't Win	United Art. 424
6/16/62	**11**	10	27. Waltz Of The Angels (a)	Mercury 71955
7/21/62	**13**	11	28. Open Pit Mine	United Art. 462
8/25/62	**28**	1	29. You're Still On My Mind	Mercury 72010
10/6/62	**3**	18	30. **A Girl I Used To Know/**	
10/13/62	**13**	9	31. Big Fool Of The Year written by Justin Tubb	United Art. 500
2/9/63	**7**	18	32. **Not What I Had In Mind/**	
4/6/63	**29**	1	33. I Saw Me **GEORGE JONES & The Jones Boys (above 4)**	United Art. 528
5/4/63	**3**	28	34. **We Must Have Been Out Of Our Minds** (b)	United Art. 575
7/13/63	**5**	22	35. **You Comb Her Hair** flip side "Ain't It Funny What Love Will Do" Bubbled Under at #124	United Art. 578
12/7/63	**17**	7	36. Let's Invite Them Over (b)/	
11/30/63	**20**	5	37. What's In Our Heart (b)	United Art. 635

DATE	POS	WKS	ARTIST–RECORD TITLE	LABEL & NO.
2/1/64	5	18	38. **Your Heart Turned Left (And I Was On The Right)/**	
2/8/64	15	9	39. My Tears Are Overdue	United Art. 683
3/28/64	39	2	40. The Last Town I Painted	Mercury 72233
6/27/64	10	15	41. **Where Does A Little Tear Come From/**	
7/18/64	31	4	42. Something I Dreamed	United Art. 724
9/5/64	31	5	43. Please Be My Love (b)	United Art. 732
9/26/64	3	28	44. **The Race Is On**	United Art. 751
12/19/64+	25	10	45. Multiply The Heartaches (b)	United Art. 784
2/6/65	15	14	46. Least Of All	United Art. 804
3/20/65	9	19	47. **Things Have Gone To Pieces**	Musicor 1067
5/1/65	16	9	48. I've Got Five Dollars And It's Saturday Night (c)	Musicor 1066
6/19/65	14	10	49. Wrong Number	United Art. 858
7/10/65	25	6	50. Louisiana Man (c)	Musicor 1097
			flip side "I'm A Fool To Care" Bubbled Under at #115	
9/4/65	6	17	51. **Love Bug**	Musicor 1098
10/16/65	40	2	52. What's Money	United Art. 901
11/20/65+	8	16	53. **Take Me**	Musicor 1117
3/19/66	6	16	54. **I'm A People**	Musicor 1143
7/9/66	30	5	55. Old Brush Arbors	Musicor 1174
7/30/66	5	16	56. **Four-O-Thirty Three**	Musicor 1181
2/11/67	1 (2)	19	57. **Walk Through This World With Me**	Musicor 1226
6/10/67	5	14	58. **I Can't Get There From Here**	Musicor 1243
9/23/67	24	8	59. Party Pickin' (b)	Musicor 1238
10/28/67	7	14	60. **If My Heart Had Windows**	Musicor 1267
2/24/68	8	11	61. **Say It's Not You**	Musicor 1289
5/4/68	35	5	62. Small Time Laboring Man	Musicor 1297
7/6/68	3	13	63. **As Long As I Live**	Musicor 1298
10/19/68	12	9	64. Milwaukee, Here I Come	Musicor 1325
			GEORGE JONES & BRENDA CARTER	
11/23/68+	2 (2)	17	65. **When The Grass Grows Over Me**	Musicor 1333
4/12/69	2 (2)	16	66. **I'll Share My World With You**	Musicor 1351
7/26/69	6	13	67. **If Not For You**	Musicor 1366
11/22/69+	6	13	68. **She's Mine**	Musicor 1381
3/28/70	28	7	69. Where Grass Won't Grow	Musicor 1392
7/11/70	13	12	70. Tell Me My Lying Eyes Are Wrong	Musicor 1408
			GEORGE JONES And The Jones Boys	
11/28/70+	2 (1)	13	71. **A Good Year For The Roses**	Musicor 1425
3/27/71	10	11	72. **Sometimes You Just Can't Win** [R]	Musicor 1432
			new version of #26 above	
6/26/71	7	11	73. **Right Won't Touch A Hand**	Musicor 1440
10/23/71	13	9	74. I'll Follow You (Up To Our Cloud)	Musicor 1446
1/8/72	9	11	75. **Take Me (d)**	Epic 10815
			new version of #53 above	
3/4/72	6	10	76. **We Can Make It**	Epic 10831
3/4/72	30	2	77. A Day In The Life Of A Fool	RCA 0625
6/3/72	2 (1)	12	78. **Loving You Could Never Be Better**	Epic 10858
7/22/72	6	13	79. **The Ceremony (d)**	Epic 10881
11/11/72	5	14	80. **A Picture Of Me (Without You)**	Epic 10917
1/6/73	38	1	81. Old Fashioned Singing (d)	Epic 10923

DATE	POS	WKS	ARTIST– RECORD TITLE	LABEL & NO.
3/24/73	6	11	82. **What My Woman Can't Do**	Epic 10959
5/5/73	32	5	83. Let's Build A World Together (d)	Epic 10963
7/7/73	7	11	84. **Nothing Ever Hurt Me (Half As Bad As Losing You)**	Epic 11006
9/15/73	1 (2)	14	85. **We're Gonna Hold On** (d)	Epic 11031
12/15/73+	3	12	86. **Once You've Had The Best**	Epic 11053
3/9/74	15	8	87. (We're Not) The Jet Set (d)	Epic 11083
5/11/74	25	6	88. The Telephone Call	Epic 11099
			TINA & DADDY (Jones & his stepdaughter)	
6/29/74	1 (1)	14	89. **The Grand Tour**	Epic 11122
8/17/74	8	7	90. **We Loved It Away** (d)	Epic 11151
11/16/74+	1 (1)	10	91. **The Door**	Epic 50038
4/19/75	10	9	92. **These Days (I Barely Get By)**	Epic 50088
6/21/75	25	5	93. God's Gonna Get'cha (For That) (d)	Epic 50099
8/16/75	21	6	94. Memories Of Us	Epic 50127
2/28/76	16	8	95. The Battle	Epic 50187
6/19/76	1 (1)	12	96. **Golden Ring** (d)	Epic 50235
6/26/76	37	2	97. You Always Look Your Best (Here In My Arms)	Epic 50227
9/18/76	3	13	98. **Her Name Is...**	Epic 50271
12/25/76+	1 (2)	12	99. **Near You** (d)	Epic 50314
			#1 Pop hit (17 weeks) for Francis Craig in 1947	
6/11/77	34	4	100. Old King Kong	Epic 50385
7/23/77	5	10	101. **Southern California** (d)	Epic 50418
9/3/77	24	5	102. If I Could Put Them All Together (I'd Have You)	Epic 50423
1/21/78	6	9	103. **Bartender's Blues**	Epic 50495
			James Taylor (guest vocal)	
7/15/78	11	7	104. I'll Just Take It Out In Love	Epic 50564
12/23/78+	7	8	105. **Mabellene** (e)	Epic 50647
			#5 Pop hit for Chuck Berry in 1955	
6/16/79	14	6	106. You Can Have Her (e)	Epic 50708
			#12 Pop hit for Roy Hamilton in 1961	
7/21/79	22	6	107. Someday My Day Will Come	Epic 50684
3/8/80	2 (1)	11	108. **Two Story House** (d)	Epic 50849
5/3/80	1 (1)	13	109. **He Stopped Loving Her Today**	Epic 50867
			CMA Award: Single of the Year	
7/19/80	31	4	110. When You're Ugly Like Us (You Just Naturally Got To Be Cool) (e)	Epic 50891
9/13/80	2 (1)	11	111. **I'm Not Ready Yet**	Epic 50922
9/27/80	19	5	112. A Pair Of Old Sneakers (d)	Epic 50930
1/10/81	18	5	113. You Better Move On (e)	Epic 50949
			#24 Pop hit for Arthur Alexander in 1962	
1/31/81	8	11	114. **If Drinkin' Don't Kill Me (Her Memory Will)**	Epic 50968
10/17/81	1 (1)	10	115. **Still Doin' Time**	Epic 02526
2/13/82	5	14	116. **Same Ole Me**	Epic 02696
			The Oak Ridge Boys (backing vocals)	
8/21/82	1 (1)	10	117. **Yesterday's Wine**	Epic 03072
			MERLE HAGGARD/GEORGE JONES	
1/8/83	10	10	118. C.C. Waterback	Epic 03405
			GEORGE JONES/MERLE HAGGARD	
1/29/83	3	11	119. Shine On (Shine All Your Sweet Love On Me)	Epic 03489
5/21/83	1 (1)	13	120. **I Always Get Lucky With You**	Epic 03883

DATE	POS	WKS	ARTIST– RECORD TITLE	LABEL & NO.
9/24/83	2 (1)	13	121. **Tennessee Whiskey**	Epic 04082
1/21/84	6	10	122. **We Didn't See A Thing** **RAY CHARLES & GEORGE JONES featuring Chet Atkins**	Columbia 04297
4/21/84	3	13	123. **You've Still Got A Place In My Heart**	Epic 04413
10/13/84	2 (3)	15	124. **She's My Rock**	Epic 04609
1/26/85	15	9	125. Hallelujah, I Love You So **GEORGE JONES with BRENDA LEE** #5 R&B hit for Ray Charles in 1956	Epic 04723
5/25/85	19	7	126. Size Seven Round (Made Of Gold) **GEORGE JONES and LACY J. DALTON**	Epic 04876
8/24/85	3	12	127. **Who's Gonna Fill Their Shoes**	Epic 05439
12/14/85+	3	14	128. **The One I Loved Back Then (The Corvette Song)**	Epic 05698
5/17/86	9	11	129. **Somebody Wants Me Out Of The Way**	Epic 05862
10/11/86	10	10	130. **Wine Colored Roses**	Epic 06296
2/7/87	8	11	131. **The Right Left Hand**	Epic 06593
6/13/87	26	6	132. I Turn To You	Epic 07107
1/16/88	26	6	133. The Bird	Epic 07655
1/21/89	5	12	134. **I'm A One Woman Man**	Epic 08509
6/3/89	26	5	135. The King Is Gone (So Are You) originally shown as "Ya Ba Da Ba Do (So Are You)"	Epic 68743
9/9/89	31	3	136. Writing On The Wall	Epic 68991
9/15/90	8	17	137. **A Few Ole Country Boys** **RANDY TRAVIS & GEORGE JONES**	Warner 19586
10/5/91	32	7	138. You Couldn't Get The Picture	MCA 54187
12/26/92+	34	5	139. I Don't Need Your Rockin' Chair with special guests Vince Gill, Mark Chesnutt, Garth Brooks, Travis Tritt, Joe Diffie, Alan Jackson, Pam Tillis, T. Graham Brown, Patty Loveless and Clint Black	MCA 54470
12/18/93+	24	8	140. High-Tech Redneck	MCA 54749

JONES, Grandpa

Born Louis Marshall Jones on 10/20/13 in Niagra, Kentucky. Raised in Akron, Ohio, where he had his own radio show in the early 1930s. Worked with Bradley Kincaid in 1935 and began appearing as "Grandpa" Jones. Own band, the Granchildren, in 1937. Served in U.S. Army, 1944-46. With the *Grand Ole Opry* since 1946. Regular on the *Hee-Haw* TV series since 1969. Elected to the Country Music Hall of Fame in 1978.

DATE	POS	WKS	ARTIST– RECORD TITLE	LABEL & NO.
2/23/59	21	2	1. The All-American Boy #2 Pop hit for Bobby Bare (Bill Parsons) in 1959	Decca 30823
12/15/62+	5	16	2. **T For Texas** #2 Pop hit for Jimmie Rodgers in 1928 as "Blue Yodel"	Monument 801

JONES, Tom

Born Thomas Jones Woodward on 6/7/40 in Pontypridd, South Wales. Worked local clubs as Tommy Scott; formed own trio, The Senators, in 1963. Began solo career in London in 1964. Won the 1965 Best New Artist Grammy Award. Host of own TV musical variety series, 1969-71.

DATE	POS	WKS	ARTIST– RECORD TITLE	LABEL & NO.
1/22/77	1 (1)	10	1. **Say You'll Stay Until Tomorrow**	Epic 50308
5/16/81	19	7	2. Darlin'	Mercury 76100
8/29/81	25	5	3. What In The World's Come Over You #5 Pop hit for Jack Scott in 1960	Mercury 76115
12/26/81+	26	6	4. Lady Lay Down	Mercury 76125
10/16/82	16	8	5. A Woman's Touch	Mercury 76172

DATE	POS	WKS	ARTIST– RECORD TITLE	LABEL & NO.
3/19/83	**4**	11	6. **Touch Me (I'll Be Your Fool Once More)**	Mercury 810445
8/20/83	**34**	3	7. It'll Be Me	Mercury 812631
1/28/84	**13**	10	8. I've Been Rained On Too	Mercury 814820
5/26/84	**30**	4	9. This Time	Mercury 818801
1/11/86	**36**	4	10. It's Four In The Morning	Mercury 884252

JORDAN, Louis, and His Tympany Five

Jordan born on 7/8/08 in Brinkley, Arkansas. Died of a heart attack on 2/4/75. R&B vocalist/saxophonist. First recorded for Brunswick in 1929, with the Jungle Band. Innovative, extremely popular vocal style paved the way for later R&B styles. Inducted into the Rock and Roll Hall of Fame in 1987 as a forefather of rock and roll.

DATE	POS	WKS	ARTIST– RECORD TITLE	LABEL & NO.
1/15/44	**1 (3)**	13	1. **Ration Blues/**	
1/29/44	**7**	1	2. **Deacon Jones**	Decca 8654
7/1/44	**1 (5)**	9	3. **Is You Is Or Is You Ain't (Ma' Baby)**	Decca 8659
			from the movie *Follow The Boys* starring Marlene Dietrich	

JUDD, Wynonna

Born Christina Ciminella on 5/30/64 in Ashland, Kentucky. Moved to Hollywood in 1968. Appeared in the movie *More American Graffiti*. To Nashville in May 1979. Half of The Judds duo with her mother, Naomi, 1983-91. Her sister is actress Ashley Judd of the TV show *Sisters*.

DATE	POS	WKS	ARTIST– RECORD TITLE	LABEL & NO.
2/22/92	**1 (1)**	16	1. **She Is His Only Need**	Curb/MCA 54320
5/23/92	**1 (3)**	18	2. **I Saw The Light**	Curb/MCA 54407
9/5/92	**1 (4)**	17	3. **No One Else On Earth**	Curb/MCA 54449
12/19/92+	**4**	14	4. **My Strongest Weakness**	Curb/MCA 54516
4/10/93	**3**	14	5. **Tell Me Why**	Curb/MCA 54606
5/22/93	**2 (1)**	15	6. **A Bad Goodbye**	RCA 62503
			CLINT BLACK (with Wynonna)	
7/31/93	**3**	14	7. **Only Love**	Curb/MCA 54689
11/13/93+	**6**	14	8. **Is It Over Yet**	Curb/MCA 54754
2/26/94	**2 (1)**	15	9. **Rock Bottom**	Curb/MCA 54809
6/25/94	**10**	11	10. **Girls With Guitars**	Curb/MCA 54875
			written by Mary Chapin Carpenter	
1/20/96	**1 (1)**	18	11. **To Be Loved By You**	Curb/MCA 55084
5/4/96	**14** ↑	12↑	12. Heaven Help My Heart	Curb/MCA 55194

JUDDS, The

Family duo from Ashland, Kentucky consisting of Naomi (born Diana Ellen Judd on 1/11/46) and daughter Wynonna (born Christina Ciminella on 5/30/64). Moved to Hollywood in 1968. Both appeared in the movie *More American Graffiti*. Moved to Nashville in May 1979. Added guitarist Don Potter and made stage debut in Omaha, Nebraska, in mid-1984. Naomi's chronic hepatitis forced duo split at the end of 1991. Sang theme of the NBC-TV show *The Torkelsons*. CMA Awards: 1984 Horizon Award; 1985, 1986 and 1987 Vocal Group of the Year; 1988, 1989, 1990 and 1991 Vocal Duo of the Year. Naomi's daughter and Wynonna's sister is actress Ashley Judd.

THE JUDDS (WYNONNA & NAOMI):

DATE	POS	WKS	ARTIST– RECORD TITLE	LABEL & NO.
1/21/84	**17**	10	1. **Had A Dream (For The Heart)**	RCA/Curb 13673
			hit for Elvis Presley in 1976 as "For The Heart"	
5/26/84	**1 (1)**	14	2. **Mama He's Crazy**	RCA/Curb 13772

DATE	POS	WKS	ARTIST – RECORD TITLE	LABEL & NO.
10/20/84	1 (2)	15	3. **Why Not Me** CMA Award: Single of the Year	RCA/Curb 13923
2/16/85	1 (1)	14	4. **Girls Night Out**	RCA/Curb 13991
6/22/85	1 (1)	14	5. **Love Is Alive**	RCA/Curb 14093
10/19/85	1 (2)	14	6. **Have Mercy**	RCA/Curb 14193
3/1/86	1 (1)	15	7. **Grandpa (Tell Me 'Bout The Good Old Days)**	RCA/Curb 14290
6/7/86	1 (1)	12	8. **Rockin' With The Rhythm Of The Rain**	RCA/Curb 14362
10/25/86+	1 (1)	16	9. **Cry Myself To Sleep**	RCA/Curb 5000
2/21/87	10	9	10. **Don't Be Cruel** #1 Pop/Country/R&B hit for Elvis Presley in 1956	RCA/Curb 5094
5/16/87	1 (1)	13	11. **I Know Where I'm Going**	RCA/Curb 5164
8/29/87	1 (1)	14	12. **Maybe Your Baby's Got The Blues**	RCA/Curb 5255
1/23/88	1 (1)	12	13. **Turn It Loose**	RCA/Curb 5329
6/18/88	2 (2)	13	14. **Give A Little Love**	RCA/Curb 8300
			THE JUDDS:	
10/29/88+	1 (1)	15	15. **Change Of Heart**	RCA/Curb 8715
3/11/89	1 (1)	13	16. **Young Love**	RCA/Curb 8820
7/15/89	1 (1)	15	17. **Let Me Tell You About Love**	RCA/Curb 8947
12/2/89+	8	15	18. **One Man Woman**	RCA/Curb 9077
4/21/90	16	12	19. Guardian Angels	Curb/RCA 2524
8/18/90	5	14	20. **Born To Be Blue**	Curb/RCA 2597
12/15/90+	5	15	21. **Love Can Build A Bridge**	Curb/RCA 2708
4/20/91	6	15	22. **One Hundred And Two**	Curb/RCA 2782
11/2/91	29	5	23. John Deere Tractor originally appeared on The Judds' debut mini-LP in 1984	Curb/RCA 62038
			JURGENS, Dick, and his Orchestra Jurgens born on 1/9/10 in Sacramento. Died on 10/5/95. Own big band from 1928. Wrote "Elmer's Tune," "Careless," "One Dozen Roses," "If I Knew Then" and many others. Vocalist Eddy Howard had over 40 Pop hits. Started an electronics business with brother Will in the mid-1950s.	
3/8/47	4	2	1. **(Oh Why, Oh Why, Did I Ever Leave) Wyoming** Jimmy Castle, Al Galante and Band (vocals)	Columbia 37210
			JUSTIS, Bill Born on 10/14/26 in Birmingham, Alabama. Died on 7/15/82 in Nashville. Session saxophonist/arranger/producer. Led house band for Sun Records.	
11/25/57+	6	16	● 1. **Raunchy** [I] Best Seller #6 / Jockey #14; Sid Manker (guitar); Bill Justis (sax)	Phillips 3519

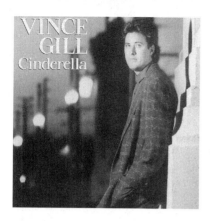

Vince Gill's "Cinderella" reached No. 5 in 1987 and briefly became the highest-charting record of the singer's career. The former singer with the Pop group Pure Prairie League has since become one of the biggest concert attractions in the industry, and was twice named the Country Music Association's Entertainer Of The Year.

Mickey Gilley—who co-owned the famous Gilley's nightclub in Texas featured in the film *Urban Cowboy*—spent the mid-'70s making records for the short-lived Playboy Records label. "Roll You Like A Wheel," his duet with former Playmate/later singer Barbi Benton, reached No. 32 in 1975.

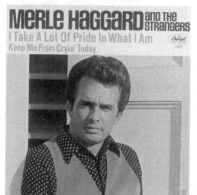

Lee Greenwood, a former Las Vegas casino dealer, enjoyed a four-song streak of No. 1 hits in the mid-'80s, including 1985's "Don't Underestimate My Love For You."

Merle Haggard, among the most popular performers in all of Country music, followed up his massively successful No. 1 hit "Mama Tried" with "I Take A Lot Of Pride In What I Am" in 1968. The song rose to No. 3—and within a year, his pride-filled "Okie From Muskogee" made headlines everywhere.

Emmylou Harris's first major acclaim came via her pairing with the Flying Burrito Brothers and influential Country-Rock figure Gram Parsons, but solo success quickly followed. Her "Wayfaring Stranger" reached No. 7 in 1980. Harris issued a much-praised collaborative album with Dolly Parton and Linda Ronstadt in 1987.

Becky Hobbs, a one-time Los Angeles-based writer for such Pop artists as Helen Reddy and Jane Olivor, moved to Nashville in the '80s and had a respectable career as a hitmaker. Her "Hottest 'Ex' In Texas" reached No. 37 in 1985.

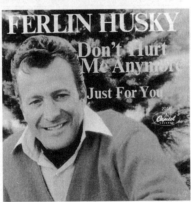

Homer And Jethro, a renowned musical comedy duo, had a firm grasp of the essentials of '60s Pop culture, as their dual 1964 remakes of the Beatles' "I Want To Hold Your Hand" and "She Loves You" indicate. Who did their hair?

Johnny Horton, the one-time "Singing Fisherman," had a No. 7 hit with 1956's "I'm A One-Woman Man." Horton's later hits took a noticeable historical/geographical turn; among them were "The Battle Of New Orleans," "North To Alaska," "Sink The Bismarck" and "When It's Springtime In Alaska (It's Forty Below)."

Ferlin Husky, a former merchant marine, was a commanding chart presence throughout much of the '60s. His 1967 track "Just For You," which reached No. 4, was one of eight Top 10 records he recorded between 1953 and 1967.

Stonewall Jackson—and that's his real name—released 43 charting hits on Columbia between 1958 and 1973. After 1968's "I Believe In Love," which climbed to No. 31, his sole Top 10 hit was a remake of Lobo's Pop hit "Me And You And A Dog Named Boo."

Sonny James, the "Southern Gentleman," scored a No. 2 hit with his 1966 single "Room in Your Heart," after which each of his next 16 singles—all the way through 1971—climbed to the very top of the chart. Alabama would break that record a decade later.

George Jones, one of the most profoundly influential figures in all of Country music, has scored nearly 140 Top 40 hits since his the release of "Why, Baby, Why" in 1955. His classic 1962 hit "She Thinks I Still Care"—his first hit for United Artists—stayed at No. 1 for six weeks.

DATE	POS	WKS	ARTIST– RECORD TITLE	LABEL & NO.
			# K	
			KALIN TWINS	
8/4/58	13	7	Herbert and Harold Kalin, born on 2/16/34 in Port Jervis, New York. ● 1. When Best Seller #13	Decca 30642
			KANDY, Jim	
9/11/65	29	4	1. I'm The Man	K-Ark 647
			KANE, Kieran	
			Born on 10/7/49 in Queens, New York. Drummer in rock band from age nine. Moved to Los Angeles in the early '70s, worked as a session musician. Moved to Nashville in 1979, teamed with songwriter Jamie O'Hara. Kane and O'Hara formed singing duo, The O'Kanes, in 1986.	
7/11/81	14	9	1. You're The Best	Elektra 47148
11/28/81+	16	11	2. It's Who You Love	Elektra 47228
4/3/82	26	8	3. I Feel It With You	Elektra 47415
8/7/82	26	6	4. I'll Be Your Man Around The House	Elektra 47478
6/11/83	30	4	5. It's You	Warner 29711
4/21/84	28	4	6. Dedicate	Warner 29336
			KEITH, Toby	
			Born Toby Keith Covel on 7/8/61 in Clinton, Oklahoma. Former rodeo hand, oil field worker and semi-pro football player.	
4/10/93	1 (2)	15	1. **Should've Been A Cowboy**	Mercury 864990
8/7/93	5	15	2. **He Ain't Worth Missing**	Mercury 862262
12/4/93+	2 (1)	17	3. **A Little Less Talk And A Lot More Action**	Mercury 862844
4/2/94	2 (1)	17	4. **Wish I Didn't Know Now**	Mercury 858290
8/13/94	1 (1)	17	5. **Who's That Man**	Polydor 853358
12/31/94+	10	14	6. **Upstairs Downtown**	Polydor 851136
4/8/95	2 (3)	18	7. **You Ain't Much Fun**	Polydor 851728
8/5/95	15	10	8. Big Ol' Truck	Polydor 579574
3/30/96	2 (2)	17	9. **Does That Blue Moon Ever Shine On You**	Polydor 576140
			KELLUM, Murry	
			Born in Jackson, Tennessee; raised in Plain, Texas. Died in a plane crash on 9/30/90 (age 47).	
7/10/71	26	6	1. Joy To The World #1 Pop hit for Three Dog Night in 1971	Epic 10741
			KEMP, Wayne	
			Born on 6/1/41 in Greenwood, Arkansas. Auto racer while a teenager. Own band in early '60s. Wrote hit "Love Bug" for George Jones, "The Image Of Me" and other hits for Conway Twitty and Ricky Van Shelton.	
4/14/73	17	10	1. Honky Tonk Wine	MCA 40019
3/16/74	32	3	2. Listen	MCA 40176

DATE	POS	WKS	ARTIST– RECORD TITLE	LABEL & NO.
5/16/81	**35**	3	3. Your Wife Is Cheatin' On Us Again	Mercury 57047
			KENDALLS, The	
			Father-and-daughter duo from St. Louis, consisting of Royce (born 9/25/34) and Jeannie (born 11/30/54) Kendall. Royce and his brother Floyce had worked together as the Austin Brothers in the late '50s.	
8/27/77	**1 (4)**	13	1. **Heaven's Just A Sin Away**	Ovation 1103
			CMA Award: Single of the Year	
2/18/78	**2 (2)**	10	2. **It Don't Feel Like Sinnin' To Me**	Ovation 1106
6/10/78	**6**	9	3. **Pittsburgh Stealers**	Ovation 1109
9/30/78	**1 (1)**	10	4. **Sweet Desire/**	
		10	5. Old Fashioned Love	Ovation 1112
1/20/79	**5**	11	6. **I Had A Lovely Time**	Ovation 1119
5/12/79	**11**	8	7. Just Like Real People	Ovation 1125
9/1/79	**16**	7	8. I Don't Do Like That No More/	
		7	9. Never My Love	Ovation 1129
12/1/79+	**5**	10	10. **You'd Make An Angel Wanna Cheat**	Ovation 1136
4/5/80	**5**	11	11. **I'm Already Blue**	Ovation 1143
8/16/80	**9**	10	12. **Put It Off Until Tomorrow**	Ovation 1154
			written by Dolly Parton and Dolly's uncle, Bill Owens	
4/18/81	**26**	5	13. Heart Of The Matter	Ovation 1169
9/5/81	**7**	10	14. **Teach Me To Cheat**	Mercury 57055
1/16/82	**10**	9	15. **If You're Waiting On Me (You're Backing Up)**	Mercury 76131
7/10/82	**30**	5	16. Cheater's Prayer	Mercury 76155
10/23/82	**35**	3	17. That's What I Get For Thinking	Mercury 76178
6/25/83	**19**	7	18. Precious Love	Mercury 812300
			Emmylou Harris (harmony vocal)	
10/8/83	**20**	8	19. Movin' Train	Mercury 814195
2/11/84	**1 (1)**	12	20. **Thank God For The Radio**	Mercury 818056
7/7/84	**15**	8	21. My Baby's Gone	Mercury 822203
12/1/84+	**20**	8	22. I'd Dance Every Dance With You	Mercury 880306
3/30/85	**27**	6	23. Four Wheel Drive	Mercury 880588
7/6/85	**26**	6	24. If You Break My Heart	Mercury 880828
			KENNEDY, Ray	
			Born on 5/13/54 in Buffalo, New York. His father, Ray Sr., was the national credit manager for Sears and conceptualized the Discover credit card.	
1/5/91	**10**	12	1. **What A Way To Go**	Atlantic 87960
			KENT, George	
			Born on 6/12/35 in Dallas. Moved to Metaire, Louisiana; worked on WARB-Covington, Louisiana. Owner of the Cow Palace in Ft. Collins, Colorado.	
2/14/70	**26**	5	1. Hello, I'm A Jukebox	Mercury 72985
			Diana Duke (female vocal)	

DATE	POS	WKS	ARTIST– RECORD TITLE	LABEL & NO.
			KENTUCKY HEADHUNTERS, The	
			Rock-country quintet from Edmonton, Kentucky. Founded by brothers Richard (born 1/27/55) and Fred (born 7/8/58) Young with their cousin Greg Martin (born 3/31/54). Brothers Doug (born 2/16/60) and Ricky Lee (born 10/8/53) Phelps left in 1992 to form Brother Phelps; replaced by Mark Orr (born 11/16/49) and Anthony Kenney (born 10/8/53). Group hosted own show on WLOC-FM radio, *The Chitlin' Show*. CMA Awards: 1990 and 1991 Vocal Group of the Year.	
11/11/89	25	9	1. Walk Softly On This Heart Of Mine	Mercury 874744
3/17/90	15	14	2. Dumas Walker	Mercury 876536
			title refers to the owner of Walker's Package Store in Moss, Tennessee (d: 4/22/91, age 75)	
6/23/90	8	16	3. **Oh Lonesome Me**	Mercury 875450
11/10/90	23	9	4. Rock 'N' Roll Angel	Mercury 878214
			KENYON, Joe	
			Pseudonym of producer/guitarist Jerry Kennedy and pianist David Briggs.	
8/8/87	33	5	1. Hymne [I]	Mercury 888642
			tune written by Vangelis and featured in Gallo Wine commercials	
			KERSHAW, Doug	
			Born on 1/24/36 in Tiel Ridge, Louisiana. Sang with his mother from age eight. At 12 years old, had own band, the Continental Playboys, with brothers Russell "Rusty" and Nelson "Pee Wee." Teamed with Rusty in duo Rusty & Doug; recorded for Feature in 1953. Went solo in 1964. Appeared in the movies *Zachariah*, *Medicine Ball Caravan* and *Days Of Heaven*.	
8/1/81	29	4	1. Hello Woman	Scotti Br. 02137
			KERSHAW, Sammy	
			Native of Kaplan, Louisiana. Began singing in clubs at age 12. One-time member of the group Blackwater. Third cousin of Cajun fiddler Doug Kershaw. Appeared in the 1995 movie *Fall Time*.	
11/16/91+	3	15	1. **Cadillac Style**	Mercury 868812
3/14/92	12	12	2. Don't Go Near The Water	Mercury 866324
7/18/92	17	11	3. Yard Sale	Mercury 866754
11/7/92+	10	13	4. **Anywhere But Here**	Mercury 864316
2/27/93	1 (1)	18	5. **She Don't Know She's Beautiful**	Mercury 864854
6/5/93	9	13	6. **Haunted Heart**	Mercury 862096
10/9/93	7	14	7. **Queen Of My Double Wide Trailer**	Mercury 862600
2/12/94	3	16	8. **I Can't Reach Her Anymore**	Mercury 858102
6/11/94	2 (1)	15	9. **National Working Woman's Holiday**	Mercury 858722
9/10/94	2 (2)	16	10. **Third Rate Romance**	Mercury 858922
			#11 Country hit for The Amazing Rhythm Aces in 1975	
1/21/95	27	6	11. Southbound	Mercury 856410
4/15/95	18	9	12. If You're Gonna Walk, I'm Gonna Crawl	Mercury 856686
4/27/96	5	13↑	13. Meant To Be	Mercury 852874
			KETCHUM, Hal	
			Born on 4/9/53 in Greenwich, New York. Singer/guitarist. Began as a drummer in an R&B band at age 15. Later moved to Florida and worked as a carpenter's helper. Moved to Gruene, Texas, in 1981. Joined the *Grand Ole Opry* in 1994.	
6/29/91	2 (1)	14	1. **Small Town Saturday Night**	Curb 76865

DATE	POS	WKS	ARTIST–RECORD TITLE	LABEL & NO.
11/30/91+	**13**	12	2. I Know Where Love Lives	Curb 76892
3/7/92	**2** (1)	17	3. **Past The Point Of Rescue**	Curb LP Cut
7/4/92	**16**	9	4. Five O'Clock World	Curb 76903
			#4 Pop hit for The Vogues in 1966;	
			above 4 from the album *Past The Point Of Rescue* on Curb 77450	
10/17/92+	**3**	17	5. **Sure Love**	Curb LP Cut
			later available as the B side of #7 below	
3/6/93	**2** (1)	17	6. **Hearts Are Gonna Roll**	Curb LP Cut
7/3/93	**8**	12	7. **Mama Knows The Highway**	Curb 76915
11/13/93	**24**	9	8. Someplace Far Away (Careful What You're Dreamin')	Curb LP Cut
			above 4 from the album *Sure Love* on Curb 77581	
5/14/94	**20**	13	9. (Tonight We Just Might) Fall In Love Again	Curb 76922
10/22/94	**22**	8	10. That's What I Get (For Losin' You)	Curb LP Cut
3/25/95	**8**	13	11. **Stay Forever**	MCG/Curb 76929
			above 3 from the album *Every Little Word* on Curb 77660	

KILGORE, Merle

Born Wyatt Merle Kilgore on 9/8/34 in Chickasha, Oklahoma; raised in Shreveport, Louisiana. Worked as a DJ at KENT-Shreveport in 1950. Appeared on the *Louisiana Hayride* and the *Grand Ole Opry* in the early '50s. Wrote many hits for other artists, including "More And More" for Webb Pierce, "Wolverton Mountain" for Claude King, "Johnny Reb" for Johnny Horton and "Ring Of Fire" for Johnny Cash. Appeared in the movies *Nevada Smith* and *Five Card Stud*. Longtime opening act for Hank Williams, Jr., whom he now manages.

DATE	POS	WKS	ARTIST–RECORD TITLE	LABEL & NO.
2/1/60	**12**	13	1. Dear Mama	Starday 469
7/4/60	**10**	11	2. **Love Has Made You Beautiful/**	
7/18/60	**29**	1	3. Getting Old Before My Time	Starday 497

KIMBERLYS, The—see JENNINGS, Waylon

KING, Claude

Born on 2/5/33 in Shreveport, Louisiana. Guitarist from age 12. Attended University of Idaho on a baseball scholarship. Worked on the *Louisiana Hayride* from 1952. First recorded for Gotham in 1952. Appeared in the movies *Swamp Girl* and *Year Of The Wahoo*. Acted in the TV miniseries *The Blue And The Gray* in 1982.

DATE	POS	WKS	ARTIST–RECORD TITLE	LABEL & NO.
7/3/61	**7**	16	1. **Big River, Big Man**	Columbia 42043
11/13/61+	**7**	15	2. **The Comancheros**	Columbia 42196
			inspired by the movie starring John Wayne	
5/5/62	**1** (9)	26	● 3. **Wolverton Mountain**	Columbia 42352
			title is an actual place in Arkansas where Clifton Clowers lived	
10/20/62	**10**	7	4. **The Burning Of Atlanta**	Columbia 42581
12/22/62+	**11**	9	5. I've Got The World By The Tail	Columbia 42630
3/9/63	**12**	9	6. Sheepskin Valley	Columbia 42688
6/29/63	**12**	5	7. Building A Bridge	Columbia 42782
8/17/63	**13**	5	8. Hey Lucille!	Columbia 42833
3/7/64	**33**	2	9. That's What Makes The World Go Around	Columbia 42959
8/29/64	**11**	16	10. Sam Hill	Columbia 43083
6/26/65	**6**	18	11. **Tiger Woman**	Columbia 43298
12/4/65+	**17**	10	12. Little Buddy	Columbia 43416
4/23/66	**13**	12	13. Catch A Little Raindrop	Columbia 43510
5/27/67	**32**	4	14. The Watchman	Columbia 44035

DATE	POS	WKS	ARTIST– RECORD TITLE	LABEL & NO.
6/7/69	**9**	12	15. **All For The Love Of A Girl**	Columbia 44833
12/6/69	**18**	6	16. Friend, Lover, Woman, Wife	Columbia 45015
7/4/70	**33**	2	17. I'll Be Your Baby Tonight written by Bob Dylan	Columbia 45142
12/5/70+	**17**	10	18. Mary's Vineyard	Columbia 45248
5/8/71	**23**	8	19. Chip 'N' Dale's Place	Columbia 45340

KING, Don

Born on 5/1/54 in Omaha, Nebraska. Singer/songwriter/guitarist. To Nashville in 1974. Own Don King Music Group publishing company in Nashville.

DATE	POS	WKS	ARTIST– RECORD TITLE	LABEL & NO.
3/19/77	**16**	7	1. I've Got You (To Come Home To)	Con Brio 116
7/2/77	**17**	7	2. She's The Girl Of My Dreams	Con Brio 120
2/18/78	**29**	4	3. Music Is My Woman	Con Brio 129
6/3/78	**29**	5	4. Don't Make No Promises (You Can't Keep)	Con Brio 133
9/2/78	**26**	5	5. The Feelings So Right Tonight	Con Brio 137
1/6/79	**28**	4	6. You Were Worth Waiting For	Con Brio 142
4/7/79	**39**	2	7. Live Entertainment	Con Brio 149
3/22/80	**40**	1	8. Lonely Hotel	Epic 50840
6/28/80	**32**	4	9. Here Comes That Feeling Again	Epic 50877
6/20/81	**38**	2	10. I Still Miss Someone written by Johnny Cash	Epic 02046
10/10/81	**27**	5	11. The Closer You Get	Epic 02468
2/20/82	**40**	1	12. Running On Love	Epic 02674

KING, Donny

Born Joseph Mier in Crowley, Louisiana. Singer/guitarist.

DATE	POS	WKS	ARTIST– RECORD TITLE	LABEL & NO.
3/29/75	**20**	6	1. Mathilda #47 Pop hit for Cookie & His Cupcakes in 1959	Warner 8074

KING, Pee Wee

Born Julius Frank Kuczynski on 2/18/14 in Abrams, Wisconsin; raised in Milwaukee. Played fiddle and accordion. With the Log Cabin Boys in Louisville, 1935-36. Led own band, the Golden West Cowboys, from 1936. On the *Grand Ole Opry*, 1937-47. Own radio and TV series on WAVE-Louisville, 1947-57. Wrote "Slow Poke," "Tennessee Waltz," "Bonaparte's Retreat," "You Belong To Me," "Bimbo" and "Changing Partners." Worked with Minnie Pearl, 1959-63; continued touring until 1968. Elected to the Country Music Hall of Fame in 1974. Redd Stewart was lead singer on most of King's hits.

PEE WEE KING AND HIS GOLDEN WEST COWBOYS:

DATE	POS	WKS	ARTIST– RECORD TITLE	LABEL & NO.
4/3/48	**3**	35	1. **Tennessee Waltz** Best Seller #3 / Juke Box #4; 45 rpm: 48-0003	RCA Victor 2680
6/18/49	**12**	2	2. Tennessee Tears Best Seller #12; 45 rpm: 48-0037; Dave Denney (vocal)	RCA Victor 0037
9/10/49	**3**	3	3. **Tennessee Polka** Juke Box #3; 45 rpm: 48-0085; Gene Stewart (vocal)	RCA Victor 0086
1/21/50	**10**	1	4. **Bonaparte's Retreat** Jockey #10; 45 rpm: 48-0114	RCA Victor 0111
2/17/51	**6**	4	5. **Tennessee Waltz** [R] Jockey #6 / Juke Box #7	RCA 0407

DATE	POS	WKS	ARTIST– RECORD TITLE	LABEL & NO.
9/15/51	**1** (15)	31	● 6. **Slow Poke**	RCA 0489
			Juke Box #1(15) / Best Seller #1(14) / Jockey #1(9)	
			PEE WEE KING AND HIS BAND FEATURING REDD STEWART:	
2/16/52	**5**	14	7. **Silver And Gold**	RCA 4458
			Juke Box #5 / Best Seller #5 / Jockey #7	
5/17/52	**8**	3	8. **Busybody**	RCA 4655
			Juke Box #8 / Jockey #9	
1/2/54	**4**	10	9. **Changing Partners/**	
			Jockey #4	
1/23/54	**9**	2	10. **Bimbo**	RCA 5537
			Juke Box #9 / Best Seller #10 / Jockey #10	
7/10/54	**15**	1	11. Backward, Turn Backward	RCA 5694
			Jockey #15; Redd Stewart (vocal, all of above - except #2 & 3)	
			KING COLE TRIO, The	
			Jazz trio: Nat "King" Cole (piano), Oscar Moore (guitar) and Wesley Prince (bass). After the trio's long series of top-selling records, Cole (born 3/17/17, Montgomery, Alabama; died 2/15/65) went solo in 1950. With his "smooth" vocal style, Cole was one of the first black performers to be hugely popular with white audiences.	
5/13/44	**1** (6)	15	1. **Straighten Up And Fly Right/**	
5/20/44	**2** (1)	5	2. **I Can't See For Lookin'**	Capitol 154
			KING SISTERS, The	
			Family vocal group from Salt Lake City. Consisted of sisters Alyce, Yvonne, Donna and Louise Driggs. Own TV series, *The King Family*, in the '60s.	
12/28/46	**5**	1	1. **Divorce Me C.O.D.**	Victor 20-2018
			Buddy Cole (orch.)	
			KIRBY, Dave	
			Wrote "Is Anybody Goin' To San Antone" for Charley Pride, and many more. Married singer Leona Williams.	
6/20/81	**37**	3	1. North Alabama	Dimension 1019
			KIRK, Eddie	
			Born Edward Merle Kirk on 3/21/19 in Greeley, Colorado. With the Beverly Hillbillies in the early '30s. National Yodeling Champion in 1935 and 1936. Appeared on the Gene Autry radio shows and *Town Hall Party* in Compton, California, during the late '40s. Appeared in Western movies.	
10/2/48	**9**	6	1. **The Gods Were Angry With Me**	Capitol 15176
			Juke Box #9 / Best Seller #10; Tex Ritter (recitation)	
3/12/49	**9**	3	2. **Candy Kisses**	Capitol 15391
			Best Seller #9 / Juke Box #10	
			KIRK, Red	
			Worked on WNOX-Knoxville with Archie Campbell in 1947. Worked on WIMA-Lima, Ohio, in 1951. Known as "The Voice Of The Country."	
6/25/49	**14**	1	1. **Lovesick Blues**	Mercury 6189
			Juke Box #14	
7/22/50	**7**	7	2. **Lose Your Blues**	Mercury 6257
			Jockey #7; Jerry Byrd (lead vocal)	

DATE	POS	WKS	ARTIST–RECORD TITLE	LABEL & NO.
			KNIGHT, Evelyn	
			Born in Reedsville, Virginia, in 1920. Singer with Paul Whiteman, Tony Martin and Gordon MacRae. Also worked with the Herman Chittison Trio. Nicknamed "The Lass With The Delicate Air."	
2/17/51	6	1	1. **My Heart Cries For You** **EVELYN KNIGHT and RED FOLEY** Jockey #6; Alcyone Beasley Singers (backing vocals)	Decca 27378
			KNOBLOCK, Fred	
			Born in Jackson, Mississippi. With the rock band Let's Eat in the late 1970s. Member of the Country singing/songwriter trios Schuyler, Knobloch & Overstreet (SKO) and Schuyler, Knobloch & Bickhardt (SKB).	
9/6/80	30	3	1. Why Not Me	Scotti Br. 518
12/27/80+	10	11	2. **Killin' Time** **FRED KNOBLOCK AND SUSAN ANTON** Anton is an actress/model	Scotti Br. 609
9/12/81	10	8	3. **Memphis** written by Chuck Berry; Lonnie Mack and Johnny Rivers had Pop hits	Scotti Br. 02434
4/17/82	33	4	4. I Had It All	Scotti Br. 02752
			KRAUSS, Alison	
			Born on 7/23/71 in Champaign, Illinois. Singer/bluegrass fiddler. CMA Awards: 1995 Horizon Award; 1995 Female Vocalist of the Year.	
12/31/94+	7	16	1. **Somewhere In The Vicinity Of The Heart** **SHENANDOAH With Alison Krauss** from Shenandoah's album *In The Vicinity Of The Heart* on Liberty 31109; later available as the B-side of Shenandoah's single "Darned If I Don't (Danged If I Do)" on Liberty 18484	Liberty LP Cut
4/22/95	3	12	2. **When You Say Nothing At All** **ALISON KRAUSS & UNION STATION** CMA Award: Single of the Year	BNA 64277
			KRISTOFFERSON, Kris	
			Born on 6/22/36 in Brownsville, Texas. Attended Pomona College and earned Rhodes Scholarship to Oxford University in England; attended 1958-59. Wrote "Me And Bobby McGee," "For The Good Times" and "Help Me Make It Through The Night." Moved to Nashville in 1965. Married to Rita Coolidge, 1973-80. Has starred in many movies since 1972.	
5/12/73	1 (1)	14	● 1. **Why Me** Rita Coolidge and Larry Gatlin (backing vocals)	Monument 8571
			WAYLON JENNINGS, WILLIE NELSON, JOHNNY CASH, KRIS KRISTOFFERSON:	
6/1/85	1 (1)	14	2. **Highwayman**	Columbia 04881
10/5/85	15	9	3. Desperados Waiting For A Train	Columbia 05594
3/31/90	25	7	4. Silver Stallion	Columbia 73233

DATE	POS	WKS	ARTIST– RECORD TITLE	LABEL & NO.

L

LA COSTA

Born LaCosta Tucker on 4/6/51 in Seminole, Texas. Elder sister of Tanya Tucker. With Tanya in the Country Westerners in Phoenix in the '60s. Left music for a career in medicine, returned to show business in 1972.

DATE	POS	WKS	ARTIST– RECORD TITLE	LABEL & NO.
6/8/74	25	6	1. I Wanta Get To You	Capitol 3856
10/5/74	3	13	2. **Get On My Love Train**	Capitol 3945
3/8/75	10	9	3. **He Took Me For A Ride**	Capitol 4022
7/5/75	19	6	4. This House Runs On Sunshine	Capitol 4082
11/1/75	11	9	5. Western Man	Capitol 4139
2/21/76	28	5	6. I Just Got A Feeling	Capitol 4209
6/5/76	23	7	7. Lovin' Somebody On A Rainy Night	Capitol 4264
10/16/76	37	3	8. What'll I Do	Capitol 4327

LANA RAE—see RAE

LANDERS, Dave

Uncle of Rich Landers.

DATE	POS	WKS	ARTIST– RECORD TITLE	LABEL & NO.
7/9/49	10	7	1. **Before You Call** Best Seller #10 / Juke Box #12	MGM 10427

LANDERS, Rich

Born in St. Louis. Played piano and guitar from age eight, worked professionally from age 16. Nephew of Dave Landers. Wrote Vern Gosdin's "Your Bedroom Eyes."

DATE	POS	WKS	ARTIST– RECORD TITLE	LABEL & NO.
8/15/81	40	1	1. Hold On	Ovation 1173
3/19/83	40	1	2. Take It All	AMI 1311

LANE, Cristy

Born Eleanor Johnston on 1/8/40 in Peoria, Illinois. Owned a nightclub in Peoria. Moved to Nashville in 1972. Her husband, Lee Stoller, formed LS Records in 1976.

DATE	POS	WKS	ARTIST– RECORD TITLE	LABEL & NO.
9/17/77	7	10	1. **Let Me Down Easy**	LS 131
1/14/78	16	6	2. Shake Me I Rattle	LS 148
4/15/78	10	9	3. **I'm Gonna Love You Anyway**	LS 156
8/5/78	7	10	4. **Penny Arcade**	LS 167
12/16/78+	5	12	5. **I Just Can't Stay Married To You**	LS 169
5/19/79	10	10	6. **Simple Little Words** also released on LS 172	United Art. 1304
9/8/79	17	8	7. Slippin' Up, Slippin' Around	United Art. 1314
1/5/80	16	7	8. Come To My Love	United Art. 1328
4/12/80	1 (1)	14	9. **One Day At A Time**	United Art. 1342
9/6/80	8	8	10. **Sweet Sexy Eyes**	United Art. 1369
2/7/81	17	9	11. I Have A Dream first recorded by Abba on their *Voulez-Vous* album in 1979	Liberty 1396
5/23/81	21	7	12. Love To Love You	Liberty 1406
11/14/81	38	2	13. Cheatin' Is Still On My Mind	Liberty 1432

DATE	POS	WKS	ARTIST–RECORD TITLE	LABEL & NO.
2/6/82	22	5	14. Lies On Your Lips	Liberty 1443
			LANE, Red	
			Real name: Hollis R. DeLaughter. Born on 2/9/39 in Bogalusa, Louisiana; raised in Michigan. Singer/songwriter. Did session work in Nashville from the early '60s.	
5/29/71	32	5	1. The World Needs A Melody	RCA 9970
			LANE, Terri	
			Female singer born in Joelton, Tennessee. Vocalist with studio band on WSM-Nashville. Made numerous radio and TV commercials.	
4/28/73	37	4	1. Daisy May (And Daisy May Not)	Monument 8565
			LANG, k.d.	
			Born Kathryn Dawn Lang on 11/2/61 in Consort, Alberta, Canada. Named her group The Reclines, in honor of of Patsy Cline.	
6/18/88	21	9	1. I'm Down To My Last Cigarette	Sire 27919
8/12/89	22	7	2. Full Moon Full Of Love	Sire 22932
			k.d. lang and the reclines	
			LARKIN, Billy	
			Born in Huntland, Tennessee. Attended Middle Tennessee State University.	
2/22/75	22	6	1. Leave It Up To Me	Bryan 1010
6/7/75	23	5	2. The Devil In Mrs. Jones	Bryan 1018
10/4/75	34	4	3. Indian Giver	Bryan 1026
9/25/76	36	3	4. Kiss And Say Goodbye	Casino 076
			#1 Pop hit for the Manhattans in 1976	
3/7/81	35	3	5. 20/20 Hindsight	Sunbird 7557
6/27/81	24	6	6. Longing For The High	Sunbird 7562
			LARSON, Nicolette	
			Born on 7/17/52 in Helena, Montana; raised in Kansas City. Attended the University of Missouri. Moved to California in 1974; worked with the Nocturnes. Worked as backup singer for Hoyt Axton, Neil Young, Linda Ronstadt, Emmylou Harris, the Doobie Brothers, Van Halen, Graham Nash and many others.	
7/12/86	9	11	1. **That's How You Know When Love's Right**	MCA 52839
			Steve Wariner (guest vocal)	
			LAWRENCE, Tracy	
			Born on 1/27/68 in Atlanta, Texas; raised in Foreman, Arkansas. Male singer. In May 1991, he was shot four times in an attempted holdup in Nashville; fully recovered. In April 1994, arrested for possession of a prohibited weapon and for impersonating a police officer.	
11/23/91+	1 (1)	18	1. **Sticks And Stones**	Atlantic 87588
2/29/92	3	17	2. **Today's Lonely Fool**	Atlantic LP Cut
7/4/92	4	18	3. **Runnin' Behind**	Atlantic LP Cut
10/31/92+	8	14	4. **Somebody Paints The Wall**	Atlantic LP Cut
			later available as the B-side of #5 below; above 4 from the album *Sticks And Stones* on Atlantic 82326	
3/13/93	1 (2)	17	5. **Alibis**	Atlantic 87372

DATE	POS	WKS	ARTIST–RECORD TITLE	LABEL & NO.
6/19/93	**1** (1)	18	6. **Can't Break It To My Heart**	Atlantic 87330
10/2/93	**1** (1)	14	7. **My Second Home**	Atlantic 87312
2/19/94	**1** (2)	17	8. **If The Good Die Young**	Atlantic LP Cut
			above 4 from the album *Alibis* on Atlantic 82483	
6/11/94	7	13	9. **Renegades, Rebels And Rogues**	Atlantic LP Cut
			from the movie *Maverick* starring Mel Gibson and Jodie Foster, and from the soundtrack album on Atlantic 82595	
9/24/94	**2** (1)	18	10. **I See It Now**	Atlantic 87199
1/21/95	**2** (2)	17	11. **As Any Fool Can See**	Atlantic 87180
4/29/95	**1** (1)	17	12. **Texas Tornado**	Atlantic LP Cut
8/12/95	**2** (1)	18	13. **If The World Had A Front Porch**	Atlantic 87119
			above 4 from the album *I See It Now* on Atlantic 82656	
12/30/95+	4	18	14. If You Loved Me	Atlantic LP Cut
4/20/96	**1** (3)	14 ↑	15. Time Marches On	Atlantic LP Cut
			above 2 from the album *Time Marches On* on Atlantic 82866	
			LAWRENCE, Vicki	
			Born on 5/26/49 in Inglewood, California. Regular on Carol Burnett's CBS-TV series, 1967-78. Also starred in TV's *Mama's Family*, 1982-87. Married songwriter/singer Bobby Russell in 1972.	
6/2/73	36	3	● 1. The Night The Lights Went Out In Georgia	Bell 45303
			LEAPY LEE	
			Born Lee Graham on 7/2/42 in Eastbourne, England. Acted on stage and TV in England.	
10/26/68	11	12	1. Little Arrows	Decca 32380
			LEATHERWOOD, Bill	
7/11/60	11	13	1. The Long Walk	Country Jub. 539
			LeDOUX, Chris	
			Born on 10/2/48 in Biloxi, Mississippi. Moved to Austin in 1960. Inter-Collegiate National Champion Bareback Rider; World Bareback Champion in 1976. After several years of independent label success, big fan Garth Brooks helped to get him signed to Capitol. Mentioned in lyrics of Brooks's first hit "Much Too Young (To Feel This Damn Old)."	
8/1/92	7	12	1. **Whatcha Gonna Do With A Cowboy**	Liberty 57885
			Garth Brooks (backing vocal)	
12/5/92+	18	11	2. Cadillac Ranch	Liberty 56787
			LEE, Billy—see NUNN, Earl	
			LEE, Brenda	
			Born Brenda Mae Tarpley on 12/11/44 in Lithonia, Georgia. Professional singer since age six. Signed to Decca Records in 1956. Became known as "Little Miss Dynamite."	
4/6/57	15	1	1. One Step At A Time	Decca 30198
			Best Seller #15	
9/11/71	30	6	2. If This Is Our Last Time	Decca 32848
3/4/72	37	4	3. Misty Memories	Decca 32918
3/17/73	5	11	4. **Nobody Wins**	MCA 40003
9/8/73	6	11	5. **Sunday Sunrise**	MCA 40107

DATE	POS	WKS	ARTIST– RECORD TITLE	LABEL & NO.
2/16/74	6	9	6. **Wrong Ideas**	MCA 40171
8/17/74	4	9	7. **Big Four Poster Bed**	MCA 40262
12/7/74+	6	8	8. **Rock On Baby**	MCA 40318
5/3/75	8	9	9. **He's My Rock**	MCA 40385
			The Holladays (vocal accompaniment)	
9/13/75	23	5	10. Bringing It Back	MCA 40442
3/13/76	38	1	11. Find Yourself Another Puppet	MCA 40511
11/3/79	8	11	12. **Tell Me What It's Like**	MCA 41130
3/1/80	10	9	13. **The Cowgirl And The Dandy**	MCA 41187
10/11/80	9	8	14. **Broken Trust**	MCA 41322
			The Oak Ridge Boys (vocal accompaniment)	
2/21/81	26	5	15. Every Now And Then	MCA 51047
11/28/81	32	3	16. Only When I Laugh	MCA 51195
			title song from the movie starring Marsha Mason	
2/27/82	33	3	17. From Levis To Calvin Klein Jeans	MCA 51230
9/8/84	22	6	18. A Sweeter Love (I'll Never Know)	MCA 52394
1/26/85	15	9	19. Hallelujah, I Love You So	Epic 04723
			GEORGE JONES with BRENDA LEE	
			#5 R&B hit for Ray Charles in 1956	

LEE, Dickey

Born Dickey Lipscomb on 9/21/36 in Memphis. First recorded for Sun Records in 1957.

DATE	POS	WKS	ARTIST– RECORD TITLE	LABEL & NO.
10/9/71	8	11	1. **Never Ending Song Of Love**	RCA 1013
			#13 Pop hit for Delaney & Bonnie in 1971	
3/4/72	25	7	2. I Saw My Lady	RCA 0623
7/1/72	15	11	3. Ashes Of Love	RCA 0710
11/11/72	31	5	4. Baby, Bye Bye	RCA 0798
7/28/73	30	2	5. Put Me Down Softly	RCA 0980
1/11/75	22	5	6. The Busiest Memory In Town	RCA 10091
9/13/75	1 (1)	14	7. **Rocky**	RCA 10361
			#9 Pop hit for Austin Roberts in 1975	
2/21/76	9	9	8. **Angels, Roses, And Rain**	RCA 10543
7/10/76	35	3	9. Makin' Love Don't Always Make Love Grow	RCA 10684
10/2/76	3	12	10. **9,999,999 Tears**	RCA 10764
			written by Razzy Bailey	
4/9/77	20	7	11. If You Gotta Make A Fool Of Somebody	RCA 10914
			#22 Pop hit for James Ray in 1962	
7/30/77	22	5	12. Virginia, How Far Will You Go	RCA 11009
11/5/77	21	6	13. Peanut Butter	RCA 11125
2/25/78	27	6	14. Love Is A Word	RCA 11191
9/6/80	30	4	15. Workin' My Way To Your Heart	Mercury 57027
12/20/80+	30	4	16. Lost In Love	Mercury 57036
			DICKEY LEE with KATHY BURDICK	
			#3 Pop hit for Air Supply in 1980	
8/1/81	37	2	17. Honky Tonk Hearts	Mercury 57052

DATE	POS	WKS	ARTIST– RECORD TITLE	LABEL & NO.
			LEE, Johnny	
			Born John Lee Ham on 7/3/46 in Texas City; raised in Alta Loma, Texas. Played in rock bands in the early '60s. Own band, the Road Runners, in high school. Served in U.S. Navy during Vietnam conflict. Worked at Gilley's nightclub; later opened his own club a few miles away. Married to actress Charlene Tilton, 1982-84.	
9/4/76	**22**	6	1. Red Sails In The Sunset	GRT 065
			#1 Pop hit for both Bing Crosby and Guy Lombardo in 1935	
1/22/77	**37**	1	2. Ramblin' Rose	GRT 096
			#2 Pop hit for Nat King Cole in 1962	
6/11/77	**15**	9	3. Country Party	GRT 125
			Country version of Rick Nelson's "Garden Party"	
8/2/80	**1 (3)**	10	● 4. **Lookin' For Love**	Full Moon 47004
			from the movie *Urban Cowboy* starring John Travolta	
10/25/80	**1 (2)**	13	5. **One In A Million**	Asylum 47076
2/14/81	**3**	12	6. **Pickin' Up Strangers**	Full Moon 47105
6/6/81	**3**	12	7. **Prisoner Of Hope**	Full Moon 47138
10/10/81	**1 (1)**	10	8. **Bet Your Heart On Me**	Full Moon 47215
2/6/82	**10**	10	9. **Be There For Me Baby**	Full Moon 47301
5/29/82	**14**	8	10. When You Fall In Love	Full Moon 47444
11/6/82	**10**	11	11. Cherokee Fiddle	Full Moon 69945
			JOHNNY LEE AND FRIENDS	
			Michael Martin Murphey and Charlie Daniels (backing vocals)	
2/19/83	**6**	12	12. **Sounds Like Love**	Full Moon 69848
7/2/83	**2 (2)**	13	13. **Hey Bartender**	Full Moon 29605
11/12/83	**23**	5	14. My Baby Don't Slow Dance	Full Moon 29486
2/25/84	**1 (1)**	12	15. **The Yellow Rose**	Warner 29375
			JOHNNY LEE with LANE BRODY	
			theme song from the TV series starring Cybill Shepherd	
9/15/84	**1 (1)**	14	16. **You Could've Heard A Heart Break**	Warner 29206
2/2/85	**9**	12	17. **Rollin' Lonely**	Warner 29110
6/1/85	**12**	12	18. Save The Last Chance	Warner 29021
11/2/85	**19**	7	19. They Never Had To Get Over You	Warner 28901
			LEE, Joni	
			Born Joni Lee Jenkins in 1957 in Arkansas; raised in Oklahoma City. Eldest daughter of Conway Twitty. Singing since age four. Also see Conway Twitty.	
1/3/76	**16**	8	1. I'm Sorry Charlie	MCA 40501
			LEE, Robin	
			Born Robin Lee Irwin on 11/7/53 in Nashville. Female vocalist. Graduate of Overton High School.	
5/10/86	**37**	2	1. I'll Take Your Love Anytime	Evergreen 1039
4/7/90	**12**	10	2. Black Velvet	Atlantic 87979
			#1 Pop hit for Alannah Myles in 1990	
			LEHR, Zella	
			Born on 3/14/51 in Burbank, California. Worked in family vaudeville team, the Crazy Lehrs, from age six. Act later renamed the Young Lehrs. Regular on the TV series *Hee-Haw*. Reno-area favorite.	
1/21/78	**7**	11	1. **Two Doors Down**	RCA 11174
6/24/78	**31**	5	2. When The Fire Gets Hot	RCA 11265

DATE	POS	WKS	ARTIST– RECORD TITLE	LABEL & NO.
9/16/78	**20**	8	3. Danger, Heartbreak Ahead	RCA 11359
1/27/79	**24**	5	4. Play Me A Memory	RCA 11433
8/11/79	**34**	3	5. Once In A Blue Moon	RCA 11648
1/26/80	**26**	4	6. Love Has Taken Its' Time	RCA 11754
5/17/80	**25**	5	7. Rodeo Eyes	RCA 11953
11/8/80	**34**	3	8. Love Crazy Love	RCA 12073
9/12/81	**16**	7	9. Feedin' The Fire	Columbia 02431
			LEWIS, Bobby	
			Guitarist/lute player born in Hodgenville, Kentucky. On radio and TV shows from age 13. Worked on the TV series *High Varieties, Old Kentucky Barn Dance, Saturday Night Country Style* and *Hayloft Hoedown*.	
11/12/66	**6**	14	1. **How Long Has It Been**	United Art. 50067
7/1/67	**12**	11	2. Love Me And Make It All Better written by Eddie Rabbitt	United Art. 50161
11/18/67	**26**	7	3. I Doubt It	United Art. 50208
4/13/68	**29**	7	4. Ordinary Miracle	United Art. 50263
8/17/68	**10**	11	5. **From Heaven To Heartache**	United Art. 50327
2/8/69	**27**	6	6. Each And Every Part Of Me	United Art. 50476
10/4/69	**25**	6	7. Things For You And I	United Art. 50573
6/27/70	**14**	10	8. Hello Mary Lou #9 Pop hit for Ricky Nelson in 1961	United Art. 50668
12/1/73	**21**	6	9. Too Many Memories	Ace of Hearts 0472
3/30/74	**32**	4	10. I Never Get Through Missing You	Ace of Hearts 0480
6/2/79	**39**	2	11. She's Been Keepin' Me Up Nights	Capricorn 0318
			LEWIS, Hugh X.	
			Born Hubert Brad Lewis on 12/7/32 in Yeaddiss, Kentucky. Worked on CBC-TV's *Tennessee Barn Dance* in 1963; *Grand Ole Opry* in 1964; ABC-TV's *American Swingaround* in 1967. Appeared in the movies *40-Acre Feud, Gold Guitar* and *Cottonpickin' Chicken-Pluckers*. Wrote "B.J. The D.J." for Stonewall Jackson.	
1/2/65	**21**	15	1. What I Need Most	Kapp 622
9/18/65	**32**	3	2. Out Where The Ocean Meets The Sky	Kapp 673
1/22/66	**30**	5	3. I'd Better Call The Law On Me	Kapp 717
8/5/67	**38**	5	4. You're So Cold (I'm Turning Blue)	Kapp 830
5/4/68	**36**	3	5. Evolution And The Bible	Kapp 895
			LEWIS, Jerry Lee	
			Born on 9/29/35 in Ferriday, Louisiana. Played piano since age nine, professionally since age 15. First recorded for Sun in 1956. Appeared in the 1957 movie *Jamboree!* Career waned in 1958 after marriage to 13-year-old cousin, Myra Gale Brown, daughter of his bass player. Made comeback in Country music beginning in 1968. Nicknamed "The Killer," Lewis has been surrounded by personal tragedies in the past two decades and survived several serious illnesses. Cousin to Country singer Mickey Gilley and TV evangelist Jimmy Swaggart. Had several duets with his sister, Linda Gail Lewis. Inducted into the Rock and Roll Hall of Fame in 1986. Jerry's early career is documented in the 1989 movie *Great Balls Of Fire* starring Dennis Quaid.	
6/17/57	**1** (2)	23	● 1. **Whole Lot Of Shakin' Going On** Best Seller #1 / Jockey #6	Sun 267

DATE	POS	WKS	ARTIST– RECORD TITLE	LABEL & NO.
12/2/57+	1 (2)	19	● 2. **Great Balls Of Fire/** Best Seller #1 / Jockey #4	
12/23/57+	2 (2)	10	3. **You Win Again** Best Seller #2 / Jockey #4	Sun 281
3/17/58	4	13	4. **Breathless** Best Seller #4 / Jockey #12	Sun 288
6/9/58	9	10	5. **High School Confidential** Best Seller #9	Sun 296
10/13/58	19	1	6. I'll Make It All Up To You Best Seller #19	Sun 303
5/8/61	27	1	7. What'd I Say	Sun 356
8/7/61	22	5	8. Cold Cold Heart **JERRY LEE LEWIS And His Pumping Piano** (all of above, except #1)	Sun 364
2/1/64	36	2	9. Pen And Paper flip side "Hit The Road Jack" Bubbled Under at #103	Smash 1857
3/23/68	4	15	10. **Another Place Another Time**	Smash 2146
6/15/68	2 (2)	15	11. **What's Made Milwaukee Famous (Has Made A Loser Out Of Me)**	Smash 2164
10/12/68	2 (2)	10	12. **She Still Comes Around (To Love What's Left Of Me)**	Smash 2186
1/11/69	1 (1)	13	13. **To Make Love Sweeter For You**	Smash 2202
6/7/69	3	13	14. **One Has My Name (The Other Has My Heart)**	Smash 2224
6/14/69	9	8	15. **Don't Let Me Cross Over** **JERRY LEE LEWIS & LINDA GAIL LEWIS**	Smash 2220
9/6/69	6	9	16. **Invitation To Your Party**	Sun 1101
10/11/69	2 (2)	12	17. **She Even Woke Me Up To Say Goodbye**	Smash 2244
12/13/69+	2 (2)	14	18. **One Minute Past Eternity**	Sun 1107
2/28/70	2 (2)	12	19. **Once More With Feeling**	Smash 2257
5/9/70	7	13	20. **I Can't Seem To Say Goodbye**	Sun 1115
8/29/70	1 (2)	14	21. **There Must Be More To Love Than This**	Mercury 73099
12/12/70+	11	9	22. Waiting For A Train (All Around The Watertank) #14 Pop hit for Jimmie Rodgers in 1929	Sun 1119
4/10/71	3	13	23. **Touching Home**	Mercury 73192
7/3/71	31	6	24. Love On Broadway	Sun 1125
8/7/71	11	11	25. When He Walks On You (Like You Have Walked On Me)	Mercury 73227
11/13/71+	1 (1)	16	26. **Would You Take Another Chance On Me/**	
		15	27. Me And Bobby McGee	Mercury 73248
3/18/72	1 (3)	14	28. **Chantilly Lace/** #6 Pop hit for the Big Bopper in 1958	
		14	29. Think About It Darlin'	Mercury 73273
7/1/72	11	9	30. Lonely Weekends flip side "Turn On Your Love Light" made #95 on the *Hot 100*	Mercury 73296
10/28/72	14	10	31. Who's Gonna Play This Old Piano	Mercury 73328
3/10/73	19	7	32. No More Hanging On	Mercury 73361
5/19/73	20	7	33. Drinking Wine Spo-Dee O'Dee #2 R&B hit for Stick McGhee in 1949	Mercury 73374
10/20/73	6	10	34. **Sometimes A Memory Ain't Enough**	Mercury 73423
3/9/74	21	7	35. I'm Left, You're Right, She's Gone recorded by Elvis Presley on Sun 217 in 1955	Mercury 73452
7/20/74	18	6	36. Tell Tale Signs	Mercury 73491

DATE	POS	WKS	ARTIST– RECORD TITLE	LABEL & NO.
11/9/74	8	8	37. **He Can't Fill My Shoes**	Mercury 73618
3/22/75	13	8	38. I Can Still Hear The Music In The Restroom	Mercury 73661
7/26/75	24	6	39. Boogie Woogie Country Man	Mercury 73685
8/21/76	6	11	40. **Let's Put It Back Together Again**	Mercury 73822
1/15/77	27	4	41. The Closest Thing To You	Mercury 73872
11/19/77+	4	13	42. **Middle Age Crazy** title of 1980 movie, based on this song	Mercury 55011
4/1/78	10	7	43. **Come On In**	Mercury 55021
7/1/78	10	9	44. **I'll Find It Where I Can**	Mercury 55028
1/20/79	26	5	45. Save The Last Dance For Me #1 Pop hit for The Drifters in 1960	Sun 1139
4/21/79	18	6	46. Rockin' My Life Away/	
		6	47. I Wish I Was Eighteen Again	Elektra 46030
8/11/79	20	5	48. Who Will The Next Fool Be	Elektra 46067
2/23/80	11	8	49. When Two Worlds Collide	Elektra 46591
6/21/80	28	5	50. Honky Tonk Stuff	Elektra 46642
9/27/80	10	8	51. **Over The Rainbow** Judy Garland, Glenn Miller and Bob Crosby had hit versions in 1939	Elektra 47026
2/7/81	4	10	52. **Thirty Nine And Holding**	Elektra 47095

LEWIS, Linda Gail

Born on 7/18/47 in Ferriday, Louisiana. Youngest sister of Jerry Lee Lewis. Appeared on the TV series *Shindig* with Jerry Lee. Retired from music in 1977.

DATE	POS	WKS	ARTIST– RECORD TITLE	LABEL & NO.
6/14/69	9	8	1. **Don't Let Me Cross Over** **JERRY LEE LEWIS & LINDA GAIL LEWIS**	Smash 2220
9/16/72	39	3	2. Smile, Somebody Loves You	Mercury 73316

LEWIS, Texas Jim, and His Lone Star Cowboys

Born on 10/15/09 in Meigs, Georgia. Died on 1/23/90. Moved to Bedias, Texas, in 1928. Worked in New York City with the Lone Star Cowboys, 1935. Has appeared in 42 movies, beginning in 1937. First recorded for Vocalion in 1937. Own Kiddie TV series, *Safety Junction*, in Seattle, 1950-57.

DATE	POS	WKS	ARTIST– RECORD TITLE	LABEL & NO.
9/2/44	3	6	1. **Too Late To Worry Too Blue To Cry**	Decca 6099

LIGHTFOOT, Gordon

Born on 11/17/38 in Orilla, Ontario. Worked on CBC-TV series *Country Hoedown*. Teamed with Jim Whalen as the Two Tones in the mid-1960s. Wrote hits "Early Morning Rain" for Peter, Paul and Mary, "Ribbon Of Darkness" for Marty Robbins, and many others. First recorded for Chateau in 1965.

DATE	POS	WKS	ARTIST– RECORD TITLE	LABEL & NO.
7/13/74	13	7	● 1. Sundown	Reprise 1194

LINDSEY, LaWanda

Born on 1/12/53 in Tampa, Florida; raised in Savannah, Georgia. Debuted with father's band, the Dixie Showboys, in 1962. First recorded at age 14.

DATE	POS	WKS	ARTIST– RECORD TITLE	LABEL & NO.
4/18/70	27	4	1. Pickin' Wild Mountain Berries **LaWANDA LINDSEY & KENNY VERNON** #27 Pop hit for Peggy Scott & Jo Jo Benson in 1968	Chart 5055

DATE	POS	WKS	ARTIST– RECORD TITLE	LABEL & NO.
8/25/73	**38**	2	2. Today Will Be The First Day Of The Rest Of My Life	Capitol 3652
6/29/74	**28**	7	3. Hello Out There	Capitol 3875

LITTLE, Peggy

Born in Marlin, Texas; raised in Waco. On radio at age 10. Appeared on the TV series *Shindig*. Married at age 16. Regular on TV's *The Mike Douglas Show*.

DATE	POS	WKS	ARTIST– RECORD TITLE	LABEL & NO.
5/10/69	**40**	1	1. Son Of A Preacher Man #10 Pop hit for Dusty Springfield in 1969	Dot 17199
4/4/70	**37**	2	2. Mama, I Won't Be Wearing A Ring	Dot 17338
10/6/73	**37**	2	3. Sugarman	Epic 11028

LITTLE TEXAS

Six-man group: Texans Tim Rushlow (vocals), Dwayne O'Brien, Porter Howell and Duane Propes, with Del Gray and Brady Seals (nephew of Troy Seals and cousin of singers Jim [of Seals & Crofts] and Dan Seals). Seals was replaced by Jeff Huskins in 1995.

DATE	POS	WKS	ARTIST– RECORD TITLE	LABEL & NO.
10/12/91	**8**	15	1. **Some Guys Have All The Love** later available as the B-side of #2 below	Warner LP Cut
3/21/92	**13**	13	2. First Time For Everything	Warner 19024
7/18/92	**5**	15	3. **You And Forever And Me**	Warner 18867
11/21/92+	**17**	10	4. What Were You Thinkin'	Warner 18741
2/20/93	**16**	13	5. I'd Rather Miss You all of above from the album *First Time For Everything* on Warner 26820	Warner 18668
6/26/93	**2** (1)	16	6. **What Might Have Been**	Warner 18516
10/9/93	**4**	13	7. **God Blessed Texas**	Warner 18385
2/5/94	**1** (2)	17	8. **My Love**	Warner 18295
6/4/94	**14**	11	9. Stop On A Dime above 4 from the album *Big Time* on Warner 45276	Warner LP Cut
9/10/94	**5**	17	10. **Kick A Little**	Warner 18103
1/14/95	**4**	15	11. **Amy's Back In Austin**	Warner 18001
5/27/95	**27**	7	12. Southern Grace above 3 from the album *Kick A Little* on Warner 45739	Warner LP Cut
9/23/95	**5**	17	13. **Life Goes On**	Warner 17770

LOBO

Born Roland Kent Lavoie on 7/31/43 in Tallahassee, Florida. Played with Legends in Tampa in 1961. This group included Jim Stafford, Gerald Chambers and Gram Parsons. Own publishing company, Boo Publishing, since 1974. Member of The Wolfpack.

DATE	POS	WKS	ARTIST– RECORD TITLE	LABEL & NO.
1/30/82	**40**	1	1. I Don't Want To Want You	Lobo I

LOCKLIN, Hank

Born Lawrence Hankins Locklin on 2/15/18 in McLellan, Florida. Worked on WCOA-Pensacola in 1942. Joined the *Louisiana Hayride* in the late '40s. With the *Grand Ole Opry* since 1960. Toured Europe in 1957. Elected mayor of McLellan in the early '60s. Own TV series in Houston and Dallas in the '70s.

DATE	POS	WKS	ARTIST– RECORD TITLE	LABEL & NO.
6/25/49	**8**	5	1. **The Same Sweet Girl** Juke Box #8 / Best Seller #15	4 Star 1313
9/5/53	**1** (3)	32	2. **Let Me Be The One** Jockey #1(3) / Juke Box #1(2) / Best Seller #2	4 Star 1641

DATE	POS	WKS	ARTIST – RECORD TITLE	LABEL & NO.
3/24/56	9	1	3. **Why Baby Why** Jockey #9	RCA 6347
8/19/57	4	39	4. **Geisha Girl/** Best Seller #4 / Jockey #6	
		6	5. Livin' Alone Best Seller flip	RCA 6984
3/31/58	5	35	6. **Send Me The Pillow You Dream On** Jockey #5 / Best Seller #5	RCA 7127
4/28/58	3	23	7. **It's A Little More Like Heaven/** Jockey #3 / Best Seller #8	
		7	8. Blue Glass Skirt Best Seller flip	RCA 7203
3/7/60	1 (14)	36	9. **Please Help Me, I'm Falling**	RCA 7692
12/31/60+	14	12	10. One Step Ahead Of My Past	RCA 7813
6/5/61	12	7	11. From Here To There To You	RCA 7871
10/2/61	7	14	12. **Happy Birthday To Me/**	
9/11/61	14	12	13. You're The Reason	RCA 7921
1/13/62	10	14	14. **Happy Journey**	RCA 7965
6/23/62	14	11	15. We're Gonna Go Fishin'	RCA 8034
4/20/63	23	4	16. Flyin' South	RCA 8156
4/25/64	15	11	17. Followed Closely By My Teardrops	RCA 8318
5/29/65	32	6	18. Forty Nine, Fifty One	RCA 8560
2/12/66	35	2	19. The Girls Get Prettier (Every Day)	RCA 8695
11/11/67+	8	17	20. **The Country Hall Of Fame**	RCA 9323
4/27/68	40	3	21. Love Song For You	RCA 9476
3/1/69	34	6	22. Where The Blue Of The Night Meets The Gold Of The Day	RCA 9710
			LOGAN, Bud, & Wilma Burgess	
			Logan is former lead singer of The Blue Boys (vocal backing group for Jim Reeves).	
2/9/74	14	10	1. Wake Me Into Love	Shannon 816
			LONESOME STRANGERS, The	
			Los Angeles-based quartet: Jeff Rymes, Randy Weeks, Lorne Rall and Mike McLean.	
4/1/89	32	4	1. Goodbye Lonesome, Hello Baby Doll	Hightone 508
			LONESTAR	
			Nashville-based band: Richey McDonald (vocals, guitar), John Rich (vocals, bass), Michael Britt (guitar), Dean Sams (keyboards) and Keech Rainwater (drums).	
2/3/96	1 (3)	17	1. **No News/**	
9/23/95	8	15	2. **Tequila Talkin'**	BNA 64386
			LONG, Shorty, And The Santa Fe Rangers	
			Born Emidio Vagnoni on 10/11/23 in Reading, Pennsylvania. Worked on the WLS National Barn Dance and the Hayloft Hoedown in Philadelphia.	
10/30/48	12	1	1. Sweeter Than The Flowers Best Seller #12	Decca 46139

DATE	POS	WKS	ARTIST– RECORD TITLE	LABEL & NO.
			LONZO & OSCAR	
			Originally a comedy duo consisting of Rollin Sullivan (born 1/19/19, Edmonton, Kentucky) and Ken Marvin. Marvin was replaced in 1945 by Rollin's brother John (born 7/7/17; died 6/5/67). Joined the *Grand Ole Opry* in 1947. After John's death, Rollin teamed with David Hooten.	
1/31/48	5	7	1. **I'm My Own Grandpa** [N]	Victor 20-2563
			Juke Box #5; Winston County Pea Pickers (instrumental backing)	
6/5/61	26	1	2. Country Music Time	Starday 543
2/23/74	29	5	3. Traces Of Life	GRC 1006
			LORD, Bobby	
			Born on 1/6/34 in Sanford, Florida. Featured on Paul Whiteman's TV shows in the early '50s. Worked on Red Foley's *Jubilee USA* TV series in the late '50s. Own *Bobby Lord Show* in the mid-1960s.	
9/8/56	10	2	1. **Without Your Love**	Columbia 21539
			Juke Box #10 / Jockey #15	
1/11/64	21	9	2. Life Can Have Meaning	Hickory 1232
3/29/69	40	2	3. Yesterday's Letters	Decca 32431
12/20/69+	28	7	4. Rainbow Girl	Decca 32578
5/23/70	15	10	5. You And Me Against The World	Decca 32657
9/19/70	21	10	6. Wake Me Up Early In The Morning	Decca 32718
			LORRIE, Myrna-Buddy DeVal	
			Myrna was born Myrna Petrunke on 8/6/40 in Fort William, Ontario. Vocalist from age nine. Wrote "Are You Mine" at age 13. Own TV series at age 15. Buddy was born on 4/15/15 in Port Arthur, Ontario.	
1/1/55	6	14	1. **Are You Mine**	Abbott 172
			Jockey #6 / Juke Box #7 / Best Seller #12	
			LOU, Bonnie—see BONNIE	
			LOUDERMILK, John D.	
			Born on 3/31/34 in Durham, North Carolina. First cousin of The Louvin Brothers. Recorded as Johnny Dee and Ebe Sneezer on Colonial in 1957. Prolific songwriter; wrote "A Rose And A Baby Ruth," "Sittin' In The Balcony," "Tobacco Road," "Then You Can Tell Me Goodbye," "Waterloo," "Abilene," "Talk Back Trembling Lips," "Ebony Eyes," "Sad Movies," "Norman" and many others.	
6/29/63	23	4	1. Bad News	RCA 8154
7/10/65	20	9	2. That Ain't All	RCA 8579
			LOUVIN, Charlie	
			Born on 7/7/27. Younger of The Louvin Brothers.	
6/27/64	4	26	1. **I Don't Love You Anymore**	Capitol 5173
12/19/64+	27	14	2. Less And Less	Capitol 5296
4/10/65	7	14	3. **See The Big Man Cry**	Capitol 5369
10/30/65	26	7	4. Think I'll Go Somewhere And Cry Myself To Sleep	Capitol 5475
12/25/65+	15	11	5. You Finally Said Something Good (When You Said Goodbye)	Capitol 5550
1/21/67	38	2	6. Off And On	Capitol 5791
12/23/67+	36	4	7. The Only Way Out (Is To Walk Over Me)	Capitol 2007
3/30/68	20	11	8. Will You Visit Me On Sundays?	Capitol 2106

DATE	POS	WKS	ARTIST– RECORD TITLE	LABEL & NO.
8/31/68	**15**	9	9. Hey Daddy	Capitol 2231
12/21/68+	**19**	12	10. What Are Those Things (With Big Black Wings)	Capitol 2350
5/17/69	**27**	7	11. Let's Put Our World Back Together	Capitol 2448
10/18/69	**29**	5	12. Little Reasons	Capitol 2612
11/14/70	**18**	9	13. Something To Brag About	Capitol 2915
3/20/71	**26**	6	14. Did You Ever	Capitol 3029
7/10/71	**30**	3	15. Baby, You've Got What It Takes	Capitol 3111
			CHARLIE LOUVIN & MELBA MONTGOMERY (above 3)	
			#5 Pop hit for Dinah Washington & Brook Benton in 1960	
3/23/74	**36**	1	16. You're My Wife, She's My Woman	United Art. 368

LOUVIN BROTHERS, The

Duo of brothers (real name: Loudermilk) Lonnie Ira (born 4/21/24; died 6/28/65 in car crash) and Charlie Elzer (born 7/7/27). Worked with the Foggy Mountain Boys in Chattanooga in 1943, then had own radio show. Ira was in Charlie Monroe's Kentucky Partners in the mid-1940s. First known as The Louvin Brothers in 1947 when they worked on WROL-Knoxville. First recorded for Decca in 1949. On the *Grand Ole Opry*, 1955-57; returned in 1959. Disbanded in 1963. Charlie appeared in the movies *Music City USA* and *The Golden Guitar*.

DATE	POS	WKS	ARTIST– RECORD TITLE	LABEL & NO.
9/10/55	**8**	13	1. **When I Stop Dreaming** *Jockey #8 / Best Seller #13*	Capitol 3177
1/14/56	**1** (2)	24	2. **I Don't Believe You've Met My Baby** *Jockey #1 / Best Seller #5 / Juke Box #5*	Capitol 3300
5/26/56	**7**	10	3. **Hoping That You're Hoping** *Jockey #7 / Best Seller #8*	Capitol 3413
10/6/56	**7**	12	4. **You're Running Wild/** *Best Seller #7 / Jockey #11*	
10/6/56	**7**	11	5. **Cash On The Barrel Head** *Best Seller #7 / Jockey #10*	Capitol 3523
3/9/57	**11**	4	6. Don't Laugh *Jockey #11*	Capitol 3630
7/15/57	**14**	1	7. Plenty Of Everything But You **IRA and CHARLEY LOUVIN** *Jockey #14*	Capitol 3715
10/20/58+	**9**	22	8. **My Baby's Gone**	Capitol 4055
2/16/59	**19**	7	9. Knoxville Girl	Capitol 4117
3/13/61	**12**	14	10. I Love You Best Of All	Capitol 4506
9/25/61	**26**	1	11. How's The World Treating You	Capitol 4628
11/17/62	**21**	6	12. Must You Throw Dirt In My Face	Capitol 4822

LOVELESS, Patty

Born Patricia Ramey on 1/4/57 in Pikeville, Kentucky. Worked in duo with brother Roger from age 14. Toured with the Wilburn Brothers while still in high school. Worked clubs in North Carolina, 1973-85. Staff writer for Acuff-Rose. Joined the *Grand Ole Opry* in 1988. Married producer Emory Gordy, Jr., in February 1989. Distant cousin of Loretta Lynn, Crystal Gayle, Peggy Sue and Jay Lee Webb.

DATE	POS	WKS	ARTIST– RECORD TITLE	LABEL & NO.
3/12/88	**10**	10	1. **If My Heart Had Windows**	MCA 53270
6/18/88	**2** (1)	15	2. **A Little Bit In Love** *written by Steve Earle*	MCA 53333
11/5/88+	**4**	13	3. **Blue Side Of Town**	MCA 53418
2/18/89	**5**	14	4. **Don't Toss Us Away**	MCA 53477
6/10/89	**1** (1)	13	5. **Timber, I'm Falling In Love**	MCA 53641

DATE	POS	WKS	ARTIST– RECORD TITLE	LABEL & NO.
9/30/89	6	14	6. **The Lonely Side Of Love**	MCA 53702
1/27/90	1 (1)	20	7. **Chains**	MCA 53764
6/2/90	5	13	8. **On Down The Line**	MCA 79004
11/10/90	20	9	9. The Night's Too Long	MCA 53895
1/26/91	5	16	10. **I'm That Kind Of Girl**	MCA 53977
6/22/91	22	8	11. Blue Memories	MCA 54075
10/5/91	3	13	12. **Hurt Me Bad (In A Real Good Way)**	MCA 54178
2/1/92	13	11	13. Jealous Bone	MCA 54271
6/6/92	30	6	14. Can't Stop Myself From Loving You	MCA 54371
4/17/93	1 (2)	18	15. **Blame It On Your Heart**	Epic 74906
9/4/93	20	10	16. Nothin' But The Wheel	Epic 77076
12/4/93+	6	14	17. **You Will**	Epic 77271
4/9/94	3	15	18. **How Can I Help You Say Goodbye**	Epic 77416
8/13/94	3	17	19. **I Try To Think About Elvis**	Epic 77609
12/10/94+	4	16	20. **Here I Am**	Epic 77734
4/8/95	5	17	21. **You Don't Even Know Who I Am**	Epic 77856
7/29/95	6	14	22. **Halfway Down**	Epic 77956
1/13/96	1 (2)	18	23. **You Can Feel Bad**	Epic 78209
5/4/96	16 ↑	12 ↑	24. A Thousand Times A Day	Epic 78309

LOVETT, Lyle

Born on 11/1/56 in Houston; raised in Klein, Texas. Graduate of Texas A&M with degrees in German and journalism. Acted in the movies *The Player* and *Short Cuts*. Married actress Julia Roberts on 6/26/93; separated in March 1995.

DATE	POS	WKS	ARTIST– RECORD TITLE	LABEL & NO.
8/23/86	21	7	1. Farther Down The Line	Curb/MCA 52818
11/22/86+	10	12	2. **Cowboy Man**	Curb/MCA 52951
3/28/87	18	7	3. God Will	Curb/MCA 53030
6/27/87	15	9	4. Why I Don't Know	Curb/MCA 53102
10/24/87	13	12	5. Give Back My Heart	Curb/MCA 53157
3/5/88	17	8	6. She's No Lady	Curb/MCA 53246
6/18/88	24	6	7. I Loved You Yesterday	Curb/MCA 53316

LOWE, Jim

Born on 5/7/27 in Springfield, Missouri. DJ/vocalist/pianist/composer. DJ in New York City when he recorded the Pop hit "The Green Door" in 1956.

DATE	POS	WKS	ARTIST– RECORD TITLE	LABEL & NO.
5/20/57	8	3	1. **Talkin' To The Blues/** Best Seller #8; from the TV production *Modern Romances*	
		1	2. Four Walls Best Seller flip	Dot 15569

LOWRY, Ron

DATE	POS	WKS	ARTIST– RECORD TITLE	LABEL & NO.
4/25/70	39	2	1. Marry Me	Republic 1409

LUKE THE DRIFTER, JR.—see WILLIAMS, Hank Jr.

DATE	POS	WKS	ARTIST-RECORD TITLE		LABEL & NO.
			LUMAN, Bob		
			Born on 4/15/37 in Nacogdoches, Texas. Died on 12/27/78. Country-rockabilly singer/songwriter/guitarist. Member of the *Grand Ole Opry* from 1965 until his death.		
10/10/60	**9**	10	1. **Let's Think About Living**		Warner 5172
2/22/64	**24**	14	2. The File		Hickory 1238
2/5/66	**39**	2	3. Five Miles From Home (Soon I'll See Mary)		Hickory 1355
6/25/66	**39**	1	4. Poor Boy Blues		Hickory 1382
			written by Carl Perkins		
6/8/68	**19**	9	5. Ain't Got Time To Be Unhappy		Epic 10312
3/29/69	**24**	7	6. Come On Home And Sing The Blues To Daddy		Epic 10439
8/9/69	**23**	6	7. Every Day I Have To Cry Some		Epic 10480
			#45 Pop hit for Arthur Alexander in 1975		
8/1/70	**22**	8	8. Honky Tonk Man		Epic 10631
8/21/71	**40**	2	9. I Got A Woman		Epic 10755
			#1 R&B hit for Ray Charles in 1955		
11/27/71	**30**	6	10. A Chain Don't Take To Me		Epic 10786
2/19/72	**6**	13	11. **When You Say Love**		Epic 10823
			#32 Pop hit for Sonny & Cher in 1972		
6/24/72	**21**	6	12. It Takes You		Epic 10869
9/30/72	**4**	15	13. **Lonely Women Make Good Lovers**		Epic 10905
2/17/73	**7**	11	14. **Neither One Of Us**		Epic 10943
			#2 Pop hit for Gladys Knight & The Pips in 1973		
7/7/73	**23**	7	15. A Good Love Is Like A Good Song		Epic 10994
11/17/73+	**7**	11	16. **Still Loving You**	[R]	Epic 11039
4/13/74	**23**	6	17. Just Enough To Make Me Stay		Epic 11087
8/10/74	**25**	6	18. Let Me Make The Bright Lights Shine For You		Epic 11138
3/15/75	**22**	7	19. Proud Of You Baby		Epic 50065
9/3/77	**33**	3	20. I'm A Honky-Tonk Woman's Man		Polydor 14408
10/29/77	**13**	10	21. The Pay Phone		Polydor 14431
			LUNSFORD, Mike		
			Born on 6/30/50 in Guyman, Oklahoma. Graduated from Panhandle State University in 1973, then moved to Nashville and worked at local clubs.		
8/28/76	**16**	7	1. Honey Hungry		Starday 143
12/18/76+	**28**	5	2. Stealin' Feelin'		Starday 146
			LYNN, Judy		
			Born Judy Lynn Voiten on 4/12/36 in Boise, Idaho. For 21 years a featured artist in Nevada casinos. Retired in 1980 to become an ordained minister.		
8/18/62	**7**	16	1. **Footsteps Of A Fool**		United Art. 472
1/26/63	**29**	1	2. My Secret		United Art. 519
4/6/63	**16**	15	3. My Father's Voice		United Art. 571

DATE	POS	WKS	ARTIST–RECORD TITLE	LABEL & NO.
			LYNN, Loretta	
			Born Loretta Webb on 4/14/34 in Butcher Holler, Kentucky. Married to Oliver "Moonshine" Lynn on 1/10/48. Moved to Custer, Washington, and worked in a band with her brother Jay Lee Webb. Joined the *Grand Ole Opry* in 1962. Toured with the Wilburn Brothers Show, 1960-68. Her autobiography *Coal Miner's Daughter* made into a movie. Elected to the Country Music Hall of Fame in 1988. Sister of Crystal Gayle and Peggy Sue; distant cousin of Patty Loveless. Her son Ernest Ray also recorded. CMA Awards: 1967, 1972 and 1973 Female Vocalist of the Year; 1972 Entertainer of the Year; 1972, 1973, 1974 and 1975 Vocal Duo of the Year (with Conway Twitty). (a) ERNEST TUBB and LORETTA LYNN (b) LORETTA LYNN/CONWAY TWITTY	
6/13/60	14	9	1. I'm A Honky Tonk Girl	Zero 107
7/7/62	6	16	2. **Success**	Decca 31384
6/8/63	13	11	3. The Other Woman	Decca 31471
11/16/63+	4	25	4. **Before I'm Over You**	Decca 31541
5/9/64	3	20	5. **Wine Women And Song**	Decca 31608
8/8/64	11	19	6. Mr. And Mrs. Used To Be (a)	Decca 31643
12/5/64+	3	22	7. **Happy Birthday**	Decca 31707
5/22/65	7	17	8. **Blue Kentucky Girl**	Decca 31769
8/7/65	24	9	9. Our Hearts Are Holding Hands	Decca 31793
9/25/65	10	15	10. **The Home You're Tearin' Down**	Decca 31836
2/5/66	4	14	11. **Dear Uncle Sam**	Decca 31893
6/4/66	2 (2)	22	12. **You Ain't Woman Enough**	Decca 31966
12/10/66+	1 (1)	15	13. **Don't Come Home A'Drinkin' (With Lovin' On Your Mind)**	Decca 32045
6/3/67	7	14	14. **If You're Not Gone Too Long**	Decca 32127
10/7/67	5	14	15. **What Kind Of A Girl (Do You Think I Am?)**	Decca 32184
3/9/68	1 (1)	15	16. **Fist City**	Decca 32264
6/22/68	2 (1)	15	17. **You've Just Stepped In (From Stepping Out On Me)**	Decca 32332
11/2/68	3	15	18. **Your Squaw Is On The Warpath**	Decca 32392
3/1/69	1 (1)	15	19. **Woman Of The World (Leave My World Alone)**	Decca 32439
6/28/69	18	8	20. Who's Gonna Take The Garbage Out (a)	Decca 32496
7/26/69	3	14	21. **To Make A Man (Feel Like A Man)**	Decca 32513
12/13/69+	11	13	22. Wings Upon Your Horns	Decca 32586
3/14/70	4	12	23. **I Know How**	Decca 32637
7/4/70	6	14	24. **You Wanna Give Me A Lift**	Decca 32693
11/7/70	1 (1)	14	25. **Coal Miner's Daughter**	Decca 32749
2/6/71	1 (2)	14	26. **After The Fire Is Gone** (b)	Decca 32776
3/27/71	3	14	27. **I Wanna Be Free**	Decca 32796
7/31/71	5	15	28. **You're Lookin' At Country**	Decca 32851
10/9/71	1 (1)	15	29. **Lead Me On** (b)	Decca 32873
12/18/71+	1 (2)	14	30. **One's On The Way** first released on Decca 32900 as "Here In Topeka"	Decca 32900
7/8/72	3	15	31. **Here I Am Again**	Decca 32974
12/23/72+	1 (1)	14	32. **Rated "X"**	Decca 33039
6/2/73	1 (2)	13	33. **Love Is The Foundation**	MCA 40058
6/30/73	1 (1)	13	34. **Louisiana Woman, Mississippi Man** (b)	MCA 40079
12/1/73+	3	13	35. **Hey Loretta**	MCA 40150

DATE	POS	WKS	ARTIST– RECORD TITLE	LABEL & NO.
5/25/74	**4**	9	36. **They Don't Make 'Em Like My Daddy**	MCA 40223
7/6/74	**1** (1)	11	37. **As Soon As I Hang Up The Phone** (b)	MCA 40251
9/28/74	**1** (1)	13	38. **Trouble In Paradise**	MCA 40283
3/1/75	**5**	9	39. **The Pill**	MCA 40358
7/5/75	**1** (1)	13	40. **Feelins'** (b)	MCA 40420
8/16/75	**10**	10	41. **Home**	MCA 40438
11/29/75+	**2** (1)	11	42. **When The Tingle Becomes A Chill**	MCA 40484
5/1/76	**20**	7	43. Red, White And Blue	MCA 40541
6/26/76	**3**	10	44. **The Letter**	MCA 40572
9/25/76	**1** (2)	12	45. **Somebody Somewhere (Don't Know What He's Missin' Tonight)**	MCA 40607
3/5/77	**1** (1)	13	46. **She's Got You**	MCA 40679
6/11/77	**2** (3)	11	47. **I Can't Love You Enough** (b)	MCA 40728
8/20/77	**7**	9	48. **Why Can't He Be You**	MCA 40747
12/10/77+	**1** (2)	11	49. **Out Of My Head And Back In My Bed**	MCA 40832
6/10/78	**12**	9	50. Spring Fever	MCA 40910
7/1/78	**6**	8	51. **From Seven Till Ten** (b)/	
		7	52. You're The Reason Our Kids Are Ugly (b)	MCA 40920
11/11/78	**10**	10	53. **We've Come A Long Way, Baby**	MCA 40954
5/19/79	**3**	10	54. **I Can't Feel You Anymore**	MCA 41021
10/27/79	**5**	10	55. **I've Got A Picture Of Us On My Mind**	MCA 41129
11/24/79+	**9**	10	56. **You Know Just What I'd Do** (b)/	
		10	57. The Sadness Of It All (b)	MCA 41141
3/29/80	**35**	2	58. Pregnant Again	MCA 41185
5/31/80	**5**	10	59. **It's True Love** (b)	MCA 41232
7/5/80	**30**	4	60. Naked In The Rain	MCA 41250
11/15/80	**20**	6	61. Cheatin' On A Cheater	MCA 51015
2/14/81	**7**	10	62. **Lovin' What Your Lovin' Does To Me** (b)	MCA 51050
3/21/81	**20**	6	63. Somebody Led Me Away	MCA 51058
6/20/81	**2** (2)	11	64. **I Still Believe In Waltzes** (b)	MCA 51114
2/13/82	**9**	14	65. **I Lie**	MCA 52005
9/11/82	**19**	8	66. Making Love From Memory	MCA 52092
3/5/83	**39**	1	67. Breakin' It/	
		1	68. There's All Kinds Of Smoke (In The Barroom)	MCA 52158
8/31/85	**19**	6	69. Heart Don't Do This To Me	MCA 52621

LYNN, Rebecca

8/12/78	**39**	1	1. Music, Music, Music #1 Pop hit for Teresa Brewer in 1950	Scorpion 0550

LYNNE, Shelby

Born on 10/22/68 in Quantico, Virginia; raised in Jackson, Alabama. Female singer.

8/5/89	**38**	2	1. The Hurtin' Side	Epic 68942
8/4/90	**26**	7	2. I'll Lie Myself To Sleep	Epic 73319
1/5/91	**23**	9	3. Things Are Tough All Over	Epic 73521

DATE	POS	WKS	ARTIST—RECORD TITLE	LABEL & NO.

M

MacGREGOR, Mary

Born on 5/6/48 in St. Paul, Minnesota. Pop singer.

DATE	POS	WKS	ARTIST—RECORD TITLE	LABEL & NO.
2/5/77	3	9	● 1. **Torn Between Two Lovers**	Ariola Am. 7638
5/28/77	36	2	2. This Girl (Has Turned Into A Woman)	Ariola Am. 7662

MACK, Warner

Born Warner MacPherson on 4/2/38 in Nashville; raised in Vicksburg, Mississippi. Began playing while in high school and worked in local clubs. Appeared on the TV series *Louisiana Hayride* and *Ozark Jubilee* in the mid-1950s.

DATE	POS	WKS	ARTIST—RECORD TITLE	LABEL & NO.
8/12/57+	9	36	1. **Is It Wrong (For Loving You)**	Decca 30301
			Best Seller #9 / Jockey #11	
1/11/64	34	4	2. Surely	Decca 31559
12/5/64+	4	23	3. **Sittin' In An All Nite Cafe**	Decca 31684
6/5/65	1 (1)	22	4. **The Bridge Washed Out**	Decca 31774
11/6/65+	3	19	5. **Sittin' On A Rock (Crying In A Creek)**	Decca 31853
4/9/66	3	18	6. **Talkin' To The Wall**	Decca 31911
9/10/66	4	16	7. **It Takes A Lot Of Money**	Decca 32004
3/4/67	8	14	8. **Drifting Apart**	Decca 32082
7/15/67	4	14	9. **How Long Will It Take**	Decca 32142
12/9/67+	11	11	10. I'd Give The World (To Be Back Loving You)	Decca 32211
6/1/68	7	14	11. **I'm Gonna Move On**	Decca 32308
12/21/68+	23	14	12. Don't Wake Me I'm Dreaming	Decca 32394
5/17/69	6	13	13. **Leave My Dream Alone**	Decca 32473
10/11/69	8	11	14. **I'll Still Be Missing You**	Decca 32547
4/25/70	19	7	15. Love Hungry	Decca 32646
10/10/70	16	8	16. Live For The Good Times	Decca 32725
3/20/71	34	6	17. You Make Me Feel Like A Man	Decca 32781

MADDOX, Rose

Born Roselea Arbana Brogdon on 8/15/25 near Boaz, Alabama; raised in Bakersfield. Worked with family band on KTRB-Modesto in the mid-1940s. First recorded with brothers Cal, Henry, Fred and Don as the Maddox Brothers and Sister Rose for Four Star in 1947. Appeared on the *Louisiana Hayride* and *Grand Ole Opry* before the group disbanded in 1959.

(a) BUCK OWENS And ROSE MADDOX

DATE	POS	WKS	ARTIST—RECORD TITLE	LABEL & NO.
5/18/59	22	3	1. Gambler's Love	Capitol 4177
1/30/61	14	13	2. Kissing My Pillow/	
2/13/61	15	7	3. I Want To Live Again	Capitol 4487
5/22/61	4	14	4. **Loose Talk** (a)/	
5/15/61	8	12	5. **Mental Cruelty** (a)	Capitol 4550
8/14/61	14	6	6. Conscience, I'm Guilty	Capitol 4598
11/10/62+	3	18	7. **Sing A Little Song Of Heartache**	Capitol 4845
3/16/63	18	8	8. Lonely Teardrops	Capitol 4905

DATE	POS	WKS	ARTIST– RECORD TITLE	LABEL & NO.
6/15/63	**18**	13	9. Down To The River	Capitol 4975
8/3/63	**15**	6	10. We're The Talk Of The Town (a)/	
8/10/63	**19**	6	11. Sweethearts In Heaven (a)	Capitol 4992
11/23/63	**18**	4	12. Somebody Told Somebody	Capitol 5038
8/15/64	**30**	4	13. Blue Bird Let Me Tag Along	Capitol 5186

MAGGARD, Cledus, And The Citizen's Band

Maggard born Jay Huguely in Quick Sand, Kentucky. Worked at Leslie Advertising in Greenville, South Carolina, when he recorded "The White Knight."

DATE	POS	WKS	ARTIST– RECORD TITLE	LABEL & NO.
1/3/76	**1** (1)	11	1. **The White Knight** [N]	Mercury 73751

MAINES BROTHERS BAND, The

Family band: Kenny (guitar, harmonica), Steve (guitar), Lloyd (steel guitar) and Donnie (drums) Maines. With Richard Bowden (fiddle), Gary Banks (keyboards) and Jerry Brownlow (bass).

DATE	POS	WKS	ARTIST– RECORD TITLE	LABEL & NO.
3/23/85	**24**	6	1. Everybody Needs Love On Saturday Night	Mercury 880536

MALCHAK, Tim

Born on 6/25/57 in Binghamton, New York. Worked as a folk singer in California and New York City. Teamed with Dwight Rucker in 1980.

DATE	POS	WKS	ARTIST– RECORD TITLE	LABEL & NO.
4/25/87	**37**	2	1. Colorado Moon	Alpine 006
9/12/87	**39**	2	2. Restless Angel	Alpine 007
3/12/88	**35**	4	3. It Goes Without Saying	Alpine 008

MANCINI, Henry—see PRIDE, Charley

MANDRELL, Barbara

Born on 12/25/48 in Houston; raised in Oceanside, California. Plays steel guitar, bass, banjo and saxophone. Worked in the family band and appeared on the TV series *Town Hall Party*, *Johnny Cash Show* and *Red Foley Show* in the early '60s. First recorded for Mosrite in 1963. Moved to Nashville in 1971. Own TV series, 1980-82, with sisters Louise and Irlene and other family members. Suffered severe injuries in an auto accident in 1984, from which she fully recovered. Joined the *Grand Ole Opry* in 1972. CMA Awards: 1979 and 1981 Female Vocalist of the Year; 1980 and 1981 Entertainer of the Year.

(a) DAVID HOUSTON and BARBARA MANDRELL

DATE	POS	WKS	ARTIST– RECORD TITLE	LABEL & NO.
6/13/70	**18**	9	1. Playin' Around With Love	Columbia 45143
10/17/70	**6**	11	2. **After Closing Time** (a)	Epic 10656
2/6/71	**17**	10	3. Do Right Woman - Do Right Man	Columbia 45307
7/17/71	**12**	9	4. Treat Him Right #2 Pop hit for Roy Head ("Treat Her Right") in 1965	Columbia 45391
10/30/71	**20**	7	5. We've Got Everything But Love (a)	Epic 10779
1/1/72	**10**	9	6. **Tonight My Baby's Coming Home**	Columbia 45505
5/6/72	**11**	9	7. Show Me #35 Pop hit for Joe Tex in 1967	Columbia 45580
10/7/72	**24**	10	8. A Perfect Match (a)	Epic 10908
11/25/72	**27**	7	9. Holdin' On (To The Love I Got)	Columbia 45702
5/12/73	**24**	8	10. Give A Little, Take A Little	Columbia 45819
9/1/73	**7**	14	11. **The Midnight Oil**	Columbia 45904
1/19/74	**6**	12	12. **I Love You, I Love You** (a)	Epic 11068

DATE	POS	WKS	ARTIST–RECORD TITLE	LABEL & NO.
7/6/74	40	2	13. Lovin' You Is Worth It (a)	Epic 11120
7/27/74	12	8	14. This Time I Almost Made It	Columbia 46054
9/21/74	14	9	15. Ten Commandments Of Love (a) #22 Pop hit for Harvey & The Moonglows in 1958	Epic 20005
4/12/75	39	1	16. Wonder When My Baby's Comin' Home	Columbia 10082
1/10/76	5	12	17. **Standing Room Only**	ABC/Dot 17601
5/29/76	16	8	18. That's What Friends Are For	ABC/Dot 17623
9/11/76	24	7	19. Love Is Thin Ice	ABC/Dot 17644
1/15/77	16	7	20. Midnight Angel	ABC/Dot 17668
4/16/77	3	13	21. **Married But Not To Each Other** #16 R&B hit for Denise LaSalle in 1976	ABC/Dot 17688
9/17/77	12	9	22. Hold Me	ABC/Dot 17716
1/7/78	4	11	23. **Woman To Woman** #22 Pop hit for Shirley Brown in 1974	ABC/Dot 17736
5/27/78	5	11	24. **Tonight**	ABC 12362
9/16/78	1 (3)	11	25. **Sleeping Single In A Double Bed**	ABC 12403
2/17/79	1 (1)	11	26. **(If Loving You Is Wrong) I Don't Want To Be Right** #3 Pop hit for Luther Ingram in 1972	ABC 12451
8/25/79	4	10	27. **Fooled By A Feeling**	MCA 41077
1/5/80	1 (1)	10	28. **Years** #35 Pop hit for Wayne Newton in 1980	MCA 41162
7/12/80	3	11	29. **Crackers**	MCA 41263
10/25/80	6	12	30. **The Best Of Strangers**	MCA 51001
2/14/81	13	9	31. Love Is Fair/	
		9	32. Sometime, Somewhere, Somehow	MCA 51062
5/23/81	1 (1)	8	33. **I Was Country When Country Wasn't Cool** George Jones (guest vocal)	MCA 51107
9/26/81	2 (1)	10	34. **Wish You Were Here**	MCA 51171
5/8/82	1 (1)	14	35. **'Till You're Gone**	MCA 52038
9/25/82	9	10	36. **Operator, Long Distance Please**	MCA 52111
5/7/83	4	12	37. **In Times Like These**	MCA 52206
9/10/83	1 (1)	14	38. **One Of A Kind Pair Of Fools**	MCA 52258
3/3/84	3	12	39. **Happy Birthday Dear Heartache**	MCA 52340
6/30/84	2 (1)	13	40. **Only A Lonely Heart Knows**	MCA 52397
7/28/84	3	14	41. **To Me** **BARBARA MANDRELL/LEE GREENWOOD**	MCA 52415
11/3/84	11	11	42. Crossword Puzzle	MCA 52465
2/23/85	19	7	43. It Should Have Been Love By Now **BARBARA MANDRELL/LEE GREENWOOD**	MCA 52525
4/6/85	7	11	44. **There's No Love In Tennessee**	MCA 52537
9/7/85	8	12	45. **Angel In Your Arms** #6 Pop hit for the group Hot in 1977	MCA 52645
12/28/85+	4	13	46. **Fast Lanes And Country Roads**	MCA 52737
4/19/86	20	6	47. When You Get To The Heart **BARBARA MANDRELL with the OAK RIDGE BOYS**	MCA 52802
9/6/86	6	13	48. **No One Mends A Broken Heart Like You**	MCA 52900
7/25/87	13	11	49. **Child Support**	EMI America 43032
9/24/88	5	13	50. **I Wish That I Could Fall In Love Today**	Capitol 44220
3/11/89	19	8	51. My Train Of Thought	Capitol 44276

DATE	POS	WKS	ARTIST–RECORD TITLE	LABEL & NO.
			MANDRELL, Louise	
			Born on 7/13/54 in Corpus Christi, Texas. Younger sister of Barbara Mandrell. Guitarist/bassist, worked with Barbara's band, the Do-Rights, at age 15. Toured with Merle Haggard in the early '70s. Previously married to R.C. Bannon and Gary Buck.	
6/16/79	13	7	1. Reunited #1 Pop hit for Peaches & Herb in 1979	Epic 50717
1/16/82	35	2	2. Where There's Smoke There's Fire	RCA 12359
3/20/82	35	4	3. (You Sure Know Your Way) Around My Heart	RCA 13039
8/21/82	20	9	4. Some Of My Best Friends Are Old Songs	RCA 13278
12/18/82+	22	7	5. Romance	RCA 13373
12/25/82	35	2	6. Christmas Is Just A Song For Us This Year [X] flip side of Alabama's Christmas single	RCA 13358
3/12/83	6	12	7. **Save Me**	RCA 13450
8/13/83	10	9	8. **Too Hot To Sleep**	RCA 13567
11/26/83+	13	10	9. Runaway Heart	RCA 13649
4/21/84	7	12	10. **I'm Not Through Loving You Yet**	RCA 13752
9/22/84	24	7	11. Goodbye Heartache	RCA 13850
5/4/85	8	10	12. **Maybe My Baby**	RCA 14039
9/7/85	5	12	13. **I Wanna Say Yes**	RCA 14151
1/25/86	22	6	14. Some Girls Have All The Luck #10 Pop hit for Rod Stewart as "Some Guys Have All The Luck" in 1984	RCA 14251
8/2/86	35	3	15. I Wanna Hear It From Your Lips #35 Pop hit for Eric Carmen in 1985	RCA 14364
4/4/87	28	4	16. Do I Have To Say Goodbye	RCA 5115
			MANN, Lorene	
			Born on 1/4/37 in Huntland, Tennessee. Singer/songwriter. Wrote "Don't Go Near The Indians" for Rex Allen and "Left To Right" for Kitty Wells.	
10/23/65	23	5	1. Hurry, Mr. Peters **JUSTIN TUBB & LORENE MANN** answer to Roy Drusky & Priscilla Mitchell's "Yes, Mr. Peters"	RCA 8659
2/10/68	24	9	2. The Dark End Of The Street	RCA 9401
7/27/68	31	6	3. Tell It Like It Is #2 Pop hit for Aaron Neville in 1967	RCA 9549
1/18/69	36	6	4. My Special Prayer **ARCHIE CAMPBELL and LORENE MANN (above 3)**	RCA 9691
			MANNERS, Zeke, and his Band	
			Manners born on 10/10/11 in San Francisco. Pianist/accordionist. Founder of the Beverly Hillbillies band with brother Tom in 1928. Worked on KELK-Beverly Hills. Moved to New York City; worked with Elton Britt in 1935.	
2/16/46	2 (9)	19	1. **Sioux City Sue** Curly Gribbs (vocal)	Victor 20-1797
12/14/46	5	2	2. **Inflation** The Singing Lariateers (backing vocals)	Victor 20-2013
			MARCY BROS., The	
			Kevin, Kris and Kendall Marcy from Oroville, California. The brothers were raised in Hay Springs, Nebraska.	
6/24/89	34	3	1. Cotton Pickin' Time	Warner 22956

DATE	POS	WKS	ARTIST– RECORD TITLE	LABEL & NO.
			MARLIN SISTERS, The—see YANKOVIC, Frankie	
			MARTELL, Linda	
			Born in Leesville, South Carolina. Worked R&B clubs in Columbia, South Carolina. First black female Country singer on the *Grand Ole Opry*, 1969.	
8/23/69	22	7	1. Color Him Father	Plantation 24
			#7 Pop hit for The Winstons in 1969	
1/3/70	33	2	2. Before The Next Teardrop Falls	Plantation 35
			MARTIN, Benny	
			Born on 5/8/28 in Sparta, Tennessee. Worked on WNOX-Knoxville Mid-Day Merry-Go-Round. Moved to WLAC-Nashville in 1944.	
5/25/63	28	1	1. Rosebuds And You	Starday 623
			MARTIN, Dean	
			Born Dino Crocetti on 6/7/17 in Steubenville, Ohio. Died on 12/25/95. Vocalist/actor. Teamed with comedian Jerry Lewis, 1946-56; made 16 movies together. Martin hosted own TV show, 1965-74.	
8/20/83	35	3	1. My First Country Song	Warner 29584
			written by Conway Twitty, who also does a guest vocal	
			MARTIN, Jimmy	
			Born on 8/10/27 in Sneedville, Tennessee. Played with Bill Monroe's Bluegrass Boys, 1949-54. Worked with the Osborne Brothers in the mid-1950s. Own band, the Sunny Mountain Boys, and worked the WJR-Detroit *Barn Dance* and *Louisiana Hayride*.	
12/8/58	14	6	1. Rock Hearts	Decca 30703
5/25/59	26	3	2. Night	Decca 30877
2/15/64	19	14	3. Widow Maker	Decca 31558
			MARTINDALE, Wink	
			Born Winston Martindale on 12/4/33 in Jackson, Tennessee. DJ since 1950. Own TV shows starting with *Teenage Dance Party*. Host of *Tic Tac Dough*, *Gambit* and other TV game shows.	
10/19/59	11	10	● 1. Deck Of Cards [S]	Dot 15968
			MASON DIXON	
			Trio from Lamar University, Beaumont, Texas. Consisted of Frank Gilligan (born 11/2/55, Queens, New York), lead vocals; Jerry Dengler (born 5/29/55, Colorado Springs), guitar, banjo, and Rick Henderson (born 5/29/53, Beaumont, Texas), vocalist.	
6/6/87	39	1	1. 3935 West End Avenue	Premier One 112
3/25/89	35	3	2. Exception To The Rule	Capitol 44331
			MASSEY, Wayne	
			Singer/actor from Glendale, California. Played Johnny Drummond on TV's daytime soap opera *One Life To Live*. Married to Charly McClain.	
			CHARLY MCCLAIN WITH WAYNE MASSEY:	
7/27/85	5	13	1. **With Just One Look In Your Eyes**	Epic 05398
12/14/85+	10	12	2. **You Are My Music, You Are My Song**	Epic 05693

DATE	POS	WKS	ARTIST– RECORD TITLE	LABEL & NO.
4/26/86	17	8	3. When It's Down To Me And You	Epic 05842
			MATHIS, Country Johnny	
			Born on 9/28/33 in Maud, Texas. Worked on the Big D Jamboree, *Louisiana Hayride* and *Grand Ole Opry*. Recorded with Jimmy Lee Fautheree as Jimmy & Johnny.	
3/9/63	14	13	1. Please Talk To My Heart	United Art. 536
			MATTEA, Kathy	
			Born on 6/21/59 in Cross Lane, West Virginia. Guitarist since high school. Attended West Virginia University, played in the bluegrass group Pennsboro. Moved to Nashville and worked as a tour guide at the Country Music Hall Of Fame. Toured with Bobby Goldsboro, Don Williams, Oak Ridge Boys and Gary Morris. CMA Awards: 1989 and 1990 Female Vocalist of the Year.	
11/26/83	25	7	1. Street Talk	Mercury 814375
4/7/84	26	5	2. Someone Is Falling In Love	Mercury 818289
4/27/85	34	4	3. It's Your Reputation Talkin'	Mercury 880595
8/17/85	22	7	4. He Won't Give In	Mercury 880867
5/10/86	3	13	5. **Love At The Five & Dime**	Mercury 884573
10/25/86	10	12	6. **Walk The Way The Wind Blows**	Mercury 884978
2/21/87	5	13	7. **You're The Power**	Mercury 888319
6/20/87	6	12	8. **Train Of Memories**	Mercury 888574
11/7/87+	1 (1)	15	9. **Goin' Gone**	Mercury 888874
3/19/88	1 (2)	14	10. **Eighteen Wheels And A Dozen Roses** CMA Award: Single of the Year	Mercury 870148
7/23/88	4	13	11. **Untold Stories**	Mercury 870476
11/26/88+	4	15	12. **Life As We Knew It**	Mercury 872082
5/13/89	1 (1)	14	13. **Come From The Heart**	Mercury 872766
8/26/89	1 (1)	14	14. **Burnin' Old Memories**	Mercury 874672
12/9/89+	10	16	15. **Where've You Been**	Mercury 876262
4/21/90	2 (1)	17	16. **She Came From Fort Worth**	Mercury 876746
8/4/90	9	15	17. **The Battle Hymn Of Love** **KATHY MATTEA * TIM O'BRIEN**	Mercury 875692
11/24/90+	9	14	18. **A Few Good Things Remain**	Mercury 878246
3/23/91	7	12	19. **Time Passes By**	Mercury 878934
7/20/91	18	11	20. Whole Lotta Holes	Mercury 868394
11/30/91+	27	6	21. Asking Us To Dance	Mercury 868866
10/10/92	11	12	22. Lonesome Standard Time	Mercury 864318
2/13/93	19	11	23. Standing Knee Deep In A River (Dying Of Thirst)	Mercury 864810
4/16/94	3	16	24. **Walking Away A Winner**	Mercury 858464
8/20/94	13	11	25. Nobody's Gonna Rain On Our Parade	Mercury 858800
12/31/94+	34	5	26. Maybe She's Human	Mercury 856262
4/29/95	20	8	27. Clown In Your Rodeo	Mercury 856484
			MAVERICKS, The	
			Four-man band from Miami: Raul Malo (vocals), Robert Reynolds, Paul Deakin and David Lee Holt. Reynolds married Trisha Yearwood on 5/21/94. CMA Award: 1995 Vocal Group of the Year.	
3/26/94	25	7	1. What A Crying Shame	MCA 54748
8/6/94	18	8	2. O What A Thrill	MCA 54780

DATE	POS	WKS	ARTIST–RECORD TITLE	LABEL & NO.
10/29/94	**20**	10	3. There Goes My Heart	MCA 54909
3/4/95	**30**	6	4. I Should Have Been True	MCA 54975
10/14/95	**22**	12	5. Here Comes The Rain	MCA 55080
2/17/96	**13**	16	6. All You Ever Do Is Bring Me Down	MCA 55154

McANALLY, Mac

Born Lyman McAnally, Jr., on 7/15/57 in Red Bay, Alabama. Session singer/songwriter/guitarist. Wrote Shenandoah's "Two Dozen Roses," Ricky Van Shelton's "Crime of Passion," Alabama's "Old Flame" and Sawyer Brown's "Cafe On The Corner."

DATE	POS	WKS	ARTIST–RECORD TITLE	LABEL & NO.
3/17/90	**14**	9	1. Back Where I Come From	Warner 22662

McAULIFF, Leon

Born William Leon McAuliff on 1/3/17 in Houston. Died on 8/20/88. Worked with Texas Jim Lewis, and The Light Crust Doughboys; recorded for Brunswick in 1933. With Bob Wills' Texas Playboys, 1935-42. In the service, 1942-46. Own band, the Cimarron Boys, from 1946. Appeared in 10 Western movies. Wrote "Steel Guitar Rag," "Blue Bonnet Rag," "Pan Handle Rag" and "San Antonio Rose." One of the first to play electric steel guitar.

DATE	POS	WKS	ARTIST–RECORD TITLE	LABEL & NO.
6/4/49	**6**	5	1. **Panhandle Rag** [I] **LEON McAULIFFE and his WESTERN SWING BAND** Best Seller #6 / Juke Box #10	Columbia 20546
8/21/61	**16**	15	2. Cozy Inn	Cimarron 4050
12/22/62+	**22**	11	3. Faded Love [I]	Cimarron 4057
1/11/64	**35**	1	4. Shape Up Or Ship Out **LEON McAULIFFE**	Capitol 5066
7/3/71	**22**	4	5. Faded Love [R] **TOMPALL AND THE GLASER BROTHERS WITH LEON McAULIFFE AND THE CIMARRON BOYS** new version of #3 above	MGM 14249

McBRIDE, Dale

Born on 12/18/36 in Bell County, Texas; raised in Lampasas, Texas. Died on 11/30/92 of a brain tumor. Played guitar since age 13. Original member of the Downbeats; worked with Jimmy Heap. Dale's son Terry fronts McBride & The Ride.

DATE	POS	WKS	ARTIST–RECORD TITLE	LABEL & NO.
12/25/76+	**26**	6	1. Ordinary Man	Con Brio 114
1/21/78	**37**	2	2. Always Lovin Her Man	Con Brio 127

McBRIDE, Martina

Born Martina Schifft on 7/29/66 in Medicine Lodge, Kansas; raised in Sharon, Kansas.

DATE	POS	WKS	ARTIST–RECORD TITLE	LABEL & NO.
5/23/92	**23**	8	1. The Time Has Come	RCA 62215
10/9/93	**2** (1)	11	2. **My Baby Loves Me**	RCA 62599
1/29/94	**6**	16	3. **Life #9**	RCA 62697
6/18/94	**12**	14	4. Independence Day	RCA 62828
12/3/94+	**21**	10	5. Heart Trouble	RCA 62961
8/26/95	**4**	16	6. **Safe In The Arms Of Love**	RCA 64345
12/30/95+	**1** (1)	16	7. **Wild Angels**	RCA 64437
5/18/96	**28**	10 ↑	8. Phones Are Ringin' All Over Town	RCA 64487

DATE	POS	WKS	ARTIST– RECORD TITLE	LABEL & NO.
			McBRIDE & THE RIDE	
			Band of notable Nashville session musicians: Terry McBride (born 9/16/58, Lampasas, Texas; vocals, bass), Ray Herndon (guitar) and Billy Thomas (drums). Herndon and Thomas left in 1993; Kenny Vaughn (guitar), Randy Frazier (bass) and Keith Edwards (drums) joined. Gary Morse and Jeff Roach also joined by 1994. McBride is the son of Dale McBride.	
5/4/91	15	13	1. Can I Count On You	MCA 54022
9/21/91	28	6	2. Same Old Star	MCA 54125
4/11/92	2 (2)	16	3. **Sacred Ground**	MCA 54356
8/15/92	5	16	4. **Going Out Of My Mind**	MCA 54413
12/26/92+	5	14	5. **Just One Night**	MCA 54494
4/24/93	3	16	6. **Love On The Loose, Heart On The Run**	MCA 54601
9/4/93	17	10	7. Hurry Sundown	MCA 54688
1/8/94	26	8	8. No More Cryin'	MCA 54761
			from the movie *8 Seconds* starring Luke Perry	
			McCALL, C.W.	
			Born William Fries on 11/15/28 in Audubon, Iowa. The character C.W. McCall was created for the Mertz Bread Company; Fries was its advertising man. Elected mayor of Ouray, Colorado, in the early '80s.	
8/10/74	19	6	1. Old Home Filler-Up An' Keep On-A-Truckin' Cafe [N]	MGM 14738
1/18/75	12	8	2. Wolf Creek Pass [N]	MGM 14764
5/31/75	13	7	3. Classified [N]	MGM 14801
10/18/75	24	5	4. Black Bear Road [N]	MGM 14825
12/6/75	1 (6)	13	● 5. **Convoy** [N]	MGM 14839
4/10/76	19	7	6. There Won't Be No Country Music (There Won't Be No Rock 'N' Roll) [S]	Polydor 14310
7/31/76	32	3	7. Crispy Critters [N]	Polydor 14331
1/22/77	40	1	8. 'Round The World With The Rubber Duck [N]	Polydor 14365
			sequel to #5 above	
10/1/77	2 (2)	10	9. **Roses For Mama** [S]	Polydor 14420
			McCALL, Darrell	
			Born on 4/30/40 in New Jasper, Ohio. Lead tenor with the Little Dippers. Toured with Faron Young and Ray Price. Co-writer of the hit "Eleven Roses" for Hank Williams, Jr.	
1/12/63	17	8	1. A Stranger Was Here **DARRELL McCALL with The Milestones**	Philips 40079
4/16/77	32	5	2. Lily Dale **DARRELL McCALL & WILLIE NELSON**	Columbia 10480
8/20/77	35	3	3. Dreams Of A Dreamer	Columbia 10576
			McCARTERS, The	
			Trio of sisters from Sevierville, Tennessee: Jennifer (born 3/1/64) and twins Lisa and Teresa (born 11/21/66).	
2/13/88	5	12	1. **Timeless And True Love**	Warner 28125
7/2/88	4	13	2. **The Gift**	Warner 27868
11/12/88	28	4	3. I Give You Music	Warner 27721
5/6/89	9	12	4. **Up And Gone**	Warner 22991
12/9/89+	26	5	5. Quit While I'm Behind **JENNIFER McCARTER & THE McCARTERS**	Warner 22763

DATE	POS	WKS	ARTIST– RECORD TITLE	LABEL & NO.
			McCLAIN, Charly	
			Born Charlotte Denise McClain on 3/26/56 in Jackson, Tennessee. Sang in band with brother at age nine. Worked on the Mid-South Jamboree, 1973-75. Toured with O.B. McClinton. Appeared on the TV series *Hart To Hart, CHiPs, Austin City Limits* and *Solid Gold*. Married actor Wayne Massey in July 1984.	
			(a) CHARLY McCLAIN & MICKEY GILLEY	
			(b) CHARLY McCLAIN with WAYNE MASSEY	
5/13/78	13	8	1. Let Me Be Your Baby	Epic 50525
9/30/78	8	10	2. **That's What You Do To Me**	Epic 50598
2/10/79	24	7	3. Take Me Back	Epic 50653
6/2/79	11	9	4. When A Love Ain't Right	Epic 50706
9/29/79	20	7	5. You're A Part Of Me	Epic 50759
11/10/79	16	9	6. I Hate The Way I Love It	Epic 50791
			JOHNNY RODRIGUEZ and CHARLY McCLAIN	
2/2/80	7	9	7. **Men**	Epic 50825
5/31/80	23	7	8. Let's Put Our Love In Motion	Epic 50873
8/30/80	18	7	9. Women Get Lonely	Epic 50916
12/13/80+	1 (1)	12	10. **Who's Cheatin' Who**	Epic 50948
5/2/81	5	12	11. **Surround Me With Love**	Epic 01045
9/5/81	4	10	12. **Sleepin' With The Radio On**	Epic 02421
1/16/82	5	12	13. **The Very Best Is You**	Epic 02656
7/10/82	3	14	14. **Dancing Your Memory Away**	Epic 02975
11/13/82+	7	13	15. **With You**	Epic 03308
5/7/83	20	8	16. Fly Into Love	Epic 03808
8/6/83	1 (1)	13	17. **Paradise Tonight** (a)	Epic 04007
11/26/83+	3	14	18. **Sentimental Ol' You**	Epic 04172
3/10/84	5	11	19. **Candy Man** (a)	Epic 04368
			#25 Pop hit for Roy Orbison in 1961	
5/5/84	22	7	20. Band Of Gold	Epic 04423
			#3 Pop hit for Freda Payne in 1970	
7/14/84	14	9	21. The Right Stuff (a)	Epic 04489
10/20/84	25	6	22. Some Hearts Get All The Breaks	Epic 04586
3/16/85	1 (1)	14	23. **Radio Heart**	Epic 04777
7/27/85	5	13	24. **With Just One Look In Your Eyes** (b)	Epic 05398
12/14/85+	10	12	25. **You Are My Music, You Are My Song** (b)	Epic 05693
4/26/86	17	8	26. When It's Down To Me And You (b)	Epic 05842
4/4/87	20	9	27. Don't Touch Me There	Epic 06980
			McCLINTON, O.B.	
			Born Obie Burnett McClinton on 4/25/40 in Senatobia, Mississippi. Died of abdominal cancer on 9/23/87. Worked on WDIA-Memphis and as a staff writer for Stax/Volt Records. First recorded for Stax in 1971. One of the few black Country stars.	
1/13/73	37	2	1. Don't Let The Green Grass Fool You	Enterprise 9059
			#17 Pop hit for Wilson Pickett in 1971	
4/14/73	36	3	2. My Whole World Is Falling Down	Enterprise 9062

DATE	POS	WKS	ARTIST– RECORD TITLE	LABEL & NO.
			McCOY, Charlie	
			Born on 3/28/41 in Oak Hill, West Virginia. Toured with Stonewall Jackson in the early '60s. Worked with the band Area Code 615 in 1969. Top Nashville harmonica player and session musician.	
3/4/72	**16**	11	1. I Started Loving You Again [I]	Monument 8529
7/29/72	**23**	9	2. I'm So Lonesome I Could Cry [I]	Monument 8546
11/25/72	**19**	7	3. I Really Don't Want To Know [I]	Monument 8554
3/31/73	**26**	7	4. Orange Blossom Special [I]	Monument 8566
8/25/73	**33**	2	5. Shenandoah [I]	Monument 8576
12/22/73	**33**	2	6. Release Me [I]	Monument 8589
7/6/74	**22**	6	7. Boogie Woogie (A/K/A T.D.'s Boogie Woogie) [I]	Monument 8611
			CHARLIE McCOY & BAREFOOT JERRY	
9/9/78	**30**	4	8. Fair And Tender Ladies	Monument 258
			McCOY, Neal	
			Real name: Hubert Neal McGauhey, Jr. Native of Jacksonville, Texas.	
6/27/92	**40**	1	1. Where Forever Begins	Atlantic LP Cut
3/13/93	**26**	7	2. Now I Pray For Rain	Atlantic LP Cut
			above 2 from the album *Where Forever Begins* on Atlantic 82396	
1/15/94	**1 (2)**	16	3. **No Doubt About It**	Atlantic 87287
5/7/94	**1 (4)**	18	4. **Wink**	Atlantic 87247
8/20/94	**5**	17	5. **The City Put The Country Back In Me**	Atlantic 87213
1/7/95	**3**	17	6. **For A Change**	Atlantic 87176
5/13/95	**3**	16	7. **They're Playin' Our Song**	Atlantic LP Cut
1/27/96	**3**	17	8. **You Gotta Love That/**	
9/2/95	**16**	14	9. If I Was A Drinkin' Man	Atlantic 87120
			above 3 from the album *You Gotta Love That!* on Atlantic 82727	
			McCREADY, Mindy	
			Female singer from Fort Myers, Florida.	
3/23/96	**6**	16	1. **Ten Thousand Angels**	BNA 64470
			McDANIEL, Mel	
			Born on 9/6/42 in Checotah, Oklahoma. Performing since age 14. Worked clubs in Oklahoma, Arkansas and Kansas. Worked in Anchorage, Alaska, 1970-72. Moved to Nashville in 1973 and worked as staff writer and demo singer for Combine Music. Joined the *Grand Ole Opry* in 1986.	
3/5/77	**39**	2	1. All The Sweet	Capitol 4373
7/2/77	**18**	7	2. Gentle To Your Senses	Capitol 4430
10/15/77	**27**	5	3. Soul Of A Honky Tonk Woman	Capitol 4481
1/14/78	**11**	8	4. God Made Love	Capitol 4520
9/16/78	**26**	6	5. Bordertown Woman	Capitol 4597
4/14/79	**33**	3	6. Love Lies	Capitol 4691
7/28/79	**24**	6	7. Play Her Back To Yesterday	Capitol 4740
11/3/79	**27**	6	8. Lovin' Starts Where Friendship Ends	Capitol 4784
8/16/80	**39**	2	9. Hello Daddy, Good Morning Darling	Capitol 4886
12/27/80+	**23**	7	10. Countryfied	Capitol 4949
4/11/81	**7**	10	11. **Louisiana Saturday Night**	Capitol 4983
8/8/81	**10**	9	12. **Right In The Palm Of Your Hand**	Capitol 5022

DATE	POS	WKS	ARTIST–RECORD TITLE	LABEL & NO.
11/28/81+	**19**	10	13. Preaching Up A Storm	Capitol 5059
4/10/82	**10**	10	14. **Take Me To The Country**	Capitol 5095
			MEL McDANIELS	
7/17/82	**4**	14	15. **Big Ole Brew**	Capitol 5138
12/11/82+	**20**	8	16. I Wish I Was In Nashville	Capitol 5169
5/14/83	**22**	7	17. Old Man River (I've Come To Talk Again)	Capitol 5218
9/10/83	**39**	1	18. Hot Time In Old Town Tonight	Capitol 5259
12/3/83+	**9**	12	19. **I Call It Love**	Capitol 5298
12/8/84+	**1** (1)	15	20. **Baby's Got Her Blue Jeans On**	Capitol 5418
4/13/85	**6**	12	21. **Let It Roll (Let It Rock)**	Capitol 5458
			#64 Pop hit for Chuck Berry in 1960	
10/5/85	**5**	15	22. **Stand Up**	Capitol 5513
2/22/86	**22**	8	23. Shoe String	Capitol 5544
10/25/86	**12**	12	24. Stand On It	Capitol 5620
			written by Bruce Springsteen	
6/18/88	**9**	12	25. **Real Good Feel Good Song**	Capitol 44158

McDONALD, Skeets

Born Enos William McDonald on 10/1/15 in Greenway, Arkansas. Died of a heart attack on 3/31/68. Worked clubs in Michigan in the early '40s. Moved to California in 1951 and appeared on the series *Town Hall Party* in Compton.

DATE	POS	WKS	ARTIST–RECORD TITLE	LABEL & NO.
10/25/52	**1** (3)	18	1. **Don't Let The Stars Get In Your Eyes**	Capitol 2216
			Juke Box #1 / Best Seller #2 / Jockey #3; #1 Pop hit for Perry Como in 1953	
10/24/60	**21**	6	2. This Old Heart	Columbia 41773
9/28/63	**9**	18	3. **Call Me Mr. Brown**	Columbia 42807
1/1/66	**29**	4	4. Big Chief Buffalo Nickel (Desert Blues)	Columbia 43425
			written and recorded by Jimmie Rodgers in 1929 as "Desert Blues"	
2/11/67	**28**	4	5. Mabel	Columbia 43946

McDOWELL, Ronnie

Born on 3/26/50 in Fountain Head, Tennessee; raised in Portland, Tennessee. Began singing while in the service. Worked as a commercial sign painter. Sang on the soundtrack for the 1979 TV movie *Elvis*.

DATE	POS	WKS	ARTIST–RECORD TITLE	LABEL & NO.
9/24/77	**13**	5	● 1. The King Is Gone	Scorpion 135
			a tribute to Elvis Presley	
1/21/78	**5**	10	2. **I Love You, I Love You, I Love You**	Scorpion 149
5/20/78	**15**	7	3. Here Comes The Reason I Live	Scorpion 159
11/11/78	**39**	1	4. This Is A Holdup	Scorpion 0560
5/26/79	**18**	7	5. World's Most Perfect Woman	Epic 50696
9/15/79	**26**	6	6. Love Me Now/	
1/26/80	**29**	4	7. Never Seen A Mountain So High	Epic 50753
4/19/80	**37**	4	8. Lovin' A Livin' Dream	Epic 50857
10/4/80	**36**	2	9. Gone	Epic 50925
1/31/81	**2** (1)	9	10. **Wandering Eyes**	Epic 50962
7/18/81	**1** (1)	10	11. **Older Women**	Epic 02129
11/28/81+	**4**	12	12. **Watchin' Girls Go By**	Epic 02614
6/5/82	**11**	11	13. I Just Cut Myself	Epic 02884
10/2/82	**7**	11	14. **Step Back**	Epic 03203

DATE	POS	WKS	ARTIST – RECORD TITLE	LABEL & NO.
2/26/83	**10**	11	15. **Personally** #19 Pop hit for Karla Bonoff in 1982	Epic 03526
7/2/83	**1** (1)	12	16. **You're Gonna Ruin My Bad Reputation**	Epic 03946
11/12/83+	**3**	14	17. **You Made A Wanted Man Of Me**	Epic 04167
3/24/84	**7**	11	18. **I Dream Of Women Like You**	Epic 04367
7/21/84	**8**	11	19. **I Got A Million Of 'Em**	Epic 04499
3/16/85	**5**	13	20. **In A New York Minute**	Epic 04816
8/10/85	**9**	12	21. **Love Talks**	Epic 05404
5/24/86	**6**	12	22. **All Tied Up**	Curb/MCA 52816
10/11/86	**37**	3	23. When You Hurt, I Hurt	Curb/MCA 52907
1/31/87	**30**	4	24. Lovin' That Crazy Feelin'	Curb/MCA 52994
2/6/88	**8**	12	25. **It's Only Make Believe** Conway Twitty (guest vocal)	Curb 10501
8/20/88	**27**	6	26. Suspicion/ #3 Pop hit for Terry Stafford in 1964	
6/25/88	**36**	3	27. I'm Still Missing You	Curb 10508
5/20/89	**39**	2	28. Sea Of Heartbreak	Curb 10525
1/26/91	**26**	9	29. Unchained Melody #4 Pop hit for The Righteous Brothers in 1965	Curb 76850
			McENTIRE, Pake	
			Born Dale Stanley McEntire in 6/23/53 in Chockie, Oklahoma. Older brother of Reba and Susie; sang with them as the Singing McEntires at rodeos until 1975. Member of the Professional Rodeo Cowboys Association since 1971. Continues to compete in roping events. Recorded for own Old Cross Records. Sang backup harmony for Reba.	
2/22/86	**20**	7	1. Every Night	RCA 14220
5/31/86	**3**	14	2. **Savin' My Love For You**	RCA 14336
11/8/86	**12**	10	3. Bad Love	RCA 5004
3/14/87	**25**	5	4. Heart Vs. Heart Reba McEntire (harmony vocal)	RCA 5092
10/31/87	**29**	4	5. Good God, I Had It Good	RCA 5256
			McENTIRE, Reba	
			Born on 3/28/54 on a ranch in Chockie, Oklahoma. Sang with older brother Pake and younger sister Susie at rodeos as the Singing McEntires while still a teenager. Competed in rodeos as a horseback barrel rider. Family trio recorded for Boss in 1972. Discovered by Red Steagall when she sang the National Anthem at the National Rodeo Finals in Oklahoma City in 1974. Married rodeo champion Charlie Battles on 6/21/76; divorced in 1987. Married her manager, Narvel Blackstock, in 1989. First worked on the *Grand Ole Opry* in 1977, became a member in 1985. Acted in the 1990 movie *Tremors* and several TV movies. Seven members of her band plus her tour manager were killed in a plane crash on 3/16/91. CMA Awards: 1984, 1985, 1986 and 1987 Female Vocalist of the Year; 1986 Entertainer of the Year.	
6/17/78	**20**	7	1. Three Sheets In The Wind/	
		7	2. I'd Really Love To See You Tonight #2 Pop hit for England Dan & John Ford Coley in 1976	Mercury 55026
10/14/78	**28**	4	3. Last Night, Ev'ry Night	Mercury 55036
5/26/79	**36**	4	4. Runaway Heart	Mercury 55058
8/4/79	**26**	5	5. That Makes Two Of Us **JACKY WARD & REBA McENTIRE (#1, 2, 5)**	Mercury 55054
10/20/79	**19**	6	6. Sweet Dreams	Mercury 57003

DATE	POS	WKS	ARTIST–RECORD TITLE	LABEL & NO.
2/16/80	40	1	7. (I Still Long To Hold You) Now And Then	Mercury 57014
6/28/80	8	11	8. **(You Lift Me) Up To Heaven**	Mercury 57025
11/8/80	18	7	9. I Can See Forever In Your Eyes	Mercury 57034
4/4/81	13	10	10. I Don't Think Love Ought To Be That Way	Mercury 57046
8/1/81	5	11	11. **Today All Over Again**	Mercury 57054
12/19/81+	13	10	12. Only You (And You Alone) #5 Pop hit for the Platters in 1955	Mercury 57062
6/19/82	3	15	13. **I'm Not That Lonely Yet**	Mercury 76157
10/30/82+	1 (1)	14	14. **Can't Even Get The Blues**	Mercury 76180
2/19/83	1 (1)	14	15. **You're The First Time I've Thought About Leaving**	Mercury 810338
8/27/83	7	11	16. **Why Do We Want (What We Know We Can't Have)**	Mercury 812632
1/14/84	12	10	17. There Ain't No Future In This	Mercury 814629
4/14/84	5	10	18. **Just A Little Love**	MCA 52349
7/28/84	15	9	19. He Broke Your Mem'ry Last Night	MCA 52404
11/3/84+	1 (1)	14	20. **How Blue**	MCA 52468
3/2/85	1 (1)	13	21. **Somebody Should Leave**	MCA 52527
7/6/85	6	12	22. **Have I Got A Deal For You**	MCA 52604
10/26/85	5	14	23. **Only In My Mind**	MCA 52691
3/15/86	1 (1)	15	24. **Whoever's In New England**	MCA 52767
7/12/86	1 (1)	13	25. **Little Rock**	MCA 52848
10/25/86+	1 (1)	15	26. **What Am I Gonna Do About You**	MCA 52922
2/14/87	4	12	27. **Let The Music Lift You Up**	MCA 52990
5/30/87	1 (1)	14	28. **One Promise Too Late**	MCA 53092
10/3/87	1 (1)	14	29. **The Last One To Know**	MCA 53159
1/30/88	1 (1)	13	30. **Love Will Find Its Way To You**	MCA 53244
5/28/88	5	12	31. **Sunday Kind Of Love** #15 Pop hit for Jo Stafford in 1947	MCA 53315
10/1/88	1 (1)	14	32. **I Know How He Feels**	MCA 53402
1/14/89	1 (1)	14	33. **New Fool At An Old Game**	MCA 53473
5/20/89	1 (1)	14	34. **Cathy's Clown** #1 Pop hit for The Everly Brothers in 1960	MCA 53638
9/16/89	4	13	35. 'Til Love Comes Again	MCA 53694
1/13/90	7	13	36. **Little Girl**	MCA 53763
2/17/90	13	11	37. Oklahoma Swing **VINCE GILL with Reba McEntire**	MCA 53780
5/5/90	2 (2)	18	38. **Walk On** originally the B-side of #34 above	MCA 79009
9/1/90	1 (1)	19	39. **You Lie**	MCA 79071
12/8/90+	3	19	40. **Rumor Has It**	MCA 53970
3/16/91	8	11	41. **Fancy**	MCA 54042
6/8/91	2 (1)	18	42. **Fallin' Out Of Love**	MCA 54108
10/26/91	1 (2)	19	43. **For My Broken Heart**	MCA 54223
2/1/92	1 (2)	19	44. **Is There Life Out There**	MCA 54319
5/16/92	12	12	45. The Night The Lights Went Out In Georgia	MCA 54386
8/29/92	3	14	46. **The Greatest Man I Never Knew**	MCA 54441
11/28/92+	5	14	47. **Take It Back**	MCA 54544
2/27/93	1 (2)	16	48. **The Heart Won't Lie** **REBA McENTIRE and VINCE GILL** co-written by Kim Carnes	MCA 54599

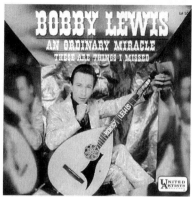

The Judds' amazingly successful career took off swiftly with their 1984 single "Mama He's Crazy." The track was the first of eight consecutive chart toppers for the famous mother-daughter team. By the time they split in 1991, the duo had scored a total of 14 No. 1 hits.

Bobby Lewis's "An Ordinary Miracle" reached No. 29 in 1968. The Kentucky-born singer later scored hits by remaking songs by such artists as Rick Nelson, Dinah Washington and the Pop act Gallery.

Linda Gail Lewis, younger sister of the famous Jerry Lee, scored her sole Top 10 hit in 1969 with "Don't Let Me Cross Over." Like follow-up hit "Roll Over Beethoven," the song was a duet with her well-known sibling.

Patty Loveless—a former rock and roll singer whose actual married name was Lovelace—received songwriting encouragment as a teenager from both Dolly Parton and Porter Wagoner. "Lonely Days, Lonely Nights," her first charting single, reached No. 46 in early 1986.

Loretta Lynn—prolific Country legend and the very same coal miner's daughter immortalized via autobiography and film—saw her 1985 single "Heart Don't Do This To Me" climb into the Top 20 a full 25 years after her initial charting single, "Honky Tonk Girl."

Barbara Mandrell—voted Entertainer of the Year by the Country Music Association in 1980 and 1981—was a highly conspicuous chart presence in the early '80s. Her "Fast Lanes And Country Roads," which reached No. 4 in early 1986, was the 24th Top 10 record of her career.

Louise Mandrell—Barbara's younger sister—managed considerable chart success of her own in the '80s. Her 1984 single "This Bed's Not Big Enough" reached No. 52. Mandrell married R.C. Bannon in 1979 and recorded a series of duets with him for Epic and RCA.

The Marcy Bros.' first charting single, 1988's "The Things I Didn't Say," spent five weeks on the charts and peaked at No. 68. The three brothers—Kendal, Kevin and Kris—are California natives.

Kathy Mattea scored her second No. 1 single in 1988 with "Eighteen Wheels And A Dozen Roses." The tune would become the Country Music Association's Single Of The Year for 1988.

The McCarters—Tennessee twins Lisa and Teresa and their sister Jennifer—met dual Top 5 success in 1988 with "Timeless And True Love" and "The Gift."

Charlie McClain, a gifted singer who appeared on "Hart To Hart" and "CHiPS," among other TV shows, married actor Wayne Massey in 1984 and soon recorded a series of duets with him, including 1985's Top 5 hit "With Just One Look In Your Eyes."

Mel McDaniel's 1986 single "Stand On It" doubtlessly appeared in the record collections of rock and roll fanatics: The track, a No. 12 hit, was penned by none other than Bruce Springsteen.

DATE	POS	WKS	ARTIST– RECORD TITLE	LABEL & NO.
5/29/93	**5**	15	49. **It's Your Call**	MCA 54496
9/4/93	**1** (1)	16	50. **Does He Love You**	MCA 54719
			REBA McENTIRE (with Linda Davis)	
1/1/94	**7**	14	51. **They Asked About You**	MCA 54769
4/23/94	**5**	14	52. **Why Haven't I Heard From You**	MCA 54823
8/13/94	**15**	11	53. She Thinks His Name Was John	MCA 54899
11/19/94+	**2** (1)	16	54. **Till You Love Me**	MCA 54888
2/25/95	**1** (1)	17	55. **The Heart Is A Lonely Hunter**	MCA 54987
6/3/95	**2** (1)	15	56. **And Still**	MCA 55047
9/23/95	**20**	7	57. On My Own	MCA 55100
			Trisha Yearwood, Martina McBride and Linda Davis (backing vocals); #1 Pop and R&B hit for Patti LaBelle & Michael McDonald in 1986	
12/2/95+	**9**	14	58. **Ring On Her Finger, Time On Her Hands**	MCA 55161
4/20/96	**19**	12	59. Starting Over Again	MCA 55183
			written by Donna Summer and her husband, Bruce Sudano	

McGRAW, Tim

Born on 5/1/67 in Delhi, Louisiana; raised in Start, Louisiana. His father, Tug McGraw, was a professional baseball player, 1964-84. Tim attended Northeast Louisiana University on several sports scholarships.

DATE	POS	WKS	ARTIST– RECORD TITLE	LABEL & NO.
2/19/94	**8**	12	● 1. **Indian Outlaw**	Curb 76920
			includes a verse from the #1 1971 Pop hit "Indian Reservation"	
4/30/94	**1** (2)	14	● 2. **Don't Take The Girl**	Curb 76925
8/6/94	**2** (3)	17	3. **Down On The Farm**	Curb LP Cut
11/5/94+	**1** (2)	19	4. **Not A Moment Too Soon/**	
3/11/95	**5**	13	5. **Refried Dreams**	Curb 76931
			all of above from the album *Not A Moment Too Soon* on Curb 77659	
8/19/95	**1** (5)	19	6. **I Like It, I Love It**	Curb 76961
11/11/95	**2** (2)	16	7. **Can't Be Really Gone**	Curb 76971
3/16/96	**5**	12	8. **All I Want Is A Life**	Curb LP Cut
			above 3 from the album *All I Want* on Curb 77800	

McGUINN, Roger—see HILLMAN, Chris

McLEAN, Don

Born on 10/2/45 in New Rochelle, New York. Singer/songwriter/poet. He was the inspiration for the Pop hit "Killing Me Softly."

DATE	POS	WKS	ARTIST– RECORD TITLE	LABEL & NO.
2/14/81	**6**	9	1. **Crying**	Millennium 11799

MEDLEY, Bill

Born on 9/19/40 in Santa Ana, California. Baritone of The Righteous Brothers duo. Co-owner of a Las Vegas nightclub named Kicks with Paul Revere of The Raiders.

DATE	POS	WKS	ARTIST– RECORD TITLE	LABEL & NO.
1/28/84	**28**	6	1. Till Your Memory's Gone	RCA 13692
5/19/84	**17**	9	2. I Still Do	RCA 13753
9/8/84	**26**	6	3. I've Always Got The Heart To Sing The Blues	RCA 13851

MELLONS, Ken

Born in Kingsport, Tennessee; moved to Nashville at age three.

DATE	POS	WKS	ARTIST– RECORD TITLE	LABEL & NO.
9/10/94	**8**	14	1. **Jukebox Junkie**	Epic 77579

DATE	POS	WKS	ARTIST– RECORD TITLE	LABEL & NO.
5/6/95	40	1	2. Workin' For The Weekend	Epic 77861
12/16/95	39	1	3. Rub-A-Dubbin'	Epic 78066
			MEREDITH, Buddy	
			Born William G. Meredith on 4/13/26 in Beaver Falls, Pennsylvania.	
5/12/62	27	2	1. I May Fall Again	Nashville 5042
			MESSINA, Jo Dee	
3/9/96	2 (1)	14	1. **Heads Carolina, Tails California**	Curb 76982
			MESSNER, Bud, & his Sky Line Boys	
			Born Norman Messner on 10/9/17 in Luray, Virginia. Teamed with Molly Darr; worked state fairs. On WJEJ-Hagerstown and the *Grand Ole Opry*. The Sky Line Boys included Buddy Allen, Jack Throckmorton, Jimmy Throckmorton and Ray Ingram.	
6/3/50	7	6	1. **Slippin' Around With Jole Blon** Juke Box #7 / Best Seller #9; Bill Franklin (vocal)	Abbey 15004
			MIDDLETON, Eddie	
			Born in Albany, Georgia. In R.C. & The Moonpies with Mickey Thomas (of rock group Jefferson Starship).	
10/22/77	38	2	1. Endlessly #12 Pop hit for Brook Benton in 1959	Epic 50431
			MILES, Dick	
3/30/68	17	8	1. The Last Goodbye	Capitol 2113
			MILLER, Frankie	
			Born on 12/17/30 in Victoria, Texas. Singer/songwriter. Attended St. Joseph High School and Victoria College. Worked on KNAL-Victoria and appeared on *Jubilee USA* on ABC-TV. Regular on *Cowtown Hoedown*, Fort Worth, in 1959.	
4/13/59	5	19	1. **Black Land Farmer**	Starday 424
10/5/59	7	21	2. **Family Man**	Starday 457
5/23/60	15	14	3. Baby Rocked Her Dolly	Starday 496
7/17/61	16	5	4. Black Land Farmer [R]	Starday 424
2/29/64	34	4	5. A Little South Of Memphis	Starday 655
			MILLER, Jody	
			Born Myrna Joy Miller on 11/29/41 in Phoenix and raised in Blanchard, Oklahoma. In vocal trio, the Melodies, while still in high school. Worked local clubs. Appeared on Tom Paxton's TV show in the early '60s. Moved to Los Angeles in 1963. Owns an 1100-acre ranch in Blanchard and raises quarter horses.	
6/5/65	5	9	1. **Queen Of The House** answer to Roger Miller's "King Of The Road"	Capitol 5402
9/19/70	21	7	2. Look At Mine	Epic 10641
1/16/71	19	10	3. If You Think I Love You Now (I've Just Started)	Epic 10692
7/3/71	5	12	4. **He's So Fine**	Epic 10734
10/30/71	5	9	5. **Baby I'm Yours**	Epic 10785

DATE	POS	WKS	ARTIST– RECORD TITLE	LABEL & NO.
4/15/72	**15**	10	6. Be My Baby #2 Pop hit for The Ronettes in 1963	Epic 10835
6/10/72	**13**	8	7. Let's All Go Down To The River **JODY MILLER and JOHNNY PAYCHECK**	Epic 10863
7/8/72	**4**	11	8. **There's A Party Goin' On**	Epic 10878
11/25/72	**18**	9	9. To Know Him Is To Love Him #1 Pop hit for The Teddy Bears in 1958	Epic 10916
4/7/73	**9**	9	10. **Good News**	Epic 10960
7/28/73	**5**	10	11. **Darling, You Can Always Come Back Home**	Epic 11016
12/29/73+	**29**	7	12. The House Of The Rising Sun #1 Pop hit for The Animals in 1964	Epic 11056
1/8/77	**25**	5	13. When The New Wears Off Our Love	Epic 50304

MILLER, Mary K.

Born in Houston. First recorded at age 14 for Reprise.

DATE	POS	WKS	ARTIST– RECORD TITLE	LABEL & NO.
1/28/78	**33**	3	1. The Longest Walk #6 Pop hit for Jaye P. Morgan in 1955	Inergi 304
6/17/78	**28**	6	2. I Can't Stop Loving You #1 Pop hit for Ray Charles in 1962	Inergi 307
10/7/78	**19**	6	3. Handcuffed To A Heartache	Inergi 310
4/7/79	**17**	8	4. Next Best Feeling	Inergi 312

MILLER, Ned

Born Henry Ned Miller on 4/12/25 in Raines, Utah. Singer/songwriter. To California in 1956. Signed with Fabor in 1956. Wrote the Gale Storm and Bonnie Guitar Pop hit "Dark Moon."

DATE	POS	WKS	ARTIST– RECORD TITLE	LABEL & NO.
12/15/62+	**2** (4)	19	1. **From A Jack To A King**	Fabor 114
5/25/63	**27**	3	2. One Among The Many	Fabor 116
9/14/63	**28**	1	3. Another Fool Like Me	Fabor 121
5/2/64	**13**	18	4. Invisible Tears	Fabor 128
1/23/65	**7**	18	5. **Do What You Do Do Well**	Fabor 137
8/21/65	**28**	7	6. Whistle Walkin'	Capitol 5431
9/3/66	**39**	2	7. Summer Roses	Capitol 5661
6/6/70	**39**	2	8. The Lover's Song	Republic 1411

MILLER, Roger

Born on 1/2/36 in Fort Worth, Texas; raised in Erick, Oklahoma. Died of cancer on 10/25/92. Vocalist/humorist/guitarist/composer. To Nashville in the mid-1950s; began songwriting career. With Faron Young as writer/drummer in 1962. Won six Grammys in 1965. Own TV show in 1966. Songwriter of 1985's Tony Award-winning Broadway musical *Big River*. Elected to the Country Music Hall of Fame in 1995.

DATE	POS	WKS	ARTIST– RECORD TITLE	LABEL & NO.
10/31/60+	**14**	16	1. You Don't Want My Love	RCA 7776
6/5/61	**6**	18	2. **When Two Worlds Collide**	RCA 7878
6/1/63	**26**	1	3. Lock, Stock And Teardrops	RCA 8175
6/13/64	**1** (6)	22	4. **Dang Me** [N]	Smash 1881
9/19/64	**3**	17	5. **Chug-A-Lug** [N]	Smash 1926
12/19/64+	**15**	9	6. Do-Wacka-Do [N]	Smash 1947
2/13/65	**1** (5)	20	● 7. **King Of The Road**	Smash 1965
5/29/65	**2** (2)	15	8. **Engine Engine #9**	Smash 1983
7/24/65	**10**	12	9. One Dyin' And A Buryin'	Smash 1994

DATE	POS	WKS	ARTIST- RECORD TITLE	LABEL & NO.
10/2/65	7	13	10. **Kansas City Star** [N]	Smash 1998
12/4/65+	3	14	11. **England Swings**	Smash 2010
2/26/66	5	14	12. **Husbands And Wives/**	
2/26/66	13	10	13. I've Been A Long Time Leavin' (But I'll Be A Long Time Gone)	Smash 2024
7/23/66	35	3	14. You Can't Roller Skate In A Buffalo Herd [N]	Smash 2043
10/15/66	39	3	15. My Uncle Used To Love Me But She Died [N]	Smash 2055
4/15/67	7	15	16. **Walkin' In The Sunshine**	Smash 2081
11/18/67	27	8	17. The Ballad Of Waterhole #3 (Code Of The West)	Smash 2121
			from the movie *Waterhole #3* starring James Coburn	
3/16/68	6	12	18. **Little Green Apples**	Smash 2148
12/28/68+	15	9	19. Vance	Smash 2197
8/2/69	12	11	20. Me And Bobby McGee	Smash 2230
			#1 Pop hit for Janis Joplin in 1971	
11/1/69	14	8	21. Where Have All The Average People Gone	Smash 2246
4/4/70	36	2	22. The Tom Green County Fair	Smash 2258
9/19/70	15	8	23. South/	
		8	24. Don't We All Have The Right	Mercury 73102
5/8/71	11	10	25. Tomorrow Night In Baltimore	Mercury 73190
8/28/71	28	4	26. Loving Her Was Easier (Than Anything I'll Ever Do Again)	Mercury 73230
5/6/72	34	5	27. We Found It In Each Other's Arms	Mercury 73268
8/11/73	14	9	28. Open Up Your Heart	Columbia 45873
12/22/73+	24	4	29. I Believe In The Sunshine	Columbia 45948
11/7/81	36	2	30. Everyone Gets Crazy Now And Then	Elektra 47192
6/26/82	19	9	31. Old Friends	Columbia 02681
			ROGER MILLER & WILLIE NELSON (with RAY PRICE)	
11/16/85	36	2	32. River In The Rain	MCA 52663
			from the Broadway musical *Big River* starring Daniel H. Jenkins	

MILLINDER, Lucky, And His Orchestra

Millinder born Lucius Millinder on 8/8/1900 in Anniston, Alabama. Died on 9/28/66 in New York City. R&B bandleader.

DATE	POS	WKS	ARTIST- RECORD TITLE	LABEL & NO.
1/15/44	4	5	1. **Sweet Slumber**	Decca 18569
			Trevor Bacon (vocal)	
7/29/44	4	2	2. **Hurry, Hurry**	Decca 18609
			Wynonie "Mr. Blues" Harris (vocal)	

MILSAP, Ronnie

Born on 1/16/46 in Robbinsville, North Carolina. Singer/pianist/guitarist. Blind since birth; multi-instrumentalist by age 12. With J.J. Cale band; own band from 1965. Joined the *Grand Ole Opry* in 1976. CMA Awards: 1974, 1976 and 1977 Male Vocalist of the Year; 1977 Entertainer of the Year.

DATE	POS	WKS	ARTIST- RECORD TITLE	LABEL & NO.
8/4/73	10	9	1. **I Hate You/**	
		9	2. (All Together Now) Let's Fall Apart	RCA 0969
12/8/73+	11	12	3. That Girl Who Waits On Tables	RCA 0097
4/20/74	1 (1)	12	4. **Pure Love**	RCA 0237
			written by Eddie Rabbitt	
8/17/74	1 (2)	9	5. **Please Don't Tell Me How The Story Ends**	RCA 0313
12/14/74+	1 (1)	10	6. **(I'd Be) A Legend In My Time**	RCA 10112

DATE	POS	WKS	ARTIST– RECORD TITLE	LABEL & NO.
4/5/75	**6**	10	7. **Too Late To Worry, Too Blue To Cry**	RCA 10228
8/9/75	**1 (2)**	11	8. **Daydreams About Night Things**	RCA 10335
10/18/75	**15**	8	9. She Even Woke Me Up To Say Goodbye	Warner 8127
11/22/75+	**4**	11	10. **Just In Case**	RCA 10420
4/3/76	**1 (1)**	11	11. **What Goes On When The Sun Goes Down**	RCA 10593
7/24/76	**1 (2)**	11	12. **(I'm A) Stand By My Woman Man**	RCA 10724
12/11/76+	**1 (1)**	12	13. **Let My Love Be Your Pillow**	RCA 10843
6/4/77	**1 (3)**	12	14. **It Was Almost Like A Song**	RCA 10976
11/19/77+	**1 (1)**	14	15. **What A Difference You've Made In My Life**	RCA 11146
6/3/78	**1 (3)**	11	16. **Only One Love In My Life**	RCA 11270
9/2/78	**1 (1)**	10	17. **Let's Take The Long Way Around The World**	RCA 11369
12/23/78+	**2 (3)**	12	18. **Back On My Mind Again/**	
		12	19. Santa Barbara	RCA 11421
4/28/79	**1 (1)**	12	20. **Nobody Likes Sad Songs**	RCA 11553
8/25/79	**6**	10	21. **In No Time At All/**	
		10	22. Get It Up	RCA 11695
1/26/80	**1 (1)**	11	23. **Why Don't You Spend The Night**	RCA 11909
4/12/80	**1 (3)**	13	24. **My Heart/**	
		13	25. Silent Night (After The Fight)	RCA 11952
7/5/80	**1 (1)**	12	26. **Cowboys And Clowns/**	
			from the movie *Bronco Billy* starring Clint Eastwood	
		12	27. Misery Loves Company	RCA 12006
10/11/80	**1 (1)**	10	28. **Smoky Mountain Rain**	RCA 12084
3/28/81	**1 (1)**	9	29. **Am I Losing You**	RCA 12194
7/11/81	**1 (2)**	11	30. **(There's) No Gettin' Over Me**	RCA 12264
11/14/81+	**1 (1)**	11	31. **I Wouldn't Have Missed It For The World**	RCA 12342
5/15/82	**1 (1)**	11	32. **Any Day Now**	RCA 13216
8/28/82	**1 (1)**	12	33. **He Got You**	RCA 13286
12/4/82+	**1 (1)**	13	34. **Inside/**	
		13	35. Carolina Dreams	RCA 13362
4/23/83	**5**	11	36. **Stranger In My House**	RCA 13470
8/6/83	**1 (1)**	12	37. **Don't You Know How Much I Love You**	RCA 13564
11/26/83+	**1 (1)**	14	38. **Show Her**	RCA 13658
6/2/84	**1 (1)**	14	39. **Still Losing You**	RCA 13805
9/22/84	**6**	11	40. **Prisoner Of The Highway**	RCA 13847
			flip side "She Loves My Car" made #84 on the *Hot 100*	
4/20/85	**1 (1)**	13	41. **She Keeps The Home Fires Burning**	RCA 14034
7/27/85	**1 (2)**	14	42. **Lost In The Fifties Tonight (In the Still of the Night)**	RCA 14135
3/22/86	**1 (1)**	14	43. **Happy, Happy Birthday Baby**	RCA 14286
			#5 Pop hit for The Tune Weavers in 1957	
7/12/86	**1 (1)**	14	44. **In Love**	RCA 14365
12/6/86+	**1 (1)**	13	45. **How Do I Turn You On**	RCA 5033
5/30/87	**1 (1)**	12	46. **Snap Your Fingers**	RCA 5169
			#8 Pop hit for Joe Henderson in 1962	
7/4/87	**1 (1)**	13	47. **Make No Mistake, She's Mine**	RCA 5209
			RONNIE MILSAP & KENNY ROGERS	
			#51 Pop hit for Barbra Streisand & Kim Carnes in 1985 as "Make No Mistake, He's Mine"	

DATE	POS	WKS	ARTIST–RECORD TITLE	LABEL & NO.
11/7/87+	**1** (1)	13	48. **Where Do The Nights Go**	RCA 5259
3/19/88	**2** (1)	13	49. **Old Folks**	RCA 6896
			RONNIE MILSAP & MIKE REID	
8/6/88	**4**	13	50. **Button Off My Shirt**	RCA 8389
1/7/89	**1** (1)	13	51. **Don't You Ever Get Tired (Of Hurting Me)**	RCA 8746
5/13/89	**4**	13	52. **Houston Solution**	RCA 8868
10/7/89	**1** (2)	24	53. **A Woman In Love**	RCA 9027
2/24/90	**2** (2)	18	54. **Stranger Things Have Happened**	RCA 9120
3/16/91	**3**	19	55. **Are You Lovin' Me Like I'm Lovin' You**	RCA 2509
7/27/91	**6**	14	56. **Since I Don't Have You**	RCA 2848
			#12 Pop hit for The Skyliners in 1959	
12/21/91+	**4**	13	57. **Turn That Radio On**	RCA 62104
4/18/92	**11**	13	58. All Is Fair In Love And War	RCA 62217
8/14/93	30	6	59. True Believer	Liberty 17595

MINNIE PEARL

Born Sarah Ophelia Colley on 10/25/12 in Centerville, Tennessee. Died on 3/4/96 after suffering a stroke. Comedienne/actress; taught drama in Atlanta in 1934. With the *Grand Ole Opry* from 1940. Elected to the Country Music Hall of Fame in 1975. Trademark was her straw hat with its $1.98 price tag still attached.

3/5/66	10	12	1. **Giddyup Go - Answer** [S]	Starday 754
			answer to Red Sovine's "Giddyup Go"	

MITCHELL, Charles, and his Orchestra

Steel guitarist with Jimmie Davis, co-writer of "You Are My Sunshine." Worked for the State of Louisiana while Davis was governor.

4/29/44	4	1	1. **If It's Wrong To Love You**	Bluebird 33-0508

MITCHELL, Marty

From Birmingham, Alabama. Recorded for Atlantic at age 17.

3/18/78	34	3	1. You Are The Sunshine Of My Life	MC 5005
			#1 Pop hit for Stevie Wonder in 1973	

MITCHELL, Price

5/31/75	29	4	1. Personality	GRT 020
			#2 Pop hit for Lloyd Price in 1959	

MITCHELL, Priscilla

Born on 9/18/41 in Marietta, Georgia. Sang on WFOM-Marietta at age four. First recorded as a rock and roll singer under the name Sadina in the late '50s. Married to Jerry Reed; worked as a backup singer.

5/29/65	**1** (2)	23	1. **Yes, Mr. Peters**	Mercury 72416

MITCHUM, Robert

Born on 8/6/17 in Bridgeport, Connecticut. Since 1943, leading man in movies, including *Not As A Stranger, The Longest Day, Heaven Knows, Mr. Allison* and many others. Starred in the 1983 TV mini-series *The Winds Of War*. Father of actor Chris Mitchum.

6/10/67	9	13	1. **Little Old Wine Drinker Me**	Monument 1006

DATE	POS	WKS	ARTIST–RECORD TITLE	LABEL & NO.
			MIZE, Billy	
			Born on 4/29/29 in Kansas City, Kansas; raised in California. Steel guitarist. Worked as a DJ on KPMC. On KERO-TV *Trading Post Show*, 1953-66. Host of Gene Autry's Melody Ranch shows, 1966-67. A TV producer with his own production company. Recorded as Billy & Cliff on the Challenge label.	
6/7/69	**40**	2	1. Make It Rain	Imperial 66365
11/13/76	**31**	4	2. It Hurts To Know The Feeling's Gone	Zodiac 1011
			MONROE, Bill, and His Blue Grass Boys	
			Monroe known as "The Father Of Bluegrass." Born on 9/13/11 in Rosine, Kentucky. Moved to Indiana in 1929. In band with brothers Birch and Charlie in East Chicago, 1929-34. Worked on WLS *Barn Dance*. Toured with Charlie as the Monroe Brothers and recorded for Victor in 1936. Duo split up in 1938. Formed own band, the Kentuckians, later named the Blue Grass Boys. On the *Grand Ole Opry* since 1939. Wrote "Blue Moon Of Kentucky," "Gotta Travel On," "Kentucky Waltz." Elected to the Country Music Hall of Fame in 1970. Won Grammy's Lifetime Achievement Award in 1993.	
3/23/46	**3**	6	1. **Kentucky Waltz**	Columbia 36907
12/7/46	**5**	4	2. **Footprints In The Snow**	Columbia 37151
6/19/48	**11**	1	3. Sweetheart, You Done Me Wrong Juke Box #11	Columbia 38172
11/6/48	**13**	1	4. Wicked Path Of Sin Best Seller #13	Columbia 20503
11/27/48	**11**	5	5. Little Community Church Best Seller #11 / Juke Box #12	Columbia 20488
4/16/49	**12**	5	6. Toy Heart Best Seller #12	Columbia 20552
8/6/49	**12**	1	7. When You Are Lonely Juke Box #12; Lester Flatt (guest vocal: 3,6,7)	Columbia 20526
11/3/58	**27**	1	8. Scotland [I] **BILL MONROE**	Decca 30739
3/2/59	**15**	6	9. Gotta Travel On	Decca 30809
			MONROE, Vaughn, and his Orchestra	
			Monroe born on 10/7/11 in Akron, Ohio. Died on 5/21/73. Trumpeter/band leader/singer. Very popular in TV, radio and movies.	
5/14/49	**2 (1)**	5	● 1. **Riders In The Sky (A Cowboy Legend)** Best Seller #2 / Juke Box #10; 45 rpm: 47-2902; #30 Pop hit for The Ramrods in 1961	RCA Victor 3411
			MONTANA, Billy, & The Long Shots	
			Quintet from Voorheesville, New York: Billy (real name: William Schlappi) and Kyle Montana, Dave Flint, Bobby Kendall and Doug Bernhard.	
10/3/87	**40**	1	1. Baby I Was Leaving Anyhow	Warner 28256
			MONTGOMERY, John Michael	
			Born on 1/20/65 in Danville, Kentucky. Singer/guitarist. Discovered while playing at the Austin City Saloon in Lexington, Kentucky. CMA Award: 1994 Horizon Award.	
11/14/92+	**4**	14	1. **Life's A Dance** later available as the B-side of #2 below	Atlantic LP Cut
4/3/93	**1 (3)**	17	2. **I Love The Way You Love Me**	Atlantic 87371
7/24/93	**21**	10	3. Beer And Bones above 3 from the album *Life's A Dance* on Atlantic 82420	Atlantic 87326

DATE	POS	WKS	ARTIST–RECORD TITLE	LABEL & NO.
12/18/93+	**1 (4)**	18	● 4. **I Swear**	Atlantic 87288
			CMA Award: Single of the Year	
4/2/94	**4**	13	5. **Rope The Moon**	Atlantic 87248
7/2/94	**1 (2)**	14	6. **Be My Baby Tonight**	Atlantic 87236
10/8/94	**1 (1)**	18	7. **If You've Got Love**	Atlantic 87198
3/11/95	**1 (3)**	17	8. **I Can Love You Like That**	Atlantic LP Cut
			#5 Pop hit for All-4-One in 1995	
5/27/95	**1 (3)**	17	9. **Sold (The Grundy County Auction Incident)**	Atlantic LP Cut
9/9/95	**3**	13	10. **No Man's Land**	Atlantic 87105
12/2/95+	**4**	17	11. **Cowboy Love**	Atlantic LP Cut
3/9/96	**4**	17	12. **Long As I Live**	Atlantic LP Cut
			above 5 from the album *John Michael Montgomery* on Atlantic 82728	

MONTGOMERY, Melba

Born on 10/14/38 in Iron City, Tennessee; raised in Florence, Alabama. Guitarist/fiddle player. Won Pet Milk Amateur contest in Nashville, 1958. Toured with Roy Acuff's Smoky Mountain Boys, 1958-62. Solo work since 1962.

(a) GEORGE JONES & MELBA MONTGOMERY
(b) CHARLIE LOUVIN & MELBA MONTGOMERY

DATE	POS	WKS	ARTIST–RECORD TITLE	LABEL & NO.
5/4/63	**3**	28	1. **We Must Have Been Out Of Our Minds** (a)	United Art. 575
8/24/63	**26**	6	2. Hall Of Shame	United Art. 576
12/7/63	**17**	7	3. Let's Invite Them Over (a)/	
11/30/63	**20**	5	4. What's In Our Heart (a)	United Art. 635
12/7/63+	**22**	8	5. The Greatest One Of All	United Art. 652
9/5/64	**31**	5	6. Please Be My Love (a)	United Art. 732
12/19/64+	**25**	10	7. Multiply The Heartaches (a)	United Art. 784
1/22/66	**15**	11	8. Baby, Ain't That Fine	Musicor 1135
			GENE PITNEY and MELBA MONTGOMERY	
9/23/67	**24**	8	9. Party Pickin' (a)	Musicor 1238
11/14/70	**18**	9	10. Something To Brag About (b)	Capitol 2915
3/20/71	**26**	6	11. Did You Ever (b)	Capitol 3029
7/10/71	**30**	3	12. Baby, You've Got What It Takes (b)	Capitol 3111
			#5 Pop hit for Dinah Washington & Brook Benton in 1960	
11/17/73	**38**	1	13. Wrap Your Love Around Me	Elektra 45866
4/6/74	**1 (1)**	12	14. **No Charge**	Elektra 45883
3/1/75	**15**	7	15. Don't Let The Good Times Fool You	Elektra 45229
1/21/78	**22**	6	16. Angel Of The Morning	United Art. 1115
			#7 Pop hit for Merrilee Rush in 1968	

MOODY, Clyde

Born on 9/19/14 on a Cherokee Reservation in North Carolina; raised in Marion, North Carolina. Died on 4/7/89. Guitarist from age eight. With J. Hugh Hall as Bill & Joe on WSPA-Spartanburg in 1929. First recorded for ARC in 1935. Worked with Mainer's Sons Of The Mountaineers, Bill Monroe and Roy Acuff to the mid-1940s. Own TV shows in Washington, D.C., and North Carolina. Known as "The Hillbilly Waltz King."

DATE	POS	WKS	ARTIST–RECORD TITLE	LABEL & NO.
8/14/48	**8**	1	1. **Red Roses Tied In Blue**/	
			Best Seller #8	
6/19/48	**15**	1	2. Carolina Waltz	King 706
			Best Seller #15	
3/11/50	**8**	2	3. **I Love You Because**	King 837
			Jockey #8	

DATE	POS	WKS	ARTIST– RECORD TITLE	LABEL & NO.
			MOORE, Lattie	
			Born on 10/17/24 in Scotsville, Kentucky. Toured with Lash LaRue in the late '40s. Own radio show, *Midwest Jamboree*, in Indianapolis in 1951. First recorded for Speed in 1952. Considered by many to be the original rockabilly artist.	
1/30/61	**25**	3	1. Drunk Again	King 5413
			MORGAN, Al	
			Pianist from Chicago. Own Dumont TV series in 1947. Known as "Mr. Flying Fingers."	
9/17/49	**8**	1	1. **Jealous Heart**	London 500
			Best Seller #8; first released on Universal 148 in 1949;	
			45 rpm: London 3001; #47 Pop hit for Connie Francis in 1965	
			MORGAN, Billie	
			Born on 12/13/22 in Nashville. Worked on KAMD-Camden, Arkansas, 1945-46.	
3/23/59	**22**	3	1. Life To Live	Starday 420
			MORGAN, George	
			Born George Thomas Morgan on 6/28/24 in Waverly, Tennessee. Died of a heart attack in July 1975. Raised in Barberton, Ohio. Worked on WWVA-Wheeling *Jamboree* in the late '40s. Wrote "Candy Kisses." On the *Grand Ole Opry*, 1948-56, and again from 1959. Own show on WLAC-TV, Nashville, 1956-59. Father of Lorrie Morgan.	
2/26/49	**1** (3)	23	1. **Candy Kisses/**	
			Best Seller #1 / Juke Box #2	
3/19/49	**4**	14	2. **Please Don't Let Me Love You**	Columbia 20547
			Best Seller #4 / Juke Box #4	
4/30/49	**8**	6	3. **Rainbow In My Heart/**	
			Best Seller #8 / Juke Box #10	
5/7/49	**11**	1	4. All I Need Is Some More Lovin'	Columbia 20563
			Best Seller #11	
7/23/49	**4**	12	5. **Room Full Of Roses**	Columbia 20594
			Best Seller #4 / Juke Box #10	
12/10/49	**4**	4	6. **I Love Everything About You/**	
			Jockey #4 / Best Seller #14	
10/29/49	**5**	9	7. **Cry-Baby Heart**	Columbia 20627
			Best Seller #5 / Juke Box #6 / Jockey #7	
4/19/52	**2** (6)	23	8. **Almost**	Columbia 20906
			Best Seller #2 / Jockey #2 / Juke Box #2	
3/7/53	**10**	1	9. **(I Just Had A Date) A Lover's Quarrel**	Columbia 21070
			Juke Box #10	
1/26/57	**15**	1	10. There Goes My Love	Columbia 40792
			Jockey #15	
2/16/59	**3**	23	11. **I'm In Love Again**	Columbia 41318
8/17/59	**20**	9	12. Little Dutch Girl/	
8/24/59	**26**	1	13. The Last Thing I Want To Know	Columbia 41420
1/11/60	**4**	20	14. **You're The Only Good Thing (That's Happened To Me)**	Columbia 41523
2/1/64	**23**	4	15. One Dozen Roses (And Our Love)	Columbia 42882
6/6/64	**23**	12	16. Slipping Around	Columbia 43020
			MARION WORTH & GEORGE MORGAN	

DATE	POS	WKS	ARTIST – RECORD TITLE	LABEL & NO.
10/31/64	37	2	17. Tears And Roses	Columbia 43098
12/18/65+	27	9	18. A Picture That's New	Columbia 43393
6/10/67	40	1	19. I Couldn't See	Starday 804
9/28/68	31	4	20. Sounds Of Goodbye	Starday 850
5/3/69	30	7	21. Like A Bird	Stop 252
5/2/70	17	9	22. Lilacs And Fire	Stop 365
2/2/74	21	6	23. Red Rose From The Blue Side Of Town	MCA 40159

MORGAN, Lorrie

Born Loretta Lynn Morgan on 6/27/59. Youngest daughter of George Morgan. Worked on the *Grand Ole Opry* since 1984. Married Keith Whitley (died 5/9/89) in November 1986.

DATE	POS	WKS	ARTIST – RECORD TITLE	LABEL & NO.
1/28/89	20	8	1. Trainwreck Of Emotion	RCA 8638
5/20/89	9	13	2. **Dear Me**	RCA 8866
10/7/89	2 (3)	22	3. **Out Of Your Shoes**	RCA 9016
2/10/90	1 (1)	20	4. **Five Minutes**	RCA 9118
6/16/90	4	15	5. **He Talks To Me**	RCA 2508
8/11/90	13	12	6. 'Til A Tear Becomes A Rose	RCA 2619
			KEITH WHITLEY and LORRIE MORGAN	
4/13/91	3	18	7. **We Both Walk**	RCA 2748
8/24/91	9	17	8. **A Picture Of Me (Without You)**	RCA 62014
1/11/92	4	16	9. **Except For Monday**	RCA 62105
5/30/92	14	11	10. Something In Red	RCA 62219
9/19/92	2 (2)	18	11. **Watch Me**	BNA 62333
1/2/93	1 (3)	18	12. **What Part Of No**	BNA 62414
5/15/93	14	11	13. I Guess You Had To Be There	BNA 62415
9/11/93	8	14	14. **Half Enough**	BNA 62576
5/7/94	31	1	15. My Night To Howl	BNA 62767
9/10/94	39	2	16. Heart Over Mind	BNA 62946
6/3/95	1 (1)	16	17. **I Didn't Know My Own Strength**	BNA 64287
9/23/95	4	17	18. **Back In Your Arms Again**	BNA 64353
2/10/96	32	6	19. Standing Tall	BNA LP Cut
			above 3 from the album Greatest Hits *on BNA 66508*	
5/18/96	18 ↑	10 ↑	20. By My Side	BNA 64512
			LORRIE MORGAN with Jon Randall	

MORRIS, Gary

Born on 12/7/48 in Fort Worth, Texas. Sang in duo with twin sister, Carrie, while in the third grade. Appeared on the *Ted Mack Amateur Hour* while in high school. Own band, Breakaway, in Colorado. Moved to Nashville in 1979. Had lead part with Linda Ronstadt in *La Boheme*, New York City, in 1984; and in *Les Miserables* in 1988. Appeared as Wayne Masterson, a blind country singer, on TV's *The Colbys*.

(a) CRYSTAL GAYLE & GARY MORRIS

DATE	POS	WKS	ARTIST – RECORD TITLE	LABEL & NO.
12/13/80	40	1	1. Sweet Red Wine	Warner 49564
4/25/81	40	1	2. Fire In Your Eyes	Warner 49668
10/24/81	8	14	3. **Headed For A Heartache**	Warner 49829
3/13/82	12	12	4. Don't Look Back	Warner 50017
7/31/82	15	9	5. Dreams Die Hard	Warner 29967
12/25/82+	9	12	6. **Velvet Chains**	Warner 29853

DATE	POS	WKS	ARTIST– RECORD TITLE	LABEL & NO.
5/7/83	5	13	7. **The Love She Found In Me**	Warner 29683
9/3/83	4	12	8. **The Wind Beneath My Wings** #1 Pop hit for Bette Midler in 1989	Warner 29532
12/17/83+	4	12	9. **Why Lady Why**	Warner 29450
1/28/84	9	10	10. **You're Welcome To Tonight** **LYNN ANDERSON & GARY MORRIS**	Permian 82003
5/5/84	7	11	11. **Between Two Fires**	Warner 29321
8/18/84	7	12	12. **Second Hand Heart**	Warner 29230
12/8/84+	1 (1)	15	13. **Baby Bye Bye**	Warner 29131
5/25/85	9	12	14. **Lasso The Moon** from the movie *Rustler's Rhapsody* starring Tom Berenger	Warner 29028
9/7/85	1 (1)	15	15. **I'll Never Stop Loving You**	Warner 28947
11/30/85+	1 (1)	14	16. **Makin' Up For Lost Time (The Dallas Lovers' Song)** (a) from the TV series *Dallas* starring Larry Hagman	Warner 28856
1/25/86	1 (1)	13	17. **100% Chance Of Rain**	Warner 28823
6/14/86	28	4	18. Anything Goes	Warner 28713
8/9/86	27	5	19. Honeycomb #1 Pop hit for Jimmie Rodgers in 1957	Warner 28654
11/15/86+	1 (1)	15	20. **Leave Me Lonely**	Warner 28542
3/21/87	9	10	21. **Plain Brown Wrapper**	Warner 28468
5/9/87	4	12	22. **Another World** (a) theme song from the daytime-TV serial	Warner 28373
3/12/88	26	6	23. All Of This & More (a)	Warner 28106

MORRIS, Lamar

Born in Andalusia, Alabama. Leader of The Bama Band since 1976. Formerly married to Hank Williams, Jr.'s stepsister, Lucretia.

DATE	POS	WKS	ARTIST– RECORD TITLE	LABEL & NO.
5/15/71	27	7	1. If You Love Me (Really Love Me) #4 Pop hit for Kay Starr in 1954	MGM 14236

MORRISON, Kathy—see WILBOURN, Bill

MOSBY, Johnny and Jonie

Husband-and-wife team of Johnny (born Fort Smith, Arkansas) and Jonie (real name: Janice Irene Shields; born 8/10/40 in Van Nuys, California) Mosby.

DATE	POS	WKS	ARTIST– RECORD TITLE	LABEL & NO.
5/18/63	13	9	1. Don't Call Me From A Honky Tonk	Columbia 42668
10/12/63+	12	15	2. Trouble In My Arms/	
11/2/63	27	1	3. Who's Been Cheatin' Who	Columbia 42841
5/16/64	16	9	4. Keep Those Cards And Letters Coming In	Columbia 43005
10/17/64	21	9	5. How The Other Half Lives	Columbia 43100
12/2/67	36	3	6. Make A Left And Then A Right	Capitol 5980
2/22/69	12	14	7. Just Hold My Hand	Capitol 2384
8/9/69	38	4	8. Hold Me, Thrill Me, Kiss Me #8 Pop hit for Mel Carter in 1965	Capitol 2505
11/8/69	26	7	9. I'll Never Be Free	Capitol 2608
3/28/70	34	3	10. Third World	Capitol 2730
5/30/70	18	9	11. I'm Leavin' It Up To You #1 Pop hit for Dale & Grace in 1963	Capitol 2796
4/3/71	40	2	12. Oh, Love Of Mine	Capitol 3039

DATE	POS	WKS	ARTIST–RECORD TITLE	LABEL & NO.
			MULLICAN, Moon	
			Born Aubrey Mullican on 3/27/09 near Corrigan, Texas. Died of a heart attack on 1/1/67. Toured Texas and Louisiana with own band in the mid-1930s. Worked with the Blue Ridge Playboys and the Texas Wanderers in the early '40s. Went solo in 1946. Worked on the *Grand Ole Opry*, 1949-55. Toured with Jimmie Davis, 1960-63. His distinctive two finger, right-hand style won him fame as the "King of The Hillbilly Piano Players."	
2/8/47	2 (1)	15	1. **New Pretty Blonde (Jole Blon)** **MOON MULLICAN And the Showboys**	King 578
7/26/47	4	1	2. **Jole Blon's Sister**	King 632
5/15/48	3	26	3. **Sweeter Than The Flowers** Best Seller #3 / Juke Box #3	King 673
3/18/50	1 (4)	36	4. **I'll Sail My Ship Alone** Juke Box #1(4) / Best Seller #1(1) / Jockey #2	King 830
8/26/50	4	11	5. **Mona Lisa/** Juke Box #4 / Jockey #7 / Best Seller #8	
8/26/50	5	7	6. **Goodnight Irene** Juke Box #5 / Best Seller #10 / Jockey #10	King 886
8/4/51	7	2	7. **Cherokee Boogie (Eh-Oh-Aleena)** Best Seller #7 / Juke Box #10	King 965
5/29/61	15	4	8. Ragged But Right	Starday 545
			MUNDY, Jim	
			Born James L. White on 2/8/34 in Muldrow, Oklahoma. Professional singer since 1950. Wrote commercials for Miller Beer, Kentucky Fried Chicken and Pizza Hut. Brother of Ann J. Morton and Bill White.	
12/29/73+	13	10	1. The River's Too Wide	ABC 11400
5/24/75	37	2	2. She's Already Gone	ABC 12074
			MURPHEY, Michael Martin	
			Born on 5/5/38 in Dallas. Sang in the Texas Twosome while still in high school. Toured as Travis Lewis of The Lewis & Clarke Expedition in 1967. Worked as a staff writer for Screen Gems. Lived in Austin, 1971-74; Colorado, 1974-79. Based in Taos, New Mexico, since 1979. Appeared in the movies *Take This Job And Shove It* and *Hard Country*.	
			MICHAEL MURPHEY:	
4/3/76	36	2	1. A Mansion On The Hill flip side "Renegade" made #39 on the *Hot 100*	Epic 50184
7/10/82	1 (1)	16	2. **What's Forever For**	Liberty 1466
12/11/82+	3	13	3. **Still Taking Chances**	Liberty 1486
4/23/83	11	10	4. Love Affairs	Liberty 1494
10/8/83	9	11	5. **Don't Count The Rainy Days**	Liberty 1505
2/11/84	7	12	6. **Will It Be Love By Morning**	Liberty 1514
			MICHAEL MARTIN MURPHEY:	
6/9/84	12	9	7. Disenchanted	Liberty 1517
9/29/84	19	8	8. Radio Land	Liberty 1523
1/5/85	8	12	9. **What She Wants**	EMI America 8243
6/22/85	9	12	10. **Carolina In The Pines** [R] new version of Murphey's #21 Pop hit from 1975	EMI America 8265
3/1/86	26	6	11. Tonight We Ride	Warner 28797
6/14/86	15	9	12. Rollin' Nowhere	Warner 28694

DATE	POS	WKS	ARTIST–RECORD TITLE	LABEL & NO.
9/27/86	40	2	13. Fiddlin' Man	Warner 28598
2/14/87	4	14	14. **A Face In The Crowd** **MICHAEL MARTIN MURPHEY and HOLLY DUNN**	Warner 28471
6/13/87	1 (1)	13	15. **A Long Line Of Love**	Warner 28370
12/19/87+	3	15	16. **I'm Gonna Miss You, Girl**	Warner 28168
5/7/88	4	13	17. **Talkin' To The Wrong Man** **MICHAEL MARTIN MURPHEY with RYAN MURPHEY** **(Michael's son)**	Warner 27947
10/15/88	29	4	18. Pilgrims On The Way (Matthew's Song)	Warner 27810
1/21/89	3	14	19. **From The Word Go**	Warner 27668
6/17/89	9	12	20. **Never Givin' Up On Love** from the movie *Pink Cadillac* starring Clint Eastwood	Warner 22970

MURPHY, David Lee

Singer/songwriter/guitarist from Herrin, Illinois.

DATE	POS	WKS	ARTIST–RECORD TITLE	LABEL & NO.
5/28/94	36	3	1. Just Once from the movie *8 Seconds* starring Luke Perry	MCA 54794
5/6/95	6	15	2. **Party Crowd**	MCA 54977
9/2/95	1 (2)	17	3. **Dust On The Bottle**	MCA 54944
12/23/95+	13	14	4. Out With A Bang	MCA 55153
4/20/96	2 (1)	14↑	5. **Every Time I Get Around You**	MCA 55186

MURRAY, Anne

Born Morna Anne Murray on 6/20/45 in Springhill, Nova Scotia. High school teacher for one year after college. With CBC-TV show *Sing Along Jubilee*. First recorded for ARC in 1969. Regular on Glen Campbell's TV series *Goodtime Hour*. Currently resides in Toronto. CMA Award: 1985 Vocal Duo of the Year (with Dave Loggins).

DATE	POS	WKS	ARTIST–RECORD TITLE	LABEL & NO.
8/22/70	10	13	● 1. **Snowbird**	Capitol 2738
4/10/71	27	6	2. A Stranger In My Place written by Kenny Rogers	Capitol 3059
11/20/71	40	2	3. I Say A Little Prayer/By The Time I Get To Phoenix **GLEN CAMPBELL/ANNE MURRAY**	Capitol 3200
2/12/72	11	12	4. Cotton Jenny written by Gordon Lightfoot	Capitol 3260
1/20/73	10	13	5. **Danny's Song** written by Kenny Loggins for his nephew	Capitol 3481
6/30/73	20	6	6. What About Me	Capitol 3600
1/5/74	5	12	7. **Love Song**	Capitol 3776
5/18/74	1 (2)	14	8. **He Thinks I Still Care** flip side "You Won't See Me" made #8 on the *Hot 100*	Capitol 3867
10/26/74	5	11	9. **Son Of A Rotten Gambler** flip side "Just One Look" made #86 on the *Hot 100*	Capitol 3955
3/15/75	28	4	10. Uproar	Capitol 4025
3/6/76	19	7	11. The Call	Capitol 4207
10/2/76+	22	7	12. Things	Capitol 4329
2/4/78	4	11	13. **Walk Right Back** #7 Pop hit for The Everly Brothers in 1961	Capitol 4527
6/10/78	4	11	● 14. **You Needed Me**	Capitol 4574
1/27/79	1 (3)	12	15. **I Just Fall In Love Again**	Capitol 4675
6/2/79	1 (1)	10	16. **Shadows In The Moonlight**	Capitol 4716
10/6/79	1 (1)	11	17. **Broken Hearted Me**	Capitol 4773

DATE	POS	WKS	ARTIST-RECORD TITLE	LABEL & NO.
1/12/80	3	11	18. **Daydream Believer** #1 Pop hit for The Monkees in 1967	Capitol 4813
4/19/80	9	9	19. **Lucky Me**	Capitol 4848
7/26/80	23	5	20. I'm Happy Just To Dance With You #95 Pop hit for The Beatles in 1964	Capitol 4878
9/27/80	1 (1)	10	21. **Could I Have This Dance** from the movie *Urban Cowboy* starring John Travolta	Capitol 4920
4/18/81	1 (1)	12	22. **Blessed Are The Believers**	Capitol 4987
7/25/81	16	7	23. We Don't Have To Hold Out	Capitol 5013
10/3/81	9	8	24. **It's All I Can Do**	Capitol 5023
1/30/82	4	13	25. **Another Sleepless Night**	Capitol 5083
8/14/82	7	11	26. **Hey! Baby!** #1 Pop hit for Bruce Channel in 1962	Capitol 5145
12/25/82+	7	11	27. **Somebody's Always Saying Goodbye**	Capitol 5183
10/1/83	1 (1)	14	28. **A Little Good News** CMA Award: Single of the Year	Capitol 5264
5/19/84	1 (1)	13	29. **Just Another Woman In Love**	Capitol 5344
10/6/84	1 (1)	13	30. **Nobody Loves Me Like You Do** **ANNE MURRAY (with Dave Loggins)**	Capitol 5401
2/9/85	2 (1)	14	31. **Time Don't Run Out On Me**	Capitol 5436
6/1/85	7	13	32. **I Don't Think I'm Ready For You** from the movie *Stick* starring Burt Reynolds	Capitol 5472
2/8/86	1 (1)	14	33. **Now And Forever (You And Me)**	Capitol 5547
9/13/86	26	8	34. My Life's A Dance	Capitol 5610
1/31/87	23	6	35. On And On	Capitol 5655
6/6/87	20	9	36. Are You Still In Love With Me	Capitol 44005
10/10/87	27	4	37. Anyone Can Do The Heartbreak	Capitol 44053
1/7/89	36	3	38. Slow Passin' Time	Capitol 44272
10/21/89	28	6	39. If I Ever Fall In Love Again **ANNE MURRAY with Kenny Rogers**	Capitol 44432
9/22/90	5	16	40. **Feed This Fire**	Capitol LP Cut
2/23/91	39	1	41. Bluebird above 2 from the album *You Will* on Capitol 94102	Capitol LP Cut

N

NAYLOR, Jerry

Born on 3/6/39 in Stephenville, Texas. Own band at age 14; worked on the *Louisiana Hayride*. Worked as a DJ in San Angelo, Texas. Replaced Joe B. Mauldin in The Crickets in 1961. Suffered a heart attack in 1964, but fully recovered. Had award-winning radio series, *Continental Country*, in the early '70s.

DATE	POS	WKS	ARTIST-RECORD TITLE	LABEL & NO.
3/15/75	27	4	1. Is This All There Is To A Honky Tonk?	Melodyland 6003
3/18/78	37	1	2. If You Don't Want To Love Her	MC/Curb 5004

NEEDMORE CREEK SINGERS—see ARNOLD, Eddy

DATE	POS	WKS	ARTIST– RECORD TITLE	LABEL & NO.
			## NELSON, Ricky	
			Born Eric Hilliard Nelson on 5/8/40 in Teaneck, New Jersey. Died on 12/31/85 in a plane crash in DeKalb, Texas. Son of bandleader Ozzie Nelson and vocalist Harriet Hilliard. Rick and brother David appeared on Nelson's radio show from March 1949, later on TV, 1952-66. Formed own Stone Canyon Band in 1969. In movies *Rio Bravo*, *The Wackiest Ship In The Army* and *Love And Kisses*. Married Kristin Harmon (sister of actor Mark Harmon) in 1963; divorced in 1982. Their daughter Tracy is a movie/TV actress. Their twin sons began recording as Nelson in 1990. Ricky was one of the first teen idols of the rock era. Inducted into the Rock and Roll Hall of Fame in 1987.	
1/20/58	8	12	● 1. **Stood Up/** Best Seller #8	
1/20/58	12	6	2. Waitin' In School Best Seller #12	Imperial 5483
4/14/58	10	11	3. **My Bucket's Got A Hole In It/** Best Seller #10	
4/14/58	10	10	● 4. **Believe What You Say** Best Seller #10	Imperial 5503
7/7/58	3	15	● 5. **Poor Little Fool** Best Seller #3 / Jockey #8	Imperial 5528
			## NELSON, Willie	
			Born on 4/30/33 in Fort Worth, Texas; raised in Abbott, Texas. Learned guitar at age 10. In U.S. Air Force during the Korean War, then worked as a DJ in Waco, San Antonio and Houston. Played bass for Ray Price. Moved to Nashville in 1960. Wrote hits "Crazy" for Patsy Cline, "Night Life" for Ray Price, "Hello Walls" for Faron Young and "Funny How Time Slips Away" for Billy Walker. Moved back to Texas in 1970. In the movies *Electric Horseman*, *Honeysuckle Rose*, *Barbarosa*, *Coming Out Of The Ice*, *Songwriter* and *Red-Headed Stranger*. Host of the legendary Fourth of July picnic concerts in Austin, Texas, since 1972. President of Farm Aid, Inc. CMA Awards: 1976 Vocal Duo of the Year (with Waylon Jennings); 1979 Entertainer of the Year; 1983 Vocal Duo of the Year (with Merle Haggard); 1984 Vocal Duo of the Year (with Julio Iglesias). Won Grammy's Living Legends Award in 1989. Elected to the Country Music Hall of Fame in 1993. (a) WAYLON & WILLIE (b) WILLIE NELSON and RAY PRICE (c) WAYLON JENNINGS, WILLIE NELSON, JOHNNY CASH, KRIS KRISTOFFERSON	
3/17/62	10	13	1. **Willingly** **WILLIE NELSON & SHIRLEY COLLIE**	Liberty 55403
5/26/62	7	13	2. **Touch Me**	Liberty 55439
4/6/63	25	5	3. Half A Man	Liberty 55532
1/18/64	33	3	4. You Took My Happy Away	Liberty 55638
10/22/66	19	10	5. One In A Row	RCA 8933
4/8/67	24	9	6. The Party's Over	RCA 9100
7/8/67	21	9	7. Blackjack County Chain	RCA 9202
3/2/68	22	7	8. Little Things	RCA 9427
10/5/68	36	3	9. Johnny One Time	RCA 9605
12/28/68+	13	12	10. Bring Me Sunshine	RCA 9684
1/24/70	36	2	11. I Hope So	Liberty 56143
3/6/71	28	6	12. I'm A Memory	RCA 9951
11/3/73	22	7	13. Stay All Night (Stay A Little Longer)	Atlantic 2979
5/4/74	17	9	14. Bloody Mary Morning	Atlantic 3020

DATE	POS	WKS	ARTIST–RECORD TITLE	LABEL & NO.
9/14/74	**17**	7	15. After The Fire Is Gone **WILLIE NELSON & TRACY NELSON** Willie and Tracy are not related	Atlantic 4028
8/9/75	**1 (2)**	12	16. **Blue Eyes Crying In The Rain**	Columbia 10176
12/13/75+	**29**	5	17. Fire And Rain #3 Pop hit for James Taylor in 1970	RCA 10429
1/10/76	**1 (3)**	13	18. **Good Hearted Woman** (a) CMA Award: Single of the Year	RCA 10529
1/24/76	**2 (1)**	11	19. **Remember Me**	Columbia 10275
5/15/76	**11**	9	20. I'd Have To Be Crazy	Columbia 10327
8/7/76	**1 (1)**	12	21. **If You've Got The Money I've Got The Time**	Columbia 10383
12/25/76+	**4**	12	22. **Uncloudy Day**	Columbia 10453
4/16/77	**32**	5	23. Lily Dale **DARRELL McCALL & WILLIE NELSON**	Columbia 10480
6/4/77	**22**	6	24. I'm A Memory [R]	RCA 10969
8/13/77	**9**	8	25. **I Love You A Thousand Ways**	Columbia 10588
10/1/77	**16**	8	26. You Ought To Hear Me Cry	RCA 11061
12/10/77+	**9**	11	27. **Something To Brag About** **MARY KAY PLACE with WILLIE NELSON**	Columbia 10644
1/21/78	**1 (4)**	12	28. **Mammas Don't Let Your Babies Grow Up To Be Cowboys** (a)/	
		11	29. I Can Get Off On You (a)	RCA 11198
4/1/78	**5**	9	30. **If You Can Touch Her At All**	RCA 11235
4/15/78	**1 (1)**	11	31. **Georgia On My Mind** written in 1930 by Hoagy Carmichael	Columbia 10704
7/29/78	**1 (1)**	9	32. **Blue Skies** written in 1927 by Irving Berlin	Columbia 10784
10/28/78	**3**	10	33. **All Of Me** #1 Pop hit for both Louis Armstrong and Paul Whiteman in 1932	Columbia 10834
1/13/79	**12**	8	34. Whiskey River	Columbia 10877
2/24/79	**4**	10	35. **Sweet Memories**	RCA 11465
4/28/79	**15**	8	36. September Song	Columbia 10929
7/14/79	**1 (1)**	9	37. **Heartbreak Hotel** **WILLIE NELSON and LEON RUSSELL** #1 Pop hit for Elvis Presley in 1956	Columbia 11023
9/8/79	**16**	8	38. Crazy Arms	RCA 11673
11/24/79+	**4**	9	39. **Help Me Make It Through The Night**	Columbia 11126
1/26/80	**1 (2)**	10	40. **My Heroes Have Always Been Cowboys** from the movie The Electric Horseman starring Robert Redford	Columbia 11186
3/1/80	**20**	7	41. Night Life **DANNY DAVIS and WILLIE NELSON with THE NASHVILLE BRASS**	RCA 11893
5/17/80	**6**	10	42. **Midnight Rider** #19 Pop hit for Gregg Allman in 1974	Columbia 11257
8/23/80	**3**	11	43. **Faded Love** (b)	Columbia 11329
9/13/80	**1 (1)**	11	44. **On The Road Again** from the movie Honeysuckle Rose starring Nelson	Columbia 11351
12/27/80+	**11**	8	45. Don't You Ever Get Tired (Of Hurting Me) (b)	Columbia 11405
1/24/81	**1 (1)**	11	46. **Angel Flying Too Close To The Ground** from the movie Honeysuckle Rose starring Nelson	Columbia 11418
5/9/81	**11**	6	47. Mona Lisa #1 Pop hit for Nat King Cole in 1950	Columbia 02000

DATE	POS	WKS	ARTIST– RECORD TITLE	LABEL & NO.
7/18/81	25	6	48. Good Times [R]	RCA 12254
8/22/81	26	4	49. I'm Gonna Sit Right Down And Write Myself A Letter #3 Pop hit for Billy Williams in 1957	Columbia 02187
10/24/81	23	6	50. Mountain Dew	RCA 12328
12/19/81	39	1	51. Heartaches Of A Fool	Columbia 02558
3/20/82	1 (2)	15	▲ 52. **Always On My Mind** CMA Award: Single of the Year	Columbia 02741
3/27/82	1 (2)	12	53. **Just To Satisfy You** (a)	RCA 13073
6/26/82	19	9	54. Old Friends **ROGER MILLER & WILLIE NELSON (with RAY PRICE)**	Columbia 02681
8/28/82	2 (2)	12	55. **Let It Be Me** #7 Pop hit for The Everly Brothers in 1960	Columbia 03073
11/6/82	13	11	56. (Sittin' On) The Dock Of The Bay (a) #1 Pop hit for Otis Redding in 1968	RCA 13319
1/8/83	2 (2)	11	57. **Last Thing I Needed First Thing This Morning**	Columbia 03385
1/15/83	7	10	58. **Everything's Beautiful (In It's Own Way)** **DOLLY PARTON WILLIE NELSON**	Monument 03408
2/5/83	6	11	59. **Reasons To Quit** **MERLE HAGGARD and WILLIE NELSON**	Epic 03494
4/2/83	10	9	60. **Little Old Fashioned Karma**	Columbia 03674
5/14/83	1 (1)	14	61. **Pancho And Lefty** **WILLIE NELSON and MERLE HAGGARD**	Epic 03842
7/16/83	3	12	62. **Why Do I Have To Choose**	Columbia 03965
10/29/83	8	11	63. **Take It To The Limit** (a) #4 Pop hit for the Eagles in 1976	Columbia 04131
1/21/84	11	9	64. Without A Song #6 Pop hit for Paul Whiteman in 1930	Columbia 04263
3/17/84	1 (2)	13	● 65. **To All The Girls I've Loved Before** **JULIO IGLESIAS & WILLIE NELSON**	Columbia 04217
9/1/84	1 (1)	12	66. **City Of New Orleans** #18 Pop hit for Arlo Guthrie in 1972	Columbia 04568
1/26/85	1 (1)	12	67. **Seven Spanish Angels** **RAY CHARLES with WILLIE NELSON**	Columbia 04715
5/4/85	1 (1)	14	68. **Forgiving You Was Easy**	Columbia 04847
6/1/85	1 (1)	14	69. **Highwayman** (c)	Columbia 04881
10/5/85	15	9	70. Desperados Waiting For A Train (c)	Columbia 05594
10/12/85	14	9	71. Me And Paul [R]	Columbia 05597
4/12/86	1 (1)	14	72. **Living In The Promiseland**	Columbia 05834
8/30/86	21	7	73. I'm Not Trying To Forget You	Columbia 06246
1/10/87	24	5	74. Partners After All	Columbia 06530
8/1/87	27	4	75. Island In The Sea	Columbia 07202
10/15/88	8	12	76. **Spanish Eyes** **WILLIE NELSON with JULIO IGLESIAS**	Columbia 08066
7/1/89	1 (1)	15	77. **Nothing I Can Do About It Now**	Columbia 68923
11/4/89+	8	15	78. **There You Are**	Columbia 73015
3/31/90	25	7	79. Silver Stallion (c)	Columbia 73233
10/13/90	17	12	80. Ain't Necessarily So	Columbia 73518

NESBITT, Jim

Born on 12/1/31 in Bishopville, South Carolina. Worked with Slim Mims & His Dream Ranch Boys. DJ at WAGS-Bishopville. Nickname: the 'Lasses Sopper'.

DATE	POS	WKS	ARTIST–RECORD TITLE	LABEL & NO.
4/3/61	11	7	1. Please Mr. Kennedy [N] also released on Country Jubilee 549 and Ace 621; melody is the same as "Davy Crockett"	Dot 16197
2/2/63	28	1	2. Livin' Offa Credit [N]	Dot 16424
4/11/64	7	21	3. **Looking For More In '64** [N]	Chart 1065
9/26/64	20	9	4. Mother-In-Law [N]	Chart 1100
2/6/65	15	11	5. A Tiger In My Tank [N]	Chart 1165
7/3/65	34	4	6. Still Alive In '65 [N]	Chart 1200
9/4/65	21	8	7. The Friendly Undertaker [N]	Chart 1240
9/24/66	38	3	8. Heck Of A Fix In 66 [N]	Chart 1350
3/21/70	20	8	9. Runnin' Bare [N] novelty version of Johnny Preston's "Running Bear"	Chart 5052
			NETTLES, Bill, and his Dixie Blue Boys Born on 3/13/07 in Natchitoches, Louisiana. Died of a heart attack on 4/5/67. First recorded for Brunswick in 1937.	
6/25/49	9	6	1. **Hadacol Boogie** Juke Box #9	Mercury 6190
			NEVILLE, Aaron Born on 1/24/41 in New Orleans. Member of the New Orleans family group The Neville Brothers. Brother Art was keyboardist of The Meters. Bassist/singer Ivan Neville is his son.	
10/16/93	38	2	1. The Grand Tour	A&M 0312
			NEW GRASS REVIVAL Quartet consisting of Sam Bush (fiddle, mandolin), John Cowan (vocals, bass), Pat Flynn (guitar) and Bela Fleck (banjo). All are accomplished studio and solo artists.	
7/15/89	37	2	1. Callin' Baton Rouge	Capitol 44357
			NEWMAN, Jack	
8/24/59	24	1	1. House Of Blue Lovers	TNT 170
			NEWMAN, Jimmy Born Jimmy Yeve Newman on 8/27/27 near Big Mamou, Louisiana. Own show on KPLC-Lake Charles. On the *Louisiana Hayride* in the early '50s. Member of the *Grand Ole Opry* since 1956. The "C" in his stage name stands for "Cajun."	
5/22/54	4	11	1. **Cry, Cry, Darling** [R] Jockey #4 / Juke Box #8 / Best Seller #9; first recorded by Newman on Khoury 530	Dot 1195
3/26/55	7	7	2. **Daydreamin'** Juke Box #7 / Jockey #9 / Best Seller #13	Dot 1237
7/9/55	7	10	3. **Blue Darlin'** Jockey #7 / Juke Box #8 / Best Seller #13	Dot 1260
12/17/55+	9	2	4. **God Was So Good** Jockey #9	Dot 1270
4/7/56	9	6	5. **Seasons Of My Heart** Juke Box #9 / Jockey #10	Dot 1278
7/7/56	13	4	6. Come Back To Me Jockey #13	Dot 1283

DATE	POS	WKS	ARTIST– RECORD TITLE	LABEL & NO.
5/20/57	2 (2)	21	7. **A Fallen Star** Jockey #2 / Best Seller #4 / Juke Box #9; also released on Dot 15574 (Pop series)	Dot 1289
11/3/58+	7	16	8. **You're Makin' A Fool Out Of Me**	MGM 12707
4/13/59	19	4	9. So Soon	MGM 12749
6/22/59	30	1	10. Lonely Girl	MGM 12790
7/27/59	9	13	11. **Grin And Bear It**	MGM 12812
11/2/59	29	1	12. Walkin' Down The Road	MGM 12830
3/7/60	21	7	13. I Miss You Already	MGM 12864
6/20/60	6	14	14. **A Lovely Work Of Art**	MGM 12894
11/7/60	11	18	15. Wanting You With Me Tonight	MGM 12945
4/17/61	14	8	16. Everybody's Dying For Love	Decca 31217
12/25/61+	22	2	17. Alligator Man	Decca 31324
12/22/62+	12	9	18. Bayou Talk	Decca 31440
12/14/63+	9	19	19. **D.J. For A Day**	Decca 31553
5/16/64	34	3	20. Angel On Leave/	
5/30/64	34	3	21. Summer Skies And Golden Sands **JIMMY "C." NEWMAN (above 4)**	Decca 31609
5/8/65	13	14	22. Back In Circulation/	
4/17/65	37	5	23. City Of The Angels	Decca 31745
10/16/65	8	18	24. **Artificial Rose**	Decca 31841
4/23/66	10	12	25. **Back Pocket Money**	Decca 31916
10/15/66	25	6	26. Bring Your Heart Home	Decca 31994
2/25/67	32	5	27. Dropping Out Of Sight	Decca 32067
6/24/67	24	7	28. Louisiana Saturday Night	Decca 32130
12/2/67+	11	12	29. Blue Lonely Winter	Decca 32202
9/14/68	20	11	30. Born To Love You	Decca 32366
6/21/69	31	5	31. Boo Dan	Decca 32484

NEWTON, Juice

Born Judy Kay Newton on 2/18/52 in New Jersey; raised in Virginia Beach. Performed folk music from age 13. Moved to Los Angeles with own Silver Spur band in 1974; recorded for RCA in 1975. Group disbanded in 1978. Newton is an accomplished equestrienne.

DATE	POS	WKS	ARTIST– RECORD TITLE	LABEL & NO.
3/17/79	37	2	1. Let's Keep It That Way	Capitol 4679
3/1/80	35	3	2. Sunshine #4 Pop hit for Jonathan Edwards in 1972	Capitol 4818
4/4/81	22	4	● 3. Angel Of The Morning	Capitol 4976
7/11/81	14	8	● 4. Queen Of Hearts	Capitol 4997
11/14/81+	1 (1)	13	5. **The Sweetest Thing (I've Ever Known)**	Capitol 5046
6/19/82	30	3	6. Love's Been A Little Bit Hard On Me	Capitol 5120
9/18/82	2 (2)	12	7. **Break It To Me Gently**	Capitol 5148
9/15/84	32	4	8. Ride 'Em Cowboy originally released as the B-side of #5 above	Capitol 5379
8/10/85	1 (1)	13	9. **You Make Me Want To Make You Mine**	RCA 14139
11/30/85+	1 (1)	13	10. **Hurt** #4 Pop hit for Timi Yuro in 1961	RCA 14199
4/26/86	5	13	11. **Old Flame**	RCA 14295
8/2/86	1 (1)	14	12. **Both To Each Other (Friends & Lovers)** **EDDIE RABBITT and JUICE NEWTON** #2 Pop hit for Gloria Loring & Carl Anderson in 1986	RCA 14377

DATE	POS	WKS	ARTIST–RECORD TITLE	LABEL & NO.
9/6/86	9	12	13. **Cheap Love** *written by Del Shannon*	RCA 14417
1/10/87	9	11	14. **What Can I Do With My Heart**	RCA 5068
8/15/87	24	6	15. First Time Caller	RCA 5170
12/12/87+	8	14	16. **Tell Me True**	RCA 5283
6/17/89	40	1	17. When Love Comes Around The Bend	RCA 8815

NEWTON-JOHN, Olivia

Born on 9/26/48 in Cambridge, England. To Australia in 1953. At age 16, won talent contest trip to England; sang with Pat Carroll as Pat & Olivia. With the group Toomorrow, in a British movie of the same name. Granddaughter of Nobel Prize-winning German physicist Max Born. Appeared in the movies *Grease*, *Xanadu* and *Two Of A Kind*. Married actor Matt Lattanzi in 1984. Opened own chain of clothing boutiques called Koala Blue in 1984. Battled breast cancer in 1992. CMA Award: 1974 Female Vocalist of the Year.

DATE	POS	WKS	ARTIST–RECORD TITLE	LABEL & NO.
10/27/73	7	12	● 1. **Let Me Be There**	MCA 40101
5/4/74	2 (2)	14	● 2. **If You Love Me (Let Me Know)**	MCA 40209
9/14/74	6	13	● 3. **I Honestly Love You**	MCA 40280
2/22/75	3	11	● 4. **Have You Never Been Mellow**	MCA 40349
6/28/75	5	11	● 5. **Please Mr. Please**	MCA 40418
10/25/75	19	6	6. Something Better To Do	MCA 40459
12/20/75+	5	9	7. **Let It Shine**	MCA 40495
3/27/76	5	10	8. **Come On Over**	MCA 40525
8/28/76	14	7	9. Don't Stop Believin'	MCA 40600
11/20/76	21	5	10. Every Face Tells A Story	MCA 40642
3/12/77	40	2	11. Sam	MCA 40670
8/26/78	20	5	● 12. **Hopelessly Devoted To You** *from the movie Grease starring Newton-John*	RSO 903
9/1/79	29	5	13. Dancin' 'Round And 'Round *flip side "Totally Hot" made #52 on the Hot 100*	MCA 41074

NIGHTSTREETS

Nashville-based trio: Rick Taylor, Jerry Taylor (no relation) and Joyce Hawthorne. Also recorded as simply Streets.

DATE	POS	WKS	ARTIST–RECORD TITLE	LABEL & NO.
2/23/80	32	3	1. Love In The Meantime **STREETS**	Epic 50827

NITTY GRITTY DIRT BAND

Group formed as the Illegitimate Jug Band in 1966. Consisted of Jeff Hanna (born 7/11/47), Jimmie Fadden, Ralph Barr, Leslie Thompson, John McEuen and Bruce Kunkel. Kunkel replaced by Chris Darrow in 1968. Barr replaced by Jim Ibbotson in 1971. Changed name to The Dirt Band in 1976. Resumed using Nitty Gritty Dirt Band name in 1982. Ex-Eagle Bernie Leadon briefly replaced McEuen in early 1987. Revamped lineup since late 1987: Hanna, Ibbotson, Fadden and Bob Carpenter. Appeared in the movies *For Singles Only* and *Paint Your Wagon*.

DATE	POS	WKS	ARTIST–RECORD TITLE	LABEL & NO.
7/16/83	19	8	1. Shot Full Of Love	Liberty 1499
10/29/83	9	13	2. **Dance Little Jean**	Liberty 1507
6/16/84	1 (1)	13	3. **Long Hard Road (The Sharecropper's Dream)**	Warner 29282
10/13/84	3	15	4. **I Love Only You**	Warner 29203
2/2/85	2 (2)	14	5. **High Horse**	Warner 29099
6/22/85	1 (1)	15	6. **Modern Day Romance**	Warner 29027

DATE	POS	WKS	ARTIST–RECORD TITLE	LABEL & NO.
11/2/85+	**3**	14	7. **Home Again In My Heart**	Warner 28897
3/22/86	**6**	12	8. **Partners, Brothers And Friends**	Warner 28780
7/5/86	**5**	13	9. **Stand A Little Rain**	Warner 28690
11/29/86+	**7**	13	10. Fire In The Sky [R]	Warner 28547
			first made #76 on the *Hot 100* in 1981 on Liberty 1429	
4/11/87	**2** (1)	12	11. **Baby's Got A Hold On Me**	Warner 28443
7/25/87	**1** (1)	15	12. **Fishin' In The Dark**	Warner 28311
12/5/87+	**5**	15	13. **Oh What A Love**	Warner 28173
5/7/88	**4**	12	14. **Workin' Man (Nowhere To Go)**	Warner 27940
9/17/88	**2** (1)	13	15. **I've Been Lookin'**	Warner 27750
1/21/89	**6**	13	16. **Down That Road Tonight**	Warner 27679
6/24/89	**27**	5	17. Turn Of The Century	Universal 66009
7/1/89	**14**	10	18. And So It Goes	Universal 66008
			JOHN DENVER and THE NITTY GRITTY DIRT BAND	
11/4/89+	**10**	13	19. **When It's Gone**	Universal 66023

DATE	POS	WKS	ARTIST–RECORD TITLE	LABEL & NO.
			## NIXON, Nick	
			Born Hershel Paul Nixon on 3/20/41 in Poplar Bluff, Missouri. Co-wrote Barbara Fairchild's "Teddy Bear Song." Longtime St. Louis area favorite.	
8/23/75	**38**	3	1. I'm Too Use To Loving You	Mercury 73691
4/24/76	**28**	4	2. Rocking In Rosalee's Boat	Mercury 73772
12/17/77+	**34**	4	3. I'll Get Over You	Mercury 55010

DATE	POS	WKS	ARTIST–RECORD TITLE	LABEL & NO.
			## NOACK, Eddie	
			Born Armona A. Noack on 4/29/30 in Houston. Died on 2/5/78. Recorded rockabilly under pseudonym Tommy Wood.	
12/15/58	**14**	2	1. Have Blues—Will Travel	D 1019

DATE	POS	WKS	ARTIST–RECORD TITLE	LABEL & NO.
			## NOBLE, Nick	
			Born Nicholas Valkan on 6/21/36 in Chicago. Attended Loyola University. Pop singer.	
10/14/78	**40**	1	1. Stay With Me	Churchill 7713
5/19/79	**36**	3	2. The Girl On The Other Side	TMS 601
			NICK NOBLE & LEW DOUGLASS	
3/8/80	**35**	3	3. Big Man's Cafe	Churchill 7755

DATE	POS	WKS	ARTIST–RECORD TITLE	LABEL & NO.
			## NORMA JEAN	
			Born Norma Jean Beasler on 1/30/38 in Wellston, Oklahoma. Own show on KLPR-Oklahoma City by age 13. Worked on Red Foley's *Ozark Jubilee* TV series in 1958. On Porter Wagoner's TV series, 1960-67.	
1/4/64	**11**	15	1. Let's Go All The Way	RCA 8261
6/20/64	**25**	16	2. Put Your Arms Around Her/	
7/4/64	**32**	5	3. I'm A Walkin' Advertisement (For the Blues)	RCA 8328
10/17/64	**8**	21	4. **Go Cat Go**	RCA 8433
4/17/65	**21**	7	5. I Cried All The Way To The Bank	RCA 8518
8/7/65	**8**	13	6. **I Wouldn't Buy A Used Car From Him**	RCA 8623
4/16/66	**28**	8	7. The Shirt	RCA 8790
8/27/66	**28**	6	8. Pursuing Happiness	RCA 8887
10/29/66	**5**	14	9. **The Game Of Triangles**	RCA 8963
			BOBBY BARE, NORMA JEAN, LIZ ANDERSON	

DATE	POS	WKS	ARTIST–RECORD TITLE	LABEL & NO.
12/24/66+	24	7	10. Don't Let That Doorknob Hit You	RCA 8989
9/16/67	38	3	11. Jackson Ain't A Very Big Town	RCA 9258
12/9/67+	18	9	12. Heaven Help The Working Girl	RCA 9362
8/24/68	35	2	13. You Changed Everything About Me But My Name	RCA 9558

NORWOOD, Daron

Born in Lubbock; raised in Tahoka, Texas. Played piano for Jim Ed Brown, Rex Allen Jr. and Shelly West. Regular at the Buckboard Country Music Showcase in Atlanta.

DATE	POS	WKS	ARTIST–RECORD TITLE	LABEL & NO.
2/5/94	26	8	1. If It Wasn't For Her I Wouldn't Have You	Giant 18386
5/14/94	24	8	2. Cowboys Don't Cry	Giant 18216

NUNN, Earl, and his Alabama Ramblers feat. Billy Lee

DATE	POS	WKS	ARTIST–RECORD TITLE	LABEL & NO.
4/9/49	13	1	1. Double Talkin' Woman Juke Box #13	Specialty 701

OAK RIDGE BOYS

Group's roots go back to early 1940s when they were a gospel-Country quartet performing in Oak Ridge, Tennessee. Joined the *Grand Ole Opry* in 1945. Fluctuating lineup of 40-plus members has survived two disbandonments, one in 1946 and again in 1956. Known as the Oak Ridge Quartet until 1964. Switched to country-pop style in 1977. Consistent lineup, 1973-87: Duane Allen (born 4/29/43; lead singer), Joe Bonsall (born 5/18/48; tenor), William Lee Golden (born 1/12/35; baritone) and Richard Sterban (born 4/24/43; bass). All had previously sung in gospel groups. Steve Sanders replaced Golden from 1987 until Golden returned in 1996. CMA Award: 1978 Vocal Group of the Year.

DATE	POS	WKS	ARTIST–RECORD TITLE	LABEL & NO.
8/6/77	3	12	1. **Y'All Come Back Saloon**	ABC/Dot 17710
12/17/77+	2 (2)	11	2. **You're The One**	ABC/Dot 17732
4/29/78	1 (1)	11	3. **I'll Be True To You**	ABC 12350
9/9/78	3	11	4. **Cryin' Again**	ABC 12397
12/16/78+	3	10	5. **Come On In**	ABC 12434
4/7/79	2 (2)	11	6. **Sail Away**	MCA 12463
8/25/79	7	9	7. **Dream On** #32 Pop hit for The Righteous Brothers in 1974	MCA 41078
12/15/79+	1 (1)	11	8. **Leaving Louisiana In The Broad Daylight**	MCA 41154
4/26/80	1 (1)	12	9. **Trying To Love Two Women**	MCA 41217
8/2/80	3	11	10. **Heart Of Mine**	MCA 41280
11/22/80+	3	12	11. **Beautiful You**	MCA 51022
4/18/81	1 (1)	9	▲ 12. **Elvira** CMA Award: Single of the Year	MCA 51084
9/19/81	1 (1)	9	13. **Fancy Free**	MCA 51169
1/30/82	1 (1)	12	14. **Bobbie Sue**	MCA 51231
6/12/82	22	7	15. So Fine	MCA 52065
8/14/82	2 (2)	12	16. **I Wish You Could Have Turned My Head (And Left My Heart Alone)**	MCA 52095

DATE	POS	WKS	ARTIST– RECORD TITLE	LABEL & NO.
12/11/82+	**3**	10	17. Thank God For Kids	MCA 52145
2/26/83	**1** (1)	13	18. American Made	MCA 52179
6/18/83	**1** (1)	12	19. Love Song	MCA 52224
11/5/83+	**5**	13	20. Ozark Mountain Jubilee	MCA 52288
3/10/84	**1** (1)	12	21. I Guess It Never Hurts To Hurt Sometimes	MCA 52342
7/28/84	**1** (1)	13	22. Everyday	MCA 52419
12/1/84+	**1** (1)	14	23. Make My Life With You	MCA 52488
4/13/85	**1** (1)	13	24. Little Things	MCA 52556
8/17/85	**1** (1)	13	25. Touch A Hand, Make A Friend	MCA 52646
			#23 Pop hit for The Staple Singers in 1974	
12/7/85+	**3**	14	26. Come On In (You Did The Best You Could Do)	MCA 52722
4/5/86	**15**	8	27. Juliet	MCA 52801
4/19/86	**20**	6	28. When You Get To The Heart	MCA 52802
			BARBARA MANDRELL with the OAK RIDGE BOYS	
8/2/86	**24**	7	29. You Made A Rock Of A Rolling Stone	MCA 52873
3/7/87	**1** (1)	14	30. It Takes A Little Rain (To Make Love Grow)	MCA 53010
6/27/87	**1** (1)	15	31. This Crazy Love	MCA 53023
11/7/87	**17**	7	32. Time In	MCA 53175
3/19/88	**5**	13	33. True Heart	MCA 53272
8/13/88	**1** (1)	15	34. Gonna Take A Lot Of River	MCA 53381
12/24/88+	**10**	12	35. Bridges And Walls	MCA 53460
4/22/89	**7**	13	36. Beyond Those Years	MCA 53625
9/2/89	**4**	12	37. An American Family	MCA 53705
1/6/90	**1** (1)	21	38. No Matter How High	MCA 53757
12/22/90+	**31**	6	39. (You're My) Soul And Inspiration	RCA 2665
			from the movie My Heroes Have Always Been Cowboys *starring Scott Glenn*	
4/13/91	**6**	17	40. Lucky Moon	RCA 2779

O'CONNOR, Mark, & The New Nashville Cats

Former child prodigy fiddle player from Seattle. Highly prolific studio musician. Member of rock group The Dregs in early '80s. The New Nashville Cats are an assemblage of 53 prominent studio musicians including Ricky Skaggs, Vince Gill, Marty Stuart and Steve Wariner on vocals.

DATE	POS	WKS	ARTIST– RECORD TITLE	LABEL & NO.
4/27/91	25	8	1. Restless	Warner 19354
			MARK O'CONNOR-THE NEW NASHVILLE CATS Featuring STEVE WARINER, RICKY SKAGGS AND VINCE GILL	

O'DELL, Doye

Born Allen Doye O'Dell on 11/22/12 in Plainview, Texas. Worked with Uncle John Wills Band and the Sons Of The Pioneers. Own TV series, Western Varieties.

DATE	POS	WKS	ARTIST– RECORD TITLE	LABEL & NO.
7/24/48	12	3	1. Dear Oakie	Exclusive 33
			Juke Box #12 / Best Seller #13	

O'DELL, Kenny

Born Kenneth Gist, Jr., in Oklahoma (early 1940s). Singer/songwriter/guitarist. Worked with Duane Eddy and own band, Guys And Dolls. Moved to Nashville in 1969. Wrote Charlie Rich's "Behind Closed Doors."

DATE	POS	WKS	ARTIST– RECORD TITLE	LABEL & NO.
2/22/75	18	5	1. Soulful Woman	Capricorn 0219

DATE	POS	WKS	ARTIST– RECORD TITLE	LABEL & NO.
7/12/75	37	2	2. My Honky Tonk Ways	Capricorn 0233
7/22/78	9	9	3. **Let's Shake Hands And Come Out Lovin'**	Capricorn 0301
11/25/78+	12	8	4. As Long As I Can Wake Up In Your Arms	Capricorn 0309
4/14/79	32	3	5. Medicine Woman	Capricorn 0317

O'GWYNN, James

Born on 1/26/28 in Winchester, Mississippi; raised in Hattiesburg, Mississippi. Worked on the *Houston Jamboree*, 1954-56, and the *Louisiana Hayride*, 1956-60. Moved to Nashville in 1961 and worked on the *Grand Ole Opry* for two years. Known as "The Smiling Irishman Of Country Music."

DATE	POS	WKS	ARTIST– RECORD TITLE	LABEL & NO.
10/20/58	16	3	1. Talk To Me Lonesome Heart	D 1006
12/29/58	28	3	2. Blue Memories	D 1022
4/27/59	13	4	3. How Can I Think Of Tomorrow	Mercury 71419
12/21/59+	26	4	4. Easy Money	Mercury 71513
2/20/61	21	6	5. House Of Blue Lovers	Mercury 71731
4/21/62	7	10	6. **My Name Is Mud**	Mercury 71935

O'KANES, The

Duo of Jamie O'Hara (born 8/8/50; Toledo, Ohio) and Kieran Kane (born 10/7/49; Queens, New York). Wrote "Grandpa (Tell Me 'Bout The Good Old Days)" for The Judds, and many others.

DATE	POS	WKS	ARTIST– RECORD TITLE	LABEL & NO.
11/1/86	10	12	1. **Oh Darlin'**	Columbia 06242
2/28/87	1 (1)	14	2. **Can't Stop My Heart From Loving You**	Columbia 06606
7/25/87	9	11	3. **Daddies Need To Grow Up Too**	Columbia 07187
11/7/87+	5	14	4. **Just Lovin' You**	Columbia 07611
3/26/88	4	12	5. **One True Love**	Columbia 07736
8/6/88	10	11	6. **Blue Love**	Columbia 07943

O'NEAL, Coleman

DATE	POS	WKS	ARTIST– RECORD TITLE	LABEL & NO.
1/5/63	8	16	1. **Mr. Heartache, Move On**	Chancellor 108

ORBISON, Roy

Born on 4/23/36 in Vernon, Texas. Died of a heart attack on 12/6/88 in Madison, Tennessee. Had own band, the Wink Westerners, in 1952. Attended North Texas State University with Pat Boone. First recorded for Je-Wel in early 1956 as leader of The Teen Kings. Toured with Sun Records shows to 1958. Wife Claudette killed in a motorcycle accident on 6/7/66; two sons died in a fire, 1968. Member of the supergroup Traveling Wilburys in 1988.

DATE	POS	WKS	ARTIST– RECORD TITLE	LABEL & NO.
7/19/80	6	9	1. **That Lovin' You Feelin' Again** **ROY ORBISON & EMMYLOU HARRIS** from the movie *Roadie* starring Meat Loaf	Warner 49262
2/25/89	7	11	2. **You Got It**	Virgin 99245

ORRALL, Robert Ellis

Born on 5/4/55 in Winthrop, Massachusetts. Wrote hits "Next To You, Next To Me" and "Give Me Five Minutes" by Shenandoah, "The Sweetest Thing" by Carlene Carter and others.

DATE	POS	WKS	ARTIST– RECORD TITLE	LABEL & NO.
1/2/93	19	11	1. Boom! It Was Over	RCA 62335
5/8/93	31	4	2. A Little Bit Of Her Love	RCA 62475

DATE	POS	WKS	ARTIST– RECORD TITLE	LABEL & NO.
			OSBORNE, Jimmie	
			Born on 4/8/23 in Winchester, Kentucky. Committed suicide on 12/26/57. Made appearances on the *Louisiana Hayride, Grand Ole Opry* and the WLS *National Barn Dance.*	
7/10/48	10	2	1. **My Heart Echoes** Juke Box #10	King 715
6/25/49	7	6	2. **The Death Of Little Kathy Fiscus** Best Seller #7	King 788
10/7/50	9	3	3. **God Please Protect America** Jockey #9	King 893
			OSBORNE BROTHERS	
			Originally a bluegrass duo from Hyden, Kentucky, consisting of brothers Bobby Van (born 12/7/31; mandolin) and Sonny (born 10/29/37; banjo) Osborne. On WROL-Knoxville in 1953. Recorded with Jimmy Martin in the mid-1950s. On WWVA-Wheeling *Jamboree,* 1956-59. Benny Birchfield (banjo) was added in 1959. Member of the *Grand Ole Opry* since 1964. Birchfield was later replaced by Ronnie Reno, then Dale Sledd, Jim Brock and Bob's son, Bobby. CMA Award: 1971 Vocal Group of the Year.	
3/24/58	13	2	1. Once More **OSBORNE BROTHERS & RED ALLEN** Jockey #13 Harley "Red" Allen was leader of own bluegrass band; later a bluegrass DJ in Dayton, Ohio; died on 4/3/93	MGM 12583
2/4/67	33	3	2. The Kind Of Woman I Got	Decca 32052
3/16/68	33	2	3. Rocky Top	Decca 32242
9/6/69	28	7	4. Tennessee Hound Dog	Decca 32516
4/17/71	37	3	5. Georgia Pineywoods	Decca 32794
			OSLIN, K.T.	
			Born Kay Toinette Oslin on 5/15/41 in Crossitt, Arkansas; raised in Mobile, Alabama. Vocalist/songwriter/actress. In folk trio with Guy Clark and David Jones in Houston in the mid-1960s. Teamed with Frank Davis. Appeared in the musicals *Hello Dolly, West Side Story* and *Promises Promises.* Made commercials in New York City. To Nashville in 1985. Underwent quadruple-bypass heart surgery on 8/29/95. CMA Award: 1988 Female Vocalist of the Year.	
2/28/87	40	1	1. Wall Of Tears	RCA 5066
5/23/87	7	12	2. **80's Ladies**	RCA 5154
10/3/87	1 (1)	16	3. **Do Ya'**	RCA 5239
2/20/88	1 (1)	13	4. **I'll Always Come Back**	RCA 5330
7/23/88	13	10	5. Money	RCA 8388
10/29/88+	1 (1)	14	6. **Hold Me**	RCA 8725
2/25/89	2 (1)	13	7. **Hey Bobby**	RCA 8865
6/24/89	5	13	8. **This Woman**	RCA 8943
11/18/89	23	7	9. Didn't Expect It To Go Down This Way	RCA 9029
10/13/90	1 (2)	18	10. **Come Next Monday**	RCA 2667
3/23/91	28	5	11. Mary And Willie	RCA 2746
			OSMOND, Donny And Marie	
			Brother-and-sister co-hosts of own musical/variety TV series, 1976-78. Starred in the movie *Goin' Coconuts.*	
8/31/74	17	6	● 1. I'm Leaving It (All) Up To You	MGM 14735

DATE	POS	WKS	ARTIST–RECORD TITLE	LABEL & NO.
			OSMOND, Marie	
			Born Olive Marie Osmond on 10/13/59 in Ogden, Utah. Began performing in concert with her brothers at age 14. Co-hosted the TV series *Ripley's Believe It Or Not*, 1985-86. CMA Award: 1986 Vocal Duo of the Year (with Dan Seals).	
9/29/73	**1** (2)	12	● 1. **Paper Roses**	MGM 14609
9/28/74	**33**	2	2. In My Little Corner Of The World	MGM 14694
3/29/75	**29**	4	3. Who's Sorry Now	MGM 14786
8/3/85	**1** (1)	14	4. **Meet Me In Montana** **MARIE OSMOND with DAN SEALS**	Curb/Capitol 5478
11/30/85+	**1** (1)	15	5. **There's No Stopping Your Heart**	Curb/Capitol 5521
4/26/86	**4**	12	6. **Read My Lips**	Curb/Capitol 5563
9/13/86	**1** (1)	13	7. **You're Still New To Me** **MARIE OSMOND with PAUL DAVIS**	Curb/Capitol 5613
1/17/87	**14**	9	8. I Only Wanted You	Curb/Capitol 5663
5/9/87	**24**	5	9. Everybody's Crazy 'Bout My Baby	Curb/Capitol 5703
			OSMOND BROTHERS, The	
			Family group from Ogden, Utah: Alan (born 6/22/49), Wayne (born 8/28/51), Merrill (born 4/30/53) and Jay (born 3/2/55). Began as a quartet in 1959, singing religious and barbershop-quartet songs. Regulars on Andy Williams' TV show, 1962-67. With brother Donny, had several Pop hits in the early '70s.	
5/22/82	**17**	9	1. I Think About Your Lovin' **THE OSMONDS**	Elektra/Curb 47438
10/2/82	**28**	5	2. It's Like Falling In Love (Over And Over)	Elektra/Curb 69969
6/23/84	**39**	2	3. If Every Man Had A Woman Like You	Warner/Curb 29312
			OVERSTREET, Paul	
			Born on 3/17/56 in Newton, Mississippi. Wrote "Same Old Me" for George Jones and "A Long Line Of Love" for Michael Martin Murphey. Part of Schuyler, Knobloch & Overstreet (SKO). Went solo in 1987. Briefly married to Dolly Parton's sister, Freida.	
12/12/87+	**1** (1)	15	1. **I Won't Take Less Than Your Love** **TANYA TUCKER with PAUL DAVIS & PAUL OVERSTREET**	Capitol 44100
10/15/88	**3**	14	2. **Love Helps Those**	MTM 72113
4/29/89	**9**	11	3. **Sowin' Love**	RCA 8919
9/16/89	**5**	16	4. **All The Fun**	RCA 9015
2/3/90	**2** (1)	19	5. **Seein' My Father In Me**	RCA 9116
6/16/90	**3**	13	6. **Richest Man On Earth**	RCA 2505
12/8/90+	**1** (1)	18	7. **Daddy's Come Around**	RCA 2707
3/30/91	**4**	18	8. **Heroes**	RCA 2780
8/10/91	**5**	17	9. **Ball And Chain**	RCA 62012
1/25/92	**30**	4	10. If I Could Bottle This Up	RCA 62106
8/1/92	**22**	9	11. Me And My Baby	RCA 62254
			OVERSTREET, Tommy	
			Born on 9/10/37 in Oklahoma City. On TV in Houston in the early '60s. Worked with Slim Willet in the mid-1960s: own band thereafter. Managed the Nashville office of Dot Records from 1967. His niece is singer Susan St. Marie.	
5/15/71	**5**	13	1. **Gwen (Congratulations)**	Dot 17375

DATE	POS	WKS	ARTIST – RECORD TITLE	LABEL & NO.
8/28/71	5	13	2. **I Don't Know You (Anymore)**	Dot 17387
1/22/72	2 (1)	13	3. **Ann (Don't Go Runnin')**	Dot 17402
6/17/72	16	10	4. A Seed Before The Rose	Dot 17418
10/14/72	3	15	5. **Heaven Is My Woman's Love**	Dot 17428
5/5/73	7	12	6. **Send Me No Roses**	Dot 17455
10/6/73	7	14	7. **I'll Never Break These Chains**	Dot 17474
3/2/74	3	13	8. **(Jeannie Marie) You Were A Lady**	Dot 17493
8/24/74	8	11	9. **If I Miss You Again Tonight**	Dot 17515
1/11/75	9	9	10. **I'm A Believer**	ABC/Dot 17533
5/31/75	6	10	11. **That's When My Woman Begins**	ABC/Dot 17552
11/1/75	16	8	12. From Woman To Woman	ABC/Dot 17580
7/4/76	15	9	13. Here Comes That Girl Again	ABC/Dot 17630
10/30/76	29	6	14. Young Girl #2 Pop hit for Gary Puckett & The Union Gap in 1968	ABC/Dot 17657
1/22/77	11	9	15. If Love Was A Bottle Of Wine	ABC/Dot 17672
5/21/77	5	10	16. **Don't Go City Girl On Me**	ABC/Dot 17697
10/8/77	20	6	17. This Time I'm In It For The Love	ABC/Dot 17721
2/4/78	12	8	18. Yes Ma'am	ABC/Dot 17737
7/8/78	20	6	19. Better Me	ABC 12367
10/7/78	11	8	20. Fadin' In, Fadin' Out	ABC 12408
6/2/79	27	5	21. I'll Never Let You Down	Elektra 46023
9/8/79	23	6	22. What More Could A Man Need	Elektra 46516
12/22/79+	36	4	23. Fadin' Renegade	Elektra 46564

OWENS, Bonnie

Born Bonnie Campbell on 10/1/32 in Blanchard, Oklahoma. Worked clubs in Arizona, then joined Buck Owens in Mac's Skillet Lickers in Mesa, Arizona, 1946. Married to Buck, 1948-53. Married to Merle Haggard, 1965-78. Mother of Buddy Alan.

DATE	POS	WKS	ARTIST – RECORD TITLE	LABEL & NO.
6/22/63	25	1	1. Why Don't Daddy Live Here Anymore	Tally 149
4/18/64	27	4	2. Don't Take Advantage Of Me	Tally 156
9/19/64	28	24	3. Just Between The Two Of Us **MERLE HAGGARD and BONNIE OWENS**	Tally 181

OWENS, Buck

Born Alvis Edgar Owens on 8/12/29 in Sherman, Texas; raised in Mesa, Arizona. On the Buck & Britt show, KTYL-Mesa, in 1946. Married to Bonnie Campbell, 1948-53. Moved to Bakersfield, California, in 1951. Formed band, the Schoolhouse Playboys, and played saxophone and trumpet. Did session work with Wanda Jackson, Sonny James and Faron Young. Played lead guitar with Tommy Collins in the mid-1950s. First recorded for Pep in 1955 as Corky Jones. Co-host of the TV series *Hee-Haw*, 1969-86. Buck and Bonnie's son, Buddy Alan, began recording in 1968. Also see The Buckaroos.

(a) BUCK OWENS And ROSE MADDOX
(b) BUCK OWENS & SUSAN RAYE

DATE	POS	WKS	ARTIST – RECORD TITLE	LABEL & NO.
5/11/59	24	2	1. Second Fiddle	Capitol 4172
10/5/59	4	22	2. **Under Your Spell Again**	Capitol 4245
3/7/60	3	30	3. **Above And Beyond**	Capitol 4337
9/19/60	2 (3)	24	4. **Excuse Me (I Think I've Got A Heartache)**/	
10/24/60	25	3	5. I've Got A Right To Know	Capitol 4412

DATE	POS	WKS	ARTIST–RECORD TITLE	LABEL & NO.
1/30/61	**2 (8)**	26	6. **Foolin' Around/**	
3/27/61	**27**	1	7. High As The Mountains	Capitol 4496
5/22/61	**4**	14	8. **Loose Talk** (a)/	
5/15/61	**8**	12	9. **Mental Cruelty** (a)	Capitol 4550
8/7/61	**2 (1)**	24	10. **Under The Influence Of Love**	Capitol 4602
2/24/62	**11**	16	11. Nobody's Fool But Yours	Capitol 4679
7/28/62	**11**	11	12. Save The Last Dance For Me	Capitol 4765
10/27/62	**8**	8	13. **Kickin' Our Hearts Around/**	
10/27/62	**17**	5	14. I Can't Stop (My Lovin' You)	Capitol 4826
12/29/62+	**10**	14	15. **You're For Me/**	
1/5/63	**24**	3	16. House Down The Block	Capitol 4872
4/13/63	**1 (4)**	28	17. **Act Naturally**	Capitol 4937
			#47 Pop hit for The Beatles (Ringo Starr) in 1965	
8/3/63	**15**	6	18. We're The Talk Of The Town (a)/	
8/10/63	**19**	6	19. Sweethearts In Heaven (a)	Capitol 4992
9/21/63	**1 (16)**	30	20. **Love's Gonna Live Here**	Capitol 5025
3/28/64	**1 (7)**	26	21. **My Heart Skips A Beat/**	
4/4/64	**1 (2)**	27	22. **Together Again**	Capitol 5136
8/29/64	**1 (6)**	27	23. **I Don't Care (Just as Long as You Love Me)/**	
10/31/64	**33**	5	24. Don't Let Her Know	Capitol 5240
1/30/65	**1 (5)**	19	25. **I've Got A Tiger By The Tail**	Capitol 5336
5/15/65	**1 (6)**	20	26. **Before You Go**	Capitol 5410
8/14/65	**1 (1)**	17	27. **Only You (Can Break My Heart)/**	
8/14/65	**10**	12	28. **Gonna Have Love**	Capitol 5465

BUCK OWENS & THE BUCKAROOS:

DATE	POS	WKS	ARTIST–RECORD TITLE	LABEL & NO.
11/6/65	**1 (2)**	16	29. **Buckaroo/** [I]	
12/25/65+	**24**	5	30. If You Want A Love	Capitol 5517
1/22/66	**1 (7)**	18	31. **Waitin' In Your Welfare Line**	Capitol 5566
5/28/66	**1 (6)**	20	32. **Think Of Me**	Capitol 5647
9/3/66	**1 (4)**	20	33. **Open Up Your Heart**	Capitol 5705
1/28/67	**1 (4)**	14	34. **Where Does The Good Times Go**	Capitol 5811
4/15/67	**1 (3)**	13	35. **Sam's Place**	Capitol 5865
7/29/67	**1 (1)**	14	36. **Your Tender Loving Care**	Capitol 5942
10/28/67+	**2 (1)**	15	37. **It Takes People Like You (To Make People Like Me)**	Capitol 2001
2/10/68	**1 (1)**	13	38. **How Long Will My Baby Be Gone**	Capitol 2080
4/27/68	**2 (1)**	13	39. **Sweet Rosie Jones**	Capitol 2142
8/10/68	**7**	12	40. **Let The World Keep On A Turnin'**	Capitol 2237
			BUCK OWENS AND BUDDY ALAN AND THE BUCKAROOS	
10/26/68	**5**	15	41. **I've Got You On My Mind Again**	Capitol 2300
2/8/69	**1 (2)**	14	42. **Who's Gonna Mow Your Grass**	Capitol 2377
5/31/69	**1 (2)**	14	43. **Johnny B. Goode**	Capitol 2485
			#8 Pop hit for Chuck Berry in 1958	
8/23/69	**1 (1)**	13	44. **Tall Dark Stranger**	Capitol 2570
11/22/69	**5**	12	45. **Big In Vegas**	Capitol 2646
3/7/70	**13**	9	46. We're Gonna Get Together (b)	Capitol 2731
5/16/70	**12**	10	47. Togetherness (b)	Capitol 2791
6/20/70	**2 (2)**	12	48. **The Kansas City Song**	Capitol 2783

DATE	POS	WKS	ARTIST–RECORD TITLE	LABEL & NO.
9/12/70	8	11	49. **The Great White Horse** (b)	Capitol 2871
11/14/70	9	11	50. **I Wouldn't Live In New York City (If They Gave Me The Whole Dang Town)**	Capitol 2947
2/13/71	9	11	51. **Bridge Over Troubled Water** #1 Pop hit for Simon & Garfunkel in 1970	Capitol 3023
5/22/71	3	13	52. **Ruby (Are You Mad)**	Capitol 3096
9/11/71	2 (2)	13	53. **Rollin' In My Sweet Baby's Arms**	Capitol 3164
12/25/71+	29	5	54. Too Old To Cut The Mustard **BUCK & BUDDY**	Capitol 3215
2/26/72	8	9	55. **I'll Still Be Waiting For You**	Capitol 3262
5/13/72	1 (1)	13	56. **Made In Japan**	Capitol 3314
8/5/72	13	11	57. Looking Back To See (b)	Capitol 3368
10/7/72	13	11	58. You Ain't Gonna Have Ol' Buck To Kick Around No More	Capitol 3429
1/20/73	23	6	59. In The Palm Of Your Hand [R] originally made #43 as the B-side of #31 above	Capitol 3504
4/14/73	14	9	60. Ain't It Amazing, Gracie	Capitol 3563

BUCK OWENS:

DATE	POS	WKS	ARTIST–RECORD TITLE	LABEL & NO.
7/21/73	35	2	61. The Good Old Days (Are Here Again) (b)	Capitol 3601
9/15/73	27	6	62. Arms Full Of Empty	Capitol 3688
12/22/73+	8	9	63. **Big Game Hunter**	Capitol 3769
4/13/74	9	10	64. **On The Cover Of The Music City News** take-off on Dr. Hook's Pop hit "The Cover Of 'Rolling Stone'"	Capitol 3841
8/10/74	6	8	65. **(It's A) Monsters' Holiday**	Capitol 3907
12/28/74+	8	10	66. **Great Expectations**	Capitol 3976
4/26/75	19	5	67. 41st Street Lonely Hearts' Club/	
		5	68. Weekend Daddy	Capitol 4043
8/2/75	20	7	69. Love Is Strange (b) #11 Pop hit for Mickey & Sylvia in 1957	Capitol 4100
9/23/78	27	5	70. Nights Are Forever Without You #10 Pop hit for England Dan & John Ford Coley in 1976	Warner 8614
5/26/79	11	9	71. Play Together Again Again **BUCK OWENS with EMMYLOU HARRIS** title refers to #22 above	Warner 8830
10/6/79	30	4	72. Hangin' In And Hangin' On	Warner 49046
1/19/80	22	5	73. Let Jesse Rob The Train	Warner 49118
7/23/88	1 (1)	14	74. **Streets Of Bakersfield** **DWIGHT YOAKAM & BUCK OWENS**	Reprise 27964
7/29/89	27	6	75. Act Naturally [R] **BUCK OWENS and RINGO STARR** new version of #17 above	Capitol 44409

OXFORD, Vernon

Born on 6/8/41 near Rogers, Arkansas; raised in Wichita, Kansas. His father was a champion fiddler. Own band in the late '50s.

DATE	POS	WKS	ARTIST–RECORD TITLE	LABEL & NO.
7/17/76	17	6	1. Redneck! (The Redneck National Anthem)	RCA 10693

DATE	POS	WKS	ARTIST–RECORD TITLE	LABEL & NO.

P

PAGE, Patti

Born Clara Ann Fowler on 11/8/27 in Muskogee, Oklahoma; raised in Tulsa. One of 11 children. On radio KTUL with Al Klauser & His Oklahomans, as Ann Fowler, late 1940s. Another singer was billed as "Patti Page" for the Page Milk Company show on KTUL. When she left, Fowler took her place and name. With the Jimmy Joy band in 1947. On *Breakfast Club*, Chicago radio in 1947; signed by Mercury Records. Used multi-voice effect on records, 1947. Own TV series *The Patti Page Show*, 1955-58, and *The Big Record*, 1957-58. Appeared in the 1960 movie *Elmer Gantry*.

DATE	POS	WKS	ARTIST–RECORD TITLE	LABEL & NO.
5/7/49	**15**	1	1. Money, Marbles And Chalk Juke Box #15; Zeb Masher (orch.)	Mercury 5251
1/6/51	**2 (3)**	12	● 2. **The Tennessee Waltz** Juke Box #2 / Best Seller #5 / Jockey #5; Jack Rael (orch.)	Mercury 5534
7/17/61	**21**	3	3. Mom And Dad's Waltz	Mercury 71823
2/17/62	**13**	15	4. Go On Home	Mercury 71906
6/13/70	**22**	8	5. I Wish I Had A Mommy Like You	Columbia 45159
2/6/71	**24**	7	6. Give Him Love	Mercury 73162
6/5/71	**37**	3	7. Make Me Your Kind Of Woman	Mercury 73199
12/18/71	**38**	2	8. Think Again/	
		1	9. A Woman Left Lonely	Mercury 73249
1/13/73	**14**	8	10. Hello We're Lonely **PATTI PAGE & TOM T. HALL**	Mercury 73347
2/9/74	**29**	4	11. You're Gonna Hurt Me (One More Time)	Epic 11072
4/18/81	**39**	2	12. No Aces	Plantation 197

PARNELL, Lee Roy

Born on 12/21/56 in Abilene, Texas. To Nashville in 1987.

DATE	POS	WKS	ARTIST–RECORD TITLE	LABEL & NO.
7/4/92	**2 (2)**	13	1. **What Kind Of Fool Do You Think I Am**	Arista 12431
11/7/92+	**8**	14	2. **Love Without Mercy**	Arista 12462
3/20/93	**2 (1)**	18	3. **Tender Moment**	Arista 12523
9/25/93	**6**	14	4. **On The Road**	Arista 12588
1/29/94	**3**	17	5. **I'm Holding My Own**	Arista 12642
6/11/94	**17**	11	6. Take These Chains From My Heart	Arista 12695
6/17/95	**2 (1)**	16	7. **A Little Bit Of You**	Career 12823
10/28/95+	**12**	13	8. When A Woman Loves A Man	Career 12862
2/10/96	**3**	17	9. **Heart's Desire**	Career 12952

DATE	POS	WKS	ARTIST– RECORD TITLE	LABEL & NO.
			PARTON, Dolly	
			Born on 1/19/46 in Sevier County, Tennessee. Worked on Knoxville radio show at age 11. First recorded for Gold Band in 1957. To Nashville in 1964. Replaced Norma Jean on the Porter Wagoner TV show, 1967-74. Joined the *Grand Ole Opry* in 1969. Starred in the movies *9 To 5, The Best Little Whorehouse In Texas, Steel Magnolias* and *Straight Talk*. Hosted own variety show in 1987. CMA Awards: 1968 Vocal Group of the Year (with Porter Wagoner); 1970 and 1971 Vocal Duo of the Year (with Porter Wagoner); 1975 and 1976 Female Vocalist of the Year; 1978 Entertainer of the Year. (a) PORTER WAGONER & DOLLY PARTON (b) KENNY ROGERS & DOLLY PARTON (c) DOLLY PARTON, LINDA RONSTADT, EMMYLOU HARRIS	
2/25/67	24	9	1. Dumb Blonde	Monument 982
7/1/67	17	8	2. Something Fishy	Monument 1007
12/30/67+	7	13	3. **The Last Thing On My Mind** (a)	RCA 9369
5/4/68	7	12	4. **Holding On To Nothin'** (a)	RCA 9490
7/20/68	17	11	5. Just Because I'm A Woman	RCA 9548
8/10/68	5	11	6. **We'll Get Ahead Someday** (a)	RCA 9577
11/30/68	25	9	7. In The Good Old Days (When Times Were Bad)	RCA 9657
3/15/69	9	13	8. **Yours Love** (a)	RCA 0104
5/31/69	40	1	9. Daddy	RCA 0132
7/5/69	16	8	10. Always, Always (a)	RCA 0172
11/1/69	5	14	11. **Just Someone I Used To Know** (a)	RCA 0247
2/28/70	9	12	12. **Tomorrow Is Forever** (a)	RCA 9799
3/7/70	40	2	13. Daddy Come And Get Me	RCA 9784
7/11/70	3	15	14. **Mule Skinner Blues (Blue Yodel No. 8)** #5 Pop hit for The Fendermen in 1960	RCA 9863
8/8/70	7	13	15. **Daddy Was An Old Time Preacher Man** (a)	RCA 9875
12/19/70+	1 (1)	14	16. **Joshua**	RCA 9928
2/27/71	7	12	17. **Better Move It On Home** (a)	RCA 9958
5/1/71	23	7	18. Comin' For To Carry Me Home based on the American spiritual "Swing Low, Sweet Chariot"	RCA 9971
7/17/71	14	9	19. The Right Combination (a)	RCA 9994
7/31/71	17	10	20. My Blue Tears	RCA 9999
11/13/71	4	12	21. **Coat Of Many Colors**	RCA 0538
11/27/71+	11	11	22. Burning The Midnight Oil (a)	RCA 0565
3/25/72	6	12	23. **Touch Your Woman**	RCA 0662
4/22/72	9	12	24. **Lost Forever In Your Kiss** (a)	RCA 0675
8/19/72	20	7	25. Washday Blues	RCA 0757
9/16/72	14	11	26. Together Always (a)	RCA 0773
1/27/73	15	10	27. My Tennessee Mountain Home	RCA 0868
4/7/73	30	4	28. We Found It (a)	RCA 0893
6/2/73	20	8	29. Traveling Man	RCA 0950
7/14/73	3	14	30. **If Teardrops Were Pennies** (a)	RCA 0981
12/8/73+	1 (1)	13	31. **Jolene**	RCA 0145
4/27/74	1 (1)	12	32. **I Will Always Love You** #1 Pop hit for Whitney Houston in 1992	RCA 0234
8/31/74	1 (1)	10	33. **Please Don't Stop Loving Me** (a)	RCA 10010
9/28/74	1 (1)	12	34. **Love Is Like A Butterfly**	RCA 10031
2/15/75	1 (1)	9	35. **The Bargain Store**	RCA 10164

DATE	POS	WKS	ARTIST – RECORD TITLE		LABEL & NO.
6/28/75	2 (1)	10	36. **The Seeker**		RCA 10310
8/9/75	5	12	37. **Say Forever You'll Be Mine** (a)		RCA 10328
10/18/75	9	10	38. **We Used To**		RCA 10396
3/20/76	19	7	39. Hey, Lucky Lady		RCA 10564
6/5/76	8	10	40. **Is Forever Longer Than Always** (a)		RCA 10652
8/7/76	3	13	41. **All I Can Do**		RCA 10730
4/23/77	11	10	42. Light Of A Clear Blue Morning		RCA 10935
10/22/77	1 (5)	14	● 43. **Here You Come Again**		RCA 11123
3/25/78	1 (2)	10	44. **It's All Wrong, But It's All Right/**		
		9	45. Two Doors Down		RCA 11240
8/19/78	1 (3)	12	46. **Heartbreaker**		RCA 11296
12/2/78+	1 (1)	10	47. **I Really Got The Feeling**		RCA 11420
6/9/79	1 (2)	10	48. **You're The Only One**		RCA 11577
9/8/79	7	10	49. **Sweet Summer Lovin'/**		
		10	50. Great Balls Of Fire		RCA 11705
3/29/80	1 (1)	11	51. **Starting Over Again**		RCA 11926
			written by Donna Summer and her husband, Bruce Sudano		
7/12/80	2 (2)	12	52. **Making Plans** (a)		RCA 11983
8/9/80	1 (1)	10	53. **Old Flames Can't Hold A Candle To You**		RCA 12040
11/22/80+	12	10	54. If You Go, I'll Follow You (a)		RCA 12119
12/6/80+	1 (1)	9	● 55. **9 To 5**		RCA 12133
			title song from the movie starring Parton		
4/18/81	1 (1)	13	56. **But You Know I Love You**		RCA 12200
9/19/81	14	7	57. The House Of The Rising Sun		RCA 12282
			#1 Pop hit for The Animals in 1964		
3/13/82	8	12	58. **Single Women**		RCA 13057
6/5/82	7	11	59. **Heartbreak Express**		RCA 13234
8/21/82	1 (1)	13	60. **I Will Always Love You/**	[R]	
			new version of #32 above; from the movie *The Best Little Whorehouse In Texas* starring Parton		
		13	61. Do I Ever Cross Your Mind		RCA 13260
12/4/82	8	9	62. **Hard Candy Christmas**	[X]	RCA 13361
1/15/83	7	10	63. **Everything's Beautiful (In It's Own Way)**		Monument 03408
			DOLLY PARTON WILLIE NELSON		
6/4/83	20	7	64. Potential New Boyfriend		RCA 13514
9/10/83	1 (2)	15	▲ 65. **Islands In The Stream** (b)		RCA 13615
			written by the Bee Gees		
1/21/84	3	12	66. **Save The Last Dance For Me**		RCA 13703
			The Jordanaires (backing vocals); #1 Pop hit for The Drifters in 1960		
5/5/84	36	3	67. Downtown		RCA 13756
			#1 Pop hit for Petula Clark in 1965		
6/23/84	1 (1)	13	68. **Tennessee Homesick Blues**		RCA 13819
10/6/84	10	11	69. **God Won't Get You**		RCA 13883
			above 2 from the movie *Rhinestone* starring Parton		
2/16/85	3	14	70. **Don't Call It Love**		RCA 13987
6/1/85	1 (1)	16	71. **Real Love** (b)		RCA 14058
12/21/85+	1 (1)	14	72. **Think About Love**		RCA 14218
5/24/86	17	8	73. Tie Our Love (In a Double Knot)		RCA 14297
10/4/86	31	3	74. We Had It All		RCA 5001

DATE	POS	WKS	ARTIST– RECORD TITLE	LABEL & NO.
2/28/87	**1** (1)	14	75. **To Know Him Is To Love Him** (c) #1 Pop hit for The Teddy Bears in 1958	Warner 28492
6/13/87	**3**	11	76. **Telling Me Lies** (c)	Warner 28371
10/10/87	**5**	13	77. **Those Memories Of You** (c)	Warner 28248
4/16/88	**6**	11	78. **Wildflowers** (c)	Warner 27970
5/27/89	**1** (1)	13	79. **Why'd You Come In Here Lookin' Like That**	Columbia 68760
9/9/89	**1** (1)	17	80. **Yellow Roses**	Columbia 69040
1/13/90	**39**	1	81. He's Alive	Columbia 73200
3/24/90	**39**	1	82. Time For Me To Fly #56 Pop hit for REO Speedwagon in 1978	Columbia 73226
6/16/90	**29**	5	83. White Limozeen	Columbia 73341
8/25/90	**21**	9	84. Love Is Strange (b)	Reprise 19760
3/16/91	**1** (1)	17	85. **Rockin' Years** **DOLLY PARTON with RICKY VAN SHELTON**	Columbia 73711
7/6/91	**15**	11	86. Silver And Gold	Columbia 73826
11/23/91	**33**	6	87. Eagle When She Flies	Columbia 74011
3/6/93	**27**	6	88. Romeo **DOLLY PARTON AND FRIENDS** (Billy Ray Cyrus, Tanya Tucker, Kathy Mattea, Mary-Chapin Carpenter and Pam Tillis)	Columbia 74876
9/30/95	**15**	11	89. I Will Always Love You [R] **DOLLY PARTON WITH SPECIAL GUEST VINCE GILL** new version of #32 & #60 above	Columbia 78079
			PARTON, Randy	
			Born on 12/15/55 in Sevierville, Tennessee. Younger brother of Dolly Parton. Worked with Jean Shepard in 1974, then with Dolly, 1974-79.	
4/18/81	**30**	3	1. Hold Me Like You Never Had Me	RCA 12137
8/29/81	**30**	3	2. Shot Full Of Love	RCA 12271
			PARTON, Stella	
			Born on 5/4/49 in Sevierville, Tennessee. Younger sister of Dolly Parton. Sang with Stella Carroll & The Gospel Carrolls. Own gospel group, the Stella Parton Singers.	
6/21/75	**9**	11	1. **I Want To Hold You In My Dreams Tonight**	Country Soul 039
8/27/77	**15**	7	2. The Danger Of A Stranger	Elektra 45410
12/3/77+	**14**	10	3. Standard Lie Number One	Elektra 45437
4/15/78	**20**	5	4. Four Little Letters	Elektra 45468
7/29/78	**28**	4	5. Undercover Lovers	Elektra 45490
10/28/78	**21**	6	6. Stormy Weather	Elektra 45533
5/19/79	**26**	5	7. Steady As The Rain	Elektra 46029
8/25/79	**36**	3	8. The Room At The Top Of The Stairs	Elektra 46502
			PAUL, Buddy	
			DJ at KCIJ-Shreveport at the time of his hit.	
8/1/60	**22**	4	1. This Old Town	Murco 1018
			PAUL, Joyce	
8/10/68	**36**	2	1. Phone Call To Mama	United Art. 50315

DATE	POS	WKS	ARTIST–RECORD TITLE	LABEL & NO.
			PAUL, Les, and Mary Ford	
			Paul (born Lester Polsfuss, 6/9/16, Waukesha, Wisconsin) and Ford (born Colleen Summer, 7/7/28, Pasadena; died 9/30/77) were married, 1949-63. Paul was an innovator in electric guitar and multi-track recordings.	
3/10/51	7	1	● 1. **Mockin' Bird Hill** Jockey #7	Capitol 1373
			PAYCHECK, Johnny	
			Born Donald Eugene Lytle on 5/31/37 in Greenfield, Ohio. Guitarist/steel guitarist. Moved to Nashville in 1955, worked with Porter Wagoner, Faron Young, George Jones and Ray Price. Recorded as Donnie Young for Decca in 1959. Changed name in 1965. Wrote "Apartment No. 9" for Tammy Wynette and "Touch My Heart" for Ray Price. Toured with Merle Haggard, 1981-83.	
11/6/65	26	9	1. A-11	Hilltop 3007
3/5/66	40	1	2. Heartbreak Tennessee	Hilltop 3009
6/18/66	8	17	3. **The Lovin' Machine**	Little Dar. 008
12/17/66+	13	9	4. Motel Time Again	Little Dar. 0016
5/6/67	15	10	5. Jukebox Charlie	Little Dar. 0020
9/30/67	32	6	6. The Cave	Little Dar. 0032
8/2/69	31	7	7. Wherever You Are	Little Dar. 0060
10/23/71	2 (1)	16	8. **She's All I Got** #39 Pop hit for Freddie North in 1971	Epic 10783
3/25/72	4	12	9. **Someone To Give My Love To**	Epic 10836
6/10/72	13	8	10. Let's All Go Down To The River **JODY MILLER and JOHNNY PAYCHECK**	Epic 10863
7/8/72	12	9	11. Love Is A Good Thing	Epic 10876
11/4/72	21	8	12. Somebody Loves Me	Epic 10912
3/17/73	10	9	13. **Something About You I Love**	Epic 10947
6/23/73	2 (3)	13	14. **Mr. Lovemaker**	Epic 10999
11/24/73+	8	11	15. **Song And Dance Man**	Epic 11046
4/20/74	19	6	16. My Part Of Forever	Epic 11090
8/10/74	23	5	17. Keep On Lovin' Me	Epic 11142
11/23/74+	12	9	18. For A Minute There	Epic 50040
4/5/75	26	5	19. Loving You Beats All I've Ever Seen	Epic 50073
7/12/75	38	3	20. I Don't Love Her Anymore	Epic 50111
10/25/75	23	6	21. All-American Man	Epic 50146
8/21/76	34	4	22. 11 Months And 29 Days	Epic 50249
2/26/77	7	12	23. **Slide Off Of Your Satin Sheets**	Epic 50334
6/25/77	8	10	24. **I'm The Only Hell (Mama Ever Raised)**	Epic 50391
11/19/77+	1 (2)	13	25. **Take This Job And Shove It** the 1981 movie starring Art Carney was based on this song	Epic 50469
4/29/78	17	6	26. Georgia In A Jug/	
4/29/78	33	6	27. Me And The I.R.S.	Epic 50539
10/28/78	7	10	28. **Friend, Lover, Wife**	Epic 50621

12/23/78+	7	8	29. **Mabellene**
			       GEORGE JONES & JOHNNY PAYCHECK
			         #5 Pop hit for Chuck Berry in 1955
				Epic 50647

2/17/79	27	5	30. The Outlaw's Prayer	Epic 50655

DATE	POS	WKS	ARTIST– RECORD TITLE	LABEL & NO.
6/16/79	**14**	6	31. You Can Have Her **GEORGE JONES & JOHNNY PAYCHECK** #12 Pop hit for Roy Hamilton in 1961	Epic 50708
1/19/80	**17**	7	32. Drinkin' And Drivin'	Epic 50818
5/10/80	**40**	2	33. Fifteen Beers	Epic 50863
7/19/80	**31**	4	34. When You're Ugly Like Us (You Just Naturally Got To Be Cool) **GEORGE JONES & JOHNNY PAYCHECK**	Epic 50891
9/27/80	**22**	6	35. In Memory Of A Memory	Epic 50923
1/10/81	**18**	5	36. You Better Move On **GEORGE JONES and JOHNNY PAYCHECK** #24 Pop hit for Arthur Alexander in 1962	Epic 50949
1/12/85	**30**	6	37. I Never Got Over You	AMI 1322
6/21/86	**21**	9	38. Old Violin	Mercury 884720

PAYNE, Leon

Born on 6/15/17 in Alba, Texas. Died of a heart attack on 9/11/69. Blind since early childhood. Guitarist/pianist/drummer. Played with Jack Rhodes's Rhythm Boys. Own Band, the Lone Star Buddies, from 1949. Wrote "I Love You Because," "Lost Highway" and "Blue Side Of Lonesome." Initial member of the Songwriter's Hall of Fame. Also recorded as Rock Rogers.

DATE	POS	WKS	ARTIST– RECORD TITLE	LABEL & NO.
11/5/49+	**1 (2)**	32	1. **I Love You Because** Jockey #1 / Best Seller #4 / Juke Box #10	Capitol 40238

PEARL, Minnie—see MINNIE

PEGGY SUE

Born Peggy Sue Webb on 3/24/47 in Butcher Holler, Kentucky. Sister of Loretta Lynn, Crystal Gayle and Jay Lee Webb; distant cousin of Patty Loveless. Wrote "Don't Come Home A'Drinkin'" with Loretta, performed on tours with her. Married to Sonny Wright.

DATE	POS	WKS	ARTIST– RECORD TITLE	LABEL & NO.
7/5/69	**28**	6	1. I'm Dynamite	Decca 32485
11/29/69	**30**	2	2. I'm Gettin' Tired Of Babyin' You	Decca 32571
8/15/70	**37**	2	3. All American Husband	Decca 32698
2/12/77	**34**	5	4. Every Beat Of My Heart	Door Knob 021
1/13/79	**37**	3	5. How I Love You In The Morning	Door Knob 079
4/21/79	**30**	4	6. I Want To See Me In Your Eyes	Door Knob 094

PENNINGTON, Ray

Born Ramon Daniel Pennington in Clay County, Kentucky, 1933. On TV in Cincinnati at age 16. Own band by 1952. Worked on local TV shows in Kentucky, Indiana and Ohio from the late '50s.

DATE	POS	WKS	ARTIST– RECORD TITLE	LABEL & NO.
6/3/67	**29**	4	1. Ramblin' Man	Capitol 5855

PENNY, Hank

Born Herbert Clayton Penny on 8/18/18 in Birmingham, Alabama. Died on 4/17/92 of heart failure. Accomplished banjo player. Performed on WWL-New Orleans and WLW-Cincinnati before moving to Los Angeles and forming own band in the mid-1940s. Worked as a comedian on Spade Cooley's TV series, KTLA-TV. Married to Sue Thompson, 1953-63.

DATE	POS	WKS	ARTIST– RECORD TITLE	LABEL & NO.
6/15/46	**4**	6	1. **Steel Guitar Stomp** [I]	King 528
9/14/46	**4**	4	2. **Get Yourself A Red Head**	King 540
2/25/50	**4**	12	3. **Bloodshot Eyes** Juke Box #4	King 828

DATE	POS	WKS	ARTIST–RECORD TITLE	LABEL & NO.
			PERFECT STRANGER	
			Quartet from Texas: Shayne Morrison, Richard Raines, Steve Murray and Andy Ginn. Group named after the 1985 hit by Southern Pacific.	
6/24/95	4	12	1. **You Have The Right To Remain Silent**	Curb 76956
			PERKINS, Carl	
			Born on 4/9/32 near Tiptonville, Tennessee. Rockabilly singer/guitarist/ songwriter. The Beatles recorded his songs "Matchbox," "Honey Don't" and "Everybody's Trying To Be My Baby." Inducted into the Rock and Roll Hall of Fame in 1987.	
2/18/56	1 (3)	24	1. **Blue Suede Shoes** Juke Box #1 / Best Seller #2 / Jockey #2; Grammy Hall of Fame Award winner in 1986	Sun 234
6/30/56	7	6	2. **Boppin' The Blues** Juke Box #7 / Best Seller #9	Sun 243
10/6/56	10	2	3. **Dixie Fried/** Best Seller #10	
		2	4. I'm Sorry, I'm Not Sorry Best Seller flip	Sun 249
3/9/57	13	8	5. Your True Love Best Seller #13	Sun 261
3/31/58	17	9	6. Pink Pedal Pushers Best Seller #17	Columbia 41131
1/21/67	22	10	7. Country Boy's Dream	Dollie 505
7/1/67	40	2	8. Shine, Shine, Shine	Dollie 508
2/1/69	20	9	9. Restless	Columbia 44723
7/12/86	31	5	10. Birth Of Rock And Roll	America 884760
			PERRY, Brenda Kaye	
3/4/78	35	3	1. Deeper Water	MRC 1010
5/20/78	37	3	2. I Can't Get Up By Myself	MRC 1013
			PFEIFER, Diane	
			Born on 11/4/50 in St. Louis. Own all-girl rock band while in college.	
12/26/81+	35	3	1. Play Something We Could Love To	Capitol 5060
			PHILLIPS, Bill	
			Born on 1/28/36 in Canton, North Carolina. Worked on the *Old Southern Jamboree*, WMIL-Miami, in 1955. Moved to Nashville in 1957. Worked with Johnny Wright and Kitty Wells from the early '70s.	
8/24/59	27	2	1. Sawmill	Columbia 41416
2/8/60	24	4	2. Georgia Town Blues **MEL TILLIS and BILL PHILLIPS (above 2)**	Columbia 41530
4/18/64	22	8	3. I Can Stand It (As Long As She Can)	Decca 31584
10/24/64	26	9	4. Stop Me	Decca 31648
4/2/66	6	18	5. **Put It Off Until Tomorrow** Dolly Parton (harmony vocal)	Decca 31901
8/20/66	8	17	6. **The Company You Keep** above 2 written by Dolly Parton and Bill Owens	Decca 31996
2/18/67	10	11	7. **The Words I'm Gonna Have To Eat**	Decca 32074
8/12/67	39	3	8. I Learn Something New Everyday	Decca 32141

DATE	POS	WKS	ARTIST– RECORD TITLE	LABEL & NO.
12/23/67+	**25**	6	9. Love's Dead End	Decca 32207
11/8/69	**10**	11	10. **Little Boy Sad**	Decca 32565
			#17 Pop hit for Johnny Burnette in 1961	
			### PHILLIPS, Charlie	
			Born on 7/2/37 in Clovis, New Mexico. Worked on the *Ozark Jubilee*, *Louisiana Hayride* and the *Big D Jamboree*. Own band, the Sugartimers, from 1957.	
4/14/62	**9**	7	1. **I Guess I'll Never Learn**	Columbia 42289
10/12/63	**30**	1	2. This Is The House	Columbia 42851
			### PHILLIPS, Stu	
			Born on 1/19/33 in Montreal, Canada. Member of the *Grand Ole Opry* since 1967.	
5/21/66	**39**	1	1. Bracero	RCA 8771
9/10/66	**32**	7	2. The Great El Tigre (The Tiger)	RCA 8868
7/8/67	**21**	11	3. Vin Rose	RCA 9219
11/4/67	**13**	10	4. Juanita Jones	RCA 9333
			### PIERCE, Webb	
			Born on 8/8/21 in West Monroe, Louisiana. Died on 2/24/91 of heart failure. Worked on KMLB-Monroe, then on the *Louisiana Hayride* from the early '50s to 1955. First recorded on Pacemaker. Own band that included Faron Young, Jimmy Day and Floyd Cramer. Moved to Nashville in 1955 and joined the *Grand Ole Opry*. Formerly one of the owners of the Cedarwood Publishing Company. Appeared in the movies *Buffalo Guns*, *Music City USA* and *Road To Nashville*. His daughter Debbie was a member of Chantilly.	
1/5/52	**1 (4)**	27	1. **Wondering** Jockey #1 / Best Seller #4 / Juke Box #4	Decca 46364
6/7/52	**1 (3)**	20	2. **That Heart Belongs To Me** Jockey #1 / Juke Box #2 / Best Seller #5	Decca 28091
10/4/52	**1 (4)**	23	3. **Back Street Affair** Jockey #1(4) / Juke Box #1(3) / Best Seller #1(2)	Decca 28369
1/31/53	**4**	7	4. **I'll Go On Alone/** Juke Box #4 / Best Seller #7 / Jockey #8	
2/14/53	**4**	6	5. **That's Me Without You** Jockey #4 / Juke Box #4 / Best Seller #9	Decca 28534
3/28/53	**4**	14	6. **The Last Waltz/** Best Seller #4 / Jockey #5 / Juke Box #5	
4/18/53	**5**	6	7. **I Haven't Got The Heart** Juke Box #5 / Jockey #6	Decca 28594
7/4/53	**1 (8)**	22	8. **It's Been So Long/** Jockey #1(8) / Best Seller #1(6) / Juke Box #1(1)	
7/4/53	**9**	2	9. **Don't Throw Your Life Away** Juke Box #9	Decca 28725
10/24/53	**1 (12)**	27	10. **There Stands The Glass/** Best Seller #1(12) / Juke Box #1(9) / Jockey #1(6)	
10/24/53+	**3**	17	11. **I'm Walking The Dog** Juke Box #3 / Jockey #4 / Best Seller #6	Decca 28834
2/6/54	**1 (17)**	36	12. **Slowly** Best Seller #1(17) / Juke Box #1(17) / Jockey #1(15)	Decca 28991

DATE	POS	WKS	ARTIST– RECORD TITLE	LABEL & NO.
6/5/54	1 (2)	31	13. **Even Tho/** *Jockey #1 / Juke Box #2 / Best Seller #3*	
6/12/54	4	18	14. **Sparkling Brown Eyes** **WEBB PIERCE with WILBURN BROTHERS** *Best Seller #4 / Jockey #4 / Juke Box #4*	Decca 29107
10/9/54	1 (10)	29	15. **More And More/** *Juke Box #1(10) / Best Seller #1(9) / Jockey #1(8)*	
10/9/54	4	12	16. **You're Not Mine Anymore** *Jockey #4 / Best Seller #8*	Decca 29252
2/5/55	1 (21)	37	17. **In The Jailhouse Now/** *Juke Box #1(21) / Best Seller #1(20) / Jockey #1(15)*	
2/12/55	10	2	18. **I'm Gonna Fall Out Of Love With You** *Jockey #10 / Best Seller #14*	Decca 29391
6/18/55	1 (12)	32	19. **I Don't Care/** *Best Seller #1(12) / Jockey #1(12) / Juke Box #1(12)*	
		6	20. Your Good For Nothing Heart *Jockey flip / Juke Box flip*	Decca 29480
9/24/55	1 (13)	32	21. **Love, Love, Love/** *Jockey #1(13) / Juke Box #1(9) / Best Seller #1(8)*	
10/29/55	7	5	22. **If You Were Me** *Jockey #7*	Decca 29662
12/17/55+	1 (4)	25	23. **Why Baby Why** **RED SOVINE & WEBB PIERCE** *Jockey #1(4) / Best Seller #1(1) / Juke Box #1(1);* *also released on Decca 29739*	Decca 29755
3/3/56	2 (7)	21	24. **Yes I Know Why/** *Jockey #2 / Best Seller #3 / Juke Box #3*	
3/10/56	3	13	25. **'Cause I Love You** *Juke Box #3 / Best Seller #5 / Jockey #12*	Decca 29805
4/21/56	5	14	26. **Little Rosa** **RED SOVINE and WEBB PIERCE** *Best Seller #5 / Jockey #5 / Juke Box #5*	Decca 29876
7/21/56	7	11	27. **Any Old Time/** *Jockey #7 / Juke Box #7 / Best Seller #10*	
		6	28. We'll Find A Way *Juke Box flip / Best Seller flip*	Decca 29974
10/13/56	10	8	29. **Teenage Boogie/** *Best Seller #10 / Jockey #15*	
		5	30. I'm Really Glad You Hurt Me *Best Seller flip*	Decca 30045
1/5/57	3	22	31. **I'm Tired/** *Best Seller #3 / Jockey #4 / Juke Box #4*	
		4	32. It's My Way	Decca 30155
3/30/57	1 (1)	22	33. **Honky Tonk Song** *Jockey #1 / Best Seller #2 / Juke Box #7*	Decca 30255
4/6/57	8	9	34. **Oh, So Many Years** **KITTY WELLS and WEBB PIERCE** *Jockey #8*	Decca 30183
4/13/57	12	2	35. Someday *Jockey #12*	Decca 30255
5/27/57	7	15	36. **Bye Bye, Love/** *Jockey #7 / Best Seller #8*	
6/10/57	7	12	37. **Missing You** *Jockey #7 / Best Seller #13*	Decca 30321

DATE	POS	WKS	ARTIST– RECORD TITLE	LABEL & NO.
9/30/57	3	17	38. **Holiday For Love/** Jockey #3 / Best Seller #6	
11/18/57	12	1	39. Don't Do It Darlin' Jockey #12	Decca 30419
1/20/58	12	1	40. One Week Later **WEBB PIERCE and KITTY WELLS** Jockey #12	Decca 30489
5/5/58	3	17	41. **Cryin' Over You/** Jockey #3 / Best Seller #12	
6/2/58	10	4	42. **You'll Come Back** Jockey #10	Decca 30623
10/20/58	7	10	43. **Tupelo County Jail/**	
9/29/58	10	12	44. **Falling Back To You** Jockey #10 / Hot C&W #10 / Best Seller #18	Decca 30711
1/19/59	22	3	45. I'm Letting You Go	Decca 30789
4/6/59	6	16	46. **A Thousand Miles Ago**	Decca 30858
7/20/59	2 (9)	25	47. **I Ain't Never**	Decca 30923
12/21/59+	4	18	48. **No Love Have I**	Decca 31021
5/23/60	11	8	49. Is It Wrong (For Loving You)/	
4/11/60	17	10	50. (Doin' The) Lovers Leap	Decca 31058
9/12/60	11	8	51. Drifting Texas Sand	Decca 31118
11/14/60	4	18	52. **Fallen Angel**	Decca 31165
2/20/61	5	15	53. **Let Forgiveness In** flip side "There's More Pretty Girls Than One" Bubbled Under at #118	Decca 31197
5/29/61	3	21	54. **Sweet Lips**	Decca 31249
9/25/61	5	22	55. **Walking The Streets/**	
10/2/61	7	19	56. **How Do You Talk To A Baby**	Decca 31298
2/10/62	5	16	57. **Alla My Love**	Decca 31347
6/2/62	7	13	58. **Take Time/**	
5/26/62	8	13	59. **Crazy Wild Desire**	Decca 31380
10/6/62	5	15	60. **Cow Town/**	
10/13/62	19	10	61. Sooner Or Later	Decca 31421
1/5/63	25	3	62. How Come Your Dog Don't Bite Nobody But Me **WEBB PIERCE and MEL TILLIS**	Decca 31445
3/2/63	15	8	63. Sawmill/	
4/6/63	21	3	64. If I Could Come Back	Decca 31451
6/22/63	7	15	65. **Sands Of Gold**	Decca 31488
11/9/63	9	13	66. **Those Wonderful Years/**	
10/26/63+	13	15	67. If The Back Door Could Talk	Decca 31544
2/22/64	25	11	68. Waiting A Lifetime	Decca 31582
5/30/64	2 (1)	21	69. **Memory #1** flip side "French Riviera" Bubbled Under at #126	Decca 31617
9/26/64	9	15	70. **Finally** **KITTY WELLS and WEBB PIERCE**	Decca 31663
2/13/65	26	11	71. That's Where My Money Goes	Decca 31704
3/27/65	22	12	72. Loving You Then Losing You	Decca 31737
9/4/65	13	11	73. Who Do I Think I Am	Decca 31816
9/3/66	25	8	74. Love's Something (I Can't Understand)	Decca 31982
11/26/66	14	10	75. Where'd Ya Stay Last Night	Decca 32033
6/3/67	39	2	76. Goodbye City, Goodbye Girl	Decca 32098

DATE	POS	WKS	ARTIST–RECORD TITLE	LABEL & NO.
9/2/67	**6**	14	77. **Fool Fool Fool**	Decca 32167
2/24/68	**24**	8	78. Luzianna	Decca 32246
7/27/68	**26**	5	79. Stranger In A Strange, Strange City	Decca 32339
11/9/68	**22**	8	80. Saturday Night	Decca 32388
3/15/69	**32**	6	81. If I Had Last Night To Live Over	Decca 32438
8/2/69	**14**	9	82. This Thing	Decca 32508
12/27/69+	**38**	3	83. Love Ain't Never Gonna Be No Better	Decca 32577
4/17/71	**31**	3	84. Tell Him That You Love Him	Decca 32787

PILLOW, Ray

Born on 7/4/37 in Lynchburg, Virginia. Sang in college rock band in the late '50s. Moved to Nashville in 1961. Toured with the Martha White Show. With the *Grand Ole Opry* since 1966.

DATE	POS	WKS	ARTIST–RECORD TITLE	LABEL & NO.
1/1/66	**17**	9	1. Thank You Ma'am	Capitol 5518
4/30/66	**32**	5	2. Common Colds And Broken Hearts	Capitol 5597
5/28/66	**9**	13	3. **I'll Take The Dog** **JEAN SHEPARD & RAY PILLOW**	Capitol 5633
10/22/66	**26**	8	4. Volkswagen	Capitol 5735
12/31/66+	**25**	6	5. Mr. Do-It-Yourself **JEAN SHEPARD & RAY PILLOW**	Capitol 5769
9/27/69	**38**	2	6. Reconsider Me	Plantation 25

PINETOPPERS, The

Group formed by brothers Roy (bass) and Vaughn (mandolin, guitar) Horton from Broadtop Mountain, Pennsylvania. Moved to New York City in 1935. Own shows on NBC and CBS radio. Added Ray Smith, Rusty Keefer and Johnny Browers to form The Pinetoppers. Vocals by Trudy and Gloria Marlin (the Beaver Valley Sweethearts). Roy elected to the Country Music Hall of Fame in 1982.

DATE	POS	WKS	ARTIST–RECORD TITLE	LABEL & NO.
12/23/50+	**3**	13	1. **Mockin' Bird Hill** Juke Box #3 / Jockey #4 / Best Seller #5; Beaver Valley Sweethearts (vocal)	Coral 64061

PINKARD & BOWDEN

Comedy team of Sandy Pinkard and Richard Bowden. Pinkard (real name: James Sanford Pinkard, Jr., from Gueydan, Louisiana) was a staff writer for Jim Ed Norman; wrote "You're The Reason God Made Oklahoma." Bowden (guitarist from Linden, Texas) was with own band, Blue Steel, and Shiloh, with Don Henley.

DATE	POS	WKS	ARTIST–RECORD TITLE	LABEL & NO.
10/13/84	**39**	1	1. Mama, She's Lazy [N] parody of The Judds' "Mama He's Crazy"	Warner 29205

PIRATES OF THE MISSISSIPPI

Alabama-based band: Bill McCorvey (lead singer), Rich Alves (guitar), Pat Severs (steel guitar), Dean Townson (bass) and Jimmy Lowe (drums).

DATE	POS	WKS	ARTIST–RECORD TITLE	LABEL & NO.
8/18/90	**26**	7	1. Honky Tonk Blues	Capitol 44579
4/20/91	**15**	11	2. Feed Jake also available as the B-side of #4 below	Capitol LP Cut
8/31/91	**29**	6	3. Speak Of The Devil also available as the B-side of #5 below; above 3 from the album *Pirates Of The Mississippi* on Capitol 94389	Capitol LP Cut
4/4/92	**22**	8	4. Til I'm Holding You Again	Liberty 57704
8/8/92	**36**	3	5. Too Much	Liberty 57767

DATE	POS	WKS	ARTIST– RECORD TITLE	LABEL & NO.
			PITNEY, Gene	
			Born on 2/17/41 in Hartford, Connecticut; raised in Rockville, Connecticut. Own band at Rockville High School. Recorded for Decca in 1959 with Ginny Arnell as Jamie & Jane. Recorded for Blaze in 1960 as Billy Bryan. First recorded under own name for Festival in 1960. Wrote "Hello Mary Lou," "He's A Rebel" and "Rubber Ball."	
5/1/65	16	9	1. I've Got Five Dollars And It's Saturday Night	Musicor 1066
7/10/65	25	6	2. Louisiana Man **GEORGE & GENE** (above 2) flip side "I'm A Fool To Care" Bubbled Under at #115	Musicor 1097
1/22/66	15	11	3. Baby, Ain't That Fine **GENE PITNEY and MELBA MONTGOMERY**	Musicor 1135
			PLACE, Mary Kay, as Loretta Haggers	
			Born on 8/23/47 in Tulsa. Singer/composer/comedienne. Script writer for many TV comedy shows. Played Loretta Haggers on TV's *Mary Hartman, Mary Hartman*, 1976-78.	
11/6/76	3	11	1. **Baby Boy**	Columbia 10422
12/10/77+	9	11	2. **Something To Brag About** **MARY KAY PLACE with WILLIE NELSON**	Columbia 10644
			POINTER, Anita—see CONLEY, Earl Thomas	
			POINTER SISTERS	
			Soul group formed in Oakland in 1971, consisting of sisters Ruth, Bonnie, June and Anita Pointer.	
10/5/74	37	3	1. Fairytale	Blue Thumb 254
			POOLE, Cheryl	
			Born in Tyler, Texas.	
9/28/68	39	2	1. Three Playing Love	Paula 309
			POSEY, Sandy	
			Born on 6/18/44 in Jasper, Alabama; raised in West Memphis, Arkansas. Worked as a session singer in Nashville and Memphis in the early '60s. Left music, 1968-70.	
11/20/71+	18	11	1. Bring Him Safely Home To Me	Columbia 45458
12/2/72	36	3	2. Happy, Happy Birthday Baby #5 Pop hit for The Tune Weavers in 1957	Columbia 45703
6/9/73	39	1	3. Don't	Columbia 45828
4/8/78	21	7	4. Born To Be With You #5 Pop hit for The Chordettes in 1956	Warner 8540
9/2/78	26	3	5. Love, Love, Love/Chapel Of Love	Warner 8610
3/3/79	26	7	6. Love Is Sometimes Easy	Warner 8731
			PRADO, Perez	
			Born Damaso Perez Prado on 12/11/16 in Mantanzas, Cuba. Died on 9/14/89. Known as "The King Of Mambo."	
8/18/58	18	1	● 1. Patricia [I] Best Seller #18	RCA 7245

DATE	POS	WKS	ARTIST– RECORD TITLE	LABEL & NO.
			PRESLEY, Elvis	
			"The King of Rock & Roll." Ranked as the #1 artist in the book *Joel Whitburn's Top Pop Singles*. Born on 1/8/35 in Tupelo, Mississippi. Died at his Graceland Mansion in Memphis on 8/16/77 of heart failure caused by prescription drug abuse. Won talent contest at age eight, singing "Old Shep." First recorded for Sun in 1954. Signed to RCA Records on 11/22/55. In U.S. Army, 3/24/58 to 3/5/60. Starred in 33 movies, beginning with *Love Me Tender* in 1956. NBC-TV special in 1968. Married Priscilla Beaulieu on 5/1/67; divorced on 10/11/73. Priscilla pursued acting in the 1980s with roles in TV's *Dynasty* and the *Naked Gun* movies. Their only child, Lisa Marie, (born 2/1/68) married Michael Jackson on 5/26/94 and filed for divorce in January 1996. Elvis's last live performance was in Indianapolis on 6/26/77. Won Grammy's Lifetime Achievement Award in 1971. Inducted into the Rock and Roll Hall of Fame in 1986. The U.S. Postal Service issued an Elvis commemorative stamp on 1/8/93.	
7/16/55	**5**	15	1. **Baby Let's Play House/** Jockey #5 / Best Seller #10	
		3	2. I'm Left, You're Right, She's Gone Best Seller flip; #12 R&B hit for Arthur Gunter in 1955	Sun 217
9/17/55+	**1 (5)**	39	3. **I Forgot To Remember To Forget/** Juke Box #1(5) / Best Seller #1(2) / Jockey #4	
12/31/55+	**11**	4	4. Mystery Train Jockey #11	Sun 223
3/3/56	**1 (17)**	27	▲ 5. **Heartbreak Hotel/** Best Seller #1(17) / Juke Box #1(13) / Jockey #1(12)	
3/31/56	**8**	6	6. **I Was The One** Jockey #8	RCA 47-6420
6/2/56	**1 (2)**	20	▲ 7. **I Want You, I Need You, I Love You/** Best Seller #1(2) / Juke Box #1(1) / Jockey #5	
6/2/56	**13**	13	8. My Baby Left Me Best Seller #13; written and recorded on RCA by Arthur "Big Boy" Crudup in 1950	RCA 47-6540
8/4/56	**1 (10)**	28	▲³ 9. **Hound Dog/** Juke Box #1(10) / Best Seller #1(5) / Jockey #6; Grammy Hall of Fame winner (1988); #1 R&B hit for Big Mama Thornton in 1953	
8/11/56	**1 (10)**	28	▲³ 10. **Don't Be Cruel** Juke Box #1(10) / Best Seller #1(5) / Jockey #2; the Juke Box and Best Seller charts combined "Don't Be Cruel" and "Hound Dog" as one listing; "Don't Be Cruel" had more #1 weeks as the top side on both Juke Box (7 weeks A-side, 3 weeks B-side) and Best Seller charts (5 weeks A-side)	RCA 47-6604
10/20/56	**3**	18	▲² 11. **Love Me Tender/** Best Seller #3 / Jockey #4 / Juke Box #4; from Presley's first movie; tune adapted from "Aura Lee" of 1861	
		6	12. Anyway You Want Me (That's How I Will Be) Best Seller flip	RCA 47-6643
12/29/56	**10**	3	13. **Love Me** Jockey #10 / Juke Box #10; from the E.P. *Elvis*; 2 other cuts from the E.P. made the Pop charts: "When My Blue Moon Turns To Gold Again" (#19) and "Paralyzed" (#59)	RCA EPA-992
2/2/57	**3**	14	▲ 14. **Too Much/** Juke Box #3 / Best Seller #5 / Jockey #6	
3/2/57	**8**	1	15. **Playing For Keeps** Juke Box #8	RCA 47-6800
4/13/57	**1 (1)**	16	▲² 16. **All Shook Up** Juke Box #1 / Best Seller #3 / Jockey #3; flip side "That's When Your Heartaches Begin" made #58 on the Pop charts	RCA 47-6870

DATE	POS	WKS	ARTIST– RECORD TITLE	LABEL & NO.
7/1/57	**1** (1)	16	▲ 17. **(Let Me Be Your) Teddy Bear/** Best Seller #1 / Jockey #4	
9/16/57	**15**	2	18. Loving You Jockey #15	RCA 47-7000
8/19/57	**11**	2	19. Mean Woman Blues Jockey #11; from the E.P. *Loving You, Vol. II*; #5 Pop hit for Roy Orbison in 1963; above 3 from the movie *Loving You* starring Presley	RCA EPA 2-1515
10/14/57	**1** (1)	24	▲² 20. **Jailhouse Rock/** Best Seller #1 / Jockey #3	
10/28/57	**11**	4	21. Treat Me Nice Jockey #11; above 2 from the movie *Jailhouse Rock* starring Presley	RCA 47-7035
2/3/58	**2** (5)	18	▲ 22. **Don't/** Best Seller #2 / Jockey #3	
2/3/58	**4**	13	23. **I Beg Of You** Best Seller #4 / Jockey #5	RCA 47-7150
4/21/58	**3**	15	▲ 24. **Wear My Ring Around Your Neck/** Best Seller #3 / Jockey #4	
		2	25. Doncha' Think It's Time Best Seller flip	RCA 47-7240
6/30/58	**2** (2)	16	▲ 26. **Hard Headed Woman/** Best Seller #2 / Jockey #8	
		3	27. Don't Ask Me Why Best Seller flip; above 2 from the movie *King Creole* starring Presley	RCA 47-7280
12/22/58	**24**	3	28. One Night #11 R&B hit for Smiley Lewis in 1956; flip side "I Got Stung" made #8 on the *Hot 100*	RCA 47-7410
5/30/60	**27**	2	▲ 29. Stuck On You recorded 15 days after Presley's Army discharge; flip side "Fame And Fortune" made #17 on the *Hot 100*	RCA 47-7740
12/12/60+	**22**	6	▲² 30. Are You Lonesome To-night? Vaughn Deleath and Henry Burr both had top 10 versions in 1927; flip side "I Gotta Know" made #20 on the *Hot 100*	RCA 47-7810
1/3/70	**13**	10	▲ 31. Don't Cry Daddy flip side "Rubberneckin'" made the *Hot 100* as a B-side "tag-along"	RCA 47-9768
3/21/70	**31**	6	● 32. Kentucky Rain written by Eddie Rabbitt	RCA 47-9791
7/18/70	**37**	3	● 33. The Wonder Of You recorded "live" in Las Vegas; #25 Pop hit for Ray Peterson in 1959; flip side "Mama Liked The Roses" made the *Hot 100* as a B-side "tag-along"	RCA 47-9835
1/23/71	**9**	11	34. **There Goes My Everything/** #20 Pop hit for Engelbert Humperdinck in 1967	
1/23/71	**23**	11	● 35. I Really Don't Want To Know #11 Pop hit for Les Paul & Mary Ford in 1954	RCA 47-9960
6/19/71	**34**	5	36. Life flip side "Only Believe" made the *Hot 100* as a B-side "tag-along"	RCA 47-9985
11/4/72	**36**	4	37. It's A Matter Of Time flip side "Burning Love" made #2 on the *Hot 100*	RCA 74-0769
1/13/73	**16**	8	38. Always On My Mind/	
		8	● 39. Separate Ways from the movie *Elvis on Tour*	RCA 74-0815
6/2/73	**31**	5	40. Fool/	
		5	41. Steamroller Blues recorded "live" in Hawaii (written by James Taylor in 1970)	RCA 74-0910

DATE	POS	WKS	ARTIST– RECORD TITLE	LABEL & NO.
3/2/74	**4**	10	42. **I've Got A Thing About You Baby/**	
		10	43. Take Good Care Of Her	RCA APBO-0196
			#7 Pop hit for Adam Wade in 1961	
6/29/74	**6**	10	44. **Help Me/**	
		10	45. If You Talk In Your Sleep	RCA APBO-0280
11/23/74+	**9**	9	46. **It's Midnight/**	
		4	47. Promised Land	RCA PB-10074
			#41 Pop hit for Chuck Berry in 1965	
3/1/75	**14**	5	48. My Boy	RCA PB-10191
			#41 Pop hit for Richard Harris in 1972	
6/7/75	**11**	7	49. T-R-O-U-B-L-E	RCA PB-10278
11/22/75	**33**	4	50. Pieces Of My Life	RCA PB-10401
			flip side "Bringing It Back" made #65 on the *Hot 100*	
4/24/76	**6**	10	51. Hurt	RCA PB-10601
			#4 Pop hit for Timi Yuro in 1961	
1/15/77	**1 (1)**	10	52. **Moody Blue/**	
		10	53. She Thinks I Still Care	RCA PB-10857
7/9/77	**1 (1)**	12	● 54. **Way Down/**	
		12	55. Pledging My Love	RCA PB-10998
			#1 R&B hit for Johnny Ace in 1955	
11/26/77+	**2 (1)**	12	● 56. **My Way**	RCA PB-11165
			recorded "live" from Presley's tour; written in 1969 by Paul Anka	
4/8/78	**6**	7	57. **Unchained Melody/**	
			#4 Pop hit for The Righteous Brothers in 1965	
		7	58. Softly, As I Leave You [S]	RCA PB-11212
			Presley talks, with vocal by Sherrill Neilsen;	
			#27 Pop hit for Frank Sinatra in 1964	
5/12/79	**10**	7	59. **Are You Sincere/**	
			#3 Pop hit for Andy Williams in 1958	
		7	60. Solitaire	RCA PB-11533
			#17 Pop hit for the Carpenters in 1975; written by Neil Sedaka	
8/25/79	**6**	7	61. **There's A Honky Tonk Angel (Who Will Take Me Back In)/**	
		7	62. I Got A Feelin' In My Body	RCA PB-11679
1/31/81	**1 (1)**	8	63. **Guitar Man** [R]	RCA PB-12158
			re-mix by Felton Jarvis (died 1/3/81) of Presley's 1968 Pop hit	
5/2/81	**8**	10	64. **Lovin' Arms/**	
			#61 Pop hit for Dobie Gray in 1973	
		10	65. You Asked Me To	RCA PB-12205
12/11/82	**31**	4	66. The Elvis Medley	RCA PB-13351
			Jailhouse Rock/Teddy Bear/Hound Dog/Don't Be Cruel/Burning Love/Suspicious Minds	
			PRICE, David	
			Rodeo rider from Odessa, Texas. Band leader for Red Stegall, 1977-79.	
2/29/64	**29**	4	1. The World Lost A Man	Rice 1001

DATE	POS	WKS	ARTIST– RECORD TITLE	LABEL & NO.
			PRICE, Kenny	
			Born on 5/27/31 in Florence, Kentucky. Died of a heart attack on 8/4/87. In the service, 1952-54, and appeared with the Horace Heidt USO shows in Korea. Worked on WLW-TV *Hometowneers* show and *Midwestern Hayride* in 1957. Appeared on TV's *Hee-Haw* from 1976. Known as "The Round Mound Of Sound."	
9/3/66	7	14	1. **Walking On New Grass**	Boone 1042
1/14/67	7	13	2. **Happy Tracks**	Boone 1051
6/10/67	26	8	3. Pretty Girl, Pretty Clothes, Pretty Sad	Boone 1056
9/30/67	24	9	4. Grass Won't Grow On A Busy Street	Boone 1063
1/6/68	11	11	5. My Goal For Today	Boone 1067
5/11/68	31	6	6. Going Home For The Last Time	Boone 1070
10/5/68	37	2	7. Southern Bound	Boone 1075
2/14/70	17	10	8. Northeast Arkansas Mississippi County Bootlegger	RCA 9787
8/1/70	10	11	9. **Biloxi**	RCA 9869
1/2/71	8	12	10. **The Sheriff Of Boone County**	RCA 9932
10/23/71	38	2	11. Charlotte Fever	RCA 1015
2/26/72	37	2	12. Super Sideman	RCA 0617
10/7/72	24	8	13. Sea Of Heartbreak	RCA 0781
2/9/74	29	4	14. Turn On Your Light (And Let It Shine)	RCA 0198
			PRICE, Ray	
			Born on 1/12/26 in Perryville, Texas; raised in Dallas. In the service, 1944-46, then attended veterinary college. Worked on KRBC-Abilene *Hillbilly Circus* in 1948, and *Big D Jamboree* in Dallas. First recorded for Bullet in 1950. Appeared on the soundtrack of the movie *Honky Tonk Man*. Known as "The Cherokee Cowboy" (also the name of his backing band).	
5/17/52	3	11	1. **Talk To Your Heart** Jockey #3 / Juke Box #6 / Best Seller #10	Columbia 20913
11/8/52	4	9	2. **Don't Let The Stars Get In Your Eyes** Best Seller #4 / Jockey #6 / Juke Box #7; #1 Pop hit for Perry Como in 1953	Columbia 21025
3/6/54	2 (2)	19	3. **I'll Be There (If You Ever Want Me)**/ Best Seller #2 / Jockey #2 / Juke Box #3	
4/10/54	6	13	4. **Release Me** Juke Box #6 / Best Seller #7; #4 Pop hit for Engelbert Humperdinck in 1967	Columbia 21214
6/26/54	13	4	5. Much Too Young To Die Best Seller #13 / Jockey #13	Columbia 21249
10/30/54	8	13	6. **If You Don't, Somebody Else Will** Best Seller #8 / Juke Box #10 / Jockey #14	Columbia 21315
1/7/56	5	11	7. **Run Boy** Jockey #5 / Juke Box #10 / Best Seller #15	Columbia 21474
5/26/56	1 (20)	45	8. **Crazy Arms**/ Jockey #1(20) / Best Seller #1 (11) / Juke Box #1(1)	
6/9/56	7	7	9. **You Done Me Wrong** Jockey #7	Columbia 21510
11/10/56	2 (2)	21	10. **I've Got A New Heartache**/ Jockey #2 / Juke Box #2 / Best Seller #3	
11/17/56	4	21	11. **Wasted Words** Best Seller #4 / Jockey #6 / Juke Box #9	Columbia 21562
6/10/57	12	4	12. I'll Be There (When You Get Lonely) Jockey #12 / Best Seller #13; title also shown as simply "I'll Be There"	Columbia 40889

DATE	POS	WKS	ARTIST– RECORD TITLE	LABEL & NO.
7/29/57	1 (4)	37	13. **My Shoes Keep Walking Back To You** Jockey #1(4) / Best Seller #3	Columbia 40951
3/3/58	3	18	14. **Curtain In The Window/** Jockey #3 / Best Seller #6	
		4	15. It's All Your Fault Best Seller flip	Columbia 41105
7/14/58	1 (13)	34	16. **City Lights/** Hot C&W #1 / Jockey #2	
7/21/58	3	19	17. **Invitation To The Blues** Jockey #3 / Best Seller #8	Columbia 41191
1/5/59	7	19	18. **That's What It's Like To Be Lonesome**	Columbia 41309
5/11/59	2 (1)	40	19. **Heartaches By The Number** #1 Pop hit for Guy Mitchell in 1959	Columbia 41374
10/12/59	1 (2)	30	20. **The Same Old Me/**	
11/23/59	5	15	21. **Under Your Spell Again**	Columbia 41477
4/4/60	2 (8)	27	22. **One More Time**	Columbia 41590
10/3/60	5	17	23. **I Wish I Could Fall In Love Today/**	
10/24/60	23	3	24. I Can't Run Away From Myself	Columbia 41767
3/20/61	5	21	25. **Heart Over Mind/**	
3/27/61	13	11	26. The Twenty-Fourth Hour	Columbia 41947
10/9/61	3	23	27. **Soft Rain/**	
11/13/61	26	2	28. Here We Are Again	Columbia 42132
6/2/62	12	8	29. I've Just Destroyed The World (I'm Living In)/	
6/2/62	22	1	30. Big Shoes	Columbia 42310
9/22/62	5	15	31. **Pride**	Columbia 42518
2/9/63	7	20	32. **Walk Me To The Door/**	
3/2/63	11	16	33. You Took Her Off My Hands (Now Please Take Her Off My Mind)	Columbia 42658
8/10/63	2 (1)	21	34. **Make The World Go Away/**	
10/5/63	28	2	35. Night Life	Columbia 42827
4/4/64	2 (4)	22	36. **Burning Memories/**	
4/4/64	34	3	37. That's All That Matters	Columbia 42971
9/5/64	7	17	38. **Please Talk To My Heart**	Columbia 43086
1/23/65	38	1	39. A Thing Called Sadness	Columbia 43162
5/15/65	2 (2)	22	40. **The Other Woman**	Columbia 43264
12/4/65+	11	13	41. Don't You Ever Get Tired Of Hurting Me	Columbia 43427
4/30/66	7	17	42. **A Way To Survive/**	
6/25/66	28	4	43. I'm Not Crazy Yet	Columbia 43560
10/15/66	3	17	44. **Touch My Heart**	Columbia 43795
4/22/67	9	13	45. **Danny Boy**	Columbia 44042
8/5/67	6	15	46. **I'm Still Not Over You**	Columbia 44195
1/20/68	8	12	47. **Take Me As I Am (Or Let Me Go)**	Columbia 44374
5/18/68	11	13	48. I've Been There Before	Columbia 44505
10/5/68	6	13	49. **She Wears My Ring**	Columbia 44628
4/5/69	11	10	50. Sweetheart Of The Year	Columbia 44761
8/23/69	14	11	51. Raining In My Heart #88 Pop hit for Buddy Holly in 1959	Columbia 44931
12/6/69	14	9	52. April's Fool	Columbia 45005
3/21/70	8	13	53. **You Wouldn't Know Love**	Columbia 45095

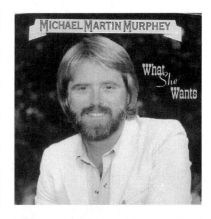

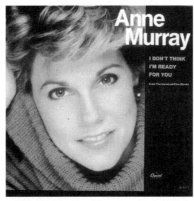

Reba McEntire's hugely successful career began at Mercury Records in 1976. Eight years and six Top 10 hits later, she signed to a new label and released "Just A Little Love," which reached No. 5 and initiated her lengthy stay at MCA Records.

Ronnie Milsap's huge impact on Country music has been deeply felt since the early '70s. Blind since birth, the talented singer/multi-instrumentalist has had a slew of No. 1 hits. "Lost In The Fifties Tonight (In The Still Of The Night)" of 1985 was his 27th.

Michael Martin Murphey began his career as a Pop singer: He was in 1967 Pop group the Lewis & Clarke Expedition, then scored solo hits in the early '70s with such songs as "Geronimo's Cadillac" and "Wildfire." "What She Wants," which reached no. 8 in 1985, was his fifth Top 10 Country hit.

Anne Murray, Nova Scotia-born and popular in both the Pop and Country fields, saw "I Don't Think I'm Ready For You"—her 40th charting Country single—reach No. 7 in 1985. Murray had regularly appeared on Glen Campbell's popular "Goodtime Hour" TV show 15 years earlier.

Willie Nelson's 1968 single "Good Times" was reissued by RCA on the 1981 collection of early Nelson recordings, *Minstrel Man*. The same song would later pop up on the soundtrack to the 1984 Nelson/Kris Kristofferson film *Songwriter*.

Juice Newton's music career climbed both the Country and Pop charts in the early '80s. By the time of her 1985 No. 1 hit "You Make Me Want To Make You Mine," however, the pop crossover had completely faded—and Judy Kay Newton was Country through and through.

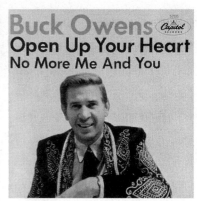

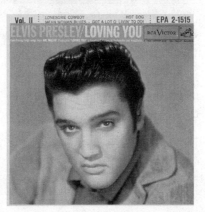

The Oak Ridge Boys' third No. 1 hit, "Trying To Love Two Women," stayed on the charts for a total of 15 weeks—as did its predecessor "Leaving Louisiana In the Daylight," also a No. 1 smash.

Marie Osmond's prior status as a teenybopper queen with brother Donnie by no means affected her level of acceptance to Country fans. "I Only Wanted You," her No. 14 hit of 1986, had followed four consecutive Top 5 singles, three of which had reached No. 1.

Buck Owens's spectacular contribution to Country music—evidenced by 21 No. 1 hits, including 1966's "Open Up Your Heart"—was superbly captured on Rhino Records' memorable 1992 boxed set *The Buck Owens Collection.*

Dolly Parton's 1987 "The River Unbroken" was the singer's first charting single for Columbia Records, with whom she signed after a historic, hit-filled and lengthy stint at RCA.

Stella Parton, younger sister of Dolly, signed with Elektra Records on 1977 and by 1982 was recording for the small Town House label. "I'll Miss You" reached No. 65 in 1982.

Elvis Presley's 1957 EP *Loving You*— from the film of the same name—followed his No. 1 smash "(Let Me Be Your) Teddy Bear," and contained the dual hits "Loving You" and "Mean Woman Blues," which peaked at Nos. 15 and 11 respectively.

DATE	POS	WKS	ARTIST– RECORD TITLE	LABEL & NO.
7/4/70	**1** (1)	19	54. **For The Good Times/**	
		18	55.　Grazin' In Greener Pastures	Columbia 45178
3/27/71	**1** (3)	17	56. **I Won't Mention It Again**	Columbia 45329
8/14/71	**2** (1)	15	57. **I'd Rather Be Sorry**	Columbia 45425
4/29/72	**2** (1)	12	58. **The Lonesomest Lonesome**	Columbia 45583
11/18/72	**1** (3)	14	59. **She's Got To Be A Saint**	Columbia 45724
8/11/73	**1** (1)	14	60. **You're The Best Thing That Ever Happened To Me**	Columbia 45889
			#3 Pop hit for Gladys Knight & The Pips in 1974	
4/13/74	25	8	61.　Storms Of Troubled Times	Columbia 46015
9/14/74	15	6	62.　Like A First Time Thing	Columbia 10006
11/23/74+	**4**	11	63. **Like Old Times Again**	Myrrh 146
3/1/75	**3**	10	64. **Roses And Love Songs**	Myrrh 150
6/28/75	17	7	65.　Farthest Thing From My Mind	ABC 12095
9/20/75	31	4	66.　If You Ever Change Your Mind	Columbia 10150
			above 7 written by Jim Weatherly	
12/20/75	40	1	67.　Say I Do	ABC/Dot 17588
4/24/76	34	4	68.　That's All She Wrote	ABC/Dot 17616
1/8/77	14	9	69.　A Mansion On The Hill	ABC/Dot 17666
5/7/77	38	2	70.　Help Me	Columbia 10503
6/25/77	28	6	71.　Different Kind Of Flower	ABC/Dot 17690
			RAY PRICE AND THE CHEROKEE COWBOYS	
10/22/77	21	6	72.　Born To Love Me	ABC/Dot 17718
			also released on Columbia 10631	
11/25/78+	19	8	73.　Feet	Monument 267
3/31/79	30	5	74.　There's Always Me	Monument 277
			#56 Pop hit for Elvis Presley in 1967	
6/30/79	18	7	75.　That's The Only Way To Say Good Morning	Monument 283
8/23/80	**3**	11	76. **Faded Love**	Columbia 11329
12/27/80+	11	8	77.　Don't You Ever Get Tired (Of Hurting Me)	Columbia 11405
			WILLIE NELSON and RAY PRICE (above 2)	
5/2/81	28	5	78.　Getting Over You Again	Dimension 1018
8/8/81	**6**	10	79. **It Don't Hurt Me Half As Bad**	Dimension 1021
12/5/81+	**9**	11	80. **Diamonds In The Stars**	Dimension 1024
5/1/82	18	8	81.　Forty And Fadin'	Dimension 1031
6/26/82	19	9	82.　Old Friends	Columbia 02681
			ROGER MILLER & WILLIE NELSON (with RAY PRICE)	
			PRIDE, Charley	
			Born on 3/18/38 in Sledge, Mississippi. Played baseball for the Memphis Red Sox in the Negro American League, 1954-56. In service, 1956-58. Worked in construction in Montana and played semi-pro baseball in the Pioneer League. Discovered by Red Sovine in 1963. The most successful black Country performer. CMA Awards: 1971 and 1972 Male Vocalist of the Year; 1971 Entertainer of the Year.	
12/31/66+	**9**	14	1. **Just Between You And Me**	RCA 9000
5/20/67	**6**	14	2. **I Know One**	RCA 9162
9/23/67	**4**	16	3. **Does My Ring Hurt Your Finger**	RCA 9281
			COUNTRY CHARLEY PRIDE (above 3)	
1/27/68	**4**	14	4. **The Day The World Stood Still**	RCA 9403
5/25/68	**2** (2)	14	5. **The Easy Part's Over**	RCA 9514
10/5/68	**4**	13	6. **Let The Chips Fall**	RCA 9622

DATE	POS	WKS	ARTIST–RECORD TITLE	LABEL & NO.
2/15/69	**3**	14	7. Kaw-Liga	RCA 9716
6/21/69	**1 (1)**	16	8. All I Have To Offer You (Is Me)	RCA 0167
11/15/69	**1 (3)**	15	9. (I'm So) Afraid Of Losing You Again	RCA 0265
3/14/70	**1 (2)**	16	10. Is Anybody Goin' To San Antone	RCA 9806
6/20/70	**1 (2)**	15	11. Wonder Could I Live There Anymore	RCA 9855
10/3/70	**1 (2)**	15	12. I Can't Believe That You've Stopped Loving Me	RCA 9902
2/13/71	**1 (3)**	13	13. I'd Rather Love You	RCA 9952
5/15/71	**21**	7	14. Let Me Live	RCA 9974
7/3/71	**1 (4)**	14	15. I'm Just Me	RCA 9996
10/30/71	**1 (5)**	18	● 16. Kiss An Angel Good Mornin'	RCA 0550
2/26/72	**2 (2)**	13	17. All His Children	RCA 0624
			CHARLEY PRIDE with HENRY MANCINI	
			from the movie *Sometimes A Great Notion* starring Paul Newman	
6/10/72	**1 (3)**	14	18. It's Gonna Take A Little Bit Longer	RCA 0707
10/21/72	**1 (3)**	14	19. She's Too Good To Be True	RCA 0802
2/24/73	**1 (1)**	12	20. A Shoulder To Cry On	RCA 0884
			written by Merle Haggard	
5/19/73	**1 (1)**	13	21. Don't Fight The Feelings Of Love	RCA 0942
10/27/73	**1 (1)**	13	22. Amazing Love	RCA 0073
5/11/74	**3**	11	23. We Could	RCA 0257
9/14/74	**3**	14	24. Mississippi Cotton Picking Delta Town	RCA 10030
12/28/74+	**1 (1)**	9	25. Then Who Am I	RCA 10126
4/19/75	**6**	10	26. I Ain't All Bad	RCA 10236
8/23/75	**1 (1)**	11	27. Hope You're Feelin' Me (Like I'm Feelin' You)	RCA 10344
12/20/75+	**3**	11	28. The Happiness Of Having You	RCA 10455
3/27/76	**1 (1)**	10	29. My Eyes Can Only See As Far As You	RCA 10592
9/11/76	**2 (2)**	11	30. A Whole Lotta Things To Sing About	RCA 10757
2/5/77	**1 (1)**	10	31. She's Just An Old Love Turned Memory	RCA 10875
5/28/77	**1 (1)**	12	32. I'll Be Leaving Alone	RCA 10975
9/24/77	**1 (1)**	11	33. More To Me	RCA 11086
2/18/78	**1 (2)**	12	34. Someone Loves You Honey	RCA 11201
7/1/78	**3**	10	35. When I Stop Leaving (I'll Be Gone)	RCA 11287
10/28/78	**2 (3)**	11	36. Burgers And Fries	RCA 11391
3/3/79	**1 (1)**	11	37. Where Do I Put Her Memory	RCA 11477
7/21/79	**1 (1)**	10	38. You're My Jamaica	RCA 11655
11/3/79+	**2 (1)**	12	39. Missin' You	RCA 11751
2/23/80	**1 (1)**	10	40. Honky Tonk Blues	RCA 11912
5/24/80	**1 (1)**	10	41. You Win Again	RCA 12002
10/11/80	**4**	11	42. You Almost Slipped My Mind	RCA 12100
3/21/81	**7**	9	43. Roll On Mississippi	RCA 12178
8/29/81	**1 (2)**	11	44. Never Been So Loved (In All My Life)	RCA 12294
1/16/82	**1 (1)**	11	45. Mountain Of Love	RCA 13014
			#9 Pop hit for Johnny Rivers in 1964	
5/8/82	**2 (2)**	13	46. I Don't Think She's In Love Anymore	RCA 13096
9/11/82	**1 (1)**	12	47. You're So Good When You're Bad	RCA 13293
12/25/82+	**1 (1)**	12	48. Why Baby Why	RCA 13397
3/26/83	**7**	10	49. More And More	RCA 13451
7/9/83	**1 (1)**	13	50. Night Games	RCA 13542
11/5/83+	**2 (1)**	14	51. Ev'ry Heart Should Have One	RCA 13648

DATE	POS	WKS	ARTIST– RECORD TITLE	LABEL & NO.
7/7/84	9	11	52. **The Power Of Love**	RCA 13821
12/8/84	32	4	53. Missin' Mississippi	RCA 13936
5/18/85	25	5	54. Down On The Farm	RCA 14045
8/10/85	34	3	55. Let A Little Love Come In	RCA 14134
4/11/87	14	10	56. Have I Got Some Blues For You	16th Ave. 70400
8/22/87	31	4	57. If You Still Want A Fool Around	16th Ave. 70402
1/16/88	5	13	58. **Shouldn't It Be Easier Than This**	16th Ave. 70408
6/4/88	13	11	59. I'm Gonna Love Her On The Radio	16th Ave. 70414
12/16/89+	28	5	60. Amy's Eyes	16th Ave. 70435
			PROPHET, Ronnie	
			Born on 12/26/43 in Calumet, Quebec. Worked clubs in Ottawa and Montreal in the late '50s. Performed in the Bahamas and Fort Lauderdale in the mid-1960s. Moved to Nashville in 1969; toured with Danny Thomas in 1979. Own TV series in England.	
10/4/75	26	5	1. Sanctuary	RCA 50027
2/7/76	36	3	2. Shine On	RCA 50136
			PRUETT, Jeanne	
			Born Norma Jean Bowman on 1/30/37 in Pell City, Alabama. Moved to Nashville in 1956 with husband Jack Pruett (guitarist for Marty Robbins). Songwriter for Robbins from 1963. On the *Grand Ole Opry* since 1973.	
4/15/72	34	4	1. Love Me	Decca 32929
4/21/73	1 (3)	15	2. **Satin Sheets**	MCA 40015
10/6/73	8	11	3. **I'm Your Woman**	MCA 40116
4/20/74	15	9	4. You Don't Need To Move A Mountain	MCA 40207
10/12/74	22	8	5. Welcome To The Sunshine (Sweet Baby Jane)	MCA 40284
2/15/75	25	7	6. Just Like Your Daddy	MCA 40340
8/30/75	24	7	7. A Poor Man's Woman	MCA 40440
3/19/77	30	3	8. I'm Living A Lie	MCA 40678
12/15/79+	6	11	9. **Back To Back**	IBC 0005
3/29/80	5	11	10. **Temporarily Yours**	IBC 0008
7/26/80	9	8	11. **It's Too Late**	IBC 00010
			PRUITT, Lewis	
			Longtime lead guitarist for Carl Smith.	
12/7/59+	10	21	1. **Timbrook**	Peach 725
6/27/60	4	17	2. **Softly And Tenderly (I'll Hold You In My Arms)**	Decca 31095
4/3/61	11	9	3. Crazy Bullfrog	Decca 31201
			PRYOR, Cactus, And His Pricklypears	
			Richard "Cactus" Pryor, longtime DJ at KTBC-Austin, Texas. Member of the Country Music DJ Hall of Fame.	
6/3/50	7	1	1. **Cry Of The Dying Duck In A Thunder-Storm** [N] Jockey #7	Four Star 1459
			PULLINS, Leroy	
			Born Carl Leroy Pullins on 11/12/40 in Elgin, Illinois.	
7/2/66	18	10	1. I'm A Nut [N]	Kapp 758

DATE	POS	WKS	ARTIST– RECORD TITLE	LABEL & NO.
			PUTMAN, Curly	
			Born Claude Putman, Jr., on 11/20/30 in Princeton, Alabama. Prolific songwriter, wrote "Green Green Grass Of Home" for Tom Jones, "He Stopped Loving Her Today" for George Jones and "My Elusive Dreams" for David Houston and Tammy Wynette.	
2/29/60	23	1	1. The Prison Song	Cherokee 504

R

DATE	POS	WKS	ARTIST– RECORD TITLE	LABEL & NO.
			RABBITT, Eddie	
			Born Edward Thomas Rabbitt on 11/27/44 in Brooklyn; raised in East Orange, New Jersey. Singer/songwriter/guitarist. First recorded for 20th Century in 1964. Moved to Nashville in 1968. Became established after Elvis Presley recorded his song "Kentucky Rain."	
11/9/74	34	3	1. You Get To Me	Elektra 45895
5/3/75	12	9	2. Forgive And Forget	Elektra 45237
9/27/75	11	9	3. I Should Have Married You	Elektra 45269
2/28/76	1 (1)	12	4. **Drinkin' My Baby (Off My Mind)**	Elektra 45301
6/19/76	5	12	5. **Rocky Mountain Music/**	
		12	6. Do You Right Tonight	Elektra 45315
11/20/76+	3	12	7. **Two Dollars In The Jukebox**	Elektra 45357
4/16/77	2 (1)	12	8. **I Can't Help Myself**	Elektra 45390
8/27/77	6	11	9. **We Can't Go On Living Like This**	Elektra 45418
2/25/78	2 (2)	13	10. **Hearts On Fire**	Elektra 45461
6/17/78	1 (1)	10	11. **You Don't Love Me Anymore**	Elektra 45488
9/30/78	1 (1)	11	12. **I Just Want To Love You**	Elektra 45531
12/23/78+	1 (3)	12	13. **Every Which Way But Loose**	Elektra 45554
			title song from the movie starring Clint Eastwood	
6/23/79	1 (1)	10	14. **Suspicions**	Elektra 46053
11/17/79+	5	10	15. **Pour Me Another Tequilla**	Elektra 46558
3/22/80	1 (1)	11	16. **Gone Too Far**	Elektra 46613
6/28/80	1 (1)	12	● 17. **Drivin' My Life Away**	Elektra 46656
			from the movie Roadie starring Meat Loaf	
11/15/80+	1 (1)	12	● 18. **I Love A Rainy Night**	Elektra 47066
8/15/81	1 (1)	11	19. **Step By Step**	Elektra 47174
12/5/81+	1 (1)	12	20. **Someone Could Lose A Heart Tonight**	Elektra 47239
4/17/82	2 (3)	12	21. **I Don't Know Where To Start**	Elektra 47435
10/23/82	1 (1)	12	22. **You And I**	Elektra 69936
			EDDIE RABBITT with CRYSTAL GAYLE	
4/16/83	1 (1)	13	23. **You Can't Run From Love**	Warner 29712
9/17/83	10	9	24. **You Put The Beat In My Heart**	Warner 29512
1/14/84	10	8	25. **Nothing Like Falling In Love**	Warner 29431
5/26/84	3	13	26. **B-B-B-Burnin' Up With Love**	Warner 29279
10/27/84+	1 (1)	14	27. **The Best Year Of My Life**	Warner 29186
3/9/85	4	12	28. **Warning Sign**	Warner 29089
7/27/85	6	12	29. **She's Comin' Back To Say Goodbye**	Warner 28976
11/9/85	10	11	30. **A World Without Love**	RCA 14192

DATE	POS	WKS	ARTIST– RECORD TITLE	LABEL & NO.
4/5/86	4	13	31. **Repetitive Regret**	RCA 14317
8/2/86	1 (1)	14	32. **Both To Each Other (Friends & Lovers)** **EDDIE RABBITT and JUICE NEWTON** #2 Pop hit for Gloria Loring & Carl Anderson in 1986	RCA 14377
11/22/86+	9	13	33. **Gotta Have You**	RCA 5012
1/30/88	1 (1)	14	34. **I Wanna Dance With You**	RCA 5238
6/11/88	1 (1)	14	35. **The Wanderer** #2 Pop hit for Dion in 1961	RCA 8306
10/29/88	7	12	36. **We Must Be Doin' Somethin' Right**	RCA 8716
12/16/89+	1 (2)	24	37. **On Second Thought**	Universal 66025
4/28/90	8	12	38. **Runnin' With The Wind**	Capitol 44538
9/1/90	32	4	39. It's Lonely Out Tonite	Capitol LP Cut
10/6/90	11	11	40. American Boy	Capitol LP Cut

RAE, Lana

Female singer from Oklahoma. Was a runner-up in the Miss Oklahoma beauty pageant.

DATE	POS	WKS	ARTIST– RECORD TITLE	LABEL & NO.
3/25/72	26	8	1. You're My Shoulder To Lean On	Decca 32927

RAINFORD, Tina

Pop singer in Germany.

DATE	POS	WKS	ARTIST– RECORD TITLE	LABEL & NO.
5/21/77	25	6	1. Silver Bird	Epic 50304

RAINWATER, Marvin

Born Marvin Karlton Percy on 7/2/25 in Wichita, Kansas. Worked in logging camps in Oregon. Performed in clubs in Washington, D.C., with Roy Clark in 1953. Appeared on Red Foley's *Ozark Jubilee* in the early '50s. Worked on Arthur Godfrey's TV show in 1955. Marvin is one-quarter Cherokee Indian.

DATE	POS	WKS	ARTIST– RECORD TITLE	LABEL & NO.
4/6/57	3	28	● 1. **Gonna Find Me A Bluebird/** Best Seller #3 / Jockey #3 / Juke Box #5	
		1	2. So You Think You've Got Troubles Best Seller flip	MGM 12412
4/14/58	15	3	3. Whole Lotta Woman Best Seller #15	MGM 12609
9/15/58	11	1	4. Nothin' Needs Nothin' (Like I Need You) Jockey #11	MGM 12701
7/6/59	16	6	5. Half-Breed	MGM 12803

RAKES, Pal

Born Palmer Crawford Rakes III in Tampa, Florida. While a teenager in Philadelphia, played in band with singer Daryl Hall (of Pop duo Hall & Oates).

DATE	POS	WKS	ARTIST– RECORD TITLE	LABEL & NO.
4/30/77	24	6	1. That's When The Lyin' Stops (And The Lovin' Starts)	Warner 8340
8/27/77	31	4	2. 'Til I Can't Take It Anymore	Warner 8416

RAMBLING ROGUE, The

Nickname of songwriter/publisher/producer/executive Fred Rose. Born on 8/24/1897 in Evansville, Indiana. Died on 12/1/54. First recorded for Brunswick in the 1920s. In 1942, formed Acuff-Rose music publishing company with Roy Acuff; they also formed the Hickory label in 1953. One of first three elected to the Country Music Hall of Fame.

DATE	POS	WKS	ARTIST– RECORD TITLE	LABEL & NO.
10/27/45	5	1	1. **Tender Hearted Sue**	Okeh 6747

DATE	POS	WKS	ARTIST– RECORD TITLE	LABEL & NO.
			RANDALL, Jon—see MORGAN, Lorrie	
			RANEY, Wayne	
			Born on 8/17/21 in Wolf Bayou, Arkansas. Died on 1/23/93 of cancer. Harmonica wizard; worked with the Raney Family gospel singers and the Delmore Brothers in the late '40s.	
10/30/48	11	1	1. Lost John Boogie Juke Box #11 / Best Seller #14	King 719
11/20/48	13	2	2. Jack And Jill Boogie Juke Box #13	King 732
7/30/49	1 (3)	22	3. **Why Don't You Haul Off And Love Me** Juke Box #1(3) / Best Seller #1(2) / Jockey #5	King 791
			RAVEN, Eddy	
			Born Edward Garvin Futch on 8/19/44 in Lafayette, Louisiana. Performed with blues rockers Johnny and Edgar Winter and the Rocking Cajuns. First recorded for Cosmos in 1962. Toured with the Jimmie Davis Band. Moved to Nashville in 1970; worked as a staff writer for Acuff-Rose.	
5/24/75	27	5	1. Good News, Bad News	ABC 12083
1/17/76	34	5	2. Free To Be	ABC/Dot 17595
4/5/80	25	6	3. Dealin' With The Devil	Dimension 1005
7/12/80	30	4	4. You've Got Those Eyes	Dimension 1007
10/25/80	34	3	5. Another Texas Song	Dimension 1011
2/7/81	23	7	6. Peace Of Mind	Dimension 1017
6/13/81	13	9	7. I Should've Called	Elektra 47136
11/14/81+	11	12	8. Who Do You Know In California	Elektra 47216
3/13/82	14	11	9. A Little Bit Crazy	Elektra 47413
7/10/82	10	9	10. **She's Playing Hard To Forget**	Elektra 47469
12/18/82+	25	7	11. San Antonio Nights	Elektra 69929
4/7/84	1 (1)	13	12. **I Got Mexico**	RCA 13746
8/11/84	9	11	13. **I Could Use Another You**	RCA 13839
12/8/84+	9	12	14. **She's Gonna Win Your Heart**	RCA 13939
5/11/85	9	11	15. **Operator, Operator**	RCA 14044
8/24/85	8	12	16. **I Wanna Hear It From You**	RCA 14164
1/11/86	3	12	17. **You Should Have Been Gone By Now**	RCA 14250
6/21/86	3	14	18. **Sometimes A Lady**	RCA 14319
12/6/86+	3	15	19. **Right Hand Man**	RCA 5032
4/11/87	3	13	20. **You're Never Too Old For Young Love**	RCA 5128
8/15/87	1 (1)	13	21. **Shine, Shine, Shine**	RCA 5221
2/27/88	1 (1)	14	22. **I'm Gonna Get You**	RCA 6831
7/2/88	1 (1)	15	23. **Joe Knows How To Live**	RCA 8303
12/24/88+	4	13	24. **'Til You Cry**	RCA 8798
5/6/89	1 (1)	14	25. **In A Letter To You**	Universal 66003
9/2/89	1 (1)	14	26. **Bayou Boys**	Universal 66016
1/27/90	6	13	27. **Sooner Or Later** originally released on Universal 66029	Capitol 44528
5/26/90	10	10	28. **Island**	Capitol 44537

DATE	POS	WKS	ARTIST– RECORD TITLE	LABEL & NO.
			RAYE, Collin	
			Born Floyd Collin Wray on 8/22/59 in DeQueen, Arkansas. Was "Bubba" Wray in The Wrays.	
8/3/91	29	6	1. All I Can Be (Is A Sweet Memory)	Epic 73831
11/9/91+	1 (3)	17	2. **Love, Me**	Epic 74051
3/21/92	2 (1)	17	3. **Every Second**	Epic 74242
8/8/92	1 (2)	19	4. **In This Life**	Epic 74421
12/26/92+	7	17	5. **I Want You Bad (And That Ain't Good)**	Epic 74786
5/1/93	5	14	6. **Somebody Else's Moon**	Epic 74912
9/11/93	4	15	7. **That Was A River**	Epic 77118
1/1/94	6	15	8. **That's My Story** co-written by Lee Roy Parnell	Epic 77308
4/30/94	2 (1)	17	9. **Little Rock**	Epic 77436
8/27/94	8	14	10. **Man Of My Word**	Epic 77632
12/17/94+	1 (1)	18	11. **My Kind Of Girl**	Epic 77773
4/29/95	4	16	12. **If I Were You**	Epic 77859
8/5/95	2 (2)	16	13. **One Boy, One Girl**	Epic 77973
12/16/95+	3	16	14. **Not That Different**	Epic 78189
3/30/96	3	17	15. **I Think About You**	Epic 78238
			RAYE, Susan	
			Born on 10/8/44 in Eugene, Oregon. Appeared on the TV show *Hoedown* in Portland. Worked with Buck Owens, 1968-76, and on the TV series *Hee-Haw* from 1969. Appeared in the movie *From Nashville With Music* 1971.	
2/7/70	30	7	1. Put A Little Love In Your Heart #4 Pop hit for Jackie DeShannon in 1969	Capitol 2701
3/7/70	13	9	2. We're Gonna Get Together	Capitol 2731
5/16/70	12	10	3. Togetherness **BUCK OWENS & SUSAN RAYE (above 2)**	Capitol 2791
7/25/70	35	4	4. One Night Stand	Capitol 2833
9/12/70	8	11	5. **The Great White Horse** **BUCK OWENS & SUSAN RAYE**	Capitol 2871
12/5/70+	10	8	6. **Willy Jones**	Capitol 2950
3/13/71	9	11	7. **L.A. International Airport**	Capitol 3035
7/31/71	6	13	8. **Pitty, Pitty, Patter**	Capitol 3129
11/20/71+	3	13	9. **(I've Got A) Happy Heart**	Capitol 3209
6/10/72	10	10	10. **My Heart Has A Mind Of Its Own** #1 Pop hit for Connie Francis in 1960	Capitol 3327
8/5/72	13	11	11. Looking Back To See **BUCK OWENS & SUSAN RAYE**	Capitol 3368
10/14/72	16	9	12. Wheel Of Fortune #1 Pop hit for Kay Starr in 1952	Capitol 3438
1/13/73	17	11	13. Love Sure Feels Good In My Heart	Capitol 3499
4/28/73	18	9	14. Cheating Game	Capitol 3569
7/21/73	35	2	15. The Good Old Days (Are Here Again) **BUCK OWENS & SUSAN RAYE**	Capitol 3601
9/29/73	23	7	16. Plastic Trains, Paper Planes	Capitol 3699
5/4/74	18	9	17. Stop The World (And Let Me Off)	Capitol 3850
1/4/75	9	8	18. **Whatcha Gonna Do With A Dog Like That**	Capitol 3980

DATE	POS	WKS	ARTIST– RECORD TITLE	LABEL & NO.
8/2/75	20	7	19. Love Is Strange **BUCK OWENS & SUSAN RAYE** #11 Pop hit for Mickey & Sylvia in 1957	Capitol 4100

REED, Jerry

Born Jerry Reed Hubbard on 3/20/37 in Atlanta. Accomplished actor. First recorded for Capitol in 1955. Did guitar session work in Nashville in the early '60s. Worked on the TV series *Glen Campbell's Goodtime Hour* in the early '70s. Appeared in the movies *W.W. and the Dixie Dancekings, Smokey and the Bandit I, II & III, Gator, Hot Stuff* and *Bat 21*. Own TV series *Concrete Cowboys*. Married to Priscilla Mitchell. Appeared on the TV series *Nashville 99*. Elected to the Georgia Music Hall of Fame in 1986.

DATE	POS	WKS	ARTIST– RECORD TITLE	LABEL & NO.
12/9/67+	15	9	1. Tupelo Mississippi Flash	RCA 9334
5/18/68	14	10	2. Remembering	RCA 9493
5/3/69	20	6	3. There's Better Things In Life	RCA 0124
9/20/69	11	10	4. Are You From Dixie (Cause I'm From Dixie Too)	RCA 0211
3/21/70	14	10	5. Talk About The Good Times	RCA 9804
8/29/70	16	7	6. Georgia Sunshine	RCA 9870
11/14/70	16	10	● 7. Amos Moses/ [N]	
		10	8. The Preacher And The Bear	RCA 9904
5/22/71	1 (5)	13	9. **When You're Hot, You're Hot** [N]	RCA 9976
9/18/71	11	11	10. Ko-Ko Joe	RCA 1011
2/12/72	27	4	11. Another Puff [N]	RCA 0613
4/22/72	24	7	12. Smell The Flowers	RCA 0667
8/12/72	22	8	13. Alabama Wild Man [R] originally hit #48 in 1968 on RCA 9623	RCA 0738
1/13/73	18	6	14. You Took All The Ramblin' Out Of Me	RCA 0857
6/9/73	1 (1)	13	15. **Lord, Mr. Ford** [N]	RCA 0960
1/19/74	25	5	16. The Uptown Poker Club	RCA 0194
3/2/74	13	6	17. The Crude Oil Blues [N]	RCA 0224
6/8/74	12	7	18. A Good Woman's Love	RCA 0273
1/11/75	18	6	19. Let's Sing Our Song	RCA 10132
3/26/77	19	7	20. Semolita	RCA 10893
8/27/77	2 (2)	12	21. **East Bound And Down/** from the movie *Smokey and the Bandit* starring Burt Reynolds	
		11	22. (I'm Just A) Redneck In A Rock And Roll Bar	RCA 11056
1/21/78	20	6	23. You Know What **JERRY REED and SEIDINA (Reed's daughter)**	RCA 11164
4/29/78	39	1	24. Sweet Love Feelings	RCA 11232
6/24/78	10	9	25. **(I Love You) What Can I Say/**	
		6	26. High Rollin' from the movie *High-Ballin'* starring Reed	RCA 11281
11/25/78+	14	8	27. Gimme Back My Blues	RCA 11407
3/17/79	18	6	28. Second-Hand Satin Lady (And A Bargain Basement Boy)	RCA 11472
7/7/79	40	2	29. (Who Was The Man Who Put) The Line In Gasoline [N]	RCA 11638
12/22/79+	12	8	30. Sugar Foot Rag	RCA 11764
4/26/80	36	4	31. Age/	
		4	32. Workin' At The Carwash Blues #32 Pop hit for Jim Croce in 1974	RCA 11944
10/4/80	26	5	33. Texas Bound And Flyin' from the movie *Smokey and the Bandit II* starring Burt Reynolds	RCA 12083

DATE	POS	WKS	ARTIST– RECORD TITLE	LABEL & NO.
10/31/81	30	4	34. Patches *#4 Pop hit for Clarence Carter in 1970*	RCA 12318
5/22/82	32	4	35. The Man With The Golden Thumb	RCA 13081
7/24/82	**1** (2)	12	36. **She Got The Goldmine (I Got The Shaft)** [N]	RCA 13268
11/6/82	**2** (3)	10	37. **The Bird** [N] **JERRY REED and Friends** *impressions of Willie Nelson's "Whiskey River" & "On The Road Again" and George Jones's "He Stopped Loving Her Today"*	RCA 13355
2/19/83	13	9	38. Down On The Corner *#3 Pop hit for Creedence Clearwater Revival in 1969*	RCA 13422
6/18/83	16	9	39. Good Ole Boys/	
		9	40. She's Ready For Someone To Love Her	RCA 13527
9/3/83	20	6	41. Hold On, I'm Comin' **WAYLON JENNINGS & JERRY REED** *#21 Pop hit for Sam & Dave in 1966*	RCA 13580

REEVES, Del

Born Franklin Delano Reeves on 7/14/33 in Sparta, North Carolina. Own radio show at age 12. Appeared on the *Chester Smith Show* and own TV shows in California in the late '50s. Moved to Nashville in 1966. Member of the *Grand Ole Opry* since 1966. Own TV show, *Country Carnival*. Appeared in the movies *Second Fiddle To A Steel Guitar*, *Sam Whiskey*, *Cotton Pickin' Chicken-Pluckers* and *Forty-Acre Feud*.

DATE	POS	WKS	ARTIST– RECORD TITLE	LABEL & NO.
11/6/61	9	17	1. **Be Quiet Mind**	Decca 31307
10/27/62	11	11	2. He Stands Real Tall	Decca 31417
4/27/63	13	14	3. The Only Girl I Can't Forget	Reprise 20158
3/27/65	**1** (2)	18	4. **Girl On The Billboard**	United Art. 824
8/21/65	4	16	5. **The Belles Of Southern Bell**	United Art. 890
12/11/65+	9	12	6. **Women Do Funny Things To Me**	United Art. 940
7/9/66	37	3	7. Gettin' Any Feed For Your Chickens	United Art. 50035
11/26/66	27	6	8. This Must Be The Bottom	United Art. 50081
7/15/67	33	5	9. The Private	United Art. 50157
10/28/67	12	15	10. A Dime At A Time	United Art. 50210
4/20/68	18	8	11. Wild Blood	United Art. 50270
8/24/68	5	13	12. **Looking At The World Through A Windshield**	United Art. 50332
1/11/69	3	15	13. **Good Time Charlies** *title also shown as "Good Time Charlie's"*	United Art. 50487
5/31/69	5	13	14. **Be Glad**	United Art. 50531
10/25/69	12	9	15. There Wouldn't Be A Lonely Heart In Town	United Art. 50564
11/22/69	31	3	16. Take A Little Good Will Home **BOBBY GOLDSBORO & DEL REEVES**	United Art. 50591
2/21/70	14	9	17. A Lover's Question **DEL REEVES and The Goodtime Charlies** *#6 Pop hit for Clyde McPhatter in 1959*	United Art. 50622
6/27/70	20	7	18. Land Mark Tavern **DEL REEVES & PENNY DeHAVEN**	United Art. 50669
10/31/70	22	5	19. Right Back Loving You Again	United Art. 50714
1/30/71	30	5	20. Bar Room Talk	United Art. 50743
5/15/71	33	5	21. Working Like The Devil (For The Lord)	United Art. 50763
7/17/71	9	11	22. **The Philadelphia Fillies**	United Art. 50802
12/4/71	31	3	23. A Dozen Pairs Of Boots	United Art. 50840
2/26/72	29	6	24. The Best Is Yet To Come	United Art. 50877

DATE	POS	WKS	ARTIST– RECORD TITLE	LABEL & NO.
11/3/73	**22**	6	25. Lay A Little Lovin' On Me	United Art. 308
5/29/76	**29**	5	26. On The Rebound	United Art. 797
			DEL REEVES & BILLIE JO SPEARS	

REEVES, Jim

Born James Travis Reeves on 8/20/24 in Panola County, Texas. Killed in a plane crash on 7/31/64 in Nashville. Aspirations of a professional baseball career cut short by an ankle injury. DJ at KWKH-Shreveport, Louisiana, home of the *Louisiana Hayride*, early '50s. First recorded for Macy's in 1950. Joined *Hayride* cast in 1953. Joined the *Grand Ole Opry* in 1955. Own ABN-Radio series in 1957. Appeared in the 1963 movie *Kimberley Jim*. Elected to the Country Music Hall of Fame in 1967.

DATE	POS	WKS	ARTIST– RECORD TITLE	LABEL & NO.
3/28/53	**1** (9)	26	1. **Mexican Joe** **JIM REEVES and The Circle O Ranch Boys** Juke Box #1(9) / Jockey #1(7) / Best Seller #1(6)	Abbott 116
12/5/53+	**1** (3)	21	2. **Bimbo** Jockey #1 / Best Seller #2 / Juke Box #2	Abbott 148
1/9/54	**3**	22	3. **I Love You** **GINNY WRIGHT/JIM REEVES** Jockey #3 / Juke Box #7 / Best Seller #8	Fabor 101
6/26/54	**15**	1	4. Then I'll Stop Loving You Jockey #15	Abbott 160
10/23/54+	**5**	12	5. **Penny Candy** **JIM REEVES with The Louisiana Hayride Band** Juke Box #5 / Jockey #8	Abbott 170
4/30/55	**9**	1	6. **Drinking Tequila** Juke Box #9	Abbott 178
8/20/55	**4**	20	7. **Yonder Comes A Sucker/** Juke Box #4 / Jockey #6 / Best Seller #8	
		2	8. I'm Hurtin' Inside Juke Box flip	RCA 6200
6/23/56	**8**	13	9. **My Lips Are Sealed** Jockey #8 / Juke Box #8 / Best Seller #10	RCA 6517
9/29/56	**4**	19	10. **According To My Heart/** Jockey #4 / Best Seller #9 / Juke Box #10	
		1	11. The Mother Of A Honky Tonk Girl Best Seller flip	RCA 6620
1/12/57	**3**	18	12. **Am I Losing You/** Jockey #3 / Juke Box #5 / Best Seller #8	
		5	13. Waitin' For A Train Juke Box flip	RCA 6749
4/29/57	**1** (8)	26	14. **Four Walls** Jockey #1 / Best Seller #2 / Juke Box #4	RCA 6874
8/19/57	**9**	6	15. **Two Shadows On Your Window/** Jockey #9	
8/26/57	**12**	1	16. Young Hearts Best Seller #12 / Jockey #14	RCA 6973
12/2/57+	**3**	18	17. **Anna Marie** Jockey #3 / Best Seller #10	RCA 7070
5/12/58	**8**	7	18. **I Love You More/** Jockey #8 / Best Seller #14	
4/21/58	**10**	3	19. Overnight Jockey #10	RCA 7171
7/14/58	**2** (3)	22	20. **Blue Boy** Jockey #2 / Best Seller #4	RCA 7266

DATE	POS	WKS	ARTIST– RECORD TITLE	LABEL & NO.
11/10/58+	**1 (5)**	25	21. **Billy Bayou/** *written by Roger Miller*	
11/17/58+	18	7	22. I'd Like To Be	RCA 7380
3/30/59	**2 (4)**	20	23. **Home**	RCA 7479
7/27/59	**5**	16	24. **Partners/**	
8/17/59	17	7	25. I'm Beginning To Forget You	RCA 7557
12/7/59+	**1 (14)**	34	● 26. **He'll Have To Go**	RCA 7643
7/18/60	**3**	18	27. **I'm Gettin' Better/**	
7/25/60	**6**	16	28. **I Know One**	RCA 7756
10/31/60	**3**	25	29. **I Missed Me/**	
11/21/60	**8**	14	30. **Am I Losing You** [R]	RCA 7800
3/27/61	**4**	12	31. **The Blizzard**	RCA 7855
7/17/61	15	11	32. What Would You Do?/	
10/2/61	16	6	33. Stand At Your Window	RCA 7905
12/11/61+	**2 (2)**	21	34. **Losing Your Love/**	
12/11/61+	7	16	35. **(How Can I Write On Paper) What I Feel In My Heart**	RCA 7950
5/26/62	**2 (9)**	21	36. **Adios Amigo/**	
5/19/62	20	3	37. A Letter To My Heart	RCA 8019
9/1/62	**2 (3)**	21	38. **I'm Gonna Change Everything/**	
9/8/62	18	3	39. Pride Goes Before A Fall	RCA 8080
2/9/63	**3**	23	40. **Is This Me?** *written by Dottie West*	RCA 8127
7/13/63	**3**	18	41. **Guilty/**	
7/27/63	11	18	42. Little Ole You	RCA 8193
1/25/64	**2 (2)**	26	43. **Welcome To My World**	RCA 8289
3/28/64	7	18	44. **Love Is No Excuse** **JIM REEVES & DOTTIE WEST** *flip side "Look Who's Talking" Bubbled Under at #121*	RCA 8324
7/18/64	**1 (7)**	24	45. **I Guess I'm Crazy**	RCA 8383
11/28/64+	**3**	19	46. **I Won't Forget You**	RCA 8461
3/6/65	**1 (3)**	22	47. **This Is It**	RCA 8508
8/7/65	**1 (3)**	19	48. **Is It Really Over?**	RCA 8625
1/15/66	**2 (3)**	16	49. **Snow Flake**	RCA 8719
4/9/66	**1 (4)**	19	50. **Distant Drums**	RCA 8789
8/13/66	**1 (1)**	19	51. **Blue Side Of Lonesome**	RCA 8902
2/11/67	**1 (1)**	12	52. **I Won't Come In While He's There**	RCA 9057
7/15/67	16	12	53. The Storm	RCA 9238
11/25/67+	**9**	13	54. **I Heard A Heart Break Last Night**	RCA 9343
3/23/68	**9**	11	55. **That's When I See The Blues (In Your Pretty Brown Eyes)**	RCA 9455
9/21/68	**7**	15	56. **When You Are Gone**	RCA 9614
5/3/69	**6**	11	57. **When Two Worlds Collide**	RCA 0135
12/20/69+	**10**	11	58. **Nobody's Fool/**	
		11	59. Why Do I Love You (Melody of Love) [S] *#2 Pop hit for Billy Vaughn in 1955*	RCA 0286
8/22/70	**4**	14	60. **Angels Don't Lie**	RCA 9880
5/1/71	16	8	61. Gypsy Feet	RCA 9969
2/26/72	15	8	62. The Writing's On The Wall	RCA 0626

DATE	POS	WKS	ARTIST– RECORD TITLE	LABEL & NO.
8/12/72	**8**	14	63. **Missing You** #29 Pop hit for Ray Peterson in 1961	RCA 0744
6/30/73	**12**	10	64. Am I That Easy To Forget #25 Pop hit for Debbie Reynolds in 1960	RCA 0963
6/1/74	**19**	5	65. I'd Fight The World	RCA 0255
5/14/77	**14**	8	66. It's Nothin' To Me	RCA 10956
9/17/77	**23**	6	67. Little Ole Dime	RCA 11060
2/25/78	**29**	5	68. You're The Only Good Thing (That's Happened to Me)	RCA 11187
7/7/79	**10**	8	69. **Don't Let Me Cross Over**	RCA 11564
11/17/79+	**6**	11	70. **Oh, How I Miss You Tonight**	RCA 11737
5/3/80	**10**	10	71. **Take Me In Your Arms And Hold Me** **JIM REEVES/DEBORAH ALLEN (above 3)**	RCA 11946
12/27/80+	**35**	3	72. There's Always Me #56 Pop hit for Elvis Presley in 1967	RCA 12118
11/28/81+	**5**	11	73. **Have You Ever Been Lonely (Have You Ever Been Blue)** **JIM REEVES and PATSY CLINE** Cline and Reeves never recorded together; their voices were spliced together electronically	RCA 12346
			REID, Mike	
			Born on 5/24/47 in Altoona, Pennsylvania. Former professional football player. First-round draft pick of the Cincinnati Bengals, AFC/NFL Defensive Rookie of the Year, and NFL All-Pro. During the off-season, classical pianist with the Cincinnati, Dallas, San Antonio and Utah symphonies. Grammy-winning songwriter. Hits recorded by Ronnie Milsap, Bonnie Raitt, Barbara Mandrell and others.	
3/19/88	**2** (1)	13	1. **Old Folks** **RONNIE MILSAP & MIKE REID**	RCA 6896
12/15/90+	**1** (2)	17	2. **Walk On Faith**	Columbia 73623
4/20/91	**17**	12	3. Till You Were Gone	Columbia 73736
8/17/91	**14**	12	4. As Simple As That	Columbia 73888
12/7/91+	**23**	12	5. I'll Stop Loving You	Columbia 74102
			REMINGTONS, The	
			Trio of pop veterans Jimmy Griffin (Bread), and Richard Mainegra and Rick Yancey (both of Cymarron). Griffin was also a member of Black Tie. Mainegra wrote songs for Reba McEntire and others. Yancey left in 1992, replaced by Denny Henson.	
11/9/91+	**10**	13	1. **A Long Time Ago**	BNA 62063
4/11/92	**33**	5	2. I Could Love You (With My Eyes Closed)	BNA 62201
7/18/92	**18**	8	3. Two-Timin' Me	BNA 62276
			RENO, Jack	
			Born on 11/30/35 in Bloomfield, Iowa. Prominent DJ. Worked on KCOG-Centerville at age 16. Appeared on the *Ozark Jubilee* in 1955. DJ on many stations since 1958.	
1/13/68	**10**	12	1. **Repeat After Me**	JAB 9009
11/23/68+	**19**	11	2. I Want One	Dot 17169
6/14/69	**34**	6	3. I'm A Good Man (In A Bad Frame Of Mind)	Dot 17233
10/18/69	**22**	5	4. We All Go Crazy	Dot 17293
10/30/71	**12**	10	5. Hitchin' A Ride #5 Pop hit for Vanity Fare in 1970	Target 0137

DATE	POS	WKS	ARTIST–RECORD TITLE	LABEL & NO.
3/4/72	26	7	6. Heartaches By The Numbers	Target 0141
7/15/72	38	2	7. Do You Want To Dance	Target 0150
			#5 Pop hit for Bobby Freeman in 1958	

RENO & SMILEY

Duo of Don Reno and Red Smiley. Also recorded as Chick & His Hot Rods.

DATE	POS	WKS	ARTIST–RECORD TITLE	LABEL & NO.
5/29/61	14	10	1. Don't Let Your Sweet Love Die	King 5469
8/28/61	23	5	2. Love Oh Love, Oh Please Come Home	King 5520
9/18/61	27	2	3. Jimmy Caught The Dickens (Pushing Ernest In The Tub) [N] **CHICK & HIS HOT RODS**	King 5537

RESTLESS HEART

Group from Nashville consisting of former session musicians Larry Stewart (lead vocals, guitar, keyboards), Dave Innis (guitar, keyboards), Greg Jennings (guitar), Paul Gregg (bass) and John Dittrich (drums). Stewart went solo in early 1992. Innis left in early 1993. The remaining three continued with two backing musicians.

DATE	POS	WKS	ARTIST–RECORD TITLE	LABEL & NO.
3/2/85	23	7	1. Let The Heartache Ride	RCA 13969
6/22/85	10	12	2. **I Want Everyone To Cry**	RCA 14086
11/16/85+	7	12	3. **(Back to the) Heartbreak Kid**	RCA 14190
4/12/86	10	11	4. **Til I Loved You**	RCA 14292
8/30/86	1 (1)	14	5. **That Rock Won't Roll**	RCA 14376
1/10/87	1 (1)	13	6. **I'll Still Be Loving You**	RCA 5065
6/13/87	1 (1)	14	7. **Why Does It Have To Be (Wrong or Right)**	RCA 5132
11/21/87+	1 (1)	14	8. **Wheels**	RCA 5280
6/4/88	1 (1)	14	9. **Bluest Eyes In Texas**	RCA 8386
10/8/88	1 (1)	14	10. **A Tender Lie**	RCA 8714
3/11/89	3	13	11. **Big Dreams In A Small Town**	RCA 8816
8/5/89	4	14	12. **Say What's In Your Heart**	RCA 9034
1/6/90	4	18	13. **Fast Movin' Train**	RCA 9115
5/12/90	5	14	14. **Dancy's Dream**	RCA 2503
9/22/90	21	8	15. When Somebody Loves You	RCA 2663
1/12/91	16	15	16. Long Lost Friend	RCA 2709
11/2/91+	3	18	17. **You Can Depend On Me**	RCA 62129
4/11/92	40	2	18. Familiar Pain	RCA 62054
10/10/92	9	16	19. **When She Cries**	RCA 62412
2/13/93	13	12	20. Mending Fences	RCA 62419
6/19/93	11	12	21. We Got The Love	RCA 62510

RICE, Bill

Producer/songwriter from Gallo, Arkansas. Teamed with Jerry Foster.

DATE	POS	WKS	ARTIST–RECORD TITLE	LABEL & NO.
4/10/71	33	5	1. Travelin' Minstrel Man	Capitol 3049

RICE, Bobby G.

Born Robert Gene Rice on 7/13/44 in Boscobel, Wisconsin. Plays guitar and banjo. Made professional debut at age five. His family operated the Circle D Dance Hall, and family band worked on WRCO-Richmond, Wisconsin, for seven years. Worked in duo with sister Lorraine in 1964, then had own band.

DATE	POS	WKS	ARTIST– RECORD TITLE	LABEL & NO.
5/16/70	32	4	1. Sugar Shack #1 Pop hit for Jimmy Gilmer & The Fireballs in 1963	Royal Amer. 6
9/12/70	35	5	2. Hey Baby #1 Pop hit for Bruce Channel in 1962	Royal Amer. 18
6/26/71	20	9	3. Mountain Of Love #9 Pop hit for Johnny Rivers in 1964	Royal Amer. 32
1/22/72	33	6	4. Suspicion #3 Pop hit for Terry Stafford in 1964	Royal Amer. 48
2/3/73	3	10	5. **You Lay So Easy On My Mind**	Metromedia 902
6/2/73	8	11	6. **You Give Me You**	Metromedia 0107
10/20/73	13	9	7. The Whole World's Making Love Again Tonight	Metromedia 0075
11/30/74	30	4	8. Make It Feel Like Love Again	GRT 009
2/8/75	9	9	9. **Write Me A Letter**	GRT 014
5/31/75	10	9	10. **Freda Comes, Freda Goes**	GRT 021
2/7/76	35	3	11. Pick Me Up On Your Way Down	GRT 036
12/2/78	30	5	12. The Softest Touch In Town	Republic 031

RICH, Charlie

Born on 12/14/32 in Colt, Arkansas. Died of an acute blood clot on 7/25/95. Rockabilly-Country singer/pianist/songwriter. First played jazz and blues. Own jazz group, the Velvetones, mid-1950s, while in U.S. Air Force. Session work with Sun Records in 1958. Known as "The Silver Fox." CMA Awards: 1973 Male Vocalist of the Year; 1974 Entertainer of the Year.

DATE	POS	WKS	ARTIST– RECORD TITLE	LABEL & NO.
12/5/70	37	2	1. Nice 'N' Easy [R] originally "Bubbled Under" at #131 in 1964 on Groove 0041; #60 Pop hit for Frank Sinatra in 1964	Epic 10662
1/15/72	35	5	2. A Part Of Your Life	Epic 10809
9/30/72	6	12	3. **I Take It On Home**	Epic 10867
3/10/73	1 (2)	16	● 4. **Behind Closed Doors** CMA Award: Single of the Year	Epic 10950
8/18/73	29	6	5. Tomorrow Night	RCA 0983
10/13/73	1 (3)	14	● 6. **The Most Beautiful Girl**	Epic 11040
1/12/74	1 (2)	14	7. **There Won't Be Anymore**	RCA 0195
3/16/74	1 (3)	11	8. **A Very Special Love Song**	Epic 11091
5/18/74	1 (1)	9	9. **I Don't See Me In Your Eyes Anymore**	RCA 0260
7/20/74	23	6	10. A Field Of Yellow Daisies	Mercury 73498
8/31/74	1 (1)	10	11. **I Love My Friend**	Epic 20006
10/26/74	1 (1)	10	12. **She Called Me Baby**	RCA 10062
2/22/75	3	8	13. **My Elusive Dreams**	Epic 50064
5/10/75	23	6	14. It's All Over Now originally released as the B-side of #7 above	RCA 10256
6/21/75	3	10	15. **Every Time You Touch Me (I Get High)**	Epic 50103
9/27/75	4	12	16. **All Over Me**	Epic 50142
1/10/76	10	8	17. **Since I Fell For You** #4 Pop hit for Lenny Welch in 1963	Epic 50182
5/15/76	22	6	18. America, The Beautiful (1976)	Epic 50222
10/2/76	27	4	19. Road Song	Epic 50268
2/5/77	24	6	20. My Mountain Dew Charlie's RCA and Mercury hits were recorded 1963-66	RCA 10859
2/26/77	12	8	21. Easy Look	Epic 50328
6/18/77	1 (2)	13	22. **Rollin' With The Flow**	Epic 50392

DATE	POS	WKS	ARTIST– RECORD TITLE	LABEL & NO.
4/22/78	8	9	23. Puttin' In Overtime At Home	United Art. 1193
7/15/78	10	8	24. Beautiful Woman	Epic 50562
10/14/78	1 (1)	10	25. On My Knees	Epic 50616
			CHARLIE RICH with JANIE FRICKE	
1/6/79	3	10	26. I'll Wake You Up When I Get Home	Elektra 45553
			from the movie *Every Which Way But Loose* starring Clint Eastwood	
4/7/79	26	5	27. I Lost My Head	United Art. 1280
6/9/79	20	7	28. Spanish Eyes	Epic 50701
			#15 Pop hit for Al Martino in 1966	
12/15/79+	22	7	29. You're Gonna Love Yourself In The Morning	United Art. 1325
10/25/80	12	8	30. A Man Just Don't Know What A Woman Goes Through	Elektra 47047
3/14/81	26	4	31. Are We Dreamin' The Same Dream	Elektra 47104

RICHARDS, Earl

Born Henry Earl Sinks in Amarillo. Owned Ace of Hearts label.

DATE	POS	WKS	ARTIST– RECORD TITLE	LABEL & NO.
10/25/69	39	1	1. The House Of Blue Lights	United Art. 50561
			#9 Pop hit for Chuck Miller in 1955	
2/24/73	23	6	2. Margie, Who's Watching The Baby	Ace of Hearts 0461
			#115 Pop hit for R.B. Greaves in 1972	

RICHARDS, Sue

Born in Muscle Shoals. Sang in family gospel group from age four. Recorded for Sun at age 11. Later worked with her daughters as backup vocalists for Tammy Wynette.

DATE	POS	WKS	ARTIST– RECORD TITLE	LABEL & NO.
10/11/75	32	5	1. Tower Of Strength	ABC/Dot 17572
			#5 Pop hit for Gene McDaniels in 1961	
2/21/76	25	5	2. Sweet Sensuous Feelings	ABC/Dot 17600

RICHIE, Lionel

Born on 6/20/49 in Tuskegee, Alabama. Former lead singer of R&B-pop group the Commodores.

DATE	POS	WKS	ARTIST– RECORD TITLE	LABEL & NO.
8/18/84	24	6	1. Stuck On You	Motown 1746
12/6/86+	10	9	2. Deep River Woman	Motown 1873
			LIONEL RICHIE with Alabama	
			flip side "Ballerina Girl" by Richie made #7 on the *Hot 100*	

RICOCHET

Six-man group: Heath Wright (vocals, guitar), Teddy Carr (guitar), Junior Bryant (fiddle), Eddie Kilgallon (keyboards), Greg Cook (bass) and Jeff Bryant (drums).

DATE	POS	WKS	ARTIST– RECORD TITLE	LABEL & NO.
1/27/96	5	14	1. What Do I Know	Columbia 78088
5/18/96	1 (1)↑	10↑	2. Daddy's Money	Columbia 78097

RIDDLE, Allan

DATE	POS	WKS	ARTIST– RECORD TITLE	LABEL & NO.
11/7/60	16	12	1. The Moon Is Crying	Plaid 1001

RILEY, Jeannie C.

Born Jeanne Carolyn Stephenson on 10/19/45 in Anson, Texas. Moved to Nashville in the mid-1960s. Sang on demo records and worked as a secretary.

DATE	POS	WKS	ARTIST – RECORD TITLE		LABEL & NO.
8/31/68	1 (3)	13	● 1. **Harper Valley P.T.A.**		Plantation 3
			CMA Award: Single of the Year		
12/28/68+	6	12	2. **The Girl Most Likely**		Plantation 7
3/1/69	35	3	3. The Price I Pay To Stay		Capitol 2378
4/12/69	5	11	4. **There Never Was A Time**		Plantation 16
7/19/69	32	3	5. The Rib		Plantation 22
11/1/69	33	6	6. The Back Side Of Dallas/		
11/22/69	34	3	7. Things Go Better With Love		Plantation 29
2/14/70	7	10	8. **Country Girl**		Plantation 44
7/18/70	21	8	9. Duty Not Desire		Plantation 59
4/17/71	4	12	10. **Oh, Singer**		Plantation 72
11/13/71	15	10	11. Roses And Thorns		Plantation 79
1/29/72	12	10	12. Give Myself A Party		MGM 14341
6/24/72+	7	5	13. **Good Enough To Be Your Wife**		Plantation 75
6/24/72	30	5	14. Good Morning Country Rain		MGM 14382

RITTER, Tex

Born Maurice Woodward Ritter on 1/12/05 near Murvaul, Texas. Died of a heart attack on 1/2/74. Spent two years in law school, then left for a career on Broadway. Acted in the play *Green Grow The Lilacs* in 1931. Worked on the radio shows *Lone-Star Rangers, Country Tom's Round-Up* and WHN *Barn Dance* in the 1930s. Moved to Hollywood in 1936 and starred in 85 Western movies until 1945. Co-host of the radio and TV series *Town Hall Party,* 1953-60. Sang title song on soundtrack of *High Noon* in 1953, which won an Academy Award. Moved to Nashville in 1965; worked on the *Grand Ole Opry.* Elected to the Country Music Hall of Fame in 1964. His son, John Ritter, starred in the TV series *Three's Company, Hearts Afire* and others, plus many movies.

TEX RITTER AND HIS TEXANS:

DATE	POS	WKS	ARTIST – RECORD TITLE		LABEL & NO.
11/11/44	1 (6)	20	1. **I'm Wastin' My Tears On You/**		
11/11/44+	2 (1)	22	2. There's A New Moon Over My Shoulder		Capitol 174
12/16/44+	2 (2)	23	3. **Jealous Heart**		Capitol 179
8/4/45	1 (11)	20	4. **You Two-Timed Me One Time Too Often**		Capitol 206

TEX RITTER:

DATE	POS	WKS	ARTIST – RECORD TITLE		LABEL & NO.
12/8/45+	1 (3)	7	5. **You Will Have To Pay/**		
12/29/45	2 (1)	3	6. **Christmas Carols By The Old Corral**	[X]	Capitol 223
5/18/46	5	6	7. **Long Time Gone**		Capitol 253
10/19/46	3	10	8. **When You Leave Don't Slam The Door/**		
12/7/46	3	2	9. Have I Told You Lately That I Love You		Capitol 296
3/13/48	9	1	10. **Rye Whiskey**		Capitol A. 40084
6/12/48	10	7	11. **Deck of Cards**	[S]	Capitol A. 40114
			Best Seller #10 / Juke Box #13		
6/12/48	15	1	12. Pecos Bill		Capitol A. 40106
			TEX RITTER with Andy Parker And The Plainsmen		
			Juke Box #15; from the movie *Melody Time* starring Roy Rogers		
7/10/48	5	7	13. **Rock And Rye**		Capitol 15119
			Best Seller #5 / Juke Box #8		
11/18/50	6	3	14. **Daddy's Last Letter (Private First Class John H. McCormick)**	[S]	Capitol 1267
			Jockey #6 / Best Seller #8; an actual letter from a soldier killed in the Korean War		

DATE	POS	WKS	ARTIST– RECORD TITLE	LABEL & NO.
6/19/61	**5**	21	15. **I Dreamed Of A Hill-Billy Heaven** [S]	Capitol 4567
4/15/67	**13**	11	16. Just Beyond The Moon	Capitol 5839
9/6/69	**39**	2	17. Growin' Up	Capitol 2541
2/16/74	**35**	3	18. The Americans (A Canadian's Opinion) [S]	Capitol 3814
			RIVERS, Jack	
			Longtime session guitarist. Played on Gene Autry's "Rudolph, The Red-Nosed Reindeer," "Peter Cottontail," and many others. Died on 2/11/89.	
9/18/48	**12**	2	1. Dear Oakie Juke Box #12	Capitol 15169
			ROBBINS, Dennis	
			Born in Hazelwood, North Carolina. Former member of the Michigan pop group Rockets. Lead vocalist/guitarist of the group Billy Hill.	
6/20/92	**34**	4	1. Home Sweet Home	Giant 18982
			ROBBINS, Marty	
			Born Martin David Robinson on 9/26/25 in Glendale, Arizona. Died of a heart attack on 12/8/82. Singer/guitarist/composer. Own radio show with K-Bar Cowboys, late 1940s. Own TV show, *Western Caravan*, KPHO-Phoenix, 1951. First recorded for Columbia in 1952. Joined the *Grand Ole Opry* in 1953. Own Robbins label in 1958. Stock car racer. Appeared in the movies *Road To Nashville* and *Guns Of A Stranger*.	
12/20/52+	**1** (2)	18	1. **I'll Go On Alone** Jockey #1 / Best Seller #10	Columbia 21022
3/28/53	**5**	11	2. **I Couldn't Keep From Crying** Juke Box #5 / Best Seller #6 / Jockey #6	Columbia 21075
7/3/54	**12**	3	3. Pretty Words Jockey #12 / Best Seller #14	Columbia 21246
11/20/54	**14**	1	4. Call Me Up (And I'll Come Calling On You) Jockey #14	Columbia 21291
1/8/55	**14**	1	5. Time Goes By Jockey #14	Columbia 21324
2/12/55	**7**	11	6. **That's All Right** Jockey #7 / Best Seller #9; cover version of Elvis Presley's first Sun recording	Columbia 21351
10/1/55	**9**	7	7. **Maybelline** Jockey #9; #5 Pop hit for Chuck Berry in 1955	Columbia 21446
9/22/56	**1** (13)	30	8. **Singing The Blues/** Best Seller #1(13) / Juke Box #1(13) / Jockey #1(11)	Columbia 21545
10/6/56	**7**	10	9. **I Can't Quit (I've Gone Too Far)** Jockey #7	
2/2/57	**3**	15	10. **Knee Deep In The Blues/** Jockey #3 / Best Seller #5 / Juke Box #7	Columbia 40815
3/2/57	**14**	2	11. The Same Two Lips Jockey #14	
4/20/57	**1** (5)	22	● 12. **A White Sport Coat (And A Pink Carnation)** Best Seller #1(5) / Juke Box #1(5) / Jockey #1(1)	Columbia 40864
9/9/57	**11**	3	13. Please Don't Blame Me/ Best Seller #11	Columbia 40969
9/9/57	**15**	1	14. Teen-Age Dream Jockey #15 / Best Seller #15	
11/25/57+	**1** (4)	23	15. **The Story Of My Life** Best Seller #1(4) / Jockey #1(4)	Columbia 41013

DATE	POS	WKS	ARTIST–RECORD TITLE	LABEL & NO.
4/7/58	**1 (2)**	25	16. **Just Married/**	
			Jockey #1 / Best Seller #3	
4/7/58	**2 (2)**	25	17. **Stairway Of Love**	Columbia 41143
			Best Seller #2 / Jockey #8	
8/18/58	**4**	10	18. **She Was Only Seventeen (He Was One Year More)**	Columbia 41208
			Best Seller #4 / Jockey #13	
12/15/58	**23**	5	19. Ain't I The Lucky One	Columbia 41282
3/9/59	**15**	9	20. The Hanging Tree	Columbia 41325
			title song from the movie starring Gary Cooper	
11/9/59	**1 (7)**	26	21. **El Paso**	Columbia 41511
3/21/60	**5**	14	22. **Big Iron**	Columbia 41589
9/26/60	**26**	4	23. Five Brothers	Columbia 41771
2/6/61	**1 (10)**	19	24. **Don't Worry**	Columbia 41922
6/5/61	**24**	4	25. Jimmy Martinez	Columbia 42008
9/18/61	**3**	20	26. **It's Your World**	Columbia 42065
2/3/62	**12**	13	27. Sometimes I'm Tempted	Columbia 42246
			flip side "I Told The Brook" made #81 on the *Hot 100*	
6/2/62	**12**	9	28. Love Can't Wait	Columbia 42375
8/4/62	**1 (8)**	21	29. **Devil Woman**	Columbia 42486
12/8/62+	**1 (1)**	14	30. **Ruby Ann**	Columbia 42614
3/23/63	**14**	9	31. Cigarettes And Coffee Blues	Columbia 42701
9/7/63	**13**	11	32. Not So Long Ago	Columbia 42831
11/30/63+	**1 (3)**	23	33. **Begging To You**	Columbia 42890
3/14/64	**15**	9	34. Girl From Spanish Town	Columbia 42968
6/27/64	**3**	19	35. **The Cowboy In The Continental Suit**	Columbia 43049
11/7/64	**8**	15	36. **One Of These Days**	Columbia 43134
4/24/65	**1 (1)**	19	37. **Ribbon Of Darkness**	Columbia 43258
			written by Gordon Lightfoot	
12/11/65+	**21**	6	38. While You're Dancing	Columbia 43428
2/19/66	**14**	11	39. Count Me Out/	
3/5/66	**21**	7	40. Private Wilson White	Columbia 43500
7/16/66	**3**	17	41. **The Shoe Goes On The Other Foot Tonight**	Columbia 43680
12/17/66+	**16**	9	42. Mr. Shorty	Columbia 43870
2/25/67	**16**	8	43. No Tears Milady/	
4/8/67	**34**	4	44. Fly Butterfly Fly	Columbia 43845
6/17/67	**1 (1)**	14	45. **Tonight Carmen**	Columbia 44128
10/7/67	**9**	11	46. **Gardenias In Her Hair**	Columbia 44271
5/18/68	**10**	13	47. **Love Is In The Air**	Columbia 44509
10/5/68	**1 (2)**	15	48. **I Walk Alone**	Columbia 44633
2/22/69	**5**	12	49. **It's A Sin**	Columbia 44739
7/19/69	**8**	12	50. **I Can't Say Goodbye**	Columbia 44895
11/29/69+	**10**	11	51. **Camelia**	Columbia 45024
2/28/70	**1 (1)**	15	52. **My Woman, My Woman, My Wife**	Columbia 45091
9/26/70	**7**	11	53. **Jolie Girl**	Columbia 45215
12/19/70+	**5**	11	54. **Padre**	Columbia 45273
			#13 Pop hit for Toni Arden in 1958	
6/12/71	**7**	10	55. **The Chair/**	
		8	56. Seventeen Years	Columbia 45377
10/23/71	**9**	10	57. **Early Morning Sunshine**	Columbia 45442

DATE	POS	WKS	ARTIST– RECORD TITLE	LABEL & NO.
1/15/72	**6**	13	58. **The Best Part Of Living**	Columbia 45520
9/30/72	**32**	6	59. I've Got A Woman's Love	Columbia 45668
10/21/72	**11**	11	60. This Much A Man	Decca 33006
3/24/73	**6**	12	61. **Walking Piece Of Heaven**	MCA 40012
8/4/73	**40**	1	62. A Man And A Train	MCA 40067
			from the movie Emperor of the North Pole starring Lee Marvin	
11/10/73	**9**	9	63. **Love Me/**	
		9	64. Crawling On My Knees	MCA 40134
2/23/74	**10**	9	65. **Twentieth Century Drifter**	MCA 40172
6/22/74	**12**	10	66. Don't You Think	MCA 40236
11/23/74	**39**	1	67. Two Gun Daddy	MCA 40296
2/15/75	**23**	5	68. Life	MCA 40342
5/8/76	**1** (2)	11	69. **El Paso City**	Columbia 10305
9/18/76	**1** (1)	11	70. **Among My Souvenirs**	Columbia 10396
			#7 Pop hit for Connie Francis in 1959	
2/19/77	**4**	9	71. **Adios Amigo**	Columbia 10472
6/4/77	**10**	10	72. **I Don't Know Why (I Just Do)**	Columbia 10536
			#12 Pop hit for Linda Scott in 1961	
10/29/77	**6**	11	73. **Don't Let Me Touch You**	Columbia 10629
2/4/78	**6**	9	74. **Return To Me**	Columbia 10673
			#4 Pop hit for Dean Martin in 1958	
11/18/78	**17**	7	75. Please Don't Play A Love Song	Columbia 10821
3/3/79	**15**	8	76. Touch Me With Magic	Columbia 10905
7/7/79	**16**	7	77. All Around Cowboy	Columbia 11016
11/3/79	**25**	5	78. Buenos Dias Argentina	Columbia 11102
5/17/80	**37**	2	79. She's Made Of Faith	Columbia 11240
11/29/80	**28**	4	80. An Occasional Rose	Columbia 11372
6/12/82	**10**	11	81. **Some Memories Just Won't Die**	Columbia 02854
10/30/82	**24**	7	82. Tie Your Dream To Mine	Columbia 03236
1/22/83	**10**	9	83. **Honkytonk Man**	Warner 29847
			title song from the movie starring Clint Eastwood	

ROBERTS, Kenny

Born on 10/14/26 in Lenoir City, Tennessee. Yodeler; worked with the Down Homers.

DATE	POS	WKS	ARTIST– RECORD TITLE	LABEL & NO.
9/17/49	**4**	11	1. **I Never See Maggie Alone/**	
			Juke Box #4 / Best Seller #5	
10/8/49	**15**	1	2. Wedding Bells	Coral 64012
			Juke Box #15	
11/19/49	**14**	1	3. Jealous Heart	Coral 64021
			Juke Box #14	
5/13/50	**8**	4	4. **Choc'late Ice Cream Cone**	Coral 64032
			Jockey #8 / Juke Box #10	

ROBERTS, Pat

Born in Seattle. Male singer. Worked in uncle Jack Roberts's band.

DATE	POS	WKS	ARTIST– RECORD TITLE	LABEL & NO.
12/9/72	**34**	4	1. Rhythm Of The Rain	Dot 17434
			#3 Pop hit for The Cascades in 1963	

DATE	POS	WKS	ARTIST– RECORD TITLE	LABEL & NO.
			ROBERTSON, Texas Jim, and The Panhandle Punchers	
			Robertson was born near Batesville, Texas on 2/27/09. Died on 11/11/66.	
12/28/46	5	1	1. **Filipino Baby/**	
2/15/47	5	1	2. **Rainbow At Midnight**	RCA Victor 1975
2/28/48	8	1	3. **Signed, Sealed And Delivered**	RCA Victor 2651
1/7/50	13	1	4. Slipping Around Best Seller #13; 45 rpm: 48-0071	RCA Victor 0074
			ROBISON, Carson	
			Born on 8/4/1890 in Oswego, Kansas. Died on 3/24/57 in Pleasant Valley, New York. Moved to Kansas City in 1920 and worked with Jack Riley, 1920-24. Moved to New York City in 1924 and worked on radio shows. Known as "The Kansas Jaybird."	
6/30/45	5	1	1. **Hitler's Last Letter To Hirohito** [N]	Victor 20-1665
8/14/48	3	28	2. **Life Gits Tee-Jus Don't It** [N] **CARSON ROBISON with His Pleasant Valley Boys** Best Seller #3 / Juke Box #3	MGM 10224
			ROCKIN' SIDNEY	
			Born Sidney Simien on 4/9/38 in Lebeau, Louisiana. Recorded blues and soul as Count Rockin' Sidney in the early '60s. Own Zydeco band, the Dukes.	
7/6/85	19	8	1. My Toot-Toot	Epic 05430
			RODGERS, Jimmie	
			Born on 9/18/33 in Camas, Washington. Pop vocalist/guitarist/pianist. Own NBC-TV series in 1959. Career hampered following mysterious assault in Los Angeles on 12/1/67, which left him with a fractured skull. Returned to performing on 1/28/69.	
10/14/57	7	13	● 1. **Honeycomb** Best Seller #7 / Jockey #11	Roulette 4015
12/2/57	6	16	● 2. **Kisses Sweeter Than Wine** Best Seller #6 / Jockey #8	Roulette 4031
3/3/58	5	11	● 3. **Oh-Oh, I'm Falling In Love Again** Best Seller #5 / Jockey #15	Roulette 4045
5/19/58	5	17	● 4. **Secretly/** Best Seller #5 / Jockey #14	
		9	5. Make Me A Miracle Best Seller flip	Roulette 4070
8/25/58	13	8	6. Are You Really Mine Best Seller #13	Roulette 4090
			RODGERS, Jimmie, and the Rainbow Ranch Boys	
			Rodgers, "The Father Of Country Music," born James Charles Rodgers on 9/8/1897 in Meridian, Mississippi. Contracted tuberculosis while working as a railroad brakeman. During recuperation, began singing and writing songs for a living. By merging hillbilly and blues, he developed a new style that made him a legend following his death on 5/26/33. Elected to the Country Music Hall of Fame in 1961. Inducted into the Rock and Roll Hall of Fame in 1986 as a forefather of rock and roll.	
5/14/55	7	12	1. **In The Jailhouse Now No. 2** [R] Juke Box #7 / Best Seller #8 / Jockey #9; first released on Victor 22523 in 1930; new overdubbed backing includes Chet Atkins and Hank Snow	RCA 6092

DATE	POS	WKS	ARTIST–RECORD TITLE	LABEL & NO.
			RODMAN, Judy	
			Born Judy M. Robbins on 5/23/51 in Riverside, California; raised in Miami and Jacksonville. Worked as a jingle singer from age 17. Moved to Memphis in 1971. Worked with Janie Fricke and Karen Taylor-Good as Phase II. Married drummer John Rodman in 1975. Moved to Nashville in 1980; made commercials, sang backup vocals.	
5/11/85	**40**	1	1. I've Been Had By Love Before	MTM 72050
9/21/85	**33**	3	2. You're Gonna Miss Me When I'm Gone	MTM 72054
12/28/85+	**30**	5	3. I Sure Need Your Lovin'	MTM 72061
5/3/86	**1** (1)	14	4. **Until I Met You**	MTM 72065
11/8/86+	**9**	12	5. **She Thinks That She'll Marry**	MTM 72076
3/14/87	**7**	12	6. **Girls Ride Horses Too**	MTM 72083
7/18/87	**5**	13	7. **I'll Be Your Baby Tonight** written by Bob Dylan	MTM 72089
12/5/87+	**18**	10	8. I Want A Love Like That	MTM 72092
			RODRIGUEZ, Johnny	
			Born Juan Rodriguez on 12/10/51 in Sabinal, Texas. Guitarist from age seven. Performed with high school rock band in the late '60s. Moved to Nashville in 1971; worked with the Tom T. Hall band, 1971-72. First solo recording in 1972.	
12/23/72+	**9**	11	1. **Pass Me By (If You're Only Passing Through)**	Mercury 73334
4/21/73	**1** (1)	12	2. **You Always Come Back (To Hurting Me)**	Mercury 73368
9/8/73	**1** (2)	13	3. **Ridin' My Thumb To Mexico**	Mercury 73416
1/12/74	**1** (1)	11	4. **That's The Way Love Goes**	Mercury 73446
4/27/74	**6**	9	5. **Something** #1 Pop hit for The Beatles in 1969	Mercury 73471
7/27/74	**2** (1)	10	6. **Dance With Me (Just One More Time)**	Mercury 73493
11/9/74	**3**	9	7. **We're Over**	Mercury 73621
3/1/75	**1** (1)	9	8. **I Just Can't Get Her Out Of My Mind**	Mercury 73659
6/14/75	**1** (1)	10	9. **Just Get Up And Close The Door**	Mercury 73682
10/25/75	**1** (1)	11	10. **Love Put A Song In My Heart**	Mercury 73715
3/13/76	**3**	11	11. **I Couldn't Be Me Without You**	Mercury 73769
7/24/76	**2** (2)	10	12. **I Wonder If I Ever Said Goodbye**	Mercury 73815
10/23/76	**5**	11	13. **Hillbilly Heart**	Mercury 73855
1/29/77	**5**	10	14. **Desperado** written and recorded by the Eagles in 1973	Mercury 73878
5/28/77	**5**	10	15. **If Practice Makes Perfect**	Mercury 73914
9/24/77	**25**	6	16. Eres Tu #9 Pop hit for Mocedades in 1974	Mercury 55004
11/19/77	**14**	8	17. Savin' This Love Song For You	Mercury 55012
3/11/78	**7**	10	18. **We Believe In Happy Endings**	Mercury 55020
7/15/78	**7**	9	19. **Love Me With All Your Heart (Cuando Calienta El Sol)** #3 Pop hit for The Ray Charles Singers in 1964	Mercury 55029
1/6/79	**16**	7	20. Alibis	Mercury 55050
3/24/79	**6**	10	21. **Down On The Rio Grande**	Epic 50671
7/28/79	**17**	7	22. Fools For Each Other	Epic 50735
11/10/79	**16**	9	23. I Hate The Way I Love It **JOHNNY RODRIGUEZ and CHARLY McCLAIN**	Epic 50791
12/22/79+	**19**	7	24. What'll I Tell Virginia	Epic 50808
5/10/80	**29**	4	25. Love, Look At Us Now	Epic 50859

DATE	POS	WKS	ARTIST– RECORD TITLE	LABEL & NO.
10/18/80	17	8	26. North Of The Border	Epic 50932
5/2/81	22	7	27. I Want You Tonight	Epic 01033
9/5/81	30	4	28. Trying Not To Love You	Epic 02411
3/19/83	4	13	29. **Foolin'**	Epic 03598
8/6/83	6	11	30. **How Could I Love Her So Much**	Epic 03972
12/24/83+	35	3	31. Back On Her Mind Again	Epic 04206
2/25/84	15	9	32. Too Late To Go Home	Epic 04336
6/16/84	30	4	33. Let's Leave The Lights On Tonight	Epic 04460
1/23/88	12	11	34. I Didn't (Every Chance I Had)	Capitol 44071
			ROE, Tommy	
			Born on 5/9/42 in Atlanta. Pop-rock singer/guitarist/composer. Formed band The Satins in the late '50s. Moved to Britain in the mid-1960s; returned in 1969.	
2/14/87	38	2	1. Let's Be Fools Like That Again	Mercury 888206
			ROGERS, David	
			Born on 3/27/36 in Atlanta. Died on 8/10/93. Worked clubs in Atlanta, 1952-67, staying at the Egyptian Ballroom for six years. Worked on the WWVA-Wheeling *Jamboree* in 1967.	
9/7/68	38	3	1. I'm In Love With My Wife	Columbia 44561
1/4/69	37	5	2. You Touched My Heart	Columbia 44668
12/13/69+	23	8	3. A World Called You	Columbia 45007
11/7/70	26	6	4. I Wake Up In Heaven	Columbia 45226
6/19/71	19	11	5. She Don't Make Me Cry	Columbia 45383
12/4/71+	21	9	6. Ruby You're Warm	Columbia 45478
3/18/72	9	10	7. **Need You**	Columbia 45551
			#25 Pop hit for Donnie Owens in 1958	
9/2/72	38	3	8. Goodbye	Columbia 45642
12/9/72	35	6	9. All Heaven Breaks Loose	Columbia 45714
5/26/73	17	7	10. Just Thank Me	Atlantic 2957
9/15/73	22	8	11. It'll Be Her	Atlantic 4005
1/26/74	9	10	12. **Loving You Has Changed My Life**	Atlantic 4012
6/22/74	21	6	13. Hey There Girl	Atlantic 4022
2/12/77	21	7	14. I'm Gonna Love You Right Out Of This World	Republic 343
12/17/77+	24	6	15. You And Me Alone	Republic 011
3/25/78	22	5	16. I'll Be There (When You Get Lonely)	Republic 015
7/1/78	32	4	17. Let's Try To Remember	Republic 020
9/30/78	31	4	18. When A Woman Cries	Republic 029
3/24/79	18	8	19. Darlin'	Republic 038
8/4/79	36	3	20. You Are My Rainbow	Republic 042
1/19/80	39	2	21. You're Amazing	Republic 048
			ROGERS, Jesse, and His '49ers	
			Rogers born in Meridian, Mississippi. Worked on local radio from age 17. Own NBC-TV series for children in 1949. Known as "The Western Balladeer."	
9/10/49	15	1	1. Wedding Bells	Bluebird 32-0002
			Juke Box #15	

DATE	POS	WKS	ARTIST– RECORD TITLE	LABEL & NO.
			ROGERS, Kenny	
			Born Kenneth Donald Rogers on 8/21/38 in Houston. With high school band The Scholars in 1958. Bass player of jazz group The Bobby Doyle Trio, recorded for Columbia. In Kirby Stone Four and The New Christy Minstrels, mid-1960s. Formed The First Edition in 1967. Went solo in 1973. Starred in the movies *The Gambler I, II & III, Coward Of The County* and *Six Pack*. Married Marianne Gordon of TV's *Hee-Haw* in 1977. His nephew Dann Rogers also records. CMA 1978 and 1979 Vocal Duo of the Year (with Dottie West); 1979 Male Vocalist of the Year.	
			(a) KENNY ROGERS & DOTTIE WEST	
8/30/69	39	1	1. Ruby, Don't Take Your Love To Town	Reprise 0829
			KENNY ROGERS AND THE FIRST EDITION	
			written by Mel Tillis	
1/17/76	19	7	2. Love Lifted Me	United Art. 746
11/6/76	19	7	3. Laura (What's He Got That I Ain't Got?)	United Art. 868
2/12/77	1 (2)	14	● 4. **Lucille**	United Art. 929
			CMA Award: Single of the Year	
8/13/77	1 (1)	12	5. **Daytime Friends**	United Art. 1027
11/5/77	9	10	6. **Sweet Music Man**	United Art. 1095
3/4/78	1 (2)	11	7. **Every Time Two Fools Collide** (a)	United Art. 1137
6/10/78	1 (1)	10	8. **Love Or Something Like It**	United Art. 1210
9/9/78	2 (1)	11	9. **Anyone Who Isn't Me Tonight** (a)	United Art. 1234
10/28/78	1 (3)	11	10. **The Gambler**	United Art. 1250
2/24/79	1 (1)	11	11. **All I Ever Need Is You** (a)	United Art. 1276
			#7 Pop hit for Sonny & Cher in 1971	
5/5/79	1 (2)	11	● 12. **She Believes In Me**	United Art. 1273
7/14/79	3	10	13. **Til I Can Make It On My Own** (a)	United Art. 1299
9/22/79	1 (2)	9	14. **You Decorated My Life**	United Art. 1315
12/1/79+	1 (3)	9	● 15. **Coward Of The County**	United Art. 1327
4/19/80	3	10	16. **Don't Fall In Love With A Dreamer**	United Art. 1345
			KENNY ROGERS with Kim Carnes	
7/5/80	4	10	17. **Love The World Away**	United Art. 1359
			from the movie *Urban Cowboy* starring John Travolta	
10/18/80	1 (1)	8	● 18. **Lady**	Liberty 1380
			written by Lionel Richie	
4/18/81	1 (1)	10	19. **What Are We Doin' In Love** (a)	Liberty 1404
6/27/81	1 (2)	10	20. **I Don't Need You**	Liberty 1415
10/3/81	5	7	21. **Share Your Love With Me**	Liberty 1430
11/28/81+	9	11	22. **Blaze Of Glory**	Liberty 1441
2/13/82	5	11	23. **Through The Years**	Liberty 1444
			above 6 (except #19) produced by Lionel Richie	
7/10/82	1 (1)	14	24. **Love Will Turn You Around**	Liberty 1471
			from the movie *Six Pack* starring Rogers	
10/30/82	3	13	25. **A Love Song**	Liberty 1485
2/5/83	1 (1)	13	26. **We've Got Tonight**	Liberty 1492
			KENNY ROGERS and SHEENA EASTON	
5/21/83	13	9	27. All My Life	Liberty 1495
8/20/83	5	11	28. **Scarlet Fever**	Liberty 1503
9/10/83	1 (2)	15	▲ 29. **Islands In The Stream** (b)	RCA 13615
			written by the Bee Gees	
12/10/83+	20	8	30. You Were A Good Friend	Liberty 1511

DATE	POS	WKS	ARTIST– RECORD TITLE	LABEL & NO.
1/28/84	**3**	12	31. **Buried Treasure**	RCA 13710
			flip side "This Woman" made #23 on the *Hot 100*	
4/21/84	**19**	7	32. Together Again (a)	Liberty 1516
5/12/84	**30**	5	33. Eyes That See In The Dark	RCA 13774
7/21/84	**11**	11	34. Evening Star/	
		9	35. Midsummer Nights	RCA 13832
1/26/85	**1** (1)	13	36. **Crazy**	RCA 13975
5/25/85	**37**	2	37. Love Is What We Make It	Liberty 1524
6/1/85	**1** (1)	16	38. **Real Love** (b)	RCA 14058
10/26/85+	**1** (1)	14	39. **Morning Desire**	RCA 14194
3/8/86	**1** (1)	14	40. **Tomb Of The Unknown Love**	RCA 14298
1/17/87	**2** (2)	14	41. **Twenty Years Ago**	RCA 5078
7/4/87	**1** (1)	13	42. **Make No Mistake, She's Mine**	RCA 5209
			RONNIE MILSAP & KENNY ROGERS	
			#51 Pop hit for Barbra Streisand & Kim Carnes in 1985 as "Make No Mistake, He's Mine"	
10/17/87	**2** (2)	14	43. **I Prefer The Moonlight**	RCA 5258
3/19/88	**6**	11	44. **The Factory**	RCA 6832
9/10/88	**26**	7	45. When You Put Your Heart In It	Reprise 27812
6/24/89	**30**	5	46. Planet Texas	Reprise 27690
9/16/89	**8**	12	47. **The Vows Go Unbroken (Always True To You)**	Reprise 22828
10/21/89	**28**	6	48. If I Ever Fall In Love Again	Capitol 44432
			ANNE MURRAY with Kenny Rogers	
2/24/90	**25**	6	49. Maybe	Reprise 19972
			KENNY ROGERS with Holly Dunn	
8/25/90	**21**	9	50. Love Is Strange (b)	Reprise 19760
12/21/91+	**11**	14	51. If You Want To Find Love	Reprise 19080
			Linda Davis (backing vocal)	

ROGERS, Ronnie

Born Randall J. Rogers in Nashville. Wrote "Keep On Truckin'" hit for Dave Dudley.

DATE	POS	WKS	ARTIST– RECORD TITLE	LABEL & NO.
1/9/82	**39**	1	1. Gonna Take My Angel Out Tonight	Lifesong 45094
4/24/82	**37**	2	2. My Love Belongs To You	Lifesong 45095

ROGERS, Roy

Popular "singing cowboy" who starred in over 90 movies. Born Leonard Franklin Slye on 11/5/11 in Cincinnati. Moved to California in 1930. Member of Hollywood Hillbillies, Rocky Mountaineers and Texas Outlaws. Own group, the International Cowboys. Formed the Pioneer Trio in 1934 with Bob Nolan and Tim Spencer, which evolved into the Sons Of The Pioneers; group appeared in several movies. Went solo in 1937; briefly known as "Dick Weston." By 1938, known as "Roy Rogers" and starred in his first movie, *Under Western Stars*. Married his co-star Dale Evans (born Frances Octavia Smith, 10/31/12, Uvalde, Texas) on 12/31/47; they starred in the TV series *The Roy Rogers Show*, 1951-57, and *The Roy Rogers & Dale Evans Show*, 1962. Elected to the Country Music Hall of Fame in 1980 as a member of the Sons of The Pioneers, and individually in 1988.

DATE	POS	WKS	ARTIST– RECORD TITLE	LABEL & NO.
7/6/46	**7**	1	1. **A Little White Cross On The Hill**	Victor 20-1872
			Morton Scott (orch.)	
3/15/47	**4**	1	2. **My Chickashay Gal**	Victor 20-2124
			Country Washburne (orch.)	

DATE	POS	WKS	ARTIST– RECORD TITLE	LABEL & NO.
6/12/48	6	14	3. **Blue Shadows On The Trail/** Best Seller #6 / Juke Box #7	
6/12/48	13	4	4. (There'll Never Be Another) Pecos Bill Best Seller #13; from the movie *Melody Time* starring Rogers	Victor 20-2780
2/4/50	8	1	5. **Stampede** Jockey #8; 45 rpm: 48-0161; Sons Of The Pioneers (backing vocals, above 3)	RCA Victor 0154
10/17/70	35	3	6. Money Can't Buy Love	Capitol 2895
2/6/71	12	10	7. Lovenworth	Capitol 3016
1/25/75	15	6	8. Hoppy, Gene And Me [N] tribute to Hopalong Cassidy, Gene Autry and Roy Rogers	20th Century 2154

ROGERS, Smokey

Born on 3/23/27. Western swing banjoist. Performed with Spade Cooley and later with Tex Williams. Wrote Ferlin Husky's #1 hit "Gone."

DATE	POS	WKS	ARTIST– RECORD TITLE	LABEL & NO.
1/1/49	8	4	1. **A Little Bird Told Me** Juke Box #8	Capitol 15326

ROLAND, Adrian

Born in Lamarque, Texas. Died on 7/1/66 in Baton Rouge, Louisiana.

DATE	POS	WKS	ARTIST– RECORD TITLE	LABEL & NO.
9/19/60	19	4	1. Imitation Of Love	Allstar 7207

RONSTADT, Linda

Born on 7/15/46 in Tucson, Arizona. While in high school formed folk trio The Three Ronstadts (with sister and brother). To Los Angeles in 1964. Formed the Stone Poneys with Bobby Kimmel (guitar) and Ken Edwards (keyboards); recorded for Sidewalk in 1966. Went solo in 1968. In 1971 formed backing band with Glenn Frey, Don Henley, Randy Meisner and Bernie Leadon (later became the Eagles). Starred in the operetta *Pirates Of Penzance* in New York City in 1980, also in movie of same name in 1983. Also see Hoyt Axton.

DATE	POS	WKS	ARTIST– RECORD TITLE	LABEL & NO.
4/6/74	20	6	1. Silver Threads And Golden Needles	Asylum 11032
1/18/75	2 (1)	12	2. **I Can't Help It (If I'm Still In Love With You)** flip side "You're No Good" made #1 on the *Hot 100*	Capitol 3990
5/3/75	1 (1)	10	3. **When Will I Be Loved**	Capitol 4050
10/4/75	5	11	4. **Love Is A Rose** originally released on Asylum 45271; flip side "Heat Wave" made #5 on the *Hot 100*	Asylum 45282
1/17/76	11	8	5. Tracks Of My Tears/	
1/17/76	12	8	6. The Sweetest Gift **LINDA RONSTADT and EMMYLOU HARRIS**	Asylum 45295
10/2/76	27	5	7. That'll Be The Day	Asylum 45340
1/8/77	6	10	8. **Crazy** flip side "Someone To Lay Down Beside Me" made #42 on the *Hot 100*	Asylum 45361
10/1/77	2 (2)	12	▲ 9. **Blue Bayou**	Asylum 45431
5/27/78	8	9	10. **I Never Will Marry** flip side "Tumbling Dice" made #32 on the *Hot 100*	Asylum 45479
11/13/82	27	5	11. Sometimes You Just Can't Win **LINDA RONSTADT and JOHN DAVID SOUTHER** flip side "Get Closer" by Ronstadt made #29 on the *Hot 100*	Asylum 69948

DATE	POS	WKS	ARTIST– RECORD TITLE	LABEL & NO.
			DOLLY PARTON, LINDA RONSTADT, EMMYLOU HARRIS:	
2/28/87	**1** (1)	14	12. **To Know Him Is To Love Him** #1 Pop hit for The Teddy Bears in 1958	Warner 28492
6/13/87	**3**	11	13. **Telling Me Lies**	Warner 28371
10/10/87	**5**	13	14. **Those Memories Of You**	Warner 28248
4/16/88	**6**	11	15. **Wildflowers**	Warner 27970
			ROOFTOP SINGERS, The	
			Folk trio consisting of Erik Darling, Willard Svanoe and Lynne Taylor (died 1982). Darling was a member of The Tarriers in 1956 and The Weavers, 1958-62.	
2/23/63	**23**	4	● 1. **Walk Right In**	Vanguard 35017
			ROSE, Fred—see RAMBLING ROGUE, The	
			ROSS, Charlie	
			Born in Greenville, Mississippi. DJ on WDDT radio. Moved to California in the late 1960s, worked with Eternity's Children. DJ at KFJZ-Ft. Worth in the mid-1970s.	
3/20/76	**13**	8	1. Without Your Love (Mr. Jordan)	Big Tree 16056
7/17/82	**33**	4	2. The High Cost Of Loving	Town House 1057
			ROSS, Jeris	
			Female vocalist from East Alton, Illinois. Worked as a Pop singer in St. Louis.	
5/31/75	**17**	7	1. Pictures On Paper	ABC 12064
			ROY, Bobbie	
			Born Barbara Elaine Roy on 7/27/53 in Landstuhl, Germany, where her father was in the Army. Moved to Elkins, West Virginia, in 1960.	
7/1/72	**32**	4	1. One Woman's Trash (Another Woman's Treasure)	Capitol 3301
			ROYAL, Billy Joe	
			Born on 4/3/42 in Valdosta, Georgia; raised in Marietta, Georgia. Guitarist/pianist/drummer. Own band, the Corvettes, while in high school. First recorded for Fairlane in 1961. Moved to Cincinnati in 1963.	
11/30/85+	**10**	12	1. **Burned Like A Rocket**	Atln. Am. 99599
9/27/86	**14**	11	2. I Miss You Already	Atln. Am. 99519
3/7/87	**11**	12	3. Old Bridges Burn Slow	Atln. Am. 99485
8/1/87	**23**	7	4. Members Only **DONNA FARGO and BILLY JOE ROYAL**	Mercury 888680
11/14/87+	**5**	14	5. **I'll Pin A Note On Your Pillow**	Atln. Am. 99404
4/9/88	**10**	12	6. **Out Of Sight And On My Mind**	Atln. Am. 99364
9/17/88	**17**	9	7. It Keeps Right On Hurtin' #3 Pop hit for Johnny Tillotson in 1962	Atln. Am. 99295
2/11/89	**2** (2)	14	8. **Tell It Like It Is** #2 Pop hit for Aaron Neville in 1967	Atln. Am. 99242
6/10/89	**4**	14	9. **Love Has No Right**	Atln. Am. 99217
10/14/89+	**2** (1)	18	10. **Till I Can't Take It Anymore**	Atlantic 88815
6/9/90	**17**	9	11. Searchin' For Some Kind Of Clue	Atlantic 87933
11/17/90	**33**	1	12. Ring Where A Ring Used To Be	Atlantic 87867
3/2/91	**29**	5	13. If The Jukebox Took Teardrops	Atlantic 87770

DATE	POS	WKS	ARTIST– RECORD TITLE	LABEL & NO.
			RUSSELL, Bobby	
			Born on 4/19/41 in Nashville. Died of a heart attack on 11/19/92. Wrote "The Night The Lights Went Out In Georgia," "Honey," "Little Green Apples" and "The Joker Went Wild." First husband of Vicki Lawrence.	
9/6/69	**34**	5	1. Better Homes And Gardens	Elf 90031
8/14/71	**24**	7	2. Saturday Morning Confusion	United Art. 50788
			RUSSELL, Johnny	
			Born on 1/23/40 in Sunflower County, Mississippi; raised in California. Worked as the manager of the Wilburn Brothers music company. Wrote "Act Naturally," hit for The Beatles and Buck Owens. Member of the *Grand Ole Opry* since 1985. Once married to Beverly Heckel.	
8/12/72	**36**	5	1. Rain Falling On Me	RCA 0729
12/2/72+	**12**	12	2. Catfish John	RCA 0810
4/21/73	**31**	6	3. Chained	RCA 0908
9/1/73	**4**	13	4. **Rednecks, White Socks And Blue Ribbon Beer**	RCA 0021
12/8/73+	**14**	8	5. The Baptism Of Jesse Taylor	RCA 0165
5/25/74	**39**	2	6. She's In Love With A Rodeo Man	RCA 0248
11/2/74	**38**	1	7. She Burn't The Little Roadside Tavern Down	RCA 10038
2/1/75	**23**	4	8. That's How My Baby Builds A Fire	RCA 10135
6/7/75	**13**	8	9. Hello I Love You	RCA 10258
			The Jordanaires (backing vocals, all of above - except #8)	
2/5/77	**32**	3	10. The Son Of Hickory Holler's Tramp/	
			#40 Pop hit for O.C. Smith in 1968	
		3	11. I Wonder How She's Doing Now	RCA 10853
			The Jordanaires with Janie Fricke and Laverna Moore (backing vocals, above 2)	
6/10/78	**24**	6	12. You'll Be Back (Every Night In My Dreams)	Polydor 14475
12/23/78+	**29**	5	13. How Deep In Love Am I?	Mercury 55045
			RUSSELL, Leon—see NELSON, Willie	
			RUSTY & DOUG	
			Duo of brothers Russell Lee "Rusty" (born 2/2/38) and Doug (born 1/24/36) Kershaw. Both from Tiel Ridge, Louisiana.	
8/13/55	**14**	2	1. So Lovely, Baby	Hickory 1027
			Jockey #14	
9/23/57	**14**	1	2. Love Me To Pieces	Hickory 1068
			Jockey #14; #11 Pop hit for Jill Corey in 1957	
10/20/58	**22**	2	3. Hey Sheriff	Hickory 1083
2/6/61	**10**	15	4. **Louisiana Man**	Hickory 1137
8/21/61	**14**	10	5. Diggy Liggy Lo	Hickory 1151
			RYAN, Charlie, and the Timberline Riders	
			Born on 12/19/15 in Graceville, Minnesota; raised in Montana.	
9/5/60	**14**	6	1. Hot Rod Lincoln [S-N]	4 Star 1733
			first recorded on Ryan's Souvenir label in 1955	

DATE	POS	WKS	ARTIST– RECORD TITLE	LABEL & NO.
			RYLES, John Wesley	
			Born on 12/2/50 in Bastrop, Louisiana. Moved to Fort Worth, Texas, and worked on the Cowtown Hoedown Show. Moved to Dallas and performed on the *Big D Jamboree* in 1963. Moved to Nashville in 1966.	
			JOHN WESLEY RYLES I:	
1/4/69	9	12	1. **Kay**	Columbia 44682
5/16/70	17	8	2. I've Just Been Wasting My Time	Columbia 45119
12/25/71	39	1	3. Reconsider Me	Plantation 81
			JOHN WESLEY RYLES:	
6/4/77	18	8	4. Fool	ABC/Dot 17679
9/10/77	5	10	5. **Once In A Lifetime Thing**	ABC/Dot 17698
1/14/78	13	7	6. Shine On Me (The Sun Still Shines When It Rains)	ABC/Dot 17733
1/27/79	33	4	7. Love Ain't Made For Fools	ABC 12432
6/16/79	14	9	8. Liberated Woman	MCA 41033
11/3/79	20	7	9. You Are Always On My Mind	MCA 41124
3/15/80	24	5	10. Perfect Strangers	MCA 41184
6/6/87	36	3	11. Midnight Blue	Warner 28377
1/9/88	20	9	12. Louisiana Rain	Warner 28228
			S	
			SADLER, SSgt Barry	
			Born on 11/1/40 in Carlsbad, New Mexico. Died of heart failure on 11/5/89 in Tennessee. Staff Sergeant of U.S. Army Special Forces (aka Green Berets). Served in Vietnam until injuring leg in booby trap. Shot in the head during a 1988 robbery attempt at his Guatemala home; suffered brain damage.	
2/26/66	2 (2)	12	● 1. **The Ballad Of The Green Berets**	RCA 8739
			SANDERS, Ray	
			Born Raymon Sanders on 10/1/35 in St. John, Kentucky. Radio performer since age 15.	
10/31/60	18	11	1. A World So Full Of Love	Liberty 55267
4/3/61	20	8	2. Lonelyville	Liberty 55304
6/28/69	22	8	3. Beer Drinkin' Music	Imperial 66366
8/29/70	36	3	4. Blame It On Rosey	United Art. 50689
1/16/71	38	3	5. Judy	United Art. 50732
11/13/71	18	9	6. All I Ever Need Is You	United Art. 50827
			#7 Pop hit for Sonny & Cher in 1971	
			SAWYER, Ray	
			Born on 2/1/37 in Monroeville, Alabama; raised in Chickasaw, Alabama. Eye-patched singer from Dr. Hook.	
12/4/76	28	5	1. (One More Year Of) Daddy's Little Girl	Capitol 4344

DATE	POS	WKS	ARTIST– RECORD TITLE	LABEL & NO.
			SAWYER BROWN	
			Group formed in Nashville in the late '70s by Mark Miller (born 10/25/58, Dayton, Ohio; lead singer) and Bobby Randall (born Midland, Michigan; vocals, lead guitar), with Gregg "Hobie" Hubbard (keyboards), Jim Scholten (bass) and "Curly" Joe Smyth (drums). Originally named Savannah, renamed after a street in Nashville. Won $100,000 on *Star Search* TV series in 1984. Randall left in 1992 to host the TNN show *Be A Star*, replaced by guitarist Duncan Cameron. CMA Award: 1985 Horizon Award.	
11/24/84+	**16**	10	1. Leona	Capitol/Curb 5403
3/2/85	**1** (1)	14	2. **Step That Step**	Capitol/Curb 5446
6/29/85	**3**	14	3. **Used To Blue**	Capitol/Curb 5477
10/19/85	**5**	14	4. **Betty's Bein' Bad**	Capitol/Curb 5517
2/22/86	**14**	9	5. Heart Don't Fall Now	Capitol/Curb 5548
5/31/86	**15**	9	6. Shakin'	Capitol/Curb 5585
10/4/86	**11**	10	7. Out Goin' Cattin'	Capitol/Curb 5629
			SAWYER BROWN with "CAT" JOE BONSALL	
2/7/87	**25**	6	8. Gypsies On Parade	Capitol/Curb 5677
9/19/87	**29**	5	9. Somewhere In The Night	Capitol/Curb 44054
12/26/87+	**2** (1)	15	10. **This Missin' You Heart Of Mine**	Capitol/Curb 44108
5/21/88	**27**	5	11. Old Photographs	Capitol/Curb 44143
10/22/88	**11**	11	12. My Baby's Gone	Capitol/Curb 44218
9/16/89	**5**	13	13. **The Race Is On**	Capitol/Curb 44431
4/7/90	**33**	3	14. Did It For Love	Capitol/Curb 44483
7/7/90	**33**	3	15. Puttin' The Dark Back Into The Night	Capitol/Curb LP Cut
			above 3 from the album *The Boys Are Back* on Capitol/Curb 92358	
11/24/90	**40**	1	16. When Love Comes Callin'	Curb/Cap. LP Cut
			from the album *Greatest Hits* on Curb/Capitol 94259	
8/10/91	**2** (1)	17	17. **The Walk**	Curb/Cap. LP Cut
			from the album *Buick* on Curb/Capitol 94260	
12/7/91+	**3**	18	18. **The Dirt Road**	Curb/Cap. LP Cut
3/21/92	**1** (1)	18	19. **Some Girls Do**	Curb/Cap. LP Cut
			later available as the B-side of #21 below; above 2 from the album *The Dirt Road* on Curb/Capitol 95624	
8/22/92	**5**	15	20. **Cafe On The Corner**	Curb LP Cut
12/26/92+	**3**	16	21. **All These Years**	Curb 76912
4/10/93	**5**	14	22. **Trouble On The Line**	Curb LP Cut
			above 3 from the album *Cafe On The Corner* on Curb 77574	
7/17/93	**1** (2)	18	23. **Thank God For You**	Curb 76914
10/30/93+	**4**	17	24. **The Boys And Me**	Curb LP Cut
4/9/94	**40**	1	25. Outskirts Of Town	Curb LP Cut
7/16/94	**5**	13	26. **Hard To Say**	Curb LP Cut
			above 4 from the album *Outskirts Of Town* on Curb 77626	
12/10/94+	**2** (2)	17	27. **This Time**	Curb 76930
4/1/95	**4**	13	28. **I Don't Believe In Goodbye**	Curb 76936
8/12/95	**11**	14	29. (This Thing Called) Wantin' And Havin' It All	Curb 76955
12/23/95+	**19**	10	30. 'Round Here	Curb 76975
4/27/96	**3** ↑	13↑	31. **Treat Her Right**	Curb 76987

DATE	POS	WKS	ARTIST– RECORD TITLE	LABEL & NO.
			SCHNEIDER, John	
			Born on 4/8/59 in Mount Kisco, New York. Actor from age eight. Wrote the score for the musical *Under Odin's Eye*. Played Bo Duke on the TV series *Dukes Of Hazzard*. Appeared in the movies *Dream House, Happy Endings, Gus Brown And Midnight Brewster, Eddie Macon's Run, Fine White Line* and *Stagecoach*. Scriptwriter/director.	
7/4/81	**4**	9	1. **It's Now Or Never**	Scotti Br. 02105
10/17/81	**13**	8	2. Them Good Ol' Boys Are Bad	Scotti Br. 02489
			flip side "Still" made #69 on the *Hot 100*	
6/12/82	**32**	3	3. Dreamin'	Scotti Br. 02889
8/25/84	**1** (1)	15	4. **I've Been Around Enough To Know**	MCA 52407
1/26/85	**1** (1)	14	5. **Country Girls**	MCA 52510
5/18/85	**10**	10	6. **It's A Short Walk From Heaven To Hell**	MCA 52567
8/31/85	**10**	12	7. **I'm Going To Leave You Tomorrow**	MCA 52648
1/11/86	**1** (1)	14	8. **What's A Memory Like You (Doing In A Love Like This)**	MCA 52723
5/24/86	**1** (1)	15	9. **You're The Last Thing I Needed Tonight**	MCA 52827
9/13/86	**5**	13	10. **At The Sound Of The Tone**	MCA 52901
1/17/87	**10**	11	11. **Take The Long Way Home**	MCA 52989
4/18/87	**6**	13	12. **Love, You Ain't Seen The Last Of Me**	MCA 53069
8/29/87	**32**	2	13. When The Right One Comes Along	MCA 53144
			SCHUYLER, KNOBLOCH & OVERSTREET	
			Trio of prolific songwriters: Thom Schuyler, J. Fred Knoblock and Paul Overstreet. Also known as S-K-O. Overstreet replaced by Craig Bickhardt in 1987.	
8/16/86	**9**	12	1. **You Can't Stop Love**	MTM 72071
			S-K-O:	
12/27/86+	**1** (1)	14	2. **Baby's Got A New Baby**	MTM 72081
5/9/87	**16**	8	3. American Me	MTM 72086
			SCHUYLER, KNOBLOCH & BICKHARDT:	
9/19/87	**19**	8	4. No Easy Horses	MTM 72090
12/26/87+	**24**	8	5. This Old House	MTM 72100
5/21/88	**8**	12	6. **Givers And Takers**	MTM 72099
			SCOTT, Earl	
			Born Earl Batdorf on 9/9/36 in Youngstown, Ohio. Son is John Batdorf of the rock group Batdorf & Rodney.	
11/3/62	**8**	10	1. **Then A Tear Fell**	Kapp 854
7/27/63	**23**	7	2. Loose Lips	Mercury 72110
1/4/64	**30**	1	3. Restless River	Mercury 72190
1/30/65	**30**	10	4. I'll Wander Back To You	Decca 31693
			SCRUGGS, Earl	
			Born Earl Eugene Scruggs on 1/6/24. See Flatt & Scruggs for complete bio.	
8/4/79	**30**	4	1. I Could Sure Use The Feeling	Columbia 10992

DATE	POS	WKS	ARTIST– RECORD TITLE	LABEL & NO.
			SEA, Johnny	
			Born on 7/15/40 in Gulfport, Mississippi. (Real last name: Seay.) Joined the *Louisiana Hayride* while still in high school.	
4/20/59	**13**	9	1. Frankie's Man, Johnny	NRC 019
2/8/60	**13**	8	2. Nobody's Darling But Mine	NRC 049
5/30/64	**27**	7	3. My Baby Walks All Over Me	Philips 40164
5/1/65	**19**	12	4. My Old Faded Rose	Philips 40267
6/25/66	**14**	9	5. Day For Decision　　　　　　　　　　[S]	Warner 5820
			patriotic answer to Barry McGuire's "Eve Of Destruction"	
11/23/68	**32**	6	6. Three Six Packs, Two Arms And A Juke Box **JOHNNY SEAY**	Columbia 44634
			SEALS, Dan	
			Born on 2/8/48 in McCamey, Texas; raised in Iraan and Rankin, Texas. Played in family band with brother Jim Seals (of Seals & Crofts) at age four. Formed Southwest F.O.B. with John Ford Coley and Shane Keister in 1967; recorded for GPC. Teamed with Coley as England Dan & John Ford Coley. Recorded solo for Atlantic as England Dan in 1980. Cousin of Troy Seals, Johnny Duncan and Brady Seals (Little Texas). CMA Award: 1986 Vocal Duo of the Year (with Marie Osmond).	
6/4/83	**18**	7	1. Everybody's Dream Girl	Liberty 1496
9/17/83	**28**	4	2. After You	Liberty 1504
1/7/84	**37**	2	3. You Really Go For The Heart	Liberty 1512
3/24/84	**10**	10	4. **God Must Be A Cowboy**	Liberty 1515
8/25/84	**9**	10	5. **(You Bring Out) The Wild Side Of Me**	EMI America 8220
12/22/84+	**2** (2)	14	6. **My Baby's Got Good Timing**	EMI America 8245
4/27/85	**9**	10	7. **My Old Yellow Car**	EMI America 8261
8/3/85	**1** (1)	14	8. **Meet Me In Montana** **MARIE OSMOND with DAN SEALS**	Capitol 5478
11/16/85+	**1** (1)	13	9. **Bop** CMA Award: Single of the Year	EMI America 8289
4/26/86	**1** (1)	14	10. **Everything That Glitters (Is Not Gold)**	EMI America 8311
11/8/86+	**1** (1)	16	11. **You Still Move Me**	EMI America 8343
3/21/87	**1** (1)	14	12. **I Will Be There**	EMI America 8377
7/11/87	**1** (1)	14	13. **Three Time Loser**	EMI America 43023
10/31/87+	**1** (1)	14	14. **One Friend**	Capitol 44077
7/16/88	**1** (1)	14	15. **Addicted**	Capitol 44130
11/26/88+	**1** (1)	16	16. **Big Wheels In The Moonlight**	Capitol 44267
4/8/89	**5**	14	17. **They Rage On**	Capitol 44345
3/10/90	**1** (3)	16	18. **Love On Arrival**	Capitol 44435
6/23/90	**1** (2)	17	19. **Good Times** #11 Pop hit for Sam Cooke in 1964	Capitol 44577
			SEELY, Jeannie	
			Born Marilyn Jeanne Seely on 7/6/40 in Titusville, Pennsylvania. Worked on local radio shows from age 11, later worked on the *Midwestern Hayride*. Staff writer for Four Star Music in Los Angeles. Married briefly to Hank Cochran; moved to Nashville in 1965. On the *Grand Ole Opry* since 1967, and worked for a time with the Jack Greene show.	
4/23/66	**2** (3)	20	1. **Don't Touch Me**	Monument 933
9/10/66	**15**	14	2. It's Only Love	Monument 965
12/31/66+	**13**	11	3. A Wanderin' Man	Monument 987

DATE	POS	WKS	ARTIST-RECORD TITLE	LABEL & NO.
5/6/67	39	1	4. When It's Over	Monument 999
11/18/67+	10	10	5. **I'll Love You More (Than You Need)**	Monument 1029
3/23/68	24	7	6. Welcome Home To Nothing	Monument 1054
7/13/68	23	6	7. How Is He?	Monument 1075
11/29/69+	2 (2)	13	8. **Wish I Didn't Have To Miss You**	Decca 32580
1/1/72	15	9	9. Much Oblige	Decca 32898
9/2/72	19	9	10. What In The World Has Gone Wrong With Our Love	Decca 32991
			JACK GREENE/JEANNIE SEELY (above 3)	
8/11/73	6	13	11. **Can I Sleep In Your Arms**	MCA 40074
1/5/74	11	9	12. Lucky Ladies	MCA 40162
6/29/74	37	2	13. I Miss You	MCA 40225
10/19/74	26	7	14. He Can Be Mine	MCA 40287
			SEGER, Bob	
			Born on 5/6/45 in Dearborn, Michigan; raised in Detroit. Rock singer/songwriter.	
2/12/83	15	8	1. Shame On The Moon	Capitol 5187
			written by Rodney Crowell	
			SELF, Ted	
7/4/60	20	10	1. Little Angel (Come Rock Me To Sleep)	Plaid 115
			SELLARS, Marilyn	
			From Northfield, Minnesota. Worked as an airline stewardess.	
6/8/74	19	7	1. One Day At A Time	Mega 1205
2/22/75	39	1	2. He's Everywhere	Mega 1221
			SERATT, Kenny	
			Born in Manila, Arkansas; raised in Dyess, Arkansas, and in California. Appeared at the Ramada in Hemet, California, for 11 years. Out of music, 1967-72.	
10/11/80	39	2	1. Until The Bitter End	MDJ 1005
			SESSIONS, Ronnie	
			Born on 12/7/48 in Henrietta, Oklahoma; raised in Bakersfield, California. First recorded at age nine, and performed on the TV series *Herb Henson's Trading Post*. Toured with Buck Owens, Merle Haggard and Glen Campbell. Moved to Nashville in 1971; worked as a staff writer for Tree Publishing.	
9/9/72	36	4	1. Never Been To Spain	MGM 14394
			#5 Pop hit for Three Dog Night in 1972	
12/18/76+	16	8	2. Wiggle Wiggle	MCA 40624
4/30/77	15	8	3. Me And Millie (Stompin' Grapes And Gettin' Silly)	MCA 40705
9/3/77	30	3	4. Ambush	MCA 40758
10/28/78	25	5	5. Juliet And Romeo	MCA 40952
			SHARPE, Sunday	
			(Her real name.) Born in 1946 in Orlando, Florida. Worked as a caterer. First female country singer to perform at West Point Academy.	
9/21/74	11	8	1. I'm Having Your Baby	United Art. 507
			answer song to Paul Anka's "(You're) Having My Baby"	

DATE	POS	WKS	ARTIST– RECORD TITLE	LABEL & NO.
11/27/76	**18**	7	2. A Little At A Time	Playboy 6090
			SHAW, Brian	
			Born in 1949 in Grove City, Pennsylvania. Played bass from age 16. Worked on WWVA-Wheeling *Jamboree* and the *Grand Ole Opry*.	
11/23/74	**17**	7	1. Here We Go Again	RCA 10071
			SHAW, Ron	
			Singer from Anaheim, California.	
11/25/78	**36**	2	1. Save The Last Dance For Me	Pacific C. 1631
			#1 Pop hit for The Drifters in 1960	
			SHAY, Dorothy	
			Born Dorothy Sims in 1923 in Jacksonville, Florida. Died on 10/22/78 of a heart attack. Comedienne. Made regular appearances on the Spike Jones radio series in 1947. Billed as "The Park Avenue Hillbilly." Appeared in the 1951 movie *Comin' 'Round The Mountain*. Appeared on *The Waltons* TV series.	
8/16/47	**4**	7	1. **Feudin' And Fightin'**	Columbia 37189
			Mischa Russell (orch.); from the Broadway musical *Laffing Room Only* starring Betty Garrett	
			SHELTON, Ricky Van	
			Born Richard Van Shelton on 1/12/52 in Danville, Virginia; raised in Grit, Virginia. Worked as a pipefitter. Joined the *Grand Ole Opry* in 1988. CMA Awards: 1988 Horizon Award; 1989 Male Vocalist of the Year.	
2/7/87	**24**	6	1. Wild-Eyed Dream	Columbia 06542
5/9/87	**7**	12	2. **Crime Of Passion**	Columbia 07025
9/12/87	**1** (1)	15	3. **Somebody Lied**	Columbia 07311
1/23/88	**1** (1)	13	4. **Life Turned Her That Way**	Columbia 07672
5/21/88	**1** (1)	14	5. **Don't We All Have The Right**	Columbia 07798
			first released as the B-side of #2 above	
9/24/88	**1** (2)	15	6. **I'll Leave This World Loving You**	Columbia 08022
1/14/89	**1** (1)	12	7. **From A Jack To A King**	Columbia 08529
4/29/89	**4**	12	8. **Hole In My Pocket**	Columbia 68694
8/5/89	**1** (1)	15	9. **Living Proof**	Columbia 68994
12/2/89+	**2** (2)	18	10. **Statue Of A Fool**	Columbia 73077
3/31/90	**1** (1)	21	11. **I've Cried My Last Tear For You**	Columbia 73263
7/21/90	**2** (2)	18	12. **I Meant Every Word He Said**	Columbia 73413
11/10/90+	**4**	18	13. **Life's Little Ups And Downs**	Columbia 73587
3/16/91	**1** (1)	17	14. **Rockin' Years**	Columbia 73711
			DOLLY PARTON with RICKY VAN SHELTON	
5/18/91	**1** (1)	18	15. **I Am A Simple Man**	Columbia 73780
8/24/91	**1** (2)	20	16. **Keep It Between The Lines**	Columbia 73956
12/7/91+	**13**	15	17. After The Lights Go Out	Columbia 74104
4/4/92	**2** (1)	18	18. **Backroads**	Columbia 74258
8/22/92	**26**	8	19. Wear My Ring Around Your Neck	Columbia 74418
			from the movie *Honeymoon In Vegas* starring James Caan	
11/14/92+	**5**	17	20. **Wild Man**	Columbia 74748
4/17/93	**26**	8	21. Just As I Am	Columbia 74896
2/19/94	**20**	9	22. Where Was I	Columbia 77334

DATE	POS	WKS	ARTIST–RECORD TITLE	LABEL & NO.
			SHENANDOAH	
			Quintet formed in Muscle Shoals, Alabama, as the MGM Band: Marty Raybon (vocals), Mike McGuire (drums), Ralph Ezell (bass), Stan Thorn (keyboards) and Jim Seales (former guitarist of the funk group Funkadelic). McGuire married actress Teresa Blake (of TV soap *All My Children*) on 7/9/94. In 1995, Ezell was replaced by Rocky Thacker.	
2/6/88	28	5	1. Stop The Rain	Columbia 07654
5/21/88	9	12	2. **She Doesn't Cry Anymore**	Columbia 07779
10/22/88	5	12	3. **Mama Knows**	Columbia 08042
2/18/89	1 (2)	13	4. **The Church On Cumberland Road**	Columbia 68550
6/10/89	1 (1)	14	5. **Sunday In The South**	Columbia 68892
9/30/89	1 (1)	24	6. **Two Dozen Roses**	Columbia 69061
3/17/90	6	11	7. **See If I Care**	Columbia 73237
6/30/90	1 (3)	18	8. **Next To You, Next To Me**	Columbia 73373
10/20/90	5	18	9. **Ghost In This House**	Columbia 73520
2/2/91	7	16	10. **I Got You**	Columbia 73672
6/1/91	9	14	11. **The Moon Over Georgia**	Columbia 73777
10/26/91	38	1	12. When You Were Mine	Columbia 73957
4/25/92	2 (1)	17	13. **Rock My Baby**	RCA 62199
9/12/92	28	6	14. Hey Mister (I Need This Job)	RCA 62290
12/26/92+	15	12	15. Leavin's Been A Long Time Comin'	RCA 62397
6/26/93	15	11	16. Janie Baker's Love Slave	RCA 62504
11/20/93+	3	14	17. **I Want To Be Loved Like That**	RCA 62642
3/5/94	1 (1)	17	18. **If Bubba Can Dance (I Can Too)**	RCA 62761

12/31/94+	7	16	19. **Somewhere In The Vicinity Of The Heart**
			     SHENANDOAH With Alison Krauss
			     from Shenandoah's album *In The Vicinity Of The Heart* on Liberty
			     31109; later available as the B-side #20 below
				Liberty LP Cut

5/13/95	4	16	20. **Darned If I Don't (Danged If I Do)**	Liberty 18484
9/9/95	24	8	21. Heaven Bound (I'm Ready)	Capitol 18730
2/3/96	40	1	22. Always Have, Always Will	Capitol 18903
			SHEPARD, Jean	
			Born Ollie Imogene Shepard on 11/21/33 in Pauls Valley, Oklahoma; raised in Visalia, California. Formed all-girl band, the Melody Ranch Girls, in the late 1940s. Discovered by Hank Thompson. Worked with Red Foley's *Ozark Jubilee*, 1955-57. Member of the *Grand Ole Opry* since 1955. Husband Hawkshaw Hawkins died in a plane crash on 3/5/63.	
7/25/53	1 (6)	23	1. **A Dear John Letter** Best Seller #1(6) / Juke Box #1(4) / Jockey #2	Capitol 2502

10/10/53	4	7	2. **Forgive Me John**
			     JEAN SHEPARD & FERLIN HUSKEY (above 2)
			     Best Seller #4 / Juke Box #6 / Jockey #8
				Capitol 2586

6/25/55	4	22	3. **A Satisfied Mind/** Best Seller #4 / Juke Box #4 / Jockey #10	
7/16/55	13	1	4. Take Possession Jockey #13	Capitol 3118
10/8/55	4	19	5. **Beautiful Lies/** Best Seller #4 / Juke Box #4 / Jockey #12	
10/22/55	10	3	6. **I Thought Of You** Jockey #10	Capitol 3222
12/22/58	18	2	7. I Want To Go Where No One Knows Me	Capitol 4068

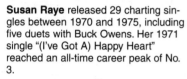

Susan Raye released 29 charting singles between 1970 and 1975, including five duets with Buck Owens. Her 1971 single "(I've Got A) Happy Heart" reached an all-time career peak of No. 3.

Del Reeves's 12th charting single came in 1967 with the No. 33 hit "The Private." The singer's full name? None other than Franklin Delano Reeves.

Jim Reeves's career was tragically cut short by a 1964 plane crash, though he continued to score posthumous hits well into the '80s. Eerily, the three hits to follow his death were "I Won't Forget You," "This Is It," and "Is It Really Over?"

Restless Heart's first Top 10 hit came via 1985's "I Want Everyone To Cry." That and three other Top 10 entries were found on the Nashville-based quintet's eponymous debut album.

Charlie Rich, the so-called "Silver Fox," began his career at Sun Records, then in 1963 signed to RCA's Groove subsidiary—for whom he recorded "She Loved Everybody But Me." His greatest success would come 10 years later, with 1973's No. 1 hit "Behind Closed Doors."

Tex Ritter's truly legendary career included its share of decided non-smashes—such as his late '60s single "Bump Tiddil Dee Bum Bum," which, despite its delightful title, failed to make an impression on the charts.

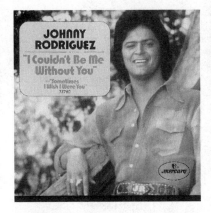

Johnny Rodriguez, a former member of Tom T. Hall's band and—with Freddy Fender—one of Country's biggest Latino stars, boasted 15 consecutive Top 10 hits between 1972 and 1977. His "I Couldn't Be Me Without You" climbed to No. 3 in 1976.

Kenny Rogers's longstanding role as a hitmaker features a peculiar quirk. Of the 53 chart hits he recorded between 1969 and 1980, only the first, the second and—oddly—the 40th were released on Reprise Records.

Billy Joe Royal's '60s Pop roots have never been totally out of the picture. The Georgia-born singer—who had a Top 10 Pop hit in 1965 with "Down In The Boondocks"—remade Johnny Tillotson's 1962 Pop hit "It Keeps Right On Hurtin'" in 1988. It rose to No. 17 on the Country charts.

Sawyer Brown is living proof that TV's "Star Search" did what it claimed. First the Nashville-based quintet appeared on the show in 1984, then, a year later—with a contract with Capitol under its belt—the group shot to the top of the charts with "Step That Step."

John Schneider, known to TV fans as Bo Duke from "The Dukes Of Hazzard," met equal success in the recording studio: His "Country Girls" became the second No. 1 single of his career in 1985.

Dan Seals, formerly half of '70s Pop duo England Dan & John Ford Coley, enjoyed a hot streak of 11 No. 1 hits between 1985 and 1990. Count 1986's "Everything That Glitters (Is Not Gold)" among them.

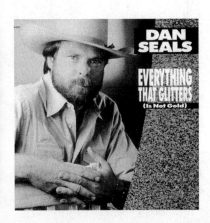

DATE	POS	WKS	ARTIST– RECORD TITLE	LABEL & NO.
4/20/59	30	1	8. Have Heart, Will Love	Capitol 4129
6/6/64	5	23	9. **Second Fiddle (To An Old Guitar)**	Capitol 5169
3/13/65	38	2	10. A Tear Dropped By	Capitol 5304
6/12/65	30	5	11. Someone's Gotta Cry	Capitol 5392
3/12/66	13	13	12. Many Happy Hangovers To You	Capitol 5585
5/28/66	9	13	13. **I'll Take The Dog**	Capitol 5633
7/23/66	10	14	14. **If Teardrops Were Silver**	Capitol 5681
12/31/66+	25	6	15. Mr. Do-It-Yourself	Capitol 5769
			JEAN SHEPARD & RAY PILLOW (#13 & #15)	
2/25/67	12	11	16. Heart, We Did All That We Could	Capitol 5822
6/24/67	17	7	17. Your Forevers (Don't Last Very Long)	Capitol 5899
11/11/67	40	1	18. I Don't See How I Can Make It	Capitol 5983
7/13/68	36	4	19. A Real Good Woman	Capitol 2180
9/27/69	18	8	20. Seven Lonely Days	Capitol 2585
1/17/70	8	12	21. **Then He Touched Me**	Capitol 2694
5/16/70	23	8	22. A Woman's Hand	Capitol 2779
9/5/70	22	8	23. I Want You Free	Capitol 2847
11/28/70	12	10	24. Another Lonely Night	Capitol 2941
2/27/71	24	8	25. With His Hand In Mine	Capitol 3033
7/7/73	4	13	26. **Slippin' Away**	United Art. 248
1/5/74	36	3	27. Come On Phone	United Art. 317
3/30/74	13	7	28. At The Time	United Art. 384
8/3/74	17	6	29. I'll Do Anything It Takes (To Stay With You)	United Art. 442
11/30/74+	14	7	30. Poor Sweet Baby	United Art. 552
3/22/75	16	8	31. The Tip Of My Fingers	United Art. 591

SHEPPARD, T.G.

Born William Neal Browder on 7/20/42 in Alamo, Tennessee. Moved to Memphis in 1960. Worked as backup singer with Travis Wammack's band. Recorded as Brian Stacey for Atlantic in 1966. Invented his stage name; initials do not signify "The German Sheppard" or "The Good Sheppard," as commonly thought.

DATE	POS	WKS	ARTIST– RECORD TITLE	LABEL & NO.
12/28/74+	1 (1)	10	1. **Devil In The Bottle**	Melodyland 6002
4/26/75	1 (1)	12	2. **Tryin' To Beat The Morning Home**	Melodyland 6006
9/13/75	14	10	3. Another Woman	Melodyland 6016
1/17/76	7	11	4. **Motels And Memories**	Melodyland 6028
6/12/76	14	10	5. Solitary Man	Hitsville 6032
			#21 Pop hit for Neil Diamond in 1970	
10/2/76	8	10	6. **Show Me A Man**	Hitsville 6040
1/22/77	37	3	7. May I Spend Every New Years With You	Hitsville 6048
3/19/77	20	5	8. Lovin' On	Hitsville 6053
11/26/77+	13	8	9. Mister D.J.	Warner/Curb 8490
3/18/78	13	7	10. Don't Ever Say Good-Bye	Warner/Curb 8525
6/3/78	5	10	11. **When Can We Do This Again**	Warner/Curb 8593
9/30/78	7	8	12. **Daylight**	Warner/Curb 8678
12/23/78+	8	11	13. **Happy Together**	Warner/Curb 8721
			#1 Pop hit for The Turtles in 1967	
4/28/79	4	10	14. **You Feel Good All Over**	Warner/Curb 8808
8/18/79	1 (2)	10	15. **Last Cheater's Waltz**	Warner/Curb 49024

DATE	POS	WKS	ARTIST– RECORD TITLE	LABEL & NO.
12/15/79+	1 (2)	11	16. **I'll Be Coming Back For More**	Warner/Curb 49110
4/26/80	6	11	17. **Smooth Sailin'**	Warner/Curb 49214
8/9/80	1 (1)	11	18. **Do You Wanna Go To Heaven**	Warner/Curb 49515
12/6/80+	1 (1)	10	19. **I Feel Like Loving You Again**	Warner/Curb 49615
3/21/81	1 (1)	10	20. **I Loved 'Em Every One**	Warner/Curb 49690
7/25/81	1 (1)	13	21. **Party Time**	Warner/Curb 49761
12/5/81+	1 (1)	13	22. **Only One You**	Warner/Curb 49858
4/17/82	1 (1)	10	23. **Finally**	Warner/Curb 50041
9/18/82	1 (1)	13	24. **War Is Hell (On The Homefront Too)**	Warner/Curb 29934
12/18/82+	1 (1)	13	25. **Faking Love**	Warner/Curb 29854
			T.G. SHEPPARD and KAREN BROOKS	
4/30/83	12	9	26. Without You	Warner/Curb 29695
			#1 Pop hit for Nilsson in 1972	
11/5/83+	1 (1)	14	27. **Slow Burn**	Warner/Curb 29469
3/10/84	12	8	28. Make My Day [N]	Warner/Curb 29343
			T.G. SHEPPARD with CLINT EASTWOOD	
			from the movie *Sudden Impact* starring Clint Eastwood	
6/16/84	3	13	29. **Somewhere Down The Line**	Warner/Curb 29369
12/1/84+	4	13	30. **One Owner Heart**	Warner/Curb 29167
3/23/85	10	10	31. **You're Going Out Of My Mind**	Warner/Curb 29071
6/15/85	21	7	32. Fooled Around And Fell In Love	Columbia 04890
			#3 Pop hit for Elvin Bishop in 1976	
9/28/85	8	11	33. **Doncha?**	Columbia 05591
1/25/86	9	10	34. **In Over My Heart**	Columbia 05747
6/7/86	1 (1)	14	35. **Strong Heart**	Columbia 05905
11/8/86+	2 (2)	15	36. **Half Past Forever (Till I'm Blue In The Heart)**	Columbia 06347
4/11/87	2 (1)	13	37. **You're My First Lady**	Columbia 06999
9/26/87	2 (1)	16	38. **One For The Money**	Columbia 07312
1/14/89	14	9	39. **You Still Do**	Columbia 08119
			SHIBLEY, Arkie, and his Mountain Dew Boys	
			Shibley born in Van Buren, Arkansas, in 1915. His Mountain Dew Boys are Leon Kelly, Jack Hays and Phil Fregon.	
1/20/51	5	7	1. **Hot Rod Race** [N]	Gilt Edge 5021
			Jockey #5 / Juke Box #6	
			SHINER, Mervin	
			Born on 2/20/21 in Bethlehem, Pennsylvania. Played guitar from age 16, teamed with his mother. Appeared on WFIL-Philadelphia in 1945.	
10/8/49	5	11	1. **Why Don't You Haul Off And Love Me**	Decca 46178
			Juke Box #5 / Best Seller #11	
4/1/50	6	3	2. **Peter Cottontail**	Decca 46221
			Jockey #6 / Best Seller #7	
			SHIRLEY & SQUIRRELY	
			Novelty studio production featuring squirrels instead of chipmunks. Conceived and produced by Bob Milsap.	
7/10/76	28	5	1. Hey Shirley (This Is Squirrely) [N]	GRT 054

DATE	POS	WKS	ARTIST—RECORD TITLE	LABEL & NO.
			SHOOTERS, The	
			Quintet led by vocalist/guitarist Walt Aldridge, featuring Gary Baker (bass), Barry Billings (guitar), Chalmers Davis (keyboards) and Michael Dillon (drums). Aldridge is a prolific producer/songwriter at Muscle Shoals Fame Studios.	
2/28/87	21	7	1. They Only Come Out At Night	Epic 06623
11/7/87	34	4	2. Tell It To Your Teddy Bear	Epic 07367
3/12/88	31	4	3. I Taught Her Everything She Knows About Love	Epic 07684
11/26/88+	13	10	4. Borderline	Epic 08082
4/8/89	17	8	5. If I Ever Go Crazy	Epic 68587
8/26/89	39	1	6. You Just Can't Lose 'Em All	Epic 68955
			SHOPPE, The	
			Band formed in Dallas in 1968. Consisted of Clarke Wilcox (guitar, banjo), Jack Wilcox (bass), Mark Cathey and Kevin Bailey (vocals), Mike Caldwell (harmonica), Lou Chavez (drums) and Roger Ferguson (guitar).	
3/28/81	33	2	1. Doesn't Anybody Get High On Love Anymore	NSD 80
			SHRUM, Walter, and his Colorado Hillbillies	
10/6/45	3	1	1. **Triflin' Gal**	Coast 2010
			SIMON, Carly	
			Born on 6/25/45 in New York City. Prolific pop singer/songwriter. Father is co-founder of Simon & Schuster publishing. Won the 1971 Best New Artist Grammy Award. Married to James Taylor, 1972-83.	
10/14/78	33	3	1. Devoted To You **CARLY SIMON & JAMES TAYLOR**	Elektra 45506
			SIMPSON, Red	
			Born Joseph Simpson in Higby, Arizona. Moved to Bakersfield in the late '40s and performed at the Blackboard Club. Co-wrote several hit songs with Buck Owens, including "Sam's Place," "Gonna Have Love," "Heart Of Glass" and "Kansas City Song."	
4/23/66	38	1	1. Roll Truck Roll	Capitol 5577
6/4/66	39	3	2. The Highway Patrol	Capitol 5637
12/25/71+	4	12	3. **I'm A Truck**	Capitol 3236
			SINGLETARY, Daryle	
			Born on a small farm outside of Whigham, Georgia. Singer/songwriter.	
5/27/95	39	1	1. I'm Living Up To Her Low Expectations	Giant 17902
9/2/95	2 (1)	15	2. **I Let Her Lie**	Giant 17818
1/20/96	4	14	3. **Too Much Fun** above 3 from the album *Daryle Singletary* on Giant 24606	Giant LP Cut
			SINGLETON, Margie	
			Born on 10/5/35 in Coushatta, Louisiana. Worked on the *Louisiana Hayride*, 1957-59. Performed on ABC-TV's *Jubilee USA* from 1960. Married to music business executive/producer Shelby Singleton and then to Leon Ashley.	
8/3/59	25	5	1. Nothin' But True Love	Starday 443

DATE	POS	WKS	ARTIST–RECORD TITLE	LABEL & NO.
2/1/60	**12**	14	2. The Eyes Of Love	Starday 472
9/18/61	**15**	3	3. Did I Ever Tell You	Mercury 71856
6/16/62	**11**	10	4. Waltz Of The Angels	Mercury 71955
			GEORGE JONES & MARGIE SINGLETON (above 2)	
12/28/63+	**11**	14	5. Old Records	Mercury 72213
3/21/64	**5**	22	6. **Keeping Up With The Joneses/**	
4/4/64	**40**	1	7. No Thanks, I Just Had One	Mercury 72237
12/26/64	**38**	2	8. Another Woman's Man Another Man's Woman	Mercury 72312
			FARON YOUNG & MARGIE SINGLETON (above 3)	
10/7/67	**39**	4	9. Ode To Billie Joe	Ashley 2011

SKAGGS, Ricky

Born on 7/18/54 in Cordell, Kentucky. Played mandolin from age five. Worked with the Clinch Mountain Boys in 1969, Country Gentlemen in 1974. Own group, Boone Creek, in 1975. In Emmylou Harris's Hot Band in 1977. Moved to Nashville in 1980 and worked with The Whites. Married Sharon White in 1981. On the *Grand Ole Opry* since 1982. CMA Awards: 1982 Horizon Award; 1982 Male Vocalist of the Year; 1985 Entertainer of the Year; 1987 Vocal Duo of the Year (with Sharon White).

DATE	POS	WKS	ARTIST–RECORD TITLE	LABEL & NO.
6/6/81	**16**	8	1. Don't Get Above Your Raising	Epic 02034
10/3/81	**9**	11	2. **You May See Me Walkin'**	Epic 02499
2/13/82	**1 (1)**	13	3. **Crying My Heart Out Over You**	Epic 02692
6/5/82	**1 (1)**	13	4. **I Don't Care**	Epic 02931
9/25/82	**1 (1)**	11	5. **Heartbroke**	Epic 03212
1/22/83	**1 (1)**	12	6. **I Wouldn't Change You If I Could**	Epic 03482
5/14/83	**1 (1)**	12	7. **Highway 40 Blues**	Epic 03812
8/27/83	**2 (1)**	13	8. **You've Got A Lover**	Epic 04044
12/24/83+	**1 (1)**	12	9. **Don't Cheat In Our Hometown**	Sugar Hill 04245
4/7/84	**1 (1)**	11	10. **Honey (Open That Door)**	Sugar Hill 04394
8/4/84	**1 (1)**	13	11. **Uncle Pen**	Sugar Hill 04527
			written by Bill Monroe in tribute to his musically influential uncle, Pen Vandiver	
11/24/84+	**2 (1)**	14	12. **Something In My Heart**	Epic 04668
4/6/85	**1 (1)**	13	13. **Country Boy**	Epic 04831
10/5/85	**7**	12	14. **You Make Me Feel Like A Man**	Epic 05585
2/1/86	**1 (1)**	13	15. **Cajun Moon**	Epic 05748
6/14/86	**10**	11	16. **I've Got A New Heartache**	Epic 05898
10/18/86	**4**	15	17. **Love's Gonna Get You Someday**	Epic 06327
3/7/87	**30**	4	18. I Wonder If I Care As Much	Epic 06650
5/16/87	**10**	12	19. **Love Can't Ever Get Better Than This**	Epic 07060
			RICKY SKAGGS & SHARON WHITE	
11/14/87+	**18**	10	20. I'm Tired	Epic 07416
4/2/88	**33**	2	21. (Angel On My Mind) That's Why I'm Walkin'	Epic 07721
			same tune as Stonewall Jackson's "Why I'm Walkin'"	
7/2/88	**17**	9	22. Thanks Again	Epic 07924
11/19/88	**30**	4	23. Old Kind Of Love	Epic 08063
4/22/89	**1 (1)**	15	24. **Lovin' Only Me**	Epic 68693
9/9/89	**5**	11	25. **Let It Be You**	Epic 68995
1/6/90	**13**	12	26. Heartbreak Hurricane	Epic 73078
6/2/90	**20**	7	27. Hummingbird	Epic 73312
9/29/90	**25**	10	28. He Was On To Somethin' (So He Made You)	Epic 73496

DATE	POS	WKS	ARTIST– RECORD TITLE	LABEL & NO.
4/27/91	25	8	29. Restless **MARK O'CONNOR-THE NEW NASHVILLE CATS Featuring STEVE WARINER, RICKY SKAGGS AND VINCE GILL**	Warner 19354
10/12/91	37	3	30. Life's Too Long (To Live Like This)	Epic 73947
2/8/92	12	13	31. Same Ol' Love	Epic 74147

SKINNER, Jimmie

Born on 4/27/09 in Blue Lick, Ohio. Died of a heart attack on 10/27/79. Own show on WNOP-Newport, Kentucky. Worked as a DJ on WNOX-Knoxville and WPEB-Middleton, Ohio, in the mid-1940s. First recorded for Red Barn. Owned a famous mail-order record shop in Cincinnati.

DATE	POS	WKS	ARTIST– RECORD TITLE	LABEL & NO.
4/30/49	15	1	1. Tennessee Border Best Seller #15	Radio Artist 244
11/4/57+	5	17	2. **I Found My Girl In The USA** Jockey #5 / Best Seller #9; answer song to "Fraulein" and "Geisha Girl"	Mercury 71192
3/24/58	8	8	3. **What Makes A Man Wander** Jockey #8 / Best Seller #14	Mercury 71256
1/19/59	7	10	4. **Dark Hollow/**	
1/12/59	21	8	5. Walkin' My Blues Away	Mercury 71387
8/3/59	17	11	6. John Wesley Hardin	Mercury 71470
1/18/60	14	11	7. Riverboat Gambler	Mercury 71539
5/16/60	21	4	8. Lonesome Road Blues	Mercury 71606
8/29/60	13	8	9. Reasons To Live	Mercury 71663
12/19/60	30	1	10. Careless Love	Mercury 71704

S-K-O—see SCHUYLER, KNOBLOCH & OVERSTREET

SLATER, David

Born on 11/22/62 in Dallas. Winner on TV's *Star Search* in 1987.

DATE	POS	WKS	ARTIST– RECORD TITLE	LABEL & NO.
5/14/88	36	2	1. I'm Still Your Fool	Capitol 44129
8/6/88	30	4	2. The Other Guy #11 Pop hit for the Little River Band in 1983	Capitol 44184

SLEDD, Patsy

Born on 1/29/44 in Falcon, Missouri. In family vocal group, the Randolph Singers. Did solo work on the *Grand Ole Opry*. Moved to Nashville in 1965. Toured with Roy Acuff in 1967. Appeared on *Hee Haw* and *Midwestern Hayride* TV shows.

DATE	POS	WKS	ARTIST– RECORD TITLE	LABEL & NO.
3/2/74	33	4	1. Chip Chip #10 Pop hit for Gene McDaniels in 1962	Mega 203

SMART, Jimmy

Native of Terrell, Texas.

DATE	POS	WKS	ARTIST– RECORD TITLE	LABEL & NO.
10/10/60	18	2	1. Broken Dream	Allstar 7211
3/13/61	16	7	2. Shorty	Plaid 1004

SMILEY, Red—see RENO & SMILEY

DATE	POS	WKS	ARTIST– RECORD TITLE	LABEL & NO.
			SMITH, Arthur "Guitar Boogie," and His Cracker-Jacks	
			Smith born on 4/1/21 in Clinton, South Carolina. Guitarist/banjo/mandolin. Long run of radio shows on WBT-Charlotte from the '30s. Operator of a recording studio in Charlotte since the '50s.	
9/25/48	9	2	1. **Banjo Boogie** [I] Juke Box #9	MGM 10229
12/25/48+	8	7	2. **Guitar Boogie/** [I] Juke Box #8	
1/1/49	8	4	3. **Boomerang** [I] Juke Box #8	MGM 10293
10/19/63	29	3	4. Tie My Hunting Dog Down, Jed [N] **ARTHUR "GUITAR BOOGIE" SMITH** same tune as "Tie Me Kangaroo Down, Sport" by Rolf Harris	Starday 642
			SMITH, Bobby	
			Born in 1946 in Balch Springs, Texas. Sang in the University of Texas choir.	
9/19/81	30	4	1. Just Enough Love (For One Woman)	Liberty 1417
1/9/82	40	1	2. Too Many Hearts In The Fire	Liberty 1439
			SMITH, Cal	
			Born Calvin Grant Shofner on 4/7/32 in Gans, Oklahoma; raised in Oakland. Worked clubs in San Jose and as a DJ on KEEN-San Jose. Regular member of the *California Hayride*. Worked with Ernest Tubb, 1962-68.	
10/5/68	35	6	1. Drinking Champagne	Kapp 938
5/27/72	4	11	2. **I've Found Someone Of My Own** #5 Pop hit for Free Movement in 1971	Decca 32959
12/30/72+	1 (1)	15	3. **The Lord Knows I'm Drinking**	Decca 33040
6/23/73	25	7	4. I Can Feel The Leavin' Coming On/	
		7	5. I've Loved You All Over The World	MCA 40061
4/6/74	1 (1)	10	6. **Country Bumpkin** CMA Award: Single of the Year	MCA 40191
9/7/74	11	7	7. Between Lust And Watching TV	MCA 40265
12/28/74+	1 (1)	12	8. **It's Time To Pay The Fiddler**	MCA 40335
5/17/75	13	8	9. She Talked A Lot About Texas	MCA 40394
11/22/75	12	8	10. Jason's Farm	MCA 40467
3/20/76	33	3	11. Thunderstorms	MCA 40517
11/13/76	38	3	12. Woman Don't Try To Sing My Song	MCA 40618
2/12/77	15	7	13. I Just Came Home To Count The Memories	MCA 40671
5/21/77	23	6	14. Come See About Me	MCA 40714
			SMITH, Carl	
			Born on 3/15/27 in Maynardsville, Tennessee. Worked on WROL-Knoxville in the 1940s. Joined WSM-Nashville in 1950, then signed by Columbia Records. With the Phillip Morris Country Music Show troupe in 1957, then served as host for ABC-TV's *Four Star Jubilee* in 1961. Hosted CTV of Canada's *Carl Smith's Country Music Hall* for five years. Married to June Carter for a time; father of Carlene Carter. Married to singer Goldie Hill since 1957. Retired to his Tennessee ranch in 1977.	
6/2/51	2 (1)	20	1. **Let's Live A Little** Jockey #2 / Best Seller #3 / Juke Box #3	Columbia 20796

DATE	POS	WKS	ARTIST- RECORD TITLE	LABEL & NO.
8/4/51	4	17	2. **Mr. Moon/** *Jockey #4 / Juke Box #5 / Best Seller #8*	
8/4/51	8	3	3. **If Teardrops Were Pennies** *Juke Box #8 / Best Seller #9 / Jockey #9*	Columbia 20825
10/27/51	1 (8)	33	4. **Let Old Mother Nature Have Her Way** *Juke Box #1(8) / Best Seller #1(6) / Jockey #1(3)*	Columbia 20862
3/1/52	1 (8)	24	5. **(When You Feel Like You're In Love) Don't Just Stand There** *Jockey #1(8) / Best Seller #1(5) / Juke Box #1(3)*	Columbia 20893
5/24/52	1 (1)	19	6. **Are You Teasing Me/** *Jockey #1 / Juke Box #2 / Best Seller #2*	
5/31/52	5	10	7. **It's A Lovely, Lovely World** *Jockey #5 / Best Seller #8 / Juke Box #9*	Columbia 20922
10/25/52	6	6	8. **Our Honeymoon** *Jockey #6 / Juke Box #6 / Best Seller #7*	Columbia 21008
1/31/53	9	1	9. **That's The Kind Of Love I'm Looking For** *Juke Box #9*	Columbia 21051
5/9/53	4	6	10. **Orchids Mean Goodbye/** *Juke Box #4 / Best Seller #7 / Jockey #7*	
5/2/53	7	3	11. **Just Wait 'Til I Get You Alone** *Jockey #7 / Juke Box #7 / Best Seller #9*	Columbia 21087
7/4/53	2 (2)	10	12. **Trademark/** *Best Seller #2 / Juke Box #5 / Jockey #6*	
7/18/53	6	1	13. **Do I Like It?** *Jockey #6*	Columbia 21119
7/25/53	1 (8)	26	14. **Hey Joe!** *Juke Box #1(8) / Jockey #1(4) / Best Seller #1(2)*	Columbia 21129
11/7/53	7	6	15. **Satisfaction Guaranteed** *Best Seller #7 / Jockey #7 / Juke Box #8*	Columbia 21166
2/13/54	7	4	16. **Dog-Gone It, Baby, I'm In Love** *Jockey #7 / Best Seller #8*	Columbia 21197
5/1/54	2 (1)	16	17. **Back Up Buddy** *Jockey #2 / Best Seller #4 / Juke Box #4*	Columbia 21226
8/7/54	4	11	18. **Go, Boy, Go**	Columbia 21266
11/6/54+	1 (7)	32	19. **Loose Talk/** *Best Seller #1(7) / Jockey #1(6) / Juke Box #1(4)*	
11/6/54+	5	10	20. **More Than Anything Else In The World** *Jockey #5 / Best Seller #15*	Columbia 21317
1/22/55	5	16	21. **Kisses Don't Lie/** *Best Seller #5 / Juke Box #7 / Jockey #8*	
1/29/55	13	2	22. **No, I Don't Believe I Will** *Best Seller #13 / Jockey #15*	Columbia 21340
4/23/55	12	3	23. Wait A Little Longer Please, Jesus *Jockey #12*	Columbia 21368
5/14/55	3	25	24. **There She Goes/** *Jockey #3 / Best Seller #5 / Juke Box #8; #26 Pop hit for Jerry Wallace in 1961*	
5/14/55	11	7	25. Old Lonesome Times *Best Seller #11 / Jockey #13*	Columbia 21382
10/15/55	11	4	26. Don't Tease Me *Jockey #11 / Best Seller #13*	Columbia 21429

DATE	POS	WKS	ARTIST– RECORD TITLE	LABEL & NO.
12/3/55+	**6**	14	27. **You're Free To Go/** Best Seller #6 / Juke Box #6 / Jockey #7	
12/3/55+	**7**	15	28. **I Feel Like Cryin'** Best Seller #7 / Juke Box #9 / Jockey #11	Columbia 21462
3/31/56	**11**	3	29. I've Changed Jockey #11 / Best Seller #14	Columbia 21493
6/23/56	**4**	23	30. **You Are The One/** Jockey #4 / Juke Box #5 / Best Seller #6	
8/4/56	**6**	6	31. **Doorstep To Heaven** Best Seller #6	Columbia 21522
10/13/56	**6**	12	32. **Before I Met You/** **CARL SMITH with The Tunesmiths** (above 3) Juke Box #6 / Jockey #7 / Best Seller #9	
10/20/56	**9**	10	33. **Wicked Lies** Best Seller #9	Columbia 21552
3/2/57	**15**	1	34. You Can't Hurt Me Anymore Best Seller #15	Columbia 40823
9/16/57	**2 (2)**	19	35. **Why, Why** Jockey #2 / Best Seller #7	Columbia 40984
3/3/58	**6**	14	36. **Your Name Is Beautiful** Jockey #6 / Best Seller #9	Columbia 41092
12/15/58	**28**	1	37. Walking The Slow Walk	Columbia 41243
1/19/59	**15**	11	38. The Best Years Of Your Life	Columbia 41290
6/1/59	**19**	3	39. It's All My Heartache	Columbia 41344
7/20/59	**5**	12	40. **Ten Thousand Drums**	Columbia 41417
12/14/59	**24**	4	41. Tomorrow Night	Columbia 41489
3/21/60	**30**	1	42. Make The Waterwheel Roll	Columbia 41557
6/20/60	**28**	2	43. Cut Across Shorty	Columbia 41642
2/20/61	**29**	2	44. You Make Me Live Again	Columbia 41819
7/10/61	**11**	9	45. Kisses Never Lie	Columbia 42042
1/13/62	**11**	15	46. Air Mail To Heaven/	
1/27/62	**24**	2	47. Things That Mean The Most	Columbia 42222
5/12/62	**16**	7	48. The Best Dressed Beggar (In Town)	Columbia 42349
4/20/63	**28**	1	49. Live For Tomorrow	Columbia 42686
8/24/63	**17**	8	50. In The Back Room Tonight	Columbia 42768
12/21/63+	**16**	9	51. Triangle/	
11/9/63+	**23**	5	52. I Almost Forgot Her Today	Columbia 42858
2/29/64	**17**	11	53. The Pillow That Whispers	Columbia 42949
6/20/64	**15**	18	54. Take My Ring Off Your Finger	Columbia 43033
10/24/64	**14**	13	55. Lonely Girl/	
1/2/65	**26**	5	56. When It's Over	Columbia 43124
5/1/65	**32**	2	57. She Called Me Baby	Columbia 43200
7/17/65	**33**	5	58. Be Good To Her	Columbia 43266
10/30/65	**36**	4	59. Let's Walk Away Strangers	Columbia 43361
9/16/67	**10**	15	60. **Deep Water**	Columbia 44233
2/10/68	**18**	6	61. Foggy River	Columbia 44396
2/8/69	**25**	8	62. Faded Love And Winter Roses	Columbia 44702
6/7/69	**18**	7	63. Good Deal, Lucille	Columbia 44816
9/6/69	**14**	8	64. I Love You Because	Columbia 44939
1/10/70	**35**	3	65. Heartbreak Avenue	Columbia 45031

DATE	POS	WKS	ARTIST– RECORD TITLE	LABEL & NO.
3/21/70	**18**	9	66. Pull My String And Wind Me Up	Columbia 45086
10/31/70	**20**	6	67. How I Love Them Old Songs	Columbia 45225
10/2/71	**21**	10	68. Red Door	Columbia 45436
2/12/72	**34**	2	69. Don't Say You're Mine	Columbia 45497

SMITH, Connie

Born Constance June Meadows on 8/14/41 in Elkhart, Indiana; raised in West Virginia and Ohio. Appeared with Floyd Miller's Square Dance Band while still a teenager. Worked on the TV series *Saturday Night Jamboree*, WSAZ-Huntingdon, West Virginia. Discovered by Bill Anderson. Member of the *Grand Ole Opry* since 1971. Appeared in the movies *Las Vegas Hillbillies, Road To Nashville* and *Second Fiddle To A Steel Guitar*.

DATE	POS	WKS	ARTIST– RECORD TITLE	LABEL & NO.
9/26/64	**1** (8)	27	1. **Once A Day**	RCA 8416
1/23/65	**4**	22	2. **Then And Only Then/**	
2/27/65	**25**	12	3. Tiny Blue Transistor Radio	RCA 8489
6/5/65	**9**	16	4. **I Can't Remember**	RCA 8551
10/9/65	**4**	17	5. **If I Talk To Him**	RCA 8663
2/12/66	**4**	17	6. **Nobody But A Fool (Would Love You)**	RCA 8746
6/11/66	**2** (2)	17	7. **Ain't Had No Lovin'**	RCA 8842
10/22/66	**3**	18	8. **The Hurtin's All Over**	RCA 8964
3/25/67	**10**	13	9. **I'll Come Runnin'**	RCA 9108
7/1/67	**4**	13	10. **Cincinnati, Ohio**	RCA 9214
11/11/67	**5**	13	11. **Burning A Hole In My Mind**	RCA 9335
2/17/68	**7**	11	12. **Baby's Back Again**	RCA 9413
5/25/68	**10**	13	13. **Run Away Little Tears**	RCA 9513
10/26/68	**20**	7	14. Cry, Cry, Cry	RCA 9624
3/15/69	**13**	12	15. Ribbon Of Darkness	RCA 0101
7/19/69	**20**	8	16. Young Love	RCA 0181
			CONNIE SMITH and NAT STUCKEY	
			#1 Pop hit for Tab Hunter in 1957	
11/8/69	**6**	15	17. **You And Your Sweet Love**	RCA 0258
5/30/70	**5**	12	18. **I Never Once Stopped Loving You**	RCA 9832
9/26/70	**14**	8	19. Louisiana Man	RCA 9887
1/9/71	**11**	12	20. Where Is My Castle	RCA 9938
5/22/71	**2** (2)	14	21. **Just One Time**	RCA 9981
11/13/71	**14**	10	22. I'm Sorry If My Love Got In Your Way	RCA 0535
3/18/72	**5**	13	23. **Just For What I Am**	RCA 0655
8/19/72	**7**	13	24. **If It Ain't Love (Let's Leave It Alone)**	RCA 0752
1/13/73	**8**	11	25. **Love Is The Look You're Looking For**	RCA 0860
4/28/73	**21**	8	26. You've Got Me (Right Where You Want Me)	Columbia 45816
7/21/73	**23**	5	27. Dream Painter	RCA 0971
12/8/73+	**10**	9	28. **Ain't Love A Good Thing**	Columbia 45954
5/4/74	**35**	3	29. Dallas	Columbia 46008
7/27/74	**13**	8	30. I Never Knew (What That Song Meant Before)	Columbia 46058
12/7/74+	**13**	8	31. I've Got My Baby On My Mind	Columbia 10051
3/22/75	**30**	6	32. I Got A Lot Of Hurtin' Done Today	Columbia 10086
6/7/75	**15**	7	33. Why Don't You Love Me	Columbia 10135
11/1/75	**29**	6	34. The Song We Fell In Love To	Columbia 10210
2/21/76	**10**	10	35. **('Til) I Kissed You**	Columbia 10277

DATE	POS	WKS	ARTIST–RECORD TITLE	LABEL & NO.
6/26/76	**31**	6	36. So Sad (To Watch Good Love Go Bad) #7 Pop hit for The Everly Brothers in 1960	Columbia 10345
9/18/76	**13**	9	37. I Don't Wanna Talk It Over Anymore	Columbia 10393
11/26/77+	**14**	8	38. I Just Want To Be Your Everything #1 Pop hit for Andy Gibb in 1977	Monument 231
3/25/78	**34**	3	39. Lovin' You Baby	Monument 241

SMITH, Kate

Born on 5/1/07 in Greenville, Virginia. Died on 6/17/86. Tremendously popular soprano who was for years one of the most-listened-to of all radio singers, and later hosted own TV variety series.

DATE	POS	WKS	ARTIST–RECORD TITLE	LABEL & NO.
10/30/48	**10**	1	1. **Foggy River** Best Seller #10; Jack Miller (orch.)	MGM 30059

SMITH, Lou

DATE	POS	WKS	ARTIST–RECORD TITLE	LABEL & NO.
8/15/60	**9**	17	1. **Cruel Love**	KRCO 105
4/17/61	**21**	5	2. I'm Wondering	Salvo 2862

SMITH, Margo

Born Bette Lou Miller on 4/9/42 in Dayton, Ohio. Sang with the Apple Sisters vocal group while in high school. Writes almost all of her hits.

DATE	POS	WKS	ARTIST–RECORD TITLE	LABEL & NO.
5/10/75	**8**	10	1. **There I Said It**	20th Century 2172
10/11/75	**30**	6	2. Paper Lovin'	20th Century 2222
6/12/76	**10**	11	3. **Save Your Kisses For Me** #27 Pop hit for The Brotherhood Of Man in 1976	Warner 8213
10/16/76	**7**	10	4. **Take My Breath Away**	Warner 8261
3/26/77	**12**	9	5. Love's Explosion	Warner 8339
7/16/77	**23**	5	6. My Weakness	Warner 8399
12/24/77+	**1 (2)**	14	7. **Don't Break The Heart That Loves You** #1 Pop hit for Connie Francis in 1962	Warner 8508
5/6/78	**1 (1)**	12	8. **It Only Hurts For A Little While** #11 Pop hit for The Ames Brothers in 1956	Warner 8555
9/16/78	**3**	10	9. **Little Things Mean A Lot** #1 Pop hit for Kitty Kallen in 1954	Warner 8653
1/20/79	**7**	10	10. **Still A Woman**	Warner 8726
5/19/79	**10**	9	11. **If I Give My Heart To You** #3 Pop hit for Doris Day in 1954	Warner 8806
9/15/79	**27**	6	12. Baby My Baby	Warner 49038
12/22/79+	**13**	9	13. The Shuffle Song	Warner 49109
1/17/81	**12**	7	14. Cup Of Tea	Warner 49626
7/4/81	**26**	6	15. While The Feeling's Good **REX ALLEN, JR. & MARGO SMITH (above 2)**	Warner 49738

SMITH, Russell

Born Howard Russell Smith on 6/17/49 in Nashville. Worked on WREN-Lafayette while a teenager. Former lead singer of the Amazing Rhythm Aces. Went solo in 1982. Now with group Run C&W.

DATE	POS	WKS	ARTIST–RECORD TITLE	LABEL & NO.
4/29/89	**37**	3	1. I Wonder What She's Doing Tonight	Epic 68615

DATE	POS	WKS	ARTIST– RECORD TITLE	LABEL & NO.
			SMITH, Sammi	
			Born on 8/5/43 in Orange, California; raised in Oklahoma. Female singer. Performing since age 12. Moved to Nashville in 1967.	
10/10/70	25	5	1. He's Everywhere	Mega 1
1/2/71	1 (3)	18	● 2. **Help Me Make It Through The Night** CMA Award: Single of the Year	Mega 0015
6/12/71	10	8	3. **Then You Walk In**	Mega 0026
10/16/71	27	8	4. For The Kids	Mega 0039
1/29/72	38	5	5. Kentucky	Mega 0056
5/20/72	36	2	6. Girl In New Orleans	Mega 0068
6/24/72	13	14	7. I've Got To Have You	Mega 0079
2/16/74	16	8	8. The Rainbow In Daddy's Eyes	Mega 204
10/12/74	26	7	9. Long Black Veil	Mega 1214
3/8/75	33	4	10. Cover Me	Mega 1222
10/4/75	9	11	11. **Today I Started Loving You Again**	Mega 1236
8/21/76	29	3	12. Sunday School To Broadway	Elektra 45334
3/5/77	19	6	13. Loving Arms	Elektra 45374
6/11/77	27	5	14. I Can't Stop Loving You #1 Pop hit for Ray Charles in 1962	Elektra 45398
10/15/77	23	5	15. Days That End In "Y"	Elektra 45429
3/31/79	16	8	16. What A Lie	Cyclone 100
8/11/79	27	6	17. The Letter #1 Pop hit for The Box Tops in 1967	Cyclone 104
1/24/81	36	2	18. I Just Want To Be With You	Snd. Factory 425
3/28/81	16	7	19. Cheatin's A Two Way Street	Snd. Factory 427
9/12/81	34	3	20. Sometimes I Cry When I'm Alone	Snd. Factory 446
			SMITH, Warren	
			Born on 2/7/33 in Humphreys County, Mississippi. Died of a heart attack on 1/30/80. Rockabilly singer/songwriter. Served in U.S. Air Force until 1950. Discovered by Carl Perkins. Involved in automobile accident on 8/17/65; left music until the mid-1970s.	
9/5/60	5	17	1. **I Don't Believe I'll Fall In Love Today**	Liberty 55248
2/20/61	7	15	2. **Odds And Ends (Bits And Pieces)**	Liberty 55302
9/11/61	23	3	3. Why, Baby, Why **WARREN SMITH and SHIRLEY COLLIE**	Liberty 55361
9/11/61	26	3	4. Call Of The Wild	Liberty 55336
11/2/63	25	3	5. That's Why I Sing In A Honky Tonk	Liberty 55615
			SNODGRASS, Elmer, and The Musical Pioneers	
			DJ on WAKE-Bakersfield, California.	
1/18/60	20	10	1. Until Today	Decca 31048
1/30/61	25	1	2. What A Terrible Feeling	Decca 31145

DATE	POS	WKS	ARTIST—RECORD TITLE	LABEL & NO.
			SNOW, Hank	
			Born Clarence Eugene Snow on 5/9/14 in Liverpool, Nova Scotia. Worked as a cabin boy in the Merchant Marine from age 12. Performed at clubs in Halifax and appeared on CHNS-Halifax from 1934. First recorded for Victor in 1936. Moved to the U.S. in the mid-1940s; worked on the WWVA-Wheeling *Jamboree*. Worked in Hollywood with his performing horse, Shawnee. On KRLD-Dallas in the late 1940s; with the *Grand Ole Opry* since 1950. Backing group: The Rainbow Ranch Boys. Known as The Singing Ranger. Elected to the Country Music Hall of Fame in 1979.	
			HANK SNOW (THE SINGING RANGER) AND HIS RAINBOW RANCH BOYS:	
12/31/49	**10**	1	1. **Marriage Vow** Best Seller #10; 45 rpm: 48-0056	RCA Victor 0062
7/1/50	**1** (21)	44	2. **I'm Moving On** Best Seller #1(21) / Jockey #1(18) / Juke Box #1(14)	RCA Victor 0328
11/25/50+	**1** (2)	23	3. **The Golden Rocket** Best Seller #1(2) / Jockey #1(1) / Juke Box #2	RCA Victor 0400
3/3/51	**1** (8)	27	4. **The Rhumba Boogie** Best Seller #1(8) / Juke Box #1(5) / Jockey #1(2)	RCA 0431
5/12/51	**2** (1)	14	5. **Down The Trail Of Achin' Hearts/** Juke Box #2 / Best Seller #7 / Jockey #7	
4/21/51	**4**	11	6. **Bluebird Island** **HANK SNOW (The Singing Ranger) with ANITA CARTER and The Rainbow Ranch Boys** (above 2) Best Seller #4 / Juke Box #7	RCA 0441
9/15/51	**6**	6	7. **Unwanted Sign Upon Your Heart** Best Seller #6 / Jockey #9	RCA 0498
12/15/51+	**4**	9	8. **Music Makin' Mama From Memphis** Juke Box #4 / Jockey #5 / Best Seller #6	RCA 4346
4/5/52	**2** (3)	18	9. **The Gold Rush Is Over** Juke Box #2 / Best Seller #4 / Jockey #4	RCA 4522
7/5/52	**2** (1)	14	10. **Lady's Man/** Best Seller #2 / Juke Box #5 / Jockey #6	
7/26/52	**8**	3	11. **Married By The Bible, Divorced By The Law** Juke Box #8 / Best Seller #10	RCA 4733
9/27/52	**3**	11	12. **I Went To Your Wedding** Juke Box #3 / Best Seller #4 / Jockey #4	RCA 4909
12/27/52+	**3**	16	13. **(Now and Then, There's) A Fool Such As I/** Jockey #3 / Juke Box #3 / Best Seller #4	
12/13/52+	**4**	10	14. **The Gal Who Invented Kissin'** Best Seller #4 / Juke Box #5 / Jockey #9	RCA 5034
4/4/53	**9**	2	15. **Honeymoon On A Rocket Ship** Best Seller #9 / Jockey #9 / Juke Box #9	RCA 5155
6/6/53	**3**	11	16. **Spanish Fire Ball** Best Seller #3 / Juke Box #4 / Jockey #5	RCA 5296
10/3/53	**10**	1	17. **For Now And Always** Jockey #10	RCA 5380
11/28/53	**6**	6	18. **When Mexican Joe Met Jole Blon** Best Seller #6 / Juke Box #9	RCA 5490
5/29/54	**1** (20)	41	19. **I Don't Hurt Anymore** Best Seller #1(20) / Juke Box #1(20) / Jockey #1(18)	RCA 5698
12/4/54	**10**	6	20. **That Crazy Mambo Thing** Juke Box #10 / Best Seller #11	RCA 5912

DATE	POS	WKS	ARTIST– RECORD TITLE	LABEL & NO.
12/25/54+	1 (2)	16	21. **Let Me Go, Lover!** Jockey #1 / Juke Box #2 / Best Seller #3	RCA 5960
1/1/55	15	1	22. The Next Voice You Hear Best Seller #15	RCA 5912
4/2/55	15	1	23. Silver Bell [I] **HANK SNOW and CHET ATKINS** Best Seller #15	RCA 5995
4/9/55	3	27	24. **Yellow Roses/** Best Seller #3 / Jockey #3 / Juke Box #3	
4/16/55	3	17	25. **Would You Mind?** Jockey #3 / Juke Box #4	RCA 6057
7/23/55	7	8	26. **Cryin', Prayin', Waitin', Hopin'/** Juke Box #7 / Best Seller #9 / Jockey #10	
7/23/55	7	2	27. **I'm Glad I Got To See You Once Again** Juke Box #7 / Best Seller #12	RCA 6154
11/5/55	5	9	28. **Born To Be Happy/** Juke Box #5 / Jockey #10 / Best Seller #14	
11/5/55	5	8	29. **Mainliner (The Hawk with Silver Wings)** Juke Box #5 / Best Seller #8	RCA 6269
2/4/56	5	10	30. **These Hands/** Juke Box #5 / Jockey #6 / Best Seller #8	
2/18/56	11	4	31. I'm Moving In Best Seller #11	RCA 6379
8/4/56	4	22	32. **Conscience I'm Guilty/** Juke Box #4 / Best Seller #8 / Jockey #9	
8/4/56	5	4	33. **Hula Rock** Juke Box #5	RCA 6578
12/15/56+	7	9	34. **Stolen Moments** Juke Box #7 / Best Seller #8 / Jockey #9	RCA 6715
			HANK SNOW:	
7/22/57	4	19	35. **Tangled Mind/** Jockey #4 / Best Seller #9	
7/22/57	8	14	36. **My Arms Are A House** Jockey #8 / Best Seller #13	RCA 6955
3/31/58	15	1	37. Whispering Rain Jockey #15 / Best Seller #18	RCA 7154
6/23/58	7	9	38. **Big Wheels** Jockey #7 / Best Seller #18	RCA 7233
11/3/58	16	5	39. A Woman Captured Me	RCA 7325
3/16/59	19	6	40. Doggone That Train	RCA 7448
6/1/59	6	11	41. **Chasin' A Rainbow** **HANK SNOW and The Rainbow Ranch Boys**	RCA 7524
10/19/59	3	20	42. **The Last Ride**	RCA 7586
4/11/60	22	5	43. Rockin', Rollin' Ocean	RCA 7702
7/18/60	9	15	44. **Miller's Cave**	RCA 7748
5/15/61	5	20	45. **Beggar To A King** written by The Big Bopper (J.P. Richardson)	RCA 7869
10/9/61	11	9	46. The Restless One	RCA 7933
6/2/62	15	10	47. You Take The Future (And I'll Take the Past)	RCA 8009
9/15/62	1 (2)	22	48. **I've Been Everywhere**	RCA 8072
4/27/63	9	11	49. **The Man Who Robbed The Bank At Santa Fe**	RCA 8151
10/26/63	2 (3)	22	50. **Ninety Miles An Hour (Down a Dead End Street)**	RCA 8239

DATE	POS	WKS	ARTIST– RECORD TITLE	LABEL & NO.
4/11/64	11	14	51. Breakfast With The Blues/	
7/11/64	21	11	52. I Stepped Over The Line	RCA 8334
2/20/65	7	18	53. **The Wishing Well (Down in the Well)**	RCA 8488
11/6/65	28	4	54. The Queen Of Draw Poker Town	RCA 8655
1/8/66	18	12	55. I've Cried A Mile	RCA 8713
5/7/66	22	11	56. The Count Down	RCA 8808
12/31/66+	21	10	57. Hula Love	RCA 9012
6/10/67	18	9	58. Down At The Pawn Shop	RCA 9188
10/28/67	20	9	59. Learnin' A New Way Of Life	RCA 9300
6/15/68	20	12	60. The Late And Great Love (Of My Heart)	RCA 9523
1/4/69	16	15	61. The Name Of The Game Was Love	RCA 9685
6/14/69	26	6	62. Rome Wasn't Built In A Day	RCA 0151
3/16/74	1 (1)	10	63. **Hello Love**	RCA 0215
8/31/74	36	1	64. That's You And Me	RCA 0307
12/14/74+	26	6	65. Easy To Love	RCA 10108

SNYDER, Jimmy

DATE	POS	WKS	ARTIST– RECORD TITLE	LABEL & NO.
3/28/70	30	3	1. The Chicago Story	Wayside 009

SOME OF CHET'S FRIENDS

Tribute to Chet Atkins by RCA artists: Jerry Reed, Floyd Cramer, Eddy Arnold, Dottie West, Archie Campbell, Bobby Bare, Norma Jean, George Hamilton IV, Skeeter Davis, Jimmy Dean, Hank Locklin, Jim Ed Brown, Hank Snow, John D. Loudermilk, Connie Smith, Homer & Jethro, Waylon Jennings, Willie Nelson, Porter Wagoner and Don Bowman.

DATE	POS	WKS	ARTIST– RECORD TITLE	LABEL & NO.
7/22/67	38	2	1. Chet's Tune	RCA 9229

SONNIER, Jo-el

Born on 10/2/46 in Rayne, Louisiana. Cajun accordianist. First recorded for Swallow in 1960. Won first prize in the Mamou Mardi Gras Competition in 1968. Worked in Nashville, 1974-79. Once known as the "Cajun Valentino." Bit part in the movie *Mask*.

DATE	POS	WKS	ARTIST– RECORD TITLE	LABEL & NO.
1/9/88	39	2	1. Come On Joe	RCA 5282
4/2/88	7	11	2. **No More One More Time**	RCA 6895
8/13/88	9	12	3. **Tear-Stained Letter**	RCA 8304
12/24/88+	35	4	4. Rainin' In My Heart	RCA 8726
			#34 Pop hit for Slim Harpo in 1961	
12/2/89+	24	8	5. If Your Heart Should Ever Roll This Way Again	RCA 9014

SONS OF THE PIONEERS

Originally a trio consisting of Bob Nolan (born 4/1/08, died 6/15/80), Leonard Slye (also known as Dick Weston and Roy Rogers) and Tim Spencer (died 6/26/74, age 65). Formed in 1934 and first called the Pioneers; recorded for Decca in 1934. Brothers Karl (died 9/20/61, age 52; guitar) and Hugh (fiddle) Farr were added in 1936. Appeared in the movie *Rhythm On The Range* and many others. Rogers and Spencer left in 1937, replaced by Lloyd Perryman and Pat Brady. Spencer returned shortly thereafter. Nolan wrote "Cool Water" and "Tumbling Tumbleweeds." Elected to the Country Music Hall of Fame in 1980.

DATE	POS	WKS	ARTIST– RECORD TITLE	LABEL & NO.
10/6/45	4	2	1. **Stars And Stripes On Iwo Jima**	RCA Victor 1724
6/29/46	6	1	2. **No One To Cry To**	RCA Victor 1868
2/15/47	5	1	3. **Baby Doll**	RCA Victor 2086

DATE	POS	WKS	ARTIST– RECORD TITLE	LABEL & NO.
3/8/47	**4**	1	4. **Cool Water** [R] first recorded as by the Sons in 1936; also on the flip side of #1 above	Decca 46027
7/12/47	**5**	1	5. **Cigareetes, Whusky, And Wild, Wild Women**	RCA Victor 2199
7/26/47	**4**	2	6. **Teardrops In My Heart**	RCA Victor 2276
8/21/48	**11**	1	7. Tumbling Tumbleweeds [R] Juke Box #11; 45 rpm: 48-0005; recorded on Decca 5047 in 1934	RCA Victor 1904
9/4/48	**7**	11	8. **Cool Water** [R] Best Seller #7 / Juke Box #11; 45 rpm: 48-0004; first recorded on Decca 5939 in 1941	Decca 46027
2/19/49	**12**	1	9. My Best To You Juke Box #12	RCA Victor 2199
9/10/49	**10**	1	10. **Room Full Of Roses** Juke Box #10; 45 rpm: 48-0060	RCA Victor 0065
			SOSEBEE, Tommy	
			Born Bud Thomas Sosebee on 5/23/23 in Duncan, South Carolina. Died on 10/23/67 in Greenville, South Carolina. Known as "The Voice Of The Hills."	
3/14/53	**7**	2	1. **Till I Waltz Again With You** Jockey #7	Coral 60916
			SOUTH, Joe	
			Born Joe Souter on 2/28/40 in Atlanta. Successful Nashville session guitarist/songwriter in the mid-1960s. Wrote "Down In The Boondocks," "Hush" and "Rose Garden."	
8/28/61	**16**	6	1. You're The Reason	Fairlane 21006
10/25/69	**27**	6	2. Don't It Make You Want To Go Home **JOE SOUTH & THE BELIEVERS**	Capitol 2592
			SOUTHER, J.D.—see RONSTADT, Linda	
			SOUTHERN PACIFIC	
			Band formed in Los Angeles in 1985. Consisted of John McFee (formerly with The Doobie Brothers; guitar, fiddle), Stu Cook (formerly with Creedence Clearwater Revival; bass), Keith Knudsen (formerly with The Doobie Brothers; drums), Kurt Howell (keyboards), and lead vocalist Tim Goodman. Goodman replaced by David Jenkins (formerly with Pablo Cruise) in 1986. Jenkins left in early 1989. Group disbanded in 1991.	
9/7/85	**14**	10	1. Thing About You Emmylou Harris (guest vocal); written by Tom Petty	Warner 28943
12/21/85+	**18**	9	2. Perfect Stranger	Warner 28870
5/10/86	**9**	10	3. **Reno Bound** originally the B-side of #2 above	Warner 28722
8/30/86	**17**	9	4. A Girl Like Emmylou	Warner 28647
1/17/87	**37**	2	5. Killbilly Hill	Warner 28554
4/25/87	**26**	5	6. Don't Let Go Of My Heart	Warner 28408
5/14/88	**14**	10	7. Midnight Highway	Warner 27952
8/27/88	**2** (2)	16	8. **New Shade Of Blue**	Warner 27790
1/7/89	**5**	12	9. **Honey I Dare You**	Warner 27691
6/17/89	**4**	13	10. **Any Way The Wind Blows** from the movie *Pink Cadillac* starring Clint Eastwood	Warner 22965
1/13/90	**26**	8	11. Time's Up **SOUTHERN PACIFIC and CARLENE CARTER**	Warner 22714

DATE	POS	WKS	ARTIST–RECORD TITLE	LABEL & NO.
5/19/90	**31**	3	12. I Go To Pieces #9 Pop hit for Peter and Gordon in 1965	Warner 19860
9/15/90	**32**	5	13. Reckless Heart	Warner 19871

SOVINE, Red

Born Woodrow Wilson Sovine on 7/17/18 in Charleston, West Virginia. Died of a heart attack on 4/4/80. Worked on WCHS-Charleston with Jim Pike's Carolina Tarheels from 1935. Own band, the Echo Valley Boys, in 1947. On the *Louisiana Hayride*, 1949-54. On the *Grand Ole Opry* from 1954. Known as "The Old Syrup Sopper" from a radio series he did for Johnny Fair Syrup.

DATE	POS	WKS	ARTIST–RECORD TITLE	LABEL & NO.
3/26/55	**14**	2	1. Are You Mine **RED SOVINE - GOLDIE HILL** Best Seller #14	Decca 29411
12/17/55+	**1 (4)**	25	2. **Why Baby Why** **RED SOVINE and WEBB PIERCE** Jockey #1(4) / Best Seller #1(1) / Juke Box #1(1); also released on Decca 29739	Decca 29755
3/24/56	**15**	1	3. If Jesus Came To Your House Jockey #15	Decca 29825
4/21/56	**5**	14	4. **Little Rosa/** **RED SOVINE and WEBB PIERCE** Best Seller #5 / Jockey #5 / Juke Box #5	
5/19/56	**5**	8	5. **Hold Everything (Till I Get Home)** Juke Box #5	Decca 29876
1/11/64	**22**	11	6. Dream House For Sale	Starday 650
11/27/65+	**1 (6)**	21	7. **Giddyup Go** [S]	Starday 737
3/11/67	**17**	9	8. I Didn't Jump The Fence	Starday 794
8/19/67	**9**	13	9. **Phantom 309/** [S]	
7/22/67	**33**	5	10. In Your Heart	Starday 811
1/13/68	**33**	8	11. Tell Maude I Slipped	Starday 823
8/17/74	**16**	8	12. It'll Come Back	Chart 5220
7/4/76	**1 (3)**	8	● 13. **Teddy Bear** [S]	Starday 142

SPACEK, Sissy

Born Mary Elizabeth Spacek on 12/25/49 in Quitman, Texas. Singer/actress. Won Academy Award portraying Loretta Lynn in the movie *Coal Miner's Daughter*.

DATE	POS	WKS	ARTIST–RECORD TITLE	LABEL & NO.
5/24/80	**24**	4	1. Coal Miner's Daughter title song from the movie starring Sissy Spacek	MCA 41221
9/24/83	**15**	9	2. Lonely But Only For You	Atln. Am. 99847

SPEARS, Billie Jo

Born Billie Jean Spears on 1/14/37 in Beaumont, Texas. Worked on the *Louisiana Hayride* at age 13. Moved to Nashville in 1964. Very popular in England since 1977.

DATE	POS	WKS	ARTIST–RECORD TITLE	LABEL & NO.
5/3/69	**4**	11	1. **Mr. Walker, It's All Over**	Capitol 2436
2/7/70	**40**	1	2. Daddy, I Love You	Capitol 2690
8/8/70	**17**	11	3. Marty Gray	Capitol 2844
12/26/70	**30**	4	4. I Stayed Long Enough written by Tammy Wynette	Capitol 2964
4/17/71	**23**	6	5. It Could 'A Been Me	Capitol 3055
3/15/75	**1 (1)**	10	6. **Blanket On The Ground**	United Art. 584

DATE	POS	WKS	ARTIST– RECORD TITLE	LABEL & NO.
8/2/75	**20**	10	7. Stay Away From The Apple Tree	United Art. 653
11/29/75+	**20**	8	8. Silver Wings And Golden Rings	United Art. 712
3/20/76	**5**	12	9. **What I've Got In Mind**	United Art. 764
5/29/76	**29**	5	10. On The Rebound	United Art. 797
			DEL REEVES & BILLIE JO SPEARS	
7/10/76	**5**	11	11. **Misty Blue**	United Art. 813
			#3 Pop hit for Dorothy Moore in 1976	
11/13/76	**18**	6	12. Never Did Like Whiskey	United Art. 880
2/19/77	**11**	8	13. I'm Not Easy	United Art. 935
5/21/77	**8**	11	14. **If You Want Me**	United Art. 985
9/10/77	**18**	8	15. Too Much Is Not Enough	United Art. 1041
2/4/78	**18**	5	16. Lonely Hearts Club	United Art. 1127
5/6/78	**17**	6	17. I've Got To Go	United Art. 1190
9/2/78	**16**	7	18. '57 Chevrolet	United Art. 1229
12/9/78+	**24**	6	19. Love Ain't Gonna Wait For Us	United Art. 1251
5/12/79	**21**	6	20. I Will Survive	United Art. 1292
			#1 Pop hit for Gloria Gaynor in 1979	
9/1/79	**23**	5	21. Livin' Our Love Together	United Art. 1309
12/1/79+	**21**	7	22. Rainy Days And Stormy Nights	United Art. 1326
3/15/80	**15**	8	23. Standing Tall	United Art. 1336
8/2/80	**39**	2	24. Natural Attraction	United Art. 1358
1/31/81	**13**	7	25. Your Good Girl's Gonna Go Bad	Liberty 1395
2/25/84	**39**	1	26. Midnight Blue	Parliament 1801
			SPRINGFIELDS, The	
			English folk trio: Dusty Springfield and brother Tom Springfield and Tim Feild.	
8/25/62	**16**	10	1. Silver Threads And Golden Needles	Philips 40038
			STAFF, Bobbi	
			Born in 1946 in Kingston, North Carolina. She appeared on Arthur Smith's Talent Show while in third grade. Toured Europe with the U.S.O. in 1958.	
7/2/66	**31**	4	1. Chicken Feed	RCA 8833
			STAFFORD, Jo	
			Born on 11/12/20 in Coalinga, California. Member of Tommy Dorsey's vocal group The Pied Pipers, 1940-43. Married to orchestra leader Paul Weston. Also see Red Ingle.	
9/20/47	**5**	2	1. **Feudin' And Fightin'** [N]	Capitol 443
			vocal similar to Jo's "Cinderella G. Stump" with Red Ingle in 1947	
			STAFFORD, Terry	
			Born in Hollis, Oklahoma; raised in Amarillo, Texas. Died on 3/17/96. Worked in the Eugene Nelson band as a teenager. Moved to California in 1960; played with the Lively Ones and the Surfmen. Appeared in the movie *Wild Wheels*. Wrote "Big In Vegas" for Buck Owens.	
1/26/74	**31**	5	1. Amarillo By Morning/	
10/13/73	**35**	4	2. Say, Has Anybody Seen My Sweet Gypsy Rose	Atlantic 4006
			#3 Pop hit for Tony Orlando & Dawn in 1973	
4/27/74	**24**	7	3. Captured	Atlantic 4015

DATE	POS	WKS	ARTIST–RECORD TITLE	LABEL & NO.
			STAMPLEY, Joe	
			Born on 6/6/43 in Springhill, Louisiana. First recorded for Imperial in 1957. Lead singer of The Uniques in the mid-1960s. Staff writer for Gallico Music. CMA Award: 1980 Vocal Duo of the Year (with Moe Bandy).	
			(a) MOE BANDY & JOE STAMPLEY	
7/8/72	**9**	14	1. **If You Touch Me (You've Got To Love Me)**	Dot 17421
11/18/72+	**1** (1)	14	2. **Soul Song**	Dot 17442
4/14/73	**7**	11	3. **Bring It On Home (To Your Woman)**	Dot 17452
9/15/73	**12**	12	4. Too Far Gone	Dot 17469
12/29/73+	**3**	13	5. **I'm Still Loving You**	Dot 17485
5/25/74	**11**	9	6. How Lucky Can One Man Be	Dot 17502
10/5/74	**5**	12	7. **Take Me Home To Somewhere**	Dot 17522
2/8/75	**8**	7	8. **Penny**	ABC/Dot 17537
3/22/75	**1** (1)	10	9. **Roll On Big Mama**	Epic 50075
7/5/75	**11**	9	10. Dear Woman	Epic 50114
10/4/75	**12**	8	11. Billy, Get Me A Woman	Epic 50147
1/10/76	**25**	6	12. She's Helping Me Get Over Loving You	Epic 50179
5/8/76	**1** (1)	13	13. **All These Things**	ABC/Dot 17624
			#97 Pop hit for Stampley's group, The Uniques in 1966	
8/14/76	**16**	7	14. The Night Time And My Baby	ABC/Dot 17642
9/4/76	**18**	9	15. Whiskey Talkin'	Epic 50259
11/13/76	**12**	8	16. Everything I Own	ABC/Dot 17654
			#5 Pop hit for Bread in 1972	
1/22/77	**11**	9	17. There She Goes Again	Epic 50316
4/30/77	**26**	5	18. She's Long Legged	Epic 50361
7/16/77	**15**	9	19. Baby, I Love You So	Epic 50410
11/5/77	**14**	7	20. Everyday I Have To Cry Some	Epic 50453
			#45 Pop hit for Arthur Alexander in 1975	
4/1/78	**6**	10	21. **Red Wine And Blue Memories**	Epic 50517
7/29/78	**6**	9	22. **If You've Got Ten Minutes (Let's Fall In Love)**	Epic 50575
11/18/78+	**5**	10	23. **Do You Ever Fool Around**	Epic 50626
5/12/79	**12**	10	24. I Don't Lie	Epic 50694
7/28/79	**1** (1)	11	25. **Just Good Ol' Boys** (a)	Columbia 11027
9/15/79	**9**	9	26. **Put Your Clothes Back On**	Epic 50754
12/1/79+	**7**	9	27. **Holding The Bag** (a)	Columbia 11147
3/29/80	**17**	8	28. After Hours	Epic 50854
5/3/80	**11**	10	29. Tell Ole I Ain't Here, He Better Get On Home (a)	Columbia 11244
8/9/80	**32**	2	30. Haven't I Loved You Somewhere Before	Epic 50893
11/1/80	**18**	7	31. There's Another Woman	Epic 50934
2/14/81	**9**	9	32. **I'm Gonna Love You Back To Loving Me Again**	Epic 50972
3/28/81	**10**	9	33. **Hey Joe (Hey Moe)** (a)	Columbia 60508
6/20/81	**18**	7	34. Whiskey Chasin'	Epic 02097
8/15/81	**12**	8	35. Honky Tonk Queen (a)	Columbia 02198
4/17/82	**18**	9	36. I'm Goin' Hurtin'	Epic 02791
8/14/82	**30**	4	37. I Didn't Know You Could Break A Broken Heart	Epic 03016
11/27/82+	**25**	7	38. Backslidin'	Epic 03290
3/12/83	**24**	7	39. Finding You	Epic 03558

DATE	POS	WKS	ARTIST– RECORD TITLE	LABEL & NO.
7/23/83	**12**	9	40. Poor Side Of Town #1 Pop hit for Johnny Rivers in 1966	Epic 03966
11/26/83+	**8**	12	41. **Double Shot (Of My Baby's Love)** #17 Pop hit for the Swingin' Medallions in 1966	Epic 04173
3/17/84	**29**	5	42. Brown Eyed Girl #10 Pop hit for Van Morrison in 1967	Epic 04366
6/9/84	**39**	1	43. Memory Lane **JOE STAMPLEY and JESSICA BOUCHER**	Epic 04446
6/23/84	**8**	9	44. **Where's The Dress** (a)　　　　　　　　[N] parody about Pop singer Boy George of the group Culture Club	Columbia 04477
11/10/84	**36**	2	45. The Boy's Night Out (a)	Columbia 04601
			STANLEY BROTHERS	
			Bluegrass duo of Carter Glen (born 8/27/25, McClure, Virginia; died 12/1/66) and brother Ralph Edmond Stanley (born 2/25/27, Stratton, Virginia). Formed own band, the Clinch Mountain Boys, in 1946. First recorded for Rich-R-Tone in 1947.	
3/21/60	**17**	12	1. How Far To Little Rock　　　　　　　　[N]	King 5306
			STARCHER, Buddy	
			Born Oby Edgar Starcher on 3/16/06 near Ripley, West Virginia. Worked on WFBR-Baltimore in 1928. Worked as a DJ on WCAU, WIBG-Philadelphia. Own band from 1937. Managed KWBA-Bayton, Texas, in the early '70s.	
2/12/49	**8**	1	1. **I'll Still Write Your Name In The Sand** Juke Box #8	4 Star 1145
4/16/66	**2** (1)	14	2. **History Repeats Itself**　　　　　　　　[S]	Boone 1038
			STARR, Kay	
			Born Katherine Starks on 7/21/22 in Dougherty, Oklahoma; raised in Dallas and Memphis. With Joe Venuti's orchestra at age 15, and sang briefly with Glenn Miller, Charlie Barnet and Bob Crosby before launching solo career in 1945. Appeared in the movies *Make Believe Ballroom* and *When You're Smiling*.	
9/16/50	**2** (1)	16	1. **I'll Never Be Free/** Jockey #2 / Juke Box #2 / Best Seller #4	
8/26/50	**5**	6	2. **Ain't Nobody's Business But My Own** **KAY STARR and TENNESSEE ERNIE** (above 2) Jockey #5 / Juke Box #10	Capitol 1124
			STARR, Kenny	
			Born Kenneth Trebbe on 9/21/52 in Topeka; raised in Burlingame, Kansas. Own band, The Rockin' Rebels, at age nine. Toured with Loretta Lynn, 1968-75.	
11/29/75+	**2** (2)	11	1. **The Blind Man In The Bleachers** #18 Pop hit for David Geddes in 1975	MCA 40474
4/3/76	**26**	5	2. Tonight I'll Face The Man (Who Made It Happen)	MCA 40524
12/17/77+	**25**	8	3. Hold Tight	MCA 40817
			STARR, Ringo—see OWENS, Buck	

DATE	POS	WKS	ARTIST–RECORD TITLE	LABEL & NO.
			STATLER, Darrell	
			Born R. Darrell Staedtler on 12/27/40 in Llano, Texas. Staff songwriter for the Wilburn Brothers, Chappell Music and others since 1963.	
10/11/69	**40**	1	1. Blue Collar Job	Dot 17275
			STATLER BROTHERS, The	
			Group from Staunton, Virginia, formed as the Kingsmen in 1955. Consisted of Lew DeWitt (born 3/8/38; died 8/15/90 from Crohn's disease; tenor), Don Reid (born 6/5/45; lead), Philip Balsley (born 8/8/39; baritone) and Harold Reid (born 8/21/39; bass). Worked with Johnny Cash, 1963-71. DeWitt, who wrote their first hit, "Flowers On The Wall," retired from the group in 1982; replaced by Jimmy Fortune. Also recorded under comic persona as Lester "Roadhog" Moran & His Cadillac Cowboys. CMA Awards: 1972, 1973, 1974, 1975, 1976, 1977, 1979, 1980 and 1984 Vocal Group of the Year.	
10/9/65+	**2 (4)**	25	1. **Flowers On The Wall**	Columbia 43315
7/23/66	**30**	6	2. The Right One	Columbia 43624
12/24/66+	**37**	4	3. That'll Be The Day	Columbia 43868
5/27/67	**10**	12	4. **Ruthless**	Columbia 44070
9/16/67	**10**	12	5. **You Can't Have Your Kate And Edith, Too**	Columbia 44245
12/12/70+	**9**	14	6. **Bed Of Rose's**	Mercury 73141
5/29/71	**19**	8	7. New York City	Mercury 73194
9/4/71	**13**	10	8. Pictures	Mercury 73229
1/8/72	**23**	8	9. You Can't Go Home	Mercury 73253
3/18/72	**2 (4)**	14	10. **Do You Remember These**	Mercury 73275
9/2/72	**6**	13	11. **The Class Of '57**	Mercury 73315
3/3/73	**20**	7	12. Monday Morning Secretary	Mercury 73360
6/30/73	**29**	6	13. Woman Without A Home	Mercury 73392
10/6/73	**26**	8	14. Carry Me Back	Mercury 73415
2/9/74	**22**	6	15. Whatever Happened To Randolph Scott	Mercury 73448
7/27/74	**31**	4	16. Thank You World	Mercury 73485
12/7/74+	**15**	9	17. Susan When She Tried	Mercury 73625
4/12/75	**31**	3	18. All American Girl	Mercury 73665
7/26/75	**3**	12	19. **I'll Go To My Grave Loving You**	Mercury 73687
2/14/76	**39**	1	20. How Great Thou Art	Mercury 73732
5/8/76	**13**	8	21. Your Picture In The Paper	Mercury 73785
10/16/76	**10**	9	22. **Thank God I've Got You**	Mercury 73846
1/29/77	**10**	9	23. **The Movies**	Mercury 73877
5/14/77	**8**	10	24. **I Was There**	Mercury 73906
8/27/77	**18**	8	25. Silver Medals And Sweet Memories	Mercury 55000
12/24/77+	**17**	8	26. Some I Wrote	Mercury 55013
4/1/78	**1 (2)**	11	27. **Do You Know You Are My Sunshine**	Mercury 55022
8/12/78	**3**	11	28. **Who Am I To Say**	Mercury 55037
12/2/78+	**5**	10	29. **The Official Historian On Shirley Jean Berrell**	Mercury 55048
4/14/79	**7**	8	30. **How To Be A Country Star**	Mercury 55057
7/21/79	**11**	7	31. Here We Are Again	Mercury 55066
11/10/79	**10**	8	32. **Nothing As Original As You**	Mercury 57007
2/2/80	**8**	10	33. **(I'll Even Love You) Better Than I Did Then**	Mercury 57012
8/2/80	**5**	10	34. **Charlotte's Web**	Mercury 57031
			from the movie *Smokey and the Bandit II* starring Burt Reynolds	

DATE	POS	WKS	ARTIST– RECORD TITLE	LABEL & NO.
11/22/80+	**13**	10	35. Don't Forget Yourself	Mercury 57037
5/2/81	**35**	2	36. In The Garden	Mercury 57048
7/4/81	**5**	11	37. **Don't Wait On Me**	Mercury 57051
11/7/81+	**12**	11	38. Years Ago	Mercury 57059
3/27/82	**3**	13	39. **You'll Be Back (Every Night In My Dreams)**	Mercury 76142
7/17/82	**7**	12	40. Whatever	Mercury 76162
11/20/82+	**17**	10	41. A Child Of The Fifties	Mercury 76184
5/7/83	**2** (1)	12	42. **Oh Baby Mine (I Get So Lonely)** #2 Pop hit for The Four Knights in 1954	Mercury 811488
9/10/83	**9**	10	43. **Guilty**	Mercury 812988
1/14/84	**1** (1)	13	44. **Elizabeth**	Mercury 814881
5/12/84	**3**	13	45. **Atlanta Blue**	Mercury 818700
9/15/84	**8**	11	46. **One Takes The Blame**	Mercury 880130
1/5/85	**1** (1)	13	47. **My Only Love**	Mercury 880411
5/11/85	**3**	13	48. **Hello Mary Lou** #9 Pop hit for Ricky Nelson in 1961	Mercury 880685
9/14/85	**1** (1)	14	49. **Too Much On My Heart**	Mercury 884016
2/8/86	**8**	11	50. **Sweeter And Sweeter**	Mercury 884317
6/14/86	**5**	12	51. **Count On Me**	Mercury 884721
11/1/86	**36**	3	52. Only You #5 Pop hit for The Platters in 1955	Mercury 888042
12/27/86+	**7**	15	53. **Forever**	Mercury 888219
7/11/87	**10**	12	54. **I'll Be The One**	Mercury 888650
3/19/88	**15**	10	55. The Best I Know How	Mercury 870164
7/23/88	**27**	7	56. Am I Crazy?	Mercury 870442
11/12/88+	**12**	11	57. Let's Get Started If We're Gonna Break My Heart	Mercury 870681
3/18/89	**36**	2	58. Moon Pretty Moon	Mercury 872604
6/3/89	**6**	13	59. **More Than A Name On A Wall**	Mercury 874196

STEAGALL, Red

Born Russell Steagall on 12/22/37 in Gainesville, Texas. Guitarist and mandolin player since age 15, when he was recovering from polio. Moved to California in 1965. Staff writer for Tree and Combine Music. First recorded for Dot in 1969. Rodeo rider, and breeder of quarterhorses. Discovered Reba McEntire.

DATE	POS	WKS	ARTIST– RECORD TITLE	LABEL & NO.
3/4/72	**31**	2	1. Party Dolls And Wine **RED STEGALL**	Capitol 3244
1/6/73	**22**	6	2. Somewhere My Love	Capitol 3461
12/21/74+	**17**	8	3. Someone Cares For You	Capitol 3965
3/20/76	**11**	11	4. Lone Star Beer And Bob Wills Music	ABC/Dot 17610
7/24/76	**29**	5	5. Truck Drivin' Man	ABC/Dot 17634
3/8/80	**31**	4	6. 3 Chord Country Song	Elektra 46590
9/27/80	**30**	4	7. Hard Hat Days And Honky Tonk Nights	Elektra 47014

STEARNS, June—see DUNCAN, Johnny

STEGALL, Keith

Born Robert Keith Stegall on 11/1/54 in Wichita Falls, Texas. Third cousin of Johnny Horton. Pianist from age four; guitarist from age 12. Own band, the Pacesetters, at age 12. Toured overseas with folk group The Cheerful Givers. Worked as staff writer for CBS Music. Appeared in the movies *Killing At Hell's Gate* and *Country Gold*. Cousin of Jimmie Peters.

DATE	POS	WKS	ARTIST–RECORD TITLE	LABEL & NO.
6/16/84	25	6	1. I Want To Go Somewhere	Epic 04442
11/3/84	19	9	2. Whatever Turns You On	Epic 04590
3/16/85	13	10	3. California	Epic 04771
7/13/85	10	11	4. **Pretty Lady**	Epic 04934
4/5/86	36	3	5. I Think I'm In Love	Epic 05815
			STEPHENS, Ott	
			Born on 9/21/41 in Ringold, Georgia.	
1/19/63	15	7	1. Robert E. Lee	Chancellor 107
7/11/64	23	10	2. Be Quiet Mind	Reprise 0272
7/17/65	36	6	3. Enough Man For You	Chart 1205
			STEVENS, Even	
			Born in Lewiston, Ohio; raised in Cincinnati. Accomplished songwriter often teamed with Eddie Rabbitt and Dan Tyler.	
8/9/75	38	2	1. Let The Little Boy Dream	Elektra 45254
			STEVENS, Ray	
			Born Ray Ragsdale on 1/24/39 in Clarksdale, Georgia. Production work in the mid-1960s. Numerous appearances on Andy Williams's TV show in the late '60s. Own TV show in summer of 1970. Featured on *Music Country* TV show, 1973-74. The #1 novelty recording artist of the past 30 years. Also recorded as Henhouse Five Plus Too.	
5/23/70	39	2	● 1. Everything Is Beautiful	Barnaby 2011
1/1/72	17	8	2. Turn Your Radio On	Barnaby 2048
9/1/73	37	3	3. Nashville	Barnaby 5020
5/4/74	3	9	● 4. **The Streak** [N]	Barnaby 600
1/11/75	37	3	5. Everybody Needs A Rainbow	Barnaby 610
4/19/75	3	11	6. **Misty** written and recorded by Erroll Garner in 1954	Barnaby 614
11/1/75	38	3	7. Indian Love Call #3 Pop hit for Paul Whiteman in 1925	Barnaby 616
5/22/76	16	8	8. You Are So Beautiful #5 Pop hit for Joe Cocker in 1975	Warner 8198
8/28/76	27	5	9. Honky Tonk Waltz	Warner 8237
1/29/77	39	2	10. In The Mood [N] **HENHOUSE FIVE PLUS TOO** novelty version of Glenn Miller's 1940 #1 classic	Warner 8301
9/23/78	36	2	11. Be Your Own Best Friend	Warner 8603
2/23/80	7	8	12. **Shriner's Convention** [N]	RCA 11911
10/11/80	20	7	13. Night Games	RCA 12069
3/7/81	33	4	14. One More Last Chance	RCA 12170
3/6/82	35	2	15. Written Down In My Heart	RCA 13038
1/5/85	20	7	16. Mississippi Squirrel Revival [N]	MCA 52492
			STEWART, Gary	
			Born on 5/28/45 in Letcher County, Kentucky. First recorded for Cory in 1964. In the rock band The Amps in the mid-1960s. Toured with Charley Pride in 1976.	
7/20/74	10	11	1. **Drinkin' Thing**	RCA 0281

DATE	POS	WKS	ARTIST- RECORD TITLE	LABEL & NO.
11/23/74+	**4**	11	2. **Out Of Hand**	RCA 10061
3/29/75	**1** (1)	9	3. **She's Actin' Single (I'm Drinkin' Doubles)**	RCA 10222
7/19/75	**15**	8	4. You're Not The Woman You Use To Be	MCA 40414
11/22/75	**20**	5	5. Flat Natural Born Good-Timin' Man	RCA 10351
2/28/76	**23**	7	6. Oh, Sweet Temptation	RCA 10550
6/12/76	**15**	10	7. In Some Room Above The Street	RCA 10680
12/4/76+	**11**	10	8. Your Place Or Mine	RCA 10833
6/4/77	**16**	9	9. Ten Years Of This	RCA 10957
11/19/77	**26**	4	10. Quits	RCA 11131
4/1/78	**16**	7	11. Whiskey Trip	RCA 11224
8/19/78	**36**	3	12. Single Again	RCA 11297
12/12/81	**36**	2	13. She's Got A Drinking Problem	RCA 12343
			STEWART, Larry	
			Lead singer of Restless Heart, 1986-91.	
3/27/93	**5**	16	1. **Alright Already**	RCA 62474
8/28/93	**34**	3	2. I'll Cry Tomorrow	RCA 62546
			STEWART, Vernon	
1/12/63	**17**	6	1. The Way It Feels To Die	Chart 501
			STEWART, Wynn	
			Born Wynnford Lindsey Stewart on 6/7/34 in Morrisville, Missouri. Died of a heart attack on 7/17/85. Worked on KWTO-Springfield in 1947. Moved to California in 1949 and recorded for Intro at age 16. Own club and TV series in Las Vegas in the late '50s. With band The Tourists, in Hacienda Heights, California, in the late '60s.	
7/21/56	**14**	1	1. Waltz Of The Angels	Capitol 3408
12/28/59+	**5**	22	2. **Wishful Thinking**	Challenge 9061
5/30/60	**26**	2	3. Wrong Company	Challenge 59071
			WYNN STEWART and JAN HOWARD	
12/25/61	**18**	7	4. Big, Big Love	Challenge 9121
11/24/62	**27**	3	5. Another Day, Another Dollar	Challenge 9164
12/19/64	**30**	10	6. Half Of This, Half Of That	Challenge 5271
3/25/67	**1** (2)	18	7. **It's Such A Pretty World Today**	Capitol 5831
			#1 Easy Listening hit for Andy Russell in 1967	
8/19/67	**9**	11	8. 'Cause I Have You	Capitol 5937
11/25/67+	**7**	14	9. **Love's Gonna Happen To Me**	Capitol 2012
5/4/68	**10**	10	10. **Something Pretty**	Capitol 2137
9/14/68	**16**	8	11. In Love	Capitol 2240
1/4/69	**29**	8	12. Strings	Capitol 2341
5/3/69	**20**	8	13. Let The Whole World Sing It With Me	Capitol 2421
8/16/69	**19**	7	14. World-Wide Travelin' Man	Capitol 2549
			WYNN STEWART and The Tourists (above 6)	
9/26/70	**13**	10	15. It's A Beautiful Day	Capitol 2888
1/23/71	**32**	4	16. Heavenly	Capitol 3000
8/21/76	**8**	10	17. **After The Storm**	Playboy 6080
12/11/76+	**19**	7	18. Sing A Sad Song	Playboy 6091
2/10/79	**37**	3	19. Eyes Big As Dallas	WIN 126

DATE	POS	WKS	ARTIST– RECORD TITLE	LABEL & NO.
			STONE, Cliffie, and His Orchestra	
			Stone born Clifford Snyder on 3/1/17 in Burbank. Bass player, worked with the Anson Weeks and Freddie Slack bands in the late 1930s. Became a country DJ and hosted *Hollywood Barn Dance* and *Lucky Stars* in the mid-1940s. Worked as country A&R for Capitol Records, discovered Tennessee Ernie Ford. Wrote "No Vacancy," "Divorce Me C.O.D." and "New Steel Guitar Rag." Own record label, Granite Records. Elected to the Country Music Hall of Fame in 1989.	
3/15/47	**4**	1	1. **Silver Stars, Purple Sage, Eyes Of Blue**	Capitol 354
3/6/48	**4**	8	2. **Peepin' Thru The Keyhole (Watching Jole Blon)** **CLIFFIE STONE and His Barn Dance Band**	Capitol A. 40083
8/28/48	**11**	3	3. When My Blue Moon Turns To Gold Again Juke Box #11; #19 Pop hit for Elvis Presley in 1956	Capitol 15108
11/5/66	**30**	3	4. Little Pink Mack **KAY ADAMS with The Cliffie Stone Group**	Tower 269
			STONE, Doug	
			Born Doug Brooks on 6/19/56 in Atlanta. Changed name to avoid confusion with Garth Brooks. At age seven, opened on guitar for a Loretta Lynn concert. Starred in the 1995 movie *Gordy*.	
3/31/90	**4**	18	1. **I'd Be Better Off (In A Pine Box)**	Epic 73246
7/28/90	**6**	15	2. **Fourteen Minutes Old**	Epic 73425
12/1/90+	**5**	17	3. **These Lips Don't Know How To Say Goodbye**	Epic 73570
4/6/91	**1 (1)**	17	4. **In A Different Light**	Epic 73741
8/3/91	**4**	18	5. **I Thought It Was You**	Epic 73895
11/30/91+	**1 (2)**	18	6. **A Jukebox With A Country Song**	Epic 74089
4/11/92	**3**	16	7. **Come In Out Of The Pain**	Epic 74259
7/18/92	**4**	19	8. **Warning Labels**	Epic 74399
11/21/92+	**1 (1)**	18	9. **Too Busy Being In Love**	Epic 74761
3/20/93	**6**	15	10. **Made For Lovin' You**	Epic 74885
7/3/93	**1 (1)**	18	11. **Why Didn't I Think Of That**	Epic 77025
11/6/93+	**2 (2)**	18	12. **I Never Knew Love**	Epic 77228
3/12/94	**4**	14	13. **Addicted To A Dollar**	Epic 77375
7/16/94	**6**	14	14. **More Love**	Epic 77549
11/26/94+	**7**	15	15. **Little Houses**	Epic 77716
4/1/95	**13**	12	16. Faith In Me, Faith In You	Columbia 77837
10/21/95+	**12**	15	17. Born In The Dark	Columbia 78039
			STONEMANS, The	
			Family group formed in the late 1940s by Ernest "Pop" Stoneman (born 5/25/1893, Monorat, Virginia; died 6/14/68). Debuted on the *Grand Ole Opry* in 1962. On the Jimmy Dean TV shows in 1964 and had own series, *Those Stonemans*, in 1966. Group then consisted of Pop (autoharp, guitar), Scotty (fiddle), Van (guitar), Donna (mandolin), Roni (banjo) and Jim (bass). Pop first recorded for Okeh in 1924. CMA Award: 1967 Vocal Group of the Year.	
6/18/66	**40**	1	1. Tupelo County Jail	MGM 13466
10/15/66	**21**	10	2. The Five Little Johnson Girls	MGM 13557
5/20/67	**40**	1	3. Back To Nashville, Tennessee	MGM 13667

DATE	POS	WKS	ARTIST–RECORD TITLE	LABEL & NO.
			STRAIT, George	
			Born on 5/18/52 in Poteet, Texas; raised in Pearsall, Texas. Self-taught on guitar while in U.S. Army in 1971. Sang in a service band in Hawaii. Graduated from Southwest Texas State with a degree in agriculture. Own special, *Strait From The Heart*, on TNN. Starred in the movie *Pure Country*. CMA Awards: 1985 and 1986 Male Vocalist of the Year; 1989 and 1990 Entertainer of the Year.	
6/13/81	6	11	1. **Unwound**	MCA 51104
10/10/81	16	8	2. Down And Out	MCA 51170
2/20/82	3	15	3. **If You're Thinking You Want A Stranger (There's One Coming Home)**	MCA 51228
7/3/82	1 (1)	13	4. **Fool Hearted Memory**	MCA 52066
			from the movie *The Soldier* starring Klaus Kinski	
11/6/82+	6	12	5. **Marina Del Rey**	MCA 52120
2/26/83	4	12	6. **Amarillo By Morning**	MCA 52162
7/2/83	1 (1)	13	7. **A Fire I Can't Put Out**	MCA 52225
10/22/83+	1 (1)	15	8. **You Look So Good In Love**	MCA 52279
2/25/84	1 (1)	12	9. **Right Or Wrong**	MCA 52337
6/23/84	1 (1)	13	10. **Let's Fall To Pieces Together**	MCA 52392
10/20/84+	1 (1)	15	11. **Does Fort Worth Ever Cross Your Mind**	MCA 52458
2/23/85	5	12	12. **The Cowboy Rides Away**	MCA 52526
6/15/85	5	12	13. **The Fireman**	MCA 52586
10/12/85	1 (1)	15	14. **The Chair**	MCA 52667
2/1/86	4	13	15. **You're Something Special To Me**	MCA 52764
5/31/86	1 (1)	13	16. **Nobody In His Right Mind Would've Left Her**	MCA 52817
9/20/86	1 (1)	14	17. **It Ain't Cool To Be Crazy About You**	MCA 52914
1/24/87	1 (1)	14	18. **Ocean Front Property**	MCA 53021
5/2/87	1 (1)	13	19. **All My Ex's Live In Texas**	MCA 53087
8/29/87	1 (1)	13	20. **Am I Blue**	MCA 53165
2/13/88	1 (1)	13	21. **Famous Last Words Of A Fool**	MCA 53248
5/28/88	1 (1)	14	22. **Baby Blue**	MCA 53340
10/1/88	1 (1)	14	23. **If You Ain't Lovin' (You Ain't Livin')**	MCA 53400
1/28/89	1 (1)	13	24. **Baby's Gotten Good At Goodbye**	MCA 53486
5/6/89	1 (1)	15	25. **What's Going On In Your World**	MCA 53648
8/19/89	1 (1)	14	26. **Ace In The Hole**	MCA 53693
12/9/89+	8	16	27. **Overnight Success**	MCA 53755
5/5/90	1 (5)	20	28. **Love Without End, Amen**	MCA 79015
8/18/90	4	13	29. **Drinking Champagne**	MCA 79070
11/10/90	1 (5)	19	30. **I've Come To Expect It From You**	MCA 53969
3/30/91	1 (2)	19	31. **If I Know Me**	MCA 54052
6/22/91	1 (3)	19	32. **You Know Me Better Than That**	MCA 54127
10/12/91	3	19	33. **The Chill Of An Early Fall**	MCA 54180
2/1/92	24	7	34. Lovesick Blues	MCA 54318
4/25/92	5	14	35. **Gone As A Girl Can Get**	MCA 54379
7/25/92	3	15	36. **So Much Like My Dad**	MCA 54439
10/17/92	1 (2)	18	37. **I Cross My Heart**	MCA 54478
1/30/93	1 (1)	15	38. **Heartland**	MCA 54563
5/22/93	6	14	39. **When Did You Stop Loving Me**	MCA 54642
			above 3 from the movie *Pure Country* starring Strait	

DATE	POS	WKS	ARTIST–RECORD TITLE	LABEL & NO.
8/28/93	**1 (2)**	18	40. **Easy Come, Easy Go**	MCA 54717
12/18/93+	**3**	15	41. **I'd Like To Have That One Back**	MCA 54767
4/2/94	**8**	12	42. **Lovebug**	MCA 54819
7/16/94	**4**	13	43. **The Man In Love With You**	MCA 54854
10/15/94	**1 (1)**	16	44. **The Big One**	MCA 54938
1/7/95	**1 (1)**	16	45. **You Can't Make A Heart Love Somebody**	MCA 54964
4/8/95	**3**	12	46. **Adalida**	MCA 55019
7/15/95	**7**	11	47. **Lead On**	MCA 55064
10/7/95	**1 (4)**	18	48. **Check Yes Or No**	MCA 55127
12/30/95+	**5**	17	49. **I Know She Still Loves Me**	MCA 55163
4/13/96	**1 (2)**	15↑	50. **Blue Clear Sky**	MCA 55187

STREET, Mel

Born King Malachi Street on 10/21/33 near Grundy, West Virginia. Committed suicide on 10/21/78. Worked local radio as a teenager. Worked outside of music in Niagara Falls, New York. Own TV series, *Country Showcase*, in Bluefield, West Virginia, in the late '60s. First recorded for Tandem in 1970.

DATE	POS	WKS	ARTIST–RECORD TITLE	LABEL & NO.
6/17/72	**7**	13	1. **Borrowed Angel**	Royal Amer. 64
11/11/72+	**5**	15	2. **Lovin' On Back Streets**	Metro. Cnt. 901
4/7/73	**11**	12	3. Walk Softly On The Bridges	Metro. Cnt. 906
9/8/73	**38**	2	4. The Town Where You Live	Metro. Cnt. 0018
12/1/73+	**11**	9	5. Lovin' On Borrowed Time	Metro. Cnt. 0143
6/8/74	**15**	10	6. You Make Me Feel More Like A Man	GRT 002
12/7/74+	**16**	6	7. Forbidden Angel	GRT 012
4/5/75	**13**	8	8. Smokey Mountain Memories	GRT 017
7/26/75	**17**	9	9. Even If I Have To Steal	GRT 025
11/15/75	**23**	5	10. (This Ain't Just Another) Lust Affair	GRT 030
3/6/76	**32**	4	11. The Devil In Your Kisses (And The Angel In Your Eyes)	GRT 043
7/4/76	**10**	9	12. **I Met A Friend Of Your's Today**	GRT 057
11/20/76	**24**	7	13. Looking Out My Window Through The Pain	GRT 083
7/16/77	**19**	6	14. Barbara Don't Let Me Be The Last To Know	Polydor 14399
10/8/77	**15**	8	15. Close Enough For Lonesome	Polydor 14421
1/28/78	**9**	9	16. **If I Had A Cheating Heart**	Polydor 14448
5/6/78	**24**	5	17. Shady Rest	Polydor 14468
10/20/79	**17**	7	18. The One Thing My Lady Never Puts Into Words	Sunset 100
3/1/80	**30**	3	19. Tonight Let's Sleep On It Baby	Sunbird 103
12/6/80	**36**	3	20. Who'll Turn Out The Lights	Sunbird 7555

STREETS—see NIGHTSTREETS

STRUNK, Jud

Born Justin Strunk, Jr., on 6/11/36 in Jamestown, New York; raised in Farmington, Maine. Died in a plane crash on 10/15/81. Toured as a one-man show for U.S. Armed Forces. Worked in the Broadway musical *Beautiful Dreamer* and as a regular on TV's *Laugh-In*.

DATE	POS	WKS	ARTIST–RECORD TITLE	LABEL & NO.
4/21/73	**33**	6	1. Daisy A Day	MGM 14463

DATE	POS	WKS	ARTIST– RECORD TITLE	LABEL & NO.
			STUART, Marty	
			Born John Marty Stuart on 9/30/58 in Philadelphia, Mississippi. Worked with the Sullivan Family. Toured with Lester Flatt (Flatt & Scruggs) and Nashville Grass from age 13. Toured with the Johnny Cash Band, 1979-85. Did much session work in Nashville. Once married to Cash's daughter Cindy.	
2/15/86	19	7	1. Arlene	Columbia 05724
9/20/86	39	1	2. All Because Of You	Columbia 06230
9/30/89	32	3	3. Cry Cry Cry	MCA 53687
6/9/90	8	14	4. **Hillbilly Rock**	MCA 79001
10/6/90	20	10	5. Western Girls	MCA 79068
1/12/91	8	16	6. **Little Things**	MCA 53975
5/25/91	12	14	7. Till I Found You	MCA 54065
9/14/91	5	14	8. **Tempted**	MCA 54145
12/14/91+	2 (1)	17	9. **The Whiskey Ain't Workin'** **TRAVIS TRITT Featuring Marty Stuart**	Warner 19097
2/29/92	7	17	10. **Burn Me Down**	MCA 54253
6/20/92	7	12	11. **This One's Gonna Hurt You (For A Long, Long Time)** **MARTY STUART AND TRAVIS TRITT**	MCA 54405
10/10/92	18	9	12. Now That's Country	MCA 54477
1/16/93	24	8	13. High On A Mountain Top	MCA 54538
6/12/93	38	2	14. Hey Baby	MCA 54607
3/5/94	26	9	15. Kiss Me, I'm Gone	MCA 54777
5/11/96	23	11 ↑	16. Honky Tonkin's What I Do Best **MARTY STUART & TRAVIS TRITT**	MCA 55197
			STUBBY AND THE BUCCANEERS—see CAPTAIN STUBBY	
			STUCKEY, Nat	
			Born Nathan Wright Stuckey on 12/17/34 in Cass County, Texas. Died of lung cancer on 8/24/88. DJ on KALT-Atlanta, Texas, and KWKH-Shreveport. Own band, The Cornhuskers, 1958-59. On the *Louisiana Hayride*, 1962-66. Own band, The Sweet Thangs, from 1967. Wrote "Pop A Top" and "Waitin' In Your Welfare Line."	
9/24/66	4	16	1. **Sweet Thang**	Paula 243
2/4/67	17	7	2. Oh! Woman	Paula 257
5/13/67	27	8	3. All My Tomorrows	Paula 267
1/20/68	17	9	4. My Can Do Can't Keep Up With My Want To	Paula 287
11/2/68	9	13	5. **Plastic Saddle**	RCA 9631
2/22/69	13	10	6. Joe And Mabel's 12th Street Bar And Grill	RCA 9720
6/28/69	15	10	7. Cut Across Shorty	RCA 0163
7/19/69	20	8	8. Young Love **CONNIE SMITH & NAT STUCKEY** #1 Pop hit for Tab Hunter in 1957	RCA 0181
10/11/69	8	10	9. **Sweet Thang And Cisco**	RCA 0238
2/14/70	33	2	10. Sittin' In Atlanta Station	RCA 9786
6/6/70	31	4	11. Old Man Willis	RCA 9833
10/17/70	31	2	12. Whiskey, Whiskey	RCA 9884
1/2/71	11	11	13. She Wakes Me With A Kiss Every Morning (And She Loves Me to Sleep Every Night)	RCA 9929
5/29/71	24	7	14. Only A Woman Like You	RCA 9977

DATE	POS	WKS	ARTIST–RECORD TITLE	LABEL & NO.
9/25/71	17	7	15. I'm Gonna Act Right	RCA 1010
1/1/72	16	11	16. Forgive Me For Calling You Darling	RCA 0590
5/20/72	26	7	17. Is It Any Wonder That I Love You	RCA 0687
9/16/72	18	9	18. Don't Pay The Ransom	RCA 0761
3/3/73	10	10	19. **Take Time To Love Her**	RCA 0879
7/14/73	22	7	20. I Used It All On You	RCA 0973
11/17/73	14	7	21. Got Leaving On Her Mind	RCA 0115
3/30/74	31	4	22. You Never Say You Love Me Anymore	RCA 0222
1/4/75	36	3	23. You Don't Have To Go Home	RCA 10090
3/13/76	13	9	24. Sun Comin' Up	MCA 40519
8/5/78	26	4	25. The Days Of Sand And Shovels	MCA 40923
			#34 Pop hit for Bobby Vinton in 1969	

SULLIVAN, Gene

Born on 11/6/14 in Carbon Hill, Alabama. Also see Wiley & Gene.

DATE	POS	WKS	ARTIST–RECORD TITLE	LABEL & NO.
12/9/57+	9	8	1. **Please Pass The Biscuits**　　　　　　　[N]	Columbia 40971
			Jockey #9 / Best Seller #16	

SULLIVAN, Phil

DATE	POS	WKS	ARTIST–RECORD TITLE	LABEL & NO.
6/8/59	26	6	1. Hearts Are Lonely	Starday 437

SUN, Joe

Born James J. Paulson on 9/25/43 in Rochester, Minnesota. Worked as a DJ in Key West and Madison, Wisconsin. Worked clubs in Chicago as Jack Daniels. Own band, the Branded Men, in the late 1960s. Moved to Nashville in 1975 and worked as promo man for The Kendalls and Ovation Records.

DATE	POS	WKS	ARTIST–RECORD TITLE	LABEL & NO.
7/22/78	14	8	1. Old Flames (Can't Hold A Candle To You)	Ovation 1107
11/25/78	20	6	2. High And Dry	Ovation 1117
4/21/79	27	5	3. On Business For The King/	
		5	4. Blue Ribbon Blues	Ovation 1122
9/29/79	20	6	5. I'd Rather Go On Hurtin'	Ovation 1127
1/12/80	34	3	6. Out Of Your Mind	Ovation 1137
4/19/80	23	6	7. Shotgun Rider	Ovation 1141
9/6/80	21	6	8. Bombed, Boozed, And Busted	Ovation 1152
4/17/82	40	2	9. Holed Up In Some Honky Tonk	Elektra 47417

SUNSHINE RUBY

Ruby Bateman from Texas. Thirteen years old in 1953.

DATE	POS	WKS	ARTIST–RECORD TITLE	LABEL & NO.
6/20/53	4	1	1. **Too Young To Tango**	RCA 5250
			Jockey #4; Sonny James (fiddle)	

SUPERNAW, Doug

Singer/songwriter/guitarist from Houston. Briefly attended college in Houston on a golf scholarship.

DATE	POS	WKS	ARTIST–RECORD TITLE	LABEL & NO.
6/26/93	4	15	1. **Reno**	BNA 62537
10/23/93	1 (2)	17	2. **I Don't Call Him Daddy**	BNA 62638
3/12/94	23	8	3. Red And Rio Grande	BNA 62757
2/4/95	16	9	4. What'll You Do About Me	BNA 64214

DATE	POS	WKS	ARTIST– RECORD TITLE	LABEL & NO.
12/9/95+	3	13	5. **Not Enough Hours In The Night**	Giant 17764

SWAN, Billy

Born on 5/12/42 in Cape Girardeau, Missouri. Own band, Mirt Mitley & The Rhythm Steppers, in the late '50s. Writer for Bill Black's Combo in Memphis. Produced the first album by Tony Joe White. Toured with Kris Kristofferson from the early '70s. Formed the band Black Tie with Randy Meisner in 1986.

DATE	POS	WKS	ARTIST– RECORD TITLE	LABEL & NO.
11/9/74	1 (2)	9	● 1. **I Can Help**	Monument 8621
9/27/75	17	8	2. Everything's The Same (Ain't Nothing Changed)	Monument 8661
8/19/78	30	4	3. Hello! Remember Me	A&M 2046
5/2/81	18	6	4. Do I Have To Draw A Picture	Epic 51000
8/15/81	18	7	5. I'm Into Lovin' You	Epic 02196
12/19/81+	19	8	6. Stuck Right In The Middle Of Your Love	Epic 02601
5/15/82	32	4	7. With Their Kind Of Money And Our Kind Of Love	Epic 02841
3/5/83	39	2	8. Rainbows And Butterflies	Epic 03505

SWEETHEARTS OF THE RODEO

Duo of sisters from California: Janis (guitar, vocals) and Kristine (vocals) Oliver. Moved to Nashville in 1983. Winners of the Wrangler Country Showdown Talent Contest in 1985. Janis is married to Vince Gill.

DATE	POS	WKS	ARTIST– RECORD TITLE	LABEL & NO.
5/17/86	21	6	1. **Hey Doll Baby** #8 R&B hit for The Clovers in 1956	Columbia 05824
8/16/86	7	13	2. **Since I Found You**	Columbia 06166
12/20/86+	4	13	3. **Midnight Girl/Sunset Town**	Columbia 06525
4/18/87	4	13	4. **Chains Of Gold**	Columbia 07023
10/10/87	10	10	5. **Gotta Get Away** originally the B-side of #4 above	Columbia 07314
4/23/88	5	12	6. **Satisfy You**	Columbia 07757
8/27/88	5	13	7. **Blue To The Bone**	Columbia 07985
1/7/89	9	11	8. **I Feel Fine** #1 Pop hit for The Beatles in 1964	Columbia 08504
5/27/89	39	1	9. If I Never See Midnight Again	Columbia 68684
3/10/90	25	6	10. This Heart	Columbia 73213

SYLVIA

Born Sylvia Kirby on 12/9/56 in Kokomo, Indiana. Sang in church choir from age three. Moved to Nashville in 1975; worked as a secretary for producer Tom Collins. Did session backup vocals. Made stage debut as a soloist in the fall of 1979. Curently performs as Sylvia Hutton.

DATE	POS	WKS	ARTIST– RECORD TITLE	LABEL & NO.
11/17/79	36	3	1. You Don't Miss A Thing	RCA 11735
5/31/80	35	4	2. It Don't Hurt To Dream	RCA 11958
10/4/80	10	9	3. **Tumbleweed**	RCA 12077
1/31/81	1 (1)	11	4. **Drifter**	RCA 12164
5/16/81	7	9	5. **The Matador**	RCA 12214
10/3/81	8	8	6. **Heart On The Mend**	RCA 12302
2/6/82	12	9	7. Sweet Yesterday	RCA 13020
6/19/82	1 (1)	14	● 8. **Nobody**	RCA 13223
11/20/82+	2 (2)	13	9. **Like Nothing Ever Happened**	RCA 13330
5/21/83	5	12	10. **Snapshot**	RCA 13501
9/24/83	18	8	11. The Boy Gets Around	RCA 13589

DATE	POS	WKS	ARTIST– RECORD TITLE	LABEL & NO.
1/7/84	3	11	12. **I Never Quite Got Back (From Loving You)**	RCA 13689
5/5/84	24	6	13. Victims Of Goodbye	RCA 13755
8/11/84	36	2	14. Love Over Old Times	RCA 13838
3/9/85	2 (2)	15	15. **Fallin' In Love**	RCA 13997
7/20/85	9	11	16. **Cry Just A Little Bit**	RCA 14107
			#67 hit for Shakin' Stevens in 1984	
12/21/85+	9	11	17. **I Love You By Heart**	RCA 14217
			SYLVIA & MICHAEL JOHNSON	
8/2/86	33	4	18. Nothin' Ventured Nothin' Gained	RCA 14375

T

TALL, Tom

Born Tommie Lee Guthrie on 12/17/37 in Amarillo. Worked on *Town Hall Party*, 1955; *Grand Ole Opry*, 1956; *Louisiana Hayride*, 1956-59, and *Big D Jamboree*, 1955-59.

DATE	POS	WKS	ARTIST– RECORD TITLE	LABEL & NO.
1/1/55	2 (3)	26	1. **Are You Mine**	Fabor 117
			GINNY WRIGHT/TOM TALL	
			Jockey #2 / Juke Box #4 / Best Seller #5; also released on Zero 106	
1/4/64	25	1	2. Bad, Bad Tuesday	Petal 1210

TAYLOR, Carmol

Born on 9/5/31 in Brilliant, Alabama. Died of lung cancer on 12/5/86. Worked at local shows and square dances from age 15. Wrote "Wild As A Wildcat" for Charlie Walker, "The Grand Tour" for George Jones, "He Loves Me All The Way" for Tammy Wynette, "There's A Song On My Jukebox" for David Wills, and many others. Staff writer for Al Gallico Music; producer for Country International Records.

DATE	POS	WKS	ARTIST– RECORD TITLE	LABEL & NO.
3/27/76	35	3	1. Play The Saddest Song On The Juke Box	Elektra 45299
5/29/76	23	6	2. I Really Had A Ball Last Night	Elektra 45312

TAYLOR, Chip

Born James Wesley Voigt in 1940 in Westchester County, New York. Brother of actor Jon Voight. Worked in a trio with Al Georgoni and Trade Martin in the early '70s. Wrote "Angel of The Morning" and "Wild Thing."

DATE	POS	WKS	ARTIST– RECORD TITLE	LABEL & NO.
6/14/75	28	4	1. Early Sunday Morning	Warner 8090

TAYLOR, Frank

DATE	POS	WKS	ARTIST– RECORD TITLE	LABEL & NO.
6/1/63	28	1	1. Snow White Cloud	Parkway 869

TAYLOR, James

Born on 3/12/48 in Boston. Prolific Pop singer/songwriter/guitarist. Married to Carly Simon, 1972-83. His siblings Kate, Alex and Livingston Taylor also recorded.

DATE	POS	WKS	ARTIST– RECORD TITLE	LABEL & NO.
10/14/78	33	3	1. Devoted To You	Elektra 45506
			CARLY SIMON & JAMES TAYLOR	
1/11/86	26	6	2. Everyday	Columbia 05681
			written by Buddy Holly	

DATE	POS	WKS	ARTIST– RECORD TITLE	LABEL & NO.
			TAYLOR-GOOD, Karen	
			Born Karen Berke in El Paso, Texas. Worked as a folk singer. In Phase II with Janie Fricke and Judy Rodman in Memphis in 1971. Married to musician Dennis Good. Made many commercial jingles.	
4/24/82	38	2	1. Diamond In The Rough **KAREN TAYLOR**	Mesa 1111
			TENNESSEE EXPRESS	
			Nashville vocal group evolved from the group The Sound 70's Singers. Sang harmony on John Anderson's "Swingin'."	
9/19/81	31	3	1. Big Like A River	RCA 12277
			TERRY, Al	
			Born Allison Joseph Theriot, Jr., on 1/14/22 in Kaplan, Louisiana. Leader of the Southerners, 1946-52. Toured with Red Foley. Own band from 1954.	
4/24/54	8	5	1. **Good Deal, Lucille** Jockey #8 / Juke Box #8	Hickory 1003
2/29/60	28	1	2. Watch Dog	Hickory 1111
			THOMAS, B.J.	
			Born Billy Joe Thomas on 8/7/42 in Hugo, Oklahoma; raised in Rosenberg, Texas. Sang in church choir as a teenager. Joined band, The Triumphs, while in high school. Thomas has featured gospel music since 1976.	
3/29/75	1 (1)	10	● 1. **(Hey Won't You Play) Another Somebody Done Somebody Wrong Song**	ABC 12054
11/8/75	37	3	2. Help Me Make It (To My Rockin' Chair)	ABC 12121
2/25/78	25	6	3. Everybody Loves A Rain Song	MCA 40854
5/16/81	27	5	4. Some Love Songs Never Die	MCA 51087
9/5/81	22	5	5. I Recall A Gypsy Woman	MCA 51151
3/5/83	1 (1)	14	6. **Whatever Happened To Old Fashioned Love**	Clev. Int. 03492
7/30/83	1 (1)	13	7. **New Looks From An Old Lover**	Columbia 03985
12/24/83+	3	12	8. **Two Car Garage**	Clev. Int. 04237
5/12/84	10	11	9. **The Whole World's In Love When You're Lonely**	Clev. Int. 04431
9/1/84	14	9	10. Rock And Roll Shoes **RAY CHARLES with B.J. THOMAS**	Columbia 04531
11/24/84+	17	10	11. The Girl Most Likely To	Clev. Int. 04608
			THOMAS, Dick	
			Born Richard Thomas Goldhahn on 9/4/15 in Philadelphia. Violinist/accordionist. On radio since 1934. Appeared in Western movies from 1941.	
9/29/45	1 (4)	23	1. **Sioux City Sue**	National 5007
12/8/45	4	1	2. **Honestly**	National 5008
			DICK THOMAS AND HIS NASHVILLE RAMBLERS:	
9/25/48	13	1	3. The Beaut From Butte Juke Box #13	Decca 46132
2/12/49	12	1	4. The Sister Of Sioux City Sue Juke Box #12 / Best Seller #14	Decca 46147

DATE	POS	WKS	ARTIST– RECORD TITLE	LABEL & NO.
			THOMPSON, Hank	
			Born Henry William Thompson on 9/3/25 in Waco, Texas. On WACO-Waco as a teenager, billed as "Hank, The Hired Hand." Served in U.S. Navy during World War II. Attended Southern Methodist, University of Texas and Princeton. Formed own band, His Brazos Valley Boys. First recorded for Globe in 1946. Elected to the Country Music Hall of Fame in 1989.	
			HANK THOMPSON AND HIS BRAZOS VALLEY BOYS:	
1/31/48	**2** (2)	38	1. **Humpty Dumpty Heart** Juke Box #2 / Best Seller #3	Capitol A. 40065
2/5/49	**10**	1	2. **What Are We Gonna Do About The Moonlight/** Juke Box #10	
9/4/48	**12**	2	3. Yesterday's Mail Juke Box #12	Capitol 15132
10/16/48	**7**	10	4. **Green Light** Juke Box #7 / Best Seller #8	Capitol 15187
2/5/49	**14**	1	5. I Find You Cheatin' On Me/ Best Seller #14	
2/12/49	**15**	1	6. You Broke My Heart (In Little Bitty Pieces) Juke Box #15	Capitol 15345
10/1/49	**6**	7	7. **Whoa Sailor** Juke Box #6 / Best Seller #8	Capitol 40218
10/1/49	**10**	1	8. **Soft Lips/** Juke Box #10	
11/5/49	**15**	1	9. The Grass Looks Greener Over Yonder Juke Box #15	Capitol 40211
3/15/52	**1** (15)	30	10. **The Wild Side Of Life** Best Seller #1(15) / Juke Box #1(15) / Jockey #1(8)	Capitol 1942
6/28/52	**3**	15	11. **Waiting In The Lobby Of Your Heart** Juke Box #3 / Best Seller #5 / Jockey #7	Capitol 2063
12/13/52	**10**	1	12. **The New Wears Off Too Fast** Juke Box #10	Capitol 2269
3/28/53	**9**	2	13. **No Help Wanted** Juke Box #9 / Best Seller #10 / Jockey #10	Capitol 2376
5/23/53	**1** (3)	20	14. **Rub-A-Dub-Dub** Juke Box #1 / Jockey #2 / Best Seller #5	Capitol 2445
9/19/53	**8**	4	15. **Yesterday's Girl** Best Seller #8 / Jockey #8	Capitol 2553
12/12/53+	**1** (2)	19	16. **Wake Up, Irene** Juke Box #1 / Best Seller #3 / Jockey #4; answer song to "Goodnight, Irene"	Capitol 2646
5/22/54	**9**	1	17. **A Fooler, A Faker/** Juke Box #9 / Best Seller #15	
5/8/54	**10**	2	18. **Breakin' The Rules** Best Seller #10	Capitol 2758
7/3/54	**9**	12	19. **Honky-Tonk Girl/** Best Seller #9 / Juke Box #10 / Jockey #11	
7/17/54	**10**	4	20. **We've Gone Too Far** Best Seller #10 / Jockey #15	Capitol 2823
10/16/54	**3**	20	21. **The New Green Light** Juke Box #3 / Best Seller #7 / Jockey #8	Capitol 2920

DATE	POS	WKS	ARTIST– RECORD TITLE	LABEL & NO.
2/26/55	**12**	4	22. If Lovin' You Is Wrong/ Best Seller #12 / Jockey #14	
3/12/55	**13**	2	23. Annie Over Best Seller #13	Capitol 3030
6/4/55	**5**	9	24. **Wildwood Flower/** [I] **HANK THOMPSON and His Brazos Valley Boys with MERLE TRAVIS** Juke Box #5 / Best Seller #8 / Jockey #13	
6/4/55	**7**	8	25. **Breakin' In Another Heart** Best Seller #7	Capitol 3106
8/20/55	**6**	11	26. **Most Of All** Jockey #6 / Best Seller #11	Capitol 3188
12/10/55	**5**	7	27. **Don't Take It Out On Me/** Best Seller #5 / Juke Box #9 / Jockey #13	
		5	28. Honey, Honey Bee Ball Best Seller flip / Juke Box flip	Capitol 3275
3/24/56	**4**	22	29. **The Blackboard Of My Heart/** Jockey #4 / Best Seller #6 / Juke Box #6	
3/24/56	**14**	5	30. I'm Not Mad, Just Hurt Best Seller #14	Capitol 3347
2/23/57	**13**	4	31. Rockin' In The Congo/ Best Seller #13	
		2	32. I Was The First One Best Seller flip	Capitol 3623
10/14/57	**14**	2	33. Tears Are Only Rain Jockey #14	Capitol 3781
6/9/58	**11**	3	34. How Do You Hold A Memory Jockey #11	Capitol 3950
8/18/58	**2 (4)**	22	35. **Squaws Along The Yukon**	Capitol 4017
12/1/58+	**7**	23	36. **I've Run Out Of Tomorrows/**	
2/2/59	**26**	3	37. You're Going Back To Your Old Ways Again	Capitol 4085
5/11/59	**13**	10	38. Anybody's Girl/	
6/29/59	**25**	1	39. Total Strangers	Capitol 4182
11/9/59+	**22**	10	40. I Didn't Mean To Fall In Love	Capitol 4269
3/21/60	**10**	16	41. **A Six Pack To Go**	Capitol 4334
8/1/60	**14**	14	42. She's Just A Whole Lot Like You	Capitol 4386
5/29/61	**7**	11	43. **Oklahoma Hills/**	
5/29/61	**25**	2	44. Teach Me How To Lie	Capitol 4556
9/18/61	**12**	10	45. Hangover Tavern	Capitol 4605
9/7/63	**23**	1	46. I Wasn't Even In The Running	Capitol 4968
9/28/63	**22**	5	47. Too In Love	Capitol 5008
11/12/66	**15**	10	48. Where Is The Circus	Warner 5858
3/11/67	**16**	7	49. He's Got A Way With Women	Warner 5886
			HANK THOMPSON:	
8/3/68	**7**	11	50. **On Tap, In The Can, Or In The Bottle**	Dot 17108
10/26/68+	**5**	15	51. **Smoky The Bar** **HANK THOMPSON And The Brazos Valley Boys**	Dot 17163
3/27/71	**15**	10	52. Next Time I Fall In Love (I Won't)	Dot 17365
8/21/71	**18**	9	53. The Mark Of A Heel	Dot 17385
9/18/71+	**11**	11	54. I've Come Awful Close	Dot 17399

DATE	POS	WKS	ARTIST– RECORD TITLE	LABEL & NO.
5/20/72	**16**	8	55. Cab Driver	Dot 17410
			#23 Pop hit for The Mills Brothers in 1968	
3/9/74	**8**	10	56. **The Older The Violin, The Sweeter The Music**	Dot 17490
8/24/74	**10**	10	57. **Who Left The Door To Heaven Open**	Dot 17512
3/8/75	**29**	3	58. Mama Don't 'Low	ABC/Dot 17535
9/29/79	**29**	5	59. I Hear The South Callin' Me	MCA 41079
2/23/80	**32**	4	60. Tony's Tank-Up, Drive-In Cafe	MCA 41176

THOMPSON, Sue

Born Eva Sue McKee on 7/19/26 in Nevada, Missouri; raised in San Jose, California. Worked on the KGO-San Francisco TV series *Hometown Hayride* while still a teenager. Worked with Red Foley on the *Grand Ole Opry* in the late '50s. Married to Hank Penny, 1953-63.

DON GIBSON & SUE THOMPSON:

DATE	POS	WKS	ARTIST– RECORD TITLE	LABEL & NO.
9/23/72	**37**	4	1. I Think They Call It Love	Hickory 1646
9/21/74	**31**	5	2. Good Old Fashioned Country Love	Hickory 324
9/6/75	**36**	4	3. Oh, How Love Changes	Hickory 350

THREE SUNS, The

Instrumental trio from Philadelphia: brothers Al (died 1965; guitar) and Morty (died 7/20/90 of cancer; accordion) Nevins, with cousin Artie Dunn (died 1989; organ). With Don Kirshner, Al Nevins founded Aldon Music, the famed publishing company largely responsible for the "Brill Building" rock and roll sound.

DATE	POS	WKS	ARTIST– RECORD TITLE	LABEL & NO.
2/4/50	**7**	4	1. **Beyond The Sunset**	RCA Victor 3599
			THE THREE SUNS with ROSALIE ALLEN and ELTON BRITT	
			Jockey #7; 45 rpm: 47-3105	

THUNDERKLOUD, Billy, & The Chieftones

Group of Indian musicians from British Columbia: Billy Thunderkloud (real name: Vincent Clifford), Jack Wolf, Barry Littlestar and Richard Grayowl.

DATE	POS	WKS	ARTIST– RECORD TITLE	LABEL & NO.
6/14/75	**16**	8	1. What Time Of Day	20th Century 2181
12/20/75	**37**	1	2. Pledging My Love	20th Century 2239
			#17 Pop hit for Johnny Ace in 1955	

TILLIS, Mel

Born Lonnie Melvin Tillis on 8/8/32 in Tampa, Florida; raised in Pahokee, Florida. Football player and drummer while in high school. Served in U.S. Air Force, then worked on the railroads. Moved to Nashville in 1957. Wrote "Detroit City" and "Ruby Don't Take Your Love To Town." Appeared in the movies *W.W. and the Dixie Dancekings, Smokey and the Bandit II, Uphill All The Way* and *Murder In Music City*. Owner of Sawgrass, Cedarwood and several other publishing companies until late 1987. Autobiography titled *Stutterin' Boy*. Backing band: The Statesiders. Father of Pam Tillis. CMA Award: 1976 Entertainer of the Year.

(a) MEL TILLIS & The Statesiders
(b) MEL TILLIS & SHERRY BRYCE with The Statesiders

DATE	POS	WKS	ARTIST– RECORD TITLE	LABEL & NO.
11/10/58	**24**	4	1. The Violet And A Rose	Columbia 41189
1/5/59	**28**	4	2. Finally	Columbia 41277
8/24/59	**27**	2	3. Sawmill	Columbia 41416
2/8/60	**24**	4	4. Georgia Town Blues	Columbia 41530
			MEL TILLIS and BILL PHILLIPS (above 2)	

DATE	POS	WKS	ARTIST – RECORD TITLE		LABEL & NO.
1/5/63	25	3	5. How Come Your Dog Don't Bite Nobody But Me **WEBB PIERCE and MEL TILLIS**		Decca 31445
7/10/65	14	15	6. Wine		RIC 158
10/22/66	17	13	7. Stateside		Kapp 772
3/18/67	11	14	8. Life Turned Her That Way		Kapp 804
8/12/67	20	10	9. Goodbye Wheeling		Kapp 837
2/10/68	26	7	10. All Right (I'll Sign The Papers)		Kapp 881
6/8/68	17	11	11. Something Special		Kapp 905
10/12/68	31	6	12. Destroyed By Man		Kapp 941
1/18/69	10	13	13. **Who's Julie**		Kapp 959
5/3/69	13	13	14. Old Faithful		Kapp 986
8/30/69	9	13	15. **These Lonely Hands Of Mine**		Kapp 2031
2/7/70	10	7	16. **She'll Be Hanging 'Round Somewhere**		Kapp 2072
5/9/70	3	14	17. **Heart Over Mind** (a)		Kapp 2086
7/25/70	5	14	18. **Heaven Everyday** (a)		MGM 14148
11/14/70	25	5	19. To Lonely, Too Long		Kapp 2103
11/21/70	8	11	20. **Commercial Affection** (a)		MGM 14176
2/13/71	4	13	21. **The Arms Of A Fool** (a)		MGM 14211
6/12/71	8	12	22. **Take My Hand** (b)		MGM 14255
8/21/71	8	11	23. **Brand New Mister Me** (a)		MGM 14275
11/20/71	9	10	24. **Living And Learning** (b)		MGM 14303
1/22/72	14	9	25. Untouched (a)		MGM 14329
5/6/72	38	3	26. Anything's Better Than Nothing (b)		MGM 14365
5/27/72	12	8	27. Would You Want The World To End		MGM 14372
8/26/72	1 (2)	13	28. **I Ain't Never** (a)		MGM 14418
12/30/72+	3	13	29. **Neon Rose** (a)		MGM 14454
5/26/73	21	8	30. Thank You For Being You (a)		MGM 14522
9/15/73	2 (1)	14	31. **Sawmill** (a)	[R]	MGM 14585
12/22/73+	26	6	32. Let's Go All The Way Tonight (b)		MGM 14660
2/2/74	2 (1)	14	33. **Midnight, Me And The Blues** (a)		MGM 14689
5/4/74	11	9	34. Don't Let Go (b) #13 Pop hit for Roy Hamilton in 1958		MGM 14714
6/8/74	3	12	35. **Stomp Them Grapes** (a)		MGM 14720
10/26/74	3	10	36. **Memory Maker** (a)		MGM 14744
2/1/75	14	7	37. You Are The One (b)		MGM 14776
3/1/75	7	11	38. **Best Way I Know How** (a)		MGM 14782
6/28/75	32	6	39. Mr. Right And Mrs. Wrong (b)		MGM 14803
7/5/75	4	13	40. **Woman In The Back Of My Mind** (a)		MGM 14804
11/29/75+	16	8	41. Lookin' For Tomorrow (And Findin' Yesterdays) (a)		MGM 14835
4/3/76	15	7	42. Mental Revenge (a)		MGM 14846
6/12/76	11	10	43. Love Revival		MCA 40559
10/16/76	1 (2)	12	44. **Good Woman Blues**		MCA 40627
1/29/77	1 (1)	9	45. **Heart Healer**		MCA 40667
5/7/77	9	8	46. **Burning Memories**		MCA 40710
8/27/77	3	10	47. **I Got The Hoss**		MCA 40764
1/7/78	4	10	48. **What Did I Promise Her Last Night**		MCA 40836
5/20/78	1 (1)	11	49. **I Believe In You**		MCA 40900
9/9/78	4	11	50. **Ain't No California**		MCA 40946

DATE	POS	WKS	ARTIST– RECORD TITLE	LABEL & NO.
1/20/79	2 (3)	11	51. **Send Me Down To Tucson/**	
		11	52. Charlie's Angel	MCA 40983
6/23/79	1 (1)	11	53. **Coca Cola Cowboy**	MCA 41041
			from the movie *Every Which Way But Loose* starring Clint Eastwood (also #51 above)	
9/29/79	6	11	54. **Blind In Love**	Elektra 46536
1/26/80	6	10	55. **Lying Time Again**	Elektra 46583
5/17/80	3	10	56. **Your Body Is An Outlaw**	Elektra 46628
9/13/80	9	9	57. **Steppin' Out** (a)	Elektra 47015
12/27/80+	1 (1)	11	58. **Southern Rains**	Elektra 47082
4/11/81	8	10	59. **A Million Old Goodbyes**	Elektra 47116
8/8/81	23	5	60. Texas Cowboy Night	Elektra 47157
			MEL TILLIS & NANCY SINATRA	
9/26/81	10	9	61. **One-Night Fever**	Elektra 47178
3/20/82	36	4	62. It's A Long Way To Daytona	Elektra 47412
6/26/82	37	2	63. The One That Got Away	Elektra 47453
10/16/82	17	8	64. Stay A Little Longer	Elektra 69963
4/9/83	10	11	65. **In The Middle Of The Night**	MCA 52182
5/26/84	10	11	66. **New Patches**	MCA 52373
7/6/85	37	2	67. You Done Me Wrong	RCA 14061
4/16/88	31	4	68. You'll Come Back (You Always Do)	Mercury 870192

TILLIS, Pam

Born on 7/24/57 in Plant City, Florida. Daughter of Mel Tillis. Married to Bob DiPiero (of Billy Hill). CMA Award: 1994 Female Vocalist of the Year.

DATE	POS	WKS	ARTIST– RECORD TITLE	LABEL & NO.
1/12/91	5	14	1. **Don't Tell Me What To Do**	Arista 2129
5/4/91	6	16	2. **One Of Those Things**	Arista 2203
			originally released on Warner 28984 in 1985	
9/7/91	11	11	3. Put Yourself In My Place	Arista 12268
1/4/92	3	17	4. **Maybe It Was Memphis**	Arista 12371
5/16/92	21	9	5. Blue Rose Is	Arista 12408
9/12/92	3	17	6. **Shake The Sugar Tree**	Arista 12454
1/30/93	4	14	7. **Let That Pony Run**	Arista 12506
5/29/93	11	11	8. Cleopatra, Queen Of Denial	Arista 12552
10/2/93	16	11	9. Do You Know Where Your Man Is	Arista 12606
4/9/94	5	15	10. **Spilled Perfume**	Arista 12676
8/20/94	2 (1)	16	11. **When You Walk In The Room**	Arista 12726
			#35 Pop hit for The Searchers in 1964	
12/3/94+	1 (2)	15	12. **Mi Vida Loca (My Crazy Life)**	Arista 12759
3/25/95	16	8	13. I Was Blown Away	Arista 12802
6/24/95	3	15	14. **In Between Dances**	Arista 12833
10/21/95+	6	16	15. **Deep Down**	Arista 12878
3/2/96	8	15	16. **The River And The Highway**	Arista 12958

Shenandoah's first entry into the charts, 1987's "They Don't Make Love Like We Used To," held fast at No. 54. Within a year, the Muscle Shoals-based band scored two Top 10 hits. Legal squabbles over the rights to their name later forced the group into bankruptcy.

T.G. Sheppard's remake of the Elvin Bishop Group's Pop hit "Fooled Around And Fell In Love" served as his less-than-auspicious label debut for Columbia in 1985. His lowest-charting single in nine years, it peaked at No. 21. But the hitmaker followed it up with six consecutive Top 10 hits.

Connie Smith—who appeared in such films as *Las Vegas Hillbillies* and *Road To Nashville*—made the Buckeye State proud in 1967 with her No. 4 hit "Cincinnati, Ohio."

Hank Snow, the legendary Country music figure born in Nova Scotia, produced an astounding 85 chart hits between 1949 and 1980. "The Man Who Robbed The Bank At Santa Fe"—his 49th hit—reached No. 9 in 1963.

Southern Pacific's success on the Country chart—with hits such as 1988's No. 5 single "Honey I Dare You"—was the second time around for most band members. Former rockers, the quintet consisted of past members of The Doobie Brothers, Creedence Clearwater Revival and Pablo Cruise.

The Statlers have been nothing if not enormously prolific: "Atlanta Blue," their No. 3 hit from 1984, was their 48th chart hit since their 1965 debut smash "Flowers On The Wall."

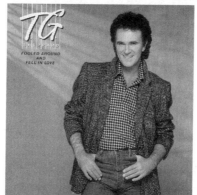

Wynn Stewart, who claimed 31 chart hits before dying of a heart attack in 1985, scored a No. 7 hit with 1967's "Love's Gonna Happen To Me." Though 20 more hits would come, none surpassed that mark.

George Strait's no-nonsense approach to Country has garnered him one of the most steadfast fan bases in Country music. His seventh No. 1 single, 1985's "The Chair," was one of countless hits included on *Strait Out Of The Box,* a 4-CD box set issued by MCA in 1995.

Marty Stuart, a distinguished picker with a resume that included work with Lester Flatt and Johnny Cash, made his debut chart appearance in 1985 via his No. 19 hit "Arlene."

Sweethearts Of The Rodeo—who took their name from 1968's pioneering Country-Rock album by the Byrds—features Kristine and Janis Oliver, two California-bred sisters, the latter of whom married singer Vince Gill.

Sylvia—born Sylvia Kirby Allen—was a former secretary whose singing talents did not go unnoticed by producer Tom Collins. Of her two No. 1 hits, 1981's "Drifter" was the first.

Hank Thompson's prolific hit-making ability—he released 79 charting singles—let him down somewhat with 1962's "I've Convinced Everybody But Myself." It never made a chart appearance.

DATE	POS	WKS	ARTIST—RECORD TITLE	LABEL & NO.
			TILLMAN, Floyd	
			Born on 12/8/14 in Ryan, Oklahoma; raised in Post, Texas. Moved to San Antonio; played with the Mark Clark Orchestra and the Blue Ridge Playboys, and in Houston with Ted Daffan and Moon Mullican in the '30s. Wrote "Slipping Around." Elected to the Country Music Hall of Fame in 1984.	
			FLOYD TILLMAN AND HIS FAVORITE PLAYBOYS:	
1/8/44	**1** (1)	13	1. **They Took The Stars Out Of Heaven**	Decca 6090
12/30/44	**4**	8	2. **Each Night At Nine/**	
12/16/44	**5**	3	3. G.I. Blues	Decca 6104
			FLOYD TILLMAN:	
8/3/46	**2** (1)	7	4. **Drivin' Nails In My Coffin**	Columbia 36998
7/10/48	**5**	19	5. **I Love You So Much, It Hurts**	Columbia 20430
			Juke Box #5 / Best Seller #6	
1/29/49	**14**	1	6. Please Don't Pass Me By	Columbia 20496
			Best Seller #14	
7/2/49	**5**	12	7. **Slipping Around**	Columbia 20581
			Best Seller #5 / Jockey #6 / Juke Box #6	
10/8/49	**6**	8	8. **I'll Never Slip Around Again**	Columbia 20615
			Best Seller #6 / Juke Box #8	
12/31/49+	**4**	3	9. **I Gotta Have My Baby Back**	Columbia 20641
			Jockey #4	
12/19/60	**29**	1	10. It Just Tears Me Up	Liberty 55280
			TILLOTSON, Johnny	
			Born on 4/20/39 in Jacksonville, Florida; raised in Palatka, Florida. On local radio *Young Folks Revue* from age nine. DJ on WWPF. Appeared on the TV show *Toby Dowdy* in Jacksonville, then own show. Signed by Cadence Records in 1958. Appeared in the movie *Just For Fun*.	
6/23/62	**4**	13	1. **It Keeps Right On A-Hurtin'**	Cadence 1418
9/8/62	**11**	10	2. Send Me The Pillow You Dream On	Cadence 1424
			TILTON, Sheila	
			Born in 1951 in Kailua, Hawaii. Sang at rodeos with sisters Muriel and Gwen.	
8/14/76	**23**	6	1. Half As Much	Con Brio 110
			#1 Pop hit for Rosemary Clooney in 1952	
			TINA & DADDY—see JONES, George	
			TIPPIN, Aaron	
			Born on 7/3/58 in Pensacola, Florida; raised in South Carolina. Worked as a corporate airplane pilot before turning to songwriting. With Mark Collie, co-wrote Collie's "Something With A Ring To It."	
12/15/90+	**6**	14	1. **You've Got To Stand For Something**	RCA 2664
6/8/91	**40**	2	2. I Wonder How Far It Is Over You	RCA 2747
2/29/92	**1** (3)	18	3. **There Ain't Nothin' Wrong With The Radio**	RCA 62181
7/18/92	**5**	13	4. **I Wouldn't Have It Any Other Way**	RCA 62241
12/12/92	**38**	1	5. I Was Born With A Broken Heart	RCA 62338
2/20/93	**7**	17	6. **My Blue Angel**	RCA 62430
7/10/93	**7**	15	7. **Working Man's Ph.D.**	RCA 62520

DATE	POS	WKS	ARTIST—RECORD TITLE	LABEL & NO.
11/13/93+	**17**	12	8. The Call Of The Wild	RCA 62657
6/4/94	**30**	7	9. Whole Lotta Love On The Line	RCA 62832
11/19/94+	**15**	13	10. I Got It Honest	RCA 62947
4/15/95	**39**	2	11. She Feels Like A Brand New Man Tonight	RCA 64272
9/30/95	**1** (2)	17	12. **That's As Close As I'll Get To Loving You**	RCA 64392
2/24/96	**22**	8	13. Without Your Love	RCA 64471

TOROK, Mitchell

Born on 10/28/29 in Houston. Played guitar since age 12. First recorded in 1948. Wrote "Mexican Joe" for Jim Reeves, "Pledge Of Love" and "Caribbean."

DATE	POS	WKS	ARTIST—RECORD TITLE	LABEL & NO.
8/22/53	**1** (2)	24	1. **Caribbean** Juke Box #1 / Best Seller #4 / Jockey #5; reissue on Guyden made #27 on the *Hot 100* in 1959	Abbott 140
1/23/54	**9**	3	2. **Hootchy Kootchy Henry (From Hawaii)** Juke Box #9	Abbott 150

TRACTORS, The

Country-rock band formed in Tulsa, Oklahoma, of veteran sidemen: Steve Ripley (guitar), Walt Richmond (keyboards), Ron Getman (guitar), Casey Van Beek (vocals) and Jamie Oldaker (drums).

DATE	POS	WKS	ARTIST—RECORD TITLE	LABEL & NO.
10/1/94	**11**	14	1. Baby Likes To Rock It	Arista 12717

TRASK, Diana

Born on 6/23/40 in Melbourne, Australia. One of the most popular stars in Australia by the age of 16. Moved to the U.S. in 1959. Appeared on Don McNeil's Breakfast Club and the Jack Benny TV shows. Regular on the TV series *Sing Along With Mitch*. Toured with Hank Williams, Jr., in the late '60s. Returned to Australia in 1975.

DATE	POS	WKS	ARTIST—RECORD TITLE	LABEL & NO.
12/27/69+	**37**	2	1. I Fall To Pieces	Dot 17316
4/25/70	**38**	3	2. Beneath Still Waters	Dot 17342
3/4/72	**30**	6	3. We've Got To Work It Out Between Us	Dot 17404
9/2/72	**33**	4	4. It Meant Nothing To Me	Dot 17424
3/31/73	**15**	9	5. Say When	Dot 17448
8/11/73	**20**	7	6. It's A Man's World (If You Had A Man Like Mine)	Dot 17467
1/12/74	**16**	9	7. When I Get My Hands On You	Dot 17486
4/20/74	**13**	9	8. Lean It All On Me	Dot 17496
10/5/74	**32**	2	9. (If You Wanna Hold On) Hold On To Your Man	Dot 17520
2/22/75	**21**	6	10. Oh Boy	Dot 17536

TRAVIS, Merle

Born on 11/29/17 in Rosewood, Kentucky. Died on 10/20/83 in Tahlequah, Oklahoma. Gifted songwriter with a highly influential guitar style. Worked with The Tennessee Tomcats and The Georgia Wildcats. Performed on WLW-Cincinnati, *Boone County Jamboree*, and NBC-Radio *Plantation Party* in the late '30s. Served in U.S. Marines, then settled in California in 1946. Appeared in the movie *From Here to Eternity*. Wrote "Sixteen Tons" and "Smoke, Smoke, Smoke (That Cigarette)." Regular on the TV shows *Hometown Jamboree* and *Town Hall Party*. Elected to the Country Music Hall of Fame in 1977.

DATE	POS	WKS	ARTIST—RECORD TITLE	LABEL & NO.
6/8/46	**2** (4)	11	1. **Cincinnati Lou/**	
6/15/46	**3**	9	2. **No Vacancy**	Capitol 258

DATE	POS	WKS	ARTIST– RECORD TITLE	LABEL & NO.
9/21/46	1 (14)	23	3. **Divorce Me C.O.D./**	
1/11/47	5	2	4. **Missouri**	Capitol 290
1/25/47	1 (14)	22	5. **So Round, So Firm, So Fully Packed**	Capitol 349
5/17/47	4	3	6. **Steel Guitar Rag/**	
5/24/47	4	4	7. **Three Times Seven**	Capitol 384
11/1/47	4	2	8. **Fat Gal/**	
3/20/48	7	1	9. **Merle's Boogie Woogie**	Capitol A. 40026
8/28/48	11	3	10. Crazy Boogie	Capitol 15143
			Juke Box #11 / Best Seller #12	
2/5/49	13	1	11. What A Shame	Capitol 15317
			Juke Box #13	
6/4/55	5	9	12. **Wildwood Flower** [I]	Capitol 3106
			HANK THOMPSON and His Brazos Valley Boys with MERLE TRAVIS	
			Juke Box #5 / Best Seller #8 / Jockey #13	

TRAVIS, Randy

Born Randy Bruce Traywick on 5/4/59 in Marshville, North Carolina. Sang with brother in a band at age 10, worked local clubs from age 14. Worked at Country City USA, Charlotte, 1976-81. First recorded for Paula in 1978. Moved to Nashville in 1981; worked as singer/dishwasher/cook at Lib Hatcher's Nashville Palace. Recorded as Randy Traywick and Randy Ray before adopting stage name, Randy Travis, in 1985. Married Hatcher, his longtime manager, on 5/31/91. Joined the *Grand Ole Opry* in 1986. CMA Awards: 1986 Horizon Award; 1987 and 1988 Male Vocalist of the Year. Acted in the movies *Young Guns, Frank And Jesse, Dead Man's Revenge, The Legend Of O.B. Taggart, At Risk, Maverick* and TV's *Matlock.*

DATE	POS	WKS	ARTIST– RECORD TITLE	LABEL & NO.
2/8/86	6	12	1. **1982**	Warner 28828
5/17/86	1 (1)	14	2. **On The Other Hand** [R]	Warner 28962
8/30/86	1 (1)	14	3. **Diggin' Up Bones**	Warner 28649
12/20/86+	2 (2)	15	4. **No Place Like Home**	Warner 28525
5/2/87	1 (3)	13	5. **Forever And Ever, Amen**	Warner 28384
			CMA Award: Single of the Year	
9/5/87	1 (1)	14	6. **I Won't Need You Anymore (Always And Forever)**	Warner 28246
12/19/87+	1 (1)	15	7. **Too Gone Too Long**	Warner 28286
4/16/88	1 (2)	12	8. **I Told You So**	Warner 27969
8/6/88	1 (1)	13	9. **Honky Tonk Moon**	Warner 27833
11/26/88+	1 (1)	13	10. **Deeper Than The Holler**	Warner 27689
3/18/89	1 (1)	13	11. **Is It Still Over?**	Warner 27551
7/8/89	17	9	12. Promises	Warner 22917
9/30/89	1 (1)	15	13. **It's Just A Matter Of Time**	Warner 22841
2/10/90	1 (4)	22	14. **Hard Rock Bottom Of Your Heart**	Warner 19935
5/26/90	2 (2)	19	15. **He Walked On Water**	Warner 19878
9/15/90	8	17	16. **A Few Ole Country Boys**	Warner 19586
			RANDY TRAVIS & GEORGE JONES	
2/9/91	3	17	17. **Heroes And Friends**	Warner 19469
5/11/91	3	18	18. **Point Of Light**	Warner 19283
			written by Don Schlitz and Thom Schuyler at the request of President Bush for his Points Of Light program, which recognized people for outstanding community service	
10/5/91	1 (1)	17	19. **Forever Together**	Warner 19158
1/4/92	2 (3)	18	20. **Better Class Of Losers**	Warner 19069
5/2/92	20	7	21. I'd Surrender All	Warner 18943

DATE	POS	WKS	ARTIST–RECORD TITLE	LABEL & NO.
8/22/92	**1** (1)	18	22. **If I Didn't Have You**	Warner 18792
12/5/92+	**1** (2)	18	23. **Look Heart, No Hands**	Warner 18709
5/1/93	**21**	10	24. An Old Pair Of Shoes	Warner 18616
3/26/94	**2** (1)	16	25. **Before You Kill Us All**	Warner 18208
7/2/94	**1** (1)	17	26. **Whisper My Name**	Warner 18153
10/29/94	**5**	17	27. **This Is Me**	Warner 18062
2/25/95	**7**	13	28. **The Box**	Warner 17970

TREVINO, Rick

Born in 1971 in Austin, Texas. Records in both Spanish and English.

DATE	POS	WKS	ARTIST–RECORD TITLE	LABEL & NO.
4/16/94	35	4	1. Honky Tonk Crowd written by Marty Stuart	Columbia 77373
7/9/94	**3**	15	2. **She Can't Say I Didn't Cry**	Columbia 77535
11/5/94+	**5**	16	3. **Doctor Time**	Columbia 77708
6/10/95	**6**	14	4. **Bobbie Ann Mason**	Columbia 77903

TREVOR, Van

Born on 11/12/40 in Lewiston, Maine. Made professional debut at age seven. Moved to Nashville in the mid-1960s. Worked as a producer/songwriter, 1973-76.

DATE	POS	WKS	ARTIST–RECORD TITLE	LABEL & NO.
6/11/66	22	11	1. Born To Be In Love With You	Band Box 367
12/31/66+	27	7	2. Our Side	Band Box 371
11/4/67	26	7	3. You've Been So Good To Me	Date 1565
5/25/68	31	7	4. Take Me Along With You	Date 1594

TRIPP, Allen

Born in Fort Worth. Sang with the Texas Boys Choir.

DATE	POS	WKS	ARTIST–RECORD TITLE	LABEL & NO.
5/1/82	39	2	1. Love Is	Nashville 1001

TRITT, Travis

Born James Travis Tritt on 2/9/63 in Marietta, Georgia. Joined the *Grand Ole Opry* in 1992. CMA Award: 1991 Horizon Award.

DATE	POS	WKS	ARTIST–RECORD TITLE	LABEL & NO.
9/30/89	**9**	16	1. **Country Club**	Warner 22882
3/17/90	**1** (1)	20	2. **Help Me Hold On**	Warner 19918
6/30/90	**2** (1)	19	3. **I'm Gonna Be Somebody**	Warner 19797
11/3/90	**28**	6	4. Put Some Drive In Your Country	Warner 19715
3/2/91	**3**	18	5. **Drift Off To Dream**	Warner 19431
6/8/91	**2** (1)	19	6. **Here's A Quarter (Call Someone Who Cares)**	Warner 19310
9/14/91	**1** (2)	20	7. **Anymore**	Warner 19190
12/14/91+	**2** (1)	17	8. **The Whiskey Ain't Workin'** **TRAVIS TRITT Featuring Marty Stuart**	Warner 19097
4/4/92	**4**	16	9. **Nothing Short Of Dying**	Warner 18984
6/20/92	**7**	12	10. **This One's Gonna Hurt You (For A Long, Long Time)** **MARTY STUART AND TRAVIS TRITT**	MCA 54405
9/5/92	**5**	15	11. **Lord Have Mercy On The Working Man** **TRAVIS TRITT & FRIENDS** Little Texas, T. Graham Brown, Porter Wagoner, George Jones, Tanya Tucker, Brooks & Dunn and Dana McVicker (guest vocalists)	Warner 18779
12/19/92+	**1** (2)	18	12. **Can I Trust You With My Heart**	Warner 18669

DATE	POS	WKS	ARTIST— RECORD TITLE	LABEL & NO.
4/3/93	**13**	12	13. T-R-O-U-B-L-E	Warner 18588
7/31/93	**11**	11	14. Looking Out For Number One	Warner 18463
12/4/93	**30**	5	15. Worth Every Mile	Warner LP Cut
			above 5 from the album T-R-O-U-B-L-E on Warner 45058	
2/5/94	**21**	8	16. Take It Easy	Warner 18240
			#12 Pop hit for the Eagles in 1972	
5/7/94	**1** (1)	18	17. **Foolish Pride**	Warner 18180
8/27/94	**22**	9	18. Ten Feet Tall And Bulletproof	Warner 18104
12/24/94+	**11**	14	19. Between An Old Memory And Me	Warner 18003
5/6/95	**2** (1)	16	20. **Tell Me I Was Dreaming**	Warner LP Cut
			above 4 from the album Ten Feet Tall And Bulletproof on Warner 45603	
9/2/95	**7**	16	21. **Sometimes She Forgets**	Warner 17792
			written by Steve Earle	
5/11/96	**23**	11↑	22. Honky Tonkin's What I Do Best	MCA 55197
			MARTY STUART & TRAVIS TRITT	

TUBB, Ernest

Born on 2/9/14 in Crisp, Texas. Died of emphysema on 9/6/84. Worked on KONO-San Antonio and KGKO-Fort Worth in the mid-1930s. First recorded for Bluebird in 1936. Wrote "I'm Walking The Floor Over You" in 1941. Moved to Nashville in 1943; joined the *Grand Ole Opry*. Appeared in the movies *Fighting Buckaroo, Hollywood Barn Dance, Ridin' West* and *Jamboree*. Broadcast from his own Ernest Tubb Record Shop beginning in 1947. Elected to the Country Music Hall of Fame in 1965. Nicknamed "The Texas Troubadour."

(a) ERNEST TUBB & RED FOLEY

DATE	POS	WKS	ARTIST— RECORD TITLE	LABEL & NO.
1/8/44	**2** (3)	17	1. **Try Me One More Time**	Decca 6093
5/27/44	**1** (4)	29	2. **Soldier's Last Letter/**	
6/3/44	**4**	3	3. Yesterday's Tears	Decca 6098
3/31/45	**3**	14	4. **Tomorrow Never Comes/**	
3/17/45	**6**	1	5. Keep My Mem'ry In Your Heart	Decca 6106
8/4/45	**3**	8	6. **Careless Darlin'**	Decca 6110
11/17/45	**1** (4)	13	7. **It's Been So Long Darling**	Decca 6112
11/16/46+	**1** (2)	20	8. **Rainbow At Midnight**	Decca 46018
11/16/46	**2** (4)	12	9. **Filipino Baby/**	
12/21/46	**5**	2	10. Drivin' Nails In My Coffin	Decca 46019
5/17/47	**4**	6	11. **Don't Look Now (But Your Broken Heart Is Showing)/**	
6/28/47	**5**	1	12. So Round, So Firm, So Fully Packed	Decca 46040
7/19/47	**4**	1	13. **I'll Step Aside**	Decca 46041
5/15/48	**5**	14	14. **Seaman's Blues**	Decca 46119
			Best Seller #5 / Juke Box #8	
7/17/48	**15**	1	15. You Nearly Lose Your Mind	Decca 46125
			Juke Box #15	
8/7/48	**5**	13	16. **Forever Is Ending Today/**	
			Best Seller #5 / Juke Box #6	
9/4/48	**9**	6	17. **That Wild And Wicked Look In Your Eye**	Decca 46134
			Juke Box #9	
12/11/48+	**2** (1)	17	18. **Have You Ever Been Lonely? (Have You Ever Been Blue)/**	
			Juke Box #2 / Best Seller #9	
12/11/48+	**5**	17	19. **Let's Say Goodbye Like We Said Hello**	Decca 46144
			Best Seller #5 / Juke Box #6	

DATE	POS	WKS	ARTIST-RECORD TITLE		LABEL & NO.
3/19/49	4	9	20. **Till The End Of The World/** *Juke Box #4 / Best Seller #11*		
5/7/49	15	1	21. Daddy, When Is Mommy Coming Home *Juke Box #15*		Decca 46150
4/9/49	2 (1)	16	22. **I'm Biting My Fingernails And Thinking Of You/** **ANDREWS SISTERS & ERNEST TUBB with The Texas Troubadors** *Juke Box #2 / Best Seller #4*		
4/16/49	6	5	23. **Don't Rob Another Man's Castle** **ERNEST TUBB & ANDREWS SISTERS with The Texas Troubadors** *Juke Box #6 / Best Seller #10*		Decca 24592
5/28/49	6	4	24. **Mean Mama Blues** *Juke Box #6*		Decca 46162
7/30/49	1 (1)	20	25. **Slipping Around/** *Juke Box #1 / Best Seller #4*		
9/17/49	10	3	26. **My Tennessee Baby** *Juke Box #10*		Decca 46173
9/3/49	6	10	27. **My Filipino Rose/** *Juke Box #6 / Best Seller #11*		
9/3/49	8	8	28. **Warm Red Wine** *Best Seller #8 / Juke Box #9*		Decca 46175
12/3/49	1 (1)	6	29. **Blue Christmas/** *Juke Box #1 / Best Seller #2 / Jockey #2*	[X]	
12/24/49	7	1	30. **White Christmas** *Juke Box #7 / Best Seller #15*	[X]	Decca 46186
12/31/49+	2 (2)	10	31. **Tennessee Border No. 2** (a)/ *Best Seller #2 / Juke Box #2*		
1/21/50	7	2	32. **Don't Be Ashamed Of Your Age** (a) *Juke Box #7 / Jockey #9*		Decca 46200
2/4/50	2 (1)	17	33. **Letters Have No Arms/** *Juke Box #2 / Jockey #3 / Best Seller #5*		
2/25/50	8	1	34. **I'll Take A Back Seat For You** *Juke Box #8*		Decca 46207
2/25/50	2 (1)	20	35. **I Love You Because/** *Juke Box #2 / Best Seller #4 / Jockey #6*		
3/18/50	8	2	36. **Unfaithful One** *Juke Box #8*		Decca 46213
6/24/50	3	15	37. **Throw Your Love My Way/** *Jockey #3 / Juke Box #4 / Best Seller #5*		
8/5/50	9	4	38. **Give Me A Little Old Fashioned Love** *Juke Box #9*		Decca 46243
8/12/50	1 (3)	15	39. Goodnight Irene (a)/ *Juke Box #1(3) / Best Seller #1(2) / Jockey #2;* *The Sunshine Trio (female backing vocals)*		
9/2/50	9	2	40. Hillbilly Fever No. 2 (a) *Juke Box #9*		Decca 46255
10/28/50	10	2	41. **You Don't Have To Be A Baby To Cry** *Juke Box #10*		Decca 46257
11/4/50	5	9	42. **(Remember Me) I'm The One Who Loves You** *Juke Box #5 / Best Seller #7*		Decca 46269
12/30/50	9	1	43. **Blue Christmas** *Jockey #9 / Juke Box #10*	[X-R]	Decca 46186
5/19/51	9	1	44. **The Strange Little Girl** (a) *Juke Box #9; Anita Kerr Singers (backing vocals)*		Decca 46311

DATE	POS	WKS	ARTIST- RECORD TITLE		LABEL & NO.
6/2/51	9	3	45. **Don't Stay Too Long** Jockey #9		Decca 46296
9/15/51	6	2	46. **Hey La La** Juke Box #6; Anita Kerr Singers (backing vocals)		Decca 46338
12/15/51	7	2	47. **Driftwood On The River** Juke Box #7		Decca 46377
12/29/51	5	1	48. **Blue Christmas** Jockey #5	[X-R]	Decca 46186
2/2/52	5	9	49. **Too Old To Cut The Mustard** (a) Best Seller #5 / Juke Box #8 / Jockey #10		Decca 46387
2/9/52	3	11	50. **Missing In Action** Best Seller #3 / Jockey #5 / Juke Box #9		Decca 46389
5/17/52	9	2	51. **Somebody's Stolen My Honey** Juke Box #9 / Best Seller #10		Decca 28067
9/13/52	5	11	52. **Fortunes In Memories** Juke Box #5 / Jockey #7		Decca 28310
4/18/53	7	2	53. **No Help Wanted #2** (a) Best Seller #7 / Juke Box #9		Decca 28634
12/12/53	9	2	54. **Divorce Granted** Juke Box #9		Decca 28869
10/16/54	11	5	55. Two Glasses, Joe Best Seller #11		Decca 29220
9/17/55	7	11	56. **The Yellow Rose Of Texas** Jockey #7 / Best Seller #13		Decca 29633
12/17/55	7	4	57. **Thirty Days (To Come Back Home)** Juke Box #7 / Jockey #10; written by Chuck Berry		Decca 29731
7/8/57	8	2	58. **Mister Love** **ERNEST TUBB & THE WILBURN BROTHERS** Jockey #8		Decca 30305
4/28/58	13	4	59. House Of Glass Jockey #13		Decca 30549
5/26/58	9	10	60. **Hey, Mr. Bluebird** **ERNEST TUBB and THE WILBURN BROTHERS** Jockey #9 / Best Seller #14		Decca 30610
10/20/58	8	11	61. **Half A Mind/**		
10/20/58	21	1	62. The Blues		Decca 30685
1/5/59	19	3	63. What Am I Living For		Decca 30759
5/4/59	12	13	64. I Cried A Tear		Decca 30872
9/28/59	14	14	65. Next Time		Decca 30952
9/5/60	16	7	66. Ev'rybody's Somebody's Fool		Decca 31119
6/5/61	16	9	67. Thoughts Of A Fool		Decca 31241
11/13/61	14	11	68. Through That Door		Decca 31300
8/18/62	16	9	69. I'm Looking High And Low For My Baby/		
9/8/62	30	1	70. Show Her Lots Of Gold		Decca 31399
6/22/63	28	1	71. Mr. Juke Box		Decca 31476
9/28/63	3	23	72. **Thanks A Lot**		Decca 31526
5/30/64	26	15	73. Be Better To Your Baby		Decca 31614
8/8/64	11	19	74. Mr. And Mrs. Used To Be **ERNEST TUBB and LORETTA LYNN**		Decca 31643
1/30/65	15	9	75. Pass The Booze		Decca 31706
3/13/65	29	9	76. Do What You Do Do Well		Decca 31742
8/7/65	24	9	77. Our Hearts Are Holding Hands **ERNEST TUBB and LORETTA LYNN**		Decca 31793

DATE	POS	WKS	ARTIST- RECORD TITLE	LABEL & NO.
11/13/65	**34**	4	78. Waltz Across Texas	Decca 31824
4/9/66	**32**	6	79. Till My Getup Has Gotup And Gone	Decca 31908
			ERNEST TUBB and His Texas Troubadours (above 2)	
11/12/66	**16**	12	80. Another Story	Decca 32022
6/28/69	**18**	8	81. Who's Gonna Take The Garbage Out	Decca 32496
			ERNEST TUBB and LORETTA LYNN	
11/10/79	**31**	3	82. Walkin' The Floor Over You [R]	Cachet 4507
			ERNEST TUBB & FRIENDS	
			Merle Haggard, Chet Atkins and Charlie Daniels (guest vocals)	

TUBB, Justin

Born Justin Wayne Tubb on 8/20/35 in San Antonio, Texas. Eldest son of Ernest Tubb. On the *Grand Ole Opry* since 1955. Manager of the *Ernest Tubb Midnight Jamboree Radio Show* and his own publishing company. Wrote "Lonesome 7-7203" for Hawkshaw Hawkins, "Be Glad" for Del Reeves, and many others.

DATE	POS	WKS	ARTIST- RECORD TITLE	LABEL & NO.
7/3/54	**4**	21	1. **Looking Back To See**	Decca 29145
			GOLDIE HILL - JUSTIN TUBB	
			Juke Box #4 / Best Seller #5 / Jockey #5	
1/8/55	**11**	2	2. Sure Fire Kisses	Decca 29349
			JUSTIN TUBB - GOLDIE HILL	
			Jockey #11 / Best Seller #13	
2/19/55	**8**	7	3. **I Gotta Go Get My Baby**	Decca 29401
			Jockey #8	
4/13/63	**6**	16	4. **Take A Letter, Miss Gray**	Groove 0017
10/23/65	**23**	5	5. Hurry, Mr. Peters	RCA 8659
			JUSTIN TUBB & LORENE MANN	
			answer song to Roy Drusky & Priscilla Mitchell's "Yes, Mr. Peters"	

TUCKER, Tanya

Born on 10/10/58 in Seminole, Texas; raised in Wilcox, Arizona. Appeared on the *Lew King* TV series in Phoenix from 1969. Appeared in the movie *Jeremiah Johnson*. Had her first charted record at age 13. CMA Award: 1991 Female Vocalist of the Year. Recording artist LaCosta Tucker is her older sister.

DATE	POS	WKS	ARTIST- RECORD TITLE	LABEL & NO.
6/3/72	**6**	14	1. **Delta Dawn**	Columbia 45588
			#1 Pop hit for Helen Reddy in 1973	
12/2/72+	**5**	13	2. **Love's The Answer/**	
		13	3. The Jamestown Ferry	Columbia 45721
4/7/73	**1** (1)	14	4. **What's Your Mama's Name**	Columbia 45799
8/11/73	**1** (1)	12	5. **Blood Red And Goin' Down**	Columbia 45892
2/2/74	**1** (1)	13	6. **Would You Lay With Me (In A Field Of Stone)**	Columbia 45991
			written by David Allan Coe	
7/6/74	**4**	9	7. **The Man That Turned My Mama On**	Columbia 46047
1/25/75	**18**	6	8. I Believe The South Is Gonna Rise Again	Columbia 10069
5/10/75	**1** (1)	12	9. **Lizzie And The Rainman**	MCA 40402
7/12/75	**18**	7	10. Spring	Columbia 10127
9/6/75	**1** (1)	11	11. **San Antonio Stroll**	MCA 40444
11/29/75	**23**	6	12. Greener Than The Grass (We Laid On)	Columbia 10236
12/27/75+	**4**	12	13. **Don't Believe My Heart Can Stand Another You**	MCA 40497
5/1/76	**3**	11	14. **You've Got Me To Hold On To**	MCA 40540
8/14/76	**1** (1)	12	15. **Here's Some Love**	MCA 40598
1/15/77	**12**	8	16. Ridin' Rainbows	MCA 40650

DATE	POS	WKS	ARTIST– RECORD TITLE	LABEL & NO.
4/30/77	**7**	11	17. **It's A Cowboy Lovin' Night**	MCA 40708
8/20/77	**40**	1	18. You Are So Beautiful *#5 Pop hit for Joe Cocker in 1975*	Columbia 10577
9/3/77	**16**	6	19. Dancing The Night Away	MCA 40755
12/2/78+	**5**	11	20. **Texas (When I Die)** *flip side "Not Fade Away" made #70 on the Hot 100*	MCA 40976
4/28/79	**18**	7	21. I'm The Singer, You're The Song *flip side "Lover Goodbye" Bubbled Under at #103*	MCA 41005
9/13/80	**10**	8	22. **Pecos Promenade** *from the movie Smokey and the Bandit II starring Burt Reynolds*	MCA 41305
1/10/81	**4**	9	23. **Can I See You Tonight**	MCA 51037
5/30/81	**40**	2	24. Love Knows We Tried	MCA 51096
1/29/83	**10**	9	25. **Feel Right**	Arista 0677
8/20/83	**22**	6	26. Baby I'm Yours *#11 Pop hit for Barbara Lewis in 1965*	Arista 9046
3/8/86	**3**	15	27. **One Love At A Time**	Capitol 5533
8/2/86	**1 (1)**	14	28. **Just Another Love**	Capitol 5604
11/22/86+	**2 (1)**	15	29. **I'll Come Back As Another Woman**	Capitol 5652
4/18/87	**8**	13	30. **It's Only Over For You** *some records were printed as "It's Only For You"*	Capitol 5694
8/15/87	**2 (2)**	15	31. **Love Me Like You Used To**	Capitol 44036
12/12/87+	**1 (1)**	15	32. **I Won't Take Less Than Your Love** **TANYA TUCKER with PAUL DAVIS & PAUL OVERSTREET**	Capitol 44100
4/16/88	**1 (1)**	14	33. **If It Don't Come Easy**	Capitol 44142
8/6/88	**1 (1)**	15	34. **Strong Enough To Bend**	Capitol 44188
12/17/88+	**2 (1)**	15	35. **Highway Robbery**	Capitol 44271
4/15/89	**4**	13	36. **Call On Me**	Capitol 44348
8/19/89	**27**	6	37. Daddy And Home	Capitol 44401
11/11/89+	**2 (2)**	20	38. **My Arms Stay Open All Night**	Capitol 44469
4/14/90	**3**	16	39. **Walking Shoes**	Capitol 44520
7/14/90	**6**	14	40. **Don't Go Out** **TANYA TUCKER with T. Graham Brown**	Capitol 44586
11/24/90+	**6**	12	41. **It Won't Be Me**	Capitol LP Cut
3/30/91	**12**	13	42. Oh What It Did To Me *later available as the B-side of #44 below; above 4 from the album* *Tennessee Woman on Capitol 91821*	Capitol LP Cut
7/6/91	**2 (1)**	18	43. **Down To My Last Teardrop** *also released as the B-side of #46 below*	Capitol LP Cut
11/9/91+	**2 (1)**	16	44. **(Without You) What Do I Do With Me**	Capitol 44774
2/29/92	**3**	18	45. **Some Kind Of Trouble**	Liberty 57703
6/27/92	**4**	16	46. **If Your Heart Ain't Busy Tonight** *above 4 from the album What Do I Do With Me on Capitol 95562*	Liberty 57768
10/17/92	**2 (1)**	17	47. **Two Sparrows In A Hurricane**	Liberty 56825
2/6/93	**2 (2)**	14	48. **It's A Little Too Late**	Liberty 56953
5/8/93	**4**	14	49. **Tell Me About It** **TANYA TUCKER with Delbert McClinton**	Liberty 56985
10/23/93	**2 (1)**	15	50. **Soon**	Liberty 17594
2/12/94	**11**	12	51. We Don't Have To Do This	Liberty 17803
7/2/94	**4**	14	52. **Hangin' In**	Liberty 17908
10/15/94	**20**	9	53. You Just Watch Me	Liberty 18135
3/25/95	**27**	6	54. Between The Two Of Them	Liberty 18485

DATE	POS	WKS	ARTIST— RECORD TITLE	LABEL & NO.
7/15/95	40	2	55. Find Out What's Happenin' *above 2 from the album* Fire To Fire *on Liberty 28943*	Liberty LP Cut
			TURNER, Mary Lou	
			Born in Hazard, Kentucky. Singer with the Bill Anderson Show.	
12/20/75+	**1** (1)	11	1. **Sometimes**	MCA 40488
4/10/76	7	9	2. **That's What Made Me Love You** **BILL ANDERSON & MARY LOU TURNER (above 2)**	MCA 40533
7/10/76	25	7	3. It's Different With You	MCA 40566
11/6/76	30	3	4. Love It Away	MCA 40620
3/12/77	40	2	5. Cheatin' Overtime	MCA 40674
8/6/77	18	7	6. Where Are You Going, Billy Boy	MCA 40753
2/18/78	25	4	7. I'm Way Ahead Of You **BILL ANDERSON & MARY LOU TURNER (above 2)**	MCA 40852
			TURNER, Zeb	
			Born William Edward Grishaw on 6/23/15 in Lynchburg, Virginia. Now deceased. Wrote "It's A Sin" and "That's When Your Heartaches Begin."	
9/17/49	**11**	1	1. Tennessee Boogie *Juke Box #11*	King 790
4/21/51	8	2	2. **Chew Tobacco Rag** *Juke Box #8 / Jockey #9*	King 950
			TUTTLE, Wesley, and His Texas Stars	
			Tuttle born on 12/30/17 in Lamar, Colorado. Worked on WLW-Cincinnati, then moved to California. Appeared with the Sons Of The Pioneers in Western movies. Regular performances on the *Town Hall Party.* Duets with wife Marilyn, a former member of the Sunshine Girls who appeared in Shirley Temple movies.	
10/6/45	**1** (4)	14	1. **With Tears In My Eyes**	Capitol 216
3/9/46	**3**	4	2. **Detour/**	
3/16/46	**5**	2	3. **I Wish I Had Never Met Sunshine**	Capitol 233
7/20/46	**4**	5	4. **Tho' I Tried (I Can't Forget You)**	Capitol 267
11/20/54	**15**	1	5. Never **MARILYN & WESLEY TUTTLE** *Best Seller #15*	Capitol 2850
			TWAIN, Shania	
			Shania pronounced: shu-NYE-uh. Born on 8/28/65 in Windsor, Ontario; raised in Timmons, Ontario. Married Robert John "Mutt" Lange (producer of rock bands Def Leppard, The Cars and Foreigner) on 12/28/93.	
6/3/95	**1** (2)	17	1. **Any Man Of Mine/**	
3/11/95	**11**	11	● 2. Whose Bed Have Your Boots Been Under?	Mercury 856448
12/2/95+	**1** (2)	18	3. **(If You're Not In It For Love) I'm Outta Here!/**	
9/2/95	**14**	12	4. The Woman In Me (Needs The Man In You)	Mercury 852206
3/2/96	**1** (2)	18	5. **You Win My Love**	Mercury 852138
5/25/96	**1** (1)	9 ↑	6.. **No One Needs To Know**	Mercury 852986

DATE	POS	WKS	ARTIST–RECORD TITLE	LABEL & NO.
			## TWITTY, Conway	
			Born Harold Lloyd Jenkins on 9/1/33 in Friars Point, Mississippi; raised in Helena, Arkansas. Died of an abdominal aneurysm on 6/5/93. Formed own group, The Phillips County Ramblers, at age 10. Offered a professional contract with the Philadelphia Phillies when drafted into the Army. With service band Cimmarons in Japan, early 1950s. Changed name in 1957 (derived from Conway, Arkansas, and Twitty, Texas) and first recorded for Sun (unissued recordings). Appeared in the movies *Sexpot Goes To College* and *College Confidential*. Switched from Pop to Country music in 1965. Moved to Nashville in 1968. Own tourist complex, Twitty City, in Hendersonville, Tennessee. CMA Awards: 1972, 1973, 1974 and 1975 Vocal Duo of the Year (with Loretta Lynn). (a) LORETTA LYNN/CONWAY TWITTY	
4/23/66	18	8	1. Guess My Eyes Were Bigger Than My Heart	Decca 31897
10/1/66	36	6	2. Look Into My Teardrops	Decca 31983
3/11/67	21	10	3. I Don't Want To Be With Me	Decca 32081
7/29/67	32	6	4. Don't Put Your Hurt In My Heart	Decca 32147
4/6/68	5	16	5. **The Image Of Me**	Decca 32272
9/14/68	1 (1)	13	6. **Next In Line**	Decca 32361
1/4/69	2 (2)	16	7. **Darling, You Know I Wouldn't Lie**	Decca 32424
5/24/69	1 (1)	15	8. **I Love You More Today**	Decca 32481
9/27/69	1 (1)	13	9. **To See My Angel Cry**	Decca 32546
1/10/70	3	12	10. **That's When She Started To Stop Loving You**	Decca 32599
4/25/70	1 (4)	18	11. **Hello Darlin'**	Decca 32661
10/17/70	1 (1)	16	12. **Fifteen Years Ago**	Decca 32742
2/6/71	1 (2)	14	13. **After The Fire Is Gone** (a)	Decca 32776
3/27/71	1 (1)	15	14. **How Much More Can She Stand**	Decca 32801
7/24/71	4	12	15. **I Wonder What She'll Think About Me Leaving** written by Merle Haggard	Decca 32842
10/9/71	1 (1)	15	16. **Lead Me On** (a)	Decca 32873
12/11/71+	4	14	17. **I Can't See Me Without You**	Decca 32895
4/15/72	1 (1)	13	18. **(Lost Her Love) On Our Last Date** same tune as Floyd Cramer's "Last Date"	Decca 32945
8/5/72	1 (1)	14	19. **I Can't Stop Loving You**	Decca 32988
12/9/72+	1 (2)	14	20. **She Needs Someone To Hold Her (When She Cries)** first released as the B-side of #19 above	Decca 33033
4/7/73	2 (1)	13	21. **Baby's Gone**	MCA 40027
6/30/73	1 (1)	13	22. **Louisiana Woman, Mississippi Man** (a)	MCA 40079
8/4/73	1 (3)	16	23. **You've Never Been This Far Before**	MCA 40094
2/9/74	1 (1)	12	24. **There's A Honky Tonk Angel (Who'll Take Me** **Back In)**	MCA 40173
5/25/74	3	13	25. **I'm Not Through Loving You Yet**	MCA 40224
7/6/74	1 (1)	11	26. **As Soon As I Hang Up The Phone** (a)	MCA 40251
9/14/74	1 (2)	13	27. **I See The Want To In Your Eyes**	MCA 40282
2/1/75	1 (1)	8	28. **Linda On My Mind**	MCA 40339
6/7/75	1 (2)	10	29. **Touch The Hand/**	
9/6/75	4	9	30. **Don't Cry Joni** Joni Lee Twitty (Conway's daughter; guest vocal)	MCA 40407
7/5/75	1 (1)	13	31. **Feelins'** (a)	MCA 40420
12/20/75+	1 (1)	10	32. **This Time I've Hurt Her More Than She Loves Me**	MCA 40492
4/10/76	1 (1)	11	33. **After All The Good Is Gone**	MCA 40534

DATE	POS	WKS	ARTIST—RECORD TITLE	LABEL & NO.
6/26/76	3	10	34. **The Letter** (a)	MCA 40572
8/28/76	1 (1)	11	35. **The Games That Daddies Play**	MCA 40601
11/27/76+	1 (1)	12	36. **I Can't Believe She Gives It All To Me**	MCA 40649
3/12/77	1 (1)	13	37. **Play, Guitar Play**	MCA 40682
6/11/77	2 (3)	11	38. **I Can't Love You Enough** (a)	MCA 40728
7/30/77	1 (1)	11	39. **I've Already Loved You In My Mind**	MCA 40754
11/5/77	3	11	40. **Georgia Keeps Pulling On My Ring**	MCA 40805
3/4/78	16	6	41. **The Grandest Lady Of Them All**	MCA 40857
			salute to the *Grand Ole Opry*	
7/1/78	6	8	42. **From Seven Till Ten** (a)/	
		7	43. You're The Reason Our Kids Are Ugly (a)	MCA 40920
7/22/78	2 (1)	10	44. **Boogie Grass Band**	MCA 40929
11/25/78+	3	11	45. **Your Love Had Taken Me That High**	MCA 40963
3/31/79	1 (1)	9	46. **Don't Take It Away**	MCA 41002
7/21/79	1 (1)	10	47. **I May Never Get To Heaven**	MCA 41059
11/3/79	1 (3)	11	48. **Happy Birthday Darlin'**	MCA 41135
11/24/79+	9	10	49. **You Know Just What I'd Do** (a)/	
		10	50. The Sadness Of It All (a)	MCA 41141
2/2/80	1 (1)	12	51. **I'd Love To Lay You Down**	MCA 41174
5/31/80	5	10	52. **It's True Love** (a)	MCA 41232
7/12/80	6	9	53. **I've Never Seen The Likes Of You**	MCA 41271
11/1/80+	3	12	54. **A Bridge That Just Won't Burn**	MCA 51011
2/14/81	7	10	55. **Lovin' What Your Lovin' Does To Me** (a)	MCA 51050
3/7/81	1 (1)	10	56. **Rest Your Love On Me/**	
			written by Barry Gibb (of the Bee Gees)	
		10	57. I Am The Dreamer (You Are The Dream)	MCA 51059
6/20/81	2 (2)	11	58. **I Still Believe In Waltzes** (a)	MCA 51114
7/25/81	1 (1)	10	59. **Tight Fittin' Jeans**	MCA 51137
11/14/81+	1 (1)	12	60. **Red Neckin' Love Makin' Night**	MCA 51199
2/6/82	1 (1)	13	61. **The Clown**	Elektra 47302
5/8/82	1 (2)	10	62. **Slow Hand**	Elektra 47443
			#2 Pop hit for the Pointer Sisters in 1981	
10/2/82	2 (2)	12	63. **We Did But Now You Don't**	Elektra 69964
1/15/83	1 (1)	12	64. **The Rose**	Elektra 69854
			#3 Pop hit for Bette Midler in 1980	
6/11/83	2 (2)	14	65. **Lost In The Feeling**	Warner 29636
			Ricky Skaggs (backing vocal)	
10/15/83	6	10	66. **Heartache Tonight**	Warner 29505
			#1 Pop hit for the Eagles in 1979	
1/21/84	7	11	67. **Three Times A Lady**	Warner 29395
			#1 Pop hit for the Commodores in 1978	
4/28/84	1 (1)	14	68. **Somebody's Needin' Somebody**	Warner 29308
8/11/84	1 (1)	14	69. **I Don't Know A Thing About Love (The Moon Song)**	Warner 29227
			Joni Lee Twitty (guest vocal)	
11/24/84+	1 (1)	14	70. **Ain't She Somethin' Else**	Warner 29137
3/30/85	1 (1)	13	71. **Don't Call Him A Cowboy**	Warner 29057
7/20/85	3	13	72. **Between Blue Eyes And Jeans**	Warner 28966
11/23/85	19	8	73. The Legend And The Man	Warner 28866
3/29/86	26	5	74. You'll Never Know How Much I Needed You Today	Warner 28772
6/28/86	1 (1)	13	75. **Desperado Love**	Warner 28692

DATE	POS	WKS	ARTIST– RECORD TITLE	LABEL & NO.
11/8/86+	2 (1)	14	76. **Fallin' For You For Years**	Warner 28577
3/21/87	2 (2)	14	77. **Julia**	MCA 53034
8/1/87	2 (1)	14	78. **I Want To Know You Before We Make Love**	MCA 53134
12/19/87+	6	13	79. **That's My Job**	MCA 53200
4/30/88	7	12	80. **Goodbye Time**	MCA 53276
8/27/88	9	12	81. **Saturday Night Special**	MCA 53373
			Vince Gill (harmony vocal)	
12/24/88+	4	14	82. **I Wish I Was Still In Your Dreams**	MCA 53456
5/13/89	2 (1)	14	83. **She's Got A Single Thing In Mind**	MCA 53633
9/23/89	19	7	84. House On Old Lonesome Road	MCA 53688
6/2/90	30	4	85. Fit To Be Tied Down	MCA 79000
10/6/90	2 (2)	16	86. **Crazy In Love**	MCA 79067
1/19/91	3	18	87. **I Couldn't See You Leavin'**	MCA 53983
9/21/91	22	8	88. She's Got A Man On Her Mind	MCA 54186

TYLER, Bonnie

Born Gaynor Hopkins on 6/8/53 in Swansea, Wales. Worked local clubs until the mid-1970s. Distinctive raspy vocals caused by operation to remove throat nodules in 1976.

DATE	POS	WKS	ARTIST– RECORD TITLE	LABEL & NO.
5/20/78	10	7	● 1. **It's A Heartache**	RCA 11249

TYLER, "T" Texas

Born David Luke Myrick on 6/20/16 in Mena, Arkansas. Died on 1/28/72. Raised in Texas, educated in Philadelphia. Appeared on the *Major Bowes Amateur Hour* in New York in the late '30s. Worked on the *Louisiana Hayride* in 1942. Moved to California after the service in 1946. Appeared in the 1949 movie *Horseman Of The Sierras*. Own TV series, *Range Round-Up*, in Los Angeles. Billed as "The Man With A Million Friends."

DATE	POS	WKS	ARTIST– RECORD TITLE	LABEL & NO.
8/24/46	5	1	1. **Filipino Baby**	4 Star 1009
			"T" TEXAS TYLER and his Oklahoma Melody Boys	
4/10/48	2 (1)	13	2. **Deck Of Cards** [S]	4 Star 1228
			Best Seller #2 / Juke Box #3	
7/3/48	10	2	3. **Dad Gave My Dog Away**	4 Star 1248
			Best Seller #10 / Juke Box #13	
9/25/48	9	4	4. **Memories Of France/**	4 Star 1249
			Juke Box #9	
11/13/48	11	1	5. Honky Tonk Gal	
			Juke Box #11	
11/26/49	4	5	6. **My Bucket's Got A Hole In It**	4 Star 1383
			Juke Box #4 / Jockey #8	
4/18/53	5	15	7. **Bumming Around**	Decca 28579
			Best Seller #5 / Juke Box #5	
7/17/54	3	19	8. **Courtin' In The Rain**	4 Star 1660
			T. TEXAS TYLER and His Band	
			Jockey #3 / Juke Box #4	

DATE	POS	WKS	ARTIST— RECORD TITLE	LABEL & NO.

V

VAN DYKE, Leroy

Born on 10/4/29 in Spring Fork, Missouri. Worked as a newspaper reporter. Served in U.S. Army in the early '50s. Worked as an auctioneer; wrote "Auctioneer" with Buddy Black. Appeared on Red Foley's TV shows and the *Grand Ole Opry*. Appeared in the movie *What Am I Bid?* in 1967.

DATE	POS	WKS	ARTIST— RECORD TITLE	LABEL & NO.
1/5/57	9	2	1. **Auctioneer** Jockey #9 / Juke Box #10	Dot 15503
9/4/61	1 (19)	37	2. **Walk On By**	Mercury 71834
3/31/62	3	12	3. **If A Woman Answers (Hang Up The Phone)**	Mercury 71926
12/29/62	16	7	4. Black Cloud The Merry Melody Singers (backing vocals)	Mercury 72057
1/23/65	40	1	5. Anne Of A Thousand Days	Mercury 72360
10/29/66	34	5	6. Roses From A Stranger	Warner 5841
2/3/68	23	6	7. Louisville	Warner 7155

VASSY, Kin

Born Charles Kindred Vassy. Died of cancer on 6/23/94 (age 50). Formerly with The Back Porch Majority, and Kenny Rogers and The First Edition.

DATE	POS	WKS	ARTIST— RECORD TITLE	LABEL & NO.
6/27/81	39	1	1. Likin' Him And Lovin' You	Liberty 1407
1/16/82	21	5	2. When You Were Blue And I Was Green	Liberty 1440

VAUGHN, Sharon—see FELTS, Narvel

VERNON, Kenny

Born on 7/19/40 in Jackson, Tennessee. On WDXI radio with Carl Perkins in 1956. Worked in San Diego and Las Vegas, including eight years at the Golden Nugget.

DATE	POS	WKS	ARTIST— RECORD TITLE	LABEL & NO.
4/18/70	27	4	1. Pickin' Wild Mountain Berries #27 Pop hit for Peggy Scott & Jo Jo Benson in 1968	Chart 5055

VINCENT, Gene, and His Blue Caps

Vincent born Vincent Eugene Craddock on 2/11/35 in Norfolk, Virginia. Died from an ulcer hemorrhage on 10/12/71. Innovative rock and roll singer/songwriter/guitarist.

DATE	POS	WKS	ARTIST— RECORD TITLE	LABEL & NO.
7/7/56	5	17	1. **Be-Bop-A-Lula** Best Seller #5 / Juke Box #5 / Jockey #9	Capitol 3450

VINCENT, Rick

Born in San Bernadino; raised in Bakersfield, California.

DATE	POS	WKS	ARTIST— RECORD TITLE	LABEL & NO.
2/20/93	39	1	1. The Best Mistakes I Ever Made	Curb LP Cut

VINTON, Bobby

Born Stanley Robert Vinton on 4/16/35 in Canonsburg, Pennsylvania. Father was a bandleader. Formed own band while in high school; toured as backing band for Dick Clark's "Caravan of Stars" in 1960. Left band for a singing career in 1962. Own musical variety TV series, 1975-78.

DATE	POS	WKS	ARTIST— RECORD TITLE	LABEL & NO.
3/14/70	27	6	1. My Elusive Dreams	Epic 10576

DATE	POS	WKS	ARTIST– RECORD TITLE	LABEL & NO.
			# W	
			## WAGONER, Porter	
			Born on 8/12/27 in West Plains, Missouri. Broadcast from a grocery store in West Plains in the late 1940s. Worked on KWTO-Springfield in 1951. Performed on Red Foley's TV series *Ozark Jubilee* in the early '50s. On the *Grand Ole Opry* since 1957. Own TV series with Norma Jean starting in 1960; the show featured Dolly Parton, 1967-74. CMA Awards: 1968 Vocal Group of the Year (with Dolly Parton); 1970 and 1971 Vocal Duo of the Year (with Dolly Parton).	
			(a) PORTER WAGONER & DOLLY PARTON	
10/30/54+	7	12	1. **Company's Comin'** Jockey #7	RCA 5848
5/28/55	1 (4)	33	2. **A Satisfied Mind** Jockey #1 / Juke Box #2 / Best Seller #2	RCA 6105
12/3/55+	3	22	3. **Eat, Drink, And Be Merry (Tomorrow You'll Cry)** Best Seller #3 / Juke Box #3 / Jockey #5	RCA 6289
3/31/56	8	11	4. **What Would You Do? (If Jesus Came To Your House)** Best Seller #8 / Jockey #14	RCA 6421
5/26/56	14	4	5. Uncle Pen Jockey #14; written by Bill Monroe in tribute to his musically influential uncle, Pen Vandiver	RCA 6494
11/17/56	11	2	6. Tryin' To Forget The Blues Jockey #11	RCA 6598
8/19/57	11	3	7. I Thought I Heard You Call My Name Jockey #11	RCA 6964
5/4/59	29	1	8. Me And Fred And Joe And Bill	RCA 7457
1/18/60	26	4	9. The Girl Who Didn't Need Love	RCA 7638
10/31/60	26	1	10. Falling Again/	RCA 7770
10/31/60	30	1	11. An Old Log Cabin For Sale	
3/6/61	10	13	12. **Your Old Love Letters**	RCA 7837
1/13/62	1 (2)	29	13. **Misery Loves Company** written by Jerry Reed	RCA 7967
6/23/62	10	10	14. **Cold Dark Waters**	RCA 8026
12/8/62+	7	15	15. **I've Enjoyed As Much Of This As I Can Stand**	RCA 8105
6/22/63	20	7	16. My Baby's Not Here (In Town Tonight)/	RCA 8178
7/20/63	29	1	17. In The Shadows Of The Wine	
1/18/64	19	12	18. Howdy Neighbor Howdy	RCA 8257
4/25/64	5	21	19. **Sorrow On The Rocks**	RCA 8338
10/10/64	11	23	20. I'll Go Down Swinging	RCA 8432
5/15/65	21	6	21. I'm Gonna Feed You Now	RCA 8524
8/7/65	4	18	22. **Green, Green Grass Of Home**	RCA 8622
1/8/66	3	15	23. **Skid Row Joe**	RCA 8723
5/7/66	21	12	24. I Just Came To Smell The Flowers	RCA 8800
2/18/67	2 (1)	16	25. **The Cold Hard Facts Of Life**	RCA 9067
8/19/67	15	11	26. Julie written by Waylon Jennings	RCA 9243
12/30/67+	7	13	27. **The Last Thing On My Mind** (a)	RCA 9369
1/6/68	24	9	28. Woman Hungry	RCA 9379

DATE	POS	WKS	ARTIST– RECORD TITLE		LABEL & NO.
5/4/68	7	12	29. **Holding On To Nothin'** (a)		RCA 9490
6/22/68	16	12	30. Be Proud Of Your Man		RCA 9530
8/10/68	5	11	31. **We'll Get Ahead Someday** (a)		RCA 9577
11/9/68+	2 (4)	20	32. **The Carroll County Accident**		RCA 9651
3/15/69	9	13	33. **Yours Love** (a)		RCA 0104
6/28/69	3	13	34. **Big Wind**		RCA 0168
7/5/69	16	8	35. Always, Always (a)		RCA 0172
11/1/69	5	14	36. **Just Someone I Used To Know** (a)		RCA 0247
12/6/69	21	8	37. When You're Hot You're Hot		RCA 0267
2/28/70	9	12	38. **Tomorrow Is Forever** (a)		RCA 9799
8/8/70	7	13	39. **Daddy Was An Old Time Preacher Man** (a)		RCA 9875
1/16/71	18	12	40. The Last One To Touch Me		RCA 9939
2/27/71	7	12	41. **Better Move It On Home** (a)		RCA 9958
6/5/71	15	8	42. Charley's Picture		RCA 9979
7/17/71	14	9	43. The Right Combination (a)		RCA 9994
9/11/71	11	12	44. Be A Little Quieter		RCA 1007
11/27/71+	11	11	45. Burning The Midnight Oil (a)		RCA 0565
3/18/72	8	11	46. **What Ain't To Be, Just Might Happen**		RCA 0648
4/22/72	9	12	47. **Lost Forever In Your Kiss** (a)		RCA 0675
8/19/72	14	10	48. A World Without Music		RCA 0753
9/16/72	14	11	49. Together Always (a)		RCA 0773
11/25/72	16	9	50. Katy Did		RCA 0820
4/7/73	30	4	51. We Found It (a)		RCA 0893
7/14/73	3	14	52. **If Teardrops Were Pennies** (a)		RCA 0981
8/25/73	37	2	53. Wake Up, Jacob		RCA 0013
8/31/74	1 (1)	10	54. **Please Don't Stop Loving Me** (a)		RCA 10010
8/31/74	15	6	55. Highway Headin' South		RCA 0328
1/18/75	19	6	56. Carolina Moonshiner		RCA 10124
8/9/75	5	12	57. **Say Forever You'll Be Mine** (a)		RCA 10328
6/5/76	8	10	58. **Is Forever Longer Than Always** (a)		RCA 10652
12/23/78+	31	4	59. Ole Slew Foot/	[R]	
		4	60. I'm Gonna Feed 'Em Now	[R]	RCA 11411
4/7/79	34	3	61. I Want To Walk You Home		RCA 11491
9/8/79	32	3	62. Everything I've Always Wanted		RCA 11671
7/12/80	2 (2)	12	63. **Making Plans** (a)		RCA 11983
11/22/80+	12	10	64. If You Go, I'll Follow You (a)		RCA 12119
4/16/83	35	3	65. This Cowboy's Hat		Warner 29772

WAKELY, Jimmy

Born on 2/16/14 near Mineola, Arkansas; raised in Oklahoma. Died on 9/25/82. Guitarist/pianist. Own Jimmy Wakely Trio with Johnny Bond and Scotty Harrell on WKY-Oklahoma City in 1937. Worked on Gene Autry's *Melody Ranch* series on CBS radio in the early 1940s. Nicknamed "The Melody Kid." Starred in over 70 Western movies. Own radio series, 1952-57, and a TV series with Tex Ritter in 1961. Own record label, Shasta, in the mid-1960s.

(a) MARGARET WHITING & JIMMY WAKELY

DATE	POS	WKS	ARTIST– RECORD TITLE	LABEL & NO.
4/15/44	2 (1)	4	1. **I'm Sending You Red Roses**	Decca 6095

DATE	POS	WKS	ARTIST– RECORD TITLE	LABEL & NO.
4/3/48	**9**	6	2. **Signed, Sealed And Delivered** Best Seller #9 / Juke Box #9	Capitol A. 40088
9/4/48	**1 (11)**	32	3. **One Has My Name (The Other Has My Heart)** Best Seller #1(11) / Juke Box #1(7)	Capitol 15162
10/30/48+	**1 (5)**	28	4. **I Love You So Much It Hurts** Juke Box #1(5) / Best Seller #1(4)	Capitol 15243
11/13/48+	**8**	5	5. **Mine All Mine** Juke Box #8	Capitol 15236
2/5/49	**10**	1	6. **Forever More** Juke Box #10	Capitol 15333
2/19/49	**9**	6	7. **Till The End Of The World** Best Seller #9 / Juke Box #15	Capitol 15368
5/14/49	**4**	9	8. **I Wish I Had A Nickel/** Juke Box #4 / Best Seller #10	
6/18/49	**10**	3	9. **Someday You'll Call My Name** Juke Box #10; Velma Williams (harmony vocal)	Capitol 40153
8/6/49	**14**	2	10. Tellin' My Troubles To My Old Guitar Juke Box #14	Capitol 40187
9/10/49	**1 (17)**	28	● 11. **Slipping Around** (a)/ Best Seller #1(17) / Juke Box #1(12) / Jockey #2	
9/10/49	**6**	8	12. **Wedding Bells** (a) Juke Box #6 / Best Seller #7	Capitol 40224
11/5/49	**2 (3)**	13	13. **I'll Never Slip Around Again** (a) Juke Box #2 / Best Seller #2 / Jockey #10	Capitol 40246
2/11/50	**2 (1)**	9	14. **Broken Down Merry-Go-Round** (a)/ Best Seller #2 / Juke Box #3 / Jockey #5	
2/11/50	**3**	7	15. **The Gods Were Angry With Me** (a) Best Seller #3 / Juke Box #4	Capitol 800
4/8/50	**7**	3	16. **Peter Cottontail** Jockey #7	Capitol 929
4/22/50	**2 (1)**	10	17. **Let's Go To Church (Next Sunday Morning)** (a) Best Seller #2 / Jockey #6 / Juke Box #6	Capitol 960
9/23/50	**10**	1	18. Mona Lisa Jockey #10; from the movie *Captain Carey, U.S.A.* starring Alan Ladd	Capitol 1151
11/18/50	**6**	1	19. **A Bushel And A Peck** (a) Best Seller #6 / Juke Box #10; from the Broadway musical *Guys And Dolls*	Capitol 1234
1/20/51	**7**	1	20. **My Heart Cries For You** Best Seller #7 / Jockey #10; Les Baxter Chorus (backing vocals)	Capitol 1328
3/17/51	**5**	12	21. **Beautiful Brown Eyes** **JIMMY WAKELY and the LES BAXTER CHORUS** Best Seller #5 / Juke Box #5 / Jockey #9	Capitol 1393
6/2/51	**7**	2	22. **When You And I Were Young Maggie Blues** (a) Juke Box #7	Capitol 1500
12/8/51	**5**	5	23. **I Don't Want To Be Free** (a) Juke Box #5	Capitol 1816
			WALKER, Billy Born on 1/14/29 in Ralls, Texas. Own radio show on KICA-Clovis, New Mexico, at age 15. Worked on the *Big D Jamboree* in Dallas as "The Masked Singer" in 1949. Performed on the *Louisiana Hayride* and *Ozark Jubilee* until 1960, on the *Grand Ole Opry* since 1960. Own TV series, *Country Carnival*. Appeared in the movies *Second Fiddle To A Steel Guitar* and *Red River Round Up*. Known as "The Tall Texan."	

DATE	POS	WKS	ARTIST–RECORD TITLE	LABEL & NO.
6/26/54	8	13	1. **Thank You For Calling** *Jockey #8 / Best Seller #12*	Columbia 21256
6/24/57	12	6	2. On My Mind Again *Jockey #12*	Columbia 40920
11/7/60	19	8	3. I Wish You Love	Columbia 41763
10/16/61	23	2	4. Funny How Time Slips Away *#22 Pop hit for Jimmy Elledge in 1962*	Columbia 42050
3/3/62	1 (2)	23	5. **Charlie's Shoes**	Columbia 42287
9/1/62	5	12	6. **Willie The Weeper**	Columbia 42492
8/17/63	21	12	7. Heart, Be Careful	Columbia 42794
12/28/63+	22	14	8. The Morning Paper	Columbia 42891
5/23/64	7	19	9. **Circumstances**	Columbia 43010
10/10/64	2 (2)	22	10. **Cross The Brazos At Waco**	Columbia 43120
4/10/65	8	17	11. **Matamoros**	Columbia 43223
9/18/65	16	9	12. If It Pleases You	Columbia 43327
6/25/66	2 (4)	20	13. **A Million And One**	Monument 943
12/10/66+	3	13	14. **Bear With Me A Little Longer**	Monument 980
3/25/67	10	12	15. **Anything Your Heart Desires** [R] *first recorded on Columbia 41008 in 1957*	Monument 997
7/15/67	18	10	16. In Del Rio	Monument 1013
10/14/67	11	10	17. I Taught Her Everything She Knows	Monument 1024
3/23/68	18	10	18. Sundown Mary	Monument 1055
7/13/68	8	10	19. **Ramona** *#1 Pop hit for both Gene Austin and Paul Whiteman in 1928*	Monument 1079
11/16/68	20	8	20. Age Of Worry	Monument 1098
3/1/69	20	9	21. From The Bottle To The Bottom **BILLY WALKER and The Tennessee Walkers**	Monument 1123
5/31/69	12	9	22. Smoky Places *#12 Pop hit for The Corsairs in 1962*	Monument 1140
9/27/69	37	4	23. Better Homes And Gardens	Monument 1154
12/27/69+	9	10	24. **Thinking 'Bout You, Babe**	Monument 1174
4/18/70	23	6	25. Darling Days	Monument 1189
7/4/70	3	16	26. **When A Man Loves A Woman (The Way That I Love You)**	MGM 14134
11/7/70	3	11	27. **She Goes Walking Through My Mind**	MGM 14173
2/6/71	3	12	28. **I'm Gonna Keep On Keep On Lovin' You**	MGM 14210
5/29/71	28	6	29. It's Time To Love Her *from the movie Lookin' Good starring Robert Blake*	MGM 14239
8/14/71	22	8	30. Don't Let Him Make A Memory Out Of Me	MGM 14268
12/4/71	25	6	31. Traces Of A Woman	MGM 14305
6/24/72	24	6	32. Gone (Our Endless Love) **BILLY WALKER with The Mike Curb Congregation**	MGM 14377
10/21/72	3	12	33. **Sing Me A Love Song To Baby**	MGM 14422
4/7/73	34	3	34. My Mind Hangs On To You	MGM 14488
3/9/74	39	1	35. I Changed My Mind *written by Conway Twitty*	MGM 14693
4/26/75	10	11	36. **Word Games**	RCA 10205
10/11/75	25	5	37. If I'm Losing You	RCA 10345
1/17/76	19	8	38. Don't Stop In My World (If You Don't Mean To Stay)	RCA 10466

DATE	POS	WKS	ARTIST– RECORD TITLE	LABEL & NO.
			WALKER, Charlie	
			Born on 11/2/26 in Copeville, Texas. Played with the Cowboy Ramblers in 1943. During World War II, worked as a DJ with the Armed Forces Radio Network. Top country DJ in the early '50s. Worked as an emcee at the Golden Nugget in Las Vegas. On the *Grand Ole Opry* since 1967. Excellent golfer, also a golf event broadcaster. Appeared in the movie *Country Music*.	
1/28/56	9	2	1. **Only You, Only You** Juke Box #9	Decca 29715
10/20/58	2 (4)	22	2. **Pick Me Up On Your Way Down**	Columbia 41211
6/8/59	16	9	3. I'll Catch You When You Fall	Columbia 41388
10/26/59	22	2	4. When My Conscience Hurts The Most	Columbia 41467
5/16/60	11	16	5. Who Will Buy The Wine	Columbia 41633
2/6/61	25	3	6. Facing The Wall	Columbia 41820
1/9/65	17	12	7. Close All The Honky Tonks	Epic 9727
6/26/65	8	15	8. **Wild As A Wildcat**	Epic 9799
1/15/66	39	1	9. He's A Jolly Good Fellow	Epic 9852
3/26/66	37	2	10. The Man In The Little White Suit	Epic 9875
3/25/67	38	2	11. The Town That Never Sleeps	Epic 10118
7/1/67	8	12	12. **Don't Squeeze My Sharmon**	Epic 10174
12/2/67	33	4	13. I Wouldn't Take Her To A Dogfight	Epic 10237
8/24/68	31	7	14. San Diego	Epic 10349
			WALKER, Cindy	
			Born in Mexia, Texas. First recorded for Decca in 1942. Wrote "You Don't Know Me" and "Take Me In Your Arms And Hold Me" for Eddy Arnold, "I Don't Care" for Webb Pierce, "Distant Drums" for Jim Reeves, and many others.	
11/4/44	5	1	1. **When My Blue Moon Turns To Gold Again** #19 Pop hit for Elvis Presley in 1956	Decca 6103
			WALKER, Clay	
			Native of Beaumont, Texas. Diagnosed with multiple sclerosis in April 1996.	
8/7/93	1 (1)	16	1. **What's It To You**	Giant 18450
11/13/93+	1 (1)	18	2. **Live Until I Die**	Giant 18332
3/26/94	11	11	3. Where Do I Fit In The Picture	Giant 18210
6/25/94	1 (1)	18	4. **Dreaming With My Eyes Open**	Giant 18139
10/1/94	1 (1)	19	5. **If I Could Make A Living**	Giant 18068
1/28/95	1 (2)	17	6. **This Woman And This Man**	Giant 17995
5/20/95	16	12	7. My Heart Will Never Know	Giant 17887
9/30/95	2 (2)	18	8. **Who Needs You Baby**	Giant 17771
1/27/96	2 (1)	18	9. **Hypnotize The Moon**	Giant 17704
			WALKER, Wiley—see WILEY & GENE	
			WALLACE, Jerry	
			Born on 12/15/28 in Guilford, Missouri; raised in Glendale, Arizona. First recorded for Allied in 1951. Appeared on the TV shows *Night Gallery* and *Hec Ramsey*.	
10/9/65	23	11	1. Life's Gone And Slipped Away	Mercury 72461
1/13/68	36	3	2. This One's On The House	Liberty 56001
10/5/68	22	7	3. Sweet Child Of Sunshine	Liberty 56059

DATE	POS	WKS	ARTIST – RECORD TITLE	LABEL & NO.
3/13/71	**22**	9	4. After You	Decca 32777
9/18/71	**19**	10	5. The Morning After	Decca 32859
2/5/72	**12**	13	6. To Get To You	Decca 32914
7/29/72	**1** (2)	16	7. **If You Leave Me Tonight I'll Cry**	Decca 32989
			from TV's *Rod Serling's Night Gallery: The Tune In Dan's Cafe*	
12/23/72+	**2** (1)	13	8. **Do You Know What It's Like To Be Lonesome**	Decca 33036
5/5/73	**21**	9	9. Sound Of Goodbye/	
		9	10. The Song Nobody Sings	MCA 40037
9/8/73	**3**	13	11. **Don't Give Up On Me**	MCA 40111
3/9/74	**18**	7	12. Guess Who	MCA 40183
7/13/74	**9**	9	13. **My Wife's House**	MCA 40248
12/14/74+	**20**	7	14. I Wonder Whose Baby (You Are Now)	MCA 40321
4/19/75	**32**	4	15. Comin' Home To You	MGM 14788
8/6/77	**26**	5	16. I Miss You Already	BMA 002
12/10/77+	**28**	6	17. I'll Promise You Tomorrow	BMA 005
3/18/78	**24**	4	18. At The End Of A Rainbow	BMA 006
			#7 Pop hit for Earl Grant in 1958	
11/25/78	**38**	1	19. I Wanna Go To Heaven	4 Star 1035

WARD, Jacky

Born on 11/18/46 in Groveton, Texas. Supporting act on tours with Ronnie Milsap and Crystal Gayle.

DATE	POS	WKS	ARTIST – RECORD TITLE	LABEL & NO.
8/5/72	**39**	1	1. Big Blue Diamond	Target 0146
12/27/75+	**38**	2	2. Dance Her By Me (One More Time)	Mercury 73716
10/2/76	**24**	7	3. I Never Said It Would Be Easy	Mercury 73826
3/12/77	**31**	4	4. Texas Angel	Mercury 73880
10/1/77	**9**	11	5. **Fools Fall In Love**	Mercury 55003
2/18/78	**3**	9	6. **A Lover's Question**	Mercury 55018
			#6 Pop hit for Clyde McPhatter in 1959	
6/17/78	**20**	7	7. Three Sheets In The Wind/	
		7	8. I'd Really Love To See You Tonight	Mercury 55026
			#2 Pop hit for England Dan & John Ford Coley in 1976	
8/26/78	**24**	5	9. I Want To Be In Love	Mercury 55038
11/18/78	**11**	9	10. Rhythm Of The Rain	Mercury 55047
			#3 Pop hit for The Cascades in 1963	
3/3/79	**8**	9	11. **Wisdom Of A Fool**	Mercury 55055
8/4/79	**26**	5	12. That Makes Two Of Us	Mercury 55054
			JACKY WARD & REBA McENTIRE (#7, 8, 12)	
10/6/79	**14**	8	13. You're My Kind Of Woman	Mercury 57004
2/2/80	**32**	4	14. I'd Do Anything For You	Mercury 57013
6/14/80	**8**	11	15. **Save Your Heart For Me**	Mercury 57022
10/4/80	**7**	9	16. **That's The Way A Cowboy Rocks And Rolls**	Mercury 57032
2/7/81	**13**	9	17. Somethin' On The Radio	Mercury 57044
4/17/82	**32**	4	18. Travelin' Man	Asylum 47424
			#1 Pop hit for Ricky Nelson in 1961	

DATE	POS	WKS	ARTIST– RECORD TITLE	LABEL & NO.
			WARINER, Steve	
			Born Steve Noel Wariner on 12/25/54 in Noblesville, Indiana. Played bass while a teenager. Wrote songs from age 16. Bass player with Dottie West, 1971-74. Worked with Bob Luman and Chet Atkins. Joined the *Grand Ole Opry* in 1996. Also see Nicolette Larson.	
12/13/80+	7	9	1. **Your Memory**	RCA 12139
5/2/81	6	11	2. **By Now**	RCA 12204
10/17/81	1 (1)	12	3. **All Roads Lead To You**	RCA 12307
3/27/82	15	11	4. Kansas City Lights	RCA 13072
10/2/82	30	3	5. Don't It Break Your Heart	RCA 13308
1/22/83	27	4	6. Don't Plan On Sleepin' Tonight	RCA 13395
6/4/83	23	7	7. Don't Your Mem'ry Ever Sleep At Night	RCA 13515
9/3/83	5	11	8. **Midnight Fire**	RCA 13588
1/14/84	4	12	9. **Lonely Women Make Good Lovers**	RCA 13691
4/28/84	12	11	10. Why Goodbye	RCA 13768
1/12/85	3	13	11. **What I Didn't Do**	MCA 52506
5/4/85	8	11	12. **Heart Trouble**	MCA 52562
8/17/85	1 (1)	15	13. **Some Fools Never Learn**	MCA 52644
12/7/85+	1 (1)	15	14. **You Can Dream Of Me**	MCA 52721
3/29/86	1 (1)	14	15. **Life's Highway**	MCA 52786
9/6/86	4	12	16. **Starting Over Again**	MCA 52837
1/17/87	1 (1)	13	17. **Small Town Girl**	MCA 53006
5/9/87	1 (1)	14	18. **The Weekend**	MCA 53068
7/4/87	6	14	19. **The Hand That Rocks The Cradle**	MCA 53108
			GLEN CAMPBELL with STEVE WARINER	
9/19/87	1 (1)	13	20. Lynda	MCA 53160
3/5/88	2 (1)	14	21. **Baby I'm Yours**	MCA 53287
7/9/88	2 (2)	15	22. **I Should Be With You**	MCA 53347
11/12/88+	6	14	23. **Hold On (A Little Longer)**	MCA 53419
3/25/89	1 (1)	14	24. **Where Did I Go Wrong**	MCA 53504
7/15/89	1 (1)	15	25. **I Got Dreams**	MCA 53665
11/11/89+	5	23	26. **When I Could Come Home To You**	MCA 53738
4/7/90	7	13	27. **The Domino Theory**	MCA 53733
8/4/90	8	16	28. **Precious Thing**	MCA 79051
12/22/90+	17	11	29. There For Awhile	MCA 53936
4/27/91	25	8	30. Restless	Warner 19354
			MARK O'CONNOR-THE NEW NASHVILLE CATS Featuring STEVE WARINER, RICKY SKAGGS AND VINCE GILL	
10/26/91+	6	16	31. **Leave Him Out Of This**	Arista 12349
2/29/92	3	16	32. **The Tips Of My Fingers**	Arista 12393
7/4/92	9	14	33. **A Woman Loves**	Arista 12426
10/24/92	32	4	34. Crash Course In The Blues	Arista 12461
3/13/93	30	6	35. Like A River To The Sea	Arista 12510
7/31/93	8	15	36. **If I Didn't Love You**	Arista 12578
12/18/93+	24	8	37. Drivin' And Cryin'	Arista 12609
5/14/94	18	9	38. It Won't Be Over You	Arista 12672

DATE	POS	WKS	ARTIST– RECORD TITLE	LABEL & NO.
			WARNES, Jennifer	
			Born in Seattle; raised in Orange County, California. Pop/MOR-styled vocalist. Lead actress in the Los Angeles production of *Hair*. Also recorded as Jennifer Warren and simply as Jennifer.	
3/26/77	17	7	1. Right Time Of The Night	Arista 0223
7/28/79	10	8	2. **I Know A Heartache When I See One**	Arista 0430
			WATSON, B.B.	
			Born Haskill Watson on 7/10/53 in Tyler, Texas; raised in La Porte, Texas. B.B. stands for Bad Boy.	
9/21/91	23	6	1. Light At The End Of The Tunnel	BNA 62039
			WATSON, Gene	
			Born Gary Gene Watson on 10/11/43 in Palestine, Texas; raised in Paris, Texas. Worked professionally since age 13. Own band, Gene Watson & The Other Four. Recorded for Tonka in 1965. Played for many years at the Dynasty Club in Houston.	
6/21/75	3	14	1. **Love In The Hot Afternoon**	Capitol 4076
11/8/75	5	9	2. **Where Love Begins**	Capitol 4143
3/6/76	10	10	3. **You Could Know As Much About A Stranger**	Capitol 4214
7/10/76	20	7	4. Because You Believed In Me	Capitol 4279
2/26/77	3	12	5. **Paper Rosie**	Capitol 4378
9/10/77	11	9	6. The Old Man And His Horn	Capitol 4458
12/24/77+	8	10	7. **I Don't Need A Thing At All**	Capitol 4513
4/22/78	11	9	8. Cowboys Don't Get Lucky All The Time	Capitol 4556
9/9/78	8	9	9. **One Sided Conversation**	Capitol 4616
3/10/79	5	10	10. **Farewell Party**	Capitol 4680
6/23/79	5	10	11. **Pick The Wildwood Flower**	Capitol 4723
9/22/79	3	10	12. **Should I Come Home (Or Should I Go Crazy)**	Capitol 4772
1/19/80	4	10	13. **Nothing Sure Looked Good On You**	Capitol 4814
5/17/80	18	7	14. Bedroom Ballad	Capitol 4854
8/23/80	15	6	15. Raisin' Cane In Texas	Capitol 4898
11/22/80	13	7	16. No One Will Ever Know	Capitol 4940
2/28/81	33	3	17. Any Way You Want Me	Warner 49648
			from the movie *Any Which Way You Can* starring Clint Eastwood	
4/4/81	17	6	18. Between This Time And The Next Time	MCA 51039
7/18/81	23	6	19. Maybe I Should Have Been Listening	MCA 51127
10/17/81+	1 (1)	15	20. **Fourteen Carat Mind**	MCA 51183
3/20/82	9	12	21. **Speak Softly (You're Talking To My Heart)**	MCA 52009
7/24/82	8	11	22. **This Dream's On Me**	MCA 52074
12/4/82+	5	12	23. **What She Don't Know Won't Hurt Her**	MCA 52131
4/9/83	2 (1)	12	24. **You're Out Doing What I'm Here Doing Without**	MCA 52191
8/20/83	9	10	25. **Sometimes I Get Lucky And Forget**	MCA 52243
12/24/83+	10	9	26. **Drinkin' My Way Back Home**	MCA 52309
4/21/84	10	10	27. **Forever Again**	MCA 52356
8/4/84	33	4	28. Little By Little	MCA 52410
			GENE WATSON with The Farewell Party Band (above 5)	
11/10/84+	7	13	29. **Got No Reason Now For Goin' Home**	Curb/MCA 52457
			written by Johnny Russell	
7/20/85	24	7	30. Cold Summer Day In Georgia	Epic 05407

DATE	POS	WKS	ARTIST— RECORD TITLE	LABEL & NO.
11/9/85+	5	14	31. **Memories To Burn**	Epic 05633
3/29/86	32	4	32. Carmen	Epic 05817
10/11/86	29	6	33. Everything I Used To Do	Epic 06290
9/12/87	28	6	34. Everybody Needs A Hero	Epic 07308
12/10/88+	5	13	35. **Don't Waste It On The Blues**	Warner 27692
4/15/89	20	7	36. Back In The Fire	Warner 27532
8/19/89	24	6	37. The Jukebox Played Along	Warner 22912
			WAYNE, Nancy	
11/16/74	34	3	1. Gone	20th Century 2124
			WEATHERLY, Jim	
			Born on 3/17/43 in Pontotoc, Mississippi. Accomplished songwriter; wrote "Midnight Train To Georgia," "Best Thing That Ever Happened To Me" and "Neither One Of Us (Wants To Be The First To Say Goodbye)." Played quarterback for the University of Mississippi.	
2/22/75	9	8	1. **I'll Still Love You**	Buddah 444
8/20/77	27	5	2. All That Keeps Me Going	ABC 12288
12/8/79	32	4	3. Smooth Sailin'	Elektra 46547
3/15/80	34	3	4. Gift From Missouri	Elektra 46592
			WEAVERS, The, & Terry Gilkyson	
			Folk group consisting of Pete Seeger, Veronica "Ronnie" Gilbert, Lee Hays (died 1981) and Fred Kellerman, backing Hamilton Henry "Terry" Gilkyson.	
6/2/51	8	2	● 1. **On Top Of Old Smoky** Juke Box #8	Decca 27515
			WEBB, Jay Lee	
			Born in Van Lear, Kentucky. Brother of Loretta Lynn, Crystal Gayle and Peggy Sue; distant cousin of Patty Loveless.	
3/4/67	37	2	1. I Come Home A-Drinkin' (To A Worn-Out Wife Like You) **JACK WEBB** answer song to Loretta Lynn's "Don't Come Home A'Drinkin'"	Decca 32087
3/1/69	21	9	2. She's Lookin' Better By The Minute	Decca 32430
			WEBB, June	
			Born on 9/22/34 in L'Anse, Michigan. Worked on WLAC-Nashville from 1947.	
11/3/58	29	3	1. A Mansion On The Hill	Hickory 1086
			WEISSBERG, Eric, & Steve Mandell	
			Prominent session musicians. Both had worked with Judy Collins and John Denver. Weissberg was a member of The Tarriers.	
3/3/73	5	8	● 1. **Dueling Banjos** [I] tune written in 1955 by Arthur Smith and Don Reno as "Feudin' Banjos"; featured in the movie *Deliverance* starring Burt Reynolds	Warner 7659

DATE	POS	WKS	ARTIST–RECORD TITLE	LABEL & NO.
			WELCH, Kevin	
			Born on 8/17/55 in Los Angeles. Wrote Moe Band's "Til I'm Too Old To Die Young," Gary Morris's "Velvet Chains" and Don Williams's "Desperately."	
7/21/90	**39**	1	1. Till I See You Again	Reprise 19873
			WELK, Lawrence	
			Born on 3/11/03 in Strasburg, North Dakota. Died on 5/17/92 of pneumonia. Accordion player and polka/sweet band leader since the mid-1920s. Band's style labeled "champagne music." Own national TV musical variety show began on 7/2/55 and ran on ABC until 9/4/71. New episodes in syndication, 1971-82. Reruns are still enjoying immense popularity.	
9/8/45	**1** (1)	14	1. **Shame On You/**	
11/10/45	**3**	2	2. **At Mail Call Today**	Decca 18698
			LAWRENCE WELK AND HIS ORCHESTRA with RED FOLEY (above 2)	
			WELLER, Freddy	
			Born Wilton F. Weller on 9/9/47 in Atlanta. Worked on the *Atlanta Jubilee* in East Point, Georgia, with Jerry Reed, Ray Stevens and Joe South. Performed with Billy Joe Royal in the mid-1960s. Worked with Paul Revere & The Raiders, 1967-71. Co-wrote pop hits "Dizzy" and "Jam Up Jelly Tight" with Tommy Roe. Worked as a bassist/guitarist with Joe South.	
5/3/69	**2** (2)	13	1. **Games People Play**	Columbia 44800
			#12 Pop hit for Joe South in 1969	
8/9/69	**5**	13	2. **These Are Not My People**	Columbia 44916
12/13/69+	**25**	6	3. Down In The Boondocks	Columbia 45026
			#9 Pop hit for Billy Joe Royal in 1965	
1/2/71	**3**	14	4. **The Promised Land**	Columbia 45276
			written by Chuck Berry	
6/19/71	**3**	13	5. **Indian Lake**	Columbia 45388
			#10 Pop hit for The Cowsills in 1968	
10/16/71	**5**	11	6. **Another Night Of Love**	Columbia 45451
3/11/72	**26**	8	7. Ballad Of A Hillbilly Singer	Columbia 45542
7/8/72	**17**	10	8. The Roadmaster	Columbia 45624
12/2/72+	**11**	11	9. She Loves Me (Right Out Of My Mind)	Columbia 45723
5/12/73	**8**	11	10. **Too Much Monkey Business**	Columbia 45827
			written by Chuck Berry	
9/8/73	**13**	9	11. The Perfect Stranger	Columbia 45902
1/5/74	**11**	12	12. I've Just Got To Know (How Loving You Would Be)	Columbia 45968
6/29/74	**21**	7	13. Sexy Lady	Columbia 46040
10/12/74	**16**	9	14. You're Not Getting Older (You're Getting Better)	Columbia 10016
8/5/78	**32**	4	15. Bar Wars	Columbia 10769
11/18/78	**23**	5	16. Love Got In The Way	Columbia 10837
2/24/79	**27**	5	17. Fantasy Island	Columbia 10890
6/23/79	**40**	2	18. Nadine	Columbia 10973
			#23 Pop hit for Chuck Berry in 1964	
12/22/79+	**33**	5	19. Go For The Night	Columbia 11149

DATE	POS	WKS	ARTIST– RECORD TITLE	LABEL & NO.
			WELLS, Kitty	
			Born Muriel Ellen Deason on 8/30/19 in Nashville. Singing on WSIX-Nashville at age 16. Married Johnny Wright in 1938 and he changed her stage name to Kitty Wells. Toured with Johnnie & Jack; appeared on WBIG-Greensboro and WNOX-Knoxville. Worked on the *Louisiana Hayride*, 1948-53. First recorded for RCA in 1949. Formed the Kitty Wells/Johnny Wright Family Show in 1969; Bobby and Ruby Wright are Kitty and Johnny's children. Elected to the Country Music Hall of Fame in 1976. Won Grammy's Lifetime Achievement Award in 1991. Known as "The Queen Of Country Music."	
			(a) KITTY WELLS and RED FOLEY	
7/19/52	1 (6)	18	1. **It Wasn't God Who Made Honky Tonk Angels** Best Seller #1(6) / Juke Box #1(5) / Jockey #2; answer to Hank Thompson's "The Wild Side Of Life"	Decca 28232
3/7/53	6	4	2. **Paying For That Back Street Affair** Best Seller #6 / Juke Box #9; answer song to Webb Pierce's "Back Street Affair"	Decca 28578
9/12/53	8	2	3. **Hey Joe** Juke Box #8; answer song to the same-titled tune by Carl Smith	Decca 28797
1/23/54	9	1	4. **Cheatin's A Sin** Juke Box #9	Decca 28931
4/3/54	8	1	5. **Release Me** Juke Box #8	Decca 29023
5/22/54	1 (1)	41	6. **One By One** (a)/ Juke Box #1 / Best Seller #2 / Jockey #2	
7/10/54	12	1	7. I'm A Stranger In My Home (a) Jockey #12 / Best Seller #15	Decca 29065
12/4/54	14	1	8. Thou Shalt Not Steal Best Seller #14; written by Don Everly (of The Everly Brothers)	Decca 29313
2/26/55	3	16	9. **As Long As I Live** (a)/ Juke Box #3 / Best Seller #7 / Jockey #8	
2/26/55	6	17	10. **Make Believe ('Til We Can Make It Come True)** (a) Juke Box #6 / Best Seller #7 / Jockey #14	Decca 29390
3/12/55	2 (15)	28	11. **Makin' Believe**/ Best Seller #2 / Juke Box #2 / Jockey #2	
4/9/55	7	11	12. **Whose Shoulder Will You Cry On** Jockey #7	Decca 29419
7/30/55	9	13	13. **There's Poison In Your Heart**/ Juke Box #9 / Best Seller #11	
9/24/55	12	1	14. I'm In Love With You Jockey #12	Decca 29577
12/17/55+	7	8	15. **Lonely Side Of Town**/ Juke Box #7 / Best Seller #13	
12/24/55	7	9	16. **I've Kissed You My Last Time** Best Seller #7 / Jockey #10	Decca 29728
1/28/56	3	31	17. **You And Me** (a)/ Best Seller #3 / Jockey #3 / Juke Box #6	
		6	18. No One But You (a) Best Seller flip / Juke Box flip	Decca 29740
5/12/56	11	5	19. How Far Is Heaven Jockey #11 / Best Seller #15; Carol Sue (Kitty's daughter; guest vocal)	Decca 29823
7/7/56	3	34	20. **Searching (For Someone Like You)**/ Juke Box #3 / Best Seller #4 / Jockey #4	
9/22/56	13	1	21. I'd Rather Stay Home Jockey #13	Decca 29956

DATE	POS	WKS	ARTIST–RECORD TITLE	LABEL & NO.
12/1/56+	**6**	13	22. **Repenting/** *Juke Box #6 / Best Seller #9 / Jockey #11*	
		7	23. I'm Counting On You *Juke Box flip / Best Seller flip*	Decca 30094

4/6/57	**8**	9	24. **Oh, So Many Years**
			    KITTY WELLS and WEBB PIERCE
			    Jockey #8
				Decca 30183

6/3/57	**7**	9	25. **Three Ways (To Love You)** *Jockey #7 / Best Seller #15*	Decca 30288

9/23/57	**10**	6	26. **(I'll Always Be Your) Fraulein**
			    Best Seller #10 / Jockey #13; answer song to Bobby Helms's
			    "Fraulein"
				Decca 30415

1/20/58	**12**	1	27. One Week Later
			    WEBB PIERCE and KITTY WELLS
			    Jockey #12
				Decca 30489

3/3/58	**3**	19	28. **I Can't Stop Loving You/** *Jockey #3 / Best Seller #8*	
		11	29. She's No Angel *Best Seller flip*	Decca 30551
7/7/58	**7**	14	30. **Jealousy** *Jockey #7 / Best Seller #11*	Decca 30662
10/6/58	**15**	11	31. Touch And Go Heart/	
11/10/58	**16**	7	32. He's Lost His Love For Me	Decca 30736
2/16/59	**5**	14	33. **Mommy For A Day/**	
3/9/59	**18**	2	34. All The Time	Decca 30804
7/6/59	**12**	10	35. Your Wild Life's Gonna Get You Down	Decca 30890
11/9/59+	**5**	25	36. **Amigo's Guitar**	Decca 30987
4/18/60	**5**	22	37. **Left To Right**	Decca 31065
9/5/60	**16**	9	38. Carmel By The Sea	Decca 31123
12/19/60	**26**	3	39. I Can't Tell My Heart That **KITTY WELLS and ROY DRUSKY**	Decca 31164
3/6/61	**19**	10	40. The Other Cheek/	
3/20/61	**29**	2	41. Fickle Fun	Decca 31192
5/29/61	**1 (4)**	23	42. **Heartbreak U.S.A./**	
6/26/61	**20**	5	43. There Must Be Another Way To Live	Decca 31246
12/4/61+	**10**	12	44. **Day Into Night/**	
1/6/62	**21**	3	45. Our Mansion Is A Prison Now	Decca 31313
3/3/62	**5**	14	46. **Unloved Unwanted**	Decca 31349
8/4/62	**8**	11	47. **Will Your Lawyer Talk To God**	Decca 31392
11/3/62	**7**	13	48. **We Missed You**	Decca 31422
3/30/63	**13**	9	49. Cold And Lonely (Is The Forecast For Tonight)	Decca 31457
8/3/63	**29**	2	50. A Heartache For A Keepsake/	
8/17/63	**22**	6	51. I Gave My Wedding Dress Away	Decca 31501
2/1/64	**7**	25	52. **This White Circle On My Finger**	Decca 31580
6/6/64	**4**	23	53. **Password/**	
6/20/64	**34**	4	54. I've Thought Of Leaving You	Decca 31622
9/26/64	**9**	15	55. **Finally** **KITTY WELLS and WEBB PIERCE**	Decca 31663
1/2/65	**8**	14	56. **I'll Repossess My Heart**	Decca 31705
4/24/65	**4**	16	57. **You Don't Hear/**	
4/10/65	**27**	10	58. Six Lonely Hours	Decca 31749

DATE	POS	WKS	ARTIST– RECORD TITLE	LABEL & NO.
8/21/65	**9**	15	59. **Meanwhile, Down At Joe's**	Decca 31817
2/5/66	**15**	13	60. A Woman Half My Age	Decca 31881
7/30/66	**14**	12	61. It's All Over (But The Crying)	Decca 31957
4/1/67	**34**	5	62. Love Makes The World Go Around	Decca 32088
9/16/67	**28**	8	63. Queen Of Honky Tonk Street	Decca 32163
3/2/68	**35**	4	64. My Big Truck Drivin' Man	Decca 32247
			WELLS, Ruby—see JOHNNIE & JACK	

WEST, Dottie

Born Dorothy Marie Marsh on 10/11/32 in McMinnville, Tennessee. Died on 9/4/91 from injuries suffered in a car accident. Worked on local TV in Cleveland in the mid-1950s. Married steel guitarist Bill West; their daughter is Shelly West. On the *Grand Ole Opry* from 1964 until her death. Made commercials for Coca-Cola, including the award-winning "Country Sunshine," which she wrote. Appeared in the movies *Second Fiddle To A Steel Guitar* and *There's A Still On The Hill*. CMA Awards: 1978 and 1979 Vocal Duo of the Year (with Kenny Rogers).

(a) KENNY ROGERS & DOTTIE WEST

DATE	POS	WKS	ARTIST– RECORD TITLE	LABEL & NO.
11/30/63	**29**	2	1. Let Me Off At The Corner	RCA 8225
3/28/64	**7**	18	2. **Love Is No Excuse** **JIM REEVES & DOTTIE WEST** flip side "Look Who's Talking" Bubbled Under at #121	RCA 8324
8/29/64	**10**	14	3. **Here Comes My Baby**	RCA 8374
3/13/65	**32**	5	4. Didn't I	RCA 8467
6/19/65	**30**	5	5. Gettin' Married Has Made Us Strangers	RCA 8525
8/28/65	**32**	3	6. No Sign Of Living	RCA 8615
12/25/65+	**22**	10	7. Before The Ring On Your Finger Turns Green	RCA 8702
3/12/66	**5**	21	8. **Would You Hold It Against Me**	RCA 8770
9/3/66	**24**	7	9. Mommy, Can I Still Call Him Daddy Dale West (Dottie's 4-year-old son; guest vocal)	RCA 8900
1/14/67	**17**	8	10. What's Come Over My Baby	RCA 9011
4/1/67	**8**	14	11. **Paper Mansions**	RCA 9118
9/9/67	**13**	12	12. Like A Fool	RCA 9267
2/3/68	**24**	5	13. Childhood Places	RCA 9377
5/11/68	**15**	10	14. Country Girl	RCA 9497
9/28/68	**19**	9	15. Reno	RCA 9604
3/8/69	**2** (1)	15	16. **Rings Of Gold**	RCA 9715
8/16/69	**32**	4	17. Sweet Memories	RCA 0178
12/20/69+	**7**	11	18. **There's A Story (Goin' 'Round)** **DOTTIE WEST & DON GIBSON (above 3)**	RCA 0291
9/12/70	**37**	3	19. It's Dawned On Me You're Gone	RCA 9872
11/21/70	**21**	6	20. Forever Yours	RCA 9911
2/27/71	**29**	5	21. Slowly **JIMMY DEAN and DOTTIE WEST**	RCA 9947
1/6/73	**28**	6	22. If It's All Right With You	RCA 0828
10/6/73	**2** (1)	12	23. **Country Sunshine**	RCA 0072
4/20/74	**8**	10	24. **Last Time I Saw Him** #14 Pop hit for Diana Ross in 1974	RCA 0231
8/24/74	**21**	6	25. House Of Love	RCA 0321
1/25/75	**35**	4	26. Lay Back Lover	RCA 10125

DATE	POS	WKS	ARTIST– RECORD TITLE	LABEL & NO.
12/11/76+	19	8	27. When It's Just You And Me	United Art. 898
4/16/77	28	6	28. Every Word I Write	United Art. 946
7/30/77	30	4	29. Tonight You Belong To Me	United Art. 1010
			#4 Pop hit for Patience & Prudence in 1956	
3/4/78	**1 (2)**	11	30. **Every Time Two Fools Collide** (a)	United Art. 1137
7/8/78	17	6	31. Come See Me And Come Lonely	United Art. 1209
9/9/78	**2 (1)**	11	32. **Anyone Who Isn't Me Tonight** (a)	United Art. 1234
2/24/79	**1 (1)**	11	33. **All I Ever Need Is You** (a)	United Art. 1276
			#7 Pop hit for Sonny & Cher in 1971	
7/14/79	**3**	10	34. **Til I Can Make It On My Own** (a)	United Art. 1299
11/10/79	12	9	35. You Pick Me Up (And Put Me Down)	United Art. 1324
2/23/80	**1 (1)**	12	36. **A Lesson In Leavin'**	United Art. 1339
6/21/80	13	9	37. Leavin's For Unbelievers	United Art. 1352
12/27/80+	**1 (1)**	11	38. **Are You Happy Baby?**	Liberty 1392
4/18/81	**1 (1)**	10	39. **What Are We Doin' In Love** (a)	Liberty 1404
8/1/81	16	7	40. (I'm Gonna) Put You Back On The Rack	Liberty 1419
11/21/81+	16	8	41. It's High Time	Liberty 1436
3/13/82	26	7	42. You're Not Easy To Forget	Liberty 1451
10/16/82	29	3	43. She Can't Get My Love Off The Bed	Liberty 1479
7/30/83	40	1	44. Tulsa Ballroom	Liberty 1500
4/21/84	19	7	45. Together Again (a)	Liberty 1516

WEST, Shelly

Born on 5/23/58 in Cleveland; raised in Nashville. Daughter of Dottie West and steel guitarist Bill West. Toured with Dottie, 1975-77. Worked with Allen Frizzell from 1977; married to him until 1985; successful duo partnership with Allen's brother, David. CMA Awards: 1981 and 1982 Vocal Duo of the Year (with David Frizzell).

(a) DAVID FRIZZELL & SHELLY WEST

DATE	POS	WKS	ARTIST– RECORD TITLE	LABEL & NO.
2/7/81	**1 (1)**	11	1. **You're The Reason God Made Oklahoma** (a)	Warner 49650
			from the movie *Any Which Way You Can* starring Clint Eastwood	
7/11/81	**9**	8	2. **A Texas State Of Mind** (a)	Warner 49745
10/31/81	**16**	10	3. **Husbands And Wives** (a)	Warner 49825
2/20/82	**8**	13	4. **Another Honky-Tonk Night On Broadway** (a)	Warner 50007
7/31/82	**4**	13	5. **I Just Came Here To Dance** (a)	Warner 29980
3/12/83	**1 (1)**	13	6. **Jose Cuervo**	Warner 29778
7/23/83	**4**	11	7. **Flight 309 To Tennessee**	Viva 29597
12/3/83+	**10**	10	8. **Another Motel Memory**	Viva 29461
3/3/84	20	7	9. Silent Partners (a)	Viva 29404
7/7/84	34	3	10. Somebody Buy This Cowgirl A Beer	Viva 29265
10/20/84	13	9	11. It's A Be Together Night (a)	Viva 29187
2/23/85	21	7	12. Now There's You	Viva 29106

WHEELER, Billy Edd

Born on 12/9/32 in Whitesville, West Virginia. Singer/songwriter/playwright. Wrote "Reverend Mr. Black" for the Kingston Trio, "Jackson" for Johnny Cash & June Carter, and "Coward Of The County" for Kenny Rogers. Co-owner of Sleepy Hollow Music.

DATE	POS	WKS	ARTIST– RECORD TITLE	LABEL & NO.
12/5/64+	**3**	21	1. **Ode To The Little Brown Shack Out Back** [N]	Kapp 617

DATE	POS	WKS	ARTIST– RECORD TITLE	LABEL & NO.
			WHEELER, Karen	
			Born in Sikeston, Missouri. Daughter of Onie Wheeler. Worked in The Harden Trio for a time. Appeared on the *Renfro Valley Barn Dance* and WWVA-Wheeling *Jamboree*.	
4/27/74	31	5	1. Born To Love And Satisfy	RCA 0223
			WHIPPLE, Sterling	
			Native of Eugene, Oregon. Moved to Nashville in 1974. Wrote "The Blind Man In The Bleachers."	
5/6/78	26	4	1. Dirty Work	Warner 8552
11/11/78	25	5	2. Then You'll Remember	Warner 8632
			WHITE, Bryan	
			Born in 1974 in Oklahoma City. Singer/guitarist.	
2/11/95	24	9	1. Look At Me Now	Asylum 64489
7/15/95	1 (1)	11	2. **Someone Else's Star**	Asylum 64435
11/4/95+	1 (1)	16	3. **Rebecca Lynn**	Asylum 64360
3/30/96	4	16	4. **I'm Not Supposed To Love You Anymore**	Asylum 64313
			WHITE, Lari	
			Born on 5/13/65 in Dunedin, Florida. (First name pronounced: Laurie.) Attended the University of Miami. In 1988, she won first prize on TNN's *You Can Be A Star!* Tour singer for Rodney Crowell in 1991.	
5/21/94	10	12	1. **That's My Baby**	RCA 62764
10/15/94	5	14	2. **Now I Know**	RCA 62896
2/18/95	10	14	3. **That's How You Know (When You're In Love)**	RCA 64233
2/10/96	20	11	4. Ready, Willing And Able	RCA 64455
			WHITE, Mack	
			Born in Dothan, Georgia.	
2/2/74	34	2	1. Too Much Pride	Commercial 1314
4/17/76	35	3	2. Let Me Be Your Friend	Commercial 1317
9/18/76	34	5	3. Take Me As I Am (Or Let Me Go)	Commercial 1319
			WHITE, Michael	
			Native of Knoxville, Tennessee; raised in Nashville. Popular demo singer/songwriter. Conway Twitty recorded two songs White wrote at age 12, one of which was "You Make It Hard To Take The Easy Way Out" (flip side of "You've Never Been This Far Before"). Son of L.E. White.	
2/22/92	32	5	1. Professional Fool	Reprise 19128
			WHITES, The	
			Family group formed in 1971 as The Down Home Folks. Consisted of Buck White (guitar, mandolin, piano) and his wife Patty, and daughters Sharon (guitar) and Cheryl (bass). Buck worked as a session man in the early '50s and played with the Blue Sage Boys in 1952. Buck and Patty had been in the original Down Home Folks with Arnold and Peggy Johnston (1962); Sharon and Cheryl were in the Down Home Kids with Teddy and Eddie Johnston (1966). Patty retired from music in 1973. Sharon is married to Ricky Skaggs. Members of the *Grand Ole Opry* since 1984.	
9/25/82	10	10	1. **You Put The Blue In Me**	Elektra/Curb 69980

DATE	POS	WKS	ARTIST – RECORD TITLE	LABEL & NO.
1/29/83	9	9	2. **Hangin' Around**	Elektra/Curb 69855
5/28/83	9	11	3. **I Wonder Who's Holding My Baby Tonight**	Warner/Curb 29659
10/8/83	25	7	4. When The New Wears Off Of Our Love	Warner/Curb 29513
1/21/84	10	9	5. **Give Me Back That Old Familiar Feeling**	Warner/Curb 29411
6/16/84	14	9	6. Forever You	MCA/Curb 52381
9/22/84	10	10	7. **Pins And Needles**	MCA/Curb 52432
3/30/85	12	9	8. If It Ain't Love (Let's Leave It Alone)	MCA/Curb 52535
7/27/85	27	5	9. Hometown Gossip	MCA/Curb 52615
12/7/85	33	3	10. I Don't Want To Get Over You	MCA/Curb 52697
			all of above (except #1) produced by Ricky Skaggs	
6/28/86	36	3	11. Love Won't Wait	MCA/Curb 52825
12/13/86+	30	6	12. It Should Have Been Easy	MCA/Curb 52953

WHITING, Margaret

Born on 7/22/24 in Detroit; raised in Hollywood. Daughter of popular composer Richard Whiting ("Till We Meet Again"). Very popular 1946-54, with over 40 charted Pop hits.

MARGARET WHITING & JIMMY WAKELY:

DATE	POS	WKS	ARTIST – RECORD TITLE	LABEL & NO.
9/10/49	1 (17)	28	● 1. **Slipping Around/** Best Seller #1(17) / Juke Box #1(12) / Jockey #2	
9/10/49	6	8	2. **Wedding Bells** Juke Box #6 / Best Seller #7	Capitol 40224
11/5/49	2 (3)	13	3. **I'll Never Slip Around Again** Juke Box #2 / Best Seller #2 / Jockey #10	Capitol 40246
2/11/50	2 (1)	9	4. **Broken Down Merry-Go-Round/** Best Seller #2 / Juke Box #3 / Jockey #5	
2/11/50	3	7	5. **The Gods Were Angry With Me** Best Seller #3 / Juke Box #4	Capitol 800
4/22/50	2 (1)	10	6. **Let's Go To Church (Next Sunday Morning)** Best Seller #2 / Jockey #6 / Juke Box #6	Capitol 960
11/18/50	6	1	7. **A Bushel And A Peck** Best Seller #6 / Juke Box #10; from the Broadway musical *Guys And Dolls*	Capitol 1234
6/2/51	7	2	8. **When You And I Were Young Maggie Blues** Juke Box #7	Capitol 1500
12/8/51	5	5	9. **I Don't Want To Be Free** Juke Box #5	Capitol 1816

WHITLEY, Keith

Born Jessie Keith Whitley on 7/1/55 in Sandy Hook, Kentucky. Died on 5/9/89 of alcohol abuse. Appeared with Buddy Starcher on radio in Charleston, West Virginia, at age eight. Own band, The East Kentucky Mountain Boys, with Ricky Skaggs, from 1968 to the early '70s. Played in Ralph Stanley's Clinch Mountain Boys in the mid-1970s. Also recorded with own New Tradition, and Country Store in 1972. With J.D. Crowe and New South in 1978. Married Lorrie Morgan in 1986.

DATE	POS	WKS	ARTIST – RECORD TITLE	LABEL & NO.
3/8/86	14	10	1. Miami, My Amy	RCA 14285
7/19/86	9	12	2. **Ten Feet Away**	RCA 14363
11/29/86+	9	14	3. **Homecoming '63**	RCA 5013
4/4/87	10	10	4. **Hard Livin'**	RCA 5116
10/3/87	36	2	5. Would These Arms Be In Your Way	RCA 5237
12/19/87+	16	11	6. Some Old Side Road	RCA 5326

DATE	POS	WKS	ARTIST– RECORD TITLE	LABEL & NO.
5/21/88	**1** (1)	16	7. **Don't Close Your Eyes**	RCA 6901
10/8/88	**1** (2)	14	8. **When You Say Nothing At All**	RCA 8637
2/4/89	**1** (2)	14	9. **I'm No Stranger To The Rain**	RCA 8797
			CMA Award: Single of the Year	
7/1/89	**1** (1)	14	10. **I Wonder Do You Think Of Me**	RCA 8940
10/28/89+	**1** (1)	17	11. **It Ain't Nothin'**	RCA 9059
3/24/90	**3**	18	12. **I'm Over You**	RCA 9122
8/11/90	**13**	12	13. **'Til A Tear Becomes A Rose**	RCA 2619
			KEITH WHITLEY and LORRIE MORGAN	
9/21/91	**2** (1)	18	14. **Brotherly Love**	RCA 62037
			KEITH WHITLEY & EARL THOMAS CONLEY	
2/8/92	**15**	11	15. **Somebody's Doin' Me Right**	RCA 62166

WHITMAN, Slim

Born Otis Dewey Whitman on 1/20/24 in Tampa. Guitarist/yodeller. Worked in a shipyard and served in U.S. Navy, 1943-46. Played semi-pro baseball with the Plant City Berries. On radio WDAE-Tampa in 1946 and worked local clubs. Played with the Light Crust Doughboys in 1949. Worked on the *Louisiana Hayride* in 1950. First recorded for RCA in 1950. First played the London Palladium in 1952 and remains very popular in Great Britain.

DATE	POS	WKS	ARTIST– RECORD TITLE	LABEL & NO.
5/17/52	**10**	1	1. **Love Song Of The Waterfall**	Imperial 8134
			SLIM WHITMAN, The Smilin' Star Duster	
			Jockey #10	
7/5/52	**2** (3)	24	● 2. **Indian Love Call**	Imperial 8156
			Best Seller #2 / Juke Box #2 / Jockey #3	
12/6/52+	**3**	13	3. **Keep It A Secret/**	
			Jockey #3 / Juke Box #3 / Best Seller #5	
12/20/52	**10**	1	4. **My Heart Is Broken In Three**	Imperial 8169
			Juke Box #10	
11/14/53	**8**	5	5. **North Wind**	Imperial 8208
			Best Seller #8 / Jockey #8 / Juke Box #8	
1/23/54	**2** (1)	18	● 6. **Secret Love**	Imperial 8223
			Jockey #2 / Best Seller #3 / Juke Box #3; from the movie *Calamity Jane* starring Doris Day; #1 Pop hit for Doris Day in 1954	
5/1/54	**4**	23	● 7. **Rose-Marie**	Imperial 8236
			Juke Box #4 / Best Seller #5 / Jockey #7	
11/6/54	**4**	3	8. **Singing Hills**	Imperial 8267
			Juke Box #4	
1/15/55	**11**	2	9. Cattle Call	Imperial 8281
			Best Seller #11	
7/3/61	**30**	1	10. The Bells That Broke My Heart	Imperial 5746
11/6/65	**8**	16	11. **More Than Yesterday**	Imperial 66130
3/26/66	**17**	10	12. The Twelfth Of Never	Imperial 66153
			#9 Pop hit for Johnny Mathis in 1957	
4/13/68	**17**	10	13. Rainbows Are Back In Style	Imperial 66283
9/7/68	**22**	7	14. Happy Street	Imperial 66311
5/16/70	**27**	5	15. Tomorrow Never Comes	Imperial 66441
9/5/70	**26**	7	16. Shutters And Boards	United Art. 50697
			#24 Pop hit for Jerry Wallace in 1963	
12/26/70+	**7**	12	17. **Guess Who**	United Art. 50731
			#31 Pop hit for Jesse Belvin in 1959	
5/22/71	**6**	11	18. **Something Beautiful (To Remember)**	United Art. 50775

DATE	POS	WKS	ARTIST—RECORD TITLE	LABEL & NO.
9/11/71	**21**	7	19. It's A Sin To Tell A Lie *#7 Pop hit for Somethin' Smith & The Redheads in 1955*	United Art. 50806
8/30/80	**15**	6	20. When	Clev. Int. 50912

WICKHAM, Lewie

4/25/70	**36**	3	1. Little Bit Late [N]	Starday 888

WIGGINS, John & Audrey

Brother-and-sister duo from Waynesville, North Carolina. In the early '60s, their father, Johnny Wiggins (died January 1993), was Ernest Tubb's tour bus driver/mechanic and opened his shows as "The Singing Bus Driver." John (born 10/13/62) and Audrey (born 12/26/67) worked with Clinton Gregory, 1979-87.

9/10/94	**22**	9	1. Has Anybody Seen Amy	Mercury 858920

WILBOURN, Bill, & Kathy Morrison

Wilbourn is a former DJ from Aliceville, Alabama.

6/13/70	**34**	5	1. A Good Thing	United Art. 50660

WILBURN BROTHERS

Duo from Hardy, Arkansas: brothers Virgil Doyle (born 7/7/30, died 10/16/82) and Thurman Theodore "Teddy" (born 11/30/31) Wilburn. Raised in Arkansas, first sang with the Wilburn Family group on the *Grand Ole Opry* in 1941. Worked on the *Louisiana Hayride*, 1948-51. Both served in U.S. Army, 1951-53, then formed duo. On the *Grand Ole Opry* since 1953. Own TV series featuring Loretta Lynn. Owners of Surefire Music. Doyle married for a time to Margie Bowes.

6/12/54	**4**	18	1. **Sparkling Brown Eyes** **WEBB PIERCE with WILBURN BROTHERS** *Best Seller #4 / Jockey #4 / Juke Box #4*	Decca 29107
6/11/55	**13**	2	2. I Wanna Wanna Wanna *Jockey #13*	Decca 29459
1/21/56	**13**	3	3. You're Not Play Love *Jockey #13*	Decca 29747
8/11/56	**10**	8	4. **I'm So In Love With You** *Jockey #10*	Decca 29887
12/1/56	**6**	11	5. **Go Away With Me** *Jockey #6*	Decca 30087
7/8/57	**8**	2	6. **Mister Love** *Jockey #8*	Decca 30305
5/26/58	**9**	10	7. **Hey, Mr. Bluebird** **ERNEST TUBB and THE WILBURN BROTHERS** (above 2) *Jockey #9 / Best Seller #14*	Decca 30610
1/5/59	**4**	19	8. **Which One Is To Blame/**	
1/19/59	**18**	4	9. The Knoxville Girl	Decca 30787
5/18/59	**6**	19	10. **Somebody's Back In Town**	Decca 30871
10/26/59	**9**	13	11. **A Woman's Intuition**	Decca 30968
12/19/60	**27**	2	12. The Best Of All My Heartaches	Decca 31152
7/31/61	**14**	6	13. Blue Blue Day	Decca 31276
5/12/62	**4**	22	14. **Trouble's Back In Town**	Decca 31363
11/17/62	**21**	5	15. The Sound Of Your Footsteps	Decca 31425
5/11/63	**4**	13	16. **Roll Muddy River**	Decca 31464

DATE	POS	WKS	ARTIST– RECORD TITLE	LABEL & NO.
9/14/63	**10**	13	17. **Tell Her So**	Decca 31520
3/7/64	**34**	2	18. Hangin' Around	Decca 31578
12/12/64+	**19**	9	19. I'm Gonna Tie One On Tonight	Decca 31674
6/26/65	**30**	8	20. I Had One Too Many	Decca 31764
10/2/65	**5**	18	21. **It's Another World**	Decca 31819
2/19/66	**8**	15	22. **Someone Before Me**	Decca 31894
7/23/66	**13**	12	23. I Can't Keep Away From You	Decca 31974
12/17/66+	**3**	14	24. **Hurt Her Once For Me**	Decca 32038
5/27/67	**13**	10	25. Roarin' Again	Decca 32117
10/28/67	**24**	6	26. Goody, Goody Gumdrop	Decca 32169
4/26/69	**38**	5	27. It Looks Like The Sun's Gonna Shine	Decca 32449
2/28/70	**37**	3	28. Little Johnny From Down The Street	Decca 32608

WILD CHOIR

Short-lived Nashville group: Gail Davies, Pete Pendras, Denny Bixby, Larry Chaney and Bob Mummert.

DATE	POS	WKS	ARTIST– RECORD TITLE	LABEL & NO.
11/29/86	**40**	1	1. Heart To Heart	RCA 5011

WILD ROSE

Female quintet: Pamela Gadd (vocals), Wanda Vick (lead guitar), Pam Perry (mandolin; left in 1992), Kathy Mac (bass) and Nancy Given Prout (drums). Vick was a guitarist with Lynn Anderson's band. Prout's husband, Brian, is drummer for Diamond Rio.

DATE	POS	WKS	ARTIST– RECORD TITLE	LABEL & NO.
10/7/89	**15**	10	1. Breaking New Ground	Universal 66018
3/10/90	**38**	2	2. Go Down Swingin' originally released on Universal 66033	Capitol 44529

WILEY & GENE

Wiley Walker (born 11/17/11, Florida) and Gene Sullivan (born 11/6/14, Alabama); formed duet in Dallas in 1939. Wrote and originally recorded "When My Blue Moon Turns To Gold Again."

DATE	POS	WKS	ARTIST– RECORD TITLE	LABEL & NO.
1/5/46	**2 (1)**	1	1. **Make Room In Your Heart For A Friend**	Columbia 36869

WILKINS, Little David

Born in Parsons, Tennessee. Recorded for Sun Records at the age of 15.

DATE	POS	WKS	ARTIST– RECORD TITLE	LABEL & NO.
2/8/75	**14**	7	1. Whoever Turned You On, Forgot To Turn You Off	MCA 40345
8/23/75	**11**	8	2. One Monkey Don't Stop No Show	MCA 40427
2/28/76	**18**	8	3. The Good Night Special	MCA 40510
2/19/77	**21**	6	4. He'll Play The Music (But You Can't Make Him Dance)	MCA 40668
11/19/77	**21**	7	5. Agree To Disagree	Playboy 5822

WILLET, Slim, with The Brush Cutters

Willet born Winston Lee Moore on 12/1/19 near Dublin, Texas. Died of a heart attack on 7/1/66. Worked on radio in Abilene, 1949-66. First recorded for Star Talent in 1950. Own band, the Hired Hands, 1950-55.

DATE	POS	WKS	ARTIST– RECORD TITLE	LABEL & NO.
9/27/52	**1 (1)**	23	1. **Don't Let The Stars (Get In Your Eyes)** Jockey #1 / Best Seller #2 / Juke Box #2; #1 Pop hit for Perry Como in 1953	4 Star 1614

DATE	POS	WKS	ARTIST–RECORD TITLE	LABEL & NO.
			WILLIAMS, Cootie	
			Born Charles Melvin Williams on 7/24/08 in Mobile, Alabama. Died on 9/15/85. Jazz trumpet star. With Duke Ellington, 1929-40; Benny Goodman, 1940-41.	
7/8/44	4	6	1. **Red Blues** Eddie "Cleanhead" Vinson (vocal)	Hit 7084
			WILLIAMS, Don	
			Born on 5/27/39 in Floydada, Texas. Made professional debut in 1957. Moved to Corpus Christi; formed the Pozo-Seco Singers with Susan Taylor and Lofton Cline in 1964. Moved to Nashville in 1967; went solo in 1971. Became staff writer for Jack Clement. Appeared in the movies *W.W. and the Dixie Dancekings* and *Smokey and the Bandit II*. Also extremely popular in Europe, where he was named Country Music Star Of The Decade in England in 1980. CMA Award: 1978 Male Vocalist of the Year.	
1/20/73	14	11	1. The Shelter Of Your Eyes	JMI 12
5/26/73	12	13	2. Come Early Morning/	
7/28/73	33	6	3. Amanda	JMI 24
12/8/73+	13	10	4. Atta Way To Go	JMI 32
3/30/74	5	10	5. **We Should Be Together**	JMI 36
8/3/74	1 (1)	12	6. **I Wouldn't Want To Live If You Didn't Love Me**	Dot 17516
12/28/74+	4	12	7. **The Ties That Bind** #37 Pop hit for Brook Benton in 1960	ABC/Dot 17531
5/3/75	1 (1)	12	8. **You're My Best Friend**	ABC/Dot 17550
9/6/75	1 (1)	12	9. **(Turn Out The Light And) Love Me Tonight**	ABC/Dot 17568
2/14/76	1 (1)	12	10. **Til The Rivers All Run Dry**	ABC/Dot 17604
6/19/76	1 (1)	12	11. **Say It Again**	ABC/Dot 17631
10/30/76	2 (2)	11	12. **She Never Knew Me**	ABC/Dot 17658
3/19/77	1 (1)	12	13. **Some Broken Hearts Never Mend**	ABC/Dot 17683
9/10/77	1 (1)	11	14. **I'm Just A Country Boy**	ABC/Dot 17717
2/25/78	7	9	15. **I've Got A Winner In You**	ABC 12332
7/8/78	3	10	16. **Rake And Ramblin' Man**	ABC 12373
11/11/78+	1 (1)	11	17. **Tulsa Time** #30 Pop hit for Eric Clapton in 1980	ABC 12425
3/31/79	3	10	18. **Lay Down Beside Me** also released on ABC 12458	MCA 12458
8/11/79	1 (1)	10	19. **It Must Be Love**	MCA 41069
12/15/79+	1 (1)	12	20. **Love Me Over Again**	MCA 41155
4/5/80	2 (3)	12	21. **Good Ole Boys Like Me**	MCA 41205
8/30/80	1 (2)	12	22. **I Believe In You**	MCA 41304
3/7/81	6	11	23. **Falling Again**	MCA 51065
7/18/81	4	10	24. **Miracles**	MCA 51134
10/10/81	3	9	25. **If I Needed You** **EMMYLOU HARRIS & DON WILLIAMS**	Warner 49809
12/5/81+	1 (1)	14	26. **Lord, I Hope This Day Is Good**	MCA 51207
5/1/82	3	12	27. **Listen To The Radio**	MCA 52037
9/4/82	3	12	28. **Mistakes**	MCA 52097
1/8/83	1 (1)	12	29. **If Hollywood Don't Need You**	MCA 52152
4/30/83	1 (1)	12	30. **Love Is On A Roll**	MCA 52205
8/13/83	2 (1)	13	31. **Nobody But You**	MCA 52245
12/24/83+	1 (1)	12	32. **Stay Young**	MCA 52310

DATE	POS	WKS	ARTIST– RECORD TITLE	LABEL & NO.
6/2/84	**1** (1)	13	33. **That's The Thing About Love**	MCA 52389
9/29/84	**11**	10	34. Maggie's Dream	MCA 52448
2/2/85	**2** (1)	12	35. **Walkin' A Broken Heart**	MCA 52514
11/9/85	**20**	9	36. It's Time For Love	MCA 52692
2/1/86	**3**	14	37. **We've Got A Good Fire Goin'**	Capitol 5526
6/21/86	**1** (1)	13	38. **Heartbeat In The Darkness**	Capitol 5588
11/1/86+	**3**	14	39. **Then It's Love**	Capitol 5638
2/21/87	**9**	12	40. Senorita	Capitol 5683
6/27/87	**4**	14	41. **I'll Never Be In Love Again**	Capitol 44019
11/21/87+	**9**	13	42. **I Wouldn't Be A Man**	Capitol 44066
4/9/88	**5**	13	43. **Another Place, Another Time**	Capitol 44131
9/3/88	**7**	13	44. **Desperately**	Capitol 44216
2/4/89	**5**	13	45. **Old Coyote Town**	Capitol 44274
5/20/89	**4**	14	46. **One Good Well**	RCA 8867
9/30/89	**4**	23	47. **I've Been Loved By The Best**	RCA 9017
2/17/90	**4**	18	48. **Just As Long As I Have You**	RCA 9119
7/21/90	**22**	8	49. Maybe That's All It Takes	RCA 2507
9/29/90	**2** (2)	18	50. **Back In My Younger Days**	RCA 2677
2/9/91	**4**	17	51. **True Love**	RCA 2745
6/8/91	**7**	17	52. **Lord Have Mercy On A Country Boy**	RCA 2820

WILLIAMS, Hank, with His Drifting Cowboys

Williams born Hiram King Williams on 9/17/23 in Mount Olive, Alabama. Died on 1/1/53 en route to a concert in Canton, Ohio. Moved to Montgomery in the late 1930s. Own radio show on WSFA-Montgomery; billed as "The Singing Kid." Formed his own band, The Drifting Cowboys, as a teenager. Married Audrey Sheppard in 1944; their son is Hank Williams, Jr. First recorded for Sterling in 1946. Worked on the *Louisiana Hayride*, 1948-49; with the *Grand Ole Opry*, 1949-52. Toured with Bob Hope, Jack Benny and Minnie Pearl in the Hadacol Caravan in 1951. In 1952, divorced Audrey, was fired from the Opry in August and married Billie Jean Jones Eshlimar (Billie Jean Horton), who later married Johnny Horton. Elected to the Country Music Hall of Fame in 1961. Also recorded as Luke The Drifter. Won Grammy's Lifetime Achievement Award in 1987. Inducted into the Rock and Roll Hall of Fame in 1987 as a forefather of rock and roll. The premier country songwriter. George Hamilton portrayed Hank in his movie biography, *Your Cheatin' Heart*.

DATE	POS	WKS	ARTIST– RECORD TITLE	LABEL & NO.
8/9/47	**4**	3	1. **Move It On Over**	MGM 10033
7/3/48	**14**	1	2. Honky Tonkin' [R] Juke Box #14; first released in 1947 on Sterling 210	MGM 10171
7/24/48	**6**	3	3. **I'm A Long Gone Daddy** **HANK WILLIAMS and his Guitar** Juke Box #6	MGM 10212
3/5/49	**1** (16)	42	● 4. **Lovesick Blues/** Best Seller #1(16) / Juke Box #1(10)	
7/9/49	**6**	2	5. **Never Again** [R] Juke Box #6; first released in 1947 on Sterling 201	MGM 10352
3/5/49	**12**	2	6. Mansion On The Hill Juke Box #12	MGM 10328
5/14/49	**2** (2)	29	7. **Wedding Bells** Best Seller #2 / Juke Box #2	MGM 10401
7/23/49	**5**	11	8. **Mind Your Own Business** Juke Box #5 / Best Seller #6	MGM 10461

DATE	POS	WKS	ARTIST–RECORD TITLE	LABEL & NO.
10/1/49	**4**	9	9. **You're Gonna Change (Or I'm Gonna Leave)/** Best Seller #4 / Juke Box #8	
10/8/49	**12**	3	10. Lost Highway Best Seller #12 / Juke Box #14	MGM 10506
11/26/49	**2 (1)**	12	11. **My Bucket's Got A Hole In It** Best Seller #2 / Juke Box #2 / Jockey #5; flip side is the classic tune "I'm So Lonesome I Could Cry"	MGM 10560
2/18/50	**5**	5	12. **I Just Don't Like This Kind Of Livin'** Best Seller #5 / Juke Box #5 / Jockey #8	MGM 10609
3/25/50	**1 (8)**	21	13. **Long Gone Lonesome Blues/** Jockey #1(8) / Best Seller #1(5) / Juke Box #1(4)	
4/15/50	**9**	1	14. **My Son Calls Another Man Daddy** Juke Box #9	MGM 10645
5/27/50	**1 (10)**	25	15. **Why Don't You Love Me** Jockey #1(10) / Best Seller #1(6) / Juke Box #1(5)	MGM 10696
10/7/50	**5**	6	16. **They'll Never Take Her Love From Me/** Jockey #5	
10/14/50	**9**	1	17. **Why Should We Try Anymore** Best Seller #9	MGM 10760
11/18/50	**1 (1)**	15	18. **Moanin' The Blues/** Jockey #1 / Best Seller #2 / Juke Box #3	
11/18/50	**9**	4	19. **Nobody's Lonesome For Me** Jockey #9	MGM 10832
3/17/51	**1 (1)**	46	● 20. **Cold, Cold Heart/** Jockey #1 / Best Seller #2 / Juke Box #4	
3/3/51	**8**	4	21. **Dear John** Juke Box #8 / Best Seller #10	MGM 10904
6/9/51	**2 (2)**	13	22. **I Can't Help It (If I'm Still In Love With You)/** Jockey #2 / Juke Box #3 / Best Seller #6	
5/26/51	**3**	10	23. **Howlin' At The Moon** Juke Box #3 / Best Seller #4 / Jockey #6	MGM 10961
7/14/51	**1 (8)**	25	24. **Hey, Good Lookin'** Jockey #1 / Juke Box #2 / Best Seller #2	MGM 11000
10/20/51	**4**	18	25. **Crazy Heart/** Juke Box #4 / Jockey #6 / Best Seller #7	
10/20/51	**9**	2	26. **Lonesome Whistle** Jockey #9	MGM 11054
12/22/51+	**4**	15	27. **Baby, We're Really In Love** Jockey #4 / Juke Box #4 / Best Seller #8	MGM 11100
3/1/52	**2 (1)**	12	28. **Honky Tonk Blues** Juke Box #2 / Best Seller #7 / Jockey #10	MGM 11160
5/3/52	**2 (2)**	16	29. **Half As Much** Best Seller #2 / Juke Box #4 / Jockey #7	MGM 11202
8/16/52	**1 (14)**	29	● 30. **Jambalaya (On The Bayou)** Best Seller #1(14) / Jockey #1(14) / Juke Box #1(12)	MGM 11283
10/11/52	**2 (1)**	12	31. **Settin' The Woods On Fire/** Jockey #2 / Juke Box #4 / Best Seller #5	
11/15/52	**10**	1	32. **You Win Again** Juke Box #10	MGM 11318
12/20/52+	**1 (1)**	13	33. **I'll Never Get Out Of This World Alive** Best Seller #1 / Juke Box #4 / Jockey #7	MGM 11366
2/21/53	**1 (13)**	19	34. **Kaw-Liga/** Best Seller #1(13) / Jockey #1(8) / Juke Box #1(8)	
2/21/53	**1 (6)**	23	35. **Your Cheatin' Heart** Jockey #1(6) / Juke Box #1(2) / Best Seller #2	MGM 11416

DATE	POS	WKS	ARTIST– RECORD TITLE	LABEL & NO.
5/16/53	1 (4)	13	36. **Take These Chains From My Heart** Best Seller #1 / Juke Box #2 / Jockey #3	MGM 11479
7/25/53	4	9	37. **I Won't Be Home No More** Best Seller #4 / Juke Box #4 / Jockey #5	MGM 11533
10/10/53	7	2	38. **Weary Blues From Waitin'** Best Seller #7 / Juke Box #7 / Jockey #9	MGM 11574
4/30/55	9	3	39. **Please Don't Let Me Love You** Juke Box #9	MGM 11928
2/11/89	7	10	40. **There's A Tear In My Beer** **HANK WILLIAMS, JR. with HANK WILLIAMS, SR.** Hank Sr.'s vocals dubbed in from an obscure single-copy vinyl recording	Warner/Curb 27584

WILLIAMS, Hank, Jr.

Born Randall Hank Williams on 5/26/49 in Shreveport, Louisiana; son of Hank and Audrey Williams. Raised in Nashville; a star athlete in high school. Toured with Audrey's Caravan Of Stars from age 13. On the *Grand Ole Opry* since 1962. Appeared on the soundtrack of the movie *Your Cheatin' Heart* in 1964. Moved to Cullman, Alabama, in 1974. Injured in a climbing accident on 8/8/75 in Montana; returned to performing in 1977. Richard Thomas starred as Hank in his 1983 biographical TV movie, *Living Proof: The Hank Williams Story*. Starred in the movie *A Time To Sing*. Now lives near Aris, Tennessee. Also recorded as Luke The Drifter, Jr. His father gave him the nickname "Bocephus." CMA Awards: 1987 and 1988 Entertainer of the Year.

(a) LUKE THE DRIFTER, JR.
(b) HANK WILLIAMS, JR. and LOIS JOHNSON
(c) HANK WILLIAMS, JR. With THE MIKE CURB CONGREGATION

DATE	POS	WKS	ARTIST– RECORD TITLE	LABEL & NO.
2/15/64	5	18	1. **Long Gone Lonesome Blues**	MGM 13208
6/4/66	5	18	2. **Standing In The Shadows**	MGM 13504
2/17/68	31	5	3. I Wouldn't Change A Thing About You (But Your Name)	MGM 13857
9/14/68	3	14	4. **It's All Over But The Crying** from the movie *A Time to Sing* starring Williams	MGM 13968
12/14/68	39	3	5. I Was With Red Foley (The Night He Passed Away) (a)	MGM 14002
1/25/69	14	11	6. Custody (a)	MGM 14020
3/8/69	16	8	7. A Baby Again	MGM 14024
5/17/69	3	12	8. **Cajun Baby**	MGM 14047
7/26/69	37	3	9. Be Careful Of Stones That You Throw (a) #31 Pop hit for Dion in 1963	MGM 14062
9/20/69	4	12	10. **I'd Rather Be Gone**	MGM 14077
2/7/70	36	2	11. Something To Think About	MGM 14095
3/21/70	12	10	12. I Walked Out On Heaven	MGM 14107
6/13/70	36	3	13. It Don't Take But One Mistake (a)	MGM 14120
7/18/70	23	7	14. Removing The Shadow (b)	MGM 14136
8/1/70	1 (2)	15	15. **All For The Love Of Sunshine** (c) from the movie *Kelly's Heroes* starring Clint Eastwood	MGM 14152
10/24/70	12	9	16. So Sad (To Watch Good Love Go Bad) (b) #7 Pop hit for The Everly Brothers in 1960	MGM 14164
12/26/70+	3	13	17. **Rainin' In My Heart** (c) #34 Pop hit for Slim Harpo in 1961	MGM 14194
5/15/71	6	11	18. **I've Got A Right To Cry**	MGM 14240

DATE	POS	WKS	ARTIST– RECORD TITLE	LABEL & NO.
9/11/71	18	10	19. After All They All Used To Belong To Me	MGM 14277
1/1/72	7	11	20. **Ain't That A Shame** (c)	MGM 14317
			#1 R&B hit for Fats Domino in 1955	
4/22/72	14	11	21. Send Me Some Lovin' (b)	MGM 14356
5/6/72	1 (2)	14	22. **Eleven Roses**	MGM 14371
9/30/72	3	14	23. **Pride's Not Hard To Swallow**	MGM 14421
12/2/72+	22	8	24. Whole Lotta Loving (b)	MGM 14443
			#6 Pop hit for Fats Domino in 1959	
3/24/73	23	9	25. After You	MGM 14486
7/14/73	12	9	26. Hank	MGM 14550
			a tribute to Hank Williams, Sr.	
11/17/73	4	14	27. **The Last Love Song**	MGM 14656
3/30/74	13	8	28. Rainy Night In Georgia	MGM 14700
			#4 Pop hit for Brook Benton in 1970	
7/27/74	7	9	29. **I'll Think Of Something**	MGM 14731
11/30/74	19	6	30. Angels Are Hard To Find	MGM 14755
5/10/75	26	5	31. Where He's Going, I've Already Been/	
		3	32. The Kind Of Woman I Got	MGM 14794
8/16/75	29	4	33. The Same Old Story	MGM 14813
12/6/75	19	7	34. Stoned At The Jukebox	MGM 14833
5/15/76	38	2	35. Living Proof	MGM 14845
5/7/77	27	5	36. Mobile Boogie	Warner/Curb 8361
2/11/78	38	2	37. Feelin' Better	Warner/Curb 8507
8/26/78	15	8	38. I Fought The Law	Warner/Curb 8641
			#9 Pop hit for the Bobby Fuller Four in 1966	
6/23/79	4	9	39. **Family Tradition**	Elektra/Curb 46046
10/20/79	2 (2)	9	40. **Whiskey Bent And Hell Bound**	Elektra/Curb 46535
2/23/80	5	9	41. **Women I've Never Had**	Elektra/Curb 46593
6/7/80	12	8	42. Kaw-Liga	Elektra/Curb 46636
9/13/80	6	9	43. **Old Habits**	Elektra/Curb 47016
2/7/81	1 (1)	10	44. **Texas Women**	Elektra/Curb 47102
6/13/81	1 (1)	9	45. **Dixie On My Mind**	Elektra/Curb 47137
9/26/81	1 (1)	10	46. **All My Rowdy Friends (Have Settled Down)**	Elektra/Curb 47191
2/6/82	2 (3)	15	47. **A Country Boy Can Survive**	Elektra/Curb 47257
6/12/82	1 (1)	12	48. **Honky Tonkin'**	Elektra/Curb 47462
10/23/82	5	11	49. **The American Dream/**	
		11	50. If Heaven Ain't A Lot Like Dixie	Elektra/Curb 69960
2/12/83	4	12	51. **Gonna Go Huntin' Tonight**	Elektra/Curb 69846
6/18/83	6	11	52. **Leave Them Boys Alone**	Warner/Curb 29633
			Waylon Jennings and Ernest Tubb (guest vocals)	
10/22/83	5	12	53. **Queen Of My Heart**	Warner/Curb 29500
11/19/83	15	9	54. The Conversation	RCA 13631
			WAYLON JENNINGS with HANK WILLIAMS, JR.	
3/10/84	3	12	55. **Man Of Steel**	Warner/Curb 29382
6/30/84	5	11	56. **Attitude Adjustment**	Warner/Curb 29253
10/27/84	10	11	57. **All My Rowdy Friends Are Coming Over Tonight**	Warner/Curb 29184
2/16/85	10	11	58. **Major Moves**	Warner/Curb 29095
5/25/85	1 (1)	15	59. **I'm For Love**	Warner/Curb 29022
9/21/85	4	12	60. **This Ain't Dallas**	Warner/Curb 28912

DATE	POS	WKS	ARTIST– RECORD TITLE	LABEL & NO.
9/28/85	**14**	8	61. Two Old Cats Like Us **RAY CHARLES with HANK WILLIAMS, JR.**	Columbia 05575
3/8/86	**1** (1)	14	62. **Ain't Misbehavin'** written and popularized in 1929 by Fats Waller	Warner/Curb 28794
6/28/86	**2** (2)	14	63. **Country State Of Mind**	Warner/Curb 28691
10/18/86	**1** (2)	14	64. **Mind Your Own Business** Willie Nelson, Reba McEntire, Tom Petty and Reverend Ike (guest vocals)	Warner/Curb 28581
3/21/87	**31**	3	65. When Something Is Good (Why Does It Change)	Warner/Curb 28452
6/20/87	**1** (1)	14	66. **Born To Boogie**	Warner/Curb 28369
10/24/87+	**4**	14	67. **Heaven Can't Be Found**	Warner/Curb 28227
3/5/88	**2** (1)	13	68. **Young Country** Butch Baker, T. Graham Brown, Highway 101, Dana McVicker, Steve Earle, Keith Whitley and Marty Stuart (celebrity chorus)	Warner/Curb 28120
7/9/88	**8**	10	69. **If The South Woulda Won**	Warner/Curb 27862
10/29/88	**21**	8	70. That Old Wheel **JOHNNY CASH with HANK WILLIAMS, JR.**	Mercury 870688
11/19/88+	**14**	10	71. Early In The Morning And Late At Night	Warner/Curb 27722
2/11/89	**7**	10	72. **There's A Tear In My Beer** **HANK WILLIAMS, JR. with HANK WILLIAMS, SR.** Hank Sr.'s vocals dubbed in from an obscure single copy vinyl recording	Warner/Curb 27584
7/29/89	**6**	13	73. **Finders Are Keepers**	Warner/Curb 22945
2/24/90	**15**	11	74. Ain't Nobody's Business	Warner/Curb 19957
6/9/90	**10**	11	75. **Good Friends, Good Whiskey, Good Lovin'**	Warner/Curb 19872
9/15/90	**27**	3	76. Don't Give Us A Reason recorded as a message to Iraq's leader, Saddam Hussein, during the Persian Gulf crisis before war broke out	Warner/Curb 19542
2/23/91	**39**	3	77. I Mean I Love You	Warner/Curb 19463
6/1/91	**26**	9	78. If It Will It Will	Warner/Curb 19352
			WILLIAMS, Lawton	
			Born on 7/29/22 in Troy, Tennessee. Worked as a DJ in Detroit and Dearborn in the '40s. Own TV series in Fort Worth in the late '40s. Wrote "Fraulein" for Bobby Helms and "Geisha Girl" for Hank Locklin.	
10/23/61+	**13**	25	1. Anywhere There's People	Mercury 71867
10/10/64	**40**	1	2. Everything's O.K. On The LBJ	RCA 8407
			WILLIAMS, Leona—see HAGGARD, Merle	
			WILLIAMS, Tex	
			Born Sollie Paul Williams on 8/23/17 near Ramsey, Illinois. Died of lung cancer on 10/11/85. Worked on WJBL-Decatur, Illinois, in 1930. Moved to California with his band, the Reno Racketeers, in the mid-1930s. Appeared in many Western movies. Worked as vocalist with the Spade Cooley band. Own band, the Western Caravan, in 1946. Own TV series in the '60s. **TEX WILLIAMS AND HIS WESTERN CARAVAN:**	
11/30/46	**4**	2	1. **The California Polka**	Capitol 302
7/5/47	**1** (16)	23	● 2. **Smoke! Smoke! Smoke! (That Cigarette)** [N] Capitol's first million-selling record	Capitol A. 40001
10/4/47	**4**	8	3. **That's What I Like About The West**	Capitol A. 40031
12/13/47	**2** (8)	15	4. **Never Trust A Woman**	Capitol A. 40054

DATE	POS	WKS	ARTIST– RECORD TITLE	LABEL & NO.
2/14/48	2 (2)	11	5. **Don't Telephone - Don't Telegraph (Tell A Woman)**	Capitol A. 40081
5/15/48	4	12	6. **Suspicion**	Capitol A. 40109
			Best Seller #4 / Juke Box #4	
6/19/48	5	15	7. **Banjo Polka**	Capitol A. 15101
			Juke Box #5 / Best Seller #11	
6/26/48	6	8	8. **Who? Me?/**	
			Best Seller #6 / Juke Box #11	
7/31/48	15	1	9. Foolish Tears	Capitol 15113
			Juke Box #15	
9/11/48	6	5	10. **Talking Boogie/**	
			Juke Box #6 / Best Seller #12	
11/13/48	13	3	11. Just A Pair Of Blue Eyes	Capitol 15175
			Juke Box #13 / Best Seller #14	
11/20/48	5	8	12. **Life Gits Tee-Jus, Don't It?** [N]	Capitol 15271
			Juke Box #5 / Best Seller #9	
10/22/49	11	2	13. (There's A) Bluebird On Your Windowsill	Capitol 40225
			Juke Box #11 / Best Seller #12	
			TEX WILLIAMS:	
6/12/65	26	8	14. Too Many Tigers	Boone 1028
10/9/65	30	7	15. Big Tennessee	Boone 1032
1/29/66	18	5	16. Bottom Of A Mountain	Boone 1036
3/16/68	32	5	17. Smoke, Smoke, Smoke-'68 [R]	Boone 1069
			new version of #2 above	
10/9/71	29	5	18. The Night Miss Nancy Ann's Hotel For Single Girls	
			Burned Down [N]	Monument 8503

WILLIAMS BROS. (Jimmy & Bobby)

Jimmy and Bobby Williams.

DATE	POS	WKS	ARTIST– RECORD TITLE	LABEL & NO.
6/15/63	28	1	1. Bad Old Memories	Del-Mar 1008

WILLING, Foy, and His Riders of The Purple Sage

Willing born Foy Willingham in 1915 in Bosque County, Texas. Died on 7/24/78. Worked on local radio shows while still a teenager. On radio in New York City, 1933-35. Returned to Texas; worked as a DJ. Moved to California in 1940 and formed band, The Riders Of The Purple Sage. Regular appearances on the *Hollywood Barn Dance*; appeared in several movies. Group disbanded in 1952; Willing continued as a solo artist.

DATE	POS	WKS	ARTIST– RECORD TITLE	LABEL & NO.
7/15/44	3	5	1. **Texas Blues**	Capitol 162
3/16/46	6	1	2. **Detour**	Decca 9000
12/14/46	4	1	3. **Have I Told You Lately (That I Love You)**	Majestic 6000
6/19/48	14	2	4. Anytime	Capitol A. 40108
			Juke Box #14	
1/1/49	15	1	5. Brush Those Tears From Your Eyes	Capitol 15290
			Best Seller #15	

WILLIS, Hal

Born Leonard Francis Gauthier in Roslyn, Quebec. Moved to Nashville in 1958.

DATE	POS	WKS	ARTIST– RECORD TITLE	LABEL & NO.
11/7/64	5	15	1. **The Lumberjack**	Sims 207

DATE	POS	WKS	ARTIST– RECORD TITLE	LABEL & NO.
			WILLIS BROTHERS, The	
			Family group consisting of James "Guy" (born 7/15/15, died 4/13/81; guitar), Charles "Skeeter" (born 12/20/07, died 1976; fiddle) and Richard "Vic" (born 5/31/22, died 1/15/95; accordion) Willis. Worked as the Oklahoma Wranglers on KGEF-Shawnee in 1932. Appeared on the Brush Creek Follie, KMBC-Kansas City, 1940-42. On the *Grand Ole Opry*, 1946-49; returned to the Opry in 1960. Backed Hank Williams on his first recordings. With Eddy Arnold to 1957. Vic later led the Vic Willis Trio.	
9/12/64	9	19	1. **Give Me 40 Acres (To Turn This Rig Around)**	Starday 681
3/25/67	14	11	2. Bob	Starday 796
			WILLS, Bob, & His Texas Playboys	
			Wills born James Robert Wills on 3/6/05 near Kosse, Texas. Died on 5/13/75. Fiddle player for square dances in Memphis, Texas, while still a teenager. Own group, the Wills Fiddle Band, in 1929 (later became the Light Crust Doughboys). Formed the Texas Playboys in 1933; his brother Johnnie Lee Wills was a member until 1940. Band featured Tommy Duncan (vocals) and Leon McAuliffe (steel guitar). Wrote "San Antonio Rose" and "My Shoes Keep Walking Back To You." Own radio show on KVOO-Tulsa, 1934-58. Appeared in many Western movies. Had heart attacks in 1962, 1964, 1969 and 1973. In a coma from December 1973 until his death. Elected to the Country Music Hall of Fame in 1968. Known as "The King Of Western Swing." His band recorded as the Original Texas Playboys in 1977.	
1/8/44	3	1	1. **New San Antonio Rose** [R] vocal version of Wills's 1938 classic tune; essentially the same song as his 1935 "Spanish Two Step"	Okeh 05694
9/9/44	2 (5)	11	2. **We Might As Well Forget It/**	
9/23/44	2 (2)	17	3. **You're From Texas**	Okeh 6722
3/24/45	1 (2)	15	4. **Smoke On The Water/**	
3/24/45	3	18	5. **Hang Your Head In Shame**	Okeh 6736
6/16/45	1 (1)	11	6. **Stars And Stripes On Iwo Jima/**	
7/21/45	5	4	7. **You Don't Care What Happens To Me**	Okeh 6742
11/17/45	1 (3)	14	8. **Silver Dew On The Blue Grass Tonight/**	
11/3/45+	2 (1)	8	9. **Texas Playboy Rag** [I]	Columbia 36841
12/29/45+	1 (1)	5	10. **White Cross On Okinawa**	Columbia 36881
5/4/46	1 (16)	23	11. **New Spanish Two Step/** [R] vocal version of Wills's 1935 recording	
5/11/46	3	18	12. **Roly-Poly**	Columbia 36966
11/30/46	2 (2)	8	13. **Stay A Little Longer/**	
11/30/46	4	1	14. **I Can't Go On This Way**	Columbia 37097
3/29/47	5	1	15. **I'm Gonna Be Boss From Now On** Jesse Ashlock (vocal)	Columbia 37205
5/17/47	1 (1)	6	16. **Sugar Moon**	Columbia 37313
7/12/47	4	1	17. **Bob Wills Boogie** [I]	Columbia 37357
1/31/48	4	17	18. **Bubbles In My Beer**	MGM 10116
7/3/48	8	2	19. **Keeper Of My Heart** Juke Box #8	MGM 10175
7/24/48	15	1	20. Texarkana Baby Best Seller #15	Columbia 38179
9/18/48	10	1	21. **Thorn In My Heart** Juke Box #10	MGM 10236
1/21/50	10	1	22. **Ida Red Likes The Boogie** Juke Box #10; Tiny Moore (vocal)	MGM 10570
11/4/50	8	5	23. **Faded Love** Jockey #8; Rusty McDonald and The Playboy Trio (vocals)	MGM 10786

DATE	POS	WKS	ARTIST – RECORD TITLE	LABEL & NO.
8/8/60	5	17	24. **Heart To Heart Talk**	Liberty 55260
1/23/61	26	1	25. The Image Of Me	Liberty 55264
			BOB WILLS & TOMMY DUNCAN	
			WILLS, David	
			Born on 10/23/51 in Pulaski, Tennessee. Toured with Charlie Rich and Charley Pride.	
1/11/75	10	7	1. **There's A Song On The Jukebox**	Epic 50036
4/19/75	10	8	2. **From Barrooms To Bedrooms**	Epic 50090
8/2/75	31	5	3. The Barmaid	Epic 50118
12/6/75	35	3	4. She Deserves My Very Best	Epic 50154
7/30/83	19	7	5. The Eyes Of A Stranger	RCA 13541
12/17/83+	26	6	6. Miss Understanding	RCA 13653
4/7/84	31	3	7. Lady In Waiting	RCA 13737
			WILLS, Johnnie Lee, And His Boys	
			Born on 9/2/12 in Jewett, Texas. Died on 10/25/84. Younger brother of Bob Wills. With Bob in the Texas Playboys, 1933-40. Fiddle/banjo player. Own band, 1940-64.	
1/28/50	2 (5)	11	1. **Rag Mop** Juke Box #2 / Best Seller #2 / Jockey #3	Bullet 696
4/1/50	7	2	2. **Peter Cotton Tail** Juke Box #7 / Jockey #8	Bullet 700
			WILSON, Coleman	
7/31/61	23	5	1. Passing Zone Blues	King 5512
			WILSON, Jim	
			Native of Bowling Green, Kentucky. Popular DJ in Texas.	
7/23/55	8	9	1. **Daddy, You Know What?** Jockey #8; Wilson's daughter June speaks a few words	Mercury 70635
			WILSON, Norro	
			Born Norris D. Wilson on 4/4/38 in Scottsville, Kentucky. Outstanding songwriter. Credits include "A Very Special Love Song," "I Love My Friend" and "The Most Beautiful Girl" for Charlie Rich; "I'll See Him Through" for Tammy Wynette; "Baby, Baby (I Know You're A Lady)" for David Houston, and "Soul Song" for Joe Stampley.	
7/18/70	20	9	1. Do It To Someone You Love	Mercury 73077
12/23/72+	28	7	2. Everybody Needs Lovin'	RCA 0824
10/27/73	35	3	3. Ain't It Good (To Feel This Way)	RCA 0062
			WINSLOW, Stephanie	
			Born on 8/27/56 in Yankton, South Dakota. Accomplished fiddler, made professional debut at age 10. Stephanie Winslow is a stage name taken from the town of Winslow, Arizona. Formerly married to the owner of Oak Records, Ray Ruff, who was also married to Susie Allanson and Carlette.	
10/6/79	10	9	1. **Say You Love Me** #11 Pop hit for Fleetwood Mac in 1976	Warner/Curb 49074
1/26/80	14	6	2. Crying #2 Pop hit for Roy Orbison in 1961	Warner/Curb 49146

DATE	POS	WKS	ARTIST– RECORD TITLE	LABEL & NO.
4/26/80	38	2	3. I Can't Remember	Warner/Curb 49201
7/19/80	36	4	4. Try It On	Warner/Curb 49257
10/18/80	35	3	5. Baby, I'm A Want You	Warner/Curb 49557
			#3 Pop hit for Bread in 1971	
1/17/81	25	5	6. Anything But Yes Is Still A No	Warner/Curb 49628
4/11/81	36	3	7. Hideaway Healing	Warner/Curb 49693
7/25/81	39	2	8. I've Been A Fool/	
		2	9. Sometimes When We Touch	Warner/Curb 49753
			#3 Pop hit for Dan Hill in 1978	
10/24/81	29	5	10. When You Walk In The Room	Warner/Curb 49831
			#35 Pop hit for The Searchers in 1964	
8/7/82	40	1	11. Don't We Belong In Love	Primero 1007
10/22/83	25	6	12. Kiss Me Darling	Curb/MCA 52291
2/18/84	29	5	13. Dancin' With The Devil	Curb 52327

WINTERS, Don

Born on 4/17/29 in Tampa. Worked with Marty Robbins, 1960-82.

DATE	POS	WKS	ARTIST– RECORD TITLE	LABEL & NO.
7/3/61	10	10	1. **Too Many Times/**	
7/17/61	27	2	2. Shake Hands With A Loser	Decca 31253

WISEMAN, Mac

Born Malcolm Wiseman on 5/23/25 in Waynesboro, Virginia. Played banjo and guitar with the Hungry Five while in high school. Worked as a DJ at WSVA-Harrisburg. Worked with Molly O'Day, Bill Monroe and Flatt & Scruggs. First recorded for Dot in 1951. Country A&R director for Dot Records in 1957.

DATE	POS	WKS	ARTIST– RECORD TITLE	LABEL & NO.
5/28/55	10	2	1. **The Ballad Of Davy Crockett**	Dot 1240
			Jockey #10	
8/10/59	5	20	2. **Jimmy Brown The Newsboy**	Dot 15946
9/21/63	12	8	3. Your Best Friend And Me	Capitol 5011
1/3/70	38	3	4. Johnny's Cash & Charley's Pride [N]	RCA 0283

WOOD, Danny

Born in Grand Prairie, Texas. First recorded for London in 1972.

DATE	POS	WKS	ARTIST– RECORD TITLE	LABEL & NO.
7/26/80	30	3	1. A Heart's Been Broken	RCA 11968
1/24/81	37	2	2. It Took Us All Night Long To Say Goodbye	RCA 12123

WOOD, Del

Born Adelaide Hendricks on 2/22/20 in Nashville. Died on 10/3/89. Popular female ragtime pianist on the *Grand Ole Opry* from 1953.

DATE	POS	WKS	ARTIST– RECORD TITLE	LABEL & NO.
9/8/51	5	12	1. **Down Yonder** [I]	Tennessee 775
			Juke Box #5 / Jockey #7 / Best Seller #9	

WOODS, Gene

DATE	POS	WKS	ARTIST– RECORD TITLE	LABEL & NO.
10/10/60	7	13	1. **The Ballad Of Wild River**	Hap 1004

DATE	POS	WKS	ARTIST– RECORD TITLE	LABEL & NO.

WOOLEY, Sheb/Ben Colder

Born Shelby F. Wooley on 4/10/21 near Erick, Oklahoma. Singer/ songwriter/actor. Played Pete Nolan in the TV series *Rawhide*. Also made comical recordings under the pseudonym Ben Colder. Appeared in the movies *High Noon*, *Rocky Mountain*, *Giant* and *Hoosiers*. Wrote *Hee Haw*'s theme song.

(a) BEN COLDER

DATE	POS	WKS	ARTIST– RECORD TITLE	LABEL & NO.
1/13/62	**1** (1)	17	1. **That's My Pa** [N]	MGM 13046
12/29/62	**18**	1	2. Don't Go Near The Eskimos (a) [N] parody of "Don't Go Near The Indians"	MGM 13104
3/2/63	**30**	2	3. Hello Wall No. 2 (a) [N]	MGM 13122
7/18/64	**33**	7	4. Blue Guitar [R] originally recorded in 1954 on MGM 11717	MGM 13241
6/4/66	**34**	5	5. I'll Leave The Singin' To The Bluebirds	MGM 13477
10/1/66	**6**	13	6. **Almost Persuaded No. 2** (a) [N]	MGM 13590
7/6/68	**22**	10	7. Tie A Tiger Down	MGM 13938
10/26/68	**24**	6	8. Harper Valley P.T.A. (Later That Same Day) (a) [N]	MGM 13997

WOPAT, Tom

Born on 9/9/51 in Lodi, Wisconsin. Played Luke Duke on TV's *The Dukes Of Hazzard*. Host of TNN's *Prime Time Country* in 1996.

DATE	POS	WKS	ARTIST– RECORD TITLE	LABEL & NO.
6/7/86	**39**	1	1. True Love (Never Did Run Smooth)	EMI America 8316
1/24/87	**16**	9	2. The Rock And Roll Of Love	EMI America 8364
6/20/87	**28**	5	3. Put Me Out Of My Misery	EMI America 43010
10/10/87	**20**	8	4. Susannah	EMI America 43034
2/13/88	**18**	9	5. A Little Bit Closer	EMI-Man. 50112
7/30/88	**40**	1	6. Hey Little Sister	Capitol 44144
11/19/88	**29**	5	7. Not Enough Love	Capitol 44243

WORK, Jimmy

Born in Akron in 1924; raised in Dukedom, Tennessee. Worked on WCAR-Pontiac, Michigan, in the mid-1940s. First recorded for Trophy in 1947.

DATE	POS	WKS	ARTIST– RECORD TITLE	LABEL & NO.
2/19/55	**5**	13	1. **Making Believe** Juke Box #5 / Jockey #7 / Best Seller #11	Dot 1221
7/2/55	**6**	4	2. **That's What Makes The Juke Box Play** Juke Box #6	Dot 1245

WORTH, Marion

Born Mary Ann Ward in Birmingham, Alabama. Worked on Dallas radio shows in 1947.

DATE	POS	WKS	ARTIST– RECORD TITLE	LABEL & NO.
10/19/59+	**12**	20	1. Are You Willing, Willie	Cherokee 503
5/23/60	**5**	15	2. **That's My Kind Of Love**	Guyden 2033
11/14/60	**7**	23	3. **I Think I Know**	Columbia 41799
5/22/61	**21**	1	4. There'll Always Be Sadness	Columbia 41972
2/2/63	**14**	5	5. Shake Me I Rattle (Squeeze Me I Cry)	Columbia 42640
6/8/63	**18**	3	6. Crazy Arms	Columbia 42703
5/9/64	**33**	4	7. You Took Him Off My Hands (Now Please Take Him Off My Mind)	Columbia 42992

DATE	POS	WKS	ARTIST– RECORD TITLE	LABEL & NO.
6/6/64	23	12	8. Slipping Around **MARION WORTH & GEORGE MORGAN**	Columbia 43020
10/24/64	25	5	9. The French Song #54 Pop hit for Lucille Starr in 1964	Columbia 43119
12/18/65+	32	5	10. I Will Not Blow Out The Light	Columbia 43405
			## WRIGHT, B.J.	
6/7/80	36	3	Born in Gallatin, Tennessee. Male singer. 1. J.R. title refers to J.R. Ewing of TV's *Dallas*	Soundwaves 4604
			## WRIGHT, Bobby	
			Born Johnnie R. Wright, Jr., on 3/30/42 in Charleston, West Virginia. Son of Johnny Wright and Kitty Wells; brother of Ruby Wright. On the *Louisiana Hayride* at age eight; recording since 1953. Appeared as Willie in the TV series *McHale's Navy*. Tours with the family show.	
7/5/69	40	1	1. Upstairs In The Bedroom	Decca 32464
7/31/71	13	12	2. Here I Go Again	Decca 32839
12/22/73	39	1	3. Lovin' Someone On My Mind	ABC 11390
3/30/74	24	6	4. Seasons In The Sun #1 Pop hit for Terry Jacks in 1974	ABC 11418
			## WRIGHT, Curtis	
			Born on 6/6/55 in Huntington, Pennsylvania. Former member of the Super Grit Cowboy Band. Backing singer for Vern Gosdin. Jingle singer for Burger King and Maxwell House. Co-wrote "Next To You, Next To Me" and "Rock My Baby" for Shenandoah.	
12/23/89	38	4	1. She's Got A Man On Her Mind	Airborne 75746
			## WRIGHT, Ginny	
			Born in Twin City, Georgia.	
1/9/54	3	22	1. **I Love You** **GINNY WRIGHT/JIM REEVES** Jockey #3 / Juke Box #7 / Best Seller #8	Fabor 101
10/1/55	2 (3)	26	2. **Are You Mine** **GINNY WRIGHT/TOM TALL** Jockey #2 / Juke Box #4 / Best Seller #5; also released on Zero 106	Fabor 117
			## WRIGHT, Johnny	
			Born on 5/13/14 in Mount Juliet, Tennessee; raised in Nashville. Banjo/fiddle player. Teamed with Jack Anglin, 1938-63, as Johnnie & Jack. Married Kitty Wells in 1938; Bobby and Ruby Wright are their children. Worked on WSIX-Nashville in the late '30s. Own band, the Tennessee Mountain Boys, in the early '40s. Went solo after the death of Anglin in March 1963. Formed the Kitty Wells/Johnny Wright Family Show in 1969.	
5/9/64	22	13	1. Walkin', Talkin', Cryin', Barely Beatin' Broken Heart **JOHNNY WRIGHT And The Tennessee Mountain Boys**	Decca 31593
1/16/65	37	2	2. Don't Give Up The Ship	Decca 31679
5/22/65	28	8	3. Blame It On The Moonlight	Decca 31740
8/28/65	1 (3)	20	4. **Hello Vietnam** written by Tom T. Hall	Decca 31821

DATE	POS	WKS	ARTIST– RECORD TITLE	LABEL & NO.
1/8/66	**31**	7	5. Keep The Flag Flying	Decca 31875
6/11/66	**31**	5	6. Nickels, Quarters And Dimes	Decca 31927
			WRIGHT, Michelle	
			Born on 7/1/61 in Morpeth, Ontario, Canada.	
7/14/90	**32**	4	1. New Kind Of Love	Arista 2002
5/9/92	**10**	15	2. **Take It Like A Man**	Arista 12406
12/12/92	**31**	4	3. He Would Be Sixteen	Arista 12480
			WRIGHT, Ruby	
			Born on 10/27/39 in Nashville. Daughter of Kitty Wells and Johnny Wright. Member of Nita, Rita & Ruby.	
9/12/64	**13**	11	1. Dern Ya	RIC 126
			answer song to Roger Miller's "Dang Me"	
			WRIGHT BROTHERS, The	
			Trio from Bedford, Indiana, formed in high school in 1972. Consisted of C. Thomas Wright, William Timothy Wright and Karl Hinkle. Hinkle replaced by John McDowell in 1975. Disbanded in 1977, but re-formed with Hinkle in the group, 1978-84. Hinkle was again replaced by McDowell in 1984.	
12/5/81	**35**	2	1. Family Man	Warner 49837
10/9/82	**40**	1	2. Made In The U.S.A.	Warner 29926
5/19/84	**33**	3	3. Southern Women	Mercury 818653
			WYNETTE, Tammy	
			Born Virginia Wynette Pugh on 5/5/42 in Itawamba County, Mississippi. Worked as a beautician in Birmingham in the early '60s. On the *Country Boy Eddy* TV show, WBRC-Birmingham, in 1965. Moved to Nashville in 1966 and hooked up with her producer, Billy Sherrill. Married to George Jones, 1969-75. Married her manager, George Richey (brother of Wyley McPherson), on 7/6/78. Plagued by ill health most of her life, has endured 17 major operations. Known as "The First Lady Of Country Music." CMA Awards: 1968, 1969 and 1970 Female Vocalist of the Year.	
			(a) GEORGE JONES & TAMMY WYNETTE	
4/1/67	**3**	19	1. **Your Good Girl's Gonna Go Bad**	Epic 10134
7/29/67	**1 (2)**	16	2. **My Elusive Dreams**	Epic 10194
			DAVID HOUSTON & TAMMY WYNETTE	
9/9/67	**1 (3)**	18	3. **I Don't Wanna Play House**	Epic 10211
1/27/68	**1 (1)**	14	4. **Take Me To Your World**	Epic 10269
2/10/68	**11**	11	5. It's All Over	Epic 10274
			DAVID HOUSTON & TAMMY WYNETTE	
5/25/68	**1 (3)**	16	6. **D-I-V-O-R-C-E**	Epic 10315
10/26/68	**1 (3)**	18	7. **Stand By Your Man**	Epic 10398
4/12/69	**1 (2)**	14	8. **Singing My Song**	Epic 10462
9/6/69	**1 (2)**	15	9. **The Ways To Love A Man**	Epic 10512
1/31/70	**2 (2)**	13	10. **I'll See Him Through**	Epic 10571
5/30/70	**1 (3)**	14	11. **He Loves Me All The Way**	Epic 10612
9/19/70	**1 (2)**	13	12. **Run, Woman, Run**	Epic 10653
12/12/70+	**5**	11	13. **The Wonders You Perform**	Epic 10687
3/6/71	**2 (3)**	14	14. **We Sure Can Love Each Other**	Epic 10707

DATE	POS	WKS	ARTIST– RECORD TITLE	LABEL & NO.
7/17/71	**1 (2)**	15	15. **Good Lovin' (Makes It Right)**	Epic 10759
1/8/72	**1 (1)**	13	16. **Bedtime Story**	Epic 10818
1/8/72	**9**	11	17. **Take Me** (a)	Epic 10815
5/27/72	**2 (2)**	12	18. **Reach Out Your Hand** originally the B-side of #16 above	Epic 10856
7/22/72	**6**	13	19. **The Ceremony** (a)	Epic 10881
9/30/72	**1 (1)**	12	20. **My Man**	Epic 10909
1/6/73	**38**	1	21. Old Fashioned Singing (a)	Epic 10923
1/20/73	**1 (1)**	12	22. **'Til I Get It Right**	Epic 10940
4/28/73	**1 (1)**	13	23. **Kids Say The Darndest Things**	Epic 10969
5/5/73	**32**	5	24. Let's Build A World Together (a)	Epic 10963
9/15/73	**1 (2)**	14	25. **We're Gonna Hold On** (a)	Epic 11031
1/12/74	**1 (2)**	12	26. **Another Lonely Song**	Epic 11079
3/9/74	**15**	8	27. (We're Not) The Jet Set (a)	Epic 11083
8/17/74	**8**	7	28. **We Loved It Away** (a)	Epic 11151
9/7/74	**4**	11	29. **Woman To Woman**	Epic 50008
3/8/75	**4**	12	30. **(You Make Me Want To Be) A Mother**	Epic 50071
6/21/75	**25**	5	31. God's Gonna Get'cha (For That) (a)	Epic 50099
10/18/75	**13**	8	32. I Still Believe In Fairy Tales	Epic 50145
2/28/76	**1 (1)**	11	33. **'Til I Can Make It On My Own**	Epic 50196
6/19/76	**1 (1)**	12	34. **Golden Ring** (a)	Epic 50235
9/4/76	**1 (2)**	12	35. **You And Me**	Epic 50264
12/25/76+	**1 (2)**	12	36. **Near You** (a) #1 Pop hit (17 weeks) for Francis Craig in 1947	Epic 50314
4/2/77	**6**	10	37. **(Let's Get Together) One Last Time**	Epic 50349
7/23/77	**5**	10	38. **Southern California** (a)	Epic 50418
10/15/77	**6**	10	39. **One Of A Kind**	Epic 50450
5/20/78	**26**	5	40. I'd Like To See Jesus (On The Midnight Special)	Epic 50538
7/29/78	**3**	10	41. **Womanhood**	Epic 50574
3/3/79	**6**	8	42. **They Call It Making Love**	Epic 50661
6/23/79	**7**	9	43. **No One Else In The World**	Epic 50722
3/8/80	**2 (1)**	11	44. **Two Story House** (a)	Epic 50849
5/17/80	**17**	8	45. He Was There (When I Needed You)	Epic 50868
8/30/80	**17**	7	46. Starting Over all of above produced by Billy Sherrill	Epic 50915
9/27/80	**19**	5	47. A Pair Of Old Sneakers (a)	Epic 50930
4/11/81	**21**	6	48. Cowboys Don't Shoot Straight (Like They Used To)	Epic 51011
10/3/81	**18**	6	49. Crying In The Rain #6 Pop hit for The Everly Brothers in 1962	Epic 02439
4/17/82	**8**	11	50. **Another Chance**	Epic 02770
9/11/82	**16**	8	51. You Still Get To Me In My Dreams	Epic 03064
1/15/83	**19**	6	52. A Good Night's Love	Epic 03384
7/14/84	**40**	1	53. Lonely Heart	Epic 04467
3/23/85	**6**	12	54. **Sometimes When We Touch** **MARK GRAY and TAMMY WYNETTE** #3 Pop hit for Dan Hill in 1978	Columbia 04782
9/5/87	**12**	10	55. Your Love Ricky Skaggs (harmony vocal)	Epic 07226
1/9/88	**16**	10	56. Talkin' To Myself Again The O'Kanes (harmony vocals)	Epic 07635

DATE	POS	WKS	ARTIST–RECORD TITLE	LABEL & NO.
6/4/88	**25**	6	57. Beneath A Painted Sky Emmylou Harris (harmony vocal)	Epic 07788

WYNONNA—see JUDD, Wynonna

Y

YANKOVIC, Frankie, & His Yanks

Born on 7/28/15 in Davis, West Virginia; raised in Cleveland. Accordionist/polka band leader. First recorded with the Slovene Folk Orchestra in 1932 on his own Yankee label. Member of the International Polka Hall of Fame.

DATE	POS	WKS	ARTIST–RECORD TITLE	LABEL & NO.
5/8/48	**7**	1	1. **Just Because**	Columbia 12359
1/1/49	**13**	1	2. The Iron Range [I] Best Seller #13	Columbia 12381
4/30/49	**7**	7	● 3. **Blue Skirt Waltz** **FRANKIE YANKOVIC & HIS YANKS** with **THE MARLIN SISTERS** Best Seller #7 / Juke Box #10	Columbia 12394

YARBROUGH, Bob

Born in Chattanooga, Tennessee, in 1940.

DATE	POS	WKS	ARTIST–RECORD TITLE	LABEL & NO.
7/10/71	**38**	2	1. You're Just More A Woman	Sugar Hill 013

YEARWOOD, Trisha

Born on 9/19/64 in Monticello, Georgia. Backing singer on Garth Brooks's first album. Married Robert Reynolds of The Mavericks on 5/21/94.

DATE	POS	WKS	ARTIST–RECORD TITLE	LABEL & NO.
6/15/91	**1 (2)**	16	1. **She's In Love With The Boy**	MCA 54076
9/28/91	**4**	15	2. **Like We Never Had A Broken Heart** co-written by Garth Brooks	MCA 54172
1/11/92	**8**	14	3. **That's What I Like About You**	MCA 54270
4/18/92	**4**	16	4. **The Woman Before Me**	MCA 54362
8/15/92	**5**	13	5. **Wrong Side Of Memphis**	MCA 54414
11/21/92+	**2 (1)**	17	6. **Walkaway Joe** **TRISHA YEARWOOD** with **Don Henley**	MCA 54495
3/20/93	**12**	10	7. You Say You Will	MCA 54600
7/3/93	**19**	9	8. Down On My Knees	MCA 54670
10/30/93	**2 (1)**	16	9. **The Song Remembers When**	MCA 54734
2/26/94	**21**	10	10. Better Your Heart Than Mine	MCA 54786
7/30/94	**1 (2)**	17	11. **XXX's And OOO's (An American Girl)**	MCA 54898
1/28/95	**1 (2)**	18	12. **Thinkin' About You**	MCA 54973
5/20/95	**23**	9	13. You Can Sleep While I Drive written by Melissa Etheridge	MCA 55025
8/26/95	**9**	14	14. **I Wanna Go Too Far**	MCA 55078

DATE	POS	WKS	ARTIST– RECORD TITLE	LABEL & NO.
			## YOAKAM, Dwight	
			Born on 10/23/56 in Pikesville, Kentucky. Singer/songwriter. Played in southern Ohio before moving to Los Angeles in the early '80s. First recorded for Oak Records. Member of the Buzzin' Cousins, group that appeared in the 1992 movie *Falling From Grace*. In Spring 1993, had the lead in the play *Southern Rapture*, directed by Peter Fonda in Los Angeles.	
4/5/86	3	13	1. **Honky Tonk Man**	Reprise 28793
7/19/86	4	14	2. **Guitars, Cadillacs**	Reprise 28688
12/13/86	31	6	3. It Won't Hurt	Reprise 28565
4/18/87	7	12	4. **Little Sister**	Reprise 28432
			#5 Pop hit for Elvis Presley in 1961	
8/15/87	8	11	5. **Little Ways**	Reprise 28310
12/5/87+	6	13	6. **Please, Please Baby**	Reprise 28174
3/19/88	9	11	7. **Always Late With Your Kisses**	Reprise 27994
7/23/88	1 (1)	14	8. **Streets Of Bakersfield**	Reprise 27964
			DWIGHT YOAKAM & BUCK OWENS	
11/26/88+	1 (1)	16	9. **I Sang Dixie**	Reprise 27715
3/25/89	5	13	10. **I Got You**	Reprise 27567
10/14/89	35	4	11. Long White Cadillac	Reprise 22799
12/1/90+	11	11	12. Turn It On, Turn It Up, Turn Me Loose	Reprise 19543
3/30/91	5	16	13. **You're The One**	Reprise 19405
8/31/91	15	13	14. Nothing's Changed Here	Reprise 19256
1/25/92	7	15	15. **It Only Hurts When I Cry**	Reprise 19148
5/30/92	18	11	16. The Heart That You Own	Reprise 18966
12/5/92	35	2	17. Suspicious Minds	Epic Snd. 74753
			#1 Pop hit for Elvis Presley in 1969; from the movie *Honeymoon In Vegas* starring James Caan	
3/27/93	2 (3)	18	18. **Ain't That Lonely Yet**	Reprise 18590
7/17/93	2 (1)	17	19. **A Thousand Miles From Nowhere**	Reprise 18528
10/30/93+	2 (1)	14	20. **Fast As You**	Reprise 18341
3/19/94	14	10	21. Try Not To Look So Pretty	Reprise 18239
7/23/94	22	10	22. Pocket Of A Clown	Reprise LP Cut
			above 5 from the album *This Time* on Reprise 45241	
11/4/95	20	10	23. Nothing	Reprise 17734
			## YOUNG, Faron	
			Born on 2/25/32 in Shreveport, Louisiana. Worked with Webb Pierce on the *Louisiana Hayride* in 1951. First recorded with Tillman Franks & His Rainbow Boys for Gotham in 1951. Went solo in 1952. Appeared in the 1956 movie *Hidden Guns* and got his nickname, "The Young Sheriff," and band name, "His Country Deputies," from that movie. Other movies include *Stampede*, *Daniel Boone, Raiders Of Old California* and *That's Country*. Founder and one-time publisher of the *Music City News* in Nashville.	
1/10/53	2 (1)	18	1. **Goin' Steady**	Capitol 2299
			Jockey #2 / Juke Box #7 / Best Seller #10	
6/6/53	5	5	2. **I Can't Wait (For The Sun To Go Down)**	Capitol 2461
			Jockey #5	
9/4/54	8	9	3. **A Place For Girls Like You**	Capitol 2859
			Jockey #8 / Best Seller #13	
11/20/54+	2 (3)	27	4. **If You Ain't Lovin'**	Capitol 2953
			Juke Box #2 / Jockey #2 / Best Seller #3	

DATE	POS	WKS	ARTIST—RECORD TITLE	LABEL & NO.
4/2/55	1 (3)	22	5. **Live Fast, Love Hard, Die Young/** Jockey #1 / Juke Box #2 / Best Seller #3	
		12	6. Forgive Me, Dear Juke Box flip	Capitol 3056
8/13/55	2 (4)	28	7. **All Right/** Jockey #2 / Juke Box #3 / Best Seller #4	
8/6/55	11	9	8. Go Back You Fool Best Seller #11	Capitol 3169
11/19/55+	5	13	9. **It's A Great Life (If You Don't Weaken)/** Jockey #5 / Juke Box #6 / Best Seller #7	
		1	10. For The Love Of A Woman Like You Juke Box flip	Capitol 3258
4/14/56	3	10	11. **You're Still Mine/** Jockey #3 / Best Seller #5	
4/7/56	4	16	12. **I've Got Five Dollars And It's Saturday Night** Best Seller #4 / Juke Box #4 / Jockey #10	Capitol 3369
6/23/56	2 (1)	33	13. **Sweet Dreams/** Jockey #2 / Juke Box #4 / Best Seller #5	
		3	14. Until I Met You Juke Box flip	Capitol 3443
11/10/56	9	6	15. **Turn Her Down/** Jockey #9 / Best Seller #13	
		1	16. I'll Be Satisfied With Love Best Seller flip	Capitol 3549
2/23/57	5	13	17. **I Miss You Already (And You're Not Even Gone)/** Jockey #5 / Best Seller #8	
		1	18. I'm Gonna Live Some Before I Die Best Seller flip	Capitol 3611
5/20/57	15	1	19. The Shrine Of St. Cecilia Jockey #15	Capitol 3696
8/5/57	12	1	20. Love Has Finally Come My Way Jockey #12	Capitol 3753
6/23/58	1 (13)	29	21. **Alone With You/** Jockey #1 / Best Seller #2	
6/30/58	10	2	22. **Every Time I'm Kissing You** Jockey #10	Capitol 3982
10/20/58	9	17	23. **That's The Way I Feel/**	
10/27/58	22	5	24. I Hate Myself	Capitol 4050
2/2/59	16	9	25. A Long Time Ago/	
1/26/59	20	10	26. Last Night At A Party	Capitol 4113
4/13/59	14	8	27. That's The Way It's Gotta Be	Capitol 4164
7/20/59	1 (4)	32	28. **Country Girl/**	
7/27/59	27	6	29. I Hear You Talkin'	Capitol 4233
11/16/59+	4	21	30. **Riverboat/**	
11/16/59+	10	18	31. **Face To The Wall**	Capitol 4291
4/11/60	5	17	32. **Your Old Used To Be**	Capitol 4351
10/24/60	21	5	33. There's Not Any Like You Left	Capitol 4410
12/26/60+	20	7	34. Forget The Past/	
1/16/61	28	3	35. A World So Full Of Love	Capitol 4463
3/20/61	1 (9)	23	36. **Hello Walls/**	
5/15/61	28	2	37. Congratulations above 2 written by Willie Nelson	Capitol 4533

DATE	POS	WKS	ARTIST– RECORD TITLE	LABEL & NO.
10/2/61	8	17	38. **Backtrack**	Capitol 4616
3/24/62	7	13	39. **Three Days**	Capitol 4696
6/16/62	4	19	40. **The Comeback**	Capitol 4754
12/22/62+	9	10	41. **Down By The River**	Capitol 4868
3/2/63	4	16	42. **The Yellow Bandana**	Mercury 72085
6/8/63	14	7	43. Nightmare/	
6/1/63	30	1	44. I've Come To Say Goodbye	Mercury 72114
10/26/63	13	7	45. We've Got Something In Common	Mercury 72167
12/21/63+	10	12	46. **You'll Drive Me Back (Into Her Arms Again)**	Mercury 72201
3/21/64	5	22	47. **Keeping Up With The Joneses/**	
4/4/64	40	1	48. No Thanks, I Just Had One	Mercury 72237
8/8/64	23	5	49. Rhinestones	Mercury 72271
10/17/64	11	14	50. My Friend On The Right	Mercury 72313
12/26/64	38	2	51. Another Woman's Man Another Man's Woman	Mercury 72312
			FARON YOUNG & MARGIE SINGLETON (#47, 48, 51)	
2/6/65	10	16	52. **Walk Tall**	Mercury 72375
8/14/65	34	3	53. Nothing Left To Lose	Mercury 72440
12/11/65+	14	11	54. My Dreams	Mercury 72490
11/5/66	7	13	55. **Unmitigated Gall**	Mercury 72617
11/18/67+	14	13	56. Wonderful World Of Women	Mercury 72728
3/30/68	14	13	57. She Went A Little Bit Farther	Mercury 72774
8/24/68	8	13	58. **I Just Came To Get My Baby**	Mercury 72827
4/5/69	25	7	59. I've Got Precious Memories	Mercury 72889
7/26/69	2 (2)	14	60. **Wine Me Up**	Mercury 72936
11/8/69	4	13	61. **Your Time's Comin'**	Mercury 72983
2/14/70	6	12	62. **Occasional Wife**	Mercury 73018
6/13/70	4	12	63. **If I Ever Fall In Love (With A Honky Tonk Girl)**	Mercury 73065
10/17/70	5	11	64. **Goin' Steady** [R]	Mercury 73112
4/10/71	6	14	65. **Step Aside**	Mercury 73191
8/14/71	9	12	66. **Leavin' And Sayin' Goodbye**	Mercury 73220
12/25/71+	1 (2)	16	67. **It's Four In The Morning**	Mercury 73250
7/29/72	5	15	68. **This Little Girl Of Mine**	Mercury 73308
2/24/73	15	8	69. She Fights That Lovin' Feeling	Mercury 73359
8/18/73	9	11	70. **Just What I Had In Mind**	Mercury 73403
3/30/74	8	10	71. **Some Kind Of A Woman**	Mercury 73464
8/17/74	20	5	72. The Wrong In Loving You	Mercury 73500
12/28/74+	23	7	73. Another You	Mercury 73633
8/23/75	16	7	74. Here I Am In Dallas	Mercury 73692
1/3/76	21	8	75. Feel Again	Mercury 73731
5/15/76	33	4	76. I'd Just Be Fool Enough	Mercury 73782
11/6/76	30	5	77. (The Worst You Ever Gave Me Was) The Best I Ever Had	Mercury 73847
8/6/77	25	4	78. Crutches	Mercury 73925
4/8/78	38	1	79. Loving Here And Living There And Lying In Between	Mercury 55019

YOUNG, Neil

Born on 11/12/45 in Toronto. Rock singer/songwriter/guitarist.

11/9/85	33	5	1. Get Back To The Country	Geffen 28883

DATE	POS	WKS	ARTIST–RECORD TITLE	LABEL & NO.
			YOUNGER BROTHERS	
7/31/82	**19**	9	James and Michael Williams from Edinburg, Texas. Changed named to James & Michael Younger to avoid conflict with a band from Leola, Pennsylvania. 1. Nothing But The Radio On	MCA 52076
			Z	
			ZACA CREEK	
10/28/89	**38**	1	Quartet of brothers: Gates (vocals), Scot (guitar), Jeff (keyboards) and James (bass) Foss. Zaca Creek is an underground stream in their hometown of Santa Ynez, California. 1. Sometimes Love's Not A Pretty Thing	Columbia 69062

Randy Travis became a hit-making dynamo in the mid-'80s. The former Randy Bruce Traywick issued three No. 1 singles in 1987, of which "Too Gone Too Long" was the third.

Justin Tubb, son of Country legend Ernest Tubb, reached the charts seven times on his own. "Take A Letter, Miss Gray," issued on RCA-distributed Groove Records, reached No. 6 in 1963.

Tanya Tucker's lengthy residency in the charts—which began with 1971's No. 6 hit "Delta Dawn"—is all the more remarkable considering her relative youth. Born in 1958, the colorful star enjoyed her 38th hit with 1987's No. 2 smash "Love Me Like You Used To."

Conway Twitty's 1982 hit "The Clown" was his first for Elektra. It reached No. 1—his 28th solo chart-topper overall—as did its immediate predecessor on MCA, "Red Neckin' Love Makin' Night."

Billy Walker, nicknamed "The Tall Texan," scored 65 chart hits between 1954 and 1980. "Heart, Be Careful" came a year after his first No. 1 hit, 1962's "Charlie's Shoes."

Steve Wariner's six-year stretch at RCA—successful by any standard—ended in 1984. The same year, the Indiana-born singer-songwriter signed to MCA and soon reached No. 3 with "What I Didn't Do."

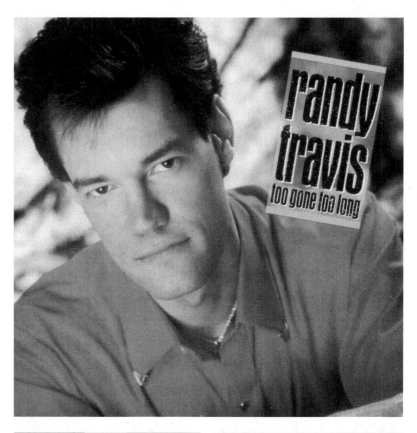

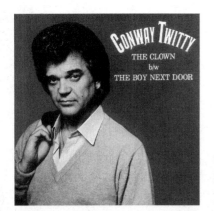

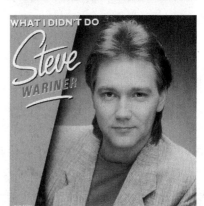

Dottie West's "Are You Happy Baby?," the second No. 1 of her career, was the singer's first release on Liberty Records—due to the name-change of her former label, United Artists, in 1980.

Don Williams, one-time founder of '60s act the Pozo-Seco Singers, enjoyed a long streak of Top 10 singles beginning with 1974's "We Should Be Together." 1987's "I Wouldn't Be A Man," which reached No. 9, was his 36th.

Hank Williams, universally regarded as the finest of all Country songwriters, not only reached the top of the charts with 1953's "Your Cheatin' Heart"—the classic song lent its title to the 1964 film adaptation of Williams's life, which starred actor George Hamilton and featured the singing of Hank, Jr.

Hank Williams, Jr.'s 1988 take on Civil War possibilities—"If The South Woulda Won"—became the 75th charting solo hit of Bocephus's lengthy and distinguished career.

Dwight Yoakam's "Always Late With Your Kisses," a No. 9 hit in 1988, was immediately followed by the Kentucky-born singer's first No. 1 smash "Streets Of Bakersfield"—a duet with no less a Bakersfield sensation than Buck Owens.

Faron Young's massive string of hits took him to the Top 10 42 times, beginning with 1953's "Goin' Steady" and extending through 1964's "Keeping Up With The Joneses," recorded with Margie Singleton. "Three Days" zoomed to No. 7 in 1962.

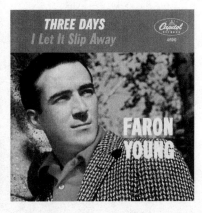

THE SONGS

Lists, alphabetically, all titles in the artist section. The artist's name is listed next to each title along with the highest position attained and year of peak popularity. Some titles show the letter F as a position, indicating the title was listed as a flip side and did not chart on its own.

A song with more than one charted version is listed once, with the artists' names listed below the title in chronological order. Songs that have the same title but are different tunes are listed separately, with the most popular title listed first. This will make it easy to determine which songs are the same composition, the number of charted versions of a particular song, and which of these are the most popular.

Cross references have been used throughout to aid in finding a title.

Please keep the following in mind when searching for titles:

Titles such a "I.O.U.," "J.R.," and "S.O.S." will be found at the beginning of their respective letters; however, titles such as "T-R-O-U-B-L-E," and "C-H-R-I-S-T-M-A-S," which are spellings of words, are listed with their regular spellings.

Titles are alphabetized word by word, rather than letter by letter, so "Blue Train" precedes "Bluebird," "Can You" precedes "Candy," and so on.

Titles that are identical except for an apostrophized word in one of the titles, are shown together. ("Lovin'" appears immediately above "Loving.")

POS/YR	RECORD TITLE/ARTIST

A

POS/YR	RECORD TITLE/ARTIST
26/65	A-11...Johnny Paycheck
	Abilene
1/63	George Hamilton IV
24/77	Sonny James
	Above And Beyond
3/60	Buck Owens
1/89	Rodney Crowell
16/81	**Acapulco**...Johnny Duncan
16/60	**Accidently On Purpose**...George Jones
4/56	**According To My Heart**...Jim Reeves
1/89	**Ace In The Hole**...George Strait
9/92	**Aces**...Suzy Bogguss
5/62	**Aching, Breaking Heart**...George Jones
1/92	**Achy Breaky Heart**...Billy Ray Cyrus
	Act Naturally
1/63	Buck Owens
27/89	Buck Owens & Ringo Starr
3/95	**Adalida**...George Strait
1/88	**Addicted**...Dan Seals
4/94	**Addicted To A Dollar**...Doug Stone
2/62	**Adios Amigo**...Jim Reeves
4/77	**Adios Amigo**...Marty Robbins
14/49	**Afraid**...Rex Allen with Jerry Byrd
22/73	**Afraid I'll Want To Love Her One More Time**...Billy "Crash" Craddock
	Afraid Of Losing You Again ..see: (I'm So)
4/84	**After All**...Ed Bruce
1/76	**After All The Good Is Gone**...Conway Twitty
	(After All These Years) ..see: I Still Love You
18/71	**After All They All Used To Belong To Me**...Hank Williams, Jr.
1/89	**After All This Time**...Rodney Crowell
6/70	**After Closing Time**...David Houston & Barbara Mandrell
17/80	**After Hours**...Joe Stampley
7/62	**After Loving You**...Eddy Arnold
10/77	**(After Sweet Memories) Play Born To Lose Again**...Dottsy
32/77	**After The Ball**...Johnny Cash
	After The Fire Is Gone
1/71	Conway Twitty & Loretta Lynn
17/74	Willie Nelson & Tracy Nelson
19/83	**After The Great Depression**...Razzy Bailey
10/83	**After The Last Goodbye**...Gus Hardin

POS/YR	RECORD TITLE/ARTIST
13/92	**After The Lights Go Out**...Ricky Van Shelton
16/82	**After The Love Slips Away**...Earl Thomas Conley
40/77	**After The Lovin'**...Engelbert Humperdinck
8/76	**After The Storm**...Wynn Stewart
22/71	**After You**...Jerry Wallace
23/73	**After You**...Hank Williams, Jr.
28/83	**After You**...Dan Seals
9/76	**Afternoon Delight**...Johnny Carver
19/65	**Again**...Don Gibson
36/80	**Age**...Jerry Reed
20/68	**Age Of Worry**...Billy Walker
21/77	**Agree To Disagree**...Little David Wilkins
1/93	**Ain't Going Down (Til The Sun Comes Up)**...Garth Brooks
23/63	**Ain't Got Time For Nothin'**...Bob Gallion
19/68	**Ain't Got Time To Be Unhappy**...Bob Luman
2/66	**Ain't Had No Lovin'**...Connie Smith
23/58	**Ain't I The Lucky One**...Marty Robbins
15/72	**Ain't It All Worth Living For**...Tompall/Glaser Brothers
14/73	**Ain't It Amazing, Gracie**...Buck Owens
35/73	**Ain't It Good (To Feel This Way)**...Norro Wilson
10/74	**Ain't Love A Good Thing**...Connie Smith
1/86	**Ain't Misbehavin'**...Hank Williams, Jr.
17/90	**Ain't Necessarily So**...Willie Nelson
4/78	**Ain't No California**...Mel Tillis
4/82	**Ain't No Money**...Rosanne Cash
7/83	**Ain't No Trick (It Takes Magic)**...Lee Greenwood
15/90	**Ain't Nobody's Business**...Hank Williams, Jr.
5/50	**Ain't Nobody's Business But My Own**...Kay Starr & Tennessee Ernie
10/72	**Ain't Nothin' Shakin' (But the Leaves on the Trees)**...Billy "Crash" Craddock
1/85	**Ain't She Somethin' Else**...Conway Twitty
7/72	**Ain't That A Shame**...Hank Williams, Jr.
2/93	**Ain't That Lonely Yet**...Dwight Yoakam
11/62	**Air Mail To Heaven**...Carl Smith
37/83	**Air That I Breathe**...Rex Allen, Jr.
1/60	**Alabam**...Cowboy Copas
3/51	**Alabama Jubilee**...Red Foley
22/72	**Alabama Wild Man**...Jerry Reed
1/93	**Alibis**...Tracy Lawrence
16/79	**Alibis**...Johnny Rodriguez

POS/YR	RECORD TITLE/ARTIST
20/81	**Alice Doesn't Love Here Anymore**...Bobby Goldsboro
18/75	**Alimony**...Bobby Bare
34/88	**Alive And Well**...Gatlin Bros.
7/46	**All Alone In This World Without You**...Eddy Arnold
21/59	**All-American Boy**...Grandpa Jones
31/75	**All American Girl**...Statler Brothers
37/70	**All American Husband**...Peggy Sue
23/75	**All-American Man**...Johnny Paycheck
16/79	**All Around Cowboy**...Marty Robbins
39/86	**All Because Of You**...Marty Stuart
9/69	**All For The Love Of A Girl**...Claude King
1/70	**All For The Love Of Sunshine**...Hank Williams, Jr.
	All Grown Up
8/58	Johnny Horton
26/63	Johnny Horton
35/72	**All Heaven Breaks Loose**...David Rogers
2/72	**All His Children**...Charley Pride/Henry Mancini
29/91	**All I Can Be (Is A Sweet Memory)**...Collin Raye
3/76	**All I Can Do**...Dolly Parton
	All I Ever Need Is You
18/71	Ray Sanders
1/79	Kenny Rogers & Dottie West
	All I Have To Do Is Dream
1/58	Everly Brothers
6/70	Bobbie Gentry & Glen Campbell
1/69	**All I Have To Offer You (Is Me)**...Charley Pride
11/49	**All I Need Is Some More Lovin'**...George Morgan
8/95	**All I Need To Know**...Kenny Chesney
21/79	**All I Want And Need Forever**...Vern Gosdin
5/96	**All I Want Is A Life**...Tim McGraw
30/82	**All I'm Missing Is You**...Eddy Arnold
13/73	**All In The Name Of Love**...Narvel Felts
11/92	**All Is Fair In Love And War**...Ronnie Milsap
1/87	**All My Ex's Live In Texas**...George Strait
9/70	**All My Hard Times**...Roy Drusky
13/83	**All My Life**...Kenny Rogers
23/67	**All My Love**...Don Gibson
10/84	**All My Rowdy Friends Are Coming Over Tonight**...Hank Williams, Jr.
1/81	**All My Rowdy Friends (Have Settled Down)**...Hank Williams, Jr.
27/67	**All My Tomorrows**...Nat Stuckey

POS/YR	RECORD TITLE/ARTIST
40/81	**All Night Long**...Johnny Duncan
	All Of ..also see: Alla
3/78	**All Of Me**...Willie Nelson
28/67	**All Of Me Belongs To You**...Dick Curless
26/88	**All Of This & More**...Crystal Gayle/Gary Morris
4/58	**All Over Again**...Johnny Cash
4/75	**All Over Me**...Charlie Rich
2/55	**All Right**...Faron Young
26/68	**All Right (I'll Sign The Papers)**...Mel Tillis
1/81	**All Roads Lead To You**...Steve Wariner
1/57	**All Shook Up**...Elvis Presley
8/85	**All Tangled Up In Love**...Gus Hardin with Earl Thomas Conley
27/77	**All That Keeps Me Going**...Jim Weatherly
33/70	**All That Keeps Ya Goin'**...Tompall/Glaser Brothers
5/89	**All The Fun**...Paul Overstreet
1/79	**All The Gold In California**...Larry Gatlin & The Gatlin Brothers Band
20/76	**All The King's Horses**...Lynn Anderson
5/72	**All The Lonely Women In The World**...Bill Anderson
5/89	**All The Reasons Why**...Highway 101
39/77	**All The Sweet**...Mel McDaniel
	All The Time
18/59	Kitty Wells
1/67	Jack Greene
(also see: I Need You)	
1/76	**All These Things**...Joe Stampley
3/93	**All These Years**...Sawyer Brown
6/86	**All Tied Up**...Ronnie McDowell
F/73	**(All Together Now) Let's Fall Apart**...Ronnie Milsap
13/96	**All You Ever Do Is Bring Me Down**...Mavericks
5/62	**Alla My Love**...Webb Pierce
22/62	**Alligator Man**...Jimmy Newman
2/52	**Almost**...George Morgan
11/96	**Almost A Memory Now**...BlackHawk
20/83	**Almost Called Her Baby By Mistake**...Gatlin Bros.
1/93	**Almost Goodbye**...Mark Chesnutt
	Almost Persuaded
1/66	David Houston
6/66	Ben Colder (No. 2)
1/58	**Alone With You**...Faron Young
1/68	**Already It's Heaven**...David Houston
5/93	**Alright Already**...Larry Stewart

POS/YR	RECORD TITLE/ARTIST
18/80	**Always**...Patsy Cline
16/69	**Always, Always**...Porter Wagoner & Dolly Parton
	(Always And Forever) ..see: I Won't Need You Anymore
1/86	**Always Have Always Will**...Janie Fricke
40/96	**Always Have, Always Will**...Shenandoah
	Always Late (With Your Kisses)
1/51	Lefty Frizzell
9/88	Dwight Yoakam
37/78	**Always Lovin Her Man**...Dale McBride
	Always On My Mind
16/73	Elvis Presley
20/79	John Wesley Ryles
1/82	Willie Nelson
6/71	**Always Remember**...Bill Anderson
1/75	**Always Wanting You**...Merle Haggard
1/87	**Am I Blue**...George Strait
27/88	**Am I Crazy?**...Statler Brothers
	Am I Losing You
3/57	Jim Reeves
8/60	Jim Reeves
1/81	Ronnie Milsap
	Am I That Easy To Forget
9/59	Carl Belew
11/60	Skeeter Davis
12/73	Jim Reeves
	Amanda
33/73	Don Williams
1/79	Waylon Jennings
	Amarillo By Morning
31/74	Terry Stafford
4/83	George Strait
9/76	**Amazing Grace (Used To Be Her Favorite Song)**...Amazing Rhythm Aces
1/73	**Amazing Love**...Charley Pride
36/85	**Amber Waves Of Grain**...Merle Haggard
30/77	**Ambush**...Ronnie Sessions
6/84	**America**...Waylon Jennings
22/76	**America The Beautiful**...Charlie Rich
11/90	**American Boy**...Eddie Rabbitt
5/82	**American Dream**...Hank Williams, Jr.
4/89	**American Family**...Oak Ridge Boys
1/93	**American Honky-Tonk Bar Association**...Garth Brooks
1/83	**American Made**...Oak Ridge Boys
16/87	**American Me**...Schuyler, Knobloch & Overstreet
8/88	**Americana**...Moe Bandy
35/74	**Americans**...Tex Ritter
5/60	**Amigo's Guitar**...Kitty Wells

POS/YR	RECORD TITLE/ARTIST
1/76	**Among My Souvenirs**...Marty Robbins
16/70	**Amos Moses**...Jerry Reed
4/95	**Amy's Back In Austin**...Little Texas
28/90	**Amy's Eyes**...Charley Pride
14/89	**And So It Goes**...John Denver & The Nitty Gritty Dirt Band
2/95	**And Still**...Reba McEntire
1/81	**Angel Flying Too Close To The Ground**...Willie Nelson
1/84	**Angel In Disguise**...Earl Thomas Conley
8/85	**Angel In Your Arms**...Barbara Mandrell
	Angel Of The Morning
34/70	Connie Eaton
22/78	Melba Montgomery
22/81	Juice Newton
34/64	**Angel On Leave**...Jimmy "C" Newman
33/88	**(Angel On My Mind) That's Why I'm Walkin'**...Ricky Skaggs
13/71	**Angel's Sunday**...Jim Ed Brown
32/81	**Angela**...Mundo Earwood
28/94	**Angels Among Us**...Alabama
19/74	**Angels Are Hard To Find**...Hank Williams, Jr.
4/70	**Angels Don't Lie**...Jim Reeves
9/76	**Angels, Roses, And Rain**...Dickey Lee
16/68	**Angry Words**...Stonewall Jackson
17/66	**Anita, You're Dreaming**...Waylon Jennings
2/72	**Ann (Don't Go Runnin')**...Tommy Overstreet
28/68	**Anna, I'm Taking You Home**...Leon Ashley
3/58	**Anna Marie**...Jim Reeves
40/65	**Anne Of A Thousand Days**...Leroy Van Dyke
13/55	**Annie Over**...Hank Thompson
9/74	**Annie's Song**...John Denver
2/60	**Another**...Roy Drusky
28/63	**Another Bridge To Burn**..."Little" Jimmy Dickens
8/82	**Another Chance**...Tammy Wynette
27/62	**Another Day, Another Dollar**...Wynn Stewart
25/69	**Another Day, Another Mile, Another Highway**...Clay Hart
25/79	**Another Easy Lovin' Night**...Randy Barlow
21/78	**Another Fine Mess**...Glen Campbell
28/63	**Another Fool Like Me**...Ned Miller
10/78	**Another Goodbye**...Donna Fargo
31/74	**Another Goodbye Song**...Rex Allen, Jr.
8/82	**Another Honky-Tonk Night On Broadway**...David Frizzell & Shelly West

POS/YR	RECORD TITLE/ARTIST
12/70	**Another Lonely Night**...Jean Shepard
1/74	**Another Lonely Song**...Tammy Wynette
24/76	**Another Morning**...Jim Ed Brown
10/84	**Another Motel Memory**...Shelly West
5/71	**Another Night Of Love**...Freddy Weller
4/68	**Another Place Another Time**...Jerry Lee Lewis
5/88	**Another Place, Another Time**...Don Williams
27/72	**Another Puff**...Jerry Reed
4/82	**Another Sleepless Night**...Anne Murray
	Another Somebody Done Somebody Wrong Song ..see: (Hey Won't You Play)
16/66	**Another Story**...Ernest Tubb
34/80	**Another Texas Song**...Eddy Raven
14/75	**Another Woman**...T.G. Sheppard
38/64	**Another Woman's Man Another Man's Woman**...Faron Young & Margie Singleton
4/87	**Another World**...Crystal Gayle & Gary Morris
23/75	**Another You**...Faron Young
3/49	**Anticipation Blues**...Tennessee Ernie Ford
	Any Day Now
26/79	Don Gibson
1/82	Ronnie Milsap
1/95	**Any Man Of Mine**...Shania Twain
7/56	**Any Old Time**...Webb Pierce
32/67	**Any Old Way You Do**...Jan Howard
3/73	**Any Old Wind That Blows**...Johnny Cash
4/89	**Any Way The Wind Blows**...Southern Pacific
33/81	**Any Way You Want Me**...Gene Watson
10/81	**Any Which Way You Can**...Glen Campbell
17/83	**Anybody Else's Heart But Mine**...Terri Gibbs
13/59	**Anybody's Girl**...Hank Thompson
1/91	**Anymore**...Travis Tritt
3/60	**Anymore**...Roy Drusky
27/87	**Anyone Can Do The Heartbreak**...Anne Murray
2/78	**Anyone Who Isn't Me Tonight**...Kenny Rogers & Dottie West
12/77	**Anything But Leavin'**...Larry Gatlin
25/81	**Anything But Yes Is Still A No**...Stephanie Winslow
28/86	**Anything Goes**...Gary Morris
12/68	**Anything Leaving Town Today**...Dave Dudley
22/63	**Anything New Gets Old (Except My Love For You)**...Don Gibson

POS/YR	RECORD TITLE/ARTIST
10/67	**Anything Your Heart Desires**...Billy Walker
38/72	**Anything's Better Than Nothing**...Mel Tillis & Sherry Bryce
	Anytime
1/48	Eddy Arnold
14/48	Foy Willing
13/71	**Anyway**...George Hamilton IV
F/56	**Anyway You Want Me (That's How I Will Be)**...Elvis Presley
10/93	**Anywhere But Here**...Sammy Kershaw
F/81	**Anywhere There's A Jukebox**...Razzy Bailey
13/62	**Anywhere There's People**...Lawton Williams
21/66	**Apartment #9**...Bobby Austin
14/69	**April's Fool**...Ray Price
2/82	**Are The Good Times Really Over**...Merle Haggard
26/81	**Are We Dreamin' The Same Dream**...Charlie Rich
1/89	**Are You Ever Gonna Love Me**...Holly Dunn
11/69	**Are You From Dixie (Cause I'm From Dixie Too)**...Jerry Reed
1/81	**Are You Happy Baby?**...Dottie West
22/61	**Are You Lonesome To-night?**...Elvis Presley
3/91	**Are You Lovin' Me Like I'm Lovin' You**...Ronnie Milsap
	Are You Mine
2/55	Ginny Wright/Tom Tall
6/55	Myrna Lorrie-Buddy DeVal
14/55	Red Sovine - Goldie Hill
1/80	**Are You On The Road To Lovin' Me Again**...Debby Boone
7/77	**Are You Ready For The Country**...Waylon Jennings
13/58	**Are You Really Mine**...Jimmie Rodgers
32/87	**Are You Satisfied**...Janie Fricke
10/79	**Are You Sincere**...Elvis Presley
20/87	**Are You Still In Love With Me**...Anne Murray
1/75	**Are You Sure Hank Done It This Way**...Waylon Jennings
1/52	**Are You Teasing Me**...Carl Smith
12/60	**Are You Willing, Willie**...Marion Worth
19/86	**Arlene**...Marty Stuart
27/73	**Arms Full Of Empty**...Buck Owens
4/71	**Arms Of A Fool**...Mel Tillis
	Around ..see: 'Round
	Around My Heart ..see: (You Sure Know Your Way)
8/65	**Artificial Rose**...Jimmy Newman
2/95	**As Any Fool Can See**...Tracy Lawrence

POS/YR	RECORD TITLE/ARTIST
8/54	**As Far As I'm Concerned**...Red Foley & Betty Foley
12/79	**As Long As I Can Wake Up In Your Arms**...Kenny O'Dell
3/55	**As Long As I Live**...Kitty Wells & Red Foley
3/68	**As Long As I Live**...George Jones
1/84	**As Long As I'm Rockin' With You**...John Conlee
30/66	**As Long As The Wind Blows**...Johnny Darrell
14/91	**As Simple As That**...Mike Reid
1/74	**As Soon As I Hang Up The Phone**...Conway Twitty & Loretta Lynn
	Ashes Of Love
37/68	Don Gibson
15/72	Dickey Lee
26/87	Desert Rose Band
19/82	**Ashes To Ashes**...Terri Gibbs
19/64	**Ask Marie**...Sonny James
27/92	**Asking Us To Dance**...Kathy Mattea
6/50	**A-Sleeping At The Foot Of The Bed**..."Little" Jimmy Dickens
13/66	**At Ease Heart**...Ernest Ashworth
	At Mail Call Today
1/45	Gene Autry
3/45	Lawrence Welk with Red Foley
24/78	**At The End Of A Rainbow**...Jerry Wallace
5/86	**At The Sound Of The Tone**...John Schneider
13/74	**At The Time**...Jean Shepard
3/84	**Atlanta Blue**...Statler Brothers
9/83	**Atlanta Burned Again Last Night**...Atlanta
36/68	**Atlanta Georgia Stray**...Sonny Curtis
6/46	**Atomic Power**...Buchanan Brothers
13/74	**Atta Way To Go**...Don Williams
5/84	**Attitude Adjustment**...Hank Williams, Jr.
9/57	**Auctioneer, The**...Leroy Van Dyke
15/68	**Autumn Of My Life**...Bobby Goldsboro

B

POS/YR	RECORD TITLE/ARTIST
3/84	**B-B-B-Burnin' Up With Love**...Eddie Rabbitt
1/64	**B.J. The D.J.**...Stonewall Jackson
7/66	**Baby**...Wilma Burgess
16/69	**Baby Again**...Hank Williams, Jr.
15/66	**Baby, Ain't That Fine**...Gene Pitney & Melba Montgomery
40/68	**Baby, Ain't That Love**...Jack Barlow

POS/YR	RECORD TITLE/ARTIST
1/70	**Baby, Baby (I Know You're A Lady)**...David Houston
1/88	**Baby Blue**...George Strait
3/76	**Baby Boy**...Mary Kay Place
1/85	**Baby Bye Bye**...Gary Morris
31/72	**Baby, Bye Bye**...Dickey Lee
5/47	**Baby Doll**...Sons Of The Pioneers
6/74	**Baby Doll**...Barbara Fairchild
26/72	**Baby Don't Get Hooked On Me**...Mac Davis
23/77	**Baby, Don't Keep Me Hangin' On**...Susie Allanson
4/83	**Baby I Lied**...Deborah Allen
15/77	**Baby, I Love You So**...Joe Stampley
31/70	**Baby, I Tried**...Jim Ed Brown
26/86	**Baby I Want It**...Girls Next Door
40/87	**Baby I Was Leaving Anyhow**...Billy Montana
35/80	**Baby, I'm A Want You**...Stephanie Winslow
33/83	**Baby I'm Gone**...Terri Gibbs
22/92	**Baby, I'm Missing You**...Highway 101
2/88	**Baby I'm Yours**...Steve Wariner
	Baby I'm Yours
5/71	Jody Miller
33/78	Debby Boone
22/83	Tanya Tucker
9/49	**Baby, It's Cold Outside**...Homer & Jethro/June Carter
21/78	**Baby It's You**...Janie Fricke
20/78	**Baby, Last Night Made My Day**...Susie Allanson
5/55	**Baby Let's Play House**...Elvis Presley
11/94	**Baby Likes To Rock It**...Tractors
27/79	**Baby My Baby**...Margo Smith
15/60	**Baby Rocked Her Dolly**...Frankie Miller
28/61	**Baby Sittin' Boogie**...Buzz Clifford
36/90	**Baby, Walk On**...Matraca Berg
4/52	**Baby, We're Really In Love**...Hank Williams
1/83	**Baby, What About You**...Crystal Gayle
22/77	**Baby, You Look Good To Me Tonight**...John Denver
7/80	**Baby, You're Something**...John Conlee
30/71	**Baby, You've Got What It Takes**...Charlie Louvin & Melba Montgomery
7/68	**Baby's Back Again**...Connie Smith
2/73	**Baby's Gone**...Conway Twitty
2/87	**Baby's Got A Hold On Me**...Nitty Gritty Dirt Band
1/87	**Baby's Got A New Baby**...S-K-O

POS/YR	RECORD TITLE/ARTIST
	Battle Of New Orleans
1/59	Johnny Horton
24/59	Jimmie Driftwood
1/89	**Bayou Boys**...Eddy Raven
12/63	**Bayou Talk**...Jimmy "C" Newman
11/71	**Be A Little Quieter**...Porter Wagoner
26/64	**Be Better To Your Baby**...Ernest Tubb
5/56	**Be-Bop-A-Lula**...Gene Vincent
37/69	**Be Careful Of Stones That You Throw**...Hank Williams, Jr.
5/69	**Be Glad**...Del Reeves
33/65	**Be Good To Her**...Carl Smith
15/72	**Be My Baby**...Jody Miller
1/94	**Be My Baby Tonight**...John Michael Montgomery
16/68	**Be Proud Of Your Man**...Porter Wagoner
	Be Quiet Mind
9/61	Del Reeves
23/64	Ott Stephens
10/82	**Be There For Me Baby**...Johnny Lee
36/78	**Be Your Own Best Friend**...Ray Stevens
1/96	**Beaches Of Cheyenne**...Garth Brooks
3/67	**Bear With Me A Little Longer**...Billy Walker
13/48	**Beaut From Butte**...Dick Thomas
5/51	**Beautiful Brown Eyes**...Jimmy Wakely & the Les Baxter Chorus
4/55	**Beautiful Lies**...Jean Shepard
10/78	**Beautiful Woman**...Charlie Rich
3/81	**Beautiful You**...Oak Ridge Boys
	Because ..also see: Cuzz
18/65	**Because I Cared**...Ernest Ashworth
28/66	**Because It's You**...Wanda Jackson
20/76	**Because You Believed In Me**...Gene Watson
9/71	**Bed Of Rose's**...Statler Brothers
4/87	**Bed You Made For Me**...Highway 101
24/80	**Bedroom, The**...Jim Ed Brown/Helen Cornelius
18/80	**Bedroom Ballad**...Gene Watson
18/78	**Bedroom Eyes**...Don Drumm
36/81	**Bedtime Stories**...Jim Chesnut
1/72	**Bedtime Story**...Tammy Wynette
21/93	**Beer And Bones**...John Michael Montgomery
22/69	**Beer Drinkin' Music**...Ray Sanders
6/56	**Before I Met You**...Carl Smith
4/64	**Before I'm Over You**...Loretta Lynn
2/79	**Before My Time**...John Conlee

POS/YR	RECORD TITLE/ARTIST
	Before The Next Teardrop Falls
33/70	Linda Martell
1/75	Freddy Fender
22/66	**Before The Ring On Your Finger Turns Green**...Dottie West
	Before This Day Ends
4/60	George Hamilton IV
23/61	Eddy Arnold
10/49	**Before You Call**...Dave Landers
1/65	**Before You Go**...Buck Owens
2/94	**Before You Kill Us All**...Randy Travis
5/61	**Beggar To A King**...Hank Snow
1/64	**Begging To You**...Marty Robbins
32/77	**Behind Blue Eyes**...Mundo Earwood
1/73	**Behind Closed Doors**...Charlie Rich
1/65	**Behind The Tear**...Sonny James
10/58	**Believe What You Say**...Ricky Nelson
4/65	**Belles Of Southern Bell**...Del Reeves
30/61	**Bells That Broke My Heart**...Slim Whitman
3/95	**Bend It Until It Breaks**...John Anderson
25/88	**Beneath A Painted Sky**...Tammy Wynette
1/80	**Beneath Still Waters**...Emmylou Harris
38/70	**Beneath Still Waters**...Diana Trask
16/62	**Best Dressed Beggar (In Town)**...Carl Smith
15/88	**Best I Know How**...Statler Brothers
29/72	**Best Is Yet To Come**...Del Reeves
39/93	**Best Mistakes I Ever Made**...Rick Vincent
27/60	**Best Of All My Heartaches**...Wilburn Brothers
6/80	**Best Of Strangers**...Barbara Mandrell
6/72	**Best Part Of Living**...Marty Robbins
7/75	**Best Way I Know How**...Mel Tillis
1/85	**Best Year Of My Life**...Eddie Rabbitt
15/59	**Best Years Of Your Life**...Carl Smith
1/81	**Bet Your Heart On Me**...Johnny Lee
2/92	**Better Class Of Losers**...Randy Travis
	Better Homes And Gardens
34/69	Bobby Russell
37/69	Billy Walker
4/89	**Better Love Next Time**...Merle Haggard
1/89	**Better Man**...Clint Black
20/78	**Better Me**...Tommy Overstreet
7/71	**Better Move It On Home**...Porter Wagoner & Dolly Parton
26/84	**Better Our Hearts Should Bend (Than Break)**...Bandana
	Better Than I Did Then ..see: (I'll Even Love You)
3/95	**Better Things To Do**...Terri Clark

POS/YR	RECORD TITLE/ARTIST
	Better Times A Comin'
20/63	Ray Godfrey
39/65	Jim & Jesse
21/94	**Better Your Heart Than Mine**...Trisha Yearwood
5/85	**Betty's Bein' Bad**...Sawyer Brown
11/95	**Between An Old Memory And Me**...Travis Tritt
3/85	**Between Blue Eyes And Jeans**...Conway Twitty
11/74	**Between Lust And Watching TV**...Cal Smith
27/95	**Between The Two Of Them**...Tanya Tucker
17/81	**Between This Time And The Next Time**...Gene Watson
7/84	**Between Two Fires**...Gary Morris
9/54	**Beware Of "It"**...Johnnie & Jack
11/59	**Beyond The Shadow**...Browns
7/50	**Beyond The Sunset**...Three Suns/Elton Britt/Rosalie Allen
7/89	**Beyond Those Years**...Oak Ridge Boys
27/75	**Beyond You**...Crystal Gayle
22/74	**Biff, The Friendly Purple Bear**...Dick Feller
1/61	**Big Bad John**...Jimmy Dean
24/62	**Big Battle**...Johnny Cash
18/61	**Big, Big Love**...Wynn Stewart
39/72	**Big Blue Diamond**...Jacky Ward
29/66	**Big Chief Buffalo Nickel (Desert Blues)**...Skeets McDonald
1/82	**Big City**...Merle Haggard
3/89	**Big Dreams In A Small Town**...Restless Heart
13/62	**Big Fool Of The Year**...George Jones
4/74	**Big Four Poster Bed**...Brenda Lee
8/74	**Big Game Hunter**...Buck Owens
12/68	**Big Girls Don't Cry**...Lynn Anderson
19/59	**Big Harlan Taylor**...George Jones
37/93	**Big Heart**...Gibson/Miller Band
29/60	**Big Hearted Me**...Don Gibson
5/69	**Big In Vegas**...Buck Owens
5/60	**Big Iron**...Marty Robbins
31/81	**Big Like A River**...Tennessee Express
5/89	**Big Love**...Bellamy Brothers
23/70	**Big Mama's Medicine Show**...Buddy Alan
39/75	**Big Mamou**...Fiddlin' Frenchie Bourque
35/80	**Big Man's Cafe**...Nick Noble
4/59	**Big Midnight Special**...Wilma Lee & Stoney Cooper
15/95	**Big Ol' Truck**...Toby Keith
4/82	**Big Ole Brew**...Mel McDaniel

POS/YR	RECORD TITLE/ARTIST
1/94	**Big One**...George Strait
4/58	**Big River**...Johnny Cash
7/61	**Big River, Big Man**...Claude King
22/62	**Big Shoes**...Ray Price
30/65	**Big Tennessee**...Tex Williams
38/85	**Big Train (From Memphis)**...John Fogerty
27/70	**Big Wheel Cannonball**...Dick Curless
7/58	**Big Wheels**...Hank Snow
1/89	**Big Wheels In The Moonlight**...Dan Seals
3/69	**Big Wind**...Porter Wagoner
1/96	**Bigger Than The Beatles**...Joe Diffie
27/76	**Biggest Airport In The World**...Moe Bandy
1/59	**Billy Bayou**...Jim Reeves
12/75	**Billy, Get Me A Woman**...Joe Stampley
4/92	**Billy The Kid**...Billy Dean
10/70	**Biloxi**...Kenny Price
	Bimbo
1/54	Jim Reeves
9/54	Pee Wee King
14/91	**Bing Bang Boom**...Highway 101
2/82	**Bird, The**...Jerry Reed & Friends
26/88	**Bird, The**...George Jones
1/58	**Bird Dog**...Everly Brothers
1/50	**Birmingham Bounce**...Red Foley
31/86	**Birth Of Rock And Roll**...Carl Perkins
37/89	**Black And White**...Rosanne Cash
24/75	**Black Bear Road**...C.W. McCall
16/62	**Black Cloud**...Leroy Van Dyke
15/90	**Black Coffee**...Lacy J. Dalton
	Black Land Farmer
5/59	Frankie Miller
16/61	Frankie Miller
1/83	**Black Sheep**...John Anderson
21/59	**Black Sheep**...Ferlin Husky
12/90	**Black Velvet**...Robin Lee
6/52	**Blackberry Boogie**...Tennessee Ernie Ford
4/56	**Blackboard Of My Heart**...Hank Thompson
21/67	**Blackjack County Chain**...Willie Nelson
31/91	**Blame, The**...Highway 101
36/70	**Blame It On Rosey**...Ray Sanders
5/91	**Blame It On Texas**...Mark Chesnutt
28/65	**Blame It On The Moonlight**...Johnny Wright
1/93	**Blame It On Your Heart**...Patty Loveless
1/75	**Blanket On The Ground**...Billie Jo Spears
9/82	**Blaze Of Glory**...Kenny Rogers
1/72	**Bless Your Heart**...Freddie Hart
1/81	**Blessed Are The Believers**...Anne Murray

POS/YR	RECORD TITLE/ARTIST
6/79	**Blind In Love**...Mel Tillis
2/76	**Blind Man In The Bleachers**...Kenny Starr
4/69	**Blistered**...Johnny Cash
4/61	**Blizzard, The**...Jim Reeves
1/73	**Blood Red And Goin' Down**...Tanya Tucker
4/50	**Bloodshot Eyes**...Hank Penny
17/74	**Bloody Mary Morning**...Willie Nelson
27/80	**Blue Baby Blue**...Lynn Anderson
2/77	**Blue Bayou**...Linda Ronstadt
30/64	**Blue Bird Let Me Tag Along**...Rose Maddox
	Blue Blue Day
1/58	Don Gibson
14/61	Wilburn Brothers
2/58	**Blue Boy**...Jim Reeves
	Blue Christmas
1/49	Ernest Tubb
9/50	Ernest Tubb
5/51	Ernest Tubb
1/96	**Blue Clear Sky**...George Strait
40/81	**Blue Collar Blues**...Mundo Earwood
40/69	**Blue Collar Job**...Darrell Statler
	Blue Darlin'
7/55	Jimmy Newman
F/78	Narvel Felts
1/75	**Blue Eyes Crying In The Rain**...Willie Nelson
F/58	**Blue Glass Skirt**...Hank Locklin
33/64	**Blue Guitar**...Sheb Wooley
7/80	**Blue Heartache**...Gail Davies
15/85	**Blue Highway**...John Conlee
	Blue Kentucky Girl
7/65	Loretta Lynn
6/79	Emmylou Harris
11/68	**Blue Lonely Winter**...Jimmy Newman
10/88	**Blue Love**...O'Kanes
22/91	**Blue Memories**...Patty Loveless
28/58	**Blue Memories**...James O'Gwynn
1/82	**Blue Moon With Heartache**...Rosanne Cash
32/82	**Blue Rendezvous**...Lloyd David Foster
F/79	**Blue Ribbon Blues**...Joe Sun
21/92	**Blue Rose Is**...Pam Tillis
6/48	**Blue Shadows On The Trail**...Roy Rogers
8/80	**Blue Side**...Crystal Gayle
1/66	**Blue Side Of Lonesome**...Jim Reeves
4/89	**Blue Side Of Town**...Patty Loveless
1/78	**Blue Skies**...Willie Nelson
7/49	**Blue Skirt Waltz**...Frankie Yankovic/Marlin Sisters
1/56	**Blue Suede Shoes**...Carl Perkins

POS/YR	RECORD TITLE/ARTIST
6/46	**Blue Texas Moonlight**...Elton Britt
5/88	**Blue To The Bone**...Sweethearts Of The Rodeo
22/73	**Blue Train (Of The Heartbreak Line)**...George Hamilton IV
	(Blue Yodel) ..see: T For Texas, & Mule Skinner Blues
4/46	**Blueberry Lane**...Elton Britt
39/91	**Bluebird**...Anne Murray
4/51	**Bluebird Island**...Hank Snow with Anita Carter
	Bluebird On Your Windowsill ..see: (There's A)
21/58	**Blues**...Ernest Tubb
15/49	**Blues In My Heart**...Red Foley
12/66	**Blues Plus Booze (Means I Lose)**...Stonewall Jackson
	Blues, Stay Away From Me
7/49	Eddie Crosby
1/50	Delmore Brothers
7/50	Owen Bradley Quintet
1/88	**Bluest Eyes In Texas**...Restless Heart
11/77	**Bluest Heartache Of The Year**...Kenny Dale
39/66	**Boa Constrictor**...Johnny Cash
14/67	**Bob**...Willis Brothers
4/47	**Bob Wills Boogie**...Bob Wills
F/75	**Bob Wills Is Still The King**...Waylon Jennings
6/95	**Bobbie Ann Mason**...Rick Trevino
1/82	**Bobbie Sue**...Oak Ridge Boys
29/75	**Boilin' Cabbage**...Bill Black's Combo
21/80	**Bombed, Boozed, And Busted**...Joe Sun
	Bonaparte's Retreat
10/50	Pee Wee King
3/74	Glen Campbell
8/74	**Boney Fingers**...Hoyt Axton
10/87	**Bonnie Jean (Little Sister)**...David Lynn Jones
31/69	**Boo Dan**...Jimmy Newman
2/78	**Boogie Grass Band**...Conway Twitty
22/74	**Boogie Woogie**...Charlie McCoy & Barefoot Jerry
24/75	**Boogie Woogie Country Man**...Jerry Lee Lewis
10/88	**Boogie Woogie Fiddle Country Blues**...Charlie Daniels Band
19/93	**Boom! It Was Over**...Robert Ellis Orrall
8/49	**Boomerang**...Arthur "Guitar Boogie" Smith
1/92	**Boot Scootin' Boogie**...Brooks & Dunn
1/86	**Bop**...Dan Seals

POS/YR	RECORD TITLE/ARTIST
7/56	**Boppin' The Blues**...Carl Perkins
13/89	**Borderline**...Shooters
26/78	**Bordertown Woman**...Mel McDaniel
21/68	**Born A Fool**...Freddie Hart
12/77	**Born Believer**...Jim Ed Brown/Helen Cornelius
2/92	**Born Country**...Alabama
12/96	**Born In The Dark**...Doug Stone
12/66	**Born Loser**...Don Gibson
5/90	**Born To Be Blue**...Judds
5/55	**Born To Be Happy**...Hank Snow
22/66	**Born To Be In Love With You**...Van Trevor
	Born To Be With You
1/68	Sonny James
21/78	Sandy Posey
1/87	**Born To Boogie**...Hank Williams, Jr.
3/44	**Born To Lose**...Ted Daffan
31/74	**Born To Love And Satisfy**...Karen Wheeler
	Born To Love Me
21/77	Ray Price
20/83	Ray Charles
6/93	**Born To Love You**...Mark Collie
20/68	**Born To Love You**...Jimmy Newman
40/84	**Born To Love You**...Karen Brooks
3/82	**Born To Run**...Emmylou Harris
17/86	**Born Yesterday**...Everly Brothers
7/72	**Borrowed Angel**...Mel Street
21/67	**Both Sides Of The Line**...Wanda Jackson
1/86	**Both To Each Other (Friends & Lovers)**...Eddie Rabbitt & Juice Newton
13/67	**Bottle, Bottle**...Jim Ed Brown
3/66	**Bottle Let Me Down**...Merle Haggard
21/60	**Bottle Or Me**...Connie Hall
35/66	**Bottles**...Billy Grammer
18/66	**Bottom Of A Mountain**...Tex Williams
	Bouquet Of Roses
1/48	Eddy Arnold
11/75	Mickey Gilley
33/72	**Bowling Green**...Hank Capps
7/95	**Box, The**...Randy Travis
18/66	**Box It Came In**...Wanda Jackson
13/80	**Boxer, The**...Emmylou Harris
18/83	**Boy Gets Around**...Sylvia
1/69	**Boy Named Sue**...Johnny Cash
36/84	**Boy's Night Out**...Moe Bandy & Joe Stampley
4/94	**Boys And Me**...Sawyer Brown
19/84	**Boys Like You**...Gail Davies
39/66	**Bracero**...Stu Phillips

POS/YR	RECORD TITLE/ARTIST
1/91	**Brand New Man**...Brooks & Dunn
8/71	**Brand New Mister Me**...Mel Tillis
1/67	**Branded Man**...Merle Haggard
5/75	**Brass Buckles**...Barbi Benton
15/85	**Break Away**...Gail Davies
2/82	**Break It To Me Gently**...Juice Newton
	Break My Mind
6/67	George Hamilton IV
13/78	Vern Gosdin
11/64	**Breakfast With The Blues**...Hank Snow
10/83	**Breakin' Down**...Waylon Jennings
25/79	**Breakin' In A Brand New Broken Heart**...Debby Boone
7/55	**Breakin' In Another Heart**...Hank Thompson
39/83	**Breakin' It**...Loretta Lynn
10/54	**Breakin' The Rules**...Hank Thompson
15/89	**Breaking New Ground**...Wild Rose
4/58	**Breathless**...Jerry Lee Lewis
12/48	**Breeze**...Cowboy Copas
9/71	**Bridge Over Troubled Water**...Buck Owens
3/81	**Bridge That Just Won't Burn**...Conway Twitty
1/65	**Bridge Washed Out**...Warner Mack
10/89	**Bridges And Walls**...Oak Ridge Boys
11/65	**Bright Lights And Country Music**...Bill Anderson
1/71	**Bright Lights, Big City**...Sonny James
9/87	**Brilliant Conversationalist**...T. Graham Brown
9/74	**Bring Back Your Love To Me**...Don Gibson
11/90	**Bring Back Your Love To Me**...Earl Thomas Conley
18/72	**Bring Him Safely Home To Me**...Sandy Posey
20/80	**Bring It On Home**...Big Al Downing
1/76	**Bring It On Home To Me**...Mickey Gilley
7/73	**Bring It On Home (To Your Woman)**...Joe Stampley
13/69	**Bring Me Sunshine**...Willie Nelson
25/66	**Bring Your Heart Home**...Jimmy Newman
	Bring Your Sweet Self Back To Me ..see: (Honey, Baby, Hurry!)
23/75	**Bringing It Back**...Brenda Lee
15/73	**Broad-Minded Man**...Jim Ed Brown
1/77	**Broken Down In Tiny Pieces**...Billy "Crash" Craddock
2/50	**Broken Down Merry-Go-Round**...Margaret Whiting & Jimmy Wakely

POS/YR	RECORD TITLE/ARTIST
18/60	**Broken Dream**...Jimmy Smart
1/79	**Broken Hearted Me**...Anne Murray
5/76	**Broken Lady**...Larry Gatlin
10/92	**Broken Promise Land**...Mark Chesnutt
9/80	**Broken Trust**...Brenda Lee
1/91	**Brother Jukebox**...Mark Chesnutt
2/91	**Brotherly Love**...Keith Whitley & Earl Thomas Conley
29/84	**Brown Eyed Girl**...Joe Stampley
3/70	**Brown Eyed Handsome Man**...Waylon Jennings
15/49	**Brush Those Tears From Your Eyes**...Foy Willing
16/95	**Bubba Hyde**...Diamond Rio
4/92	**Bubba Shot The Jukebox**...Mark Chesnutt
4/48	**Bubbles In My Beer**...Bob Wills
1/65	**Buckaroo**...Buck Owens
14/78	**Bucket To The South**...Ava Barber
25/79	**Buenos Dias Argentina**...Marty Robbins
16/93	**Bug, The**...Mary-Chapin Carpenter
12/63	**Building A Bridge**...Claude King
30/79	**Building Memories**...Sonny James
8/78	**Bull And The Beaver**...Merle Haggard/Leona Williams
	Bumming Around
5/53	Jimmie Dean
5/53	"T" Texas Tyler
31/76	**Bump Bounce Boogie**...Asleep At The Wheel
4/52	**Bundle Of Southern Sunshine**...Eddy Arnold
2/78	**Burgers And Fries**...Charley Pride
3/84	**Buried Treasure**...Kenny Rogers
7/92	**Burn Me Down**...Marty Stuart
4/92	**Burn One Down**...Clint Black
10/86	**Burned Like A Rocket**...Billy Joe Royal
3/89	**Burnin' A Hole In My Heart**...Skip Ewing
1/89	**Burnin' Old Memories**...Kathy Mattea
31/75	**Burnin' Thing**...Mac Davis
37/75	**Burning**...Ferlin Husky
5/67	**Burning A Hole In My Mind**...Connie Smith
18/67	**Burning Bridges**...Glen Campbell
	Burning Memories
2/64	Ray Price
9/77	Mel Tillis
10/62	**Burning Of Atlanta**...Claude King
11/72	**Burning The Midnight Oil**...Porter Wagoner & Dolly Parton

POS/YR	RECORD TITLE/ARTIST
21/71	**Bus Fare To Kentucky**...Skeeter Davis
6/50	**Bushel And A Peck**...Margaret Whiting & Jimmy Wakely
22/75	**Busiest Memory In Town**...Dickey Lee
	Busted
13/63	Johnny Cash with The Carter Family
6/82	John Conlee
8/52	**Busybody**...Pee Wee King
19/69	**But For Love**...Eddy Arnold
35/94	**But I Will**...Faith Hill
30/82	**But It's Cheating**...Family Brown
26/80	**But Love Me**...Janie Fricke
	But You Know I Love You
2/69	Bill Anderson
1/81	Dolly Parton
16/60	**But You Use To**...Laverne Downs
22/76	**Butterfly For Bucky**...Bobby Goldsboro
4/88	**Button Off My Shirt**...Ronnie Milsap
6/48	**Buttons And Bows**...Gene Autry
18↑/96	**By My Side**...Lorrie Morgan & Jon Randall
6/81	**By Now**...Steve Wariner
2/68	**By The Time I Get To Phoenix**...Glen Campbell
	Bye Bye Love
1/57	Everly Brothers
7/57	Webb Pierce

POS/YR	RECORD TITLE/ARTIST
23/77	**C.B. Savage**...Rod Hart
10/83	**C.C. Waterback**...George Jones/Merle Haggard
	C'est La Vie ..see: (You Never Can Tell)
16/72	**Cab Driver**...Hank Thompson
9/59	**Cabin In The Hills**...Flatt & Scruggs
18/93	**Cadillac Ranch**...Chris LeDoux
3/92	**Cadillac Style**...Sammy Kershaw
5/92	**Cafe On The Corner**...Sawyer Brown
26/95	**Cain's Blood**...4 Runner
3/69	**Cajun Baby**...Hank Williams, Jr.
1/86	**Cajun Moon**...Ricky Skaggs
16/62	**Cajun Queen**...Jimmy Dean
23/68	**Cajun Stripper**...Jim Ed Brown
11/48	**Calico Rag**...Al Dexter
13/85	**California**...Keith Stegall
11/69	**California Girl (And The Tennessee Square)**...Tompall/Glaser Brothers

POS/YR	RECORD TITLE/ARTIST
17/59	**Chain Gang**...Freddie Hart
21/80	**Chain Gang Of Love**...Roy Clark
31/73	**Chained**...Johnny Russell
3/46	**Chained To A Memory**...Eddy Arnold
1/90	**Chains**...Patty Loveless
35/75	**Chains**...Buddy Alan
4/87	**Chains Of Gold**...Sweethearts Of The Rodeo
9/77	**Chains Of Love**...Mickey Gilley
1/85	**Chair, The**...George Strait
7/71	**Chair, The**...Marty Robbins
22/80	**Champ, The**...Moe Bandy
34/75	**Champagne Ladies And Blue Ribbon Babies**...Ferlin Husky
1/84	**Chance Of Lovin' You**...Earl Thomas Conley
19/96	**Change, The**...Garth Brooks
1/89	**Change Of Heart**...Judds
24/77	**Changes In Latitudes, Changes In Attitudes**...Jimmy Buffett
16/87	**Changin' Partners**...Gatlin Bros.
4/54	**Changing Partners**...Pee Wee King
1/72	**Chantilly Lace**...Jerry Lee Lewis
	Chapel Of Love ..see: Love, Love, Love
16/67	**Charleston Railroad Tavern**...Bobby Bare
15/71	**Charley's Picture**...Porter Wagoner
16/70	**Charlie Brown**...Compton Brothers
F/79	**Charlie's Angel**...Mel Tillis
1/62	**Charlie's Shoes**...Billy Walker
38/71	**Charlotte Fever**...Kenny Price
5/80	**Charlotte's Web**...Statler Brothers
6/59	**Chasin' A Rainbow**...Hank Snow
2/90	**Chasin' That Neon Rainbow**...Alan Jackson
1/93	**Chattahoochee**...Alan Jackson
1/50	**Chattanoogie Shoe Shine Boy**...Red Foley
9/86	**Cheap Love**...Juice Newton
7/77	**Cheap Perfume And Candlelight**...Bobby Borchers
13/94	**Cheap Seats**...Alabama
14/56	**Cheated Too**...Wilma Lee & Stoney Cooper
30/82	**Cheater's Prayer**...Kendalls
15/76	**Cheatin' Is**...Barbara Fairchild
38/81	**Cheatin' Is Still On My Mind**...Cristy Lane
20/80	**Cheatin' On A Cheater**...Loretta Lynn
40/77	**Cheatin' Overtime**...Mary Lou Turner
9/54	**Cheatin's A Sin**...Kitty Wells
16/81	**Cheatin's A Two Way Street**...Sammi Smith
18/73	**Cheating Game**...Susan Raye
1/95	**Check Yes Or No**...George Strait

POS/YR	RECORD TITLE/ARTIST
7/51	**Cherokee Boogie (Eh-Oh-Aleena)**...Moon Mullican
10/82	**Cherokee Fiddle**...Johnny Lee & Friends
1/76	**Cherokee Maiden**...Merle Haggard
	Chet Atkins ..see: Chit Akins
38/67	**Chet's Tune**...Some Of Chet's Friends
8/51	**Chew Tobacco Rag**...Zeb Turner
30/70	**Chicago Story**...Jimmy Snyder
17/64	**Chickashay**...David Houston
31/66	**Chicken Feed**...Bobbi Staff
8/81	**Chicken Truck**...John Anderson
17/83	**Child Of The Fifties**...Statler Brothers
13/87	**Child Support**...Barbara Mandrell
24/68	**Childhood Places**...Dottie West
30/73	**Children**...Johnny Cash
9/88	**Chill Factor**...Merle Haggard
3/91	**Chill Of An Early Fall**...George Strait
6/48	**Chime Bells**...Elton Britt
22/62	**China Doll**...George Hamilton IV
33/74	**Chip Chip**...Patsy Sledd
23/71	**Chip 'N' Dale's Place**...Claude King
12/59	**Chip Off The Old Block**...Eddy Arnold
6/88	**Chiseled In Stone**...Vern Gosdin
14/64	**Chit Akins, Make Me A Star**...Don Bowman
	Choc'late Ice Cream Cone
5/50	Red Foley
8/50	Kenny Roberts
8/67	**Chokin' Kind**...Waylon Jennings
7/49	**C-H-R-I-S-T-M-A-S**...Eddy Arnold
12/54	**Christmas Can't Be Far Away**...Eddy Arnold
2/45	**Christmas Carols By The Old Corral**...Tex Ritter
35/82	**Christmas In Dixie**...Alabama
35/82	**Christmas Is Just A Song For Us This Year**...Louise Mandrell/RC Bannon
3/64	**Chug-A-Lug**...Roger Miller
1/89	**Church On Cumberland Road**...Shenandoah
5/47	**Cigareetes, Whusky, And Wild, Wild Women**...Sons Of The Pioneers
	Cigarettes And Coffee Blues
13/59	Lefty Frizzell
14/63	Marty Robbins
2/50	**Cincinnati Dancing Pig**...Red Foley
2/46	**Cincinnati Lou**...Merle Travis
4/67	**Cincinnati, Ohio**...Connie Smith
5/87	**Cinderella**...Vince Gill

POS/YR	RECORD TITLE/ARTIST
7/64	Circumstances...Billy Walker
	City Lights
1/58	Ray Price
1/75	Mickey Gilley
1/84	City Of New Orleans...Willie Nelson
37/65	City Of The Angels...Jimmy Newman
5/94	City Put The Country Back In Me...Neal McCoy
6/72	Class Of '57...Statler Brothers
13/75	Classified...C.W. McCall
15/58	Claudette...Everly Brothers
11/93	Cleopatra, Queen Of Denial...Pam Tillis
17/65	Close All The Honky Tonks...Charlie Walker
15/77	Close Enough For Lonesome...Mel Street
1/82	Close Enough To Perfect...Alabama
40/82	Closer To You...Burrito Brothers
	Closer You Get
27/81	Don King
1/83	Alabama
27/77	Closest Thing To You...Jerry Lee Lewis
1/82	Clown, The...Conway Twitty
20/95	Clown In Your Rodeo...Kathy Mattea
7/80	Clyde...Waylon Jennings
	Coal Miner's Daughter
1/70	Loretta Lynn
24/80	Sissy Spacek
15/89	Coast Of Colorado...Skip Ewing
4/71	Coat Of Many Colors...Dolly Parton
1/79	Coca Cola Cowboy...Mel Tillis
15/48	Cocaine Blues...Roy Hogsed
13/63	Cold And Lonely (Is The Forecast For Tonight)...Kitty Wells
	Cold, Cold Heart
1/51	Hank Williams
22/61	Jerry Lee Lewis
10/62	Cold Dark Waters...Porter Wagoner
2/67	Cold Hard Facts Of Life...Porter Wagoner
24/85	Cold Summer Day In Georgia...Gene Watson
30/75	Colinda...Fiddlin' Frenchie Burke
22/69	Color Him Father...Linda Martell
38/72	Color My World...Barbara Fairchild
7/58	Color Of The Blues...George Jones
37/87	Colorado Moon...Tim Malchak
7/62	Comancheros, The...Claude King
4/78	Come A Little Bit Closer...Johnny Duncan with Janie Fricke
20/59	Come And Knock (On The Door Of My Heart)...Roy Acuff

POS/YR	RECORD TITLE/ARTIST
7/89	Come As You Were...T. Graham Brown
13/56	Come Back To Me...Jimmy Newman
12/73	Come Early Morning...Don Williams
1/89	Come From The Heart...Kathy Mattea
3/92	Come In Out Of The Pain...Doug Stone
6/58	Come In Stranger...Johnny Cash
14/67	Come Kiss Me Love...Bobby Bare
1/73	Come Live With Me...Roy Clark
1/90	Come Next Monday...K.T. Oslin
3/91	Come On Back...Carlene Carter
24/76	Come On Down (To Our Favorite Forget-About-Her Place)...David Houston
24/69	Come On Home And Sing The Blues To Daddy...Bob Luman
3/79	Come On In...Oak Ridge Boys
8/76	Come On In...Sonny James
10/78	Come On In...Jerry Lee Lewis
19/74	Come On In And Let Me Love You...Lois Johnson
3/86	Come On In (You Did The Best You Could Do)...Oak Ridge Boys
39/88	Come On Joe...Jo-el Sonnier
5/76	Come On Over...Olivia Newton-John
36/74	Come On Phone...Jean Shepard
23/77	Come See About Me...Cal Smith
17/78	Come See Me And Come Lonely...Dottie West
37/67	Come See What's Left Of Your Man...Johnny Darrell
7/71	Come Sundown...Bobby Bare
16/78	Come To Me...Roy Head
16/80	Come To My Love...Cristy Lane
4/59	Come Walk With Me...Wilma Lee & Stoney Cooper
14/49	Come Wet Your Mustache With Me...Stubby & The Buccaneers
1/79	Come With Me...Waylon Jennings
4/62	Comeback, The...Faron Young
8/71	Comin' Down...Dave Dudley
23/71	Comin' For To Carry Me Home...Dolly Parton
32/75	Comin' Home To You...Jerry Wallace
19/66	Coming Back To You...Browns
8/70	Commercial Affection...Mel Tillis
32/66	Common Colds And Broken Hearts...Ray Pillow
1/83	Common Man...John Conlee
8/66	Company You Keep...Bill Phillips
7/55	Company's Comin'...Porter Wagoner

POS/YR	RECORD TITLE/ARTIST
39/94	**Confessin' My Love**...Shawn Camp
28/61	**Congratulations**...Faron Young
	Conscience I'm Guilty
4/56	Hank Snow
14/61	Rose Maddox
15/83	**Conversation, The**...Waylon Jennings with Hank Williams, Jr.
1/75	**Convoy**...C.W. McCall
	Cool Water
4/47	Sons Of The Pioneers
7/48	Sons Of The Pioneers
2/73	**Corner Of My Life**...Bill Anderson
	(Corvette Song) ..see: One I Loved Back Then
11/72	**Cotton Jenny**...Anne Murray
34/89	**Cotton Pickin' Time**...Marcy Bros.
1/80	**Could I Have This Dance**...Anne Murray
26/81	**Could You Love Me (One More Time)**...John Conlee
2/92	**Could've Been Me**...Billy Ray Cyrus
15/80	**Couldn't Do Nothin' Right**...Rosanne Cash
22/66	**Count Down**...Hank Snow
14/66	**Count Me Out**...Marty Robbins
5/86	**Count On Me**...Statler Brothers
16/68	**Count Your Blessings, Woman**...Jan Howard
23/96	**C-O-U-N-T-R-Y**...Joe Diffie
1/85	**Country Boy**...Ricky Skaggs
7/49	**Country Boy**..."Little" Jimmy Dickens
2/82	**Country Boy Can Survive**...Hank Williams, Jr.
3/75	**Country Boy (You Got Your Feet In L.A.)**...Glen Campbell
22/67	**Country Boy's Dream**...Carl Perkins
1/74	**Country Bumpkin**...Cal Smith
9/89	**Country Club**...Travis Tritt
36/75	**Country D.J.**...Bill Anderson
1/59	**Country Girl**...Faron Young
7/70	**Country Girl**...Jeannie C. Riley
15/68	**Country Girl**...Dottie West
1/85	**Country Girls**...John Schneider
5/71	**Country Green**...Don Gibson
16/65	**Country Guitar**...Phil Baugh
8/68	**Country Hall Of Fame**...Hank Locklin
1/74	**Country Is**...Tom T. Hall
14/49	**Country Junction**...Tennessee Ernie Ford
23/78	**Country Lovin'**...Eddy Arnold
27/74	**Country Lullabye**...Johnny Carver

POS/YR	RECORD TITLE/ARTIST
2/59	**Country Music Is Here To Stay**...Simon Crum
23/67	**Country Music Lover**..."Little" Jimmy Dickens
26/61	**Country Music Time**...Lonzo & Oscar
15/77	**Country Party**...Johnny Lee
31/87	**Country Rap**...Bellamy Brothers
2/86	**Country State Of Mind**...Hank Williams, Jr.
2/73	**Country Sunshine**...Dottie West
35/94	**Country 'Til I Die**...John Anderson
23/81	**Countryfied**...Mel McDaniel
35/71	**Countryfied**...George Hamilton IV
3/54	**Courtin' In The Rain**..."T" Texas Tyler
33/75	**Cover Me**...Sammi Smith
5/62	**Cow Town**...Webb Pierce
1/80	**Coward Of The County**...Kenny Rogers
13/76	**Cowboy**...Eddy Arnold
	(Cowboy And The Poet) ..see: Faster Horses
24/94	**Cowboy Band**...Billy Dean
23/92	**Cowboy Beat**...Bellamy Brothers
3/63	**Cowboy Boots**...Dave Dudley
19/70	**Cowboy Convention**...Buddy Alan & Don Rich
36/89	**Cowboy Hat In Dallas**...Charlie Daniels Band
3/64	**Cowboy In The Continental Suit**...Marty Robbins
4/96	**Cowboy Love**...John Michael Montgomery
10/87	**Cowboy Man**...Lyle Lovett
5/85	**Cowboy Rides Away**...George Strait
	(Cowboy Tune) ..see: End Is Not In Sight
12/93	**Cowboy's Born With A Broken Heart**...Boy Howdy
13/77	**Cowboys Ain't Supposed To Cry**...Moe Bandy
1/80	**Cowboys And Clowns**...Ronnie Milsap
29/75	**Cowboys And Daddys**...Bobby Bare
24/94	**Cowboys Don't Cry**...Daron Norwood
11/78	**Cowboys Don't Get Lucky All The Time**...Gene Watson
21/81	**Cowboys Don't Shoot Straight (Like They Used To)**...Tammy Wynette
10/80	**Cowgirl And The Dandy**...Brenda Lee
38/86	**Cowpoke**...Glen Campbell
16/61	**Cozy Inn**...Leon McAuliff
3/80	**Crackers**...Barbara Mandrell
32/92	**Crash Course In The Blues**...Steve Wariner
F/73	**Crawling On My Knees**...Marty Robbins

POS/YR	RECORD TITLE/ARTIST
1/85	**Crazy**...Kenny Rogers
	Crazy
2/62	Patsy Cline
6/77	Linda Ronstadt
	Crazy Arms
1/56	Ray Price
18/63	Marion Worth
16/79	Willie Nelson
17/79	**Crazy Blue Eyes**...Lacy J. Dalton
11/48	**Crazy Boogie**...Merle Travis
11/61	**Crazy Bullfrog**...Lewis Pruitt
4/47	**Crazy 'Cause I Love You**...Spade Cooley
1/85	**Crazy For Your Love**...Exile
3/87	**Crazy From The Heart**...Bellamy Brothers
4/51	**Crazy Heart**...Hank Williams
2/90	**Crazy In Love**...Conway Twitty
4/87	**Crazy Over You**...Foster & Lloyd
8/62	**Crazy Wild Desire**...Webb Pierce
10/74	**Credit Card Song**...Dick Feller
7/87	**Crime Of Passion**...Ricky Van Shelton
32/76	**Crispy Critters**...C.W. McCall
14/89	**Cross My Broken Heart**...Suzy Bogguss
2/64	**Cross The Brazos At Waco**...Billy Walker
11/84	**Crossword Puzzle**...Barbara Mandrell
13/74	**Crude Oil Blues**...Jerry Reed
9/60	**Cruel Love**...Lou Smith
25/77	**Crutches**...Faron Young
	Cry
3/72	Lynn Anderson
1/86	Crystal Gayle
5/49	**Cry-Baby Heart**...George Morgan
1/88	**Cry, Cry, Cry**...Highway 101
	Cry! Cry! Cry!
14/55	Johnny Cash
32/89	Marty Stuart
20/68	**Cry, Cry, Cry**...Connie Smith
	Cry, Cry, Darling
4/54	Jimmy Newman
34/78	Con Hunley
9/85	**Cry Just A Little Bit**...Sylvia
1/87	**Cry Myself To Sleep**...Judds
7/50	**Cry Of The Dying Duck In A Thunder-Storm**...Cactus Pryor
2/50	**Cry Of The Wild Goose**...Tennessee Ernie Ford
	Cryin' ..also see: Crying
3/78	**Cryin' Again**...Oak Ridge Boys
5/51	**Cryin' Heart Blues**...Johnnie & Jack
11/48	**Cryin' In My Beer**...Jerry Irby

POS/YR	RECORD TITLE/ARTIST
7/55	**Cryin', Prayin', Waitin', Hopin'**...Hank Snow
	Crying
28/70	Arlene Harden
14/80	Stephanie Winslow
6/81	Don McLean
	Crying In The Chapel
4/53	Rex Allen
4/53	Darrell Glenn
18/81	**Crying In The Rain**...Tammy Wynette
	Crying My Heart Out Over You
21/60	Flatt & Scruggs
1/82	Ricky Skaggs
3/58	**Crying Over You**...Webb Pierce
4/88	**Crying Shame**...Michael Johnson
12/65	**Crystal Chandelier**...Carl Belew
	(Cuando Calienta El Sol) ..see: Love Me With All Your Heart
2/50	**Cuddle Buggin' Baby**...Eddy Arnold
12/81	**Cup Of Tea**...Rex Allen, Jr. & Margo Smith
3/58	**Curtain In The Window**...Ray Price
14/69	**Custody**...Hank Williams, Jr.
	Cut Across Shorty
28/60	Carl Smith
15/69	Nat Stuckey
5/55	**Cuzz Yore So Sweet**...Simon Crum

D

POS/YR	RECORD TITLE/ARTIST
8/65	**DJ Cried**...Ernest Ashworth
9/64	**D.J. For A Day**...Jimmy "C" Newman
10/48	**Dad Gave My Dog Away**..."T" Texas Tyler
9/87	**Daddies Need To Grow Up Too**...O'Kanes
14/79	**Daddy**...Donna Fargo
40/69	**Daddy**...Dolly Parton
27/89	**Daddy And Home**...Tanya Tucker
40/70	**Daddy Come And Get Me**...Dolly Parton
1/71	**Daddy Frank (The Guitar Man)**...Merle Haggard
40/70	**Daddy, I Love You**...Billie Jo Spears
9/94	**Daddy Never Was The Cadillac Kind**...Confederate Railroad
1/69	**Daddy Sang Bass**...Johnny Cash
20/62	**Daddy Stopped In**...Claude Gray
7/70	**Daddy Was An Old Time Preacher Man**...Porter Wagoner & Dolly Parton
2/74	**Daddy What If**...Bobby Bare

POS/YR	RECORD TITLE/ARTIST
15/49	**Daddy, When Is Mommy Coming Home**...Ernest Tubb
8/55	**Daddy, You Know What?**...Jim Wilson
1/91	**Daddy's Come Around**...Paul Overstreet
7/86	**Daddy's Hands**...Holly Dunn
6/50	**Daddy's Last Letter**...Tex Ritter
	Daddy's Little Girl ..see: (One More Year Of)
1↑/96	**Daddy's Money**...Ricochet
33/73	**Daisy A Day**...Jud Strunk
37/73	**Daisy May (And Daisy May Not)**...Terri Lane
1/92	**Dallas**...Alan Jackson
32/80	**Dallas**...Floyd Cramer
35/74	**Dallas**...Connie Smith
	(Dallas Lovers' Song) ..see: Makin' Up For Lost Time
1/90	**Dance, The**...Garth Brooks
38/76	**Dance Her By Me (One More Time)**...Jacky Ward
9/83	**Dance Little Jean**...Nitty Gritty Dirt Band
23/81	**Dance The Two Step**...Susie Allanson
2/74	**Dance With Me (Just One More Time)**...Johnny Rodriguez
1/80	**Dancin' Cowboys**...Bellamy Brothers
29/79	**Dancin' 'Round And 'Round**...Olivia Newton-John
29/84	**Dancin' With The Devil**...Stephanie Winslow
16/77	**Dancing The Night Away**...Tanya Tucker
3/82	**Dancing Your Memory Away**...Charly McClain
5/90	**Dancy's Dream**...Restless Heart
1/64	**Dang Me**...Roger Miller
(also see: Dern Ya)	
20/78	**Danger, Heartbreak Ahead**...Zella Lehr
15/77	**Danger Of A Stranger**...Stella Parton
9/67	**Danny Boy**...Ray Price
10/73	**Danny's Song**...Anne Murray
24/68	**Dark End Of The Street**...Archie Campbell & Lorene Mann
	Dark Hollow
7/59	Jimmie Skinner
13/59	Luke Gordon
14/57	**Dark Moon**...Bonnie Guitar
1/88	**Darlene**...T. Graham Brown
	Darlin'
18/79	David Rogers
19/81	Tom Jones
26/73	**Darlin' (Don't Come Back)**...Dorsey Burnette

POS/YR	RECORD TITLE/ARTIST
23/70	**Darling Days**...Billy Walker
5/73	**Darling, You Can Always Come Back Home**...Jody Miller
2/69	**Darling, You Know I Wouldn't Lie**...Conway Twitty
4/95	**Darned If I Don't (Danged If I Do)**...Shenandoah
4/47	**Daughter Of Jole Blon**...Johnny Bond
	Davy Crockett ..see: Ballad Of
23/70	**Day Drinkin'**...Dave Dudley & Tom T. Hall
14/66	**Day For Decision**...Johnny Sea
30/72	**Day In The Life Of A Fool**...George Jones
10/62	**Day Into Night**...Kitty Wells
18/72	**Day That Love Walked In**...David Houston
4/68	**Day The World Stood Still**...Charley Pride
3/80	**Daydream Believer**...Anne Murray
7/55	**Daydreamin'**...Jimmy Newman
1/75	**Daydreams About Night Things**...Ronnie Milsap
7/78	**Daylight**...T.G. Sheppard
	Days Of Sand And Shovels
20/69	Waylon Jennings
26/78	Nat Stuckey
23/77	**Days That End In "Y"**...Sammi Smith
1/77	**Daytime Friends**...Kenny Rogers
7/44	**Deacon Jones**...Louis Jordan
19/60	**Dead Or Alive**...Bill Anderson
8/75	**Deal**...Tom T. Hall
25/80	**Dealin' With The Devil**...Eddy Raven
9/62	**Dear Ivan**...Jimmy Dean
7/53	**Dear Joan**...Jack Cardwell
8/51	**Dear John**...Hank Williams
	Dear John Letter
1/53	Jean Shepard & Ferlin Huskey
11/65	Skeeter Davis & Bobby Bare
12/60	**Dear Mama**...Merle Kilgore
9/89	**Dear Me**...Lorrie Morgan
	Dear Oakie
12/48	Doye O'Dell
12/48	Jack Rivers
4/66	**Dear Uncle Sam**...Loretta Lynn
11/75	**Dear Woman**...Joe Stampley
3/53	**Death Of Hank Williams**...Jack Cardwell
7/49	**Death Of Little Kathy Fiscus**...Jimmie Osborne
	Deck Of Cards
2/48	"T" Texas Tyler
10/48	Tex Ritter
11/59	Wink Martindale
28/84	**Dedicate**...Kieran Kane

POS/YR	RECORD TITLE/ARTIST
6/96	**Deep Down**...Pam Tillis
10/87	**Deep River Woman**...Lionel Richie with Alabama
10/67	**Deep Water**...Carl Smith
1/89	**Deeper Than The Holler**...Randy Travis
35/78	**Deeper Water**...Brenda Kaye Perry
37/69	**Delia's Gone**...Waylon Jennings
17/79	**Della And The Dealer**...Hoyt Axton
6/72	**Delta Dawn**...Tanya Tucker
14/74	**Delta Dirt**...Larry Gatlin
7/84	**Denver**...Gatlin Bros.
13/64	**Dern Ya**...Ruby Wright
(also see: Dang Me)	
	(Desert Blues) ..see: Big Chief Buffalo Nickel
5/77	**Desperado**...Johnny Rodriguez
1/86	**Desperado Love**...Conway Twitty
15/85	**Desperados Waiting For A Train**...Waylon Jennings/Willie Nelson/Johnny Cash/Kris Kristofferson
7/88	**Desperately**...Don Williams
31/68	**Destroyed By Man**...Mel Tillis
	Detour
2/46	Spade Cooley
3/46	Wesley Tuttle
5/46	Elton Britt
6/46	Foy Willing
6/63	**Detroit City**...Bobby Bare
23/75	**Devil In Mrs. Jones**...Billy Larkin
1/75	**Devil In The Bottle**...T.G. Sheppard
32/76	**Devil In Your Kisses (And The Angel In Your Eyes)**...Mel Street
1/79	**Devil Went Down To Georgia**...Charlie Daniels Band
1/62	**Devil Woman**...Marty Robbins
13/86	**Devil's On The Loose**...Waylon Jennings
	Devoted To You
7/58	Everly Brothers
33/78	Carly Simon & James Taylor
9/84	**Diamond In The Dust**...Mark Gray
38/82	**Diamond In The Rough**...Karen Taylor
9/82	**Diamonds In The Stars**...Ray Price
21/80	**Diane**...Ed Bruce
15/61	**Did I Ever Tell You**...George Jones & Margie Singleton
25/63	**Did I Miss You?**...Orville Couch
33/90	**Did It For Love**...Sawyer Brown
26/71	**Did You Ever**...Charlie Louvin & Melba Montgomery

POS/YR	RECORD TITLE/ARTIST
23/89	**Didn't Expect It To Go Down This Way**...K.T. Oslin
32/65	**Didn't I**...Dottie West
10/86	**Didn't We**...Lee Greenwood
18/67	**Diesel On My Tail**...Jim & Jesse
28/77	**Different Kind Of Flower**...Ray Price
1/86	**Diggin' Up Bones**...Randy Travis
14/61	**Diggy Liggy Lo**...Rusty & Doug
20/85	**Dim Lights, Thick Smoke (And Loud, Loud Music)**...Vern Gosdin
25/61	**Dime A Dozen**...Shirley Collie
12/67	**Dime At A Time**...Del Reeves
3/92	**Dirt Road**...Sawyer Brown
38/73	**Dirty Old Man**...George Hamilton IV
26/78	**Dirty Work**...Sterling Whipple
4/71	**Dis-Satisfied**...Bill Anderson & Jan Howard
12/84	**Disenchanted**...Michael Martin Murphey
1/66	**Distant Drums**...Jim Reeves
1/68	**D-I-V-O-R-C-E**...Tammy Wynette
9/53	**Divorce Granted**...Ernest Tubb
	Divorce Me C.O.D.
1/46	Merle Travis
5/46	King Sisters
4/47	Johnny Bond
11/83	**Dixie Dreaming**...Atlanta
10/56	**Dixie Fried**...Carl Perkins
25/81	**Dixie Man**...Randy Barlow
1/81	**Dixie On My Mind**...Hank Williams, Jr.
1/85	**Dixie Road**...Lee Greenwood
1/83	**Dixieland Delight**...Alabama
F/82	**Do I Ever Cross Your Mind**...Dolly Parton
18/81	**Do I Have To Draw A Picture**...Billy Swan
28/87	**Do I Have To Say Goodbye**...Louise Mandrell
6/53	**Do I Like It?**...Carl Smith
2/78	**Do I Love You (Yes In Every Way)**...Donna Fargo
13/78	**Do It Again Tonight**...Larry Gatlin
20/70	**Do It To Someone You Love**...Norro Wilson
4/82	**Do Me With Love**...Janie Fricke
17/71	**Do Right Woman - Do Right Man**...Barbara Mandrell
15/65	**Do-Wacka-Do**...Roger Miller
	Do What You Do Do Well
7/65	Ned Miller
29/65	Ernest Tubb
1/87	**Do Ya'**...K.T. Oslin
4/88	**Do You Believe Me Now**...Vern Gosdin
5/79	**Do You Ever Fool Around**...Joe Stampley

POS/YR	RECORD TITLE/ARTIST
39/89	**Do You Feel The Same Way Too?**...Becky Hobbs
2/73	**Do You Know What It's Like To Be Lonesome**...Jerry Wallace
16/93	**Do You Know Where Your Man Is**...Pam Tillis
1/78	**Do You Know You Are My Sunshine**...Statler Brothers
1/81	**Do You Love As Good As You Look**...Bellamy Brothers
1/88	**(Do You Love Me) Just Say Yes**...Highway 101
2/72	**Do You Remember These**...Statler Brothers
F/76	**Do You Right Tonight**...Eddie Rabbitt
1/80	**Do You Wanna Go To Heaven**...T.G. Sheppard
38/72	**Do You Want To Dance**...Jack Reno
	Dock Of The Bay ..see: (Sittin' On)
5/95	**Doctor Time**...Rick Trevino
1/85	**Does Fort Worth Ever Cross Your Mind**...George Strait
32/84	**Does He Ever Mention My Name**...Rick & Janis Carnes
1/93	**Does He Love You**...Reba McEntire (with Linda Davis)
5/63	**Does He Mean That Much To You?**...Eddy Arnold
4/67	**Does My Ring Hurt Your Finger**...Charley Pride
20/81	**Does She Wish She Was Single Again**...Burrito Brothers
2/96	**Does That Blue Moon Ever Shine On You**...Toby Keith
33/81	**Doesn't Anybody Get High On Love Anymore**...Shoppe
7/54	**Dog-Gone It, Baby, I'm In Love**...Carl Smith
6/48	**Dog House Boogie**...Hawkshaw Hawkins
19/59	**Doggone That Train**...Hank Snow
17/60	**(Doin' The) Lovers Leap**...Webb Pierce
39/76	**Doing My Time**...Don Gibson
4/87	**Domestic Life**...John Conlee
7/90	**Domino Theory**...Steve Wariner
	Don't
2/58	Elvis Presley
39/73	Sandy Posey
13/75	**Don't Anyone Make Love At Home Anymore**...Moe Bandy
F/58	**Don't Ask Me Why**...Elvis Presley

POS/YR	RECORD TITLE/ARTIST
	Don't Be Angry
4/64	Stonewall Jackson
33/73	Billy "Crash" Craddock
3/77	Donna Fargo
7/50	**Don't Be Ashamed Of Your Age**...Ernest Tubb & Red Foley
	Don't Be Cruel
1/56	Elvis Presley
10/87	Judds
4/76	**Don't Believe My Heart Can Stand Another You**...Tanya Tucker
13/81	**Don't Bother To Knock**...Jim Ed Brown/Helen Cornelius
1/78	**Don't Break The Heart That Loves You**...Margo Smith
1/85	**Don't Call Him A Cowboy**...Conway Twitty
3/85	**Don't Call It Love**...Dolly Parton
13/63	**Don't Call Me From A Honky Tonk**...Johnny & Jonie Mosby
1/84	**Don't Cheat In Our Hometown**...Ricky Skaggs
1/88	**Don't Close Your Eyes**...Keith Whitley
1/67	**Don't Come Home A'Drinkin' (With Lovin' On Your Mind)**...Loretta Lynn
(also see: I Come Home A-Drinkin')	
28/82	**Don't Come Knockin**...Cindy Hurt
9/83	**Don't Count The Rainy Days**...Michael Martin Murphey
6/44	**Don't Cry, Baby**...Erskine Hawkins
13/70	**Don't Cry Daddy**...Elvis Presley
29/85	**Don't Cry Darlin'**...David Allan Coe
4/75	**Don't Cry Joni**...Conway Twitty
12/57	**Don't Do It Darlin'**...Webb Pierce
4/54	**Don't Drop It**...Terry Fell
28/82	**Don't Ever Leave Me Again**...Vern Gosdin
13/78	**Don't Ever Say Good-Bye**...T.G. Sheppard
3/80	**Don't Fall In Love With A Dreamer**...Kenny Rogers with Kim Carnes
33/79	**Don't Feel Like The Lone Ranger**...Leon Everette
4/45	**Don't Fence Me In**...Gene Autry
1/73	**Don't Fight The Feelings Of Love**...Charley Pride
12/55	**Don't Forget**...Eddy Arnold
13/81	**Don't Forget Yourself**...Statler Brothers
16/81	**Don't Get Above Your Raising**...Ricky Skaggs
4↑/96	**Don't Get Me Started**...Rhett Akins
10/88	**Don't Give Candy To A Stranger**...Larry Boone

POS/YR	RECORD TITLE/ARTIST
3/73	**Don't Give Up On Me**...Jerry Wallace
37/65	**Don't Give Up The Ship**...Johnny Wright
27/90	**Don't Give Us A Reason**...Hank Williams, Jr.
5/77	**Don't Go City Girl On Me**...Tommy Overstreet
18/62	**Don't Go Near The Eskimos**...Ben Colder
4/62	**Don't Go Near The Indians**...Rex Allen
12/92	**Don't Go Near The Water**...Sammy Kershaw
6/90	**Don't Go Out**...Tanya Tucker with T.Graham Brown
1/87	**Don't Go To Strangers**...T. Graham Brown
4/45	**Don't Hang Around Me Anymore**...Gene Autry
30/82	**Don't It Break Your Heart**...Steve Wariner
1/77	**Don't It Make My Brown Eyes Blue**...Crystal Gayle
27/69	**Don't It Make You Want To Go Home**...Joe South
	Don't Just Stand There ..see: (When You Feel Like You're In Love)
1/70	**Don't Keep Me Hangin' On**...Sonny James
11/57	**Don't Laugh**...Louvin Brothers
11/74	**Don't Let Go**...Mel Tillis & Sherry Bryce
26/87	**Don't Let Go Of My Heart**...Southern Pacific
33/64	**Don't Let Her Know**...Buck Owens
30/63	**Don't Let Her See Me Cry**...Lefty Frizzell
22/71	**Don't Let Him Make A Memory Out Of Me**...Billy Walker
	Don't Let Me Cross Over
1/62	Carl Butler & Pearl
9/69	Jerry Lee Lewis & Linda Gail Lewis
10/79	Jim Reeves/Deborah Allen
6/77	**Don't Let Me Touch You**...Marty Robbins
1/92	**Don't Let Our Love Start Slippin' Away**...Vince Gill
24/67	**Don't Let That Doorknob Hit You**...Norma Jean
15/75	**Don't Let The Good Times Fool You**...Melba Montgomery
37/73	**Don't Let The Green Grass Fool You**...O.B. McClinton
	Don't Let The Stars Get In Your Eyes
1/52	Skeets McDonald
1/52	Slim Willet
4/52	Ray Price
8/53	Red Foley
(also see: I Let The Stars Get In My Eyes)	
14/61	**Don't Let Your Sweet Love Die**...Reno & Smiley

POS/YR	RECORD TITLE/ARTIST
16/71	**(Don't Let the Sun Set on You) Tulsa**...Waylon Jennings
4/45	**Don't Live A Lie**...Gene Autry
12/82	**Don't Look Back**...Gary Morris
11/81	**Don't Look Now (But We Just Fell In Love)**...Eddy Arnold
4/47	**Don't Look Now (But Your Broken Heart Is Showing)**...Ernest Tubb
1/84	**Don't Make It Easy For Me**...Earl Thomas Conley
F/57	**Don't Make Me Go**...Johnny Cash
29/78	**Don't Make No Promises (You Can't Keep)**...Don King
18/72	**Don't Pay The Ransom**...Nat Stuckey
27/83	**Don't Plan On Sleepin' Tonight**...Steve Wariner
23/63	**Don't Pretend**...Bobby Edwards
4/76	**Don't Pull Your Love (medley)**...Glen Campbell
32/67	**Don't Put Your Hurt In My Heart**...Conway Twitty
25/89	**Don't Quit Me Now**...James House
	Don't Rob Another Man's Castle
1/49	Eddy Arnold
6/49	Ernest Tubb & Andrews Sisters
1/91	**Don't Rock The Jukebox**...Alan Jackson
15/77	**Don't Say Goodbye**...Rex Allen, Jr.
34/72	**Don't Say You're Mine**...Carl Smith
2/72	**Don't She Look Good**...Bill Anderson
8/67	**Don't Squeeze My Sharmon**...Charlie Walker
2/52	**Don't Stay Away (Till Love Grows Cold)**...Lefty Frizzell
9/51	**Don't Stay Too Long**...Ernest Tubb
10/95	**Don't Stop**...Wade Hayes
14/76	**Don't Stop Believin'**...Olivia Newton-John
19/76	**Don't Stop In My World (If You Don't Mean To Stay)**...Billy Walker
10/57	**Don't Stop The Music**...George Jones
27/64	**Don't Take Advantage Of Me**...Bonnie Owens
17/70	**Don't Take All Your Loving**...Don Gibson
1/79	**Don't Take It Away**...Conway Twitty
5/55	**Don't Take It Out On Me**...Hank Thompson
1/94	**Don't Take The Girl**...Tim McGraw
1/59	**Don't Take Your Guns To Town**...Johnny Cash
11/55	**Don't Tease Me**...Carl Smith
2/48	**Don't Telephone - Don't Telegraph (Tell A Woman)**...Tex Williams

POS/YR	RECORD TITLE/ARTIST
5/91	**Don't Tell Me What To Do**...Pam Tillis
5/59	**Don't Tell Me Your Troubles**...Don Gibson
10/74	**Don't Tell (That Sweet Ole Lady Of Mine)**...Johnny Carver
1/76	**Don't The Girls All Get Prettier At Closing Time**...Mickey Gilley
5/77	**Don't Throw It All Away**...Dave & Sugar
9/53	**Don't Throw Your Life Away**...Webb Pierce
5/89	**Don't Toss Us Away**...Patty Loveless
	Don't Touch Me
2/66	Jeannie Seely
12/66	Wilma Burgess
20/87	**Don't Touch Me There**...Charly McClain
1/86	**Don't Underestimate My Love For You**...Lee Greenwood
5/81	**Don't Wait On Me**...Statler Brothers
23/69	**Don't Wake Me I'm Dreaming**...Warner Mack
5/89	**Don't Waste It On The Blues**...Gene Watson
	Don't We All Have The Right
F/70	Roger Miller
1/88	Ricky Van Shelton
40/82	**Don't We Belong In Love**...Stephanie Winslow
1/61	**Don't Worry**...Marty Robbins
1/82	**Don't Worry 'Bout Me Baby**...Janie Fricke
9/89	**Don't You**...Forester Sisters
8/85	**Doncha?**...T.G. Sheppard
	Don't You Ever Get Tired Of Hurting Me
11/66	Ray Price
11/81	Willie Nelson & Ray Price
1/89	Ronnie Milsap
1/83	**Don't You Know How Much I Love You**...Ronnie Milsap
12/74	**Don't You Think**...Marty Robbins
F/58	**Doncha' Think It's Time**...Elvis Presley
5/78	**Don't You Think This Outlaw Bit's Done Got Out Of Hand**...Waylon Jennings
23/83	**Don't Your Mem'ry Ever Sleep At Night**...Steve Wariner
	Doncha ..see: Don't You
6/86	**Doo-Wah Days**...Mickey Gilley
1/75	**Door, The**...George Jones
28/76	**Door I Used To Close**...Roy Head
1/76	**Door Is Always Open**...Dave & Sugar
6/56	**Doorstep To Heaven**...Carl Smith
34/64	**Double Life**...Joe Carson
30/78	**Double S**...Bill Anderson
8/84	**Double Shot (Of My Baby's Love)**...Joe Stampley

POS/YR	RECORD TITLE/ARTIST
13/49	**Double Talkin' Woman**...Earl Nunn feat. Billy Lee
16/81	**Down And Out**...George Strait
18/67	**Down At The Pawn Shop**...Hank Snow
36/77	**Down At The Pool**...Johnny Carver
4/47	**Down At The Roadside Inn**...Al Dexter
2/91	**Down At The Twist And Shout**...Mary-Chapin Carpenter
9/63	**Down By The River**...Faron Young
1/91	**Down Home**...Alabama
10/95	**Down In Flames**...BlackHawk
38/70	**Down In New Orleans**...Buddy Alan
	Down In Tennessee
12/86	John Anderson
23/95	Mark Chesnutt
	Down In The Boondocks
37/69	Penny DeHaven
25/70	Freddy Weller
19/93	**Down On My Knees**...Trisha Yearwood
13/83	**Down On The Corner**...Jerry Reed
25/85	**Down On The Farm**...Charley Pride
2/94	**Down On The Farm**...Tim McGraw
6/79	**Down On The Rio Grande**...Johnny Rodriguez
6/89	**Down That Road Tonight**...Nitty Gritty Dirt Band
33/85	**Down The Road Mountain Pass**...Dan Fogelberg
2/51	**Down The Trail Of Achin' Hearts**...Hank Snow with Anita Carter
16/79	**Down To Earth Woman**...Kenny Dale
2/81	**Down To My Last Broken Heart**...Janie Fricke
2/91	**Down To My Last Teardrop**...Tanya Tucker
18/63	**Down To The River**...Rose Maddox
5/51	**Down Yonder**...Del Wood
32/73	**Downfall Of Me**...Sonny James
36/84	**Downtown**...Dolly Parton
31/71	**Dozen Pairs Of Boots**...Del Reeves
29/70	**Drag 'Em Off The Interstate, Sock It To 'Em, J.P. Blues**...Dick Curless
11/59	**Draggin' The River**...Ferlin Husky
	Dream ..see: All I Have To Do Is
	Dream Baby (How Long Must I Dream)
7/71	Glen Campbell
9/83	Lacy J. Dalton
22/64	**Dream House For Sale**...Red Sovine
5/71	**Dream Lover**...Billy "Crash" Craddock
40/79	**Dream Never Dies**...Bill Anderson
7/81	**Dream Of Me**...Vern Gosdin

POS/YR	RECORD TITLE/ARTIST
7/79	**Dream On**...Oak Ridge Boys
18/84	**Dream On Texas Ladies**...Rex Allen, Jr.
23/73	**Dream Painter**...Connie Smith
32/82	**Dreamin'**...John Schneider
32/79	**Dreamin's All I Do**...Earl Thomas Conley
10/75	**Dreaming My Dreams With You**...Waylon Jennings
1/94	**Dreaming With My Eyes Open**...Clay Walker
9/86	**Dreamland Express**...John Denver
15/82	**Dreams Die Hard**...Gary Morris
35/77	**Dreams Of A Dreamer**...Darrell McCall
3/68	**Dreams Of The Everyday Housewife**...Glen Campbell
8/73	**Drift Away**...Narvel Felts
3/91	**Drift Off To Dream**...Travis Tritt
1/81	**Drifter**...Sylvia
8/67	**Drifting Apart**...Warner Mack
11/60	**Drifting Texas Sand**...Webb Pierce
7/51	**Driftwood On The River**...Ernest Tubb
F/70	**Drink Boys, Drink**...Jim Ed Brown
25/80	**Drink It Down, Lady**...Rex Allen, Jr.
2/85	**Drinkin' And Dreamin'**...Waylon Jennings
17/80	**Drinkin' And Drivin'**...Johnny Paycheck
8/86	**Drinkin' My Baby Goodbye**...Charlie Daniels Band
1/76	**Drinkin' My Baby (Off My Mind)**...Eddie Rabbitt
10/84	**Drinkin' My Way Back Home**...Gene Watson
10/74	**Drinkin' Thing**...Gary Stewart
	Drinking Champagne
35/68	Cal Smith
4/90	George Strait
9/55	**Drinking Tequila**...Jim Reeves
20/73	**Drinking Wine Spo-Dee O'Dee**...Jerry Lee Lewis
2/93	**Drive South**...Suzy Bogguss
24/94	**Drivin' And Cryin'**...Steve Wariner
1/80	**Drivin' My Life Away**...Eddie Rabbitt
	Drivin' Nails In My Coffin
2/46	Floyd Tillman
5/46	Ernest Tubb
26/84	**Drivin' Wheel**...Emmylou Harris
17/76	**Dropkick Me, Jesus**...Bobby Bare
	Dropping Out Of Sight
32/67	Jimmy Newman
35/81	Bobby Bare
39/85	**Drowning In Memories**...T. Graham Brown

POS/YR	RECORD TITLE/ARTIST
25/61	**Drunk Again**...Lattie Moore
5/73	**Dueling Banjos**...Eric Weissberg & Steve Mandell
	(Dukes Of Hazzard) ..see: Theme From The
15/90	**Dumas Walker**...Kentucky Headhunters
24/67	**Dumb Blonde**...Dolly Parton
1/95	**Dust On The Bottle**...David Lee Murphy
21/70	**Duty Not Desire**...Jeannie C. Riley

E

POS/YR	RECORD TITLE/ARTIST
27/69	**Each And Every Part Of Me**...Bobby Lewis
5/45	**Each Minute Seems A Million Years**...Eddy Arnold
4/60	**Each Moment ('Spent With You)**...Ernest Ashworth
4/44	**Each Night At Nine**...Floyd Tillman
16/69	**Each Time**...Johnny Bush
22/91	**Eagle, The**...Waylon Jennings
33/91	**Eagle When She Flies**...Dolly Parton
35/70	**Early In The Morning**...Mac Curtis
14/89	**Early In The Morning And Late At Night**...Hank Williams, Jr.
9/66	**Early Morning Rain**...George Hamilton IV
9/71	**Early Morning Sunshine**...Marty Robbins
28/75	**Early Sunday Morning**...Chip Taylor
20/93	**Easier Said Than Done**...Radney Foster
2/77	**East Bound And Down**...Jerry Reed
2/75	**Easy As Pie**...Billy "Crash" Craddock
1/93	**Easy Come, Easy Go**...George Strait
14/64	**Easy Come-Easy Go**...Bill Anderson
12/78	**Easy From Now On**...Emmylou Harris
12/77	**Easy Look**...Charlie Rich
1/71	**Easy Loving**...Freddie Hart
26/60	**Easy Money**...James O'Gwynn
32/83	**Easy On The Eye**...Gatlin Bros.
1/52	**Easy On The Eyes**...Eddy Arnold
2/68	**Easy Part's Over**...Charley Pride
26/75	**Easy To Love**...Hank Snow
5/86	**Easy To Please**...Janie Fricke
3/56	**Eat, Drink, And Be Merry (Tomorrow You'll Cry)**...Porter Wagoner
25/61	**Ebony Eyes**...Everly Brothers
2/49	**Echo Of Your Footsteps**...Eddy Arnold
1/53	**Eddy's Song**...Eddy Arnold
2/63	**8 X 10**...Bill Anderson
1/88	**Eighteen Wheels And A Dozen Roses**...Kathy Mattea

POS/YR	RECORD TITLE/ARTIST
7/87	80's Ladies...K.T. Oslin
1/59	El Paso...Marty Robbins
1/76	El Paso City...Marty Robbins
34/76	11 Months And 29 Days...Johnny Paycheck
1/72	Eleven Roses...Hank Williams, Jr.
1/84	Elizabeth...Statler Brothers
1/81	Elvira...Oak Ridge Boys
20/94	Elvis And Andy...Confederate Railroad
31/82	Elvis Medley...Elvis Presley
3/73	Emptiest Arms In The World...Merle Haggard
1/71	Empty Arms...Sonny James
6/50	Enclosed, One Broken Heart...Eddy Arnold
12/76	End Is Not In Sight (The Cowboy Tune)...Amazing Rhythm Aces
2/63	End Of The World...Skeeter Davis
	Endlessly
1/70	Sonny James
38/77	Eddie Middleton
13/68	Enemy, The...Jim Ed Brown
2/65	Engine Engine #9...Roger Miller
3/66	England Swings...Roger Miller
36/65	Enough Man For You...Ott Stephens
25/77	Eres Tu...Johnny Rodriguez
2/84	Ev'ry Heart Should Have One...Charley Pride
	Ev'rybody's Somebody's Fool ..see: Everybody's Somebody's Fool
37/80	Evangelina...Hoyt Axton
	Even Cowgirls Get The Blues
26/80	Lynn Anderson
35/86	Johnny Cash & Waylon Jennings
17/75	Even If I Have To Steal...Mel Street
16/91	Even Now...Exile
5/92	Even The Man In The Moon Is Crying...Mark Collie
1/54	Even Tho...Webb Pierce
11/84	Evening Star...Kenny Rogers
30/69	Ever Changing Mind...Don Gibson
4/82	Ever, Never Lovin' You...Ed Bruce
37/66	Ever Since My Baby Went Away...Jack Greene
14/79	Everlasting Love...Narvel Felts
34/77	Every Beat Of My Heart...Peggy Sue
	Every Day ..see: Everyday
21/76	Every Face Tells A Story...Olivia Newton-John
3/93	Every Little Thing...Carlene Carter
20/86	Every Night...Pake McEntire

POS/YR	RECORD TITLE/ARTIST
26/81	Every Now And Then...Brenda Lee
34/76	Every Now And Then...Mac Davis
2/94	Every Once In A While...BlackHawk
2/92	Every Second...Collin Raye
21/69	Every Step Of The Way...Ferlin Husky
2/96	Every Time I Get Around You...David Lee Murphy
7/74	Every Time I Turn The Radio On...Bill Anderson
10/58	Every Time I'm Kissing You...Faron Young
34/96	Every Time My Heart Calls Your Name...John Berry
1/78	Every Time Two Fools Collide...Kenny Rogers & Dottie West
3/75	Every Time You Touch Me (I Get High)...Charlie Rich
1/79	Every Which Way But Loose...Eddie Rabbitt
28/77	Every Word I Write...Dottie West
3/62	Everybody But Me...Ernest Ashworth
17/66	Everybody Loves A Nut...Johnny Cash
25/78	Everybody Loves A Rain Song...B.J. Thomas
5/82	Everybody Makes Mistakes...Lacy J. Dalton
37/75	Everybody Needs A Rainbow...Ray Stevens
28/87	Everybody Needs A Hero...Gene Watson
24/85	Everybody Needs Love On Saturday Night...Maines Brothers Band
28/73	Everybody Needs Lovin'...Norro Wilson
28/68	Everybody Oughta Sing A Song...Dallas Frazier
24/87	Everybody's Crazy 'Bout My Baby...Marie Osmond
40/64	Everybody's Darlin', Plus Mine...Browns
18/83	Everybody's Dream Girl...Dan Seals
14/61	Everybody's Dying For Love...Jimmy Newman
1/73	Everybody's Had The Blues...Merle Haggard
20/72	Everybody's Reaching Out For Someone...Pat Daisy
	Everybody's Somebody's Fool
16/60	Ernest Tubb
24/60	Connie Francis
11/88	Everybody's Sweetheart...Vince Gill
1/84	Everyday...Oak Ridge Boys
26/86	Everyday...James Taylor
	Everyday I Have To Cry Some
23/69	Bob Luman
14/77	Joe Stampley

POS/YR	RECORD TITLE/ARTIST
36/81	**Everyone Gets Crazy Now And Then**...Roger Miller
5/70	**Everything A Man Could Ever Need**...Glen Campbell
12/76	**Everything I Own**...Joe Stampley
29/86	**Everything I Used To Do**...Gene Watson
32/79	**Everything I've Always Wanted**...Porter Wagoner
39/70	**Everything Is Beautiful**...Ray Stevens
1/86	**Everything That Glitters (Is Not Gold)**...Dan Seals
40/70	**Everything Will Be Alright**...Claude Gray
	Everything's A Waltz ..see: (When You Fall In Love)
7/83	**Everything's Beautiful (In It's Own Way)**...Dolly Parton Willie Nelson
40/64	**Everything's O.K. On The LBJ**...Lawton Williams
17/75	**Everything's The Same (Ain't Nothing Changed)**...Billy Swan
10/82	**Everytime You Cross My Mind (You Break My Heart)**...Razzy Bailey
23/88	**Everytime You Go Outside I Hope It Rains**...Burch Sisters
24/81	**Evil Angel**...Ed Bruce
5/66	**Evil On Your Mind**...Jan Howard
36/68	**Evolution And The Bible**...Hugh X. Lewis
4/92	**Except For Monday**...Lorrie Morgan
35/89	**Exception To The Rule**...Mason Dixon
2/60	**Excuse Me (I Think I've Got A Heartache)**...Buck Owens
20/85	**Eye Of A Hurricane**...John Anderson
37/79	**Eyes Big As Dallas**...Wynn Stewart
19/83	**Eyes Of A Stranger**...David Wills
12/60	**Eyes Of Love**...Margie Singleton
30/84	**Eyes That See In The Dark**...Kenny Rogers

F

POS/YR	RECORD TITLE/ARTIST
4/87	**Face In The Crowd**...Michael Martin Murphey & Holly Dunn
1/88	**Face To Face**...Alabama
10/60	**Face To The Wall**...Faron Young
25/61	**Facing The Wall**...Charlie Walker
6/88	**Factory, The**...Kenny Rogers

POS/YR	RECORD TITLE/ARTIST
	Faded Love
8/50	Bob Wills
7/63	Patsy Cline
22/63	Leon McAuliff
22/71	Tompall/Glaser Brothers
3/80	Willie Nelson & Ray Price
	Faded Love And Winter Roses
25/69	Carl Smith
33/79	David Houston
11/78	**Fadin' In, Fadin' Out**...Tommy Overstreet
36/80	**Fadin' Renegade**...Tommy Overstreet
	Fair And Tender Ladies
28/64	George Hamilton IV
30/78	Charlie McCoy
5/89	**Fair Shake**...Foster & Lloyd
37/74	**Fairytale**...Pointer Sisters
13/95	**Faith In Me, Faith In You**...Doug Stone
10/84	**Faithless Love**...Glen Campbell
1/83	**Faking Love**...T.G. Sheppard & Karen Brooks
6/95	**Fall In Love**...Kenny Chesney
10/79	**Fall In Love With Me Tonight**...Randy Barlow
4/60	**Fallen Angel**...Webb Pierce
	Fallen Star
2/57	Jimmy Newman
8/57	Ferlin Husky
1/88	**Fallin' Again**...Alabama
26/60	**Falling Again**...Porter Wagoner
6/81	**Falling Again**...Don Williams
2/87	**Fallin' For You For Years**...Conway Twitty
2/85	**Fallin' In Love**...Sylvia
39/93	**Fallin' Never Felt So Good**...Shawn Camp
8/87	**Fallin' Out**...Waylon Jennings
2/91	**Fallin' Out Of Love**...Reba McEntire
10/58	**Falling Back To You**...Webb Pierce
40/92	**Familiar Pain**...Restless Heart
	Family Bible
10/60	Claude Gray
16/61	George Jones
7/59	**Family Man**...Frankie Miller
35/81	**Family Man**...Wright Brothers
4/79	**Family Tradition**...Hank Williams, Jr.
1/88	**Famous Last Words Of A Fool**...George Strait
30/77	**Fan The Flame, Feed The Fire**...Don Gibson
	Fancy
26/70	Bobbie Gentry
8/91	Reba McEntire
1/81	**Fancy Free**...Oak Ridge Boys

POS/YR	RECORD TITLE/ARTIST
13/71	**Fancy Satin Pillows**...Wanda Jackson
27/79	**Fantasy Island**...Freddy Weller
	Far, Far Away
11/60	Don Gibson
12/72	Don Gibson
5/79	**Farewell Party**...Gene Watson
21/86	**Farther Down The Line**...Lyle Lovett
17/75	**Farthest Thing From My Mind**...Ray Price
2/94	**Fast As You**...Dwight Yoakam
4/86	**Fast Lanes And Country Roads**...Barbara Mandrell
4/90	**Fast Movin' Train**...Restless Heart
1/76	**Faster Horses (The Cowboy And The Poet)**...Tom T. Hall
4/47	**Fat Gal**...Merle Travis
15/91	**Feed Jake**...Pirates Of The Mississippi
5/90	**Feed This Fire**...Anne Murray
16/81	**Feedin' The Fire**...Zella Lehr
21/76	**Feel Again**...Faron Young
10/83	**Feel Right**...Tanya Tucker
38/78	**Feelin' Better**...Hank Williams, Jr.
2/86	**Feelin' The Feelin'**...Bellamy Brothers
1/75	**Feelins'**...Conway Twitty & Loretta Lynn
19/77	**Feeling's Right**...Narvel Felts
26/78	**Feelings So Right Tonight**...Don King
1/81	**Feels So Right**...Alabama
19/79	**Feet**...Ray Price
30/79	**Fell Into Love**...Foxfire
	Feudin' And Fightin'
4/47	Dorothy Shay
5/47	Jo Stafford
23/95	**Fever, The**...Garth Brooks
9/91	**Few Good Things Remain**...Kathy Mattea
8/90	**Few Ole Country Boys**...Randy Travis & George Jones
29/61	**Fickle Fun**...Kitty Wells
40/86	**Fiddlin' Man**...Michael Martin Murphey
23/74	**Field Of Yellow Daisies**...Charlie Rich
40/80	**Fifteen Beers**...Johnny Paycheck
24/67	**Fifteen Days**...Wilma Burgess
1/70	**Fifteen Years Ago**...Conway Twitty
16/78	**'57 Chevrolet**...Billie Jo Spears
1/70	**Fightin' Side Of Me**...Merle Haggard
27/92	**Fighting Fire With Fire**...Davis Daniel
24/64	**File, The**...Bob Luman

POS/YR	RECORD TITLE/ARTIST
	Filipino Baby
2/46	Ernest Tubb
4/46	Cowboy Copas
5/46	Texas Jim Robertson
5/46	"T" Texas Tyler
1/82	**Finally**...T.G. Sheppard
	Finally
28/59	Mel Tillis
9/64	Kitty Wells & Webb Pierce
40/95	**Find Out What's Happenin'**...Tanya Tucker
15/68	**Find Out What's Happening**...Bobby Bare
38/76	**Find Yourself Another Puppet**...Brenda Lee
6/89	**Finders Are Keepers**...Hank Williams, Jr.
24/83	**Finding You**...Joe Stampley
19/95	**Finish What We Started**...Diamond Rio
29/76	**Fire And Rain**...Willie Nelson
1/81	**Fire & Smoke**...Earl Thomas Conley
1/83	**Fire I Can't Put Out**...George Strait
7/87	**Fire In The Sky**...Nitty Gritty Dirt Band
40/81	**Fire In Your Eyes**...Gary Morris
21/75	**Fireball Rolled A Seven**...Dave Dudley
5/85	**Fireman, The**...George Strait
9/57	**First Date, First Kiss, First Love**...Sonny James
5/95	**First Step**...Tracy Byrd
32/64	**First Step Down (Is The Longest)**...Bob Jennings
29/79	**First Thing Each Morning (Last Thing at Night)**...Cliff Cochran
1/65	**First Thing Ev'ry Morning (And The Last Thing Ev'ry Night)**...Jimmy Dean
2/75	**First Time**...Freddie Hart
10/78	**First Time**...Billy "Crash" Craddock
24/87	**First Time Caller**...Juice Newton
13/92	**First Time For Everything**...Little Texas
7/85	**First Word In Memory Is Me**...Janie Fricke
1/87	**Fishin' In The Dark**...Nitty Gritty Dirt Band
1/68	**Fist City**...Loretta Lynn
30/90	**Fit To Be Tied Down**...Conway Twitty
26/60	**Five Brothers**...Marty Robbins
14/59	**Five Feet High And Rising**...Johnny Cash
5/64	**Five Little Fingers**...Bill Anderson
21/66	**Five Little Johnson Girls**...Stonemans
39/66	**Five Miles From Home (Soon I'll See Mary)**...Bob Luman
1/90	**Five Minutes**...Lorrie Morgan
16/92	**Five O'Clock World**...Hal Ketchum
5/64	**500 Miles Away From Home**...Bobby Bare
18/89	**5:01 Blues**...Merle Haggard

POS/YR	RECORD TITLE/ARTIST
18/76	**Flash Of Fire**...Hoyt Axton
20/75	**Flat Natural Born Good-Timin' Man**...Gary Stewart
33/69	**Flat River, Mo.**...Ferlin Husky
9/61	**Flat Top**...Cowboy Copas
11/69	**Flattery Will Get You Everywhere**...Lynn Anderson
1/71	**Flesh And Blood**...Johnny Cash
4/83	**Flight 309 To Tennessee**...Shelly West
8/68	**Flower Of Love**...Leon Ashley
2/66	**Flowers On The Wall**...Statler Brothers
12/76	**Fly Away**...John Denver
8/71	**Fly Away Again**...Dave Dudley
34/67	**Fly Butterfly Fly**...Marty Robbins
20/83	**Fly Into Love**...Charly McClain
23/63	**Flyin' South**...Hank Locklin
	Foggy River
10/48	Kate Smith
18/68	Carl Smith
15/64	**Followed Closely By My Teardrops**...Hank Locklin
10/81	**Following The Feeling**...Moe Bandy/Judy Bailey
	Folsom Prison Blues
4/56	Johnny Cash
1/68	Johnny Cash
	Fool, The
14/56	Sanford Clark
22/78	Don Gibson
18/77	**Fool**...John Wesley Ryles
31/73	**Fool**...Elvis Presley
6/81	**Fool By Your Side**...Dave & Sugar
6/67	**Fool Fool Fool**...Webb Pierce
1/83	**Fool For Your Love**...Mickey Gilley
1/82	**Fool Hearted Memory**...George Strait
40/73	**Fool I've Been Today**...Jack Greene
33/83	**Fool In Me**...Sonny James
4/72	**Fool Me**...Lynn Anderson
14/63	**Fool Me Once**...Connie Hall
	Fool Such As I
3/53	Hank Snow
5/90	Baillie & the Boys
3/84	**Fool's Gold**...Lee Greenwood
39/89	**Fool's Paradise**...Larry Boone
21/85	**Fooled Around And Fell In Love**...T.G. Sheppard
25/79	**Fooled Around And Fell In Love**...Mundo Earwood
4/79	**Fooled By A Feeling**...Barbara Mandrell
9/54	**Fooler, A Faker**...Hank Thompson

POS/YR	RECORD TITLE/ARTIST
4/83	**Foolin'**...Johnny Rodriguez
2/61	**Foolin' Around**...Buck Owens
1/94	**Foolish Pride**...Travis Tritt
15/48	**Foolish Tears**...Tex Williams
	Fools
19/72	Johnny Duncan
3/79	Jim Ed Brown/Helen Cornelius
9/77	**Fools Fall In Love**...Jacky Ward
17/79	**Fools For Each Other**...Johnny Rodriguez
5/46	**Footprints In The Snow**...Bill Monroe
7/62	**Footsteps Of A Fool**...Judy Lynn
3/95	**For A Change**...Neal McCoy
12/75	**For A Minute There**...Johnny Paycheck
1/82	**For All The Wrong Reasons**...Bellamy Brothers
13/91	**For Crying Out Loud**...Davis Daniel
36/76	**For Love's Own Sake**...Ed Bruce
	For Loving Me ..see: (That's What You Get)
1/67	**For Loving You**...Bill Anderson & Jan Howard
1/91	**For My Broken Heart**...Reba McEntire
10/53	**For Now And Always**...Hank Snow
7/56	**For Rent (One Empty Heart)**...Sonny James
1/70	**For The Good Times**...Ray Price
27/71	**For The Kids**...Sammi Smith
F/55	**For The Love Of A Woman Like You**...Faron Young
16/75	**Forbidden Angel**...Mel Street
23/63	**Forbidden Lovers**...Lefty Frizzell
23/64	**Forbidden Street**...Carl Butler & Pearl
12/48	**'Fore Day In The Morning**...Roy Brown
7/87	**Forever**...Statler Brothers
10/84	**Forever Again**...Gene Watson
6/52	**Forever (And Always)**...Lefty Frizzell
1/87	**Forever And Ever, Amen**...Randy Travis
15/61	**Forever Gone**...Ernest Ashworth
5/48	**Forever Is Ending Today**...Ernest Tubb
17/76	**Forever Lovers**...Mac Davis
10/49	**Forever More**...Jimmy Wakely
37/79	**Forever One Day At A Time**...Don Gibson
1/91	**Forever Together**...Randy Travis
14/84	**Forever You**...Whites
21/70	**Forever Yours**...Dottie West
1/91	**Forever's As Far As I'll Go**...Alabama
5/84	**Forget About Me**...Bellamy Brothers
20/61	**Forget The Past**...Faron Young
12/75	**Forgive And Forget**...Eddie Rabbitt
23/63	**Forgive Me**...Beverly Buff

POS/YR	RECORD TITLE/ARTIST
6/53	**Gambler's Guitar**...Rusty Draper
22/59	**Gambler's Love**...Rose Maddox
8/49	**Gamblin' Polka Dot Blues**...Tommy Duncan
5/66	**Game Of Triangles**...Bobby Bare, Norma Jean, Liz Anderson
2/69	**Games People Play**...Freddy Weller
1/76	**Games That Daddies Play**...Conway Twitty
9/67	**Gardenias In Her Hair**...Marty Robbins
4/57	**Geisha Girl**...Hank Locklin
(also see: I Found My Girl In The USA, & Lost To A)	
26/82	**General Lee**...Johnny Cash
30/67	**Gentle On My Mind**...Glen Campbell
18/77	**Gentle To Your Senses**...Mel McDaniel
10/69	**George (And The North Woods)**...Dave Dudley
17/78	**Georgia In A Jug**...Johnny Paycheck
3/77	**Georgia Keeps Pulling On My Ring**...Conway Twitty
1/78	**Georgia On My Mind**...Willie Nelson
37/71	**Georgia Pineywoods**...Osborne Brothers
16/70	**Georgia Sunshine**...Jerry Reed
24/60	**Georgia Town Blues**...Mel Tillis & Bill Phillips
14/62	**Get A Little Dirt On Your Hands**...Bill Anderson
33/85	**Get Back To The Country**...Neil Young
21/82	**Get Into Reggae Cowboy**...Bellamy Brothers
F/79	**Get It Up**...Ronnie Milsap
3/74	**Get On My Love Train**...La Costa
	Get Rhythm
F/56	Johnny Cash
23/69	Johnny Cash
27/91	Martin Delray
34/70	**Get Together**...Gwen & Jerry Collins
5/67	**Get While The Gettin's Good**...Bill Anderson
14/66	**Get Your Lie The Way You Want It**...Bonnie Guitar
4/46	**Get Yourself A Red Head**...Hank Penny
37/66	**Gettin' Any Feed For Your Chickens**...Del Reeves
30/65	**Gettin' Married Has Made Us Strangers**...Dottie West
29/60	**Getting Old Before My Time**...Merle Kilgore
28/81	**Getting Over You Again**...Ray Price
5/90	**Ghost In This House**...Shenandoah
	(Ghost) Riders In The Sky ..see: Riders In The Sky

POS/YR	RECORD TITLE/ARTIST
1/66	**Giddyup Go**...Red Sovine
10/66	**Giddyup Go - Answer**...Minnie Pearl
4/88	**Gift, The**...McCarters
34/80	**Gift From Missouri**...Jim Weatherly
14/79	**Gimme Back My Blues**...Jerry Reed
35/70	**Ginger Is Gentle And Waiting For Me**...Jim Ed Brown
40/78	**Girl At The End Of The Bar**...John Anderson
22/68	**Girl Don't Have To Drink To Have Fun**...Wanda Jackson
15/64	**Girl From Spanish Town**...Marty Robbins
F/78	**Girl I Can Tell (You're Trying To Work It Out)**...Waylon
3/62	**Girl I Used To Know**...George Jones
36/72	**Girl In New Orleans**...Sammi Smith
17/86	**Girl Like Emmylou**...Southern Pacific
6/69	**Girl Most Likely**...Jeannie C. Riley
17/85	**Girl Most Likely To**...B.J. Thomas
1/65	**Girl On The Billboard**...Del Reeves
36/79	**Girl On The Other Side**...Nick Nobel & Lew Douglass
26/60	**Girl Who Didn't Need Love**...Porter Wagoner
26/70	**Girl Who'll Satisfy Her Man**...Barbara Fairchild
35/66	**Girls Get Prettier (Every Day)**...Hank Locklin
1/85	**Girls Night Out**...Judds
7/87	**Girls Ride Horses Too**...Judy Rodman
10/94	**Girls With Guitars**...Wynonna Judd
14/81	**Girls, Women And Ladies**...Ed Bruce
2/88	**Give A Little Love**...Judds
24/73	**Give A Little, Take A Little**...Barbara Mandrell
13/87	**Give Back My Heart**...Lyle Lovett
24/71	**Give Him Love**...Patti Page
	Give Me ..also see: Gimme
15/49	**Give Me A Hundred Reasons**...Ann Jones
9/50	**Give Me A Little Old Fashioned Love**...Ernest Tubb
10/84	**Give Me Back That Old Familiar Feeling**...Whites
9/64	**Give Me 40 Acres (To Turn This Rig Around)**...Willis Brothers
3/89	**Give Me His Last Chance**...Lionel Cartwright
1/52	**Give Me More, More, More (Of Your Kisses)**...Lefty Frizzell
1/84	**Give Me One More Chance**...Exile

POS/YR	RECORD TITLE/ARTIST
3/95	**Give Me One More Shot**...Alabama
1/87	**Give Me Wings**...Michael Johnson
13/57	**Give My Love To Rose**...Johnny Cash
	Give Myself A Party
5/58	Don Gibson
12/72	Jeannie C. Riley
8/88	**Givers And Takers**...Schuyler, Knobloch & Bickhardt
5/81	**Giving Up Easy**...Leon Everette
6/56	**Go Away With Me**...Wilburn Brothers
11/55	**Go Back You Fool**...Faron Young
4/54	**Go, Boy, Go**...Carl Smith
8/64	**Go Cat Go**...Norma Jean
38/90	**Go Down Swingin'**...Wild Rose
33/80	**Go For The Night**...Freddy Weller
10/61	**Go Home**...Flatt & Scruggs
23/66	**Go Now Pay Later**...Liz Anderson
13/62	**Go On Home**...Patti Page
14/95	**Go Rest High On That Mountain**...Vince Gill
16/69	**God Bless America Again**...Bobby Bare
7/84	**God Bless The USA**...Lee Greenwood
4/93	**God Blessed Texas**...Little Texas
32/68	**God Help You Woman**...Jim Glaser
22/78	**God Knows**...Debby Boone
11/78	**God Made Love**...Mel McDaniel
10/84	**God Must Be A Cowboy**...Dan Seals
39/78	**God Must Have Blessed America**...Glen Campbell
9/50	**God Please Protect America**...Jimmie Osborne
9/56	**God Was So Good**...Jimmy Newman
18/87	**God Will**...Lyle Lovett
10/84	**God Won't Get You**...Dolly Parton
25/75	**God's Gonna Get'cha (For That)**...George Jones & Tammy Wynette
	Gods Were Angry With Me
9/48	Eddie Kirk
3/50	Margaret Whiting & Jimmy Wakely
5/83	**Goin' Down Hill**...John Anderson
36/66	**Goin' Down The Road (Feelin' Bad)**...Skeeter Davis
1/88	**Goin' Gone**...Kathy Mattea
	Goin' Steady
2/53	Faron Young
5/70	Faron Young
2/95	**Goin' Through The Big D**...Mark Chesnutt
1/84	**Going, Going, Gone**...Lee Greenwood
31/68	**Going Home For The Last Time**...Kenny Price

POS/YR	RECORD TITLE/ARTIST
5/92	**Going Out Of My Mind**...McBride & The Ride
14/92	**Going Out Tonight**...Mary-Chapin Carpenter
17/63	**Going Through The Motions (Of Living)**...Sonny James
1/83	**Going Where The Lonely Go**...Merle Haggard
2/52	**Gold Rush Is Over**...Hank Snow
11/66	**Golden Guitar**...Bill Anderson
1/76	**Golden Ring**...George Jones & Tammy Wynette
	Golden Rocket
1/51	Hank Snow
38/70	Jim & Jesse
1/79	**Golden Tears**...Dave & Sugar
	Gone
1/57	Ferlin Husky
36/80	Ronnie McDowell
34/74	**Gone**...Nancy Wayne
5/92	**Gone As A Girl Can Get**...George Strait
1/95	**Gone Country**...Alan Jackson
23/70	**Gone Girl**...Tompall/Glaser Brothers
24/67	**Gone, On The Other Hand**...Tompall/Glaser Brothers
24/72	**Gone (Our Endless Love)**...Billy Walker
1/80	**Gone Too Far**...Eddie Rabbitt
2/45	**Gonna Build A Big Fence Around Texas**...Gene Autry
F/56	**Gonna Come Get You**...George Jones
	Gonna Find Me A Bluebird
3/57	Marvin Rainwater
12/57	Eddy Arnold
1/95	**Gonna Get A Life**...Mark Chesnutt
8/64	**Gonna Get Along Without You Now**...Skeeter Davis
4/83	**Gonna Go Huntin' Tonight**...Hank Williams, Jr.
10/65	**Gonna Have Love**...Buck Owens
1/88	**Gonna Take A Lot Of River**...Oak Ridge Boys
39/82	**Gonna Take My Angel Out Tonight**...Ronnie Rogers
25/63	**Good Country Song**...Hank Cochran
	Good Deal, Lucille
8/54	Al Terry
18/69	Carl Smith
7/71	**Good Enough To Be Your Wife**...Jeannie C. Riley
10/90	**Good Friends, Good Whiskey, Good Lovin'**...Hank Williams, Jr.

POS/YR	RECORD TITLE/ARTIST
29/87	**Good God, I Had It Good**...Pake McEntire
	Good Hearted Woman
3/72	Waylon Jennings
1/76	Waylon & Willie
23/73	**Good Love Is Like A Good Song**...Bob Luman
1/71	**Good Lovin' (Makes It Right)**...Tammy Wynette
21/80	**Good Lovin' Man**...Gail Davies
27/71	**Good Man**...June Carter Cash
30/72	**Good Morning Country Rain**...Jeannie C. Riley
37/77	**Good 'N' Country**...Kathy Barnes
9/73	**Good News**...Jody Miller
27/75	**Good News, Bad News**...Eddy Raven
18/76	**Good Night Special**...Little David Wilkins
19/83	**Good Night's Love**...Tammy Wynette
	(Good Ol' Boys) ..see: Good Ole Boys, & Theme From The Dukes Of Hazzard
15/81	**Good Ol' Girls**...Sonny Curtis
35/73	**Good Old Days (Are Here Again)**...Buck Owens & Susan Raye
31/74	**Good Old Fashioned Country Love**...Don Gibson & Sue Thompson
16/83	**Good Ole Boys**...Jerry Reed
2/80	**Good Ole Boys Like Me**...Don Williams
1/94	**Good Run Of Bad Luck**...Clint Black
34/70	**Good Thing**...Bill Wilbourn & Kathy Morrison
2/73	**Good Things**...David Houston
3/69	**Good Time Charlies**...Del Reeves
1/90	**Good Times**...Dan Seals
25/81	**Good Times**...Willie Nelson
1/76	**Good Woman Blues**...Mel Tillis
12/74	**Good Woman's Love**...Jerry Reed
2/71	**Good Year For The Roses**...George Jones
22/59	**Goodby Little Darlin'**...Johnny Cash
	Goodbye
19/74	Rex Allen, Jr.
22/79	Eddy Arnold
38/72	**Goodbye**...David Rogers
39/67	**Goodbye City, Goodbye Girl**...Webb Pierce
24/84	**Goodbye Heartache**...Louise Mandrell
12/63	**Goodbye Kisses**...Cowboy Copas
32/89	**Goodbye Lonesome, Hello Baby Doll**...Lonesome Strangers
17/81	**Goodbye Marie**...Bobby Goldsboro
11/94	**Goodbye Says It All**...BlackHawk
7/88	**Goodbye Time**...Conway Twitty

POS/YR	RECORD TITLE/ARTIST
20/67	**Goodbye Wheeling**...Mel Tillis
8/87	**Goodbyes All We've Got Left**...Steve Earle
	Goodnight Irene
1/50	Red Foley-Ernest Tubb
5/50	Moon Mullican
(also see: Wake Up, Irene)	
3/54	**Goodnight, Sweetheart, Goodnight**...Johnnie & Jack
24/67	**Goody, Goody Gumdrop**...Wilburn Brothers
10/89	**Gospel According To Luke**...Skip Ewing
14/73	**Got Leaving On Her Mind**...Nat Stuckey
1/86	**Got My Heart Set On You**...John Conlee
7/85	**Got No Reason Now For Goin' Home**...Gene Watson
1/72	**Got The All Overs For You (All Over Me)**...Freddie Hart
10/87	**Gotta Get Away**...Sweethearts Of The Rodeo
4/46	**Gotta Get Together With My Gal**...Elton Britt
9/87	**Gotta Have You**...Eddie Rabbitt
12/86	**Gotta Learn To Love Without You**...Michael Johnson
4/78	**Gotta' Quit Lookin' At You Baby**...Dave & Sugar
	Gotta Travel On
5/59	Billy Grammer
15/59	Bill Monroe
	Grand Tour
1/74	George Jones
38/93	Aaron Neville
16/78	**Grandest Lady Of Them All**...Conway Twitty
1/72	**Grandma Harp**...Merle Haggard
	(Grandma's Diary) ..see: Johnny, My Love
9/81	**Grandma's Song**...Gail Davies
1/86	**Grandpa (Tell Me 'Bout The Good Old Days)**...Judds
23/96	**Grandpa Told Me So**...Kenny Chesney
15/49	**Grass Looks Greener Over Yonder**...Hank Thompson
24/67	**Grass Won't Grow On A Busy Street**...Kenny Price
F/70	**Grazin' In Greener Pastures**...Ray Price
	Great Balls Of Fire
1/58	Jerry Lee Lewis
F/79	Dolly Parton
12/74	**Great Divide**...Roy Clark
32/66	**Great El Tigre (The Tiger)**...Stu Phillips
8/75	**Great Expectations**...Buck Owens
10/48	**Great Long Pistol**...Jerry Irby

POS/YR	RECORD TITLE/ARTIST
8/70	**Great White Horse**...Buck Owens & Susan Raye
3/92	**Greatest Man I Never Knew**...Reba McEntire
22/64	**Greatest One Of All**...Melba Montgomery
	Green Berets ..see: Ballad Of
37/82	**Green Eyes**...Tom Carlile
4/65	**Green, Green Grass Of Home**...Porter Wagoner
7/48	**Green Light**...Hank Thompson
11/67	**Green River**...Waylon Jennings
26/61	**Greener Pastures**...Stonewall Jackson
23/75	**Greener Than The Grass (We Laid On)**...Tanya Tucker
4/46	**Grievin' My Heart Out For You**...Jimmie Davis
9/59	**Grin And Bear It**...Jimmy Newman
	(Grits And Groceries) ..see: If I Don't Love You
39/69	**Growin' Up**...Tex Ritter
16/90	**Guardian Angels**...Judds
19/71	**Guess Away The Blues**...Don Gibson
18/66	**Guess My Eyes Were Bigger Than My Heart**...Conway Twitty
1/58	**Guess Things Happen That Way**...Johnny Cash
7/71	**Guess Who**...Slim Whitman
18/74	**Guess Who**...Jerry Wallace
3/63	**Guilty**...Jim Reeves
9/83	**Guilty**...Statler Brothers
37/82	**Guilty Eyes**...Bandana
8/49	**Guitar Boogie**...Arthur "Guitar Boogie" Smith
1/81	**Guitar Man**...Elvis Presley
(also see: Daddy Frank)	
	Guitar Polka
1/46	Al Dexter
3/46	Rosalie Allen
7/86	**Guitar Town**...Steve Earle
4/86	**Guitars, Cadillacs**...Dwight Yoakam
5/71	**Gwen (Congratulations)**...Tommy Overstreet
25/87	**Gypsies On Parade**...Sawyer Brown
16/71	**Gypsy Feet**...Jim Reeves

H

17/84	**Had A Dream (For The Heart)**...Judds
9/49	**Hadacol Boogie**...Bill Nettles
25/63	**Half A Man**...Willie Nelson
8/58	**Half A Mind**...Ernest Tubb

POS/YR	RECORD TITLE/ARTIST
	Half As Much
2/52	Hank Williams
23/76	Sheila Tilton
16/59	**Half-Breed**...Marvin Rainwater
8/93	**Half Enough**...Lorrie Morgan
30/64	**Half Of This, Half Of That**...Wynn Stewart
2/87	**Half Past Forever (Till I'm Blue In The Heart)**...T.G. Sheppard
4/94	**Half The Man**...Clint Black
2/79	**Half The Way**...Crystal Gayle
6/95	**Halfway Down**...Patty Loveless
26/63	**Hall Of Shame**...Melba Montgomery
15/85	**Hallelujah, I Love You So**...George Jones with Brenda Lee
22/68	**Hammer And Nails**...Jimmy Dean
34/93	**Hammer And Nails**...Radney Foster
6/87	**Hand That Rocks The Cradle**...Glen Campbell with Steve Wariner
11/61	**Hand You're Holding Now**...Skeeter Davis
19/78	**Handcuffed To A Heartache**...Mary K. Miller
2/74	**Hang In There Girl**...Freddie Hart
1/85	**Hang On To Your Heart**...Exile
	Hang Your Head In Shame
3/45	Bob Wills
4/45	Red Foley
9/83	**Hangin' Around**...Whites
34/64	**Hangin' Around**...Wilburn Brothers
4/94	**Hangin' In**...Tanya Tucker
30/79	**Hangin' In And Hangin' On**...Buck Owens
	Hangin' On
37/67	Gosdin Bros.
16/77	Vern Gosdin
26/71	**Hanging Over Me**...Jack Greene
15/59	**Hanging Tree**...Marty Robbins
14/49	**Hangman's Boogie**...Cowboy Copas
12/61	**Hangover Tavern**...Hank Thompson
12/73	**Hank**...Hank Williams, Jr.
39/73	**Hank And Lefty Raised My Country Soul**...Stoney Edwards
23/65	**Hank Williams' Guitar**...Freddie Hart
2/76	**Hank Williams, You Wrote My Life**...Moe Bandy
1/72	**Happiest Girl In The Whole U.S.A.**...Donna Fargo
3/76	**Happiness Of Having You**...Charley Pride
3/65	**Happy Birthday**...Loretta Lynn
1/79	**Happy Birthday Darlin'**...Conway Twitty
3/84	**Happy Birthday Dear Heartache**...Barbara Mandrell

POS/YR	RECORD TITLE/ARTIST
7/61	**Happy Birthday To Me**...Hank Locklin
	Happy, Happy Birthday Baby
36/72	Sandy Posey
1/86	Ronnie Milsap
	Happy Heart ..see: (I've Got A)
10/62	**Happy Journey**...Hank Locklin
2/68	**Happy State Of Mind**...Bill Anderson
22/68	**Happy Street**...Slim Whitman
11/63	**Happy To Be Unhappy**...Gary Buck
9/66	**Happy To Be With You**...Johnny Cash
8/79	**Happy Together**...T.G. Sheppard
7/67	**Happy Tracks**...Kenny Price
8/82	**Hard Candy Christmas**...Dolly Parton
36/92	**Hard Days And Honky Tonk Nights**...Earl Thomas Conley
31/70	**Hard, Hard Traveling Man**...Dick Curless
30/80	**Hard Hat Days And Honky Tonk Nights**...Red Steagall
2/58	**Hard Headed Woman**...Elvis Presley
10/87	**Hard Livin'**...Keith Whitley
13/95	**Hard Lovin' Woman**...Mark Collie
38/89	**Hard Luck Ace**...Lacy J. Dalton
1/90	**Hard Rock Bottom Of Your Heart**...Randy Travis
7/80	**Hard Times**...Lacy J. Dalton
5/94	**Hard To Say**...Sawyer Brown
11/93	**Hard Way**...Mary-Chapin Carpenter
4/93	**Hard Workin' Man**...Brooks & Dunn
10/86	**Harmony**...John Conlee
1/68	**Harper Valley P.T.A.**...Jeannie C. Riley
24/68	**Harper Valley P.T.A. (Later That Same Day)**...Ben Colder
4/46	**Harriet**...Red Foley with Roy Ross
35/65	**Harvest Of Sunshine**...Jimmy Dean
22/94	**Has Anybody Seen Amy**...John & Audrey Wiggins
9/93	**Haunted Heart**...Sammy Kershaw
11/69	**Haunted House**...Compton Brothers
1/68	**Have A Little Faith**...David Houston
14/58	**Have Blues—Will Travel**...Eddie Noack
30/59	**Have Heart, Will Love**...Jean Shepard
6/85	**Have I Got A Deal For You**...Reba McEntire
14/87	**Have I Got Some Blues For You**...Charley Pride
	Have I Told You Lately That I Love You
3/46	Gene Autry
3/46	Tex Ritter
4/46	Foy Willing
5/46	Red Foley with Roy Ross

POS/YR	RECORD TITLE/ARTIST
1/85	**Have Mercy**...Judds
	Have You Ever Been Lonely? (Have You Ever Been Blue)
2/49	Ernest Tubb
5/82	Jim Reeves & Patsy Cline
32/84	**Have You Loved Your Woman Today**...Craig Dillingham
3/75	**Have You Never Been Mellow**...Olivia Newton-John
32/80	**Haven't I Loved You Somewhere Before**...Joe Stampley
5/93	**He Ain't Worth Missing**...Toby Keith
19/77	**He Ain't You**...Lynn Anderson
15/84	**He Broke Your Mem'ry Last Night**...Reba McEntire
29/85	**He Burns Me Up**...Lane Brody
23/64	**He Called Me Baby**...Patsy Cline
26/74	**He Can Be Mine**...Jeannie Seely
8/74	**He Can't Fill My Shoes**...Jerry Lee Lewis
1/82	**He Got You**...Ronnie Milsap
1/70	**He Loves Me All The Way**...Tammy Wynette
17/64	**He Says The Same Things To Me**...Skeeter Davis
	He Stands Real Tall
11/62	Del Reeves
21/65	"Little" Jimmy Dickens
1/80	**He Stopped Loving Her Today**...George Jones
4/90	**He Talks To Me**...Lorrie Morgan
2/94	**He Thinks He'll Keep Her**...Mary-Chapin Carpenter
10/75	**He Took Me For A Ride**...La Costa
13/75	**He Turns It Into Love Again**...Lynn Anderson
2/90	**He Walked On Water**...Randy Travis
25/90	**He Was On To Somethin' (So He Made You)**...Ricky Skaggs
17/80	**He Was There (When I Needed You)**...Tammy Wynette
22/85	**He Won't Give In**...Kathy Mattea
31/92	**He Would Be Sixteen**...Michelle Wright
15/70	**He'd Still Love Me**...Lynn Anderson
1/60	**He'll Have To Go**...Jim Reeves
6/60	**He'll Have To Stay**...Jeanne Black
21/77	**He'll Play The Music (But You Can't Make Him Dance)**...Little David Wilkins
32/68	**He's A Good Ole Boy**...Arlene Harden
1/83	**He's A Heartache (Looking For A Place To Happen)**...Janie Fricke

POS/YR	RECORD TITLE/ARTIST
39/66	**He's A Jolly Good Fellow**...Charlie Walker
39/90	**He's Alive**...Dolly Parton
1/88	**He's Back And I'm Blue**...Desert Rose Band
	He's Everywhere
25/70	Sammi Smith
39/75	Marilyn Sellars
16/67	**He's Got A Way With Women**...Hank Thompson
18/87	**He's Letting Go**...Baillie & The Boys
16/58	**He's Lost His Love For Me**...Kitty Wells
	He's My Rock ..see: She's My Rock
17/80	**He's Out Of My Life**...Johnny Duncan & Janie Fricke
5/71	**He's So Fine**...Jody Miller
29/81	**He's The Fire**...Diana
12/63	**Head Over Heels In Love With You**...Don Gibson
7/77	**Head To Toe**...Bill Anderson
1/81	**Headache Tomorrow (Or A Heartache Tonight)**...Mickey Gilley
8/81	**Headed For A Heartache**...Gary Morris
2/45	**Headin' Down The Wrong Highway**...Ted Daffan
2/96	**Heads Carolina, Tails California**...Jo Dee Messina
23/79	**Healin'**...Bobby Bare
13/89	**Heart, The**...Lacy J. Dalton
21/63	**Heart, Be Careful**...Billy Walker
19/85	**Heart Don't Do This To Me**...Loretta Lynn
33/76	**Heart Don't Fail Me Now**...Randy Cornor
14/86	**Heart Don't Fall Now**...Sawyer Brown
19/91	**Heart Full Of Love**...Holly Dunn
1/48	**Heart Full Of Love (For a Handful of Kisses)**...Eddy Arnold
21/96	**Heart Half Empty**...Ty Herndon Featuring Stephanie Bentley
1/77	**Heart Healer**...Mel Tillis
1/95	**Heart Is A Lonely Hunter**...Reba McEntire
3/80	**Heart Of Mine**...Oak Ridge Boys
	Heart Of Stone ..see: (I Wish I Had A)
26/81	**Heart Of The Matter**...Kendalls
8/81	**Heart On The Mend**...Sylvia
	Heart Over Mind
5/61	Ray Price
3/70	Mel Tillis
39/94	**Heart Over Mind**...Lorrie Morgan
5/51	**Heart Strings**...Eddy Arnold
18/92	**Heart That You Own**...Dwight Yoakam
16/75	**Heart To Heart**...Roy Clark

POS/YR	RECORD TITLE/ARTIST
40/86	**Heart To Heart**...Wild Choir
5/60	**Heart To Heart Talk**...Bob Wills
8/85	**Heart Trouble**...Steve Wariner
21/95	**Heart Trouble**...Martina McBride
25/87	**Heart Vs. Heart**...Pake McEntire
12/67	**Heart, We Did All That We Could**...Jean Shepard
1/93	**Heart Won't Lie**...Reba McEntire & Vince Gill
30/80	**Heart's Been Broken**...Danny Wood
3/96	**Heart's Desire**...Lee Roy Parnell
23/93	**Heartache**...Suzy Bogguss
23/84	**Heartache And A Half**...Deborah Allen
29/63	**Heartache For A Keepsake**...Kitty Wells
6/83	**Heartache Tonight**...Conway Twitty
	Heartaches By The Number
2/59	Ray Price
26/72	Jack Reno
39/81	**Heartaches Of A Fool**...Willie Nelson
1/86	**Heartbeat In The Darkness**...Don Williams
35/70	**Heartbreak Avenue**...Carl Smith
7/82	**Heartbreak Express**...Dolly Parton
8/89	**Heartbreak Hill**...Emmylou Harris
	Heartbreak Hotel
1/56	Elvis Presley
1/79	Willie Nelson & Leon Russell
13/90	**Heartbreak Hurricane**...Ricky Skaggs
	Heartbreak Kid ..see: (Back to the)
40/66	**Heartbreak Tennessee**...Johnny Paycheck
1/61	**Heartbreak U.S.A.**...Kitty Wells
1/78	**Heartbreaker**...Dolly Parton
1/82	**Heartbroke**...Ricky Skaggs
1/93	**Heartland**...George Strait
2/93	**Hearts Are Gonna Roll**...Hal Ketchum
26/59	**Hearts Are Lonely**...Phil Sullivan
1/86	**Hearts Aren't Made To Break (They're Made To Love)**...Lee Greenwood
4/55	**Hearts Of Stone**...Red Foley
2/78	**Hearts On Fire**...Eddie Rabbitt
24/95	**Heaven Bound (I'm Ready)**...Shenandoah
4/88	**Heaven Can't Be Found**...Hank Williams, Jr.
5/70	**Heaven Everyday**...Mel Tillis
14↑/96	**Heaven Help My Heart**...Wynonna Judd
18/68	**Heaven Help The Working Girl**...Norma Jean
14/96	**Heaven In My Woman's Eyes**...Tracy Byrd
3/72	**Heaven Is My Woman's Love**...Tommy Overstreet
16/89	**Heaven Only Knows**...Emmylou Harris

POS/YR	RECORD TITLE/ARTIST
1/68	Heaven Says Hello...Sonny James
F/79	Heaven Was A Drink Of Wine...Merle Haggard
1/77	Heaven's Just A Sin Away...Kendalls
32/71	Heavenly...Wynn Stewart
8/82	Heavenly Bodies...Earl Thomas Conley
11/70	Heavenly Sunshine...Ferlin Husky
38/66	Heck Of A Fix In 66...Jim Nesbitt
1/86	Hell And High Water...T. Graham Brown
39/80	Hello Daddy, Good Morning Darling...Mel McDaniel
1/70	Hello Darlin'...Conway Twitty
4/61	Hello Fool...Ralph Emery
(also see: Hello Walls)	
13/75	Hello I Love You...Johnny Russell
26/70	Hello, I'm A Jukebox...George Kent
14/75	Hello Little Bluebird...Donna Fargo
1/74	Hello Love...Hank Snow
	Hello Mary Lou
14/70	Bobby Lewis
3/85	Statler Brothers
4/78	Hello Mexico (And Adios Baby To You)...Johnny Duncan
	Hello Out There
8/62	Carl Belew
28/74	LaWanda Lindsey
30/78	Hello! Remember Me...Billy Swan
	Hello Trouble
5/63	Orville Couch
11/89	Desert Rose Band
1/65	Hello Vietnam...Johnny Wright
30/63	Hello Wall No. 2...Ben Colder
1/61	Hello Walls...Faron Young
(also see: Hello Fool)	
14/73	Hello We're Lonely...Patti Page & Tom T. Hall
29/81	Hello Woman...Doug Kershaw
6/74	Help Me...Elvis Presley
38/77	Help Me...Ray Price
1/90	Help Me Hold On...Travis Tritt
	Help Me Make It Through The Night
1/71	Sammi Smith
4/80	Willie Nelson
37/75	Help Me Make It (To My Rockin' Chair)...B.J. Thomas
19/64	Helpless...Joe Carson
7/54	Hep Cat Baby...Eddy Arnold
3/76	Her Name Is......George Jones
2/68	Here Comes Heaven...Eddy Arnold
1/71	Here Comes Honey Again...Sonny James

POS/YR	RECORD TITLE/ARTIST
10/64	Here Comes My Baby...Dottie West
	Here Comes Santa Claus (Down Santa Claus Lane)
5/47	Gene Autry
4/48	Gene Autry
8/49	Gene Autry
32/80	Here Comes That Feeling Again...Don King
15/76	Here Comes That Girl Again...Tommy Overstreet
10/76	Here Comes The Freedom Train...Merle Haggard
9/78	Here Comes The Hurt Again...Mickey Gilley
22/95	Here Comes The Rain...Mavericks
4/68	Here Comes The Rain, Baby...Eddy Arnold
15/78	Here Comes The Reason I Live...Ronnie McDowell
38/73	Here Comes The World Again...Johnny Bush
4/95	Here I Am...Patty Loveless
3/72	Here I Am Again...Loretta Lynn
	Here I Am Drunk Again
13/60	Clyde Beavers
11/76	Moe Bandy
16/75	Here I Am In Dallas...Faron Young
13/71	Here I Go Again...Bobby Wright
20/78	Here In Love...Dottsy
3/90	Here In The Real World...Alan Jackson
7/55	Here Today And Gone Tomorrow...Browns
2/91	Here We Are...Alabama
11/79	Here We Are Again...Statler Brothers
26/61	Here We Are Again...Ray Price
17/74	Here We Go Again...Brian Shaw
1/77	Here You Come Again...Dolly Parton
2/91	Here's A Quarter (Call Someone Who Cares)...Travis Tritt
1/76	Here's Some Love...Tanya Tucker
14/54	Hernando's Hideaway...Homer & Jethro
4/91	Heroes...Paul Overstreet
3/91	Heroes And Friends...Randy Travis
	Hey Baby
35/70	Bobby G. Rice
7/82	Anne Murray
38/93	Hey Baby...Marty Stuart
2/83	Hey Bartender...Johnny Lee
2/89	Hey Bobby...K.T. Oslin
5/94	Hey Cinderella...Suzy Bogguss
15/68	Hey Daddy...Charlie Louvin
33/77	Hey Daisy (Where Have All The Good Times Gone)...Tom Bresh

POS/YR	RECORD TITLE/ARTIST
21/86	Hey Doll Baby...Sweethearts Of The Rodeo
1/51	Hey, Good Lookin'...Hank Williams
1/53	Hey Joe!...Carl Smith
8/53	Hey Joe...Kitty Wells
10/81	Hey Joe (Hey Moe)...Moe Bandy & Joe Stampley
6/51	Hey La La...Ernest Tubb
13/68	Hey Little One...Glen Campbell
40/88	Hey Little Sister...Tom Wopat
3/74	Hey Loretta...Loretta Lynn
13/63	Hey Lucille!...Claude King
19/76	Hey, Lucky Lady...Dolly Parton
9/58	Hey, Mr. Bluebird...Ernest Tubb & The Wilburn Brothers
8/53	Hey, Mr. Cotton Picker...Tennessee Ernie Ford
28/92	Hey Mister (I Need This Job)...Shenandoah
22/58	Hey Sheriff...Rusty & Doug
28/76	Hey Shirley (This Is Squirrely)...Shirley & Squirrely
21/74	Hey There Girl...David Rogers
1/75	(Hey Won't You Play) Another Somebody Done Somebody Wrong Song...B.J. Thomas
9/65	Hicktown...Tennessee Ernie Ford
36/81	Hideaway Healing...Stephanie Winslow
20/78	High And Dry...Joe Sun
27/61	High As The Mountains...Buck Owens
27/83	High Cost Of Leaving...Exile
33/82	High Cost Of Loving...Charlie Ross
1/89	High Cotton...Alabama
2/85	High Horse...Nitty Gritty Dirt Band
12/96	High Lonesome Sound...Vince Gill
24/93	High On A Mountain Top...Marty Stuart
14/88	High Ridin' Heroes...David Lynn Jones
20/93	High Rollin'...Gibson/Miller Band
F/78	High Rollin'...Jerry Reed
9/58	High School Confidential...Jerry Lee Lewis
24/94	High-Tech Redneck...George Jones
1/83	Highway 40 Blues...Ricky Skaggs
15/74	Highway Headin' South...Porter Wagoner
39/66	Highway Patrol...Red Simpson
2/89	Highway Robbery...Tanya Tucker
1/85	Highwayman...Waylon Jennings/Willie Nelson/Johnny Cash/Kris Kristofferson
	Hillbilly Fever
3/50	"Little" Jimmy Dickens
9/50	Ernest Tubb-Red Foley (No. 2)
8/81	Hillbilly Girl With The Blues...Lacy J. Dalton

POS/YR	RECORD TITLE/ARTIST
5/76	Hillbilly Heart...Johnny Rodriguez
37/86	Hillbilly Highway...Steve Earle
8/90	Hillbilly Rock...Marty Stuart
	Hillbilly Singer ..see: Ballad Of
23/63	His And Hers...Tony Douglas
13/55	His Hands...Tennessee Ernie Ford
2/66	History Repeats Itself...Buddy Starcher
12/71	Hitchin' A Ride...Jack Reno
5/45	Hitler's Last Letter To Hirohito...Carson Robison
8/51	Hobo Boogie...Red Foley
5/56	Hold Everything (Till I Get Home)...Red Sovine
1/89	Hold Me...K.T. Oslin
12/77	Hold Me...Barbara Mandrell
30/81	Hold Me Like You Never Had Me...Randy Parton
38/69	Hold Me, Thrill Me, Kiss Me...Johnny & Jonie Mosby
32/69	Hold Me Tight...Johnny Carver
5/86	Hold On...Rosanne Cash
24/83	Hold On...Gail Davies
40/81	Hold On...Rich Landers
6/89	Hold On (A Little Longer)...Steve Wariner
20/83	Hold On, I'm Comin'...Waylon Jennings & Jerry Reed
	Hold On To Your Man ..see: (If You Wanna Hold On)
25/78	Hold Tight...Kenny Starr
36/79	Hold What You've Got...Sonny James
2/90	Holdin' A Good Hand...Lee Greenwood
1/93	Holdin' Heaven...Tracy Byrd
27/72	Holdin' On (To The Love I Got)...Barbara Mandrell
6/96	Holdin' Onto Something...Jeff Carson
1/83	Holding Her And Loving You...Earl Thomas Conley
7/68	Holding On To Nothin'...Porter Wagoner & Dolly Parton
7/80	Holding The Bag...Moe Bandy & Joe Stampley
4/89	Hole In My Pocket...Ricky Van Shelton
40/82	Holed Up In Some Honky Tonk...Joe Sun
3/57	Holiday For Love...Webb Pierce
	Home
3/96	Alan Jackson
1/90	Joe Diffie
2/59	Home...Jim Reeves
10/75	Home...Loretta Lynn

POS/YR	RECORD TITLE/ARTIST
3/86	**Home Again In My Heart**...Nitty Gritty Dirt Band
6/76	**Home Made Love**...Tom Bresh
3/57	**Home Of The Blues**...Johnny Cash
32/71	**Home Sweet Home**...David Houston
34/92	**Home Sweet Home**...Dennis Robbins
10/65	**Home You're Tearin' Down**...Loretta Lynn
15/59	**Homebreaker**...Skeeter Davis
5/69	**Homecoming**...Tom T. Hall
9/87	**Homecoming '63**...Keith Whitley
38/66	**Homesick**...Bobby Bare
27/85	**Hometown Gossip**...Whites
3/93	**Hometown Honeymoon**...Alabama
4/45	**Honestly**...Dick Thomas
1/68	**Honey**...Bobby Goldsboro
8/53	**(Honey, Baby, Hurry!) Bring Your Sweet Self Back To Me**...Lefty Frizzell
2/70	**Honey Come Back**...Glen Campbell
2/46	**Honey Do You Think It's Wrong**...Al Dexter
F/55	**Honey, Honey Bee Ball**...Hank Thompson
16/76	**Honey Hungry**...Mike Lunsford
5/89	**Honey I Dare You**...Southern Pacific
15/54	**Honey, I Need You**...Johnnie & Jack
17/69	**Honey, I'm Home**...Stan Hitchcock
12/54	**Honey Love**...Carlisles
1/84	**Honey (Open That Door)**...Ricky Skaggs
	Honeycomb
7/57	Jimmie Rodgers
27/86	Gary Morris
4/74	**Honeymoon Feelin'**...Roy Clark
9/53	**Honeymoon On A Rocket Ship**...Hank Snow
24/74	**Honky Tonk Amnesia**...Moe Bandy
5/93	**Honky Tonk Attitude**...Joe Diffie
	Honky Tonk Blues
2/52	Hank Williams
1/80	Charley Pride
26/90	Pirates Of The Mississippi
10/86	**Honky Tonk Crowd**...John Anderson
35/94	**Honky Tonk Crowd**...Rick Trevino
11/48	**Honky Tonk Gal**..."T" Texas Tyler
9/54	**Honky-Tonk Girl**...Hank Thompson
6/89	**Honky Tonk Heart**...Highway 101
37/81	**Honky Tonk Hearts**...Dickey Lee
	Honky-Tonk Man
9/56	Johnny Horton
11/62	Johnny Horton
22/70	Bob Luman
3/86	Dwight Yoakam

POS/YR	RECORD TITLE/ARTIST
10/83	**Honkytonk Man**...Marty Robbins
4/77	**Honky Tonk Memories**...Mickey Gilley
1/88	**Honky Tonk Moon**...Randy Travis
12/81	**Honky Tonk Queen**...Moe Bandy & Joe Stampley
1/57	**Honky Tonk Song**...Webb Pierce
28/80	**Honky Tonk Stuff**...Jerry Lee Lewis
27/76	**Honky Tonk Waltz**...Ray Stevens
17/73	**Honky Tonk Wine**...Wayne Kemp
32/76	**Honky Tonk Women Love Red Neck Men**...Jerry Jaye
	Honky Tonkin'
14/48	Hank Williams
1/82	Hank Williams, Jr.
37/65	**Honky Tonkin' Again**...Buddy Cagle
23/96	**Honky Tonkin's What I Do Best**...Marty Stuart & Travis Tritt
25/61	**Honky Tonkitis**...Carl Butler
	Honkytonk ..see: Honky Tonk
1/85	**Honor Bound**...Earl Thomas Conley
2/81	**Hooked On Music**...Mac Davis
9/54	**Hootchy Kootchy Henry (From Hawaii)**...Mitchell Torok
1/75	**Hope You're Feelin' Me (Like I'm Feelin' You)**...Charley Pride
20/78	**Hopelessly Devoted To You**...Olivia Newton-John
12/91	**Hopelessly Yours**...Lee Greenwood with Suzy Bogguss
7/56	**Hoping That You're Hoping**...Louvin Brothers
15/75	**Hoppy, Gene And Me**...Roy Rogers
40/89	**Hot Nights**...Canyon
14/60	**Hot Rod Lincoln**...Charlie Ryan
	Hot Rod Race
5/51	Arkie Shibley
7/51	Ramblin' Jimmie Dolan
7/51	Red Foley
7/51	Tiny Hill
39/83	**Hot Time In Old Town Tonight**...Mel McDaniel
6/53	**Hot Toddy**...Red Foley
37/85	**Hottest "Ex" In Texas**...Becky Hobbs
1/56	**Hound Dog**...Elvis Presley
25/79	**Hound Dog Man**...Glen Campbell
24/63	**House Down The Block**...Buck Owens
	House Of Blue Lights
39/69	Earl Richards
17/87	Asleep At The Wheel

413

POS/YR	RECORD TITLE/ARTIST
	House Of Blue Lovers
24/59	Jack Newman
21/61	James O'Gwynn
21/95	**House Of Cards**...Mary-Chapin Carpenter
13/58	**House Of Glass**...Ernest Tubb
21/74	**House Of Love**...Dottie West
	House Of The Rising Sun
29/74	Jody Miller
14/81	Dolly Parton
19/89	**House On Old Lonesome Road**...Conway Twitty
20/74	**Houston (I'm Comin' To See You)**...Glen Campbell
1/83	**Houston (Means I'm One Day Closer To You)**...Larry Gatlin & The Gatlin Brothers Band
4/89	**Houston Solution**...Ronnie Milsap
1/85	**How Blue**...Reba McEntire
3/94	**How Can I Help You Say Goodbye**...Patty Loveless
22/78	**How Can I Leave You Again**...John Denver
13/59	**How Can I Think Of Tomorrow**...James O'Gwynn
1/71	**How Can I Unlove You**...Lynn Anderson
7/62	**(How Can I Write On Paper) What I Feel In My Heart**...Jim Reeves
36/71	**How Can You Mend A Broken Heart**...Duane Dee
25/63	**How Come Your Dog Don't Bite Nobody But Me**...Webb Pierce & Mel Tillis
6/83	**How Could I Love Her So Much**...Johnny Rodriguez
29/79	**How Deep In Love Am I?**...Johnny Russell
19/89	**How Do**...Mary-Chapin Carpenter
1/87	**How Do I Turn You On**...Ronnie Milsap
11/58	**How Do You Hold A Memory**...Hank Thompson
7/61	**How Do You Talk To A Baby**...Webb Pierce
11/56	**How Far Is Heaven**...Kitty Wells
17/60	**How Far To Little Rock**...Stanley Brothers
12/67	**How Fast Them Trucks Can Go**...Claude Gray
39/76	**How Great Thou Art**...Statler Brothers
3/70	**How I Got To Memphis**...Bobby Bare
20/70	**How I Love Them Old Songs**...Carl Smith
37/79	**How I Love You In The Morning**...Peggy Sue
23/68	**How Is He?**...Jeannie Seely
6/66	**How Long Has It Been**...Bobby Lewis
4/67	**How Long Will It Take**...Warner Mack

POS/YR	RECORD TITLE/ARTIST
7/52	**How Long Will It Take (To Stop Loving You)**...Lefty Frizzell
1/68	**How Long Will My Baby Be Gone**...Buck Owens & The Buckaroos
11/74	**How Lucky Can One Man Be**...Joe Stampley
38/88	**How Much Is It Worth To Live In L.A.**...Waylon Jennings
2/53	**(How Much Is) That Hound Dog In The Window**...Homer & Jethro
1/71	**How Much More Can She Stand**...Conway Twitty
21/64	**How The Other Half Lives**...Johnny & Jonie Mosby
7/79	**How To Be A Country Star**...Statler Brothers
	How's The World Treating You
4/53	Eddy Arnold
26/61	Louvin Brothers
19/64	**Howdy Neighbor Howdy**...Porter Wagoner
3/51	**Howlin' At The Moon**...Hank Williams
14/78	**Hubba Hubba**...Billy "Crash" Craddock
21/67	**Hula Love**...Hank Snow
5/56	**Hula Rock**...Hank Snow
20/90	**Hummingbird**...Ricky Skaggs
5/70	**Humphrey The Camel**...Jack Blanchard & Misty Morgan
2/48	**Humpty Dumpty Heart**...Hank Thompson
1/69	**Hungry Eyes**...Merle Haggard
27/61	**Hungry For Love**...Stonewall Jackson
4/81	**Hurricane**...Leon Everette
	Hurry, Hurry!
2/44	Benny Carter
4/44	Lucky Millinder
23/65	**Hurry, Mr. Peters**...Justin Tubb & Lorene Mann
(also see: Yes, Mr. Peters)	
17/93	**Hurry Sundown**...McBride & The Ride
	Hurt
14/75	Connie Cato
6/76	Elvis Presley
1/86	Juice Newton
3/67	**Hurt Her Once For Me**...Wilburn Brothers
3/91	**Hurt Me Bad (In A Real Good Way)**...Patty Loveless
38/89	**Hurtin' Side**...Shelby Lynne
3/66	**Hurtin's All Over**...Connie Smith
26/70	**Husband Hunting**...Liz Anderson
	Husbands And Wives
5/66	Roger Miller
16/81	David Frizzell & Shelly West
33/87	**Hymne**...Joe Kenyon
2/96	**Hypnotize The Moon**...Clay Walker

POS/YR	RECORD TITLE/ARTIST

I

POS/YR	RECORD TITLE/ARTIST
6/83	I.O.U....Lee Greenwood
9/76	I.O.U....Jimmy Dean
6/75	I Ain't All Bad...Charley Pride
27/68	I Ain't Buying...Johnny Darrell
10/79	I Ain't Got No Business Doin' Business Today...Razzy Bailey
34/68	I Ain't Got Nobody...Dick Curless
1/80	I Ain't Living Long Like This...Waylon Jennings
	I Ain't Never
2/59	Webb Pierce
1/72	Mel Tillis
23/64	I Almost Forgot Her Today...Carl Smith
35/72	I Already Know (What I'm Getting For My Birthday)...Wanda Jackson
1/83	I Always Get Lucky With You...George Jones
1/91	I Am A Simple Man...Ricky Van Shelton
F/81	I Am The Dreamer (You Are The Dream)...Conway Twitty
4/58	I Beg Of You...Elvis Presley
10/68	I Believe In Love...Bonnie Guitar
31/68	I Believe In Love...Stonewall Jackson
24/74	I Believe In The Sunshine...Roger Miller
1/78	I Believe In You...Mel Tillis
1/80	I Believe In You...Don Williams
18/75	I Believe The South Is Gonna Rise Again...Tanya Tucker
36/95	I Brake For Brunettes...Rhett Akins
9/84	I Call It Love...Mel McDaniel
25/73	I Can Feel The Leavin' Coming On...Cal Smith
F/78	I Can Get Off On You...Waylon & Willie
1/74	I Can Help...Billy Swan
1/95	I Can Love You Like That...John Michael Montgomery
5/62	I Can Mend Your Broken Heart...Don Gibson
36/73	I Can See Clearly Now...Lloyd Green
18/80	I Can See Forever In Your Eyes...Reba McEntire
38/80	I Can See Forever Loving You...Foxfire
22/64	I Can Stand It (As Long As She Can)...Bill Phillips
13/75	I Can Still Hear The Music In The Restroom...Jerry Lee Lewis
1/84	I Can Tell By The Way You Dance...Vern Gosdin
3/70	I Can't Be Myself...Merle Haggard
1/77	I Can't Believe She Gives It All To Me...Conway Twitty
12/73	I Can't Believe That It's All Over...Skeeter Davis
1/70	I Can't Believe That You've Stopped Loving Me...Charley Pride
34/80	I Can't Cheat...Larry G. Hudson
3/79	I Can't Feel You Anymore...Loretta Lynn
1/88	I Can't Get Close Enough...Exile
5/80	I Can't Get Enough Of You...Razzy Bailey
29/83	I Can't Get Over You (Getting Over Me)...Bandana
5/67	I Can't Get There From Here...George Jones
37/78	I Can't Get Up By Myself...Brenda Kaye Perry
37/71	I Can't Go On Loving You...Roy Drusky
4/46	I Can't Go On This Way...Bob Wills
	I Can't Help It (If I'm Still In Love With You)
2/51	Hank Williams
2/75	Linda Ronstadt
2/77	I Can't Help Myself (Here Comes The Feeling)...Eddie Rabbitt
2/60	(I Can't Help You) I'm Falling Too...Skeeter Davis
(also see: Please Help Me, I'm Falling)	
13/66	I Can't Keep Away From You...Wilburn Brothers
2/77	I Can't Love You Enough...Conway Twitty & Loretta Lynn
7/56	I Can't Quit (I've Gone Too Far)...Marty Robbins
3/94	I Can't Reach Her Anymore...Sammy Kershaw
9/65	I Can't Remember...Connie Smith
38/80	I Can't Remember...Stephanie Winslow
23/60	I Can't Run Away From Myself...Ray Price
8/69	I Can't Say Goodbye...Marty Robbins
30/82	I Can't Say Goodbye To You...Terry Gregory
2/44	I Can't See For Lookin'...King Cole Trio
4/72	I Can't See Me Without You...Conway Twitty
7/70	I Can't Seem To Say Goodbye...Jerry Lee Lewis
14/63	I Can't Stay Mad At You...Skeeter Davis

POS/YR	RECORD TITLE/ARTIST
	I Can't Stop Loving You
3/58	Kitty Wells
7/58	Don Gibson
1/72	Conway Twitty
27/77	Sammi Smith
28/78	Mary K. Miller
17/62	**I Can't Stop (My Lovin' You)**...Buck Owens
26/60	**I Can't Tell My Heart That**...Kitty Wells & Roy Drusky
9/90	**I Can't Turn The Tide**...Baillie & The Boys
4/78	**I Can't Wait Any Longer**...Bill Anderson
5/53	**I Can't Wait (For The Sun To Go Down)**...Faron Young
1/87	**I Can't Win For Losin' You**...Earl Thomas Conley
1/75	**I Care**...Tom T. Hall
39/74	**I Changed My Mind**...Billy Walker
1/79	**I Cheated Me Right Out Of You**...Moe Bandy
4/78	**I Cheated On A Good Woman's Love**...Billy "Crash" Craddock
37/67	**I Come Home A-Drinkin' (To A Worn-Out Wife Like You)**...Jay Lee Webb
(also see: Don't Come Home A'Drinkin')	
7/90	**I Could Be Persuaded**...Bellamy Brothers
1/86	**I Could Get Used To You**...Exile
33/92	**I Could Love You (With My Eyes Closed)**...Remingtons
27/66	**I Could Sing All Night**...Ferlin Husky
30/79	**I Could Sure Use The Feeling**...Earl Scruggs Revue
9/84	**I Could Use Another You**...Eddy Raven
6/84	**I Could'a Had You**...Leon Everette
3/76	**I Couldn't Be Me Without You**...Johnny Rodriguez
4/47	**I Couldn't Believe It Was True**...Eddy Arnold
5/53	**I Couldn't Keep From Crying**...Marty Robbins
1/88	**I Couldn't Leave You If I Tried**...Rodney Crowell
40/67	**I Couldn't See**...George Morgan
3/91	**I Couldn't See Leavin'**...Conway Twitty
12/59	**I Cried A Tear**...Ernest Tubb
21/65	**I Cried All The Way To The Bank**...Norma Jean
1/92	**I Cross My Heart**...George Strait
12/88	**I Didn't (Every Chance I Had)**...Johnny Rodriguez
17/67	**I Didn't Jump The Fence**...Red Sovine
1/95	**I Didn't Know My Own Strength**...Lorrie Morgan

POS/YR	RECORD TITLE/ARTIST
30/82	**I Didn't Know You Could Break A Broken Heart**...Joe Stampley
22/60	**I Didn't Mean To Fall In Love**...Hank Thompson
3/70	**I Do My Swinging At Home**...David Houston
5/60	**I Don't Believe I'll Fall In Love Today**...Warren Smith
4/95	**I Don't Believe In Goodbye**...Sawyer Brown
1/56	**I Don't Believe You've Met My Baby**...Louvin Brothers
1/93	**I Don't Call Him Daddy**...Doug Supernaw
	I Don't Care
1/55	Webb Pierce
1/82	Ricky Skaggs
1/64	**I Don't Care (Just as Long as You Love Me)**...Buck Owens
16/79	**I Don't Do Like That No More**...Kendalls
1/95	**I Don't Even Know Your Name**...Alan Jackson
8/88	**I Don't Have Far To Fall**...Skip Ewing
	I Don't Hurt Anymore
1/54	Hank Snow
37/77	Narvel Felts
1/84	**I Don't Know A Thing About Love (The Moon Song)**...Conway Twitty
2/82	**I Don't Know Where To Start**...Eddie Rabbitt
10/77	**I Don't Know Why (I Just Do)**...Marty Robbins
1/85	**I Don't Know Why You Don't Want Me**...Rosanne Cash
5/71	**I Don't Know You (Anymore)**...Tommy Overstreet
12/79	**I Don't Lie**...Joe Stampley
38/75	**I Don't Love Her Anymore**...Johnny Paycheck
4/64	**I Don't Love You Anymore**...Charlie Louvin
1/85	**I Don't Mind The Thorns (If You're The Rose)**...Lee Greenwood
8/78	**I Don't Need A Thing At All**...Gene Watson
1/81	**I Don't Need You**...Kenny Rogers
34/93	**I Don't Need Your Rockin' Chair**...George Jones
10/83	**I Don't Remember Loving You**...John Conlee
40/67	**I Don't See How I Can Make It**...Jean Shepard
1/74	**I Don't See Me In Your Eyes Anymore**...Charlie Rich

POS/YR	RECORD TITLE/ARTIST
7/85	**I Don't Think I'm Ready For You**...Anne Murray
13/81	**I Don't Think Love Ought To Be That Way**...Reba McEntire
2/82	**I Don't Think She's In Love Anymore**...Charley Pride
3/77	**I Don't Wanna Cry**...Larry Gatlin
2/84	**I Don't Wanna Lose Your Love**...Crystal Gayle
1/67	**I Don't Wanna Play House**...Tammy Wynette
13/76	**I Don't Wanna Talk It Over Anymore**...Connie Smith
1/84	**I Don't Want To Be A Memory**...Exile
5/51	**I Don't Want To Be Free**...Margaret Whiting & Jimmy Wakely
	I Don't Want To Be Right ..see: (If Loving You Is Wrong)
21/67	**I Don't Want To Be With Me**...Conway Twitty
33/85	**I Don't Want To Get Over You**...Whites
1/76	**I Don't Want To Have To Marry You**...Jim Ed Brown/Helen Cornelius
30/80	**I Don't Want To Lose**...Leon Everette
20/80	**I Don't Want To Lose You**...Con Hunley
1/89	**I Don't Want To Spoil The Party**...Rosanne Cash
40/82	**I Don't Want To Want You**...Lobo
26/67	**I Doubt It**...Bobby Lewis
7/84	**I Dream Of Women Like You**...Ronnie McDowell
	I Dreamed Of A Hill-Billy Heaven
10/55	Eddie Dean
5/61	Tex Ritter
	I Fall To Pieces
1/61	Patsy Cline
37/70	Diana Trask
6/55	**I Feel Better All Over (More Than Anywhere's Else)**...Ferlin Husky
9/89	**I Feel Fine**...Sweethearts Of The Rodeo
26/82	**I Feel It With You**...Kieran Kane
7/56	**I Feel Like Cryin'**...Carl Smith
1/81	**I Feel Like Loving You Again**...T.G. Sheppard
4/92	**I Feel Lucky**...Mary-Chapin Carpenter
14/49	**I Feel That Old Age Creeping On**...Homer & Jethro
34/85	**I Feel The Country Callin' Me**...Mac Davis
3/90	**I Fell In Love**...Carlene Carter
1/85	**I Fell In Love Again Last Night**...Forester Sisters

POS/YR	RECORD TITLE/ARTIST
13/93	**I Fell In The Water**...John Anderson
14/49	**I Find You Cheatin' On Me**...Hank Thompson
1/53	**I Forgot More Than You'll Ever Know**...Davis Sisters
	(also see: I Found Out More Than You Ever Knew)
1/56	**I Forgot To Remember To Forget**...Elvis Presley
15/78	**I Fought The Law**...Hank Williams, Jr.
5/58	**I Found My Girl In The USA**...Jimmie Skinner
	(also see: Fraulein, & Geisha Girl)
10/53	**I Found Out More Than You Ever Knew**...Betty Cody
	(also see: I Forgot More Than You'll Ever Know)
F/70	**I Found You Just In Time**...Lynn Anderson
22/63	**I Gave My Wedding Dress Away**...Kitty Wells
	(I Gave You The Best Years Of My Life) ..see: Rock N' Roll
	I Get So Lonely ..see: (Oh Baby Mine)
1/66	**I Get The Fever**...Bill Anderson
28/88	**I Give You Music**...McCarters
	I Go To Pieces
39/88	Dean Dillon
31/90	Southern Pacific
F/79	**I Got A Feelin' In My Body**...Elvis Presley
30/75	**I Got A Lot Of Hurtin' Done Today**...Connie Smith
8/84	**I Got A Million Of 'Em**...Ronnie McDowell
40/71	**I Got A Woman**...Bob Luman
1/89	**I Got Dreams**...Steve Wariner
15/95	**I Got It Honest**...Aaron Tippin
1/84	**I Got Mexico**...Eddy Raven
4/59	**I Got Stripes**...Johnny Cash
3/77	**I Got The Hoss**...Mel Tillis
4/68	**I Got You**...Waylon Jennings & Anita Carter
5/89	**I Got You**...Dwight Yoakam
7/91	**I Got You**...Shenandoah
27/63	**I Gotta Get Drunk (And I Shore Do Dread It)**...Joe Carson
8/55	**I Gotta Go Get My Baby**...Justin Tubb
	I Gotta Have My Baby Back
4/50	Floyd Tillman
10/50	Red Foley
15/56	**I Gotta Know**...Wanda Jackson
9/62	**I Guess I'll Never Learn**...Charlie Phillips

POS/YR	RECORD TITLE/ARTIST
	I Guess I'm Crazy
13/55	Tommy Collins
1/64	Jim Reeves
1/84	**I Guess It Never Hurts To Hurt Sometimes**...Oak Ridge Boys
14/93	**I Guess You Had To Be There**...Lorrie Morgan
5/86	**I Had A Beautiful Time**...Merle Haggard
5/79	**I Had A Lovely Time**...Kendalls
33/82	**I Had It All**...Fred Knoblock
30/65	**I Had One Too Many**...Wilburn Brothers
4/44	**I Hang My Head And Cry**...Gene Autry
	I Hate Goodbyes
25/73	Bobby Bare
40/77	Lois Johnson
22/58	**I Hate Myself**...Faron Young
16/79	**I Hate The Way I Love It**...Johnny Rodriguez & Charly McClain
10/73	**I Hate You**...Ronnie Milsap
17/81	**I Have A Dream**...Cristy Lane
26/77	**I Have A Dream, I Have A Dream**...Roy Clark
2/83	**I Have Loved You, Girl (But Not Like This Before)**...Earl Thomas Conley
7/88	**I Have You**...Glen Campbell
5/53	**I Haven't Got The Heart**...Webb Pierce
17/66	**I Hear Little Rock Calling**...Ferlin Husky
29/79	**I Hear The South Callin' Me**...Hank Thompson
27/59	**I Hear You Talkin'**...Faron Young
9/68	**I Heard A Heart Break Last Night**...Jim Reeves
12/49	**I Heard About You**...Bud Hobbs
33/65	**I Heard From A Memory Last Night**...Jim Edward Brown
	(I Heard That) Lonesome Whistle ..see: Lonesome Whistle
4/57	**I Heard The Bluebirds Sing**...Browns
6/74	**I Honestly Love You**...Olivia Newton-John
36/70	**I Hope So**...Willie Nelson
10/84	**I Hurt For You**...Deborah Allen
16/89	**I Just Called To Say Goodbye Again**...Larry Boone
4/82	**I Just Came Here To Dance**...David Frizzell & Shelly West
	I Just Came Home To Count The Memories
15/77	Cal Smith
7/82	John Anderson
8/68	**I Just Came To Get My Baby**...Faron Young
21/66	**I Just Came To Smell The Flowers**...Porter Wagoner

POS/YR	RECORD TITLE/ARTIST
1/75	**I Just Can't Get Her Out Of My Mind**...Johnny Rodriguez
36/70	**I Just Can't Help Believing**...David Frizzell
21/88	**I Just Can't Say No To You**...Moe Bandy
5/79	**I Just Can't Stay Married To You**...Cristy Lane
40/72	**I Just Couldn't Let Her Walk Away**...Dorsey Burnette
11/82	**I Just Cut Myself**...Ronnie McDowell
5/50	**I Just Don't Like This Kind Of Livin'**...Hank Williams
1/79	**I Just Fall In Love Again**...Anne Murray
28/76	**I Just Got A Feeling**...La Costa
10/53	**(I Just Had A Date) A Lover's Quarrel**...George Morgan
	I Just Had You On My Mind
21/78	Dottsy
22/80	Billy "Crash" Craddock
11/81	**I Just Need You For Tonight**...Billy "Crash" Craddock
17/74	**I Just Started Hatin' Cheatin' Songs Today**...Moe Bandy
36/81	**I Just Want To Be With You**...Sammi Smith
14/78	**I Just Want To Be Your Everything**...Connie Smith
1/78	**I Just Want To Love You**...Eddie Rabbitt
1/94	**I Just Wanted You To Know**...Mark Chesnutt
1/78	**I Just Wish You Were Someone I Love**...Larry Gatlin with Brothers & Friends
1/81	**I Keep Coming Back**...Razzy Bailey
14/68	**I Keep Coming Back For More**...Dave Dudley
	I Kissed You ..see: ('Til)
37/88	**I Knew Love**...Nanci Griffith
10/79	**I Know A Heartache When I See One**...Jennifer Warnes
4/70	**I Know How**...Loretta Lynn
1/88	**I Know How He Feels**...Reba McEntire
	I Know One
6/60	Jim Reeves
6/67	Charley Pride
5/96	**I Know She Still Loves Me**...George Strait
35/85	**I Know The Way To You By Heart**...Vern Gosdin
21/89	**I Know What I've Got**...J.C. Crowley
1/87	**I Know Where I'm Going**...Judds
13/92	**I Know Where Love Lives**...Hal Ketchum
29/66	**I Know You're Married (But I Love You Still)**...Bill Anderson & Jan Howard

POS/YR	RECORD TITLE/ARTIST
39/67	**I Learn Something New Everyday**...Bill Phillips
2/44	**I Learned A Lesson, I'll Never Forget**...5 Red Caps
2/95	**I Let Her Lie**...Daryle Singletary
1/53	**I Let The Stars Get In My Eyes**...Goldie Hill
	(also see: Don't Let The Stars Get In Your Eyes)
9/82	**I Lie**...Loretta Lynn
4/75	**I Like Beer**...Tom T. Hall
1/95	**I Like It, I Love It**...Tim McGraw
23/78	**I Like Ladies In Long Black Dresses**...Bobby Borchers
26/79	**I Lost My Head**...Charlie Rich
1/74	**I Love**...Tom T. Hall
1/81	**I Love A Rainy Night**...Eddie Rabbitt
4/49	**I Love Everything About You**...George Morgan
4/83	**I Love Her Mind**...Bellamy Brothers
	I Love How You Love Me
18/79	Lynn Anderson
17/83	Glen Campbell
1/74	**I Love My Friend**...Charlie Rich
15/81	**I Love My Truck**...Glen Campbell
3/84	**I Love Only You**...Nitty Gritty Dirt Band
28/80	**I Love That Woman (Like The Devil Loves Sin)**...Leon Everette
10/75	**I Love The Blues And The Boogie Woogie**...Billy "Crash" Craddock
40/76	**I Love The Way That You Love Me**...Ray Griff
15/71	**I Love The Way That You've Been Lovin' Me**...Roy Drusky
1/93	**I Love The Way You Love Me**...John Michael Montgomery
4/64	**I Love To Dance With Annie**...Ernest Ashworth
22/77	**I Love What Love Is Doing To Me**...Lynn Anderson
3/54	**I Love You**...Ginny Wright/Jim Reeves
	I Love You A Thousand Ways
1/51	Lefty Frizzell
8/51	Hawkshaw Hawkins
9/77	Willie Nelson
	I Love You Because
1/50	Leon Payne
2/50	Ernest Tubb
8/50	Clyde Moody
20/60	Johnny Cash
14/69	Carl Smith
12/61	**I Love You Best Of All**...Louvin Brothers
9/86	**I Love You By Heart**...Sylvia & Michael Johnson

POS/YR	RECORD TITLE/ARTIST
4/66	**I Love You Drops**...Bill Anderson
6/74	**I Love You, I Love You**...David Houston & Barbara Mandrell
5/78	**I Love You, I Love You, I Love You**...Ronnie McDowell
8/58	**I Love You More**...Jim Reeves
4/73	**I Love You More And More Everyday**...Sonny James
1/69	**I Love You More Today**...Conway Twitty
11/55	**I Love You Mostly**...Lefty Frizzell
	I Love You So Much, It Hurts
5/48	Floyd Tillman
1/49	Jimmy Wakely
10/78	**(I Love You) What Can I Say**...Jerry Reed
1/81	**I Loved 'Em Every One**...T.G. Sheppard
24/88	**I Loved You Yesterday**...Lyle Lovett
4/84	**I May Be Used (But Baby I Ain't Used Up)**...Waylon Jennings
27/62	**I May Fall Again**...Buddy Meredith
1/79	**I May Never Get To Heaven**...Conway Twitty
39/91	**I Mean I Love You**...Hank Williams, Jr.
2/90	**I Meant Every Word He Said**...Ricky Van Shelton
10/76	**I Met A Friend Of Your's Today**...Mel Street
37/89	**I Might Be What You're Looking For**...Larry Gatlin & The Gatlin Brothers
37/74	**I Miss You**...Jeannie Seely
26/77	**I Miss You Already**...Jerry Wallace
	I Miss You Already (And You're Not Even Gone)
5/57	Faron Young
21/60	Jimmy Newman
14/86	Billy Joe Royal
3/60	**I Missed Me**...Jim Reeves
38/80	**I Must Be Crazy**...Susie Allanson
32/73	**I Must Be Doin' Something Right**...Roy Drusky
7/46	**I Must Have Been Wrong**...Bob Atcher
F/79	**I Must Have Done Something Bad**...Merle Haggard
34/89	**I Need A Wife**...Joni Harms
1/85	**I Need More Of You**...Bellamy Brothers
11/73	**I Need Somebody Bad**...Jack Greene
22/77	**(I Need You) All The Time**...Eddy Arnold
32/74	**I Never Get Through Missing You**...Bobby Lewis
25/74	**I Never Go Around Mirrors**...Lefty Frizzell
30/85	**I Never Got Over You**...Johnny Paycheck

POS/YR	RECORD TITLE/ARTIST
9/67	**I Never Had The One I Wanted**...Claude Gray
2/94	**I Never Knew Love**...Doug Stone
13/74	**I Never Knew (What That Song Meant Before)**...Connie Smith
10/85	**I Never Made Love (Till I Made Love With You)**...Mac Davis
5/70	**I Never Once Stopped Loving You**...Connie Smith
5/70	**I Never Picked Cotton**...Roy Clark
3/84	**I Never Quite Got Back (From Loving You)**...Sylvia
24/76	**I Never Said It Would Be Easy**...Jacky Ward
4/49	**I Never See Maggie Alone**...Kenny Roberts
8/78	**I Never Will Marry**...Linda Ronstadt
14/87	**I Only Wanted You**...Marie Osmond
1/74	**I Overlooked An Orchid**...Mickey Gilley
2/87	**I Prefer The Moonlight**...Kenny Rogers
18/78	**I Promised Her A Rainbow**...Bobby Borchers
26/68	**I Promised You The World**...Ferlin Husky
	I Really Don't Want To Know
1/54	Eddy Arnold
23/71	Elvis Presley
19/72	Charlie McCoy
1/79	**I Really Got The Feeling**...Dolly Parton
23/76	**I Really Had A Ball Last Night**...Carmol Taylor
	I Recall A Gypsy Woman
16/73	Tommy Cash
22/81	B.J. Thomas
32/88	**I Remember You**...Glen Campbell
1/89	**I Sang Dixie**...Dwight Yoakam
29/63	**I Saw Me**...George Jones
7/52	**I Saw Mommy Kissing Santa Claus**...Jimmy Boyd
25/72	**I Saw My Lady**...Dickey Lee
1/92	**I Saw The Light**...Wynonna Judd
40/71	**I Say A Little Prayer (medley)**...Glen Campbell/Anne Murray
2/94	**I See It Now**...Tracy Lawrence
1/74	**I See The Want To In Your Eyes**...Conway Twitty
2/88	**I Should Be With You**...Steve Wariner
30/95	**I Should Have Been True**...Mavericks
11/75	**I Should Have Married You**...Eddie Rabbitt
13/81	**I Should've Called**...Eddy Raven
27/72	**I Start Thinking About You**...Johnny Carver
16/72	**I Started Loving You Again**...Charlie McCoy

POS/YR	RECORD TITLE/ARTIST
30/70	**I Stayed Long Enough**...Billie Jo Spears
21/64	**I Stepped Over The Line**...Hank Snow
12/88	**I Still Believe**...Lee Greenwood
13/75	**I Still Believe In Fairy Tales**...Tammy Wynette
27/68	**I Still Believe In Love**...Jan Howard
2/81	**I Still Believe In Waltzes**...Conway Twitty & Loretta Lynn
1/89	**I Still Believe In You**...Desert Rose Band
1/92	**I Still Believe In You**...Vince Gill
17/84	**I Still Do**...Bill Medley
14/75	**I Still Feel The Same About You**...Bill Anderson
40/80	**(I Still Long To Hold You) Now And Then**...Reba McEntire
28/82	**I Still Love You (After All These Years)**...Tompall/Glaser Brothers
19/83	**I Still Love You In The Same Ol' Way**...Moe Bandy
38/81	**I Still Miss Someone**...Don King
9/94	**I Sure Can Smell The Rain**...BlackHawk
30/86	**I Sure Need Your Lovin'**...Judy Rodman
1/94	**I Swear**...John Michael Montgomery
3/69	**I Take A Lot Of Pride In What I Am**...Merle Haggard
6/72	**I Take It On Home**...Charlie Rich
2/94	**I Take My Chances**...Mary Chapin Carpenter
	I Take The Chance
2/56	Browns
7/63	Ernest Ashworth
11/67	**I Taught Her Everything She Knows**...Billy Walker
31/88	**I Taught Her Everything She Knows About Love**...Shooters
7/86	**I Tell It Like It Used To Be**...T. Graham Brown
8/65	**I Thank My Lucky Stars**...Eddy Arnold
4/95	**I Think About It All The Time**...John Berry
3/96	**I Think About You**...Collin Raye
17/82	**I Think About Your Lovin'**...Osmond Brothers
7/60	**I Think I Know**...Marion Worth
1/81	**I Think I'll Just Stay Here And Drink**...Merle Haggard
36/86	**I Think I'm In Love**...Keith Stegall
	(I Think I've Got A Heartache) ..see: Excuse Me
37/72	**I Think They Call It Love**...Don Gibson & Sue Thompson

POS/YR	RECORD TITLE/ARTIST
	I Thought I Heard You Call My Name
11/57	Porter Wagoner
29/76	Jessi Colter
4/91	**I Thought It Was You**...Doug Stone
10/55	**I Thought Of You**...Jean Shepard
2/67	**I Threw Away The Rose**...Merle Haggard
1/88	**I Told You So**...Randy Travis
25/59	**I Traded Her Love (For Deep Purple Wine)**...Roland Johnson
3/94	**I Try To Think About Elvis**...Patty Loveless
26/87	**I Turn To You**...George Jones
22/73	**I Used It All On You**...Nat Stuckey
26/70	**I Wake Up In Heaven**...David Rogers
1/68	**I Walk Alone**...Marty Robbins
1/56	**I Walk The Line**...Johnny Cash
6/55	**I Walked Alone Last Night**...Eddy Arnold
12/70	**I Walked Out On Heaven**...Hank Williams, Jr.
38/81	**I Wanna Be Around**...Terri Gibbs
3/71	**I Wanna Be Free**...Loretta Lynn
33/79	**I Wanna' Come Over**...Alabama
1/88	**I Wanna Dance With You**...Eddie Rabbitt
18/63	**I Wanna Go Home**...Billy Grammer
38/78	**I Wanna Go To Heaven**...Jerry Wallace
9/95	**I Wanna Go Too Far**...Trisha Yearwood
8/85	**I Wanna Hear It From You**...Eddy Raven
35/86	**I Wanna Hear It From Your Lips**...Louise Mandrell
1/68	**I Wanna Live**...Glen Campbell
1/51	**I Wanna Play House With You**...Eddy Arnold
5/85	**I Wanna Say Yes**...Louise Mandrell
22/93	**I Wanna Take Care Of You**...Billy Dean
13/55	**I Wanna Wanna Wanna**...Wilburn Brothers
18/88	**I Want A Love Like That**...Judy Rodman
10/85	**I Want Everyone To Cry**...Restless Heart
7/95	**I Want My Goodbye Back**...Ty Herndon
19/69	**I Want One**...Jack Reno
	I Want To ..also see: I Wanna, & I Wanta
5/46	**I Want To Be A Cowboy's Sweetheart**...Rosalie Allen
24/78	**I Want To Be In Love**...Jacky Ward
13/56	**I Want To Be Loved**...Johnnie & Jack
3/94	**I Want To Be Loved Like That**...Shenandoah
4/45	**I Want To Be Sure**...Gene Autry
1/51	**I Want To Be With You Always**...Lefty Frizzell
25/84	**I Want To Go Somewhere**...Keith Stegall

POS/YR	RECORD TITLE/ARTIST
18/58	**I Want To Go Where No One Knows Me**...Jean Shepard
1/66	**I Want To Go With You**...Eddy Arnold
9/75	**I Want To Hold You In My Dreams Tonight**...Stella Parton
2/87	**I Want To Know You Before We Make Love**...Conway Twitty
15/61	**I Want To Live Again**...Rose Maddox
30/79	**I Want To See Me In Your Eyes**...Peggy Sue
26/74	**I Want To Stay**...Narvel Felts
35/79	**I Want To Thank You**...Kim Charles
34/79	**I Want To Walk You Home**...Porter Wagoner
35/72	**I Want You**...Johnny Carver
7/93	**I Want You Bad (And That Ain't Good)**...Collin Raye
22/70	**I Want You Free**...Jean Shepard
1/56	**I Want You, I Need You, I Love You**...Elvis Presley
22/81	**I Want You Tonight**...Johnny Rodriguez
25/74	**I Wanta Get To You**...La Costa
16/95	**I Was Blown Away**...Pam Tillis
38/92	**I Was Born With A Broken Heart**...Aaron Tippin
1/81	**I Was Country When Country Wasn't Cool**...Barbara Mandrell
F/57	**I Was The First One**...Hank Thompson
8/56	**I Was The One**...Elvis Presley
8/77	**I Was There**...Statler Brothers
39/68	**I Was With Red Foley (The Night He Passed Away)**...Hank Williams, Jr.
30/67	**I Washed My Face In The Morning Dew**...Tom T. Hall
8/65	**I Washed My Hands In Muddy Water**...Stonewall Jackson
23/63	**I Wasn't Even In The Running**...Hank Thompson
15/49	**I Wasted A Nickel**...Hawkshaw Hawkins
8/90	**I Watched It All (On My Radio)**...Lionel Cartwright
9/61	**I Went Out Of My Way (To Make You Happy)**...Roy Drusky
3/52	**I Went To Your Wedding**...Hank Snow
23/58	**I Will**...Ferlin Husky
21/69	**I Will Always**...Don Gibson
	I Will Always Love You
1/74	Dolly Parton
1/82	Dolly Parton
15/95	Dolly Parton With Vince Gill
30/77	**I'll Always Love You**...Cates Sisters
1/87	**I Will Be There**...Dan Seals

POS/YR	RECORD TITLE/ARTIST
32/66	**I Will Not Blow Out The Light**...Marion Worth
21/79	**I Will Rock And Roll With You**...Johnny Cash
21/79	**I Will Survive**...Billie Jo Spears
7/88	**I Will Whisper Your Name**...Michael Johnson
28/66	**I Wish**...Ernest Ashworth
	(I Wish A Buck Was Still Silver) ..see: Are The Good Times Really Over
	I Wish Her Well ..see: (There She Goes)
	I Wish I Could Fall In Love Today
5/60	Ray Price
5/88	Barbara Mandrell
4/94	**I Wish I Could Have Been There**...John Anderson
14/84	**I Wish I Could Write You A Song**...John Anderson
4/89	**(I Wish I Had A) Heart Of Stone**...Baillie & The Boys
22/70	**I Wish I Had A Mommy Like You**...Patti Page
4/49	**I Wish I Had A Nickel**...Jimmy Wakely
	I Wish I Had Never Met Sunshine
3/46	Gene Autry
5/46	Wesley Tuttle
8/49	**I Wish I Knew**...Dolph Hewitt
13/78	**I Wish I Loved Somebody Else**...Tom T. Hall
27/63	**I Wish I Was A Single Girl Again**...Jan Howard
22/80	**I Wish I Was Crazy Again**...Johnny Cash & Waylon Jennings
	I Wish I Was Eighteen Again
F/79	Jerry Lee Lewis
15/80	George Burns
20/83	**I Wish I Was In Nashville**...Mel McDaniel
4/89	**I Wish I Was Still In Your Dreams**...Conway Twitty
	I Wish That I Could Fall In Love Today ..see: I Wish I Could
3/86	**I Wish That I Could Hurt That Way Again**...T. Graham Brown
19/74	**I Wish That I Had Loved You Better**...Eddy Arnold
2/82	**I Wish You Could Have Turned My Head (And Left My Heart Alone)**...Oak Ridge Boys
24/73	**I Wish (You Had Stayed)**...Brian Collins
19/60	**I Wish You Love**...Billy Walker
4/53	**I Won't Be Home No More**...Hank Williams

POS/YR	RECORD TITLE/ARTIST
1/67	**I Won't Come In While He's There**...Jim Reeves
3/65	**I Won't Forget You**...Jim Reeves
3/50	**(I Won't Go Huntin', Jake) But I'll Go Chasin' Women**...Stuart Hamblen
1/71	**I Won't Mention It Again**...Ray Price
1/87	**I Won't Need You Anymore (Always And Forever)**...Randy Travis
1/88	**I Won't Take Less Than Your Love**...Tanya Tucker/Paul Davis/Paul Overstreet
8/83	**I Wonder**...Rosanne Cash
1/89	**I Wonder Do You Think Of Me**...Keith Whitley
40/91	**I Wonder How Far It Is Over You**...Aaron Tippin
F/77	**I Wonder How She's Doing Now**...Johnny Russell
30/87	**I Wonder If I Care As Much**...Ricky Skaggs
2/76	**I Wonder If I Ever Said Goodbye**...Johnny Rodriguez
1/73	**I Wonder If They Ever Think Of Me**...Merle Haggard
4/71	**I Wonder What She'll Think About Me Leaving**...Conway Twitty
37/89	**I Wonder What She's Doing Tonight**...Russell Smith
10/83	**I Wonder Where We'd Be Tonight**...Vern Gosdin
9/83	**I Wonder Who's Holding My Baby Tonight**...Whites
20/75	**I Wonder Whose Baby (You Are Now)**...Jerry Wallace
	I Wore A Tie Today ..see: (Jim)
12/78	**I Would Like To See You Again**...Johnny Cash
9/88	**I Wouldn't Be A Man**...Don Williams
8/65	**I Wouldn't Buy A Used Car From Him**...Norma Jean
31/68	**I Wouldn't Change A Thing About You (But Your Name)**...Hank Williams, Jr.
1/83	**I Wouldn't Change You If I Could**...Ricky Skaggs
5/92	**I Wouldn't Have It Any Other Way**...Aaron Tippin
1/82	**I Wouldn't Have Missed It For The World**...Ronnie Milsap
9/70	**I Wouldn't Live In New York City**...Buck Owens
33/67	**I Wouldn't Take Her To A Dogfight**...Charlie Walker

POS/YR	RECORD TITLE/ARTIST
1/74	**I Wouldn't Want To Live If You Didn't Love Me**...Don Williams
1/75	**(I'd Be) A Legend In My Time**...Ronnie Milsap
4/90	**I'd Be Better Off (In A Pine Box)**...Doug Stone
30/66	**I'd Better Call The Law On Me**...Hugh X. Lewis
20/85	**I'd Dance Every Dance With You**...Kendalls
32/80	**I'd Do Anything For You**...Jacky Ward
	I'd Fight The World
23/62	Hank Cochran
19/74	Jim Reeves
11/68	**I'd Give The World (To Be Back Loving You)**...Warner Mack
	I'd Go Crazy ..see: (If It Weren't For Country Music)
11/76	**I'd Have To Be Crazy**...Willie Nelson
	I'd Just Be Fool Enough
16/66	Browns
33/76	Faron Young
18/59	**I'd Like To Be**...Jim Reeves
3/94	**I'd Like To Have That One Back**...George Strait
26/78	**I'd Like To See Jesus (On The Midnight Special)**...Tammy Wynette
5/75	**I'd Like To Sleep Til I Get Over You**...Freddie Hart
1/80	**I'd Love To Lay You Down**...Conway Twitty
1/91	**I'd Love You All Over Again**...Alan Jackson
4/69	**I'd Rather Be Gone**...Hank Williams, Jr.
2/71	**I'd Rather Be Sorry**...Ray Price
20/79	**I'd Rather Go On Hurtin'**...Joe Sun
32/80	**I'd Rather Leave While I'm In Love**...Rita Coolidge
10/61	**I'd Rather Loan You Out**...Roy Drusky
1/71	**I'd Rather Love You**...Charley Pride
16/93	**I'd Rather Miss You**...Little Texas
13/56	**I'd Rather Stay Home**...Kitty Wells
F/78	**I'd Really Love To See You Tonight**...Jacky Ward & Reba McEntire
20/92	**I'd Surrender All**...Randy Travis
9/52	**I'd Trade All Of My Tomorrows (For Just One Yesterday)**...Eddy Arnold
10/57	**(I'll Always Be Your) Fraulein**...Kitty Wells (also see: Fraulein)
1/88	**I'll Always Come Back**...K.T. Oslin
14/55	**I'll Baby Sit With You**...Ferlin Husky
7/45	**I'll Be Back**...Gene Autry

POS/YR	RECORD TITLE/ARTIST
1/80	**I'll Be Coming Back For More**...T.G. Sheppard
1/77	**I'll Be Leaving Alone**...Charley Pride
16/89	**I'll Be Lovin' You**...Lee Greenwood
F/56	**I'll Be Satisfied With Love**...Faron Young
10/87	**I'll Be The One**...Statler Brothers
	I'll Be There (If You Ever Want Me)
2/54	Ray Price
17/72	Johnny Bush
4/81	Gail Davies
	I'll Be There (When You Get Lonely)
12/57	Ray Price
22/78	David Rogers
1/78	**I'll Be True To You**...Oak Ridge Boys
	I'll Be Your Baby Tonight
33/70	Claude King
5/87	Judy Rodman
26/82	**I'll Be Your Man Around The House**...Kieran Kane
12/76	**I'll Be Your San Antone Rose**...Dottsy
40/75	**I'll Be Your Steppin' Stone**...David Houston
16/59	**I'll Catch You When You Fall**...Charlie Walker
2/87	**I'll Come Back As Another Woman**...Tanya Tucker
10/67	**I'll Come Runnin'**...Connie Smith
34/93	**I'll Cry Tomorrow**...Larry Stewart
17/74	**I'll Do Anything It Takes**...Jean Shepard
2/77	**I'll Do It All Over Again**...Crystal Gayle
8/80	**(I'll Even Love You) Better Than I Did Then**...Statler Brothers
10/78	**I'll Find It Where I Can**...Jerry Lee Lewis
13/71	**I'll Follow You (Up To Our Cloud)**...George Jones
3/44	**I'll Forgive You But I Can't Forget**...Roy Acuff
1/76	**I'll Get Over You**...Crystal Gayle
34/78	**I'll Get Over You**...Nick Nixon
6/88	**I'll Give You All My Love Tonight**...Bellamy Brothers
F/76	**I'll Go Back To Her**...Waylon Jennings
11/64	**I'll Go Down Swinging**...Porter Wagoner
	I'll Go On Alone
1/53	Marty Robbins
4/53	Webb Pierce
3/75	**I'll Go To My Grave Loving You**...Statler Brothers
1/47	**I'll Hold You In My Heart (Till I Can Hold You In My Arms)**...Eddy Arnold (also see: Take Me In Your Arms And Hold Me)

POS/YR	RECORD TITLE/ARTIST
4/61	I'll Just Have A Cup Of Coffee (Then I'll Go)...Claude Gray
11/78	I'll Just Take It Out In Love...George Jones
2/65	I'll Keep Holding On (Just To Your Love)...Sonny James
34/66	I'll Leave The Singin' To The Bluebirds...Sheb Wooley
1/88	I'll Leave This World Loving You...Ricky Van Shelton
26/90	I'll Lie Myself To Sleep...Shelby Lynne
14/79	I'll Love Away Your Troubles For Awhile...Janie Fricke
10/68	I'll Love You More (Than You Need)...Jeannie Seely
11/70	I'll Make Amends...Roy Drusky
19/58	I'll Make It All Up To You...Jerry Lee Lewis
4/81	I'll Need Someone To Hold Me (When I Cry)...Janie Fricke
	I'll Never Be Free
2/50	Kay Starr & Tennessee Ernie
26/69	Johnny & Jonie Mosby
11/78	Jim Ed Brown/Helen Cornelius
4/87	I'll Never Be In Love Again...Don Williams
7/73	I'll Never Break These Chains...Tommy Overstreet
1/67	I'll Never Find Another You...Sonny James
6/95	I'll Never Forgive My Heart...Brooks & Dunn
1/53	I'll Never Get Out Of This World Alive...Hank Williams
27/79	I'll Never Let You Down...Tommy Overstreet
5/45	I'll Never Let You Worry My Mind...Red Foley
	I'll Never Slip Around Again
2/49	Margaret Whiting & Jimmy Wakely
6/49	Floyd Tillman
1/85	I'll Never Stop Loving You...Gary Morris
5/88	I'll Pin A Note On Your Pillow...Billy Joe Royal
28/78	I'll Promise You Tomorrow...Jerry Wallace
8/65	I'll Repossess My Heart...Kitty Wells
	I'll Sail My Ship Alone
1/50	Moon Mullican
10/51	Tiny Hill
2/70	I'll See Him Through...Tammy Wynette
2/69	I'll Share My World With You...George Jones
22/63	I'll Sign...Beverly Buff
27/75	I'll Sing For You...Don Gibson
21/92	I'll Start With You...Paulette Carlson

POS/YR	RECORD TITLE/ARTIST
4/47	I'll Step Aside...Ernest Tubb
1/87	I'll Still Be Loving You...Restless Heart
8/69	I'll Still Be Missing You...Warner Mack
8/72	I'll Still Be Waiting For You...Buck Owens & The Buckaroos
9/75	I'll Still Love You...Jim Weatherly
8/49	I'll Still Write Your Name In The Sand...Buddy Starchin
23/92	I'll Stop Loving You...Mike Reid
8/50	I'll Take A Back Seat For You...Ernest Tubb
9/66	I'll Take The Dog...Jean Shepard & Ray Pillow
37/86	I'll Take Your Love Anytime...Robin Lee
	I'll Think Of Something
7/74	Hank Williams, Jr.
1/92	Mark Chesnutt
1/96	I'll Try...Alan Jackson
6/74	I'll Try A Little Bit Harder...Donna Fargo
2/45	I'll Wait For You Dear...Al Dexter
3/79	I'll Wake You Up When I Get Home...Charlie Rich
30/65	I'll Wander Back To You...Earl Scott
9/75	I'm A Believer...Tommy Overstreet
5/45	I'm A Brandin' My Darlin' With My Heart...Jack Guthrie
7/45	I'm A Convict With Old Glory In My Heart...Elton Britt
22/69	I'm A Drifter...Bobby Goldsboro
34/69	I'm A Good Man (In A Bad Frame Of Mind)...Jack Reno
14/60	I'm A Honky Tonk Girl...Loretta Lynn
33/77	I'm A Honky-Tonk Woman's Man...Bob Luman
6/48	I'm A Long Gone Daddy...Hank Williams
9/70	I'm A Lover (Not a Fighter)...Skeeter Davis
	I'm A Memory
28/71	Willie Nelson
22/77	Willie Nelson
18/66	I'm A Nut...Leroy Pullins
	I'm A One-Woman Man
7/56	Johnny Horton
5/89	George Jones
6/66	I'm A People...George Jones
1/74	I'm A Ramblin' Man...Waylon Jennings
1/76	(I'm A) Stand By My Woman Man...Ronnie Milsap
12/54	I'm A Stranger In My Home...Kitty Wells & Red Foley
30/68	I'm A Swinger...Jimmy Dean
4/72	I'm A Truck...Red Simpson

POS/YR	RECORD TITLE/ARTIST
32/64	I'm A Walkin' Advertisement...Norma Jean
23/76	I'm All Wrapped Up In You...Don Gibson
5/80	I'm Already Blue...Kendalls
20/70	I'm Alright...Lynn Anderson
2/78	I'm Always On A Mountain When I Fall...Merle Haggard
3/53	I'm An Old, Old Man...Lefty Frizzell
17/59	I'm Beginning To Forget You...Jim Reeves
2/49	I'm Biting My Fingernails And Thinking Of You...Andrews Sisters & Ernest Tubb
38/68	I'm Coming Back Home To Stay...Buckaroos
11/57	I'm Coming Home...Johnny Horton
F/57	I'm Counting On You...Kitty Wells
21/88	I'm Down To My Last Cigarette...k.d. lang
3/69	I'm Down To My Last "I Love You"...David Houston
39/82	I'm Drinkin' Canada Dry...Burrito Brothers
28/69	I'm Dynamite...Peggy Sue
	I'm Falling Too ..see: (I Can't Help You)
1/85	I'm For Love...Hank Williams, Jr.
3/60	I'm Gettin' Better...Jim Reeves
30/69	I'm Gettin' Tired Of Babyin' You...Peggy Sue
10/77	I'm Getting Good At Missing You (Solitaire)...Rex Allen, Jr.
7/55	I'm Glad I Got To See You Once Again...Hank Snow
18/82	I'm Goin' Hurtin'...Joe Stampley
10/85	I'm Going To Leave You Tomorrow...John Schneider
17/71	I'm Gonna Act Right...Nat Stuckey
5/47	I'm Gonna Be Boss From Now On...Bob Wills
2/90	I'm Gonna Be Somebody...Travis Tritt
2/62	I'm Gonna Change Everything...Jim Reeves
10/55	I'm Gonna Fall Out Of Love With You...Webb Pierce
	I'm Gonna Feed You Now
21/65	Porter Wagoner
F/79	Porter Wagoner
1/88	I'm Gonna Get You...Eddy Raven
1/82	I'm Gonna Hire A Wino To Decorate Our Home...David Frizzell
3/71	I'm Gonna Keep On Keep On Lovin' You...Billy Walker
5/72	I'm Gonna Knock On Your Door...Billy "Crash" Craddock
F/57	I'm Gonna Live Some Before I Die...Faron Young

POS/YR	RECORD TITLE/ARTIST
13/88	I'm Gonna Love Her On The Radio...Charley Pride
3/76	I'm Gonna Love You...Dave & Sugar
13/79	I'm Gonna Love You...Glen Campbell
10/78	I'm Gonna Love You Anyway...Cristy Lane
9/81	I'm Gonna Love You Back To Loving Me Again...Joe Stampley
21/77	I'm Gonna Love You Right Out Of This World...David Rogers
17/80	I'm Gonna Love You Tonight (In My Dreams)...Johnny Duncan
3/88	I'm Gonna Miss You, Girl...Michael Martin Murphey
7/68	I'm Gonna Move On...Warner Mack
16/81	(I'm Gonna) Put You Back On The Rack...Dottie West
26/81	I'm Gonna Sit Right Down And Write Myself A Letter...Willie Nelson
19/65	I'm Gonna Tie One On Tonight...Wilburn Brothers
28/71	I'm Gonna Write A Song...Tommy Cash
14/64	I'm Hanging Up The Phone...Carl Butler & Pearl
23/80	I'm Happy Just To Dance With You...Anne Murray
11/74	I'm Having Your Baby...Sunday Sharpe
3/94	I'm Holding My Own...Lee Roy Parnell
F/55	I'm Hurtin' Inside...Jim Reeves
	I'm Hurting ..see: (Yes)
1/92	I'm In A Hurry (And Don't Know Why)...Alabama
3/59	I'm In Love Again...George Morgan
21/95	I'm In Love With A Capital "U"...Joe Diffie
38/68	I'm In Love With My Wife...David Rogers
12/55	I'm In Love With You...Kitty Wells
18/81	I'm Into Lovin' You...Billy Swan
30/80	I'm Into The Bottle...Dean Dillon
	I'm Just A Country Boy
37/65	Jim Edward Brown
1/77	Don Williams
F/77	(I'm Just A) Redneck In A Rock And Roll Bar...Jerry Reed
4/81	I'm Just An Old Chunk Of Coal...John Anderson
1/71	I'm Just Me...Charley Pride
2/77	I'm Knee Deep In Loving You...Dave & Sugar

POS/YR	RECORD TITLE/ARTIST
	I'm Leavin' It (All) Up To You
18/70	Johnny & Jonie Mosby
17/74	Donny & Marie Osmond
26/78	Freddy Fender
	I'm Left, You're Right, She's Gone
F/55	Elvis Presley
21/74	Jerry Lee Lewis
15/65	**I'm Letting You Go**...Eddy Arnold
22/59	**I'm Letting You Go**...Webb Pierce
30/77	**I'm Living A Lie**...Jeanne Pruett
9/66	**I'm Living In Two Worlds**...Bonnie Guitar
39/95	**I'm Living Up To Her Low Expectations**...Daryle Singletary
16/62	**I'm Looking High And Low For My Baby**...Ernest Tubb
1/45	**I'm Losing My Mind Over You**...Al Dexter
5/45	**I'm Lost Without You**...Al Dexter
11/56	**I'm Moving In**...Hank Snow
	I'm Moving On
1/50	Hank Snow
14/60	Don Gibson
5/83	Emmylou Harris
5/48	**I'm My Own Grandpa**...Lonzo & Oscar
1/89	**I'm No Stranger To The Rain**...Keith Whitley
37/82	**(I'm Not) A Candle In The Wind**...Bobby Bare
34/93	**I'm Not Built That Way**...Billy Dean
28/66	**I'm Not Crazy Yet**...Ray Price
11/77	**I'm Not Easy**...Billie Jo Spears
1/75	**I'm Not Lisa**...Jessi Colter
14/56	**I'm Not Mad, Just Hurt**...Hank Thompson
2/80	**I'm Not Ready Yet**...George Jones
2/95	**I'm Not Strong Enough To Say No**...BlackHawk
4/96	**I'm Not Supposed To Love You Anymore**...Bryan White
3/82	**I'm Not That Lonely Yet**...Reba McEntire
F/84	**I'm Not That Way Anymore**...Alabama
3/74	**I'm Not Through Loving You Yet**...Conway Twitty
7/84	**I'm Not Through Loving You Yet**...Louise Mandrell
21/86	**I'm Not Trying To Forget You**...Willie Nelson
1/83	**I'm Only In It For The Love**...John Conlee
3/90	**I'm Over You**...Keith Whitley
F/56	**I'm Really Glad You Hurt Me**...Webb Pierce
9/63	**I'm Saving My Love**...Skeeter Davis
2/44	**I'm Sending You Red Roses**...Jimmy Wakely

POS/YR	RECORD TITLE/ARTIST
1/69	**(I'm So) Afraid Of Losing You Again**...Charley Pride
10/56	**I'm So In Love With You**...Wilburn Brothers
	I'm So Lonesome I Could Cry
23/72	Charlie McCoy
17/76	Terry Bradshaw
1/75	**I'm Sorry**...John Denver
16/76	**I'm Sorry Charlie**...Joni Lee
9/77	**I'm Sorry For You, My Friend**...Moe Bandy
F/56	**I'm Sorry, I'm Not Sorry**...Carl Perkins
14/71	**I'm Sorry If My Love Got In Your Way**...Connie Smith
1/89	**I'm Still Crazy**...Vern Gosdin
4/95	**I'm Still Dancin' With You**...Wade Hayes
39/80	**I'm Still In Love With You**...Larry G. Hudson
3/74	**I'm Still Loving You**...Joe Stampley
36/88	**I'm Still Missing You**...Ronnie McDowell
6/67	**I'm Still Not Over You**...Ray Price
36/88	**I'm Still Your Fool**...David Slater
5/91	**I'm That Kind Of Girl**...Patty Loveless
24/62	**(I'm The Girl On) Wolverton Mountain**...Jo Ann Campbell
(also see: Wolverton Mountain)	
29/65	**I'm The Man**...Jim Kandy
28/72	**I'm The Man On Susie's Mind**...Glenn Barber
10/85	**I'm The One Mama Warned You About**...Mickey Gilley
	I'm The One Who Loves You ..see: (Remember Me)
8/77	**I'm The Only Hell (Mama Ever Raised)**...Johnny Paycheck
18/79	**I'm The Singer, You're The Song**...Tanya Tucker
3/44	**I'm Thinking Tonight Of My Blue Eyes**...Gene Autry
	I'm Throwing Rice (At the Girl That I Love)
1/49	Eddy Arnold
11/49	Red Foley
	I'm Tired
3/57	Webb Pierce
18/88	Ricky Skaggs
38/75	**I'm Too Use To Loving You**...Nick Nixon
8/51	**I'm Waiting Just For You**...Hawkshaw Hawkins
3/54	**I'm Walking The Dog**...Webb Pierce
12/49	**I'm Waltzing With Tears In My Eyes**...Cowboy Copas
1/44	**I'm Wastin' My Tears On You**...Tex Ritter

POS/YR	RECORD TITLE/ARTIST
25/78	**I'm Way Ahead Of You**...Bill Anderson & Mary Lou Turner
21/61	**I'm Wondering**...Lou Smith
8/73	**I'm Your Woman**...Jeanne Pruett
1/77	**I've Already Loved You In My Mind**...Conway Twitty
34/74	**I've Already Stayed Too Long**...Don Adams
1/78	**I've Always Been Crazy**...Waylon Jennings
26/84	**I've Always Got The Heart To Sing The Blues**...Bill Medley
39/81	**I've Been A Fool**...Stephanie Winslow
13/66	**I've Been A Long Time Leavin' (But I'll Be A Long Time Gone)**...Roger Miller
1/84	**I've Been Around Enough To Know**...John Schneider
	I've Been Everywhere
1/62	Hank Snow
16/70	Lynn Anderson
40/85	**I've Been Had By Love Before**...Judy Rodman
2/88	**I've Been Lookin'**...Nitty Gritty Dirt Band
29/78	**I've Been Loved**...Cates Sisters
4/89	**I've Been Loved By The Best**...Don Williams
13/84	**I've Been Rained On Too**...Tom Jones
11/68	**I've Been There Before**...Ray Price
2/55	**I've Been Thinking**...Eddy Arnold
28/78	**I've Been Too Long Lonely Baby**...Billy "Crash" Craddock
14/79	**I've Been Waiting For You All Of My Life**...Con Hunley
2/84	**I've Been Wrong Before**...Deborah Allen
11/56	**I've Changed**...Carl Smith
11/72	**I've Come Awful Close**...Hank Thompson
1/90	**I've Come To Expect It From You**...George Strait
30/63	**I've Come To Say Goodbye**...Faron Young
18/66	**I've Cried A Mile**...Hank Snow
1/90	**I've Cried My Last Tear For You**...Ricky Van Shelton
	I've Cried (The Blues Right Out Of My Eyes)
23/70	Crystal Gayle
40/78	Crystal Gayle
7/79	**I've Done Enough Dyin' Today**...Larry Gatlin
7/63	**I've Enjoyed As Much Of This As I Can Stand**...Porter Wagoner
4/72	**I've Found Someone Of My Own**...Cal Smith
3/72	**(I've Got A) Happy Heart**...Susan Raye

POS/YR	RECORD TITLE/ARTIST
	I've Got A New Heartache
2/56	Ray Price
10/86	Ricky Skaggs
5/79	**I've Got A Picture Of Us On My Mind**...Loretta Lynn
6/71	**I've Got A Right To Cry**...Hank Williams, Jr.
25/60	**I've Got A Right To Know**...Buck Owens
4/74	**I've Got A Thing About You Baby**...Elvis Presley
1/65	**I've Got A Tiger By The Tail**...Buck Owens
7/78	**I've Got A Winner In You**...Don Williams
32/72	**I've Got A Woman's Love**...Marty Robbins
	I've Got Five Dollars And It's Saturday Night
4/56	Faron Young
16/65	George & Gene
3/94	**I've Got It Made**...John Anderson
13/75	**I've Got My Baby On My Mind**...Connie Smith
25/69	**I've Got Precious Memories**...Faron Young
11/63	**I've Got The World By The Tail**...Claude King
17/78	**I've Got To Go**...Billie Jo Spears
13/72	**I've Got To Have You**...Sammi Smith
5/68	**I've Got You On My Mind Again**...Buck Owens
16/77	**I've Got You (To Come Home To)**...Don King
17/70	**I've Just Been Wasting My Time**...John Wesley Ryles
12/62	**I've Just Destroyed The World (I'm Living In)**...Ray Price
11/74	**I've Just Got To Know (How Loving You Would Be)**...Freddy Weller
7/55	**I've Kissed You My Last Time**...Kitty Wells
F/73	**I've Loved You All Over The World**...Cal Smith
15/76	**I've Loved You All The Way**...Donna Fargo
14/75	**I've Never Loved Anyone More**...Lynn Anderson
6/80	**I've Never Seen The Likes Of You**...Conway Twitty
7/59	**I've Run Out Of Tomorrows**...Hank Thompson
4/45	**I've Taken All I'm Gonna Take From You**...Spade Cooley
34/64	**I've Thought Of Leaving You**...Kitty Wells
10/50	**Ida Red Likes The Boogie**...Bob Wills
3/62	**If A Woman Answers (Hang Up The Phone)**...Leroy Van Dyke
9/84	**If All The Magic Is Gone**...Mark Gray

POS/YR	RECORD TITLE/ARTIST
1/94	**If Bubba Can Dance (I Can Too)**...Shenandoah
8/81	**If Drinkin' Don't Kill Me (Her Memory Will)**...George Jones
39/84	**If Every Man Had A Woman Like You**...Osmond Brothers
13/79	**If Everyone Had Someone Like You**...Eddy Arnold
F/82	**If Heaven Ain't A Lot Like Dixie**...Hank Williams, Jr.
1/83	**If Hollywood Don't Need You**...Don Williams
30/92	**If I Could Bottle This Up**...Paul Overstreet
21/63	**If I Could Come Back**...Webb Pierce
1/94	**If I Could Make A Living**...Clay Walker
10/84	**If I Could Only Dance With You**...Jim Glaser
4/75	**If I Could Only Win Your Love**...Emmylou Harris
24/77	**If I Could Put Them All Together (I'd Have You)**...George Jones
4/79	**If I Could Write A Song As Beautiful As You**...Billy "Crash" Craddock
28/62	**If I Cried Every Time You Hurt Me**...Wanda Jackson
1/92	**If I Didn't Have You**...Randy Travis
8/93	**If I Didn't Love You**...Steve Wariner
26/83	**If I Didn't Love You**...Gus Hardin
29/58	**If I Don't Love You (Grits Ain't Groceries)**...George Jones
4/70	**If I Ever Fall In Love**...Faron Young
28/89	**If I Ever Fall In Love Again**...Anne Murray & Kenny Rogers
17/89	**If I Ever Go Crazy**...Shooters
28/80	**If I Ever Had To Say Goodbye To You**...Eddy Arnold
18/79	**If I Fell In Love With You**...Rex Allen, Jr.
10/79	**If I Give My Heart To You**...Margo Smith
	If I Had A Cheating Heart
9/78	Mel Street
36/93	Ricky Lynn Gregg
29/72	**If I Had A Hammer**...Johnny Cash & June Carter Cash
25/95	**If I Had Any Pride Left At All**...John Berry
2/76	**If I Had It To Do All Over Again**...Roy Clark
32/69	**If I Had Last Night To Live Over**...Webb Pierce
1/89	**If I Had You**...Alabama
11/81	**If I Keep On Going Crazy**...Leon Everette

POS/YR	RECORD TITLE/ARTIST
5/67	**If I Kiss You (Will You Go Away)**...Lynn Anderson
1/91	**If I Know Me**...George Strait
11/76	**If I Let Her Come In**...Ray Griff
8/74	**If I Miss You Again Tonight**...Tommy Overstreet
3/81	**If I Needed You**...Emmylou Harris & Don Williams
39/89	**If I Never See Midnight Again**...Sweethearts Of The Rodeo
1/79	**If I Said You Have A Beautiful Body Would You Hold It Against Me**...Bellamy Brothers
4/65	**If I Talk To Him**...Connie Smith
16/95	**If I Was A Drinkin' Man**...Neal McCoy
2/70	**If I Were A Carpenter**...Johnny Cash & June Carter
4/95	**If I Were You**...Collin Raye
8/96	**If I Were You**...Terri Clark
25/75	**If I'm Losing You**...Billy Walker
35/88	**If It Ain't Broke Don't Fix It**...John Anderson
20/85	**If It Ain't Love**...Ed Bruce
12/77	**If It Ain't Love By Now**...Jim Ed Brown/Helen Cornelius
7/72	**If It Ain't Love (Let's Leave It Alone)**...Connie Smith
12/85	**If It Ain't Love (Let's Leave It Alone)**...Whites
1/88	**If It Don't Come Easy**...Tanya Tucker
14/72	**If It Feels Good Do It**...Dave Dudley
16/65	**If It Pleases You**...Billy Walker
19/83	**If It Was Easy**...Ed Bruce
26/94	**If It Wasn't For Her I Wouldn't Have You**...Daron Norwood
26/91	**(If It Weren't For Country Music) I'd Go Crazy**...Clinton Gregory
10/85	**If It Weren't For Him**...Vince Gill
26/91	**If It Will It Will**...Hank Williams, Jr.
28/73	**If It's All Right With You**...Dottie West
2/70	**If It's All The Same To You**...Bill Anderson & Jan Howard
4/44	**If It's Wrong To Love You**...Charles Mitchell
6/90	**If Looks Could Kill**...Rodney Crowell
6/79	**If Love Had A Face**...Razzy Bailey
11/77	**If Love Was A Bottle Of Wine**...Tommy Overstreet
12/55	**If Lovin' You Is Wrong**...Hank Thompson
1/79	**(If Loving You Is Wrong) I Don't Want To Be Right**...Barbara Mandrell

POS/YR	RECORD TITLE/ARTIST
	If My Heart Had Windows
7/67	George Jones
10/88	Patty Loveless
6/69	**If Not For You**...George Jones
26/77	**If Not You**...Dr. Hook
16/88	**If Ole Hank Could Only See Us Now**...Waylon Jennings
5/77	**If Practice Makes Perfect**...Johnny Rodriguez
15/73	**If She Just Helps Me Get Over You**...Sonny James
27/82	**If Something Should Come Between Us**...Burrito Brothers
	If Teardrops Were Pennies
8/51	Carl Smith
3/73	Porter Wagoner & Dolly Parton
10/66	**If Teardrops Were Silver**...Jean Shepard
15/85	**If That Ain't Love**...Lacy J. Dalton
21/83	**If That's What You're Thinking**...Karen Brooks
13/64	**If The Back Door Could Talk**...Webb Pierce
1/91	**If The Devil Danced (In Empty Pockets)**...Joe Diffie
8/84	**If The Fall Don't Get You**...Janie Fricke
1/94	**If The Good Die Young**...Tracy Lawrence
29/91	**If The Jukebox Took Teardrops**...Billy Joe Royal
16/85	**If The Phone Doesn't Ring, It's Me**...Jimmy Buffett
8/88	**If The South Woulda Won**...Hank Williams, Jr.
12/67	**If The Whole World Stopped Lovin'**...Roy Drusky
2/95	**If The World Had A Front Porch**...Tracy Lawrence
6/78	**If The World Ran Out Of Love Tonight**...Jim Ed Brown/Helen Cornelius
3/92	**If There Hadn't Been You**...Billy Dean
21/80	**If There Were No Memories**...John Anderson
9/87	**If There's Any Justice**...Lee Greenwood
24/66	**If This House Could Talk**...Stonewall Jackson
F/70	**If This Is Love**...Jack Greene
30/71	**If This Is Our Last Time**...Brenda Lee
1/89	**If Tomorrow Never Comes**...Garth Brooks
1/73	**If We Make It Through December**...Merle Haggard
2/77	**If We're Not Back In Love By Monday**...Merle Haggard
31/82	**If You Ain't Got Nothin' (You Ain't Got Nothin' To Lose)**...Bobby Bare

POS/YR	RECORD TITLE/ARTIST
	If You Ain't Lovin'
2/55	Faron Young
1/88	George Strait
26/85	**If You Break My Heart**...Kendalls
2/73	**If You Can Live With It (I Can Live Without It)**...Bill Anderson
5/78	**If You Can Touch Her At All**...Willie Nelson
7/66	**If You Can't Bite, Don't Growl**...Tommy Collins
3/73	**If You Can't Feel It (It Ain't There)**...Freddie Hart
1/88	**If You Change Your Mind**...Rosanne Cash
6/90	**If You Could Only See Me Now**...T. Graham Brown
40/79	**If You Could See You Through My Eyes**...Tom Grant
6/62	**If You Don't Know I Ain't Gonna Tell You**...George Hamilton IV
11/77	**If You Don't Love Me (Why Don't You Just Leave Me Alone)**...Freddy Fender
	If You Don't Somebody Else Will
3/54	Jimmy & Johnny
8/54	Ray Price
37/78	**If You Don't Want To Love Her**...Jerry Naylor
1/80	**If You Ever Change Your Mind**...Crystal Gayle
31/75	**If You Ever Change Your Mind**...Ray Price
16/77	**If You Ever Get To Houston (Look Me Down)**...Don Gibson
31/72	**If You Ever Need My Love**...Jack Greene
12/81	**If You Go, I'll Follow You**...Porter Wagoner & Dolly Parton
20/77	**If You Gotta Make A Fool Of Somebody**...Dickey Lee
1/72	**If You Leave Me Tonight I'll Cry**...Jerry Wallace
2/74	**If You Love Me (Let Me Know)**...Olivia Newton-John
27/71	**If You Love Me (Really Love Me)**...Lamar Morris
4/96	**If You Loved Me**...Tracy Lawrence
31/87	**If You Still Want A Fool Around**...Charley Pride
F/74	**If You Talk In Your Sleep**...Elvis Presley
19/71	**If You Think I Love You Now (I've Just Started)**...Jody Miller
F/77	**If You Think I'm Crazy Now**...Bobby Bare
34/71	**If You Think That It's All Right**...Johnny Carver
9/72	**If You Touch Me (You've Got To Love Me)**...Joe Stampley

POS/YR	RECORD TITLE/ARTIST
32/74	**(If You Wanna Hold On) Hold On To Your Man**...Diana Trask
24/66	**If You Want A Love**...Buck Owens
8/77	**If You Want Me**...Billie Jo Spears
2/91	**If You Want Me To**...Joe Diffie
23/90	**If You Want To Be My Woman**...Merle Haggard
11/92	**If You Want To Find Love**...Kenny Rogers
7/55	**If You Were Me**...Webb Pierce
26/73	**If You're Goin' Girl**...Don Gibson
5/83	**If You're Gonna Do Me Wrong (Do It Right)**...Vern Gosdin
1/84	**If You're Gonna Play In Texas**...Alabama
18/95	**If You're Gonna Walk, I'm Gonna Crawl**...Sammy Kershaw
34/78	**If You're Looking For A Fool**...Freddy Fender
7/67	**If You're Not Gone Too Long**...Loretta Lynn
1/96	**(If You're Not In It For Love) I'm Outta Here!**...Shania Twain
3/82	**If You're Thinking You Want A Stranger**...George Strait
10/82	**If You're Waiting On Me (You're Backing Up)**...Kendalls
1/94	**If You've Got Love**...John Michael Montgomery
6/78	**If You've Got Ten Minutes (Let's Fall In Love)**...Joe Stampley
	If You've Got The Money I've Got The Time
1/50	Lefty Frizzell
1/76	Willie Nelson
4/92	**If Your Heart Ain't Busy Tonight**...Tanya Tucker
24/90	**If Your Heart Should Ever Roll This Way Again**...Jo-el Sonnier
29/59	**Igmoo (The Pride Of South Central High)**...Stonewall Jackson
5/68	**Image Of Me**...Conway Twitty
26/61	**Image Of Me**...Bob Wills & Tommy Duncan
21/62	**Imagine That**...Patsy Cline
19/60	**Imitation Of Love**...Adrian Roland
1/91	**In A Different Light**...Doug Stone
1/89	**In A Letter To You**...Eddy Raven
5/85	**In A New York Minute**...Ronnie McDowell
2/93	**In A Week Or Two**...Diamond Rio
13/80	**In America**...Charlie Daniels Band
13/90	**In Another Lifetime**...Desert Rose Band
27/85	**In Another Minute**...Jim Glaser
3/95	**In Between Dances**...Pam Tillis

POS/YR	RECORD TITLE/ARTIST
38/64	**In Case You Ever Change Your Mind**...Bill Anderson
18/67	**In Del Rio**...Billy Walker
15/82	**In Like With Each Other**...Gatlin Bros.
1/86	**In Love**...Ronnie Milsap
16/68	**In Love**...Wynn Stewart
22/80	**In Memory Of A Memory**...Johnny Paycheck
17/61	**In Memory Of Johnny Horton**...Johnny Hardy
9/84	**In My Dreams**...Emmylou Harris
1/84	**In My Eyes**...John Conlee
12/90	**In My Eyes**...Lionel Cartwright
33/74	**In My Little Corner Of The World**...Marie Osmond
19/94	**In My Own Backyard**...Joe Diffie
6/79	**In No Time At All**...Ronnie Milsap
9/86	**In Over My Heart**...T.G. Sheppard
4/95	**In Pictures**...Alabama
15/76	**In Some Room Above The Street**...Gary Stewart
17/63	**In The Back Room Tonight**...Carl Smith
35/81	**In The Garden**...Statler Brothers
25/68	**In The Good Old Days**...Dolly Parton
3/93	**In The Heart Of A Woman**...Billy Ray Cyrus
	In The Jailhouse Now
1/55	Webb Pierce
7/55	Jimmie Rodgers (No. 2)
8/62	Johnny Cash
15/77	Sonny James
6/62	**In The Middle Of A Heartache**...Wanda Jackson
23/64	**In The Middle Of A Memory**...Carl Belew
10/83	**In The Middle Of The Night**...Mel Tillis
14/84	**In The Midnight Hour**...Razzy Bailey
39/77	**In The Mood**...Henhouse Five Plus Too
23/73	**In The Palm Of Your Hand**...Buck Owens
34/66	**In The Same Old Way**...Bobby Bare
29/63	**In The Shadows Of The Wine**...Porter Wagoner
21/72	**In The Spring (The Roses Always Turn Red)**...Dorsey Burnette
	(In The Still Of The Night) ..see: Lost In The Fifties Tonight
1/92	**In This Life**...Collin Raye
21/63	**In This Very Same Room**...George Hamilton IV
6/55	**In Time**...Eddy Arnold
4/83	**In Times Like These**...Barbara Mandrell
33/67	**In Your Heart**...Red Sovine

POS/YR	RECORD TITLE/ARTIST
21/72	**It Takes You**...Bob Luman
5/55	**It Tickles**...Tommy Collins
31/84	**It Took A Lot Of Drinkin' (To Get That Woman Over Me)**...Moe Bandy
37/81	**It Took Us All Night Long To Say Goodbye**...Danny Wood
17/82	**It Turns Me Inside Out**...Lee Greenwood
1/77	**It Was Almost Like A Song**...Ronnie Milsap
7/75	**It Was Always So Easy (To Find An Unhappy Woman)**...Moe Bandy
21/62	**It Was You**...Ferlin Husky
37/81	**It Was You**...Billy "Crash" Craddock
	It Wasn't God Who Made Honky Tonk Angels
1/52	Kitty Wells
20/71	Lynn Anderson
(also see: Wild Side Of Life)	
6/91	**It Won't Be Me**...Tanya Tucker
18/94	**It Won't Be Over You**...Steve Wariner
31/86	**It Won't Hurt**...Dwight Yoakam
19/96	**It Works**...Alabama
7/96	**It Wouldn't Hurt To Have Wings**...Mark Chesnutt
	It'll Be Her [Him]
22/73	David Rogers
19/82	Tompall/Glaser Brothers
1/86	**It'll Be Me**...Exile
34/83	**It'll Be Me**...Tom Jones
16/74	**It'll Come Back**...Red Sovine
13/84	**It's A Be Together Night**...Frizzell & West
13/70	**It's A Beautiful Day**...Wynn Stewart
2/79	**It's A Cheating Situation**...Moe Bandy
7/77	**It's A Cowboy Lovin' Night**...Tanya Tucker
30/83	**It's A Dirty Job**...Bobby Bare & Lacy J. Dalton
5/56	**It's A Great Life (If You Don't Weaken)**...Faron Young
	It's A Heartache
10/78	Bonnie Tyler
32/81	Dave & Sugar
3/58	**It's A Little More Like Heaven**...Hank Locklin
2/93	**It's A Little Too Late**...Tanya Tucker
12/68	**It's A Long, Long Way To Georgia**...Don Gibson
36/82	**It's A Long Way To Daytona**...Mel Tillis
	It's A Lovely, Lovely World
5/52	Carl Smith
5/81	Gail Davies
20/73	**It's A Man's World**...Diana Trask

POS/YR	RECORD TITLE/ARTIST
36/72	**It's A Matter Of Time**...Elvis Presley
6/74	**(It's A) Monsters' Holiday**...Buck Owens
10/85	**It's A Short Walk From Heaven To Hell**...John Schneider
	It's A Sin
1/47	Eddy Arnold
5/69	Marty Robbins
21/71	**It's A Sin To Tell A Lie**...Slim Whitman
16/75	**It's A Sin When You Love Somebody**...Glen Campbell
9/81	**It's All I Can Do**...Anne Murray
12/77	**It's All In The Game**...Tom T. Hall
1/75	**It's All In The Movies**...Merle Haggard
19/59	**It's All My Heartache**...Carl Smith
11/68	**It's All Over**...David Houston & Tammy Wynette
3/68	**It's All Over But The Crying**...Hank Williams, Jr.
14/66	**It's All Over (But The Crying)**...Kitty Wells
15/85	**It's All Over Now**...John Anderson
23/75	**It's All Over Now**...Charlie Rich
1/78	**It's All Wrong, But It's All Right**...Dolly Parton
F/58	**It's All Your Fault**...Ray Price
7/65	**It's Alright**...Bobby Bare
11/89	**(It's Always Gonna Be) Someday**...Holly Dunn
5/65	**It's Another World**...Wilburn Brothers
2/78	**It's Been A Great Afternoon**...Merle Haggard
1/53	**It's Been So Long**...Webb Pierce
1/45	**It's Been So Long Darling**...Ernest Tubb
37/70	**It's Dawned On Me You're Gone**...Dottie West
25/76	**It's Different With You**...Mary Lou Turner
	It's Four In The Morning
1/72	Faron Young
36/86	Tom Jones
1/72	**It's Gonna Take A Little Bit Longer**...Charley Pride
10/80	**It's Hard To Be Humble**...Mac Davis
40/82	**It's Hard To Be The Dreamer (When I Used to be the Dream)**...Donna Fargo
F/77	**It's Heaven Loving You**...Freddie Hart
16/82	**It's High Time**...Dottie West
	It's Just A Matter Of Time
1/70	Sonny James
7/86	Glen Campbell
1/89	Randy Travis
30/59	**It's Just About Time**...Johnny Cash

POS/YR	RECORD TITLE/ARTIST
28/82	**It's Like Falling In Love (Over And Over)**...Osmond Brothers
1/80	**It's Like We Never Said Goodbye**...Crystal Gayle
32/90	**It's Lonely Out Tonite**...Eddie Rabbitt
9/75	**It's Midnight**...Elvis Presley
11/76	**It's Morning (And I Still Love You)**...Jessi Colter
F/57	**It's My Way**...Webb Pierce
8/51	**It's No Secret**...Stuart Hamblen
1/72	**It's Not Love (But It's Not Bad)**...Merle Haggard
27/95	**It's Not The End Of The World**...Emilio
17/60	**It's Not Wrong**...Connie Hall
(also see: Is It Wrong)	
14/77	**It's Nothin' To Me**...Jim Reeves
4/81	**It's Now Or Never**...John Schneider
15/66	**It's Only Love**...Jeannie Seely
	It's Only Make Believe
3/70	Glen Campbell
8/88	Ronnie McDowell
8/87	**It's Only Over For You**...Tanya Tucker
4/68	**It's Over**...Eddy Arnold
14/80	**It's Over**...Rex Allen, Jr.
1/67	**It's Such A Pretty World Today**...Wynn Stewart
1/88	**It's Such A Small World**...Rodney Crowell & Rosanne Cash
10/74	**It's That Time Of Night**...Jim Ed Brown
1/67	**It's The Little Things**...Sonny James
20/85	**It's Time For Love**...Don Williams
13/74	**It's Time To Cross That Bridge**...Jack Greene
28/71	**It's Time To Love Her**...Billy Walker
1/75	**It's Time To Pay The Fiddler**...Cal Smith
12/79	**It's Time We Talk Things Over**...Rex Allen, Jr.
9/80	**It's Too Late**...Jeanne Pruett
5/80	**It's True Love**...Conway Twitty & Loretta Lynn
3/46	**It's Up To You**...Al Dexter
5/96	**It's What I Do**...Billy Dean
16/82	**It's Who You Love**...Kieran Kane
30/83	**It's You**...Kieran Kane
5/90	**It's You Again**...Skip Ewing
21/88	**It's You Again**...Exile
5/93	**It's Your Call**...Reba McEntire
34/85	**It's Your Reputation Talkin'**...Kathy Mattea
3/61	**It's Your World**...Marty Robbins

POS/YR	RECORD TITLE/ARTIST
	J
36/80	**J.R.**...B.J. Wright
13/48	**Jack And Jill Boogie**...Wayne Raney
2/67	**Jackson**...Johnny Cash & June Carter
	Jackson Ain't A Very Big Town
38/67	Norma Jean
21/68	Johnny Duncan & June Stearns
5/58	**Jacqueline**...Bobby Helms
20/84	**Jagged Edge Of A Broken Heart**...Gail Davies
1/57	**Jailhouse Rock**...Elvis Presley
1/52	**Jambalaya (On The Bayou)**...Hank Williams
F/73	**Jamestown Ferry**...Tanya Tucker
15/93	**Janie Baker's Love Slave**...Shenandoah
34/72	**January, April And Me**...Dick Curless
39/75	**January Jones**...Johnny Carver
12/75	**Jason's Farm**...Cal Smith
13/92	**Jealous Bone**...Patty Loveless
	Jealous Heart
2/45	Tex Ritter
8/49	Al Morgan
14/49	Kenny Roberts
12/64	**Jealous Hearted Me**...Eddy Arnold
7/58	**Jealousy**...Kitty Wells
3/74	**(Jeannie Marie) You Were A Lady**...Tommy Overstreet
	Jed Clampett ..see: Ballad Of
22/60	**Jenny Lou**...Sonny James
4/92	**Jesus And Mama**...Confederate Railroad
F/80	**Jesus On The Radio (Daddy on the Phone)**...Tom T. Hall
3/70	**Jesus, Take A Hold**...Merle Haggard
	Jet Set ..see: (We're Not)
7/54	**Jilted**...Red Foley
27/61	**(Jim) I Wore A Tie Today**...Eddy Arnold
26/68	**Jimmie Rodgers Blues**...Elton Britt
5/59	**Jimmy Brown The Newsboy**...Mac Wiseman
27/61	**Jimmy Caught The Dickens (Pushing Ernest In The Tub)**...Chick & His Hot Rods
24/61	**Jimmy Martinez**...Marty Robbins
13/57	**Jingle Bell Rock**...Bobby Helms
26/75	**Jo And The Cowboy**...Johnny Duncan
24/68	**Jody And The Kid**...Roy Drusky
13/69	**Joe And Mabel's 12th Street Bar And Grill**...Nat Stuckey

POS/YR	RECORD TITLE/ARTIST
5/69	**Just Someone I Used To Know**...Porter Wagoner & Dolly Parton
17/73	**Just Thank Me**...David Rogers
22/65	**Just Thought I'd Let You Know**...Carl Butler & Pearl
	Just To Satisfy You
31/65	Bobby Bare
1/82	Waylon & Willie
7/53	**Just Wait 'Til I Get You Alone**...Carl Smith
9/73	**Just What I Had In Mind**...Faron Young
40/79	**Just When I Needed You Most**...Diana

K

POS/YR	RECORD TITLE/ARTIST
15/82	**Kansas City Lights**...Steve Wariner
2/70	**Kansas City Song**...Buck Owens
7/65	**Kansas City Star**...Roger Miller
	(Karneval) ..see: One More Time
2/72	**Kate**...Johnny Cash
16/72	**Katy Did**...Porter Wagoner
11/59	**Katy Too**...Johnny Cash
	Kaw-Liga
1/53	Hank Williams
3/69	Charley Pride
12/80	Hank Williams, Jr.
9/69	**Kay**...John Wesley Ryles
3/53	**Keep It A Secret**...Slim Whitman
1/91	**Keep It Between The Lines**...Ricky Van Shelton
17/90	**Keep It In The Middle Of The Road**...Exile
1/73	**Keep Me In Mind**...Lynn Anderson
6/45	**Keep My Mem'ry In Your Heart**...Ernest Tubb
23/74	**Keep On Lovin' Me**...Johnny Paycheck
19/73	**Keep On Truckin'**...Dave Dudley
31/66	**Keep The Flag Flying**...Johnny Wright
16/64	**Keep Those Cards And Letters Coming In**...Johnny & Jonie Mosby
8/48	**Keeper Of My Heart**...Bob Wills
2/95	**Keeper Of The Stars**...Tracy Byrd
5/64	**Keeping Up With The Joneses**...Faron Young & Margie Singleton
8/55	**Kentuckian Song**...Eddy Arnold
38/72	**Kentucky**...Sammi Smith
1/75	**Kentucky Gambler**...Merle Haggard
20/62	**Kentucky Means Paradise**...Green River Boys/Glen Campbell
31/70	**Kentucky Rain**...Elvis Presley

POS/YR	RECORD TITLE/ARTIST
	Kentucky Waltz
3/46	Bill Monroe
1/51	Eddy Arnold
26/77	**Kentucky Woman**...Randy Barlow
10/85	**Kern River**...Merle Haggard
	Key's In The Mailbox
18/60	Freddie Hart
15/72	Tony Booth
5/94	**Kick A Little**...Little Texas
8/62	**Kickin' Our Hearts Around**...Buck Owens
2/73	**Kid Stuff**...Barbara Fairchild
1/87	**Kids Of The Baby Boom**...Bellamy Brothers
1/73	**Kids Say The Darndest Things**...Tammy Wynette
37/87	**Killbilly Hill**...Southern Pacific
17/82	**Killin' Kind**...Bandana
1/89	**Killin' Time**...Clint Black
10/81	**Killin' Time**...Fred Knoblock & Susan Anton
	Kind Of Woman I Got
33/67	Osborne Brothers
F/75	Hank Williams, Jr.
13/77	**King Is Gone**...Ronnie McDowell
26/89	**King Is Gone (So Are You)**...George Jones
1/65	**King Of The Road**...Roger Miller
(also see: Queen Of The House)	
1/71	**Kiss An Angel Good Mornin'**...Charley Pride
36/76	**Kiss And Say Goodbye**...Billy Larkin
7/55	**Kiss-Crazy Baby**...Johnnie & Jack
29/73	**Kiss It And Make It Better**...Mac Davis
25/83	**Kiss Me Darling**...Stephanie Winslow
26/94	**Kiss Me, I'm Gone**...Marty Stuart
22/93	**Kiss Me In The Car**...John Berry
24/69	**Kissed By The Rain, Warmed By The Sun**...Glenn Barber
5/55	**Kisses Don't Lie**...Carl Smith
11/61	**Kisses Never Lie**...Carl Smith
6/57	**Kisses Sweeter Than Wine**...Jimmie Rodgers
14/61	**Kissing My Pillow**...Rose Maddox
3/57	**Knee Deep In The Blues**...Marty Robbins
18/63	**Knock Again, True Love**...Claude Gray
29/84	**Knock On Wood**...Razzy Bailey
3/71	**Knock Three Times**...Billy "Crash" Craddock
3/53	**Knothole**...Carlisles
	Knoxville Girl
18/59	Wilburn Brothers
19/59	Louvin Brothers
39/72	**Knoxville Station**...Bobby Austin

POS/YR	RECORD TITLE/ARTIST
11/71	**Ko-Ko Joe**...Jerry Reed
4/47	**Kokomo Island**...Al Dexter

L

POS/YR	RECORD TITLE/ARTIST
9/71	**L.A. International Airport**...Susan Raye
1/80	**Lady**...Kenny Rogers
14/75	**Lady Came From Baltimore**...Johnny Cash
1/83	**Lady Down On Love**...Alabama
9/79	**Lady In The Blue Mercedes**...Johnny Duncan
31/84	**Lady In Waiting**...David Wills
	Lady Lay Down
1/79	John Conlee
26/82	Tom Jones
4/85	**Lady Like You**...Glen Campbell
22/73	**Lady Of The Night**...David Houston
31/83	**Lady, She's Right**...Leon Everette
3/84	**Lady Takes The Cowboy Everytime**...Gatlin Bros.
2/52	**Lady's Man**...Hank Snow
20/70	**Land Mark Tavern**...Del Reeves & Penny DeHaven
9/85	**Lasso The Moon**...Gary Morris
1/79	**Last Cheater's Waltz**...T.G. Sheppard
12/80	**Last Cowboy Song**...Ed Bruce
	Last Date
5/61	Skeeter Davis (My Last Date)
11/61	Floyd Cramer
1/72	Conway Twitty
1/83	Emmylou Harris
7/64	**Last Day In The Mines**...Dave Dudley
17/68	**Last Goodbye**...Dick Miles
38/77	**Last Gunfighter Ballad**...Johnny Cash
4/73	**Last Love Song**...Hank Williams, Jr.
20/59	**Last Night At A Party**...Faron Young
28/78	**Last Night, Ev'ry Night**...Reba McEntire
27/77	**Last Of The Winfield Amateurs**...Ray Griff
1/87	**Last One To Know**...Reba McEntire
18/71	**Last One To Touch Me**...Porter Wagoner
4/88	**Last Resort**...T. Graham Brown
3/59	**Last Ride**...Hank Snow
2/83	**Last Thing I Needed First Thing This Morning**...Willie Nelson
26/59	**Last Thing I Want To Know**...George Morgan
7/68	**Last Thing On My Mind**...Porter Wagoner & Dolly Parton

POS/YR	RECORD TITLE/ARTIST
25/72	**Last Time I Called Somebody Darlin'**...Roy Drusky
21/71	**Last Time I Saw Her**...Glen Campbell
8/74	**Last Time I Saw Him**...Dottie West
39/64	**Last Town I Painted**...George Jones
4/53	**Last Waltz**...Webb Pierce
2/66	**Last Word In Lonesome Is Me**...Eddy Arnold
20/68	**Late And Great Love (Of My Heart)**...Hank Snow
	Laura (What's He Got That I Ain't Got)
1/67	Leon Ashley
19/76	Kenny Rogers
13/49	**Lavender Blue (Dilly Dilly)**...Burl Ives with Captain Stubby
3/76	**Lawdy Miss Clawdy**...Mickey Gilley
9/72	**Lawrence Welk - Hee Haw Counter-Revolution Polka**...Roy Clark
22/73	**Lay A Little Lovin' On Me**...Del Reeves
13/80	**Lay Back In The Arms Of Someone**...Randy Barlow
35/75	**Lay Back Lover**...Dottie West
3/79	**Lay Down Beside Me**...Don Williams
26/78	**Lay Down Sally**...Eric Clapton
13/48	**Lazy Mary**...Bud Hobbs
1/71	**Lead Me On**...Conway Twitty & Loretta Lynn
7/95	**Lead On**...George Strait
13/74	**Lean It All On Me**...Diana Trask
1/91	**Leap Of Faith**...Lionel Cartwright
20/67	**Learnin' A New Way Of Life**...Hank Snow
2/93	**Learning To Live Again**...Garth Brooks
28/81	**Learning To Live Again**...Bobby Bare
15/65	**Least Of All**...George Jones
34/64	**Leave A Little Play (In The Chain Of Love)**...Bob Jennings
6/92	**Leave Him Out Of This**...Steve Wariner
7/90	**Leave It Alone**...Forester Sisters
22/75	**Leave It Up To Me**...Billy Larkin
1/87	**Leave Me Lonely**...Gary Morris
6/69	**Leave My Dream Alone**...Warner Mack
6/83	**Leave Them Boys Alone**...Hank Williams, Jr.
9/71	**Leavin' And Sayin' Goodbye**...Faron Young
8/63	**Leavin' On Your Mind**...Patsy Cline
15/93	**Leavin's Been A Long Time Comin'**...Shenandoah
13/80	**Leavin's For Unbelievers**...Dottie West
1/80	**Leaving Louisiana In The Broad Daylight**...Oak Ridge Boys
10/84	**Left Side Of The Bed**...Mark Gray

POS/YR	RECORD TITLE/ARTIST
5/60	**Left To Right**...Kitty Wells
19/85	**Legend And The Man**...Conway Twitty
	Legend In My Time ..see: (I'd Be)
1/68	**Legend Of Bonnie And Clyde**...Merle Haggard
27/62	**Legend Of The Johnson Boys**...Flatt & Scruggs
38/72	**Legendary Chicken Fairy**...Jack Blanchard & Misty Morgan
9/62	**Leona**...Stonewall Jackson
16/85	**Leona**...Sawyer Brown
9/81	**Leonard**...Merle Haggard
33/95	**Leroy The Redneck Reindeer**...Joe Diffie
27/65	**Less And Less**...Charlie Louvin
1/80	**Lesson In Leavin'**...Dottie West
34/85	**Let A Little Love Come In**...Charley Pride
5/61	**Let Forgiveness In**...Webb Pierce
6/93	**Let Go**...Brother Phelps
7/93	**Let Go Of The Stone**...John Anderson
18/91	**Let Her Go**...Mark Collie
	Let It Be Me
14/69	Glen Campbell & Bobbie Gentry
2/82	Willie Nelson
5/89	**Let It Be You**...Ricky Skaggs
6/85	**Let It Roll (Let It Rock)**...Mel McDaniel
5/76	**Let It Shine**...Olivia Newton-John
22/80	**Let Jesse Rob The Train**...Buck Owens
1/53	**Let Me Be The One**...Hank Locklin
7/73	**Let Me Be There**...Olivia Newton-John
13/78	**Let Me Be Your Baby**...Charly McClain
35/76	**Let Me Be Your Friend**...Mack White
1/57	**(Let Me Be Your) Teddy Bear**...Elvis Presley
7/77	**Let Me Down Easy**...Cristy Lane
16/85	**Let Me Down Easy**...Jim Glaser
1/55	**Let Me Go, Lover!**...Hank Snow
27/70	**Let Me Go (Set Me Free)**...Johnny Duncan
23/80	**Let Me In**...Kenny Dale
21/71	**Let Me Live**...Charley Pride
22/77	**Let Me Love You Once Before You Go**...Barbara Fairchild
25/74	**Let Me Make The Bright Lights Shine For You**...Bob Luman
29/63	**Let Me Off At The Corner**...Dottie West
1/89	**Let Me Tell You About Love**...Judds
1/77	**Let My Love Be Your Pillow**...Ronnie Milsap
1/51	**Let Old Mother Nature Have Her Way**...Carl Smith
10/84	**Let Somebody Else Drive**...John Anderson

POS/YR	RECORD TITLE/ARTIST
4/93	**Let That Pony Run**...Pam Tillis
4/68	**Let The Chips Fall**...Charley Pride
23/85	**Let The Heartache Ride**...Restless Heart
38/75	**Let The Little Boy Dream**...Even Stevens
4/87	**Let The Music Lift You Up**...Reba McEntire
20/69	**Let The Whole World Sing It With Me**...Wynn Stewart
7/68	**Let The World Keep On A Turnin'**...Buck Owens & Buddy Alan
21/76	**Let Your Love Flow**...Bellamy Brothers
13/72	**Let's All Go Down To The River**...Jody Miller & Johnny Paycheck
F/75	**Let's All Help The Cowboys (Sing The Blues)**...Waylon Jennings
38/87	**Let's Be Fools Like That Again**...Tommy Roe
32/73	**Let's Build A World Together**...George Jones & Tammy Wynette
1/84	**Let's Chase Each Other Around The Room**...Merle Haggard
16/87	**Let's Do Something**...Vince Gill
26/62	**Let's End It Before It Begins**...Claude Gray
	Let's Fall Apart ..see: (All Together Now)
1/84	**Let's Fall To Pieces Together**...George Strait
6/80	**Let's Get It While The Gettin's Good**...Eddy Arnold
10/83	**Let's Get Over Them Together**...Moe Bandy/Becky Hobbs
12/89	**Let's Get Started If We're Gonna Break My Heart**...Statler Brothers
6/77	**(Let's Get Together) One Last Time**...Tammy Wynette
11/64	**Let's Go All The Way**...Norma Jean
26/74	**Let's Go All The Way Tonight**...Mel Tillis & Sherry Bryce
2/50	**Let's Go To Church (Next Sunday Morning)**...Margaret Whiting & Jimmy Wakely
5/95	**Let's Go To Vegas**...Faith Hill
17/63	**Let's Invite Them Over**...George Jones & Melba Montgomery
	Let's Keep It That Way
37/79	Juice Newton
10/80	Mac Davis
30/84	**Let's Leave The Lights On Tonight**...Johnny Rodriguez
2/51	**Let's Live A Little**...Carl Smith
6/76	**Let's Put It Back Together Again**...Jerry Lee Lewis
23/80	**Let's Put Our Love In Motion**...Charly McClain

POS/YR	RECORD TITLE/ARTIST
27/69	Let's Put Our World Back Together...Charlie Louvin
5/49	Let's Say Goodbye Like We Said Hello...Ernest Tubb
9/78	Let's Shake Hands And Come Out Lovin'...Kenny O'Dell
18/75	Let's Sing Our Song...Jerry Reed
1/84	Let's Stop Talkin' About It...Janie Fricke
1/78	Let's Take The Long Way Around The World...Ronnie Milsap
27/79	Let's Take The Time To Fall In Love Again...Jim Chesnut
9/60	Let's Think About Living...Bob Luman
28/79	Let's Try Again...Janie Fricke
32/78	Let's Try To Remember...David Rogers
36/65	Let's Walk Away Strangers...Carl Smith
3/76	Letter, The...Conway Twitty & Loretta Lynn
27/79	Letter, The...Sammi Smith
9/88	Letter Home...Forester Sisters
10/75	Letter That Johnny Walker Read...Asleep At The Wheel
	Letter To Home ..see: (Love Always)
20/62	Letter To My Heart...Jim Reeves
2/50	Letters Have No Arms...Ernest Tubb
6/92	Letting Go...Suzy Bogguss
6/77	Liars One, Believers Zero...Bill Anderson
14/79	Liberated Woman...John Wesley Ryles
2/85	Lie To You For Your Love...Bellamy Brothers
22/82	Lies On Your Lips...Cristy Lane
23/75	Life...Marty Robbins
6/94	Life #9...Martina McBride
34/71	Life...Elvis Presley
4/89	Life As We Knew It...Kathy Mattea
21/64	Life Can Have Meaning...Bobby Lord
4/95	Life Gets Away...Clint Black
	Life Gits Tee-Jus Don't It
3/48	Carson Robison
5/48	Tex Williams
5/95	Life Goes On...Little Texas
15/60	Life Of A Poor Boy...Stonewall Jackson
2/59	Life To Go...Stonewall Jackson
22/59	Life To Live...Billie Morgan
	Life Turned Her That Way
11/67	Mel Tillis
1/88	Ricky Van Shelton
4/93	Life's A Dance...John Michael Montgomery
23/65	Life's Gone And Slipped Away...Jerry Wallace
1/86	Life's Highway...Steve Wariner

POS/YR	RECORD TITLE/ARTIST
4/91	Life's Little Ups And Downs...Ricky Van Shelton
37/91	Life's Too Long (To Live Like This)...Ricky Skaggs
4/94	Lifestyles Of The Not So Rich And Famous...Tracy Byrd
23/91	Light At The End Of The Tunnel...B.B. Watson
11/77	Light Of A Clear Blue Morning...Dolly Parton
35/88	Light Years...Glen Campbell
40/86	Lights Of Albuquerque...Jim Glaser
30/69	Like A Bird...George Morgan
15/74	Like A First Time Thing...Ray Price
13/67	Like A Fool...Dottie West
30/93	Like A River To The Sea...Steve Wariner
34/76	Like A Sad Song...John Denver
14/89	Like Father Like Son...Lionel Cartwright
2/83	Like Nothing Ever Happened...Sylvia
4/75	Like Old Times Again...Ray Price
21/80	Like Strangers...Gail Davies
3/96	Like There Ain't No Yesterday...BlackHawk
4/91	Like We Never Had A Broken Heart...Trisha Yearwood
39/81	Likin' Him And Lovin' You...Kin Vassy
17/73	Lila...Doyle Holly
17/70	Lilacs And Fire...George Morgan
32/77	Lily Dale...Darrell McCall & Willie Nelson
	Lincoln Park Inn ..see: (Margie's At)
1/75	Linda On My Mind...Conway Twitty
25/64	Linda With The Lonely Eyes...George Hamilton IV
	Line In Gasoline ..see: (Who Was The Man Who Put)
9/95	Lipstick Promises...George Ducas
24/72	Listen...Tommy Cash
32/74	Listen...Wayne Kemp
15/71	Listen Betty...Dave Dudley
4/72	Listen To A Country Song...Lynn Anderson
3/82	Listen To The Radio...Don Williams
20/60	Little Angel (Come Rock Me To Sleep)...Ted Self
3/50	Little Angel With The Dirty Face...Eddy Arnold
11/68	Little Arrows...Leapy Lee
18/76	Little At A Time...Sunday Sharpe
5/75	Little Band Of Gold...Sonny James
8/49	Little Bird Told Me...Smokey Rogers
18/88	Little Bit Closer...Tom Wopat

POS/YR	RECORD TITLE/ARTIST
14/82	**Little Bit Crazy**...Eddy Raven
2/88	**Little Bit In Love**...Patty Loveless
36/70	**Little Bit Late**...Lewie Wickham
14/68	**Little Bit Later On Down The Line**...Bobby Bare
31/93	**Little Bit Of Her Love**...Robert Ellis Orrall
2/95	**Little Bit Of You**...Lee Roy Parnell
6/75	**Little Bit South Of Saskatoon**...Sonny James
2/62	**Little Bitty Tear**...Burl Ives
10/62	**Little Black Book**...Jimmy Dean
10/69	**Little Boy Sad**...Bill Phillips
17/66	**Little Buddy**...Claude King
33/84	**Little By Little**...Gene Watson
25/95	**Little By Little**...James House
11/48	**Little Community Church**...Bill Monroe
24/59	**Little Drummer Boy**...Johnny Cash
20/59	**Little Dutch Girl**...George Morgan
17/80	**Little Getting Used To**...Mickey Gilley
7/90	**Little Girl**...Reba McEntire
31/74	**Little Girl Feeling**...Barbara Fairchild
2/73	**Little Girl Gone**...Donna Fargo
1/83	**Little Good News**...Anne Murray
6/68	**Little Green Apples**...Roger Miller
29/80	**Little Ground In Texas**...Capitals
13/60	**Little Guy Called Joe**...Stonewall Jackson
3/62	**Little Heartache**...Eddy Arnold
7/95	**Little Houses**...Doug Stone
37/70	**Little Johnny From Down The Street**...Wilburn Brothers
2/94	**Little Less Talk And A Lot More Action**...Toby Keith
21/61	**Little Miss Belong To No One**...Margie Bowes
1/95	**Little Miss Honky Tonk**...Brooks & Dunn
22/62	**Little Music Box**...Skeeter Davis
10/83	**Little Old Fashioned Karma**...Willie Nelson
9/67	**Little Old Wine Drinker Me**...Robert Mitchum
23/77	**Little Ole Dime**...Jim Reeves
11/63	**Little Ole You**...Jim Reeves
31/66	**Little Pedro**...Carl Butler & Pearl
30/66	**Little Pink Mack**...Kay Adams with The Cliffie Stone Group
29/69	**Little Reasons**...Charlie Louvin
1/86	**Little Rock**...Reba McEntire
2/94	**Little Rock**...Collin Raye
5/56	**Little Rosa**...Red Sovine & Webb Pierce

POS/YR	RECORD TITLE/ARTIST
7/87	**Little Sister**...Dwight Yoakam
	(also see: Bonnie Jean)
34/64	**Little South Of Memphis**...Frankie Miller
1/85	**Little Things**...Oak Ridge Boys
8/91	**Little Things**...Marty Stuart
22/68	**Little Things**...Willie Nelson
3/78	**Little Things Mean A Lot**...Margo Smith
7/55	**Little Tom**...Ferlin Husky
36/65	**Little Unfair**...Lefty Frizzell
8/87	**Little Ways**...Dwight Yoakam
7/46	**Little White Cross On The Hill**...Roy Rogers
18/68	**Little World Girl**...George Hamilton IV
32/76	**Littlest Cowboy Rides Again**...Ed Bruce
39/79	**Live Entertainment**...Don King
1/55	**Live Fast, Love Hard, Die Young**...Faron Young
16/70	**Live For The Good Times**...Warner Mack
28/63	**Live For Tomorrow**...Carl Smith
1/94	**Live Until I Die**...Clay Walker
F/57	**Livin' Alone**...Hank Locklin
3/65	**Livin' In A House Full Of Love**...David Houston
9/82	**Livin' In These Troubled Times**...Crystal Gayle
28/63	**Livin' Offa Credit**...Jim Nesbitt
1/94	**Livin' On Love**...Alan Jackson
23/79	**Livin' Our Love Together**...Billie Jo Spears
9/71	**Living And Learning**...Mel Tillis & Sherry Bryce
1/86	**Living In The Promiseland**...Willie Nelson
2/76	**Living It Down**...Freddy Fender
29/77	**Living Next Door To Alice**...Johnny Carver
1/89	**Living Proof**...Ricky Van Shelton
38/76	**Living Proof**...Hank Williams, Jr.
F/70	**Living Under Pressure**...Eddy Arnold
7/91	**Liza Jane**...Vince Gill
1/75	**Lizzie And The Rainman**...Tanya Tucker
30/79	**Lo Que Sea (What Ever May The Future Be)**...Jess Garron
26/63	**Lock, Stock And Teardrops**...Roger Miller
23/69	**Lodi**...Buddy Alan
11/76	**Lone Star Beer And Bob Wills Music**...Red Steagall
36/87	**Lone Star State Of Mind**...Nanci Griffith
1/67	**Lonely Again**...Eddy Arnold
2/86	**Lonely Alone**...Forester Sisters
15/83	**Lonely But Only For You**...Sissy Spacek
39/77	**Lonely Eyes**...Rayburn Anthony

POS/YR	RECORD TITLE/ARTIST
14/64	**Lonely Girl**...Carl Smith
30/59	**Lonely Girl**...Jimmy Newman
40/84	**Lonely Heart**...Tammy Wynette
18/78	**Lonely Hearts Club**...Billie Jo Spears
40/80	**Lonely Hotel**...Don King
18/58	**Lonely Island Pearl**...Johnnie & Jack
23/75	**Lonely Men, Lonely Women**...Connie Eaton
1/82	**Lonely Nights**...Mickey Gilley
38/72	**Lonely People**...Eddy Arnold
16/60	**Lonely River Rhine**...Bobby Helms
6/89	**Lonely Side Of Love**...Patty Loveless
7/56	**Lonely Side Of Town**...Kitty Wells
8/78	**Lonely Street**...Rex Allen, Jr.
5/76	**Lonely Teardrops**...Narvel Felts
18/63	**Lonely Teardrops**...Rose Maddox
11/72	**Lonely Weekends**...Jerry Lee Lewis
	Lonely Women Make Good Lovers
4/72	Bob Luman
4/84	Steve Wariner
13/66	**Lonelyville**...Dave Dudley
20/61	**Lonelyville**...Ray Sanders
	Lonesome 7-7203
1/63	Hawkshaw Hawkins
16/72	Tony Booth
24/84	Darrell Clanton
2/62	**Lonesome Number One**...Don Gibson
11/59	**Lonesome Old House**...Don Gibson
21/60	**Lonesome Road Blues**...Jimmie Skinner
11/92	**Lonesome Standard Time**...Kathy Mattea
	Lonesome Whistle
9/51	Hank Williams
29/71	Don Gibson
2/72	**Lonesomest Lonesome**...Ray Price
5/85	**Long And Lasting Love**...Crystal Gayle
4/96	**Long As I Live**...John Michael Montgomery
	Long Black Veil
6/59	Lefty Frizzell
26/74	Sammi Smith
	Long Gone Lonesome Blues
1/50	Hank Williams
5/64	Hank Williams, Jr.
27/80	**Long Haired Country Boy**...Charlie Daniels Band
1/84	**Long Hard Road (The Sharecropper's Dream)**...Nitty Gritty Dirt Band
6/67	**Long-Legged Guitar Pickin' Man**...Johnny Cash & June Carter
1/87	**Long Line Of Love**...Michael Martin Murphey
5/70	**Long Long Texas Road**...Roy Drusky

POS/YR	RECORD TITLE/ARTIST
16/91	**Long Lost Friend**...Restless Heart
5/89	**Long Shot**...Baillie & The Boys
10/92	**Long Time Ago**...Remingtons
16/59	**Long Time Ago**...Faron Young
5/46	**Long Time Gone**...Tex Ritter
15/66	**Long Time Gone**...Dave Dudley
11/60	**Long Walk**...Bill Leatherwood
35/89	**Long White Cadillac**...Dwight Yoakam
35/69	**Longest Beer Of The Night**...Jim Ed Brown
33/78	**Longest Walk**...Mary K. Miller
17/76	**Longhaired Redneck**...David Allan Coe
24/81	**Longing For The High**...Billy Larkin
24/95	**Look At Me Now**...Bryan White
21/70	**Look At Mine**...Jody Miller
17/75	**Look At Them Beans**...Johnny Cash
4/92	**Look At Us**...Vince Gill
1/93	**Look Heart, No Hands**...Randy Travis
36/66	**Look Into My Teardrops**...Conway Twitty
11/95	**Look What Followed Me Home**...David Ball
4/51	**Look What Thoughts Will Do**...Lefty Frizzell
21/77	**Look Who I'm Cheating On Tonight**...Bobby Bare
8/58	**Look Who's Blue**...Don Gibson
4/44	**Look Who's Talkin'**...Ted Daffan
F/77	**Lookin' For A Feeling**...Waylon Jennings
1/80	**Lookin' For Love**...Johnny Lee
16/76	**Lookin' For Tomorrow (And Findin' Yesterdays)**...Mel Tillis
37/71	**Lookin' Out My Back Door**...Buddy Alan
5/68	**Looking At The World Through A Windshield**...Del Reeves
	Looking Back To See
4/54	Goldie Hill - Justin Tubb
8/54	Browns
13/72	Buck Owens & Susan Raye
7/64	**Looking For More In '64**...Jim Nesbitt
30/76	**Looking For Space**...John Denver
11/93	**Looking Out For Number One**...Travis Tritt
24/76	**Looking Out My Window Through The Pain**...Mel Street
35/90	**Looks Aren't Everything**...Mark Collie
23/63	**Loose Lips**...Earl Scott
	Loose Talk
1/55	Carl Smith
4/61	Buck Owens & Rose Maddox
7/91	**Lord Have Mercy On A Country Boy**...Don Williams
5/92	**Lord Have Mercy On The Working Man**...Travis Tritt

POS/YR	RECORD TITLE/ARTIST
1/82	**Lord, I Hope This Day Is Good**...Don Williams
16/70	**Lord Is That Me**...Jack Greene
1/73	**Lord Knows I'm Drinking**...Cal Smith
1/73	**Lord, Mr. Ford**...Jerry Reed
7/50	**Lose Your Blues**...Red Kirk
28/78	**Loser, The**...Kenny Dale
3/67	**Loser's Cathedral**...David Houston
36/71	**Loser's Cocktail**...Dick Curless
37/81	**Loser's Night Out**...Jack Grayson & Blackjack
14/80	**Losing Kind Of Love**...Lacy J. Dalton
2/62	**Losing Your Love**...Jim Reeves
6/92	**Lost And Found**...Brooks & Dunn
9/72	**Lost Forever In Your Kiss**...Porter Wagoner & Dolly Parton
12/49	**Lost Highway**...Hank Williams
	Lost His [Her] Love On Our Last Date ..see: Last Date
30/81	**Lost In Love**...Dickey Lee/Kathy Burdick
2/83	**Lost In The Feeling**...Conway Twitty
1/85	**Lost In The Fifties Tonight (In the Still of the Night)**...Ronnie Milsap
22/65	**Lost In The Shuffle**...Stonewall Jackson
11/48	**Lost John Boogie**...Wayne Raney
5/83	**Lost My Baby Blues**...David Frizzell
15/58	**Lost To A Geisha Girl**...Skeeter Davis
(also see: Geisha Girl)	
	Louisiana Man
10/61	Rusty & Doug
25/65	George & Gene
14/70	Connie Smith
20/88	**Louisiana Rain**...John Wesley Ryles
7/81	**Louisiana Saturday Night**...Mel McDaniel
24/67	**Louisiana Saturday Night**...Jimmy Newman
1/73	**Louisiana Woman, Mississippi Man**...Conway Twitty & Loretta Lynn
23/68	**Louisville**...Leroy Van Dyke
2/94	**Love A Little Stronger**...Diamond Rio
11/83	**Love Affairs**...Michael Martin Murphey
24/79	**Love Ain't Gonna Wait For Us**...Billie Jo Spears
33/79	**Love Ain't Made For Fools**...John Wesley Ryles
38/70	**Love Ain't Never Gonna Be No Better**...Webb Pierce
19/81	**Love Ain't Never Hurt Nobody**...Bobby Goldsboro
14/85	**(Love Always) Letter To Home**...Glen Campbell

POS/YR	RECORD TITLE/ARTIST
3/86	**Love At The Five & Dime**...Kathy Mattea
6/65	**Love Bug**...George Jones
12/58	**Love Bug Crawl**...Jimmy Edwards
28/82	**Love Busted**...Billy "Crash" Craddock
5/91	**Love Can Build A Bridge**...Judds
10/87	**Love Can't Ever Get Better Than This**...Ricky Skaggs & Sharon White
12/62	**Love Can't Wait**...Marty Robbins
34/80	**Love Crazy Love**...Zella Lehr
13/81	**Love Dies Hard**...Randy Barlow
1/85	**Love Don't Care (Whose Heart It Breaks)**...Earl Thomas Conley
23/78	**Love Got In The Way**...Freddy Weller
12/57	**Love Has Finally Come My Way**...Faron Young
10/60	**Love Has Made You Beautiful**...Merle Kilgore
4/89	**Love Has No Right**...Billy Joe Royal
26/80	**Love Has Taken Its' Time**...Zella Lehr
3/88	**Love Helps Those**...Paul Overstreet
19/70	**Love Hungry**...Warner Mack
1/81	**Love In The First Degree**...Alabama
3/75	**Love In The Hot Afternoon**...Gene Watson
32/80	**Love In The Meantime**...Streets
39/82	**Love Is**...Allen Tripp
12/72	**Love Is A Good Thing**...Johnny Paycheck
5/75	**Love Is A Rose**...Linda Ronstadt
5/70	**Love Is A Sometimes Thing**...Bill Anderson
27/78	**Love Is A Word**...Dickey Lee
1/85	**Love Is Alive**...Judds
29/80	**Love Is All Around**...Sonny Curtis
13/81	**Love Is Fair**...Barbara Mandrell
10/68	**Love Is In The Air**...Marty Robbins
3/77	**Love Is Just A Game**...Larry Gatlin
1/74	**Love Is Like A Butterfly**...Dolly Parton
36/72	**Love Is Like A Spinning Wheel**...Jan Howard
7/64	**Love Is No Excuse**...Jim Reeves & Dottie West
1/83	**Love Is On A Roll**...Don Williams
26/79	**Love Is Sometimes Easy**...Sandy Posey
	Love Is Strange
20/75	Buck Owens & Susan Raye
21/90	Kenny Rogers & Dolly Parton
1/73	**Love Is The Foundation**...Loretta Lynn
8/73	**Love Is The Look You're Looking For**...Connie Smith
24/76	**Love Is Thin Ice**...Barbara Mandrell
37/85	**Love Is What We Make It**...Kenny Rogers

POS/YR	RECORD TITLE/ARTIST
30/76	**Love It Away**...Mary Lou Turner
40/81	**Love Knows We Tried**...Tanya Tucker
9/95	**Love Lessons**...Tracy Byrd
33/79	**Love Lies**...Mel McDaniel
19/76	**Love Lifted Me**...Kenny Rogers
29/80	**Love, Look At Us Now**...Johnny Rodriguez
17/64	**Love Looks Good On You**...David Houston
1/55	**Love, Love, Love**...Webb Pierce
26/78	**Love, Love, Love/Chapel Of Love**...Sandy Posey
34/67	**Love Makes The World Go Around**...Kitty Wells
1/92	**Love, Me**...Collin Raye
	Love Me
34/72	Jeanne Pruett
9/73	Marty Robbins
10/56	**Love Me**...Elvis Presley
12/67	**Love Me And Make It All Better**...Bobby Lewis
24/79	**Love Me Like A Stranger**...Cliff Cochran
2/87	**Love Me Like You Used To**...Tanya Tucker
14/68	**Love Me, Love Me**...Bobby Barnett
26/79	**Love Me Now**...Ronnie McDowell
1/80	**Love Me Over Again**...Don Williams
3/56	**Love Me Tender**...Elvis Presley
14/57	**Love Me To Pieces**...Rusty & Doug
	Love Me Tonight ..see: (Turn Out The Light And)
F/78	**Love Me When You Can**...Merle Haggard
7/78	**Love Me With All Your Heart**...Johnny Rodriguez
4/88	**Love Of A Lifetime**...Gatlin Bros.
23/61	**Love Oh Love, Oh Please Come Home**...Reno & Smiley
1/90	**Love On Arrival**...Dan Seals
31/71	**Love On Broadway**...Jerry Lee Lewis
3/93	**Love On The Loose, Heart On The Run**...McBride & The Ride
1/78	**Love Or Something Like It**...Kenny Rogers
1/89	**Love Out Loud**...Earl Thomas Conley
36/84	**Love Over Old Times**...Sylvia
1/75	**Love Put A Song In My Heart**...Johnny Rodriguez
6/87	**Love Reunited**...Desert Rose Band
11/76	**Love Revival**...Mel Tillis
5/83	**Love She Found In Me**...Gary Morris
2/87	**Love Someone Like Me**...Holly Dunn
1/83	**Love Song**...Oak Ridge Boys
3/82	**Love Song**...Kenny Rogers

POS/YR	RECORD TITLE/ARTIST
5/74	**Love Song**...Anne Murray
40/80	**Love Song**...Dave & Sugar
40/68	**Love Song For You**...Hank Locklin
8/50	**Love Song In 32 Bars**...Johnny Bond
10/52	**Love Song Of The Waterfall**...Slim Whitman
27/79	**Love Songs Just For You**...Glenn Barber
17/73	**Love Sure Feels Good In My Heart**...Susan Raye
4/68	**Love Takes Care Of Me**...Jack Greene
9/85	**Love Talks**...Ronnie McDowell
4/80	**Love The World Away**...Kenny Rogers
21/81	**Love To Love You**...Cristy Lane
30/82	**Love Was Born**...Randy Barlow
39/76	**Love Was (Once Around The Dance Floor)**...Linda Hargrove
7/89	**Love Will**...Forester Sisters
12/91	**Love Will Bring Her Around**...Rob Crosby
1/88	**Love Will Find Its Way To You**...Reba McEntire
14/86	**Love Will Get You Through Times With No Money**...Girls Next Door
1/82	**Love Will Turn You Around**...Kenny Rogers
1/90	**Love Without End, Amen**...George Strait
8/93	**Love Without Mercy**...Lee Roy Parnell
36/86	**Love Won't Wait**...Whites
6/87	**Love, You Ain't Seen The Last Of Me**...John Schneider
30/82	**Love's Been A Little Bit Hard On Me**...Juice Newton
25/68	**Love's Dead End**...Bill Phillips
12/77	**Love's Explosion**...Margo Smith
13/82	**Love's Found You And Me**...Ed Bruce
8/82	**Love's Gonna Fall Here Tonight**...Razzy Bailey
4/86	**Love's Gonna Get You Someday**...Ricky Skaggs
7/68	**Love's Gonna Happen To Me**...Wynn Stewart
1/63	**Love's Gonna Live Here**...Buck Owens
1/92	**Love's Got A Hold On You**...Alan Jackson
28/71	**Love's Old Song**...Barbara Fairchild
25/66	**Love's Something (I Can't Understand)**...Webb Pierce
5/73	**Love's The Answer**...Tanya Tucker
8/94	**Lovebug**...George Strait
2/50	**Lovebug Itch**...Eddy Arnold
6/60	**Lovely Work Of Art**...Jimmy Newman
12/71	**Lovenworth**...Roy Rogers

POS/YR	RECORD TITLE/ARTIST
	Lover's Leap ..see: (Doin' The)
	Lover's Quarrel ..see: (I Just Had A Date)
	Lover's Question
14/70	Del Reeves
3/78	Jacky Ward
39/70	**Lover's Song**...Ned Miller
3/80	**Lovers Live Longer**...Bellamy Brothers
	Lovesick Blues
1/49	Hank Williams
14/49	Red Kirk
15/57	Sonny James
24/92	George Strait
	Lovin' ..also see: Loving
37/80	**Lovin' A Livin' Dream**...Ronnie McDowell
10/92	**Lovin' All Night**...Rodney Crowell
	Lovin' Her Was Easier (Than Anything I'll Ever Do Again)
28/71	Roger Miller
2/81	Tompall/Glaser Brothers
8/66	**Lovin' Machine**...Johnny Paycheck
	Lovin' Man ..see: Oh Pretty Woman
	Lovin' On
20/77	T.G. Sheppard
16/79	Bellamy Brothers
5/73	**Lovin' On Back Streets**...Mel Street
11/74	**Lovin' On Borrowed Time**...Mel Street
1/89	**Lovin' Only Me**...Ricky Skaggs
23/76	**Lovin' Somebody On A Rainy Night**...La Costa
39/73	**Lovin' Someone On My Mind**...Bobby Wright
27/79	**Lovin' Starts Where Friendship Ends**...Mel McDaniel
30/87	**Lovin' That Crazy Feelin'**...Ronnie McDowell
	Lovin' Up A Storm ..see: Loving Up
7/81	**Lovin' What Your Lovin' Does To Me**...Conway Twitty & Loretta Lynn
34/78	**Lovin' You Baby**...Connie Smith
40/74	**Lovin' You Is Worth It**...David Houston & Barbara Mandrell
39/78	**Lovin' You Off My Mind**...Cates Sisters
	Loving Arms
19/77	Sammi Smith
8/81	Elvis Presley
14/63	**Loving Arms**...Carl Butler & Pearl
1/91	**Loving Blind**...Clint Black
27/73	**Loving Gift**...Johnny Cash & June Carter Cash
38/78	**Loving Here And Living There And Lying In Between**...Faron Young

POS/YR	RECORD TITLE/ARTIST
37/85	**Lovin' Up A Storm**...Bandana
1/80	**Loving Up A Storm**...Razzy Bailey
15/57	**Loving You**...Elvis Presley
26/75	**Loving You Beats All I've Ever Seen**...Johnny Paycheck
2/72	**Loving You Could Never Be Better**...George Jones
9/74	**Loving You Has Changed My Life**...David Rogers
32/83	**Loving You Hurts**...Gus Hardin
31/79	**Loving You Is A Natural High**...Larry G. Hudson
33/71	**(Loving You Is) Sunshine**...Barbara Fairchild
22/65	**Loving You Then Losing You**...Webb Pierce
7/61	**Loving You (Was Worth This Broken Heart)**...Bob Gallion
6/75	**Loving You Will Never Grow Old**...Lois Johnson
31/79	**Low Dog Blues**...John Anderson
1/77	**Lucille**...Kenny Rogers
1/83	**Lucille (You Won't Do Your Daddy's Will)**...Waylon Jennings
1/77	**Luckenbach, Texas**...Waylon Jennings
21/74	**Lucky Arms**...Lefty Frizzell
11/74	**Lucky Ladies**...Jeannie Seely
9/80	**Lucky Me**...Anne Murray
6/91	**Lucky Moon**...Oak Ridge Boys
5/64	**Lumberjack, The**...Hal Willis
	Lust Affair ..see: (This Ain't Just Another)
8/59	**Luther Played The Boogie**...Johnny Cash
24/68	**Luzianna**...Webb Pierce
8/75	**Lyin' Eyes**...Eagles
5/88	**Lyin' In His Arms Again**...Forester Sisters
27/61	**Lying Again**...Freddie Hart
2/79	**Lying In Love With You**...Jim Ed Brown/Helen Cornelius
6/80	**Lying Time Again**...Mel Tillis
1/87	**Lynda**...Steve Wariner

M

28/67	**Mabel**...Skeets McDonald
7/79	**Mabellene**...George Jones & Johnny Paycheck
23/69	**MacArthur Park**...Waylon Jennings & The Kimberlys
6/64	**Mad**...Dave Dudley

POS/YR	RECORD TITLE/ARTIST
6/93	**Made For Lovin' You**...Doug Stone
1/72	**Made In Japan**...Buck Owens
40/82	**Made In The U.S.A.**....Wright Brothers
11/84	**Maggie's Dream**...Don Williams
39/71	**Magnificent Sanctuary Band**...Roy Clark
10/71	**Maiden's Prayer**...David Houston
5/55	**Mainliner (The Hawk with Silver Wings)**...Hank Snow
10/85	**Major Moves**...Hank Williams, Jr.
36/67	**Make A Left And Then A Right**...Johnny & Jonie Mosby
6/55	**Make Believe ('Til We Can Make It Come True)**...Kitty Wells & Red Foley
30/74	**Make It Feel Like Love Again**...Bobby G. Rice
40/69	**Make It Rain**...Billy Mize
F/58	**Make Me A Miracle**...Jimmie Rodgers
37/71	**Make Me Your Kind Of Woman**...Patti Page
35/80	**Make Mine Night Time**...Bill Anderson
12/84	**Make My Day**...T.G. Sheppard/Clint Eastwood
1/85	**Make My Life With You**...Oak Ridge Boys
1/87	**Make No Mistake, She's Mine**...Ronnie Milsap & Kenny Rogers
2/46	**Make Room In Your Heart For A Friend**...Wiley & Gene
30/60	**Make The Waterwheel Roll**...Carl Smith
	Make The World Go Away
2/63	Ray Price
1/65	Eddy Arnold
	Makin' Believe ..see: Making
35/76	**Makin' Love Don't Always Make Love Grow**...Dickey Lee
11/74	**Makin' The Best Of A Bad Situation**...Dick Feller
1/86	**Makin' Up For Lost Time (The Dallas Lovers' Song)**...Crystal Gayle & Gary Morris
F/71	**Makin' Up His Mind**...Jack Greene
	Making Believe
2/55	Kitty Wells
5/55	Jimmy Work
8/77	Emmylou Harris
F/78	Merle Haggard
19/82	**Making Love From Memory**...Loretta Lynn
2/80	**Making Plans**...Porter Wagoner & Dolly Parton
6/50	**Mama And Daddy Broke My Heart**...Eddy Arnold
4/53	**Mama, Come Get Your Baby Boy**...Eddy Arnold

POS/YR	RECORD TITLE/ARTIST
9/92	**Mama Don't Forget To Pray For Me**...Diamond Rio
29/75	**Mama Don't 'Low**...Hank Thompson
1/84	**Mama He's Crazy**...Judds
	(also see: Mama, She's Lazy)
37/70	**Mama, I Won't Be Wearing A Ring**...Peggy Little
5/88	**Mama Knows**...Shenandoah
8/93	**Mama Knows The Highway**...Hal Ketchum
34/69	**Mama Lou**...Penny DeHaven
1/62	**Mama Sang A Song**...Bill Anderson
39/84	**Mama, She's Lazy**...Pinkard & Bowden
	(also see: Mama He's Crazy)
5/67	**Mama Spank**...Liz Anderson
1/68	**Mama Tried**...Merle Haggard
1/86	**Mama's Never Seen Those Eyes**...Forester Sisters
11/87	**Mama's Rockin' Chair**...John Conlee
	Mammas Don't Let Your Babies Grow Up To Be Cowboys
15/76	Ed Bruce
1/78	Waylon & Willie
40/73	**Man And A Train**...Marty Robbins
17/69	**Man And Wife Time**...Jim Ed Brown
3/71	**Man In Black**...Johnny Cash
4/94	**Man In Love With You**...George Strait
37/66	**Man In The Little White Suit**...Charlie Walker
17/83	**Man In The Mirror**...Jim Glaser
12/80	**Man Just Don't Know What A Woman Goes Through**...Charlie Rich
36/75	**Man Needs Love**...David Houston
8/94	**Man Of My Word**...Collin Raye
3/84	**Man Of Steel**...Hank Williams, Jr.
30/75	**Man On Page 602**...Zoot Fenster
4/74	**Man That Turned My Mama On**...Tanya Tucker
9/63	**Man Who Robbed The Bank At Santa Fe**...Hank Snow
32/82	**Man With The Golden Thumb**...Jerry Reed
28/70	**Man's Kind Of Woman**...Eddy Arnold
38/87	**Mandolin Rain**...Bruce Hornsby & The Range
6/72	**Manhattan Kansas**...Glen Campbell
	Mansion On The Hill
12/49	Hank Williams
29/58	June Webb
14/77	Ray Price
36/76	**Mansion On The Hill**...Michael Martin Murphey

POS/YR	RECORD TITLE/ARTIST
3/90	**Many A Long & Lonesome Highway**...Rodney Crowell
13/66	**Many Happy Hangovers To You**...Jean Shepard
34/89	**Many Mansions**...Moe Bandy
10/49	**Many Tears Ago**...Eddy Arnold
13/77	**Margaritaville**...Jimmy Buffett
23/73	**Margie, Who's Watching The Baby**...Earl Richards
4/69	**(Margie's At) The Lincoln Park Inn**...Bobby Bare
1/74	**Marie Laveau**...Bobby Bare
6/83	**Marina Del Rey**...George Strait
21/61	**Marines, Let's Go**...Rex Allen
18/71	**Mark Of A Heel**...Hank Thompson
10/53	**Marriage Of Mexican Joe**...Carolyn Bradshaw
10/49	**Marriage Vow**...Hank Snow
3/77	**Married But Not To Each Other**...Barbara Mandrell
8/52	**Married By The Bible, Divorced By The Law**...Hank Snow
25/71	**Married To A Memory**...Arlene Harden
33/81	**Married Women**...Sonny Curtis
39/70	**Marry Me**...Ron Lowry
17/70	**Marty Gray**...Billie Jo Spears
28/91	**Mary And Willie**...K.T. Oslin
12/63	**Mary Ann Regrets**...Burl Ives
12/60	**Mary Don't You Weep**...Stonewall Jackson
17/71	**Mary's Vineyard**...Claude King
2/63	**Matador, The**...Johnny Cash
7/81	**Matador**...Sylvia
8/65	**Matamoros**...Billy Walker
20/75	**Mathilda**...Donny King
	(Matthew's Song) ..see: Pilgrims On The Way
35/79	**May I**...Terri Hollowell
37/77	**May I Spend Every New Years With You**...T.G. Sheppard
1/65	**May The Bird Of Paradise Fly Up Your Nose**..."Little" Jimmy Dickens
13/78	**May The Force Be With You Always**...Tom T. Hall
8/51	**May The Good Lord Bless And Keep You**...Eddy Arnold
25/90	**Maybe**...Kenny Rogers with Holly Dunn
7/78	**Maybe Baby**...Susie Allanson
28/61	**Maybe I Do**...Dave Dudley

POS/YR	RECORD TITLE/ARTIST
	Maybe I [You] Should've Been Listening
31/78	Rayburn Anthony
23/81	Gene Watson
3/92	**Maybe It Was Memphis**...Pam Tillis
8/85	**Maybe My Baby**...Louise Mandrell
34/95	**Maybe She's Human**...Kathy Mattea
22/90	**Maybe That's All It Takes**...Don Williams
1/87	**Maybe Your Baby's Got The Blues**...Judds
9/55	**Maybelline**...Marty Robbins
8/64	**Me**...Bill Anderson
4/85	**Me Against The Night**...Crystal Gayle
	Me And Bobby McGee
12/69	Roger Miller
F/72	Jerry Lee Lewis
29/59	**Me And Fred And Joe And Bill**...Porter Wagoner
8/72	**Me And Jesus**...Tom T. Hall
15/77	**Me And Millie**...Ronnie Sessions
22/92	**Me And My Baby**...Paul Overstreet
9/79	**Me And My Broken Heart**...Rex Allen, Jr.
12/76	**Me And Ole C.B.**...Dave Dudley
14/85	**Me And Paul**...Willie Nelson
33/78	**Me And The I.R.S.**...Johnny Paycheck
29/87	**Me And You**...Donna Fargo
7/71	**Me And You And A Dog Named Boo**...Stonewall Jackson
30/60	**Mean Eyed Cat**...Johnny Cash
6/49	**Mean Mama Blues**...Ernest Tubb
22/66	**Mean Old Woman**...Claude Gray
11/57	**Mean Woman Blues**...Elvis Presley
5/96	**Meant To Be**...Sammy Kershaw
9/65	**Meanwhile, Down At Joe's**...Kitty Wells
32/79	**Medicine Woman**...Kenny O'Dell
1/91	**Meet In The Middle**...Diamond Rio
1/85	**Meet Me In Montana**...Marie Osmond with Dan Seals
38/64	**Meet Me Tonight Outside Of Town**...Jim Howard
23/87	**Members Only**...Donna Fargo & Billy Joe Royal
9/48	**Memories Of France**..."T" Texas Tyler
21/75	**Memories Of Us**...George Jones
5/86	**Memories To Burn**...Gene Watson
39/84	**Memory Lane**...Joe Stampley & Jessica Boucher
3/74	**Memory Maker**...Mel Tillis
2/64	**Memory #1**...Webb Pierce
10/81	**Memphis**...Fred Knoblock
7/80	**Men**...Charly McClain

POS/YR	RECORD TITLE/ARTIST
8/91	**Men**...Forester Sisters
16/66	**Men In My Little Girl's Life**...Archie Campbell
13/93	**Mending Fences**...Restless Heart
8/61	**Mental Cruelty**...Buck Owens & Rose Maddox
14/68	**Mental Journey**...Leon Ashley
	Mental Revenge
12/67	Waylon Jennings
15/76	Mel Tillis
2/93	**Mercury Blues**...Alan Jackson
7/48	**Merle's Boogie Woogie**...Merle Travis
1/53	**Mexican Joe**...Jim Reeves
4/44	**Mexico Joe**...Ivie Anderson
4/74	**Mi Esposa Con Amor (To My Wife With Love)**...Sonny James
1/95	**Mi Vida Loca (My Crazy Life)**...Pam Tillis
14/86	**Miami, My Amy**...Keith Whitley
4/78	**Middle Age Crazy**...Jerry Lee Lewis
1/53	**Midnight**...Red Foley
16/77	**Midnight Angel**...Barbara Mandrell
36/87	**Midnight Blue**...John Wesley Ryles
39/84	**Midnight Blue**...Billie Jo Spears
5/83	**Midnight Fire**...Steve Wariner
4/87	**Midnight Girl/Sunset Town**...Sweethearts Of The Rodeo
1/81	**Midnight Hauler**...Razzy Bailey
14/88	**Midnight Highway**...Southern Pacific
3/92	**Midnight In Montgomery**...Alan Jackson
2/74	**Midnight, Me And The Blues**...Mel Tillis
7/73	**Midnight Oil**...Barbara Mandrell
6/80	**Midnight Rider**...Willie Nelson
9/82	**Midnight Rodeo**...Leon Everette
F/84	**Midsummer Nights**...Kenny Rogers
38/77	**Miles And Miles Of Texas**...Asleep At The Wheel
8/52	**Milk Bucket Boogie**...Red Foley
	Miller's Cave
9/60	Hank Snow
4/64	Bobby Bare
2/66	**Million And One**...Billy Walker
39/83	**Million Light Beers Ago**...David Frizzell
8/81	**Million Old Goodbyes**...Mel Tillis
13/63	**Million Years Or So**...Eddy Arnold
12/68	**Milwaukee, Here I Come**...George Jones & Brenda Carter
	Mind Your Own Business
5/49	Hank Williams
35/64	Jimmy Dean
1/86	Hank Williams, Jr.

POS/YR	RECORD TITLE/ARTIST
8/49	**Mine All Mine**...Jimmy Wakely
24/66	**Minute Men (Are Turning In Their Graves)**...Stonewall Jackson
9/63	**Minute You're Gone**...Sonny James
4/81	**Miracles**...Don Williams
3/91	**Mirror Mirror**...Diamond Rio
12/82	**Mis'ry River**...Terri Gibbs
3/80	**Misery And Gin**...Merle Haggard
	Misery Loves Company
1/62	Porter Wagoner
F/80	Ronnie Milsap
2/81	**Miss Emily's Picture**...John Conlee
26/84	**Miss Understanding**...David Wills
32/84	**Missin' Mississippi**...Charley Pride
3/52	**Missing In Action**...Ernest Tubb
2/80	**Missin' You**...Charley Pride
	Missing You
7/57	Webb Pierce
8/72	Jim Reeves
1/50	**Mississippi**...Red Foley
19/79	**Mississippi**...Charlie Daniels Band
31/76	**Mississippi**...Barbara Fairchild
3/74	**Mississippi Cotton Picking Delta Town**...Charley Pride
15/95	**Mississippi Moon**...John Anderson
20/85	**Mississippi Squirrel Revival**...Ray Stevens
14/71	**Mississippi Woman**...Waylon Jennings
20/75	**Mississippi You're On My Mind**...Stoney Edwards
5/47	**Missouri**...Merle Travis
3/82	**Mistakes**...Don Williams
	Mister ..see: Mr.
13/55	**Mister Sandman**...Chet Atkins
3/75	**Misty**...Ray Stevens
	Misty Blue
4/66	Wilma Burgess
3/67	Eddy Arnold
5/76	Billie Jo Spears
37/72	**Misty Memories**...Brenda Lee
	Misunderstanding ..see: Miss Understanding
1/50	**Moanin' The Blues**...Hank Williams
27/77	**Mobile Boogie**...Hank Williams, Jr.
	Mockin' Bird Hill
3/51	Pinetoppers
7/51	Les Paul & Mary Ford
9/77	Donna Fargo
1/85	**Modern Day Romance**...Nitty Gritty Dirt Band
5/64	**Molly**...Eddy Arnold & The Needmore Creek Singers

POS/YR	RECORD TITLE/ARTIST
10/48	**Molly Darling**...Eddy Arnold
28/75	**Molly (I Ain't Gettin' Any Younger)**...Dorsey Burnette
	Mom And Dad's Waltz
2/51	Lefty Frizzell
21/61	Patti Page
24/66	**Mommy, Can I Still Call Him Daddy**...Dottie West
5/59	**Mommy For A Day**...Kitty Wells
	Mona Lisa
4/50	Moon Mullican
10/50	Jimmy Wakely
11/81	Willie Nelson
2/84	**Mona Lisa Lost Her Smile**...David Allan Coe
20/73	**Monday Morning Secretary**...Statler Brothers
13/88	**Money**...K.T. Oslin
15/57	**Money**...Browns
35/70	**Money Can't Buy Love**...Roy Rogers
1/93	**Money In The Bank**...John Anderson
	Money, Marbles And Chalk
12/49	Stubby & The Buccaneers
15/49	Patti Page
15/60	**Money To Burn**...George Jones
11/72	**Monkey That Became President**...Tom T. Hall
	Monsters' Holiday ..see: (It's A)
1/77	**Moody Blue**...Elvis Presley
16/60	**Moon Is Crying**...Allan Riddle
1/87	**Moon Is Still Over Her Shoulder**...Michael Johnson
9/91	**Moon Over Georgia**...Shenandoah
36/89	**Moon Pretty Moon**...Statler Brothers
	(Moon Song) ..see: I Don't Know A Thing About Love
18/90	**Moonshadow Road**...T. Graham Brown
26/72	**More About John Henry**...Tom T. Hall
	More And More
1/54	Webb Pierce
7/83	Charley Pride
6/94	**More Love**...Doug Stone
6/89	**More Than A Name On A Wall**...Statler Brothers
5/55	**More Than Anything Else In The World**...Carl Smith
8/65	**More Than Yesterday**...Slim Whitman
1/77	**More To Me**...Charley Pride
14/72	**Mornin' After Baby Let Me Down**...Ray Griff

POS/YR	RECORD TITLE/ARTIST
1/87	**Mornin' Ride**...Lee Greenwood
4/70	**Morning**...Jim Ed Brown
19/71	**Morning After**...Jerry Wallace
5/80	**Morning Comes Too Early**...Jim Ed Brown/Helen Cornelius
1/86	**Morning Desire**...Kenny Rogers
22/64	**Morning Paper**...Billy Walker
1/73	**Most Beautiful Girl**...Charlie Rich
6/55	**Most Of All**...Hank Thompson
18/70	**Most Uncomplicated Goodbye I've Ever Heard**...Henson Cargill
19/75	**Most Wanted Woman In Town**...Roy Head
13/67	**Motel Time Again**...Johnny Paycheck
7/76	**Motels And Memories**...T.G. Sheppard
	Mother ..see: (You Make Me Want To Be) A
17/77	**Mother Country Music**...Vern Gosdin
20/64	**Mother-In-Law**...Jim Nesbitt
21/68	**Mother, May I**...Liz Anderson & Lynn Anderson
F/56	**Mother Of A Honky Tonk Girl**...Jim Reeves
23/81	**Mountain Dew**...Willie Nelson
1/82	**Mountain Music**...Alabama
	Mountain Of Love
20/71	Bobby G. Rice
1/82	Charley Pride
2/63	**Mountain Of Love**...David Houston
4/47	**Move It On Over**...Hank Williams
10/77	**Movies, The**...Statler Brothers
1/75	**Movin' On**...Merle Haggard
20/83	**Movin' Train**...Kendalls
2/51	**Mr. And Mississippi**...Tennessee Ernie Ford
11/64	**Mr. And Mrs. Used To Be**...Ernest Tubb & Loretta Lynn
13/78	**Mister D.J.**...T.G. Sheppard
34/90	**Mister DJ**...Charlie Daniels Band
25/67	**Mr. Do-It-Yourself**...Jean Shepard & Ray Pillow
20/76	**Mr. Doodles**...Donna Fargo
15/57	**Mister Fire Eyes**...Bonnie Guitar
15/65	**Mister Garfield**...Johnny Cash
8/63	**Mr. Heartache, Move On**...Coleman O'Neal
20/79	**Mr. Jones**...Big Al Downing
28/63	**Mr. Juke Box**...Ernest Tubb
8/57	**Mister Love**...Ernest Tubb & The Wilburn Brothers
2/73	**Mr. Lovemaker**...Johnny Paycheck
4/51	**Mr. Moon**...Carl Smith
32/75	**Mr. Right And Mrs. Wrong**...Mel Tillis & Sherry Bryce

POS/YR	RECORD TITLE/ARTIST
10/81	**Mister Sandman**...Emmylou Harris
16/67	**Mr. Shorty**...Marty Robbins
4/69	**Mr. Walker, It's All Over**...Billie Jo Spears
15/72	**Much Oblige**...Jack Greene/Jeannie Seely
13/54	**Much Too Young To Die**...Ray Price
8/89	**Much Too Young (To Feel This Damn Old)**...Garth Brooks
15/69	**Muddy Mississippi Line**...Bobby Goldsboro
	Mule Skinner Blues
16/60	Fendermen
3/70	Dolly Parton (Blue Yodel No. 8)
1/49	**Mule Train**...Tennessee Ernie Ford
25/65	**Multiply The Heartaches**...George Jones & Melba Montgomery
29/78	**Music Is My Woman**...Don King
4/52	**Music Makin' Mama From Memphis**...Hank Snow
39/78	**Music, Music, Music**...Rebecca Lynn
21/62	**Must You Throw Dirt In My Face**...Louvin Brothers
8/57	**My Arms Are A House**...Hank Snow
2/90	**My Arms Stay Open All Night**...Tanya Tucker
23/83	**My Baby Don't Slow Dance**...Johnny Lee
13/56	**My Baby Left Me**...Elvis Presley
2/93	**My Baby Loves Me**...Martina McBride
1/81	**My Baby Thinks He's A Train**...Rosanne Cash
34/68	**My Baby Walked Right Out On Me**...Wanda Jackson
27/64	**My Baby Walks All Over Me**...Johnny Sea
	My Baby's Gone
9/59	Louvin Brothers
15/84	Kendalls
11/88	**My Baby's Gone**...Sawyer Brown
2/85	**My Baby's Got Good Timing**...Dan Seals
20/63	**My Baby's Not Here (In Town Tonight)**...Porter Wagoner
12/49	**My Best To You**...Sons Of The Pioneers
20/69	**My Big Iron Skillet**...Wanda Jackson
35/68	**My Big Truck Drivin' Man**...Kitty Wells
7/93	**My Blue Angel**...Aaron Tippin
17/71	**My Blue Tears**...Dolly Parton
14/75	**My Boy**...Elvis Presley
	My Bucket's Got A Hole In It
2/49	Hank Williams
4/49	"T" Texas Tyler
10/58	Ricky Nelson
17/68	**My Can Do Can't Keep Up With My Want To**...Nat Stuckey

POS/YR	RECORD TITLE/ARTIST
4/47	**My Chickashay Gal**...Roy Rogers
26/69	**My Cup Runneth Over**...Johnny Bush
5/48	**My Daddy Is Only A Picture**...Eddy Arnold
14/66	**My Dreams**...Faron Young
3/61	**My Ears Should Burn (When Fools Are Talked About)**...Claude Gray
	My Elusive Dreams
1/67	David Houston & Tammy Wynette
27/70	Bobby Vinton
3/75	Charlie Rich
7/54	**My Everything**...Eddy Arnold
1/76	**My Eyes Can Only See As Far As You**...Charley Pride
16/63	**My Father's Voice**...Judy Lynn
1/81	**My Favorite Memory**...Merle Haggard
6/49	**My Filipino Rose**...Ernest Tubb
35/83	**My First Country Song**...Dean Martin
6/83	**My First Taste Of Texas**...Ed Bruce
11/64	**My Friend On The Right**...Faron Young
	(My Friends Are Gonna Be) Strangers ..see: (From Now On My Friends Are Gonna Be)
11/68	**My Goal For Today**...Kenny Price
20/77	**My Good Thing's Gone**...Narvel Felts
14/69	**My Grass Is Green**...Roy Drusky
1/72	**My Hang-Up Is You**...Freddie Hart
1/80	**My Heart**...Ronnie Milsap
	My Heart Cries For You
6/51	Evelyn Knight & Red Foley
7/51	Jimmy Wakely
10/48	**My Heart Echoes**...Jimmie Osborne
5↑/96	**My Heart Has A History**...Paul Brandt
	My Heart Has A Mind Of Its Own
10/72	Susan Raye
11/79	Debby Boone
10/52	**My Heart Is Broken In Three**...Slim Whitman
38/79	**My Heart Is Not My Own**...Mundo Earwood
7/90	**My Heart Is Set On You**...Lionel Cartwright
1/64	**My Heart Skips A Beat**...Buck Owens
16/95	**My Heart Will Never Know**...Clay Walker
10/49	**My Heart's Bouquet**..."Little" Jimmy Dickens
1/80	**My Heroes Have Always Been Cowboys**...Willie Nelson
17/80	**My Home's In Alabama**...Alabama
37/75	**My Honky Tonk Ways**...Kenny O'Dell
1/95	**My Kind Of Girl**...Collin Raye
12/67	**My Kind Of Love**...Dave Dudley

POS/YR	RECORD TITLE/ARTIST
40/79	**My Lady**...Freddie Hart
9/83	**My Lady Loves Me (Just As I Am)**...Leon Everette
	My Last Date ..see: Last Date
37/73	**My Last Day**...Tony Douglas
1/69	**My Life (Throw It Away If I Want To)**...Bill Anderson
26/86	**My Life's A Dance**...Anne Murray
8/56	**My Lips Are Sealed**...Jim Reeves
1/70	**My Love**...Sonny James
1/94	**My Love**...Little Texas
15/59	**My Love And Little Me**...Margie Bowes
37/82	**My Love Belongs To You**...Ronnie Rogers
28/79	**My Mama Never Heard Me Sing**...Billy "Crash" Craddock
1/72	**My Man**...Tammy Wynette
1/96	**My Maria**...Brooks & Dunn
34/73	**My Mind Hangs On To You**...Billy Walker
24/77	**My Mountain Dew**...Charlie Rich
7/62	**My Name Is Mud**...James O'Gwynn
1/91	**My Next Broken Heart**...Brooks & Dunn
31/94	**My Night To Howl**...Lorrie Morgan
19/65	**My Old Faded Rose**...Johnny Sea
9/85	**My Old Yellow Car**...Dan Seals
1/85	**My Only Love**...Statler Brothers
4/79	**My Own Kind Of Hat**...Merle Haggard
19/74	**My Part Of Forever**...Johnny Paycheck
22/90	**My Past Is Present**...Rodney Crowell
14/76	**My Prayer**...Narvel Felts
14/59	**My Reason For Living**...Ferlin Husky
6/87	**My Rough And Rowdy Days**...Waylon Jennings
40/64	**My Saro Jane**...Flatt & Scruggs
1/93	**My Second Home**...Tracy Lawrence
29/63	**My Secret**...Judy Lynn
1/57	**My Shoes Keep Walking Back To You**...Ray Price
8/79	**My Silver Lining**...Mickey Gilley
15/69	**My Son**...Jan Howard
9/50	**My Son Calls Another Man Daddy**...Hank Williams
1/57	**My Special Angel**...Bobby Helms
36/69	**My Special Prayer**...Archie Campbell & Lorene Mann
4/93	**My Strongest Weakness**...Wynonna Judd
38/89	**My Sweet Love Ain't Around**...Suzy Bogguss
15/64	**My Tears Are Overdue**...George Jones
36/64	**My Tears Don't Show**...Carl Butler & Pearl

POS/YR	RECORD TITLE/ARTIST
10/49	**My Tennessee Baby**...Ernest Tubb
15/73	**My Tennessee Mountain Home**...Dolly Parton
19/85	**My Toot-Toot**...Rockin' Sidney
19/89	**My Train Of Thought**...Barbara Mandrell
39/66	**My Uncle Used To Love Me But She Died**...Roger Miller
2/78	**My Way**...Elvis Presley
23/77	**My Weakness**...Margo Smith
36/73	**My Whole World Is Falling Down**...O.B. McClinton
9/74	**My Wife's House**...Jerry Wallace
15/81	**My Woman Loves The Devil Out Of Me**...Moe Bandy
1/70	**My Woman, My Woman, My Wife**...Marty Robbins
4/69	**My Woman's Good To Me**...David Houston
3/75	**My Woman's Man**...Freddie Hart & The Heartbeats
4/79	**My World Begins And Ends With You**...Dave & Sugar
11/56	**Mystery Train**...Elvis Presley

N

POS/YR	RECORD TITLE/ARTIST
40/79	**Nadine**...Freddy Weller
30/80	**Naked In The Rain**...Loretta Lynn
16/69	**Name Of The Game Was Love**...Hank Snow
9/71	**Nashville**...David Houston
37/73	**Nashville**...Ray Stevens
2/94	**National Working Woman's Holiday**...Sammy Kershaw
39/80	**Natural Attraction**...Billie Jo Spears
1/85	**Natural High**...Merle Haggard
20/82	**Natural Love**...Petula Clark
1/77	**Near You**...George Jones & Tammy Wynette
34/87	**Need A Little Time Off For Bad Behavior**...David Allan Coe
1/67	**Need You**...Sonny James
9/72	**Need You**...David Rogers
24/76	**Negatory Romance**...Tom T. Hall
7/73	**Neither One Of Us**...Bob Luman
1/92	**Neon Moon**...Brooks & Dunn
3/73	**Neon Rose**...Mel Tillis
28/64	**Nester, The**...Lefty Frizzell
15/54	**Never**...Marilyn & Wesley Tuttle
6/49	**Never Again**...Hank Williams

POS/YR	RECORD TITLE/ARTIST
22/89	Never Alone...Vince Gill
36/80	Never Be Anyone Else...R.C. Bannon
1/86	Never Be You...Rosanne Cash
1/81	Never Been So Loved (In All My Life)...Charley Pride
36/72	Never Been To Spain...Ronnie Sessions
36/75	Never Coming Back Again...Rex Allen, Jr.
6/84	Never Could Toe The Mark...Waylon Jennings
18/76	Never Did Like Whiskey...Billie Jo Spears
8/71	Never Ending Song Of Love...Dickey Lee
9/89	Never Givin' Up On Love...Michael Martin Murphey
8/89	Never Had It So Good...Mary-Chapin Carpenter
3/90	Never Knew Lonely...Vince Gill
25/69	"Never More" Quote The Raven...Stonewall Jackson
9/78	Never My Love...Vern Gosdin
F/79	Never My Love...Kendalls
30/89	Never Say Never...T. Graham Brown
29/80	Never Seen A Mountain So High...Ronnie McDowell
	Never Trust A Woman
2/47	Red Foley
2/47	Tex Williams
5/48	Tiny Hill
18/82	New Cut Road...Bobby Bare
1/89	New Fool At An Old Game...Reba McEntire
3/54	New Green Light...Hank Thompson
39/68	New Heart...Ernest Ashworth
	New Jolie Blonde (New Pretty Blonde)
1/47	Red Foley
2/47	Moon Mullican
(also see: Jole Blon)	
32/90	New Kind Of Love...Michelle Wright
25/67	New Lips...Roy Drusky
1/83	New Looks From An Old Lover...B.J. Thomas
28/69	New Orleans...Anthony Armstrong Jones
10/84	New Patches...Mel Tillis
	New Pretty Blonde ..see: New Jolie Blonde
26/59	New River Train...Bobby Helms
3/44	New San Antonio Rose...Bob Wills
2/88	New Shade Of Blue...Southern Pacific
1/46	New Spanish Two Step...Bob Wills
5/46	New Steel Guitar Rag...Bill Boyd
17/82	New Way Out...Karen Brooks
2/91	New Way (To Light Up An Old Flame)...Joe Diffie

POS/YR	RECORD TITLE/ARTIST
10/52	New Wears Off Too Fast...Hank Thompson
19/71	New York City...Statler Brothers
26/63	New York Town...Flatt & Scruggs
18/80	New York Wine And Tennessee Shine...Dave & Sugar
17/79	Next Best Feeling...Mary K. Miller
1/68	Next In Line...Conway Twitty
9/57	Next In Line...Johnny Cash
16/92	Next Thing Smokin'...Joe Diffie
14/59	Next Time...Ernest Tubb
15/71	Next Time I Fall In Love (I Won't)...Hank Thompson
1/90	Next To You, Next To Me...Shenandoah
15/55	Next Voice You Hear...Hank Snow
37/70	Nice 'N' Easy...Charlie Rich
31/66	Nickels, Quarters And Dimes...Johnny Wright
26/59	Night...Jimmy Martin
1/83	Night Games...Charley Pride
20/80	Night Games...Ray Stevens
9/95	Night Is Fallin' In My Heart...Diamond Rio
	Night Life
28/63	Ray Price
31/68	Claude Gray
20/80	Danny Davis/Willie Nelson/The Nashville Brass
29/71	Night Miss Nancy Ann's Hotel For Single Girls Burned Down...Tex Williams
	Night The Lights Went Out In Georgia
36/73	Vicki Lawrence
12/92	Reba McEntire
33/71	Night They Drove Old Dixie Down...Alice Creech
16/76	Night Time And My Baby...Joe Stampley
2/78	Night Time Magic...Larry Gatlin
20/90	Night's Too Long...Patty Loveless
14/63	Nightmare...Faron Young
4/86	Nights...Ed Bruce
27/78	Nights Are Forever Without You...Buck Owens
1/81	9 To 5...Dolly Parton
2/63	Ninety Miles An Hour...Hank Snow
13/59	Ninety-Nine...Bill Anderson
7/81	1959...John Anderson
6/86	1982...Randy Travis
3/76	9,999,999 Tears...Dickey Lee
39/81	No Aces...Patti Page
8/68	No Another Time...Lynn Anderson
1/74	No Charge...Melba Montgomery

POS/YR	RECORD TITLE/ARTIST
1/94	No Doubt About It...Neal McCoy
19/87	No Easy Horses...Schuyler, Knobloch & Bickhardt
3/93	No Future In The Past...Vince Gill
	No Gettin' Over Me ..see: (There's)
	No Help Wanted
1/53	Carlisles
9/53	Hank Thompson
7/53	No Help Wanted #2...Ernest Tubb
13/55	No, I Don't Believe I Will...Carl Smith
2/44	No Letter Today...Ted Daffan
15/70	No Love At All...Lynn Anderson
	No Love Have I
4/60	Webb Pierce
26/78	Gail Davies
3/95	No Man's Land...John Michael Montgomery
1/90	No Matter How High...Oak Ridge Boys
17/79	No Memories Hangin' Round...Rosanne Cash/Bobby Bare
26/94	No More Cryin'...McBride & The Ride
19/73	No More Hanging On...Jerry Lee Lewis
7/88	No More One More Time...Jo-el Sonnier
15/71	No Need To Worry...Johnny Cash & June Carter
1/96	No News...Lonestar
8/78	No, No, No (I'd Rather Be Free)...Rex Allen, Jr.
F/56	No One But You...Kitty Wells & Red Foley
14/55	No One Dear But You...Johnnie & Jack
7/79	No One Else In The World...Tammy Wynette
1/92	No One Else On Earth...Wynonna Judd
6/86	No One Mends A Broken Heart Like You...Barbara Mandrell
1/96	No One Needs To Know...Shania Twain
6/46	No One To Cry To...Sons Of The Pioneers
13/80	No One Will Ever Know...Gene Watson
10/67	No One's Gonna Hurt You Anymore...Bill Anderson
2/87	No Place Like Home...Randy Travis
20/82	No Relief In Sight...Con Hunley
32/65	No Sign Of Living...Dottie West
10/78	No Sleep Tonight...Randy Barlow
16/67	No Tears Milady...Marty Robbins
40/64	No Thanks, I Just Had One...Faron Young & Margie Singleton
3/93	No Time To Kill...Clint Black
3/46	No Vacancy...Merle Travis
1/82	Nobody...Sylvia

POS/YR	RECORD TITLE/ARTIST
4/66	Nobody But A Fool (Would Love You)...Connie Smith
2/83	Nobody But You...Don Williams
1/85	Nobody Falls Like A Fool...Earl Thomas Conley
	Nobody In His Right Mind Would've Left Her
25/81	Dean Dillon
1/86	George Strait
1/79	Nobody Likes Sad Songs...Ronnie Milsap
1/84	Nobody Loves Me Like You Do...Anne Murray (with Dave Loggins)
26/87	Nobody Should Have To Love This Way...Crystal Gayle
3/85	Nobody Wants To Be Alone...Crystal Gayle
2/93	Nobody Wins...Radney Foster
5/73	Nobody Wins...Brenda Lee
22/88	Nobody's Angel...Crystal Gayle
13/60	Nobody's Darling But Mine...Johnny Sea
10/70	Nobody's Fool...Jim Reeves
24/81	Nobody's Fool...Deborah Allen
11/62	Nobody's Fool But Yours...Buck Owens
13/94	Nobody's Gonna Rain On Our Parade...Kathy Mattea
1/90	Nobody's Home...Clint Black
9/50	Nobody's Lonesome For Me...Hank Williams
2/90	Nobody's Talking...Exile
8/69	None Of My Business...Henson Cargill
2/92	Norma Jean Riley...Diamond Rio
37/81	North Alabama...Dave Kirby
17/80	North Of The Border...Johnny Rodriguez
1/61	North To Alaska...Johnny Horton
8/53	North Wind...Slim Whitman
17/70	Northeast Arkansas Mississippi County Bootlegger...Kenny Price
1/95	Not A Moment Too Soon...Tim McGraw
2/90	Not Counting You...Garth Brooks
3/96	Not Enough Hours In The Night...Doug Supernaw
29/88	Not Enough Love...Tom Wopat
24/64	Not My Kind Of People...Stonewall Jackson
1/95	Not On Your Love...Jeff Carson
13/63	Not So Long Ago...Marty Robbins
3/96	Not That Different...Collin Raye
15/92	Not Too Much To Ask...Mary-Chapin Carpenter with Joe Diffie
7/63	Not What I Had In Mind...George Jones
20/93	Nothin' But The Wheel...Patty Loveless

POS/YR	RECORD TITLE/ARTIST
25/59	**Nothin' But True Love**...Margie Singleton
11/58	**Nothin' Needs Nothin' (Like I Need You)**...Marvin Rainwater
35/76	**Nothin' Takes The Place Of You**...Asleep At The Wheel
33/86	**Nothin' Ventured Nothin' Gained**...Sylvia
20/95	**Nothing**...Dwight Yoakam
10/79	**Nothing As Original As You**...Statler Brothers
26/82	**Nothing Behind You, Nothing In Sight**...John Conlee
19/82	**Nothing But The Radio On**...James & Michael Younger
12/86	**Nothing But Your Love Matters**...Gatlin Bros.
37/85	**Nothing Can Hurt Me Now**...Gail Davies
7/73	**Nothing Ever Hurt Me (Half As Bad As Losing You)**...George Jones
1/89	**Nothing I Can Do About It Now**...Willie Nelson
34/65	**Nothing Left To Lose**...Faron Young
10/84	**Nothing Like Falling In Love**...Eddie Rabbitt
4/92	**Nothing Short Of Dying**...Travis Tritt
4/80	**Nothing Sure Looked Good On You**...Gene Watson
39/68	**Nothing Takes The Place Of Loving You**...Stonewall Jackson
15/91	**Nothing's Changed Here**...Dwight Yoakam
3/90	**Nothing's News**...Clint Black
1/86	**Now And Forever (You And Me)**...Anne Murray
	Now And Then ..see: (I Still Long To Hold You)
	(Now And Then There's) A Fool Such As I ..see: Fool Such As I
5/94	**Now I Know**...Lari White
26/93	**Now I Pray For Rain**...Neal McCoy
38/81	**Now That The Feeling's Gone**...Billy "Crash" Craddock
17/91	**Now That We're Alone**...Rodney Crowell
18/92	**Now That's Country**...Marty Stuart
21/85	**Now There's You**...Shelly West
19/78	**Now You See 'Em, Now You Don't**...Roy Head
7/92	**Nowhere Bound**...Diamond Rio
20/87	**Nowhere Road**...Steve Earle
11/80	**Numbers**...Bobby Bare

POS/YR	RECORD TITLE/ARTIST
18/94	**O What A Thrill**...Mavericks
3/47	**Oakie Boogie**...Jack Guthrie
28/80	**Occasional Rose**...Marty Robbins
6/70	**Occasional Wife**...Faron Young
1/87	**Ocean Front Property**...George Strait
29/61	**Ocean Of Tears**...Billie Jean Horton
7/61	**Odds And Ends (Bits And Pieces)**...Warren Smith
21/71	**Ode To A Half A Pound Of Ground Round**...Tom T. Hall
	Ode To Billie Joe
17/67	Bobbie Gentry
39/67	Margie Singleton
3/65	**Ode To The Little Brown Shack Out Back**...Billy Edd Wheeler
38/67	**Off And On**...Charlie Louvin
5/79	**Official Historian On Shirley Jean Berrell**...Statler Brothers
	(Oh Baby Mine) I Get So Lonely
1/54	Johnnie & Jack
2/83	Statler Brothers
21/75	**Oh Boy**...Diana Trask
38/84	**Oh Carolina**...Vince Gill
10/86	**Oh Darlin'**...O'Kanes
12/82	**Oh Girl**...Con Hunley
25/70	**Oh Happy Day**...Glen Campbell
9/87	**Oh Heart**...Baillie & The Boys
6/80	**Oh, How I Miss You Tonight**...Jim Reeves/Deborah Allen
36/75	**Oh, How Love Changes**...Don Gibson & Sue Thompson
	Oh Lonesome Me
1/58	Don Gibson
13/61	Johnny Cash
8/90	Kentucky Headhunters
40/71	**Oh, Love Of Mine**...Johnny & Jonie Mosby
5/93	**Oh Me, Oh My, Sweet Baby**...Diamond Rio
	Oh-Oh, I'm Falling In Love Again
5/58	Jimmie Rodgers
29/73	Eddy Arnold
13/70	**Oh Pretty Woman**...Arlene Harden (Lovin' Man)
4/71	**Oh, Singer**...Jeannie C. Riley
8/57	**Oh, So Many Years**...Kitty Wells & Webb Pierce
23/76	**Oh, Sweet Temptation**...Gary Stewart
5/88	**Oh What A Love**...Nitty Gritty Dirt Band

POS/YR	RECORD TITLE/ARTIST
12/91	**Oh What It Did To Me**...Tanya Tucker
4/47	**(Oh Why, Oh Why, Did I Ever Leave) Wyoming**...Dick Jurgens
17/67	**Oh! Woman**...Nat Stuckey
1/69	**Okie From Muskogee**...Merle Haggard
9/86	**Oklahoma Borderline**...Vince Gill
	Oklahoma Hills
1/45	Jack Guthrie
7/61	Hank Thompson
15/72	**Oklahoma Sunday Morning**...Glen Campbell
13/90	**Oklahoma Swing**...Vince Gill with Reba McEntire
9/48	**Oklahoma Waltz**...Johnny Bond
38/73	**Old Betsy Goes Boing, Boing, Boing**...Hummers
11/87	**Old Bridges Burn Slow**...Billy Joe Royal
30/66	**Old Brush Arbors**...George Jones
4/93	**Old Country**...Mark Chesnutt
5/89	**Old Coyote Town**...Don Williams
1/73	**(Old Dogs-Children And) Watermelon Wine**...Tom T. Hall
1/95	**Old Enough To Know Better**...Wade Hayes
13/69	**Old Faithful**...Mel Tillis
F/78	**Old Fashioned Love**...Kendalls
38/73	**Old Fashioned Singing**...George Jones & Tammy Wynette
1/81	**Old Flame**...Alabama
5/86	**Old Flame**...Juice Newton
	Old Flames (Can't Hold A Candle To You)
14/78	Joe Sun
1/80	Dolly Parton
5/92	**Old Flames Have New Names**...Mark Chesnutt
2/88	**Old Folks**...Ronnie Milsap & Mike Reid
19/82	**Old Friends**...Roger Miller/Willie Nelson/Ray Price
6/80	**Old Habits**...Hank Williams, Jr.
2/85	**Old Hippie**...Bellamy Brothers
19/74	**Old Home Filler-Up An' Keep On-A-Truckin' Cafe**...C.W. McCall
30/88	**Old Kind Of Love**...Ricky Skaggs
34/77	**Old King Kong**...George Jones
20/60	**Old Lamplighter**...Browns
30/60	**Old Log Cabin For Sale**...Porter Wagoner
11/55	**Old Lonesome Times**...Carl Smith
11/77	**Old Man And His Horn**...Gene Watson
1/74	**Old Man From The Mountain**...Merle Haggard

POS/YR	RECORD TITLE/ARTIST
22/83	**Old Man River (I've Come To Talk Again)**...Mel McDaniel
31/70	**Old Man Willis**...Nat Stuckey
7/59	**Old Moon**...Betty Foley
21/93	**Old Pair Of Shoes**...Randy Travis
27/88	**Old Photographs**...Sawyer Brown
11/64	**Old Records**...Margie Singleton
3/62	**Old Rivers**...Walter Brennan
5/86	**Old School**...John Conlee
8/63	**Old Showboat**...Stonewall Jackson
9/80	**Old Side Of Town**...Tom T. Hall
9/51	**Old Soldiers Never Die**...Gene Autry
26/77	**Old Time Feeling**...Johnny Cash & June Carter Cash
21/86	**Old Violin**...Johnny Paycheck
3/52	**Older And Bolder**...Eddy Arnold
8/74	**Older The Violin, The Sweeter The Music**...Hank Thompson
1/81	**Older Women**...Ronnie McDowell
31/79	**Ole Slew Foot**...Porter Wagoner
10↑/96	**On A Good Night**...Wade Hayes
23/87	**On And On**...Anne Murray
27/79	**On Business For The King**...Joe Sun
5/90	**On Down The Line**...Patty Loveless
1/78	**On My Knees**...Charlie Rich with Janie Fricke
12/57	**On My Mind Again**...Billy Walker
20/95	**On My Own**...Reba McEntire
1/90	**On Second Thought**...Eddie Rabbitt
7/68	**On Tap, In The Can, Or In The Bottle**...Hank Thompson
9/74	**On The Cover Of The Music City News**...Buck Owens
1/86	**On The Other Hand**...Randy Travis
29/76	**On The Rebound**...Del Reeves & Billie Jo Spears
6/93	**On The Road**...Lee Roy Parnell
1/80	**On The Road Again**...Willie Nelson
8/51	**On Top Of Old Smoky**...Weavers & Terry Gilkyson
4/67	**Once**...Ferlin Husky
1/64	**Once A Day**...Connie Smith
1/86	**Once In A Blue Moon**...Earl Thomas Conley
34/79	**Once In A Blue Moon**...Zella Lehr
5/77	**Once In A Lifetime Thing**...John Wesley Ryles
	Once More
8/58	Roy Acuff
13/58	Osborne Brothers & Red Allen

POS/YR	RECORD TITLE/ARTIST
2/70	**Once More With Feeling**...Jerry Lee Lewis
3/93	**Once Upon A Lifetime**...Alabama
3/74	**Once You've Had The Best**...George Jones
27/63	**One Among The Many**...Ned Miller
2/95	**One Boy, One Girl**...Collin Raye
1/54	**One By One**...Kitty Wells & Red Foley
	One Day At A Time
19/74	Marilyn Sellars
1/80	Cristy Lane
8/74	**One Day At A Time**...Don Gibson
23/64	**One Dozen Roses (And Our Love)**...George Morgan
10/65	**One Dyin' And A Buryin'**...Roger Miller
2/95	**One Emotion**...Clint Black
2/87	**One For The Money**...T.G. Sheppard
1/88	**One Friend**...Dan Seals
4/89	**One Good Well**...Don Williams
17/61	**One Grain Of Sand**...Eddy Arnold
	One Has My Name (The Other Has My Heart)
1/48	Jimmy Wakely
11/48	Eddie Dean
8/49	Bob Eberly
3/69	Jerry Lee Lewis
6/91	**One Hundred And Two**...Judds
14/71	**One Hundred Children**...Tom T. Hall
1/86	**100% Chance Of Rain**...Gary Morris
3/86	**One I Loved Back Then (The Corvette Song)**...George Jones
11/64	**One If For Him, Two If For Me**...David Houston
1/80	**One In A Million**...Johnny Lee
19/66	**One In A Row**...Willie Nelson
1/49	**One Kiss Too Many**...Eddy Arnold
33/73	**One Last Time**...Glen Campbell
(also see: Let's Get Together)	
11/62	**One Look At Heaven**...Stonewall Jackson
33/91	**One Love**...Carlene Carter
3/86	**One Love At A Time**...Tanya Tucker
27/65	**One Man Band**...Phil Baugh
8/90	**One Man Woman**...Judds
2/70	**One Minute Past Eternity**...Jerry Lee Lewis
11/75	**One Monkey Don't Stop No Show**...Little David Wilkins
1/93	**One More Last Chance**...Vince Gill
33/81	**One More Last Chance**...Ray Stevens
12/69	**One More Mile**...Dave Dudley
7/91	**One More Payment**...Clint Black
2/60	**One More Time**...Ray Price

POS/YR	RECORD TITLE/ARTIST
28/71	**One More Time**...Ferlin Husky
31/76	**One More Time (Karneval)**...Crystal Gayle
28/76	**(One More Year Of) Daddy's Little Girl**...Ray Sawyer
24/58	**One Night**...Elvis Presley
7/94	**One Night A Day**...Garth Brooks
10/81	**One-Night Fever**...Mel Tillis
39/71	**One Night Of Love**...Johnny Duncan
35/70	**One Night Stand**...Susan Raye
6/77	**One Of A Kind**...Tammy Wynette
13/80	**One Of A Kind**...Moe Bandy
1/83	**One Of A Kind Pair Of Fools**...Barbara Mandrell
28/60	**One Of Her Fools**...Paul Davis
3/76	**One Of These Days**...Emmylou Harris
8/64	**One Of These Days**...Marty Robbins
36/68	**One Of These Days**...Tompall/Glaser Brothers
6/91	**One Of Those Things**...Pam Tillis
2/66	**One On The Right Is On The Left**...Johnny Cash
4/85	**One Owner Heart**...T.G. Sheppard
1/76	**One Piece At A Time**...Johnny Cash
1/87	**One Promise Too Late**...Reba McEntire
26/78	**One Run For The Roses**...Narvel Felts
8/78	**One Sided Conversation**...Gene Watson
9/70	**One Song Away**...Tommy Cash
14/61	**One Step Ahead Of My Past**...Hank Locklin
15/57	**One Step At A Time**...Brenda Lee
2/88	**One Step Forward**...Desert Rose Band
8/84	**One Takes The Blame**...Statler Brothers
37/82	**One That Got Away**...Mel Tillis
17/79	**One Thing My Lady Never Puts Into Words**...Mel Street
4/88	**One True Love**...O'Kanes
20/61	**One Way Street**...Bob Gallion
12/58	**One Week Later**...Webb Pierce & Kitty Wells
32/72	**One Woman's Trash (Another Woman's Treasure)**...Bobbie Roy
38/72	**One You Say Good Mornin' To**...Jimmy Dean
13/60	**One You Slip Around With**...Jan Howard
1/72	**One's On The Way**...Loretta Lynn
2/72	**Oney**...Johnny Cash
2/84	**Only A Lonely Heart Knows**...Barbara Mandrell
24/71	**Only A Woman Like You**...Nat Stuckey
2/68	**Only Daddy That'll Walk The Line**...Waylon Jennings

POS/YR	RECORD TITLE/ARTIST
13/63	**Only Girl I Can't Forget**...Del Reeves
3/91	**Only Here For A Little While**...Billy Dean
12/83	**Only If There Is Another You**...Moe Bandy
5/85	**Only In My Mind**...Reba McEntire
3/93	**Only Love**...Wynonna Judd
	Only Love Can Break A Heart
2/72	Sonny James
7/79	Kenny Dale
11/88	**Only Love Can Save Me Now**...Crystal Gayle
1/78	**Only One Love In My Life**...Ronnie Milsap
1/82	**Only One You**...T.G. Sheppard
1/69	**Only The Lonely**...Sonny James
4/92	**Only The Wind**...Billy Dean
36/68	**Only Way Out (Is To Walk Over Me)**...Charlie Louvin
32/81	**Only When I Laugh**...Brenda Lee
4/87	**Only When I Love**...Holly Dunn
	Only You
34/78	Freddie Hart
13/82	Reba McEntire
36/86	Statler Brothers
1/65	**Only You (Can Break My Heart)**...Buck Owens
9/56	**Only You, Only You**...Charlie Walker
13/62	**Open Pit Mine**...George Jones
1/66	**Open Up Your Heart**...Buck Owens
14/73	**Open Up Your Heart**...Roger Miller
9/82	**Operator, Long Distance Please**...Barbara Mandrell
9/85	**Operator, Operator**...Eddy Raven
10/61	**Optimistic**...Skeeter Davis
	Orange Blossom Special
3/65	Johnny Cash
26/73	Charlie McCoy
4/53	**Orchids Mean Goodbye**...Carl Smith
26/77	**Ordinary Man**...Dale McBride
29/68	**Ordinary Miracle**...Bobby Lewis
19/61	**Other Cheek**...Kitty Wells
30/88	**Other Guy**...David Slater
2/65	**Other Woman**...Ray Price
13/63	**Other Woman**...Loretta Lynn
24/65	**Our Hearts Are Holding Hands**...Ernest Tubb & Loretta Lynn
6/52	**Our Honeymoon**...Carl Smith
18/69	**Our House Is Not A Home**...Lynn Anderson
8/50	**Our Lady Of Fatima**...Red Foley
1/83	**Our Love Is On The Faultline**...Crystal Gayle

POS/YR	RECORD TITLE/ARTIST
21/62	**Our Mansion Is A Prison Now**...Kitty Wells
	(Our Own) Jole Blon ..see: Jole Blon
27/67	**Our Side**...Van Trevor
33/64	**Our Things**...Margie Bowes
21/86	**Out Among The Stars**...Merle Haggard
9/54	**Out Behind The Barn**..."Little" Jimmy Dickens
11/86	**Out Goin' Cattin'**...Sawyer Brown with "Cat" Joe Bonsall
25/60	**Out Of Control**...George Jones
4/75	**Out Of Hand**...Gary Stewart
1/78	**Out Of My Head And Back In My Bed**...Loretta Lynn
10/88	**Out Of Sight And On My Mind**...Billy Joe Royal
34/80	**Out Of Your Mind**...Joe Sun
2/89	**Out Of Your Shoes**...Lorrie Morgan
32/65	**Out Where The Ocean Meets The Sky**...Hugh X. Lewis
13/96	**Out With A Bang**...David Lee Murphy
9/92	**Outbound Plane**...Suzy Bogguss
27/79	**Outlaw's Prayer**...Johnny Paycheck
18/83	**Outside Lookin' In**...Bandana
40/94	**Outskirts Of Town**...Sawyer Brown
10/80	**Over**...Leon Everette
10/80	**Over The Rainbow**...Jerry Lee Lewis
15/49	**Over Three Hills**...Ernie Benedict
15/83	**Over You**...Lane Brody
10/58	**Overnight**...Jim Reeves
7/76	**Overnight Sensation**...Mickey Gilley
8/90	**Overnight Success**...George Strait
5/84	**Ozark Mountain Jubilee**...Oak Ridge Boys

POS/YR	RECORD TITLE/ARTIST
8/84	**P.S. I Love You**...Tom T. Hall
3/62	**P.T. 109**...Jimmy Dean
5/71	**Padre**...Marty Robbins
34/86	**Pages Of My Mind**...Ray Charles
13/89	**Paint The Town And Hang The Moon Tonight**...J.C. Crowley
8/45	**Pair Of Broken Hearts**...Spade Cooley
19/80	**Pair Of Old Sneakers**...George Jones & Tammy Wynette
33/76	**Paloma Blanca**...George Baker Selection
9/48	**Pan American**...Hawkshaw Hawkins
7/50	**Pan American Boogie**...Delmore Brothers

POS/YR	RECORD TITLE/ARTIST
1/83	**Pancho And Lefty**...Willie Nelson & Merle Haggard
6/49	**Panhandle Rag**...Leon McAuliffe
3/92	**Papa Loved Mama**...Garth Brooks
16/71	**Papa Was A Good Man**...Johnny Cash
30/75	**Paper Lovin'**...Margo Smith
8/67	**Paper Mansions**...Dottie West
1/73	**Paper Roses**...Marie Osmond
3/77	**Paper Rosie**...Gene Watson
26/76	**Paradise**...Lynn Anderson
26/96	**Paradise**...John Anderson
1/83	**Paradise Tonight**...Charly McClain & Mickey Gilley
35/72	**Part Of Your Life**...Charlie Rich
38/81	**Partner Nobody Chose**...Guy Clark
5/59	**Partners**...Jim Reeves
24/87	**Partners After All**...Willie Nelson
6/86	**Partners, Brothers And Friends**...Nitty Gritty Dirt Band
6/95	**Party Crowd**...David Lee Murphy
31/72	**Party Dolls And Wine**...Red Steagall
24/67	**Party Pickin'**...George Jones & Melba Montgomery
1/81	**Party Time**...T.G. Sheppard
24/67	**Party's Over**...Willie Nelson
3/90	**Pass It On Down**...Alabama
	Pass Me By (If You're Only Passing Through)
9/73	Johnny Rodriguez
22/80	Janie Fricke
15/65	**Pass The Booze**...Ernest Tubb
28/77	**Passing Thing**...Ray Griff
37/64	**Passing Through**...David Houston
23/61	**Passing Zone Blues**...Coleman Wilson
4/93	**Passionate Kisses**...Mary-Chapin Carpenter
4/64	**Password**...Kitty Wells
2/92	**Past The Point Of Rescue**...Hal Ketchum
	Patches
26/70	Ray Griff
30/81	Jerry Reed
18/58	**Patricia**...Perez Prado
13/77	**Pay Phone**...Bob Luman
6/53	**Paying For That Back Street Affair**...Kitty Wells
	(also see: Back Street Affair)
	Peace In The Valley ..see: (There'll Be)
23/81	**Peace Of Mind**...Eddy Raven
21/77	**Peanut Butter**...Dickey Lee
10/76	**Peanuts And Diamonds**...Bill Anderson

POS/YR	RECORD TITLE/ARTIST
8/63	**Pearl Pearl Pearl**...Flatt & Scruggs
	Pecos Bill ..see: (There'll Never Be Another)
10/80	**Pecos Promenade**...Tanya Tucker
8/64	**Peel Me A Nanner**...Roy Drusky
4/48	**Peepin' Thru The Keyhole (Watching Jole Blon)**...Cliffie Stone
36/64	**Pen And Paper**...Jerry Lee Lewis
12/49	**Pennies For Papa**..."Little" Jimmy Dickens
8/75	**Penny**...Joe Stampley
7/78	**Penny Arcade**...Cristy Lane
5/55	**Penny Candy**...Jim Reeves
23/90	**Perfect**...Baillie & the Boys
23/81	**Perfect Fool**...Debby Boone
24/72	**Perfect Match**...David Houston & Barbara Mandrell
16/70	**Perfect Mountain**...Don Gibson
13/73	**Perfect Stranger**...Freddy Weller
18/86	**Perfect Stranger**...Southern Pacific
24/80	**Perfect Strangers**...John Wesley Ryles
29/75	**Personality**...Price Mitchell
10/83	**Personally**...Ronnie McDowell
	Peter Cottontail
3/50	Gene Autry
6/50	Mervin Shiner
7/50	Jimmy Wakely
7/50	Johnnie Lee Wills
14/64	**Petticoat Junction**...Flatt & Scruggs
9/67	**Phantom 309**...Red Sovine
9/71	**Philadelphia Fillies**...Del Reeves
36/68	**Phone Call To Mama**...Joyce Paul
28/96	**Phones Are Ringin' All Over Town**...Martina McBride
	Pick Me Up On Your Way Down
2/58	Charlie Walker
35/76	Bobby G. Rice
13/64	**Pick Of The Week**...Roy Drusky
	Pick The Wildwood Flower
34/74	Johnny Cash/Mother Maybelle Carter
5/79	Gene Watson
3/81	**Pickin' Up Strangers**...Johnny Lee
27/70	**Pickin' Wild Mountain Berries**...LaWanda Lindsey & Kenny Vernon
1/94	**Pickup Man**...Joe Diffie
8/60	**Picture, The**...Ray Godfrey
28/91	**Picture Me**...Davis Daniel
	Picture Of Me (Without You)
5/72	George Jones
9/91	Lorrie Morgan
27/66	**Picture That's New**...George Morgan

POS/YR	RECORD TITLE/ARTIST
13/71	**Pictures**...Statler Brothers
35/84	**Pictures**...Atlanta
17/75	**Pictures On Paper**...Jeris Ross
1/94	**Piece Of My Heart**...Faith Hill
33/75	**Pieces Of My Life**...Elvis Presley
29/88	**Pilgrims On The Way (Matthew's Song)**...Michael Martin Murphey
5/75	**Pill, The**...Loretta Lynn
17/64	**Pillow That Whispers**...Carl Smith
13/60	**Pinball Machine**...Lonnie Irving
15/67	**Piney Wood Hills**...Bobby Bare
17/58	**Pink Pedal Pushers**...Carl Perkins
10/84	**Pins And Needles**...Whites
	Pistol Packin' Mama
1/44	Bing Crosby & Andrews Sisters
1/44	Al Dexter
6/78	**Pittsburgh Stealers**...Kendalls
6/71	**Pitty, Pitty, Patter**...Susan Raye
8/54	**Place For Girls Like You**...Faron Young
1/85	**Place To Fall Apart**...Merle Haggard with Janie Fricke
9/87	**Plain Brown Wrapper**...Gary Morris
30/89	**Planet Texas**...Kenny Rogers
9/68	**Plastic Saddle**...Nat Stuckey
23/73	**Plastic Trains, Paper Planes**...Susan Raye
17/80	**Play Another Slow Song**...Johnny Duncan
	Play Born To Lose Again ..see: (After Sweet Memories)
1/77	**Play, Guitar Play**...Conway Twitty
24/79	**Play Her Back To Yesterday**...Mel McDaniel
24/79	**Play Me A Memory**...Zella Lehr
34/76	**Play Me No Sad Songs**...Rex Allen, Jr.
25/92	**Play, Ruby, Play**...Clinton Gregory
35/82	**Play Something We Could Love To**...Diane Pfeifer
35/76	**Play The Saddest Song On The Juke Box**...Carmol Taylor
11/79	**Play Together Again Again**...Buck Owens/Emmylou Harris
18/70	**Playin' Around With Love**...Barbara Mandrell
22/79	**Playin' Hard To Get**...Janie Fricke
8/57	**Playing For Keeps**...Elvis Presley
34/78	**Please**...Narvel Felts
7/86	**Please Be Love**...Mark Gray
31/64	**Please Be My Love**...George Jones & Melba Montgomery
11/57	**Please Don't Blame Me**...Marty Robbins
10/69	**Please Don't Go**...Eddy Arnold

POS/YR	RECORD TITLE/ARTIST
4/49	**Please Don't Let Me Love You**...George Morgan
9/55	**Please Don't Let Me Love You**...Hank Williams
14/49	**Please Don't Pass Me By**...Floyd Tillman
17/78	**Please Don't Play A Love Song**...Marty Robbins
1/74	**Please Don't Stop Loving Me**...Porter Wagoner & Dolly Parton
	Please Don't Tell Me How The Story Ends
8/71	Bobby Bare
1/74	Ronnie Milsap
	Please Help Me, I'm Falling
1/60	Hank Locklin
12/78	Janie Fricke
(also see: I Can't Help You)	
10/69	**Please Let Me Prove (My Love For You)**...Dave Dudley
11/61	**Please Mr. Kennedy**...Jim Nesbitt
5/75	**Please Mr. Please**...Olivia Newton-John
9/58	**Please Pass The Biscuits**...Gene Sullivan
6/88	**Please, Please Baby**...Dwight Yoakam
40/69	**Please Take Me Back**...Jim Glaser
	Please Talk To My Heart
14/63	Country Johnny Mathis
7/64	Ray Price
32/81	**Pleasure's All Mine**...Dave & Sugar
13/77	**Pleasure's Been All Mine**...Freddie Hart
	Pledging My Love
37/75	Billy Thunderkloud
F/77	Elvis Presley
9/84	Emmylou Harris
14/57	**Plenty Of Everything But You**...Ira & Charley Louvin
9/61	**Po' Folks**...Bill Anderson
7/91	**Pocket Full Of Gold**...Vince Gill
22/94	**Pocket Of A Clown**...Dwight Yoakam
3/91	**Point Of Light**...Randy Travis
25/60	**Poison In Your Hand**...Connie Hall
	Poison Love
4/51	Johnnie & Jack
27/78	Gail Davies
12/61	**Polka On A Banjo**...Flatt & Scruggs
26/87	**Ponies**...Michael Johnson
1/70	**Pool Shark**...Dave Dudley
30/83	**Poor Boy**...Razzy Bailey
39/66	**Poor Boy Blues**...Bob Luman
	Poor Folks ..see: Po' Folks
3/58	**Poor Little Fool**...Ricky Nelson
2/56	**Poor Man's Riches**...Benny Barnes

POS/YR	RECORD TITLE/ARTIST
14/57	**Poor Man's Roses (Or A Rich Man's Gold)**...Patsy Cline
24/75	**Poor Man's Woman**...Jeanne Pruett
10/59	**Poor Old Heartsick Me**...Margie Bowes
12/83	**Poor Side Of Town**...Joe Stampley
14/75	**Poor Sweet Baby**...Jean Shepard
3/67	**Pop A Top**...Jim Ed Brown
26/71	**Portrait Of My Woman**...Eddy Arnold
20/83	**Potential New Boyfriend**...Dolly Parton
5/80	**Pour Me Another Tequilla**...Eddie Rabbitt
9/84	**Power Of Love**...Charley Pride
8/78	**Power Of Positive Drinkin'**...Mickey Gilley
F/70	**Preacher And The Bear**...Jerry Reed
19/82	**Preaching Up A Storm**...Mel McDaniel
19/83	**Precious Love**...Kendalls
8/90	**Precious Thing**...Steve Wariner
35/80	**Pregnant Again**...Loretta Lynn
6/72	**Pretend I Never Happened**...Waylon Jennings
26/67	**Pretty Girl, Pretty Clothes, Pretty Sad**...Kenny Price
10/85	**Pretty Lady**...Keith Stegall
12/54	**Pretty Words**...Marty Robbins
35/69	**Price I Pay To Stay**...Jeannie C. Riley
	Pride
5/62	Ray Price
12/81	Janie Fricke
18/62	**Pride Goes Before A Fall**...Jim Reeves
	(Pride Of South Central High) ..see: Igmoo
3/72	**Pride's Not Hard To Swallow**...Hank Williams, Jr.
23/60	**Prison Song**...Curly Putman
10/50	**Prison Without Walls**...Eddy Arnold
3/81	**Prisoner Of Hope**...Johnny Lee
6/84	**Prisoner Of The Highway**...Ronnie Milsap
14/76	**Prisoner's Song**...Sonny James
30/66	**Prissy**...Chet Atkins
33/67	**Private, The**...Del Reeves
21/66	**Private Wilson White**...Marty Robbins
12/57	**Prize Possession**...Ferlin Husky
17/59	**Problems**...Everly Brothers
4/44	**Prodigal Son**...Roy Acuff
32/92	**Professional Fool**...Michael White
	Promised Land
3/71	Freddy Weller
F/75	Elvis Presley
17/89	**Promises**...Randy Travis
15/67	**Promises And Hearts (Were Made To Break)**...Stonewall Jackson

POS/YR	RECORD TITLE/ARTIST
4/68	**Promises, Promises**...Lynn Anderson
3/93	**Prop Me Up Beside The Jukebox (If I Die)**...Joe Diffie
22/69	**Proud Mary**...Anthony Armstrong Jones
22/75	**Proud Of You Baby**...Bob Luman
18/70	**Pull My String And Wind Me Up**...Carl Smith
28/68	**Punish Me Tomorrow**...Carl Butler & Pearl
1/74	**Pure Love**...Ronnie Milsap
28/66	**Pursuing Happiness**...Norma Jean
11/65	**Pushed In A Corner**...Ernest Ashworth
30/70	**Put A Little Love In Your Heart**...Susan Raye
23/76	**Put A Little Lovin' On Me**...Bobby Bare
21/75	**Put Another Log On The Fire**...Tompall
	Put It Off Until Tomorrow
6/66	Bill Phillips
9/80	Kendalls
30/73	**Put Me Down Softly**...Dickey Lee
28/87	**Put Me Out Of My Misery**...Tom Wopat
28/90	**Put Some Drive In Your Country**...Travis Tritt
	Put You Back On The Rack ..see: (I'm Gonna)
25/64	**Put Your Arms Around Her**...Norma Jean
9/79	**Put Your Clothes Back On**...Joe Stampley
1/82	**Put Your Dreams Away**...Mickey Gilley
11/91	**Put Yourself In My Place**...Pam Tillis
4/90	**Put Yourself In My Shoes**...Clint Black
8/78	**Puttin' In Overtime At Home**...Charlie Rich
33/90	**Puttin' The Dark Back Into The Night**...Sawyer Brown

POS/YR	RECORD TITLE/ARTIST
28/65	**Queen Of Draw Poker Town**...Hank Snow
14/81	**Queen Of Hearts**...Juice Newton
28/67	**Queen Of Honky Tonk Street**...Kitty Wells
2/93	**Queen Of Memphis**...Confederate Railroad
7/93	**Queen Of My Double Wide Trailer**...Sammy Kershaw
5/83	**Queen Of My Heart**...Hank Williams, Jr.
5/65	**Queen Of The House**...Jody Miller
(also see: King Of The Road)	
	Queen Of The Silver Dollar
29/73	Doyle Holly
25/76	Dave & Sugar
3/50	**Quicksilver**...Elton Britt & Rosalie Allen
36/87	**Quietly Crazy**...Ed Bruce

POS/YR	RECORD TITLE/ARTIST
26/90	**Quit While I'm Behind**...Jennifer McCarter & The McCarters
3/71	**Quits**...Bill Anderson
26/77	**Quits**...Gary Stewart
7/90	**Quittin' Time**...Mary-Chapin Carpenter

R

POS/YR	RECORD TITLE/ARTIST
	Race Is On
3/64	George Jones
5/89	Sawyer Brown
39/88	**Radio, The**...Vince Gill
1/85	**Radio Heart**...Charly McClain
19/84	**Radio Land**...Michael Martin Murphey
2/50	**Rag Mop**...Johnnie Lee Wills
19/78	**Ragamuffin Man**...Donna Fargo
15/61	**Ragged But Right**...Moon Mullican
31/74	**Ragged Old Flag**...Johnny Cash
5/47	**Ragtime Cowboy Joe**...Eddy Howard
36/72	**Rain Falling On Me**...Johnny Russell
	Rainbow At Midnight
5/46	Carlisle Brothers
1/47	Ernest Tubb
5/47	Texas Jim Robertson
28/70	**Rainbow Girl**...Bobby Lord
16/74	**Rainbow In Daddy's Eyes**...Sammi Smith
8/49	**Rainbow In My Heart**...George Morgan
4/81	**Rainbow Stew**...Merle Haggard
39/83	**Rainbows And Butterflies**...Billy Swan
20/66	**Rainbows And Roses**...Roy Drusky
17/68	**Rainbows Are Back In Style**...Slim Whitman
33/74	**Raindrops**...Narvel Felts
	Rainin' In My Heart
3/71	Hank Williams, Jr.
35/89	Jo-el Sonnier
14/69	**Raining In My Heart**...Ray Price
4/77	**Rains Came**...Freddy Fender
2/75	**Rainy Day Woman**...Waylon Jennings
21/80	**Rainy Days And Stormy Nights**...Billie Jo Spears
13/74	**Rainy Night In Georgia**...Hank Williams, Jr.
15/80	**Raisin' Cane In Texas**...Gene Watson
3/78	**Rake And Ramblin' Man**...Don Williams
2/77	**Ramblin' Fever**...Merle Haggard
29/67	**Ramblin' Man**...Ray Pennington
37/77	**Ramblin' Rose**...Johnny Lee

POS/YR	RECORD TITLE/ARTIST
8/68	**Ramona**...Billy Walker
1/73	**Rated "X"**...Loretta Lynn
1/44	**Ration Blues**...Louis Jordan
	Raunchy
6/58	Bill Justis
11/58	Ernie Freeman
3/73	**Ravishing Ruby**...Tom T. Hall
2/72	**Reach Out Your Hand**...Tammy Wynette
38/87	**Read Between The Lines**...Lynn Anderson
4/86	**Read My Lips**...Marie Osmond
1/78	**Ready For The Times To Get Better**...Crystal Gayle
20/96	**Ready, Willing And Able**...Lari White
38/80	**Real Buddy Holly Story**...Sonny Curtis
20/80	**Real Cowboy (You Say You're)**...Billy "Crash" Craddock
9/88	**Real Good Feel Good Song**...Mel McDaniel
36/68	**Real Good Woman**...Jean Shepard
1/85	**Real Love**...Kenny Rogers & Dolly Parton
30/67	**Real Thing**...Billy Grammer
13/60	**Reasons To Live**...Jimmie Skinner
6/83	**Reasons To Quit**...Merle Haggard & Willie Nelson
1/96	**Rebecca Lynn**...Bryan White
24/61	**Rebel - Johnny Yuma**...Johnny Cash
17/58	**Rebel-'Rouser**...Duane Eddy
9/88	**Rebels Without A Clue**...Bellamy Brothers
1/93	**Reckless**...Alabama
32/90	**Reckless Heart**...Southern Pacific
	Reconsider Me
38/69	Ray Pillow
39/71	John Wesley Ryles
2/75	Narvel Felts
23/94	**Red And Rio Grande**...Doug Supernaw
4/79	**Red Bandana**...Merle Haggard
4/44	**Red Blues**...Cootie Williams
21/71	**Red Door**...Carl Smith
17/78	**Red Hot Memory**...Kenny Dale
1/82	**Red Neckin' Love Makin' Night**...Conway Twitty
17/72	**Red Red Wine**...Roy Drusky
21/74	**Red Rose From The Blue Side Of Town**...George Morgan
8/48	**Red Roses Tied In Blue**...Clyde Moody
22/76	**Red Sails In The Sunset**...Johnny Lee
20/76	**Red, White And Blue**...Loretta Lynn
6/78	**Red Wine And Blue Memories**...Joe Stampley
1/82	**Redneck Girl**...Bellamy Brothers

POS/YR	RECORD TITLE/ARTIST	POS/YR	RECORD TITLE/ARTIST
	Redneck In A Rock And Roll Bar ..see: (I'm Just A)		**Ribbon Of Darkness**
17/76	**Redneck! (The Redneck National Anthem)**...Vernon Oxford	1/65	Marty Robbins
		13/69	Connie Smith
18/95	**Redneck 12 Days Of Christmas**...Jeff Foxworthy	19/81	**Rich Man**...Terri Gibbs
		10/55	**Richest Man (In The World)**...Eddy Arnold
4/73	**Rednecks, White Socks And Blue Ribbon Beer**...Johnny Russell	3/90	**Richest Man On Earth**...Paul Overstreet
5/95	**Refried Dreams**...Tim McGraw	4/83	**Ride, The**...David Allan Coe
	Release Me	32/84	**Ride 'Em Cowboy**...Juice Newton
5/54	Jimmy Heap/Perk Williams	11/73	**Ride Me Down Easy**...Bobby Bare
6/54	Ray Price	36/67	**Ride, Ride, Ride**...Lynn Anderson
8/54	Kitty Wells		**Riders In The Sky**
33/73	Charlie McCoy	2/49	Vaughn Monroe
	(Remember Me) I'm The One Who Loves You	8/49	Burl Ives
		27/73	Roy Clark
2/50	Stuart Hamblen	2/79	Johnny Cash
5/50	Ernest Tubb	1/73	**Ridin' My Thumb To Mexico**...Johnny Rodriguez
2/76	Willie Nelson		
14/68	**Remembering**...Jerry Reed	12/77	**Ridin' Rainbows**...Tanya Tucker
23/70	**Removing The Shadow**...Hank Williams, Jr. & Lois Johnson	22/70	**Right Back Loving You Again**...Del Reeves
		14/71	**Right Combination**...Porter Wagoner & Dolly Parton
7/94	**Renegades, Rebels And Rogues**...Tracy Lawrence		
		1/87	**Right From The Start**...Earl Thomas Conley
4/93	**Reno**...Doug Supernaw	3/87	**Right Hand Man**...Eddy Raven
19/68	**Reno**...Dottie West	10/81	**Right In The Palm Of Your Hand**...Mel McDaniel
9/86	**Reno Bound**...Southern Pacific		
10/68	**Repeat After Me**...Jack Reno	10/90	**Right In The Wrong Direction**...Vern Gosdin
6/57	**Repenting**...Kitty Wells		
4/86	**Repetitive Regret**...Eddie Rabbitt	8/87	**Right Left Hand**...George Jones
	Rest Your Love On Me	15/91	**Right Now**...Mary-Chapin Carpenter
39/79	Bee Gees	30/66	**Right One**...Statler Brothers
1/81	Conway Twitty	21/70	**Right Or Left At Oak Street**...Roy Clark
	Restless	1/84	**Right Or Wrong**...George Strait
20/69	Carl Perkins	9/61	**Right Or Wrong**...Wanda Jackson
25/91	Mark O'Connor	14/84	**Right Stuff**...Charly McClain & Mickey Gilley
39/74	**Restless**...Crystal Gayle		
39/87	**Restless Angel**...Tim Malchak	17/77	**Right Time Of The Night**...Jennifer Warnes
11/61	**Restless One**...Hank Snow	7/71	**Right Won't Touch A Hand**...George Jones
30/64	**Restless River**...Earl Scott	1/63	**Ring Of Fire**...Johnny Cash
6/78	**Return To Me**...Marty Robbins		**Ring On Her Finger, Time On Her Hands**
13/79	**Reunited**...Louise Mandrell & R.C. Bannon	5/82	Lee Greenwood
1/75	**Rhinestone Cowboy**...Glen Campbell	9/96	Reba McEntire
23/64	**Rhinestones**...Faron Young	33/90	**Ring Where A Ring Used To Be**...Billy Joe Royal
1/51	**Rhumba Boogie**...Hank Snow		
	Rhythm Of The Rain	21/64	**Ringo**...Lorne Greene
34/72	Pat Roberts	7/71	**Rings**...Tompall/Glaser Brothers
11/78	Jacky Ward	2/69	**Rings Of Gold**...Dottie West & Don Gibson
32/69	**Rib, The**...Jeannie C. Riley	9/70	**Rise And Shine**...Tommy Cash
		1/92	**River, The**...Garth Brooks
		8/96	**River And The Highway**...Pam Tillis
		23/69	**River Bottom**...Johnny Darrell

POS/YR	RECORD TITLE/ARTIST
36/85	**River In The Rain**...Roger Miller
9/54	**River Of No Return**...Tennessee Ernie Ford
13/74	**River's Too Wide**...Jim Mundy
4/60	**Riverboat**...Faron Young
14/60	**Riverboat Gambler**...Jimmie Skinner
27/76	**Road Song**...Charlie Rich
17/72	**Roadmaster, The**...Freddy Weller
13/67	**Roarin' Again**...Wilburn Brothers
15/63	**Robert E. Lee**...Ott Stephens
16/79	**Robinhood**...Billy "Crash" Craddock
	Rock And Roll ..see: Rock 'N' Roll
	Rock And Rye
5/48	Tex Ritter
14/48	Al Dexter
2/94	**Rock Bottom**...Wynonna Judd
14/58	**Rock Hearts**...Jimmy Martin
35/70	**Rock Island Line**...Johnny Cash
26/70	**Rock Me Back To Little Rock**...Jan Howard
29/93	**Rock Me (In The Cradle Of Love)**...Deborah Allen
2/92	**Rock My Baby**...Shenandoah
2/94	**Rock My World (Little Country Girl)**...Brooks & Dunn
29/75	**Rock N' Roll**...Mac Davis
23/90	**Rock 'N' Roll Angel**...Kentucky Headhunters
16/87	**Rock And Roll Of Love**...Tom Wopat
14/84	**Rock And Roll Shoes**...Ray Charles with B.J. Thomas
6/75	**Rock On Baby**...Brenda Lee
13/57	**Rockin' In The Congo**...Hank Thompson
18/79	**Rockin' My Life Away**...Jerry Lee Lewis
1/86	**Rockin' With The Rhythm Of The Rain**...Judds
1/91	**Rockin' Years**...Dolly Parton with Ricky Van Shelton
22/60	**Rockin', Rollin' Ocean**...Hank Snow
28/76	**Rocking In Rosalee's Boat**...Nick Nixon
1/75	**Rocky**...Dickey Lee
5/76	**Rocky Mountain Music**...Eddie Rabbitt
	Rocky Top
33/68	Osborne Brothers
17/70	Lynn Anderson
3/91	**Rodeo**...Garth Brooks
37/82	**Rodeo Clown**...Mac Davis
25/80	**Rodeo Eyes**...Zella Lehr
10/82	**Rodeo Romeo**...Moe Bandy
36/88	**Rogue, The**...David Lynn Jones
4/63	**Roll Muddy River**...Wilburn Brothers

POS/YR	RECORD TITLE/ARTIST
1/75	**Roll On Big Mama**...Joe Stampley
1/84	**Roll On (Eighteen Wheeler)**...Alabama
7/81	**Roll On Mississippi**...Charley Pride
26/67	**Roll Over And Play Dead**...Jan Howard
38/66	**Roll Truck Roll**...Red Simpson
32/75	**Roll You Like A Wheel**...Mickey Gilley & Barbi Benton
2/71	**Rollin' In My Sweet Baby's Arms**...Buck Owens
9/85	**Rollin' Lonely**...Johnny Lee
15/86	**Rollin' Nowhere**...Michael Martin Murphey
1/77	**Rollin' With The Flow**...Charlie Rich
3/46	**Roly-Poly**...Bob Wills
22/83	**Romance**...Louise Mandrell
26/69	**Rome Wasn't Built In A Day**...Hank Snow
27/93	**Romeo**...Dolly Parton
36/79	**Room At The Top Of The Stairs**...Stella Parton
	Room Full Of Roses
4/49	George Morgan
10/49	Sons Of The Pioneers
1/74	Mickey Gilley
2/66	**Room In Your Heart**...Sonny James
1/76	**Roots Of My Raising**...Merle Haggard
4/94	**Rope The Moon**...John Michael Montgomery
1/44	**Rosalita**...Al Dexter
2/68	**Rosanna's Going Wild**...Johnny Cash
1/83	**Rose, The**...Conway Twitty
5/78	**Rose Colored Glasses**...John Conlee
1/70	**Rose Garden**...Lynn Anderson
1/87	**Rose In Paradise**...Waylon Jennings
4/54	**Rose-Marie**...Slim Whitman
33/80	**Rose's Are Red**...Freddie Hart
28/63	**Rosebuds And You**...Benny Martin
3/75	**Roses And Love Songs**...Ray Price
15/71	**Roses And Thorns**...Jeannie C. Riley
2/77	**Roses For Mama**...C.W. McCall
34/66	**Roses From A Stranger**...Leroy Van Dyke
17/74	**Rosie Cries A Lot**...Ferlin Husky
19/96	**'Round Here**...Sawyer Brown
9/82	**'Round The Clock Lovin'**...Gail Davies
40/77	**'Round The World With The Rubber Duck**...C.W. McCall
31/81	**Round-Up Saloon**...Bobby Goldsboro
11/68	**Row Row Row**...Henson Cargill
1/53	**Rub-A-Dub-Dub**...Hank Thompson
39/95	**Rub-A-Dubbin'**...Ken Mellons
1/74	**Rub It In**...Billy "Crash" Craddock

POS/YR	RECORD TITLE/ARTIST
1/63	**Ruby Ann**...Marty Robbins
3/71	**Ruby (Are You Mad)**...Buck Owens
1/75	**Ruby, Baby**...Billy "Crash" Craddock
	Ruby, Don't Take Your Love To Town
9/67	Johnny Darrell
39/69	Kenny Rogers
21/72	**Ruby You're Warm**...David Rogers
	Rudolph, The Red-Nosed Reindeer
1/49	Gene Autry
5/50	Gene Autry
3/91	**Rumor Has It**...Reba McEntire
10/68	**Run Away Little Tears**...Connie Smith
5/56	**Run Boy**...Ray Price
8/54	**Run 'Em Off**...Lefty Frizzell
1/70	**Run, Woman, Run**...Tammy Wynette
30/78	**Runaway**...Narvel Felts
13/84	**Runaway Heart**...Louise Mandrell
36/79	**Runaway Heart**...Reba McEntire
1/88	**Runaway Train**...Rosanne Cash
20/70	**Runnin' Bare**...Jim Nesbitt
(also see: Running Bear)	
4/92	**Runnin' Behind**...Tracy Lawrence
8/90	**Runnin' With The Wind**...Eddie Rabbitt
1/69	**Running Bear**...Sonny James
(also see: Runnin' Bare)	
24/85	**Running Down Memory Lane**...Rex Allen, Jr.
12/78	**Running Kind**...Merle Haggard
40/82	**Running On Love**...Don King
14/79	**Rusty Old Halo**...Hoyt Axton
10/67	**Ruthless**...Statler Brothers
9/48	**Rye Whiskey**...Tex Ritter

S

POS/YR	RECORD TITLE/ARTIST
15/55	**S.O.S.**...Johnnie & Jack
2/92	**Sacred Ground**...McBride & The Ride
17/76	**Sad Country Love Song**...Tom Bresh
31/67	**Sad Face**...Ernest Ashworth
F/80	**Sadness Of It All**...Conway Twitty & Loretta Lynn
4/95	**Safe In The Arms Of Love**...Martina McBride
1/64	**Saginaw, Michigan**...Lefty Frizzell
2/79	**Sail Away**...Oak Ridge Boys
16/79	**Sail On**...Tom Grant
16/59	**Sailor Man**...Johnnie & Jack

POS/YR	RECORD TITLE/ARTIST
19/59	**Sal's Got A Sugar Lip**...Johnny Horton
20/62	**Sally Was A Good Old Girl**...Hank Cochran
8/52	**Salty Dog Rag**...Red Foley
8/70	**Salute To A Switchblade**...Tom T. Hall
40/77	**Sam**...Olivia Newton-John
11/64	**Sam Hill**...Claude King
1/67	**Sam's Place**...Buck Owens
12/92	**Same Ol' Love**...Ricky Skaggs
1/59	**Same Old Me**...Ray Price
28/91	**Same Old Star**...McBride & The Ride
29/75	**Same Old Story**...Hank Williams, Jr.
5/82	**Same Ole Me**...George Jones
8/49	**Same Sweet Girl**...Hank Locklin
14/57	**Same Two Lips**...Marty Robbins
25/83	**San Antonio Nights**...Eddy Raven
8/61	**San Antonio Rose**...Floyd Cramer
1/75	**San Antonio Stroll**...Tanya Tucker
31/68	**San Diego**...Charlie Walker
26/75	**Sanctuary**...Ronnie Prophet
7/63	**Sands Of Gold**...Webb Pierce
F/79	**Santa Barbara**...Ronnie Milsap
5/88	**Santa Fe**...Bellamy Brothers
1/73	**Satin Sheets**...Jeanne Pruett
17/73	**Satisfaction**...Jack Greene
7/53	**Satisfaction Guaranteed**...Carl Smith
	Satisfied Mind
1/55	Porter Wagoner
3/55	Red Foley & Betty Foley
4/55	Jean Shepard
25/73	Roy Drusky
5/88	**Satisfy You**...Sweethearts Of The Rodeo
24/71	**Saturday Morning Confusion**...Bobby Russell
22/68	**Saturday Night**...Webb Pierce
9/88	**Saturday Night Special**...Conway Twitty
6/83	**Save Me**...Louise Mandrell
12/85	**Save The Last Chance**...Johnny Lee
	Save The Last Dance For Me
36/78	Ron Shaw
4/79	Emmylou Harris
26/79	Jerry Lee Lewis
3/84	Dolly Parton
11/62	**Save The Last Dance For Me**...Buck Owens
8/80	**Save Your Heart For Me**...Jacky Ward
10/76	**Save Your Kisses For Me**...Margo Smith
3/86	**Savin' My Love For You**...Pake McEntire
14/77	**Savin' This Love Song For You**...Johnny Rodriguez

POS/YR	RECORD TITLE/ARTIST
	Sawmill
27/59	Mel Tillis & Bill Phillips
15/63	Webb Pierce
2/73	Mel Tillis
21/94	**Sawmill Road**...Diamond Rio
5/75	**Say Forever You'll Be Mine**...Porter Wagoner & Dolly Parton
35/73	**Say, Has Anybody Seen My Sweet Gypsy Rose**...Terry Stafford
40/75	**Say I Do**...Ray Price
1/76	**Say It Again**...Don Williams
31/91	**Say It's Not True**...Lionel Cartwright
8/68	**Say It's Not You**...George Jones
4/89	**Say What's In Your Heart**...Restless Heart
15/73	**Say When**...Diana Trask
10/79	**Say You Love Me**...Stephanie Winslow
1/77	**Say You'll Stay Until Tomorrow**...Tom Jones
2/77	**Saying Hello, Saying I Love You, Saying Goodbye**...Jim Ed Brown/Helen Cornelius
5/83	**Scarlet Fever**...Kenny Rogers
7/60	**Scarlet Ribbons (For Her Hair)**...Browns
27/58	**Scotland**...Bill Monroe
8/81	**Scratch My Back (And Whisper in My Ear)**...Razzy Bailey
	Sea Of Heartbreak
2/61	Don Gibson
24/72	Kenny Price
33/79	Lynn Anderson
39/89	Ronnie McDowell
5/48	**Seaman's Blues**...Ernest Tubb
17/90	**Searchin' For Some Kind Of Clue**...Billy Joe Royal
3/56	**Searching (For Someone Like You)**...Kitty Wells
24/74	**Seasons In The Sun**...Bobby Wright
	Seasons Of My Heart
9/56	Jimmy Newman
10/60	Johnny Cash
18/62	**Second Choice**...Stonewall Jackson
24/59	**Second Fiddle**...Buck Owens
5/64	**Second Fiddle (To An Old Guitar)**...Jean Shepard
7/84	**Second Hand Heart**...Gary Morris
3/63	**Second Hand Rose**...Roy Drusky
18/79	**Second-Hand Satin Lady (And A Bargain Basement Boy)**...Jerry Reed
15/60	**Second Honeymoon**...Johnny Cash
5/86	**Second To No One**...Rosanne Cash

POS/YR	RECORD TITLE/ARTIST
	Secret Love
2/54	Slim Whitman
1/75	Freddy Fender
5/58	**Secretly**...Jimmie Rodgers
6/90	**See If I Care**...Shenandoah
F/69	**See Ruby Fall**...Johnny Cash
7/65	**See The Big Man Cry**...Charlie Louvin
18/76	**See You On Sunday**...Glen Campbell
16/72	**Seed Before The Rose**...Tommy Overstreet
2/90	**Seein' My Father In Me**...Paul Overstreet
2/75	**Seeker, The**...Dolly Parton
2/92	**Seminole Wind**...John Anderson
19/77	**Semolita**...Jerry Reed
2/79	**Send Me Down To Tucson**...Mel Tillis
7/73	**Send Me No Roses**...Tommy Overstreet
14/72	**Send Me Some Lovin'**...Hank Williams, Jr. & Lois Johnson
	Send Me The Pillow You Dream On
5/58	Hank Locklin
23/60	Browns
11/62	Johnny Tillotson
9/87	**Senorita**...Don Williams
3/84	**Sentimental Ol' You**...Charly McClain
F/73	**Separate Ways**...Elvis Presley
	September Song
40/69	Roy Clark
15/79	Willie Nelson
1/88	**Set 'Em Up Joe**...Vern Gosdin
5/59	**Set Him Free**...Skeeter Davis
2/52	**Settin' The Woods On Fire**...Hank Williams
7/89	**Setting Me Up**...Highway 101
28/66	**Seven Days Of Crying (Makes One Weak)**...Harden Trio
	Seven Lonely Days
7/53	Bonnie Lou
18/69	Jean Shepard
1/85	**Seven Spanish Angels**...Ray Charles with Willie Nelson
1/81	**Seven Year Ache**...Rosanne Cash
F/71	**Seventeen Years**...Marty Robbins
21/74	**Sexy Lady**...Freddy Weller
8/91	**Shadow Of A Doubt**...Earl Thomas Conley
5/45	**Shadow On My Heart**...Ted Daffan
1/79	**Shadows In The Moonlight**...Anne Murray
28/79	**Shadows Of Love**...Rayburn Anthony
15/83	**Shadows Of My Mind**...Leon Everette
24/78	**Shady Rest**...Mel Street
6/53	**Shake A Hand**...Red Foley
15/54	**Shake-A-Leg**...Carlisles

POS/YR	RECORD TITLE/ARTIST
27/61	**Shake Hands With A Loser**...Don Winters
	Shake Me I Rattle (Squeeze Me I Cry)
14/63	Marion Worth
16/78	Cristy Lane
3/92	**Shake The Sugar Tree**...Pam Tillis
15/86	**Shakin'**...Sawyer Brown
	Shame On Me
18/62	Bobby Bare
8/77	Donna Fargo
15/83	**Shame On The Moon**...Bob Seger
	Shame On You
1/45	Spade Cooley
1/45	Lawrence Welk with Red Foley
4/45	Bill Boyd
11/77	**Shame, Shame On Me**...Kenny Dale
26/93	**Shame Shame Shame Shame**...Mark Collie
1/91	**Shameless**...Garth Brooks
35/64	**Shape Up Or Ship Out**...Leon McAuliff
5/81	**Share Your Love With Me**...Kenny Rogers
15/79	**Sharing**...Kenny Dale
2/95	**She Ain't Your Ordinary Girl**...Alabama
1/86	**She And I**...Alabama
1/79	**She Believes In Me**...Kenny Rogers
16/81	**She Belongs To Everyone But Me**...Burrito Brothers
3/44	**She Broke My Heart In Three Places**...Hoosier Hot Shots
38/74	**She Burn't The Little Roadside Tavern Down**...Johnny Russell
	She Called Me Baby
32/65	Carl Smith
1/74	Charlie Rich
2/90	**She Came From Fort Worth**...Kathy Mattea
1/78	**She Can Put Her Shoes Under My Bed**...Johnny Duncan
29/82	**She Can't Get My Love Off The Bed**...Dottie West
3/94	**She Can't Say I Didn't Cry**...Rick Trevino
2/80	**She Can't Say That Anymore**...John Conlee
28/70	**She Cheats On Me**...Glenn Barber
4/87	**She Couldn't Love Me Anymore**...T. Graham Brown
35/75	**She Deserves My Very Best**...David Wills
8/89	**She Deserves You**...Baillie & The Boys
9/88	**She Doesn't Cry Anymore**...Shenandoah
1/93	**She Don't Know She's Beautiful**...Sammy Kershaw
3/89	**She Don't Love Nobody**...Desert Rose Band
19/71	**She Don't Make Me Cry**...David Rogers

POS/YR	RECORD TITLE/ARTIST
14/54	**She Done Give Her Heart To Me**...Sonny James
6/94	**She Dreams**...Mark Chesnutt
	She Even Woke Me Up To Say Goodbye
2/69	Jerry Lee Lewis
15/75	Ronnie Milsap
39/95	**She Feels Like A Brand New Man Tonight**...Aaron Tippin
15/73	**She Fights That Lovin' Feeling**...Faron Young
3/70	**She Goes Walking Through My Mind**...Billy Walker
1/82	**She Got The Goldmine (I Got The Shaft)**...Jerry Reed
1/92	**She Is His Only Need**...Wynonna Judd
11/77	**She Just Loved The Cheatin' Out Of Me**...Moe Bandy
13/80	**She Just Started Liking Cheatin' Songs**...John Anderson
1/85	**She Keeps The Home Fires Burning**...Ronnie Milsap
1/82	**She Left Love All Over Me**...Razzy Bailey
11/73	**She Loves Me (Right Out Of My Mind)**...Freddy Weller
21/74	**She Met A Stranger, I Met A Train**...Tommy Cash
1/73	**She Needs Someone To Hold Her (When She Cries)**...Conway Twitty
27/94	**She Never Cried**...Confederate Railroad
2/76	**She Never Knew Me**...Don Williams
23/89	**She Reminded Me Of You**...Mickey Gilley
17/96	**She Said Yes**...Rhett Akins
2/68	**She Still Comes Around**...Jerry Lee Lewis
3/84	**She Sure Got Away With My Heart**...John Anderson
13/75	**She Talked A Lot About Texas**...Cal Smith
15/94	**She Thinks His Name Was John**...Reba McEntire
	She [He] Thinks I Still Care
1/62	George Jones
1/74	Anne Murray
F/77	Elvis Presley
39/68	**She Thinks I'm On That Train**...Henson Cargill
9/87	**She Thinks That She'll Marry**...Judy Rodman
30/85	**She Told Me Yes**...Chance
37/92	**She Took It Like A Man**...Confederate Railroad
11/77	**She Took More Than Her Share**...Moe Bandy

POS/YR	RECORD TITLE/ARTIST
1/93	**She Used To Be Mine**...Brooks & Dunn
2/86	**She Used To Be Somebody's Baby**...Gatlin Bros.
11/85	**She Used To Love Me A Lot**...David Allan Coe
19/82	**She Used To Sing On Sunday**...Gatlin Bros.
11/71	**She Wakes Me With A Kiss Every Morning**...Nat Stuckey
4/58	**She Was Only Seventeen (He Was One Year More)**...Marty Robbins
6/68	**She Wears My Ring**...Ray Price
14/68	**She Went A Little Bit Farther**...Faron Young
4/94	**She'd Give Anything**...Boy Howdy
10/70	**She'll Be Hanging 'Round Somewhere**...Mel Tillis
12/76	**She'll Throw Stones At You**...Freddie Hart
3/70	**She's A Little Bit Country**...George Hamilton IV
1/85	**She's A Miracle**...Exile
15/91	**She's A Natural**...Rob Crosby
1/75	**She's Actin' Single (I'm Drinkin' Doubles)**...Gary Stewart
2/71	**She's All I Got**...Johnny Paycheck
3/73	**She's All Woman**...David Houston
37/75	**She's Already Gone**...Jim Mundy
39/79	**She's Been Keepin' Me Up Nights**...Bobby Lewis
6/85	**She's Comin' Back To Say Goodbye**...Eddie Rabbitt
1/89	**She's Crazy For Leavin'**...Rodney Crowell
1/95	**She's Every Woman**...Garth Brooks
	She's Gone Gone Gone
12/65	Lefty Frizzell
6/89	Glen Campbell
9/85	**She's Gonna Win Your Heart**...Eddy Raven
36/81	**She's Got A Drinking Problem**...Gary Stewart
	She's Got A Man On Her Mind
38/89	Curtis Wright
22/91	Conway Twitty
26/96	**She's Got A Mind Of Her Own**...James Bonamy
2/89	**She's Got A Single Thing In Mind**...Conway Twitty
24/74	**She's Got Everything I Need**...Eddy Arnold
1/92	**She's Got The Rhythm (And I Got The Blues)**...Alan Jackson
1/72	**She's Got To Be A Saint**...Ray Price

POS/YR	RECORD TITLE/ARTIST
	She's Got You
1/62	Patsy Cline
1/77	Loretta Lynn
25/76	**She's Helping Me Get Over Loving You**...Joe Stampley
39/74	**She's In Love With A Rodeo Man**...Johnny Russell
1/91	**She's In Love With The Boy**...Trisha Yearwood
14/60	**She's Just A Whole Lot Like You**...Hank Thompson
1/77	**She's Just An Old Love Turned Memory**...Charley Pride
37/71	**She's Leavin' (Bonnie, Please Don't Go)**...Jim Ed Brown
26/77	**She's Long Legged**...Joe Stampley
21/69	**She's Lookin' Better By The Minute**...Jay Lee Webb
7/82	**She's Lying**...Lee Greenwood
37/80	**She's Made Of Faith**...Marty Robbins
6/70	**She's Mine**...George Jones
	She's [He's] My Rock
20/73	Stoney Edwards
8/75	Brenda Lee
2/84	George Jones
28/92	**She's Never Comin' Back**...Mark Collie
F/58	**She's No Angel**...Kitty Wells
17/88	**She's No Lady**...Lyle Lovett
6/93	**She's Not Cryin' Anymore**...Billy Ray Cyrus
4/82	**She's Not Really Cheatin' (She's Just Gettin' Even)**...Moe Bandy
1/94	**She's Not The Cheatin' Kind**...Brooks & Dunn
10/82	**She's Playing Hard To Forget**...Eddy Raven
1/77	**She's Pulling Me Back Again**...Mickey Gilley
F/83	**She's Ready For Someone To Love Her**...Jerry Reed
2/85	**She's Single Again**...Janie Fricke
17/81	**She's Steppin' Out**...Con Hunley
17/77	**She's The Girl Of My Dreams**...Don King
19/89	**She's There**...Daniele Alexander
1/72	**She's Too Good To Be True**...Charley Pride
1/87	**She's Too Good To Be True**...Exile
12/63	**Sheepskin Valley**...Claude King
14/73	**Shelter Of Your Eyes**...Don Williams
33/73	**Shenandoah**...Charlie McCoy
8/71	**Sheriff Of Boone County**...Kenny Price
5/82	**Shine**...Waylon Jennings
36/76	**Shine On**...Ronnie Prophet

POS/YR	RECORD TITLE/ARTIST
13/78	**Shine On Me**...John Wesley Ryles
3/83	**Shine On (Shine All Your Sweet Love On Me)**...George Jones
7/51	**Shine, Shave, Shower (It's Saturday)**...Lefty Frizzell
	Shine, Shine, Shine
40/67	Carl Perkins
1/87	Eddy Raven
19/69	**Ship In The Bottle**...Stonewall Jackson
5/92	**Ships That Don't Come In**...Joe Diffie
28/66	**Shirt, The**...Norma Jean
3/66	**Shoe Goes On The Other Foot Tonight**...Marty Robbins
22/86	**Shoe String**...Mel McDaniel
17/63	**Shoes Of A Fool**...Bill Goodwin
8/70	**Shoeshine Man**...Tom T. Hall
16/61	**Shorty**...Jimmy Smart
	Shot Full Of Love
30/81	Randy Parton
19/83	Nitty Gritty Dirt Band
1/51	**Shot Gun Boogie**...Tennessee Ernie Ford
30/84	**Shot In The Dark**...Leon Everette
23/80	**Shotgun Rider**...Joe Sun
3/79	**Should I Come Home (Or Should I Go Crazy)**...Gene Watson
10/58	**Should We Tell Him**...Everly Brothers
3/95	**Should've Asked Her Faster**...Ty England
1/93	**Should've Been A Cowboy**...Toby Keith
1/73	**Shoulder To Cry On**...Charley Pride
34/79	**Shoulder To Shoulder (Arm and Arm)**...Roy Clark
5/88	**Shouldn't It Be Easier Than This**...Charley Pride
1/84	**Show Her**...Ronnie Milsap
30/62	**Show Her Lots Of Gold**...Ernest Tubb
11/72	**Show Me**...Barbara Mandrell
8/76	**Show Me A Man**...T.G. Sheppard
7/49	**Show Me The Way Back To Your Heart**...Eddy Arnold
15/57	**Shrine Of St. Cecilia**...Faron Young
7/80	**Shriner's Convention**...Ray Stevens
13/80	**Shuffle Song**...Margo Smith
5/46	**Shut That Gate**...Ted Daffan
1/94	**Shut Up And Kiss Me**...Mary-Chapin Carpenter
26/70	**Shutters And Boards**...Slim Whitman
7/51	**Sick, Sober And Sorry**...Johnny Bond
F/70	**Sidewalks Of Chicago**...Merle Haggard

POS/YR	RECORD TITLE/ARTIST
	Signed Sealed And Delivered
2/48	Cowboy Copas
6/48	Bob Atcher
8/48	Texas Jim Robertson
9/48	Jimmy Wakely
10/61	Cowboy Copas
29/80	**Silence On The Line**...Henson Cargill
F/80	**Silent Night (After The Fight)**...Ronnie Milsap
20/84	**Silent Partners**...Frizzell & West
7/81	**Silent Treatment**...Earl Thomas Conley
5/52	**Silver And Gold**...Pee Wee King
15/91	**Silver And Gold**...Dolly Parton
15/55	**Silver Bell**...Hank Snow & Chet Atkins
25/77	**Silver Bird**...Tina Rainford
1/45	**Silver Dew On The Blue Grass Tonight**...Bob Wills
18/77	**Silver Medals And Sweet Memories**...Statler Brothers
4/46	**Silver Spurs (On The Golden Stairs)**...Gene Autry
25/90	**Silver Stallion**...Waylon Jennings/Willie Nelson/Johnny Cash/Kris Kristofferson
4/47	**Silver Stars, Purple Sage, Eyes Of Blue**...Cliffie Stone
	Silver Threads And Golden Needles
16/62	Springfields
20/74	Linda Ronstadt
20/76	**Silver Wings And Golden Rings**...Billie Jo Spears
10/79	**Simple Little Words**...Cristy Lane
12/90	**Simple Man**...Charlie Daniels Band
6/91	**Since I Don't Have You**...Ronnie Milsap
	Since I Fell For You
10/76	Charlie Rich
20/79	Con Hunley
7/86	**Since I Found You**...Sweethearts Of The Rodeo
	Since I Met You, Baby
1/69	Sonny James
10/75	Freddy Fender
8/89	**Sincerely**...Forester Sisters
3/63	**Sing A Little Song Of Heartache**...Rose Maddox
	Sing A Sad Song
26/63	Buddy Cagle
19/64	Merle Haggard
19/77	Wynn Stewart
3/73	**Sing About Love**...Lynn Anderson
3/72	**Sing Me A Love Song To Baby**...Billy Walker

POS/YR	RECORD TITLE/ARTIST
1/68	**Sing Me Back Home**...Merle Haggard
12/70	**Singer Of Sad Songs**...Waylon Jennings
29/75	**Singin' In The Kitchen**...Bobby Bare & The Family
4/54	**Singing Hills**...Slim Whitman
18/71	**Singing In Viet Nam Talking Blues**...Johnny Cash
1/69	**Singing My Song**...Tammy Wynette
	Singing The Blues
1/56	Marty Robbins
17/83	Gail Davies
36/78	**Single Again**...Gary Stewart
8/82	**Single Women**...Dolly Parton
6/60	**Sink The Bismarck**...Johnny Horton
14/48	**Sinner's Death**...Roy Acuff
	Sioux City Sue
1/45	Dick Thomas
2/46	Hoosier Hot Shots & Two Ton Baker
2/46	Zeke Manners
3/46	Tiny Hill
12/49	**Sister Of Sioux City Sue**...Dick Thomas
4/65	**Sittin' In An All Nite Cafe**...Warner Mack
33/70	**Sittin' In Atlanta Station**...Nat Stuckey
3/66	**Sittin' On A Rock (Crying In A Creek)**...Warner Mack
13/82	**(Sittin' On) The Dock Of The Bay**...Waylon & Willie
14/49	**Sittin' On The Doorstep**...Woody Carter
	Six Days On The Road
2/63	Dave Dudley
29/88	Steve Earle & The Dukes
27/65	**Six Lonely Hours**...Kitty Wells
10/60	**Six Pack To Go**...Hank Thompson
12/65	**Six Times A Day (The Trains Came Down)**...Dick Curless
4/70	**Six White Horses**...Tommy Cash
1/55	**Sixteen Tons**...Tennessee Ernie Ford
7/82	**16th Avenue**...Lacy J. Dalton
19/85	**Size Seven Round (Made Of Gold)**...George Jones & Lacy J. Dalton
3/66	**Skid Row Joe**...Porter Wagoner
1/68	**Skip A Rope**...Henson Cargill
10/48	**Slap Her Down Again Paw**...Esmereldy
8/53	**Slaves Of A Hopeless Love Affair**...Red Foley
20/61	**Sleep, Baby, Sleep**...Connie Hall
11/78	**Sleep Tight, Good Night Man**...Bobby Bare
4/81	**Sleepin' With The Radio On**...Charly McClain
	Sleeping ..also see: A-Sleeping

POS/YR	RECORD TITLE/ARTIST
1/78	**Sleeping Single In A Double Bed**...Barbara Mandrell
9/61	**Sleepy-Eyed John**...Johnny Horton
7/77	**Slide Off Of Your Satin Sheets**...Johnny Paycheck
22/79	**Slip Away**...Dottsy
14/73	**Slippin' And Slidin'**...Billy "Crash" Craddock
7/50	**Slippin' Around With Jole Blon**...Bud Messner
4/73	**Slippin' Away**...Jean Shepard
19/78	**Slippin' Away**...Bellamy Brothers
17/79	**Slippin' Up, Slippin' Around**...Cristy Lane
	Slipping Around
1/49	Ernest Tubb
1/49	Margaret Whiting & Jimmy Wakely
5/49	Floyd Tillman
13/50	Texas Jim Robertson
23/64	Marion Worth & George Morgan
10/78	**Slow And Easy**...Randy Barlow
8/86	**Slow Boat To China**...Girls Next Door
1/84	**Slow Burn**...T.G. Sheppard
10/85	**Slow Burning Memory**...Vern Gosdin
6/79	**Slow Dancing**...Johnny Duncan
13/82	**Slow Down**...Lacy J. Dalton
1/82	**Slow Hand**...Conway Twitty
36/89	**Slow Passin' Time**...Anne Murray
17/62	**Slow Poison**...Johnny & Jack
	Slow Poke
1/51	Pee Wee King
7/52	Hawkshaw Hawkins
	Slowly
1/54	Webb Pierce
29/71	Jimmy Dean & Dottie West
37/81	Kippi Brannon
35/68	**Small Time Laboring Man**...George Jones
1/87	**Small Town Girl**...Steve Wariner
2/91	**Small Town Saturday Night**...Hal Ketchum
24/72	**Smell The Flowers**...Jerry Reed
15/74	**Smile For Me**...Lynn Anderson
39/72	**Smile, Somebody Loves You**...Linda Gail Lewis
13/60	**Smiling Bill McCall**...Johnny Cash
24/59	**Smoke Along The Track**...Stonewall Jackson
	Smoke On The Water
1/44	Red Foley
1/45	Bob Wills
7/45	Boyd Heath
	Smoke! Smoke! Smoke! (That Cigarette)
1/47	Tex Williams
32/68	Tex Williams ('68)

POS/YR	RECORD TITLE/ARTIST
8/49	**Smokey Mountain Boogie**...Tennessee Ernie Ford
	Smokey Mountain Memories
13/75	Mel Street
F/82	Earl Thomas Conley
1/80	**Smoky Mountain Rain**...Ronnie Milsap
12/69	**Smoky Places**...Billy Walker
5/69	**Smoky The Bar**...Hank Thompson
6/80	**Smooth Sailin'**...T.G. Sheppard
32/79	**Smooth Sailin'**...Jim Weatherly
	Snap Your Fingers
40/71	Dick Curless
12/74	Don Gibson
1/87	Ronnie Milsap
5/83	**Snapshot**...Sylvia
16/67	**Sneaking 'Cross The Border**...Harden Trio
2/66	**Snow Flake**...Jim Reeves
28/63	**Snow White Cloud**...Frank Taylor
10/70	**Snowbird**...Anne Murray
4/56	**So Doggone Lonesome**...Johnny Cash
22/82	**So Fine**...Oak Ridge Boys
27/78	**So Good, So Rare, So Fine**...Freddie Hart
F/77	**So Good Woman**...Waylon Jennings
2/95	**So Help Me Girl**...Joe Diffie
22/62	**So How Come (No One Loves Me)**...Don Gibson
1/44	**So Long Pal**...Al Dexter
14/55	**So Lovely, Baby**...Rusty & Doug
16/59	**So Many Times**...Roy Acuff
	So Many Ways
28/73	Eddy Arnold
33/77	David Houston
3/92	**So Much Like My Dad**...George Strait
	So Round, So Firm, So Fully Packed
1/47	Merle Travis
3/47	Johnny Bond
5/47	Ernest Tubb
	So Sad (To Watch Good Love Go Bad)
12/70	Hank Williams, Jr. & Lois Johnson
31/76	Connie Smith
28/83	Emmylou Harris
19/59	**So Soon**...Jimmy Newman
20/71	**So This Is Love**...Tommy Cash
14/62	**So Wrong**...Patsy Cline
F/57	**So You Think You've Got Troubles**...Marvin Rainwater
13/78	**Soft Lights And Hard Country Music**...Moe Bandy
10/49	**Soft Lips**...Hank Thompson
3/61	**Soft Rain**...Ray Price

POS/YR	RECORD TITLE/ARTIST
8/72	**Soft, Sweet And Warm**...David Houston
30/78	**Softest Touch In Town**...Bobby G. Rice
4/60	**Softly And Tenderly (I'll Hold You In My Arms)**...Lewis Pruitt
F/78	**Softly, As I Leave You**...Elvis Presley
29/76	**Sold Out Of Flagpoles**...Johnny Cash
1/95	**Sold (The Grundy County Auction Incident)**...John Michael Montgomery
15/59	**Soldier's Joy**...Hawkshaw Hawkins
	Soldier's Last Letter
1/44	Ernest Tubb
3/71	Merle Haggard
F/79	**Solitaire**...Elvis Presley
(also see: I'm Getting Good At Missing You)	
28/69	**Solitary**...Don Gibson
14/76	**Solitary Man**...T.G. Sheppard
1/77	**Some Broken Hearts Never Mend**...Don Williams
10/81	**Some Days Are Diamonds (Some Days Are Stone)**...John Denver
1/85	**Some Fools Never Learn**...Steve Wariner
1/92	**Some Girls Do**...Sawyer Brown
22/86	**Some Girls Have All The Luck**...Louise Mandrell
8/91	**Some Guys Have All The Love**...Little Texas
25/84	**Some Hearts Get All The Breaks**...Charly McClain
17/78	**Some I Wrote**...Statler Brothers
8/74	**Some Kind Of A Woman**...Faron Young
3/92	**Some Kind Of Trouble**...Tanya Tucker
27/81	**Some Love Songs Never Die**...B.J. Thomas
10/82	**Some Memories Just Won't Die**...Marty Robbins
20/82	**Some Of My Best Friends Are Old Songs**...Louise Mandrell
28/73	**Some Old California Memory**...Henson Cargill
16/88	**Some Old Side Road**...Keith Whitley
13/96	**Some Things Are Meant To Be**...Linda Davis
34/84	**Somebody Buy This Cowgirl A Beer**...Shelly West
4/85	**Somebody Else's Fire**...Janie Fricke
5/93	**Somebody Else's Moon**...Collin Raye
10/76	**Somebody Hold Me (Until She Passes By)**...Narvel Felts
20/81	**Somebody Led Me Away**...Loretta Lynn
1/87	**Somebody Lied**...Ricky Van Shelton
1/66	**Somebody Like Me**...Eddy Arnold

POS/YR	RECORD TITLE/ARTIST
21/72	**Somebody Loves Me**...Johnny Paycheck
8/76	**Somebody Loves You**...Crystal Gayle
9/93	**Somebody New**...Billy Ray Cyrus
8/93	**Somebody Paints The Wall**...Tracy Lawrence
16/62	**Somebody Save Me**...Ferlin Husky
1/85	**Somebody Should Leave**...Reba McEntire
1/76	**Somebody Somewhere**...Loretta Lynn
6/79	**Somebody Special**...Donna Fargo
18/63	**Somebody Told Somebody**...Rose Maddox
9/86	**Somebody Wants Me Out Of The Way**...George Jones
7/83	**Somebody's Always Saying Goodbye**...Anne Murray
6/59	**Somebody's Back In Town**...Wilburn Brothers
2/51	**Somebody's Been Beating My Time**...Eddy Arnold
32/81	**Somebody's Darling, Somebody's Wife**...Dottsy
15/92	**Somebody's Doin' Me Right**...Keith Whitley
1/83	**Somebody's Gonna Love You**...Lee Greenwood
8/81	**Somebody's Knockin'**...Terri Gibbs
1/84	**Somebody's Needin' Somebody**...Conway Twitty
9/52	**Somebody's Stolen My Honey**...Ernest Tubb
1/91	**Someday**...Alan Jackson
12/57	**Someday**...Webb Pierce
28/86	**Someday**...Steve Earle
(also see: It's Always Gonna Be)	
22/79	**Someday My Day Will Come**...George Jones
	Someday Soon
39/76	Kathy Barnes
21/82	Moe Bandy
12/91	Suzy Bogguss
4/70	**Someday We'll Be Together**...Bill Anderson & Jan Howard
2/71	**Someday We'll Look Back**...Merle Haggard
1/84	**Someday When Things Are Good**...Merle Haggard
10/49	**Someday You'll Call My Name**...Jimmy Wakely
	Someday (You'll Want Me To Want You)
2/46	Elton Britt
3/46	Hoosier Hot Shots & Sally Foster
4/46	Gene Autry
5/87	**Someone**...Lee Greenwood
8/66	**Someone Before Me**...Wilburn Brothers

POS/YR	RECORD TITLE/ARTIST
17/75	**Someone Cares For You**...Red Steagall
1/82	**Someone Could Lose A Heart Tonight**...Eddie Rabbitt
3/96	**Someone Else's Dream**...Faith Hill
1/95	**Someone Else's Star**...Bryan White
14/90	**Someone Else's Trouble Now**...Highway 101
26/84	**Someone Is Falling In Love**...Kathy Mattea
11/79	**Someone Is Looking For Someone Like You**...Gail Davies
26/85	**Someone Like You**...Emmylou Harris
1/78	**Someone Loves You Honey**...Charley Pride
4/72	**Someone To Give My Love To**...Johnny Paycheck
32/67	**Someone Told My Story**...Merle Haggard
30/65	**Someone's Gotta Cry**...Jean Shepard
29/76	**Someone's With Your Wife Tonight, Mister**...Bobby Borchers
24/93	**Someplace Far Away (Careful What You're Dreamin')**...Hal Ketchum
13/81	**Somethin' On The Radio**...Jacky Ward
6/74	**Something**...Johnny Rodriguez
10/73	**Something About You I Love**...Johnny Paycheck
6/71	**Something Beautiful (To Remember)**...Slim Whitman
19/75	**Something Better To Do**...Olivia Newton-John
17/67	**Something Fishy**...Dolly Parton
31/64	**Something I Dreamed**...George Jones
2/85	**Something In My Heart**...Ricky Skaggs
14/92	**Something In Red**...Lorrie Morgan
14/90	**Something Of A Dreamer**...Mary-Chapin Carpenter
4/51	**Something Old, Something New**...Eddy Arnold
23/62	**Something Precious**...Skeeter Davis
10/68	**Something Pretty**...Wynn Stewart
17/68	**Something Special**...Mel Tillis
	Something To Brag About
18/70	Charlie Louvin & Melba Montgomery
9/78	Mary Kay Place with Willie Nelson
36/70	**Something To Think About**...Hank Williams, Jr.
15/70	**Something Unseen**...Jack Greene
24/93	**Something's Gonna Change Her Mind**...Mark Collie
19/69	**Something's Wrong In California**...Waylon Jennings

POS/YR	RECORD TITLE/ARTIST
F/81	**Sometime, Somewhere, Somehow**...Barbara Mandrell
10/74	**Sometime Sunshine**...Jim Ed Brown
1/76	**Sometimes**...Bill Anderson & Mary Lou Turner
3/86	**Sometimes A Lady**...Eddy Raven
6/73	**Sometimes A Memory Ain't Enough**...Jerry Lee Lewis
34/81	**Sometimes I Cry When I'm Alone**...Sammi Smith
9/83	**Sometimes I Get Lucky And Forget**...Gene Watson
9/76	**Sometimes I Talk In My Sleep**...Randy Cornor
12/62	**Sometimes I'm Tempted**...Marty Robbins
38/89	**Sometimes Love's Not A Pretty Thing**...Zaca Creek
7/95	**Sometimes She Forgets**...Travis Tritt
	Sometimes When We Touch
F/81	Stephanie Winslow
6/85	Mark Gray & Tammy Wynette
	Sometimes You Just Can't Win
17/62	George Jones
10/71	George Jones
27/82	Linda Ronstadt & John David Souther
37/70	**Someway**...Don Gibson
2/74	**Somewhere Between Love And Tomorrow**...Roy Clark
23/88	**Somewhere Between Ragged And Right**...John Anderson
1/82	**Somewhere Between Right And Wrong**...Earl Thomas Conley
3/84	**Somewhere Down The Line**...T.G. Sheppard
3/91	**Somewhere In My Broken Heart**...Billy Dean
29/87	**Somewhere In The Night**...Sawyer Brown
7/95	**Somewhere In The Vicinity Of The Heart**...Shenandoah With Alison Krauss
15/72	**Somewhere In Virginia In The Rain**...Jack Blanchard & Misty Morgan
22/73	**Somewhere My Love**...Red Steagall
1/93	**Somewhere Other Than The Night**...Garth Brooks
1/87	**Somewhere Tonight**...Highway 101
40/69	**Son Of A Preacher Man**...Peggy Little
5/74	**Son Of A Rotten Gambler**...Anne Murray
14/79	**Son Of Clayton Delaney**...Tom T. Hall
	Son Of Hickory Holler's Tramp
22/68	Johnny Darrell
32/77	Johnny Russell

POS/YR	RECORD TITLE/ARTIST
8/74	**Song And Dance Man**...Johnny Paycheck
6/95	**Song For The Life**...Alan Jackson
5/77	**Song In The Night**...Johnny Duncan
F/73	**Song Nobody Sings**...Jerry Wallace
1/89	**Song Of The South**...Alabama
2/93	**Song Remembers When**...Trisha Yearwood
37/71	**Song To Mama**...Carter Family
29/75	**Song We Fell In Love To**...Connie Smith
13/79	**Song We Made Love To**...Mickey Gilley
10/65	**Sons Of Katie Elder**...Johnny Cash
2/93	**Soon**...Tanya Tucker
6/90	**Sooner Or Later**...Eddy Raven
19/62	**Sooner Or Later**...Webb Pierce
5/64	**Sorrow On The Rocks**...Porter Wagoner
	Soul And Inspiration ..see: (You're My)
22/70	**Soul Deep**...Eddy Arnold
27/77	**Soul Of A Honky Tonk Woman**...Mel McDaniel
10/82	**Soul Searchin'**...Leon Everette
1/73	**Soul Song**...Joe Stampley
18/75	**Soulful Woman**...Kenny O'Dell
1/84	**Sound Of Goodbye**...Crystal Gayle
21/73	**Sound Of Goodbye**...Jerry Wallace
21/62	**Sound Of Your Footsteps**...Wilburn Brothers
6/83	**Sounds Like Love**...Johnny Lee
31/68	**Sounds Of Goodbye**...George Morgan
15/70	**South**...Roger Miller
27/95	**Southbound**...Sammy Kershaw
37/68	**Southern Bound**...Kenny Price
5/77	**Southern California**...George Jones & Tammy Wynette
27/95	**Southern Grace**...Little Texas
6/73	**Southern Loving**...Jim Ed Brown
1/77	**Southern Nights**...Glen Campbell
1/81	**Southern Rains**...Mel Tillis
1/90	**Southern Star**...Alabama
33/84	**Southern Women**...Wright Brothers
9/89	**Sowin' Love**...Paul Overstreet
	Spanish Eyes
20/79	Charlie Rich
8/88	Willie Nelson with Julio Iglesias
3/53	**Spanish Fire Ball**...Hank Snow
	Sparkling Brown Eyes
4/54	Webb Pierce with Wilburn Brothers
30/60	George Jones
10/51	**Sparrow In The Tree Top**...Rex Allen
29/91	**Speak Of The Devil**...Pirates Of The Mississippi

POS/YR	RECORD TITLE/ARTIST
9/82	**Speak Softly**...Gene Watson
29/72	**Special Day**...Arlene Harden
5/94	**Spilled Perfume**...Pam Tillis
14/58	**Splish Splash**...Bobby Darin
F/73	**Spokane Motel Blues**...Tom T. Hall
	Spring
30/69	Clay Hart
18/75	Tanya Tucker
12/78	**Spring Fever**...Loretta Lynn
2/58	**Squaws Along The Yukon**...Hank Thompson
2/58	**Stairway Of Love**...Marty Robbins
5/67	**Stamp Out Loneliness**...Stonewall Jackson
8/50	**Stampede**...Roy Rogers
5/86	**Stand A Little Rain**...Nitty Gritty Dirt Band
16/61	**Stand At Your Window**...Jim Reeves
10/66	**Stand Beside Me**...Jimmy Dean
1/80	**Stand By Me**...Mickey Gilley
	Stand By My Woman Man ..see: (I'm A)
1/68	**Stand By Your Man**...Tammy Wynette
12/86	**Stand On It**...Mel McDaniel
5/85	**Stand Up**...Mel McDaniel
28/62	**Stand Up**...Ferlin Husky
14/78	**Standard Lie Number One**...Stella Parton
5/66	**Standing In The Shadows**...Hank Williams, Jr.
17/74	**Standing In Your Line**...Barbara Fairchild
19/93	**Standing Knee Deep In A River (Dying Of Thirst)**...Kathy Mattea
2/95	**Standing On The Edge Of Goodbye**...John Berry
3/94	**Standing Outside The Fire**...Garth Brooks
5/76	**Standing Room Only**...Barbara Mandrell
	Standing Tall
15/80	Billie Jo Spears
32/96	Lorrie Morgan
	Stars And Stripes On Iwo Jima
1/45	Bob Wills
4/45	Sons Of The Pioneers
30/81	**Stars On The Water**...Rodney Crowell
6/90	**Start All Over Again**...Desert Rose Band
16/78	**Starting All Over Again**...Don Gibson
17/80	**Starting Over**...Tammy Wynette
	Starting Over Again
1/80	Dolly Parton
19/96	Reba McEntire
4/86	**Starting Over Again**...Steve Wariner
2/94	**State Of Mind**...Clint Black
17/66	**Stateside**...Mel Tillis

POS/YR	RECORD TITLE/ARTIST
	Statue Of A Fool
1/69	Jack Greene
10/74	Brian Collins
2/90	Ricky Van Shelton
5/77	**Statues Without Hearts**...Larry Gatlin
	Stay A Little Longer
2/46	Bob Wills
22/73	Willie Nelson
17/82	Mel Tillis
20/75	**Stay Away From The Apple Tree**...Billie Jo Spears
8/95	**Stay Forever**...Hal Ketchum
7/70	**Stay There 'Til I Get There**...Lynn Anderson
6/79	**Stay With Me**...Dave & Sugar
40/78	**Stay With Me**...Nick Noble
1/84	**Stay Young**...Don Williams
26/79	**Steady As The Rain**...Stella Parton
9/50	**Steal Away**...Red Foley
28/77	**Stealin' Feelin'**...Mike Lunsford
F/73	**Steamroller Blues**...Elvis Presley
4/47	**Steel Guitar Rag**...Merle Travis
9/49	**Steel Guitar Ramble**...Cecil Campbell's Tennessee Ramblers
4/46	**Steel Guitar Stomp**...Hank Penny
15/66	**Steel Rail Blues**...George Hamilton IV
6/71	**Step Aside**...Faron Young
7/82	**Step Back**...Ronnie McDowell
1/81	**Step By Step**...Eddie Rabbitt
1/85	**Step That Step**...Sawyer Brown
9/80	**Steppin' Out**...Mel Tillis
1/92	**Sticks And Stones**...Tracy Lawrence
1/63	**Still**...Bill Anderson
7/79	**Still A Woman**...Margo Smith
34/65	**Still Alive In '65**...Jim Nesbitt
20/91	**Still Burnin' For You**...Rob Crosby
1/81	**Still Doin' Time**...George Jones
33/86	**Still Hurtin' Me**...Charlie Daniels Band
1/84	**Still Losing You**...Ronnie Milsap
7/74	**Still Loving You**...Bob Luman
27/63	**Still Loving You**...Clyde Beavers
3/83	**Still Taking Chances**...Michael Martin Murphey
11/77	**Still The One**...Bill Anderson
4/75	**Still Thinkin' 'Bout You**...Billy "Crash" Craddock
5/88	**Still Within The Sound Of My Voice**...Glen Campbell
7/57	**Stolen Moments**...Hank Snow

POS/YR	RECORD TITLE/ARTIST
3/74	**Stomp Them Grapes**...Mel Tillis
	(Stompin' Grapes And Gettin' Silly) ..see: **Me And Millie**
40/94	**Stone Cold Country**...Gibson/Miller Band
19/75	**Stoned At The Jukebox**...Hank Williams, Jr.
31/72	**Stonin' Around**...Dick Curless
8/58	**Stood Up**...Ricky Nelson
	Stop And Smell The Roses
29/74	Henson Cargill
40/74	Mac Davis
26/64	**Stop Me**...Bill Phillips
14/94	**Stop On A Dime**...Little Texas
28/88	**Stop The Rain**...Shenandoah
15/66	**Stop The Start (Of Tears In My Heart)**...Johnny Dollar
13/68	**Stop The Sun**...Bonnie Guitar
	Stop The World (And Let Me Off)
7/58	Johnnie & Jack
16/65	Waylon Jennings
18/74	Susan Raye
16/67	**Storm, The**...Jim Reeves
33/94	**Storm In The Heartland**...Billy Ray Cyrus
	Storms Never Last
17/75	Dottsy
17/81	Waylon & Jessi
25/74	**Storms Of Troubled Times**...Ray Price
21/78	**Stormy Weather**...Stella Parton
33/80	**Story Behind The Story**...Big Al Downing
10/90	**Story Of Love**...Desert Rose Band
1/58	**Story Of My Life**...Marty Robbins
16/60	**Straight A's In Love**...Johnny Cash
37/68	**Straight Life**...Bobby Goldsboro
1/92	**Straight Tequila Night**...John Anderson
1/87	**Straight To The Heart**...Crystal Gayle
1/44	**Straighten Up And Fly Right**...King Cole Trio
26/79	**Stranded On A Dead End Street**...ETC Band
	Strange Little Girl
5/51	Cowboy Copas
9/51	Red Foley & Ernest Tubb
9/51	Tennessee Ernie Ford
4/76	**Stranger**...Johnny Duncan
26/68	**Stranger In A Strange, Strange City**...Webb Pierce
5/83	**Stranger In My House**...Ronnie Milsap
27/71	**Stranger In My Place**...Anne Murray
2/90	**Stranger Things Have Happened**...Ronnie Milsap
27/59	**Stranger To Me**...Don Gibson

POS/YR	RECORD TITLE/ARTIST
17/63	**Stranger Was Here**...Darrell McCall
	Strangers ..see: **(From Now On All My Friends Are Gonna Be)**
7/88	**Strangers Again**...Holly Dunn
40/69	**Strawberry Farms**...Tom T. Hall
3/74	**Streak, The**...Ray Stevens
9/70	**Street Singer**...Merle Haggard
25/83	**Street Talk**...Kathy Mattea
1/88	**Streets Of Bakersfield**...Dwight Yoakam & Buck Owens
5/66	**Streets Of Baltimore**...Bobby Bare
29/69	**Strings**...Wynn Stewart
1/88	**Strong Enough To Bend**...Tanya Tucker
1/86	**Strong Heart**...T.G. Sheppard
15/83	**Strong Weakness**...Bellamy Brothers
27/64	**Stronger Than Dirt**...Glenn Barber
24/84	**Stuck On You**...Lionel Richie
27/60	**Stuck On You**...Elvis Presley
19/82	**Stuck Right In The Middle Of Your Love**...Billy Swan
6/62	**Success**...Loretta Lynn
7/69	**Such A Fool**...Roy Drusky
F/77	**Sugar Coated Love**...Freddy Fender
1/80	**Sugar Daddy**...Bellamy Brothers
	Sugar Foot ..see: **Sugarfoot**
38/70	**Sugar In The Flowers**...Anthony Armstrong Jones
27/64	**Sugar Lump**...Sonny James
1/47	**Sugar Moon**...Bob Wills
32/70	**Sugar Shack**...Bobby G. Rice
	Sugarfoot Rag
4/50	Red Foley
12/80	Jerry Reed
37/73	**Sugarman**...Peggy Little
21/63	**Sukiyaki**...Clyde Beavers
39/66	**Summer Roses**...Ned Miller
34/64	**Summer Skies And Golden Sands**...Jimmy "C" Newman
2/88	**Summer Wind**...Desert Rose Band
1/95	**Summer's Comin'**...Clint Black
1/94	**Summertime Blues**...Alan Jackson
13/76	**Sun Comin' Up**...Nat Stuckey
30/65	**Sun Glasses**...Skeeter Davis
32/76	**Sunday Afternoon Boatride In The Park On The Lake**...R.W. Blackwood
3/50	**Sunday Down In Tennessee**...Red Foley
1/89	**Sunday In The South**...Shenandoah
5/88	**Sunday Kind Of Love**...Reba McEntire

POS/YR	RECORD TITLE/ARTIST
38/71	**Sunday Morning Christian**...Harlan Howard
1/70	**Sunday Morning Coming Down**...Johnny Cash
29/76	**Sunday School To Broadway**...Sammi Smith
6/73	**Sunday Sunrise**...Brenda Lee
13/74	**Sundown**...Gordon Lightfoot
18/68	**Sundown Mary**...Billy Walker
4/77	**Sunflower**...Glen Campbell
12/61	**Sunny Tennessee**...Cowboy Copas
	Sunset Town ..see: Midnight Girl
35/80	**Sunshine**...Juice Newton
1/73	**Super Kind Of Woman**...Freddie Hart
14/86	**Super Love**...Exile
37/72	**Super Sideman**...Kenny Price
1/73	**Superman**...Donna Fargo
33/74	**Superskirt**...Connie Cato
5/82	**Sure Feels Like Love**...Gatlin Bros.
11/55	**Sure Fire Kisses**...Justin Tubb - Goldie Hill
3/93	**Sure Love**...Hal Ketchum
8/88	**Sure Thing**...Foster & Lloyd
15/80	**Sure Thing**...Freddie Hart
34/64	**Surely**...Warner Mack
5/81	**Surround Me With Love**...Charly McClain
15/75	**Susan When She Tried**...Statler Brothers
20/87	**Susannah**...Tom Wopat
4/48	**Suspicion**...Tex Williams
	Suspicion
33/72	Bobby G. Rice
27/88	Ronnie McDowell
1/79	**Suspicions**...Eddie Rabbitt
	Suspicious Minds
25/70	Waylon Jennings & Jessi Colter
2/76	Waylon & Jessi
35/92	Dwight Yoakam
26/64	**Sweet Adorable You**...Eddy Arnold
40/73	**Sweet Becky Walker**...Larry Gatlin
40/70	**Sweet Caroline**...Anthony Armstrong Jones
22/68	**Sweet Child Of Sunshine**...Jerry Wallace
34/80	**Sweet City Woman**...Tompall/Glaser Brothers
5/84	**Sweet Country Music**...Atlanta
6/73	**Sweet Country Woman**...Johnny Duncan
1/78	**Sweet Desire**...Kendalls
7/72	**Sweet Dream Woman**...Waylon Jennings

POS/YR	RECORD TITLE/ARTIST
	Sweet Dreams
2/56	Faron Young
9/56	Don Gibson
6/61	Don Gibson
5/63	Patsy Cline
1/76	Emmylou Harris
19/79	Reba McEntire
20/78	**Sweet Fantasy**...Bobby Borchers
3/61	**Sweet Lips**...Webb Pierce
37/87	**Sweet Little '66**...Steve Earle & The Dukes
39/78	**Sweet Love Feelings**...Jerry Reed
23/72	**Sweet, Love Me Good Woman**...Tompall/Glaser Brothers
3/74	**Sweet Magnolia Blossom**...Billy "Crash" Craddock
10/79	**Sweet Melinda**...Randy Barlow
	Sweet Memories
32/69	Dottie West & Don Gibson
4/79	Willie Nelson
	Sweet Misery
16/67	Jimmy Dean
14/71	Ferlin Husky
9/77	**Sweet Music Man**...Kenny Rogers
40/80	**Sweet Red Wine**...Gary Morris
2/68	**Sweet Rosie Jones**...Buck Owens & Buddy Alan
25/76	**Sweet Sensuous Feelings**...Sue Richards
8/80	**Sweet Sexy Eyes**...Cristy Lane
4/44	**Sweet Slumber**...Lucky Millinder
7/79	**Sweet Summer Lovin'**...Dolly Parton
7/75	**Sweet Surrender**...John Denver
18/65	**Sweet, Sweet Judy**...David Houston
8/78	**Sweet, Sweet Smile**...Carpenters
23/76	**Sweet Talkin' Man**...Lynn Anderson
4/66	**Sweet Thang**...Nat Stuckey
8/69	**Sweet Thang And Cisco**...Nat Stuckey
26/69	**Sweet Wine**...Johnny Carver
12/82	**Sweet Yesterday**...Sylvia
8/86	**Sweeter And Sweeter**...Statler Brothers
22/84	**Sweeter Love (I'll Never Know)**...Brenda Lee
	Sweeter Than The Flowers
3/48	Moon Mullican
12/48	Shorty Long/The Santa Fe Rangers
12/76	**Sweetest Gift**...Linda Ronstadt & Emmylou Harris
25/91	**Sweetest Thing**...Carlene Carter
1/82	**Sweetest Thing (I've Ever Known)**...Juice Newton
11/69	**Sweetheart Of The Year**...Ray Price

POS/YR	RECORD TITLE/ARTIST
11/48	**Sweetheart, You Done Me Wrong**...Bill Monroe
20/61	**Sweethearts Again**...Bob Gallion
19/63	**Sweethearts In Heaven**...Buck Owens & Rose Maddox
1/83	**Swingin'**...John Anderson
5/66	**Swinging Doors**...Merle Haggard
12/72	**Sylvia's Mother**...Bobby Bare

T

	T For Texas
5/63	Grandpa Jones
36/76	Tompall & His Outlaw Band
7/94	**T.L.C. A.S.A.P.**...Alabama
30/63	**Tadpole**...Tillman Franks
8/51	**Tailor Made Woman**...Tennessee Ernie & Joe "Fingers" Carr
5/54	**Tain't Nice (To Talk Like That)**...Carlisles
8/70	**Take A Letter Maria**...Anthony Armstrong Jones
6/63	**Take A Letter, Miss Gray**...Justin Tubb
31/69	**Take A Little Good Will Home**...Bobby Goldsboro & Del Reeves
2/92	**Take A Little Trip**...Alabama
7/49	**Take An Old Cold 'Tater (And Wait)**...Jimmie Dickens
	Take Good Care Of Her
1/66	Sonny James
F/74	Elvis Presley
40/83	**Take It All**...Rich Landers
5/93	**Take It Back**...Reba McEntire
17/81	**Take It Easy**...Crystal Gayle
21/94	**Take It Easy**...Travis Tritt
10/92	**Take It Like A Man**...Michelle Wright
8/83	**Take It To The Limit**...Waylon & Willie
	Take Me
8/66	George Jones
9/72	George Jones & Tammy Wynette
31/68	**Take Me Along With You**...Van Trevor
2/94	**Take Me As I Am**...Faith Hill
	Take Me As I Am (Or Let Me Go)
8/68	Ray Price
34/76	Mack White
28/81	Bobby Bare
24/79	**Take Me Back**...Charly McClain
1/82	**Take Me Down**...Alabama
5/74	**Take Me Home To Somewhere**...Joe Stampley
	Take Me In Your Arms And Hold Me
1/50	Eddy Arnold
10/80	Jim Reeves/Deborah Allen
(also see: I'll Hold You In My Heart)	
25/80	**Take Me, Take Me**...Rosanne Cash
10/82	**Take Me To The Country**...Mel McDaniel
5/80	**Take Me To Your Lovin' Place**...Gatlin Bros.
1/68	**Take Me To Your World**...Tammy Wynette
7/76	**Take My Breath Away**...Margo Smith
8/71	**Take My Hand**...Mel Tillis & Sherry Bryce
38/68	**Take My Hand For Awhile**...George Hamilton IV
15/64	**Take My Ring Off Your Finger**...Carl Smith
34/69	**Take Off Time**...Claude Gray
13/55	**Take Possession**...Jean Shepard
10/87	**Take The Long Way Home**...John Schneider
	Take These Chains From My Heart
1/53	Hank Williams
17/94	Lee Roy Parnell Featuring Brooks & Dunn
1/78	**Take This Job And Shove It**...Johnny Paycheck
7/62	**Take Time**...Webb Pierce
10/73	**Take Time To Love Her**...Nat Stuckey
2/92	**Take Your Memory With You**...Vince Gill
5/70	**Taker, The**...Waylon Jennings
33/79	**Takes A Fool To Love A Fool**...Burton Cummings
2/81	**Takin' It Easy**...Lacy J. Dalton
12/80	**Taking Somebody With Me When I Fall**...Gatlin Bros.
14/70	**Talk About The Good Times**...Jerry Reed
1/63	**Talk Back Trembling Lips**...Ernest Ashworth
26/66	**Talk Me Some Sense**...Bobby Bare
	Talk To Me
13/78	Freddy Fender
1/83	Mickey Gilley
35/82	**Talk To Me Loneliness**...Cindy Hurt
16/58	**Talk To Me Lonesome Heart**...James O'Gwynn
3/52	**Talk To Your Heart**...Ray Price
16/88	**Talkin' To Myself Again**...Tammy Wynette
8/57	**Talkin' To The Blues**...Jim Lowe
4/87	**Talkin' To The Moon**...Gatlin Bros.
	Talkin' To The Wall
3/66	Warner Mack
7/74	Lynn Anderson
4/88	**Talkin' To The Wrong Man**...Michael Martin Murphey/Ryan Murphey

POS/YR	RECORD TITLE/ARTIST
	Tennessee Polka
3/49	Pee Wee King
4/49	Red Foley
1/80	**Tennessee River**...Alabama
9/82	**Tennessee Rose**...Emmylou Harris
	Tennessee Saturday Night
1/49	Red Foley
11/49	Johnny Bond
5/59	**Tennessee Stud**...Eddy Arnold
12/49	**Tennessee Tears**...Pee Wee King
	Tennessee Waltz
3/48	Cowboy Copas
3/48	Pee Wee King
12/48	Roy Acuff
2/51	Patti Page
6/51	Pee Wee King
18/80	Lacy J. Dalton
2/83	**Tennessee Whiskey**...George Jones
6/53	**Tennessee Wig Walk**...Bonnie Lou
31/80	**Tequila Sheila**...Bobby Bare
8/95	**Tequila Talkin'**...Lonestar
	Texarkana Baby
1/48	Eddy Arnold
15/48	Bob Wills
36/76	**Texas**...Charlie Daniels Band
35/76	**Texas - 1947**...Johnny Cash
31/77	**Texas Angel**...Jacky Ward
3/44	**Texas Blues**...Foy Willing
26/80	**Texas Bound And Flyin'**...Jerry Reed
23/81	**Texas Cowboy Night**...Mel Tillis & Nancy Sinatra
18/88	**Texas In 1880**...Foster & Lloyd
9/80	**Texas In My Rear View Mirror**...Mac Davis
2/46	**Texas Playboy Rag**...Bob Wills
9/81	**Texas State Of Mind**...David Frizzell & Shelly West
22/93	**Texas Tattoo**...Gibson/Miller Band
1/95	**Texas Tornado**...Tracy Lawrence
5/79	**Texas (When I Die)**...Tanya Tucker
34/76	**Texas Woman**...Pat Boone
1/81	**Texas Women**...Hank Williams, Jr.
6/70	**Thank God And Greyhound**...Roy Clark
3/83	**Thank God For Kids**...Oak Ridge Boys
1/84	**Thank God For The Radio**...Kendalls
1/93	**Thank God For You**...Sawyer Brown
1/75	**Thank God I'm A Country Boy**...John Denver
10/76	**Thank God I've Got You**...Statler Brothers
11/77	**Thank God She's Mine**...Freddie Hart
33/80	**Thank You, Ever-Lovin'**...Kenny Dale

POS/YR	RECORD TITLE/ARTIST
21/73	**Thank You For Being You**...Mel Tillis
8/54	**Thank You For Calling**...Billy Walker
35/73	**Thank You For Touching My Life**...Tony Douglas
17/66	**Thank You Ma'am**...Ray Pillow
31/74	**Thank You World**...Statler Brothers
24/75	**Thanks**...Bill Anderson
3/63	**Thanks A Lot**...Ernest Tubb
12/59	**Thanks A Lot**...Johnny Cash
40/68	**Thanks A Lot For Tryin' Anyway**...Liz Anderson
17/88	**Thanks Again**...Ricky Skaggs
29/72	**Thanks For The Mem'ries**...Barbara Fairchild
20/65	**That Ain't All**...John D. Loudermilk
3/95	**That Ain't My Truck**...Rhett Akins
1/94	**That Ain't No Way To Go**...Brooks & Dunn
22/72	**That Certain One**...Tommy Cash
10/54	**That Crazy Mambo Thing**...Hank Snow
1/55	**That Do Make It Nice**...Eddy Arnold
11/74	**That Girl Who Waits On Tables**...Ronnie Milsap
1/52	**That Heart Belongs To Me**...Webb Pierce
	That Hound Dog In The Window ..see: (How Much Is)
4/90	**That Just About Does It**...Vern Gosdin
11/76	**That Look In Her Eyes**...Freddie Hart
6/80	**That Lovin' You Feelin' Again**...Roy Orbison & Emmylou Harris
26/79	**That Makes Two Of Us**...Jacky Ward & Reba McEntire
21/88	**That Old Wheel**...Johnny Cash with Hank Williams, Jr.
40/95	**That Road Not Taken**...Joe Diffie
1/86	**That Rock Won't Roll**...Restless Heart
33/74	**That Same Ol' Look Of Love**...David Houston
36/69	**That See Me Later Look**...Bonnie Guitar
2/74	**That Song Is Driving Me Crazy**...Tom T. Hall
1/93	**That Summer**...Garth Brooks
1/87	**That Was A Close One**...Earl Thomas Conley
4/93	**That Was A River**...Collin Raye
1/77	**That Was Yesterday**...Donna Fargo
9/48	**That Wild And Wicked Look In Your Eye**...Ernest Tubb
27/76	**That'll Be The Day**...Linda Ronstadt
37/67	**That'll Be The Day**...Statler Brothers
2/69	**That's A No No**...Lynn Anderson

POS/YR	RECORD TITLE/ARTIST
12/56	**That's All**...Tennessee Ernie Ford
4/53	**That's All Right**...Autry Inman
7/55	**That's All Right**...Marty Robbins
34/76	**That's All She Wrote**...Ray Price
	That's All That Matters
34/64	Ray Price
1/80	Mickey Gilley
1/95	**That's As Close As I'll Get To Loving You**...Aaron Tippin
	That's How Much I Love You
2/46	Eddy Arnold
4/47	Red Foley
23/75	**That's How My Baby Builds A Fire**...Johnny Russell
9/86	**That's How You Know When Love's Right**...Nicolette Larson
10/95	**That's How You Know (When You're In Love)**...Lari White
7/95	**That's Just About Right**...BlackHawk
	That's Me Without You
4/53	Webb Pierce
9/53	Sonny James
10/94	**That's My Baby**...Lari White
6/88	**That's My Job**...Conway Twitty
5/60	**That's My Kind Of Love**...Marion Worth
1/62	**That's My Pa**...Sheb Wooley
6/94	**That's My Story**...Collin Raye
35/86	**That's One To Grow On**...Dobie Gray
9/88	**That's That**...Michael Johnson
9/53	**That's The Kind Of Love I'm Looking For**...Carl Smith
18/79	**That's The Only Way To Say Good Morning**...Ray Price
1/84	**That's The Thing About Love**...Don Williams
7/80	**That's The Way A Cowboy Rocks And Rolls**...Jacky Ward
9/58	**That's The Way I Feel**...Faron Young
14/59	**That's The Way It's Gotta Be**...Faron Young
	That's The Way Love Goes
1/74	Johnny Rodriguez
1/84	Merle Haggard
	That's The Way Love Should Be
23/75	Brian Collins
7/77	Dave & Sugar
16/76	**That's What Friends Are For**...Barbara Mandrell
24/76	**That's What I Get (For Doin' My Own Thinkin')**...Ray Griff
22/94	**That's What I Get (For Losin' You)**...Hal Ketchum

POS/YR	RECORD TITLE/ARTIST
8↑/96	**That's What I Get For Lovin' You**...Diamond Rio
10/80	**That's What I Get For Loving You**...Eddy Arnold
35/82	**That's What I Get For Thinking**...Kendalls
4/47	**That's What I Like About The West**...Tex Williams
8/92	**That's What I Like About You**...Trisha Yearwood
28/58	**That's What I Tell My Heart**...Bob Gallion
30/73	**That's What I'll Do**...Don Gibson
40/92	**That's What I'm Working On Tonight**...Dixiana
	That's What It's Like To Be Lonesome
7/59	Ray Price
12/59	Bill Anderson
7/76	**That's What Made Me Love You**...Bill Anderson & Mary Lou Turner
	That's What Makes The Juke Box Play
6/55	Jimmy Work
11/78	Moe Bandy
33/64	**That's What Makes The World Go Around**...Claude King
8/78	**That's What You Do To Me**...Charly McClain
10/85	**(That's What You Do) When You're In Love**...Forester Sisters
9/66	**(That's What You Get) For Lovin' Me**...Waylon Jennings
5/88	**That's What Your Love Does To Me**...Holly Dunn
9/68	**That's When I See The Blues (In Your Pretty Brown Eyes)**...Jim Reeves
6/75	**That's When My Woman Begins**...Tommy Overstreet
3/70	**That's When She Started To Stop Loving You**...Conway Twitty
24/77	**That's When The Lyin' Stops (And The Lovin' Starts)**...Pal Rakes
26/65	**That's Where My Money Goes**...Webb Pierce
1/72	**That's Why I Love You Like I Do**...Sonny James
16/69	**That's Why I Love You So Much**...Ferlin Husky
25/63	**That's Why I Sing In A Honky Tonk**...Warren Smith
	That's Why I'm Walkin' ..see: (Angel On My Mind)
36/74	**That's You And Me**...Hank Snow

POS/YR	RECORD TITLE/ARTIST
13/81	**Them Good Ol' Boys Are Bad**...John Schneider
1/80	**Theme From The Dukes Of Hazzard**...Waylon Jennings
8/62	**Then A Tear Fell**...Earl Scott
4/91	**Then Again**...Alabama
4/65	**Then And Only Then**...Connie Smith
8/70	**Then He Touched Me**...Jean Shepard
2/49	**Then I Turned And Walked Slowly Away**...Eddy Arnold
	Then I'll Stop Loving You
15/54	Jim Reeves
12/64	Browns
3/87	**Then It's Love**...Don Williams
31/70	**Then She's A Lover**...Roy Clark
32/69	**Then The Baby Came**...Henson Cargill
1/75	**Then Who Am I**...Charley Pride
1/68	**Then You Can Tell Me Goodbye**...Eddy Arnold
10/71	**Then You Walk In**...Sammi Smith
25/78	**Then You'll Remember**...Sterling Whipple
10/68	**There Ain't No Easy Run**...Dave Dudley
12/84	**There Ain't No Future In This**...Reba McEntire
2/78	**There Ain't No Good Chain Gang**...Johnny Cash & Waylon Jennings
1/92	**There Ain't Nothin' Wrong With The Radio**...Aaron Tippin
17/91	**There For Awhile**...Steve Wariner
	There Goes My Everything
1/66	Jack Greene
9/71	Elvis Presley
20/94	**There Goes My Heart**...Mavericks
4/89	**There Goes My Heart Again**...Holly Dunn
15/57	**There Goes My Love**...George Morgan
8/75	**There I Said It**...Margo Smith
20/79	**There Is A Miracle In You**...Tom T. Hall
20/61	**There Must Be Another Way To Live**...Kitty Wells
25/71	**There Must Be More To Life (Than Growing Old)**...Jack Blanchard & Misty Morgan
1/70	**There Must Be More To Love Than This**...Jerry Lee Lewis
5/69	**There Never Was A Time**...Jeannie C. Riley
3/55	**There She Goes**...Carl Smith
11/77	**There She Goes Again**...Joe Stampley
24/75	**(There She Goes) I Wish Her Well**...Don Gibson

POS/YR	RECORD TITLE/ARTIST
	There Stands The Glass
1/53	Webb Pierce
34/73	Johnny Bush
1/74	**There Won't Be Anymore**...Charlie Rich
19/76	**There Won't Be No Country Music**...C.W. McCall
12/69	**There Wouldn't Be A Lonely Heart In Town**...Del Reeves
8/90	**There You Are**...Willie Nelson
1/57	**There You Go**...Johnny Cash
32/91	**There You Go**...Exile
21/61	**There'll Always Be Sadness**...Marion Worth
5/51	**(There'll Be) Peace In The Valley (For Me)**...Red Foley
	(There'll Never Be Another) Pecos Bill
13/48	Roy Rogers
15/48	Tex Ritter
3/59	**There's A Big Wheel**...Wilma Lee & Stoney Cooper
5/44	**There's A Blue Star Shining Bright**...Red Foley
11/49	**(There's A) Bluebird On Your Windowsill**...Tex Williams
4/44	**There's A Chill On The Hill Tonight**...Jimmie Davis
1/85	**(There's A) Fire In The Night**...Alabama
16/68	**There's A Fool Born Every Minute**...Skeeter Davis
	There's A Honky Tonk Angel (Who'll Take Me Back In)
1/74	Conway Twitty
6/79	Elvis Presley
	There's A New Moon Over My Shoulder
1/45	Jimmie Davis
2/45	Tex Ritter
4/72	**There's A Party Goin' On**...Jody Miller
10/75	**There's A Song On The Jukebox**...David Wills
7/70	**There's A Story (Goin' 'Round)**...Dottie West & Don Gibson
7/89	**There's A Tear In My Beer**...Hank Williams, Jr.
13/71	**There's A Whole Lot About A Woman (A Man Don't Know)**...Jack Greene
F/83	**There's All Kinds Of Smoke (In The Barroom)**...Loretta Lynn
	There's Always Me
30/79	Ray Price
35/81	Jim Reeves
17/62	**There's Always One (Who Loves A Lot)**...Roy Drusky

POS/YR	RECORD TITLE/ARTIST
18/80	**There's Another Woman**...Joe Stampley
1/51	**There's Been A Change In Me**...Eddy Arnold
20/69	**There's Better Things In Life**...Jerry Reed
21/64	**There's More Pretty Girls Than One**...George Hamilton IV
1/81	**(There's) No Gettin' Over Me**...Ronnie Milsap
7/85	**There's No Love In Tennessee**...Barbara Mandrell
1/86	**There's No Stopping Your Heart**...Marie Osmond
1/85	**There's No Way**...Alabama
6/50	**There's No Wings On My Angel**...Eddy Arnold
3/49	**There's Not A Thing (I Wouldn't Do For You)**...Eddy Arnold
21/60	**There's Not Any Like You Left**...Faron Young
9/55	**There's Poison In Your Heart**...Kitty Wells
19/71	**There's Something About A Lady**...Johnny Duncan
5/69	**These Are Not My People**...Freddy Weller
10/75	**These Days (I Barely Get By)**...George Jones
5/56	**These Hands**...Hank Snow
5/91	**These Lips Don't Know How To Say Goodbye**...Doug Stone
9/69	**These Lonely Hands Of Mine**...Mel Tillis
7/94	**They Asked About You**...Reba McEntire
6/79	**They Call It Making Love**...Tammy Wynette
12/81	**They Could Put Me In Jail**...Bellamy Brothers
32/76	**They Don't Make 'Em Like That Anymore**...Bobby Borchers
2/94	**They Don't Make 'Em Like That Anymore**...Boy Howdy
4/74	**They Don't Make 'Em Like My Daddy**...Loretta Lynn
10/69	**They Don't Make Love Like They Used To**...Eddy Arnold
19/85	**They Never Had To Get Over You**...Johnny Lee
19/80	**They Never Lost You**...Con Hunley
21/87	**They Only Come Out At Night**...Shooters
5/89	**They Rage On**...Dan Seals
1/44	**They Took The Stars Out Of Heaven**...Floyd Tillman
5/50	**They'll Never Take Her Love From Me**...Hank Williams
3/95	**They're Playin' Our Song**...Neal McCoy

POS/YR	RECORD TITLE/ARTIST
14/85	**Thing About You**...Southern Pacific
	Thing Called Love
21/68	Jimmy Dean
2/72	Johnny Cash
38/65	**Thing Called Sadness**...Ray Price
	Things
22/71	Anne Murray
25/75	Ronnie Dove
23/91	**Things Are Tough All Over**...Shelby Lynne
1/74	**Things Aren't Funny Anymore**...Merle Haggard
25/69	**Things For You And I**...Bobby Lewis
34/69	**Things Go Better With Love**...Jeannie C. Riley
9/65	**Things Have Gone To Pieces**...George Jones
31/77	**Things I Treasure**...Dorsey Burnette
18/78	**Things I'd Do For You**...Mundo Earwood
24/62	**Things That Mean The Most**...Carl Smith
36/90	**Things You Left Undone**...Matraca Berg
F/72	**Think About It Darlin'**...Jerry Lee Lewis
1/86	**Think About Love**...Dolly Parton
18/78	**Think About Me**...Freddy Fender
38/71	**Think Again**...Patti Page
26/65	**Think I'll Go Somewhere And Cry Myself To Sleep**...Charlie Louvin
1/66	**Think Of Me**...Buck Owens
21/76	**Think Summer**...Roy Clark
1/95	**Thinkin' About You**...Trisha Yearwood
1/76	**Thinkin' Of A Rendezvous**...Johnny Duncan
2/94	**Thinkin' Problem**...David Ball
9/70	**Thinking 'Bout You, Babe**...Billy Walker
	Third Rate Romance
11/75	Amazing Rhythm Aces
2/94	Sammy Kershaw
1/94	**Third Rock From The Sun**...Joe Diffie
34/70	**Third World**...Johnny & Jonie Mosby
7/55	**Thirty Days (To Come Back Home)**...Ernest Tubb
4/81	**Thirty Nine And Holding**...Jerry Lee Lewis
39/87	**3935 West End Avenue**...Mason Dixon
4/85	**This Ain't Dallas**...Hank Williams, Jr.
23/75	**(This Ain't Just Another) Lust Affair**...Mel Street
14/90	**This Ain't My First Rodeo**...Vern Gosdin
35/83	**This Cowboy's Hat**...Porter Wagoner
1/87	**This Crazy Love**...Oak Ridge Boys
8/82	**This Dream's On Me**...Gene Watson
40/69	**This Generation Shall Not Pass**...Henson Cargill

POS/YR	RECORD TITLE/ARTIST
36/77	**This Girl (Has Turned Into A Woman)**...Mary MacGregor
25/90	**This Heart**...Sweethearts Of The Rodeo
19/75	**This House Runs On Sunshine**...La Costa
39/78	**This Is A Holdup**...Ronnie McDowell
20/79	**This Is A Love Song**...Bill Anderson
1/65	**This Is It**...Jim Reeves
5/94	**This Is Me**...Randy Travis
6/95	**This Is Me Missing You**...James House
21/75	**This Is My Year For Mexico**...Crystal Gayle
30/63	**This Is The House**...Charlie Phillips
16/78	**This Is The Love**...Sonny James
3/54	**This Is The Thanks I Get (For Loving You)**...Eddy Arnold
4/58	**This Little Girl Of Mine**...Everly Brothers
5/72	**This Little Girl Of Mine**...Faron Young
2/88	**This Missin' You Heart Of Mine**...Sawyer Brown
11/72	**This Much A Man**...Marty Robbins
32/80	**This Must Be My Ship**...Carol Chase
27/66	**This Must Be The Bottom**...Del Reeves
20/70	**This Night (Ain't Fit For Nothing But Drinking)**...Dave Dudley
	This Ol' ..see: This Old
	This Old Heart
21/60	Skeets McDonald
24/60	Bobby Barnett
24/88	**This Old House**...Schuyler, Knobloch & Bickhardt
33/87	**This Ol' Town**...Lacy J. Dalton
22/60	**This Old Town**...Buddy Paul
	This Ole House
2/54	Stuart Hamblen
16/60	Wilma Lee & Stoney Cooper
7/92	**This One's Gonna Hurt You (For A Long, Long Time)**...Marty Stuart & Travis Tritt
36/68	**This One's On The House**...Jerry Wallace
13/93	**This Romeo Ain't Got Julie Yet**...Diamond Rio
11/90	**This Side Of Goodbye**...Highway 101
14/69	**This Thing**...Webb Pierce
11/95	**(This Thing Called) Wantin' And Havin' It All**...Sawyer Brown
1/74	**This Time**...Waylon Jennings
2/95	**This Time**...Sawyer Brown
30/84	**This Time**...Tom Jones
12/74	**This Time I Almost Made It**...Barbara Mandrell
20/77	**This Time I'm In It For The Love**...Tommy Overstreet

POS/YR	RECORD TITLE/ARTIST
1/76	**This Time I've Hurt Her More Than She Loves Me**...Conway Twitty
7/64	**This White Circle On My Finger**...Kitty Wells
5/89	**This Woman**...K.T. Oslin
1/95	**This Woman And This Man**...Clay Walker
12/48	**This World Can't Stand Long**...Roy Acuff
27/67	**This World Holds Nothing (Since You're Gone)**...Stonewall Jackson
4/46	**Tho' I Tried (I Can't Forget You)**...Wesley Tuttle
10/48	**Thorn In My Heart**...Bob Wills
5/87	**Those Memories Of You**...Dolly Parton, Linda Ronstadt, Emmylou Harris
9/63	**Those Wonderful Years**...Webb Pierce
14/54	**Thou Shalt Not Steal**...Kitty Wells
16/61	**Thoughts Of A Fool**...Ernest Tubb
6/59	**Thousand Miles Ago**...Webb Pierce
2/93	**Thousand Miles From Nowhere**...Dwight Yoakam
16↑/96	**Thousand Times A Day**...Patty Loveless
8/65	**Three A.M.**...Bill Anderson
	Three Bells
1/59	Browns
29/69	Jim Ed Brown
31/80	**3 Chord Country Song**...Red Steagall
7/62	**Three Days**...Faron Young
2/61	**Three Hearts In A Tangle**...Roy Drusky
39/68	**Three Playing Love**...Cheryl Poole
37/83	**3/4 Time**...Ray Charles
20/78	**Three Sheets In The Wind**...Jacky Ward & Reba McEntire
30/63	**Three Sheets In The Wind**...Johnny Bond
32/68	**Three Six Packs, Two Arms And A Juke Box**...Johnny Sea
9/61	**Three Steps To The Phone (Millions of Miles)**...George Hamilton IV
1/87	**Three Time Loser**...Dan Seals
	Three Times A Lady
23/78	Nate Harvell
7/84	Conway Twitty
4/47	**Three Times Seven**...Merle Travis
7/52	**Three Ways Of Knowing**...Johnnie & Jack
7/57	**Three Ways (To Love You)**...Kitty Wells
25/95	**Three Words, Two Hearts, One Night**...Mark Collie
14/61	**Through That Door**...Ernest Tubb
31/64	**Through The Eyes Of A Fool**...Roy Clark
27/67	**Through The Eyes Of Love**...Tompall/Glaser Brothers
5/82	**Through The Years**...Kenny Rogers

POS/YR	RECORD TITLE/ARTIST
3/50	Throw Your Love My Way...Ernest Tubb
1/91	Thunder Rolls...Garth Brooks
33/76	Thunderstorms...Cal Smith
22/68	Tie A Tiger Down...Sheb Wooley
	Tie A Yellow Ribbon ..see: Yellow Ribbon
29/63	Tie My Hunting Dog Down, Jed...Arthur "Guitar Boogie" Smith
17/86	Tie Our Love (In a Double Knot)...Dolly Parton
24/82	Tie Your Dream To Mine...Marty Robbins
4/75	Ties That Bind...Don Williams
15/65	Tiger In My Tank...Jim Nesbitt
6/65	Tiger Woman...Claude King
1/81	Tight Fittin' Jeans...Conway Twitty
13/90	'Til A Tear Becomes A Rose...Keith Whitley & Lorrie Morgan
	'Til I Can Make It On My Own
1/76	Tammy Wynette
3/79	Kenny Rogers & Dottie West
	'Til I Can't Take It Anymore
31/77	Pal Rakes
2/90	Billy Joe Royal
1/83	'Til I Gain Control Again...Crystal Gayle
1/73	'Til I Get It Right...Tammy Wynette
	('Til) I Kissed You
8/59	Everly Brothers
10/76	Connie Smith
10/86	Til I Loved You...Restless Heart
22/92	Til I'm Holding You Again...Pirates Of The Mississippi
4/89	'Til Love Comes Again...Reba McEntire
1/76	Til The Rivers All Run Dry...Don Williams
39/83	Til You And Your Lover Are Lovers Again...Engelbert Humperdinck
4/89	'Til You Cry...Eddy Raven
12/91	Till I Found You...Marty Stuart
39/90	Till I See You Again...Kevin Welch
24/80	Till I Stop Shaking...Billy "Crash" Craddock
7/53	Till I Waltz Again With You...Tommy Sosebee
6/87	Till I'm Too Old To Die Young...Moe Bandy
32/66	Till My Getup Has Gotup And Gone...Ernest Tubb
7/77	Till The End...Vern Gosdin
	Till The End Of The World
4/49	Ernest Tubb
9/49	Jimmy Wakely
12/49	Johnny Bond
10/52	Bing Crosby & Grady Martin

POS/YR	RECORD TITLE/ARTIST
8/73	'Till The Water Stops Runnin'...Billy "Crash" Craddock
2/95	Till You Love Me...Reba McEntire
17/91	Till You Were Gone...Mike Reid
1/82	'Till You're Gone...Barbara Mandrell
28/84	Till Your Memory's Gone...Bill Medley
13/64	Timber I'm Falling...Ferlin Husky
1/89	Timber, I'm Falling In Love...Patty Loveless
10/60	Timbrook...Lewis Pruitt
2/85	Time Don't Run Out On Me...Anne Murray
39/90	Time For Me To Fly...Dolly Parton
14/55	Time Goes By...Marty Robbins
23/92	Time Has Come...Martina McBride
17/87	Time In...Oak Ridge Boys
1/96	Time Marches On...Tracy Lawrence
7/91	Time Passes By...Kathy Mattea
17/66	Time To Bum Again...Waylon Jennings
6/45	Time Won't Heal My Broken Heart...Ted Daffan
26/90	Time's Up...Southern Pacific & Carlene Carter
5/88	Timeless And True Love...McCarters
30/65	Times Are Gettin' Hard...Bobby Bare
25/65	Tiny Blue Transistor Radio...Connie Smith
24/67	Tiny Tears...Liz Anderson
	Tip Of My Fingers
7/60	Bill Anderson
10/63	Roy Clark
3/66	Eddy Arnold
16/75	Jean Shepard
3/92	Steve Wariner
2/66	Tippy Toeing...Harden Trio
	'Tis Sweet To Be Remembered
8/52	Cowboy Copas
9/52	Flatt & Scruggs
15/62	To A Sleeping Beauty...Jimmy Dean
1/84	To All The Girls I've Loved Before...Julio Iglesias & Willie Nelson
1/96	To Be Loved By You...Wynonna Judd
35/85	To Be Lovers...Chance
34/91	To Be With You...Larry Boone
3/78	To Daddy...Emmylou Harris
12/72	To Get To You...Jerry Wallace
	To Know Him Is To Love Him
18/72	Jody Miller
1/87	Dolly Parton, Linda Ronstadt, Emmylou Harris
25/70	To Lonely, Too Long...Mel Tillis
22/77	To Love Somebody...Narvel Felts
3/69	To Make A Man (Feel Like A Man)...Loretta Lynn

POS/YR	RECORD TITLE/ARTIST
1/69	**To Make Love Sweeter For You**...Jerry Lee Lewis
3/84	**To Me**...Barbara Mandrell/Lee Greenwood
2/47	**To My Sorrow**...Eddy Arnold
	(To My Wife With Love) ..see: Mi Esposa Con Amor
1/69	**To See My Angel Cry**...Conway Twitty
13/61	**To You And Yours (From Me and Mine)**...George Hamilton IV
5/81	**Today All Over Again**...Reba McEntire
9/75	**Today I Started Loving You Again**...Sammi Smith
10/83	**Today My World Slipped Away**...Vern Gosdin
38/73	**Today Will Be The First Day Of The Rest Of My Life**...LaWanda Lindsey
3/92	**Today's Lonely Fool**...Tracy Lawrence
21/78	**Toe To Toe**...Freddie Hart
	Together Again
1/64	Buck Owens
1/76	Emmylou Harris
19/84	Kenny Rogers & Dottie West
14/72	**Together Always**...Porter Wagoner & Dolly Parton
	Togetherness
24/68	Freddie Hart
12/70	Buck Owens & Susan Raye
36/70	**Tom Green County Fair**...Roger Miller
1/86	**Tomb Of The Unknown Love**...Kenny Rogers
5/65	**Tombstone Every Mile**...Dick Curless
9/70	**Tomorrow Is Forever**...Porter Wagoner & Dolly Parton
	Tomorrow Never Comes
3/45	Ernest Tubb
27/70	Slim Whitman
	Tomorrow Night
24/59	Carl Smith
29/73	Charlie Rich
11/71	**Tomorrow Night In Baltimore**...Roger Miller
5/78	**Tonight**...Barbara Mandrell
1/67	**Tonight Carmen**...Marty Robbins
4/93	**Tonight I Climbed The Wall**...Alan Jackson
26/76	**Tonight I'll Face The Man (Who Made It Happen)**...Kenny Starr
31/66	**Tonight I'm Coming Home**...Buddy Cagle
38/82	**Tonight I'm Feeling You (All Over Again)**...Jack Grayson
19/84	**Tonight I'm Here With Someone Else**...Karen Brooks

POS/YR	RECORD TITLE/ARTIST
30/80	**Tonight Let's Sleep On It Baby**...Mel Street
10/72	**Tonight My Baby's Coming Home**...Barbara Mandrell
6/79	**Tonight She's Gonna Love Me (Like There Was No Tomorrow)**...Razzy Bailey
12/74	**Tonight Someone's Falling In Love**...Johnny Carver
20/94	**(Tonight We Just Might) Fall In Love Again**...Hal Ketchum
26/86	**Tonight We Ride**...Michael Martin Murphey
30/77	**Tonight You Belong To Me**...Dottie West
28/78	**Tonight's The Night (It's Gonna Be Alright)**...Roy Head
32/80	**Tony's Tank-Up, Drive-In Cafe**...Hank Thompson
1/93	**Too Busy Being In Love**...Doug Stone
3/90	**Too Cold At Home**...Mark Chesnutt
	Too Far Gone
12/73	Joe Stampley
13/79	Emmylou Harris
1/88	**Too Gone Too Long**...Randy Travis
4/84	**Too Good To Stop Now**...Mickey Gilley
10/83	**Too Hot To Sleep**...Louise Mandrell
22/63	**Too In Love**...Hank Thompson
15/84	**Too Late To Go Home**...Johnny Rodriguez
9/64	**Too Late To Try Again**...Carl Butler & Pearl
	Too Late To Worry, Too Blue To Cry
1/44	Al Dexter
3/44	Texas Jim Lewis
6/75	Ronnie Milsap
28/81	**Too Long Gone**...Vern Gosdin
40/82	**Too Many Hearts In The Fire**...Bobby Smith
1/81	**Too Many Lovers**...Crystal Gayle
21/73	**Too Many Memories**...Bobby Lewis
29/78	**Too Many Nights Alone**...Bobby Bare
5/87	**Too Many Rivers**...Forester Sisters
26/65	**Too Many Tigers**...Tex Williams
2/86	**Too Many Times**...Earl Thomas Conley & Anita Pointer
10/61	**Too Many Times**...Don Winters
3/57	**Too Much**...Elvis Presley
36/92	**Too Much**...Pirates Of The Mississippi
4/96	**Too Much Fun**...Daryle Singletary
1/86	**Too Much Is Not Enough**...Bellamy Brothers/The Forester Sisters
18/77	**Too Much Is Not Enough**...Billie Jo Spears
8/73	**Too Much Monkey Business**...Freddy Weller
25/89	**Too Much Month At The End Of The Money**...Billy Hill

POS/YR	RECORD TITLE/ARTIST
28/67	**Too Much Of You**...Lynn Anderson
1/85	**Too Much On My Heart**...Statler Brothers
34/74	**Too Much Pride**...Mack White
19/60	**Too Much To Lose**...Carl Belew
13/57	**Too Much Water**...George Jones
	Too Old To Cut The Mustard
5/52	Ernest Tubb & Red Foley
6/52	Carlisles
29/72	Buck & Buddy
13/80	**Too Old To Play Cowboy**...Razzy Bailey
4/53	**Too Young To Tango**...Sunshine Ruby
2/73	**Top Of The World**...Lynn Anderson
3/77	**Torn Between Two Lovers**...Mary MacGregor
25/59	**Total Strangers**...Hank Thompson
1/85	**Touch A Hand, Make A Friend**...Oak Ridge Boys
5/88	**Touch And Go Crazy**...Lee Greenwood
15/58	**Touch And Go Heart**...Kitty Wells
7/62	**Touch Me**...Willie Nelson
	Touch Me (I'll Be Your Fool Once More)
18/79	Big Al Downing
4/83	Tom Jones
1/86	**Touch Me When We're Dancing**...Alabama
15/79	**Touch Me With Magic**...Marty Robbins
3/66	**Touch My Heart**...Ray Price
1/75	**Touch The Hand**...Conway Twitty
6/73	**Touch The Morning**...Don Gibson
6/72	**Touch Your Woman**...Dolly Parton
3/71	**Touching Home**...Jerry Lee Lewis
	Tower Of Strength
32/75	Sue Richards
33/79	Narvel Felts
16/68	**Town That Broke My Heart**...Bobby Bare
38/67	**Town That Never Sleeps**...Charlie Walker
38/73	**Town Where You Live**...Mel Street
12/49	**Toy Heart**...Bill Monroe
30/85	**Toyko, Oklahoma**...John Anderson
30/72	**Traces**...Sonny James
25/71	**Traces Of A Woman**...Billy Walker
29/74	**Traces Of Life**...Lonzo & Oscar
11/76	**Tracks Of My Tears**...Linda Ronstadt
2/53	**Trademark**...Carl Smith
7/57	**Train Of Love**...Johnny Cash
6/87	**Train Of Memories**...Kathy Mattea
20/89	**Trainwreck Of Emotion**...Lorrie Morgan
14/48	**Tramp On The Street**...Bill Carlisle
10/93	**Trashy Women**...Confederate Railroad
29/59	**Travelin' Man**...Red Foley

POS/YR	RECORD TITLE/ARTIST
32/82	**Travelin' Man**...Jacky Ward
20/73	**Traveling Man**...Dolly Parton
33/71	**Travelin' Minstrel Man**...Bill Rice
6/51	**Travellin' Blues**...Lefty Frizzell
6/58	**Treasure Of Love**...George Jones
3↑/96	**Treat Her Right**...Sawyer Brown
12/71	**Treat Him Right**...Barbara Mandrell
18/91	**Treat Me Like A Stranger**...Baillie & The Boys
11/57	**Treat Me Nice**...Elvis Presley
16/64	**Triangle**...Carl Smith
	Triflin' Gal
2/45	Al Dexter
3/45	Walt Shrum
1/73	**Trip To Heaven**...Freddie Hart
	T-R-O-U-B-L-E
11/75	Elvis Presley
13/93	Travis Tritt
18/95	**Trouble**...Mark Chesnutt
30/65	**Trouble And Me**...Stonewall Jackson
7/56	**Trouble In Mind**...Eddy Arnold
12/64	**Trouble In My Arms**...Johnny & Jonie Mosby
1/74	**Trouble In Paradise**...Loretta Lynn
24/60	**Trouble In The Amen Corner**...Archie Campbell
5/93	**Trouble On The Line**...Sawyer Brown
4/62	**Trouble's Back In Town**...Wilburn Brothers
3/65	**Truck Drivin' Son-Of-A-Gun**...Dave Dudley
	Truck Driving Man
11/65	George Hamilton IV
29/76	Red Steagall
23/67	**Trucker's Prayer**...Dave Dudley
30/93	**True Believer**...Ronnie Milsap
9/69	**True Grit**...Glen Campbell
5/88	**True Heart**...Oak Ridge Boys
F/81	**True Life Country Music**...Razzy Bailey
4/91	**True Love**...Don Williams
32/85	**True Love**...Vince Gill
22/71	**True Love Is Greater Than Friendship**...Arlene Harden
39/86	**True Love (Never Did Run Smooth)**...Tom Wopat
1/80	**True Love Ways**...Mickey Gilley
3/66	**True Love's A Blessing**...Sonny James
23/95	**True To His Word**...Boy Howdy
35/73	**True True Lovin'**...Ferlin Husky
2/69	**Try A Little Kindness**...Glen Campbell
36/80	**Try It On**...Stephanie Winslow

POS/YR	RECORD TITLE/ARTIST
32/81	**Try Me**...Randy Barlow
2/44	**Try Me One More Time**...Ernest Tubb
14/94	**Try Not To Look So Pretty**...Dwight Yoakam
1/75	**Tryin' To Beat The Morning Home**...T.G. Sheppard
11/56	**Tryin' To Forget The Blues**...Porter Wagoner
1/94	**Tryin' To Get Over You**...Vince Gill
6/93	**Tryin' To Hide A Fire In The Dark**...Billy Dean
12/79	**Tryin' To Satisfy You**...Dottsy
30/81	**Trying Not To Love You**...Johnny Rodriguez
1/80	**Trying To Love Two Women**...Oak Ridge Boys
	Tulsa ..also see: (Don't Let the Sun Set on You)
40/83	**Tulsa Ballroom**...Dottie West
1/79	**Tulsa Time**...Don Williams
10/80	**Tumbleweed**...Sylvia
11/48	**Tumbling Tumbleweeds**...Sons Of The Pioneers
	Tupelo County Jail
7/58	Webb Pierce
40/66	Stonemans
15/68	**Tupelo Mississippi Flash**...Jerry Reed
9/56	**Turn Her Down**...Faron Young
1/88	**Turn It Loose**...Judds
11/91	**Turn It On, Turn It Up, Turn Me Loose**...Dwight Yoakam
39/84	**Turn Me Loose**...Vince Gill
27/89	**Turn Of The Century**...Nitty Gritty Dirt Band
29/74	**Turn On Your Light (And Let It Shine)**...Kenny Price
1/75	**(Turn Out The Light And) Love Me Tonight**...Don Williams
4/92	**Turn That Radio On**...Ronnie Milsap
1/67	**Turn The World Around**...Eddy Arnold
17/72	**Turn Your Radio On**...Ray Stevens
F/72	**Turnin' Off A Memory**...Merle Haggard
1/84	**Turning Away**...Crystal Gayle
17/66	**Twelfth Of Never**...Slim Whitman
10/74	**Twentieth Century Drifter**...Marty Robbins
11/56	**Twenty Feet Of Muddy Water**...Sonny James
2/87	**Twenty Years Ago**...Kenny Rogers
35/81	**20/20 Hindsight**...Billy Larkin
18/77	**Twenty-Four Hours From Tulsa**...Randy Barlow
13/61	**Twenty-Fourth Hour**...Ray Price

POS/YR	RECORD TITLE/ARTIST
1/88	**Twinkle, Twinkle Lucky Star**...Merle Haggard
	Two Brothers ..see: Ballad Of
3/84	**Two Car Garage**...B.J. Thomas
8/49	**Two Cents, Three Eggs And A Postcard**...Red Foley
3/77	**Two Dollars In The Jukebox**...Eddie Rabbitt
	Two Doors Down
7/78	Zella Lehr
F/78	Dolly Parton
1/89	**Two Dozen Roses**...Shenandoah
11/54	**Two Glasses, Joe**...Ernest Tubb
39/74	**Two Gun Daddy**...Marty Robbins
F/81	**Two Hearts Beat Better Than One**...Eddy Arnold
18/78	**Two Hearts Tangled In Love**...Kenny Dale
9/55	**Two Kinds Of Love**...Eddy Arnold
8/77	**Two Less Lonely People**...Rex Allen, Jr.
7/78	**Two Lonely People**...Moe Bandy
1/78	**Two More Bottles Of Wine**...Emmylou Harris
1/91	**Two Of A Kind, Workin' On A Full House**...Garth Brooks
14/85	**Two Old Cats Like Us**...Ray Charles with Hank Williams, Jr.
35/70	**Two Separate Bar Stools**...Wanda Jackson
9/57	**Two Shadows On Your Window**...Jim Reeves
15/65	**Two Six Packs Away**...Dave Dudley
2/92	**Two Sparrows In A Hurricane**...Tanya Tucker
6/79	**Two Steps Forward And Three Steps Back**...Susie Allanson
2/80	**Two Story House**...George Jones & Tammy Wynette
18/92	**Two-Timin' Me**...Remingtons
39/86	**Two Too Many**...Holly Dunn

U

POS/YR	RECORD TITLE/ARTIST
9/75	**U.S. of A**...Donna Fargo
8/58	**Uh-Huh—mm**...Sonny James
F/57	**Uh, Uh, No**...George Jones
1/91	**Unanswered Prayers**...Garth Brooks
29/73	**Unbelievable Love**...Jim Ed Brown
	Unchained Melody
6/78	Elvis Presley
26/91	Ronnie McDowell

POS/YR	RECORD TITLE/ARTIST
	Uncle Pen
14/56	Porter Wagoner
1/84	Ricky Skaggs
4/77	**Uncloudy Day**...Willie Nelson
27/91	**Unconditional Love**...Glen Campbell
18/62	**Under Cover Of The Night**...Dave Dudley
24/88	**Under The Boardwalk**...Lynn Anderson
2/61	**Under The Influence Of Love**...Buck Owens
	Under Your Spell Again
4/59	Buck Owens
5/59	Ray Price
39/71	Waylon Jennings & Jessi Colter
28/78	**Undercover Lovers**...Stella Parton
26/64	**Understand Your Gal**...Margie Bowes
1/64	**Understand Your Man**...Johnny Cash
10/68	**Undo The Right**...Johnny Bush
23/72	**Unexpected Goodbye**...Glenn Barber
8/50	**Unfaithful One**...Ernest Tubb
32/83	**Unfinished Business**...Lloyd David Foster
18/63	**Unkind Words**...Kathy Dee
14/48	**Unloved And Unclaimed**...Roy Acuff
5/62	**Unloved Unwanted**...Kitty Wells
7/66	**Unmitigated Gall**...Faron Young
4/94	**Untanglin' My Mind**...Clint Black
10/55	**Untied**...Tommy Collins
1/86	**Until I Met You**...Judy Rodman
F/56	**Until I Met You**...Faron Young
1/69	**Until My Dreams Come True**...Jack Greene
39/80	**Until The Bitter End**...Kenny Seratt
39/74	**Until The End Of Time**...Narvel Felts & Sharon Vaughn
20/60	**Until Today**...Elmer Snodgrass
4/88	**Untold Stories**...Kathy Mattea
14/72	**Untouched**...Mel Tillis
6/51	**Unwanted Sign Upon Your Heart**...Hank Snow
6/81	**Unwound**...George Strait
9/89	**Up And Gone**...McCarters
	Up To Heaven ..see: (You Lift Me)
28/75	**Uproar**...Anne Murray
10/95	**Upstairs Downtown**...Toby Keith
40/69	**Upstairs In The Bedroom**...Bobby Wright
25/74	**Uptown Poker Club**...Jerry Reed
7/67	**Urge For Going**...George Hamilton IV
3/85	**Used To Blue**...Sawyer Brown

POS/YR	RECORD TITLE/ARTIST
	V
15/69	**Vance**...Roger Miller
7/76	**Vaya Con Dios**...Freddy Fender
30/77	**Vegas**...Bobby & Jeannie Bare
9/83	**Velvet Chains**...Gary Morris
5/82	**Very Best Is You**...Charly McClain
1/74	**Very Special Love Song**...Charlie Rich
40/84	**Victim Of Life's Circumstances**...Vince Gill
34/82	**Victim Or A Fool**...Rodney Crowell
24/84	**Victims Of Goodbye**...Sylvia
12/66	**Viet Nam Blues**...Dave Dudley
21/67	**Vin Rose**...Stu Phillips
	Violet And A Rose
24/58	Mel Tillis
10/62	"Little" Jimmy Dickens
36/64	Wanda Jackson
22/77	**Virginia, How Far Will You Go**...Dickey Lee
26/66	**Volkswagen**...Ray Pillow
22/63	**Volunteer, The**...Autry Inman
8/89	**Vows Go Unbroken (Always True To You)**...Kenny Rogers
	W
12/55	**Wait A Little Longer Please, Jesus**...Carl Smith
F/57	**Waitin' For A Train**...Jim Reeves
39/92	**Waitin' For The Deal To Go Down**...Dixiana
12/58	**Waitin' In School**...Ricky Nelson
1/66	**Waitin' In Your Welfare Line**...Buck Owens
25/64	**Waiting A Lifetime**...Webb Pierce
11/71	**Waiting For A Train (All Around The Watertank)**...Jerry Lee Lewis
3/52	**Waiting In The Lobby Of Your Heart**...Hank Thompson
14/74	**Wake Me Into Love**...Bud Logan & Wilma Burgess
21/70	**Wake Me Up Early In The Morning**...Bobby Lord
1/54	**Wake Up, Irene**...Hank Thompson
(also see: Goodnight Irene)	
37/73	**Wake Up, Jacob**...Porter Wagoner
1/57	**Wake Up Little Susie**...Everly Brothers
2/91	**Walk, The**...Sawyer Brown
28/87	**Walk Me In The Rain**...Girls Next Door

POS/YR	RECORD TITLE/ARTIST
7/63	**Walk Me To The Door**...Ray Price
2/90	**Walk On**...Reba McEntire
30/83	**Walk On**...Karen Brooks
1/61	**Walk On By**...Leroy Van Dyke
1/91	**Walk On Faith**...Mike Reid
5/68	**Walk On Out Of My Mind**...Waylon Jennings
9/61	**Walk Out Backwards**...Bill Anderson
4/78	**Walk Right Back**...Anne Murray
23/63	**Walk Right In**...Rooftop Singers
7/76	**Walk Softly**...Billy "Crash" Craddock
11/73	**Walk Softly On The Bridges**...Mel Street
25/89	**Walk Softly On This Heart Of Mine**...Kentucky Headhunters
10/65	**Walk Tall**...Faron Young
10/86	**Walk The Way The Wind Blows**...Kathy Mattea
1/67	**Walk Through This World With Me**...George Jones
30/70	**Walk Unashamed**...Tompall/Glaser Brothers
2/93	**Walkaway Joe**...Trisha Yearwood
2/85	**Walkin' A Broken Heart**...Don Williams
2/57	**Walkin' After Midnight**...Patsy Cline
23/69	**Walkin' Back To Birmingham**...Leon Ashley
29/59	**Walkin' Down The Road**...Jimmy Newman
7/67	**Walkin' In The Sunshine**...Roger Miller
21/59	**Walkin' My Blues Away**...Jimmie Skinner
	Walkin', Talkin', Cryin', Barely Beatin' Broken Heart
22/64	Johnny Wright
4/90	Highway 101
1/90	**Walkin' Away**...Clint Black
2/96	**Walkin' Away**...Diamond Rio
3/94	**Walking Away A Winner**...Kathy Mattea
7/66	**Walking On New Grass**...Kenny Price
	Walking Piece Of Heaven
6/73	Marty Robbins
22/79	Freddy Fender
3/90	**Walking Shoes**...Tanya Tucker
	Walking The Floor Over You
18/65	George Hamilton IV
31/79	Ernest Tubb
28/58	**Walking The Slow Walk**...Carl Smith
5/61	**Walking The Streets**...Webb Pierce
15/95	**Walking To Jerusalem**...Tracy Byrd
24/59	**Wall, The**...Freddie Hart
40/87	**Wall Of Tears**...K.T. Oslin
5/62	**Wall To Wall Love**...Bob Gallion
34/65	**Waltz Across Texas**...Ernest Tubb

POS/YR	RECORD TITLE/ARTIST
10/85	**Waltz Me To Heaven**...Waylon Jennings
	Waltz Of The Angels
14/56	Wynn Stewart
11/62	George Jones & Margie Singleton
8/48	**Waltz Of The Wind**...Roy Acuff
13/62	**Waltz You Saved For Me**...Ferlin Husky
1/88	**Wanderer, The**...Eddie Rabbitt
13/67	**Wanderin' Man**...Jeannie Seely
2/81	**Wandering Eyes**...Ronnie McDowell
	Want To Thank You ..see: I Want
3/74	**Want-To's, The**...Freddie Hart
3/90	**Wanted**...Alan Jackson
11/60	**Wanting You With Me Tonight**...Jimmy Newman
1/82	**War Is Hell (On The Homefront Too)**...T.G. Sheppard
8/49	**Warm Red Wine**...Ernest Tubb
6/75	**Warm Side Of You**...Freddie Hart
25/70	**Warmth Of The Wine**...Johnny Bush
4/92	**Warning Labels**...Doug Stone
4/85	**Warning Sign**...Eddie Rabbitt
20/72	**Washday Blues**...Dolly Parton
28/79	**Wasn't It Easy Baby**...Freddie Hart
1/75	**Wasted Days And Wasted Nights**...Freddy Fender
27/60	**Wasted Love**...Red Herring
4/56	**Wasted Words**...Ray Price
28/60	**Watch Dog**...Al Terry
2/92	**Watch Me**...Lorrie Morgan
10/65	**Watch Where You're Going**...Don Gibson
4/82	**Watchin' Girls Go By**...Ronnie McDowell
7/71	**Watching Scotty Grow**...Bobby Goldsboro
32/67	**Watchman, The**...Claude King
16/73	**Watergate Blues**...Tom T. Hall
	Waterhole #3 ..see: Ballad Of
1/59	**Waterloo**...Stonewall Jackson
4/94	**Watermelon Crawl**...Tracy Byrd
	Watermelon Wine ..see: (Old Dogs-Children And)
	Wave To Me, My Lady
3/46	Elton Britt
4/46	Gene Autry
4/84	**Way Back**...John Conlee
1/77	**Way Down**...Elvis Presley
5/83	**Way Down Deep**...Vern Gosdin
39/87	**Way Down Texas Way**...Asleep At The Wheel
2/80	**Way I Am**...Merle Haggard
17/63	**Way It Feels To Die**...Vernon Stewart

POS/YR	RECORD TITLE/ARTIST
7/66	**Way To Survive**...Ray Price
1/87	**Way We Make A Broken Heart**...Rosanne Cash
7/80	**Wayfaring Stranger**...Emmylou Harris
2/58	**Ways Of A Woman In Love**...Johnny Cash
1/69	**Ways To Love A Man**...Tammy Wynette
22/69	**We All Go Crazy**...Jack Reno
	We Believe In Happy Endings
7/78	Johnny Rodriguez
1/88	Earl Thomas Conley with Emmylou Harris
2/78	**We Belong Together**...Susie Allanson
3/91	**We Both Walk**...Lorrie Morgan
6/72	**We Can Make It**...George Jones
40/77	**We Can't Build A Fire In The Rain**...Roy Clark
6/77	**We Can't Go On Living Like This**...Eddie Rabbitt
6/94	**We Can't Love Like This Anymore**...Alabama
3/74	**We Could**...Charley Pride
2/82	**We Did But Now You Don't**...Conway Twitty
6/84	**We Didn't See A Thing**...Ray Charles/George Jones/Chet Atkins
11/94	**We Don't Have To Do This**...Tanya Tucker
16/81	**We Don't Have To Hold Out**...Anne Murray
30/73	**We Found It**...Porter Wagoner & Dolly Parton
34/72	**We Found It In Each Other's Arms**...Roger Miller
26/78	**We Got Love**...Lynn Anderson
34/79	**We Got Love**...Mundo Earwood
11/93	**We Got The Love**...Restless Heart
20/69	**We Had All The Good Things Going**...Jan Howard
	We Had It All
28/73	Waylon Jennings
31/86	Dolly Parton
9/94	**We Just Disagree**...Billy Dean
40/73	**We Know It's Over**...Dave Dudley & Karen O'Donnal
8/74	**We Loved It Away**...George Jones & Tammy Wynette
2/44	**We Might As Well Forget It**...Bob Wills
7/62	**We Missed You**...Kitty Wells
7/88	**We Must Be Doin' Somethin' Right**...Eddie Rabbitt
3/63	**We Must Have Been Out Of Our Minds**...George Jones & Melba Montgomery

POS/YR	RECORD TITLE/ARTIST
22/88	**We Never Touch At All**...Merle Haggard
12/92	**We Shall Be Free**...Garth Brooks
5/74	**We Should Be Together**...Don Williams
2/71	**We Sure Can Love Each Other**...Tammy Wynette
2/92	**We Tell Ourselves**...Clint Black
9/75	**We Used To**...Dolly Parton
38/65	**We'd Destroy Each Other**...Carl Butler & Pearl
2/93	**We'll Burn That Bridge**...Brooks & Dunn
F/56	**We'll Find A Way**...Webb Pierce
5/68	**We'll Get Ahead Someday**...Porter Wagoner & Dolly Parton
34/72	**We'll Sing In The Sunshine**...Alice Creech
37/74	**We're Back In Love Again**...Johnny Bush
13/70	**We're Gonna Get Together**...Buck Owens & Susan Raye
14/62	**We're Gonna Go Fishin'**...Hank Locklin
1/73	**We're Gonna Hold On**...George Jones & Tammy Wynette
15/74	**(We're Not) The Jet Set**...George Jones & Tammy Wynette
18/80	**We're Number One**...Gatlin Bros.
3/74	**We're Over**...Johnny Rodriguez
15/63	**We're The Talk Of The Town**...Buck Owens & Rose Maddox
10/78	**We've Come A Long Way, Baby**...Loretta Lynn
10/54	**We've Gone Too Far**...Hank Thompson
3/86	**We've Got A Good Fire Goin'**...Don Williams
20/71	**We've Got Everything But Love**...David Houston & Barbara Mandrell
14/91	**We've Got It Made**...Lee Greenwood
13/63	**We've Got Something In Common**...Faron Young
30/72	**We've Got To Work It Out Between Us**...Diana Trask
1/83	**We've Got Tonight**...Kenny Rogers & Sheena Easton
18/68	**Weakness In A Man**...Roy Drusky
	Wear My Ring Around Your Neck
3/58	Elvis Presley
26/92	Ricky Van Shelton
7/53	**Weary Blues From Waitin'**...Hank Williams
	Wedding Bells
2/49	Hank Williams
6/49	Margaret Whiting & Jimmy Wakely
15/49	Kenny Roberts
15/49	Jesse Rogers

POS/YR	RECORD TITLE/ARTIST
33/69	**Wedding Cake**...Connie Francis
13/78	**Week-End Friend**...Con Hunley
1/70	**Week In A Country Jail**...Tom T. Hall
10/64	**Week In The Country**...Ernest Ashworth
1/87	**Weekend, The**...Steve Wariner
F/75	**Weekend Daddy**...Buck Owens
24/68	**Welcome Home To Nothing**...Jeannie Seely
	Welcome To My World
2/64	Jim Reeves
34/71	Eddy Arnold
22/74	**Welcome To The Sunshine (Sweet Baby Jane)**...Jeanne Pruett
6/70	**Welfare Cadilac**...Guy Drake
28/94	**Were You Really Livin'**...Brother Phelps
23/71	**West Texas Highway**...George Hamilton IV
20/90	**Western Girls**...Marty Stuart
11/75	**Western Man**...La Costa
25/94	**What A Crying Shame**...Mavericks
1/78	**What A Difference You've Made In My Life**...Ronnie Milsap
2/48	**What A Fool I Was**...Eddy Arnold
23/61	**What A Laugh!**...Freddie Hart
16/79	**What A Lie**...Sammi Smith
1/74	**What A Man, My Man Is**...Lynn Anderson
23/62	**What A Pleasure**...Connie Hall
13/49	**What A Shame**...Merle Travis
25/61	**What A Terrible Feeling**...Elmer Snodgrass
	What A Way To Go
18/77	Bobby Borchers
10/91	Ray Kennedy
29/68	**What A Way To Live**...Johnny Bush
20/73	**What About Me**...Anne Murray
22/61	**What About Me**...Don Gibson
8/72	**What Ain't To Be, Just Might Happen**...Porter Wagoner
13/72	**What Am I Gonna Do**...Bobby Bare
1/87	**What Am I Gonna Do About You**...Reba McEntire
37/67	**What Am I Gonna Do Now**...Ferlin Husky
3/83	**What Am I Gonna Do (With The Rest Of My Life)**...Merle Haggard
38/64	**What Am I Gonna Do With You**...Skeeter Davis
19/59	**What Am I Living For**...Ernest Tubb
7/56	**What Am I Worth**...George Jones
19/69	**What Are Those Things (With Big Black Wings)**...Charlie Louvin
1/81	**What Are We Doin' In Love**...Dottie West with Kenny Rogers

POS/YR	RECORD TITLE/ARTIST
4/81	**What Are We Doin' Lonesome**...Gatlin Bros.
10/49	**What Are We Gonna Do About The Moonlight**...Hank Thompson
9/87	**What Can I Do With My Heart**...Juice Newton
	What Cha ..also see: Whatcha
30/78	**What Cha Doin' After Midnight, Baby**...Helen Cornelius
4/78	**What Did I Promise Her Last Night**...Mel Tillis
7/58	**What Do I Care**...Johnny Cash
	What Do I Do With Me ..see: (Without You)
5/96	**What Do I Know**...Ricochet
6/88	**What Do You Want From Me This Time**...Foster & Lloyd
5/67	**What Does It Take**...Skeeter Davis
	(What Ever May The Future Be) ..see: Lo Que Sea
1/76	**What Goes On When The Sun Goes Down**...Ronnie Milsap
28/80	**What Good Is A Heart**...Dean Dillon
F/76	**What Have You Got Planned Tonight Diana**...Merle Haggard
9/78	**What Have You Got To Lose**...Tom T. Hall
3/85	**What I Didn't Do**...Steve Wariner
	What I Feel In My Heart ..see: (How Can I Write On Paper)
12/81	**What I Had With You**...John Conlee
18/83	**What I Learned From Loving You**...Lynn Anderson
5/96	**What I Meant To Say**...Wade Hayes
21/65	**What I Need Most**...Hugh X. Lewis
1/89	**What I'd Say**...Earl Thomas Conley
5/76	**What I've Got In Mind**...Billie Jo Spears
21/79	**What In Her World Did I Do**...Eddy Arnold
19/72	**What In The World Has Gone Wrong With Our Love**...Jack Greene/Jeannie Seely
	What In The World's Come Over You
10/75	Sonny James
25/81	Tom Jones
1/47	**What Is Life Without Love**...Eddy Arnold
3/70	**What Is Truth**...Johnny Cash
5/67	**What Kind Of A Girl (Do You Think I Am?)**...Loretta Lynn
24/92	**What Kind Of Fool**...Lionel Cartwright
2/92	**What Kind Of Fool Do You Think I Am**...Lee Roy Parnell
11/92	**What Kind Of Love**...Rodney Crowell
4/66	**What Kinda Deal Is This**...Bill Carlisle
2/67	**What Locks The Door**...Jack Greene

POS/YR	RECORD TITLE/ARTIST
8/58	**What Makes A Man Wander**...Jimmie Skinner
25/65	**What Makes A Man Wander?**...Jan Howard
1/95	**What Mattered Most**...Ty Herndon
2/93	**What Might Have Been**...Little Texas
23/79	**What More Could A Man Need**...Tommy Overstreet
6/73	**What My Woman Can't Do**...George Jones
1/93	**What Part Of No**...Lorrie Morgan
5/83	**What She Don't Know Won't Hurt Her**...Gene Watson
1/88	**What She Is (Is A Woman In Love)**...Earl Thomas Conley
8/85	**What She Wants**...Michael Martin Murphey
1/92	**What She's Doing Now**...Garth Brooks
2/94	**What The Cowgirls Do**...Vince Gill
35/94	**What They're Talkin' About**...Rhett Akins
9/78	**What Time Do You Have To Be Back To Heaven**...Razzy Bailey
16/75	**What Time Of Day**...Billy Thunderkloud
39/90	**What We Really Want**...Rosanne Cash
4/66	**What We're Fighting For**...Dave Dudley
17/93	**What Were You Thinkin'**...Little Texas
15/61	**What Would You Do?**...Jim Reeves
	What Would You Do? (If Jesus Came To Your House)
8/56	Porter Wagoner
15/56	Red Sovine
10/84	**What Would Your Memories Do**...Vern Gosdin
8/86	**What You'll Do When I'm Gone**...Waylon Jennings
27/61	**What'd I Say**...Jerry Lee Lewis
37/76	**What'll I Do**...La Costa
19/80	**What'll I Tell Virginia**...Johnny Rodriguez
16/95	**What'll You Do About Me**...Doug Supernaw
21/77	**What're You Doing Tonight**...Janie Fricke
1/86	**What's A Memory Like You (Doing In A Love Like This)**...John Schneider
17/67	**What's Come Over My Baby**...Dottie West
1/82	**What's Forever For**...Michael Murphey
1/89	**What's Going On In Your World**...George Strait
5/75	**What's Happened To Blue Eyes**...Jessi Colter
1/65	**What's He Doing In My World**...Eddy Arnold
5/94	**What's In It For Me**...John Berry
20/63	**What's In Our Heart**...George Jones & Melba Montgomery

POS/YR	RECORD TITLE/ARTIST
1/93	**What's It To You**...Clay Walker
2/68	**What's Made Milwaukee Famous (Has Made A Loser Out Of Me)**...Jerry Lee Lewis
40/65	**What's Money**...George Jones
11/81	**What's New With You**...Con Hunley
30/78	**What's The Name Of That Song?**...Glenn Barber
1/73	**What's Your Mama's Name**...Tanya Tucker
	Whatcha ..also see: What Cha
4/54	**Whatcha Gonna Do Now**...Tommy Collins
7/92	**Whatcha Gonna Do With A Cowboy**...Chris LeDoux
9/75	**Whatcha Gonna Do With A Dog Like That**...Susan Raye
7/82	**Whatever**...Statler Brothers
1/83	**Whatever Happened To Old Fashioned Love**...B.J. Thomas
22/74	**Whatever Happened To Randolph Scott**...Statler Brothers
38/75	**Whatever I Say**...Donna Fargo
19/84	**Whatever Turns You On**...Keith Stegall
16/72	**Wheel Of Fortune**...Susan Raye
37/64	**Wheel Song**...Gary Buck
1/88	**Wheels**...Restless Heart
13/58	**When**...Kalin Twins
15/80	**When**...Slim Whitman
11/79	**When A Love Ain't Right**...Charly McClain
18/82	**When A Man Loves A Woman**...Jack Grayson & Blackjack
3/70	**When A Man Loves A Woman (The Way That I Love You)**...Billy Walker
32/73	**When A Man Loves A Woman (The Way That I Love You)**...Tony Booth
20/87	**When A Woman Cries**...Janie Fricke
31/78	**When A Woman Cries**...David Rogers
12/96	**When A Woman Loves A Man**...Lee Roy Parnell
24/95	**When And Where**...Confederate Railroad
3/96	**When Boy Meets Girl**...Terri Clark
5/78	**When Can We Do This Again**...T.G. Sheppard
6/93	**When Did You Stop Loving Me**...George Strait
17/85	**When Givin' Up Was Easy**...Ed Bruce
11/71	**When He Walks On You (Like You Have Walked On Me)**...Jerry Lee Lewis
2/90	**When I Call Your Name**...Vince Gill
5/90	**When I Could Come Home To You**...Steve Wariner

POS/YR	RECORD TITLE/ARTIST
3/79	**When I Dream**...Crystal Gayle
16/74	**When I Get My Hands On You**...Diana Trask
10/62	**When I Get Thru With You (You'll Love Me Too)**...Patsy Cline
36/78	**When I Get You Alone**...Mundo Earwood
8/55	**When I Stop Dreaming**...Louvin Brothers
3/78	**When I Stop Leaving (I'll Be Gone)**...Charley Pride
1/83	**When I'm Away From You**...Bellamy Brothers
38/87	**When I'm Free Again**...Rodney Crowell
34/79	**When I'm Gone**...Dottsy
3/92	**When It Comes To You**...John Anderson
17/86	**When It's Down To Me And You**...Charly McClain with Wayne Massey
10/90	**When It's Gone**...Nitty Gritty Dirt Band
	When It's Just You And Me
19/77	Dottie West
31/81	Kenny Dale
26/65	**When It's Over**...Carl Smith
39/67	**When It's Over**...Jeannie Seely
1/59	**When It's Springtime In Alaska**...Johnny Horton
40/89	**When Love Comes Around The Bend**...Juice Newton
40/90	**When Love Comes Callin'**...Sawyer Brown
3/94	**When Love Finds You**...Vince Gill
6/53	**When Mexican Joe Met Jole Blon**...Hank Snow
	When My Blue Moon Turns To Gold Again
5/44	Cindy Walker
11/48	Cliffie Stone
F/77	Merle Haggard
22/59	**When My Conscience Hurts The Most**...Charlie Walker
2/44	**When My Man Comes Home**...Buddy Johnson
1/93	**When My Ship Comes In**...Clint Black
2/44	**When My Sugar Walks Down The Street**...Ella Fitzgerald
9/92	**When She Cries**...Restless Heart
30/69	**When She Touches Me**...Johnny Duncan
21/90	**When Somebody Loves You**...Restless Heart
31/87	**When Something Is Good (Why Does It Change)**...Hank Williams, Jr.
6/76	**When Something Is Wrong With My Baby**...Sonny James
31/78	**When The Fire Gets Hot**...Zella Lehr
2/69	**When The Grass Grows Over Me**...George Jones

POS/YR	RECORD TITLE/ARTIST
10/74	**When The Morning Comes**...Hoyt Axton
	When The New Wears Off Of Our Love
25/77	Jody Miller
25/83	Whites
32/87	**When The Right One Comes Along**...John Schneider
27/66	**When The Ship Hit The Sand**..."Little" Jimmy Dickens
1/72	**When The Snow Is On The Roses**...Sonny James
7/94	**When The Thought Of You Catches Up With Me**...David Ball
2/76	**When The Tingle Becomes A Chill**...Loretta Lynn
37/65	**When The Wind Blows In Chicago**...Roy Clark
30/64	**When The World's On Fire**...Tillman Franks
	When Two Worlds Collide
6/61	Roger Miller
6/69	Jim Reeves
11/80	Jerry Lee Lewis
1/84	**When We Make Love**...Alabama
24/69	**When We Tried**...Jan Howard
1/75	**When Will I Be Loved**...Linda Ronstadt
7/51	**When You And I Were Young Maggie Blues**...Margaret Whiting & Jimmy Wakely
7/68	**When You Are Gone**...Jim Reeves
12/49	**When You Are Lonely**...Bill Monroe
14/82	**When You Fall In Love**...Johnny Lee
14/81	**(When You Fall In Love) Everything's A Waltz**...Ed Bruce
1/52	**(When You Feel Like You're In Love) Don't Just Stand There**...Carl Smith
20/86	**When You Get To The Heart**...Barbara Mandrell/Oak Ridge Boys
37/86	**When You Hurt, I Hurt**...Ronnie McDowell
3/46	**When You Leave Don't Slam The Door**...Tex Ritter
14/93	**When You Leave That Way You Can Never Go Back**...Confederate Railroad
26/88	**When You Put Your Heart In It**...Kenny Rogers
6/72	**When You Say Love**...Bob Luman
	When You Say Nothing At All
1/88	Keith Whitley
3/95	Alison Krauss & Union Station
	When You Walk In The Room
29/81	Stephanie Winslow
2/94	Pam Tillis
21/82	**When You Were Blue And I Was Green**...Kin Vassy

POS/YR	RECORD TITLE/ARTIST
38/91	**When You Were Mine**...Shenandoah
1/71	**When You're Hot, You're Hot**...Jerry Reed
21/69	**When You're Hot You're Hot**...Porter Wagoner
	When You're In Love ..see: (That's What You Do)
16/83	**When You're Not A Lady**...Jim Glaser
31/80	**When You're Ugly Like Us**...George Jones & Johnny Paycheck
14/74	**When Your Good Love Was Mine**...Narvel Felts
2/94	**Whenever You Come Around**...Vince Gill
23/92	**Wher'm I Gonna Live?**...Billy Ray Cyrus
18/77	**Where Are You Going, Billy Boy**...Bill Anderson & Mary Lou Turner
1/91	**Where Are You Now**...Clint Black
10/83	**Where Are You Spending Your Nights These Days**...David Frizzell
14/67	**Where Could I Go? (But To Her)**...David Houston
1/89	**Where Did I Go Wrong**...Steve Wariner
11/94	**Where Do I Fit In The Picture**...Clay Walker
1/79	**Where Do I Put Her Memory**...Charley Pride
1/88	**Where Do The Nights Go**...Ronnie Milsap
10/64	**Where Does A Little Tear Come From**...George Jones
1/67	**Where Does The Good Times Go**...Buck Owens
40/92	**Where Forever Begins**...Neal McCoy
28/70	**Where Grass Won't Grow**...George Jones
6/70	**Where Have All Our Heroes Gone**...Bill Anderson
14/69	**Where Have All The Average People Gone**...Roger Miller
	(Where Have All The Good Times Gone) ..see: Hey Daisy
26/75	**Where He's Going, I've Already Been**...Hank Williams, Jr.
9/62	**Where I Ought To Be**...Skeeter Davis
11/71	**Where Is My Castle**...Connie Smith
15/66	**Where Is The Circus**...Hank Thompson
5/75	**Where Love Begins**...Gene Watson
2/68	**Where Love Used To Live**...David Houston
10/69	**Where The Blue And Lonely Go**...Roy Drusky
34/69	**Where The Blue Of The Night Meets The Gold Of The Day**...Hank Locklin
15/62	**Where The Old Red River Flows**...Jimmie Davis

POS/YR	RECORD TITLE/ARTIST
29/94	**Where There's Smoke**...Archer Park
35/82	**Where There's Smoke There's Fire**...Louise Mandrell & RC Bannon
20/94	**Where Was I**...Ricky Van Shelton
14/66	**Where'd Ya Stay Last Night**...Webb Pierce
8/84	**Where's The Dress**...Moe Bandy & Joe Stampley
28/69	**Where's The Playground Susie**...Glen Campbell
10/90	**Where've You Been**...Kathy Mattea
20/73	**Wherefore And Why**...Glen Campbell
31/69	**Wherever You Are**...Johnny Paycheck
3/95	**Wherever You Go**...Clint Black
4/95	**Which Bridge To Cross (Which Bridge To Burn)**...Vince Gill
4/59	**Which One Is To Blame**...Wilburn Brothers
19/69	**Which One Will It Be**...Bobby Bare
28/89	**Which Way Do I Go (Now That I'm Gone)**...Waylon Jennings
31/80	**While I Was Makin' Love To You**...Susie Allanson
26/81	**While The Feeling's Good**...Rex Allen, Jr. & Margo Smith
21/66	**While You're Dancing**...Marty Robbins
25/69	**While Your Lover Sleeps**...Leon Ashley
2/92	**Whiskey Ain't Workin'**...Travis Tritt & Marty Stuart
2/79	**Whiskey Bent And Hell Bound**...Hank Williams, Jr.
18/81	**Whiskey Chasin'**...Joe Stampley
2/87	**Whiskey, If You Were A Woman**...Highway 101
	Whiskey River
14/72	Johnny Bush
12/79	Willie Nelson
18/76	**Whiskey Talkin'**...Joe Stampley
16/78	**Whiskey Trip**...Gary Stewart
5/95	**Whiskey Under The Bridge**...Brooks & Dunn
31/70	**Whiskey, Whiskey**...Nat Stuckey
10/81	**Whisper**...Lacy J. Dalton
1/94	**Whisper My Name**...Randy Travis
15/58	**Whispering Rain**...Hank Snow
12/77	**Whispers**...Bobby Borchers
28/65	**Whistle Walkin'**...Ned Miller
7/49	**White Christmas**...Ernest Tubb
1/46	**White Cross On Okinawa**...Bob Wills
25/68	**White Fences And Evergreen Trees**...Ferlin Husky
1/76	**White Knight**...Cledus Maggard

POS/YR	RECORD TITLE/ARTIST
21/65	**White Lightnin' Express**...Roy Drusky
1/59	**White Lightning**...George Jones
29/90	**White Limozeen**...Dolly Parton
14/85	**White Line**...Emmylou Harris
5/72	**White Silver Sands**...Sonny James
1/57	**White Sport Coat (And A Pink Carnation)**...Marty Robbins
3/78	**Who Am I To Say**...Statler Brothers
3/59	**Who Cares**...Don Gibson
13/65	**Who Do I Think I Am**...Webb Pierce
11/82	**Who Do You Know In California**...Eddy Raven
10/74	**Who Left The Door To Heaven Open**...Hank Thompson
6/48	**Who? Me?**...Tex Williams
29/92	**Who Needs It**...Clinton Gregory
2/95	**Who Needs You Baby**...Clay Walker
4/94	**(Who Says) You Can't Have It All**...Alan Jackson
7/59	**Who Shot Sam**...George Jones
40/79	**(Who Was The Man Who Put) The Line In Gasoline**...Jerry Reed
11/60	**Who Will Buy The Wine**...Charlie Walker
20/79	**Who Will The Next Fool Be**...Jerry Lee Lewis
2/89	**Who You Gonna Blame It On This Time**...Vern Gosdin
36/80	**Who'll Turn Out The Lights**...Mel Street
27/63	**Who's Been Cheatin' Who**...Johnny & Jonie Mosby
1/81	**Who's Cheatin' Who**...Charly McClain
3/85	**Who's Gonna Fill Their Shoes**...George Jones
37/83	**Who's Gonna Keep Me Warm**...Phil Everly
1/69	**Who's Gonna Mow Your Grass**...Buck Owens
14/72	**Who's Gonna Play This Old Piano**...Jerry Lee Lewis
18/69	**Who's Gonna Take The Garbage Out**...Ernest Tubb & Loretta Lynn
10/69	**Who's Julie**...Mel Tillis
1/90	**Who's Lonely Now**...Highway 101
29/75	**Who's Sorry Now**...Marie Osmond
32/96	**Who's That Girl**...Stephanie Bentley
1/94	**Who's That Man**...Toby Keith
37/85	**Who's The Blonde Stranger?**...Jimmy Buffett
6/49	**Whoa Sailor**...Hank Thompson
14/75	**Whoever Turned You On, Forgot To Turn You Off**...Little David Wilkins
1/86	**Whoever's In New England**...Reba McEntire
1/57	**Whole Lot Of Shakin' Going On**...Jerry Lee Lewis
18/72	**Whole Lot Of Somethin'**...Tony Booth
18/91	**Whole Lotta Holes**...Kathy Mattea
30/94	**Whole Lotta Love On The Line**...Aaron Tippin
22/73	**Whole Lotta Loving**...Hank Williams, Jr. & Lois Johnson
2/76	**Whole Lotta Things To Sing About**...Charley Pride
15/58	**Whole Lotta Woman**...Marvin Rainwater
14/70	**Whole World Comes To Me**...Jack Greene
27/70	**Whole World Holding Hands**...Freddie Hart
10/84	**Whole World's In Love When You're Lonely**...B.J. Thomas
13/73	**Whole World's Making Love Again Tonight**...Bobby G. Rice
11/95	**Whose Bed Have Your Boots Been Under?**...Shania Twain
7/55	**Whose Shoulder Will You Cry On**...Kitty Wells
	Why Baby Why
4/55	George Jones
1/56	Red Sovine & Webb Pierce
9/56	Hank Locklin
23/61	Warren Smith & Shirley Collie
1/83	Charley Pride
7/77	**Why Can't He Be You**...Loretta Lynn
F/79	**Why Did You Have To Be So Good**...Dave & Sugar
1/93	**Why Didn't I Think Of That**...Doug Stone
3/83	**Why Do I Have To Choose**...Willie Nelson
F/70	**Why Do I Love You (Melody of Love)**...Jim Reeves
7/83	**Why Do We Want (What We Know We Can't Have)**...Reba McEntire
1/87	**Why Does It Have To Be (Wrong or Right)**...Restless Heart
25/63	**Why Don't Daddy Live Here Anymore**...Bonnie Owens
39/93	**Why Don't That Telephone Ring**...Tracy Byrd
	Why Don't You Haul Off And Love Me
1/49	Wayne Raney
5/49	Mervin Shiner
9/49	Bob Atcher
	Why Don't You Love Me
1/50	Hank Williams
15/75	Connie Smith

POS/YR	RECORD TITLE/ARTIST
1/80	**Why Don't You Spend The Night**...Ronnie Milsap
12/84	**Why Goodbye**...Steve Wariner
1/79	**Why Have You Left The One You Left Me For**...Crystal Gayle
5/94	**Why Haven't I Heard From You**...Reba McEntire
15/87	**Why I Don't Know**...Lyle Lovett
6/60	**Why I'm Walkin'**...Stonewall Jackson
1/80	**Why Lady Why**...Alabama
4/84	**Why Lady Why**...Gary Morris
8/77	**Why Lovers Turn To Strangers**...Freddie Hart
1/73	**Why Me**...Kris Kristofferson
1/84	**Why Not Me**...Judds
30/80	**Why Not Me**...Fred Knoblock
3/50	**Why Should I Cry?**...Eddy Arnold
9/50	**Why Should We Try Anymore**...Hank Williams
2/57	**Why, Why**...Carl Smith
17/69	**Why You Been Gone So Long**...Johnny Darrell
1/89	**Why'd You Come In Here Lookin' Like That**...Dolly Parton
22/76	**Wichita Jail**...Charlie Daniels Band
1/68	**Wichita Lineman**...Glen Campbell
24/69	**Wicked California**...Tompall/Glaser Brothers
9/56	**Wicked Lies**...Carl Smith
13/48	**Wicked Path Of Sin**...Bill Monroe
19/64	**Widow Maker**...Jimmy Martin
22/67	**Wife Of The Party**...Liz Anderson
16/77	**Wiggle Wiggle**...Ronnie Sessions
1/82	**Wild And Blue**...John Anderson
1/96	**Wild Angels**...Martina McBride
8/65	**Wild As A Wildcat**...Charlie Walker
18/68	**Wild Blood**...Del Reeves
21/80	**Wild Bull Rider**...Hoyt Axton
24/87	**Wild-Eyed Dream**...Ricky Van Shelton
5/93	**Wild Man**...Ricky Van Shelton
14/83	**Wild Montana Skies**...John Denver & Emmylou Harris
1/94	**Wild One**...Faith Hill
	Wild River ..see: Ballad Of
	Wild Side Of Life
1/52	Hank Thompson
6/52	Burl Ives & Grady Martin
13/76	Freddy Fender
10/81	Waylon Jennings & Jessi Colter (medley)
(also see: It Wasn't God Who Made Honky Tonk Angels)	

POS/YR	RECORD TITLE/ARTIST
	Wild Side Of Me ..see: (You Bring Out)
F/82	**Wild Turkey**...Lacy J. Dalton
2/68	**Wild Week-End**...Bill Anderson
15/63	**Wild Wild Wind**...Stonewall Jackson
9/88	**Wilder Days**...Baillie & The Boys
6/88	**Wildflowers**...Dolly Parton/Linda Ronstadt/Emmylou Harris
5/55	**Wildwood Flower**...Hank Thompson with Merle Travis
7/84	**Will It Be Love By Morning**...Michael Martin Murphey
5/49	**Will Santy Come To Shanty Town**...Eddy Arnold
5/86	**Will The Wolf Survive**...Waylon Jennings
37/91	**Will This Be The Day**...Desert Rose Band
20/68	**Will You Visit Me On Sundays?**...Charlie Louvin
8/62	**Will Your Lawyer Talk To God**...Kitty Wells
19/81	**Willie Jones**...Bobby Bare
5/62	**Willie The Weeper**...Billy Walker
25/76	**Willie, Waylon And Me**...David Allan Coe
10/62	**Willingly**...Willie Nelson & Shirley Collie
23/61	**Willow Tree**...Ferlin Husky
10/71	**Willy Jones**...Susan Raye
4/83	**Wind Beneath My Wings**...Gary Morris
20/81	**Wind Is Bound To Change**...Gatlin Bros.
	Window Up Above
2/61	George Jones
1/75	Mickey Gilley
14/65	**Wine**...Mel Tillis
10/86	**Wine Colored Roses**...George Jones
	Wine Me Up
2/69	Faron Young
19/89	Larry Boone
1/46	**Wine, Women And Song**...Al Dexter
3/64	**Wine Women And Song**...Loretta Lynn
1/60	**Wings Of A Dove**...Ferlin Husky
11/70	**Wings Upon Your Horns**...Loretta Lynn
1/94	**Wink**...Neal McCoy
13/76	**Winner, The**...Bobby Bare
26/79	**Winners And Losers**...R.C. Bannon
8/79	**Wisdom Of A Fool**...Jacky Ward
2/70	**Wish I Didn't Have To Miss You**...Jack Greene & Jeannie Seely
2/94	**Wish I Didn't Know Now**...Toby Keith
2/81	**Wish You Were Here**...Barbara Mandrell
22/84	**Wishful Drinkin'**...Atlanta
5/60	**Wishful Thinking**...Wynn Stewart

POS/YR	RECORD TITLE/ARTIST
32/79	**Wishing I Had Listened To Your Song**...Bobby Borchers
7/65	**Wishing Well (Down in the Well)**...Hank Snow
24/71	**With His Hand In Mine**...Jean Shepard
5/85	**With Just One Look In Your Eyes**...Charly McClain with Wayne Massey
10/78	**With Love**...Rex Allen, Jr.
1/67	**With One Exception**...David Houston
3/68	**With Pen In Hand**...Johnny Darrell
1/45	**With Tears In My Eyes**...Wesley Tuttle
32/82	**With Their Kind Of Money And Our Kind Of Love**...Billy Swan
31/91	**With This Ring**...T. Graham Brown
7/83	**With You**...Charly McClain
33/86	**With You**...Vince Gill
11/84	**Without A Song**...Willie Nelson
12/83	**Without You**...T.G. Sheppard
2/92	**(Without You) What Do I Do With Me**...Tanya Tucker
10/56	**Without Your Love**...Bobby Lord
22/96	**Without Your Love**...Aaron Tippin
13/76	**Without Your Love (Mr. Jordan)**...Charlie Ross
1/84	**Woke Up In Love**...Exile
12/75	**Wolf Creek Pass**...C.W. McCall
1/62	**Wolverton Mountain**...Claude King
(also see: I'm The Girl On)	
2/71	**Woman Always Knows**...David Houston
4/92	**Woman Before Me**...Trisha Yearwood
16/58	**Woman Captured Me**...Hank Snow
38/76	**Woman Don't Try To Sing My Song**...Cal Smith
15/66	**Woman Half My Age**...Kitty Wells
24/68	**Woman Hungry**...Porter Wagoner
9/57	**Woman I Need**...Johnny Horton
1/89	**Woman In Love**...Ronnie Milsap
4/67	**Woman In Love**...Bonnie Guitar
3/81	**Woman In Me**...Crystal Gayle
14/95	**Woman In Me (Needs The Man In You)**...Shania Twain
4/75	**Woman In The Back Of My Mind**...Mel Tillis
F/71	**Woman Left Lonely**...Patti Page
17/70	**Woman Lives For Love**...Wanda Jackson
9/92	**Woman Loves**...Steve Wariner
1/69	**Woman Of The World (Leave My World Alone)**...Loretta Lynn
35/75	**Woman On My Mind**...David Houston

POS/YR	RECORD TITLE/ARTIST
	Woman (Sensuous Woman)
1/72	Don Gibson
21/94	Mark Chesnutt
4/74	**Woman To Woman**...Tammy Wynette
4/78	**Woman To Woman**...Barbara Mandrell
29/73	**Woman Without A Home**...Statler Brothers
20/69	**Woman Without Love**...Johnny Darrell
12/84	**Woman Your Love**...Moe Bandy
23/70	**Woman's Hand**...Jean Shepard
9/59	**Woman's Intuition**...Wilburn Brothers
16/82	**Woman's Touch**...Tom Jones
3/78	**Womanhood**...Tammy Wynette
9/66	**Women Do Funny Things To Me**...Del Reeves
4/82	**Women Do Know How To Carry On**...Waylon Jennings
18/80	**Women Get Lonely**...Charly McClain
5/80	**Women I've Never Had**...Hank Williams, Jr.
1/70	**Wonder Could I Live There Anymore**...Charley Pride
37/70	**Wonder Of You**...Elvis Presley
39/75	**Wonder When My Baby's Comin' Home**...Barbara Mandrell
14/68	**Wonderful World Of Women**...Faron Young
1/52	**Wondering**...Webb Pierce
6/70	**Wonders Of The Wine**...David Houston
5/71	**Wonders You Perform**...Tammy Wynette
10/75	**Word Games**...Billy Walker
8/79	**Words**...Susie Allanson
12/94	**Words By Heart**...Billy Ray Cyrus
10/67	**Words I'm Gonna Have To Eat**...Bill Phillips
	Workin' At The Car Wash Blues
27/74	Tony Booth
F/80	Jerry Reed
40/95	**Workin' For The Weekend**...Ken Mellons
21/64	**Workin' It Out**...Flatt & Scruggs
1/69	**Workin' Man Blues**...Merle Haggard
4/88	**Workin' Man (Nowhere To Go)**...Nitty Gritty Dirt Band
30/80	**Workin' My Way To Your Heart**...Dickey Lee
37/73	**Workin' On A Feelin'**...Tommy Cash
16/86	**Working Class Man**...Lacy J. Dalton
33/71	**Working Like The Devil (For The Lord)**...Del Reeves
7/85	**Working Man**...John Conlee
16/77	**Working Man Can't Get Nowhere Today**...Merle Haggard
7/93	**Working Man's Ph.D.**...Aaron Tippin

POS/YR	RECORD TITLE/ARTIST
7/86	**Working Without A Net**...Waylon Jennings
28/92	**Working Woman**...Rob Crosby
23/70	**World Called You**...David Rogers
10/66	**World Is Round**...Roy Drusky
29/64	**World Lost A Man**...David Price
	World Needs A Melody
32/71	Red Lane
35/72	Carter Family with Johnny Cash
1/74	**World Of Make Believe**...Bill Anderson
1/68	**World Of Our Own**...Sonny James
	World So Full Of Love
18/60	Ray Sanders
28/61	Faron Young
19/69	**World-Wide Travelin' Man**...Wynn Stewart
10/85	**World Without Love**...Eddie Rabbitt
14/72	**World Without Music**...Porter Wagoner
6/84	**World's Greatest Lover**...Bellamy Brothers
18/79	**World's Most Perfect Woman**...Ronnie McDowell
30/76	**(Worst You Ever Gave Me Was) The Best I Ever Had**...Faron Young
30/93	**Worth Every Mile**...Travis Tritt
36/87	**Would These Arms Be In Your Way**...Keith Whitley
13/58	**Would You Care**...Browns
6/82	**Would You Catch A Falling Star**...John Anderson
5/66	**Would You Hold It Against Me**...Dottie West
1/74	**Would You Lay With Me (In A Field Of Stone)**...Tanya Tucker
3/55	**Would You Mind?**...Hank Snow
1/72	**Would You Take Another Chance On Me**...Jerry Lee Lewis
21/73	**Would You Walk With Me Jimmy**...Arlene Harden
12/72	**Would You Want The World To End**...Mel Tillis
3/62	**Wound Time Can't Erase**...Stonewall Jackson
18/84	**Wounded Hearts**...Mark Gray
12/77	**Wrap Your Love All Around Your Man**...Lynn Anderson
38/73	**Wrap Your Love Around Me**...Melba Montgomery
8/61	**Wreck On The Highway**...Wilma Lee & Stoney Cooper
9/75	**Write Me A Letter**...Bobby G. Rice
16/66	**Write Me A Picture**...George Hamilton IV
6/44	**Write Me Sweetheart**...Roy Acuff
31/89	**Writing On The Wall**...George Jones

POS/YR	RECORD TITLE/ARTIST
15/72	**Writing's On The Wall**...Jim Reeves
35/82	**Written Down In My Heart**...Ray Stevens
5/90	**Wrong**...Waylon Jennings
26/60	**Wrong Company**...Wynn Stewart & Jan Howard
6/74	**Wrong Ideas**...Brenda Lee
20/74	**Wrong In Loving You**...Faron Young
14/65	**Wrong Number**...George Jones
6/75	**Wrong Road Again**...Crystal Gayle
5/92	**Wrong Side Of Memphis**...Trisha Yearwood
1/77	**Wurlitzer Prize (I Don't Want to Get Over You)**...Waylon Jennings
	Wyoming ..see: (Oh Why, Oh Why, Did I Ever Leave)

X

1/94	**XXX's And OOO's (An American Girl)**...Trisha Yearwood

Y

3/77	**Y'All Come Back Saloon**...Oak Ridge Boys
4/65	**Yakety Axe**...Chet Atkins
17/59	**Yankee, Go Home**...Goldie Hill
17/92	**Yard Sale**...Sammy Kershaw
1/71	**Year That Clayton Delaney Died**...Tom T. Hall
	Yearning
10/57	George Jones & Jeanette Hicks
22/61	Benny Barnes
1/80	**Years**...Barbara Mandrell
2/85	**Years After You**...John Conlee
12/82	**Years Ago**...Statler Brothers
4/63	**Yellow Bandana**...Faron Young
30/81	**Yellow Pages**...Roger Bowling
5/73	**Yellow Ribbon**...Johnny Carver
1/84	**Yellow Rose**...Johnny Lee with Lane Brody
7/55	**Yellow Rose Of Texas**...Ernest Tubb
1/89	**Yellow Roses**...Dolly Parton
3/55	**Yellow Roses**...Hank Snow
2/56	**Yes I Know Why**...Webb Pierce
6/66	**(Yes) I'm Hurting**...Don Gibson
12/78	**Yes Ma'am**...Tommy Overstreet
1/65	**Yes, Mr. Peters**...Roy Drusky & Priscilla Mitchell
(also see: Hurry, Mr. Peters)	

POS/YR	RECORD TITLE/ARTIST
10/80	**Yesterday Once More**...Moe Bandy
9/69	**Yesterday, When I Was Young**...Roy Clark
8/53	**Yesterday's Girl**...Hank Thompson
9/77	**Yesterday's Gone**...Vern Gosdin
40/69	**Yesterday's Letters**...Bobby Lord
12/48	**Yesterday's Mail**...Hank Thompson
11/63	**Yesterday's Memories**...Eddy Arnold
4/44	**Yesterday's Tears**...Ernest Tubb
1/82	**Yesterday's Wine**...Merle Haggard/George Jones
7/90	**Yet**...Exile
25/80	**Yippy Cry Yi**...Rex Allen, Jr.
4/55	**Yonder Comes A Sucker**...Jim Reeves
1/87	**You Again**...Forester Sisters
19/89	**You Ain't Down Home**...Jann Browne
6/89	**You Ain't Going Nowhere**...Chris Hillman & Roger McGuinn
13/72	**You Ain't Gonna Have Ol' Buck To Kick Around No More**...Buck Owens
5/79	**You Ain't Just Whistlin' Dixie**...Bellamy Brothers
2/95	**You Ain't Much Fun**...Toby Keith
2/66	**You Ain't Woman Enough**...Loretta Lynn
	You All ..also see: Y'All
7/54	**You All Come**...Arlie Duff
4/80	**You Almost Slipped My Mind**...Charley Pride
1/73	**You Always Come Back (To Hurting Me)**...Johnny Rodriguez
37/76	**You Always Look Your Best (Here In My Arms)**...George Jones
5/92	**You And Forever And Me**...Little Texas
1/82	**You And I**...Eddie Rabbitt with Crystal Gayle
1/76	**You And Me**...Tammy Wynette
3/56	**You And Me**...Kitty Wells & Red Foley **(also see: Now And Forever)**
15/70	**You And Me Against The World**...Bobby Lord
24/78	**You And Me Alone**...David Rogers
4/95	**You And Only You**...John Berry
6/69	**You And Your Sweet Love**...Connie Smith
12/64	**You Are My Flower**...Flatt & Scruggs
10/86	**You Are My Music, You Are My Song**...Charly McClain with Wayne Massey
36/79	**You Are My Rainbow**...David Rogers
1/68	**You Are My Treasure**...Jack Greene

POS/YR	RECORD TITLE/ARTIST
	You Are So Beautiful
16/76	Ray Stevens
40/77	Tanya Tucker
4/56	**You Are The One**...Carl Smith
14/75	**You Are The One**...Mel Tillis & Sherry Bryce
11/76	**You Are The Song (Inside Of Me)**...Freddie Hart
34/78	**You Are The Sunshine Of My Life**...Marty Mitchell
	You Ask Me To
8/73	Waylon Jennings
F/81	Elvis Presley
23/89	**You Babe**...Merle Haggard
20/67	**You Beat All I Ever Saw**...Johnny Cash
	You Better Move On
10/71	Billy "Crash" Craddock
18/81	George Jones & Johnny Paycheck
2/54	**You Better Not Do That**...Tommy Collins
28/68	**You Better Sit Down Kids**...Roy Drusky
2/95	**You Better Think Twice**...Vince Gill
9/84	**(You Bring Out) The Wild Side Of Me**...Dan Seals
15/49	**You Broke My Heart (In Little Bitty Pieces)**...Hank Thompson
3/92	**You Can Depend On Me**...Restless Heart
1/86	**You Can Dream Of Me**...Steve Wariner
1/96	**You Can Feel Bad**...Patty Loveless
	You Can Have Her
18/67	Jim Edward Brown
7/73	Waylon Jennings
14/79	George Jones & Johnny Paycheck
23/95	**You Can Sleep While I Drive**...Trisha Yearwood
33/67	**You Can Steal Me**...Bonnie Guitar
1/74	**You Can't Be A Beacon (If Your Light Don't Shine)**...Donna Fargo
3/46	**You Can't Break My Heart**...Spade Cooley
20/88	**You Can't Fall In Love When You're Cryin'**...Lee Greenwood
23/72	**You Can't Go Home**...Statler Brothers
8/54	**You Can't Have My Love**...Wanda Jackson & Billy Gray
10/67	**You Can't Have Your Kate And Edith, Too**...Statler Brothers
15/57	**You Can't Hurt Me Anymore**...Carl Smith
31/86	**You Can't Keep A Good Memory Down**...John Anderson
1/95	**You Can't Make A Heart Love Somebody**...George Strait
8/60	**You Can't Pick A Rose In December**...Ernest Ashworth

POS/YR	RECORD TITLE/ARTIST
35/66	**You Can't Roller Skate In A Buffalo Herd**...Roger Miller
20/85	**You Can't Run Away From Your Heart**...Lacy J. Dalton
1/83	**You Can't Run From Love**...Eddie Rabbitt
9/86	**You Can't Stop Love**...Schuyler, Knobloch & Overstreet
35/68	**You Changed Everything About Me But My Name**...Norma Jean
5/63	**You Comb Her Hair**...George Jones
10/76	**You Could Know As Much About A Stranger**...Gene Watson
1/84	**You Could've Heard A Heart Break**...Johnny Lee
32/91	**You Couldn't Get The Picture**...George Jones
1/79	**You Decorated My Life**...Kenny Rogers
10/79	**You Don't Bring Me Flowers**...Jim Ed Brown/Helen Cornelius
5/45	**You Don't Care What Happens To Me**...Bob Wills
4/91	**You Don't Count The Cost**...Billy Dean
5/95	**You Don't Even Know Who I Am**...Patty Loveless
10/50	**You Don't Have To Be A Baby To Cry**...Ernest Tubb
36/75	**You Don't Have To Go Home**...Nat Stuckey
4/65	**You Don't Hear**...Kitty Wells
4/83	**You Don't Know Love**...Janie Fricke
	You Don't Know Me
10/56	Eddy Arnold
1/81	Mickey Gilley
1/78	**You Don't Love Me Anymore**...Eddie Rabbitt
36/79	**You Don't Miss A Thing**...Sylvia
15/74	**You Don't Need To Move A Mountain**...Jeanne Pruett
14/61	**You Don't Want My Love**...Roger Miller
	You Done Me Wrong
7/56	Ray Price
37/85	Mel Tillis
13/59	**You Dreamer You**...Johnny Cash
4/79	**You Feel Good All Over**...T.G. Sheppard
15/66	**You Finally Said Something Good (When You Said Goodbye)**...Charlie Louvin
7/69	**You Gave Me A Mountain**...Johnny Bush
34/74	**You Get To Me**...Eddie Rabbitt
8/73	**You Give Me You**...Bobby G. Rice
7/89	**You Got It**...Roy Orbison
28/83	**You Got Me Running**...Jim Glaser

POS/YR	RECORD TITLE/ARTIST
7/56	**You Gotta Be My Baby**...George Jones
3/96	**You Gotta Love That**...Neal McCoy
4/95	**You Have The Right To Remain Silent**...Perfect Stranger
11/87	**You Haven't Heard The Last Of Me**...Moe Bandy
39/89	**You Just Can't Lose 'Em All**...Shooters
20/94	**You Just Watch Me**...Tanya Tucker
9/80	**You Know Just What I'd Do**...Conway Twitty & Loretta Lynn
1/91	**You Know Me Better Than That**...George Strait
20/78	**You Know What**...Jerry Reed & Seidina
30/73	**You Know Who**...Bobby Bare
19/80	**You Lay A Whole Lot Of Love On Me**...Con Hunley
3/73	**You Lay So Easy On My Mind**...Bobby G. Rice
1/90	**You Lie**...Reba McEntire
8/80	**(You Lift Me) Up To Heaven**...Reba McEntire
4/77	**You Light Up My Life**...Debby Boone
33/82	**You Look Like The One I Love**...Deborah Allen
1/84	**You Look So Good In Love**...George Strait
24/86	**You Made A Rock Of A Rolling Stone**...Oak Ridge Boys
3/84	**You Made A Wanted Man Of Me**...Ronnie McDowell
	You Make Me Feel Like A Man
34/71	Warner Mack
7/85	Ricky Skaggs
15/74	**You Make Me Feel More Like A Man**...Mel Street
29/61	**You Make Me Live Again**...Carl Smith
4/75	**(You Make Me Want To Be) A Mother**...Tammy Wynette
1/85	**You Make Me Want To Make You Mine**...Juice Newton
20/81	**You (Make Me Wonder Why)**...Deborah Allen
9/81	**You May See Me Walkin'**...Ricky Skaggs
1/67	**You Mean The World To Me**...David Houston
26/89	**You Must Not Be Drinking Enough**...Earl Thomas Conley
15/48	**You Nearly Lose Your Mind**...Ernest Tubb
4/78	**You Needed Me**...Anne Murray
6/77	**(You Never Can Tell) C'est La Vie**...Emmylou Harris

POS/YR	RECORD TITLE/ARTIST
8/75	**You Never Even Called Me By My Name**...David Allan Coe
5/82	**You Never Gave Up On Me**...Crystal Gayle
1/77	**You Never Miss A Real Good Thing (Till He Says Goodbye)**...Crystal Gayle
31/74	**You Never Say You Love Me Anymore**...Nat Stuckey
7/46	**You Only Want Me When You're Lonely**...Gene Autry
16/77	**You Ought To Hear Me Cry**...Willie Nelson
15/55	**You Oughta See Pickles Now**...Tommy Collins
12/79	**You Pick Me Up (And Put Me Down)**...Dottie West
14/67	**You Pushed Me Too Far**...Ferlin Husky
10/83	**You Put The Beat In My Heart**...Eddie Rabbitt
10/82	**You Put The Blue In Me**...Whites
F/77	**You Put The Bounce Back Into My Step**...Ray Griff
37/84	**You Really Go For The Heart**...Dan Seals
1/90	**You Really Had Me Going**...Holly Dunn
6/73	**You Really Haven't Changed**...Johnny Carver
16/75	**You Ring My Bell**...Ray Griff
4/76	**You Rubbed It In All Wrong**...Billy "Crash" Craddock
12/93	**You Say You Will**...Trisha Yearwood
3/86	**You Should Have Been Gone By Now**...Eddy Raven
11/79	**You Show Me Your Heart (And I'll Show You Mine)**...Tom T. Hall
14/89	**You Still Do**...T.G. Sheppard
16/82	**You Still Get To Me In My Dreams**...Tammy Wynette
1/87	**You Still Move Me**...Dan Seals
35/82	**(You Sure Know Your Way) Around My Heart**...Louise Mandrell
1/83	**You Take Me For Granted**...Merle Haggard
15/62	**You Take The Future (And I'll Take the Past)**...Hank Snow
18/59	**You Take The Table And I'll Take The Chairs**...Bob Gallion
18/73	**You Took All The Ramblin' Out Of Me**...Jerry Reed
	You Took Her [Him] Off My Hands (Now Please Take Her [Him] Off My Mind)
11/63	Ray Price
33/64	Marion Worth
33/64	**You Took My Happy Away**...Willie Nelson
37/69	**You Touched My Heart**...David Rogers

POS/YR	RECORD TITLE/ARTIST
17/82	**You Turn Me On I'm A Radio**...Gail Davies
3/85	**You Turn Me On (Like a Radio)**...Ed Bruce
1/45	**You Two-Timed Me One Time Too Often**...Tex Ritter
6/70	**You Wanna Give Me A Lift**...Loretta Lynn
20/84	**You Were A Good Friend**...Kenny Rogers
	You Were A Lady ..see: (Jeannie Marie)
1/73	**You Were Always There**...Donna Fargo
38/81	**You Were There**...Freddie Hart
28/79	**You Were Worth Waiting For**...Don King
6/94	**You Will**...Patty Loveless
1/46	**You Will Have To Pay**...Tex Ritter
	You Win Again
10/52	Hank Williams
2/58	Jerry Lee Lewis
1/80	Charley Pride
16/91	**You Win Again**...Mary-Chapin Carpenter
1/96	**You Win My Love**...Shania Twain
8/70	**You Wouldn't Know Love**...Ray Price
5/80	**You'd Make An Angel Wanna Cheat**...Kendalls
	You'll Be Back (Every Night In My Dreams)
24/78	Johnny Russell
3/82	Statler Brothers
10/58	**You'll Come Back**...Webb Pierce
31/88	**You'll Come Back (You Always Do)**...Mel Tillis
10/64	**You'll Drive Me Back (Into Her Arms Again)**...Faron Young
1/76	**You'll Lose A Good Thing**...Freddy Fender
10/89	**You'll Never Be Sorry**...Bellamy Brothers
26/86	**You'll Never Know How Much I Needed You Today**...Conway Twitty
18/83	**You're A Hard Dog (To Keep Under The Porch)**...Gail Davies
20/79	**You're A Part Of Me**...Charly McClain
39/80	**You're Amazing**...David Rogers
5/45	**You're Breaking My Heart**...Ted Daffan
31/81	**You're Crazy Man**...Freddie Hart
32/72	**You're Everything**...Tommy Cash
10/63	**You're For Me**...Buck Owens
	You're Free To Go
6/56	Carl Smith
9/77	Sonny James
2/44	**You're From Texas**...Bob Wills
1/84	**You're Gettin' To Me Again**...Jim Glaser
26/59	**You're Going Back To Your Old Ways Again**...Hank Thompson

POS/YR	RECORD TITLE/ARTIST
10/85	**You're Going Out Of My Mind**...T.G. Sheppard
4/49	**You're Gonna Change (Or I'm Gonna Leave)**...Hank Williams
29/74	**You're Gonna Hurt Me (One More Time)**...Patti Page
34/83	**You're Gonna Lose Her Like That**...Moe Bandy
	(You're Gonna Love Me Tonight) ..see: I Can Tell By The Way You Dance
	You're Gonna Love Yourself In The Morning
35/75	Roy Clark
22/80	Charlie Rich
33/85	**You're Gonna Miss Me When I'm Gone**...Judy Rodman
1/95	**You're Gonna Miss Me When I'm Gone**...Brooks & Dunn
39/70	**You're Gonna Need A Man**...Johnny Duncan
1/83	**You're Gonna Ruin My Bad Reputation**...Ronnie McDowell
27/80	**You're In Love With The Wrong Man**...Mundo Earwood
38/71	**You're Just More A Woman**...Bob Yarbrough
5/71	**You're Lookin' At Country**...Loretta Lynn
7/59	**You're Makin' A Fool Out Of Me**...Jimmy Newman
1/75	**You're My Best Friend**...Don Williams
5/82	**You're My Bestest Friend**...Mac Davis
7/81	**You're My Favorite Star**...Bellamy Brothers
2/87	**You're My First Lady**...T.G. Sheppard
1/79	**You're My Jamaica**...Charley Pride
14/79	**You're My Kind Of Woman**...Jacky Ward
1/71	**You're My Man**...Lynn Anderson
26/72	**You're My Shoulder To Lean On**...Lana Rae
31/91	**(You're My) Soul And Inspiration**...Oak Ridge Boys
36/74	**You're My Wife, She's My Woman**...Charlie Louvin
3/87	**You're Never Too Old For Young Love**...Eddy Raven
26/82	**You're Not Easy To Forget**...Dottie West
16/74	**You're Not Getting Older (You're Getting Better)**...Freddy Weller
21/83	**You're Not Leavin' Here Tonight**...Ed Bruce
4/54	**You're Not Mine Anymore**...Webb Pierce
3/47	**You're Not My Darlin' Anymore**...Gene Autry
13/56	**You're Not Play Love**...Wilburn Brothers
15/75	**You're Not The Woman You Use To Be**...Gary Stewart
2/83	**You're Out Doing What I'm Here Doing Without**...Gene Watson
7/56	**You're Running Wild**...Louvin Brothers
38/67	**You're So Cold (I'm Turning Blue)**...Hugh X. Lewis
1/82	**You're So Good When You're Bad**...Charley Pride
4/86	**You're Something Special To Me**...George Strait
3/56	**You're Still Mine**...Faron Young
1/86	**You're Still New To Me**...Marie Osmond with Paul Davis
28/62	**You're Still On My Mind**...George Jones
14/81	**You're The Best**...Kieran Kane
1/82	**You're The Best Break This Old Heart Ever Had**...Ed Bruce
1/73	**You're The Best Thing That Ever Happened To Me**...Ray Price
1/83	**You're The First Time I've Thought About Leaving**...Reba McEntire
1/86	**You're The Last Thing I Needed Tonight**...John Schneider
5/58	**You're The Nearest Thing To Heaven**...Johnny Cash
2/78	**You're The One**...Oak Ridge Boys
5/91	**You're The One**...Dwight Yoakam
	You're The Only Good Thing (That's Happened To Me)
4/60	George Morgan
29/78	Jim Reeves
1/79	**You're The Only One**...Dolly Parton
1/65	**You're The Only World I Know**...Sonny James
38/79	**You're The Part Of Me**...Jim Ed Brown
5/87	**You're The Power**...Kathy Mattea
	You're The Reason
4/61	Bobby Edwards
14/61	Hank Locklin
16/61	Joe South
1/81	**You're The Reason God Made Oklahoma**...David Frizzell & Shelly West
6/57	**You're The Reason I'm In Love**...Sonny James
F/78	**You're The Reason Our Kids Are Ugly**...Conway Twitty & Loretta Lynn
9/84	**You're Welcome To Tonight**...Lynn Anderson & Gary Morris
26/67	**You've Been So Good To Me**...Van Trevor

POS/YR	RECORD TITLE/ARTIST
9/85	You've Got A Good Love Comin'...Lee Greenwood
2/83	You've Got A Lover...Ricky Skaggs
21/73	You've Got Me (Right Where You Want Me)...Connie Smith
3/76	You've Got Me To Hold On To...Tanya Tucker
16/79	You've Got Somebody, I've Got Somebody...Vern Gosdin
10/85	You've Got Something On Your Mind...Mickey Gilley
1/87	"You've Got" The Touch...Alabama
30/80	You've Got Those Eyes...Eddy Raven
40/77	You've Got To Mend This Heartache...Ruby Falls
6/91	You've Got To Stand For Something...Aaron Tippin
27/70	You've Got Your Troubles (I've Got Mine)...Jack Blanchard & Misty Morgan
12/72	You've Gotta Cry Girl...Dave Dudley
2/68	You've Just Stepped In (From Stepping Out On Me)...Loretta Lynn
1/73	You've Never Been This Far Before...Conway Twitty
2/84	You've Really Got A Hold On Me...Mickey Gilley
	You've Still Got A Place In My Heart
14/78	Con Hunley
3/84	George Jones
2/88	Young Country...Hank Williams, Jr.
29/76	Young Girl...Tommy Overstreet
12/57	Young Hearts...Jim Reeves
	Young Love
1/57	Sonny James
20/69	Connie Smith & Nat Stuckey
1/89	Young Love...Judds
22/82	Your Bedroom Eyes...Vern Gosdin
12/63	Your Best Friend And Me...Mac Wiseman
3/80	Your Body Is An Outlaw...Mel Tillis
1/53	Your Cheatin' Heart...Hank Williams
17/67	Your Forevers (Don't Last Very Long)...Jean Shepard
F/55	Your Good For Nothing Heart...Webb Pierce
	Your Good Girl's Gonna Go Bad
3/67	Tammy Wynette
13/81	Billie Jo Spears

POS/YR	RECORD TITLE/ARTIST
5/64	Your Heart Turned Left (And I Was On The Right)...George Jones
1/84	Your Heart's Not In It...Janie Fricke
22/70	Your Husband, My Wife...Bobby Bare & Skeeter Davis
7/79	Your Kisses Will...Crystal Gayle
21/68	Your Lily White Hands...Johnny Carver
12/87	Your Love...Tammy Wynette
1/94	Your Love Amazes Me...John Berry
3/79	Your Love Had Taken Me That High...Conway Twitty
3/91	Your Love Is A Miracle...Mark Chesnutt
5/83	Your Love Shines Through...Mickey Gilley
1/83	Your Love's On The Line...Earl Thomas Conley
15/80	Your Lying Blue Eyes...John Anderson
4/77	Your Man Loves You, Honey...Tom T. Hall
7/81	Your Memory...Steve Wariner
5/86	Your Memory Ain't What It Used To Be...Mickey Gilley
17/88	Your Memory Wins Again...Skip Ewing
29/63	Your Mother's Prayer...Buddy Cagle
6/58	Your Name Is Beautiful...Carl Smith
5/80	Your Old Cold Shoulder...Crystal Gayle
10/61	Your Old Love Letters...Porter Wagoner
5/60	Your Old Used To Be...Faron Young
13/76	Your Picture In The Paper...Statler Brothers
11/77	Your Place Or Mine...Gary Stewart
20/77	Your Pretty Roses Came Too Late...Lois Johnson
36/73	Your Side Of The Bed...Mac Davis
3/68	Your Squaw Is On The Warpath...Loretta Lynn
1/67	Your Tender Loving Care...Buck Owens
4/69	Your Time's Comin'...Faron Young
13/57	Your True Love...Carl Perkins
35/81	Your Wife Is Cheatin' On Us Again...Wayne Kemp
12/59	Your Wild Life's Gonna Get You Down...Kitty Wells
22/79	Yours...Freddy Fender
28/80	Yours For The Taking...Jack Greene
	Yours Love
5/69	Waylon Jennings
9/69	Porter Wagoner & Dolly Parton

THE RECORD HOLDERS

TOP ARTIST AND RECORD ACHIEVEMENTS

TOP 100 SINGLES 1944-1996*

PK YR	WKS CHR	WKS T40	WKS T10	WKS @ #1	RANK TITLE...ARTIST
50	44	44	44	21	1. I'm Moving On...Hank Snow
47	46	46	41	21	2. I'll Hold You In My Heart (Till I Can Hold You In My Arms) ...Eddy Arnold
55	37	37	34	21	3. In The Jailhouse Now...Webb Pierce
56	45	45	41	20	4. Crazy Arms...Ray Price
54	41	41	40	20	5. I Don't Hurt Anymore...Hank Snow
48	54	54	53	19	6. Bouquet Of Roses...Eddy Arnold
61	37	37	29	19	7. Walk On By...Leroy Van Dyke
54	36	36	32	17	8. Slowly...Webb Pierce
49	28	28	27	17	9. Slipping Around...Margaret Whiting & Jimmy Wakely
56	27	27	26	17	10. Heartbreak Hotel...Elvis Presley
49	42	42	40	16	11. Lovesick Blues...Hank Williams with His Drifting Cowboys
46	29	29	29	16	12. Guitar Polka...Al Dexter and his Troopers
63	30	30	24	16	13. Love's Gonna Live Here...Buck Owens
46	23	23	23	16	14. New Spanish Two Step...Bob Wills & His Texas Playboys
47	23	23	23	16	15. Smoke! Smoke! Smoke! (That Cigarette). Tex Williams and His Western Caravan
51	31	31	31	15	16. Slow Poke...Pee Wee King and his Golden West Cowboys
52	30	30	30	15	17. The Wild Side Of Life...Hank Thompson
60	36	36	30	14	18. Please Help Me, I'm Falling...Hank Locklin
60	34	34	29	14	19. He'll Have To Go...Jim Reeves
52	29	29	29	14	20. Jambalaya (On The Bayou)...Hank Williams with His Drifting Cowboys
51	25	25	25	14	21. The Shot Gun Boogie...Tennessee Ernie Ford
46	23	23	23	14	22. Divorce Me C.O.D. ...Merle Travis
47	22	22	22	14	23. So Round, So Firm, So Fully Packed... Merle Travis
44	30	30	30	13	24. So Long Pal...Al Dexter and his Troopers
55	32	32	28	13	25. Love, Love, Love...Webb Pierce
56	30	30	28	13	26. Singing The Blues...Marty Robbins
44	27	27	27	13	27. Smoke On The Water...Red Foley
58	34	34	25	13	28. City Lights...Ray Price
58	29	29	20	13	29. Alone With You...Faron Young
50	20	20	20	13	30. Chattanoogie Shoe Shine Boy...Red Foley
53	19	19	19	13	31. Kaw-Liga...Hank Williams
55	32	32	28	12	32. I Don't Care...Webb Pierce
51	28	28	28	12	33. Always Late (With Your Kisses)...Lefty Frizzell
53	27	27	27	12	34. There Stands The Glass...Webb Pierce
60	34	34	26	12	35. Alabam...Cowboy Copas
49	31	31	26	12	36. Don't Rob Another Man's Castle...Eddy Arnold
48	32	32	31	11	37. One Has My Name (The Other Has My Heart)...Jimmy Wakely

PK YR	WKS CHR	WKS T40	WKS T10	WKS @ #1	RANK	TITLE...ARTIST
51	27	27	27	11	38.	I Want To Be With You Always...Lefty Frizzell
51	24	24	24	11	39.	I Wanna Play House With You...Eddy Arnold
51	23	23	23	11	40.	There's Been A Change In Me...Eddy Arnold
62	24	24	22	11	41.	Don't Let Me Cross Over...Carl Butler and Pearl
45	20	20	20	11	42.	You Two-Timed Me One Time Too Often Tex Ritter and His Texans
60	36	36	30	10	43.	Wings Of A Dove...Ferlin Husky
54	29	29	27	10	44.	More And More...Webb Pierce
56	28	28	25	10	45.	Don't Be Cruel/Hound Dog...Elvis Presley
50	32	25	25	10	46.	Why Don't You Love Me...Hank Williams with His Drifting Cowboys
57	27	27	21	10	47.	Gone...Ferlin Husky
58	23	23	19	10	48.	Ballad Of A Teenage Queen...Johnny Cash
55	21	21	18	10	49.	Sixteen Tons...Tennessee Ernie Ford
59	21	21	18	10	50.	The Battle Of New Orleans...Johnny Horton
61	19	19	18	10	51.	Don't Worry...Marty Robbins
59	19	19	17	10	52.	The Three Bells...The Browns
48	39	39	37	9	53.	Anytime...Eddy Arnold and his Tennessee Plowboys
45	31	31	31	9	54.	Shame On You...Spade Cooley
53	26	26	26	9	55.	Mexican Joe...Jim Reeves and The Circle O | Ranch Boys
62	26	26	21	9	56.	Wolverton Mountain...Claude King
57	24	24	20	9	57.	Young Love...Sonny James
61	23	23	18	9	58.	Hello Walls...Faron Young
66	25	24	13	9	59.	Almost Persuaded...David Houston
51	33	33	33	8	60.	Let Old Mother Nature Have Her Way. Carl Smith
48	32	32	27	8	61.	Just A Little Lovin' (Will Go A Long, Long Way)...Eddy Arnold
51	27	27	27	8	62.	The Rhumba Boogie...Hank Snow
58	34	34	26	8	63.	Oh Lonesome Me...Don Gibson
53	26	26	26	8	64.	Hey Joe!...Carl Smith
53	26	26	26	8	65.	I Forgot More Than You'll Ever Know... The Davis Sisters
57	26	26	25	8	66.	Four Walls...Jim Reeves
51	25	25	25	8	67.	Hey, Good Lookin'...Hank Williams with His Drifting Cowboys
52	24	24	24	8	68.	(When You Feel Like You're In Love) Don't Just Stand There...Carl Smith
45	22	22	22	8	69.	At Mail Call Today...Gene Autry
53	22	22	22	8	70.	It's Been So Long...Webb Pierce
50	21	21	21	8	71.	Long Gone Lonesome Blues...Hank Williams with His Drifting Cowboys
58	24	24	20	8	72.	Guess Things Happen That Way...Johnny Cash
57	22	22	20	8	73.	Wake Up Little Susie...The Everly Brothers
64	28	27	19	8	74.	Once A Day...Connie Smith
62	21	21	14	8	75.	Devil Woman...Marty Robbins
55	32	32	29	7	76.	Loose Talk...Carl Smith
61	32	32	24	7	77.	Tender Years...George Jones

PK YR	WKS CHR	WKS T40	WKS T10	WKS @ #1	RANK TITLE...ARTIST
64	26	26	22	7	78. My Heart Skips A Beat...Buck Owens
59	26	26	22	7	79. El Paso...Marty Robbins
62	27	27	21	7	80. Mama Sang A Song...Bill Anderson
57	26	26	21	7	81. Bye Bye Love...The Everly Brothers
45	21	21	21	7	82. I'm Losing My Mind Over You...Al Dexter and his Troopers
63	27	27	20	7	83. Still...Bill Anderson
63	26	26	19	7	84. Ring Of Fire...Johnny Cash
64	26	24	18	7	85. I Guess I'm Crazy...Jim Reeves
66	23	21	15	7	86. There Goes My Everything...Jack Greene
66	19	18	13	7	87. Waitin' In Your Welfare Line...Buck Owens
56	43	43	39	6	88. I Walk The Line...Johnny Cash
53	23	23	23	6	89. A Dear John Letter...Jean Shepard & Ferlin Huskey
53	23	23	23	6	90. Your Cheatin' Heart...Hank Williams with His Drifting Cowboys
44	20	20	20	6	91. I'm Wastin' My Tears On You...Tex Ritter and His Texans
62	23	23	19	6	92. She Thinks I Still Care...George Jones
45	19	19	19	6	93. Oklahoma Hills...Jack Guthrie
64	27	27	18	6	94. I Don't Care (Just as Long as You Love Me)....Buck Owens
52	18	18	18	6	95. It Wasn't God Who Made Honky Tonk Angels ...Kitty Wells
64	22	22	17	6	96. Understand Your Man...Johnny Cash
64	25	22	15	6	97. Dang Me...Roger Miller
59	20	20	15	6	98. Don't Take Your Guns To Town...Johnny Cash
44	15	15	15	6	99. Straighten Up And Fly Right...The King Cole Trio
66	22	21	14	6	100. Giddyup Go...Red Sovine

*Ranking period includes all #1 hits that peaked as of 5/25/96.

PK YR: Year record reached its peak position
WKS CHR: Total weeks charted in the Top 100
WKS T40: Total weeks charted in the Top 40
WKS T10: Total weeks charted in the Top 10
WKS @ #1: Total weeks record held the #1 position

Records are ranked according to the number of weeks they held the #1 position.
Ties are broken in the following order:
1. Total weeks in the Top 10
2. Total weeks in the Top 40
3. Total weeks charted in the Top 100
4. Points based on weekly chart position

TOP 100 ARTISTS 1944-1996

	ARTIST	POINTS		ARTIST	POINTS
1.	EDDY ARNOLD	11,861	51.	ANNE MURRAY	3,166
2.	GEORGE JONES	10,238	52.	STEVE WARINER	3,094
3.	CONWAY TWITTY	8,340	53.	EARL THOMAS CONLEY	3,043
4.	JOHNNY CASH	8,264	54.	DOTTIE WEST	2,981
5.	MERLE HAGGARD	8,080	55.	EMMYLOU HARRIS	2,970
6.	WEBB PIERCE	7,489	56.	BELLAMY BROTHERS	2,966
7.	DOLLY PARTON	6,945	57.	JOE STAMPLEY	2,955
8.	BUCK OWENS	6,841	58.	RANDY TRAVIS	2,927
9.	RAY PRICE	6,698	59.	TOM T. HALL	2,900
10.	MARTY ROBBINS	6,646	60.	MOE BANDY	2,867
11.	WAYLON JENNINGS	6,638	61.	FERLIN HUSKY	2,857
12.	JIM REEVES	6,449	62.	CONNIE SMITH	2,811
13.	WILLIE NELSON	6,096	63.	GARTH BROOKS	2,796
14.	ERNEST TUBB	6,095	64.	JOHN ANDERSON	2,731
15.	CHARLEY PRIDE	5,935	65.	FREDDIE HART	2,685
16.	LORETTA LYNN	5,759	66.	VINCE GILL	2,678
17.	SONNY JAMES	5,743	67.	BILLY WALKER	2,624
18.	FARON YOUNG	5,657	68.	JOHNNY RODRIGUEZ	2,570
19.	HANK WILLIAMS, JR.	5,643	69.	JANIE FRICKE	2,552
20.	HANK SNOW	5,551	70.	GENE WATSON	2,549
21.	RONNIE MILSAP	5,549	71.	RICKY SKAGGS	2,547
22.	ALABAMA	5,321	72.	LARRY GATLIN/GATLIN BROTHERS	2,463
23.	RED FOLEY	5,170	73.	CHARLIE RICH	2,422
24.	GEORGE STRAIT	5,075	74.	LEFTY FRIZZELL	2,404
25.	REBA MCENTIRE	5,032	75.	BOB WILLS	2,402
26.	CARL SMITH	5,027	76.	ALAN JACKSON	2,400
27.	TAMMY WYNETTE	4,992	77.	BILLY "CRASH" CRADDOCK	2,397
28.	DON WILLIAMS	4,784	78.	CLINT BLACK	2,375
29.	MEL TILLIS	4,754	79.	JOHN CONLEE	2,362
30.	BILL ANDERSON	4,752	80.	JERRY REED	2,345
31.	TANYA TUCKER	4,540	81.	STONEWALL JACKSON	2,336
32.	KITTY WELLS	4,496	82.	JOHNNY PAYCHECK	2,313
33.	PORTER WAGONER	4,477	83.	SAWYER BROWN	2,306
34.	ELVIS PRESLEY	4,461	84.	THE JUDDS	2,284
35.	KENNY ROGERS	4,450	85.	ROY DRUSKY	2,272
36.	DON GIBSON	4,326	86.	LEE GREENWOOD	2,251
37.	HANK WILLIAMS	4,305	87.	JIM ED BROWN	2,240
38.	THE STATLER BROTHERS	4,189	88.	DAVE DUDLEY	2,232
39.	HANK THOMPSON	4,126	89.	VERN GOSDIN	2,213
40.	CRYSTAL GAYLE	3,996	90.	JIMMY WAKELY	2,166
41.	GLEN CAMPBELL	3,903	91.	EDDY RAVEN	2,162
42.	JERRY LEE LEWIS	3,766	92.	ROGER MILLER	2,151
43.	OAK RIDGE BOYS	3,747	93.	RICKY VAN SHELTON	2,124
44.	BARBARA MANDRELL	3,724	94.	KATHY MATTEA	2,055
45.	MICKEY GILLEY	3,674	95.	GENE AUTRY	2,036
46.	EDDIE RABBITT	3,631	96.	JEAN SHEPARD	1,995
47.	DAVID HOUSTON	3,551	97.	AL DEXTER	1,986
48.	BOBBY BARE	3,545	98.	DONNA FARGO	1,982
49.	T.G. SHEPPARD	3,365	99.	PATTY LOVELESS	1,967
50.	LYNN ANDERSON	3,326	100.	CHARLY MCCLAIN	1,956

TOP ARTISTS BY DECADE

ARTIST	POINTS	ARTIST	POINTS	ARTIST	POINTS
FORTIES ('44-'49)		**FIFTIES ('50-'59)**		**SIXTIES ('60-'69)**	
1. EDDY ARNOLD	3,587	1. WEBB PIERCE	5,041	1. BUCK OWENS	4,729
2. ERNEST TUBB	2,612	2. EDDY ARNOLD	4,422	2. GEORGE JONES	3,872
3. BOB WILLS	2,143	3. HANK SNOW	3,913	3. JIM REEVES	3,311
4. AL DEXTER	1,986	4. CARL SMITH	3,519	4. JOHNNY CASH	2,898
5. RED FOLEY	1,746	5. RED FOLEY	3,424	5. EDDY ARNOLD	2,685
6. GENE AUTRY	1,741	6. HANK WILLIAMS	3,203	6. MARTY ROBBINS	2,525
7. JIMMY WAKELY	1,415	7. JOHNNY CASH	2,648	7. BILL ANDERSON	2,406
8. TEX RITTER	1,344	8. ELVIS PRESLEY	2,624	8. WEBB PIERCE	2,362
9. TEX WILLIAMS	1,203	9. KITTY WELLS	2,528	9. SONNY JAMES	2,320
10. MERLE TRAVIS	1,172	10. ERNEST TUBB	2,503	10. RAY PRICE	2,312
11. HANK WILLIAMS	1,032	11. RAY PRICE	2,290	11. FARON YOUNG	2,273
12. ELTON BRITT	703	12. HANK THOMPSON	2,267	12. PORTER WAGONER	2,116
13. TED DAFFAN	687	13. FARON YOUNG	2,192	13. KITTY WELLS	1,968
14. SONS OF THE PIONEERS	652	14. JIM REEVES	2,175	14. STONEWALL JACKSON	1,897
15. FLOYD TILLMAN	651	15. MARTY ROBBINS	2,018	15. LORETTA LYNN	1,845
16. SPADE COOLEY	606	16. LEFTY FRIZZELL	1,901	16. DAVID HOUSTON	1,807
17. HANK THOMPSON	597	17. TENNESSEE ERNIE FORD	1,365	17. ROY DRUSKY	1,749
18. COWBOY COPAS	594	18. FERLIN HUSKY	1,210	18. DON GIBSON	1,730
19. GEORGE MORGAN	579	19. THE EVERLY BROTHERS	1,070	19. MERLE HAGGARD	1,655
20. ROY ACUFF	570	20. JOHNNIE & JACK	993	20. ROGER MILLER	1,638
21. MARGARET WHITING	469	21. GEORGE JONES	988	21. BILLY WALKER	1,531
22. "T" TEXAS TYLER	426	22. DON GIBSON	932	22. BOBBY BARE	1,507
23. BILL MONROE	423	23. JIMMY NEWMAN	811	23. GEORGE HAMILTON IV	1,503
24. JIMMIE DAVIS	415	24. JOHNNY HORTON	789	24. CONNIE SMITH	1,447
25. TENNESSEE ERNIE FORD	413	25. THE BROWNS	769	25. DAVE DUDLEY	1,431
SEVENTIES ('70-'79)		**EIGHTIES ('80-'89)**		**NINTIES ('90-'96)**	
1. CONWAY TWITTY	4,082	1. WILLIE NELSON	3,219	1. GARTH BROOKS	2,599
2. MERLE HAGGARD	3,464	2. CONWAY TWITTY	3,201	2. GEORGE STRAIT	2,401
3. CHARLEY PRIDE	3,245	3. ALABAMA	3,196	3. ALAN JACKSON	2,400
4. LORETTA LYNN	3,145	4. RONNIE MILSAP	3,105	4. REBA MCENTIRE	2,147
5. DOLLY PARTON	3,124	5. KENNY ROGERS	2,916	5. CLINT BLACK	2,146
6. TAMMY WYNETTE	3,081	6. MERLE HAGGARD	2,907	6. ALABAMA	2,081
7. MEL TILLIS	2,991	7. OAK RIDGE BOYS	2,835	7. VINCE GILL	2,027
8. WAYLON JENNINGS	2,899	8. HANK WILLIAMS, JR.	2,735	8. BROOKS & DUNN	1,796
9. GEORGE JONES	2,857	9. GEORGE STRAIT	2,674	9. JOE DIFFIE	1,782
10. SONNY JAMES	2,573	10. EARL THOMAS CONLEY	2,661	10. MARK CHESNUTT	1,758
11. TOM T. HALL	2,408	11. REBA MCENTIRE	2,622	11. TRAVIS TRITT	1,739
12. LYNN ANDERSON	2,319	12. DON WILLIAMS	2,609	12. DOUG STONE	1,552
13. CHARLIE RICH	2,263	13. DOLLY PARTON	2,590	13. TANYA TUCKER	1,521
14. JOHNNY CASH	2,225	14. WAYLON JENNINGS	2,501	14. RANDY TRAVIS	1,520
15. BILL ANDERSON	2,168	15. CRYSTAL GAYLE	2,472	15. TRACY LAWRENCE	1,472
16. WILLIE NELSON	2,124	16. BELLAMY BROTHERS	2,464	16. PATTY LOVELESS	1,438
17. FREDDIE HART	2,083	17. GEORGE JONES	2,299	17. SAWYER BROWN	1,373
18. JERRY LEE LEWIS	2,045	18. T.G. SHEPPARD	2,250	18. COLLIN RAYE	1,337
19. BILLY "CRASH" CRADDOCK	2,043	19. RICKY SKAGGS	2,214	19. LORRIE MORGAN	1,310
20. RONNIE MILSAP	1,958	20. STEVE WARINER	2,210	20. PAM TILLIS	1,283
21. JOHNNY RODRIGUEZ	1,939	21. MICKEY GILLEY	2,147	21. JOHN MICHAEL MONTGOMERY	1,276
22. HANK WILLIAMS, JR.	1,928	22. EDDIE RABBITT	2,114	22. SHENANDOAH	1,236
23. JOE STAMPLEY	1,871	23. JANIE FRICKE	2,040	23. MARY-CHAPIN CARPENTER	1,229
24. GLEN CAMPBELL	1,842	24. THE STATLER BROTHERS	2,022	24. RICKY VAN SHELTON	1,225
25. DONNA FARGO	1,839	25. LEE GREENWOOD	2,018	25. TRISHA YEARWOOD	1,224

TOP 40 ARTIST ACHIEVEMENTS

ARTIST	TOTAL	ARTIST	TOTAL
MOST CHARTED SINGLES		**MOST TOP 10 SINGLES**	
1. GEORGE JONES	140	1. EDDY ARNOLD	92
2. EDDY ARNOLD	128	2. GEORGE JONES	78
3. JOHNNY CASH	104	3. CONWAY TWITTY	75
4. MERLE HAGGARD	90	4. MERLE HAGGARD	71
5. DOLLY PARTON	89	5. ERNEST TUBB	58
6. WAYLON JENNINGS	89	6. RED FOLEY	56
7. CONWAY TWITTY	88	7. WEBB PIERCE	54
8. WEBB PIERCE	84	8. DOLLY PARTON	54
9. MARTY ROBBINS	83	9. WAYLON JENNINGS	53
10. RAY PRICE	82	10. JOHNNY CASH	52
11. ERNEST TUBB	82	11. CHARLEY PRIDE	52
12. WILLIE NELSON	80	12. JIM REEVES	51
13. FARON YOUNG	79	13. LORETTA LYNN	51
14. HANK WILLIAMS, JR.	78	14. RONNIE MILSAP	49
15. BUCK OWENS	75	15. BUCK OWENS	47
16. JIM REEVES	73	16. MARTY ROBBINS	47
17. LORETTA LYNN	69	17. GEORGE STRAIT	47
18. CARL SMITH	69	18. RAY PRICE	46
19. MEL TILLIS	68	19. ALABAMA	46
20. ELVIS PRESLEY	66	20. DON WILLIAMS	45
21. HANK SNOW	65	21. SONNY JAMES	43
22. PORTER WAGONER	65	22. HANK SNOW	43
23. DON GIBSON	65	23. HANK WILLIAMS, JR.	42
24. SONNY JAMES	64	24. REBA MCENTIRE	42
25. KITTY WELLS	64	25. WILLIE NELSON	41
		26. FARON YOUNG	41
MOST #1 SINGLES		**MOST WEEKS HELD #1 POSITION**	
1. CONWAY TWITTY	40	1. EDDY ARNOLD	145
2. MERLE HAGGARD	38	2. WEBB PIERCE	111
3. RONNIE MILSAP	35	3. BUCK OWENS	82
4. ALABAMA	32	4. HANK WILLIAMS	82
5. CHARLEY PRIDE	29	5. JOHNNY CASH	69
6. EDDY ARNOLD	28	6. SONNY JAMES	66
7. GEORGE STRAIT	28	7. MARTY ROBBINS	63
8. DOLLY PARTON	24	8. JIM REEVES	58
9. SONNY JAMES	23	9. MERLE HAGGARD	57
10. BUCK OWENS	21	10. HANK SNOW	56
11. WILLIE NELSON	20	11. CONWAY TWITTY	52
12. TAMMY WYNETTE	20	12. ELVIS PRESLEY	50
13. KENNY ROGERS	20	13. CHARLEY PRIDE	49
14. REBA MCENTIRE	19	14. RAY PRICE	47
15. CRYSTAL GAYLE	18	15. RONNIE MILSAP	47
16. EARL THOMAS CONLEY	18	16. AL DEXTER	47
17. DON WILLIAMS	17	17. GEORGE STRAIT	44
18. OAK RIDGE BOYS	17	18. ALABAMA	40
19. MICKEY GILLEY	17	19. RED FOLEY	40
20. EDDIE RABBITT	17	20. TAMMY WYNETTE	37
21. MARTY ROBBINS	16	21. LEFTY FRIZZELL	36
22. WAYLON JENNINGS	16	22. DOLLY PARTON	33
23. LORETTA LYNN	16	23. WAYLON JENNINGS	33
24. RANDY TRAVIS	15	24. JIMMY WAKELY	33
25. GARTH BROOKS	15	25. CARL SMITH	32

TOP SINGLES BY DECADE

PK YR	WKS CHR	WKS T40	WKS T10	WKS @ #1	RANK TITLE...ARTIST
					FORTIES ('44-'49)
47	46	46	41	21	1. I'll Hold You In My Heart (Till I Can Hold You In My Arms)...Eddy Arnold
48	54	54	53	19	2. Bouquet Of Roses...Eddy Arnold
49	28	28	27	17	3. Slipping Around...Margaret Whiting & Jimmy Wakely
49	42	42	40	16	4. Lovesick Blues...Hank Williams with His Drifting Cowboys
46	29	29	29	16	5. Guitar Polka...Al Dexter and his Troopers
46	23	23	23	16	6. New Spanish Two Step...Bob Wills & His Texas Playboys
47	23	23	23	16	7. Smoke! Smoke! Smoke! (That Cigarette)...Tex Williams and His Western Caravan
46	23	23	23	14	8. Divorce Me C.O.D. ...Merle Travis
47	22	22	22	14	9. So Round, So Firm, So Fully Packed...Merle Travis
44	30	30	30	13	10. So Long Pal...Al Dexter and his Troopers
44	27	27	27	13	11. Smoke On The Water...Red Foley
49	31	31	26	12	12. Don't Rob Another Man's Castle...Eddy Arnold
48	32	32	31	11	13. One Has My Name (The Other Has My Heart)...Jimmy Wakely
45	20	20	20	11	14. You Two-Timed Me One Time Too Often...Tex Ritter and His Texans
48	39	39	37	9	15. Anytime...Eddy Arnold and his Tennessee Plowboys
45	31	31	31	9	16. Shame On You...Spade Cooley
48	32	32	27	8	17. Just A Little Lovin' (Will Go A Long, Long Way)...Eddy Arnold
45	22	22	22	8	18. At Mail Call Today...Gene Autry
45	21	21	21	7	19. I'm Losing My Mind Over You...Al Dexter and his Troopers
44	20	20	20	6	20. I'm Wastin' My Tears On You...Tex Ritter and His Texans
45	19	19	19	6	21. Oklahoma Hills...Jack Guthrie
44	15	15	15	6	22. Straighten Up And Fly Right...The King Cole Trio
47	38	38	38	5	23. It's A Sin...Eddy Arnold
49	28	28	26	5	24. I Love You So Much It Hurts...Jimmy Wakely
46	13	13	13	5	25. Wine, Women And Song...Al Dexter and his Troopers
					FIFTIES ('50-'59)
50	44	44	44	21	1. I'm Moving On...Hank Snow
55	37	37	34	21	2. In The Jailhouse Now...Webb Pierce
56	45	45	41	20	3. Crazy Arms...Ray Price
54	41	41	40	20	4. I Don't Hurt Anymore...Hank Snow
54	36	36	32	17	5. Slowly...Webb Pierce
56	27	27	26	17	6. Heartbreak Hotel...Elvis Presley
51	31	31	31	15	7. Slow Poke...Pee Wee King and his Golden West Cowboys
52	30	30	30	15	8. The Wild Side Of Life...Hank Thompson
52	29	29	29	14	9. Jambalaya (On The Bayou)...Hank Williams with His Drifting Cowboys

PK YR	WKS CHR	WKS T40	WKS T10	WKS @ #1	RANK TITLE...ARTIST
51	25	25	25	14	10. The Shot Gun Boogie...Tennessee Ernie Ford
55	32	32	28	13	11. Love, Love, Love...Webb Pierce
56	30	30	28	13	12. Singing The Blues...Marty Robbins
58	34	34	25	13	13. City Lights...Ray Price
58	29	29	20	13	14. Alone With You...Faron Young
50	20	20	20	13	15. Chattanoogie Shoe Shine Boy...Red Foley
53	19	19	19	13	16. Kaw-Liga...Hank Williams
55	32	32	28	12	17. I Don't Care...Webb Pierce
51	28	28	28	12	18. Always Late (With Your Kisses)...Lefty Frizzell
53	27	27	27	12	19. There Stands The Glass...Webb Pierce
51	27	27	27	11	20. I Want To Be With You Always...Lefty Frizzell
51	24	24	24	11	21. I Wanna Play House With You...Eddy Arnold
51	23	23	23	11	22. There's Been A Change In Me...Eddy Arnold
54	29	29	27	10	23. More And More...Webb Pierce
56	28	28	25	10	24. Don't Be Cruel/Hound Dog...Elvis Presley
50	25	25	25	10	25. Why Don't You Love Me...Hank Williams with His Drifting Cowboys

SIXTIES ('60-'69)

PK YR	WKS CHR	WKS T40	WKS T10	WKS @ #1	RANK TITLE...ARTIST
61	37	37	29	19	1. Walk On By...Leroy Van Dyke
63	30	30	24	16	2. Love's Gonna Live Here...Buck Owens
60	36	36	30	14	3. Please Help Me, I'm Falling...Hank Locklin
60	34	34	29	14	4. He'll Have To Go...Jim Reeves
60	34	34	26	12	5. Alabam...Cowboy Copas
62	24	24	22	11	6. Don't Let Me Cross Over...Carl Butler and Pearl
60	36	36	30	10	7. Wings Of A Dove...Ferlin Husky
61	19	19	18	10	8. Don't Worry...Marty Robbins
62	26	26	21	9	9. Wolverton Mountain...Claude King
61	23	23	18	9	10. Hello Walls...Faron Young
66	25	24	13	9	11. Almost Persuaded...David Houston
64	28	27	19	8	12. Once A Day...Connie Smith
62	21	21	14	8	13. Devil Woman...Marty Robbins
61	32	32	24	7	14. Tender Years...George Jones
64	26	26	22	7	15. My Heart Skips A Beat...Buck Owens
62	27	27	21	7	16. Mama Sang A Song...Bill Anderson
63	27	27	20	7	17. Still...Bill Anderson
63	26	26	19	7	18. Ring Of Fire...Johnny Cash
64	26	24	18	7	19. I Guess I'm Crazy...Jim Reeves
66	23	21	15	7	20. There Goes My Everything...Jack Greene
66	19	18	13	7	21. Waitin' In Your Welfare Line...Buck Owens
62	23	23	19	6	22. She Thinks I Still Care...George Jones
64	27	27	18	6	23. I Don't Care (Just as Long as You Love Me)...Buck Owens
64	22	22	17	6	24. Understand Your Man...Johnny Cash
64	25	22	15	6	25. Dang Me...Roger Miller

PK YR	WKS CHR	WKS T40	WKS T10	WKS @ #1	RANK	TITLE...ARTIST
						SEVENTIES ('70-'79)
72	19	18	12	6	1.	My Hang-Up Is You...Freddie Hart
77	18	14	10	6	2.	Luckenbach, Texas (Back to the Basics of Love)...Waylon Jennings
75	15	13	8	6	3.	Convoy...C.W. McCall
71	19	18	13	5	4.	Kiss An Angel Good Mornin'...Charley Pride
70	20	19	12	5	5.	Rose Garden...Lynn Anderson
77	19	14	10	5	6.	Here You Come Again...Dolly Parton
71	15	13	10	5	7.	When You're Hot, You're Hot...Jerry Reed
70	20	18	10	4	8.	Hello Darlin'...Conway Twitty
70	17	16	10	4	9.	Baby, Baby (I Know You're A Lady)...David Houston
71	16	15	10	4	10.	Empty Arms...Sonny James
71	16	14	9	4	11.	I'm Just Me...Charley Pride
70	15	14	9	4	12.	Don't Keep Me Hangin' On...Sonny James
77	18	15	8	4	13.	Don't It Make My Brown Eyes Blue...Crystal Gayle
78	16	12	8	4	14.	Mammas Don't Let Your Babies Grow Up To Be Cowboys ...Waylon & Willie
73	17	14	7	4	15.	If We Make It Through December...Merle Haggard
77	20	13	7	4	16.	Heaven's Just A Sin Away...The Kendalls
70	14	13	7	4	17.	It's Just A Matter Of Time...Sonny James
71	24	22	13	3	18.	Easy Loving...Freddie Hart
71	20	18	12	3	19.	Help Me Make It Through The Night...Sammi Smith
71	19	17	12	3	20.	I Won't Mention It Again...Ray Price
72	23	17	10	3	21.	The Happiest Girl In The Whole U.S.A. ...Donna Fargo
73	19	16	10	3	22.	You've Never Been This Far Before...Conway Twitty
72	16	15	10	3	23.	Carolyn...Merle Haggard
70	16	14	9	3	24.	Endlessly...Sonny James
70	16	14	9	3	25.	He Loves Me All The Way...Tammy Wynette
						EIGHTIES ('80-'89)
80	15	9	8	3	1.	Coward Of The County...Kenny Rogers
80	15	13	7	3	2.	My Heart...Ronnie Milsap
80	14	10	7	3	3.	Lookin' For Love...Johnny Lee
87	22	13	6	3	4.	Forever And Ever, Amen...Randy Travis
85	22	14	8	2	5.	Have Mercy...The Judds (Wynonna & Naomi)
83	23	15	7	2	6.	Islands In The Stream...Kenny Rogers with Dolly Parton
83	22	15	7	2	7.	Houston (Means I'm One Day Closer To You)...Larry Gatlin & The Gatlin Brothers
84	22	15	7	2	8.	Why Not Me...The Judds (Wynonna & Naomi)
85	23	14	7	2	9.	Lost In The Fifties Tonight (In the Still of the Night)...Ronnie Milsap
88	22	14	7	2	10.	When You Say Nothing At All...Keith Whitley
86	19	14	7	2	11.	Mind Your Own Business...Hank Williams, Jr.
84	20	13	7	2	12.	To All The Girls I've Loved Before...Julio Iglesias & Willie Nelson

PK YR	WKS CHR	WKS T40	WKS T10	WKS @ #1	RANK TITLE...ARTIST
80	16	12	7	2	13. I Believe In You...Don Williams
80	14	10	7	2	14. My Heroes Have Always Been Cowboys...Willie Nelson
89	26	24	6	2	15. A Woman In Love...Ronnie Milsap
88	21	15	6	2	16. I'll Leave This World Loving You...Ricky Van Shelton
82	21	15	6	2	17. Always On My Mind...Willie Nelson
87	23	14	6	2	18. Somewhere Tonight...Highway 101
89	22	14	6	2	19. I'm No Stranger To The Rain...Keith Whitley
88	20	14	6	2	20. Eighteen Wheels And A Dozen Roses..Kathy Mattea
80	16	13	6	2	21. One In A Million...Johnny Lee
81	16	11	6	2	22. Love In The First Degree...Alabama
81	15	11	6	2	23. (There's) No Gettin' Over Me...Ronnie Milsap
81	15	11	6	2	24. Never Been So Loved (In All My Life)...Charley Pride
81	15	10	6	2	25. I Don't Need You...Kenny Rogers
					NINTIES ('90-'96)
90	21	20	11	5	1. Love Without End, Amen...George Strait
90	20	19	10	5	2. I've Come To Expect It From You...George Strait
95	20	19	9	5	3. I Like It, I Love It...Tim McGraw
92	20	16	9	5	4. Achy Breaky Heart...Billy Ray Cyrus
95	20	18	11	4	5. Check Yes Or No...George Strait
90	20	19	10	4	6. Jukebox In My Mind...Alabama
90	26	22	9	4	7. Hard Rock Bottom Of Your Heart...Randy Travis
90	20	19	9	4	8. Friends In Low Places...Garth Brooks
93	20	16	9	4	9. Chattahoochee...Alan Jackson
92	20	19	8	4	10. What She's Doing Now...Garth Brooks
94	20	19	8	4	11. Pickup Man...Joe Diffie
94	20	18	8	4	12. I Swear...John Michael Montgomery
92	20	17	8	4	13. No One Else On Earth...Wynonna Judd
92	20	16	8	4	14. Boot Scootin' Boogie...Brooks & Dunn
94	20	18	7	4	15. Wink...Neal McCoy
94	20	17	7	4	16. Wild One...Faith Hill
92	20	18	10	3	17. Don't Let Our Love Start Slippin' Away...Vince Gill
92	20	17	10	3	18. Love, Me...Collin Raye
96	16+	16+	10	3	19. My Maria...Brooks & Dunn
91	20	19	9	3	20. Don't Rock The Jukebox...Alan Jackson
91	20	19	9	3	21. Down Home...Alabama
90	21	18	9	3	22. The Dance...Garth Brooks
92	20	18	9	3	23. I Saw The Light...Wynonna Judd
96	20	18	8	3	24. It Matters To Me...Faith Hill
95	20	17	8	3	25. Sold (The Grundy County Auction Incident)…John Michael Montgomery

+ still charted as of 7/20/96

#1 SINGLES LISTED CHRONOLOGICALLY 1944-1996

This section lists, in chronological order, all 1,302 singles/tracks that hit #1 on *Billboard*'s country charts from 1944 through May 25, 1996.

From May 15, 1948, through October 13, 1958, when *Billboard* published more than one weekly country chart, the chart designation and #1 weeks on each chart are listed in special columns at the right of the artist names. The chart designations are:

JB: Juke Box
BS: Best Sellers
JY: Jockeys

The date shown is the earliest date that a single/track hit #1 on any of the country charts. The weeks column lists the total weeks at #1, from whichever chart it achieved its highest total. This total is not a combined total from the various country charts.

Because of the multiple charts used for this research, some dates are duplicated, since certain #1 hits may have peaked on the same week on different charts. *Billboard* also showed ties at #1 on some of these

charts; therefore, the total weeks for each year may calculate out to more than 52.

Billboard has not published an issue for the last week of the year since 1976. For the years 1976 through 1991, *Billboard* considered the charts listed in the last published issue of the year to be "frozen" and all chart positions remained the same for the unpublished week. This frozen chart data is included in our tabulations. Since 1992, *Billboard* has compiled a country chart for the last week of the year, even though an issue is not published. This chart is only available through *Billboard*'s computerized information network (BIN) or by mail. Our tabulations include this unpublished chart data.

See the introduction pages of this book for more details on researching the country charts.

DATE: Date single/track first peaked at the #1 position
WKS: Total weeks single/track held the #1 position
↕: Indicates single/track hit #1, dropped down, and then returned to the #1 spot

DATE	WKS		RECORD TITLE	ARTIST
			1944	
			1/8/44 THROUGH 5/8/48: BILLBOARD'S ONLY	
			COUNTRY CHART IS A "JUKE BOX" CHART.	
1/8	5 ↕	1.	Pistol Packin' Mama	Bing Crosby & Andrews Sisters
2/5	3	2.	Pistol Packin' Mama	Al Dexter
2/26	3 ↕	3.	Ration Blues	Louis Jordan
3/11	1	4.	Rosalita	Al Dexter
3/18	1	5.	They Took The Stars Out Of Heaven	Floyd Tillman
3/25	13 ↕	6.	So Long Pal	Al Dexter
4/1	2 ↕	7.	Too Late To Worry, Too Blue To Cry	Al Dexter
6/10	6 ↕	8.	Straighten Up And Fly Right	King Cole Trio
7/29	5	9.	Is You Is Or Is You Ain't (Ma' Baby)	Louis Jordan
9/2	4	10.	Soldier's Last Letter	Ernest Tubb
9/23	13	11.	Smoke On The Water	Red Foley
12/23	6	12.	I'm Wastin' My Tears On You	Tex Ritter
			1945	
2/3	7 ↕	1.	I'm Losing My Mind Over You	Al Dexter
3/17	1	2.	There's A New Moon Over My Shoulder	Jimmie Davis
3/31	9 ↕	3.	Shame On You	Spade Cooley
4/14	2 ↕	4.	Smoke On The Water	Bob Wills
5/19	8 ↕	5.	At Mail Call Today	Gene Autry
7/7	1	6.	Stars And Stripes On Iwo Jima	Bob Wills
7/28	6 ↕	7.	Oklahoma Hills	Jack Guthrie

DATE	WKS	RECORD TITLE	ARTIST	CHARTS
8/25	11 ↕	8. You Two-Timed Me One Time Too Often	Tex Ritter	
10/27	4 ↕	9. With Tears In My Eyes	Wesley Tuttle	
11/24	4 ↕	10. Sioux City Sue	Dick Thomas	
11/24	1	11. Shame On You	Lawrence Welk Orchestra with Red Foley	
12/8	4 ↕	12. It's Been So Long Darling	Ernest Tubb	
12/15	3 ↕	13. Silver Dew On The Blue Grass Tonight	Bob Wills	

1946

DATE	WKS	RECORD TITLE	ARTIST	CHARTS
1/5	3 ↕	1. You Will Have To Pay	Tex Ritter	
1/5	1	2. White Cross On Okinawa	Bob Wills	
2/2	16 ↕	3. Guitar Polka	Al Dexter	
5/18	16 ↕	4. New Spanish Two Step	Bob Wills	
9/14	5 ↕	5. Wine, Women And Song	Al Dexter	
10/12	14 ↕	6. Divorce Me C.O.D.	Merle Travis	

1947

DATE	WKS	RECORD TITLE	ARTIST	CHARTS
1/18	2 ↕	1. Rainbow At Midnight	Ernest Tubb	
2/8	14	2. So Round, So Firm, So Fully Packed	Merle Travis	
5/17	2 ↕	3. New Jolie Blonde (New Pretty Blonde)	Red Foley	
5/24	1	4. What Is Life Without Love	Eddy Arnold	
6/7	1	5. Sugar Moon	Bob Wills	
6/14	5	6. It's A Sin	Eddy Arnold	
7/19	16 ↕	7. Smoke! Smoke! Smoke! (That Cigarette)	Tex Williams	
11/1	21 ↕	8. I'll Hold You In My Heart (Till I Can Hold You In My Arms)	Eddy Arnold	

1948

DATE	WKS	RECORD TITLE	ARTIST	JB	BS	JY
4/3	9	1. Anytime	Eddy Arnold			

5/15/48: BILLBOARD DEBUTS COUNTRY "BEST SELLERS" CHART.

DATE	WKS	RECORD TITLE	ARTIST	JB	BS	JY
6/5	19 ↕	2. Bouquet Of Roses	Eddy Arnold	18↕	19↕	
6/5	3 ↕	3. Texarkana Baby	Eddy Arnold	3↕	1	
9/18	8 ↕	4. Just A Little Lovin' (Will Go A Long, Long Way)	Eddy Arnold	8↕	4↕	
11/13	11 ↕	5. One Has My Name (The Other Has My Heart)	Jimmy Wakely	7↕	11↕	
12/25	1	6. A Heart Full Of Love (For a handful of Kisses)	Eddy Arnold		1	

1949

DATE	WKS	RECORD TITLE	ARTIST	JB	BS	JY
1/22	5 ↕	1. I Love You So Much It Hurts	Jimmy Wakely	5↕	4↕	
3/5	12 ↕	2. Don't Rob Another Man's Castle	Eddy Arnold	12↕	6↕	
3/19	1	3. Tennessee Saturday Night	Red Foley	1		
4/2	3 ↕	4. Candy Kisses	George Morgan		3↕	
5/7	16 ↕	5. Lovesick Blues	Hank Williams with His Drifting Cowboys	10↕	16↕	
6/18	3 ↕	6. One Kiss Too Many	Eddy Arnold	3↕		

6/25/49: "COUNTRY & WESTERN" IS SHOWN AS CHART TITLE FOR FIRST TIME.

DATE	WKS	RECORD TITLE	ARTIST	JB	BS	JY
7/30	4	7. I'm Throwing Rice (At the Girl That I Love)	Eddy Arnold	3↕	4	
9/10	3 ↕	8. Why Don't You Haul Off And Love Me	Wayne Raney	3↕	2↕	

DATE	WKS	RECORD TITLE	ARTIST	CHARTS		
9/24	1	9. Slipping Around	Ernest Tubb	1		
10/8	17	10. Slipping Around	Margaret Whiting & Jimmy Wakely	12↕	17	

12/10/49: BILLBOARD DEBUTS COUNTRY "JOCKEYS" CHART.

DATE	WKS	RECORD TITLE	ARTIST	CHARTS		
12/10	4	11. Mule Train	Tennessee Ernie Ford			4

1950

DATE	WKS	RECORD TITLE	ARTIST	CHARTS		
1/7	1	1. Rudolph, The Red-Nosed Reindeer	Gene Autry			1
1/7	1	2. Blue Christmas	Ernest Tubb	1		
1/14	2 ↕	3. I Love You Because	Leon Payne			2↕
1/14	1	4. Blues Stay Away From Me	Delmore Brothers	1		
1/21	13	5. Chattanoogie Shoe Shine Boy	Red Foley	13	12	13↕
1/28	1	6. Take Me In Your Arms And Hold Me	Eddy Arnold	1		
4/22	8 ↕	7. Long Gone Lonesome Blues	Hank Williams with His Drifting Cowboys	4	5↕	8↕
5/27	4 ↕	8. Birmingham Bounce	Red Foley	3↕	4↕	
6/17	10	9. Why Don't You Love Me	Hank Williams with His Drifting Cowboys	5	6↕	10
6/17	4	10. I'll Sail My Ship Alone	Moon Mullican	4	1	
7/15	1	11. Mississippi	Red Foley	1		
8/19	21 ↕	12. I'm Moving On	Hank Snow	14	21↕	18↕
8/26	3	13. Goodnight Irene	Red Foley-Ernest Tubb	3	2	
12/23	3	14. If You've Got The Money I've Got The Time	Lefty Frizzell	3		
12/30	1	15. Moanin' The Blues	Hank Williams with His Drifting Cowboys			1

1951

DATE	WKS	RECORD TITLE	ARTIST	CHARTS		
1/6	3 ↕	1. I Love You A Thousand Ways	Lefty Frizzell			3↕
1/6	2	2. The Golden Rocket	Hank Snow		2	1
1/13	14	3. The Shot Gun Boogie	Tennessee Ernie Ford	14	3↕	1
2/10	11 ↕	4. There's Been A Change In Me	Eddy Arnold		4↕	11↕
3/31	8 ↕	5. The Rhumba Boogie	Hank Snow	5	8↕	2↕
5/12	1	6. Cold, Cold Heart	Hank Williams with His Drifting Cowboys			1
5/19	3	7. Kentucky Waltz	Eddy Arnold	3	3↕	
5/26	11	8. I Want To Be With You Always	Lefty Frizzell	5	6↕	11
7/14	11	9. I Wanna Play House With You	Eddy Arnold	11	6↕	
8/11	8 ↕	10. Hey, Good Lookin'	Hank Williams with His Drifting Cowboys			8↕
9/1	12 ↕	11. Always Late (With Your Kisses)	Lefty Frizzell	6	12↕	6↕
11/3	15 ↕	12. Slow Poke	Pee Wee King	15↕	14	9↕
12/22	8 ↕	13. Let Old Mother Nature Have Her Way	Carl Smith	8↕	6	3↕

1952

DATE	WKS	RECORD TITLE	ARTIST	CHARTS		
2/2	3 ↕	1. Give Me More, More, More (Of Your Kisses)	Lefty Frizzell	3↕		3↕
3/1	4	2. Wondering	Webb Pierce			4
3/29	8 ↕	3. (When You Feel Like You're In Love) Don't Just Stand There	Carl Smith	3↕	5↕	8↕
5/3	1	4. Easy On The Eyes	Eddy Arnold		1	
5/10	15	5. The Wild Side Of Life	Hank Thompson	15	15	8↕

DATE	WKS	RECORD TITLE		ARTIST	CHARTS		
7/12	3 ↕	6.	That Heart Belongs To Me	Webb Pierce			3↕
7/19	1	7.	Are You Teasing Me	Carl Smith			1
8/16	4 ↕	8.	A Full Time Job	Eddy Arnold			4↕
8/23	6	9.	It Wasn't God Who Made Honky Tonk Angels	Kitty Wells	5	6	
9/6	14 ↕	10.	Jambalaya (On The Bayou)	Hank Williams with His Drifting Cowboys	12↕	14↕	14↕
12/6	4 ↕	11.	Back Street Affair	Webb Pierce	3	2↕	4↕
12/6	1	12.	Don't Let The Stars (Get In Your Eyes)	Slim Willet			1
12/27	3	13.	Don't Let The Stars Get In Your Eyes	Skeets McDonald	3		

1953

DATE	WKS	RECORD TITLE		ARTIST	CHARTS		
1/10	1	1.	Midnight	Red Foley		1	
1/24	2 ↕	2.	I'll Go On Alone	Marty Robbins			2↕
1/24	1	3.	I'll Never Get Out Of This World Alive	Hank Williams with His Drifting Cowboys		1	
1/31	4	4.	No Help Wanted	The Carlisles	4		4↕
1/31	3	5.	Eddy's Song	Eddy Arnold		3	
2/7	3	6.	I Let The Stars Get In My Eyes	Goldie Hill	3		
2/21	13	7.	Kaw-Liga	Hank Williams with His Drifting Cowboys	8↕	13	8
4/11	6 ↕	8.	Your Cheatin' Heart	Hank Williams with His Drifting Cowboys	2↕		6↕
5/9	9 ↕	9.	Mexican Joe	Jim Reeves	9↕	6↕	7↕
6/6	4 ↕	10.	Take These Chains From My Heart	Hank Williams with His Drifting Cowboys		4↕	
7/11	8 ↕	11.	It's Been So Long	Webb Pierce	1	6	8↕
8/1	3 ↕	12.	Rub-A-Dub-Dub	Hank Thompson	3↕		
8/22	8 ↕	13.	Hey Joe!	Carl Smith	8↕	2↕	4↕
8/29	6 ↕	14.	A Dear John Letter	Jean Shepard & Ferlin Huskey	4↕	6↕	
10/17	8 ↕	15.	I Forgot More Than You'll Ever Know	The Davis Sisters	2↕	6↕	8↕
11/21	12 ↕	16.	There Stands The Glass	Webb Pierce	9↕	12↕	6↕
12/12	2	17.	Caribbean	Mitchell Torok	2		
12/19	3 ↕	18.	Let Me Be The One	Hank Locklin	2↕		3↕

1954

DATE	WKS	RECORD TITLE		ARTIST	CHARTS		
1/9	3 ↕	1.	Bimbo	Jim Reeves			3↕
2/20	17	2.	Slowly	Webb Pierce	17↕	17	15
2/20	2	3.	Wake Up, Irene	Hank Thompson	2		
5/15	1	4.	I Really Don't Want To Know	Eddy Arnold	1		
6/12	2	5.	(Oh Baby Mine) I Get So Lonely	Johnnie & Jack			2
6/19	20	6.	I Don't Hurt Anymore	Hank Snow	20↕	20	18↕
7/3	2	7.	Even Tho	Webb Pierce			2
7/31	1	8.	One By One	Kitty Wells & Red Foley	1		
11/6	10 ↕	9.	More And More	Webb Pierce	10↕	9	8↕

1955

DATE	WKS	RECORD TITLE		ARTIST	CHARTS		
1/8	7	1.	Loose Talk	Carl Smith	4	7	6↕
1/29	2	2.	Let Me Go, Lover!	Hank Snow			2
2/26	21	3.	In The Jailhouse Now	Webb Pierce	21	20	15
6/18	3	4.	Live Fast, Love Hard, Die Young	Faron Young			3

DATE	WKS		RECORD TITLE	ARTIST	CHARTS		
7/9	4	5.	A Satisfied Mind	Porter Wagoner			4
7/16	12	6.	I Don't Care	Webb Pierce	12	12	12
10/8	2	7.	The Cattle Call	Eddy Arnold		2	
10/22	13 ↕	8.	Love, Love, Love	Webb Pierce	9↕	8	13↕
10/22	2	9.	That Do Make It Nice	Eddy Arnold	2		
12/17	10	10.	Sixteen Tons	Tennessee Ernie Ford	7↕	10	3↕

1956

DATE	WKS		RECORD TITLE	ARTIST	CHARTS		
2/11	4 ↕	1.	Why Baby Why	Red Sovine & Webb Pierce	1	1	4↕
2/25	5	2.	I Forgot To Remember To Forget	Elvis Presley	5	2	
3/17	17	3.	Heartbreak Hotel	Elvis Presley	13↕	17	12
3/17	2	4.	I Don't Believe You've Met My Baby	The Louvin Brothers			2
4/7	3	5.	Blue Suede Shoes	Carl Perkins	3		
6/23	20 ↕	6.	Crazy Arms	Ray Price	1	11↕	20↕
7/14	2	7.	I Want You, I Need You, I Love You	Elvis Presley	1	2	
7/21	6 ↕	8.	I Walk The Line	Johnny Cash	6↕		1
9/15	10	9.	Don't Be Cruel/		10	5	2
	10	10.	Hound Dog	Elvis Presley	10	5	
11/10	13	11.	Singing The Blues	Marty Robbins	13	13	11↕

1957

DATE	WKS		RECORD TITLE	ARTIST	CHARTS		
2/2	9	1.	Young Love	Sonny James	3↕	7	9
3/2	5 ↕	2.	There You Go	Johnny Cash	5↕		
4/6	10	3.	Gone	Ferlin Husky	5↕	10	9
5/13	1	4.	All Shook Up	Elvis Presley	1		
5/20	5	5.	A White Sport Coat (And A Pink Carnation)	Marty Robbins	5	5	1
5/20	1	6.	Honky Tonk Song	Webb Pierce			1
5/27	8 ↕	7.	Four Walls	Jim Reeves			8↕

6/24/57: BILLBOARD TERMINATES "JUKE BOX" CHART.

DATE	WKS		RECORD TITLE	ARTIST	CHARTS		
7/15	7 ↕	8.	Bye Bye Love	The Everly Brothers		7↕	7
8/5	1	9.	(Let Me Be Your) Teddy Bear	Elvis Presley		1	
9/9	2	10.	Whole Lot Of Shakin' Going On	Jerry Lee Lewis		2	
9/16	4 ↕	11.	Fraulein	Bobby Helms		3	4↕
9/16	4 ↕	12.	My Shoes Keep Walking Back To You	Ray Price			4↕
10/14	8 ↕	13.	Wake Up Little Susie	The Everly Brothers		7	8↕
12/2	1	14.	Jailhouse Rock	Elvis Presley		1	
12/9	4	15.	My Special Angel	Bobby Helms		4	1

1958

DATE	WKS		RECORD TITLE	ARTIST	CHARTS		
1/6	4	1.	The Story Of My Life	Marty Robbins		4	4
1/6	2	2.	Great Balls Of Fire	Jerry Lee Lewis		2	
2/3	10	3.	Ballad Of A Teenage Queen	Johnny Cash		8	10
4/14	8 ↕	4.	Oh Lonesome Me	Don Gibson		8↕	8↕
5/26	2 ↕	5.	Just Married	Marty Robbins			2↕
6/2	3	6.	All I Have To Do Is Dream	The Everly Brothers		3	1
6/23	8	7.	Guess Things Happen That Way	Johnny Cash		8	3↕
7/21	13	8.	Alone With You	Faron Young			13
8/25	2	9.	Blue Blue Day	Don Gibson		2	
9/8	6	10.	Bird Dog	The Everly Brothers		6	

DATE	WKS	RECORD TITLE	ARTIST

10/20/58: BILLBOARD TERMINATES THE "BEST SELLERS" AND "JOCKEYS" CHARTS AND BEGINS PUBLISHING ONE ALL-ENCOMPASSING COUNTRY CHART.

DATE	WKS	RECORD TITLE	ARTIST
10/20	13	11. City Lights	Ray Price

1959

DATE	WKS	RECORD TITLE	ARTIST
1/19	5	1. Billy Bayou	Jim Reeves
2/23	6	2. Don't Take Your Guns To Town	Johnny Cash
4/6	1	3. When It's Springtime In Alaska (It's Forty Below)	Johnny Horton
4/13	5	4. White Lightning	George Jones
5/18	10	5. The Battle Of New Orleans	Johnny Horton
7/27	5	6. Waterloo	Stonewall Jackson
8/31	10	7. The Three Bells	The Browns
11/9	4	8. Country Girl	Faron Young
12/7	2	9. The Same Old Me	Ray Price
12/21	7	10. El Paso	Marty Robbins

1960

DATE	WKS	RECORD TITLE	ARTIST
2/8	14	1. He'll Have To Go	Jim Reeves
5/16	14	2. Please Help Me, I'm Falling	Hank Locklin
8/22	12	3. Alabam	Cowboy Copas
11/14	10 ↕	4. Wings Of A Dove	Ferlin Husky

1961

DATE	WKS	RECORD TITLE	ARTIST
1/9	5	1. North To Alaska	Johnny Horton
2/27	10	2. Don't Worry	Marty Robbins
5/8	9	3. Hello Walls	Faron Young
7/10	4	4. Heartbreak U.S.A.	Kitty Wells
8/7	2	5. I Fall To Pieces	Patsy Cline
8/21	7 ↕	6. Tender Years	George Jones
9/25	19 ↕	7. Walk On By	Leroy Van Dyke
11/20	2	8. Big Bad John	Jimmy Dean

1962

DATE	WKS	RECORD TITLE	ARTIST
3/10	2 ↕	1. Misery Loves Company	Porter Wagoner
3/17	1	2. That's My Pa	Sheb Wooley
3/31	5 ↕	3. She's Got You	Patsy Cline
4/28	2 ↕	4. Charlie's Shoes	Billy Walker
5/19	6	5. She Thinks I Still Care	George Jones
6/30	9	6. Wolverton Mountain	Claude King
9/1	8	7. Devil Woman	Marty Robbins
10/27	7 ↕	8. Mama Sang A Song	Bill Anderson

11/3/62: THE "WESTERN" IS DROPPED FROM CHART TITLE. CHART NOW DESIGNATED ONLY AS "HOT COUNTRY SINGLES."

DATE	WKS	RECORD TITLE	ARTIST
11/10	2 ↕	9. I've Been Everywhere	Hank Snow
12/29	11 ↕	10. Don't Let Me Cross Over	Carl Butler & Pearl

DATE	WKS	RECORD TITLE	ARTIST

1963

DATE	WKS	RECORD TITLE	ARTIST
1/5	1	1. Ruby Ann	Marty Robbins
1/19	3 ↕	2. The Ballad Of Jed Clampett	Flatt & Scruggs
4/13	7 ↕	3. Still	Bill Anderson
5/4	4 ↕	4. Lonesome 7-7203	Hawkshaw Hawkins
6/15	4 ↕	5. Act Naturally	Buck Owens
7/27	7	6. Ring Of Fire	Johnny Cash
9/14	4	7. Abilene	George Hamilton IV
10/12	1	8. Talk Back Trembling Lips	Ernest Ashworth
10/19	16	9. Love's Gonna Live Here	Buck Owens

1964

DATE	WKS	RECORD TITLE	ARTIST
2/8	3 ↕	1. Begging To You	Marty Robbins
2/15	1	2. B.J. The D.J.	Stonewall Jackson
3/7	4	3. Saginaw, Michigan	Lefty Frizzell
4/4	6	4. Understand Your Man	Johnny Cash
5/16	7 ↕	5. My Heart Skips A Beat	Buck Owens
6/6	2	6. Together Again	Buck Owens
7/18	6	7. Dang Me	Roger Miller
8/29	7	8. I Guess I'm Crazy	Jim Reeves
10/17	6	9. I Don't Care (Just as Long as You Love Me)	Buck Owens
11/28	8	10. Once A Day	Connie Smith

1965

DATE	WKS	RECORD TITLE	ARTIST
1/23	4	1. You're The Only World I Know	Sonny James
2/20	5	2. I've Got A Tiger By The Tail	Buck Owens
3/27	5	3. King Of The Road	Roger Miller
5/1	3 ↕	4. This Is It	Jim Reeves
5/15	2	5. Girl On The Billboard	Del Reeves
6/5	2	6. What's He Doing In My World	Eddy Arnold
6/19	1	7. Ribbon Of Darkness	Marty Robbins
6/26	6	8. Before You Go	Buck Owens
8/7	2	9. The First Thing Ev'ry Morning (And The Last Thing Ev'ry Night)	Jimmy Dean
8/21	2	10. Yes, Mr. Peters	Roy Drusky & Priscilla Mitchell
9/4	1	11. The Bridge Washed Out	Warner Mack
9/11	3	12. Is It Really Over?	Jim Reeves
10/2	1	13. Only You (Can Break My Heart)	Buck Owens
10/9	3 ↕	14. Behind The Tear	Sonny James
10/23	3	15. Hello Vietnam	Johnny Wright
11/20	2	16. May The Bird Of Paradise Fly Up Your Nose	"Little" Jimmy Dickens
12/4	3	17. Make The World Go Away	Eddy Arnold
12/25	2	18. Buckaroo	Buck Owens & The Buckaroos

1966

DATE	WKS	RECORD TITLE	ARTIST
1/8	6	1. Giddyup Go	Red Sovine
2/19	7	2. Waitin' In Your Welfare Line	Buck Owens
4/9	6	3. I Want To Go With You	Eddy Arnold

DATE	WKS	RECORD TITLE		ARTIST
5/21	4	4.	Distant Drums	Jim Reeves
6/18	2	5.	Take Good Care Of Her	Sonny James
7/2	6	6.	Think Of Me	Buck Owens
8/13	9	7.	Almost Persuaded	David Houston
10/15	1	8.	Blue Side Of Lonesome	Jim Reeves
10/22	4	9.	Open Up Your Heart	Buck Owens
11/19	1	10.	I Get The Fever	Bill Anderson
11/26	4	11.	Somebody Like Me	Eddy Arnold
12/24	7	12.	There Goes My Everything	Jack Greene

1967

DATE	WKS	RECORD TITLE		ARTIST
2/11	1	1.	Don't Come Home A'Drinkin' (With Lovin' On Your Mind)	Loretta Lynn
2/18	4 ↕	2.	Where Does The Good Times Go	Buck Owens
3/4	1	3.	The Fugitive	Merle Haggard
3/25	1	4.	I Won't Come In While He's There	Jim Reeves
4/1	2	5.	Walk Through This World With Me	George Jones
4/15	2	6.	Lonely Again	Eddy Arnold
4/29	2	7.	Need You	Sonny James
5/13	3	8.	Sam's Place	Buck Owens
6/3	2	9.	It's Such A Pretty World Today	Wynn Stewart
6/17	5	10.	All The Time	Jack Greene
7/22	1	11.	With One Exception	David Houston
7/29	1	12.	Tonight Carmen	Marty Robbins
8/5	4	13.	I'll Never Find Another You	Sonny James
9/2	1	14.	Branded Man	Merle Haggard
9/9	1	15.	Your Tender Loving Care	Buck Owens
9/16	2	16.	My Elusive Dreams	David Houston
9/30	1	17.	Laura (What's He Got That I Ain't Got)	Leon Ashley
10/7	1	18.	Turn The World Around	Eddy Arnold
10/14	3	19.	I Don't Wanna Play House	Tammy Wynette
11/4	2	20.	You Mean The World To Me	David Houston
11/18	5	21.	It's The Little Things	Sonny James
12/23	4	22.	For Loving You	Bill Anderson & Jan Howard

1968

DATE	WKS	RECORD TITLE		ARTIST
1/20	2	1.	Sing Me Back Home	Merle Haggard
2/3	5	2.	Skip A Rope	Henson Cargill
3/9	1	3.	Take Me To Your World	Tammy Wynette
3/16	3	4.	A World Of Our Own	Sonny James
4/6	1	5.	How Long Will My Baby Be Gone	Buck Owens
4/13	1	6.	You Are My Treasure	Jack Greene
4/20	1	7.	Fist City	Loretta Lynn
4/27	2	8.	The Legend Of Bonnie And Clyde	Merle Haggard
5/11	1	9.	Have A Little Faith	David Houston
5/18	3 ↕	10.	I Wanna Live	Glen Campbell
5/25	3	11.	Honey	Bobby Goldsboro
6/29	3	12.	D-I-V-O-R-C-E	Tammy Wynette
7/20	4	13.	Folsom Prison Blues	Johnny Cash
8/17	1	14.	Heaven Says Hello	Sonny James

DATE	WKS	RECORD TITLE		ARTIST
8/24	1	15.	Already It's Heaven	David Houston
8/31	4	16.	Mama Tried	Merle Haggard
9/28	3	17.	Harper Valley P.T.A.	Jeannie C. Riley
10/19	2	18.	Then You Can Tell Me Goodbye	Eddy Arnold
11/2	1	19.	Next In Line	Conway Twitty
11/9	2	20.	I Walk Alone	Marty Robbins
11/23	3	21.	Stand By Your Man	Tammy Wynette
12/14	1	22.	Born To Be With You	Sonny James
12/21	2	23.	Wichita Lineman	Glen Campbell

1969

DATE	WKS	RECORD TITLE		ARTIST
1/4	6	1.	Daddy Sang Bass	Johnny Cash
2/15	2	2.	Until My Dreams Come True	Jack Greene
3/1	1	3.	To Make Love Sweeter For You	Jerry Lee Lewis
3/8	3	4.	Only The Lonely	Sonny James
3/29	2	5.	Who's Gonna Mow Your Grass	Buck Owens
4/12	1	6.	Woman Of The World (Leave My World Alone)	Loretta Lynn
4/19	3	7.	Galveston	Glen Campbell
5/10	1	8.	Hungry Eyes	Merle Haggard
5/17	2	9.	My Life (Throw It Away If I Want To)	Bill Anderson
5/31	2	10.	Singing My Song	Tammy Wynette
6/14	3	11.	Running Bear	Sonny James
7/5	2	12.	Statue Of A Fool	Jack Greene
7/19	1	13.	I Love You More Today	Conway Twitty
7/26	2	14.	Johnny B. Goode	Buck Owens
8/9	1	15.	All I Have To Offer You (Is Me)	Charley Pride
8/16	1	16.	Workin' Man Blues	Merle Haggard
8/23	5	17.	A Boy Named Sue	Johnny Cash
9/27	1	18.	Tall Dark Stranger	Buck Owens
10/4	3	19.	Since I Met You, Baby	Sonny James
10/25	2	20.	The Ways To Love A Man	Tammy Wynette
11/8	1	21.	To See My Angel Cry	Conway Twitty
11/15	4	22.	Okie From Muskogee	Merle Haggard
12/13	3	23.	(I'm So) Afraid Of Losing You Again	Charley Pride

1970

DATE	WKS	RECORD TITLE		ARTIST
1/3	4	1.	Baby, Baby (I Know You're A Lady)	David Houston
1/31	2	2.	A Week In A Country Jail	Tom T. Hall
2/14	4	3.	It's Just A Matter Of Time	Sonny James
3/14	3	4.	The Fightin' Side Of Me	Merle Haggard
4/4	2	5.	Tennessee Bird Walk	Jack Blanchard & Misty Morgan
4/18	2	6.	Is Anybody Goin' To San Antone	Charley Pride
5/2	1	7.	My Woman, My Woman, My Wife	Marty Robbins
5/9	1	8.	The Pool Shark	Dave Dudley
5/16	3	9.	My Love	Sonny James
6/6	4	10.	Hello Darlin'	Conway Twitty
7/4	3	11.	He Loves Me All The Way	Tammy Wynette
7/25	2	12.	Wonder Could I Live There Anymore	Charley Pride
8/8	4	13.	Don't Keep Me Hangin' On	Sonny James
9/5	2	14.	All For The Love Of Sunshine	Hank Williams, Jr.

DATE	WKS		RECORD TITLE	ARTIST
9/19	1	15.	For The Good Times	Ray Price
9/26	2	16.	There Must Be More To Love Than This	Jerry Lee Lewis
10/10	2	17.	Sunday Morning Coming Down	Johnny Cash
10/24	2	18.	Run, Woman, Run	Tammy Wynette
11/7	2	19.	I Can't Believe That You've Stopped Loving Me	Charley Pride
11/21	1	20.	Fifteen Years Ago	Conway Twitty
11/28	3	21.	Endlessly	Sonny James
12/19	1	22.	Coal Miner's Daughter	Loretta Lynn
12/26	5	23.	Rose Garden	Lynn Anderson

1971

DATE	WKS		RECORD TITLE	ARTIST
1/30	1	1.	Flesh And Blood	Johnny Cash
2/6	1	2.	Joshua	Dolly Parton
2/13	3	3.	Help Me Make It Through The Night	Sammi Smith
3/6	3	4.	I'd Rather Love You	Charley Pride
3/27	2	5.	After The Fire Is Gone	Conway Twitty & Loretta Lynn
4/10	4	6.	Empty Arms	Sonny James
5/8	1	7.	How Much More Can She Stand	Conway Twitty
5/15	3	8.	I Won't Mention It Again	Ray Price
6/5	2	9.	You're My Man	Lynn Anderson
6/19	5	10.	When You're Hot, You're Hot	Jerry Reed
7/24	1	11.	Bright Lights, Big City	Sonny James
7/31	4	12.	I'm Just Me	Charley Pride
8/28	2	13.	Good Lovin' (Makes It Right)	Tammy Wynette
9/11	3 ↕	14.	Easy Loving	Freddie Hart
9/18	2	15.	The Year That Clayton Delaney Died	Tom T. Hall
10/16	3	16.	How Can I Unlove You	Lynn Anderson
11/6	1	17.	Here Comes Honey Again	Sonny James
11/13	1	18.	Lead Me On	Conway Twitty & Loretta Lynn
11/20	2	19.	Daddy Frank (The Guitar Man)	Merle Haggard
12/4	5	20.	Kiss An Angel Good Mornin'	Charley Pride

1972

DATE	WKS		RECORD TITLE	ARTIST
1/8	1	1.	Would You Take Another Chance On Me	Jerry Lee Lewis
1/15	3	2.	Carolyn	Merle Haggard
2/5	2	3.	One's On The Way	Loretta Lynn
2/19	2	4.	It's Four In The Morning	Faron Young
3/4	1	5.	Bedtime Story	Tammy Wynette
3/11	6	6.	My Hang-Up Is You	Freddie Hart
4/22	3	7.	Chantilly Lace	Jerry Lee Lewis
5/13	2	8.	Grandma Harp	Merle Haggard
5/27	1	9.	(Lost Her Love) On Our Last Date	Conway Twitty
6/3	3	10.	The Happiest Girl In The Whole U.S.A.	Donna Fargo
6/24	1	11.	That's Why I Love You Like I Do	Sonny James
7/1	2	12.	Eleven Roses	Hank Williams, Jr.
7/15	1	13.	Made In Japan	Buck Owens
7/22	3	14.	It's Gonna Take A Little Bit Longer	Charley Pride
8/12	2	15.	Bless Your Heart	Freddie Hart & The Heartbeats
8/26	2 ↕	16.	If You Leave Me Tonight I'll Cry	Jerry Wallace
9/2	1	17.	Woman (Sensuous Woman)	Don Gibson

DATE	WKS	RECORD TITLE	ARTIST
9/16	1	18. When The Snow Is On The Roses	Sonny James
9/23	1	19. I Can't Stop Loving You	Conway Twitty
9/30	2	20. I Ain't Never	Mel Tillis
10/14	3	21. Funny Face	Donna Fargo
11/4	1	22. It's Not Love (But It's Not Bad)	Merle Haggard
11/11	1	23. My Man	Tammy Wynette
11/18	3	24. She's Too Good To Be True	Charley Pride
12/9	3	25. Got The All Overs For You (All Over Me)	Freddie Hart & The Heartbeats
12/30	3	26. She's Got To Be A Saint	Ray Price

1973

DATE	WKS	RECORD TITLE	ARTIST
1/20	1	1. Soul Song	Joe Stampley
1/27	1	2. (Old Dogs-Children And) Watermelon Wine	Tom T. Hall
2/3	2	3. She Needs Someone To Hold Her (When She Cries)	Conway Twitty
2/17	1	4. I Wonder If They Ever Think Of Me	Merle Haggard
2/24	1	5. Rated "X"	Loretta Lynn
3/3	1	6. The Lord Knows I'm Drinking	Cal Smith
3/10	1	7. 'Til I Get It Right	Tammy Wynette
3/17	2	8. Teddy Bear Song	Barbara Fairchild
3/31	1	9. Keep Me In Mind	Lynn Anderson
4/7	1	10. Super Kind Of Woman	Freddie Hart & The Heartbeats
4/14	1	11. A Shoulder To Cry On	Charley Pride
4/21	1	12. Superman	Donna Fargo
4/28	2	13. Behind Closed Doors	Charlie Rich
5/12	1	14. Come Live With Me	Roy Clark
5/19	1	15. What's Your Mama's Name	Tanya Tucker
5/26	3 ↕	16. Satin Sheets	Jeanne Pruett
6/9	1	17. You Always Come Back (To Hurting Me)	Johnny Rodriguez
6/16	1	18. Kids Say The Darndest Things	Tammy Wynette
6/30	1	19. Don't Fight The Feelings Of Love	Charley Pride
7/7	1	20. Why Me	Kris Kristofferson
7/14	2	21. Love Is The Foundation	Loretta Lynn
7/28	1	22. You Were Always There	Donna Fargo
8/4	1	23. Lord, Mr. Ford	Jerry Reed
8/11	1	24. Trip To Heaven	Freddie Hart & The Heartbeats
8/18	1	25. Louisiana Woman, Mississippi Man	Conway Twitty & Loretta Lynn
8/25	2	26. Everybody's Had The Blues	Merle Haggard
9/8	3	27. You've Never Been This Far Before	Conway Twitty
9/29	1	28. Blood Red And Goin' Down	Tanya Tucker
10/6	1	29. You're The Best Thing That Ever Happened To Me	Ray Price
10/13	2	30. Ridin' My Thumb To Mexico	Johnny Rodriguez
10/27	2	31. We're Gonna Hold On	George Jones & Tammy Wynette
11/10	2	32. Paper Roses	Marie Osmond
11/24	3	33. The Most Beautiful Girl	Charlie Rich
12/15	1	34. Amazing Love	Charley Pride
12/22	4	35. If We Make It Through December	Merle Haggard

1974

DATE	WKS	RECORD TITLE	ARTIST
1/19	2	1. I Love	Tom T. Hall
2/2	1	2. Jolene	Dolly Parton

DATE	WKS		RECORD TITLE	ARTIST
2/9	1	3.	World Of Make Believe	Bill Anderson
2/16	1	4.	That's The Way Love Goes	Johnny Rodriguez
2/23	2	5.	Another Lonely Song	Tammy Wynette
3/9	2	6.	There Won't Be Anymore	Charlie Rich
3/23	1	7.	There's A Honky Tonk Angel (Who'll Take Me Back In)	Conway Twitty
3/30	1	8.	Would You Lay With Me (In A Field Of Stone)	Tanya Tucker
4/6	3	9.	A Very Special Love Song	Charlie Rich
4/27	1	10.	Hello Love	Hank Snow
5/4	1	11.	Things Aren't Funny Anymore	Merle Haggard
5/11	1	12.	Is It Wrong (For Loving You)	Sonny James
5/18	1	13.	Country Bumpkin	Cal Smith
5/25	1	14.	No Charge	Melba Montgomery
6/1	1	15.	Pure Love	Ronnie Milsap
6/8	1	16.	I Will Always Love You	Dolly Parton
6/15	1	17.	I Don't See Me In Your Eyes Anymore	Charlie Rich
6/22	1	18.	This Time	Waylon Jennings
6/29	1	19.	Room Full Of Roses	Mickey Gilley
7/6	2	20.	He Thinks I Still Care	Anne Murray
7/20	1	21.	Marie Laveau	Bobby Bare
7/27	1	22.	You Can't Be A Beacon (If Your Light Don't Shine)	Donna Fargo
8/3	2	23.	Rub It In	Billy "Crash" Craddock
8/17	1	24.	As Soon As I Hang Up The Phone	Conway Twitty & Loretta Lynn
8/24	1	25.	Old Man From The Mountain	Merle Haggard
8/31	1	26.	The Grand Tour	George Jones
9/7	2	27.	Please Don't Tell Me How The Story Ends	Ronnie Milsap
9/21	1	28.	I Wouldn't Want To Live If You Didn't Love Me	Don Williams
9/28	1	29.	I'm A Ramblin' Man	Waylon Jennings
10/5	1	30.	I Love My Friend	Charlie Rich
10/12	1	31.	Please Don't Stop Loving Me	Porter Wagoner & Dolly Parton
10/19	2	32.	I See The Want To In Your Eyes	Conway Twitty
11/2	1	33.	I Overlooked An Orchid	Mickey Gilley
11/9	1	34.	Love Is Like A Butterfly	Dolly Parton
11/16	1	35.	Country Is	Tom T. Hall
11/23	1	36.	Trouble In Paradise	Loretta Lynn
11/30	1	37.	Back Home Again	John Denver
12/7	1	38.	She Called Me Baby	Charlie Rich
12/14	2	39.	I Can Help	Billy Swan
12/28	1	40.	What A Man, My Man Is	Lynn Anderson

1975

DATE	WKS		RECORD TITLE	ARTIST
1/4	1	1.	The Door	George Jones
1/11	1	2.	Ruby, Baby	Billy "Crash" Craddock
1/18	1	3.	Kentucky Gambler	Merle Haggard
1/25	1	4.	(I'd Be) A Legend In My Time	Ronnie Milsap
2/1	1	5.	City Lights	Mickey Gilley
2/8	1	6.	Then Who Am I	Charley Pride
2/15	1	7.	Devil In The Bottle	T.G. Sheppard
2/22	1	8.	I Care	Tom T. Hall
3/1	1	9.	It's Time To Pay The Fiddler	Cal Smith
3/8	1	10.	Linda On My Mind	Conway Twitty

DATE	WKS		RECORD TITLE	ARTIST
3/15	2	11.	Before The Next Teardrop Falls	Freddy Fender
3/29	1	12.	The Bargain Store	Dolly Parton
4/5	1	13.	I Just Can't Get Her Out Of My Mind	Johnny Rodriguez
4/12	2	14.	Always Wanting You	Merle Haggard
4/26	1	15.	Blanket On The Ground	Billie Jo Spears
5/3	1	16.	Roll On Big Mama	Joe Stampley
5/10	1	17.	She's Actin' Single (I'm Drinkin' Doubles)	Gary Stewart
5/17	1	18.	(Hey Won't You Play) Another Somebody Done Somebody Wrong Song	B.J. Thomas
5/24	1	19.	I'm Not Lisa	Jessi Colter
5/31	1	20.	Thank God I'm A Country Boy	John Denver
6/7	1	21.	Window Up Above	Mickey Gilley
6/14	1	22.	When Will I Be Loved	Linda Ronstadt
6/21	1	23.	You're My Best Friend	Don Williams
6/28	1	24.	Tryin' To Beat The Morning Home	T.G. Sheppard
7/5	1	25.	Lizzie And The Rainman	Tanya Tucker
7/12	1	26.	Movin' On	Merle Haggard
7/19	2	27.	Touch The Hand	Conway Twitty
8/2	1	28.	Just Get Up And Close The Door	Johnny Rodriguez
8/9	2	29.	Wasted Days And Wasted Nights	Freddy Fender
8/23	3 ↕	30.	Rhinestone Cowboy	Glen Campbell
9/6	1	31.	Feelins'	Conway Twitty & Loretta Lynn
9/20	2	32.	Daydreams About Night Things	Ronnie Milsap
10/4	2	33.	Blue Eyes Crying In The Rain	Willie Nelson
10/18	1	34.	Hope You're Feelin' Me (Like I'm Feelin' You)	Charley Pride
10/25	1	35.	San Antonio Stroll	Tanya Tucker
11/1	1	36.	(Turn Out The Light And) Love Me Tonight	Don Williams
11/8	1	37.	I'm Sorry	John Denver
11/15	1	38.	Are You Sure Hank Done It This Way	Waylon Jennings
11/22	1	39.	Rocky	Dickey Lee
11/29	1	40.	It's All In The Movies	Merle Haggard
12/6	1	41.	Secret Love	Freddy Fender
12/13	1	42.	Love Put A Song In My Heart	Johnny Rodriguez
12/20	6	43.	Convoy	C.W. McCall

1976

DATE	WKS		RECORD TITLE	ARTIST
1/31	1	1.	This Time I've Hurt Her More Than She Loves Me	Conway Twitty
2/7	1	2.	Sometimes	Bill Anderson & Mary Lou Turner
2/14	1	3.	The White Knight	Cledus Maggard & The Citizen's Band
2/21	3	4.	Good Hearted Woman	Waylon & Willie
3/13	1	5.	The Roots Of My Raising	Merle Haggard
3/20	1	6.	Faster Horses (The Cowboy And The Poet)	Tom T. Hall
3/27	1	7.	Til The Rivers All Run Dry	Don Williams
4/3	1	8.	You'll Lose A Good Thing	Freddy Fender
4/10	1	9.	'Til I Can Make It On My Own	Tammy Wynette
4/17	1	10.	Drinkin' My Baby (Off My Mind)	Eddie Rabbitt
4/24	1	11.	Together Again	Emmylou Harris
5/1	1	12.	Don't The Girls All Get Prettier At Closing Time	Mickey Gilley
5/8	1	13.	My Eyes Can Only See As Far As You	Charley Pride

DATE	WKS	RECORD TITLE	ARTIST
5/15	1	14. What Goes On When The Sun Goes Down	Ronnie Milsap
5/22	1	15. After All The Good Is Gone	Conway Twitty
5/29	2	16. One Piece At A Time	Johnny Cash
6/12	1	17. I'll Get Over You	Crystal Gayle
6/19	2	18. El Paso City	Marty Robbins
7/4	1	19. All These Things	Joe Stampley
7/10	1	20. The Door Is Always Open	Dave & Sugar
7/17	3	21. Teddy Bear	Red Sovine
8/7	1	22. Golden Ring	George Jones & Tammy Wynette
8/14	1	23. Say It Again	Don Williams
8/21	1	24. Bring It On Home To Me	Mickey Gilley
8/28	2	25. (I'm A) Stand By My Woman Man	Ronnie Milsap
9/11	2	26. I Don't Want To Have To Marry You	Jim Ed Brown/Helen Cornelius
9/25	1	27. If You've Got The Money I've Got The Time	Willie Nelson
10/2	1	28. Here's Some Love	Tanya Tucker
10/9	1	29. The Games That Daddies Play	Conway Twitty
10/16	2	30. You And Me	Tammy Wynette
10/30	1	31. Among My Souvenirs	Marty Robbins
11/6	1	32. Cherokee Maiden	Merle Haggard
11/13	2	33. Somebody Somewhere (Don't Know What He's Missin' Tonight)	Loretta Lynn
11/27	2	34. Good Woman Blues	Mel Tillis
12/11	2	35. Thinkin' Of A Rendezvous	Johnny Duncan
12/25	2	36. Sweet Dreams	Emmylou Harris

1977

DATE	WKS	RECORD TITLE	ARTIST
1/8	1	1. Broken Down In Tiny Pieces	Billy "Crash" Craddock
1/15	1	2. You Never Miss A Real Good Thing (Till He Says Goodbye)	Crystal Gayle
1/22	1	3. I Can't Believe She Gives It All To Me	Conway Twitty
1/29	1	4. Let My Love Be Your Pillow	Ronnie Milsap
2/5	2	5. Near You	George Jones & Tammy Wynette
2/19	1	6. Moody Blue	Elvis Presley
2/26	1	7. Say You'll Stay Until Tomorrow	Tom Jones
3/5	1	8. Heart Healer	Mel Tillis
3/12	1	9. She's Just An Old Love Turned Memory	Charley Pride
3/19	2	10. Southern Nights	Glen Campbell
4/2	2	11. Lucille	Kenny Rogers
4/16	1	12. It Couldn't Have Been Any Better	Johnny Duncan
4/23	1	13. She's Got You	Loretta Lynn
4/30	1	14. She's Pulling Me Back Again	Mickey Gilley
5/7	1	15. Play, Guitar Play	Conway Twitty
5/14	1	16. Some Broken Hearts Never Mend	Don Williams
5/21	6	17. Luckenbach, Texas (Back to the Basics of Love)	Waylon Jennings
7/2	1	18. That Was Yesterday	Donna Fargo
7/9	1	19. I'll Be Leaving Alone	Charley Pride
7/16	3	20. It Was Almost Like A Song	Ronnie Milsap
8/6	2	21. Rollin' With The Flow	Charlie Rich
8/20	1	22. Way Down	Elvis Presley
8/27	4	23. Don't It Make My Brown Eyes Blue	Crystal Gayle

DATE	WKS		RECORD TITLE	ARTIST
9/24	1	24.	I've Already Loved You In My Mind	Conway Twitty
10/1	1	25.	Daytime Friends	Kenny Rogers
10/8	4	26.	Heaven's Just A Sin Away	The Kendalls
11/5	1	27.	I'm Just A Country Boy	Don Williams
11/12	1	28.	More To Me	Charley Pride
11/19	2	29.	The Wurlitzer Prize (I Don't Want to Get Over You)	Waylon Jennings
12/3	5	30.	Here You Come Again	Dolly Parton

1978

DATE	WKS		RECORD TITLE	ARTIST
1/7	2	1.	Take This Job And Shove It	Johnny Paycheck
1/21	1	2.	What A Difference You've Made In My Life	Ronnie Milsap
1/28	2	3.	Out Of My Head And Back In My Bed	Loretta Lynn
2/11	1	4.	I Just Wish You Were Someone I Love	Larry Gatlin with Brothers & Friends
2/18	2	5.	Don't Break The Heart That Loves You	Margo Smith
3/4	4	6.	Mammas Don't Let Your Babies Grow Up To Be Cowboys	Waylon & Willie
4/1	1	7.	Ready For The Times To Get Better	Crystal Gayle
4/8	2	8.	Someone Loves You Honey	Charley Pride
4/22	2	9.	Every Time Two Fools Collide	Kenny Rogers & Dottie West
5/6	2	10.	It's All Wrong, But It's All Right	Dolly Parton
5/20	1	11.	She Can Put Her Shoes Under My Bed (Anytime)	Johnny Duncan
5/27	2	12.	Do You Know You Are My Sunshine	The Statler Brothers
6/10	1	13.	Georgia On My Mind	Willie Nelson
6/17	1	14.	Two More Bottles Of Wine	Emmylou Harris
6/24	1	15.	I'll Be True To You	The Oak Ridge Boys
7/1	1	16.	It Only Hurts For A Little While	Margo Smith
7/8	1	17.	I Believe In You	Mel Tillis
7/15	3	18.	Only One Love In My Life	Ronnie Milsap
8/5	1	19.	Love Or Something Like It	Kenny Rogers
8/12	1	20.	You Don't Love Me Anymore	Eddie Rabbitt
8/19	2	21.	Talking In Your Sleep	Crystal Gayle
9/2	1	22.	Blue Skies	Willie Nelson
9/9	3	23.	I've Always Been Crazy	Waylon Jennings
9/30	3	24.	Heartbreaker	Dolly Parton
10/21	1	25.	Tear Time	Dave & Sugar
10/28	1	26.	Let's Take The Long Way Around The World	Ronnie Milsap
11/4	3	27.	Sleeping Single In A Double Bed	Barbara Mandrell
11/25	1	28.	Sweet Desire	The Kendalls
12/2	1	29.	I Just Want To Love You	Eddie Rabbitt
12/9	1	30.	On My Knees	Charlie Rich with Janie Fricke
12/16	3	31.	The Gambler	Kenny Rogers

1979

DATE	WKS		RECORD TITLE	ARTIST
1/6	1	1.	Tulsa Time	Don Williams
1/13	1	2.	Lady Lay Down	John Conlee
1/20	1	3.	I Really Got The Feeling	Dolly Parton
1/27	2	4.	Why Have You Left The One You Left Me For	Crystal Gayle
2/10	3	5.	Every Which Way But Loose	Eddie Rabbitt
3/3	3	6.	Golden Tears	Dave & Sugar

DATE	WKS	RECORD TITLE	ARTIST
3/24	3	7. I Just Fall In Love Again	Anne Murray
4/14	1	8. (If Loving You Is Wrong) I Don't Want To Be Right	Barbara Mandrell
4/21	1	9. All I Ever Need Is You	Kenny Rogers & Dottie West
4/28	1	10. Where Do I Put Her Memory	Charley Pride
5/5	1	11. Backside Of Thirty	John Conlee
5/12	1	12. Don't Take It Away	Conway Twitty
5/19	3	13. If I Said You Have A Beautiful Body Would You Hold It Against Me	Bellamy Brothers
6/9	2	14. She Believes In Me	Kenny Rogers
6/23	1	15. Nobody Likes Sad Songs	Ronnie Milsap
6/30	3	16. Amanda	Waylon Jennings
7/21	1	17. Shadows In The Moonlight	Anne Murray
7/28	2	18. You're The Only One	Dolly Parton
8/11	1	19. Suspicions	Eddie Rabbitt
8/18	1	20. Coca Cola Cowboy	Mel Tillis
8/25	1	21. The Devil Went Down To Georgia	The Charlie Daniels Band
9/1	1	22. Heartbreak Hotel	Willie Nelson & Leon Russell
9/8	1	23. I May Never Get To Heaven	Conway Twitty
9/15	1	24. You're My Jamaica	Charley Pride
9/22	1	25. Just Good Ol' Boys	Moe Bandy & Joe Stampley
9/29	1	26. It Must Be Love	Don Williams
10/6	2	27. Last Cheater's Waltz	T.G. Sheppard
10/20	2	28. All The Gold In California	Larry Gatlin & The Gatlin Brothers
11/3	2	29. You Decorated My Life	Kenny Rogers
11/17	2	30. Come With Me	Waylon Jennings
12/1	1	31. Broken Hearted Me	Anne Murray
12/8	1	32. I Cheated Me Right Out Of You	Moe Bandy
12/15	3	33. Happy Birthday Darlin'	Conway Twitty

1980

DATE	WKS	RECORD TITLE	ARTIST
1/5	3	1. Coward Of The County	Kenny Rogers
1/26	2	2. I'll Be Coming Back For More	T.G. Sheppard
2/9	1	3. Leaving Louisiana In The Broad Daylight	The Oak Ridge Boys
2/16	1	4. Love Me Over Again	Don Williams
2/23	1	5. Years	Barbara Mandrell
3/1	1	6. I Ain't Living Long Like This	Waylon Jennings
3/8	2	7. My Heroes Have Always Been Cowboys	Willie Nelson
3/22	1	8. Why Don't You Spend The Night	Ronnie Milsap
3/29	1	9. I'd Love To Lay You Down	Conway Twitty
4/5	1	10. Sugar Daddy	Bellamy Brothers
4/12	1	11. Honky Tonk Blues	Charley Pride
4/19	1	12. It's Like We Never Said Goodbye	Crystal Gayle
4/26	1	13. A Lesson In Leavin'	Dottie West
5/3	1	14. Are You On The Road To Lovin' Me Again	Debby Boone
5/10	1	15. Beneath Still Waters	Emmylou Harris
5/17	1	16. Gone Too Far	Eddie Rabbitt
5/24	1	17. Starting Over Again	Dolly Parton
5/31	3	18. My Heart	Ronnie Milsap
6/21	1	19. One Day At A Time	Cristy Lane
6/28	1	20. Trying To Love Two Women	The Oak Ridge Boys

DATE	WKS		RECORD TITLE	ARTIST
7/5	1	21.	He Stopped Loving Her Today	George Jones
7/12	1	22.	You Win Again	Charley Pride
7/19	1	23.	True Love Ways	Mickey Gilley
7/26	1	24.	Bar Room Buddies	Merle Haggard & Clint Eastwood
8/2	1	25.	Dancin' Cowboys	Bellamy Brothers
8/9	1	26.	Stand By Me	Mickey Gilley
8/16	1	27.	Tennessee River	Alabama
8/23	1	28.	Drivin' My Life Away	Eddie Rabbitt
8/30	1	29.	Cowboys And Clowns	Ronnie Milsap
9/6	3	30.	Lookin' For Love	Johnny Lee
9/27	1	31.	Old Flames Can't Hold A Candle To You	Dolly Parton
10/4	1	32.	Do You Wanna Go To Heaven	T.G. Sheppard
10/11	1	33.	Loving Up A Storm	Razzy Bailey
10/18	2	34.	I Believe In You	Don Williams
11/1	1	35.	Theme From The Dukes Of Hazzard (Good Ol' Boys)	Waylon Jennings
11/8	1	36.	On The Road Again	Willie Nelson
11/15	1	37.	Could I Have This Dance	Anne Murray
11/22	1	38.	Lady	Kenny Rogers
11/29	1	39.	If You Ever Change Your Mind	Crystal Gayle
12/6	1	40.	Smoky Mountain Rain	Ronnie Milsap
12/13	1	41.	Why Lady Why	Alabama
12/20	1	42.	That's All That Matters	Mickey Gilley
12/27	2	43.	One In A Million	Johnny Lee

1981

DATE	WKS		RECORD TITLE	ARTIST
1/10	1	1.	I Think I'll Just Stay Here And Drink	Merle Haggard
1/17	1	2.	I Love A Rainy Night	Eddie Rabbitt
1/24	1	3.	9 To 5	Dolly Parton
1/31	1	4.	I Feel Like Loving You Again	T.G. Sheppard
2/7	1	5.	I Keep Coming Back	Razzy Bailey
2/14	1	6.	Who's Cheatin' Who	Charly McClain
2/21	1	7.	Southern Rains	Mel Tillis
2/28	1	8.	Are You Happy Baby?	Dottie West
3/7	1	9.	Do You Love As Good As You Look	The Bellamy Brothers
3/14	1	10.	Guitar Man	Elvis Presley
3/21	1	11.	Angel Flying Too Close To The Ground	Willie Nelson
3/28	1	12.	Texas Women	Hank Williams, Jr.
4/4	1	13.	Drifter	Sylvia
4/11	1	14.	You're The Reason God Made Oklahoma	David Frizzell & Shelly West
4/18	1	15.	Old Flame	Alabama
4/25	1	16.	A Headache Tomorrow (Or A Heartache Tonight)	Mickey Gilley
5/2	1	17.	Rest Your Love On Me	Conway Twitty
5/9	1	18.	Am I Losing You	Ronnie Milsap
5/16	1	19.	I Loved 'Em Every One	T.G. Sheppard
5/23	1	20.	Seven Year Ache	Rosanne Cash
5/30	1	21.	Elvira	The Oak Ridge Boys
6/6	1	22.	Friends	Razzy Bailey
6/13	1	23.	What Are We Doin' In Love	Dottie West with Kenny Rogers
6/20	1	24.	But You Know I Love You	Dolly Parton
6/27	1	25.	Blessed Are The Believers	Anne Murray

DATE	WKS	RECORD TITLE	ARTIST
7/4	1	26. I Was Country When Country Wasn't Cool	Barbara Mandrell
7/11	1	27. Fire & Smoke	Earl Thomas Conley
7/18	2	28. Feels So Right	Alabama
8/1	1	29. Dixie On My Mind	Hank Williams, Jr.
8/8	1	30. Too Many Lovers	Crystal Gayle
8/15	2	31. I Don't Need You	Kenny Rogers
8/29	2	32. (There's) No Gettin' Over Me	Ronnie Milsap
9/12	1	33. Older Women	Ronnie McDowell
9/19	1	34. You Don't Know Me	Mickey Gilley
9/26	1	35. Tight Fittin' Jeans	Conway Twitty
10/3	1	36. Midnight Hauler	Razzy Bailey
10/10	1	37. Party Time	T.G. Sheppard
10/17	1	38. Step By Step	Eddie Rabbitt
10/24	2	39. Never Been So Loved (In All My Life)	Charley Pride
11/7	1	40. Fancy Free	The Oak Ridge Boys
11/14	1	41. My Baby Thinks He's A Train	Rosanne Cash
11/21	1	42. All My Rowdy Friends (Have Settled Down)	Hank Williams, Jr.
11/28	1	43. My Favorite Memory	Merle Haggard
12/5	1	44. Bet Your Heart On Me	Johnny Lee
12/12	1	45. Still Doin' Time	George Jones
12/19	1	46. All Roads Lead To You	Steve Wariner
12/26	2	47. Love In The First Degree	Alabama

1982

DATE	WKS	RECORD TITLE	ARTIST
1/9	1	1. Fourteen Carat Mind	Gene Watson
1/16	1	2. I Wouldn't Have Missed It For The World	Ronnie Milsap
1/23	1	3. Red Neckin' Love Makin' Night	Conway Twitty
1/30	1	4. The Sweetest Thing (I've Ever Known)	Juice Newton
2/6	1	5. Lonely Nights	Mickey Gilley
2/13	1	6. Someone Could Lose A Heart Tonight	Eddie Rabbitt
2/20	1	7. Only One You	T.G. Sheppard
2/27	1	8. Lord, I Hope This Day Is Good	Don Williams
3/6	1	9. You're The Best Break This Old Heart Ever Had	Ed Bruce
3/13	1	10. Blue Moon With Heartache	Rosanne Cash
3/20	1	11. Mountain Of Love	Charley Pride
3/27	1	12. She Left Love All Over Me	Razzy Bailey
4/3	1	13. Bobbie Sue	The Oak Ridge Boys
4/10	1	14. Big City	Merle Haggard
4/17	1	15. The Clown	Conway Twitty
4/24	1	16. Crying My Heart Out Over You	Ricky Skaggs
5/1	1	17. Mountain Music	Alabama
5/8	2	18. Always On My Mind	Willie Nelson
5/22	2	19. Just To Satisfy You	Waylon & Willie
6/5	1	20. Finally	T.G. Sheppard
6/12	1	21. For All The Wrong Reasons	The Bellamy Brothers
6/19	2	22. Slow Hand	Conway Twitty
7/3	1	23. Any Day Now	Ronnie Milsap
7/10	1	24. Don't Worry 'Bout Me Baby	Janie Fricke
7/17	1	25. 'Till You're Gone	Barbara Mandrell
7/24	1	26. Take Me Down	Alabama

DATE	WKS	RECORD TITLE	ARTIST
7/31	1	27. I Don't Care	Ricky Skaggs
8/7	1	28. Honky Tonkin'	Hank Williams, Jr.
8/14	1	29. I'm Gonna Hire A Wino To Decorate Our Home	David Frizzell
8/21	1	30. Nobody	Sylvia
8/28	1	31. Fool Hearted Memory	George Strait
9/4	1	32. Love Will Turn You Around	Kenny Rogers
9/11	2	33. She Got The Goldmine (I Got The Shaft)	Jerry Reed
9/25	1	34. What's Forever For	Michael Murphey
10/2	1	35. Put Your Dreams Away	Mickey Gilley
10/9	1	36. Yesterday's Wine	Merle Haggard/George Jones
10/16	1	37. I Will Always Love You	Dolly Parton
10/23	1	38. He Got You	Ronnie Milsap
10/30	1	39. Close Enough To Perfect	Alabama
11/6	1	40. You're So Good When You're Bad	Charley Pride
11/13	1	41. Heartbroke	Ricky Skaggs
11/20	1	42. War Is Hell (On The Homefront Too)	T.G. Sheppard
11/27	1	43. It Ain't Easy Bein' Easy	Janie Fricke
12/4	1	44. You And I	Eddie Rabbitt with Crystal Gayle
12/11	1	45. Redneck Girl	The Bellamy Brothers
12/18	1	46. Somewhere Between Right And Wrong	Earl Thomas Conley
12/25	2	47. Wild And Blue	John Anderson

1983

DATE	WKS	RECORD TITLE	ARTIST
1/8	1	1. Can't Even Get The Blues	Reba McEntire
1/15	1	2. Going Where The Lonely Go	Merle Haggard
1/22	1	3. (Lost His Love) On Our Last Date	Emmylou Harris
1/29	1	4. Talk To Me	Mickey Gilley
2/5	1	5. Inside	Ronnie Milsap
2/12	1	6. 'Til I Gain Control Again	Crystal Gayle
2/19	1	7. Faking Love	T.G. Sheppard & Karen Brooks
2/26	1	8. Why Baby Why	Charley Pride
3/5	1	9. If Hollywood Don't Need You	Don Williams
3/12	1	10. The Rose	Conway Twitty
3/19	1	11. I Wouldn't Change You If I Could	Ricky Skaggs
3/26	1	12. Swingin'	John Anderson
4/2	1	13. When I'm Away From You	Bellamy Brothers
4/9	1	14. We've Got Tonight	Kenny Rogers & Sheena Easton
4/16	1	15. Dixieland Delight	Alabama
4/23	1	16. American Made	The Oak Ridge Boys
4/30	1	17. You're The First Time I've Thought About Leaving	Reba McEntire
5/7	1	18. Jose Cuervo	Shelly West
5/14	1	19. Whatever Happened To Old Fashioned Love	B.J. Thomas
5/21	1	20. Common Man	John Conlee
5/28	1	21. You Take Me For Granted	Merle Haggard
6/4	1	22. Lucille (You Won't Do Your Daddy's Will)	Waylon Jennings
6/11	1	23. Our Love Is On The Faultline	Crystal Gayle
6/18	1	24. You Can't Run From Love	Eddie Rabbitt
6/25	1	25. Fool For Your Love	Mickey Gilley
7/2	1	26. Love Is On A Roll	Don Williams
7/9	1	27. Highway 40 Blues	Ricky Skaggs

DATE	WKS		RECORD TITLE	ARTIST
7/16	1	28.	The Closer You Get	Alabama
7/23	1	29.	Pancho And Lefty	Willie Nelson & Merle Haggard
7/30	1	30.	I Always Get Lucky With You	George Jones
8/6	1	31.	Your Love's On The Line	Earl Thomas Conley
8/13	1	32.	He's A Heartache (Looking For A Place To Happen)	Janie Fricke
8/20	1	33.	Love Song	The Oak Ridge Boys
8/27	1	34.	You're Gonna Ruin My Bad Reputation	Ronnie McDowell
9/3	1	35.	A Fire I Can't Put Out	George Strait
9/10	1	36.	I'm Only In It For The Love	John Conlee
9/17	1	37.	Night Games	Charley Pride
9/24	1	38.	Baby, What About You	Crystal Gayle
10/1	1	39.	New Looks From An Old Lover	B.J. Thomas
10/8	1	40.	Don't You Know How Much I Love You	Ronnie Milsap
10/15	1	41.	Paradise Tonight	Charly McClain & Mickey Gilley
10/22	1	42.	Lady Down On Love	Alabama
10/29	2	43.	Islands In The Stream	Kenny Rogers with Dolly Parton
11/12	1	44.	Somebody's Gonna Love You	Lee Greenwood
11/19	1	45.	One Of A Kind Pair Of Fools	Barbara Mandrell
11/26	1	46.	Holding Her And Loving You	Earl Thomas Conley
12/3	1	47.	A Little Good News	Anne Murray
12/10	1	48.	Tell Me A Lie	Janie Fricke
12/17	1	49.	Black Sheep	John Anderson
12/24	2	50.	Houston (Means I'm One Day Closer To You)	Larry Gatlin & The Gatlin Brothers

1984

DATE	WKS		RECORD TITLE	ARTIST
1/7	1	1.	You Look So Good In Love	George Strait
1/14	1	2.	Slow Burn	T.G. Sheppard
1/21	1	3.	In My Eyes	John Conlee
1/28	1	4.	The Sound Of Goodbye	Crystal Gayle
2/4	1	5.	Show Her	Ronnie Milsap
2/11	1	6.	That's The Way Love Goes	Merle Haggard
2/18	1	7.	Don't Cheat In Our Hometown	Ricky Skaggs
2/25	1	8.	Stay Young	Don Williams
3/3	1	9.	Woke Up In Love	Exile
3/10	1	10.	Going, Going, Gone	Lee Greenwood
3/17	1	11.	Elizabeth	The Statler Brothers
3/24	1	12.	Roll On (Eighteen Wheeler)	Alabama
3/31	1	13.	Let's Stop Talkin' About It	Janie Fricke
4/7	1	14.	Don't Make It Easy For Me	Earl Thomas Conley
4/14	1	15.	Thank God For The Radio	The Kendalls
4/21	1	16.	The Yellow Rose	Johnny Lee with Lane Brody
4/28	1	17.	Right Or Wrong	George Strait
5/5	1	18.	I Guess It Never Hurts To Hurt Sometimes	The Oak Ridge Boys
5/12	2	19.	To All The Girls I've Loved Before	Julio Iglesias & Willie Nelson
5/26	1	20.	As Long As I'm Rockin' With You	John Conlee
6/2	1	21.	Honey (Open That Door)	Ricky Skaggs
6/9	1	22.	Someday When Things Are Good	Merle Haggard
6/16	1	23.	I Got Mexico	Eddy Raven
6/23	1	24.	When We Make Love	Alabama

DATE	WKS		RECORD TITLE	ARTIST
6/30	1	25.	I Can Tell By The Way You Dance (You're Gonna Love Me Tonight)	Vern Gosdin
7/7	1	26.	Somebody's Needin' Somebody	Conway Twitty
7/14	1	27.	I Don't Want To Be A Memory	Exile
7/21	1	28.	Just Another Woman In Love	Anne Murray
7/28	1	29.	Angel In Disguise	Earl Thomas Conley
8/4	1	30.	Mama He's Crazy	The Judds
8/11	1	31.	That's The Thing About Love	Don Williams
8/18	1	32.	Still Losing You	Ronnie Milsap
8/25	1	33.	Long Hard Road (The Sharecropper's Dream)	Nitty Gritty Dirt Band
9/1	1	34.	Let's Fall To Pieces Together	George Strait
9/8	1	35.	Tennessee Homesick Blues	Dolly Parton
9/15	1	36.	You're Gettin' To Me Again	Jim Glaser
9/22	1	37.	Let's Chase Each Other Around The Room	Merle Haggard
9/29	1	38.	Turning Away	Crystal Gayle
10/6	1	39.	Everyday	The Oak Ridge Boys
10/13	1	40.	Uncle Pen	Ricky Skaggs
10/20	1	41.	I Don't Know A Thing About Love (The Moon Song)	Conway Twitty
10/27	1	42.	If You're Gonna Play In Texas (You Gotta Have A Fiddle In The Band)	Alabama
11/3	1	43.	City Of New Orleans	Willie Nelson
11/10	1	44.	I've Been Around Enough To Know	John Schneider
11/17	1	45.	Give Me One More Chance	Exile
11/24	1	46.	You Could've Heard A Heart Break	Johnny Lee
12/1	1	47.	Your Heart's Not In It	Janie Fricke
12/8	1	48.	Chance Of Lovin' You	Earl Thomas Conley
12/15	1	49.	Nobody Loves Me Like You Do	Anne Murray (with Dave Loggins)
12/22	2	50.	Why Not Me	The Judds

1985

DATE	WKS		RECORD TITLE	ARTIST
1/5	1	1.	Does Fort Worth Ever Cross Your Mind	George Strait
1/12	1	2.	The Best Year Of My Life	Eddie Rabbitt
1/19	1	3.	How Blue	Reba McEntire
1/26	1	4.	(There's A) Fire In The Night	Alabama
2/2	1	5.	A Place To Fall Apart	Merle Haggard with Janie Fricke
2/9	1	6.	Ain't She Somethin' Else	Conway Twitty
2/16	1	7.	Make My Life With You	Oak Ridge Boys
2/23	1	8.	Baby's Got Her Blue Jeans On	Mel McDaniel
3/2	1	9.	Baby Bye Bye	Gary Morris
3/9	1	10.	My Only Love	The Statler Brothers
3/16	1	11.	Crazy For Your Love	Exile
3/23	1	12.	Seven Spanish Angels	Ray Charles with Willie Nelson
3/30	1	13.	Crazy	Kenny Rogers
4/6	1	14.	Country Girls	John Schneider
4/13	1	15.	Honor Bound	Earl Thomas Conley
4/20	1	16.	I Need More Of You	Bellamy Brothers
4/27	1	17.	Girls Night Out	The Judds
5/4	1	18.	There's No Way	Alabama
5/11	1	19.	Somebody Should Leave	Reba McEntire
5/18	1	20.	Step That Step	Sawyer Brown

DATE	WKS		RECORD TITLE	ARTIST
5/25	1	21.	Radio Heart	Charly McClain
6/1	1	22.	Don't Call Him A Cowboy	Conway Twitty
6/8	1	23.	Natural High	Merle Haggard
6/15	1	24.	Country Boy	Ricky Skaggs
6/22	1	25.	Little Things	The Oak Ridge Boys
6/29	1	26.	She Keeps The Home Fires Burning	Ronnie Milsap
7/6	1	27.	She's A Miracle	Exile
7/13	1	28.	Forgiving You Was Easy	Willie Nelson
7/20	1	29.	Dixie Road	Lee Greenwood
7/27	1	30.	Love Don't Care (Whose Heart It Breaks)	Earl Thomas Conley
8/3	1	31.	Forty Hour Week (For A Livin')	Alabama
8/10	1	32.	I'm For Love	Hank Williams, Jr.
8/17	1	33.	Highwayman	Waylon Jennings/Willie Nelson/ Johnny Cash Kris Kristofferson
8/24	1	34.	Real Love	Kenny Rogers & Dolly Parton
8/31	1	35.	Love Is Alive	The Judds
9/7	1	36.	I Don't Know Why You Don't Want Me	Rosanne Cash
9/14	1	37.	Modern Day Romance	Nitty Gritty Dirt Band
9/21	1	38.	I Fell In Love Again Last Night	The Forester Sisters
9/28	2	39.	Lost In The Fifties Tonight (In the Still of the Night)	Ronnie Milsap
10/12	1	40.	Meet Me In Montana	Marie Osmond with Dan Seals
10/19	1	41.	You Make Me Want To Make You Mine	Juice Newton
10/26	1	42.	Touch A Hand, Make A Friend	The Oak Ridge Boys
11/2	1	43.	Some Fools Never Learn	Steve Wariner
11/9	1	44.	Can't Keep A Good Man Down	Alabama
11/16	1	45.	Hang On To Your Heart	Exile
11/23	1	46.	I'll Never Stop Loving You	Gary Morris
11/30	1	47.	Too Much On My Heart	The Statler Brothers
12/7	1	48.	I Don't Mind The Thorns (If You're The Rose)	Lee Greenwood
12/14	1	49.	Nobody Falls Like A Fool	Earl Thomas Conley
12/21	1	50.	The Chair	George Strait
12/28	2	51.	Have Mercy	The Judds

1986

DATE	WKS		RECORD TITLE	ARTIST
1/11	1	1.	Morning Desire	Kenny Rogers
1/18	1	2.	Bop	Dan Seals
1/25	1	3.	Never Be You	Rosanne Cash
2/1	1	4.	Just In Case	The Forester Sisters
2/8	1	5.	Hurt	Juice Newton
2/15	1	6.	Makin' Up For Lost Time (The Dallas Lovers' Song)	Crystal Gayle & Gary Morris
2/22	1	7.	There's No Stopping Your Heart	Marie Osmond
3/1	1	8.	You Can Dream Of Me	Steve Wariner
3/8	1	9.	Think About Love	Dolly Parton
3/15	1	10.	I Could Get Used To You	Exile
3/22	1	11.	What's A Memory Like You (Doing In A Love Like This)	John Schneider
3/29	1	12.	Don't Underestimate My Love For You	Lee Greenwood
4/5	1	13.	100% Chance Of Rain	Gary Morris
4/12	1	14.	She And I	Alabama
4/19	1	15.	Cajun Moon	Ricky Skaggs
4/26	1	16.	Now And Forever (You And Me)	Anne Murray

DATE	WKS	RECORD TITLE		ARTIST
5/3	1	17.	Once In A Blue Moon	Earl Thomas Conley
5/10	1	18.	Grandpa (Tell Me 'Bout The Good Old Days)	The Judds
5/17	1	19.	Ain't Misbehavin'	Hank Williams, Jr.
5/24	1	20.	Tomb Of The Unknown Love	Kenny Rogers
5/31	1	21.	Whoever's In New England	Reba McEntire
6/7	1	22.	Happy, Happy Birthday Baby	Ronnie Milsap
6/14	1	23.	Life's Highway	Steve Wariner
6/21	1	24.	Mama's Never Seen Those Eyes	The Forester Sisters
6/28	1	25.	Living In The Promiseland	Willie Nelson
7/5	1	26.	Everything That Glitters (Is Not Gold)	Dan Seals
7/12	1	27.	Hearts Aren't Made To Break (They're Made To Love)	Lee Greenwood
7/19	1	28.	Until I Met You	Judy Rodman
7/26	1	29.	On The Other Hand	Randy Travis
8/2	1	30.	Nobody In His Right Mind Would've Left Her	George Strait
8/9	1	31.	Rockin' With The Rhythm Of The Rain	The Judds
8/16	1	32.	You're The Last Thing I Needed Tonight	John Schneider
8/23	1	33.	Strong Heart	T.G. Sheppard
8/30	1	34.	Heartbeat In The Darkness	Don Williams
9/6	1	35.	Desperado Love	Conway Twitty
9/13	1	36.	Little Rock	Reba McEntire
9/20	1	37.	Got My Heart Set On You	John Conlee
9/27	1	38.	In Love	Ronnie Milsap
10/4	1	39.	Always Have Always Will	Janie Fricke
10/11	1	40.	Both To Each Other (Friends & Lovers)	Eddie Rabbitt & Juice Newton
10/18	1	41.	Just Another Love	Tanya Tucker
10/25	1	42.	Cry	Crystal Gayle
11/1	1	43.	It'll Be Me	Exile
11/8	1	44.	Diggin' Up Bones	Randy Travis
11/15	1	45.	That Rock Won't Roll	Restless Heart
11/22	1	46.	You're Still New To Me	Marie Osmond with Paul Davis
11/29	1	47.	Touch Me When We're Dancing	Alabama
12/6	1	48.	It Ain't Cool To Be Crazy About You	George Strait
12/13	1	49.	Hell And High Water	T. Graham Brown
12/20	1	50.	Too Much Is Not Enough	Bellamy Brothers
12/27	2	51.	Mind Your Own Business	Hank Williams, Jr.

1987

DATE	WKS	RECORD TITLE		ARTIST
1/10	1	1.	Give Me Wings	Michael Johnson
1/17	1	2.	What Am I Gonna Do About You	Reba McEntire
1/24	1	3.	Cry Myself To Sleep	The Judds
1/31	1	4.	You Still Move Me	Dan Seals
2/7	1	5.	Leave Me Lonely	Gary Morris
2/14	1	6.	How Do I Turn You On	Ronnie Milsap
2/21	1	7.	Straight To The Heart	Crystal Gayle
2/28	1	8.	I Can't Win For Losin' You	Earl Thomas Conley
3/7	1	9.	Mornin' Ride	Lee Greenwood
3/14	1	10.	Baby's Got A New Baby	S-K-O
3/21	1	11.	I'll Still Be Loving You	Restless Heart
3/28	1	12.	Small Town Girl	Steve Wariner
4/4	1	13.	Ocean Front Property	George Strait

DATE	WKS	RECORD TITLE	ARTIST
4/11	1	14. "You've Got" The Touch	Alabama
4/18	1	15. Kids Of The Baby Boom	Bellamy Brothers
4/25	1	16. Rose In Paradise	Waylon Jennings
5/2	1	17. Don't Go To Strangers	T. Graham Brown
5/9	1	18. The Moon Is Still Over Her Shoulder	Michael Johnson
5/16	1	19. To Know Him Is To Love Him	Dolly Parton, Linda Ronstadt, Emmylou Harris
5/23	1	20. Can't Stop My Heart From Loving You	The O'Kanes
5/30	1	21. It Takes A Little Rain (To Make Love Grow)	The Oak Ridge Boys
6/6	1	22. I Will Be There	Dan Seals
6/13	3	23. Forever And Ever, Amen	Randy Travis
7/4	1	24. That Was A Close One	Earl Thomas Conley
7/11	1	25. All My Ex's Live In Texas	George Strait
7/18	1	26. I Know Where I'm Going	The Judds
7/25	1	27. The Weekend	Steve Wariner
8/1	1	28. Snap Your Fingers	Ronnie Milsap
8/8	1	29. One Promise Too Late	Reba McEntire
8/15	1	30. A Long Line Of Love	Michael Martin Murphey
8/22	1	31. Why Does It Have To Be (Wrong or Right)	Restless Heart
8/29	1	32. Born To Boogie	Hank Williams, Jr.
9/5	1	33. She's Too Good To Be True	Exile
9/12	1	34. Make No Mistake, She's Mine	Ronnie Milsap & Kenny Rogers
9/19	1	35. This Crazy Love	The Oak Ridge Boys
9/26	1	36. Three Time Loser	Dan Seals
10/3	1	37. You Again	The Forester Sisters
10/10	1	38. The Way We Make A Broken Heart	Rosanne Cash
10/17	1	39. Fishin' In The Dark	Nitty Gritty Dirt Band
10/24	1	40. Shine, Shine, Shine	Eddy Raven
10/31	1	41. Right From The Start	Earl Thomas Conley
11/7	1	42. Am I Blue	George Strait
11/14	1	43. Maybe Your Baby's Got The Blues	The Judds
11/21	1	44. I Won't Need You Anymore (Always And Forever)	Randy Travis
11/28	1	45. Lynda	Steve Wariner
12/5	1	46. Somebody Lied	Ricky Van Shelton
12/12	1	47. The Last One To Know	Reba McEntire
12/19	1	48. Do Ya'	K.T. Oslin
12/26	2	49. Somewhere Tonight	Highway 101

1988

DATE	WKS	RECORD TITLE	ARTIST
1/9	1	1. I Can't Get Close Enough	Exile
1/16	1	2. One Friend	Dan Seals
1/23	1	3. Where Do The Nights Go	Ronnie Milsap
1/30	1	4. Goin' Gone	Kathy Mattea
2/6	1	5. Wheels	Restless Heart
2/13	1	6. Tennessee Flat Top Box	Rosanne Cash
2/20	1	7. Twinkle, Twinkle Lucky Star	Merle Haggard
2/27	1	8. I Won't Take Less Than Your Love	Tanya Tucker
3/5	1	9. Face To Face	Alabama
3/12	1	10. Too Gone Too Long	Randy Travis
3/19	1	11. Life Turned Her That Way	Ricky Van Shelton

DATE	WKS		RECORD TITLE	ARTIST
3/26	1	12.	Turn It Loose	The Judds
4/2	1	13.	Love Will Find Its Way To You	Reba McEntire
4/9	1	14.	Famous Last Words Of A Fool	George Strait
4/16	1	15.	I Wanna Dance With You	Eddie Rabbitt
4/23	1	16.	I'll Always Come Back	K.T. Oslin
4/30	1	17.	It's Such A Small World	Rodney Crowell & Rosanne Cash
5/7	1	18.	Cry, Cry, Cry	Highway 101
5/14	1	19.	I'm Gonna Get You	Eddy Raven
5/21	2	20.	Eighteen Wheels And A Dozen Roses	Kathy Mattea
6/4	1	21.	What She Is (Is A Woman In Love)	Earl Thomas Conley
6/11	2	22.	I Told You So	Randy Travis
6/25	1	23.	He's Back And I'm Blue	The Desert Rose Band
7/2	1	24.	If It Don't Come Easy	Tanya Tucker
7/9	1	25.	Fallin' Again	Alabama
7/16	1	26.	If You Change Your Mind	Rosanne Cash
7/23	1	27.	Set 'Em Up Joe	Vern Gosdin
7/30	1	28.	Don't We All Have The Right	Ricky Van Shelton
8/6	1	29.	Baby Blue	George Strait
8/13	1	30.	Don't Close Your Eyes	Keith Whitley
8/20	1	31.	Bluest Eyes In Texas	Restless Heart
8/27	1	32.	The Wanderer	Eddie Rabbitt
9/3	1	33.	I Couldn't Leave You If I Tried	Rodney Crowell
9/10	1	34.	(Do You Love Me) Just Say Yes	Highway 101
9/17	1	35.	Joe Knows How To Live	Eddy Raven
9/24	1	36.	Addicted	Dan Seals
10/1	1	37.	We Believe In Happy Endings	Earl Thomas Conley with Emmylou Harris
10/8	1	38.	Honky Tonk Moon	Randy Travis
10/15	1	39.	Streets Of Bakersfield	Dwight Yoakam & Buck Owens
10/22	1	40.	Strong Enough To Bend	Tanya Tucker
10/29	1	41.	Gonna Take A Lot Of River	The Oak Ridge Boys
11/5	1	42.	Darlene	T. Graham Brown
11/12	1	43.	Runaway Train	Rosanne Cash
11/19	2	44.	I'll Leave This World Loving You	Ricky Van Shelton
12/3	1	45.	I Know How He Feels	Reba McEntire
12/10	1	46.	If You Ain't Lovin' (You Ain't Livin')	George Strait
12/17	1	47.	A Tender Lie	Restless Heart
12/24	2	48.	When You Say Nothing At All	Keith Whitley

1989

DATE	WKS		RECORD TITLE	ARTIST
1/7	1	1.	Hold Me	K.T. Oslin
1/14	1	2.	Change Of Heart	The Judds
1/21	1	3.	She's Crazy For Leavin'	Rodney Crowell
1/28	1	4.	Deeper Than The Holler	Randy Travis
2/4	1	5.	What I'd Say	Earl Thomas Conley
2/11	1	6.	Song Of The South	Alabama
2/18	1	7.	Big Wheels In The Moonlight	Dan Seals
2/25	1	8.	I Sang Dixie	Dwight Yoakam
3/4	1	9.	I Still Believe In You	The Desert Rose Band
3/11	1	10.	Don't You Ever Get Tired (Of Hurting Me)	Ronnie Milsap

DATE	WKS		RECORD TITLE	ARTIST
3/18	1	11.	From A Jack To A King	Ricky Van Shelton
3/25	1	12.	New Fool At An Old Game	Reba McEntire
4/1	1	13.	Baby's Gotten Good At Goodbye	George Strait
4/8	2	14.	I'm No Stranger To The Rain	Keith Whitley
4/22	2	15.	The Church On Cumberland Road	Shenandoah
5/6	1	16.	Young Love	The Judds
5/13	1	17.	Is It Still Over?	Randy Travis
5/20	1	18.	If I Had You	Alabama
5/27	1	19.	After All This Time	Rodney Crowell
6/3	1	20.	Where Did I Go Wrong	Steve Wariner
6/10	1	21.	Better Man	Clint Black
6/17	1	22.	Love Out Loud	Earl Thomas Conley
6/24	1	23.	I Don't Want To Spoil The Party	Rosanne Cash
7/1	1	24.	Come From The Heart	Kathy Mattea
7/8	1	25.	Lovin' Only Me	Ricky Skaggs
7/15	1	26.	In A Letter To You	Eddy Raven
7/22	1	27.	What's Going On In Your World	George Strait
7/29	1	28.	Cathy's Clown	Reba McEntire
8/5	1	29.	Why'd You Come In Here Lookin' Like That	Dolly Parton
8/12	1	30.	Timber, I'm Falling In Love	Patty Loveless
8/19	1	31.	Sunday In The South	Shenandoah
8/26	1	32.	Are You Ever Gonna Love Me	Holly Dunn
9/2	1	33.	I'm Still Crazy	Vern Gosdin
9/9	1	34.	I Wonder Do You Think Of Me	Keith Whitley
9/16	1	35.	Nothing I Can Do About It Now	Willie Nelson
9/23	1	36.	Above And Beyond	Rodney Crowell
9/30	1	37.	Let Me Tell You About Love	The Judds
10/7	1	38.	I Got Dreams	Steve Wariner
10/14	1	39.	Killin' Time	Clint Black
10/21	1	40.	Living Proof	Ricky Van Shelton
10/28	1	41.	High Cotton	Alabama
11/4	1	42.	Ace In The Hole	George Strait
11/11	1	43.	Burnin' Old Memories	Kathy Mattea
11/18	1	44.	Bayou Boys	Eddy Raven
11/25	1	45.	Yellow Roses	Dolly Parton
12/2	1	46.	It's Just A Matter Of Time	Randy Travis
12/9	1	47.	If Tomorrow Never Comes	Garth Brooks
12/16	1	48.	Two Dozen Roses	Shenandoah
12/23	2	49.	A Woman In Love	Ronnie Milsap

1990

DATE	WKS		RECORD TITLE	ARTIST
1/6	1	1.	Who's Lonely Now	Highway 101
1/13	1	2.	It Ain't Nothin'	Keith Whitley

1/20/90: BILLBOARD BEGINS COMPILING COUNTRY CHART THROUGH THEIR BDS SYSTEM (A COMPUTERIZED AIRPLAY MONITORING SYSTEM).

1/20	3	3.	Nobody's Home	Clint Black
2/10	1	4.	Southern Star	Alabama

2/17/90: CHART NOW DESIGNATED AS "HOT COUNTRY SINGLES & TRACKS."

2/17	2	5.	On Second Thought	Eddie Rabbitt
3/3	1	6.	No Matter How High	Oak Ridge Boys

DATE	WKS		RECORD TITLE	ARTIST
3/10	1	7.	Chains	Patty Loveless
3/17	4	8.	Hard Rock Bottom Of Your Heart	Randy Travis
4/14	1	9.	Five Minutes	Lorrie Morgan
4/21	3	10.	Love On Arrival	Dan Seals
5/12	1	11.	Help Me Hold On	Travis Tritt
5/19	2	12.	Walkin' Away	Clint Black
6/2	1	13.	I've Cried My Last Tear For You	Ricky Van Shelton
6/9	5	14.	Love Without End, Amen	George Strait
7/14	3	15.	The Dance	Garth Brooks
8/4	2	16.	Good Times	Dan Seals
8/18	3	17.	Next To You, Next To Me	Shenandoah
9/8	4	18.	Jukebox In My Mind	Alabama
10/6	4	19.	Friends In Low Places	Garth Brooks
11/3	1	20.	You Lie	Reba McEntire
11/10	1	21.	Home	Joe Diffie
11/17	1	22.	You Really Had Me Going	Holly Dunn
11/24	2	23.	Come Next Monday	K.T. Oslin
12/8	5	24.	I've Come To Expect It From You	George Strait

1991

DATE	WKS		RECORD TITLE	ARTIST
1/12	2	1.	Unanswered Prayers	Garth Brooks
1/26	1	2.	Forever's As Far As I'll Go	Alabama
2/2	1	3.	Daddy's Come Around	Paul Overstreet
2/9	2	4.	Brother Jukebox	Mark Chesnutt
2/23	2	5.	Walk On Faith	Mike Reid
3/9	2	6.	I'd Love You All Over Again	Alan Jackson
3/23	2	7.	Loving Blind	Clint Black
4/6	1	8.	Two Of A Kind, Workin' On A Full House	Garth Brooks
4/13	3	9.	Down Home	Alabama
5/4	1	10.	Rockin' Years	Dolly Parton with Ricky Van Shelton
5/11	2	11.	If I Know Me	George Strait
5/25	1	12.	In A Different Light	Doug Stone
6/1	2	13.	Meet In The Middle	Diamond Rio
6/15	1	14.	If The Devil Danced (In Empty Pockets)	Joe Diffie
6/22	2	15.	The Thunder Rolls	Garth Brooks
7/6	3	16.	Don't Rock The Jukebox	Alan Jackson
7/27	1	17.	I Am A Simple Man	Ricky Van Shelton
8/3	2	18.	She's In Love With The Boy	Trisha Yearwood
8/17	3	19.	You Know Me Better Than That	George Strait
9/7	2	20.	Brand New Man	Brooks & Dunn
9/21	1	21.	Leap Of Faith	Lionel Cartwright
9/28	2	22.	Where Are You Now	Clint Black
10/12	2	23.	Keep It Between The Lines	Ricky Van Shelton
10/26	2	24.	Anymore	Travis Tritt
11/9	1	25.	Someday	Alan Jackson
11/16	2	26.	Shameless	Garth Brooks
11/30	1	27.	Forever Together	Randy Travis
12/7	2	28.	For My Broken Heart	Reba McEntire
12/21	2	29.	My Next Broken Heart	Brooks & Dunn

DATE	WKS	RECORD TITLE	ARTIST
		1992	
1/4	3	1. Love, Me	Collin Raye
1/25	1	2. Sticks And Stones	Tracy Lawrence
2/1	2	3. A Jukebox With A Country Song	Doug Stone
2/15	4	4. What She's Doing Now	Garth Brooks
3/14	1	5. Straight Tequila Night	John Anderson
3/21	1	6. Dallas	Alan Jackson
3/28	2	7. Is There Life Out There	Reba McEntire
4/11	1	8. She Is His Only Need	Wynonna Judd
4/18	3	9. There Ain't Nothin' Wrong With The Radio	Aaron Tippin
5/9	2	10. Neon Moon	Brooks & Dunn
5/23	1	11. Some Girls Do	Sawyer Brown
5/30	5	12. Achy Breaky Heart	Billy Ray Cyrus
7/4	3	13. I Saw The Light	Wynonna Judd
7/25	1	14. The River	Garth Brooks
8/1	4	15. Boot Scootin' Boogie	Brooks & Dunn
8/29	1	16. I'll Think Of Something	Mark Chesnutt
9/5	2	17. I Still Believe In You	Vince Gill
9/19	2	18. Love's Got A Hold On You	Alan Jackson
10/3	2	19. In This Life	Collin Raye
10/17	1	20. If I Didn't Have You	Randy Travis
10/24	4	21. No One Else On Earth	Wynonna Judd
11/21	2	22. I'm In A Hurry (And Don't Know Why)	Alabama
12/5	2	23. I Cross My Heart	George Strait
12/19	1	24. She's Got The Rhythm (And I Got The Blues)	Alan Jackson
12/26	3	25. Don't Let Our Love Start Slippin' Away	Vince Gill
		1993	
1/16	1	1. Somewhere Other Than The Night	Garth Brooks
1/23	2	2. Look Heart, No Hands	Randy Travis
2/6	1	3. Too Busy Being In Love	Doug Stone
2/13	2	4. Can I Trust You With My Heart	Travis Tritt
2/27	3	5. What Part Of No	Lorrie Morgan
3/20	1	6. Heartland	George Strait
3/27	2	7. When My Ship Comes In	Clint Black
4/10	2	8. The Heart Won't Lie	Reba McEntire & Vince Gill
4/24	1	9. She Don't Know She's Beautiful	Sammy Kershaw
5/1	2	10. Alibis	Tracy Lawrence
5/15	3	11. I Love The Way You Love Me	John Michael Montgomery
6/5	2	12. Should've Been A Cowboy	Toby Keith
6/19	2	13. Blame It On Your Heart	Patty Loveless
7/3	1	14. That Summer	Garth Brooks
7/10	1	15. Money In The Bank	John Anderson
7/17	4	16. Chattahoochee	Alan Jackson
8/14	1	17. It Sure Is Monday	Mark Chesnutt
8/21	1	18. Why Didn't I Think Of That	Doug Stone
8/28	1	19. Can't Break It To My Heart	Tracy Lawrence
9/4	2	20. Thank God For You	Sawyer Brown
9/18	2 ↕	21. Ain't Going Down (Til The Sun Comes Up)	Garth Brooks

DATE	WKS		RECORD TITLE	ARTIST
9/25	1	22.	Holdin' Heaven	Tracy Byrd
10/9	1	23.	One More Last Chance	Vince Gill
10/16	1	24.	What's It To You	Clay Walker
10/23	2	25.	Easy Come, Easy Go	George Strait
11/6	1	26.	Does He Love You	Reba McEntire (with Linda Davis)
11/13	1	27.	She Used To Be Mine	Brooks & Dunn
11/20	1	28.	Almost Goodbye	Mark Chesnutt
11/27	1	29.	Reckless	Alabama
12/4	1	30.	American Honky-Tonk Bar Association	Garth Brooks
12/11	1	31.	My Second Home	Tracy Lawrence
12/18	2	32.	I Don't Call Him Daddy	Doug Supernaw

1994

DATE	WKS		RECORD TITLE	ARTIST
1/1	4	1.	Wild One	Faith Hill
1/29	1	2.	Live Until I Die	Clay Walker
2/5	4	3.	I Swear	John Michael Montgomery
3/5	1	4.	I Just Wanted You To Know	Mark Chesnutt
3/12	1	5.	Tryin' To Get Over You	Vince Gill
3/19	2	6.	No Doubt About It	Neal McCoy
4/2	2	7.	My Love	Little Texas
4/16	2	8.	If The Good Die Young	Tracy Lawrence
4/30	1	9.	Piece Of My Heart	Faith Hill
5/7	1	10.	A Good Run Of Bad Luck	Clint Black
5/14	1	11.	If Bubba Can Dance (I Can Too)	Shenandoah
5/21	1	12.	Your Love Amazes Me	John Berry
5/28	2	13.	Don't Take The Girl	Tim McGraw
6/11	1	14.	That Ain't No Way To Go	Brooks & Dunn
6/18	4	15.	Wink	Neal McCoy
7/16	1	16.	Foolish Pride	Travis Tritt
7/23	3	17.	Summertime Blues	Alan Jackson
8/13	2	18.	Be My Baby Tonight	John Michael Montgomery
8/27	1	19.	Dreaming With My Eyes Open	Clay Walker
9/3	1	20.	Whisper My Name	Randy Travis
9/10	2	21.	XXX's And OOO's (An American Girl)	Trisha Yearwood
9/24	2	22.	Third Rock From The Sun	Joe Diffie
10/8	1	23.	Who's That Man	Toby Keith
10/15	2	24.	She's Not The Cheatin' Kind	Brooks & Dunn
10/29	3	25.	Livin' On Love	Alan Jackson
11/19	1	26.	Shut Up And Kiss Me	Mary-Chapin Carpenter
11/26	1	27.	If I Could Make A Living	Clay Walker
12/3	1	28.	The Big One	George Strait
12/10	1	29.	If You've Got Love	John Michael Montgomery
12/17	4	30.	Pickup Man	Joe Diffie

1995

DATE	WKS		RECORD TITLE	ARTIST
1/14	2	1.	Not A Moment Too Soon	Tim McGraw
1/28	1	2.	Gone Country	Alan Jackson
2/4	2	3.	Mi Vida Loca (My Crazy Life)	Pam Tillis
2/18	1	4.	My Kind Of Girl	Collin Raye
2/25	2	5.	Old Enough To Know Better	Wade Hayes

DATE	WKS	RECORD TITLE	ARTIST
3/11	1	6. You Can't Make A Heart Love Somebody	George Strait
3/18	2	7. This Woman And This Man	Clay Walker
4/1	2	8. Thinkin' About You	Trisha Yearwood
4/15	1	9. The Heart Is A Lonely Hunter	Reba McEntire
4/22	3 ↕	10. I Can Love You Like That	John Michael Montgomery
4/29	1	11. Little Miss Honky Tonk	Brooks & Dunn
5/20	1	12. Gonna Get A Life	Mark Chesnutt
5/27	1	13. What Mattered Most	Ty Herndon
6/3	3	14. Summer's Comin'	Clint Black
6/24	1	15. Texas Tornado	Tracy Lawrence
7/1	3	16. Sold (The Grundy County Auction Incident)	John Michael Montgomery
7/22	2	17. Any Man Of Mine	Shania Twain
8/5	1	18. I Don't Even Know Your Name	Alan Jackson
8/12	1	19. I Didn't Know My Own Strength	Lorrie Morgan
8/19	2	20. You're Gonna Miss Me When I'm Gone	Brooks & Dunn
9/2	1	21. Not On Your Love	Jeff Carson
9/9	1	22. Someone Else's Star	Bryan White
9/16	5	23. I Like It, I Love It	Tim McGraw
10/21	1	24. She's Every Woman	Garth Brooks
10/28	2	25. Dust On The Bottle	David Lee Murphy
11/11	4	26. Check Yes Or No	George Strait
12/9	2	27. Tall, Tall Trees	Alan Jackson
12/23	2	28. That's As Close As I'll Get To Loving You	Aaron Tippin

1996

DATE	WKS	RECORD TITLE	ARTIST
1/6	1	1. Rebecca Lynn	Bryan White
1/13	3	2. It Matters To Me	Faith Hill
2/3	2	3. (If You're Not In It For Love) I'm Outta Here!	Shania Twain
2/17	2	4. Bigger Than The Beatles	Joe Diffie
3/2	1	5. Wild Angels	Martina McBride
3/9	1	6. I'll Try	Alan Jackson
3/16	1	7. The Beaches Of Cheyenne	Garth Brooks
3/23	2	8. You Can Feel Bad	Patty Loveless
4/6	1	9. To Be Loved By You	Wynonna Judd
4/13	3	10. No News	Lonestar
5/4	2	11. You Win My Love	Shania Twain
5/18	3	12. My Maria	Brooks & Dunn

LABEL ABBREVIATIONS

ABC/Hick. . . . . ABC/Hickory

ABC-Para. . . . . ABC-Paramount

Ariola Am. . . . . Ariola America

Atln. Am. . . . . Atlantic America

Bakers. I. . . . . Bakersfield International

Bellamy Br. . . . . Bellamy Brothers

Capitol A. . . . . Capitol Americana

Cap./SBK . . . . Capitol/SBK

Casabl. W. . . . . Casablanca West

Clev. Int. . . . . Cleveland International

Copper Mt. . . . . Copper Mountain

Country Jub. . . . . Country Jubilee

Curb/Cap. . . . . Curb/Capitol

EMI-Man. . . . . EMI-Manhattan

Epic Snd. . . . . Epic Soundtrax

Little Dar. . . . . Little Darlin'

Macy's Rec. . . . . Macy's Recordings

Metro. Cnt. . . . . Metromedia Country

Modern Mt. . . . . Modern Mountain

Pacific C. . . . . Pacific Challenger

Royal Amer. . . . . Royal American

Scotti Br. . . . . Scotti Brothers

Snd. Factory . . . . Sound Factory

United Art. . . . . United Artists

ALL THE HITS THAT EVER CHARTED!

Only Joel Whitburn's Record Research Books List Every Record Ever To Appear On Every Major Billboard Chart.

When the talk turns to music, more people turn to Joel Whitburn's Record Research Collection than to any other reference source.

That's because these are the only books that get right to the bottom of *Billboard*'s major charts, with complete, fully accurate chart data on every record ever charted. So they're quoted with confidence by DJs, music show hosts, program directors, collectors and other music enthusiasts worldwide.

Each book lists every record's significant chart data, such as peak position, debut date, peak date, weeks charted, label, record number and much more, all conveniently arranged for fast, easy reference. Most books also feature artist biographies, record notes, RIAA Platinum/Gold Record certifications, top artist and record achievements, all-time artist and record rankings, a chronological listing of all #1 hits, and additional in-depth chart information.

TOP POP SINGLES 1955-1993
Over 20,000 Pop singles—every "Hot 100" hit—arranged by artist. Features thousands of artist biographies and countless titles notes. 912 pages. $74.95 Hardcover/$64.95 Softcover.

POP ANNUAL 1955-1994
A year-by-year ranking, based on chart performance, of over 20,000 Pop hits. 880 pages. $69.95 Hardcover/ $59.95 Softcover.

POP HITS 1940-1954
Compiled strictly from *Billboard* and divided into two easy-to-use sections—one lists all the hits artist by artist and the other year by year. Filled with artist bios, title notes, and many special sections. 414 pages. Hardcover. $44.95.

POP MEMORIES 1890-1954
Unprecedented in depth and dimension. An artist-by-artist, title-by-title chronicle of the 65 formative years of recorded popular music. Fascinating facts and statistics on over 1,600 artists and 12,000 recordings, compiled directly from America's popular music charts, surveys and record listings. 660 pages. Hardcover. $59.95.

TOP POP ALBUMS 1955-1996
An artist-by-artist history of the over 18,300 albums that ever appeared on *Billboard*'s Pop albums charts, with a complete A-Z listing below each artist of every track from every charted album by that artist. Over 1,000 pages. Hardcover. $89.95.

TOP POP ALBUM TRACKS 1955-1992
An all-inclusive, alphabetical index of every song track from every charted music album, with the artist's name and the album's chart debut year. 544 pages. Hardcover. $34.95.

TOP POP ALBUM TRACKS 1993-1996
A supplement to our Top Pop Album Tracks 1955-1992 book featured above. Over 70 pages. Softcover. $14.95.

BILLBOARD HOT 100/POP SINGLES CHARTS:
THE EIGHTIES 1980-1989
THE SEVENTIES 1970-1979
THE SIXTIES 1960-1969
Three complete collections of the actual weekly "Hot 100" charts from each decade, reproduced in black and white at 70% of original size. Over 550 pages each. Deluxe Hardcover. $79.95 each.

POP CHARTS 1955-1959
Reproductions of every weekly Pop singles chart *Billboard* published from 1955 through 1959 ("Best Sellers," "Jockeys," "Juke Box," "Top 100" and "Hot 100"). 496 pages. Deluxe Hardcover. $59.95.

BILLBOARD POP ALBUM CHARTS 1965-1969
The greatest of all album eras—straight off the pages of *Billboard*! Every weekly *Billboard* Pop albums chart, shown in its entirety, from 1965 through 1969. All charts reproduced in black and white at 70% of original size. 496 pages. Deluxe Hardcover. $59.95.

TOP COUNTRY SINGLES 1944-1993
The complete history of the most genuine of American musical genres, with an artist-by-artist listing of every "Country" single ever charted. 624 pages. Hardcover. $59.95.